'Cause That's The Way It Was

'Cause That's The Way It Was

WILLIAM PHILLIPS

Exposition Press of Florida   Pompano Beach, Florida

First Edition

© 1986 by William Phillips

Library of Congress Catalog Card Number: 86-91234

ISBN 0-682-40297-4

Printed in the United States of America

Contents

'Cause That's The Way It Was

Part I
The West

Chapter 1
1926—The Beginning

Winnipeg, Manitoba was the largest city in western Canada in 1926. Located five hundred miles northwest of Minneapolis-St. Paul, the nearest U.S. center of comparable size made it an important metropolis on both sides of the border. Its citizens, like people all over the world, were slowly healing the wounds from the "Great War" that had ended just seven years previously. Due to the aura of optimism pervading society, the musical trend of that era was toward sprightly lyrical tunes such as "Baby Face," "Bye-Bye Blackbird" and "When the Red Red Robin Comes Bob Bob Bobbin' Along." Known as the Roaring Twenties and with the younger generation nicknamed "The Flaming Youth," it was a time of prosperity, gaiety and lightheartedness. After all, the Allies had just won "the war to end all wars," and the victors celebrated their winning streak in an outpouring of jubilation.

Many firsts and outstanding accomplishments occurred in 1926 as the United States reached the ripe old age of 150. Transatlantic radio-telephone was established, and the first airmail service commenced when private aviation companies were licensed to carry airmail. Charles A. Lindbergh completed the first nonstop solo flight across the Atlantic, the first talking motion picture was exhibited, and a Scottish inventor named Baird gave the first successful demonstration of television. This was also the year that the Book-of-the-Month Club came into existence and that contract bridge supplanted auction bridge as a national pastime.

The first commercial broadcasting radio station, KDKA in Pittsburgh, Pennsylvania, went on the air in 1920. By 1926, over 550 stations were licensed, and the National Broadcasting Corporation began operation. Henry Ford still produced the Model T, but he had begun to lose

3

ground to General Motors' Chevrolet as well as to the Chrysler Corporation's Imperial.

Names that would become household words for generations reached their positions of power during that fateful year. Chiang Kai-Shek fought rival warlords and unified China; Joseph Stalin established himself as a virtual dictator of the Soviet Union, beginning a twenty-seven year rule; and Japanese Emperor Yoshihito died, to be succeeded by Emperor Hirohito.

Among the prominent figures who passed away that year were Annie Oakley, famed crack shot of fact and fiction, and Rudolph Valentino, the romantic thirty-one-year-old of silent motion picture fame.

Yes, 1926 was a significant year for many people. For me, 1926 was not only important but essential. Oblivious to the momentuous events taking place in a turbulent world, I arrived on the cold bleak morning of October 19, 1926, the second son of William John and Edith Alice Phillips.

My brother Jack, born September, 1924, and I were fortunate that our mother and father ever became acquainted because their romance and subsequent marriage in 1923 could only have taken place in the New World. A monumental disparity in the social backgrounds of my grandparents, both English, made it unlikely that my parents would have met if their families had remained in Europe. In Winnipeg, however, the contrast in their heritage was inconsequential. Unquestionably, the dissimilarity in their early upbringing caused some grating in their life together, but they probably enjoyed a far happier marriage than most.

My paternal grandfather, born and reared in England, was completely illiterate. In the early 1890's, he arrived in Winnipeg with little money, one child, and a pregnant wife. The City of Winnipeg gave him a job in the waterworks department. An immensely powerful man, he had an outrageous temper, an outstanding memory, and the desire to work.

Promoted to superintendent in charge of laying water mains, he soon became responsible for a sizable work force. Laborers in those days, mostly illiterate immigrants from Europe, were almost as rugged as Grandfather Phillips, so his mountainous strength and bulldog determination came in good stead in keeping his crews in line. He memorized the hours worked by each man, and on returning home, he gave the figures to his wife who did the bookkeeping. Grandmother Phillips, a darling person also from poor English parentage, had only an elementary education. My father, the second of the Phillips clan born in Canada, was followed by five more for a total of eight.

My mother, born in England, came from a family of wealth and prominence. The Rodd family tree reaches back to King Richard II, or Richard the Lion Hearted. The family emigrated to Canada when she was nine years old, which unfortunately cost her the opportunity to obtain the excellent education that would have been available in England. Grandfather Rodd, highly intelligent, exceedingly well-educated and reasonably affluent, married beneath his station in life, which contributed to a miserable marriage and an early breakup, but not before he had sired five children.

In the early 1920's he deserted his family and emigrated to Florida where he remarried and had another daughter. Mother made contact with him in the 1930's, and from that point on, he corresponded with all his children and grandchildren individually until his death in 1949. I deeply regret not having had the opportunity to meet Grandfather Rodd, without question a brilliant individualist.

Father had to leave school after completing only grade four to help support the family which had a total of ten mouths to feed. An intelligent man and an avid reader, he kept abreast of world affairs and was considered extremely knowledgeable by his peers who often sought him out for advice and counsel.

At the time of his marriage, he and two of his brothers owned and operated a successful meat-rendering business in Winnipeg. He also owned a car, a luxury that in those days could be afforded only by an affluent few. He and Mother resided in a pleasant neighborhood in the city.

In all respects, they lived the good life. They spent most of their free time in the country as they both enjoyed picnicking, camping, hunting and other outdoor activities. Their favorite haunt was located about thirty miles east of Winnipeg in a farming community called Monominto. Mother had resided there for a few years shortly after emigrating from England, though upon their arrival, the Rodd family spent several months in a little town of Fleming, Saskatchewan, fifteen miles west of the Manitoba border.

Father, convinced there would be a Great Depression at least one year before it occurred, purchased 160 acres of land in Monominto as a sort of family refuge. Strewn with rocks, partially covered with a poor grade of white poplar bush and consisting of a light, sandy soil, it was a poor choice for farming, but no one could dispute its natural attractiveness. All the buildings on the property were in a sad state of disrepair. The dilapidated house, our living quarters during our entire stay on the farm, consisted of a two-story frame structure that had been added to a hoary one-story log cabin. Both sections of the dwelling were old, but the log segment dated back to the middle of the last century. Some idiot, years before our arrival, had used sand to insulate the frame portion. At almost any hour of the day or night, particularly when a wind shook the sagging old house, the sand, obeying the law of gravity, sounded similar to a gentle waterfall as it trickled ever downward. This might have been pleasant enough had it not constantly reminded us we were gradually running out of insulation, and even on that score it proved to be a dismal failure.

There were also other ramshackle, deteriorating log structures that could be used for horse and cattle barns, chicken houses, and pig sties. Actually, the buildings were about as unsuitable for successful farming as the land itself. I believe Father, though born and raised in the city, always secretly planned on becoming a farmer, and was looking for an excuse to move to what he considered his "Shangri-La." His later claim of sensing the onrushing Depression as his reason may not have been entirely accurate, and later events would seem to confirm my suspicions.

The first two or three years of my life were probably spent in utopian surroundings. I had doting parents with sufficient money to satisfy my every whim, plus an overly protective older brother. I surmise that Jack was solicitous because in later life he always came to my assistance when he thought it was required, often to his chagrin and dismay. We did, however, retain a close relationship throughout our lives. All dozen or so of our uncles and aunts, plus three of our grandparents lived in nearby neighborhoods. So Jack and I, two of the first three of the third generation, benefited enormously from this happy situation. On birthdays, Christmas, Easter and any other special occasions, we were the recipients of an ample supply of the good things in life. Unfortunately, dark clouds hovered on the horizon auguring a terrible downturn in the fortunes of most everyone, and I wasn't to be excluded.

Chapter 2

My World in Collapse

An epidemic of Polio—we called it infantile paralysis then—swept western Canada and northwestern United States in 1928. The medical profession did not know how to stop the spread or how to treat the afflicted. As a result, many youngsters lost their lives. I was stricken, but it was my good fortune not to die. Being too young to recall any of the circumstances, I repeat the story as related to me by my mother. One evening during the epidemic, we had a roast wild duck dinner with all the trimmings plus ice cream and cake. Although on the alert for symptoms of the scourge, especially with small children, my parents hopefully assumed when I took sick shortly after dinner that it was simply from overindulgence. The following day, however, while standing in my playpen and still violently ill, my legs suddenly caved in. They then became frightened and rushed me to the hospital where apparently I was on the brink of death for several days. At that point in my life, it wouldn't have made any difference to me whether I expired or not.

This unhappy occurrence left me partially paralyzed from my right hip to my foot. It would be several years before I discovered how extremely lucky I was not only to have survived the epidemic but also to have retained sufficient use of my right limb to be able to walk, though with a decided limp and recurring pain. I never anguished over what the situation might have been had my parents rushed me to the hospital on the first sign of sickness. It's possible I might not have suffered any serious disability. Like many other doting parents, they hesitated because they didn't want to believe their child had contacted the dreaded disease. How many times in the future would I encounter a similar dilemma? Parents faced with certain situations concerning

7

their children can only do what they believe is the best at the moment and can't torment themselves with any ill-fated results.

Sister Ruth, born in August, 1929, accompanied the family to the Monominto farm in late autumn of the same year while I convalesced from my illness at the home of Aunt Edna and Uncle Jim, my father's oldest brother.

Dad immediately stocked his farm with cattle, pigs, horses, and chickens. It was too late in the season to plant crops, and so he was forced to purchase hay and grain for the animals' winter feed, a significant factor in Father's financial demise. Nevertheless, the shocking stockmarket crash on October 29, 1929, which heralded the Great Depression and bound the world in chains of poverty for over a decade, was the principal cause.

Considered affluent by our neighbors at the time, we took up residence in Monominto. We had a truck, a new car, and modern furniture that looked sadly out of place in the dilapidated old house. I joined the family during the second winter, and by this time the Depression had taken a dreadful toll of our family's reserves. Cows that Father paid one hundred dollars apiece for the summer before the collapse were suddenly worth less than five dollars. Dad acquired four pregnant sows from which he successfully raised four large litters of healthy piglets. Regrettably, he would have been much further ahead if he had drowned the lot or shot the sows before they farrowed. The sows and their young were fed throughout the winter on high-priced grain bought before the downturn, but by the time they were ready for market, the price of pork had dropped from sixty to five cents per pound.

By the summer of 1930, the Phillipses were poorer than anyone in the community, and Father wasn't an experienced farmer. The car and truck were sold for next to nothing, and we didn't own another self-propelled wheeled vehicle until 1943 when Father bought a 1929 Graham Paige.

The reason I questioned Father's claim of clairvoyance regarding the impending financial collapse is because if he had simply moved to the farm and then waited until disaster struck before purchasing animals and equipment he not only would have remained solvent but also have been the wealthiest farmer in the area. He could have stocked his farm at a fraction of the cost to boot. I'm sure he thought of that himself many times during the next decade as he and his family struggled and suffered with everyone else through the world's worst depression. Hindsight has always been a more exact science than foresight, and he was not alone in his misery.

Following the stock market crash, the early thirties were the worst years as world trade declined, production dropped and unemployment skyrocketed. In 1931 and '32, more than 3,500 banks closed their doors. Between 1929 and '32, auto sales declined from $5 million to $1 million, and two out of three Detroit auto workers became idle. The average weekly wage across the country fell to seventeen dollars, and it took the equivalent of nine bushels of wheat to buy a pair of work boots. Financial panic and economic disintegration not only affected North America but also engulfed most of the world's two billion population.

My recollection of those first years following the crash of '29 are dim, though I know I suffered none of the hardships encountered by many of our countrymen. We endured considerable inconvenience, however, because the 20 miles that separated us from the nearest electric power meant we had no electric lights, refrigeration, running water, or any convenience appliances. During those early years we used only kerosene lamps in the house and kerosene lanterns in the outbuildings. Anyone not having experienced the use of kerosene lighting didn't miss a thing. They gave a flickering light similar to two large candles. I must admit nonetheless that on cold, dark, blustery winter evenings when I'd peek through the frost-encrusted windows and watch Father moving around the farmyard doing evening chores that the soft yellow light from a swaying lantern in his hand gave me a sense of contentment as it danced and ricocheted off the sparkling snow banks. As for refrigeration, we had more than required during the long winter months, but we suffered through the spring and summer when keeping perishable food was impossible. Bologna and smoked meat then became our staple diet.

All drinking and wash water had to be hand-pumped and hauled from a well located a hundred yards from the kitchen. This was a cumbersome chore but the least inequity of being without running water. Our outhouse situated 150 yards from the main residence meant that if nature called during the dark hours of a winter night with the wind howling, the snow blowing, and the temperature hovering around 30 degrees below zero we suddenly realized we did not live in the best of all worlds. Lacking electric appliances wasn't really much of a hardship because we never experienced the pleasure of using them. Toast from an open wood stove tasted considerably better than it ever did from an electric toaster. A large, iron cook stove heated the kitchen while the rest of the living quarters were warmed by a potbellied furnace that sat in the living room on the ground floor. Stove pipes extended from that stove through the ceiling to the second floor, the total extent of heat received on that level. Coal was unavailable, and so we used wood. Fires stoked for the night at 10 p.m. were only ashes by 2 a.m. At 6 o'clock in the morning, after a particularly frigid night, an inch of ice covered the waterpail in the kitchen and the first person out of bed to rekindle the stove was no coward indeed.

My responsibility for chore sharing started at the tender age of six. Milking cows, one of the first duties assumed by every child in the neighborhood, was a red letter day for every farmer. As much as his offspring, he detested the onerous task of hand milking twice daily and could hardly wait for those little hands to grow strong enough to grasp and squeeze. Keeping a sufficient supply of firewood in the house was a close second of dreaded daily chores. Logs had to be hand-bucked into suitable lengths, axed into pieces and toted and piled behind the stoves. On cold winter evenings, with a frosty north wind whipping icy snowflakes against our faces, the slow, torturous process of administering to the twenty-four hour needs of two hungry stoves was a chore equally loathed by both Jack and me.

One of the topics we youngsters usually discussed to keep our minds off the biting cold while performing those painful tasks, were the comics that came in the *Prairie Farmer*, our weekly newspaper. How vividly I recall worrying about whether Punjab or the Asp would show up in time to help poor little Orphan Annie or Daddy Warbucks out of whatever dilemma they found themselves in at the time, and how excited we'd get considering the outstanding help Punjab would be with our wood chores. Popeye and Olive Oyl were great conversation pieces as were Alley Oop, Dick Tracy, Mickey Mouse and L'il Abner.

We had no radio during those years, but our wind-up gramophone provided pleasure for everyone. Fortunately, Mother and Father had accumulated a large assortment of records before moving to the country. They gave us much of our evening entertainment, particularly on winter nights after the chores were completed. When I hear songs like "Dancing with Tears In My Eyes", "Embraceable You", "Goodnight Sweetheart", "In a Shanty In Old Shanty Town", "Lazy Bones", or "Tumbling Tumble Weed", sentimental memories of that bygone era come flooding back. Father, a frustrated drummer, kept time with the music by tapping a pair of table forks on a block of wood while we three kids huddled by a roaring fire, caring little about the misery that prevailed over most of the earth.

After the first snowfall in early November, all roads in the neighborhood were impassable to motorized traffic. There were no snowplows. From then until spring break up around mid-April, horses provided the only means of transportation. Those winters of the Great Depression spawned a unique bartering system in the Manitoba bush country. Farmers, either from their own land or by sneaking onto numerous off limit government tracts, would cut and haul back to their respective farms sleigh loads of full-length poplar trees. The trees were then hand sawed into four-foot lengths, split in half and reloaded onto wood racks in one cord quantities—a cord being a full 128-cubic feet or a pile of wood four feet high, eight feet long, and four feet in width. Owners of local general stores traded $1.25 worth of goods for one cord of wood, which had to be piled at the store beside a main road. Winnipeg fuel dealers bought the cordwood for resale as city firewood when the roads became passable for their trucks in the spring. The store owner made a profit, farmers obtained necessities, and the fuel dealers were happy, so it proved to be quite a satisfactory arrangement all around.

I frequently accompanied Father on his trips to the store when he went to swap his cord of wood for stock feed and household essentials. General stores were the local meeting places where farmers sat on nail kegs around potbellied stoves and discussed the sad shape of the world.

During the winter of 1933, I'd often hear the name of Adolph Hitler, newly elected Chancellor of Germany, and President Franklin D. Roosevelt. Roosevelt entered the White House that spring with 15 million Americans out of work. "The only thing we have to fear is fear itself," he said. His radio broadcasts always began, "My friends. . ." as he tried to calm Depression fears and win support for his "New Deal." Typical annual earnings were: physicians, $3,382; lawyers, $4,218; engineers, $2,250; construction workers, $907; public school teachers $1,227; and farm workers, $216, which meant farm laborers earned about $4.00 weekly, though room and board were included.

In Canada, the government instituted a plan where they paid a man $5.00 per month to work on a farm, and paid the farmer $5.00 per month to feed the worker, though most farmers gave the workman their $5.00 for tobacco and clothes. The Dow Jones Industrial Average reached its lowest historical point of 41.22 in 1932 but made a slight comeback in 1933 which indicated a tiny ray of light at the end of the tunnel.

Chapter 3

On the Farm

Exactly 2½ miles separated Pinewood School from our farmhouse by road. This distance could be shortened slightly by cutting across hay fields and through stands of hardwoods. The school building sat squeezed into one corner of a ten-acre parcel about one-third of which contained the ball field and general playground. Heavy bush covered the balance. At the edge of the bush stood the boys' and girls' toilets, with the girls' outhouse about a hundred yards from the school and the boys' twice that distance. They were what we classified as two-holers, and the boys' unit, usually in a sorry state of disarray for several reasons, never contained toilet tissue. This was probably due to the simple fact that the school teacher, always female, never inspected the boys' toilet, which made it an ideal sanctuary for smoking cigarettes made of dry leaves and wrapped in brown lunch bag paper.

The single classroom of 150 square feet could hold about thirty students with two sitting at each double desk. Throughout the ten years I attended, we never had more than eighteen students nor less than twelve, who were taught Grades I to VIII by one teacher. An adjoining cloak room resembled a second-hand clothing store, particularly in winter, due to the massive quantity of outer garments the students wore to ward off the freezing temperatures. The school board assigned to older students the tasks of keeping the drinking water bucket filled all year and the stove stoked in the winter months. Hauling the school's water requirements from a farm a half mile away earned that lucky pupil ten cents per day. The job of attending the stove included starting the fire at least a half hour before the 9 o'clock opening of classes, carrying the wood supply into the school from an outside pile, and keeping the stove fired up until the 4 o'clock bell. This pupil's contract required him to start on November first and continue until Easter, about 90 days, with any additional heating needs to be provided gratis. Like the water carrier, he was also paid a dime a day, receiving his check from the generous school board at the end of the season. This prize contract of keeping the schoolroom warm became mine for the final 3 years I attended Pinewood School, but that's getting ahead of my story.

I started walking to school in 1932, though during severe weather Mother taught me simple arithmetic and spelling at home. The paralysis in my right lower limb severely retarded its growth, and so as I grew, the rest of my body rapidly left my right leg behind. Not only the difference in length created a problem, but also the leg began twisting. My parents said I fell an average of three times every hundred yards I walked, though I was too young for that obvious inconvenience to leave any lasting impression. Naturally, as I grew taller, the situation worsened. A person such as Franklin D. Roosevelt who was stricken with polio as a grown man had to suffer mentally a great deal more than I because he lost a freedom of movement he had known all his life. This sudden restriction had to be a tremendous shock to his system. My body adjusted gradually as I matured.

Recreation at school during lunch hour and recess was vitally important. It offered about the only play time any of us ever had. Our days began before 7 a.m. After an hour of farm chores, we had breakfast and then made a dash for school. We were expected home within an hour of our final class, and except for a short snack break, we then completed another three hours of farm work before supper and homework. Free time at school was therefore precious, so we made the most of it.

Immediately after the first major snowstorm, we prepared the playing field for a game of "Fox and Goose," a form of tag. We trampled out a huge circle in the snow, with a smaller circle inside the larger. Several spokes were extended from the inner circle to the perimeter with the finished pattern resembling a gigantic wheel. The center circle became home base, and one was safe while within its confines. When outside, he was fair game to be tagged by one of the two "it" kids at which point he became "it."

While playing this game one day, I suddenly awoke to the fact I lacked the maneuverability of the others. Whenever I'd step out of the center safety zone, I'd be immediately tagged and then spend the balance of the recess period trying unsuccessfully to catch someone else. After several frustrating and embarrassing attempts, I realized the futility of the task, and so I changed my strategy. When "it," I simply stood there ignoring everyone rather than making a fool of myself in a useless chase. Now, instead of razzing and teasing me, the others became irritated because they were standing around getting cold, so eventually one of them would come and touch me just to get the game re-started. Being the only one roaming the paths without fear of being caught probably should have disturbed me, but I distinctly recall loving the immunity and roamed the snowy layout at my leisure, though often I'd be bowled into the snow by the older students as they whizzed past. We played many other winter games, including a form of snow hockey, where we used a rubber ball and curved sticks cut from a cherry tree.

In summer the main sport was softball, and due to a lack of available players, I always participated in the action. Hunting prairie gophers with homemade slingshots also took up much of our idle school hours during spring and early summer. This was an activity at which I matched the best. Gophers were great pests. They destroyed huge amounts of grain and also made it dangerous for horses that would step on burrows in the fields. Farmers paid us one cent per tail. Creating slingshots out of old rubber inner-tubes and the "y" of a willow tree was a craft, and using them with accuracy was a skill. Every farmer's son had some ability in both.

The four seasons in Manitoba, each as dissimilar as clouds in a summer sky, played significant roles in giving variation to our daily pursuits both at home and at school. Summer holidays to a farmer's child was a grave misnomer, for if we had a half day per week to ourselves during the daylight hours of our so-called "vacation," we were indeed fortunate. As a result when returning to school in September, we were gratified to have at last a little leisure time.

For the first week or two we simply relaxed in the warm autumn sun during the lunch period, and rebuilt our stamina from the contents in the brown paper bag we all carried to school. Frequently the bag and some dried poplar leaves were fashioned into crude cigarettes, a combination ranker than anything else I ever smoked including the strongest of cigars. When questioned by Mother of the bag's whereabouts, we generally complained that it furnished a terribly coarse substitute for toilet tissue. Burned eyebrows and hair were more difficult to explain.

Early fall months on the farm were especially strenuous. Haying and harvesting had to be completed, vegetables such as potatoes, carrots, turnips, and cabbages reaped and prepared for winter storage, and root crops like mangels and field turnips pulled, hauled and stored in huge root cellars to provide the stock with winter forage. Also, barns and other animal shelters needed plastering to be sealed for the rapidly approaching winter. By mid-October, following the Canadian Thanksgiving, the first heavy snow clouds began scudding across the sky, shedding lazy snowflakes that reluctantly sailed earthward before settling momentarily on a land made barren by weeks of nightly frosts but still retaining enough warmth to melt those early harbingers. By month's end, the clouds would stop fooling around and drop their loads in earnest, covering the bleak landscape with a mantle of white, hailing the onslaught of another frigid winter. This meant the stock would be billeted in stables for another five or six months. Beginning all over again was the thankless task of cleaning barns, hauling feed, and watering the animals.

Despite the swiftly approaching cold, late autumn always seemed a particularly pleasant and exhilarating time of the year. The heavy summer workload was finally over. Multitudes of Canadian geese winging their way south, gaggling and honking in gigantic V's, offered a pulse-throbbing farewell salute to those of us left behind. Also in preparation for their departure, ducks, robins, wrens, swallows, blackbirds, crows, and a multitude of others banded together in last-minute rallies before joining the massive migration. It was a soul-searching time for me as I often wondered if I would ever see those far-off lands where snow appeared only on post cards.

Both wild and domestic birds and animals played a dramatic role in every farmer's life in rural Manitoba. One of the saddest situations faced by country people was disposing of domestic animals no longer useful. A faithful horse who had labored long and hard ended up as fox meat. An old cow, no longer breedable and unable to produce milk, was shipped to the bologna factory. The farmer had no choice. Restricted barn space and pastures could nourish only a limited number of beasts. Economics had to overcome sentimentality. Many a tear was shed, however, when one of those loyal servants had to be dispatched.

Killing wildlife savagely and indiscriminately was abhorrent to most farmers. They detested those fanatics who roved the countryside practicing their marksmanship by destroying harmless birds and animals, such as robins, rabbits, or red squirrels, and calling it sport. I vividly recall Jack and I being incensed when any of our city relatives who, when visiting the farm, began shooting at any wild game that moved. They couldn't understand our hostility because they knew slaughtering animals in cold blood was commonplace to us.

On the farm we butchered pigs, chickens, turkeys, cows, and sheep either for the market or for our own consumption. Several species of birds and animals were destroyed for various reasons. Gophers and ground squirrels ravaged valuable crops; crows, owls, hawks, and skunks had insatiable appetites for turkey and chicken eggs; wolves and foxes constantly preyed on young lambs, poultry, and piglets. We undoubtedly considered hunting deer, moose, ducks, and geese for the table, a form of sport, but that was secondary to their delight of providing fresh meat for the table. Trapping and hunting coyotes, weasel, mink, fox, skunk and other fur-bearing animals added to our meager cash supply as well as ridding our farmyard of the most pestering predators.

In late fall, Jack and I acted as bird dogs for Father on hunting excursions for prairie chicken and partridge by flushing the prey to within range of his shotgun. At other times, we tramped the woods searching for deer that we'd try to chase into the sights of his 30/30 Winchester. Thoughts of roasted partridge stuffed with dressing or venison liver fried with onions and served with fresh home-baked bread would drive us to exhaustion. With few exceptions, it would be the first fresh meat we had tasted since March, and we were hungry for it.

Our attitude toward certain wild creatures, deer in particular, seemed strange and inconsistent. While working in the hay field throughout spring and summer, captivating does with spirited fawns would feed and gambol within a few hundred feet without showing fear of either us or the horses. While admiring their grace and beauty, we wouldn't consider doing them harm, and this they seemed to realize. In late autumn, however, after the first fall of snow, when keeping meat fresh without refrigeration no longer created a problem, we immediately experienced a change of heart and couldn't wait for the delicious odor of frying venison. The deer, as if sensing our altered frame of mind, now became adept at hide and seek. Dogs were outlawed for deer hunting in Manitoba, and so we had to pit our proficiency against the cunning of the deer. Generally we bagged enough to keep the larder stocked during the winter months, though we supplemented our game supply with beef, pork, and mutton from our own barnyard. Only strict vegetarians can honestly condemn the taking of an animal's life for food. Realistically, if noncarnivorous beasts were uncontrolled, there wouldn't be any vegetables. Man *is* carnivorous, and the balance of nature would be sadly affected if he suddenly lost his appetite for meat.

The daily excursions to and from school became especially invigo-rating during the months between Thanksgiving and Christmas. Our route followed the main road for a half mile and then zigzagged the final two miles through heavily wooded sections of a wide variety of soft-woods and hardwoods. Each area attracted a different species of wild-life, and they left their patchwork of footprints in the freshly fallen snow. Wildlife dramas of nature's continuous battle for survival would be graphically exhibited in the blanket of white as clearly as if you had been a spectator. Rabbit tracks in an erratic pattern signified pursuit, and if you followed a short distance, the site of the final act was generally the same. Bloodstained snow and chunks of fluff were unmistakable signs that a cottontail had reached an untimely end. At the scene of the crime, telltale tracks of fox, hawk, or owl left no doubt as to the per-petrator of the assassination. The same clues clearly identified a deer being chased by a pack of coyotes. Again, if the tracks were followed for a distance, the outcome would be obvious. Either the victim had become a meal or had foiled its pursuers and would live and learn from the ordeal. The stealth and cunning of most predators amazed me. Many times I've followed weasel's prints as it scurried in and out of stone piles and hollow logs searching for dinner, and then come upon a small bird, claws firmly clenched on a small twig, appearing natural as if in the midst of a song but frozen stiff . . . its life blood sucked out.

I added to the problems of the animal kingdom by the time I was eight years of age. Father wanted cottontails for chicken feed, and so I learned at an early age how to set snares on their runways and catch the unsuspecting and harmless little animals in an unrelenting noose. Returning home from school, I frequently had a half dozen rabbits for the hen house. I froze any surplus carcasses into bundles and sold them to fox farmers for a few pennies per pound. At that time, I never considered the torture those creatures experienced. The wonderful things I could purchase with the earned silver was of far greater significance. In the long run it made little difference. Every seven years, the cottontail population reached staggering proportions. Then the animals contracted an epidemic disease and expired by the thousands. I've seen dozens dying in the woods of this recurring illness, and they suffered much longer and more horribly than if they had perished by my primitive methods. As winter progressed, many animals did not forage as far for food, particularly deer and moose. Others, like skunks, bears, and groundhogs, hibernated until spring. So the stories related by snow graphics diminished, and only the hardier mammals, such as us humans, continued to trudge relentlessly through the deepening snow.

The most enjoyable season during those troubled years was Christmas and New Year. The excitement built slowly, beginning when we started planning the annual Christmas concert after the school Halloween party and climaxing in the pleasurable activity of Christmas morning. Several factors contributed to our high spirits, such as the concert, new toys, distinctive holiday fare, and the relaxation of our work schedule.

The limited number of students attending our school dictated that each had to participate in several roles in the concert held about a week before Christmas. The daily preparation for the annual show offered a marvelous opportunity to avoid the humdrum of school work for short durations and allow the humbug in most of us an opportunity to manifest itself. Our varied parts consisted of: singing a solo or being part of a choir for Christmas Carols, acting in a hodgepodge of roles in the several plays, reciting a story or poem, or practicing to be an adequate stage hand.

Choosing the gift we would receive from the school board at the program's completion required serious thought as it provided the first opportunity in a year to consider a plaything. Our school board allowance of 50¢ for the single gift would purchase any one of a number of items, including a small box of Tinkertoys, a single-reeded mouth organ, coloring book with crayons, games such as "Snakes and Ladders," or building blocks. We all chose carefully. At least three items in order of preference were submitted to the school teacher and frequently the two gifts we didn't receive then showed up under the tree on Christmas morning. Obviously some scheming went on between our parents and the school board.

During most of my time, the concert was held at the Pinewood Community Hall, three hundred yards from our residence. On days of rehearsal, we would hike to school in the morning and return by early afternoon. Though handy for us, it was an inconvenience for those children living miles in the opposite direction from Pinewood School. Nevertheless, those special December afternoon outings of long ago are pleasant memories.

On normal winter days, a total of six or eight students would join us somewhere along our two-and-a-half-mile route to school. But on those rare rehearsal afternoons at the Pinewood Hall site, all fifteen or so of our schoolmates made the trek together, and it was always a fun-filled jaunt. There were snowball fights, wrestling bouts, and cranberry races.

Cranberries never fall from their bushes in autumn with their leaves. They hang in clusters like small brilliant red grapes, easily spotted being so vividly silhouetted against the snow. The berries, frozen solid, had a pleasant, tart, tangy taste when allowed to melt slowly in your mouth. And so, racing through the snowy woods after sighting a cranberry bush provided another popular sport. Obviously, the spirit of the festive season played a major part in our high jinks, but they were unforgettable, happy times when not too much happiness existed in the world.

If my old school chums or myself could now see one of our Christmas concert performances, we would likely find it hilarious and not too professional. Our neighbors and families were rarely critical, however, and so the quality of our presentation didn't really matter. After the final curtain, one of our neighbors in a Santa Claus costume handed out those precious gifts and from that point every performer forgot those embarrassing moments when he or she had forgotten lines in a play or were singing the wrong words to the Christmas song. It was always a night to remember, moreso perhaps because it also officially started our Christmas break and the beginning of the final preparation for the big day itself.

Parents and neighbors came to the school concert either on foot or a horse-drawn winter conveyance. A makeshift frame building constructed two hundred feet from the dance hall protected the horses from the worst of the wintry blasts, inevitable at that time of year. Even in the shelter horses were heavily draped with thick woolen blankets that doubled as a means of warmth for their human cargo on the return home. Every farmer had sleigh bells attached to the harness with no two sets producing identical tones. They offered an enchanting and musical departure when the party broke up and all the sleigh bells blended into a cacophony of chimes as they slowly faded into the cold winter night.

Although the Canadian government never approved prohibition, the cost of store-bought whiskey was too expensive in those cash-short times. For libation, most farmers bought a bottle of "home-brew," which wasn't homemade beer but a whiskey distilled from potatoes, barley, or any ingredient that would produce alcohol. I don't know the proof of the concoction, but it certainly offered more punch than the product approved by the government. Homebrew, relatively inexpensive and purchased from the local bootlegger who of course attended all events, was usually diluted with a variety of mixes—tea, honey, soft drinks or other liquids—but some of the heartier souls drank it straight.

Farmers had little opportunity for relaxation or visitation, and so on the evening of the Christmas concert and the following dance, they made the most of the occasion. Merriment and festivities rarely stopped before 3 or 4 a.m., and morning chore time had arrived when most families reached home. I will vouch that many a cow who received unusually rough treatment at the morning milking or a horse failing to receive his morning allowance of oats had good reason to be thankful the Christmas concert happened only once a year.

The few days before Christmas were exceptionally busy ones for our family. Father raised turkeys that had to be killed, plucked, packed and delivered to Winnipeg for the holiday market. This enormous task could only be started a few days before actual delivery because we couldn't properly refrigerate the birds after they were dressed. The turkeys roosted in maple trees and along wooden fences that surrounded our farmyard. We would starve the birds at least twelve hours before preparing them for market so their craws would be empty. At dark we would sneak up behind the sleeping birds, grasp them by their legs, and then pen them up so they couldn't feed. Those captured set up a terrible squawking, badly frightening those still roosting, and so by the time we approached the last few, they were pretty skittish. Turkeys rarely fly and have little use for their wings, but I witnessed on several occasions a turkey in the ten- or twenty-pound range, frightened by the furor of the flock, soar off into the black of the night, land a quarter mile away, and then run through the deep snow for two or more miles with Jack and me and our wildly swaying kerosene lantern in hot pursuit. We always caught our quarry but not before we were all quite exhausted. We never regretted the extra effort though because money received from the sale of poultry paid for those special purchases required for a successful holiday.

On the farm we always had plenty of wholesome food, but luxury items were rare except for Christmas and New Years. The Christmas cake, usually the first treat to appear and prepared several weeks in advance of the big day, scarcely ever saw the light of Christmas morn, as every member of the family nibbled away from the moment it emerged from the oven. Christmas pudding, another delicacy of the season, wasn't offered up until Christmas dinner. At the concert, every child received a small sack of mixed candies, assorted nuts, an apple and an orange. This bag of goodies, almost as welcome as the gift, didn't last long as we were allowed to devour the contents at our discretion. From the cash realized from the sale of the turkeys, our parents bought a delightful mixture of Christmas treats: mixed nuts, candies, oranges, apples, figs, dates plus a variety of cookies and shortbread. For Christmas morning breakfast, our folks had smoked finnan-haddie, a highlight of the day for them, but one of those dishes for which I never acquired a taste.

Both holiday dinners were a masterpiece of planning and preparation. The main course consisted of turkey plus chicken or goose, at least four varieties of vegetables including red cabbage, a holiday necessity, mashed potatoes, thick brown gravy, bowls of spicy dressing and bread sauce. Bread sauce, a holdover from our English heritage, was another dish for which I never cultivated a palate. Recalling those massive feasts topped off with steaming plum pudding and rich, creamy homemade ice cream seems almost sacrilegious when during those times thousands of North Americans had no more on their Christmas platter than a bowl of broth and a crust of stale bread.

One episode of those early days remains etched in my memory. Our turkey crop had been a disaster, and the holidays were approaching with little available cash for the festivities. Jack and I still believed in Santa Claus, and so were not too concerned, though we understood our accustomed Christmas treats would be greatly diminished. Father, however, devised a plan in the middle of December to alleviate the family's financial woes. He and a neighbor, Herman Edie, hitched up a team of horses to a sleigh with a hayrack, drove to some government lands about eight miles away, and brought back a load of Christmas trees. A week prior to December 25th and again by horsepower, they hauled their cargo to Winnipeg in the hope of selling the trees either wholesale or retail.

Picture the circumstances: a team of plodding farm horses, moving at a speed of three miles per hour at most, temperatures of 20 degrees below zero during the day and plunging to 40 degrees below at night; and Father and Herman trudging behind the torturously slow-moving load of evergreens trying to keep their feet from freezing. They had to travel a distance of 40 miles to reach their destination, which meant they were on the road for eighteen hours including stops at some benevolent farmers to rest, water, and feed the weary animals. Despite the difficulties, they reached Winnipeg without a major problem and then tried to peddle their payload.

Due to the lateness of the season, the wholesalers already had their inventory, and so the two men had no other option but try to sell the trees door to door, asking from 25¢ to $1.00 depending on the size of the tree. Sales were slow as city people also had little surplus cash. By December 23rd, they had sold less than half their load, raising a meager fifty dollars. Though not exactly a financial success, it enabled them to purchase a few of the items so important to a successful holiday. They started for home early on the morning of Christmas Eve. The fierce cold worsened, and the temperature sank to 50 degrees below zero by evening.

The farm chores kept Mother, Jack, and me busy most of the day and part of the evening. On December 24th, Mother and Jack traipsed through the deep snow into the woods to locate a suitable Christmas tree for our living room. As evening approached, Mother became frantic with no sign of the travelers, and without telephones Father couldn't contact her. Jack and I, though concerned for Father's well-being, didn't worry about Christmas gifts because we trusted Santa would make it through the frigid night.

Mother recounted the final details of the episode many times in the following years, especially during the holiday season. After we went to bed, she began decorating the house and the tree. Every few minutes she would don a heavy sweater and go outside to listen for the sound of familiar sleigh bells. It was past 1 a.m. when she finally heard the faint tinkle of bells and recognized them as ours. The faithful team of horses, moving slowly in the biting cold with the two men plodding behind, seemed to take forever to reach the farmyard. As often happens in circumstances of this sort, the sudden release of pent-up emotions caused her to bawl the daylights out of Father for a few minutes before she calmed down and tearfully welcomed them both home. One of Father's feet was partially frozen, and both men were exhausted, hungry, and chilled to their marrow. Otherwise they were none the worse for wear. Santa showed up as expected, and as I relax today in my Florida environment, it is difficult to associate myself as being part of those bizarre events of a half century ago.

Another incident that became part of the saga of the Christmas tree trip occurred a few short hours after our exhausted Mother and Father finally retired for the night. Jack and I shared a large double bed with a headboard right at the edge of the open stairway leading to our second-story bedroom. Our Christmas stockings were hung on the headboard. Jack awoke before daylight, and anxious to learn if Old Saint Nick had paid us a visit, reached out in the dark to feel his stocking and he joyously discovered it had been filled to the neck. Excited and trying to determine the contents, he accidentally wakened me and at the same moment dislodged an apple tucked into the very top of the stocking. The thump, thump, thump of the errant fruit as it went bouncing down the full flight of stairs frightened us because we had been warned that if anything disturbed Santa during his visit he would disappear without leaving gifts.

Both convinced that the unfortunate accident had ruined our special day and unable to stand the anxiety, Jack tiptoed downstairs on the pretext of retrieving his apple if he got caught. On the other hand, if our exhausted parents didn't awaken, he decided to peek into the living room to discern what disaster, if any, his little faux-pas had caused. Returning to bed with an enormous sigh of relief, he whispered that Santa had already paid his visit. As a result, we did not sleep for the balance of the night. Our parents remembered that particular Christmas season for the nasty episode with the trees, but for us children, it turned out to be one of the best Christmases ever.

I don't recall having an unpleasant Christmas on the farm. Our parents were mainly responsible for creating a happy atmosphere, but Jack and I contributed as well. Before I was ten years old and Jack twelve, we spent our spare hours during December in a nearby poplar bush where we chopped down and sawed up in four-foot lengths, split and piled, a couple of cords of wood that we delivered to the local general store and swapped for three dollars worth of trade goods. The first gift I picked for Father was a pound of tea (he drank at least fifteen cups a day). I gaily wrapped it and placed it under the Christmas tree. Jack's first choice, a box of chocolates, now seems like a more logical selection.

Our parents were closer to their children than are most parents of today. Conditions, of course, were far different. Parents and children were rarely separated in our day and therefore had much greater influence on each other. Today's families are usually together for only short intervals. Both of our parents were exceptional individuals in their own special ways, although Dad had a terrible mean streak at times—which I inherited from him and from Grandfather Phillips. Despite his bad temper, he had a great zest for life and all that it encompassed.

Mom, an unsung genius in many ways, followed in her father's footsteps as an excellent artist specializing in landscapes and pastoral scenes, utilizing both oils and water colors. Most young couples in the area would request one of her pictures for a wedding gift, and many of her paintings still decorate the walls of homes in southern Manitoba. Mother had the ability to create with her hands almost anything her mind could conceive. She could construct a doll house and fill it with authentic furniture, more lifelike than anything bought at a store. With a simple piece of cardboard and a pair of scissors as her only instrument, she could assemble a miniature kitchen suite or produce a sofa and chair set for the doll house living room—and all during afternoon tea!

Mom never missed an opportunity to add a little family joy to the humdrum existence of those Depression days on the farm. Valentine's Day would find an intricately designed and decorated heart-shaped box of homemade toffee for each member of the family at the breakfast table. On individual birthdays, something special crafted by Mother always awaited the celebrant—perhaps pajamas made out of a flour sack or a picture with a large strip of birch bark as the canvas. She never tired of trying to pass on this exceptional ability to her children, but none of us had the same aptitude.

In another untiring effort to bring happiness to the Christmas holiday, Mom always spent at least an hour beautifying the dinner environment by running streamers from the table corners to the ceiling, creating fancy homemade silver paper place mats for vegetable dishes, placing party crackers beside each plate, and using any other means at her disposal to make the atmosphere Christmas-like and elegant. I often wonder if she felt all the trouble she went to for such a short period of time was worth the effort, but those artistic moods of hers were what helped make those bygone days so memorable for me.

Following the gaiety of the holidays, January became a wretched letdown, knowing we faced at least three more months of dreary frigid weather with little hope of respite. The days dragged by with morning chores completed by the light of a kerosene lantern and the winter sun shivering into view about the time we started for school. Often our footpath, covered with a fresh layer of snow, meant the first person had to break trail for the 2½ miles. If a blizzard came up during the day with swirling snow piling up in drifts, one of our neighbors usually arrived at school at closing time to lead us home. He would break trail, followed by the older students to provide a partial windbreak and a beaten track for the younger children to follow. Never a word would be spoken on those treks, as each face was buried deep in a muffler or a woolen scarf for protection from the stinging north wind and the lashing snow. The only audible sound above the howling storm would be the crisp crunch of mocassined feet plodding along the narrow path of freshly fallen snow. Sighting the smoke from our chimney swirling about in the gusty winds offered great comfort knowing warmth and sustenance were not far away.

Every winter morning each member of our family when leaving the house, would glance at the kitchen chimney to note the direction of the smoke. A shift to the south lifted our spirits with hope that warmer weather might be in the offing. But by nightfall, with the wind back blowing from the north, we were forced to accept the unhappy fact that spring still lay somewhere in the distant future. On some calm mornings, usually during a frigid spell with temperatures hovering 40- to 50-degrees below zero, the chimney smoke curled straight up until it dissipated in the clear, crisp, morning air. Cold winter nights were often enthralling, particularly with a moon and no wind to disturb the stillness. Northern lights flashing and zigzagging across the sky together with the moonlight reflecting off the snowbound land transformed it into a gigantic chest of glittering jewels. The blood-curdling howl of coyotes chasing their evening meal, though intimidating, only added to the striking scenario. Those special winter nights were mesmerizing and unforgettable but did not compare with the joy of seeing the chimney smoke drifting north on a piercing cold winter morning and wondering if perhaps relief from the cold was finally on its way.

Chickadees, snowbirds, Canada jays, sparrows, and several species of hawks and owls were the prime representation of bird life during the bleak winter season, and we were delighted with their company. But the first shrill notes of a horned lark on a mild February morning signalling the gradual return of our feathered friends set hearts bounding and spirits soaring. A late February warming trend, its duration unpredictable, offered a welcome respite. No matter how long the mild spell lasted, the sun, rapidly gaining strength, bared a few patches in the fields, and from these tiny oases of Mother Earth, the sweet warble of new arrivals would spring forth.

Chapter 4

At Shriner's

Spring usually spread slowly over Manitoba and remnants of snow-drifts often survived until early May. Our weather was described by some wit as "nine months of winter and three months of poor sledding." Nonetheless, the long melancholy stretch of frigid temperatures made spring special and exhilarating. Seeing or hearing the first crow would send us into a frenzy, and the return of robins, meadowlarks, killdeers, swallows, ducks and other birds rendered a constant source of jubilation. Our school ran a contest each year, with the winner the pupil who reported the most new signs of spring. Buttercups peeping through disappearing snowdrifts or pussywillows bursting from their buds along the banks of freshly rejuvenated streams provided a much better tonic than the doses of sulphur and molasses that were usually prescribed to wash away winter doldrums.

With the first patches of bare ground, we had an overwhelming urge to dig out the baseball and officially call a halt to winter. Jack would sooner toss a baseball those years than anything else on earth, and spring unleashed that yearning. Father, who had played some baseball as a young man and retained a great love for the sport, encouraged us to play ball when it didn't interfere with farm work. This created some conflict in my mind as a youngster. Normally, Jack and I were given one hour to return from school and begin our evening chores, with a latitude of about twenty minutes. Exceeding this earned us a sound thrashing with a stout willow switch. If an official school softball game after the four o'clock bell delayed our arrival home until seven o'clock, however, that was perfectly all right. This deviation from the rules did not apply to anything except baseball. Perhaps the prominence the sport held in our house convinced Jack to use it as an excuse to avoid his share of chores on occasion. Nevertheless, he practiced constantly and would go to any length to get into a game, particularly when he grew older.

The freedom we enjoyed in playing ball did not apply to some of our neighbor's children. Often in inter-school tournaments we would not have sufficient players to field a team, a problem caused by the uniqueness of our community. Within a radius of ten miles, several absolutely different cultures and nationalities existed, and baseball had a different priority to all of them. Ostenfeld, one of the largest Danish settlements in Canada, bordered our farm on the east. The Danes, first generation immigrants, spoke little English and were predominantly dairy farmers. With milking machines non-existent every member of the family was sorely needed to assist in tending the cows and performing other related chores. Allowing children time off to play baseball was unthinkable. Pinewood School, situated in the Danish settlement, with an enrollment never exceeding eighteen pupils ranging in age from six to sixteen, severely limited our selection for fielding a softball team of ten players. When Danish families prohibited their youngsters from participating, comical and embarrassing situations often resulted, particularly when we had to borrow a student or two from a rival school to complete our squad for inter-school competitions.

The polyglot of nationalities surrounding the small Anglo-Saxon enclave in which we resided, added a great dimension to my early life and an opportunity to become acquainted with other lifestyles. Four miles south of Monominto, the French settlements began, and the French, unlike the Danish, had been a major part of Manitoba's growth prior to its becoming a province in 1870. Many of their ancestors arrived as early as the eighteenth century as explorers and courier-de-bois. Though authentic Manitobans, they retained their French language and heritage, which created considerable animosity with their English-speaking neighbors. They taught French almost exclusively in their schools and remained aloof and divided from the non-French communities. In the 1930's, however, they became enthusiastic about playing baseball, and this altered the whole complex situation. The French rapidly attained proficiency at the sport, and soon each village had its own team. Tiring of competing against each other, they challenged teams from other communities and held tournaments on Sunday afternoons at many towns like Saltel, St. Anne des Chenes, St. Genevieve, La Broquerie, Lorette and others throughout the French community. Steinback, in southern Manitoba, predominantly German Mennonite, plus the Rosewood, Dugald, Anola, Monominto and Pinewood teams comprised mainly of Anglo-Saxon and Ukrainian nationalities also joined the weekly competition. Despite intense rivalry, baseball became the catalyst that melded these groups.

Frank Kelly, a close friend of our family and who for seven years dated Aunt Muriel, my mother's youngest sister, visited our farm every week end throughout the summer. A Winnipeg barber by trade, Frank played third base for the Pinewood team during the early years of this baseball competition. A personable and comic individual, he was fondly known to the French players as "Kelly." When on base, Frank used to delight in trying to steal, particularly from third base to home. One day Frank had a substantial lead off the bag when Saltel's third baseman shouted to the pitcher in a booming voice and in very broken English, "Watch dat Kelly on de tird." Father, catching for the team, and other Pinewood players, convulsed with laughter by the innocent remark and delayed the game a few moments while they got back their composure. The French team, though not sure of the reason for the hilarity, nevertheless joined in the mood. A minor incident, but fondly recalled over the years and an example of the role played by baseball in breaking down the barrier between our cultures.

To finalize the description of our multifarious community and to give a clearer picture of the distinctive nature of Monominto, the makeup of the balance of the surrounding communities is necessary.

During the latter part of the nineteenth century and the beginning of the twentieth, the Canadian government advertised for immigrants to settle the prairies. This attracted huge numbers of Russians, Poles, Estonians, and Hungarians from Europe. The largest single group from the Ukraine became an important part of Manitoba culture. Many Ukrainians plus a smattering of Polish settled on land immediately north and west of our farm. During those early years of baseball rivalry the Ukrainians, like the French, loved and became proficient at the game of baseball. They made up the largest percentage of teams from Monominto, Rosewood, Anola, and other communities. Again, this competition played an important part in intermingling the second generations of these varied cultures.

As a youngster, I watched these sporting events with mixed emotions. I loved the game, but it gradually dawned on me that my physical disability, worsening as I grew older, prohibited me from ever becoming a participant. My parents watched with desperation as they realized I might eventually be unable to walk at all. At the time, no hospitalization or government assistance of any kind existed, and the type of operations required, plus the length of time I would need to be hospitalized, was so far beyond Father's financial capabilities, it could not even be considered. Both parents regularly massaged my limb using different ointments and greases hoping they could make the ravaged muscles respond. Although still too young to grasp the real gravity of it all, I did know my life would be far different from those baseball players I watched with great envy. Then a miracle occurred.

Ben, my mother's younger brother and a musician, played with a band called the "Round Up Rangers" that toured western Canada, though they performed primarily in Winnipeg. Charlie Herald, the band leader and a Mason, brought his orchestra to Monominto occasionally, and because of our relationship with Uncle Ben, he visited our home several times. Therefore he became aware of my plight. To be a Shriner one has to be a Mason, and though Charlie Herald didn't belong to the Shriners, he knew their aims and purposes. One of the world's greatest philanthropic orders, the Shriners, exclusively devote their money and efforts to crippled children. One of the two Shriners' Hospitals in Canada at that time was located in Winnipeg with a thirty-six bed wing in the Children's Hospital. To be admitted, the family had to be financially unable to pay for medical assistance, and we qualified on that score without any difficulty. The largest percentage of children requiring special help were polio cases, and the doctors at the hospital determined categorically they could partially rehabilitate my leg and foot. In 1934, I began an odyssey that for three long years had a most profound effect on my life. But during those same three years, far more significant events were taking place that would have much graver consequences on millions of other lives.

By the mid 1930's, the world in terrible turmoil, continuously sank deeper into a financial morass. U.S. federal relief went into effect in 1933, and at least a million destitute farm families received direct government aid. In 1934 the U.S. Congress devalued the dollar by reducing its gold content by 41 percent, and President Roosevelt informed the country that the cost of the national economic recovery program would reach 10½ billion dollars by the following summer. To add to the woes of the world, free trade was abolished by most countries, and tariffs were imposed.

Economics wasn't mankind's only dilemma. Perhaps the most shocking event during those years occurred in 1935 when Mussolini sent Italian troops into Ethiopia. This act of unopposed aggression encouraged Adolph Hitler's dreams of expansionism and therefore was directly responsible for the terrible conflict soon to follow. In 1935, Hitler denounced the Versaille Treaty, providing for German disarmament, and organized the Luftwaffe, appointing Hermann Göering as Air Marshall. Strangely enough, during those eventful years most people were definitely concerned about the dire turn of events in Europe, and predicted the inevitability of another world conflict, though under no circumstances wanted to get involved themselves unless directly affected. The aggressor nations were quite weak, having had insufficient time to build their war machines. The western nations could easily have stopped their adventurism with little cost in lives or materials, but World War I, the "war to end all wars," had left too many horrible scars. Also, a majority of Americans were isolationists. Getting caught up in another bloody struggle in Europe was absolutely out of the question. So a further five years of increased agitation passed as the world watched and waited in trepidation, knowing another global conflict could not be avoided. Unfortunately that half decade of apprehension probably cost the lives of at least one hundred million human beings, a bitter price to pay for procrastination. Most problems can be solved easier today than tomorrow, from everyday tribulations of the rank and file to the horrendous issues faced by the world as a whole, but we never seem to learn that lesson.

The Hospital for Crippled Children was located in north-central Winnipeg and overlooked the Red River. The Shriners controlled the southern wing where disabled children, whose ages ranged from six to sixteen, came from a wide area, including Manitoba, Saskatchewan, northern Ontario, North and South Dakota, and Montana.

I had no recollection of my separation from the family while convalescing from the disease initially at age three, but now eight years old, I found the sudden detachment from my family quite a shock, particularly when first admitted in the fall of 1934. To add to my misery, I was placed in an isolation section for two weeks where I had absolutely no communication with other children. This wasn't terribly serious because within 48 hours of my arrival they performed the first operation and for ten days afterward my misery eliminated the desire to talk to anyone.

What the surgeons hoped to accomplish with the operations, except to straighten the leg and foot, always remained an enigma to me. Those were the days before sodium pentothal replaced chloroform as an anesthetic, and chloroform created a delightful euphoria while inducing sleep but certainly caused a massive dose of vomiting upon regaining consciousness. Prolonged nausea coupled with atrocious pain made visitors unwelcome, and with the exception of both grandmothers, I saw no one for the first week or two except the nurses and one patient named Marjorie.

As the effects of the anesthetic wore off following the operation and I kept slipping in and out of consciousness, I gradually became aware of a young lady, about fifteen years old and with her face and upper body hideously mutilated, standing quietly beside my bed. I found out later that a large drum of gasoline had exploded within a few feet of where she had been standing at her farm home in Saskatchewan. Unquestionably fortunate to have survived, her face, arms, and upper body were nevertheless badly burned, and several fingers were missing from her disfigured hands although her lower limbs were mostly uninjured. Assisting the nurses, she stood ready to place a container under my chin whenever my stomach heaved because moving my head more than a few inches caused great stabs of pain. She carefully raised to my lips a glass of ginger ale with a straw when I craved a drink. Her soft, soothing voice and sympathetic eyes were a panacea to the agony I felt and an unbelievable contradiction to the physical appearance of her tortured face.

Marjorie, hospitalized long before I arrived, had already experienced several operations. Skin grafting, not of today's standard, made progress in restructuring her face and limbs both painful and slow. During the several periods I spent in the hospital in the next three years, this courageous girl, always there, had endured numerous operations. I have no idea how they eventually improved her appearance or to what extent they rehabilitated her hands, but she deserved the best, and because of her positive attitude, she probably lives a happy and successful life. By accepting tragedy in the manner she did, Marjorie taught me during our years of association, the true meaning of grit and gave many of us the will and courage to accept and overcome our own disabilities. She had obviously come to terms with her life, accepted her fate, and mentally adjusted to it. She had the wonderful ability to emanate tremendous strength even without conversation.

During my three major visits to the Shriners' Hospital, I encountered plenty of children with polio afflictions far more severe than mine, many victims stricken in both legs or in some instances all four limbs. Patients with spinal meningitis, another malady that left its victims in terrible physical condition, generally were placed in a cast from the bottom of their feet to their necks for long periods. Being associated so intimately with different cases, I came to recognize a startling difference in their attitudes. Some had lost their will to survive and undoubtedly would remain a burden for the balance of their lives. The majority, however, had the tenacity to accept their disabilities and to get on with a successful life. None showed this spirit of determination more than Marjorie.

After leaving the isolation ward, I received a few visits from our city relatives. Aunt Doll, Father's only living sister and my most regular caller, was a religious fanatic with a heart of gold, and so her visits included a long boring sermon that didn't arouse much enthusiasm. Both grandmothers were a delight, and I always genuinely looked forward to seeing them. Mother and Father were able to come to see me once just prior to Christmas. But the visitors always eagerly awaited by all children were the Shriners who encouraged the patients to address them as "Uncle." A few of the more dedicated men visited regularly on Sunday afternoons, though the occasional Shriner spent an hour or two on weekday evenings. They were generous with their time and being financially responsible for our receiving free medical assistance and hospitalization, they obviously felt good about themselves and so created a jolly, pleasant atmosphere.

Uncle Art, the most popular, always had a pocketful of candies, a treat we rarely saw, that he would distribute to each patient after a lively conversation. Uncle John carried a couple of sponge rubber balls and would get a lively game of catch started with two or three bed-ridden cases. Watching Uncle John crawl under beds to retrieve the balls always amused the children, and the more they laughed, the more Uncle John enjoyed the game. Uncle Mac arrived with a pocketful of pennies, giving one cent to each child who cleaned up his supper and an additional penny for each extra slice of bread eaten with the meal. Perhaps Uncle Mac owned a flour mill, but he was tremendously popular with the patients. Though too young to understand thoroughly the significance of their benevolence, those and several other Sunday regulars with their strange red fezzes who caused so much happiness, left an indelible impression on my mind.

Miss McClaren, the hospital superintendent, worked with crippled children for many years, not only at the Shriners' wing of the Children's Hospital but also when they erected their own building. Known as one of the finest administrators in the hospital field, she was dearly respected and loved by patients and Shriners alike.

A few weeks before Christmas Miss McClaren came to me and explained that the Shriners bought a Christmas gift for all those who would be in the hospital on Christmas Day. She wanted to discuss my several choices. By persuasion and logic, she gradually shortened the list of selection to two: a 17-jewel watch and a meccano set. The dream of receiving a marvellous gift like a meccano set to wile away the hours rapidly made up my mind as I didn't care about the time. Miss McClaren had other ideas, explaining that the watch would remain a far more durable reminder of my Christmas in the hospital and would be engraved with my name, the date, and inscribed as a gift from the Shriners. Eventually she coerced me into choosing the timepiece for which I didn't forgive her immediately. At the time, I didn't realize the concern Miss McClaren placed on impressing on each child the importance of the Shriners' role in financing the hospital stay and rehabilitation of each patient.

In spite of my sadness at being parted from my family, that hospital Christmas provided a memorable experience for several reasons. In the first place, though by now quite certain Santa Claus didn't exist, I was not positive. No one had definitely destroyed the myth, and also, the hospital staff encouraged the younger children to expect a visit from Santa by hanging pillow cases at the foot of their bed for gifts. I went to sleep early on Christmas Eve, but the rustling of tissue paper awakened me in the early morning hours. I had my head under the sheet due to a chill in the ward and decided to listen for a few moments to determine the source of the sound. I lay there without moving a muscle trying to resolve whether a nurse was putting something in my pillow case or if Old Santa in fact flitted about. After a few moments of intense concentration, I couldn't stand the suspense any longer, and so I jerked off the sheet and bolted upright. Not a sign of movement disturbed the entire ward. Hearing the sound again, I turned rapidly and immediately ascertained the cause. The window behind my bed, slightly ajar, allowed a light breeze to rustle the streamers and bell hanging on the wall. Seeing gifts protruding from my pillow case offered some solace, but the illusion of a Santa Claus had vanished forever.

At 6:00 a.m., I awakened again, this time to a melodious choir of female voices singing Christmas carols. Hundreds of nurses, three abreast, came marching into our ward, circled, then proceeded down the aisle towards other wards. The front singers of the procession were out of sight before the final performers came into view, creating a stirring extravaganza as nurses from hospitals all over Winnipeg participated in the pageant. Resplendent in their starched uniforms, they left a host of Winnipeg crippled children an inspiring reminder of their Christmas morning in a hospital.

I received toys and gifts from family and relatives plus my watch from the Shriners, but the dinner party in the evening, the high point of the day, offered an excellent example of the treatment received by patients in Shriners' hospitals. Duty nurses plus Miss McClaren and several Shriners assembled all the patients into one large ward, some in wheelchairs and the others transported in their beds. Clowns, numerous singers, and other entertainers from across Winnipeg put on a wonderful live show followed by a silent movie starring Charlie Chaplin, my first glimpse at a motion picture. Dinner consisted of roast turkey with all the trimmings topped off with individual servings of ice cream, sculptured in the shape of Santa, including the red trimmings on his clothes. Miss McClaren, the Shriners, and the orderlies spent an hour setting up a complicated string of spotlights for taking movies of the gala event. Cameras, not as sophisticated in those days, were incapable of producing reproductions without strategically placed lighting, and high-speed film did not exist. With everything finally in place, Miss McClaren, the photographer, called for the overhead lights to be turned off and the spotlights switched on. After a momentary burst of brilliant light, the spots blanked out due, no doubt, to an overloaded fuse and blanketed the gala gathering in total darkness. After a moment of absolute silence, everyone heard Miss McClaren's disgruntled voice, "Oh, shit."

The orderly did not switch on the overhead lights immediately, perhaps to allow our delightful superintendent a few moments to compose herself, as children's laughter filled the room. Miss McClaren never apologized for her remark nor proceeded with the filmmaking. She just strode majestically from the ward like a queen. This reaction to the mishap endeared her even more in my memory as she proved she had human failings like the rest of us, and it bestowed a comical finale to a remarkable Christmas.

After four months in the hospital, I returned to the farm in the spring of 1935 with a walking cast to my knee. During the next two years, I returned to the hospital once for surgery, and twice for examinations and cast changes. If my stride had improved or if the doctors believed they could partially reconstruct the damaged limb, I had no way of knowing, but in the spring of 1937, they brought me back for a final major operation.

I again found myself in an isolation ward for the initial two weeks, though the doctors operated the day following my arrival. Regaining consciousness after several hours under anesthetic, I found my leg strapped in the air to a metal frame surrounded by heat lamps with the slightest movement producing intense pain. For three days I experienced the utmost misery and obtained little alleviation from the constant injections of pain-relieving drugs. The only bright spot was the presence of Marjorie. Her face, though still badly scarred, looked beautiful to me. Now seventeen, she had been home several times and would soon be leaving the hospital permanently. Fortunately for me, however, my Florence Nightingale still offered her special healing power those first few days of my last major Winnipeg operation. Harry Meyers, a boy my age from North Dakota, shared the isolation ward with me. Harry had received foot surgery for a problem not too severe, and recuperating at a rapid pace, he was looking for something to alleviate our boredom. With our beds placed end to end, Harry and I began an endurance test by tossing a rubber ball back and forth to see how long we could go without dropping it and then kept trying to establish a new record. Eventually, as I recall, we topped ten thousand, which meant we pitched the ball back and forth for about three hours nonstop. This simple game passed the days far more rapidly than had we sat staring out the window waiting to be moved from isolation to the general ward.

My several months in the hospital in 1937 turned out to be the most enjoyable of my various stay-overs in that worthy institution. The Shriners provided me with a wheelchair after my operation, allowing me to attend an elementary school located in the lower basement of the building. The school mistress, a pleasant, capable teacher, assisted me greatly, and I passed Grade IV before leaving the hospital. A wheelchair also allowed me the freedom to rove around the different wards, improving my social life. I had reached the age where I realized girls weren't boys but remained confused about the difference. The older boys taught me their interpretation in the usual crude fashion, and as a result, I found young female patients more and more intriguing. Miss McClaren supplied us with a Monopoly set, the rage of North America at the time, and I passed many pleasant hours with Harry Meyers and my new-found girl friends playing that delightful game.

Dr. Gardiner, the surgeon who had performed all my operations, decided he couldn't do more, and after removal of the cast and extrication of the wire stitches, almost as painful as the original insertion, I was ready to return to Monominto. After removing my cast and making me walk a few steps with crutches, the doctors attended a young lad named Roy, who occupied a bed close to mine. Roy, in the hospital longer than I, had been stricken with polio in both legs. Miss McClaren and Mom, who had come to take me home, sat on my bed and watched as they removed the casts off both Roy's legs. Then the doctors cautiously assisted him in taking a few steps with the aid of crutches. Roy, fifteen, raised on a Saskatchewan farm and the toughest-talking individual in the hospital, didn't seem like the type anything in the world would faze. But when he actually began walking by himself, even with the aid of crutches, tears welled in his eyes. I sensed the emotion he felt and knew by the determined look in his face, those two crippled legs would never hold Roy back and somehow I realized that Roy knew it as well. Miss McClaren accompanied me from the ward for the final time as Roy waved a farewell victory salute that I've cherished to this day.

Wheeling me through the hospital with Mother by her side, I recall Miss McClaren's final words. "Billy," she said, "you are too young to realize exactly what has happened to you these past three years. When you arrived, you were barely able to walk and your parents were unable to help. Since then, you have received free medical and surgical assistance worth thousands of dollars which will allow you to live a more normal life. Twice you have been completely outfitted with new clothes, including a new suit, the first you ever owned, plus several pairs of shoes."

She stopped the wheelchair and, with her arm around my shoulder, looked me squarely in the eyes. "Billy," she continued, "I want you to promise you will always remember that the Shriners provided everything. Also, the doctors must never be forgotten because they rendered all their medical services for free."

Miss McClaren, to me, resembled Eleanor Roosevelt, with the same strong face and positive features. When she spoke, one felt a power in her words.

As Miss McClaren and Mother assisted me into my uncle's car, she gave me a light kiss on the cheek and said, "Is it a promise?"

"I promise," I assured her as the car pulled away. Then added emphatically, "I promise, I will never forget."

And I didn't. Though I never saw Miss McClaren again, I heard about her often. When in her sixties, she married Dr. Gardiner, the man who performed all the surgery on my foot and leg. A strange coincidence, and I have no doubt that she made him a wonderful wife.

I did return to the "out patients'" clinic a few times after my discharge for further examination. Pressure had been exerted on my big toe by a vice-like device that was attached during the many months it had been in a cast in an effort to straighten out the foot. That contrivance left my big toe bent and misshaped. The doctors tried to persuade Mother to put me back into the hospital for a minor operation to repair the damage, but I pleaded with her not to approve. This turned out to be an unfortunate decision because minor corrective surgery at that point would have saved a lot of pain and inconvenience during the following years. Nevertheless, I had a great deal to be thankful for as a result of the benevolence of Winnipeg Shriners.

Chapter 5

Prelude to War

The several sojourns to the Shriners' Hospital surrounded by children of different ages, religions, and cultural backgrounds broadened my outlook on life enormously. When I arrived home permanently in the summer of 1937, I had matured well beyond my years.

Tremendous changes went sweeping across North America those years as events escalated toward one of the greatest catastrophes in history. Young and old alike continuously exchanged views about the troubles facing mankind, expressing their opinions and suggested cures, and I was a good listener.

North American politics had swung decidedly left, a trend that would continue unabated for the ensuing half century. Though this movement toward socialism to put badly needed dollars into the hands of the masses offered a solution at that time, history has proven that major political alterations in a nation's economic direction usually over corrects the ills they start out to relieve.

The Sixteenth Amendment, adopted by the United States Congress in 1913, allowing both corporate and individual income taxes to become a lawful element in federal tax structure, wasn't a high enough assessment to redistribute the wealth of the country properly. Volumes have been written and a multitude of theories expounded as to the major cause of the Great Depression. As a general consensus though, too few families and corporations in the United States had accumulated and were continuing to amass too much of the nation's wealth. As a result, available cash for the balance of the population just kept dwindling. This is an obvious oversimplification but if the government had started earlier to tax the wealthy individuals and corporations at a higher rate

36

and enacted government programs to create jobs, the "crash of '29" may have been averted.

A statistic released by the Internal Revenue Service in 1935 and reported by President Roosevelt declared that "one tenth of 1 percent of U.S. corporations own 52 percent of all corporate assets reported and earn 50 percent of all corporate income. Less than 5 percent own 87 percent of all corporate assets, and less than 4 percent earn 87 percent of all net profits reported by all U.S. corporations." This report clearly displayed the extraordinary extent that the country's assets were controlled by such a small minority.

Strikes, now common in Great Britain, had become a major bargaining tool for the working class even prior to the turn of the twentieth century. But in North America, the unions were just establishing a solid foothold. In an effort to unionize the automobile industry, the United Workers of America went on strike in Flint, Michigan, and after two months won a wage increase of 5 cents per hour. "Sit down" strikes had become a new C.I.O. weapon in both the glass and automobile industries. The "Little Steel Strike," at the Republic Steel Plant, flared into violence in 1937. Ten people were killed, ninety wounded. During the thirties, strikes in North America became rampant, and the sympathies of various segments of society differed greatly. Most of the upper middle class, together with much of the media, branded any labor dissident a Communist. However, the financially distressed laborer fought to improve the fortunes of his family, which in many cases meant simply getting enough to eat, and so it was difficult to fault him. Some 38 percent of U.S. families had incomes of less than $1,000 per annum, and the Bureau of Labor Statistics placed the poverty line at $1,330.

One of the most significant enactments of the time, the passage of the Social Security Act, provided a system of old age annuities and unemployment benefits. State funds were to be matched by federal aid, and the tax took effect on January 1, 1937. Roosevelt, popular with the masses for his "New Deal" measures undertaken to restore the nation's economic health, had been re-elected for a second term with 61 percent of the popular vote. Alf Landon, his Republican opponent, denounced the "New Deal" as an encroachment on American business and institutions. The Democrats denounced the Republicans as "economic royalists," indifferent to the needs of the people, and pointed to the economic progress made since 1933. Although progress had been made for four years, it again faltered in mid-1937 with business activity suffering another sharp drop. In early 1938, the Dow Jones Average fell to 98.95. In his second inaugural address, President Roosevelt said, "I see one third of a nation ill-housed, ill-clad, and ill-nourished." With all of the terrible economic news continually being headlined by newspapers and radio, we were also being bombarded by distressing and dramatic events from other parts of the world.

Hitler swiftly moved toward his date with destiny and forced most of mankind to join him. In 1936 he marched his armies into the Rhineland unopposed and then signed treaties with Italy and Japan. The following year he opened Buchenwald concentration camp. The first inmates were mostly political prisoners of every religious belief, but most of those ultimately sent to Buchenwald would be Jews. A ghastly percentage would eventually die in those gas chambers.

Hitler wasn't the only demon on the world stage. Mussolini was almost his equal. Italian forces captured Addis Ababa in 1936 and proclaimed the annexation of Ethiopia. Barefoot Ethiopian warriors by the hundreds of thousands had been killed by Italian bombs and mustard gas while Mussolini's son-in-law, Conte Ciano, expressed rapture at the beauty of the bombs "opening like red blossoms" on Ethiopia's highlands.

Haile Selassie, Ethiopia's leader, addressed the League of Nations in Geneva: "I am here today to claim the justice that is due my people. God and history will remember your judgement." As he left the rostrum, he was heard to murmur, "It is us today. It will be you tomorrow." A more prophetic statement has seldom been made, but nonetheless, the world watched, shuddered in horror, and did nothing.

Meanwhile, the Spanish Civil War, started in 1936, was teaching Italy and Germany valuable lessons in the art of modern warfare, providing a testing ground for many of their new weapons. Ten thousand German soldiers and 75,000 Italians aided General Franco and his Fascist cause. Franco commanded several hundred thousand insurgents against the Spanish Republican Army, which was supported by an international brigade of Russians, Britons, other Europeans, and Americans. Thirty-one hundred Americans fought in Spain, and over half of those soldiers died in a hopeless cause.

To add to the world's turmoil, Japanese forces invaded China in 1937, and before the year ended, more than 200,000 Chinese were executed in Nanking alone. This massacre, combined with the merciless bombing of Chinese cities, roused world opinion against Japan. But, like a prey frozen by the knowledge of imminent death, those nations not yet involved in the various conflicts simply awaited the inevitable, knowing full well they themselves faced an eventual attack because the warlords were dedicated to world domination.

An incident that didn't make headlines but that nevertheless soon had earth-shattering consequences took place at Columbia University in 1936. An Austrian-American physicist, Isidor Rabi, invented a magnetic resonance that could be used for observing the spectra of atoms and molecules in the radio frequency range, making it possible to deduce the mechanical and magnetic properties of atomic nuclei. This non-heralded occurrence ushered in the Nuclear Age, although the first nuclear fission of uranium wasn't introduced until 1938.

A strange paradox throughout recorded history is that the human race, has frequently produced, during times of intense stress, individuals with great artistic abilities, as if to balance the world's malaise with some optimism. Songs and music that remained popular for a half century were written in those depressing thirties. "Blue Moon," "Deep Purple," "Cocktails for Two," "Begin the Beguine," "Summertime," "Blue Hawaii," "Harbor Lights," and "Thanks for the Memories" are just a few. Books, plays, and radio programs were also of a high caliber, and many of the Hollywood movie stars, who would remain famous for generations, were at the height of their popularity.

On the farm, we had an old radio, half the size of a modern refrigerator and containing literally dozens of tubes, from which we occasionally received signals. Our most reliable radio was a crystal set. If the needle made the proper contact with the crystal a reasonable reception could be obtained through crude earphones, of which we had two sets. One of the thrills of my life occurred when Joe Louis knocked out Jimmy Braddock to win the world heavyweight championship in 1937. Jack and I each heard the bout through a single earphone. Father, of course, had the other set. From that simple radio we kept abreast of the news stories of the day, and on occasion heard the new hit songs. The first tune I learned was "The Isle of Capri," and hearing it today always brings back memories of the farm and that old crystal set that brought us some joy and, more importantly, kept us informed of happenings that would soon change the course of the world.

Two other events of that era, though not so significant, attracted global attention. These were the birth of the Dionne Quintuplets in 1934 and the abdication of England's King Edward VIII in 1937. The Dionnes, the first set of five babies ever to survive, caused a tragic confrontation between Dr. Dafoe, the obstetrician credited with saving their lives, and the quints' parents. Unfortunately, Mr. and Mrs. Dionne, mentally unprepared to cope with the worldwide publicity the event had caused, were made dupes due to bad advice. The bitter dispute between Dr. Dafoe, the Dionnes, and others trying to take advantage of the situation caused such a severe family rupture that before they were ten years old the quints were separated from their parents. Those five young ladies led extremely unhappy lives because proper authorities didn't protect the family's privacy.

The tempestuous love affair between King Edward VIII and Wallis Simpson made major headlines for a year. Mother, a true royalist, never forgave poor old Edward when he finally abdicated the British throne to marry "the woman he loved." I thought he had a lot of guts, but dared not express this feeling in front of Mom.

Aviation, always a source of excitement, constantly made news those years. In 1937, Howard Hughes set a new transcontinental speed record of 7 hours 28 minutes between Los Angeles and New York. Amelia Earhart, the sweetheart of American aviation and the first woman to cross the Atlantic, also became the first woman to make a solo flight across the Atlantic Ocean. The world mourned when this courageous woman was lost in the Pacific while attempting with co-pilot, Fred Noonan to fly around the world. Trans-Canada Airlines, making daily mail flights between Toronto and Winnipeg, used a route that took them just north of our farm. At the first sound of the engines, our family would race outside, regardless of the weather, to watch the blinking lights of the airplane moving slowly through the northern sky. That spectacle sent the same tremors of excitement through me then as I now experience watching a spacecraft take off. Sighting an aircraft of any kind always offered an enormous thrill because, like ten dollar bills, they were still few and far between.

These were dramatic and exciting times for Jack and me, rapidly approaching our teens.

During the period following my discharge from the hospital in 1937 until the summer of '43 when I left my boyhood home permanently (though I often returned for short durations), certain traits became etched into my character. I had an overpowering desire to earn money. Being exposed in the hospital to those children privileged to receive a weekly allowance left me with a tremendous yearning to acquire income of my own. Prior to my hospital experience, I thought little except at Christmas time about the important role money plays in life. Now I felt differently, and my determination to find a way to earn those precious dollars forced me into several confrontations with Father who still struggled just to put food on the table.

One day, while talking with Mother, I mentioned my resolve to become rich when I grew up. "Son," she said, "most children have dreams of grandeur, but few attain it, and you have the added difficulty of being physically handicapped, so I wouldn't set my sights too high. What would you do if you had a lot of money? Money can't buy happiness, you know."

"Mom," I replied without hesitation, "I would immediately buy some toilet tissue. After becoming accustomed to that luxury in the hospital, Eaton's catalogue in our outhouse drives me crazy."

Mom laughed but never forgot the remark. She often said over the years that her young son's struggles to become wealthy were due to his hankering for toilet paper.

Every winter I devoted many hours to trapping and snaring fur-bearing animals and became quite proficient at skinning, fleshing, and stretching the skins. Weasels, skunks, rabbits, and mink were my main objectives, and the market, quite strong, particularly for short-haired furs, enabled me to earn a few dollars.

Also, between the winters of 1940 and '42, I tended the school fires, which, as I mentioned earlier, earned me the princely sum of ten cents per day. The money, paid in one check at the end of the season, amounted to between nine and ten dollars. Unfortunately for me, Father sat on the school board and co-signed the check. He would hand it to me for endorsement, then use it to purchase badly needed provisions. Considering the misery I went through to make the few dollars, I felt this confiscation of my earnings was terribly unjust and didn't hesitate to inform him of my resentment. This usually resulted in a cuff on the ear followed by a stern lecture. One year he decided to begin raising sheep. My check would buy one of the ewes, and he said that any first-year lambs would be mine to sell. This appeared to be a chance to receive some compensation for my winter's work, and so I happily agreed, even though my consent was inconsequential. The following spring, my ewe had twin lambs, and I watched with glowing pride throughout the summer as they fattened into choice marketable mutton. I eagerly compiled a list of articles I badly wanted when I finally obtained my share of the cash. Unfortunately, at the time the truckload of lambs went to market our family again needed extra income, and I never received a penny.

Brashness, a deficiency in my character even as a boy, didn't endear me to Father. So with my impetuosity and Dad's bad temper, we frequently found ourselves on a collision course. Father only weighed 170 pounds and stood five feet ten inches, but until after I left home, I never attained any height and weighed only about 90 pounds. Father had a great weight advantage when our clashes were physical. He never broke any of my bones and rarely drew blood, but I sustained many a dandy bruise.

At the kitchen table I sat on his immediate left, within easy striking range of either his left or right hand, which he unleashed with great speed and little warning. Many times I was sent sprawling across the floor, the recipient of one of those backhands. Our arguments covered a wide range of topics, with politics a major point of discussion. Becoming quite proficient at the art of debating, I would press my advantage unmercifully and without considering the consequences if I had Father cornered on some point. No different from most men, Father wasn't happy about being thrust into a defensive position by his teen-aged son, and so a shot to the head generally ended the dialogue.

Strangely enough, I usually accompanied him to political meetings in our community. The Co-operative Commonwealth Federation, more commonly known as the C.C.F., was a new Labor Party that had established itself in our sister province of Saskatchewan and was struggling to gain a foothold in Manitoba. Father and several neighbors were convinced that this new political force might help bring us out of the terrible Depression, and so they took an interest in the activities. Anyone involved with the C.C.F. Party at that time was considered a Communist, and as a result I often found myself at odds with Father. Though I didn't have twenty-five cents in the egg cup on the kitchen shelf where Jack and I kept our worldly wealth, I guess my thinking even then leaned toward capitalism.

During those years Dad and I had a great love/hate relationship. Both parents, gravely concerned over the condition of my leg, believed exercise was the only hope to develop the withered muscles. After our daily 2½-mile hike from school, I was generally dispatched to locate and drive the cows to the barn for the evening milking. We lived in free range country, which meant all stock grazed along public road allowances during the day, thus preserving the farmer's land for night pasture. Once released onto the road allowance in the morning, nothing obstructed the cattle from wandering as far as they pleased throughout the day. When mosquitoes were bad, the animals would face into the wind to rid themselves of insects and, steadily feeding and walking, might roam for miles. The neighbors' cows, also released on the right-of-way, created a real conundrum when it came time to locate our stock. Several animals were fitted with cowbells, to enable us to hear them in the distance. But distinguishing the sound of our bells from those of our neighbors became an impossibility at times. Consequently we'd often find ourselves approaching the wrong cattle after miles of searching. Between school and hunting our stock, I walked many miles per week.

Another of my aggravations involved doing field work with our horses after school hours or on weekends. We never owned a tractor. If the machinery had a seat such as those for plowing, discing, or seeding, Jack got the assignment, but if harrowing or cultivating became the order of the day, where one had to walk every inch of the way, then I got the reins. Though Father's reasoning that exercise provided the best therapy for my damaged limb was 100 percent correct, I was too young to understand.

Father's temper, attached to an extremely short fuse, caused him to fly off the handle at the slightest provocation. Many times if I did or said something that irritated him, he would pick up a rock the size of his fist and heave it at me with all his might. Had he ever connected it would have been "curtains" for his youngest son. I never knew if he missed intentionally or was just a lousy shot.

Animals had an unbelievable way of annoying him. If a heifer got in the wrong stall when entering the barn, Father would go into a rage. Picking up a rope and accompanied by a barrage of profanity, he'd try to beat some sense into the animal who, now terrified, went dashing around the stable upsetting the rest of the stock. This resulted in absolute pandemonium, and the chaotic scene invariably struck me as so hilarious that I'd begin to laugh. Aware of his ill humor, I'd lurk in the shadows to avoid detection, but immobilized by convulsive laughter, I'd usually be spotted at which point I got a little taste of the rope.

Horses, in particular, drove Father into a fury. If they didn't gee or haw when commanded or stop on a dime when he hollered "whoa," he savagely jerked the reins which, being connected to the bit in their mouths, hurt them considerably. This cruel way of his with horses also caused friction between us, because both Jack and I were exceedingly fond of those steadfast animals. Therefore, when we reached our early teens, Jack and I handled the horses as much as possible, which led to additional problems between Dad and me. Jack would be in the fields with a four- or six-horse team cultivating or plowing, and despite being instructed to rest the animals for five minutes every half hour, Jack, a lover of wildlife, would frequently spot something interesting and five minutes stretched into thirty. Father and I, cultivating turnips, mangels, or potatoes, with Kate, a huge old mare who was a little on the clumsy side, could see Jack's standing outfit a half mile away across the open fields. Dad handled the cultivator while I drove Kate between those seemingly endless rows of root crops. Even in a good mood, Father always became irritated if the horse accidently stepped on a potato plant, and generally I received a reprimand. But when Jack extended his team's rest period, I could sense Father's anger rising in relation to the delay, and aware of the bad situation developing, would pay strict attention to my driving. Old Kate, however, not giving a hoot about the crisis, would without fail suddenly lose control of one of her back hooves and let it come smashing down on one of those tender potato plants. This accident invariably led to a severe tongue lashing aimed at both Kate and me plus a threat of bodily harm if it happened again. Bearing the brunt of Father's wrath because of Jack's dawdling irked me no end, and so when Jack and I were alone later, he was subjected to a dose of my rancor.

An episode that marked the beginning of the end of Father's physical punishment of me occurred one evening when he began singing a song to my sister Ruth, and I made the mistake of mimicking him during his performance. This harmless parody thoroughly annoyed him. Growing red in the face, he stopped singing abruptly and, in a stern voice, ordered me to continue with the song. Replying that I had work to do, I immediately left the house. During the next couple of hours while choring, I occasionally saw Father who appeared to be getting more irate as the evening progressed. I realized the matter had not been forgiven. After shedding our outdoor clothing and returning to the kitchen, Father approached me in a threatening manner. "Now, I want to hear you sing," he snorted.

"I don't feel like singing right now!" I replied.

With an obvious beating next on the agenda, I put up my fists to do battle. In one swift movement Father grabbed me by the front of my shirt, pinned me in the clothes closet and cocked his other fist menacingly about two feet from my nose. Recognizing the distinct disadvantage of my position, when he again ordered me to sing, discretion became the better part of valor and a squeaky note or two trickled from my throat. This appeased his anger, and I was let go without further punishment. However, while dangling in the closet in that very undignified position, I decided I had about reached the end of putting up with Father's abuse.

I did take a few more thrashings after that episode, but one day when nearing fifteen, I finally reached my limit. It happened one evening while I lugged hay into the barn with a pitchfork and Father was feeding the pigs. He had been in a grumpy mood all day, and for no reason, he hollered at me to stop littering hay all over the yard.

I hollered back, "You're full of crap. I didn't lose any hay."

Dropping his pails, he raced towards me like an enraged bull. With the four-tined pitchfork held menacingly in my two hands, I waited until he was within four feet, then shouted, "One more step and I'll drive this fork right through your guts. You lay a hand on me again as long as you live, and you'll regret it."

Father, no coward, didn't show the slightest bit of fear but seemed to sense I meant every word. Perhaps at that moment, he suddenly realized that I was no longer a child. From that day until his death, he never laid a hand on me, though we had many vociferous altercations. I do not believe Dad ever told anyone about our final encounter, and neither did I. For my part, I didn't want anything to get back to him that might disturb the peace. From his standpoint, I believe he was embarrassed to realize the situation between us had reached such a disastrous state that I might have killed him on the spot because my temper matched his, and he knew it.

Many years later after physically man-handling my own children while in a state of fury, I realized the ease with which we often abuse our children in the belief we are doing it to teach them manners or are improving their character. In some instances, light physical punishment probably does no harm to a child if administered without hostility. Unfortunately, most child raising occurs during the critical period in a man's life when his nerves are already rubbed raw, which is why grandparents would usually make better parents.

Father wasn't the only person I irritated. Jack rarely got annoyed with anyone, but I could raise his bristles easily. Though we were extremely close, we generally did battle at least once a week. Also, at school I tested every boy big or small. Reflecting on my attitude of those days, I am not certain whether I was just plain quarrelsome or simply determined to prove my capability in physical combat. Nevertheless, headstrong, stubborn, and demanding if I didn't get my own way, I wasn't the epitome of a gentleman.

A case in point occurred during the final semester (1938-1939) that Jack spent at school. I don't recall the exact details, but as the entire student body played ball, an older student instructed me to perform some function that went against my grain. Not only did I refuse to comply with the request but also stubbornly sat on second base and had to be bodily removed from the playing field. Generally Jack sided with me against the older students and, in fact, frequently took them on by himself in my defense. In this instance he must have considered me wrong because he assisted the others in my inelegant removal. I immediately planned revenge. Within a week I had organized all of my classmates into an Indian tribe, except the four oldest including Jack. Our encampment, set up a quarter of a mile from the school grounds in a heavily wooded public area, included several structures of dead poplars leaning against each other in wigwam style. Hundreds of trees were collected and used in construction. The largest tepee, 25 feet tall, would comfortably seat 20 children. My band of renegades included sister Ruth, always a great ally of mine and now a robust young lady of ten. She and the other oldest girls were made Indian princesses with their own tepees, while I, of course, nominated myself chief. Every youngster received an Indian name and an official title. Well organized, we had lookouts posted to detect the approach of the older students. I had convinced our group that if we were molested we would have to gang attack. The four outcasts left us alone, but for the last months of Jack's final year at Pinewood, he and the other three older students were left entirely to their own devices. Jack, thoroughly exasperated, didn't entirely forgive me for several months.

Promoted into Grade IX in the summer of 1939, Jack might have continued his education if the choice had been his, but he didn't have a voice in the decision. There were two reasons; first, Dad desperately needed help on the farm and only allowed Jack to complete his schooling as required by law, and secondly, Pinewood School's teacher didn't qualify to tutor beyond Grade VIII. I don't recall Jack being terribly disappointed because he absolutely adored nature and would devote hours to studying the flora and fauna that abounded in our section of Manitoba. Jack also liked to farm and enjoyed working with horses and other animals.

Uncle George, Mom's youngest brother, and his wife, Gladys, presented Jack with a bicycle for passing Grade VIII. This added quite a dimension to our lives because for the first time we had wheels (other than horse powered) for our personal movement. Uncle George, only twelve years older than Jack, had spent much of his young life at the farm, especially during the early years of the Depression. He and Dad remained close throughout their lives, and he was always more like an older brother than an uncle. After marrying Gladys, they visited the farm almost every weekend in summer. Later, when his children arrived, they vacationed there for a week or two most years. His residence on Home Street in the west section of Winnipeg was my home away from home all the years I lived in western Canada. "Unk", as he was fondly called, worked for the Hudson's Bay Company as a radio technician for over thirty years before moving to Toronto. Because of his close association with our family, it was not surprising that he should provide the first major improvement in our lifestyles.

I became quite jealous of Jack's sudden ability to move at the blinding speed of ten miles per hour, which shortened his travelling time immensely. Never selfish, Jack immediately invited me to ride the new vehicle, but due to my lopsided body, I took several nasty tumbles while trying to master the contraption, bruising myself severely and not doing the bicycle any good either. I gave up. Hearing about my inability to handle the bike, Father took me out to an open field, ordered me to mount the contraption, then spent two exasperating hours teaching me to balance myself and pedal at the same time. I fell frequently before finding my equilibrium, but when suddenly the forward propulsion was all mine, I reached the heights of ecstasy. Rarely in life did I experience any more exhilaration than when I triumphed over that bicycle. During my entire association with Father, he never allowed me to admit defeat on doing anything any other person could do and insisted that because I had to devote myself more stringently than others I would perform many activities more capably.

It is difficult to imagine the important role the new bicycle played in the lives of Jack, Ruth, and me. Ruth, an athletic and sturdy girl, enlisted at an early age to do her share of chores. She made at least four trips weekly to the store and post office a mile from our home. For her, the bike became a real timesaver. For Jack and me, it was a godsend. To reach the nearest swimming hole (remember we had no bath tub or shower) 2½ miles away, the same distance as the baseball practice field and dance hall, required 1½ hours of strenuous walking when taking into consideration the return journey. With the bicycle, we cut our travelling time enormously. Leaving the house together, Jack began running while I pedalled the bike a half mile or so, at which point I would leave the vehicle and begin walking. Upon reaching the bike, Jack would ride it a half mile past me, then leave it and begin walking again. We could cover the 2½ miles in twenty minutes with this method.

The bicycle also played a major part in my constant search for ways to earn income. Selling Christmas cards or spring garden seeds offered an opportunity to earn good commissions, but the distance between farm homes made it impractical when travelling by foot. The bicycle changed all that, and for three years I pedalled and sold those items over a range of ten miles. In late fall and early winter, with the roads deeply rutted and covered with ice, bike riding became exceedingly treacherous, and I took some terrifying tumbles when the wheels got caught in icy ruts. As I went sprawling one direction, my transportation went slithering another, and by the time we both came to a halt, fifty feet of slippery road separated us. They were bone-bruising expeditions, but because I made money, I considered it well worth the pain and effort. These tribulations with my daily existence, were pretty inconsequential compared to the tumultuous events occurring on the world stage, of course.

Sister Joyce, born into a world of uncertainties during the summer of 1935, completed our family. The final years of the thirties were not unkind to us. We had no surplus cash, but we had sufficient food, warm clothes to wear, and despite a few family squabbles, resided in a warm and pleasant atmosphere. This was a lot more than could be said for the majority of mankind as economic woes persisted almost unabated.

President Roosevelt asked the United States Congress in 1938 for funds to help stimulate the economy as business remained mired in recession. By 1939 17 percent of the country's work force—9½ million people—were still out of work. This was a considerable improvement over 1933 when fifteen million were unemployed, but those Americans with jobs had relatively low average incomes. Only slightly more than four million people earned more than $2000 annually, and only 3 percent made enough to pay income tax. Nearly 25 percent of all North Americans were still involved in the farming industry, with the total family cash income averaging only $1,000 per year. A new Chevy Coupe sold for $659 and a Nash Sedan for $793, but nevertheless, fewer than

60 percent of Canadians and Americans owned an automobile. While statistics are revealing, they fail to conjure the reality of wasted lives, of long lines of forlorn men stretching out from the city soup kitchens or shivering against the wind on the tops of freight cars as they rode hopelessly in search of nonexistent jobs.

Though still far behind the English in their constant movement toward socialism, Americans were creeping steadily in that direction. The Fair Labor Standards Act, passed in 1938, limited working hours to forty-four per week, and this was dropped to forty by 1940. Overtime had to be reimbursed at the rate of 1½ times regular pay. A minimum wage of 25 cents per hour prescribed for the year 1938 increased to 30 cents for the ensuing six years. The first Social Security checks issued on January 30, 1940 totalled $75,000, a figure that rose to 4.9 billion dollars in thirty-five years as some 31 million pensioners became eligible for Society Security benefits. The first check for $22.54 went to a Vermont widow, Ida May Fuller, 35, who received more than $20,000 before she died in 1975 at age 100.

Although appalling, the misery suffered by the populace on an international scale as a result of the terrible Depression was really only a minor irritation compared to the plague being caused by wars already in progress, and they were only skirmishes compared to the holocaust soon to envelop most of the planet.

Japanese forces on a rampage across China suffered several reverses as Chinese guerillas retained control of the countryside. The Spanish Civil War, ravaging that nation since 1936, finally ended in the spring of 1939 with the fall of Madrid to Fascist leader Generalissimo Francisco Franco. The estimated toll of over a million in Spain included those killed in battle, those executed, and those who died of starvation, disease, and malnutrition.

In September, 1938, Britain and France appeased Hitler at Munich by permitting him to take the Sudentenland, a 16,000-square-mile territory that comprised nearly a third of Czechoslovakia and contained a third of her inhabitants. "I believe it is peace for our time . . . peace with honor," said Neville Chamberlain, the British Prime Minister, on his return to London from Munich.

Charles A. Lindbergh wrote U.S. Ambassador to Britain Joseph P. Kennedy, after surveying British, German and Soviet airpower. "I am convinced that it is wiser to permit Germany eastward expansion than to throw England and France, unprepared, into a war at this time." He argued that Britain could not possibly win a war in Europe even with U.S. aid. So at that point in our history, Hitler was allowed to expand Germany's borders with only a slap on the wrist by those powers with the capability but not the desire to stop him. The delay in taking action against the Fuhrer worked exclusively in his nation's favor because although in full-war production, Germany had not yet built up any appreciable reserves. Despite the fact that Britain, France and the U.S. were not in any way prepared for war, those three great industrial nations would have soon rapidly surpassed Germany's performance. So the year's delay worked completely against them, and they would have to stem the Nazi menace on Hitler's terms.

Except for the *Prairie Farmer,* our weekly newspaper with news that was ten days old by the time it reached the farm, the crystal-set radio still furnished the only communication keeping us updated on current events. During 1938 and '39, the air waves permeated with the constant doom and gloom of international problems also contained a continuous flow of new songs and music.

"A Tisket A Tasket," "Beer Barrel Polka," "You Must Have Been A Beautiful Baby," "God Bless America," "Thanks For The Memories," and "The Isle of Capri" were great favorites. Others from hit movies included "Somewhere Over The Rainbow," and "We're Off To See The Wizard" from the "Wizard of Oz." Perhaps the most popular songs came from "Snow White And The Seven Dwarfs," among them "Some Day My Prince Will Come," "One Song," "Heigh Ho," and "Whistle While You Work." A New York columnist wrote, "Walt Disney's 'Snow White and the Seven Dwarfs' was the happiest thing that has happened in the world since the armistice." Mother took me to Winnipeg to see "Snow White," the second movie I had ever seen and I was absolutely mesmerized. Entering its golden era, Hollywood produced other great motion pictures during that period, like "Gone With The Wind," "Beau Geste," "Stagecoach," and "Goodbye Mr. Chips."

The power of radio was quite evident when, in 1938 the "War of the Worlds," written and produced by Orson Welles and broadcast over C.B.S. in New York, had a script dealing with a supposed invasion of Earth by the inhabitants of Mars. When the fictitious Martians attacked the 15-mile Pulaski Skyway Bridge in New Jersey, people in surrounding areas became panic stricken. A section of the listening public excitedly telephoned from all parts of the country to the radio station for information, and police had to be summoned to calm an anxious crowd that had gathered in front of the broadcast building. It is doubtful such a situation could develop today due to bizarre occurrences of the past fifty years that have left today's people with the attitude that anything can happen. Nothing surprises them.

During the summer of 1939, as we approached that fateful date in September when most countries including Canada would again be plunged into war, life on the farm continued at its same peaceful pace.

But as it became more obvious that the conflict wouldn't be averted, our thoughts and conversations constantly turned to the news from Europe.

Mackenzie King, Canada's Prime Minister throughout the conflict, committed the nation to a policy of a "United Canada" that would support British military action should the European peace be shattered in a war of aggression. Like other western leaders though, he continued to indulge in the wishful thinking that Hitler could be contained by judicious appeasement. He had talked to Hitler in 1937 and completely failed to understand the German dictator. The neutrality campaign being waged in the United States had a powerful effect on the thinking of many Canadians, and probably a majority of Canadians believed Canada could in fact remain neutral in the event of a European war. King did little to disabuse the public mind in this respect while at the same time he himself never had any doubt about the decision that would be taken quickly in the event of war. Many believed that although a declaration of war by Britain was still legally binding upon Canada, the nature and extent of involvement remained exclusively a matter for Ottawa's decision. Mackenzie King didn't have to wait long to prove he retained the reins of government and controlled the fate of Canadians.

World War II began on September 1, 1939, when German troops and aircraft attacked Poland exactly one week after the August 23rd signing of a mutual non-aggression pact between Nazi Germany and Soviet Russia. On September 3, Britain and France declared war on Germany, and Prime Minister King declared war one week later without substantial overt division in Canada. In those months preceding the outbreak of hostilities, particularly in English-speaking Canada, the supporters of neutrality began to shift their opinions as Hitler's implacable purpose became harder to deny. As the isolationist stance of the United States showed no signs of faltering, many Canadians began to harbor ill-feelings towards their southern neighbor. The extent of unity in Canada could have been exaggerated, however, because with a population of slightly over 11 million, still over one half million were unemployed. The country's economy was recovering slowly from the long depression. As a result, many enlistments for the first Canadian Division were products of relief camps and work projects for the unemployed who brought with them a feeling of resignation rather than patriotic enthusiasm. Quebecors believed that the war was only another British Imperial conflict, and few held any patriotism towards France, who they felt had given them no support in the past two hundred years.

One of the major events in the spring of 1939 that altered the neutralist feeling of many Canucks was the visit of King George VI and Queen Elizabeth. The students of Pinewood School heralded the Winnipeg stopover as a gold star event, not because we were eager to view the King and Queen but because a complete day of leisure was a unique experience. Early in the morning we were driven to the local railroad station to catch a train to the city. We arrived at our predetermined viewing position shortly after noon. Streets were lined with thousands of flag-waving children, all enthusiastic for the royal procession, but that ardor waned as the hours dragged by. Our ample supply of provisions kept dwindling until we found ourselves standing in the hot prairie summer sun with nothing to do but sit on the curb. Late in the afternoon the royal limousine whizzed by, a momentous occasion that took less than ten seconds. Arriving back at the farm at midnight, after eighteen hours of train riding, curb sitting and sun bathing and with just a momentary glimpse of the royal couple, I was slightly perplexed. Mother always insisted I didn't understand the importance of royalty, and she was a hundred percent right on that score.

On the morning of September 2 as the Nazi war machine smashed into Poland, we were seated around the kitchen table discussing the significance of the European conflict and its immediate effect on Canadians in general and our family in particular. Suddenly out of the western sky rolled a huge black cloud that smothered the daylight so thoroughly we had to light the lamps. Mother wrote in her personal diary that she had never seen the sky so dark and ominous during daylight hours, and it proved to be a prophetic sign if ever there was one.

The following morning, Ruth and I were out in the woods a half mile from the house picking saskatoon berries for Mother to preserve. We had a marvelous variety of berries in Manitoba: strawberries, black currants, gooseberries, raspberries, pincherries, chokeberries, blueberries, with saskatoons the most delicious of all. Our pails brimmed with fruit, Ruth and I became alarmed by an oncoming roar when unexpectedly from out of the west a squadron of seven single-engine Anson training aircraft swooped over us at tree-top level. We rarely ever saw two at one time, let alone seven, and we raced home in quite a frenzy. Reaching our yard, we heard Mrs. Edie, our neighbor, calling Mom and Dad to come over and listen on their radio to hear King George VI speak to the British Empire and declare war on Germany. Before year's end, we finally purchased a new loud speaker radio of our own, allowing us to keep abreast of the news. We realized the world imminently faced a dramatic change but didn't know exactly how each of us would be affected.

At the beginning of the 1939-40 school year, Pinewood had less than a dozen students in total, but our enrollment was soon to increase. The Bell family had just moved into the neighborhood, and within two weeks, their three youngest children—Jim, slightly older than I, Mar-

garet, a little younger, and Eileen, about Ruth's age—helped to swell
our ranks. They and other members of their clan had a close relationship
with our family for many years. For me, however, the Fryza family who
moved onto a farm a half mile from ours made the most noteworthy
addition to our classroom. The Fryzas emigrated to Canada from Poland
during the spring of 1938. Joe Fryza was sponsored into the country by
his brother, Konstanz, who owned the farm prior to their arrival. The
Fryza farm, located in another school district, was crowded so the
children were transferred to the almost empty Pinewood School. The
oldest boy, Henry, stayed home to assist on the farm, but Leona, the
oldest girl and one year older than I, Charlie, who was approximately
my age, and Frank, who was Ruth's age, soon became our daily travelling
companions. The Fryza children had attended the other school for
several weeks and so were able to speak some English, but with limited
fluency. When they transferred to Pinewood, therefore, the conversation
we engaged in for the initial few months (especially along the two-mile
pathway we shared) was comical to say the least. Charlie immediately
taught me to swear in Polish and would go into convulsions as I tried to
pronounce the various slang terms. After several months, I became quite
proficient at Polish profanity, so one day I tried my new language on
Leona, who though angry at Charlie for teaching me the vulgarities was
amused at my pronounciations. Eventually she taught me a couple of
oaths that even Charlie hadn't heard. Forty years later, I could still
curse in Polish.

Charlie and I became particularly good friends though we both had
hot tempers which resulted in numerous physical clashes. One winter
day, I whacked Charlie for some reason, and he didn't retaliate immediately. After school hours, he and I were given the responsibility of
cleaning the blackboards, and at the completion of our task Charlie
fired his brush across the room, striking me in the chest. On the way
home Charlie stayed about ten feet in front of me along the single lane,
snow-packed path through the woods without saying a word. Reaching
the main road, which we shared for an additional two hundred yards
before he branched off toward his home, Charlie allowed me to catch
up, whirled around and threw a haymaker that landed on my shoulder
and then squared off to do battle. We had a gentlemen's fight, unusual
for a couple of kids. Instead of the normal wrestling match, we slugged
it out toe-to-toe, and when one went down, the other waited until he got
to his feet. Both heavily padded with winter clothing and finding it
difficult to maneuver on the icy road prevented us from causing each
other much harm, but we did keep it up for at least a half hour. Ruth
and the school teacher, 15 minutes behind us, passed by and, except for
a momentary halt to voice their unflattering opinion of our spectacle,

kept walking. Finally both exhausted, Charlie said quite abruptly, "I've got to get home to do the chores." And with that, he sped off down his own trail as though nothing had happened. Charlie and I shared innumerable unique experiences over the succeeding few years, but never again had a physical contest figuring I guess we were a match.

The Fryza family had many relatives in Poland, and so they received the news with horror as the Germans poured into their country from the west and Soviet troops invaded from the east. Warsaw surrendered on September 17, and Germany and the U.S.S.R. partitioned Poland on September 28, Jack's 15th birthday. The trauma experienced by the Fryzas plus other Polish families is hard to imagine as their country became the first to be annihilated by the Nazi war machine. Many years later while visiting Warsaw, I was privileged to be shown by the Polish government a half-hour documentary of the methodical destruction of the beautiful capital city of Poland. The French prepared the presentation from film taken off captured German planes. I can understand the repugnance Polish people must have felt during the first months of the conflict.

From the outbreak of hostilities and throughout early spring of 1940, Britain and France sat smuggly behind the Maginot Line, a system of fortifications along the eastern frontier of France and extending from the Swiss border to Belgium. Though considered impregnable, its chief effect was the false sense of security it offered those sitting behind, like fortified lines throughout history, including the Great Wall of China. Germany also had a comparable defensive set-up, called the Siegfried Line. A popular song at the time called "We're Going To Hang Out The Washing On The Siegfried Line" didn't remain popular for long.

The light-hearted, cocky attitude of the Allies throughout the Twilight War, as phrased by Winston Churchill, ended in April when German troops occupied Denmark without resistance and then invaded Norway, whose forces were paralyzed by treachery. On May 10, the war began in earnest as the Blitzkrieg (Lightning War) rained destruction on Rotterdam and other Dutch cities from the air while German infantry swept without warning into the Lowlands, completely outflanking the Maginot Line from which never a shot was fired. Following the Dutch surrender on May 14, German mechanized divisions swept into Belgium and northern France toward the English Channel ports. Belgium's forces capitulated on May 28, the French army under General Weygand collapsed, and it appeared that 200,000 British troops in Flanders would be trapped. Perhaps at that point fate intervened as Winston Churchill, one of the greatest leaders in history, became Prime Minister of Great Britain, succeeding Neville Chamberlain who resigned in some disgrace. "I have nothing to offer but blood, toil, tears, and sweat," Churchill told the House of Commons in his maiden speech as British leader. But he made the British objective clear: "Victory: victory at all costs, victory in spite of all terror, victory however long and hard the road may be: for without victory there is no survival."

One of the miracles of the war began on June 4 as the bulk of the 200,000 British expeditionary force and 140,000 French (the remnants of that proud army) were evacuated from Dunkirk beaches. Swarming German armies for some inexplicable reason hesitated long enough for the evacuation to take place. Hundreds of craft, large and small and of every design, ferried the men across the English Channel, though 30,000 were killed or taken prisoner. The same day, during the evacuation, Churchill made one of his greatest fighting speeches: "We shall fight in France, we shall fight on the seas and oceans, we shall fight with growing confidence and growing strength in the air, we shall defend our island, whatever the cost may be, we shall fight on the beaches, we shall fight on the landing grounds, we shall fight in the fields and in the streets, we shall fight in the hills, we shall never surrender." He spoke with such conviction that no one doubted him, and at one of the lowest points in the conflict, he alone lifted the spirits of the free world. His words were chiefly bluff because in their retreat across France, British forces lost most of their armament and faced the immediate future nearly helpless to ward off invasion.

Italy declared war on France on June 10, and President Roosevelt said, "The hand that held the dagger has plunged it into the back of her neighbor." On June 14, German troops entered Paris, and on June 22, France signed an armistice with Hitler.

Hitler's conquests, unequalled since the days of Napoleon, shocked some Americans out of their isolationist stand. Nonetheless, most U.S. citizens still wanted their country to remain neutral. Congress enacted a law requiring alien residents to register and passed the Selective Service and Training Act, inaugurating the first peacetime military draft in American history. They also supplied Great Britain with fifty old destroyers in exchange for naval and air bases.

In Monominto, we listened in shocked disbelief as our new radio poured out the dreadful news and those traumatic events unfolded. Ruth and I, together with other students, knitted scarves and socks during recess and lunch hour, and often special classes were set aside for knitting. Everyone who could scrape together a few pennies bought saving stamps at the rate of twenty-five cents per week, and Canada Savings Bonds were being pedalled by the government at every opportunity.

During 1941, when the Nazi Luftwaffe intensified its air attacks on British cities and both Allied and Axis planes were being knocked out of the sky in unprecedented numbers, Ruth and I would race home from school to hear the latest reports. Ninety German bombers were destroyed between July 15 and 21, and on August 15 when the Battle of Britain reached its peak, British Spitfire fighters shot down 180 attacking Stukas. Referring to the R.A.F. Churchill said, "Never in the field of human conflict was so much owed by so many to so few." The loss of German bombers reached such enormous proportions that Hitler decided to change tactics, and in late August, he began his all-night air raids on London and other English cities. By September, hundreds were killed daily and thousands injured as the free world stood by and watched with grave concern. The brave British people prepared themselves to resist the expected German invasion of their homeland, and except for Commonwealth nations, they stood alone.

At the time of its declaration of war on the German Reich, Canada possessed a regular army of 4,000 men, a Militia of 50,000, an Air Force of 2,400, and a Navy of 2,000, but before the hostilities ended, over a million men were in uniform, a remarkable effort for a nation of only 12 million people. Over 58,000 were taken into the army in the first month, and the Canadian government dispatched one army division overseas before the end of 1939, so Canadian troops were on British soil to help defend the Mother country. Conscription, introduced in 1940, limited the service of conscripts to home defense.

Our radio not only provided us with up-to-the-minute news broadcasts but also dispensed our main source of entertainment. After chores, we all gathered around to listen to our favorite programs which included: "Fibber McGee and Molly," Edgar Bergen and Charlie McCarthy, Kate Smith's "Bandwagon," and "Truth or Consequences." Among the popular songs relating to the war were "There'll Always Be An England," "The Last Time I Saw Paris," "Bless 'Em All," and "The White Cliffs of Dover." Others that remained favorites for decades also written during those suspenseful times were "You Are My Sunshine," "When You Wish Upon A Star," "Blueberry Hill," and "Back In The Saddle Again." These are just a few that brightened up the air waves and our lives.

War news in the spring of 1941 overpowered all other happenings. Several of our older classmates plus neighbors' sons in the services were already overseas, and when the first local casualty, Lawrence Sweet, an Air Force officer was killed in a bombing raid over Europe, the war suddenly seemed very real indeed. British forces under General Wavell went on the offensive in North Africa against the Italians in late 1940 and drove them out of Libya. Except for the success of the Royal Air Force against Germany's Luftwaffe, the victory against the Italian Army was the first good news of the war, despite its short duration. General

Erwin Rommel, appointed to command German troops sent to Africa to repel the British advance, pushed General Wavell and his troops all the way back to Tobruk near the Egyptian border in the first few months of 1941. After two years of constant exposure to the barrage of tidings regarding the conflict, we unconsciously began to accept the war as a way of life and our existence on the farm went on much as before the whole thing started.

Chapter 6
Life Goes On

I believe the community of Monominto had more eccentrics per square mile than anywhere else in the world. That they were mostly bachelors perhaps had a major bearing on their strange lifestyles. John Wylie, a man in his seventies, lived in a one-room frame dwelling located on his nephew's farm adjacent to ours. John and his brother Andrew came from Scotland and were two of the earliest settlers in the Monominto area. Jim Wylie, Andrew's son, married Mary Oaks who taught me at Pinewood School for six years. Jim told me one day that his uncle John sold his homestead in the 1920's and received several of the first hundred dollar bills Jim had ever seen. John also had a Cree Indian girl friend. After selling his farm, he departed Monominto with both doll and dollars but returned 15 years later with neither. As a result, Jim constructed the frame cabin for his needy bachelor uncle. Affectionately called Old John by the local community, he did some trapping to supplement his old-age pension. Always on the lookout for as much information as possible about different methods of trapping, I found him good company and frequently dropped in for a visit. Also as we bypassed his shack, Ruth and I almost always stopped for a few minutes on our way home from school.

One afternoon in the spring of 1941 after Rommel had pushed the allies back toward Egypt, I was discussing the African situation with Old John while Ruth sat nearby as an interested listener. Rommel, nicknamed "The Desert Fox" because of his cunning leadership, received a lot of plaudits, even from his enemies, and I remarked to my friend John that Rommel seemed to be clever and capable. The old Scotchman exploded. He jumped up threateningly and waving his fists, hollered, "Get oot of here ye nu good **Nazi sympathizer. I'll nae hae a**

57

son-of-a-bitch like you in me hoose." Ruth and I took off like a couple of rabbits with a coyote hot on their tail and could hear Old John still yelling a quarter mile away. A few days later as Ruth and I went slithering by his cabin, he called out for us to come over. We did so with trepidation, but John had cooled off. He admonished me for saying anything good about the hated Hun, but reluctantly admitted that maybe Rommel showed some signs of brilliance. Nevertheless, he insisted that Rommel would soon get his come-uppance, and he proved prophetic.

Several others within a radius of two miles would have been prime candidates for a Hitchcock thriller because of their bizarre existence. The Wilson brothers, Tommy and Bobby, were midgets who stood slightly under four feet tall. They lived in a decrepit log shack that most dogs would have refused to enter. Originally constructed as a barn, it stood or rather sagged, within two hundred feet of an excellent two-story frame dwelling that was the original family home. For reasons known only to them, they refused to move out of their hovel. The Wilson boys made a meager living by bootlegging to patrons of Monominto Hall where dances were held every Saturday night. It was conveniently located a few hundred yards away from their shack.

The Anghelichts brothers, another unusual pair who distilled their own whiskey, farmed a mile and a half north of us. Occasionally, they requested Father's help with different tasks, and Dad reported they drank whiskey with everything, including coffee, tea, and dessert. He swore they even used moonshine on their breakfast cereal. Both Anghelichts were huge, powerful men. Henry, the oldest, would frequently ride one of their farm horses over to a neighbor's for a visit or perhaps as transportation to the store. He always toted a generous supply of booze, which in winter kept him warm and in summer served as an insect repellent. Usually drunk by the time he was ready to return home, Henry couldn't get astride his horse and so he would simply grab the animal by the tail and holler "Giddap!" The horse never became attuned to such an unorthodox and undignified exploitation, and so it would let fly with both feet catching Henry flush in his massive chest and sending him ass-over-teakettle into the ditch. This setback never deterred Henry who would eventually overcome the beast's skittishness and then stagger down the road toward home with a firm grasp on his horse's tail, creating quite an unusual spectacle. Albert, the other brother, would often hike, together with his girl friend, down the local railway right-of-way to a general store for provisions. They were also well fortified with whiskey and carried an ample supply to sustain them on the journey. From time to time Albert would get sleepy, and so then he and his girl friend would lie down on the railroad ties, which were high and dry, and have a snooze. One day a freight train almost ran over the two of them. The woman apparently awoke just in time to alert Albert who rolled out of the path of the on-coming train a split second before it passed over his resting place. Alec Hussack, the store owner, insisted that a short time later he heard Albert remark to his girl friend while sitting in his store, "You know, if we'd both got run over we'd be rich, because each of us would have collected a thousand bucks in life insurance." Alec claimed Albert looked downright melancholy about losing all that money. A few years later Albert was alone and didn't hear an on-coming train. He was killed on the same stretch of track. Someone finally collected his life insurance.

The Matterns were original settlers in the community. Fred, the oldest of the children, played the violin, and Frank, a younger brother, the accordion. Occasionally they were called on to perform at parties and dances. Fred, an outgoing person, played his fiddle with such vigorous great rocking back and forth that it seemed at times he would tumble off his seat. His head jerked so violently with the instrument tucked securely under his chin that often he'd be sawing at air with his bow missing the fiddle completely, but both feet hammered the floor in cadence with the rhythm. Meanwhile, Frank, an unobtrusive type fellow, pumped his accordian in quiet reserve, moving his arms and hands only as required. Never displaying facial expressions of any kind, he sat as rigid as a bed board. Both Fred and Frank lived alone on their individual farms, and a visit to Fred's house provided an unforgettable experience. Some rooms in his two-story home were littered with such a multitude of paraphernalia that they were almost filled to capacity. I seriously doubt if he had any notion of what was stored in them, and how he located anything puzzled me no end. Nevertheless, Fred was a happy man and good conversationalist, always popular with our family.

Donald Sutherland and his brother Frank moved from a Saskatchewan grain farm and bought 160 acres covered mainly by a softwood bush, ideal for cordwood. With saws and axes, the Sutherlands attacked their bush, a mile west of our farm, with an unusual ferocity. Unlike most people who simply thinned out a stand of trees, the Sutherlands annihilated it, as though they wanted their holdings to resemble the prairie they had left behind.

Occasionally, Donald would shyly approach our house or one of our neighbors to buy eggs or other produce, timing his arrival to coincide with the dinner hour. When invited to join in, he never refused and would shovel in more food in 10 minutes than the rest of the family did together in a half hour. One day Mom thought that after four helpings he had finally got full and asked if he'd like some chocolate pudding.

"Oh, yes!," he replied.

When Mother handed him the dessert, he filled his main plate with another helping of meat and mashed potatoes, then dumped the chocolate pudding over the lot. We believe he thought it was gravy. Nevertheless, he downed it with gusto and declared it delicious.

Emil Roy, a French Canadian who lived a mile north of us, raised a few pigs and chickens and had a cow or two to provide him with fresh milk, but he derived his main revenue from blacksmithing. Emil also distilled his own homebrew out of potatoes, barley—or both. When cooking, the mash gave off a peculiar aroma, and if not familiar with the smell, one would have no idea what befouled the air. Because Jack and I frequently took pieces of broken farm machinery to him for welding, we were accustomed to the odor.

Another old bachelor, Johnson McDole, moved in from Saskatchewan and settled within two hundred yards of Emil Roy. The two never got along right from the start, with their communal fence probably the greatest source of agitation.

McDole, like Donald Sutherland, took a great liking to Mother's cooking, and though he often helped Dad with farm work, Johnson spent so much time at our house that he became a real nuisance. Forever complaining to Father about Emil Roy, he often said how he would like to get something on Emil to bring him to heel. One evening at the supper table, McDole said to Dad, "You know that gawd-damn Frenchman is a strange one."

"Why so?" asked Father.

"Well," said McDole, "I'm often annoyed by an odd stench that drifts over when the wind is in the north, and so I moseyed over yesterday and discovered the smell coming from the granary. Flinging open the door, I found the damn fool with some kind of strange apparatus and a huge vat of grain mash and potatoes. What on earth possesses him to prepare pig feed in that fashion, I'll never know." He said Roy got exceedingly angry and ordered him out. "I guess he was damned embarrassed," added McDole.

Father, being a friend of both men, never let on to Johnson that his neighbor manufactured moonshine, and for the few years they were neighbors, McDole never woke up to the fact he had his nemesis where he wanted him.

Johnson McDole chewed tobacco and spit its juice where and when he took a hankering. One day he let fly into the kitchen wood container where Mother had to put her hands to fuel the fire. A brief but deathly silence followed this faux pas before Mom gave him a blast heard in the barnyard. We didn't see McDole much after that incident.

We had little to be enthusiastic about throughout 1941 as the war news from Europe continued to be grim. Franklin Delano Roosevelt began his third term, the first American President to be so elected, and his congressional message in January defied the widespread isolationist sentiment and recommended a massive Lend-Lease program to aid the Allies. Before the year ended, Congress had authorized more than 25 billion dollars for defense and Lend-Lease.

When Rudolph Hess, Hitler's personal aide and third ranking member of the Nazi Party, landed in Scotland in May, it caused quite a stir. The British immediately interned him despite the rumor he came with a peace proposal. On June 22 German troops invaded Soviet Russia. Utter fascination swept the world as 164 German divisions rolled eastward against a comparably sized Russian army. The Russian forces initially collapsed in front of deep plunging armoured thrusts of Nazi panzer divisions, and the Russian air force suffered severe losses with thousands of planes being destroyed on the ground by the Luftwaffe. During the first month, German troops pushed three hundred miles into the Russian homeland, and only the immense size of that nation prevented it from suffering the same fate as other occupied countries of Europe.

Until the invasion, few people in the Allied camp felt much sympathy toward the U.S.S.R. In fact, most took some delight in seeing Stalin and his Communist system taking a beating from the Nazis. Until Hitler set upon them, the Soviets cared for no one but themselves, but after the invasion, they began to scream for Allied aid. What strange bedfellows wars can create! Imagine the world's two great divergent ideologies— Capitalism and Communism—suddenly awakening to find themselves allies against the menace of Fascism. A Soviet capitulation appeared imminent within one to three months of the invasion, but as summer wore on and the Germans neared Moscow, their advance gradually slowed. Then, before winter, it stopped completely a few miles outside the Russian capital.

While these colossal battles were being waged during the summer of 1941, I faced a dilemma in my own personal affairs. Having completed Grade VIII successfully, I now faced the same problem that had confronted Jack two years earlier. To continue my studies, I either had to leave home or else complete Grade IX by correspondence from Manitoba's Department of Education, requiring a ten-dollar fee. Father, wanting me on the farm, refused to pay, and I admit that he faced a dilemma. Jack, nearing seventeen, expected his draft notice within a year. After having two sons to assist him in running the farm for several years, Father didn't relish the prospect of going it alone. In spite of his objections, Mother and several relatives strongly recommended I be allowed to continue my education, and when Uncle George offered to put up the fee, Father relented and I returned to school.

It wasn't only the continuation of my education that bothered me.

As the war continued, Jack's date with the military approached and I couldn't bear the thought of remaining home by myself. Except for my hospital experience, Jack and I had been inseparable. I also realized that he would be getting a chance to do something I couldn't. Patriotism never played a part in my longing to become involved. I simply wanted to be part of what seemed like a never-to-be-repeated adventure.

Father understood my hankering to join the fray. As a young man in Winnipeg, he played hockey, and heavily body-checked to the ice during a game, he severely twisted his right leg from knee to foot. For reasons I never thoroughly understood, the doctors that examined the x-rays didn't determine the extent of damage. Though he suffered extreme pain, he continued to walk on the injured limb. The leg swelled up to three times its normal size, and within a few months, Dad ended up totally bedridden. Eventually a German bone specialist found several bones out of place. Unfortunately, he missed a couple that were not discovered for another forty years. By correcting some of the problem, Father could walk again, but the continued use of the limb with bones out of place didn't allow the swelling to subside. For the rest of his life he had to keep his leg heavily bandaged when using it. Being of age at the outbreak of World War I, he wanted to join the army with two of his brothers—Uncle Joe, who was eventually killed in action in France, and Uncle Ernie, who returned home severely wounded. Not being in uniform but without any apparent sign of a disability subjected Father to many insults. Listening to him talk about the humiliation and frustration he suffered throughout the four years of that conflict, I could easily understand his anguish. Grandmother Phillips frequently remarked that Father's inability to enlist might have saved him from the same fate as his brothers. That didn't ease his disappointment, of course. Dad had reared me to believe I could do anything I put my mind to, but we now both knew that I, like he, was destined to watch this action from the sidelines.

On December 7, 1941, 360 carrier-based Japanese planes attacked Pearl Harbor and crippled the U.S. Pacific Fleet. This sneak assault, termed by Roosevelt as "a date that will live in infamy," disintegrated the isolationist sentiment of Americans and catapulted the United States into the struggle for freedom. Japan immediately declared war on Great Britain. Germany and Italy declared war on the United States and vice versa. So finally the sides were chosen, and the ruptured relations between Canadians and Americans were soon mended as the two countries pooled their resources to face a common enemy.

In mid-December, the Japanese attacked Hong Kong where Canadian troops were stationed, one a Winnipeg battalion led by a popular radio announcer. Mary Wylie, our Pinewood school teacher, had two brothers in the Winnipeg contingent. The troops fought gallantly against overwhelming odds, and when the final Japanese assault overran Canadian positions on Christmas Eve, it caused a bleak holiday in numerous homes in the Winnipeg area. Many other families in North America didn't have a particularly Merry Christmas either. On December 22, 100,000 Japanese troops landed for a major invasion of the Philippines defended by American and Philippine troops, and Manila fell to the enemy on January 2, 1942.

At the beginning of 1942, I did not contemplate that I had began my final full year on the farm. The appalling war news remained foremost in everyone's mind throughout the winter and early spring. Singapore fell to the Japanese February 15, and when they captured the Solomon Islands on March 13, Australia became imperiled. U.S. troops on the Bataan Peninsula surrendered April 9, and when Corregidor collapsed May 6, the Philippines were lost. The victorious Japanese completed their conquest of Burma when Mandalay fell on May 2. In Africa, British and Australian troops lost Tobruk to Field Marshall Erwin Rommel. Meanwhile, German U-boats were taking an enormous toll of Allied shipping. Dispatches of Japanese atrocities against prisoners of war, though ghastly news, didn't compare with the completely incomprehensible reports of Germany's "Final Solution" towards European Jews. Weekly accounts of the methodical annihilation and mass murder of all Jews within his reach began by Adolph Hitler and his gestapo chief, Heinrich Himmler, was accepted with stunning skepticism. We refused to believe that one race would actually perpetuate such an inhuman crime against another.

Feelings of hatred against Germans and Japanese in North America reached fever pitch. Over a hundred thousand American and Canadian Japanese living in coastal Pacific areas were moved inland or placed in concentration camps. Transplanted with minimum notice, they were generally deprived of all personal belongings and their property sold at rock-bottom prices. The panic of the time cannot be better illustrated than by the decision of Winnipeg officials to take precautions against the possible poisoning of that city's fresh water supply.

Winnipeg received its water from Shoal Lake, located on the Manitoba-Ontario boundary approximately 90 miles away. It travelled to the city through a concrete conduit, via gravity. Grandfather Rodd worked on the project as an engineer in the early part of the century, and the National Geographic Magazine published an article about the unique project many years ago. The Greater Winnipeg Water District, a department of the City of Winnipeg, owned, controlled, and maintained a 200 foot right-of-way from Shoal Lake to the city which encompassed a railway line that paralleled the conduit at a distance of 60 feet. This

G.W.W.D. right-of-way passed our farm a half mile to the north. The concrete conduit varied in size, but at our crossing, it spanned eight feet in diameter. It was buried beneath several feet of soil to protect it from winter frosts. Every two miles, a "breather" with a steel manhole cover secured by a massive padlock allowed inspection of the system. During the arid summers of the middle '30's when our wells had dried up, Father found a way to jimmy the lock, and so we'd drive our stock the half mile to the crossing and then with a rope and pail scoop out enough water to satisfy our herd. We would take home a few barrels of the precious liquid. If Winnipeg people realized that farmers were using their water supply to sate the thirst of cattle, there would have been hell to pay. Nevertheless, worse things would eventually happen.

It occurred to some G.W.W.D. official in 1942 how simple it would be for the enemy to poison Winnipeg's water supply by simply removing the manhole cover. To protect themselves against such a possibility, they converted a passenger car into an inspection vehicle, installed a powerful searchlight, and made a tour over the 90 miles every twelve hours. This would allow anyone with the desire of killing off the Winnipeg populace eleven hours and forty-five minutes between surveillances to pry off the lid of the breather and to do their dirty work. To make it more ludicrous, during daylight hours we'd often see the lone occupant of the car sound asleep as he went whizzing by.

One evening Dad and I were returning home after dark from hunting cows. Reaching the crossing, we could see and hear the inspection car coming hellbent down the tracks. Father said, "Let's sit on the manhole cover and let the spotlight pick us up to see if he'll stop. You sit on the manhole cover, and I'll get on the opposite side of the track."

"I want to see the driver's reaction when he spots you," I replied.

Our suspicions were confirmed when the powerful searchlight silhouetted Father on the breather like a moth in a lamp shade. The vehicle, clinging to the steel rails with the sentry sound asleep, sped toward the city unaware of the potential danger to Winnipeg's water.

There was no love lost between the farmers in the Monominto area and the G.W.W.D. officials. Freight trains with coal-fired steam engines used the route chiefly to haul pulpwood and gravel. Occasionally, these steam engines threw off sparks that ignited dry hay or grain fields paralleling the railway line. The farmers would band together to fight these destructive blazes and then attempt to collect damages from the water district. Generally, the city denied responsibility for starting the fire, which infuriated the farmers. It usually took a threat of court action before they reached a settlement.

The huge mound of protective soil covering the water main had flattened down over the years providing an excellent road for horse and wagons or for automobiles in the spring, particularly when other roads were flooded or impassable. It was also the shortest route to the two general stores located beside the railroad, either two miles east or a mile and a half west. Because these embankments were private property, travelling along them was strictly against the law. Damage to the underlying concrete conduit that might be caused by traffic concerned the G.W.W.D. the most. While accompanying Father or driving by myself with horses and wagon, I had numerous run-ins with G.W.W.D. officials. If we were going in opposite directions to a G.W.W.D. vehicle, they couldn't do much because by the time they could get stopped and back up, we could reach a crossing and turn off. However, when both were going in the same direction, it worked to their advantage. At the first sound of an approaching railway vehicle, we would start a wild gallop to the nearest turnoff, but if we lost the race and they passed us, an official would be waiting on the right-of-way to bawl us out and threaten to sue us for trespassing. I never knew of anyone who paid a fine for travelling on the right-of-way, but they could well have been correct that traffic would weaken the concrete.

One spring afternoon, Jack and I were working in our farmyard when John Thompson, a neighbor from the east, came dashing into our yard driving a pair of spirited broncos. John excitedly informed us that when he crossed the right-of-way a few minutes earlier, he passed a herd of cattle grazing along the top of the water line and that all at once part of the embankment caved in and one cow disappeared. He couldn't stop to investigate because of the friskiness of his team. Jack fetched Father while I raced to get our neighbor's son, Ernie Eedy, and the four of us sped to the crossing in Ernie's car. Sure enough, a chunk of the embankment about ten feet in diameter had caved in together with a large piece of the concrete conduit and the cow stood gazing up dolefully at us in three to four feet of ice cold rushing water. She was at least fourteen feet below the top of the embankment. She did not appear to be injured, but we realized that she could not survive long standing in the icy water. Father sent Ernie to the nearest phone to alert the G.W.W.D. of the catastrophe. Within two hours Winnipeg officials came racing down the railway line in their private car, but the frightened cow, numbed with the cold water, had wandered away from the cave-in. Three men were lowered into the water together with a canoe. They located the unfortunate animal about a mile from where she had fallen in, and she was already dead.

The G.W.W.D. administrators suggested it would be best for all concerned if we didn't make an issue of the tragic happening. They were gravely worried that if the Winnipeg papers got hold of the story some panic might result and perhaps heads would roll. They could imagine the reaction of Winnipeg's citizens if they knew a cow had been in their water supply for hours doing those things all animals are required to do, then dying, and later being butchered before its final removal.

The aftermath of the incident occurred a month later when the neighbor who lost the animal came to Dad complaining that the G.W.W.D. refused to compensate him for his loss. The water department claimed that the right-of-way, being Winnipeg property, was out of bounds to the cow. This was a ridiculous argument because the G.W.W.D. was responsible to have cattle guards at all crossings in this free range country. Father told him not to worry that he would accompany him on his next trip to Winnipeg to see the city about his cow.

Dad apparently went directly to the G.W.W.D. superintendent and said, "I understand you are denying responsibility for the loss of this man's cow."

The superintendent hotly retorted, "If you damn farmers would keep your stock and vehicles off the pipe line, it wouldn't have caved in. You are the people responsible for its weakened condition."

"I won't argue," Father said, "But two of my sons and a neighbor were witnesses to the tragedy, and we've been dying to inform the *Winnipeg Tribune* about the treatment to which the Winnipeg water supply is subjected."

It was blackmail without a doubt, but the neighbor received a very satisfactory price for his cow.

Though highly regarded in the community due to his willingness to assist anyone at anytime, most of our neighbors didn't consider Dad a particularly successful farmer and rightly so. He worked hard but lacked planning ability and would have been more successful with a chief administrator as an overseer. For instance, we would finish haying a month after the other farmers, who were already doing their fall plowing. As a result, our plowing didn't get completed until the following spring when crops should have been planted. He would get his priorities confused, not placing the proper emphasis on those tasks of greatest importance. I have no doubt his shortcomings probably had a bearing on his sometimes rancorous nature.

Each summer, in the late 1930's and usually while the three of us were haying (a chore we all enjoyed), a black sedan would come wheeling into the yard. It belonged to a government man who had come to try to collect the mortgage payment on the farm, always months or years in arrears. Recognizing the car and its bearer of bad news, Dad's mood changed instantly. A proud man, he was embarrassed when he couldn't meet his obligations and had to request more time to pay. After the man's departure, Father would be his old irrascible self for several days, even though he wasn't the only farmer behind in his mortgage payments during those financially distressing times. Had he confronted the decision makers in Winnipeg about his inability to meet the payment schedule before his indebtedness became so far overdue and requested a new payout within his financial means, I feel sure they would have altered his contract. The fact they never foreclosed showed their reluctance to take the farm back. In my opinion, if Father had faced the situation head-on instead of living in trepidation of seeing that black automobile, he would have been a happier man. Although a procrastinator when making his own decisions, later years would prove him to be a competent administrator when working under some direction.

As youngsters, Jack and I never really grasped the significance of the collector's visit, but for Father's sake, we hated to see his annual arrival. The misery Father sustained from those encounters taught me a lesson about dealing with fiscal obligations that would be beneficial throughout my business life. In later years, when unable to meet a financial responsibility, I went directly to the creditor before the due date, explained my circumstances, and suggested a plan I could manage. After a stern lecture, I generally was given time to sort out my affairs, provided they believed my request genuine. Few lenders want to foreclose if it can be avoided.

The non-school education young people are exposed to is invaluable if they understand and absorb the knowledge and store it away for future use. Dad's older brother Jim, ten years his senior, gave me great insight in dealing with human nature during the summer of 1942. Except for the few odd days Father spent in Winnipeg each year buying or selling farm stock or shopping for necessities, he rarely got a recreational break. This lack of free time was more difficult for him to accept than other farmers who had spent their life on the land. They knew no different. Father did. Prior to moving to Monominto, he and his brothers owned fishing and hunting camps in the vicinity of Lake Winnipeg where they spent summer week ends and enjoyed annual vacations. Photographs in the family album attest to the amount of time they holidayed in that locale.

When he left Winnipeg, Father sold his financial interest in the camps to Uncle Jim, who still owned a cottage on Devil's Creek that drained a large area of the Libau swamplands. Situated a half mile from where the creek joined the Red River, and two miles from where the Red emptied into Lake Winnipeg, the cabin did not have easy accessibility. Father's yarns of fishing and duck hunting in that locale as a young man always seemed one of the conversational topics dearest to his heart. Marshes surrounding the southern end of Lake Winnipeg were famous for their massive concentration of green-necked mallards, teal, canvasbacks, and other species, making it a renowned hunting region. Uncle Jim had guided Bing Crosby on duck hunting expeditions in the 1930s. With no bag limit in the early part of the century, we would listen in awe as Father recounted incidents when he and his brothers shot a hundred or more at a single hunt. Dad claimed the birds, sold to Winnipeg hotels and butcher shops, always ended up on someone's table. Fattened on surrounding prairie grain fields, Manitoba ducks were delicious eating. It wouldn't have been difficult for Father to have visited Uncle Jim's lodge, which from our farm didn't exceed 60 miles, but for a long time he never received an invitation. He and his older brother had a dispute when they dissolved their partnership in the meat-rendering business prior to his moving to the farm in 1929 and didn't talk to each other for several years.

Uncle Jim and Aunt Edna never had children, and they doted on all their nieces and nephews. He delivered and picked up merchandise in the several Army and Air Force camps throughout Manitoba and invited Jack to accompany him on his rounds during the spring of 1942. This broke the ice, and so Father and I were invited to spend a couple of days at his Devil's Lake fishing lodge in early June. The prospect of the venture thrilled and excited me, but no more than Dad. Though I had never been in any type of boat, large bodies of water attracted me like steel filings to a magnet. Whatever the reason, I anxiously waited the opportunity to get on a body of water, even though it was only a river.

We reached Uncle Jim's in midafternoon where he waited with food, plenty of beer, and ample live bait. The beer would play an important role in the lesson I was about to learn. Uncle Jim drove his car along the west bank of the Red River about eight miles from his Devil's Creek Camp that lay across the waterway on the east side. He parked his vehicle in a farmer's yard where he stored his canoe. The only bridge over the Red between Lake Winnipeg and the city at Lockport, a few miles north of Winnipeg, wasn't suitable because no road existed down the east bank to his cottage. We loaded the canoe with our provisions an hour before sundown and paddled down current for seven miles before crossing the mighty Red, over a mile in width at that point. We then turned up Devil's Creek the half mile to his cabin. A perfect summer evening, with hardly a ripple on the water, offered an idyllic setting for my first canoe ride, and though tiny, the cottage sparsely furnished with bunks projecting from each side wall seemed like a castle to me. Before retiring, Unk prepared night fishing lines that he strung out across the creek. I could hardly sleep in anticipation of the morning's adventure.

Up at dawn, I especially recall there not being a cloud visible on the horizon. After a delightful bacon and egg breakfast, Uncle Jim set me up on the dock with two fishing lines, a pail of minnows, and instructed me in how to catch perch. He didn't own modern rods or reels, but simply used a line, sinker, and baited hook, stringing the line through a forked willow hanging from the dock. When the willow jiggled, one had a fish and knowing no better, I thought the technique rather ingenious. The dock was built two feet below the bank and five or six feet above the water level in the creek. The fish, biting like crazy, jerked my line incessantly, and I excitedly pulled them in hand over hand and added them to my stringer. Dad and Uncle Jim sat in deck chairs under some large elms rimming the creek sipping beer while catching a few pickerel and jack pike on lines heavily weighted, baited with live crabs and tossed into the middle of the fast-moving current. The fun-filled morning slipped by too fast, and while preparing a mess of my perch for a tasty repast, we heard the ominous sound of thunder in the distance.

The storm approached slowly from out of the west but struck with unrestrained fury. Raging winds, a deluge of rain and hail, plus vivid lightning and booming thunder lasted for three hours. As the rain abated from the vicious electrical storm, the wind turned north and increased in velocity. Uncle Jim began to show some concern. We obviously couldn't canoe across the tumultuous Red, and the violent wind would soon push the waters of Lake Winnipeg back up the river, causing both the Red and Devil's Creek to spill over their banks within hours. Lake Winnipeg, the third largest fresh-water lake in Canada, has an enormous bulk of water. After supper, the three of us played cards, but every few minutes the men would go out to examine the creek level and check to see if the wind had diminished. By ten o'clock, the water in the creek had risen about five feet and neared the level of the dock. Though we couldn't see the Red, Unk said it would soon be overflowing its banks. He suggested we get some sleep but stay on the alert.

Though I slept quite soundly, I heard the others go out several times to investigate the situation because the wind kept howling from out of the north. Aroused shortly after daylight by the delicious aroma of frying bacon, I had the temporary notion the predicament had resolved itself, a thought that soon vanished when I ventured outside. Devil's Creek was spilling over its banks which meant it had risen over eight feet since the beginning of the storm. I watched Uncle Jim with amazement as he stowed gear into knapsacks in preparation to evacuate the cabin, its floor now less than a foot above the rising water. He left behind all items of food and most personal articles, but he loaded every remaining bottle of beer. In fact, they made up most of the weight in our packs. Heading south from camp, we had to wade through water up to our knees, we sloshed for about six miles before we came to higher ground and the first residence on the Red River, south of Lake Winnipeg. Uncle Jim explained to the occupants about our car on the opposite bank and asked if he could hire them to take us across in their fishing boat. They [point blank] refused but referred us to other commercial fishermen farther up the river. Trudging to two more dwellings, Unk made the same request, but they also flatly rejected his plea due to the wild condition of the water. Each family mentioned a man called Jake Dubroski who had a larger dory and might consider the undertaking. Dubroski's layout, almost directly across the river from our automobile, included several out buildings plus assorted machinery indicating an involvement in farming as well as commercial fishing. This time Uncle Jim used a different approach.

A man in his early thirties came up to us, and Unk stuck out his hand in a friendly greeting, "Are you Jake Dubroski?" he asked.

"Yes," the chap politely replied.

Unk introduced the three of us, then immediately entered into small talk about the atrocious weather. Then he asked Jake how the fishing had been.

"Fair," Jake responded. He invited us to see his previous day's catch, and while walking to the ice house he remarked that he still had a net in the river. The storm caught him by surprise, he explained, but nobody of a sound mind would venture onto the river on such a day. Unk never flinched, and suddenly I visualized spending the afternoon and night on the river bank with nothing to sustain us but beer. Looking at several varieties of fish lying in the ice house, I couldn't believe my ears when I heard Unk say, "Jake, that's a nice fish—that big bass, could I buy it from ya?" Uncle Jim, an impressive man, stood about six feet four and weighed about 225 pounds. Invariably he had a wad of chewing tobacco jammed into the side of his mouth. When he asked a question or made a statement, he would punctuate it with a stream of tobacco juice. This indicated he was through and expected an answer.

Jake looked at him quizzically for a second and then said, "You can have the fish Mr. Phillips."

"No, I wouldn't take it for nothing," Unk said as he handed the chap a two dollar bill, a lot of money those days. Jake pocketed the bill without further argument and invited us into the house for a cup of tea.

We joined six or eight other adults in the house, and I ravenously attacked the home-baked bread, generously layered with butter and raspberry jam. After the long hike, I was indeed hungry.

The Dubroski's, a Polish family, had congregated to prepare for a wedding the following day. Before long, some homemade wine and sour mash whiskey was brought forth, and at this stage in the proceedings, Uncle Jim used his coup de grâce.

"I have two dozen bottles of beer outside in our knapsacks. Would you mind if I brought them in?" he asked Jake.

"Hell no, that'd be just fine." Jake replied with obvious enthusiasm. People regarded store beer a rare delicacy, an unnecessary expenditure that few would buy.

Though Unk had not requested a ride across the raging river nor had Jake offered to transport us at this point, they were fully aware of our dilemma. As a result of the few beers mixed with wine and whiskey plus the fact that Dad and Uncle Jim were both good conversationalists, everyone got in a jovial mood. Having hunted in the general area for over thirty years, Dad and Uncle Jim had many things in common with the Dubroski's. Finally out of nowhere, Jake looked over at Unk and said, "How you figuring on getting across to your car, Jimmy?"

"That's a real conundrum," Unk retorted without hesitation.

"If you guys ain't afraid, I'll take you across in the dory."

"If you think it's safe, we're certainly not frightened, and I'll be delighted to pay you for your trouble," Unk said respectfully.

"Hell, life's too short to worry about getting paid for everything," Jake said with a big grin. "Just holler when you're ready to move."

Within an hour, we stood gazing across the turbulent river where 15-foot waves obscured the opposite shore. Father had experienced several close calls on Lake Winnipeg during inclement weather, and so he had reservations about risking the crossing. Jake, preparing the boat, however, assured us there would be no danger, though he added he would have to make two trips.

Uncle Jim went first and Dad and I watched mesmerized as Jake dexterously maneuvered the dory diagonally across the river, sometimes riding a wave like a cork, then slipping off the crest and plunging suddenly downward so that in between waves, they would disappear completely from view. Jake returned within a half hour. I could discern the apprehension in Dad's face as he seated himself on the floor in the stern. Sitting in the bow, I sensed no alarm, which wasn't an act of false bravado because I'd been frightened to death of other things many times before. Perhaps it was the confidence Jake transmitted in his handling of the craft, or possibly I had a natural inclination for rough water. Shortly after shoving off from shore, I got up from the floor to sit on the forward seat and found the spray from the monstrous rolling waves quite invigorating. When the large rowboat sank into a trough between two massive walls of water, climbed with graceful ease onto the crest of the next enormous billows, momentarily hesitated, then plunged once more into a channel of water, the abrupt descent gave the same sensation as a rapid decline on an elevator. Despite Dad's obvious relief at reaching the shore, I was keenly disappointed because I considered the roller-coaster ride the highlight of the entire adventure.

Returning to Winnipeg, I reflected on why Jake made what appeared to be a dangerous mission requiring considerable personal effort for absolutely no remuneration when those first few families flatly refused even when offered good money. By the time we'd reached Dubroski's, Unk had apparently decided to change tactics and use diplomacy instead of his previous direct approach. He applied his savoir faire to perfection, a prime example of not trying to prevail upon someone to do your bidding until you have sold yourself first. Trying to close a sale before the other party has reached a buying frame of mind, is a complete waste of time and a requisite in creating that mood is to find a common bond. Uncle Jim undeniably bought our passage across the raging Red River with twenty-four bottles of beer and the knowledge of how to close a deal.

During the 1930's, the summers were mostly dry and hot, crops burned in the fields and streams and ditches dried up. Not until the latter part of the decade did the rains come back, quench the land's thirst, and once again fill the brooks and flood meadows in the fall and spring. Ducks then returned by the multitudes to nest in inundated marshes, numerous in our area and ideally located by flourishing grain fields which in turn provided excellent feeding grounds for the birds. Duck shooting in the spring and fall offered both a means of recreation and a chance to provide a tasty meal. Though not good with a rifle, Dad, like his four brothers, was outstanding with a twelve-gauge shotgun. On many autumn evenings Jack and I accompanied him into the swamps and marveled at his ability to knock down five mallards with five shots as they swooped past our hide. According to law, his gun should have been plugged allowing only three shells, but he never paid any attention to such a dictatorial rule. Frequently when huddled in our hide for the evening shoot, we would observe other farmers also trying to obtain a duck dinner. Rarely did they get more than a couple of birds with twenty shots and were dumbfounded to see Father knock down a dozen or more with as many shells. Ed Barham, a neighbor's son, watched Dad's performance with amazement when he accompanied us on an occasional hunt, and as a result, the two of us became buddies.

The Barhams lived a mile and a half southwest of us, and because they were in a different school district, Ed and I didn't have much to do with each other in the early years. There were four Barham children: Mary, the eldest, Irene, then Ed, redheaded and freckle faced and a month or two older than I, and Annie. They were a unique family. Mr. Barham, an English gentleman, never did much physical labor. Rather, he functioned as the lord of the manor, overseeing the rigamarole of the estate. Mrs. Barham, of Belgian ancestry and the hardest-working woman I've ever known, never walked but jogged in a shuffling sort of rapid gait. I have vivid recollections of passing Mrs. Barham on the road as she would be on her way to the store, and I to visit Ed. She would begin to converse with me in a high-pitched voice at approximately a hundred yards away and never slowed her gait or her speed of conversation as she swept past. Generally the final words I heard would be a warning not to engage Eddie in any tomfoolery because he had plenty of work to do. They owned a large dairy herd, and without milking machines, every pair of hands was urgently required to milk and tend the stock. If there are six forward gears in the human body, Mrs. Barham, the prime mover in the family, used only high and always at full throttle.

Friendship is an indistinct emotion and what initiates a relationship is as difficult to define as trying to describe an apparition. Ed Barham and I became better acquainted as a result of our duck-hunting expeditions and began to pal around. Both blessed with a sense of humor, we usually found something funny in most situations, and Eddie, with his charismatic grin, made friends easily. He obtained an old 16-cylinder Packard in the early war years, allowing us to escort girls to local dances without having to make them walk or ride on our bicycle handlebars. The Packard guzzled gasoline at a prodigious rate, and if he hadn't shut the motor off when filling his gas tank, I believe we would have lost ground. Fuel wasn't too expensive, but as our pockets lacked much cash, we didn't do much travelling around.

One of our favorite pastimes on an evening was to visit our eccentric bachelor neighbors who were always delighted to see us but never certain what pranks we might pull. Pantomime, one of Ed's favorite antics, would usually goad me into spasms of laughter. While visiting Fred Mattern, our agile violinist friend, Eddie might do a parody of Fred's fiddling—not in view of Fred, of course—and when I'd burst out laughing, Fred figured surely I'd gone demented. One of Eddie's pet performances when paying a call on "Oh Gee" Culhane or Old John Wylie would be to open his pocketknife, and when they stooped over to fuel their stoves, he would sneak up behind them and perform an imitation castration. If caught in the act, he had the restraint to remain sober faced and pretend he'd just walked over and opened his knife, but with me doubled over in laughter, they knew they had been the butt of some joke. Though it was juvenile humor, we were juveniles, and the antics provided an outlet for our pent-up emotions.

With increasing regularity, our schoolmates and neighbors' boys were entering the services and departing overseas. Ed, the only able-bodied male on the Barham farm, couldn't enlist, and so we shared the helpless feeling of being left behind. Though humor furnished the mainstay in our association, each of us had a serious side to our nature and could expound theories and philosophies for hours without boring the other. Numerous things contributed to our affinity, but our mutual love for the Brokenhead River country seemed to provide the bond that cemented it all together.

Lake Agassiz covered most of Manitoba ten thousand years ago, and when it receded into Hudson Bay, numerous lakes, such as Lake Winnipeg and Lake Manitoba, remained. Many areas in the north of the province were swept bare to the rock, but covered with rich deposits of black loam, the southern section became ideal for grain farming. This abundance of good soil ended about where the western boundary of Monominto began, approximately five miles west of our farm. The narrow belt of stony, sandy terrain making up our community extended only three miles east to the edge of an area consisting mainly of marshes, swampland, and scraggly trees. This "no man's land" along the western edge of the great Canadian Shield runs for a thousand miles southeast almost completely across Ontario. It contains a region of mineral-rich rock covered with forests and is broken by a labyrinth of rivers and lakes. We lived, therefore, in an eight-mile band that divided a thousand miles of prairies, known as the "breadbasket of the world," from a thousand miles of wilderness reaching almost to the industrial heart of Canada. The main Brokenhead River, located about thirty miles east of Monominto, had a small branch called the Little Brokenhead, only seven miles east of our farm. The narrow stream ranged in width from ten to thirty feet and from two to five feet in depth when within its banks. During extreme dry spells in summer, it almost stopped running completely. When we had a rainy fall or a heavy winter snow followed by a rapid spring thaw, however, the Little Brokenhead would overflow its banks and flood 50,000 acres of surrounding terrain, primarily provincial government property. Interlaced through the wetlands were rocky ridges covered with stunted black and white poplar trees, berry bushes, and brouse, ideal habitat for deer, coyotes, timber wolves, and smaller animals. Other rises barely higher than the bog itself supported spindly balsam, spruce and yellow tamarac, in which moose, though scarce, liked to hang out. Mink, weasels, skunks, muskrats, and rabbits thrived over the entire territory. Ed and I both had a great attachment for this wild and glorious country, so returned there at every opportunity.

I first became acquainted with the Brokenhead during the dry mid-thirties when our land couldn't produce sufficient fodder to winter feed our stock. Father and other farmers obtained permits from the Manitoba government to hay along the river banks. With their tents, food and gear piled on a hay rack, mower and rake trailing behind, they would hitch their horses to the caravan and spend a week at a time cutting and staking the wild grass along the banks of the little stream. The precious feed would be hauled home by sleigh in the winter months. Though only a lad, I listened with rapt attention to their stories of deer herds, huge timber wolves, and the obvious enjoyment they got out of camping in the wilds.

My first exposure to Brokenhead came when I accompanied Father one winter day into the river country for a sleigh load of tamarac. Durable fence posts, an important commodity on the farm for separating fields, pastures, corrals, and even the farm itself, were difficult to obtain. Poplar trees that predominated our area were useless for posts because they rotted too rapidly when sunk into the moist ground. The nearest cedar groves, the choice wood, were thirty miles east, and so we had to settle for tamarac, a reasonable substitute.

With horses and sleigh, Dad and I left our house at 8:00 a.m. and spent two hours wending our way east before leaving behind the final settlement. Perched on the sleigh bunks with my eyes glued to the passing landscape, I sat thoroughly fascinated by the myriad of animal tracks crisscrossing the snow-covered countryside. Weasels, mink, deer, skunks, rabbits, squirrels, wolves, and coyotes left barely a square yard untravelled, quite a menagerie compared to the woods around home where I trapped. Half a mile from the river, Dad began to fell trees while I prepared a campfire and made tea to wash down our sandwich lunch. The entire scenario, from the pungent aroma of burning balsam in the campfire to the sound of woodpeckers hammering their bills into hardwoods that ricocheted through the frosty stillness, excited me tremendously. Though chilled to the bone by the time we reached home long after dark, I couldn't wait to return.

A few years later, Ed Barham, Jack, and I took three teams and headed into the same back country for tamarac on a gorgeous spring morning with the winter snow swiftly disappearing from the landscape. Crows were welcoming the return of the warm weather with their raucous calls, horned larks and meadowlarks warbled from fields and fence posts, and killdeers circled overhead in a joyous salute to the beautiful day. Near the Brokenhead we cut our load of trees, and while sitting around the campfire eating our lunch, we discussed the peace and beauty of our serene setting while our friends were dying in mortal combat in other parts of the world.

Rainy seasons brought the delight of duck hunting and more bountiful harvests but also caused a scourge of mosquitoes that in spring and early summer made our existence at times nearly unbearable. After milking, when released from the barn, cattle driven almost insane by the swarming insects would gallop at high speed to stand in smoke billowing from giant smudges we had lit in their evening pastures to provide them with some relief. Hordes of the pests would cover our clothes, sneak into our ears, eyes, nose and mouth, and generally make outdoors a hell on earth. Mother also had smudges outside the veranda entrance where we would stand for a few moments to rid ourselves of as many as possible before entering the house. When potholes, ditches, and swamps had dried up by midsummer, the mosquito population soon dwindled and life took on a rosier tinge.

The spring of 1942, particularly wet, encouraged the pesky mosquitoes to breed prodigiously, but by haying time in mid-July, they were only an ugly memory, and working in the fields again became a pleasure. I particularly recalled that year because I inherited the job of operating the hay mower. This machine had a seat, but it also a had right-foot lever for raising and lowering the cutting bar that posed a genuine problem for me. I had no power in the forward part of my foot and little muscle in the upper thigh, which made raising and lowering the bar on short notice a strenuous task that frequently caused me some anxious moments. If a stone or root, hidden by the growing hay, suddenly became visible when it was too late to halt the horses, I would have to raise the bar over the snag swiftly or suffer a costly breakdown. By grabbing my knees with my right hand and applying downward pressure together with using considerable concentration on my foot, I usually got the cutting bar over the obstacle without accident, but this problem wouldn't allow me to relax while we were moving. My leg and foot didn't strengthen rapidly, and it took a long while before I could control the mower with any degree of confidence. Despite my discomfort, I might never have driven a car without that experience because to control the brake and accelerator before automatic gear shifts and power brakes became common required similar motion by the right limb.

Jack and Father, both aware of my difficulty with the machinery, nevertheless forced me to persevere, and so Jack did the raking, and the three of us worked as a team to load and stack the fodder. At four o'clock in the afternoon during that memorable summer, Mom, Ruth, and Joyce would bring out a delicious snack of tea, sandwiches, and cake. Relaxing in the winnows of freshly raked hay, the smell of clover thick in the air, fleecy white clouds floating lazily in the blue summer sky and the drone of honey bees and summer bird songs accompanying our family chatter, again created a placid atmosphere that made it difficult to conceive the misery being suffered by so many. We also didn't recognize the seriousness of the affliction of one of our own, but soon learned that sister Joyce would not be blessed with a normal life. Invariably though, our conversation returned to the world conflict and Jack's determination to enlist in the military after spring planting the following year. He could easily have obtained an exemption, because of farming's status in the vital industry category. But Jack didn't feel he could stay home while others put their lives on the line for him, plus the constant induction into the services of friends disturbed him with Jim Phillips' enlistment probably the final straw.

The Ted Phillipses, our nearest neighbors after the Eedies, operated a farm immediately west of ours. Although not related, both families traced their ancestry to early English history. They had three sons— Alexis, the oldest; Alf, in the middle, and Jim, slightly less than two years older than Jack. In the family, too, was Rose Higgins, a cousin the same age as Jim. Rose had lost her mother, Ted's sister, at childbirth, and was reared by the Phillipses. A diminutive man with a fair education, Ted Phillips always seemed out of place on the farm. Injured in middle age and unable to do much physical labor, he fortunately possessed an insurance policy that kept the family in reasonable prosperity. I called him Uncle Ted and his wife, as Irish as Kerry County, Aunt Sadie.

The association between our families dated back to the first decade of the century when the Rodd family settled within a mile of the Phillipses shortly after immigrating from England. Grandmother Rodd had been mid-wife to Mrs. Phillips, and my mother babysat the children when they were infants. Dad became acquainted with Monominto and subsequently moved there as a result of visiting the Ted Phillipses after he met Mother. Before Jack and I were old enough, either Alfred or Alex always assisted Mother with chores if Dad was laid up.

Alexis joined the Air Force early in the conflict, and Alf stayed behind to manage the farm. Jack and I attended Pinewood School for several years with Jim and Rose, who were more like a brother and sister than neighbors' children. Jim, somewhat frail as a boy and man, didn't resemble Rose, who was constructed like a Notre Dame fullback and as strong as a bull elephant. She could run like an antelope and had a nature as pleasant as her adopted mother. We used to play a game at school called "Horse" where a small student got piggybacked on an older student and challenged another duo to a bout with the object of peeling the other rider from his perch or upsetting both horse and rider. With great strength in my upper body and Rose's overall power, we could have won the world Olympics had there been such a contest. Several times as a youngster, when unable to cope with deep snow or when my leg was in too much pain to walk, Jim would hoist me onto his shoulders and slowly trudge home with Rose giving him a breather now and then.

Shortly after leaving school for home one summer day, we heard a roar from the sky like a fast-approaching freight train. Suddenly just above the trees, we were dismayed to see an onrushing tornado cloud. In a panic, Jim grabbed one of my arms and Rose the other, and we took off like a motorcycle with my feet touching ground about once every ten yards. Jack and Isobel Dowie, also with us, couldn't keep up even without any encumbrance. I don't believe I ever covered ground faster without mechanical motivation. The tornado eventually touched down, luckily doing little damage, but if getting out of its path saved my life, I had only Rose and Jim to thank. Jimmy, an honor student, majored in engineering and enlisted in the artillery to eventually see action as a range-finder, receiving decorations for valor. Seeing Jim in uniform in 1942, though disquieting to me, became intolerable for Jack as they had been schoolmates and close friends throughout their entire tenure at Pinewood.

I loved my family, but distressed at the prospect of being on the farm without Jack, I again implored Father to allow my return to school. Though missing many school days while helping on the farm, I graduated from Grade IX into X in the top twenty of the thousands who took Manitoba Departmental Exams. Father wouldn't pay the tuition but didn't hassle me as much about continuing my education as the previous year. Knowing I couldn't go beyond Grade X by correspondence at Pinewood, he figured I'd have no alternative but to remain home after that semester. As usual, Father didn't allow for my stubborn determination. Again Uncle George came through with the fee for the year's course.

Returning to school in September, 1942, now the oldest student at Pinewood, I was accompanied by sisters Ruth and Joyce. We were perplexed with Joyce in those early years. We were all aware of her difficulty in physical coordination but believed she would outgrow the problem. Normal in stature but morose by nature, she rarely spoke unless spoken to and appeared reluctant to get involved in anything physical or mental. Ruth and I watched with dismay as Mary Wylie, the teacher, tried with great patience to persuade Joyce to attempt to write or print the alphabet or comprehend simple arithmetic. Joyce would simply shrink away and refuse stubbornly to comply with any request. At home, Mother and Father devoted hours trying to get some effort from the little girl, but she refused almost in a defiant manner even to hold a pencil. Father's patience grew thin at times, and as yet unaware of the severity of her condition, he would threaten her physically, though he never did touch her. Nothing would motivate her to exert herself.

We recalled an incident in late 1936, when Mom was out walking in the yard with Joyce in her arms and took a terrible spill. Mother had come to give Dad, Jack, and me a hand to get a stubborn old sow into a pen when the pig turned without warning and ran through Mother's legs, knocking her off her feet. As she tumbled backward, Joyce fell from her arms and struck her head on a stump. Mother received a terrible gash on her leg. Now we wondered in horror if something during that accident had caused Joyce's condition. Mother took her to Winnipeg where the doctors diagnosed her condition as simple mental retardation with the accident having no bearing on the girl's condition. I will always remain skeptical that the bash on her head as a ten-month-old baby may have had some relevance to her situation. Though a terrible tragedy for all the family, especially Mom and Dad, Joyce continued to school, and Mary Wylie, under extremely difficult conditions, eventually taught Joyce the fundamentals of reading and writing.

The gamut of emotions encountered in the average lifetime is amazing. Initially, we felt aggravation at Joyce's inability to grasp simple problems, but this slowly changed to empathy and then into a kind of helplessness when we were forced to face the reality of the situation. Mom and Dad had now suffered through unavoidable tragedies with 50 percent of their offsprings. The next, however, would be the cruelest of all.

My emotions regarding Joyce's permanent condition differed entirely from the sorrow I felt for a neighbor's family when I learned their son had been killed during the abortive Dieppe Raid on the coast of France. At the Canadian army's first action in the war, thousands of our countrymen were slain or taken prisoner. This untimely death of another neighbor shocked the community, and though we didn't know it at the time, the war had now reached its lowest point. Rationing, a fact of life for both Canadians and Americans, didn't affect us with such rationed articles as tires and gas because we didn't own a car, with store liquor and coffee, neither of which we consumed, or with meat and butter, which were farm products. Tea and sugar rationing created a problem, however. Half a pound of sugar each week per person didn't allow Mother sufficient for summer fruit preserving, and Father drank an enormous amount of tea. We made out, however, when we found we could trade butter and meat coupons for sugar and tea.

A principal event of 1942, eventually affecting the outcome of the war and for that matter of human life forever after, was kept secret for obvious reasons. In December at the University of Chicago's Stagg Field, they achieved the world's first controlled, self-sustaining nuclear chain reaction, and the world slipped unobtrusively into the Nuclear Age.

Of far less significance in mankind's overall affairs but of great concern to the average North American at the time was the announcement that all automobile production would be stopped to allow auto plants to manufacture tanks, jeeps, aircraft, and other war materials. In the U.S.A., 3½ million men still remained unemployed, a substantial decline from the 9½ million in 1939. The ranks of the idle dwindled rapidly as war plants, shipyards, oil fields, and recruiting offices clamoured for manpower. President Roosevelt called for and got 60,000 planes, 45,000 tanks, 20,000 antiaircraft guns, and 8 million deadweight tons of merchant shipping. The same rush to war production applied in Canada, and a huge cordite plant, constructed in Transcona, 25 miles west of Monominto, employed several neighbors who earned more money at that job than they ever did on the farm and so never returned to farming. The war became a prime factor in accelerating the transition of labor from agriculture to industry.

Although reports from the war front was predominantly grave throughout the year, a sprinkling of good news began to trickle through. Under the command of Jimmy Doolittle, B-25 bombers raided Tokyo, 1,000 R.A.F. Lancaster bombers attacked Cologne, Germany, and U.S. carrier-based planes stopped the Japanese at the Midway naval battle causing the Japs heavy losses.

On the home front, Jack and I often accompanied Mom to the local dance at Monominto hall on Saturday nights. Dad never danced in his life, preferring to remain home and listen to the "Grand Ole Opry" on the radio. Mother tried to teach me to dance, one of her favorite diversions, but my inability to get airborne when attempting to hop on my right foot made certain steps impossible to master. Despite my reluctance to ask the local belles for a dance, a few female friends would overlook my awkwardness and induce me to try. That era produced a bevy of recordings: "One Dozen Roses," "Paper Doll," "Jingle Jangle Jingle," "I left My Heart At The Stage Door Canteen," "Praise The Lord And Pass The Ammunition," "When The Lights Go On Again," "That Old Black Magic," and "You'd Be So Nice To Come Home To,"—all of which remained popular for years. "White Christmas" will likely endure forever. War weary, we entered 1943 with a slight sense of optimism, and that dramatic year would see the fortunes of war swing slowly in favor of the Allies. It also saw a premature end to my adolescence.

Good news was not long in coming. In early January, Australian, New Zealand, and Canadian forces took the southeastern tip of New Guinea, assuring the safety of Australia from Japanese invasion. On February 8, Allied forces captured Guadalcanal in the Solomon Islands after heavy fighting, and in March, U.S. bombers sank 21 Japanese transports loaded with 15,000 troops bound for New Guinea. Tripoli fell to the British 8th army on January 23, and Axis forces in Tunisia were in full retreat. Germany rushed in reserves, but American troops thrust into the battle helped to end Axis resistance in North Africa by early May.

Our exuberance with the sudden change in the tides of war is difficult to explain to those too young to remember. Three years of despair including Dunkirk, the disastrous collapse of France and the Low countries, merciless bombing of English cities, defeat in North Africa, the attack on Pearl Harbor, and the outstanding successes of the Japanese army in the Pacific, were all behind us now. Never really believing North America would be successfully invaded, we nevertheless considered it likely the world would be alienated against North and South America if Britain should collapse. Propaganda at the height of the conflict claimed all males other than Germans would be castrated to prevent any interference with the Fuhrer's dream of a German super race. Far fetched no doubt, but the constant reports of the horrible mass genocide of the Jewish race made anything originating from Hitler's demented mind a distinct possibility.

I usually greeted the return of the crows and larks and gradual disappearance of winter's snow with wild enthusiasm. The sight of pussywillows bursting into bloom, buttercups sprouting from freshly thawed earth, or quacking green-necked mallards searching for mates sent me into spirals of ecstasy, but as the spring of '43 blossomed forth, I didn't feel the same sense of elation.

Terribly restless, I had no conception of what the immediate future held for me. Despite the greatly improved news from across the seas, we had a long, hard row to hoe before winning total victory, and so Jack's days as a civilian were numbered. I had no idea whether or where to continue my schooling, but my mind was positively made up that after haying I would leave the farm, school or no school.

As fate had intervened when Charlie Herald came on the scene in 1935 to have me admitted to the Shriners' Hospital, a similar situation came to pass on the July 1st holiday weekend in 1943. Uncle Ernie and his family who farmed at Swan Lake, 125 miles west of Monominto, came for a rare visit that would change the course of my life.

On July 1st, our nation's birthday, Pinewood School held its annual field day and picnic, the only other day of the year other than the Christmas concert when the entire community joined for a day of fun and frivolity. The school board donated $20 for cash prizes to the 1st, 2nd, and 3rd place winners in all sporting events which was mostly distributed to the school children to buy ice cream, pop, or candy available on the picnic grounds. The fact that the 25-cent first-place money might disqualify the recipient from any possible participation as an Olympian because they'd lost their amateur status didn't cross their minds or dampen the competition.

The school handicap and wheelbarrow races offered me the only possibility to earn a prize. In the handicap, the fastest student started a hundred yards from the finish line, and the others were placed in between depending on their running ability. During my first few years at school before and throughout my hospital adventure, I felt slightly self-conscious at being placed several yards in front of a child much smaller than I, but the need of those coins overcame any embarrassment.

When the race started and I could hear those thundering feet closing in rapidly behind me, I invariably tripped and fell. When that occurred, a big Danish neighbor, Lute Damskov, always rushed onto the field, picked me up and hustled me over the finish line in first place. In spite of my embarrassment, I never refused the prize money. If I could get Rose Higgins as a partner, the wheelbarrow race offered another opportunity for spending money. Rose possessed such strength that if my arms and hands weren't moving fast enough along the ground, she'd hold me out at arm's length with my hands paddling thin air so we'd cross the finish line first. In the afternoon and evening there would be baseball, softball, and horseshoe tournaments. About seven o'clock everyone would race home to do their evening chores and return for the dance that lasted until the early hours of the morning.

As the fun day progressed in 1943, I sat watching the events and reminiscing. With no competition for me now except baseball, I had plenty of time to think. When I walked out of Pinewood School two days before, even after my ten-year stint, I felt no despondency but rather considered it the end of an era. My initials were carved in two desks; there was a library wall that I accidentally disfigured during a chemistry experiment and the school furnace that I had stoked hundreds of times; and there were blackboards on which I'd written "I will not talk in school" thousands of times. They would always remain symbols of that period of my life. I recalled some words from a Tennyson poem "Excalibur": "The old order changeth, yielding place to new and God fulfills Himself in many ways. . . ."

Unexpectedly, Uncle Ernie came over and sat on the grass beside me. "How you doin' boy? How was school?" he asked looking at me kind of quizzically.

"I'll finish in the top ten in the province," I replied a little flippantly.

"Where do you go from here?" he inquired.

"I wish I knew."

"You know, boy, there's a top-flight high school at Swan Lake where you could take XI and XII." He glanced to see my reaction, then continued, "I'll make you a proposition. If you help me on the farm evenings and weekends, I'll supply room and board, and it's only 1½ miles to school."

His statement dumbfounded me and it took a few minutes for his words to sink in. Finally, I looked at him increduously and asked, "Have you discussed this with Father? I don't think you'll be too popular if you do."

"No, but I will," he said as he got up and walked away.

I sat for a long time pondering Uncle Ernie's remarks. After consideration, I realized Mother must have been the motivating factor and wondered if Father knew anything about the proposal.

I'd only met Uncle Ernie and Aunt Alena a few times. Alena had been a registered nurse before they married. They had four children, who were with them on their visit—Marie, about one year younger than I; Betty, 11, Ernie Jr., called Sam, 5, and Jeanette, a babe in arms. I knew considerable about Uncle Ernie from the many stories I'd heard. A great favorite with both my parents, he would always be a hero in my books because of his World War I exploits.

As a foot soldier in the first Canadian Army Division, he fought in most of the major battles that made the Canadian army world famous for daring and bravery. Wounded twice at Pachandale and gassed at Ypres during the first major gas attack of the war, he paid quite a price for his patriotism. As a small boy, I could recall visiting him in a Winnipeg hospital where he'd had one kidney removed probably due to the mustard gas or his years in the trenches.

Nothing further was mentioned about our conversation until we'd all gathered prior to their departure. Saying good-bye, Uncle Ernie turned to me, "If you decide to take me up on my proposal boy, drop me a line and let me know when you will arrive in Swan Lake. I'll meet the bus."

Bewildered because I hadn't heard anything further about the offer until then but grateful because he had made his position clear to everyone, I quietly promised to write by mid-August.

And so with the die cast and my dilemma finally resolved, it left financing as the only major problem remaining. Shortly after his brother left, Father came to me and without rancor said he hated to see me leave the farm but wouldn't attempt to stop me. Any financial assistance would be out of the question, he added. I agreed to remain home until after haying, then would try to get a job harvesting to earn a few dollars.

Shortly after making this notable decision influencing my individual future, gigantic happenings in Europe were occurring that would affect millions. British paratroopers and U.S. airborne troops invaded Sicily on July 9, and Benito Mussolini resigned on July 25. Allied armies crossed the Straits of Messina and invaded southern Italy in the middle of August. Italy then surrendered unconditionally and declared war on Germany. Though one of the Fascist dictators had been beaten, the two remaining would be more difficult to bring to their knees.

In three months of heavy winter fighting in Russia, the Germans lost 50,000 men. The battle at Kursk that began on July 5 involved 6,000 German and Russian tanks plus 4,000 planes. It ended after a week of heavy fighting in a victory for the Soviet Fifth Army, but while the

Germans lost 70,000 men, 2,000 tanks, 1,400 planes, and 5,000 vehicles, the Russian losses were at least comparable. Everyone realized that the German nation could not longer bear up under such staggering losses but that the stubborn race would persist until the bitter end.

The price of the conflict staggered the imagination. The war cost American tax payers 8 billion dollars per month, as compared to the total cost of World War I at 35 billion dollars. Roosevelt asked Congress in 1943 for 100 billion dollars for the War Department. This was quite a contrasting figure to my total cash assets of $5.00.

The six weeks following Uncle Ernie's visit flew by as we threw ourselves into the task of haying. The results of my Grade X final exams placed me eighth in the province, and the report included a congratulatory letter from the Department of Education. Jack, anxious to enlist before he received his draft notice, had yet to decide which branch of the armed forces he would choose, an easy decision if it had been mine. Warriors blood must course through Phillips' veins because I forever fantasized about being a combat fighter pilot and found it difficult to accept the unfairness of fate. While I possessed an overpowering desire to get into the thick of the fray in any capacity, hundreds of thousands of military-age Canadians waited in trepidation for their draft call and then used every possible means to avoid getting into uniform. Throngs of draft dodgers across the nation put their future in jeopardy by hiding from the military police while I would have given ten years off my life to get involved.

By mid-August, the haying completed, I finally prepared to make the break and leave the comforts of home. Only sixteen, I realized nevertheless that from this point forward I would be completely responsible for my personal actions and financial well being. My entire worldly possessions consisted of four pairs of underclothes (two for summer and two for winter), three pairs of socks, two work shirts unsuitable for school wear, a couple of sweaters, a heavy parka, a pair of leather workboots, and less than $2.00 in cash. Jack, no better off, would soon have the government take care of his wardrobe and finances.

My right work boot caused me major concern due mostly to my self-consciousness. The big toe on my disabled foot, growing on an angle, had bent across the other toes and forced my boot into a grotesque shape. To retain the boot's shape, I molded a chunk of heavy tin and inserted it into the boot in an attempt to force the big toe to lay straight. Not only did this cause a bunion on the first knuckle but also the pressure of the metal induced considerable pain. It's amazing the suffering some of us will bear to salvage our vanity.

The Blocker family, who farmed fifteen miles west of Monominto, came to the Saturday night shindig looking for harvest help and offered me $4 per day to handle a stook wagon. I agreed to be at their place before noon on Monday.

I wrote Uncle Ernie on Sunday and told him to meet me two weeks from the date of my letter and thus officially began a new phase of my life.

85

at help and offered
be at their place

t me two weeks
next peace of my

————— **Chapter 7** —————

Swan Lake

The word "harvest" according to Webster's dictionary has several meanings: the season for gathering in agricultural crops; the act or process of gathering in a crop; a mature crop; the quantity of a natural product gathered in a single season, or the product or reward of exertion. The final definition more closely describes the average farmer's perspective of the word "harvest."

Tilling soil, planting crops, and for three months during the growing season hoping Mother Nature will cooperate while the green sprouts grow and ripen into maturity keeps the average farmer busy and anxious, but a bountiful harvest provides him the ultimate in gratification. Human beings delight in planting seeds, watching shoots mature into vegetables, then enjoying their efforts at the dinner table. The money saved is secondary to their pleasure. The discovery by our early ancestors that planting and tending crops increased their chance for survival influenced nomads to become agriculturalists. The sickle, the earliest device used for the traditional act of reaping, dates back to the Stone Age. Later employed by the ancient Jews and Egyptians, the sickle used throughout the world to the latter part of the 19th century consisted of a curved blade, usually sharpened metal, about two feet long and attached to a wooden handle. Cutting the grain by scythe, a handful at a time, was followed by binding the grain into sheaves, ready for threshing.

With the mechanization of agriculture brought about by the industrial revolution, hand reaping gradually gave way to machines. The sickle, replaced by the scythe, in turn gave way to the cradle (a frame attached to a scythe so that cut grain would lay flat), and finally to a binder drawn by animals or a tractor. The binder cut the grain and automatically tied it into sheaves with a coarse rope called "binder twine." When the binder's carrier was loaded with a half dozen or more sheaves, the operator dumped these bundles into convenient rows for hand stooking. Shocks or stooks consisted of approximately a dozen sheaves with the butt end on the ground. When cured, the stooks loaded on a wagon with a large rack were hauled to a waiting thresher where that machine separated the grain from the stalk on which it grew, and the chaff or pod that covered the kernel. The first known method of threshing was by striking the reaped ears of grain with a flail. In another early method, horses or oxen trod out the grain from stalks spread on a hard threshing floor. In both cases, after raking away the straw, the mixture of grain and chaff was "winnowed," or tossed into or poured through a current of air thereby blowing away the light chaff from the heavier grain.

In 1784, a Scotsman, Andrew Meikle, devised a threshing machine whereby sheaves of grain were fed into a revolving cylinder armed with wooden beaters. Another toothed drum raked away the loose straw and pushed the remaining chaff and grain through a sieve onto a series of rollers that further separated the chaff from the grain. The principle of Meikle's machine has been retained in all threshing machines up to and including the modern self-propelled combines. The threshing machine or "separator" had a revolving chain belt that carried the separated grain to a hopper which automatically tripped when it reached the weight of a bushel of the type of grain being harvested. In threshing oats, as an example, the machine operator would set the hopper to trip at 34 pounds; for wheat, at 60. The bushel of grain now ran by gravity down a metal tube into whatever receptacle the farmer had chosen to haul it away, which might be a jute sack, wagon box, truck, or portable granary. Heavy fans blew the straw and chaff through a long, large metal spout into a pile behind the thresher.

Separators built in various sizes were all driven by huge belts attached to the power pulley of a tractor or steam engine. The inches of a carriage width that carried the sheaves into the body of the machine designated the size of the thresher which ranged from 20 to 50 inches, though other sizes may have been manufactured. The smaller, 20- to 30-inch separators carried one row of sheaves usually fed by one to two men on one side of the machine. The larger threshers handled two rows and were fed from both sides of the carriage. A complete threshing machine crew varied from six to twenty men depending primarily on the size of the separator. Four teamsters with racks could usually keep a 20- to 30-inch machine constantly in sheaves, though a 28- to 30-inch might require a field or spike pitcher.

A field pitcher remained in the field and went from teamster to teamster to assist in loading, while spike pitchers remained at the separator and helped each newly arrived load discharge their cargo. Large machines in the 40-inch plus range might use from six to eight stook teams, two field pitchers and two spike pitchers. The size of the operation determined the manpower required to control the finished product, which also depended on whether the grain was going into a granary or was being hauled directly to market by horse and wagon or by truck. Finally, one or two men remained with the threshing machine to grease and oil the separator, fuel the tractor, and make repairs to the several drive belts and other moving parts that frequently broke down. Keeping the operation going without delays was crucial to the farmer.

A bountiful crop remained financially valueless until it had been threshed. Many prairie farmers with flourishing fields of grain would get caught by an early fall rainy season and be forced to watch their entire year's work rot in the fields. They might salvage some poor-grade grain when it dried out the following spring, but such an occurrence almost devastated them to the same extent as being totally hailed out. Farmers harvested their ripened grain as rapidly as possible, and this urgency provided me with a major portion of my finances for six years.

Father grew as much oats and barley as he had cultivated land. The grain provided stock feed, and the straw was used occasionally for fodder but was most important as animal bedding. Next to Christmas, threshing time was the most exciting season of all. A local entrepreneur with a tractor and a small separator would travel from farm to farm in our district and charge per bushel to thresh. It required only one to three days to do the threshing on most farms in Monominto. Neighbors would band together, each providing a stook team and rack, and thus eliminating the need to hire help. Neighbors wives would help each other in the preparing and serving of meals, and this made threshing get-together a party atmosphere—except for the hard work involved.

As our threshing date approached, Jack and I would impatiently listen, days in advance, for the well-known drone of a working separator and surmise whose farm it actually harvested. We never considered going to school when the machine finally arrived, and an indescribable elation overwhelmed us as the thresher started to pour precious kernels down the grain spout into our waiting wagon. Each tallied bushel indicated the yield per acre of each field, and we associated success or failure with the harvest based on that count. With only forty acres of grain, threshing time highlighted the working year for us, so what it meant to a prairie farmer with a thousand acres or more wasn't hard to imagine.

Stookers were generally hired at either an hourly or per acre rate.

Threshing crews earned their pay by the hour or day. In both cases, room and board was included.

At threshing time at home, I assisted Father in handling the finished product, such as loading the grain into jute bags when it came down the tube or shoveling it back if flowing directly into a wagon box or granary. The three-tined pitch fork, the predominant tool for loading and unloading sheaves, was no stranger to me though because for ten years I had used one while haying and also while feeding stock.

That bright autumn morning as the "gas car" clickety-clacked towards Millbrook and Blockers farm, I sat peering out the train window at the passing prairie and seemingly endless rows of stooked grain in a felicitous though slightly disturbed frame of mind. I had absolutely no fear of the future. In fact I gladly anticipated the opportunity of making my own decisions and felt determined to become financially independent. The frustration of constantly having insufficient money to buy even essentials had become unbearable. I sensed a freedom of spirit that morning that I suspect a young eagle must feel when first discovering it can fly. Happily soaring high over a canyon, it realizes despite its sudden maturity that a death plunge would be imminent unless it keeps flapping its wings. Nevertheless, the adolescent bird with the confidence that such a happening is doubtful, flies merrily on. Concern for my parents now left alone, with only Ruth to help manage the farm, tempered my euphoria to some degree and added to that was the abrupt separation from Jack whose future now seemed so cloudy. Still deep in thought when Millbrook Station appeared, I jumped off the train clutching my small knapsack of clothes, impatient to get on with my life and excited with the prospect of adventure.

A small granary, my accommodation while at Blockers, contained two single cots, a rickety old bureau, and one chair that I shared with another lad, Charlie Clayton, whom I knew from the Monominto dances. Being suddenly thrust into such crude lodgings swiftly jarred me into the realization that I was no longer home. Informed that threshing wouldn't begin until the following day, but I could earn a dollar and a half for an afternoon of stooking, I leaped at the opportunity. After tossing my few clothes into a drawer, I eagerly headed into the fields to begin earning my livelihood, and the first pay that would be exclusively mine.

Stooking grain allows stalks, partially green when cut, to ripen. Green or damp grain will not thresh properly. A heavy morning dew will delay threshing until the sun has dried it off, a shower can halt proceedings for half a day and a drenching rain may stall operations for days. When manpower was plentiful, a farmer would lay off his crew after a downpour rather than having to feed them for a few days. But as the war progressed and hiring help became more difficult, the farmer would do almost anything to encourage his crew to remain.

After two and a half days of threshing, rain halted the action and the Blockers drove Charlie and me back to Monominto for the weekend with the instructions that if the grain had dried out satisfactorily, they would pick us up Sunday evening.

I was anxious to get home to find out which branch of the armed services Jack had joined. Dad had accompanied Jack to help him find his way around the city, and apparently after hours of deliberation, Jack enlisted in the Air Force as a pilot. He wouldn't be inducted for two weeks, and so we went to Monominto Hall for a final Saturday night fling as a pair of civilians. We both started smoking cigarettes at this point in our lives as if to inform everyone we were now adults. We also bought a small bottle of homemade whiskey for 25 cents, mixed it with pop, and got slightly intoxicated for the first time. So within a week of severing the apron string, we had already adopted two major vices.

Going out to help Ruth with the milking early Sunday evening, I said it might possibly be the last time I would ever "pull tits." Grinning at the expression, she told me not to be so vulgar. Despite my sister's comment, the phrase, as common to every farm child either boy or girl, as the stars in a summer sky, marks the difference in attitude between rural kids and their sophisticated city cousins, who are often shocked by some of our earthy expressions. In the Shriners' Hospital during the latter stage of my confinement, I had a Winnipeg boy named John in the bed next to me. One day we got into a discussion about birth.

"You know John," I said, "one of the most moving sights you'll ever witness is a newborn calf taking its first gulp of air after leaving its mother's womb."

He looked at me in stunned disbelief. "Do you mean to tell me that your parents allow you to witness those things?" he asked incredulously.

"Why the hell not?" I replied sarcastically. "I was present several months before when the whole affair got started."

Looking at me like he just discovered I had leprosy and turning kind of white, he called the nurse and asked if he could change beds. John never spoke to me again. Part of our farm responsibility was to be present when animals bore young. Sows were clumsy and often trampled their piglets. New born lambs would occasionally lose their mothers, and it wasn't rare for a heifer or mare, particularly during their first delivery, to require assistance in delivering the new offspring.

A story that used to circulate when we were teenagers depicts the carnal knowledge most farm children acquired. Farmer Jenkins had a variety of pure bred stock; a prize bull, a registered boar, an award-winning ram, and a champion stallion. He also had a teenaged son and daughter, Billy and Sue. He charged area farmers a service fee which varied with each animal type. One day, Jenkins, his wife and son had to go to town for a day, and left Sue in charge. Shortly after they left, a neighbor, Paluski, came rushing into the yard in a frenzy and inquired from Sue the whereabouts of her father.

"He's in town with the rest of the family for the day," she explained politely, "but I know all the prices."

"I want to see your father," he shouted.

"Look Mr. Paluski, don't be concerned about me. Father left me in charge and I know what the service fees are," Sue insisted.

"Let me tell you something young lady," Paluski exploded. "Your brother Billy has got my daughter Irene pregnant."

Sue scratched her head for a minute then said apologetically, "Mr. Paluski, I know what Dad charges for the stallion, the ram, the bull, and the boar, but I'm damned if I know what he charges for Billy."

Blockers picked me up Sunday evening, and while hugging Mom and my two sisters, I said hopefully, if finances allowed, I would be home for Christmas. Jack needing a few bucks to tide him over until he got his first Air Force pay joined Father at a neighbor of Blockers for a few days of harvesting. It showered off and on the following week, and when it rained hard Saturday morning, I decided to go to Winnipeg to do a little shopping before leaving for Swan Lake on Sunday afternoon. I phoned to say good-bye to Dad and Jack with a lump in my throat, as neither Jack nor I had the slightest idea when we'd see each other again.

Over the two week period, I only got in 5½ days of threshing, for which I received the princely sum of $23.50. Blockers had to go to the city to obtain supplies and dropped me off at Eaton's, a huge department store. I spent hours comparing prices and eventually bought a pair of slacks, two shirts, socks, underclothing, and a jacket. After purchasing my bus ticket to Swan Lake, I had less than $8 remaining.

The ninety-mile trip to Swan Lake took three hours as we stopped at several small towns along the way. Never having travelled farther than from Monominto to Winnipeg, the vastness of the prairies punctuated only by groves of trees providing windbreaks for the houses amazed me. The thought that I would be more than halfway across the province made me feel like a world traveler, and enjoying the sensation, I wondered when I might go on an even longer journey. Gazing across the flatlands covered with enormous fields of stooks, I intently watched for grain elevators that, soaring into the autumn blue like prairie skyscrapers, always indicated an approaching town. The number of elevators, ranging from one to six, denoted the size of a community and fertility of the soil. Located by railroad tracks, grain elevators owned and operated by the country's grain buyers, were wooden buildings almost exclusively painted red. After weighing a farmer's load, the elevator operator dumps the grain, then shifts it at his discretion from one storage bin to another by conveyor belts. This allows the operator to separate the different types of grain and when necessary, draw samples for grade testing, fumigate for insects, or cool the grain down if damp. Damp grain, one of the main concerns, can lead to "hot spots" which if uncontrolled, will result in explosive combustion. Large country elevators have adjoining buildings called annexes, where they transfer the overflow during a bumper crop year, especially when the elevator company cannot dispose of grain as rapidly as they purchase it from the growers. Prairie elevators ship the grain by rail to the great bulk storage elevators at various shipping terminals in trade centers and shipping ports which can handle enormous capacities reaching millions of bushels. The largest installation of grain elevators in Canada is at Thunder Bay, Ontario, on Lake Superior. Perhaps the largest single elevator building in the world at Wichita, Kansas, consists of 240 tanks, each 120 feet high with 30 feet inside diameters. The total structure, over a half mile long, can hold 20 million bushels of wheat which is still only a drop in the bucket to the total grain storage capacity of elevators in the United States which approximates 1,500 million bushels.

Immediately after leaving Somerset, the elevators at Swan Lake, only five miles away, became visible. Swan Lake, a small town with four elevators, had the usual assortment of retailers including a hardware store, two grocery markets, two retail clothing outlets, a Chinese cafe, barber shop, three or four implement dealers, and a pool hall, conveniently close to the high school. Uncle Ernie, waiting for me at the bus depot, almost always went to town alone prior to my arrival, and I would soon discover the reason. We drove to the farm in his 1936 Essex, and after depositing my meager belongings in my room, and after greeting Aunt Alena (whom I always called Aunt Lena) and my cousins, I was taken by Unk on a short tour of the out buildings to acquaint me with my duties. To my dismay the first task he introduced me to, milking cows, meant I hadn't finished "pulling tits." Happily they milked only two cows, solely for family consumption. Cleaning and feeding stock comprised most of my chores, though hauling wagon loads of wheat to the elevator in Swan Lake on weekends would also be one of my responsibilities. The large two-story frame house contained a huge kitchen with adjoining living-dining room on the ground floor, plus four spacious bedrooms on the second. It was downright luxurious compared to our Monominto home, and with a room all my own, I felt like royalty.

Aunt Lena, short and stout and with a ready smile, appeared quite pleasant as did Uncle Ernie, who would prove to be a unique personality. Father and other members of the family often discussed Uncle Ernie, particularly his attitude after he returned from overseas. Like many veterans, he had difficulty adjusting back to civilian life. Spending his army credits and showing little concern for the future he dedicated himself to becoming one of the best pool players in Winnipeg and hung out at the Strand Snooker Hall on Main Street. Not considering this a reputable occupation, his brothers tried to persuade him to go to work. A handsome man, he didn't lack for female company and apparently dated several, but Aunt Alena, a registered nurse, captured his heart. An industrious Belgian woman, she wasn't inclined to let him idle around, so made arrangements with her father, Mr. Van Moll, to take over a Van Moll owned farm at Somerset, four miles from their layout at Swan Lake.

Located amidst some of the richest grain country in Manitoba, it provided a golden opportunity, but Uncle Ernie, like Father, had no farming experience, and some aspects of the business, like chores, he approached reluctantly and often to the chagrin of his wife. Five feet nine inches tall, he always slouched when standing and his arms hung down like they were too heavy for his shoulders. Unk only removed the cap or straw hat covering his partially bald head at bedtime. Generally in conversation, he cocked his head to one side like a spaniel waiting for a command, and invariably his face wore a magnetic grin that lit up his entire countenance. He chuckled from the back of his throat, and I giggled inwardly every time something amused him. His own man, if Unk decided to listen to a world series baseball game even if ripe wheat needed harvesting, he did so, and if Aunt Lena badgered him continuously for three hours to get on the tractor and cut the grain, he'd ignore her. He did possess a temper when pushed too far, but it took a lot to ruffle his feathers, probably the reason he lived almost to the age of ninety.

Following chores the morning after my arrival, cousins Marie and Betty walked me to school where Marie introduced me to Mr. Wilson, the principal, a rangy individual who gave the misleading impression of having a fierce temper. The school, a large two-story building, had several classrooms where Grades I through XII were taught by a half dozen teachers, though Grades XI and XII were assembled in one large chamber. The total school enrollment in excess of a hundred students seemed an emormous difference from Pinewood, but excepting the French class, Mr. Wilson did all the instruction for Grades XI and XII which consisted of two boys and two girls in Grade XI besides myself plus two girls in Grade XII.

I received my first shock when informed that essentials such as textbooks, pads, and other paraphernalia were not provided by the school. At lunch, a couple of classmates invited me to join them at the pool hall. After buying cigarettes and paying 10 cents for a game of snooker, it dawned on me that after I bought the required school supplies, I would again be broke. Inquiring about the likelihood of getting a harvesting job in the area, I was informed that due to the shortage of help, farmers were hiring two high school boys as a team and paying one man's wages of six dollars, the going rate in the area. Due to my experience at Blockers I felt convinced I wouldn't have to share that incredible sum of $6.00 per day with any partner, and so I made my plans accordingly. I attended school two more days, bought the school necessities, and then, with my cash reserves depleted to less than $2.00, sought further information regarding a job. Having no success, I decided to leave school and begin hunting harvest work seriously the next morning.

When I informed Uncle Ernie and Aunt Lena of my decision, they strongly protested, pointing out that my folks were counting on them to make certain I completed my schooling. Despite their objections, I had no alternative. I told them not to worry because I would rapidly catch up when I returned and that other students were also going to harvest for a week or two to take advantage of the wages. I went to bed early, planning on leaving at daylight.

Uncle Ernie roused me at 5 a.m. "Wake up boy, last night I arranged a job for you, and the farmer is downstairs right now."

"Is it on a stook team?" I inquired, trying to rub the sleep from my eyes.

"It's with Lena's brothers, the Van Molls, who have large acreage at Pilot Mound. I don't know what they have in mind," he said, "But hurry. They are waiting for you."

Though my aunt and uncle did me a favor, the fact they didn't determine the conditions would cause some embarrassment a little later. Nevertheless, relieved to have employment, I rapidly grabbed my clothes, and within twenty minutes left for Pilot Mound, a community about twenty miles west of Swan Lake.

Of the three Van Moll brothers: Morris, Gimp, and John, the latter two managed the family farm. Gimp, crippled far worse than I with polio, could only get around with the aid of crutches. After showing me to a bedroom, John Van Moll took me out to the threshing machine, already blowing straw and instructed me to get inside the portable granary and shovel grain back from the pouring spout. Despite my extreme disappointment at this turn of events, I couldn't get to talk to them until supper time when I confronted John about my pay. He replied they would pay three dollars per day. I told him with no uncertainty that I wanted a stook team and six dollars like the others.

"We don't need anyone in that capacity right now, and regardless, I

don't believe you could keep up with the other members of the crew,"
he responded. With a 44-inch machine, they employed eight stook teams
with two field pitchers, which meant the grain poured continuously into
the granary. Not only was it terribly dusty inside the windowless building but the work was just as strenuous as pitching sheaves as far as I
was concerned. The following evening after we'd finished eating, I approached John, "I'd like my $6.00 in earnings, because I'm leaving to
see if I can find a job on a stook team."

"I told your Aunt Lena I'd look after you," he retorted, "and I can't
let you go traipsing around the country."

"You also can't stop me," I replied. "If you think for one minute I'll
remain in that dust-laden granary shovelling wheat at three bucks per
day, you're badly mistaken. I just finished handling a stook team for a
week before leaving home, so there is no reason I can't do the same in
this country." I abruptly left the table with John and Gimp still sitting,
their mouths slightly ajar, unprepared for my outburst.

When I came out of my room with my packed knapsack, John was
waiting for me. "Sit down a minute and don't be so peppery," he said.
"I have a chap coming over who wants to talk to you."

In a few minutes, in walked a tall gangly farmer. Thrusting out his
hand, he introduced himself, "I'm Wayne Johnson, do you think you
can handle a stook team on this outfit?"

"I don't think, I know," I replied in my usual cocky manner.

"Well, as the Van Molls also do my threshing it's my responsibility
to supply an outfit, and since I'm too busy preparing for the thresher to
arrive at my place, I'll have to hire someone. If John is satisfied you are
holding up your end, I'll pay six dollars a day. Good luck, Bill," he
added as he shook hands and left the house.

John, who sat listening to the conversation and eyeing me as if trying
to decide whether in fact I could do a man's work, arose and said, "Bill,
part of your job is to feed, curry, water, and harness your own team, so
come out to the barn and I'll introduce you to your horses."

I thanked him heartily and promised to do my best. That evening
while cleaning and feeding my team of dapple grays, so delighted at the
prospect of earning the unbelieveable sum of six dollars per day, I
almost decided not to go to bed. That would have been a grave mistake,
however, because the next two weeks would take a greater toll of my
vital processes than any time in my life before or since.

At five o'clock the next morning, Jerry shook me awake to tend my
team. We breakfasted and headed into the fields half an hour before
sunup. After a long, tough day, I was glad to heave off my last load. I
headed for the barnyard without hearing any complaints about my
effort, and I didn't ask for any plaudits. On Saturday night members of

the crew invited me to join them in Pilot Mound for a few beers or a game of snooker, but bone weary, I sacked out.

A drenching rain halted threshing for a few days, and so Jerry, Gimp's son, invited me to join him in a cattle roundup along the fringes of Swan Lake. The lake bordering their cattle range on the north served as a natural barrier. He wanted to corral calves born during the late spring and grain feed them for marketable veal. They had two exceptionally docile black saddle ponies called Nip and Tuck that were thoroughly trained for the task at hand. Never having had a lot of experience riding horses, I boarded Nip rather cautiously and headed with Jerry into the Swan Lake Valley. Galloping along a twisting trail with yellowing poplar leaves reflecting the bright afternoon sun giving the unmistakable smell of fall, I began to envision myself quite a cowboy, a regular Gene Autry. Unfortunately I was due for a terrible let down.

The breeding stock had not likely seen a human since being released into the range in early spring. Calves were thoroughly unfamiliar with men on horseback and even more skittish. They would swerve and try to return to the herd as we began to cull them out. Jerry hollered for me to head off a young bull calf circling back to his mother. Nip, seeming to understand the command, whirled and took off after the stray, but unfortunately I was no longer aboard. When he swung right, I kept going straight ahead and found myself tumbling unceremoniously along the ground. Nip, realizing he'd lost his rider, turned back slowly, stuck his nose in my face, and I'm sure gave me the horse laugh. Jerry, almost tumbled from his mount in amusement at my plight. I gingerly climbed back on the pony, but despite my concentration, every time Nip veered suddenly, I toppled inelegantly to the turf. Getting a little bruised, I elected to return to the house, stick with the pitchfork, and leave cowboying to Jerry and Gene Autry.

We didn't get back on the grain fields for three days, then threshed nonstop for nine. We fed, watered, curried, and harnessed our team at 5 a.m., breakfasted at 6 a.m., and were usually loading at the threshing site anywhere from one to three miles away before daylight. Except for an hour dinner break to feed ourselves and the horses, we worked until dark. Most nights the horses stumbled over stooks on our return to the barnyard. Again, we fed, watered and unharnessed our team before sitting down to supper at 9 p.m. At ten o'clock we gave the animals some oats before finally crawling into our beds about 11 p.m. They were demanding eighteen-hour days. Excellent meals containing plenty of beef or chicken served with fresh vegetables and followed by an assortment of desserts helped preserve my strength. I started eating as soon as I sat down and continued to gorge myself as long as anyone remained at the table. Even when my stomach could hold no more, I still felt hungry, the only time in my life I experienced this strange phenomenon.

Occasionally the separator would break down. Arriving with a full load of sheaves, you pulled in behind the other loaded racks and waited for them to get the separator working again. Taking advantage of the lull, I would make myself comfortable on top of the sheaves and invariably fall sound asleep, oblivious to the surrounding bustle. A loud bang on the side of my rack would awaken me, and I would jump up astonished to find the separator waiting for my load. Gimp, who ran the outfit, knowing I was asleep, wouldn't disturb me until the last moment and then would whack my load with one of his crutches.

Though I was nearly six feet tall, I weighed only 140 pounds, twelve of which I lost during those exhausting nine days. We worked til after dark on the final Saturday to clean up a field of 80 acres of barley that we had started in the morning. Gimp announced we had threshed over five thousand bushels of barley, a one-day record volume for all the years he had been involved in the harvest. Dragging myself in the house for supper, I felt like I'd handled the whole 80 acres by myself.

After we ate, John said, "Billy, the job is finished and Jerry will tend the horses. Go to bed and I'll see you in the morning to arrange transportation back to Swan Lake." I didn't wait for a second invitation.

After a leisurely breakfast at 10 a.m. I went into the living room where Gimp and John sat waiting for me. Gimp spoke first, "My boy, considering your handicap, you did a creditable job. I've sat on the tractor these past two weeks and watched you wrestle with those heavy sheaves, and I'm damn proud of you."

John, now standing beside me with a wad of bills, said, "Here's your reward," and handed me six ten dollar bills, plus two twos, and two ones. Then he added, "Like Gimp said, you've earned your pay."

I don't know if the tears in my eyes were from the kind words or emotion I felt with the bonanza of $66.00 clutched in my hand. Though mentally calculating my earnings daily while laboring through the ordeal, it wasn't until I saw the cash that the significance of the windfall struck me.

A neighbor waited to take me to Swan Lake, so thanking the two Van Molls sincerely and tired but happy, I left the house never to see either of them again.

I stopped in the Chinese restaurant at Swan Lake for some pie-a-la-mode and a cup of coffee. Homer and Vick, my two male Grade XI classmates, dawdling in one of the booths, invited me over. They claimed I hadn't missed too much at school and could easily catch up. When I inquired if they'd done any harvesting, they boastfully responded that they had worked for six days earning eighteen bucks each, so I decided not to tell them about the $66.00 tucked safely in my trouser pocket.

I arrived back at the farm at 3 o'clock after a tiresome mile and a half walk from town. With no one home, and feeling totally exhausted, I hobbled up to my room. After safely stashing six ten dollar bills into my bureau drawer, I sprawled across my bed without even removing my work boots and fell asleep before my head hit the pillow.

"Wake up, wake up Billy," I heard a voice shouting beside me. "If you're going to be this lazy, you aren't going to stay here."

Trying to wipe the sleep from my eyes and determine my whereabouts I heard Aunt Lena continue in a loud, angry voice, "We went down to John's to pick you up and visited a while because we thought you'd have the chores all done, and here it is 9 o'clock and we find you sound asleep." That moment was the only time in my life I had malicious thoughts toward Aunt Lena. Befuddled, I mumbled something about being sorry as I dragged my weary carcass toward the stable to tend my chores. Despite the animosity I felt toward Aunt Lena, it rapidly dissipated when I recalled those six ten dollar bills lying snugly in my room.

Right from the beginning I found Uncle Ernie a delight in many ways. He loved to play cribbage and keeping score on paper became too awkward so I fabricated a cribbage board on which we played thousands of games. Though we rarely gambled, if I hit a winning streak he'd keep me up all hours of the night until luck swung his way. He said he couldn't go to bed while losing, but I guess he figured that shouldn't apply to me. I could sit fascinated for hours listening to his experiences during World War I. He enjoyed male companionship and idolized his oldest son Sam, still only a tad, and George, not born until after my departure. He and Aunt Lena didn't have an especially close relationship. She growled and nagged him constantly and mostly for good reason. Otherwise they might have ended up with nothing. Like Father, Unk was a "put off until tomorrower," but as a sixteen year old, I found his high jinks and the constant cat-and-mouse game he played with his wife thoroughly amusing. The first incident happened a few days after my return from Pilot Mound and Unk's own harvest had been completed. At the supper table he looked at me and said, "Hey boy, you got much homework when you finish your chores? I want you to come over to Buck Livingstone's and help me catch a couple of guinea hens."

"Not too much," I replied. "I can finish it when we get back."

Aunt Lena immediately piped up, "Ernie, you know damn well you're going to town to play pool. You start teaching that boy your bad habits and I'm really going to get cross with you."

"Don't be crazy woman," Unk shot back. "What the hell would I go to town for? I've got to get those guinea fowl to protect the chickens. The hawks are getting brazen."

Guinea fowl are strange-looking birds covered with a slaty plummage speckled with white and with a bald neck and head. Whenever an owl or hawk approaches, they set up a tremendous squawking, either frightening off the predator or warning of the danger. Farmers therefore keep a couple around to act as sentinels. Unk raised a lot of chickens for market and eggs, and so guinea fowl seemed like a logical necessity.

Before we left the lane leading to the main road, Unk turned to me and said, "Hey boy, got your wallet?"

"Why in the world would I need my wallet to catch guinea hens?" I asked suspiciously.

"You ain't too smart for a Phillips. Suppose we have to go to town for gas or something," he retorted, a roguish look on his face.

"I've still got my damned overalls on," I said. "I would have changed had I dreamed you were going to town."

"I've a notion you'll soon smarten up," he said as he turned into Livingstone's driveway.

Buck Livingstone came out of the house with a jute sack containing two guinea hens. After a few words of neighborly chit chat, Unk threw the birds in the trunk, and we headed for town and the pool hall. Some local farmers, a couple of townspeople and some Cree Indians were already involved in a game of "kelly pool." After a little good-natured repartee and I had been introduced, Unk selected a cue and got involved in the match. Watching them gamble at both kelly and pea pool at a few cents per cue, two things became obvious. Unk was an excellent shot, and he was no stranger to the pool. hall. We returned home at midnight. Aunt Lena, in bed, heard us in the kitchen and hollered down through the hot air vent, "Gawd damn you Ernie, teaching that boy to be deceitful and to gamble. What would your brother and sister-in-law think if they knew?" She continued berating him for another ten minutes.

By this time, Unk was already comfortably seated in an easy chair, his cap tugged down low over his head. He winked at me from under the brim and whispered, "You'd better get busy with your homework, boy. What the hell do you think your father is going to say if you don't pass Grade XI?"

Uncle Ernie pulled the same caper a dozen or more times during the next nine months, each time coming up with a new reason to visit town. Aunt Lena invariably spent ten minutes before we left and a half hour after we returned bawling the daylights out of him. At times I think he actually fooled himself. One evening after announcing we had to go to town to pick up something at the hardware store for the tractor and enduring the usual tirade from Aunt Lena, he insisted strenuously about the necessity of the trip and said he couldn't possibly get on with the cultivating the following day without the part. He satisfied me, and I believe almost convinced Aunt Lena. The hardware store was a hundred yards left on the main thoroughfare and the pool room a quarter mile to the right. Nearing the intersection he glanced left, then turning right muttered, "Can you imagine that son-of-a-bitch being closed this early! What is the world coming to?"

I distinctly saw a light in the hardware store but didn't know if he actually needed the tractor part or had removed a piece and put it in his pocket. Nonetheless I was becoming proficient at kelly pool and didn't want to waste my time shopping either.

The weeks slid by swiftly. I was comfortable with my new surroundings, but I missed the family and always waited anxiously for Mom's letter or news from Jack. Shortly after Jack's induction, they discovered he had a double hernia, and he was sent to the Air Force hospital at St. Thomas, Ontario, for an operation. Then he was moved to Trenton, Ontario to convalesce. In November, he began basic training in Toronto, and my heart leaped with joy when I received a letter stating he thought he would get Christmas leave. If I got home, we could be all together for the holidays. With the war progressing favorably, I'm certain the whole family secretly hoped Jack would never see action.

As snow fell and the holidays approached, my lighthearted mood caused me some embarrassment. I always had a habit of bursting out in laughter if something suddenly tickled my funny bone. In one instance, Principal Wilson ordered me from the classroom and told me not to return until I could control myself. Then in mid-December, Vick, sitting beside me, made a comical remark that made me explode in an uncontrollable guffaw.

"William, leave this school immediately," Wilson roared.

I stopped at the door and asked, "When should I come back?"

"I don't ever want to see you again," he replied vehemently. Walking outside and lighting up a cigarette, I stood watching the snowflakes flutter aimlessly to an already snow-covered ground and considered my rather distressing position. Though unafraid to go home, I would be damned ashamed to admit I'd been expelled. I decided that if I could get reinstated I'd better behave myself, for I was not likely to get a third chance.

I sneaked back to my seat during French class, and when Wilson returned after recess, he said nothing. As it turned out, Wilson's days at Swan Lake High were numbered, not mine. Dissatisfied with discipline throughout the school, the school board had hired a new principal to take over following Christmas holidays.

At the Christmas concert, Swan Lake students put on skits including songs from "Oklahoma," the tremendously successful Broadway musical of the time. Though I missed the show, I enjoyed listening to them rehearse their rendition of "The Surrey With the Fringe on Top."

Marie, an excellent piano player, could play most of the popular tunes of the period by ear, including "Don't Fence Me In," "Mairzy Doats," "Pistol Packin' Momma," "Sunday, Monday or Always," and others. As a result, we were invited to parties and school dances where she often provided much of the dance music. A few days before leaving for Winnipeg, we attended a Christmas dance at the school. As the evening progressed, I built up enough nerve to ask one of the young ladies for a dance. She looked up at me for a moment then said, "Wouldn't you just sort of hop around?"

Terribly embarrassed, I mumbled, "Yes, I suppose I would."

I might never have attempted to dance again, but Una, one of my classmates, overheard the remark and came directly over. "Let's try this step Willie," she said flippantly and grabbed my hand.

"I'm not sure I can manage it," I replied, my face still crimson.

"Nonsense," Una retorted, and before I could say more, she had me on the dance floor. A big strong girl, she guided me until I gained some confidence. Before long I could feel my feet keeping rhythm with the music. Una obviously told others of the incident because other young ladies soon encouraged me to try my new-found skill. I enjoyed the evening and could hardly wait to get back to Monominto to test my new capability on old schoolmates.

It was great to be home, but how small and rural our log kitchen now looked. The bedroom Jack and I shared was tiny. A double bed, small closet, plus a bureau allowed barely enough space to squeeze past one to reach the other. I had never noticed before. Nevertheless, it was home.

Jack looked splendid in his uniform but preferred to wear his old farm clothes for a change. He dressed up only when we attended social outings.

Jack had signed over a portion of his Air Force paycheck to the folks, and Dad used the new-found wealth for many purposes, including the purchase of an automobile—the first he'd owned in nearly fifteen years. He bought the 1929 Graham Paige sedan for $210, and though the car was 14 years old, it seemed like a royal chariot to all of us. Automobiles were no longer a rarity in Monominto, having gradually replaced the horse and sleigh as winter transportation. As a result, municipalities had to purchase power snowplows to keep the roads open in winter, sometimes without success. Few cars were equipped with self-starters and to start a balky engine with a hand crank in bitter cold usually created a major problem. We generally had to hitch up the horses and tow the vehicle a mile or two, sometimes getting half way to our destination before the engine caught. The horses must have thought we were nuts.

The family thoroughly enjoyed our ten days together, and New Years arrived too soon. For the first time, everyone had a few dollars, and so we exchanged gifts, added a larger selection of Christmas delicacies to the larder, and bought a small variety of government liquor. Dad loved a few spoonfuls of rum in his tea, a delicacy for which Jack and I had also acquired a taste. Close family ties furnished the principal reason for our pleasurable few days, but the sudden availability of money undoubtedly added immeasurably to the holidays.

Dad gave me ten dollars to buy a young tom turkey from around Swan Lake, believing a bird from a different part of the country would be more suitable for breeding purposes. He told me to keep anything left of the sawbuck. The tom cost $7, and the shipping charges were about $2. I netted a dollar, not much but appreciated.

Aboard the bus to Swan Lake I took stock of my finances. I didn't regret spending any of those six ten-dollar bills that had provided me with such a superior sense of financial stability four months earlier, but the last one had been cashed to buy my bus ticket. Again I had to plan some way to improve my monetary position.

Uncle Ernie had loaned me a .22 calibre rifle to hunt jack rabbits, worth a few cents a pound, but ammunition was strictly rationed and had become almost impossible to buy. I also trapped a few weasels and skunks, their pelts bringing from $3 to $5, but my money wasn't lasting quite as long as before. Besides buying cigarettes and paying pool fees, I also found young ladies weren't keen on dating paupers.

By mid-January my cash shortage reached the critical stage, forcing me to find an additional source of income. Elevator companies transfering wheat from annexes back to elevators that were now empty hired trucks equipped with augurs to shift the grain. When those annexes were half empty, shovellers were required to move the remaining grain from the rear of the building to the augur. Though dirty, dusty, the job paid 50 cents an hour, and so I hired on, working eight days from a Friday morning to a week the following Saturday, and missing only six days at school. To avoid any hassle, I asked only Unk's permission to work the two Saturdays at the elevator if I finished my chores before leaving for town, and he consented. To hoodwink Aunt Lena, I left home with my school clothes, changed into overalls at work and back into school clothes before returning to the farm. Marie told Miss Aurthur, the new principal, I suffered with a bad cold and so she sent home all missed assignments. The deception worked beautifully. I didn't fall too far behind in my schoolwork, and the $28 I earned bolstered my finances for a while.

Miss Aurthur was built like a British bulldog and had the same sort of demeanor. Both a strict disciplinarian and an outstanding educator, she brought to Swan Lake High precisely what the school needed. Toward the end of February, she asked me to remain after school for a chat.

Miss Aurthur felt I had the ability to get top marks if I dedicated myself to my studies and wanted to make an application on my behalf for a scholarship. She explained that I would have to write special final examinations in June under specific guidelines and that the upcoming Easter exams would be a superb dry run. I told her to go ahead and apply and promised to give it my best shot.

With my wallet temporarily replenished, I returned to a more pleasing social life. I loved curling, a popular sport on the prairies, and except for sweeping the rocks, I could match anyone at the game. Swan Lake had one of the best intermediate hockey teams in the province. Several of my schoolmates were on the team, and so I usually attended home games. Ice skating parties were also popular and required money to share the cost of refreshments. These activities soon depleted my $28.

Uncle Ernie's buildings were located on a large flat ridge that sloped gradually about half a mile to a small shallow marshy pond about a thousand yards in diameter. Before freeze-up, I often walked around the little lake to view the bands of ducks that either hatched in nests there or used it as a temporary stopover. The almost round pond froze over into a very smooth sheet of ice in early winter.

A dozen of my schoolmates plus a few ex-pupils in the same age bracket would congregate on moonlit nights for a skating party on the frozen pond. Despite a bonfire lit for warmth and to toast wieners and marshmallows, the boys would try to persuade their girl friends to skate away from the group to sit on one of the many mounds that jutted up through the ice for private conversation or whatever else came to mind.

One early March night I was relaxing with a friend on one of these piles of reeds, my mind absorbed with anything but dwindling cash reserves, when it struck me that the mounds were actually muskrat houses. I'd never trapped muskrats, but I knew muskrat pelts brought in the $4 range. Realizing my fiscal problems would be solved for several months if a substantial number of animals lived on the lake, I left my girl friend staring into space while I went dashing around the pond counting muskrat houses. Now I knew exactly how a prospector felt when first spotting a vein of gold.

Rat trapping season began in late March coinciding with Easter exams which would make it a tedious three weeks, especially in lieu of the promise I had made to Miss Aurthur. When I explained the potential bonanza to Unk, he offered to do my chores for half the take from the trapping enterprise, and I rapidly agreed. Arriving home from school three days before season opened, I could see someone down on the lake. Grabbing a half dozen traps, I raced down to investigate and was mortified to find the intruder, a sizable Cree Indian, opening up muskrat houses and setting traps.

"Hi, I'm Bill Phillips. My uncle owns this farm and I planned on harvesting these pelts myself when the season opens," I said impetuously.

Standing about 6 feet 3 inches tall and weighing around 225 pounds, he gave me the impression of Punjab. With his hands on his hips, he looked at me with some disdain. "I've trapped this pond for years, and it's not private property," he retorted. After a moment's hesitation to see if I got the message, he added, "And what difference does it make if the season isn't officially open? The fur is prime."

Stymied by this disastrous turn of events, I decided to at least try some bluff. "Well, I'm closer than you are, so I'll damn well get my share of pelts," I shot at him.

"Look", he spoke calmly, "I'm Clarence Cameron. Have you ever trapped muskrats before?"

"No, but I've read quite a lot, and I'm certain I'll make out." I replied.

"Well, here's what I suggest. We'll split the pond in half with willow branches stuck in the snow, and I'll teach you the easiest way to catch animals without damaging their fur," he offered politely. "There is no gain to either of us if we start springing each other's traps."

I hastily accepted his offer, delighted with the outcome of the confrontation because I didn't know very much about the muskrat trade. Clarence explained that if muskrats aren't drowned shortly after getting caught they invariably chew their foot off to escape their predicament. He cut several stout willows about three feet long, each with an extending branch lopped off, leaving a one inch spur. A steel ring on the end of a two foot chain attached to the trap was slipped onto the willow above the spur. The muskrat couldn't avoid stepping in the set trap placed inside the house near where it fed, easily detected by pieces of green reed and other vegetation. Once caught, the animal would dive for the bottom of the pond forcing the ring over the spur on the willow limb. This would prevent the muskrat from resurfacing and cause it to drown, an untimely end to a harmless little creature for the sake of fashion. But as in other similar situations, if the animals are not thinned out annually, they soon over-populate an area. Many would die of starvation, a far more lingering death.

With the territory marked out and my traps in place, I bade Clarence good night. Clarence said to meet him at 7 a.m. the following morning, and he'd give me some tips on skinning, fleshing, and stretching the animals. Happy with the turn of events, I returned to the pond at the agreed time but saw no sign of Clarence. When I reached the first of my locations, I found the trap missing, then the second, third, and all the others. At the final setting, a note crudely scribbled on a Chantecler cigarette paper packet and attached to a willow twig read:

"Beware! You have been trapping out of season and have been reported to the game warden."

Dumbfounded, I looked for Clarence but didn't really expect to see him. There was little doubt in my mind but that he committed the crime. Returning to the house, I made it clear to Unk that I wouldn't be frightened off but would now wait until the official beginning of the season. Unk informed me that Clarence Cameron, a ranking amateur heavyweight boxer and well regarded in the area, would probably try to scare me off what he regarded as his personal trapping grounds, especially with the high price of fur.

I reached the pond before daylight on opening morning, and through the breaking dawn, I could see Clarence moving around the houses. Waiting until I reached my first muskrat house, he marched over in a threatening manner and said, "Some son-of-a-bitch stole my traps by the time I'd arrived here the other morning. Did he take any of yours?"

No match for him physically, though determined to make my stand, I looked him square in the face and responded, "Yes, some son-of-a-bitch stole all mine and left a threatening note. I'm going to trap here regardless, and if it happens again, I'll steal every trap I can put my hands on and nobody will catch any rats." I whirled and walked away without further comment.

Sticking out of Clarence's shirt pocket was his tobacco and tucked into the side, a bright red packet of Chantecler cigarette papers. This was not irrefutable proof, but it removed any doubt in my mind that the Cree stole my traps. He probably hoped his action would discourage me from further participation, but he didn't know how desperately I needed cash.

I set a dozen traps in the houses on my half of the dividing line, returned home for breakfast and then went to school. By crossing a neighbor's field on my way back from school I could check my traps before going home, saving myself a trip and allowing some daylight to skin and stretch the animals. Approaching my first setting with apprehension, I was relieved to find my trap still intact, though empty. At the next I got a real surprise. On top of the house lay a dead muskrat, and in the trap another. Obviously, Clarence, not in sight, had removed the animal and reset the trap. I thanked him later that night when we were both doing our rounds. He just shrugged and mumbled something about if we were going to trap together we might as well be friends.

Everything went smoothly until the first Friday on a mild moonlit night. Clarence, who had been in the pool hall with Unk and me, asked if we would give him a ride to the farm as it had turned midnight. The Cree went directly to the pond while I changed my clothes. Nearing the pond, I could see Clarence on my side, and as I approached, he cautioned me to be quiet. "There are two sleighs and several men on the other side of the pond," he whispered, which happened to be in Clarence's territory.

"There might be trouble," he warned. "Do you want to come with me?"

"You're damn right," I said. "Let's go."

Walking stealthily behind the big Indian, I wondered how he knew there were two outfits. I could still hear only the slight tinkle of sleigh bells. I felt apprehension about the coming encounter, but knowing my partner had some fighting ability comforted me to some extent.

Clarence stopped and listened several times before we reached six men sitting on a muskrat house around a campfire with several cases of beer. Clarence marched up like a Royal Canadian Mounted Police Officer, but before he opened his mouth, one of the men shouted, "Hey, it's Clarence Cameron." And with this, they all got up and enthusiastically grabbed his hand. After preliminary salutations, Clarence introduced me. "This is Bill Phillips, a nephew of Ernie, who owns the farm on the hill."

"Hell, I know Ernie," one of the them said pleasantly, as did a couple of the others.

"Hey Clarence, will you and the kid have a beer?" A man called Bob asked as he handed us each a bottle.

As the party progressed, I noticed Clarence peering inside the sleigh boxes where piles of traps strewn on the floor made it obvious they intended an all-out campaign on our rats.

While downing our second beer, Clarence spoke in a voice loud enough for all to hear, "Me and Bill here have divided the pond and have been trapping it for a week. There are not enough animals to make it worthwhile for anyone else."

"Hell, we didn't know you were trapping here," one of the men immediately responded. "We won't interfere." The rest of the group heartily endorsed this statement.

A third beer put me into orbit, but in spite of my tipsy condition, I realized when crawling into bed at 2 a.m. that my income from muskrat trapping would expeditiously have dried up if it had not been for Clarence.

The following two weeks were tiresome but enjoyable. I visited my traps three times a day—on my way to school, when I left dead animals on top of the house to pick up on my return from school, and finally, with the aid of a flashlight, at midnight. Immediately after supper, I skinned, fleshed, and stretched the pelts, using cedar shingles as stretchers, and then I hung the freshly prepared fur in the barn to dry. I studied until midnight before my final inspection trip to my traps, and an hour or two after. Unk, keeping up his end of the bargain with the chores, was anxious to take our first bundle of hides to Swan Lake to sell. The owner of the hardware store who dealt in fur paid forty-two dollars for the first ten pelts. When I handed Unk his half for the loot in the pool hall, we both took a lot of good-natured razzing. Unk's cronies kidded us about stealing from the Cree Indians who had a reservation not far from Swan Lake and usually controlled all trapping rights.

I caught a total of fifty-two rats before the ice became too dangerous and we had to remove our traps. The pelts sold for $220 and put me into the best financial position ever from my share of the windfall.

During our time together, Clarence and I often chatted about the war and its effects on each of us. I mentioned the problem of obtaining .22 calibre bullets. Indians could buy all they wanted. A few days after the season ended Clarence, waiting for me outside the school, handed me three boxes of .22 shells. Flabbergasted, I reached for my wallet, but he absolutely refused to accept any payment. As he turned and walked away, I knew I'd just received payment for six traps.

I was bleary eyed while writing the Easter tests, but Miss Aurthur was pleased with the results and said that if I really applied myself until final exams there was a good chance I would earn a scholarship to continue my education. Manitoba had no Grade XIII in 1943-44, and until they extended high school for an extra year, they divided senior matriculation between XI and XII, with Grade XI considered the most difficult semester in high school. As the application for the scholarship had been submitted and accepted, I decided to make an effort to achieve success despite my uncertainty as to my desire or inclination to proceed with school. The constant struggle during the ten months to remain solvent had focused my thinking on earning, not learning. Determined to become financially self sufficient as rapidly as possible, I had no desire to become a doctor, lawyer, accountant, or other professional that meant at least another half dozen years of school. At that time, in fact, I wanted mostly to satisfy my compulsion to get involved in the gigantic conflict affecting all our lives.

Jack flunked in his effort to become a pilot at Links Trainer, a simulated airplane cockpit the Air Force used to test would-be pilots for potential coordination in handling flight instruments. Having never driven a car or operated equipment with similar controls or motion, Jack was at a distinct disadvantage and so failed. Still wanting to be a member of an air crew, he transferred to tail gunner and was shipped to Summerside, Prince Edward Island for training. This turn of events didn't make me or the rest of the family happy because the vulnerability of the rear turret on Lancaster Bombers made the life of a tail gunner in action measurable in minutes.

Fortunately, the war news continued encouraging throughout 1944. In Janaury, Allied troops landed in Italy, a morale booster. Soviet armies recaptured Novgorod, relieved Leningrad, and by early February had reached the borders of pre-war Poland. German cities were under intense bombardment by both the R.A.F. and the U.S.A.F. On January 20, the R.A.F. dropped 2,300 tons of bombs on Berlin. Meanwhile, in the Pacific, Allied forces took Kwajalein Island on February 6, landed on the Marshalls on February 17, and also in New Guinea on April 22. American B-29 bombers were increasing their attack on Japan's home islands. Rome fell on June 4. This was two days before the long-awaited second front opened on D-day, June 6, when 176,000 Allied troops landed successfully on Normandy beaches under the supreme command of General Eisenhower.

Trying to concentrate on final exams with such stupendous news pouring in from Europe was exceedingly difficult. We constantly huddled around radios to absorb news reports on the raging battles being fought as the Allies solidified their foothold on French soil. Almost everyone had a friend or relative in the Canadian army and was thoroughly involved in the mind-boggling operation.

Completing the final examination in late June, I believed my results would be satisfactory, although several weeks would elapse before I received the outcome. The evening before I returned to Monominto, we had a small private banquet for Grades X to XII, consisting of 15 pupils. Each student described his future plans. Three boys said they would be enlisting in one of the services during the summer, and I envied their freedom to make the choice. The Hartwell twin girls, who had taken Grade XII, didn't recommend Swan Lake High School for anyone intending to take that grade the following semester due to insufficient assistance available for the final year of senior matriculation. When Miss Aurthur agreed with their assessment, it eliminated one of my options. With Swan Lake excluded, I didn't know if I could earn sufficient money through the summer to spend a year in Winnipeg going to school.

All my newly acquired friends in Swan Lake vowed to keep in touch and vice versa, but I neither heard from nor ever saw any of them again.

How soon we forget. I almost hated to leave Aunt Lena, my cousins, and especially Unk, with whom I had a marvellous relationship. They had become as close to me as my own family. My ten months had not only been educational and enjoyable but financially rewarding. I left with considerably more than the $2 I had in my pocket when I arrived the previous August.

Chapter 8

Journey into Peace

After arriving in Winnipeg from Swan Lake and before continuing to Monominto, I went to an Army Recruitment office, still harboring the notion there might be a place for me in the fight. I explained to the captain on duty that getting a uniform wasn't important but that getting into action was imperative because I could be an asset in the cause. He listened sympathetically, and then directed me to the nearest Merchant Navy office, which he believed offered the best opportunity for me to see actual combat.

Within the hour, I went bounding into the Merchant Navy enlistment center. To my dismay they had huge lists of waiting applicants—men classified 4-F for other services because of poor vision, flat feet, fallen arches or other fairly minor problems. To be considered with my handicap would be virtually impossible, they explained.

As much as I hated to admit defeat, there now appeared little doubt I was destined to be a curious and frustrated onlooker rather than an active participant in one of the great adventures of our time.

I sensed a great change in Monominto and many of its inhabitants. Young ladies I'd known all my life now seemed unusually alluring. Sister Ruth was no longer a silly little girl in pigtails; she had matured into a healthy, vibrant, athletic teenager. Ed Barham though still freckle-faced, red-headed and full of malarkey, had become an adult with adult responsibilities. The greatest change was probably in me. I had gained more confidence in dealing with life in general and the fairer sex in particular, although I approached each request for a date or dance as cautiously as a coyote stalking a squirrel. Abhoring the thought of being turned down, I engineered each situation so that if possible, the young ladies did the asking. As an example, if sitting with a girl during a dance number I might say, "I'd like to invite you to dance, but I'm not certain I can handle the step." Invariably, the girl would reply, "Oh sure you can, Bill, let's give it a try!" Or I might say, "Mary, I'd love to take you to the dance Saturday night, but I can't pick you up before 9 p.m.!" Obviously, if Mary wanted to be my date she would agree to the 9 o'clock time, but if not and she winced about the lateness, my dignity was left intact.

Father suggested I learn to drive his car, which both surprised and delighted me. However, I concluded he probably hoped it would help persuade me to remain on the farm.

I encountered the same difficulty with my right leg and foot when handling the accelerator and brake on an automobile as I had with the cutter blade on the hay mower. After depressing the gas pedal for a while, the foot would grow numb and refuse to heed my command to move to the brake when needed. On these occasions, I had to move my left foot off the clutch, thereby putting the engine in gear while depressing the brake pedal. Accelerating and braking at the same moment gave the vehicle fits. Horses, dogs, sheep, and cows soon learned to clear the right-of-way. Closed gates, a constant menace, meant I spent most evenings repairing those enclosures I'd rolled over during the previous training session. For hours on end, with the ignition switched off, I would sit in the car forcing my foot to depress the accelerator and instantly move to the brake pedal when ordered. Eventually it strengthened, and I was capable of driving. I did not obtain a license for two years but Ruth and I were ecstatic when we finally had our own transportation to the local Saturday night shindig.

With my cash reserves again depleted, I left to go harvesting in early August. An agency called Farm Help Service, formed to encourage laborers from across Canada to assist in the western harvest, paid applicants the bus or train fare to areas requesting help. They sent me by train to Virden, Manitoba, a small town 225 miles west of Winnipeg and 25 miles east of the Saskatchewan border. Farm Help had representation in each community, and I reported to the local agent on my arrival late Friday afternoon. A farmer named Robinson sat waiting at the office to see if any help had arrived on the day's train. Within minutes I was in his truck and on my way to his farm one mile out of town.

After a few pleasantries, I looked over at the bewiskered old farmer and said, "What are you paying, Mr. Robinson?"

"Five dollars per day," he replied kind of curtly.

With obvious irritation, I responded just as brusquely, "I earned six dollars per day last year at Pilot Mount, and I'm not enthusiastic about working for less this year."

Robinson's face reddened, and he exploded, "You young whippersnappers come out here expecting to fleece the farmers, while my son Jim is overseas fighting for the likes of you for a dollar a day. You'll get five dollars per day if you work for me, and that's final," he shouted. As I would only get one day's threshing in before Sunday when I could leave and investigate the going rate, I shut my mouth. At noon the following day, while driving our horses into the farmyard for lunch, Bruce, one of Robinson's sons, who also handled a team, spoke to me as we crossed the yard. "Hey, Bill, come over here a minute." He took me to a portable granary partially filled with the wheat we'd threshed that morning.

"Look at that golden grain," he chortled, "When that bin is filled, it represents a thousand bucks, all for my brother Jim, who's in the Army. We'll have at least a dozen more before threshing is completed. You know, before the war we received less than half the price per bushel we're getting now."

I didn't comment but sincerely wished he could have heard his father's remarks the previous day. At least Bruce's words removed any guilt I felt when I told the old man after supper I needed my five dollars to go to Virden to buy tobacco. With the money in my hand, I looked Robinson square in the eye and said, "I hope you can hire enough help to get Jim's wheat into the granary, because I am going to Virden to see if I can obtain a little of the fruits of war myself." The old-timer may not have gotten my meaning, but perhaps Bruce enlightened him after I left.

The Farm Help office remained open Saturday nights because farmers and their wives came to do their week's grocery shopping, purchase necessities required for the harvest, and hire field hands. I reported to the agent and explained why I left Robinson's. He said the rate around Virden seemed to be between five and six dollars, but the agency didn't get involved in salary negotiations. While chatting, a tall, gangly chap entered the small office and inquired about the chances of getting a man.

"This is Bill Phillips," the agent said. "He's looking for a job."

"Hi! I'm Nels Heman," the man declared, offering his hand. "We got lots of work, plenty of good food and will pay six bucks a day for a good worker. Have you ever harvested before?"

"You bet," I responded. "I'm your man."

Approaching his car parked in the parking lot, I could see an elderly woman sitting in the back seat. Judging Nels to be in his thirties, and the lady in her sixties, I figured her to be his mother. As I slid into the front seat beside Nels, he turned and addressing the lady said, "Mrs. Miller, this is Bill Phillips, our new hired man. Bill, this is Mrs. Miller, my housekeeper."

Tiny in stature, about five foot four inches, she had a pleasant and attractive face, indicating she had been an extremely pretty young lady. With gray hair tied in a bun, she resembled a school teacher more than a farm woman. Her black eyes flashing, she looked at me but spoke to Nels.

"Nelson, what in the world makes you think this lad could do the heavy work you have in mind for him. It's just a waste of time to take him the fifteen miles out to the farm when you are simply going to have to bring him back again." Turning to me, she said, "I'm sorry, Mr. Phillips, perhaps Nelson didn't see you walk before he hired you, but with that leg, you would never be able to handle the tough task of harvesting."

"Mrs. Miller," I said, "Not meaning any disrespect, but you don't look big or strong enough to do much of anything yourself. Nevertheless, I'll bet you accomplish plenty when you want to. I wouldn't have accepted the position if I had any doubt about my capability. Besides, this won't be my first job pitching sheaves."

Mrs. Miller, slightly stunned by my remark, said no more. Nels, watching the two of us with a slight grin, now re-entered the conversation. "I asked Bill if he had harvested before I offered him the job, and by the look of his hands, he's not unaccustomed to hard work. Also, men are scarce, and I think we'd better give him a chance to see if he can manage."

With that he started the car and headed for his farm. Mrs. Miller said little during the hour we drove to their home, but she obviously played an important role in Nels' decisions. Whenever he made suggestions or plans about the coming harvest, he always turned to her for approval. He explained to me while driving that he and his two older, married brothers each owned their own separate farms, totalling several hundred acres. They threshed together, and as crops were exceptionally good, it would take well into October to complete the harvest, even with favorable weather. Nels mentioned they lost their mother at an early age, and their father, now also dead, had hired Mrs. Miller as a housekeeper to help raise the boys. When the others married, she moved in with Nels, who had remained a bachelor.

They lived in a two-story frame house where my bedroom, so tidy and pleasantly furnished, appeared like I visualized a high-class hotel room might look. Mrs. Miller, not seeming to hold any grudge on my being hired over her objections, served coffee and cake before we retired. As I climbed the stairs to my room, she offered some advice, "Tomorrow is Sunday," she stated, "you had best sleep as late as you can because you will need your reserves of strength in the coming weeks."

I thanked her for her concern and said no more despite my annoyance at this constant impression I seemed to give people about the difficulty they believed I faced in doing physical labor. When I walked, my leg swung considerably in an arc, particularly if I didn't pay attention. When my foot landed, instead of the toe pointing forward it faced sideways due to the twist in my leg. If I really concentrated while walking, however, I could manage a gait with a barely noticeable limp. I realized this because when strolling down the sidewalks in the city with my image reflecting from picture windows, I obtained a clear indication of how I looked to others. By paying strict attention to my reflection, I could almost eliminate the limp, if I didn't run out of windows.

The *Reader's Digest* published remarks made by Itzhak Perlman, a violinist whose legs were paralyzed by polio when he was five. Speaking at the International Year of Disabled Persons' ceremony held in New York City, he said, "Most disabled persons adjust well to their disabilities. Ask many of us who are disabled what we would like most in life, and we will say, 'To be a better father' or 'to be promoted in my job'. You would be surprised how few would say, 'not to be disabled'. We accept our limitations. It is others who have a problem dealing with our physical impediments."

Although I'd been on my own for only a year and Perlman's prophetic words had yet to be uttered, they aptly described what I'd already experienced. This concern about my physical ability made me resolve to do more than my share of anything I tackled and let those without disability see if they could compete with me.

Working with the Heman's turned out to be a delight, and every Saturday evening, I accompanied Nels and Mrs. Miller into Virden. A couple of small draws against my wages provided sufficient pocket money for tobacco plus toiletries and allowed a little for levity. While they shopped, I'd meet with other itinerant harvesters to shoot pool and quaff a few beers, though I would be certain to eliminate the smell of alcohol before returning to the farm. Mrs. Miller, like a fairy godmother to me, made it abundantly clear she abhorred the habit. She served outstanding meals, and on rainy mornings or Sundays, insisted I stay in bed to rest until noon. During these times she always brought a plate of hot biscuits spread with homemade jam, plus a pot of tea. I could readily understand why all the family admired and loved Mrs. Miller so dearly.

Shortly after arriving at the Heman's, I received mail from Mother including a notice from the Manitoba Department of Education congratulating me on being awarded the Roger Goulet Scholarship, granting me financial assistance to continue my education. The letter also praised my progress in the three years I'd been registered with the department. Miss Aurthur, already aware of my triumph, sent her best wishes as well. Pondering my future and realizing the decision would have a tremendous bearing on the balance of my life, I didn't respond to anyone for a week or more. My inclination wasn't toward further study, mostly because I had no impulsion to become a professional man. I was repelled by the thought of being cooped up in a city, in an office, or any other sort of confinement for the balance of my life. I knew that the freedom of spirit I'd experienced during the past few months would be difficult to exchange for the five or six years it would take to finish at a university. The financial struggle I would also face to provide myself with the barest essentials concerned me, too. After careful deliberation, I decided further study was an unpleasant option, and so I elected to discontinue my education.

Writing to Mother, unaware of the scholarship, was an unpleasant task because I knew she would be disappointed, as would also Miss Aurthur. I didn't expect either of them to understand my feelings. I wrote a short letter of thanks to the Department of Education, and as an explanation for turning down the honor, pointed out that I simply lacked sufficient funds to pay my tuition, room, and board, in Winnipeg.

The Heman wives, like Mrs. Miller, also served tasty meals including a delicious selection of pastries. My blood, unaccustomed to this sudden richness, reacted with a rash of painful boils. Mrs. Miller dressed them before I left for the field each morning, but dust and sweat saturated the bandage of one boil on my upper arm, and it turned to blood poison.

Mrs. Miller began soaking the arm with steaming hot towels to draw out the inflamation. On this same evening I received a second letter from the Registrar of the Manitoba Department of Education. Nels and Mrs. Miller, unaware of my winning the scholarship, read this letter, which was a stinging response to my rejection of the award. It concluded with a recommendation from the Registrar that I visit him at his office because he believed my financial dilemma could be resolved. The hot compresses slowly forced the red line to recede in my arm, but the therapy, though tedious, seemed almost pleasant compared to the dialogue from Mrs. Miller. Absolutely aghast at my not returning to school, she paid no heed to my reasoning and insisted that had she known of the scholarship before the new semester had begun she would have forced Nels to fire me. Nels listened to this harangue with usual, calm indifference, as she harped on about the difficulty I would encounter earning a living or supporting a family with my handicap unless I had additional schooling. I said little, though the more I heard how nearly impossible it would be for me to earn a livelihood without a university education, the more determined I became to prove them wrong.

Two months went by swiftly and in the second week of October, while threshing the final acres, I realized the poplar bluffs had already turned yellow, signaling the arrival of autumn as clearly as the calendar. I didn't know it then, but an enormous change would envelop the land as black gold from the earth's innards would replace the yellow gold of waving wheat. Virden became the foremost oil producing area in the province. I never learned whether the Hemans shared in the windfall. They were a fun-loving family, and though we worked hard, the good-natured banter between the crew made the days seem shorter and more pleasant, except for one careless and embarrassing accident on my part.

We operated with six stook teams and two field pitchers feeding the 42-inch separator from both sides. Nels assigned me his team of drivers. Drivers were horses not generally used for field work but rather for show, decked out with fancy harness, hitched to a two-team buggy, and shown off to the neighbors—much like some farmers would parade around town in deluxe automobiles in later years.

Though not as sturdy, drivers were more spirited than the average draft animals, and like all stook teams, they soon learned the meaning of one particular sound. When the pitchfork dropped on an empty rack floor, the sudden sharp noise signaled it was time to move. Twice a day this meant going home for oats and water, and so at the crack of metal on wood, they could be restrained only by snubbing the reins tightly to the front mast of the rack. Once released, the horses would leap into action, and only a firm grip on the reins kept the animals under control. The rein, a long, narrow leather strap, attached to the bit in the horse's mouth, is used to direct the animal. In the case of a team of two, both reins are attached with a snap to the side bits of both animals so that pressure on either rein directs both horses at the same instant.

The day of the accident, I carelessly forgot to snap one of the reins to the right side of a horse's bit. Once the team started to move, pulling back on the reins to restrict their friskiness directed them left, and I lacked control to stop or to turn them right. Where we were threshing, Nel's brother Jim had a lane leading to the main road enclosed by a page wire fence with cedar posts, a very expensive commodity on the prairie. When my horses veered left, the corner of the rack caught a post and snapped it like a match stick. Sounding like a pistol shot, the startled animals went into a wild gallop, and before we reached the main road, a dozen or more posts bit the dust. We sailed across the road, through the ditch, and out onto an open stubble field without upsetting the wagon, itself a miracle. After they had galloped a couple of miles, I could hear the team getting winded, and so I gently eased them into a circle while calling, "Whoa!" in a calm voice. Finally I urged them to halt, allowing me to attach the rein. Everyone agreed that as neither animal broke a leg or otherwise harmed themselves and the wagon hadn't upset, severely injuring or killing me, we were all fortunate. The Hemans refused to take payment for the broken posts, and soon forgot the mishap, but the thrilling journey across that open prairie would be unforgettable to me.

When we were having our final meal together, Nels asked me to stay another month to help with the fall plowing, for which he would pay four dollars per day. Despite my temptation to drive a tractor a few weeks for money, I had a couple of other ideas for the coming months, and so I grabbed a train for home.

The balance of my earnings totalled $167 which once again made me feel like a millionaire. As usual, it didn't last long, however, and this seesaw lifestyle of prince to pauper was becoming a disagreeable habit.

The mortgage on the farm was due, and so I gave Father sixty dollars. I donated thirty to Mother, now keen on raising Angora rabbits as a money-making proposition.

In November I planned to go into the Brokenhead River country to steal a hundred Christmas trees off government land to sell in Winnipeg. While in the city, I intended to look for a job, though I wouldn't start until after the holidays. I hoped Jack would again get a Christmas furlough, but due to immense happenings in Europe and in the Pacific, Jack also faced great changes in his service life.

The second front in Europe progressed slowly but favorably. In August, Allied forces crossed the Loire River, General Patton reached the Seine, French and American troops liberated Paris (after four years of German occupation), Rumania surrendered to the Russians, and the Red Army entered Bucharest on August 30. Both Antwerp and Brussels fell to the Allies in early September, and Athens was recaptured on October 13. In the Pacific, Guam had been retaken, and the Philippines were invaded by Allied forces. Superfortress raids on Tokyo had begun from Saipan in November. The only somber news, the new German "buzz" bombs were taking an increasing toll in Britain, despite efforts by Allied bombers to knock out the factories producing the bombs and to destroy the launching sites. Over a thousand landed in Britain, killing more than 2,700 people.

Optimism over the victories in Europe caused the military to switch Jack from British Lancaster bombers to American Liberators, and they transferred him to Boundary Bay, British Columbia to train for action somewhere in the Pacific. He had now seen Canada from coast to coast. Expecting embarkation leave by midwinter, he anticipated being home for the holidays. This was exciting news for all the family.

While helping Dad repair the barn roof on October 19, my eighteenth birthday, I glanced across our meadow late in the afternoon and saw a doe wandering aimlessly in the bright autumn sun. Father said excitedly, "Bill, grab the rifle. It's late enough in the season to keep the meat, and I'm sick and tired of bologna."

Jumping off the roof, I felt great elation at finally getting a chance to use the 30-30 Winchester. Father was a lousy rifle shot and decided I had a better chance to bag the deer than he. Handing me the loaded rifle, and cramming cartridges into the shotgun for himself, he shouted instructions. "You hightail it to the long field on the south fence. I'll circle through the bush and drive the deer to you. Don't miss."

Walking speedily through the open fields I disappointedly watched the doe veer east and vanish from danger. Dad, deep in the bush, couldn't see that our prey had fled. I went to my post disappointed at the lost opportunity, and with nothing else to do, knelt behind a small evergreen on the chance that another deer might inhabit the forest area Father was beating. Not too hopeful, I leaned my gun against the little fir and rolled myself a cigarette. To my astonishment, less than a hundred yards from my hiding place, a magnificent buck with an exquisite set of antlers snuck stealthily out of the woods, stopped, and sniffed the wind, his noble head lifted high. Sensing danger somewhere but unsure of the direction, the beautiful buck stood contemplating his next move. Hearing Father behind, he couldn't go back, but he seemed reluctant to cross the open field.

To my dismay, when I put the gun to my shoulder, my body shook so violently I couldn't see down the rifle barrel. I had never experienced buck fever. I started pulling the trigger and levering up bullets. The big deer, thoroughly confused as to the source of the barrage, never moved while I rapidly unloaded five shells somewhere in his general direction. Suddenly, with gigantic leaps he took off diagonally across the field. Down to two bullets, my head cleared as I reckoned if I didn't down my quarry, it might be a while before I got another chance to have the Winchester.

With nerves somewhat settled, I hit the animal in the hip with the sixth shot, and as he fell, snapped off my last, but missed again. The deer, badly wounded, hobbled a couple of hundred yards into the dense underbrush and laid down, but with no ammunition, I had to wait.

After a few minutes, Father came sneaking kind of warily out of the woods. "Did you get the doe?" he asked, catching his breath and looking around for a dead animal. Quickly relating the story, I pointed out where the wounded buck went down.

"Don't tell your Mother," he said, "but five of those 30-30 shells came within ten feet of me. After the first shot, though, I got down on my belly behind a big poplar."

This news really shook me up. I couldn't believe how careless I'd been and the little consideration I'd given Dad's position once the buck had been sighted. The near fatal mishap made it easy to understand how shooting accidents happen in the excitement of a hunt.

Father began to tease me unmercifully about missing a deer standing broadside with five shots, and how he would be telling Ed Barham and the neighbors about my great ability with a rifle. Meanwhile, slowly circling the wounded animal, he instructed me to get behind it on one side while he stayed on the other. Together, we'd direct it back to the open meadow. He handed me two more shells from his pocket, all he had grabbed at the house in the excitement.

Within minutes the badly stricken buck staggered to its feet and began to move ahead of us back to the fields. Unable to get a clear shot, I decided to let him continue in that direction until he broke into the open. Nearing the meadow, I could see Father already on the fringe cautiously peering into the bush, having lost sight of the animal momentarily. We both knew the wounded buck wouldn't cross the open field unless absolutely forced to but would try to sneak along the edge. The animal and Dad met about twenty feet from each other. Startled by the sudden confrontation, Father raised his shotgun and fired but missed the animal completely. The shock of the blast and Father's appearance I guess became too much for the deer. He dropped almost at Father's feet without any shotgun pellets in his head. I finished him off with a rifle bullet when I came up.

Dressing the buck and pleased at the prospect of venison steak, Father mentioned he would say nothing about my six misses if I kept mum about his one. I agreed, but with the proviso that the 30-30 Winchester was mine when we hunted together. I suggested that perhaps he should resort to a slingshot.

Uncle George gave me permission to sell Christmas trees from his front lawn on Home Street. This was only a few doors from Ellis Avenue, a main Winnipeg thoroughfare. Except for cartage charges and a five-dollar peddler's fee, everything was net profit, and so I offered my trees at very competitive prices. I clinched many sales by offering to deliver. Lugging the larger trees several blocks along slippery sidewalks was strenuous, but I could add a few pennies to the price.

Clearing a hundred bucks made the effort worthwhile. Uncle George and Aunt Gladys didn't do as well, of course, for they provided me with two weeks' bed and board at no charge quite willingly. The mess of needles and broken limbs I left behind in their lawn caused them some annoyance. As a result, Unk negated any repeat performance, even though I pointed out he did get a free Christmas tree.

The holidays turned out to be a disappointment. Jack's travel plans got fouled up, and he didn't arrive home until after New Year's Day.

Also, from the European battle front came staggering news. We believed the war would soon come to a successful conclusion, and so we were shocked when Hitler, in a surprise counter attack, proved that the German armies were far from finished.

The Battle of the Bulge began on December 16, when the Germans launched their counter offensive in the Ardennes Forest of Belgium. The immense engagement forced the Allies into a general retreat and took a heavy toll of lives. On December 16, too, the 101st Airborne Division of the American Army, who had held out against ovewhelming odds, was relieved by General Patton's Third Army. Patton's tank corp travelled 150 miles in 19 hours to halt the serious reversal and put an end to the Nazi hordes' last major aggression. Allied troops soon recaptured the lost territory and went speeding toward the German Fatherland.

I went to Winnipeg the first week in January to search for a job, having decided to throw away the ax and pitchfork, at least temporarily, and earn my livelihood in less physical pursuits. Despite my noticeable limp, employers wanted me to apply for enlistment to get my official rejection papers. So ironically, I offered to join the Army at Fort Osborne barracks—not because of any intention of being inducted but so I would be a more serviceable civilian. The several doctors who examined me were more interested in the history of my operations and the progress of my foot and leg since contracting polio rather than just giving me a simple discharge. They made the examination last an intolerable few hours.

Monarch Lumber Co. Ltd. a large lumber retailer and wholesaler, with head offices in the Hamilton Building on Main Street near Portage Avenue, advertised for a mailing desk clerk. Going over to inquire about the position, I pocketed the letter from the Department of Education regarding the scholarship and handed it in with my application. When Mr. James, the office manager, informed me during the interview that the starting salary would be forty dollars monthly, I thanked him for his time and got up to leave.

"Just a moment," he said. "That's a decent wage, and there's plenty of room for advancement."

"I'm sorry, but I couldn't live on it," I replied, putting on my coat.

"Don't be so impatient," Mr. James implored. "Because of your letter, we'll start you at sixty. Can you get by on that?"

Thinking for a few moments, intrigued with the prospect of being involved in big business and becoming an industrial tycoon, I responded, "Okay. I'll try to manage, but if I begin starving to death, I'll let you know."

The Y.M.C.A., within walking distance of my new job, had a small room I could share with an Air Force officer for five dollars per week. On Portage Avenue, around the corner from the "Y," the Willow Cafe served palatable food, though not exactly the generous servings to which I had been accustomed.

The cafe sold $5.50 meal tickets for $5.00. Numerals from 5 cents to 50 cents printed around the outside of the card were punched after each purchase. That 50 cent saving bought a full course meal at the time.

With little available cash for personal entertainment, I spent most evening hours listening to other people play the juke box. Such current hit tunes, "Don't Fence Me In," "Jealous Heart," "Sentimental Journey," "A Little on the Lonely Side," "Lilly Marlene," "Cruising Down the River," "It's Been a Long, Long, Time," and others gave me a great deal of listening pleasure. The song that always reminds me of those poverty stricken days, however, is "Drinking Rum and Coca Cola." It seemed to be forever blasting from the nickelodeons.

Movies only cost a quarter, and I saw a few of the popular films, such as "For Whom the Bell Tolls," with Gary Cooper and Ingrid Bergman; "This Gun for Hire," starring Alan Ladd; "Going My Way," with Bing Crosby; and "Yankee Doodle Dandy," with James Cagney.

My Air Force roommate arranged for tickets to sporting events for fellow officers and provided me with free passes to several competitions. In spite of these few diversions and my intrigue with the new job, the frigid winter days dragged by. Dressed as an inside office worker proved far different from being bundled in heavy clothes for farm work, especially at Portage and Main, one of the windiest and most bone-chilling places in Canada. Trudging daily along those icy sidewalks, I truly missed my heavy woolen underwear, woolen parka, and fleece-lined mitts.

The biting cold also caused an embarrassing incident. It was my daily responsibility, after closing, to tote the sackful of outgoing mail from Monarch Lumber's office to the main post office on Portage Avenue, a distance of half a mile. Registered mail had to be carried separately, as each letter was entered by the post office in each company's own book. One day, during a severe blizzard, a large envelope intended for registration separated from the bundle of other letters to be registered and dropped from my partially numbed, gloved fingers. When the post office couldn't locate the envelope in my passbook, I hurriedly retraced my steps back to the office despite the bitter cold but could not find it.

The following morning after I reported the displaced letter, Mr. Perkins, a company officer, summoned me to his private office. Two members of the Royal Canadian Mounted Police joined us shortly, and they all appeared extremely anxious to know if I had any inkling of the envelope's contents. The passbook, showed the destination to be Edmonton, Alberta, but I had no idea what the package contained. The envelope was scheduled to arrive at its destination before noon. Mr. Perkins told me to return to my desk and continue my work but not to leave the building without permission. For two hours I shuddered at the prospect of being involved with police for a missing letter containing I knew not what.

A few minutes before lunch a relieved Mr. Perkins called me to his office with the news that the package had arrived. When he told me the envelope contained 10,000 gas rationing coupons, I instantly understood the company's concern.

A few days later, when I was leaving with the afternoon bag of mail, I encountered Jim Bales on the elevator. Jim worked for a company in the same building and also delivered the afternoon mail. Frequently we'd stroll along Portage Avenue together. While walking to the post office, I related the story of the missing envelope to which Jim listened with rapt attention. When I finished, he stopped me in the middle of the sidewalk, forcing the multitude of homebound office workers to detour around us and with an incredulous expression, said, "Bill, are you telling me that package contained 10,000 gas coupons?"

"That's what Mr. Perkins told me," I replied.

"Well, you're one lucky son-of-a-bitch," he retorted. "I picked that envelope up right outside the post office. Seeing Monarch Lumber's name, I realized you dropped the thing, and so I put it in the mail unregistered. But let me tell you something, if I had any notion the package enclosed gas stamps, you'd be in jail, and I'd be on my way to Florida."

He laughed uproariously. But I'm not so sure he wasn't partially telling the truth, because he had an old car and couldn't buy sufficient gas to go any great distance.

In early March, we faced what every family dreads with a member in the service—embarkation leave. Jack arrived from the Pacific Coast to spend a few days before leaving for Montreal and then to somewhere in the Pacific. Mom, Dad, Ruth and I accompanied him to the Union Station, and as the train slowly eased out of the depot, Jack stood waving from between cars until he disappeared from view. Tears welled in the eyes of all, no doubt including Jack's. It seems strange now to think back to our fears and concerns of that era, memories of which have mostly faded away. Horror stories of Germany's death camps and grim reports about the extermination of the Jewish race made us look upon the Germans with great repugnance. Even so, most people would have sooner seen their loved ones taken prisoner by the hated Huns than by the barbaric Japs. Widely publicized tales of death and torture suffered by military prisoners at the hands of the Japanese made any thought of one of our own falling into their hands a constant nightmare.

We also feared the Japanese more at this time because the Germans were obviously using their final reserves and would soon be out of the conflict. The Japanese had suffered enormous defeats but gave the impression they could continue the struggle for years.

Allied armies sweeping over Europe crossed the German border, and by March 10 they controlled the west bank of the Rhine from the Netherlands to Koblenz. A week later, the U.S. 9th Army joined the 1st Army across from Dusseldorf and took 325,000 prisoners. In the air war, Goering's feared Luftwaffe was no longer a viable force. This allowed thousands of American and British bombers to level German cities with little fighter plane resistance.

In the Pacific, huge U.S. forces invaded the Philippines under the command of General Douglas McArthur, who had promised "to return" after his humiliating defeat there three years earlier. Manila was captured early in February and within a month, 100 U.S. B-24's rained incendiaries on Tokyo. Because its buildings were predominantly frame, the city was turned into a raging inferno, and 124,000 people were killed. In early spring, U.S. troops invaded Mindanao and then Iwo Jima, which fell after a month of fierce fighting that claimed the lives of thousands of Americans. In spite of these staggering setbacks, the Japanese spirit still seemed far from broken.

When Jack left Canada, he was the only gunner remaining in his crew. The other six had been removed, plus all guns. They flew their Liberator bomber, now converted into a transport plane, from Dorval in Quebec to India, with stopovers at Bermuda, Iceland, Cairo, and Iran. After Jack's departure, I felt extremely depressed. The walls of Monarch Lumber closed in on me as though each day the breathing space grew smaller and smaller.

Being unable to participate in Jack's exciting life agitated me, and the constant fight for financial survival kept lowering my self-esteem. The $60 monthly from Monarch covered only the barest essentials, and so I moved into a boarding house where for $9 per week I got a bed and two meals. The degrading environment in the cheap rooming house, however, lowered my morale even more. Finally the soft winds of spring arrived beckoning me outdoors and acted like a catharsis to my downcast attitude.

Not knowing what to attempt next, I scanned the daily papers. One evening a huge ad appeared in the Help Wanted Section offering one dollar per hour in a Kitchener, Ontario rubber factory for men with a 4F military classification. Train fare would be provided for those selected, and applicants could apply at the local Selective Service office for an interview. Excited by the possible opportunity to escape my indigence, I could barely eat dinner or get to sleep.

Kitchener, 1,400 miles away, seemed like an entirely different ambience. This thrilled me, of course, but the prospect of earning $40 per week conjured up visions of financial grandeur that far outweighed any other consideration.

During lunch hour the following day I raced to see if I qualified, and I did. But a war time measure required an employee to give his employer two week's notice, and all applicants chosen for Kitchener had to be on their way within four days. The chap who interviewed me expected I would have no problem getting an exemption because the Federal Government passed the law to protect vital industries engaged in war production, and Monarch Lumber hardly fit that category.

Dashing into Mr. James with the stupendous news, I expected congratulations instead of the reception I received.

"Bill," he said, looking at me like a professor. "I can't allow you to go. You are needed here, and I'll see if I can arrange a $10 a month raise."

"For Christ's sake, Mr. James," I exploded, "that's still less in a month than I'd make in two weeks in the rubber factory. Plus, I'm sick and tired of being cooped up at that desk doing menial tasks any fool can do."

"Look, Bill, cool down," he stated calmly. "Something I intended to tell you in a couple of weeks will have to be discussed now due to the circumstances. I am a Chartered Accountant, and at the first of May, I will be amalgamating with three other CA's and going back into private practice. I want you to join us as an apprentice. We'll start you at $100 a month, and you can enroll at the University of Manitoba for a five-year night course to get your Chartered Accountant's degree. Every six months you would be eligible for a raise. I believe it will be an excellent opportunity for you. What do you think?"

His remarks certainly shook me up. Slightly dumbfounded, I replied, "Mr. James, I thank you for your consideration which I will have to think about seriously. How about if I see you tomorrow morning?"

As I was leaving the office I asked, "If my answer is no, will I still be required to give you two week's notice?"

"We'll make that decision tomorrow morning," he retorted.

It was a gorgeous spring afternoon, the kind that made an office seem awfully confining. I strolled slowly down Portage Avenue deep in thought. The snow had disappeared, and robins and sparrows chirped their welcomes to the brilliant April sun. My head buzzed with my dilemma. I found the prospect of becoming a CA enticing, but wasn't sure I could face scrimping for money and being chained to a desk day and night for five more years. My vagabond lifestyle, except for the chronic cash shortage, appealed to me. Reflecting on the few dollars in my pocket and the thought of earning $40 per week, I made up my mind. Suddenly I couldn't wait to board the train for Kitchener.

The following morning Mr. James, though disappointed with my decision, gave me my release plus the small balance of my earnings. Racing over to the employment office, I was planning how to get to Monominto and bid farewell to the family before catching the train East. Unfortunately, they had filled their quota. Now out of luck as well as a job, I grabbed my clothes and hitchhiked a ride home to the farm with $20 in my pocket.

The folks were pleased to see me, each for a personal reason. Mother enjoyed our lively discussions. Ruth, a rapidly developing young lady, loved accompanying me to parties and dances. Dad always hoped I might finally settle down and help on the farm. Now going on nineteen, I had reached my full height of 6 feet 4 inches. The deficiency in the length of my right leg caused me to stand about 6 feet 2 inches, but I still towered over Dad at 5 feet 10½ inches. Only weighing 160 pounds, I resembled a string bean. The fact I'd grown so tall compounded the problem with my leg, though I managed reasonably well.

A few days later our neighbor Jim Wylie went with Dad and me to Winnipeg to buy horses. Old Kate, our faithful old mare, had passed away. This left Dad with only three horses, and four were required to pull the heavy farm equipment.

Over the years, most of our horses had been purchased at the McClean's Horse Auction located in the northwestern section of the city, and that's where we headed. At McClean's they auctioned off a hundred or more horses every week. The animals came from all over the West. They included wild, unbroken broncos to old crocks well past their prime, whose careers may have been pulling milk or bread delivery wagons on city streets.

The auction started at one o'clock in the afternoon, but the stables opened at 9:00 a.m. allowing ample time to examine the stock before the sale. Dad had a dapple gray mare called Maisey, and I spotted a dapple gray gelding that would make an ideal match for her. Dad got the horse for $42. I decided to call him Sparky because of his dumb but pleasant-looking face dominated by bright sparkly eyes. Jim paid $48 for a bay gelding that he named King.

Delighted with our purchases, we tried to arrange transportation to get them back to Monominto. After a frustrating hour without success, Dad and Jim asked if I would walk them home, offering me three dollars for each horse. Critically short of funds, I agreed, little realizing the enormity of the task. We had them hauled by truck to Winnipeg's southeastern outskirts about 30 miles from our house where I took over. It was now about five in the afternoon.

Each horse was equipped with only a halter and lead rope, which meant I didn't have rigid control. After a few miles of slow plodding, I decided to jump on Sparky's back. A little skittish, he reared, and having no stirrup in which to place my foot or saddle horn to grasp, I tumbled to the ground. Much to my amazement, Sparky didn't bolt and run but waited quietly for me to catch his lead rope and continue our journey. A little later I attempted the same procedure with King but suffered the same undignified result. Though tame animals, they plainly were not accustomed to carrying a rider, and so I resigned myself to a long walk.

Near dark I reached Prairie Grove, a small village a few miles south of the city. There I turned east down a road called the Centre Line (so named because it separated two townships) that ran directly to our farm 20 miles away. The mud road was pockmarked with huge potholes, as no equipment had yet been on it to improve its deplorable condition since the ravages of winter.

Through the pitch black, overcast night, with the temperature in the freezing range, I plodded along in front of the horses, the lead ropes wrapped around each arm. Every few yards, when I'd stumble into a pothole, the animals would jerk their heads up and jettison me back onto my feet. Ditches filled with water from the spring thaw, paralleled each side of the right-of-way. Ducks, alarmed by our sudden intrusion would take flight with a loud quacking and noisy flapping of wings. The unexpected furor within a few feet would frighten King and Sparky. Rearing up on their hind legs simultaneously, they would jerk me three feet off the ground like a jack-in-the-box. Crossroads, one mile apart and barely discernible in the blackness, seemed to take an eternity to reach. About midnight, I decided at the next crossroads to cross the bridge, find a fence post to tether the animals, and then huddle in my parka in some dry place to wait for daylight. My plan worked well. I got my charges tied to a barbed-wire fence; but while searching for a dry seat on the bridge, I frightened a pair of mallards.

Recoiling in alarm, King snapped a strap on his halter, leaving him completely at large in the almost total darkness. Hearing him munching on some spring shoots, I slowly moved toward him and was astounded when he allowed me to put my arms around his neck. Not having matches or flashlight, I removed the gas soaked stuffing out of my cigarette lighter, and setting it afire with the flint, got a few precious moments of light. This allowed me to repair the halter successfully, but I couldn't light a cigarette the balance of the trip.

With the two animals back in tow, I elected to continue my tortuous trek toward home. At the break of day it began to snow those huge, wet flakes that quickly saturate your clothing. Soaked to the skin, hungry and dying for a smoke, I arrived home at 9 a.m.—sixteen hours after leaving the city. A hot bath and a plate of bacon and eggs buoyed my spirits until I calculated that the six dollars I'd earned worked out to less than 40 cents per hour—almost identical to what I'd been paid at

Monarch Lumber. Jim's three dollars waited for me when I awoke, but Dad's remained outstanding for life. The trip, a physical nightmare, turned out to be a financial disaster.

Though Winnipeg had slowly converted to oil or gas heat, many furnaces still burned wood, so the cordwood industry continued to flourish. During the war the price per cord had increased to between five and six dollars. Farmers no longer traded it for merchandise but piled it in their own yards, and when roads became passable in spring, they sold it directly to the city dealers. Ed Barham acquired a small John Deere tractor with a power-driven circular saw attachment. Now full-length trees were piled in the yard and cut into four-foot lengths by power rather than the hand-activated Swede saw. Four men would carry the full-length log from the stacked pile to the carriage framework where the sawyer thrust the tree into a circular saw. The four-foot severed length caught by a sixth man, was heaved as far as possible, to keep the cutting area from getting clogged. Being far less awkward for me to stand still than struggle while carrying full-length trees, I generally became the end man who did the catching and throwing. Heaving four-foot blocks of green poplar that weighed from 30 to 150 pounds provided great exercise for developing the upper torso, so I eventually built tremendous strength in my arms and shoulders. My arrival home conveniently coincided with the spring ritual of sawing the cordwood plus cutting each family's annual supply of stovewood.

We started at the Barham's on an ideal spring day with the snow swiftly disappearing, and robins, crows, larks, killdeers and other new arrivals singing and chirping their appreciation of the warm, sunny afternoon. Sitting on the log pile and enjoying a cup of coffee, I showed the other crew members my hands, badly blistered after four months' inactivity from ax, saw, or pitchfork. In deference to me, plus the fact everyone had a trace of spring fever, we decided to relax for the balance of the afternoon. Ed and I went down to the creek that zigzagged across his farm to snare suckers that furnished excellent eating when caught in ice cold water.

Walking slowly home with my catch in the gorgeous twilight, with choruses of frogs greeting the passing of winter, I realized how deeply I'd missed the out-of-doors. Protected from frigid winds in Monarch Lumber's office had been somewhat pleasant, but I knew my future didn't lie in being trapped in an office 52 weeks of the year. Reaching home quite undecided how to correct my insolvency but in a euphoria due to the perfect weather, the sad news awaiting my arrival at the house swiftly dissipated my light mood.

President Roosevelt had died that afternoon of a cerebral hemorrhage at Warm Springs, Georgia, at the age of sixty-three. It was a strange twist of fate that one of the three leaders most responsible for the impending victory should fade from the scene, his goal so close to realization. The same reasoning, of course, applied to our warriors on the battlefield being killed every day, with ultimate triumph obviously at hand. Although both were suspicious of Stalin's intentions, the closeness between Roosevelt and Churchill is best described in Churchill's memoirs: "Indeed it may be said that Roosevelt died at the supreme climax of the war, and at the moment when his authority was most needed to guide the policy of the United States. When I received these tidings early on the morning of Friday, the 13th, I felt as if I had been struck a physical blow. My relations with this shining personality had played so large a part in the long, terrible years we had worked together. Now they had come to an end, and I was overpowered by a sense of deep and irreparable loss."

Roosevelt's character and achievements are still hotly debated between his fervent admirers and fierce detractors. Despite the controversy, however, no one ever denied his immense energy and self-confidence, his mastery of politics, and the enormous impact his presidency had on the development of the country. On the other hand, no one can dispute his performance in turning North America toward socialism in an escalating trend that wouldn't diminish until government became more instrumental in affecting peoples' everyday affairs, than business, industry or the unions, a curse that eventually destroyed every true democracy throughout history.

Roosevelt inaugurated a host of government regulations that interfered with the natural flow of business. His administration was accountable for regulating banking and finance that loosened credit and insured deposits, plus creating several agencies to govern industry and agriculture, most notably: The National Recovery Administration, The Agricultural Adjustment Administration, The Public Works Administration, and The Securities and Exchange Commission, which had been formed to control stock exchanges. He also instituted The Works Progress Administration, intended to offer work programs for the unemployed in the Depression, together with legislation for Social Security, plus a long-range plan for the future protection of the worker regarding unemployment, sickness and old age. The government also took a direct role in developing the natural resources of the country with the establishment of the Tennessee Valley Authority and the Rural Electrification Administration.

The vast, many faceted programs of the New Deal fashioned by many advisors, absolves Roosevelt from total blame, if in fact these many measures ultimately became a bane to the nation. During the time of his administration, though, Roosevelt had many conservative foes who considered him "a traitor to his class."

As a struggling young man in a different country, I wasn't aware that Roosevelt's socialistic proclivity would eventually have a profound effect on my personal life, as it would all members of the private sector on both sides of the border. At the time, Franklin D. Roosevelt, the only president ever elected for three terms, was a hero to me. Probably the fact that we both shared the same disability had a bearing on it. Not until years later when I began to realize he was principally responsible for starting the trend in the United States of burgeoning government did I look at Roosevelt in a different light. In the throes of the Depression, with so much misery encompassing the land, any attempt at improving the working man's lot would have been received with unbridled enthusiasm. But the sudden requirement for war materials, resulting in the expenditure of billions of dollars, actually put North America's labor force back to work, not the New Deal and other measures that Roosevelt's administration forced through Congress. Unfortunately, those government enactments eventually became responsible for spiralling inflation and a government debt that would escalate until it reached a trillion dollars.

These things were not apparent at Roosevelt's death in April, 1945, when momentous news constantly poured out of the war fronts. One of the most bizarre incidents occurred on April 28 when infuriated crowds, including many who had cheered him exuberantly only a few months before, executed Benito Mussolini, then hung the stupid Fascist dictator upside down in the public square so people could spit on him or pay any other form of disrespect.

Two days later as Russian troops converged on Berlin, Adolph Hitler, at the age of 56, committed suicide in his bunker with his mistress, Eva Braun, and other members of the Reichstag, including Joseph Goebels. Germany surrendered unconditionally on May 7, and President Harry S. Truman proclaimed May 8 V.E. Day.

The Pacific war, proceeding slowly, was expected to require another eighteen months of terrible bloodshed before the fierce-fighting Japanese could be completely overwhelmed. Mitigating developments of which few people were aware, however, would force the Japanese to capitulate within ninety days.

It took a half million Americans to subdue 110,000 Japanese on Okinawa, which fell June 21 after three months of intense combat. On July 5, Washington announced the reconquest of the Philippine Islands and, on July 10, began all out air war against the Japanese home islands. U.S. planes dropped leaflets over Hiroshima August 4 declaring, "Your city will be obliterated unless your government surrenders." The warning went unheeded, and the atomic bomb, code named "Little Boy," was dropped on the city August 6. Ten feet long and with the explosive power of 20,000 tons of TNT, it flattened four square miles of the city, killing 100,000 Japanese outright, and close to another 100,000 died from burns and radiation sickness. One day later leaflets were dropped on Nagasaki warning of "a rain of ruin the like of which has never been seen on earth." On August 9, the atomic bomb "Big Boy" was dropped on Nagasaki killing 75,000 people while another 75,000 died of assorted problems following the holocaust. Japan sued for peace August 10, and on August 14, the conquering Allies celebrated V.J. Day.

I find it impossible to adequately put into words even forty years later my elation and unbounded relief at the tidings—sentiments no doubt shared by millions who had loved ones involved in the fray.

Dad and I, out haying in the fields that fateful afternoon, watched Mom and my two sisters scurrying towards us with our afternoon refreshments. An air of urgency in their gait indicated something unusual, so we weren't totally surprised when they gave us the news of the surrender. Nevertheless, that particular luncheon in the meadows remains one of the most ecstatic and emotional get-togethers our family ever experienced, as we now knew that Jack would return home safely.

Jack had been in action a few months before the war unexpectedly ended. He and his crew had been flying from airfields in India, 1,000 miles across the Bay of Bengal to Burma where they dropped men and supplies behind enemy lines. Jack's responsibility involved getting these guerillas and their gear safely out of the aircraft when they reached the dropping zone. The Liberators (their transport planes) had been stripped of everything but the barest essentials so that additional gas tanks could be added to hold sufficient fuel for the 24-hour trips. Though never attacked by Japanese planes, they had been shot at several times from antiaircraft batteries, which damaged their plane on one occasion. Taking off with the overload of fuel provided their greatest danger, and Jack wrote that several aircraft had cracked up before getting off the runway. But now, though safe, we knew not when we'd see him and would anxiously await his return.

I had seen the terror a family experiences when notified one of their boys in uniform is in distress. The previous autumn I had been at Hussack's store which contained the nearest phone to families in our neighborhood. Alex Hussack advised me he had received a phone call from the war department for the Ted Phillips'. They would reveal no details to Alex saying that the message had to be given directly to one of the parents. I dashed the two miles to the Phillips', my heart in my throat, certain the message wouldn't involve Alexis in England but more likely Jim, an artillery range finder in action in France. Aunt Sadie and

Uncle Ted received the news courageously, but the strain on their faces told the agony they felt in their hearts as they raced to get the call. Fortunately, Jim, only wounded, for which he received a decoration for bravery, did recover completely. If the dispatch had been more serious, I could sense the grief they would have endured like millions of families throughout the world during the previous six horrible years when receiving that ominous message edged in black.

Approximately 55 million people died during those six traumatic years, mostly civilians. Millions more were left crippled, blind, mutilated, homeless, orphaned, and impoverished. Europe had 10 million displaced persons. The war had directly involved 57 nations, but the Soviet Union, Germany, China, and Japan had borne the lion's share of casualties. Counting only military personnel, Russia lost 7.5 million, Germany 2.9 million, China 2.2 million, Japan 1.5 million, Britain nearly 400,000, Italy 300,000, United States 290,000, and France 211,000. Canada's loss of slightly over 39,000 sounds insignificant, but it meant 39,000 Canadian homes were not nearly as happy as we were at the conclusion of the conflict.

Perhaps those who died in Germany's infamous concentration camps furnish the most gruesome figures. Nazi genocide killed an estimated 14 million "racial inferiors," including Poles, Slavs, Gypsies and 6 million Jews, a hideous slaughter that mere words will never describe. This bestiality left unanswered one of the most disturbing issues of the horrible conflict. How did a creature like Hitler obtain such a devoted following from the German populace, in general, and be allowed almost unrestrained freedom to perpetrate such mass murder?

Leadership of any kind has been a strange perplexity throughout history. Fully 99 percent of earth's inhabitants always follow the leadership of an elite group, who make the decisions affecting their lives. Except for a small company of writers, philosophers or intelligensia who occasionally pass judgement on that leadership, followers will rarely question the wisdom of those in control until, or unless, it directly affects their personal lives.

Some leaders control through power of persuasion, or financial manipulation, others rule with charisma, or dominate through fear such as Attila the Hun.

Political, religious, business, union, or any leader who dominates a group—regardless of the size of that assemblage or the purpose of its existence—will embrace traits setting him or her apart from those over whom they preside. In a democracy, those persons in power can only hold their position of prominence if they constantly improve the immediate lifestyles of their followers. The day-to-day issues count mostly with the masses. Little concern is given to any dire results that may befall them or their offspring in the future as a consequence of enhancing their present living standard.

The despot in an autocracy must also improve the lot of his serfs to retain control without violence, but a dictator has the advantage of planning future prosperity at the expense of current conditions, providing he commands a sufficient police force, or army, to support his policies.

Unfortunately, democratic forms of government frequently don't allow sufficient time for a new regime to correct an ailing economy before having to return to the citizenry for a fresh mandate. Instead of using strategy to correct previous mismanagement, newcomers in office must promise a quick fix to entice the electorate despite the fact this handout might destroy their own objectives in correcting long-term problems.

It follows, therefore, that a strong dictatorship can more successfully administer the affairs of a nation over a long haul than a democracy, where political leaders have to continuouly appease the masses to remain in power. No one can deny that Hitler performed a miracle in rebuilding Germany from economic ruin into one of the greatest industrial nations of modern times—all in less than a decade. He accomplished this miraculous recovery because from 1935 no one could interfere with his plans. The history books are filled with similar examples, such as Napoleon, Charlemagne, or Julius Caesar.

If despots can provide a more stable economy, then why we don't encourage this form of government seems absurd. The answer I guess is because we aren't willing to jeopardize our freedom. All too frequently, a dictator, due to greed, hunger for additional power, or loss of empathy for his followers, oversteps his bounds and runs amuck. We must therefore devise a system to be able to elect decision makers with no time limit on their term of office but with some kind of control so that if or when they lose sight of the goals for the common good they can be dispatched without anguish or agony.

Roosevelt was elected three times—not only because of his charisma and capable wartime leadership—but also due to his unswerving efforts to improve the lot of the common man, regardless of the price to be paid by future generations. Mussolini and Hitler came to power for similar reasons but retained their positions due to the potent armed forces they had created to enforce their edicts. Also as dictators, they didn't have to concern themselves with appeasing the general population every few years to remain in power.

Had they won the war, despite being ruthless killers, they both would have been idolized as martyrs and champions by the average German and Italian citizen, providing those same people continued to gain benefits from the ravages of the conflict and were not its victims. Hitler and Mussolini, cast in the role of tyrants, both died in the undignified fashion they did only because they lost the conflict.

Stalin, just as responsible for the cold-blooded murder of millions, retained his position of power through political expediency and a complete lack of empathy toward his fellow man. He killed without conscience and died from natural causes, not because he was a better human being than "El Duce" or "Herr Hitler" but because he ended up on the winning side of the struggle.

To sum it up, one of the great inadequacies of a free, democratic society is the average man is not intellectually capable of judging the total merits of those he elects to power. Winston Churchill certainly constitutes a prime example. He must be adjudicated one of the supreme commanders of a free people, not only of modern times but also possibly throughout history. No one knows whether Great Britain would have fallen had it not been for Churchill's spirited leadership. Had that happened, however, and Germany's entire might been thrown against Russia, Stalin would have been executed like the tyrant he was, and Communism may never have existed beyond that point. In that scenario, North America's position in today's society would be pure conjecture, but I personally doubt we would have enjoyed much prosperity over the past forty years. In my opinion, Churchill was the predominant factor in preventing North Americans from ever having to confront such a crisis. And what was his reward? On July 25, 1945, eleven weeks after accomplishing victory in Europe—and less than three weeks before achieving a complete triumph due to the collapse of the Japanese—the British people threw him out of office.

Churchill accepted this decision in his usual, unruffled manner. In his "Message to the Nation" on July 26, he said, "The decision of the British people has been recorded in the votes counted today. I have therefore laid down the charge which was placed upon me in darker times. I regret that I have not been permitted to finish the work against Japan. For this, however, all plans and preparations have been made, and the results may come much quicker than we have hitherto been entitled to expect. Immense responsibilities abroad and at home fall upon the new Government and we must all hope that they will be successful in bearing them.

"It only remains for me to express to the British people, for whom I have acted in these perilous years, my profound gratitude for the unflinching, unswerving support which they have given me during my task, and for the many expressions of kindness which they have shown towards their servant."

I wouldn't have been so benignant.

Churchill failed to gain reelection because as a staunch Conservative he held his position as Prime Minister through the perilous war years due to a coalition with the Labor Party. When that party withdrew its support, he no longer had sufficient patronization from the masses who thought that nationalization of industry and a government-controlled society would improve their living standards.

It did for a while, but as is usually the case in a democracy, the people who make the short-sighted decision to improve their present living standard end up paying a heavy price over the long term. If Churchill had been allowed to implement his conservative plans for the nation, the British populous might never have suffered their financial indignities.

Despite being brokenhearted at the early death of Roosevelt, exultant at the undignified demise of Mussolini, and believing Hitler's suicide too simple a finish for such a fiend, the passing of those three men did not affect my emotions like the unseating of Churchill. I felt a sense of betrayal and outright disgust by the actions of my British peers. Watching over the decades as the Labor government botched the economy of one of the world's greatest nations, I felt to some extent the British electorate had received their just desserts.

Chapter 9

Saskatchewan at Last!

My delight at the cessation of hostilities was tempered by my constant lack of funds. Between spring planting and the beginning of haying, I found the occasional job in the community that paid a few bucks; but since leaving Winnipeg, I never had more than ten dollars to my name, so I was anxiously waiting for the harvest season to roll around. Nels Heman had written and asked me to come back to Virden, but visiting fresh country and meeting new people was almost as important as earning money.

My Polish pal, Charlie Fryza, asked if I wanted company, as he also, wanted to earn some dough. I heartily agreed, and we left Winnipeg by bus for Carman, a prosperous prairie town, fifty miles southwest of the city in Manitoba's fertile grain belt.

Our bus broke down halfway to our destination, an unrecognized omen that our excursion was going to have an onerous beginning. The recent end of the war had the other passengers—like ourselves—in a jovial mood happily waiting for another bus to arrive from the city. Sitting on the roadside in the warm afternoon sun, I asked Charlie the state of his finances. He had a ten dollar bill, plus a few odd coins, he said, almost identical to my total wealth. Although I saw little sign of grain cutting along our route, I expected to find work immediately and so felt financially secure.

It was 8:00 p.m. on a Wednesday evening when we checked into a Carman hotel room which cost two dollars each. Charlie and I then went out and had a good dinner. Luxuriating in a hotel room was a novel experience for both of us. Taking into consideration the forthcoming hard sessions in the fields, we lazed around until mid-morning. Following a hearty breakfast, we went searching for work. Though our fare had been paid by The Farm Help Service, no agent had yet been appointed in Carman, so we visited service stations, hardware stores and other establishments generally frequented by farmers. In each place it was the same story; cutting would be starting any day, and no one knew of any farm where bindering had actually begun. Letting everyone know our hotel room number, and confident of getting offers of employment by evening, we spent the afternoon shooting pool and smoking tailor-made cigarettes.

Payment of our second night's rent and another fine supper left us each with less than three dollars of our original stake.

Friday morning after breakfast, we got serious about job hunting and revisited all the places from the previous day, but without success. Charlie and I then decided to go separate ways and arranged to meet for lunch to report any progress. It was the same story everywhere. Grain cutting was eminent, but no one was aware of any farmer who had actually started.

During lunch I said, "Charlie, my friend, there is no hotel room for us tonight, or we won't have enough money left to eat tomorrow. If we don't find work tomorrow, it's unlikely we'll get any job offers before Sunday."

"Where the hell are we gonna sleep?" Charlie asked, a little incredulously.

"Look," I replied, "you know that Imperial service station on the fringe of town with the living quarters on the second floor?"

"Yep," Charlie said, "the one with the friendly young mechanic named Jim who is trying to find us a job."

"That's the one," I stated, "I noticed a couple of small mattresses hanging from the rafters. Let's see if he'll let us use them for the night, and we'll offer to reimburse him a couple of bucks after earning some money."

Jim told us we were welcome to sleep on the mattresses inside the garage, providing we kept the door locked; and not to worry about paying any rent. Requiring no blankets due to the warm weather, and using suitcases for pillows, we spent a fairly comfortable night, except for being a little hungry. Our diminishing funds had forced us to cut back on our food consumption considerably during the day.

Saturday morning was bright and hot. Walking to the restaurant in a famished condition, we decided to throw caution to the wind and have a good breakfast. After devouring a plateful of bacon, eggs, toast and coffee and paying the bill, our total cash balance was slightly less than three dollars.

The Souris, a small river, ran through the center of town, and we followed it a short distance to where a lot of kids were shouting and having fun. It was the town's community swimming hole, a popular spot being enjoyed by dozens of youngsters due to the intense summer heat. For some reason the water reminded me of Swan Lake. Grabbing Charlie, I shouted, "Come on to the bus depot, and let's see if we have enough money for two bus fares to Swan Lake."

Walking along, I explained about Uncle Ernie and the fact that not only would we get our bellies filled, but also would likely find work.

But alas, the single fare to Swan Lake was $1.75 which meant we were 60 cents short for two tickets. Disappointed, we returned to the swimming hole and lazed dejectedly through the torrid afternoon.

As evening approached, a small carnival called "Red River Shows" began setting up their games and rides along the bank of the river. Charlie and I meandered over to watch the activity. Realizing Charlie wasn't beside me, I looked across the grounds and was amazed to see him pitching little steel rings onto a table. Racing over, I yelled at him, "What the hell are you doing; are you crazy?"

"Look, Bill," he said, looking a little hurt, "you get three rings for a dime, and if I can get one completely over that half dollar and another one over a quarter, we'll have enough for bus fare to Swan Lake."

"You damn fool," I shouted, "if you tried all afternoon you couldn't ring that half dollar, and that dime would have provided us each with a cup of coffee."

Charlie seemed to realize the futility of his gamble, and satisfied my point was made, I said no more.

We then moved toward a man inside a tent hollering, "Bingo! Bingo! Right this way, folks, for Bingo."

Gazing around the tent at the pots, pans and other paraphernalia hanging from wires as Bingo prizes, I heard Charlie call. Turning, I was positively dumbfounded to see him seated at the table with two Bingo cards.

"Here, Bill, sit down," he hollered excitedly. "This fellow will give us a dollar cash prize if we win."

"Chuck," I exploded, "you are either six parts of a gawd-damn fool or the best river boat gambler since Mississippi Jack." Charlie paid no attention, because the proprietor was already calling out the numbers. To my amazement, two minutes later I heard Charlie holler, "Bingo." Before I could interject, he had collected 80 cents and retained the two cards. Sitting beside him and boiling over his stupidity, I could scarcely concentrate on my card. "Bingo!" I heard beside me again, and, sure enough, Charlie had won another. No six men could have prevented my friend from trying one more time, and only after losing did he finally agree to leave the game. I felt as stupid as a prize French poodle at a cat show when Charlie handed me sufficient money to buy two bus tickets to Swan Lake.

Our luck still wasn't improving. We missed the last bus by an hour, but purchased two tickets for the Sunday evening bus scheduled to leave Carman at 6 p.m. I gave Charlie the balance of the money which was 80 cents, although I did have a copper in my pocket. This at least kept me from being completely without funds.

We bought some bread, butter and bologna at a cost of 65 cents and retired to our mattresses prepared for a light snack and long night—both of which came true.

The morning dawned clear and hot, and if there was anything beneficial about the burning sun pertaining to our situation, it was the obvious fact that it was speedily ripening the grain, leaving little doubt that grain cutting would begin on Monday, and the farmers should be looking for stookers.

Wandering aimlessly down the sidewalk, hunger pangs gnawing at our stomachs, Charlie suddenly stopped and was gazing through the plate glass window of a Chinese restaurant. "Look! Bill," he said, "those big juicy plums are 20 cents a pound. There would be quite a few plums in three quarters of a pound. What do you think?"

Big, blue, Italian prune plums were one of my favorites, and I could just taste their sweet, tangy flavor. "I doubt if we'll do better," I replied. "Let's get 'em."

Charlie politely asked the Chinese proprietor for 15 cents worth of plums.

"Twenny cen' a poun', twenny cen' a poun'," the Chinaman responded sarcastically.

"Yes, I know, but I only want three quarters of a pound," Charlie replied with some embarrassment.

In obvious aggravation, the Oriental grabbed a brown paper bag, tossed in some plums, set them on his scale, and said, "Sixteen cen', sixteen cen'."

A moment of frozen silence followed, as Chuck, fumbling in his pockets for his 15 cents, was pondering what to say. Recalling my penny, I placed it on the counter with a grand gesture like it was a hundred dollar bill.

Walking out of the cafe with our plums, Charlie turned to me and stated, "Geez, Bill, I was never so glad to see a cent. I'm sure if I'd had to tell that Chinaman to take a plum out of the bag, he would have thrown it at me."

Laughing uproariously at the incident, and munching the fruit, I pointed out to Chuck that now, flat busted, we were in the eyes of the law, officially classed as "vagrants."

It was a long, wearisome day as the hours dragged by, and 6 p.m. seemed like it would never arrive. Finally it did, but the bus didn't, nor did it appear at 8 p.m. or 9. Finally, the agent got word the bus had broken down again, and he wasn't certain when it would show up. Now we had another conundrum. The fact we didn't have a nickel to phone Uncle Ernie from Swan Lake wasn't a problem, if we got there before midnight I could borrow from one of the local shopkeepers whom I knew. If the stores were closed, we might find ourselves sitting in town all night, or walking to Unk's farm lugging our suitcases. It seemed as if the fates had really turned against us when, suddenly a car drove up, and someone hollered from an open window, "You guys looking for work?"

In less than a minute, with our bags in the trunk and on our way, we found out just how fast luck can change. Howard Wright was the driver, and his passenger was Steve Polinski, his Polish neighbor. Steve greeted Charlie like a long, lost cousin.

Howard and Steve's farms were side by side about ten miles from Carman. Cutting was to begin the following morning. They offered us five dollars per day for stooking, which we accepted since we were in no position to argue.

Howard Wright dropped Charlie off with Steve Polinski and continued to his home where I was shown to a bed already made up in the living room. Hungry, but satisfied I could last until morning, I climbed into bed exhausted from the week's travail.

After an excellent breakfast the following morning, I drove Howard's car into the field to begin stooking and spotted Chuck already at work. Bounding over to greet me, he shouted, "Did you eat last night?"

"No," I replied.

"I knew damn well your English friend wouldn't feed you," he chortled. "Only a Pollock knows when a man is hungry. I ate until one o'clock this morning—all the good things only a Polish woman knows how to cook."

I chuckled and was relieved the unpleasant ordeal was over for both of us.

We stayed with our benefactors for two weeks until the stooking was completed. As there would be a few days interval before threshing got under way, we decided to move on. Howard and Steve pleaded with us to stay and offered to get us a job stooking at a neighbor's, allowing us to return when they were ready to "blow straw." Both men also volunteered to increase our pay to six dollars per day, but our minds were made up. We'd heard rumors in Carman that wages were higher further west. We used our bus tickets to Swan Lake, and after a phone call to my relatives, carried on to Scarth, Manitoba, where we caught a late night train to Glenavon, Saskatchewan. The railroad cars were crammed with young men from Montreal, Toronto and other cities in Ontario and Quebec, many of whom had been aboard for up to 72 hours. There were no beds, damn poor food, and the entire surroundings stank of perspiration and dirty socks.

Most of the lads were eager to start working, but only a handful would put in sufficient time harvesting to qualify for a government reimbursed return ticket. If they had not been raised on an Eastern farm and were unaccustomed to using a pitch fork or performing similar physical labor, then either their muscles gave out in two days or their hands, which even with gloves, blistered so severely they couldn't stand the pain. The farmers became so disenchanted with the itinerants that if a man didn't have calloused hands, he wouldn't even be considered; and many small western towns had an abundance of young men doing menial jobs trying to earn enough money for fare back East.

For some strange reason, crossing into Saskatchewan was an enormous thrill. Because of Jack's globe trotting, I was constantly dreaming of world travel; and leaving Manitoba gave me the perception the doors to earth's great adventures were finally opening for me. Glenavon didn't have a Farm Help agent and not finding a job within three hours prompted us to hop the next train and move 15 miles west up the line to Montmartre where there was a Farm Help office. Montmartre, a predominantly French Canadian settlement, was sixty miles southeast of Regina.

The agent greeted us warmly and had a farmer pick us up within the hour. Henri Couvier, a happy faced young man, was delighted to discover we were experienced harvesters and offered us $6.50 per day. He boasted about his family's food and lodging. We accepted and never regretted our decision. Henri lived with his parents and two pretty sisters, Yvonne and Cecille, who were in our age bracket. There was also an attractive local school teacher who was boarding with them named Cecile Beauchemin. We were billeted with a married brother, Phil, who lived with his wife and three small children a mile from the home farm. They had a lovely two story house, and Charlie and I shared a private bedroom.

Cecile, the school teacher, was the first girl with whom I became romantically involved. Intelligent and witty, she was excellent company, and we'd spend most week ends and rainy evenings together. Her folks had a business in Montmartre, and the Couviers would lend me their car so Cecile and I could visit and have Sunday dinner with her parents. Charlie would occasionally date one of the Couvier sisters.

The Couviers worked in harmony, and our five weeks in their employ whizzed past. It was the first time I felt sadness in concluding a contract.

Upon leaving, the Couviers and Cecile Beauchemin made us promise to keep in touch and return the following harvest season. I corresponded with Cecile for several months.

With a nest egg in our pockets, we visited Regina, Saskatchewan's capital city and dropped in at the Farm Help Service to see if more work was available. Farm Help put us on a bus for Yorkton, 125 miles northeast of Regina, where there was still plenty of unthreshed grain.

Dozing in our seats at 10 p.m. as the vehicle stopped at Phonehill, a village ten miles out of Yorkton, we were startled to hear the bus driver holler, "Are there two men aboard from Farm Help Service?"

A little surprised due to the lateness of the hour, I stood up as a man approached. "I'm Tom Brownley," the grizzled, bewhiskered, old farmer said in a decided English accent. "I need two men and was instructed to grab you off this bus."

A hotel room in Yorkton for the night was more to our liking, but with little alternative, we grabbed our suitcases and followed the man to his car.

The seven dollars per day he offered us bolstered our morale for the few minutes it took to reach his farmyard about three miles from the highway.

Stopping the dilapidated old Ford touring car in front of the stable, he said, "Righto, lads, you'll find a lantern beside a couple of mattresses in an empty stall in there. My boys will call you for breakfast at five; do have a good rest." And with that, he dropped our suitcases and drove off.

Charlie and I, dressed in business suits, stood motionless like a couple of wooden Indians for a minute or two before entering the barn. We hadn't eaten since lunch, and the fact the old farmer didn't even ask if we'd have a cup of coffee left us flabbergasted.

Walking stealthily through the barn, dodging horse manure to prevent soiling our oxfords, we easily found our "bedroom" with a burning kerosene lantern sitting beside the mattresses piled with smelly old horse blankets. Not a word had been uttered between us, and sitting down on the mattress, Charlie looked at me with a shocked expression and said, "Let's free the horses into the yard and then burn down the barn."

"That's a helluva thought, old friend," I responded, "but, where would we spend the night? Don't forget it's October and getting pretty cold."

Too stunned and upset to do much laughing, we removed our shoes and decided to get a little rest because within six hours they'd be in to feed the animals.

Dousing the lanterns, we made ourselves as comfortable as possible, considering the pungent odor of horses that pervaded our sleeping quarters.

After cussing Brownley and his entire clan in English and Polish, and almost asleep, I was startled by a yelp from Charlie. "What's the matter?" I asked.

"Light the lantern," he ordered. "A gawd-damn mouse just ran up my leg, and I'm not lying here in the dark with those little bastards on the loose."

In the flickering light we dozed intermittently through the next few hours, but it wasn't easy due to our aggravation and the uncertainty of what the morning would bring in our uncompromising position.

At 5 a.m. sharp the stable door opened, and two young lads walked in carrying a lantern. Both were small in stature only standing about 5'6" in height.

Charlie bounded off the mattress like he'd been stung by a bee and met them before they took ten steps inside the door. "Either one of you a Brownley?" he stormed.

One of the boys nodded, and sensing trouble, set his lantern on the floor. "You ignorant son of a bitch," Charlie yelled, as he made a lunge at him.

The two lads wheeled and hi-tailed it back to the house like they'd seen a ghost.

"Charlie," I said quietly, "grab a pitchfork. I suspect we'll be defending ourselves in a minute."

"I hope they bring in the whole community," Chuck snarled. "I'll be ready."

We stood and watched the house for a few minutes, and except for a few lights suddenly beaming from the bedroom windows, there was no indication of an attack.

"Let's grab our suitcases and start walking," I suggested.

To leave the yard, we had to pass directly in front of the kitchen window where four men, including the two Charlie assailed, watched our departure.

I'm not sure who felt the greatest relief when the house was left behind—the Brownley clan, who possibly were convinced we were coming for a showdown, or Chuck and I, who felt certain a brawl was inevitable and we were decided underdogs.

It was a long, tough hike back to Phonehill toting our heavy bags along the gravel road in the slowly breaking dawn, but we were happy to leave the unpleasant experience behind. Reaching the store and post office where we'd been so rudely removed from the bus nine hours before, we read a sign on the door which said, "Open 8 A.M." Rolling ourselves a cigarette, we made ourselves comfortable as the slowly rising autumn sun simultaneously warmed the countryside and lifted our spirits.

Shortly before eight, a stocky man came out of the building, and sauntering over, said in a thick German accent, "Hey! Ain't you the two boys vat got off the bus last night?"

"You are right," I answered, "and I'd like to meet up with the guy who made the decision to send us to that bastard Brownley."

"I'm Hans Kruger," he laughingly responded. "Nobody lasts too long at the Brownleys, and don't blame me, it wasn't my decision."

Hans invited us into his living quarters that adjoined the store for a cup of coffee. We graciously accepted. His wife was feeding and preparing two little girls for school. Following coffee, Mrs. Kruger served us a heaping plate of fried German sausages with eggs, plus heaps of toasted homemade bread and jam. We ate heartily and without embarrassment, because we expected to pay. Hans and his wife listened to our encounter with the Brownleys with amusement, and Hans explained that Brownley had a bad reputation in the neighborhood and was surprised we were sent to him.

The Krugers absolutely refused any remuneration for the delicious breakfast, but Hans said he would charge us 50 cents each to take us to Yorkton. Thoroughly delighted with our change of fortune we thanked Mrs. Kruger for her hospitality and went merrily with Hans to Yorkton. It was less than a half hour's ride, and dropping us in front of the Farm Help office, he again refused to take money, saying he had to come to town anyway for other purposes.

My mind was in a whirl as I tried to rationalize the episode. The perplexities of life were really beginning to register on me.

We had just completed a terrible conflict where the entire German race was reputed to be the lowest form of life on earth. As a result of propaganda and a natural hatred for the enemy we visualized Germans either as arrogant and pompous imbeciles resembling Hermann Goering, or cunning and bestial such as Heinrich Himmler. Charlie had openly vowed to hate all Germans until he'd taken his last breath for ravaging his homeland, and I didn't blame him for his attitude.

All Englishmen, on the other hand, were pictured on a plane with the morality and good sense of Churchill, or brave and courageous like the British Tommy. Placing these nationalities in easily definable categories made us susceptible to shock and disappointment when the Krugers and the Brownleys didn't match those images we had created in our minds. Unfortunately, this polarization is accurate in many cases, not because the genes of one race are so different from another, but a country's citizens are generally branded with the politics of that country or its leaders. A person of pure French descent, who was born and reared in Russia would be considered a Russian, and his French ancestry would not be taken into consideration. A lifetime association with the Russians would presumably have altered any Gallic outlook as far as other nationals would be concerned. If Parisians consider Americans brash and arrogant, then it wouldn't matter if an American visitor was a Republican or Democrat, a Californian or Texan, was of Polish descent or French. The average Parisian would consider that person a brash and arrogant American until he had been proven otherwise.

The Krugers and Brownleys showed how unjust this generalization can be and proved that all people must be accepted as individuals, and we should not be blinded by their nationalistic roots.

Upon entering the Farm Help office, I refused to speak to anyone but the person in charge. In a none too gentle tone, I asked this gentleman how he would feel about spending the night in a barn dressed as we were, and, also, who was the clown that instructed Brownley to take us off the bus? The man, aghast at our account, wouldn't divulge the culprit but ordered his staff to tear up Brownley's card and further instructed them to accept no future petitions from the inane Englishman.

Due to our nasty experience, the manager said he would dispatch us to the best outfit in the area, and he was as good as his word.

Within an hour a young man, Ralph Johnson, picked us up. He still had a couple of weeks threshing paying 75 cents per hour. Ralph also assured us we wouldn't have to sleep in any stables, so we rapidly acquiesced with the terms, and by lunch were at his father's farm ten miles east of Yorkton, fed, changed, and ready for work.

It was a unique set up and unequalled from a hired hand's point of view in my years of harvesting across the west.

Four neighbors worked together on a 40" machine, each providing a team, wagon and two men, one of whom was a son who had total responsibility for the horses. The other four men, including Charlie and I, stayed with the wagons acting as both field pitchers and spike pitchers, combined, which meant we rested while driving to and from the fields, didn't get roused from bed in the morning until breakfast, rode in the truck to the house for both lunch and supper, and relaxed after meals with no chores to disturb us. All farmers in the quartet had attractive teen-age daughters who assisted at the tables and brought afternoon lunches into the fields. With a bevy of young people, the atmosphere was constantly jovial and lighthearted.

Feeding sheaves into a thresher was an art, and a key ingredient to the success of threshing. The proper placement of sheaves on a carriage was for the head of one to be overlapping the butt of the one in front. Sheaves going in sideways or butt first didn't thresh satisfactorily and often clogged the innards of the machine. Hired help looking for a rest, and providing the operator wasn't watching, could plug the separator in less than five minutes causing a costly shutdown. It was obvious when the machine was becoming clogged, because straw would quit blowing, and the tractor groaned unmercifully as it became more difficult to power the drive belt.

If there was such a thing as being a master at pitching sheaves, I was reaching that category. I could have four sheaves twisting and turning through the air in a line, and all landing in the carriage in exactly the correct position, one behind the other.

Clogging the separator wasn't in my makeup, and this kept me in good stead with my employers.

In mid-October some wet weather put a halt to the harvest for a day or two. A stiff gale came up that dried out the stooks, but the wind proved to be a blessing with ominous overtones.

On October 19, my nineteenth birthday, preparing to return to the fields, we noticed the eastern horizon clouded by billowing smoke. In the west law requires at the first sign of a prairie fire everyone must leave whatever they are doing and race toward the conflagration. Jumping into the back of Johnson's pickup with the other crew members, we sped toward the clouds of smoke. Near the action zone, a R.C.M.P. constable was directing the arriving firefighters to different sections to battle the inferno. We reached a hayfield just in time to see a wildly dancing wall of flame sweep across the meadow and engulf several stacks of hay. Had we arrived fifteen minutes sooner, the fodder might have been saved. With jute sacks doused in ditch water, we beat the flames back from reaching a field of barley stooks and some portable granaries filled with wheat standing in the path of the destruction. In the end, fast action by the community prevented a major catastrophe.

However, substantial damage was sustained over a radius of thirty miles. The origin of the disaster was traced to a field where a farmer had been burning straw when the gusty wind fanned the flames out of his ability to control. I tried to visualize the encounter between the hapless farmer and his unfortunate neighbors who had suffered heavy losses as the result of his carelessness.

It was 6 p.m. when we arrived back at the farmhouse for supper. The wind had died down, and it was a mild fall evening as the moon slowly climbed from the eastern horizon. One of the farmers stood up following the meal and said, "Gentlemen, the season is late, and we will be getting snow any day. How many of you are willing to go out and thresh a few hours by the light of the moon and a burning strawstack?"

Everyone unanimously agreed, and my nineteenth birthday was the only occasion in years on the prairies that I pitched wheat sheaves by moonlight.

It was an enjoyable and unforgettable few hours with the pungent aroma from the burning straw wafting across the fields which were bathed in the soft light of a full harvest moon. Also, it proved to be a wise decision, because within 48 hours we awoke to find six inches of snow covering the landscape and snowflakes still tumbling out of the heavens at the rate of an inch an hour. Less than a half day's threshing remained in the fields.

Charlie and I were homeward bound by early afternoon. Seated comfortably in the warm coach, and watching the freshly blanketed countryside glide past the train window, we happily admired the $250 we had each accumulated since the dark days at Carman which, though only ten weeks before, seemed like an eternity.

Chapter 10
Fred "Oh Gee" Culhane

Father had spent all of Jack's service allotment checks and his conscience was nagging him. I therefore contributed $100 to his habitual cash shortfall. It wasn't that he wasted money on unnecessary luxuries; only rarely did he buy government whiskey, and his wardrobe was meager. Dad was one of those individuals who accumulated just sufficient cash to scrape by and never built up any reserves.

One evening a few days after I'd arrived home from Saskatchewan and given Father the $100 he said, "Bill, I want to go to an auction sale tomorrow over at St. Genevieve" (a village twelve miles southeast). "Bring the two shotguns, and we'll try to get a duck dinner at the same time."

"Whatcha figuring on buying," Pop?" I asked.

"I want to pick up a heifer for Jack," he responded. "You know, I've used his money, and I want to have something to show for it when he gets home."

I was bewildered. He was using my money to purchase a cow for Jack, so Jack would feel good about having something to show for his vanished bank accounts. Father would feel less culpable for squandering Jack's dough; and as for me, I guess I was supposed to feel okay, because it was my contribution that made the whole weird affair possible. Telling Jack that Bill bought him a cow wasn't in Dad's schedule of things.

Dad was the highest bidder at $75 for a fine Shorthorn yearling which, henceforth, would be known as "Jack's Cow". For my remaining visits to the farm over the ensuing three years, it would be referred to as "Jack's Cow", and when it was eventually marketed Jack received exactly the same remuneration from the sale of his cow as I came by

147

after the sale of my fine spring lambs a decade before—zilch. Dad, a lousy businessman, was generally good company, and it was difficult to remain angry with him for long.

Driving home from the auction sale, Dad detoured down some backroads unfamiliar to me and parked the car by the side of the trail. Grabbing our guns we struck off through some heavy brush towards a small pond Dad had discovered where huge bands of mallards were congregating at night after feeding on the nearby stubble in preparation for their migration south. Placing me in the flight paths of the ducks, Dad skirted the little lake to flush the birds. He knocked down three as they left the water, and I bagged one when they passed over. It was plenty for a delicious dinner.

Shortly after leaving our car it began to snow, and by the time father rejoined me over an inch had fallen and it was now coming down like someone was shovelling it off a roof—huge, wet flakes that clung to trees, clothes or wherever they landed like burrs to a blanket.

It was only a mile back to the car, so we took off without concern, but constantly ducking snow covered branches made it impossible to move in a direct line. Neither of us had a compass, and there was no sun to give us direction. Keeping a straight line through a forest is normally quite simple by lining up the tops of three trees about 100 yards apart in the direction you want to go. Upon reaching the middle tree you pick out another in line with the other two and so on.

The falling wet snow limited visibility to ten feet making the "trees in a row" routine impossible to employ. Therefore, like anyone who tramps the woods without a system, we started walking in circles. Spotting human tracks buoyed our spirits temporarily, because we assumed they would lead to the road. Alas, not so. After following the tracks a few steps, I realized one footprint was pointing sideways. When my boot fit perfectly in the print I knew for certain we were lost and following our own spoor.

Dad looked at me with a sickly grin. "We might just as well make our minds up we're here for the night," he said. "It will only be a few minutes until dark, so we'd be wise to fashion some sort of shelter."

A tall spruce tree beside us, though covered with snow, looked like a good place to begin, and I moved towards it.

"You know, Pop," I said, "I'm going to climb up this tree a few feet and see if I can spot anything."

After scaling the fir about twenty feet, a slight breeze came up momentarily improving visibility. Not 200 feet from where we were going to spend a torturous twelve hours was the dim outline of the Graham Paige.

Climbing into our automobile, Dad remarked, "I thought you were crazy, scaling that tree. I wouldn't have believed you would see fifty feet."

"Neither did I," I replied, "but sometimes I get an impulse to do something when I'm faced with a problem, and I've learned to follow that impulse, if possible, as it often provides the solution."

"Bless your impulses," he said, as we headed home through a mantle of white.

Jack was now in England thoroughly unaware that he was the proud owner of a yearling heifer. Having joined the service halfway through the conflict, he wasn't entitled to return home until all those who had enlisted ahead of him were back in Canada. Instead of flying their aircraft directly home as they had into action, Jack and his comrades were put aboard a ship and dispatched to England via the Red and Mediterranean Seas. He had only briefly glimpsed numerous parts of the world through which he'd travelled, but as there was little purpose in training, and he had to wait for his repatriation number to come up, Jack decided to explore England at more length.

Mother informed Jack of an uncle, Burnell Rodd, living in Bournemouth on the English South Coast, and he located him with no difficulty. Burnell, Grandfather Rodd's youngest brother, was an architect and one of the wealthiest men in the city. He lived with his wife in a castle with maidservants, manservants, and a chauffeur, and they treated Jack as a celebrity. Having no children or other close relatives, Jack's arrival as a direct descendant gave Burnell ideas. He tried to persuade Jack to return to school in preparation for Oxford University with the idea of eventually taking over the business in Bournemouth. Jack declined the opportunity but suggested I be contacted about the proposal. It didn't appeal to me either, but I wrote Grandfather Rodd and mentioned the wonderful chance his younger brother had made available to us. Granddad Rodd promptly responded that he was considering purchasing 100,000 acres somewhere in Central America for a banana plantation, and wanted Jack and I as overseers. The little family jealousy might have set Jack and I up in fine shape if we'd wanted to take advantage, but neither proposition was of interest to us. Jack didn't continue to correspond with Burnell, and none of us are aware of what eventually happened to the family or their estate.

The uncertainty of when Jack would return, or his plans for the future, made it awkward for me to decide what to do temporarily until the family became whole again and could determine its destiny.

Trapping had always intrigued me, and I had accumulated an impressive library on the subject. Specialty books on trapping mink, snaring or trapping coyotes, preparing homemade lures, plus several books dealing with successful trapping in general, lined my bookshelves.

Matching wits against the cunning of the animals was a constant challenge, though earning money was the principal aim. At the time I never considered the agony those animals suffered when they paid with their lives for losing this contest of wits.

Ted Phillips had destroyed an old crippled horse, and Fred Culhane, who trapped for a living, wanted the carcass for dog food. Fred lived in a tiny log cabin a mile south of us except during the winter while trapping at the Brokenhead River, when he stayed in another deserted old log hovel that had been thrown together by some hunters. It was to this Brokenhead River cabin he wanted the dead horse delivered. I told Fred I'd accept the assignment at no charge if I could share the log hut for a few months, as I also planned to trap the River country. At first, he was reluctant, not being too pleased with competition, but agreed when he saw I wasn't to be deterred. Culhane didn't have exclusive rights to either the trapping or use of the camp.

In mid-December I delivered the carcass and examined my winter's quarters. It was a little disillusioning. The cabin, one of the most crudely constructed log dwellings I'd ever seen, was about twenty feet by twenty-four feet. A rough petition divided it into two sections, and the tiny portion that Fred used as living quarters was ten feet by twenty with the balance used as a rough shelter for horses.

A single bunk against the back wall had an old mattress belonging to Fred, so it was obvious I would have to put some spruce boughs on the floor for my berth. Two homemade seats and table constituted the balance of the furniture except for a stove made out of an iron barrel that served as a heating device and a place to cook. There was one small window and no floor except for some spruce poles laying on top of the earth.

As degrading as the camp appeared, it didn't dampen my enthusiasm to get started at my chosen winter's pursuit. I adored the Brokenhead country, and the weasel and mink tracks traversing the snow covered terrain heartened me that money could be made. If I had any uncertainties about the venture, it was not apprehension with my room, but with my roommate. Fred "Oh Gee" Culhane was an eccentric and unique individual.

Passing his Monominto cabin every day to and from school, I chatted with him frequently. Then, as teenagers, Ed Barham and I visited Fred if there was nothing else doing in the community. His permanent shack was a little improvement over his trapping cabin but not by much. A single room, it was crammed with more trapping and hunting paraphernalia than furniture. An old iron cook stove invariably had an assortment of pots and pans stewing on the back with skunk fat, animal glands or other ingredients that he used to concoct homemade animal lures. These were never removed when Fred cooked dinner. His scant supply of dishes sitting on bare wooden shelves showed little evidence of soap and water, and his tin tea cup was coated with a layer of sediment a half inch thick. A few cooking utensils hung on the walls amongst coyote, skunk or other pelts that he was curing. The balance of the furniture was so decrepit, it would have made an Eskimo blush.

Fred successfully trapped a variety of animals both at Monominto and Brokenhead, including coyote, weasel, mink, muskrat and skunk. Skunk inhabited the farming area in large numbers, and Fred earned a large portion of his meager income by catching this predator for the sale of fur, plus endearing himself to his neighbors by eradicating the striped pest from around their chicken coops.

As a result of Fred's constant association with skunks, the odor from this intimacy permeated his clothes, living quarters, and much of the community depending on the wind direction. The portion of public road bordering his cabin was known as "Skunk Alley".

A strange transformation took place when Fred attended a social function which he did occasionally. He always showed up with a clean shirt, suit and tie, and the skunk aroma was non-existent. It was a mystery how he kept his calling clothes free of smell and eliminated the skunk odor from himself when he had a mind to.

Both his living style and accommodations made Fred an eccentric, but his cultural background made him a unique eccentric. A diminutive Englishman, he had been a featherweight boxing champion in Britain as a young man. His father was a prominent London surgeon, and his younger brother a career officer in the British Army. Fred had ample proof of his background in an album of newspaper clippings and pictures that he showed to a select few of his acquaintances including myself. I also personally read current letters from his brother who was stationed in various British possessions in different parts of the world.

Remittance men—individuals who received allowances on an annual basis from their families to remain abroad because they disgraced their English parentage—were not uncommon in Canada. Whether Fred belonged to this fraternity, or if his weird lifestyle was of his own choosing, I never heard, nor did I ask. In his mid-fifties when I trapped with him he showed little sign of ambition, seeming perfectly content with his existence.

To further set him apart from his fellow human beings, Fred Culhane stuttered. This affliction could have been the predominant cause of his eccentricity, but only Fred or a psychiatrist could have answered that question.

When he began stammering in the middle of a sentence, he would hesitate and then interject "Oh Gee" in the conversation which generally got him back on track. And so he was known as "Oh Gee" Culhane, though we never used that crude nickname in his presence.

To be amused by a fellow mortal's abnormality is not very kind; nevertheless, most humans find humor in other people's deviance as I well know. Numerous times I've seen others mimic my limp if they thought I wasn't aware of their impersonation. Unknown to Fred Culhane, his speech defect was the source of considerable comical takeoffs throughout the community. Probably the most memorable utterance to me was when he bade farewell. It invariably started with a wave as he headed to his camp, and would begin: "Well s-s-s-s-s-s-, well s-s-s-s-s. Okay, Bill, well s-s-s-s-s-." This would continue for several seconds at which point we would be several hundred feet apart. After a few more s-s-s-s-s-s-'s he would stop and shout, "Well, oh gee, goodbye, Bill." "So long" simply wouldn't come out, but he never gave up trying.

And so shortly after Christmas, with a knapsack of provisions I left the warmth and comfort of the farm house and joined Fred and his two dog team and sled and headed for the Brokenhead River to living accommodations that made my bunk in the horse barn at Phonehill, Saskatchewan, seem like a Triple A motel room. My traps and other necessities had been hauled with the horse meat and were already at camp.

Arriving at our destination on a bleak, cold, windy afternoon was a true test of my spirit's adaptability to the rugged environment. I loved it all. I cut fresh balsam branches for the base of my bed and laid the old mattress that had been delivered earlier on top of the pile. A couple of small shelves were fashioned out of old boards lying in the unused section of the cabin, and I cut a few poles to improve the floor. Fred suggested I trap south from our encampment, while he would remain north in country in which he was more familiar. With traps and bait I meandered a couple of miles up the river to assess my territory and prepare sets. Mink and weasel tracks crisscrossed the frozen stream, and I located excellent sites to set traps. As I returned to the cabin at dusk the scenario was a picture I would recall and cherish throughout life. Snow swirling across open tundra; our cabin nestled amongst a thicket of spruce and balsams, with smoke curling from its chimney; our dogs howling in reply to coyotes wailing in the distance; the sound of Fred chopping the night's supply of wood—all combined to create a setting of solitude and camaraderie that was an extreme antithesis to the horrors that mankind had inflicted on himself during the past six years of conflict.

Fred inquired about my trip up river. Then said, "Bill, please light the b-b-b-b- the b-b-b-b- 'oh gee' light the bitch, Bill."

"What the hell are you talking about?" I asked in puzzlement.

He took his lighter and lit a piece of string sticking out of a tin can filled with deer fat.

"For Gawd's sake, is that the only light we got?" I asked incredulously.

"I'm afraid s-s-s-s-s-so," Fred replied.

"Why do you call it a bitch, Fred?" I inquired.

J-s-s-s-s- just t-t-t-t-t- try 'oh, gee' try reading or writing with it," he answered. "And you'll see why it's called a b-b-b-b-b-b- an 'oh gee' bitch!"

There was no argument, and I vowed on my initial trip for supplies to fetch a kerosene lantern.

Weeks passed rapidly, though our days began with the dawn. Shortly after breakfast, we shouldered knapsacks, donned snowshoes and headed to our individual trap lines. I was catching weasel without any problem, but try as I might, mink would avoid my settings and often were downright insolent. It was not unusual for them to steal the fresh rabbit bait, then urinate on the trap. Fred was catching mink regularly but didn't offer me any advice. I didn't blame him, because mink that I missed would probably travel down river to his traps, and each mink was worth up to $75 whereas a large prime ermine pelt would only bring $5.

Traveling with snowshoes was a pleasure, and I enjoyed this method of movement. Walking on anything without substantial substance like mud, snow or sand was awkward and painful. My heel sank, but the fore part of my foot, lacking muscle, would double back creating great pressure on my instep and ankle. Snowshoes overcame the obstacle, because of their large area, plus they offered the added advantage that the weight kept my leg straighter, and I didn't swing it as much.

The longest circuit, approximately ten miles in distance, which I covered twice weekly, traversed a variety of terrain ranging from open swampland, treed ridges, evergreen bluffs, and the winding banks of the river.

Crossing an open expanse of marsh covered with three feet of snow one late afternoon, my snow shoes suddenly broke through the crust, and I found myself floundering. The snow was suspended on the tops of cattails, and the warm afternoon sun had weakened the crust enough that my weight forced the snow and cattails to cave in. I sank three feet to frozen ground. When I battled to get one snowshoe back on top and applied my weight, the crust would again crumble. It took strenuous effort to move a few yards, and the river two miles in the distance was still two miles from camp. Darkness was approaching when I finally reached the river. Unlacing my snowshoes as I sat on the riverbank, I felt total exhaustion for the first and only time in my life.

Finding camp in the dark posed no problem. By simply following the river, and walking on the ice and packed snow with moccasins, it was effortless compared to my previous ordeal. Fortunately, I had my boiling up can, tea, plus a little bread and cheese. After preparing a campfire in the shelter of the riverbank, I took a half hour breather and some nourishment. Somewhat refreshed, I slowly made my way to the cabin and arrived just as Fred was leaving with the dog team to try to find out where I was. This incident forced me to admit that my disability could lead to disaster in certain circumstances. However, another event a couple of weeks later proved that a minor accident occurring in unfavorable conditions can be the demise of the sturdiest of men.

My pal, Ed Barham, enjoyed hunting and trapping and was also attached to the Brokenead River country, so he arranged to spend a weekend with Fred and I. His main purpose was to locate, cut and stack tamarac fence posts, though we planned on doing a little hunting and exploring as well.

It was a blustery, cold day as the three of us hiked from home into the no man's land. At mid-afternoon when we reached a tamarac bluff a mile from the cabin, Ed decided to stop and see if it would supply his needed posts, while Fred and I continued to camp with our fresh supply of provisions.

We didn't remove the padlock from the door, because the foodstuff was as safe on the toboggan as in the unheated hut. We were both anxious to take advantage of the balance of daylight on our traplines. I made a circle of about four miles. It was a bitter, cold, blizzardy night when I returned to camp where I was greeted by an unpleasant and unexpected reception.

While cutting a tree with his razor sharp ax, Ed had slipped and accidently sliced a chunk off his big toe. Bleeding profusely and knowing we wouldn't hear his shouts for help, he struck out for camp. Unfortunately, by the time he'd reached the cabin the loss of blood sapped his strength, and he couldn't break down the locked door. Ed was forced to lay in the snow for an hour until Fred returned, which was thirty minutes before my arrival. Although a sturdy individual, the combination of circumstances had left Ed in an extremely weakened condition. He was wearing three pairs of woolen long johns in addition to sweaters and other heavy clothes and was soaked in sweat by his effort to reach camp. This, plus the loss of blood, debilitated both his vigor and reasoning capacity. Instead of trying to start a fire, he lay huddled in the snow, and his perspiration soaked clothes soon became a refrigerator in the frigid temperature.

By the time I returned, Fred, with a roaring fire going, had removed Ed's moccasin and sock and thrust his toe in a cardboard carton of flour to stop the bleeding. It was working, and the flow of blood had almost ceased. Within minutes I was ready to head for the nearest settlement to get help, but Ed suggested we wait, make something hot to drink and see how he felt. As the cabin warmed, Ed peeled off his clothes, wrapped himself in a blanket, and we decided to make supper. Feeling considerably stronger and relieved that the toe had stopped bleeding, Ed urged me to wait until morning; and I didn't argue, as it was an arctic night with an icy wind.

Eddie put in a restless night, and by 5 a.m. I was on snowshoes and swiftly heading for home. In the moonlight I could see plentiful evidence of the blood my friend had lost. Balls of red snow dotted the path where he had dragged his foot a few hours before. I reached home by nine, and as I ate a hearty breakfast, Dad harnessed our fastest team to the sleigh. With a few ounces of whiskey Dad had saved for an emergency, plus a thermos of hot tea, we reckoned Ed ought to survive the return trip. I was back at the Brokenhead by one o'clock, and after giving the animals some hay and oats, headed to Monominto with a much relieved Ed Barham. The weather was viciously cold with the thermometer in the minus 30 degree range. It was too frosty to run the horses, so I kept warm trudging behind the sleigh. Ed, covered in blankets and sipping whiskey with hot tea, handled the team. We arrived at his house at dusk. Though both Ed and I were rugged outdoors men, it took such events to teach us a valuable lesson. No matter how tough and conditioned a person is, exhaustion, the loss of blood, or extreme cold can lower thinking capacity so rapidly that in a short period of time one's fragile hold on life can be lost with a simple, inconsequential mishap.

I remained home for two or three days, and shortly after returning to the river country Fred decided to pay a visit to Monominto for supplies. For three days I was alone.

One still, cold, bright moonlit night I heard a pack of wolves nearing the cabin. Grabbing my parka, I clambered to the roof. Though unable to distinguish their forms, the wolves, chasing a deer, passed my lookout within a hundred yards. Almost immediately, I heard a fast moving animal coming from the same direction; and silhouetted against the white background, a huge bull moose went crashing past the hut within a hundred feet. It was the first moose I'd seen, and though he was evidently not the prey of the wolves, he lumbered through the willows fringing the river and disappeared into the night. It was an unforgettable spectacle, and I sat on the roof for a long time mesmerized by the enchantment of the winter panorama.

I relished every moment of my solitude, but as the days and nights wore on, the tranquility that delighted me at the beginning began to lose its lustre and I was glad to hear the yelping of Fred's dogs as he returned to camp. It was evident I would never be a hermit.

The winter's venture had not been a financial success as I only caught 50 weasels for a total return of less than $200. By the time I deducted the cost of traps, equipment and provisions, my net profit wasn't anything to brag about. However, I wouldn't exchange those months at the Brokenhead for any other of my existence.

Spring came rapidly to the river country, and with numerous signs of muskrats, I decided to make one more trip home for supplies in early March and return for two weeks of muskrat trapping.

When I entered the house I was astounded to see Jack, who had arrived a few days before, sitting at the kitchen table. What an extreme change in both our appearances! Jack looked more mature and had filled out. At the time of Jack's embarkation leave, I was clean shaven and wearing a suit; I was now growing a beard, wearing old trapper's clothes and smoking a pipe. I was also two inches taller and much heavier than my brother.

Jack didn't greet me as enthusiastically as I welcomed him, and I soon learned why. During conversations over the ensuing two days it was obvious he didn't approve of my trapping enterprise and tried to persuade me to return home and get on with planning our future. He would be receiving his final discharge within a few days and was uncertain of what he wanted to do.

I had to go back to the Brokenhead to get my gear, and decided to make my decision after evaluating the prospects of catching rats.

The weather was unusually hot the afternoon I returned to the river, and the snow was disappearing like magic. To reach camp I had to don hip waders to cross areas of the trail flooded by the spring run off, as the Brokenhead was spilling over its banks. That evening flocks of Canadian geese came squawking and gaggling as they took refuge for the night in the rapidly expanding open water. Frogs were harmonizing in a gigantic chorus, and the fragrance of new growth imbued the warm spring air like wild roses in the summer. I had spring fever, and I knew it. The following morning could not have been more perfect. Birds of all species were welcoming the sudden surge of spring; crows, robins, larks, phoebes, and ducks harmonized in a delightful cacophony of nature's music, while red-winged blackbirds by the thousands did their utmost to drown out the melody of the others. Locating a dry hump by the flooding river, I made a resting place with willows and hay, then sprawling out in the blazing sun absorbed the glories of Mother Nature. For hours I lolled in the spring solitude, and between naps tried to envision my future.

Suddenly, as if jolted with electricity, I sprang up from my reverie.

The water had risen so fast that setting muskrat traps would be hazardous, if not impossible. I assembled my gear, bade farewell to Fred, and shouldering my load, took off for the farm. The day's reverie had cemented my mind to one important fact: I had to get on with my future, and however I proceeded—with family or alone—earning decent income would have to be the immediate objective.

After five hours traveling I arrived home just as my family and the Ted Phillips' were sitting down to dinner. Alf Phillips got out the scales and weighed the three knapsacks of traps, clothing, cooking utensils and other paraphernalia I had carried from the Brokenhead. With my rifle it totalled 68 pounds, a substantial load to backpack ten miles through spring runoff that at times reached the top of my hip waders.

I was in excellent condition, knew it, and was prepared for the next chapter of life, regardless of its course.

Chapter 11

The Three Star Mink Ranch

It was good to be back with Jack and unbelievable that the great black cloud hovering over us for seven years had now dissipated. We had a lot of catching up regarding our personal experiences over the previous three years—a span that saw us transformed from juveniles to adults. The year 1946 was one of the earliest springs on record, ideal to cleanse Jack's head of the cobwebs of war.

We both adored the physical world, the outdoors with all its living things. Hearing the morning melody of a meadowlark or the evening song of a robin was reason to stop and listen. A simple carpet of yellow dandelions or a swamp ablaze with marsh marigolds was cause to hesitate and wonder. We not only admired the whims of nature but were enraptured by it.

The first task assailed was land clearing, and though Jack was out of condition and his hands tender, it didn't take many days for him to tone up his muscles and acquire callouses. We labored long hours and talked at great lengths. After catching up with the past, we ventured into the future, seriously considering the possibility of farming as our life's calling. I was dubious about my penchant for farming as a liveli-hood; but Jack loved the land, and he applied to the Canadian govern-ment for a veteran's loan to buy 160 acres a half mile from the home farm. The application was refused on the basis that the soil was un-suitable for successful farming. I wasn't surprised, as the light sandy earth, covered with stones and boulders predominating our neighbor-hood had never impressed me for successful crop growing. However, it was country we knew and loved, and it was a naturalist's paradise with a greater variety of animals and birds than most places on earth. Mankind's willingness to struggle for a livelihood on land unsuited for agriculture is well known. Rich land available in a different environment wouldn't induce many farmers to move, because it isn't home. Good land perhaps, but not their land. People are imbued with an attachment to the origin of their roots. What other justification is there for Eskimos living in the Arctic hinterlands where they look forward eagerly to the ferocious winters so they can get relief from the swarming insects of summer?

While discussing other means of earning our living and remaining in the Monominto community, I suggested raising mink. There were several prosperous mink ranches in the general area, and the price of short-haired fur, especially mink, was skyrocketing. Jack was receptive to the proposal, so we decided to purchase three females and one male of the standard ranch mink variety. By purchasing our breeding stock in early winter, the mink would have a few months to become accustomed to their new surroundings before the March breeding season. Sufficient funds were pooled to buy wire and materials to construct a dozen cages. The new enterprise was named "The Three Star Mink Ranch."

Throughout the summer I built cages, dug a huge trench for an outdoor ice house and prepared the layout for a 48' mink shed.

Needing cash as usual to carry me over until harvest time I was lucky to land a job as head chainman with a provincial survey team working near the farm. The pay was fifty cents per hour with an additional twenty-five plus gas for using the Graham Paige as transportation for the five-man crew. The month's work netted a $150 nest egg, though I gave father $50 for the use of the car.

It was an active summer. As the spring sun dissolved the snow, Jack dug out the baseball equipment, and playing catch again became as regular as taking nourishment. Jack, better than ever, was anxious to get involved in actual competition. We contacted all possible baseball aspirants over a radius of ten miles who would be interested in resurrecting the old Monominto baseball team. After considerable effort and numerous practices, we fielded a respectable squad. I was delighted to be the catcher, and though a couple of the boys weren't happy about my being on the team, they were overruled for two reasons.

First, I was the only member of the group who could hang on to Jack's pitches, plus I had a good arm and was a fair batter. Second, but most important, I had Jack's support. Without him there was no team, because he was 80 percent of any success we might enjoy. Therefore, to keep Jack, they accepted me.

From my standpoint, I felt if I was equal to the others with an ax or a pitchfork and if the opposing teams didn't object, then I should be allowed to participate in the limited diversions available. Also, except for my leg, I was a better ball player than those that objected.

For three seasons I caught the majority of games for the Monominto baseball squad. We played tournament ball primarily on Sundays, though occasionally we engaged in competitions at fairs or on special holidays.

There were twelve to fifteen teams in our association, mostly in the French towns of southern Manitoba, but several other villages were also on our itinerary. Opposing teams allowed me a permanent runner from the plate permitting me to participate. Both Jack and I inherited our love of the game from Father, who knew more about the rules of baseball than anyone in the area.

This knowledge kept Father in constant demand as an umpire, creating an unusual situation in those tournaments where Jack and I were the battery for Monominto. Though Dad would try to disqualify himself from those games because there was substantial money at stake, the other teams trusted him implicitly. This arrangement often worked against us, as father usually gave the opposing squad the benefit of a close call. I razzed him unmercifully knowing he enjoyed the kidding.

Our team's fortunes rested almost exclusively with Jack who, with daily practice and stiffer competition, was steadily improving. His blazing fastball, in the 100 m.p.h. range, excellent control, superb curve ball, and an underarm submarine simply overpowered most batters. His weakest pitch was his changeup. If there was a major tournament and Monominto wasn't involved, other teams from fifty miles' distance would dispatch a car to fetch Jack. He was considered the best on the circuit. Jack's superior ability was apparent to me in comparison with those pitchers I batted against, but it wasn't until years later all doubt was removed regarding Jack's exceptional talent.

I had box seats close to home plate in Toronto for three years when The Maple Leafs belonged to the Triple A International League and were a farm team of the New York Yankees. Some of the finest pitchers in the Yankee organization played for Toronto, either on their way up or down from the majors, when Elston Howard was the catcher. None had better stuff than Jack. Intense desire, constant practice, and natural ability are the prime elements in making a good athlete exceptional. Jack had all three in large doses.

He practiced baseball from the first pitch of green in spring until the initial snowflakes of winter, and in the fields he constantly threw stones at any target within range. He was a fierce competitor. It was a sad reality of his life he couldn't test his skill in the Big Leagues. I believe he would have stacked up well.

However, our baseball participation with the other boys in the neighborhood contains pleasant memories, not only because of the competition but also because planning and working as a group to earn money for uniforms and equipment constituted a major part of our social life.

Charlie Fryza, who played shortstop for the ball club, approached me in mid-August about hitting the harvest trail. His older brother Henry joined us, plus John Seynck, the son of a neighbor who farmed one mile west of us. Johnny, just back from overseas, suggested we all go along in his 1935 Ford sedan.

We drove directly to Oak Lake, Manitoba, a small town twenty miles west of Brandon, and thirty miles from the Saskatchewan border. Threshing hadn't commenced, so we took a job stooking for ten days, a task we all disliked. We got to horsing around in the fields one day, and so the farmer fired us.

It was the only dismissal I was ever subjected to in my life, and it was embarrassing, although my mates and I laughed about the episode for months.

Men travelling together share events that are exclusively theirs, and a sort of secret society exists between those involved. Forever after, when certain terms, expressions or names are recalled, only those in the inner circle can enjoy remarks that specifically refer to that special segment of their existence. So it was with the four of us. The firing at Oak Lake proved to be only a minor event in our eight-week excursion.

Charlie and I persuaded John and Henry to proceed nonstop to Montmartre where we could renew relations with our French Canadian girlfriends and possibly find work. We arrived in the afternoon and soon located our feminine favorites. Chuck and I left Henry and John to their own devices, and during the next several hours, we enjoyed a delightful reunion with our friends.

After escorting the girls home and assuring them the four of us would return the following day to begin work, we started searching for the '35 Ford. We located it in a vacant lot at 4 a.m. with our two buddies sound asleep. Waking them was not appreciated, and we received a rather cool reception.

John took off like a rocket, and all our imploring to stop, because arrangements had been made for employment, fell on deaf ears. I guess John and Henry felt that Charlie and I were too well established in Montmartre and, therefore, had an unfair advantage in the social department.

With no definite destination in mind, John drove northeast across Saskatchewan to the town of Esterhazy where we arrived shortly after daybreak. While breakfasting, we inquired about the need for harvesters in the area and were directed to a farm a mile from the village where the proprietors were looking for stookers.

A young lady, grasping a flaxen-haired four-year-old boy by the hand, came out of the house to greet us. The woman, in her early twenties, was a knock out. Long, golden hair hanging down over her shoulders, framed a face so pretty that for a moment we sat entranced without speaking. Finally, I asked if they required harvest help. She said, yes, and invited us into the house. Inge Olson was her name, and her pilot husband had been killed overseas two years before. Photographs displayed prominently throughout the house indicated he was as handsome as she beautiful. They must have made an outstanding looking couple. Inge's father-in-law, returning from the fields, offered us a job stooking. Threshing wouldn't start for another week.

The other three boys shared a bedroom on the second floor, and I was given a couch in the living room. When Inge discovered my brother had served in the RCAF, it acted as a magnetism, and she sat and chatted with me at every opportunity. Her conversation revealed that, though terribly lonely, she hadn't severed her attachment to her dead husband. Inge's figure was as well proportioned as her face was gorgeous, and while sitting alone and talking, it took considerable restraint not to make a pass. I sensed, though, that any attempt at flirtation would have been received as a grave insult. So, hiding my emotions, I agonized at becoming too enamored with her. Finally, the empathy I felt toward Inge and her young son became unbearable, and I bade farewell after ten days of work. The other boys departed also, although we had second thoughts when Inge and her father-in-law pleaded with us to remain for the threshing season.

Over the ensuing years, when discussing attributes of the opposite sex, Inge, referred to as "The Widow," was the analogy with all four of us. I sincerely hope she found a second mate with whom she became as devoted as she seemed to be to her fallen war hero.

We motored twenty miles north to Saltcoats, Saskatchewan, twenty-five miles south of Yorkton and found an ideal situation. Two neighboring farmers needed two men each. The pay of eight dollars per day, plus first-rate meals and accommodations, kept us happily employed until the season ended in mid-October. When the final stooks had been threshed, two cases of beer were provided. After guzzling that down the four of us, our two employers, plus four other crew members (all neighboring farmers) piled into two cars and headed to Yorkton to continue our end of harvesting celebration. The party lasted several hours, and for the first time in my life, I became staggering drunk, then violently sick. This was minor compared to one of our bosses, who got the D.T.'s back at his farm, and in an unconscious state almost killed himself in the barn by rolling under the feet of the nervous horses. It required four of us to keep him pinned down in an empty stall until the seizures stopped and he regained sanity. It was a new and terrible insight into the terrors of alcohol that was slowly but gradually becoming a part of my life.

The journey rendered some new personal encounters—the first time fired, first time in love, and the first time drunk. The latter two would not remain firsts for long.

The trip provided my share of funds to purchase our mink. Jack's money was already in the kitty.

Early in November, after the first snowfall, I sleighed to the river country and cut two loads of spruce. The local lumber mill squared them on two sides, and they provided the main structural timber for our new mink headquarters. Before Christmas the partially constructed dwelling was ready for our animals. Three fine mature females and a large young male comprised our breeding stock at a cost of $400. The hard work now began in earnest.

Twice a day the minks' meals had to be carefully proportioned and mixed with horse meat, fish meal, tomato juice, and other ingredients, all of which went through a hand grinder. Their nest boxes were changed twice weekly and lined with fresh bedding. This was time consuming, because they were so ferocious one had to be constantly on guard. Any part of your anatomy near the wire mesh of the minks' cages was in danger of being mangled with their razor sharp teeth. When entering a nest box, I slapped the opposite end of the cage with a mitt or other item. When the mink raced out to attack and tear it apart, I dropped the metal door at the nest box entrance allowing me to complete the cleaning.

Throughout winter, I operated a trap line in a six-mile circle from the house to earn personal spending money and to purchase horse meat and other food supplies for the mink. While snowshoeing around my line, I shot a couple of deer to keep the larder supplied. Jack also bagged a couple, so venison was our principal diet. My biggest concern was how to keep horse meat fresh without refrigeration when the hot summer months arrived. I made blocks of ice and stored them in my newly erected ice house with layers of sawdust in between. Mink won't eat tainted meat, and I was worried the problem hadn't yet been solved.

I studied books on mink procreation, but as the March breeding season approached, I was as nervous as a new bride. Every article dealing with this crucial period stressed the importance of keeping strangers or animals from approaching the minks' pens. Two mongrel dogs we'd owned since pups, continuously skulked around the cages looking for small portions of ground horse meat that had filtered through the wire mesh. In desperation, I constructed a four-foot page wire fence to prohibit the dogs' entry. This stopped one, but the other succeeded in jumping the new barrier. With March fast approaching, I grabbed the rifle and shot him. Jack was so upset at this cold-blooded murder he threatened to shoot me; but Dad saved the day when he told Jack if I hadn't disposed of the animal, he would have because the dog was also stealing turkey eggs. I tried to justify my position by saying tough decisions will always confront us if we are trying to be successful in business. But Jack was a dog fancier, and mink are tough animals to love.

Mink are so savage that the moment copulation is completed, they must be separated or they will attempt to tear each other apart frequently ending in the death of the weaker of the two. If the male is dominant, he is placed in the female's cage. When their love-making is completed and she dashes to her nest box to escape his insistence on continuing the liaison, it is a simple matter to close the trap door. The male is then easily removed with a small trap box especially designed to transfer them from one cage to another.

If a young male is submissive to an old female, then the procedure is reversed, and she is placed in his cage. When finished, she will attack to frighten the male away, and he will retreat to his nest.

Several prominent signs signify when the females come into heat, but there is little notification when they have finished intercourse. At this critical point there are only seconds available to separate them before damage is done, so you dare not leave their presence.

Our three females came into heat within two days of each other during one of the worst March blizzards ever to strike the Manitoba countryside. A breeding session with mink lasts from thirty minutes to two hours, so for a large part of two days I sat huddled outdoors in a raging snowstorm while my charges decided if they wanted to raise a family. I was blessed. They did, and a few weeks later they presented us with eleven fine kits. We were now in the mink business in a big way.

"The Three Star Mink Ranch" had diversified our family's interests. Mother was enjoying moderate financial success from the sale of Angora rabbit wool, but Ruth, having now completed Grade VIII successfully—and with no desire for further education—had to be considered in future plans.

The local general store, post office, and gas pumps were for sale, and we made a bid for it. Besides expanding our financial potentiality, the property had a two-story frame house only ten years old. Though it lacked inside facilities or electric power, it made our old homestead look quite dilapidated in comparison. The money was borrowed from

Fred Ward, an old family friend, who secured the loan by placing a mortgage on the farm that had just recently been cleared of debt. The family took possession in early winter.

A small stable on the five-acre tract that accompanied the store could provide shelter for a team of horses and a couple of cows, which was about the limit of our stock. All members of the family had lost interest in milking cows and other related chores after Jack returned from overseas.

I purchased a six-acre parcel directly across the road from our new investment to relocate The Three Star Mink Ranch.

Jack and I were playing ball every weekend and attending the Saturday night dances at Monominto Hall. Ruth, a robust young lady of eighteen, loved to dance, and as we used the Graham Paige, she invariably joined us. Ruth had no steady boy friends, and like all rural young ladies at the time, she was constantly on the hunt for a prospective husband. At the community dances most young people of both sexes arrived alone or with other family members. After choring was completed, it was too late to have to travel any great distance to pick up a date, so the majority of singles went directly to the hall. Once there, though, the courting began in earnest. Any fellow could approach a girl for a dance without having any idea who the other was, nor would either be concerned a whit. If things developed to their mutual satisfaction, then perhaps the girl would allow the chap to squire her home.

One night a young man showed up at the local shindig with a Cree Indian woman from the Sandilands Reservation which was forty miles southeast of Monominto. The fellow, redheaded and with a pleasant smile, was of slight stature, while the sullen, black-haired lady was short, stocky, and appeared capable of playing defense for the Montreal Canadian Hockey Club. As the evening progressed, they both showed signs of too much whiskey. He was frequently dancing with Ruth, and the Cree lady was becoming severely agitated. Ruth, enjoying herself, was completely unaware the man had arrived with a date, and when he asked her to join him in a lively polka, she accepted with relish. After a half dozen circles of the dance floor, the Cree lady was furious. Like a ripe volcano, she had reached her boiling point. Standing fifteen feet from the front door she stood poised for action. As the two unsuspecting dancers came polkaing past, the fuming squaw caught her escort by the neck of his shirt and the ass of his pants and flung him toward the door screaming, "You lousy son of a bitch. I'll break your f---ing neck!" Ruth, suddenly finding herself with empty arms, stood, mouth open, like a wooden statue.

Fortunately for the redhead, he landed on his feet, and the forward propulsion gave him a little head start over the fast-charging Indian. He raced across the yard and, as graceful as an antelope, leaped a four-foot barbed-wire fence. The Cree, in hot pursuit but not as agile, had to crawl under. This gave the redhead a ten yard lead, and it was widening. The last we saw or heard they were in full flight through the field of waving wheat.

Ruth, dazed and embarrassed, vowed that in the future she would insist on seeing credentials from strangers. Betty Rasmussen, a girl friend, recommended that to prevent a reoccurrence she should keep her partner in the center of the dance floor.

The Rasmussens, one of the few Danish families that farmed west of us, had nine children with five daughters. They were all attractive girls, and Betty, the fourth oldest and about two years younger than I, was fast becoming the beauty of the bunch. A tall, athletic girl with long, blonde hair and a wide and ready smile, she was my favorite dancing partner, though I only attempted a few numbers in an evening. Current hits reminiscent of those dances were: "Five Minutes More," "Golden Earrings," "Now Is the Hour," "Ole Buttermilk Sky," and "The Old Lamplighter."

As sole proprietor of The Three Star Mink Ranch, the constant chores seven days a week were wearing on my nerves. Any deviation in the minks' feed could cause health problems, and I never determined if tainted meat was responsible for the illness that in early summer almost took the life of Rusty, our young male. He went off his food and wouldn't leave his nest box. Consulting my books on mink maladies, I found something that resembled Rusty's symptoms. The recommended cure required forcing some prescribed medicine, mixed with tomato juice, down his throat with a teaspoon. It was like suggesting I should stick my hand in a moving meat grinder. I had no choice, however, but to try or allow Rusty to die. Though dammed certain the big male mink would either spring at me or make a dash for freedom, the second I opened his nest box lid I reluctantly went to his aid.

Rusty eyed me suspiciously as I slowly opened the nest box door, but he made no attempt to move. Inserting my heavily gloved hand I gently fondled his nose. He seemed to enjoy the stroking, so I laid caution to the wind, and removing my hand wear, I cautiously touched his head with my bare fingers. Rusty accepted this patting, too. Gaining still more courage, I calmly touched his mouth with a spoonful of medicine and was amazed when he allowed me to raise his head with my free hand and dribble the medicine down his throat without him stirring a muscle. After duplicating this performance three successive days, Rusty showed signs of vigor, but still never shied away nor made a grab for my naked hand. Rusty completely recovered and was the only mink

I ever saw who preferred to have his nose caressed rather than lacerate a human finger like his kin.

For unexplainable reasons some animals learn to trust certain humans. I am doubtful if the Rusty incident could have happened with many other wild mink. Although a fable, Androcles and the lion is an example of how our ancestors accepted this rare relationship. Androcles could have removed a thorn from the paw of a hundred different lions that would still have devoured him, but fortunately, he performed the good deed on a beast that possessed that special quality. I encountered other examples.

In the early fifties Dad bought a filly that we named "Fly." She was the only mare we owned that supplied us with a colt. Whether she had been mistreated as a young horse we never knew, but for the first few months after her arrival, she would try to kick out our brains whenever we approached her stall. A sack of hay was held when walking past, so if she lashed out we wouldn't receive a broken leg. Eventually she calmed down, and we approached her without trepidation, but she would always shake like a leaf in a summer thunderstorm. Fly never overcame her skittishness, but she was the hardest-working horse I ever saw. Most farm horses are on the lazy side and have to be urged to keep their traces taut, but not Fly. She did everything in high gear. In a six-horse team she tried to pull the equipment by herself and drag the other five animals to boot. When hitched to a wagon or sleigh, Fly was always half a length ahead of her mate and couldn't be held back. When still a young horse, she took sick, and gradually worsened until her bones stuck out through her lusterless hide. The vet and our neighbors, as befuddled with her illness as we, could do nothing for the ailing mare. We were forced to watch her deteriorate daily.

One warm evening as Fly lay on her side in the barn yard, it was apparent the end was imminent. I sat on the ground beside her, and placing her head on my lap, I patted her perspiration-soaked forehead. For half an hour, except for my caressing, we were motionless; but Fly never took her eyes off my face nor closed her eyelids, as if she was trying to figure out something profound. Suddenly, as if on impulse, her eyelids closed, her body stiffened, then after a slight shudder, she died. I'm convinced my presence was conscious comfort to Fly in her death throes. We performed an autopsy on the young mare to ascertain her illness and discovered her heart was two times the size of a normal heart. As we were not veterinarians, it was impossible to tell if Fly's organ was diseased or a quirk of nature. She was indeed a unique animal and danced to the beat of her own drum.

Chum was another strange case. Chum was a five-year old mongrel dog we'd raised from a pup. Like all farm dogs, he loved to hunt rabbits and roved the woods at great length. One night in late March he didn't return home. This was unusual, but not serious. However, when the second night passed without a trace of Chum, we began to worry and circled the community, but our neighbors had not seen him either. After a week without sign nor sound, we decided Chum had met an untimely end and started to search for a new cow dog.

On a mild spring evening exactly two weeks after his disappearance, Mom called us outside because she thought she could hear Chum howling. Everyone listened carefully, and though we could hear coyotes yapping, nothing sounded like Chum. My hearing was impaired from polio, but Jack and Dad both had keen hearing. Nevertheless, only Mom was convinced she could hear our dog above the yelping wolves. The next morning Mom persuaded Dad to make a search in the direction she thought the howls came from. After two miles of walking slowly and listening intently, they finally heard a weak whimper, and within a hundred yards, they came upon our emaciated pet. Chum was caught by his hind leg in a wolf snare, and though not broken, his entire limb was raw to the bone. Coyote tracks had packed the snow to within five feet of where Chum could reach from his restraining wire trap. It was unbelievable the coyote pack had not attacked the helpless dog. Willows and everything within reach had been chewed to appease his hunger, and Chum was so weak Dad had to carry him home. He completely recovered, and though he lost a couple of toes and limped for many weeks, he lived several more years and continued to chase cottontails.

It was a miracle Chum was able to communicate with Mother on that particular evening. It is only logical that he howled or barked for the full two weeks of his entrapment, and certainly for the first week, we all listened frequently and attentively. However, on the fourteenth night, with sapping strength and facing certain death, Chum was able to transmit his message to Mother. Both parents were convinced he would have died the following night, either from hunger or at the hands of the coyote pack, who are mortal enemies of domestic dogs.

Then there was Candy. One spring morning a terrified doe fawn, only a few days old, came racing into the stable area. We'd heard a shot at dawn and presumed someone had killed her mother. Why the panic stricken little deer fled to the only haven that would save her life when it would have been more natural to have remained in the woods and died by her mother was a mystery. We easily caught the frightened little animal and placed her in a small pen in the stable. Mom took charge, and believing cow's milk might be too alien for the infant, she extracted milk from a nursing ewe. The fawn devoured the sheep's milk like a child gulps ice cream, and within days she was as frisky as her lamb cousins. Mom named her Candy, and she soon became the pet of the family. When only a few weeks old, Candy was transferred to our fenced back yard which was more like her natural environment. Having access to the kitchen, Candy would stroll in during meal times to nibble bread from our fingers. When taller, she would steal directly from the table showing absolutely no fear of the family nor flinching at sudden movements. Mom placed a strap and small bell around her neck to warn neighbors who might get hungry for fresh meat.

By midsummer fences no longer restrained Candy, and she grazed with the other animals in the pasture. Throughout winter Candy rarely strayed from the farmyard, preferring to eat and sleep in the sheep pens. By spring as a full-grown doe, she still showed little interest in the surrounding wilds and was as docile as a house cat. But as summer spread across the land, Candy gradually grazed farther afield and frequently by herself. She returned to the yard area at night, however, and still loved to nibble goodies from our hands. But this intimacy was slowly changing. Our fleet-footed friend was showing signs of suspicion, yet as far as we knew, we were the only humans with whom she had ever been associated.

As hardwoods turned yellow and evening frosts browned the goldenrod, Candy began staying away all night. Though we frequently heard the tinkle of her bell in the nearby woods and occasionally glimpsed her grazing in the meadows, she now remained aloof from the family. It was understandable as rutting season approached, and as she was of breeding age, she would return to her natural roots.

What puzzled us, though, was that she never knew anything but benevolence from her human benefactors but instinctively became uncomfortable and suspect of our intentions once she renewed her relationship with her own kind.

Candy was shot that winter. One of our neighbors reported to Mom they had seen her severed head with the bell still attached lying in the snowy woods a mile from her adopted home.

So Rusty, the fierce wild mink; Fly, the excitable bay mare; Chum, our faithful mongrel pet; and Candy, the lovable white-tailed doe—all could communicate in some special manner with their human superiors when facing imminent death. In ordinary conditions beasts of the wilds lack this telepathic ability, probably because they intuitively know that man, though the dominant animal in mentality, is also the cruelest and shows little concern for the lives of his fellow creatures.

Haying, which preceded grain cutting by a few weeks, was summer work, but as the final coils were hauled from the meadow, the hot weather began to fade and the field of brown-eyed susans, tiger lilies and ox-eye daisies were replaced by golden rod, purple phlox and other blooms of autumn. Crows, blackbirds and swallows gathering in noisy bands, plus frosty evenings signaled that harvest time had arrived once again. A restlessness overpowered me as the late summer of '47 turned into fall, and the daily monotony of striving to supply fresh meat to our mink plus other related chores was becoming too much. Rusty had regained his vitality, the female mothers were healthy, and the kits had almost reached full growth. As delighted as I was with our progress, the tedium of the daily routine became more odious than I could bear. Boredom and a perpetual cash deficiency finally induced me to persuade Jack to assume the duties of servicing our fur industry for a few weeks while I went harvesting at the Kruchaks. Unfortunately, I spent little time instructing him in the significance of proper food handling and other important points. It would prove to be a costly oversight.

The Kruchaks, a family who farmed 900 acres five miles west had asked me to come to work. Their holdings were on the fringe of the rich soil that extended 1000 miles intermittently west to the Rocky Mountains. I accepted their offer of employment.

Kruchaks were another nonpareil family of our neighborhood with whom I enjoyed a long and pleasurable acquaintanceship. Kruchak, Sr., a native of the Russian Ukraine, immigrated to Canada at the turn of the century. Small in stature, he had a great desire to create a Communist out of everyone with whom he came into contact.

Dearly loved by his family, respected by his neighbors, and a personal friend of mine, Kruchak was generally frustrated when he obtained few converts to his cause. Dan was his given name, and he was generally referred to as "Ol Dan."

In the late thirties and early forties when the labor movement was struggling to gain a foothold in Manitoba, my father and Jim Wylie were interested in their philosophies and attended every meeting. They took me with them, and that is when I first saw Dan Kruchak in action. The labor leaders from Winnipeg who organized and chaired the meetings always invited Dan because he was a known labor sympathizer, but undoubtedly they regretted their decision at each convocation. Dan spoke in a garbled combination of Ukranian and broken English heavily interspersed with oaths from both languages which was not easy to follow, much less understand. He always managed to get control of the microphone several times during each session. What concerned the Labor Party leaders the most was the gist of "Ol Dan's" topic even though few in the auditorium could comprehend his speech. It always contained Communist dogma from which the C.C.F. or Labor Party was trying desperately to disassociate itself. But Dan Kruchak had a message to expound and was determined to avail himself of every opening to communicate that doctrine. When the chairman, writhing in discomfort, could no longer constrain himself and tried to regain control of the "mike" and the meeting, a hilarious tug of war would result. This confrontation usually ended with Dan walking dejectedly off the dias mumbling something suggesting the whole gawd-damn lot were nothing but a bunch of capitalistic bums.

Dan and his wife raised five girls and six boys—Helen, Bill, Mary, John, Mike, Roman, Paul, Olga, Stella, Joe and Betty in that order. Each was distinctly dissimilar from his or her sibling. Mary and Stella were the only two to leave the Winnipeg area permanently. Helen married Rudolph Koski, and they farmed directly across the road from the Kruschak's. The balance of the clan either remained in the Monominto environs or moved to Winnipeg. The boys were all avid baseball players, and three of them—Bill, Mike and Roman—played with the Monominto team. John also participated when available, but he worked for the railroad and was rarely home. The other Kruchak brothers may not agree, but I understood Joe eventually became the best athlete of the family. Mike, recently discharged from the army when I went to work on the survey crew the previous summer, worked with me on the chain. Next to Jack he was the best pitcher on the Monominto squad. Bill, the oldest and better known as Willie, managed the home acreage plus his own quarter section. Roman also owned his own spread and worked at the home farm.

They threshed with a small separator, using four stook teams and usually a couple of field pitchers. Kruchak's was an excellent place to work though the pay was only average at $7 per day. Food was plentiful and tasty, the camaraderie and banter enjoyable, and we worked at a relaxed, though steady pace. No one panicked if the threshing machine occasionally ceased blowing straw. Sometimes "Ol Dan" would be field pitching, a golden opportunity for him to preach sense into my capitalistic noggin. I could load a rack of wheat sheaves by myself twice as speedily without Dan's companionship, but he was the patriarch of the clan, so I listened. Trying to drive home a point, "Ol Dan" would lean on his pitch fork in front of the wagon and not budge until I'd agreed with his argument. Only then would he allow my team to move to the next stook. Willie, waiting impatiently at the machine, knew the cause of the delay and said nothing. Other days Willie himself would be responsible for an idle machine. He'd climb up on the rack while a hired hand was feeding the separator and start a wrestling match, which invariably ended when both combatants tumbled off the load. Willie never lost a match, but he outweighed the heaviest of us by a hundred pounds.

I slept on the second floor of the main house with Roman. Our bed was separated by a curtain from Olga and Stella, both attractive girls. Being in my age bracket and good friends, they probably wondered why

I never peaked nor sneaked behind such a simple barrier, but Roman went to bed before me, got up after me and always slept on the outside. Stella and I dated a few times, and she was a beautiful young lady. Her presence and Olga's made working at the Kruchak's a little more special.

If the season wasn't closing in too fast, Bill would shut the operation down Saturday afternoon at 6 p.m., an hour earlier than usual. Roman, who also drove a stook team, and I would race our horses into the yard, unharness and turn them out to pasture in jig time. After a rapid cleanup and change of clothes, we gulped supper, and with a couple of buddies, jumped into Roman's car and hightailed it to St. Anne Des Chenes, the nearest town, ten miles away, where we could buy beer. The beer parlor, filled with our neighbors, provided a couple hours of pleasant relaxation. Then we headed for the Monominto dance hall where dancing, partying and drinking kept us from bed until daylight. We didn't care though, because we had all day on Sunday to rest and soothe our sore heads.

One Saturday late in the season Bill, concerned we might not finish the harvest before the first snowfall, notified the crew there would be threshing on Sunday. Roman and I didn't heed the warning and savored the usual Saturday night ritual without restraint, crawling into bed at 6 a.m. They allowed us to sleep until eight, and then ramrodded us out to harness our horses. Too sick to eat, we headed directly for the field not knowing that blessed relief was on the way. Ominous storm clouds were gathering in the western sky and moved steadily closer throughout the morning. I should have been conscientious enough to hope the weather would remain dry for my friends, but my aching head overpowered my conscience, and I prayed for rain.

At eleven o'clock the first drops fell, and within fifteen minutes it was a downpour. Roman and I easily beat any previous Saturday night record for getting our horses into pasture. A granary in the center of the yard contained a double bed and mattress. Neither of us informed the other of his intentions, but we both arrived at that refuge at the same moment. Without a word of protest as to possession, and not bothering to remove our heavy work boots, we slumped onto the bed; and the last thing I recall before falling into the arms of Morpheus was Stella covering us with a blanket.

I survived the ordeal, as did Roman, but we swore an oath to pay more attention to Willie in the future.

The stooks would be too wet for threshing for several days, so Roman drove me home where the awaiting tidings plunged my spirits lower than during my horrendous morning hangover.

Rusty had escaped when Jack inadvertently left open the door to his nest box. In addition, one female and five of the kits were dead, probably from food poisoning. Jack, though distraught, wasn't to blame, because he had never intended to be overseer of the animals, and I hadn't given him sufficient, detailed instructions. Distressed and brokenhearted at our loss but knowing full well I didn't possess the stick-to-itiveness needed to manage a mink ranch properly 365 days a year, I suggested to Jack he sell the remaining mink to any of the neighboring ranches that would purchase them, and we would abrogate The Three Star Mink Ranch.

The mink business was my idea. I chose the breeding stock, cut the timbers, erected the mink building and ice house, and constructed the minks' cages. I studied for hours to satisfactorily supervise their mating ceremony and suffered through five months from April to August attempting to keep the horse meat fresh without refrigeration. I saved Rusty's life. I was also totally responsible for the demise of the enterprise.

This trait of mine in being unable to stick with an undertaking for protracted periods of time would haunt me all my life. After the initial thrill of starting an enterprise, I soon grew weary of the status quo and sought new adventure. During the span of my business career, this characteristic would cause the loss of a lot of money and create many heartaches, but it also provided numerous exciting experiences.

And so it would this time. . . .

Lagniappe
The Post War Years

The war changed Western society in spectacular ways. Neither Canadians nor Americans were prepared to return to prewar conditions, particularly the younger generation—those who were teenagers in 1938 and grew from adolescence to adults in a difficult and tumultuous era. Women, who played a magnificent role in munitions, aircraft and other war production factories, were not going to return meekly to their kitchens. They were now an established factor in the labor market, which meant more jobs than ever before would be required. Much has been written about the wellspring of the feminine fight for equality, or the embryo of the sex revolution. I believe the war was the springboard for both, and, clearly, those revolutionary changes in our social attitudes toward the two topics were closely interconnected.

There was no postwar "slump" in any extreme sense after 1945. Though a slight decline in jobs occurred in 1946 from the 1944 peak, by 1947 there was again full employment. The postwar years were essentially an extension of the period of economic growth initiated by the war, and as usual, prosperity brought contentment and political stability, but only temporarily. Unfortunately, the labor class would not be content for long, and politicians rarely practice restraint or possess the aptitude to stand pat.

It was remarkable how smoothly and easily the millions of service men and women, in both nations, were absorbed back into the civilian economy. The generous veterans' benefits accorded them contributed to this, while at the same time giving the economy a boost.

Among the industries rapidly reconverted from war production to peaceful purposes, none was more notable—or more representative—than the automobile industry, whose wartime achievements had been so striking. At the end of hostilities, the demand for civilian cars was enormous, and factories in both Canada and the United States were back in full production by early 1946.

The television industry was also on the verge of colossal expansion. In 1945 only 5,000 U.S. homes had sets—bulky receivers with tiny screens that picked up what little programming was available from the handful of stations in operation. But the world was on the edge of a communications revolution that would see television sets in nearly every home of every developed country.

Automation was born in 1946. "Automation" is a word coined by D.S. Harder, a Ford Motor Company engineer, for a system he had devised to manufacture automobile engines. Harder's completely automatic process produced a new engine every fourteen minutes, reducing production time from 21 hours, and was the first complete self-regulating system applied to manufacturing. It would not be the last, as automation was to become another burgeoning business in the postwar world. It was also another significant factor in the growing unrest between management and labor.

Atomic energy was being hailed as the energy source of the future, but with much of the populace, nuclear fission raised fearsome questions. Would it end dependence on fossil fuels, or would it destroy the world? Questions still in dispute forty years later.

England was rocketing to socialism. In 1946 a National Health Service bill was enacted by Parliament making medical service free to all Britons.

Canada was also moving in the direction of the welfare state, a trend that would gradually accelerate until a quarter of a century later it ruined the financial status of a nation that, with intelligent leadership, could have been a showpiece for the Western world instead of gasping for its economic breath. Prime Minister Mackenzie King liked to think of himself as a social reformer and the friend of the working man, essentially akin to President Roosevelt. He established the Unemployment Insurance Act in 1944; then The Family Allowances Act which provided the "baby bonus," a monthly payment for each child under the age of sixteen. There were long discussions of a non-contributory system of old age pensions throughout the late 40's, though the Old Age Security Act did not become law until 1951.

By 1945 the population of the United States had topped 140 million, of which the top 8.5 percent held 20.9 percent of the country's personal wealth, down from 32.4 percent in 1929. This was an appreciable decrease in only 16 years, and a sign that the redistribution of wealth through taxation was having a positive effect. But the masses are never satisfied with the status quo, or even slow and steady improvement in their living standard. Our democratic system demands that any politician looking to get elected must offer the electorate more than the opposing party or parties. The stupidity of the arrangement is obvious. That which politicians promise to give to the people, they first must tax from the people, and a high percentage of those taxes will be absorbed by the government before the small balance trickles to the citizenry. This massive misuse by the government of its income is the groundswell of inflation.

President Roosevelt's inflation control order of April 1943 kept prices from climbing more than 29 percent from 1939-1945, but President Truman, by executive order, removed curbs in 1945. Housing shortages and pent-up demand for consumer goods led to runaway prices and rising wage claims, not only in North America but also in much of the world. In the United States strikes idled over 4½ million workers in 1946 with a loss of 116 million man days, the worst stoppage since 1919.

The Taft-Hartley Act, passed in 1946 over President Truman's veto, restricted organized labor's power to strike, outlawed the closed shop (which requires employers to hire only union members), prohibited use of union funds for political purposes, introduced an 80-day "cooling off" period before a strike or lockout could begin, and empowered the government to obtain injunctions where strikes "would imperil the national health or safety" if allowed to occur or continue.

The original purpose of strikes to force unscrupulous industrialists to improve working conditions and pay fair wages was successful. It proved to be the single most significant action workers could use to enforce compliance with their demands.

As unions strengthen financially, they are able to attract top flight leaders. These union bosses, to justify their increasingly high wages, have to constantly improve the lot of the people who elect them or be thrown out of their cushy positions. This leads to the identical pattern between workers and union leaders as with the citizenry as a whole and their various governments. In either case those seeking power are dependent on an electorate who will insist on a continuous upgrading in their lifestyle in exchange for keeping those politicians or union leaders in their position of authority.

There is only one source where money can ultimately be obtained to provide this increased living standard. That source is the money maker or producer. The primer movers, therefore, that furnish the wealth to generate both government and unions are that segment of society where the financial burden is steadily increased. Like building a fire in the woods to keep warm, if the fire gets out of control and burns the bush, the fire builder will freeze to death anyhow.

Producers, whether small independent entrepreneurs or huge industrialists, are profit oriented. All too frequently they allow the drive for increased earnings to influence decisions regarding wages and working conditions of employees who are vitally important to the success of any venture. This struggle for personal profit, however, distinguishes the primary difference between capitalism and socialism.

Capitalism is an economic system characterized by freedom of the market with increasing concentration of private and corporate ownership of production and distribution proportionate to increasing accumulation and reinvestment of profits. In contrast, socialism is a system where the producers possess both political power and the means of producing and distributing goods.

If free enterprise, or capitalism, is a superior arrangement over a completely government controlled society, or socialism, for the ultimate well being of all citizens, then a means must be found to curb the growth and power of all unions and governing bodies, while at the same time establishing a method to prevent the producers from running roughshod over the proletariat. This perplexing problem of how to balance the power of government, unions and corporations is the prominent factor in maintaining a successful democracy.

Although the war had ended, world affairs were still troublesome and disconcerting. The Nuremberg Tribunal sentenced twelve leading Nazis to death, including Ribbentrop and Hermann Goering (who committed suicide by taking poison). Rudolph Hess and Walter Funk were sentenced to life imprisonment.

Fascism was now nearly obliterated as a world peril. Communism, the next menace, was speedily threatening world order, though Marxism had been building up steam for a quarter century.

Winston Churchill described the escalating issues in his usual inimitable style. At a speech in Missouri in 1946, he said, "From Stettin in the Baltic to Trieste in the Adriatic, an iron curtain has descended across the Continent." He added that Moscow's totalitarian dominance has produced a decline of confidence in "the haggard world."

As the desperate planet prayed for deliverance from further bloodshed, people built their hopes on the United Nations that opened its first session in London on a Monday in January, 1946. Before the year was concluded, New York was selected as the permanent U.N. headquarters.

War-torn nations prayed for peace but were apprehensive as they watched the world divide into two colossal antagonistic camps. Still they began to rebuild their cities out of the rubble left by the worst destruction in the history of warfare.

The Marshall Plan was proposed by Secretary of State George C.

Marshall in 1947. It gave financial aid to European countries "willing to assist in the task of recovery." It was implemented the following year.

Warsaw was reconstructed in part from photographs to resemble its prewar appearance, and Tokyo was rebuilt as it was after the 1923 earthquake with houses numbered according to the order in which they were built.

It seems in retrospect that the world's depressing issues in the mid-forties should have overpowered any euphoria remaining from the conclusion of the world conflict, but in fact, they were mostly pleasant years with many events taking place that eventually would have just as substantial an effect on our personal lives as the present confrontation between the two super powers.

Jackie Robinson, the first black baseball player in the major leagues, signed with the Brooklyn Dodgers. This color breakdown in sports was essential in getting Black America into the mainstream of society, though it would be a long and uneasy transition. Nevertheless, within two decades black athletes would be a major influence in all North American sports.

The Flamingo Hotel was completed in Las Vegas in 1946 and began the transformation of that Nevada city into a resort of grandiose hotel casinos. It was built by "Bugsy" Siegel with backing from syndicate boss Meyer Lansky. Las Vegas was to become the gambling mecca of the world within two decades and would also appease my gambling appetite in later years.

The first unidentified flying objects made headlines in 1947, as businessman Kenneth Arnold claimed to have witnessed nine shiny pulsating objects flying over the Cascade Mountains at speeds up to 1700 miles per hour. The Civil Aeronautics Administration expressed doubts that anything would be flying that fast, but in the next 25 years, 15 million Americans will claim to have seen U.F.O.'s.

War songs were gradually disappearing, and romantic ballads flooded the air waves: "La Vie en Rose," "Seems Like Old Times," "To Each His Own," "Tenderly," and "Ballerina." There were also happy and snappy songs: "Too Fat Polka," "Ole Buttermilk Sky," and "Let It Snow, Let It Snow."

The movie industry was flourishing with a great variety of themes: "The Lost Weekend," "The Best Years of Our Lives," "Duel In The Sun," "The Razor's Edge," and "My Darling Clementine." Movie theaters were being erected at a great rate.

The year 1947 was also the year the bikini swimsuit was officially launched. It was designed by a Frenchman but wouldn't become popular in North America for another ten years. You could still buy a Hershey bar for a nickel.

In comparison to the ways and woes of the world, the dissolution of The Three Star Mink Ranch was inconsequential. The adaptability of human beings to adversity is one of the traits that allowed these creatures to survive. I was learning rapidly, though, that the spirit reacts differently depending on the dimensions of the misfortune.

So though I felt dispirited, I was far from broken, as I boarded a train for a 500-mile journey east into new adventures.

Chapter 12
Lumberjack!

In 1947 the scarcity of labor induced Ontario's paper companies to advertise for men in Winnipeg. They offered to reimburse the fare for those agreeing to work the winter in the woods. I signed up with Brompton Pulp and Paper, who arranged my train passage to Nipigon, Ontario, 400 miles east of Winnipeg. It was a picturesque journey, and I was enamored with the passing terrain. Elevations greater than a hundred feet were nonexistent across the prairie flatlands and lakes a rarity, so the panorama of soaring hillsides aflame with brilliant fall colors and sparkling lakes and rivers that seemed joined together like links in a gigantic chain had me gasping in delight.

Nipigon on Lake Superior is headquarters for several large pulp companies who also operate paper mills, the main source of employment in the area. Various companies had buses at the railway station to transport new employees to bush camps spread out over an expanse of hundreds of miles. A flurry of excitement at the station delayed things for a half hour while railroad employees and Ontario Provincial Police flushed off the train a few men who didn't disembark, and were trying to obtain a free ride to Toronto, Montreal, or other points east.

Aboard the Brompton bus, I was surprised to learn we had a 60-mile road trip to Beardmore, the regional base of operations for Brompton Pulp and Paper. Beardmore, with a permanent population of four hundred, had a commercial section much larger than comparable sized towns due to the enormous weekend influx of miners and woodsmen. Situated on the main thoroughfare were two hotels—the Northland and the Beardmore—each containing oversized beer parlors; five cafes, numerous assorted stores, a bowling alley, pool hall, and the office of Brompton Pulp and Paper. No legal hard liquor outlets were located closer than 50 miles. But at an establishment called The Hub, a few blocks off the main drag, illicit booze could be purchased with the proper credentials—money.

Within a radius of 20 miles a multitude of pulp camps were interspersed with numerous gold mines which were operating 24 hours a day. A fleet of fifty taxi cabs stationed in town were the only means of transportation, so with a phone in every camp, and lumberjacks and miners being notoriously heavy drinkers, a brisk cab business flourished between the camps and Beardmore.

I was assigned to Camp 47 located nine miles from town and three miles off the main highway on a road that almost defies description. With barely sufficient width for two vehicles to pass, it clung precariously to steep hillsides, crossed water courses over crude log bridges, zigzagged around rocky outcroppings and wound through never-ending stands of spruce, balsam and assorted hardwoods.

Relieved to arrive at Camp 47 safely, I little suspected at the time how often I would travel that torturous trail in the next seven months.

Camp 47 was not what I'd envisioned. Instead of three or four rough log cabins, nestled among tall trees, it was a self-sustaining settlement. A cleared area of at least ten acres contained twenty frame structures of various sizes such as bunkhouses, kitchen, office, stable, saunas, privies and garages. The complete encampment resembled a desert oasis but, in lieu of sand, was surrounded by a solid curtain of forest.

Although weary from the sixteen hour train journey without a sleeping berth, plus two bus trips to reach camp, I was too stirred up to rest.

It was a warm, bright mid-September afternoon as I wandered around the grounds familiarizing myself with my new surroundings. The pungent smell of fresh sawdust and new lumber, the constant crashing of falling timber, plus swarms of blackflies soon assured me I was no longer on the prairies.

It was early in the season, and the camp was half empty. At full capacity it accommodated up to 150 men, two-thirds of whom worked directly for Brompton Pulp & Paper and the balance employed by Gus Rentz, a German contractor. Gus, who owned a government lease controlling all acreage south of the camp, contracted to supply a stipulated number of cords of pulpwood annually to Brompton.

Both company and contractor employees shared most accommodations, including dining room, sauna, washing facilities, office and privies, but they were billeted in separate bunkhouses. Rentz's men were also paid directly by Brompton. I was assigned to Gus as a pulp cutter.

The main bunkhouse was built like a giant U. Each wing, with sleeping facilities for up to sixty men, was joined at the bottom of the

U by a large wash and laundry room. An array of wash tubs and basins were available to both wings, as were barrels of cold and boiling water.

The large kitchen employed one chief cook, an assistant, and four "cookies" or waiters. They shared separate living quarters, as did most of the truck drivers and machine operators.

Two hundred yards from the main buildings was the combination office and commissary where two clerks were responsible for camp records. They also acted as storekeepers, charging to each individual account any item bought from their commissary including tobacco, toiletries, confectionary, a variety of clothes, plus bush supplies such as sawblades, axes, files and other related equipment.

Close to the office was the camp manager's one-bedroom frame bungalow. It belonged to Captain Smith, recently discharged from the Army, who was married to an English war bride, the only female in camp.

The horsebarn accommodating ten animals was located next to an overflowing spring that never froze over and provided drinking water for both horses and the complex.

The bunkhouse interiors comprised only the barest essentials. Single steel cots lined each wall exactly 18 inches apart. Above each bed was a wooden apple box nailed to the wall to hold personal possessions. Suitcases went under the bed. A huge iron stove in the center of each wing provided the heat, and it was vitally important for personal comfort to carefully choose your cot's location from the stove. In frigid weather the far reaches of the building were almost like being outside, while beside the gigantic furnace, when red with heat, was similar to Dante's inferno. I was able to obtain a choice location. Stretched across the end of the room was a long plank table used mostly for cards but also as a writing desk. A small battery-operated radio, the table's only decoration, was used primarily as an alarm clock.

Remuneration was still low in the pulp industry, and all personnel, who were mostly piece workers, were covered by contract with the Wood Cutters and Sawmill Worker's Union. Pulp cutters worked for $5.85 per piled cord, haulers received $1.15 per cord, although the teamster was paid an additional $1.80 per day to look after the horses. Truckers, independent contractors, also earned on a cordage basis. They hauled from a central zone where the teamsters had unloaded to nearby rivers where in huge booms the wood was rafted in the spring down to Lake Superior and on to the paper mills.

Salaried employees earning from $5 to $8 per day, depending on the job, included dining room waiters, who also washed dishes, plus men called bull cooks who hauled water, chopped wood and stoked fires during the day, swept bunk houses and maintained wash areas. The chief cook and his assistant, plus the payroll and commissary clerks, worked on a monthly salary not covered by union contract. A charge of $1.85 daily was deducted from everyone for meals.

Andy Melnyk, Gus Rentz's second in command and "strip boss" (the man responsible for blazing and overseeing the strips), was a broad-shouldered, powerful Ukrainian. On the afternoon of my arrival, Andy inquired about my bush experience and advised me as to the equipment required. He recommended a sharp ax, a couple of Swede saw blades, files, a setter (a tool for setting saw teeth at an equal and proper width), and a pulp hook. The pulp hook was a short tool with a curved sharp steel spike that, when swung with one hand, would sink into the end of the eight-foot log providing a grip. By lifting one end of the log off the ground with one hand and placing the other arm under its length, you could balance the weight and lift and pile even the largest logs, some of which spanned twelve inches in diameter. To complete my outfit, I acquired a small haversack to tote equipment plus carry a lunch and thermos of hot coffee. Coming back for lunch would be too time con-suming, as I was informed my strip would be over two miles from camp.

Andy also informed me that the most important factor in successful pulp cutting was keeping the saw blade teeth sharp and evenly set. A dull blade requires two or three minutes of backbreaking labor to chew through a six-inch butt, while a correctly prepared blade slices through the wood as effortlessly as sawing soft butter. Unfortunately, sharpen-ing and setting a Swede saw blade is an art requiring bright light, keen eyesight, tolerable patience, and considerable practice.

The clang of the dinner bell was a welcome sound, as my food intake had been skimpy since leaving Winnipeg. Not knowing what to expect regarding meal content or serving procedure, I was delighted with my first repast. Although it was help-yourself pandemonium, with the plat-ters of victuals piled in a row along the center, the food was excellent and ample.

Large tureens of soup were served followed by several varieties of cold meat, plus a hot meat course (fish would be the main course on Friday, with roast chicken on Sunday). There were huge bowls of mashed potatoes, plus three other kinds of hot vegetables, tomatoes, onions and cucumbers, stacks of home-baked bread, plates of butter, cheese, and miscellaneous jams and jellies. Finally, for dessert there were three types of hot pies and an assortment of cakes and pastries.

At first the food disappeared as rapidly as the waiters placed it on the tables, but gradually the lumberjacks' appetites were appeased, and an ample supply of victuals still remained. Watching these huge, hungry men eat was unforgettable, and in the following weeks it was not unusual to see the occasional individual eat a dozen eggs and a pound of bacon for breakfast. Mealtime was the highpoint of the average woodsman's day.

The dinner gong rang five times daily except on Sundays. First bell was a 5 a.m. wake up call, then 6 a.m. breakfast, twelve o'clock noon lunch, 6 p.m. dinner, and 9 p.m. coffee and pastry. A large side table was heaped with lunch making provisions at the breakfast setting for those men not returning to camp for that meal. On Sunday mornings the 5 a.m. wake up call was omitted, and breakfast was at seven.

Andy was waiting the following morning to show Al and Russ Claxton, two brothers from Moose Jaw, Saskatchewan and myself our strips, which were adjoining. A pulpwood tract was divided into 80-foot strips with blazed sidelines distinguishing each cutter's exclusive territory. All trees over a four-inch butt had to be felled regardless if rotten or a variety of tree unusable for paper manufacturing. The government enforced this policy to make a cut over section more suitable for reforestation. Spruce, balsam pine, poplar and birch were acceptable for pulp and piled together, while other varieties were cut and stashed with limbs and tops. Stumps could not protrude more than three inches above ground so as not to impede sleighs during the haul. Pulp was piled on a wood base (usually formed from useless wood) beside a cleared eight-foot right-of-way and in a framework that would hold the eight-foot logs neatly in a four-foot by four-foot pile.

Sixteen-foot pulp logs, cut only in the company's sector, were skidded out by single horses to a main road where they were loaded directly on trucks. Every piece of pulp was stamped on the end by a steel hammer bearing the trademark of Brompton Pulp and Paper. Like cattle branding, the paper companies wanted to distinguish each other's logs when they were boomed to Lake Superior in the spring. My original intention was to produce two cords each day, but at the beginning it was unachievable. However, for twelve weeks before being transferred to the haul, I averaged that output. As I perfected my technique in preparing saw blades and became accustomed to handling the logs with the pulp hook, my output improved and the task became easier.

Except for the black fly menace, which lasted until the heavy frosts in early October, the days were enjoyable and the long string of pulpwood piles strung out behind attested to our productivity. The scaler, solely responsible for evaluating our yield, measured the wood (deducting any unsuitable pulp), stamped Brompton's name on each log with his steel hammer, put a six digit number on every pile with a blue crayon, and entered each cord on an individual slip with that number and recorded it in the office. It was a sensible system. If a cutter believed the scaler gave him short shrift on a pulpwood pile, he could easily pinpoint the area of contention and get a recheck. Also, everyone from the cutters to the sleigh and truck haulers were paid in accordance to the cordage stipulated on each numbered slip.

Snow fell frequently beginning in November and within a month reached three feet, requiring considerable struggle to fell the trees three inches above their roots. Though the task grew more arduous, the surroundings were invigorating, and sounds from the woods distinct with clear, calm, cold days especially sonorous. Scalers' hammers reverberating through the woods in a never-ending staccato, the ring of steel axes meeting wood, and the constant crash of falling trees was quite unique.

The Claxton brothers were good companions. We walked to and from our strips together and lunched each day beside a roaring camp-fire. Al, the eldest, was quite slim and not as rambunctious as Russ, who resembled Robert Preston, not only in his rugged good looks but also with his broad shoulders and husky build. Russ loved a vigorous wrestling match and constantly instigated a bout with me at every opportunity. Al always scolded him and insisted he stop horsing around. Generally Russ would grin sheepishly and back off.

One night in Beardmore five of us were sitting having a few beers in the Beardmore Hotel. There were the two Claxton boys; George Dubouis, a tall, strong, young French Canadian; Unas, who though not as large, was as tough as nails, and myself. Suddenly, another French Canadian came rushing in and talking excitedly in French informed George Dubouis that a Camp 47 man was getting beaten up at the Northland, the other hotel. It was a kind of understanding that camp-mates go to each other's assistance. So we rushed over. Approaching two combatants struggling on the ground, I recognized the one on the bottom as a chap from our camp. Surrounding the brawling pair were a dozen men.

"Brought your gawd-damn friends, eh!" one of them snarled as the group encircled the six of us.

Our guy, almost unconscious, was taking a vicious beating. In one motion, Unas and I grabbed the assailant under the armpits, pulled him off, and then lifted up the badly bruised Camp 47 victim. The hair was standing up on the nape of my neck, as I waited an onslaught from the ring of men. Glancing around, I saw the reason for the delay. Russ, a three-foot length of pipe held menacingly above his head and a wicked glint in his eyes, was on the verge of charging. He was restrained by Al, who, holding his arm in a vice grip, was hollering at our anticipated enemies.

"Go back to your beer, and let us take this man to a doctor, before someone gets killed."

Cautiously watching Russ the men picked the victor off the ground where Unas and I had tossed him, and with no further conversation or threatening motions, dispersed. Unas, George, and I stood helpless while Al tried to cool down Russ, who was in a rage, even though he hadn't been involved in the brawl, didn't know who was responsible, nor how it got started. Finally Al, in a calm voice, but not releasing his brother's arm, persuaded him to throw away his lethal weapon, return to the hotel and enjoy our libation. Going to a doctor, the other two discovered our man had a fractured arm and broken nose.

Al was obviously concerned about his brother's temper, and an incident a couple weeks later substantiated this conviction. In the bunk-house I was standing between the Claxton boys' cots when Russ made a flying leap intending to land on my back. From the corner of my eye I saw the coming lunge, so bracing myself and swinging my hips in a whiplike fashion, I threw him into the wall like a ragdoll with a tremendous thud. While slowly picking himself up, I saw a glint in his eyes that spelled real trouble. But before Russ could spring, Al grabbed him around the throat and wrestled him to the bed. Intending no harm I went to apologize, but Al pleaded with me to return to my bunk.

The Claxtons left camp next morning, and though we'd enjoyed excellent companionship over ten weeks, they never bade me farewell. Their strange behavior was explained by sheer coincidence two weeks later.

It was common for men to scribble names, addresses, and graffiti over the camp's lumber walls around their beds. A few days before Christmas a man arrived who noticed the Claxton boys' names. He inquired if anyone knew them, and I was pointed out as being their closest camp acquaintance.

"I'm Bob Farmer," he said, extending his hand. "I do a little writing, and I'm putting together an article on pulp camps, so I came to get some firsthand knowledge. My home is in Moose Jaw," he continued, "I understand you knew the Claxtons."

I told Bob of my relationship with the two brothers and in further discussion remarked how Russ and I frequently horsed around.

"He has a bad reputation in Saskatchewan," Bob interrupted. "After several free-for-alls at dance halls and beer parlors, Russ Claxton finally killed a man with a club. He was acquitted on the basis of self-defense, but it is generally accepted that his father's influence as a big shot on the railroad and the fact they hired the finest attorneys are the reasons he isn't behind bars."

"Well," I replied rather weakly, "I did see an indication of bad temper in Russ."

A bad temper, indeed, I thought. If it hadn't been for Al, I could easily have been another victim, but I wondered if those twelve men in

Beardmore received a mental message when Russ was brandishing his length of pipe that caused their unusual retreat.

The Claxtons' cots were not empty long. Days were strenuous, but time passed swiftly as a steady stream of men arrived and departed Camp 47. In the average pulpwood camp 25 percent of the personnel were responsible for 75 percent of production. Many men either lacked experience and couldn't cope or were alcoholics and earned just enough to get drunk for a few days. Others were just plain lazy and lasted from a few days to a month at most.

After supper and on Sundays card games flourished, and I participated in them all. Poker was the most popular, but cribbage and a crude form of bridge were also played. The stakes in poker varied from a 25-cent limit to the occasional session that reached five bucks.

Regular poker, such as stud and draw, were played plus wild-card variations including Kings and Little Ones, Wild Pansy, and Baseball. However, the most popular was Double Up, a game in which nothing was wild. Two cards were dealt to each player with five cards face down in the center, turned up one at a time between bets and used by all. No checking was permitted; you either bet the stipulated amount or folded. The first bet was a dime, second 20 cents, third 40 cents, and so on, with the wager on the fifth card being $1.60. I was uncannily lucky, but Double Up was a superb test of poker ability. Stakes were high compared to the $11.70 we earned from producing two cords of wood requiring nine hours of hard labor.

The key to success in Double Up was reading the players when the bet reached 80 cents. Greenhorns couldn't hide their reluctance in parting with their money when dealt a poor hand or their exuberance if they held a likely winner. With an average hand such as a top pair, two small pair (though a high card often won), and confident the other players didn't hold much, I tried to position myself to be the second or third better on the final card. I raised on the 80-cent card in an attempt to scare out those between me and the player under the gun on the last card. If already in that position, I avoided raising. The importance of being second better was the shock effect. After the opener laid down $1.60 and I suddenly increased it to $3.20, those behind faced a tough decision unless they held a good hand. Bluff definitely won more pots in Double Up than good cards.

One night I was dealt a Double Up hand in a situation poker players dream about. My two dealt cards were a pair of red nines, the first card turned was the nine of clubs, the second the ace of clubs, and the third the ten of clubs, at which point those players who held two clubs now had a flush and began to raise. The fourth card, the nine of spades, gave me an absolute cinch with four nines, but one player had two aces in his hand, so with a full house, aces on top, he believed he had a sure thing and raised me. I called, hoping the last card was a club. When the deuce of clubs was turned over, action was guaranteed. The player with the king of clubs felt secure, and the two players with the queen and jack (which were both dealt) dare not fold. I took enough cash out of the pot to equal twelve cords of piled pulp representing a week's strenuous exertion.

Many of us quit a little earlier on Saturday afternoons allowing time to clean up and change before supper in preparation for a night in town. It was a three-dollar cab fare to Beardmore, and the cabs loaded six, so it cost 50 cents per rider each direction. The bowling alley and pool hall were usually crowded, so we invariably ended up boozing. Normally we started off at one of the two beer parlors, but generally ended up at The Hub, the local nightclub which was built and owned by Mary Hub. It was common gossip that Mary got the money for The Hub's construction by using her body as well as her head.

The Hub really wasn't much of anything, but on the other hand it was a little bit of everything. One section used as a dance hall had a jukebox, a battered old piano, plus several tables and chairs scattered down the sides providing a place to sit and drink the watered-down rotgut sold at bootleg prices or a setup if you had your own whiskey. The refreshment counter at one side in an alcove served anything from coffee to corn whiskey, and either behind or sitting on the stools in front were half a dozen waitresses who could be persuaded to come onto the dance floor and carouse with the drunken patrons if they felt the effort would result in suitable remuneration.

The favorite activity in Beardmore on weekends, though, was brawling, and during my tenure in the area, I saw and was involved in a number of them. Several prevailing conditions were responsible, with drunkenness usually supplying the spark, but three distinctly opposing factions in the region at the time provided a combustible fuse. Miners and lumberjacks, alway antagonists, constantly engaged in free-for-alls, generally because too many men were trying to share too few women. Many houses in Beardmore were three faceted—residences, bootleggers and a brothel. However, another ingredient was present that contributed to the general chaos. Bitter feelings existed and were escalating between native Canadians, many of whom were veterans, and newly arrived displaced persons. Canada, like several other nations, had agreed to accept thousands of D.P.'s, who, looking for immediate employment, flocked to the bush camps and mines. These refugees, fresh out of internment camps from Central Europe, were as tough, rugged and spoiling for a fight as any Canadian. Thus, the stage was set for action.

The Woodcutters and Saw Mill Workers Union, as well as the Mine Workers Union, were just getting firmly established in the area. They already had improved conditions in the camps tremendously. Sacks of straw, haven for body lice, and doubled-decker bunks had been replaced by single steel cots and padded mattresses. Proper washing and laundry facilities were provided. Food inspection was enforced, and balanced diets were now the norm rather than the exception. However, the most sought after betterment was an increase in both wages and the unit price per cord to all pieceworkers. The camps were an open shop, and whether the D.P.'s had been warned not to join the unions or because of their inherent hatred of anything remotely linked to Communism, I don't know, but they rarely signed up. This infuriated both the Canadian miners and lumberjacks.

The breeding grounds for most fights was the hotel beer parlors where the different cliques assembled only a few feet apart. When alcohol heated the blood, one wrong word could provoke a riot, and with only two Ontario Provincial Police Officers stationed in Beardmore, it usually went unchecked.

One Saturday evening, short of cash, I chose not to go to town with the boys with whom I chummed around. A poker game started amongst a different group who were waiting for a taxi. Borrowing ten bucks from Gus Rentz, I cut myself in. My fortunes were never better, and by the time that taxi arrived, I'd won $70 and most of the money in the game. I was shamed into going to Beardmore with them to pay for the cab and buy a couple of rounds.

Shortly after entering the Northland Hotel my own buddies showed up and persuaded me to join them for a party at The Hub. Before leaving I gave the waiter two bucks for two rounds for the boys with whom I came and heard one in a heated debate with a group of D.P.'s at the adjoining table.

Three hours later we returned, and the Northland was in a shambles, with broken chairs, tables and shattered glasses strewn across the huge beverage room. The waiters attempting to clean the mess attested to the ferocity of the battle. The next day the Camp 47 boys, who had been involved, were badly wounded with cracked ribs, black eyes, busted noses, and cuts and bruises.

Fortunately, my luck at cards in the early evening had continued at the Northland Hotel because if my own group hadn't arrived, I'd have been a participant in another brawl that at the moment didn't interest me. What I didn't know was that the causes of the conflict already had me entwined in its complicity.

Camp 47 had a small percentage of men with union cards, but with no camp steward, there was no concentrated effort to enlist new members. The battle in Beardmore had been instigated by D.P.'s making snide remarks to union men, or vice versa, and the impetus in camp was now to become more unionized. A request was sent to the Wood-cutters and Sawmill Workers Unions' head office at the Lake Head (Port Arthur + Fort William) to dispatch an organizer. A union official arrived within a week and rapidly signed a large ratio of our men into their ranks but insisted a camp steward had to be elected immediately. The man selected had to be employed for three months prior to his nomination. This stipulation was required so that if an employer fired a newly appointed steward it was considered an objection to unionization rather than dissatisfaction with the employee. Unless there was a good reason for the dismissal, the union would close the camp.

During my three months working for Rentz, I became friends with several of the old-timers. Two of them, Gus's younger brother Paul, and his partner, Larry, prevailed upon me to join the union and take on the non-paying position, as no one else who qualified would accept the responsibility. So not by popular vote but by acclamation, I unexpectedly became the new steward of Camp 47. I was ill prepared for the role because suddenly, without any previous training, I became combination doctor, father confessor, union steward, and Joe-Boy. Many involvements were bizarre, to say the least.

Several illiterate men in camp asked me to read letters from wives containing exceedingly personal remarks, and then requested I pen their replies. As it was their only means of communicating with loved ones, their delight at news from home outweighed any embarrassment to them, but my face was damm red at times. However, that was only a minor irritation.

If someone spit on the bunkhouse floor, it was insisted I have the culprit thrown out of camp. An argument at a card game had me called on as final judge. Anyone too near or far from the stove would bring a request to reshuffle the bunkhouse beds; a pulp cutter's belief he was short changed by a scaler would automatically involve me; and complaints about the menu were always dumped on my lap. Generally, I could straighten out these situations without too much aggravation, but during one of the coldest spells of the winter, dysentery struck, and I had my hands full. It spread through camp like a prairie fire, and for three days very few men went to work.

A couple of three-hole privies located a hundred yards from the bunk house with small wood stoves and kerosene lanterns, were sufficient to handle normal traffic, but during the emergency they were not nearly adequate. It was a trying situation to make a 100-yard dash in the middle of a 40-below zero night wearing nothing but long johns and a pair of boots. But to get there and discover the outhouse filled to capacity was a catastrophe. Being forced to squat in the snow in subzero weather made men ugly, quarrelsome and looking for a scapegoat to vent their frustration. Some fellows, with a serious case of dysentery, were accused of playing cards in the privies. Others were charged with relieving themselves on the pathways and so on.

I felt certain all would be forgotten once the sickness had dissipated, and this proved correct, except for one thing. Several men contended the cause of the stomach cramps was due to soap left on dishes. This was an old camp superstition, but these men nevertheless insisted the kitchen attendants be dismissed. The cook said the charge was ridiculous, and if any of his staff were fired, he and his assistant would also walk off the job. Our meals were excellent, well prepared and of good variety, and I wasn't going to be responsible for what seemed like an unnecessary change.

I had Hank Wojik, our head clerk, telephone Brompton's doctor in Beardmore to get an opinion. He reported to me that the doctor said the camp had the flu and nothing else. Armed with this information, I called a general meeting, had Hank Wojik announce his conversation with the doctor, and then told the men if they persisted on firing the kitchen staff, I would resign as steward. The overwhelming support for my position quieted the revolt in the ranks, and I never had my authority questioned again except once by Andy.

At the time of my appointment the night watchman was Gus Rentz's eighty year old father, whose responsibility was to keep the huge wood stoves stoked during the cold winter nights. We were located in the White River District, an area that claimed to be the coldest in Canada. Several times during winter the temperature dropped to over 60 degrees below zero. Gus's old father always made certain the stoves in his son's quarters were well fueled but frequently would fall asleep on our side of the bunkhouse; and the men in the company quarters would spend a miserable night. Also on occasion, he would fail to tend the fires in the garages, and in the mornings the truck drivers and machine operators would spend an hour struggling to start their vehicles. All those affected came screaming to me to have him fired.

I warned the old fellow twice, but when it happened a third time, I had no alternative but to have him replaced. Thus I found myself in the position of firing my boss's father. Gus understood and didn't hold any hard feelings, but Andy decided to reprimand me for my action. One weekend afternoon during a camp party he became ugly and invited me out into the snow for a tussle. Following him out of the bunkhouse, I was determined to get in the first blow, so as he turned, I swung. Andy, stepping back, tripped over a pile of wood buried in the snow and went sprawling. He let out a holler, and when the boys rushed from the bunkhouse and saw big Andy sprawled in the snow, they assumed I must have decked him. Andy, quite drunk, wasn't sure whether I'd hit him or not, and I didn't let on. From then on I had no problem with troublemakers and was considered a man not to tangle with.

Gus Rentz only required two crews to haul pulp to the landing sites. The pulp haul was the prime winter money maker in a pulpwood camp, and as senior employee, I was offered first opportunity and a fine team of sturdy bay geldings. For my partner I chose Harry Lafleure, a robust Metis from St. Boniface, Manitoba, a suburb of Winnipeg. Metis is half French and half Cree Indian. Our sleighs were double bobs that fully loaded could hold up to three cords of eight-foot pulp, but this was possible only if it was a short haul of a couple hundred yards or less, with no sharp rises. Otherwise, we averaged only half that amount.

If the horses were unable to pull the load up any hill, and we were forced to partially unload the heavy pulp, it was time consuming and costly, as we were working for $1.15 per cord.

Urging our horses up inclines brought forth a stream of oaths from both myself and Doug Smith, the other teamster. One week while hauling into the main camp area we had to bypass Captain Smith's house which was situated at the top of a fairly steep knoll. Standing on top of the load of swaying pulp to better control the horses, we prodded our animals into a run within a hundred feet of the hill and into a full gallop by the time we reached the bottom. At this point, our conversation became salty and vociferous. The only language in its proper deliverance to which horses paid any heed.

"Hey, hey, get going, you f---ing pair of long-eared donkeys! Get the lead out of your ass. Hey, Hey, move it, you bastards! If I have to unload this pulp, there'll be no gawd damm oats for you tonight."

Holding the reins taut to give the horses footing but whirling the ends and occasionally slapping them on the flanks, the goading became more urgent as we neared the crest.

"Hey, hey, hey. Come on, get moving, you lazy pair of bay sons of bitches; by the lightning Jesus, if we get stalled, I'll slug you with a chunk of this gawd damm pulp."

If success was still in doubt nearing the top as the animals were laboring hard, then the final few crucial yards would bring forth a further stream of screaming curses until the sleigh was on the flat, which was within a hundred feet of the Smith's residence.

Mrs. Smith wrote a derogatory letter to the local newspaper about the colorful language of Canadian lumberjacks which was published a few weeks later. But her husband, Captain Smith, knowing of his wife's concern, came and asked if we could tone down our language for a few days.

"Smitty," I answered. "Do you realize if we don't make that hill, what we have to do?"

"I admit it would be a hell of an inconvenience," he answered.

"Then imagine me urging my horses. Please horses, don't stop, gawd darn I won't feed you no oats, if we have to unload."

"I get the message, Slim," Captain Smith responded laughing. "I'll tell the Missus to stay inside and keep the windows closed for the balance of the week."

Because time was of the essence when working on piecework, Doug Smith and I figured we could make more money when facing severe inclines if we took larger loads and helped each other up the hills. We unhitched the team from one load and hooked them to the sleigh tongue of the other, then followed the same procedure as when we were on our own, except that the teamster with the lead horses had to run beside his animals. Dashing through three feet of snow with the reins held tight, feet touching ground every ten feet was thrilling action, but today I don't know how I managed.

Coordination in the partnership was essential to making good money on the pulp haul. Each man, standing at opposite ends of the pulp pile, would swing his pulp hook setting the steel tip in the end of the log, and with a rhythm that only came from working together, would swing the eight-foot pulp simultaneously onto the sleigh. This identical motion was used when unloading.

After working together a while, each man would even sense at what pulp log the other was aiming, and this intuition made the task less laborious and more profitable.

Doug Smith and I both had first-class partners. Harry Lafleure was steady and congenial, while big John Stroeder, Doug's partner, was a strong, happy-go-lucky German D.P. We hit a stretch of weather when for three successive days the thermometer dropped at night to 60 below. The clear, frigid days were too cold for horses to work, because they would suffer lung damage in the frosty air. After two days of card playing, sleeping and reading, we got fed up with the bunkhouse and decided to go out for a few hours and shovel snow off the pulp piles. Wearing wool-lined parkas with fur trimmed hoods, the only part of our anatomy exposed to the subzero temperature was our faces. Because of the record cold, we took a camera to snap pictures of the event. The strips we wanted shovelled were two miles from camp. We'd only worked a few minutes when standing next to John having his picture taken, I noticed one of his cheeks turning white, and within seconds, so was his nose. He thawed it with his bare hands, and we immediately headed back, but the slight breeze in our faces made it impossible to keep John's face from freezing, even though we all took turns removing our mitts and warming his flesh. By the time we reached camp he was severely frostbitten. The misfortune never stopped Big John from completing the haul as Doug's partner, but I lost Harry for an entirely different and cursed circumstance.

Everyone halted work at noon on Christmas Eve, and though there was a long wait for taxis, most of our camp mates, like the men from other pulp and mining camps in the surrounding region, headed for Beardmore. Between three and four thousand bodies were milling the town streets, mostly drunk, and I often wondered where all the whiskey came from, which by midnight was selling for upwards of $50 per quart.

Some Christmas spirit was evident, but scuffles erupted in every quarter, and at one point I watched a cruiser with four Ontario Provincial Police officers drive up where a free-for-all was taking place. Before they opened the doors of the vehicle, a dozen men grabbed the squad car and were about to turn it over. When one of the police fired a shot over their heads, the mob retreated, and the Provincials simply drove away. There was no way they could have gained control without using firearms in earnest. Knives, clubs and broken bottles instead of guns, were the weapons employed in the many melees I witnessed, but life was as cheap in Beardmore those years as it ever was in Deadwood, South Dakota, in its heyday where the six-shooter was the master.

When I was ready to return to camp at midnight, Harry Lafleure was uncontrollably drunk and impossible to reason with. At daylight on Christmas morning a cab driver found him lying unconscious in the snow in freezing temperatures. He dragged him into a heated cab office. Harry survived, but his Indian blood didn't allow him to sober up for two weeks until he was stone broke and terribly ill.

I never saw Harry again after Christmas Eve, but I got the report from Gus Rentz, who knew everyone in town. Though heavy hearted with the news, because a sober Harry was a fine human being, I was to get further lessons that Christmas season about the horrors of alcohol.

Louis LaPointe, also from Winnipeg and a teamster for Brompton, was a friend with whom I played poker and bridge. Good natured and congenial, he told me he had a liquor problem and therefore never went to town. Also, with a young wife and two children, he wanted to save his dough.

Louis, in Captain Smith's company during the battle for Europe, was known as the Mad Frenchman because of his wild escapades when drunk. A quart of whiskey stashed in my suitcase had been saved for Christmas day. Going over to water and feed my horses at 7 a.m. I took the booze to give the other teamsters a Christmas drink. Louis was at the stable when I passed around the liquor.

"Go ahead and have a Christmas shot, Louis," I encouraged, passing him the bottle.

"Slim, I may be sorry," he replied, as he looked longingly at the booze.

"Aw, what he hell," he said as he took a generous slug.

Before breakfast the five of us emptied the quart, and Louis gulped his share with increasing relish.

By ten o'clock in the morning the six of us, including Louis, obtained a cab to go to Beardmore where we spent the day drinking and carousing, returning to camp at five o'clock, an hour before Christmas supper. Louis became more rambunctious as the day progressed. At first, he was just noisy but then increasingly quarrelsome.

Back in camp I tried to persuade him to have a rest, but he wanted to wrestle. Louis wasn't a big man, and I easily picked him up and in jest tossed him on his bed. Jumping up like a rubber ball he accidentally bumped his head on his own apple box. In an unbelievable display of frenzy, he smashed the crate off the wall with his bare fists. His knuckles and hands were covered with blood, though I didn't know at the time he had broken a small bone in his hand. When the dinner bell rang, I made a dash for my Christmas meal. However, I was also heading for disaster. The huge dining room heater inside the front door was red hot. Someone unwittingly jostled me, and being tipsy, I lost my balance and headed for the furnace. Sticking my hand out to save my face I grabbed the searing stove severely burning the front of my right palm.

The pain was excruciating. A waiter coaxed me to sit at the table where he placed my hand in a pan of snow that eased the agony. Feeling better I decided to eat, and because of having only one usable hand, one of my buddies filled a plate with turkey and all the trimmings. A red-headed Irishman sitting at the table, Red Flannery, generally one of the first to get drunk but strangely cold sober, came over and looked at my hand, "Slim, as soon as you eat, come with me to the office. They have some ointment up there that will hurt like hell when applied but will soon take away the pain."

I gave him no argument, and we went directly from the dining hall. Another big Irishman, Bill MacDonnell, the assistant clerk, was on duty. In his mid-sixties Bill was a retired Kingston penitentiary prison guard. He was an excellent poker player, and I liked him, though he showed no mercy in a card game and had several enemies.

The medical supplies were in a trunk under Bill's bed. Red and another chap pinned me to the bed while Bill removed my hand from the snow, dried it off and applied the salve. My hair stood straight up for a minute or two, but as Red had promised, the pain soon vanished.

I had an enormous blister for a few days but never missed an hour of work. However, I was a lucky one.

As we sat chatting, Red told Bill about Louis, who had never shown up for dinner. I hoped fervently he was asleep.

Bill promptly said, "Bring the lad up if he's awake, and let me have a look at his hand. I have some healing powders."

Returning to the bunkhouse, Red advised me to go to bed saying he would look after Louis. I was delighted to comply.

About fifteen minutes passed when Doug Smith came racing through the door yelling, "Bill, hurry over to the office, there's a problem."

I thought my eyes were deceiving me when I entered the office. It looked like a cyclone had passed through since my departure twenty minutes before. The place was a shambles, and Bill's face was bruised and bleeding. Red filled me in. Louis seemed placable enough on the way over, Red said, and was quiet when he sat on Bill's cot, but as Bill knelt down to get medication from out of his chest, Louis lashed out with both fists screaming what a son of a bitch Bill was because he took his money in poker games. Red said before he could intervene, Louis grabbed a length of steel pipe and attempted to decapitate MacDonnell, meanwhile smashing the office furniture and other items to smithereens. Red finally grabbed the weapon and shoved Louis out the door.

Bill had already phoned the Ontario Provincials, and almost incoherent with rage, told them that Louis had attempted to murder him and wanted him so charged.

Red and I tried to calm Bill down with the thought that although there was significant damage in the room, he wasn't severely hurt and to take into consideration Louis was blind drunk.

Within a half hour, two Provincial Police constables, one a sergeant, entered the office. Bill, obviously relieved at their presence, nevertheless insisted they lock Louis up and charge him with attempted murder. The five of us were discussing the best method to handle the mad Frenchman when through the door, like a charging bull, came the man in question.

Heading straight for Bill, he was hollering, "MacDonnell, you rotten old son of a bitch. I'll get even with you."

Before he reached Bill, the young cop grabbed Louis by the shoulder, spun him and threw two rapid punches; the first broke his nose, and the second knocked out two teeth. He then threw him across the bed like a rag doll. Louis, bawling like a baby, was speedily regaining his senses.

Bill, still not satisfied, insisted LaPointe be locked up.

"Mr. MacDonnell," the sergeant pleaded, "to put the man in jail we will have to drive 55 miles to Nipigon and back. Before your call we were going to sit down with our families to Christmas dinner. I am sure you'll be having no further trouble with LaPointe."

Bill was adamant, and it looked like an impasse when in walked Captain Smith. Hearing about the ruckus, he came directly over. After listening to the whole story, he asked Bill to trust him with LaPointe until morning.

Bill, who had great respect for Smitty, finally acquiesced, and we all heaved a sigh of relief—each for his own reasons. As I watched a bloody, dejected Louis follow Captain Smith from the room, my heart was heavy with the shame I felt. Perhaps he would have drank anyway—that I would never know, but I did know that I was responsible for the first one. A lesson I would never forget nor repeat. Smitty put Louis on a train for Winnipeg the following day, because with a broken hand he was no longer able to haul pulp.

The holidays had been a disaster; not only had I lost a good friend in Louis, but Harry, my working partner, was permanently gone. Between Christmas and New Year's I tried a couple of new mates on the haul but wasn't satisfied with their performance. I had been associating with three fellows who were employed directly with Brompton: Andy McDougal, Ben Bishop and Joe Levesque, all from the east coast, veterans, and enjoyable company.

Aware Harry Lafleure was gone, Joe Levesque asked if I might consider him as a partner. I was apprehensive due to his short stature but nevertheless offered him a tryout. Joe was strong, willing and pleasant company, and soon we were throwing pulpwood like a well-oiled machine. He had one strange idiosyncrasy; Joe hated the female sex.

"All dames is for the birds," he would frequently say.

Joe Levesque, Acadian French, from Sydney, Nova Scotia, had a coal black moustache that matched his black hair, and whenever he became thoughtful or excited, it gave a noticeable twitch.

One day sitting on a pile of pulp to refresh ourselves with some hot coffee, Joe heaved a sigh and said again, "Slim, all dames is for the birds."

"Joe, what caused all this bitterness in you about women?" I asked.

Twitching his moustache, and looking at me quizzically, he replied, "I didn't realize my feelings were so conspicuous, but now you ask, I'll tell you."

Joe related events of a wretched childhood caused by the escapades of an errant mother. "My mother was a real party girl, Slim, a true tramp, and I don't know how my dad put up with her as long as he did. When I was about eight years old, he kicked her out, and I was sent to live with his brother Rene."

"Were there no others in the family?" I asked.

"Yes, I had a sister Mary, about three years younger."

"What happened to her?"

"She was boarded out to one of dad's five other brothers," Joe said, as he gulped the last of his coffee. "I've never heard from her or her whereabouts since that time."

I felt like giving Joe the obvious advice about not judging all women by his mother but decided to finish my coffee and go back to work.

One Saturday night a few weeks later, Ben, Andy, Joe and I taxied to Beardmore to let off steam. After sloshing beer for a couple of hours, the four of us pooled five bucks apiece for a bottle of bootleg Scotch.

"Let's grab a cab and go down to The Hub Bar," Andy said.

"To hell with The Hub, nothing but a bunch of cruddy dames and cheap whiskey," said Joe.

"Nothing else to do," Andy insisted.

Ben and I agreed, so we hailed a cab and struck out for The Hub.

The establishment was almost empty. The waitresses were in their usual positions, with an unobstructed view of all who entered and arranged themselves so all who entered got an interesting view of them. I immediately noticed one young lady with an attractive but haggard-looking face. She was short, about 5 feet 2 inches, and had coal black hair. Andy spotted her as rapidly as I did. "That's a cute thing with the black hair," Andy said, loud enough for everybody in the place to hear.

"Nothing but a bloody pig if she works in here," Joe spat out, also very loud.

Within a few minutes Andy had the girl on the dance floor, and Joe never missed an opportunity to pass a vulgar or uncomplimentary remark whenever they were within hearing range. Ben and I tried to shut Joe up because Andy was becoming upset, and the girl was furious. But the liquor had warmed Joe to his favorite topic, and he was uncontrollable. We finally managed to get Joe to the refreshment bar for a cup of black coffee, and to my annoyance and surprise the girl immediately left Andy, followed us to the bar, and began to help serve. She brought a cup of coffee to where I was seated a half dozen stools from Joe. Sliding the cup in front of me, and nodding at Joe, she said, "Who the hell is your mouthy friend?"

"Joe Levesque" I replied. "If it's any of your affair."

She seemed startled, but at the same time looked like she already knew. Staring at Joe she continued, "Know where he's from?"

"The east coast someplace—Sydney, I believe."

"Did ya ever hear him talk about his family?"

"Some."

"Ever hear him mention Rene Levesque?"

"I believe it was his uncle."

All at once I noticed the outstanding resemblance between her and Joe, and just as suddenly realized she had recognized it some minutes before.

The moment Joe became aware I was talking to the girl he charged over. "Slim, for gawds sake! Don't tell me you're getting wrapped up with this broad, too," he snarled.

"Shut up a minute and listen," I snapped at him.

Before he could open his mouth, the girl quietly said, "Joe, what was your father's name?"

"What the hell business is that of yours?" Joe roared.

I grabbed Joe by the arm and yelled, "Answer her."

Before either of us could say more, the girl, looking straight into Joe's eyes, said, "I have an uncle in Sydney name of Rene Levesque."

It was now Joe's turn to be numbstruck. "So have I," he murmured after a moment's hesitation, his eyes suddenly riveted on the girl's face.

"What is your father's name?" she asked again, her voice trembling.

"Louis."

"Joe, that was my father's name also."

"You're Mary?" Joe whispered in shocked disbelief.

"Yes," she nodded, tears streaming down her pretty face.

The next few minutes were spent in convulsive laughter, joyful embracing and tearful apologies. The full brunt of their discovery didn't strike them immediately, but after a good cry, they sat down alone at one of the tables in the dance hall.

The emotion packed fifteen minutes sobered all of us, so Ben, Andy and myself slurped coffee and without appearing too nosy kept glancing into the next room. After about a half hour, I noticed Joe hand Mary a wad of money which she tucked into her purse. Joe immediately got up and came over, "Let's get back to camp, boys. I can't blow no more dough. I've got a sister to support."

The following day Joe left camp by cab, picked Mary up at The Hub and took her to Geraldton, a town about fifty miles east. Geraldton, also a thriving pulpwood and gold mining center, was much larger than Beardmore. Joe got Mary a job as a waitress, this time with no strings attached. He reasoned that with a decent place to live and surrounded by more permanent type families, Mary had a better chance to stay out of trouble. He was beaming with satisfaction when he arrived back in camp that evening. "Slim," he said, "now that I've got a family to take care of, we're really going to toss pulpwood."

And toss pulpwood we did. We increased our previous output by a third. Joe had never been more congenial and chatty than in those next few weeks. "Slim, when we finish here this winter, Mary and I will go with you to Winnipeg, get a cozy apartment, meet some nice people, get a decent job, and the two of us will really get straightened out," Joe said.

"Sounds like a great idea," I agreed.

Late one afternoon a few days later a car drove into camp. At the wheel was a pimply faced kid and snuggled beside him was Mary. They wanted to see Joe. Joe went away with them for a few hours, and when he returned he looked troubled. "That bloody sister of mine has traces of her mother in her," he said. "I gave her most of my money, packed her off to Winnipeg with instructions to get a nice apartment, a good job and write to me when she was settled. I got rid of that goofball she was with. I'm sure she'll be okay now," he concluded, but somehow he didn't seem as convinced as before.

We went back to throwing pulpwood. Joe was now more thoughtful. "Do you think any of these dames ever straighten themselves out, Slim?" he asked one day.

I didn't know too much about it, but I knew what he was anxious to hear. "Sure," I said, as reassuringly as I could. "If you get them in the right surroundings, and give 'em a chance."

"I'll give her all the chances in the world," Joe said, "but I hate to be taken for a sucker. She has already cleaned me out of nearly four months' pay."

When a couple of more weeks passed without word from Mary, Joe was noticeably irritable. At times he was sure she was in some kind of trouble, and other times he was positive she was giving him the business. As for me, I was uncertain; surely, I reasoned, with all the help Joe had given her and the concern he had shown, she wouldn't be so hopelessly inconsiderate as to ignore him now. My assumption was correct; she didn't.

At dusk one night as Joe and I were pulling into camp with our empty sleigh, I spotted a taxi cab drive in and park beside the office. Out hopped Mary. Joe leaped off the sleigh and raced towards her. As my rig drew closer, I was flabbergasted to see painted on the door of the cab The Winnipeg Yellow Cab Co. Winnipeg was over five hundred miles west.

Joe and Mary spent about an hour in the office. When all three emerged, Mary and the cabbie took off together, and Joe trudged wearily to the bunkhouse. He came over to where I was watching out the window. "Feel like going to town for a couple of beers?" he asked.

"Sure do, Joe." I wouldn't have turned him down at that moment for anything in the world.

An hour later as we sat down in the Beardmore Hotel with a bottle of ale, Joe began to talk. "She was in some kind of trouble, Slim," he said. "I had to give her every dime I had left to pay the cab fare and help her out of it. I promised I'd meet her in Winnipeg next week, so you'd better get yourself another partner. I'll be leaving camp tomorrow."

I didn't attempt to talk him out of it because he obviously had made up his mind; however, I did say, "Joe, are you sure that girl is really worth it? I'm getting suspicious she's just taking you for a ride."

"Don't worry, everything is going to work out fine." Then Joe added, "Slim, could you loan me fifty bucks for a month? I'll mail it to you at this camp if you're planning on staying a while."

"Sure will, and I expect I'll be here for another month," I replied.

Entering the bunkhouse after breakfast the next morning I was surprised to find Joe still with us, because the bus left Beardmore for Winnipeg at 6:30 a.m. "Change your mind, Joe?" I asked.

"No, I'm catching a later bus," he offered, his moustache dancing as he thrust his hand out in farewell.

Andy was my new partner. Heading to the bush for our first load, he said, "I never realized there were two buses to Winnipeg each day."

"I don't believe there is," I replied, "but I know there is one leaving for Montreal before noon."

A few weeks later Andy and I went to town and ended up at The Hub. To my great astonishment, behind the counter stood Mary.

"Did Joe find you?" I asked.

Her face flushed angrily. "I'd like to know where that skunk went," she said. "I waited for him in Winnipeg for three weeks. Do you know where he is? I phoned the camp and was told he'd left."

I was glad to admit that I didn't.

Ironically enough, the next morning I received an envelope from Joe which contained fifty bucks and a note. The note read simply, "Thanks a million, Slim, and remember, all dames is for the birds."

Doug Smith, his partner John, plus Andy and I completed the haul for Gus Rentz in late March as the snow was rapidly disappearing, though at the peak of winter there was an unbelievable seven feet on the flat. Doug, who was from Regina, planned to leave camp with me so we could spend a couple of days relaxing in Winnipeg. Captain Smith asked me to spend a few days with the company to help clean up some scattered piles of pulp before sledding completely vanished for the season. Requiring a partner, I offered Doug the job, and he agreed. Smith was giving us a special rate allowing us to supplement our winter's stake.

We agreed to remain a week. After four days, the bare spots in the roads were getting too numerous for hauling a decent pay load, so we were going to quit when Hank, the clerk, told me that union headquarters in Port Arthur had phoned to inquire if I was still in camp and, if so, requested I remain until the weekend. A Ralph Potter would be coming in to pay me a visit. I persuaded Doug to control his patience and promised to leave for the West as soon as I saw Potter, who arrived on Saturday afternoon.

Ralph Potter was an affable young man, and after introducing himself, looked me square in the face and said, "Mr. Phillips, we would like to talk to you about working for the union; you have an outstanding record of enlisting recruits in Camp 47, and we desperately require this kind of dedication throughout northern Ontario."

I was astounded, to say the least. It was true that almost any man remaining in camp for a week or more was signed up, but it wasn't a big deal with me. When it looked like they would stick around a while, I went and said, "Here, Jim, Tom or Bob, we want you in the union if you don't already belong, and it will cost so much. Please sign here." Very few refused or gave me an argument, so if my record was so good, I had to assume other stewards didn't put in any effort.

While I tried to comprehend the offer, Ralph continued, "I can't go into details; you'll have to go to the Lakehead and meet with the top officials for that. You would receive a monthly salary, car and a generous travel allowance."

"How far would I travel?" I asked.

"You would be assigned a territory that might contain up to a hundred camps. We believe it is vitally important to completely unionize the skeleton crews who remain in the bush year around. They will provide the incentive and sound foundation to enroll the new men who will begin pouring into the camps by the late summer. We want strong representation, because almost certainly there will be a strike called by early fall when the main cutting season is about to begin."

"Strike?" I asked increduously. The word hit me like a thunderbolt. "Why a strike?"

Ralph jumped in excitedly. "Mr. Phillips, are you satisfied with the money you earned this winter, while the greedy paper companies are making millions and gouging ordinary laborers like you to gain those profits?"

"No, Mr. Potter," I responded hesitantly, "I wasn't satisfied with the price per cord I received, either for cutting or on the winter haul. I will always strive to earn more money because that's part of my nature. But it's the most money I've ever made daily or weekly, and if we approach the companies for a higher rate per cord, how do we know they won't grant it?"

Ralph looked at me impatiently. "Bill, if I may call you that, you miss the point. If the companies grant the increase without a strike, imagine what we might get if we either threaten or go out on strike?"

"Look, Ralph," I was warming up to the subject. "It's that exact philosophy that worries me, and I have trouble accepting. Do the union officials know what the companies can afford to pay, or are negotiations like a rubber band that we keep stretching until it finally breaks, at which point we have nothing? It seems to me that you already have decided to strike before even talking to the pulp and paper companies about a new contract."

"You're too naive. It's obvious, Bill, you don't understand that to get the attention of the money-grabbing paper companies, we have to play rough."

"And it's just as obvious to me, Ralph," I retorted hotly, "you don't understand that the old adage "you can catch more flies with honey than with vinegar" has got to apply to negotiations between unions and companies, the same as between a husband and wife. I've had no experience with either, but it's only logical."

Ralph got up, extended his hand and said, "Bill Phillips, do me a favor and come into our office at Port Arthur, speak to some of our top officials, and then make a decision."

I thanked him for his time and promised to do exactly that.

That evening I discussed the offer with Paul Rentz and Doug Smith. We all agreed that pulp companies, like most corporations, are greedy and didn't give their employees a fair shake unless forced to. Now the unions were adopting that identical code, and eventually the working men would get caught in the middle. Going into a bargaining session, already knowing we were going to strike, was like telling your father if he didn't give you more money, you would poison the dairy herd. If he let you proceed with your threat, you'd have the satisfaction of beholding a lot of dead cows, but with no source of income, you not only wouldn't get an increase but no wages at all. An old Greek fable described this scenario well in *He Killed the Goose That Laid the Golden Egg.*

Still undecided when I retired Saturday night, I informed Doug, if our affairs were straightened out with Brompton, we could leave for the Lakehead the following day. Either I would stop at Port Arthur and see the union or proceed directly to Winnipeg with him.

By the time the breakfast bell rang, my mind was already made up. I sympathized with the union position. As they were just gaining power, they were anxious to test their wings, but it was already obvious they would abuse their power as badly as the money grabbing corporations had done for decades. I felt their psychology was wrong and their impetus aimed incorrectly.

I wrote a short thank you letter to union headquarters and enclosed my union card. It was my opinion at the time that unions during the previous half century were entirely responsible for improving the lot of the masses, including mine, and were still amending ills that existed in various industries. However, already having seen examples of union power being utilized as ruthless as corporate omnipotence, I elected to be an onlooker until I was more enlightened.

Doug and I arrived at Beardmore at noon and had to wait three hours for a bus. The town looked like a cyclone had struck. Garbage, including empty beer and whiskey bottles, was strewn from curb to curb. Drunks littered benches and sidewalks, some trying to gain a little relief from after-shave lotion or rubbing alcohol. Windows were broken on both sides of the main thoroughfare.

Man, I thought, is indeed a strange paradox. During the winter a team of horses had been found dead in a small stable. Abandoned, they had starved or frozen to death. It was a terrible and inexcusable tragedy, and the S.P.C.A., police, and citizens were up in arms for a week to locate the culprits and bring them to justice. Rightfully so, but somehow we fail to associate helpless drunken men in the same category as defenseless animals and show little pity or concern when their plight is as vulnerable.

Doug and I ran into three other men heading for the Lakehead, so we decided to hire a large cab. Though it was 125 miles, the cab was only a little more expensive, and we were all in a hurry to leave booming, brawling Beardmore.

Doug and I made good train connections in Port Arthur and arrived in Winnipeg by Monday noon. We got a nice hotel room, then went on a buying spree for new clothes and all the accouterments, plus a bottle of whiskey. We reminisced, relaxed and drank, and by evening decided to chase girls. We were lucky and found a couple, although I admit they weren't running too fast. The next day I returned to Monominto.

My timing in returning to Monominto was perfect. Jack and the neighbors had just begun sawing the annual output of house fuel and cordwood and desperately needed a man to catch the blocks.

Business at the store was fair, but the family was living off the shelves and dissipating the profits because there was no longer any income from the weekly sale of cream, eggs, or other farm products. Mother arranged with a Winnipeg orphanage for a little girl to live with them and provide companionship for Joyce, especially to and from school. This made a total of seven hungry mouths to feed, including mine.

The mortgage payment was behind, as usual, so I gave father $150 to take it out of arrears.

Jack had cut a little cordwood during the winter, but otherwise had no income, as his Air Force credits had dried up. He suggested we crop the farm on a partnership basis, so I put up the money for seed grain until he sold his cordwood. Dad didn't interfere with us cropping, haying or cutting wood off the home farm, but steadfastly refused to turn the title over to Jack and me. He simply couldn't abide the thought of parting outright with the ownership of his utopia.

The farm required new fencing to protect the fields from marrauding cows, and Jack consented to accept that responsibility. As there would be no income from hay or grain sales until fall, it was obvious one of us had to earn cash, so I was on the lookout for employment.

John Senyk drove over to the store one day with a shiny black 1942 Ford sedan. It was a beauty. As I was admiring the vehicle and wondering how long before I could afford one, John said,

"Bill, what are you doing this summer?"

"Looking for work," I replied. "How about you?"

"I have a job as a dragline operator and need an oiler. I think you could handle the job," John stated.

"If the pay is reasonable, I'm your man, John," I responded with enthusiasm.

John got the position through his younger brother, Pete, who was married to Ed Barham's sister, Irene. Pete had been a dragline operator for several years. They were working for a contractor who was building a section of provincial highway 15 miles west of the town of Seven Sisters Falls into a virgin lake area in the White Shell Forest Reserve. Seven Sisters was a 70-mile drive northeast of Monominto.

I started work with Johnny the second week in May and thoroughly enjoyed zooming along in his sleek new automobile. For reasons I never ascertained, the dragline and bunkhouses had laboriously been taken by bulldozers ten miles into the virgin bush. We began constructing the road grade back out to Seven Sisters. Therefore, we parked the car and walked ten miles along the freshly cleared right-of-way to reach our machine; whereas, if we had simply built the road the opposite direction, we could have brought our car along the fresh grade and saved one hell of a lot of hiking. The contractor was hired by the Manitoba government, which probably explained the strange arrangement. I never could understand government planning.

We operated two 12-hour shifts six days a week with a crew of five including Pete Senyk and his oiler, either Paul or Mike Kruchak, John Senyk and I, plus Alec, the one-eyed cook.

A small twenty foot trailer bunkhouse provided living and sleeping quarters for four of us, and a sixteen footer acted as kitchen, dining room and Alec's accommodations, so our quarters weren't exactly deluxe.

My responsibilities were simple. Every six hours the machinery was thoroughly greased and oiled which took twenty minutes. Certain parts received five-minute attention every couple of hours, but the machine wasn't stopped at those junctures. My toughest duty was assisting Johnny in moving the pads.

Although there were hardwood ridges along the route, we were digging mostly in marshy terrain where the huge, heavy piece of equipment would have sunk out of sight if not resting on pads. Pads were six logs, a minimum of twelve-inch diameters and thirty feet in length, bound together with one-inch steel cable. They resembled a raft. The cable at each end of the pad was fashioned into a loop.

Seven pads were required—three for the machine to sit on, and four for movement. The dragline cable controlling the bucket had a large attached hook, so when John wanted to move ahead, he swung the boom, lowered the bucket, and I slipped the hook into the loop at the end of the pad. He would then swing the pad in front of the machine on the newly built grade where I would unhook it after which Johnny would swing the machine around for the next pad and so on. When all four were in place, he moved forward and commenced excavating.

To save me getting soaked when it was pouring rain, John would try to grab the loop himself by maneuvering the hook. This was awkward and time consuming, but as long as the machine was in motion, it was registering on the time card, so whether we were forming road-bed or not, everybody was getting paid. The only loser was the Manitoba government, and like most governments, wasting money never seemed to concern them.

The contractor was paid by 24-hour time cards installed in the dragline cab. A clock with an attached red pencil that jiggled with the movement of the machine marked the card. One five minute down time break was allowed every hour, plus half an hour for oiling, and an hour for lunch each shift. We found a method of manipulating the card and moving it forward leaving a five-minute white space every hour. In fact, we worked 55 minutes but were credited with a full hour. When Johnny took his hour lunch break, I practiced operating the bucket, then we advanced the card the allowable hour. This meant we gained almost two hours per shift or twelve hours each week. Our agreed weekly operating schedule was from 6 a.m. Monday to 6 a.m. Sunday, and we alternated shifts weekly. When going from night to day shift, instead of a 24-hour break, we got 36, and when going from day to night duty, then in lieu of 48 hours we got 60. It was fraud, but perfectly safe, because what government inspector would walk ten miles into no man's land on a Friday afternoon or Saturday?

Returning home every weekend was a Godsend. There was no refrigeration at our campsite, so Alec could serve nothing but cold or canned meats, and Mother's meals were as tasty as ever. Also, it gave us an opportunity to get clean laundry.

Things on the farm were in poor shape. Our twenty acres of barley, sprouting beautifully, was providing excellent pasture for the neighbors' cattle. Jack was devoting his time to baseball rather than constructing the fence to protect our investment. We had harsh words over his lackadaisical attitude, but Jack always had difficulty laboring by himself. When working together, though, I couldn't keep up with his effort. By the time we got the field closed in by fencing on weekends, the grain crop was a disaster.

My earnings of about $250 monthly represented a dollar per hour for the twelve-hour stints. Though not burdensome, the task was extremely boring, particularly night duty. If anyone had suggested I could sleep in the back of a working dragline on a steel seat, I would have recommended they visit a psychiatrist. When John was swinging the boom back and forth scooping up buckets of soil to build the road base, the interior of the dragline bucked and swayed like an untamed bronco tossing me around like I was a rag doll unless I jammed myself into a corner. There was a nauseating stink of diesel fuel and constant din resembling a canning factory in full production. But once inured to the pandemonium and smell, I couldn't stay awake. Nights were chilly, and mosquitoes infested the swamp in clouds, so the warm interior of the dragline was a haven, and the constant drone of the diesel engine acted like chloroform overpowering all other discomforts.

The section of the White Shell Reserve where we were constructing the highway paralleled the fast-flowing Winnipeg River which, when reaching Seven Sisters Falls, powered generators that supplied southern Manitoba with a great deal of its electric current. It was untamed, virgin country abounding in wildlife, especially black bears. I had Dad's 30-30 Winchester to frighten these nuisances away from around the camp. We didn't shoot to kill the animals because they were harmless unless you interfered with a mother and her cubs or allowed them to become scavengers. Also we didn't want to chance having a wounded bear around the encampment.

Bears do have a frightening image to many people, and Alec was scared to death of these marauders. One evening at dusk while Johnny and I were retiring, we heard our one-eyed cook holler bloody murder. Alec kept our butter, eggs, bacon and cold meats in a wooden crate under the front steps of the cook house. He had stepped outside just as a huge black bear snatched the box with our provisions in his jaws. Grabbing the gun and glimpsing the animal at the edge of our bunkhouse ten feet away, I aimed a shot just above the bear's head but must have grazed him. He dropped his loot and went crashing through the forest like a tank.

Recovering our food supplies was simple, but prevailing upon Alec to remain as our chef after the incident took considerable persuasion. He did remain, though rarely left the sanctity of the trailer even in daylight.

John Senyck was normally a quiet, introverted person. One pitch black Sunday night while trodding the heavily wooded path back to camp, our only light provided by a myriad of stars and a million fireflies, Johnny sang or whistled every step of the way.

"You're in a particularly good mood tonight, friend," I remarked.

"Good mood, hell," Johnny retorted. "Any bears within sound of my voice will be heading for the Ontario border."

I didn't say so but felt he was probably right. His off-key caterwauling was also driving me to distraction.

I came close to meeting my maker during the summer—not as a result of being attacked by bears but by pure ignorance and stupidity.

We were camped beside a small creek that wound like a snake's back a mile before emptying into the Winnipeg River. A Cree Indian trapper had left a 12-foot birch bark canoe at our encampment and said we were welcome to use it. Dying to try my expertise at canoeing, I took off one hot July day down the stream. By the time I reached the Winnipeg River I felt comfortable in the craft, so decided to paddle out into an open expanse of water. At this point the river was a large lake at least a mile wide and three miles long with a fast current running through the center. Lazily drifting in the open water and enjoying the tranquil scenic surroundings, it suddenly occurred to me the canoe was moving swiftly toward an opening between two cliffs of rock that soared a hundred feet in height on both sides of the river. Grabbing the paddle I struggled for a quarter hour with all my strength to pull out of the rapid current but without success. Fortunately I could see the bottom of the lake so I jumped into the water and towed the canoe ashore a hundred yards from the river's mouth. Climbing the sloping rock embankment to see what would have been my fate if I'd lost the battle, left me with nightmares for a year. Raging, frothy rapids stretched from the rocky embankment upon which I was standing right across the violent water to the opposite bank that also was a sheer wall of rock.

Trembling at my close call, I lit my last cigarette and tossed the empty package into the open water a few feet from the mouth of the torrent and watched with trepidation as it was sucked along with the same motion as if I'd flushed it down a toilet. Escape for me would have been impossible. The river is no longer as treacherous, because a huge reservoir was subsequently constructed to better control the river flow before reaching Seven Sister's Falls.

The near tragedy didn't deter me from spending my idle daylight hours on the banks of the river. I was attracted to the open water, because the breeze was a refreshing diversion from the stifling summer heat we were subjected to at the trailers which were surrounded by a curtain of tall trees and a haven for insects. Though having almost no fishing experience, I purchased a silver spoon and some thirty-pound test line. Standing on a rock shelf protruding into the water and whirling the lure around my head like lassoing a heifer, I heaved it a hundred feet into the river. Lazily pulling the line in hand over hand, I was astonished to feel a tug. Within two minutes I landed a huge Northern Pike. When I returned to camp with my prize, Alec wanted to cook it for supper, but as we were leaving first thing in the morning, I decided to take it home to show the family.

It was a warm muggy night, and Saturday was hot and sultry. By the time we reached Monominto, my fish was thoroughly ripe. While I weighed the pike, Mom grabbed the camera for picture taking, and Jack the shovel for a burial service. Though I obtained a photograph of the 15-pound fish, it provided no sustenance for any of us.

Pete Senyk borrowed my crude outfit the following week and caught several fish of similar size.

Boredom was aggravating me, as usual. Johnny was teaching me to become an operator, but when the wheat fields turned golden, the lure of the harvest compelled me to quit. Roman Kruchak had asked me to return, and by early August I was back on the end of a pitchfork.

My session at Kruchak's was pleasant, but uneventful, except for one traumatic event.

One evening Willie Kruchak needed a part for the separator and asked me to accompany him to the village of Anola six miles away situated beside the Canadian Pacific Railway's main transcontinental line. While chatting with Paul Nimchuk, the store proprietor, a passenger train went whizzing by toward Winnipeg. "There goes the Minaki Special," Paul remarked nonchalantly. Minaki, Ontario, was a popular resort area with Winnipeg people, because it was handy to several large lakes and convenient to reach by rail.

Bill couldn't get the required part at Anola, so we drove six miles west to Glass where there was a machinery parts store. Leaving our vehicle I saw huge flames leaping into the sky three miles further west at the town of Dugald. Koski, the storekeeper, said he'd heard a tremendous crash a few minutes before our arrival. Bill and I jumped into his pickup, sped to Dugald and became involved in one of the most tragic train accidents in North American railroad history.

Although the calamity happened only fifteen minutes before our arrival, Dugald was a disaster area. The transcontinental passenger train from Vancouver to Halifax was standing on the main line heading east when the Minaki Special doing 70 miles per hour and racing towards Winnipeg was switched onto the same set of tracks. The two powerful engines were standing vertically on their rear wheels leaning against each other as if they were in a gigantic embrace. No passengers were seriously injured on the west bound, and the train crew had leaped to safety, but the Minaki Special was a nightmare. The engineer and fireman were instantly killed. It is believed they could have jumped from the locomotive before impact and perhaps saved themselves, but they died attempting to brake the giant machine and avert the tragic catastrophe. Five wooden passenger cars lying on their sides, completely ablaze, were surrounded by dead and injured. I immediately counted seven bodies, and one lady was lying beside her completely severed head. The worst horror was not the corpses, but the agonizing screams from those trapped inside the fiery pyre. In my memory, those muffled cries lasted for hours, but realistically, it was only moments as the heat was so intense. We couldn't approach closer than a hundred feet before being driven back. The conflagration was impossible to control, because gas was the source of heat and lighting, and the wooden coaches ignited like tinder.

The scene rapidly became total chaos. Within fifteen miles west of the crash site were three cities: Transcona, St. Boniface and Winnipeg. Ambulances, police cars and fire department vehicles from all three, sirens blaring, came tearing down the two-lane gravel road leading into Dugald.

The intense heat from the burning train ignited the adjacent elevators, and flaming grain was pouring from their crumbling walls. Forty-five gallon fuel drums stacked beside the tracks, skyrocketing hundreds of feet in the air, exploded in a gigantic display of fireworks, and upon returning to earth were setting residences aflame all over the village.

Dugald had no running water, so the fire departments had to pump from nearby ditches, which, due to the dry season, were almost empty.

Bill and I were recruited to help lug the huge hoses to any available water source. We remained with the catastrophe until the early morning hours at which point police had the entire area cordoned off.

Wandering wearily and wordless back to our truck, we passed small knots of people still huddled together, a look of thorough disbelief etched on their grief-stricken faces. One little girl, who had been hurtled through a coach window, ran through three miles of grain fields before stopping at a farmer's house. Though in an absolute daze, she must have sensed her parents were trapped in the inferno and fled the tragedy, hoping it would obliterate it from her memory. It's unlikely it would. I lost no friend or relative in the disaster, yet the nightmare would remain etched in my brain forever.

Human beings involved in war or living in a country facing constant turmoil can become impervious to death and disaster in order to retain their sanity. However, for Bill and me, unfamiliar with such catastrophes and unexpectedly encountering that fatal scene in the quiet little prairie town of Dugald, it was mind boggling.

Kruchak's harvest was almost completed when Mom got word to me a machine would be available to thresh our few stooks of barley. Jack wasn't available, so I rushed home and got Ed Barham and Jim Wylie to give me a hand. What could have been a bumper crop of 1,000 bushels was instead, less than 100, and I sold it to Jim Wylie for $70.

I knew my days in Monominto were numbered, and gazing across the fields and meadows that early autumn afternoon before returning to the store, fifteen years of pleasant reflections crossed my mind: Scenes of trapping and hunting; haying and family lunches savored in an atmosphere of tranquility; countless hours of walking behind six horses while cultivating and harrowing those fields I'd helped to clear; meadows yellow with marsh marigolds that we hauled home in buckets each Mother's Day; grasslands ablaze with tiger lilies, Indian paint brushes and purple phlox—minor matters to many, but major memories in my young life.

In the previous several years I had contributed financially to free the farm from debt and labored strenuously to improve its production, but I knew Father loved this land too much to part with its ownership. Trudging from the field, I sensed never again would the farm be part of my life.

Mom knew I was moving on and had my laundry prepared. Svend Westerguard, a Dane who farmed the quarter section immediately east of us, had told Mother he would like to join me if I was going west to harvest. The following day Farm Help Service sent Svend and me by bus to Minnedosa, Manitoba, 150 miles northwest of Winnipeg. It was a Swedish settlement, and we enjoyed a successful two-week run.

Svend accompanied me to Brandon, the second largest city in Manitoba and 90 miles east of the Saskatchewan border, to see if we could locate more work. Harvesting in the province was already completed, so Svend returned home. In Brandon I ran into a school buddy, Verner Jensen, who also played baseball on the Monominto team. We decided to visit Regina and search for work, but no threshing jobs were available in Saskatchewan either. Having nothing better to do, I elected to hit the road 500 miles west to Calgary, Alberta. Verner had commitments at home, so I traveled on alone.

Traversing Saskatchewan and Alberta that gorgeous autumn day, I perceived my days of prairie harvesting speedily coming to an end. Combines were finally propelling the binder and thresher into yesterday, just as those machines had replaced the sickle. Back in 1948 when I first started at Van Molls, there was constant talk amongst farmers about the merits of this new-fangled method of harvesting. If a combine was in the vicinity, farmers would pay a visit, watch it operate and then return to their threshing machine and discuss the pros and cons of the new mechanical device. Industrial change comes slowly, and old habits are hard to break. The combine simply 'combined' the binder and thresher by cutting the standing crop, gathering it up, threshing the seed from the stem, separating out the chaff, collecting the seed in a hopper for delivery to a truck, and finally returning the straw to the ground. One man with a self-propelled combine could harvest from 50 to 100 acres per day depending on the size of the machine, plus a trucker to haul away the grain. Two men could now produce what used to require eight or ten. Each harvest season more Western farmers overcame their reluctance to conversion, and by 1948 threshing machines were vanishing from the plains like the buffalo did a century before.

Engrossed in my thoughts of changing times and enchanted by the rolling plains of southern Alberta, I was thoroughly delighted when the big Greyhound bus lurched to a halt as a large herd of antelope went bounding across the highway. They were the first antelope I'd ever seen and a rare sight. Our bus driver announced a huge prairie fire was causing the fleet-footed animals to change habitat, and the pungent smell of smoke was indeed heavy in the air.

If a picture is worth a thousand words, then reality is worth a thousand pictures. Innumerable times I'd admired the Rocky Mountains in print—postcards, magazines, calendars, etc., but nearing Calgary as the pinnacles began looming out of the horizon, their awesome splendor was overwhelming.

I took a hotel room in Calgary overlooking the mighty Rockies. As it was nearing the weekend, I decided to relax for a day or two and enjoy the environment of the famous Stampede City.

Alberta allowed mixed beer drinking in its parlors, but separate beverage rooms for men were out of bounds for ladies. It was a unique arrangement, so I went to check it out. As the men's room was crowded, I sat at a table with another young fellow. After chatting a while and deciding he was an affable lad, I invited him up to my room for a shot of whiskey.

Stooping over to insert the key, the chap stepped behind me and thrust his hand between my thighs where no male had ever touched me before. Nausea struck me at first as I suddenly realized his motive. Then

I became enraged. He was only a short lad of slight build and obviously wasn't expecting an attack. Whirling around, I threw a roundhouse left, catching him flush on the jaw, and as he staggered back I smashed a straight right to his face.

The two rapid blows sent him staggering down the narrow corridor, blood spurting from his nose and mouth. In a fury, I started after him, but he had regained his balance and was dashing down the aisleway just as another man turned a corner and came toward us. Seeing blood smeared on the lad's face and the furor in my eyes, the man instinctively grabbed my arm, "What the hell is going on?" he shouted.

Jerking my arm free, I took a few more steps, but the unfortunate gay was long gone. Whirling, I started menacingly toward the new arrival, who was leaning against the wall, his arms folded across his chest. "I'll kill the f---ing faggot!" I stormed. "Why did you grab me?"

"I didn't want to be witness to a murder," the fellow replied. "What caused the ruckus?"

In a few words I explained the incident. "I'm Ray Dunc," the man offered with a pleasant smile. "Offer me the drink. I'm not interested in your body."

Sitting in my room, Ray, who was in his late thirties, calmed me down and explained what happened wasn't unusual. He offered some advice on how to spot a gay and indicated I must have given the kid some encouragement for him to have come to my room.

Ray Dunc, about 5 feet 8 inches tall, but stocky, had a dour face and receding hairline. From Seattle, Washington, he had recently been discharged as an officer from the United States Air Force.

Arriving home from the Pacific theater of war, he found his wife living with another man. Disenchanted with life, he was drinking heavily and bumming around. Crossing the border with his car at Vancouver, Ray had driven east to Calgary where he smashed up his vehicle in an accident. With insufficient cash to have the car repaired, he was looking for a temporary job.

We knocked around Calgary for the weekend and grew comfortable in each other's company. Ray, of Spanish descent, was not a particularly handsome fellow but had a quiet demeanor that made him well received with most people. Ray inquired about my plans. I explained about Farm Help Service and its function and told him that on Monday morning I was going to see what they had to offer.

Having dinner Sunday evening, Ray asked, "Slim, would you object if I accompany you tomorrow? Maybe I can get a job harvesting."

Ray had already informed me he was a qualified diesel mechanic and had a full set of what he called "Blue Point" tools in his luggage.

"Hell, Ray, I'd be delighted with your company," I replied enthusiastically, "but pitching sheaves is rugged work if you're not used to it. I would have thought you'd make more money at your own profession."

"Look, Slim, money at the moment isn't important. I'm more interested in straightening out my mixed-up thinking, and I've thoroughly enjoyed our two days together. I'll tell the garage in the morning they can keep the car if I'm not back, and I'll leave them the ownership, because I want no ties or responsibilities."

"You've got yourself a partner, friend," I said, "and we'll meet at the breakfast table at 8 a.m."

We were at the Farm Help office sharp at 9 a.m., and a rancher, Russ McDonald, looking for men hired us on the spot. Wages were an unbelievable one dollar per hour. The McDonald's had an enormous ranch of several thousand acres a few miles out of Cremona in the foothills of the Rockies. Cremona was about 50 miles northwest of Calgary. It was the most picturesque agricultural country I could ever imagine with undulating hills growing steadily larger until they joined the base of the first authentic mountains. Purple peaks jutting skyward like gigantic sentinels punctuated the western horizon as far as you could see with intermittent white-capped pinnacles soaring above the others.

Besides a huge herd of pure bred Shorthorns scattered over thousands of acres of range, the McDonald's had a couple more thousand acres under cultivation. Ray and I were taken to a bunkhouse, the first I'd been billeted in while harvesting. Though a little crowded, it was comfortable. A total of nine hired men shared the quarters, and each had a single steel cot. A couple of small tables for cards or writing, washing facilities and a large pot-bellied stove comprised the balance of the furnishings.

I went back on a stook team, and Ray was assigned the task of field pitching. Ray suffered like hell the first few days, mostly with blistered hands. Foreseeing the problem, I had insisted he bring two pairs of heavy gloves and healing salve, so he was able to survive. I was impressed with his gumption. It was a huge outfit with eight stook teams, two field pitchers, plus a spike pitcher, and we cleared a lot of acreage each day.

The crew, from all over the country, included one slightly built lad from Toronto which he pronounced "Trawna" and which became his nickname. Trawna was a sturdy little character, who through sheer determination had toughened himself to the task of field pitching. It was his first trip away from the big city, and like many young men, he was enamoured with the romance of cowboy life. Returning to the farmyard with my team and empty rack at dinnertime and at day's end, I picked up the two field pitchers. Trawna always requested Ray to boost him on the back of one of my horses so he could play cowboy to and from the field. He certainly seemed like a pleasant lad, and Ray and I enjoyed his company.

Three scruffy looking boys, driving stook teams, were friends from Vancouver, another two chaps hailed from Saskatchewan, and an elderly man in his mid-sixties, whom we called "Old John" was from wherever he hung his hat, as he described it. After a couple of weeks of working together, things in the bunkhouse were going smoothly, though except for Trawna, Ray and I stayed pretty much to ourselves.

One Saturday evening "Old John" got hold of a bottle of liquor and by midnight was stoned. Garbling about having plenty of money to get through the winter, he pulled out a wallet with several hundred dollars in large bills and began waving them around the room. Lying on my cot reading and paying scant attention, I heard Ray jump up and holler at "Old John." "You stupid old bastard, do you want to get rolled tonight or tomorrow? You won't have that money by morning, you gawd damn fool."

Ray jammed the bills back in "Old John's" billfold, placed the old man's bed between his and mine, then produced from his knapsack the meanest looking knife I'd ever seen. Unsheathing the weapon, he slammed it down on the little table beside his bed, and in a loud voice announced, "I ain't suggesting anybody in this camp is a thief, but if anyone is considering robbing this crazy old son of a bitch, I want you to know you'll have to take on Slim, myself and old Betsy," pointing to his knife. Everybody went to sleep, and so did I, but not before coming to the conclusion there was a lot more to Ray Dunc than met the eye.

Next morning at Sunday breakfast, Ray informed McDonald, Sr. of the episode and told him if "Old John" wasn't gone by noon, he, I and Trawna would depart before evening. Mr. McDonald wholeheartedly concurred.

It was late September with frosty nights, but the weather held perfect for threshing. At 5 a.m. when I left the bunkhouse for the stable to tend my horses, the looming mountains reaching into the starlit sky magnetized me, and I wanted to go rushing toward them like a lemming's suicidal dash to the sea. Their purple-shadowed outlines in the darkness were haunting and foreboding, and their impenetrable immensity overshadowed everything else into insignificance that surrounded those wonders of nature.

One delightful early morning, while walking to the barn, white frost covering the countryside in a mantle of silver and a myriad of twinkling stars illuminating the prairie sky like a diamond tiara, I suddenly became aware the mountains were bathed in white and had dramatically changed their appearance.

At breakfast Mr. McDonald addressed the group, "Gentlemen", he said, "we won't thresh past noon, because we'll be snowed in. As we are almost finished, we'll call it quits. I'll have your money waiting for you after lunch."

A brighter, more ideal morning never dawned as we headed for the fields, but by ten o'clock clouds drifting in from the mountains began sprinkling us with their forerunners of winter. At eleven o'clock snow was falling heavily and before noon, as McDonald had predicted, we were forced to halt.

Threshing across the western provinces over the years had been financially rewarding and provided me with many pleasant experiences. Nevertheless, I was determined when tossing the last sheaf for McDonald to permanently retire the three-tined pitchfork. I realized it was the end of an era. Within two years threshing machines on the prairies were relics of the past.

When Ray and I discussed plans for the immediate future, I mentioned that Vancouver was next on my itinerary.

"Hell, Slim, I've just come from the Coast. Let's try Edmonton," he said. "You can visit Vancouver some other time."

Having become attached to Ray, I consented, and it's amazing how minor decisions in our lives can sometimes play paramount roles in our destinies. Packing our gear, Trawna asked if he could join us, and Ray and I had no objections. Russ McDonald drove the three of us twenty miles east through the snowstorm to the main highway between Calgary and Edmonton to catch a northbound Greyhound. By mid-afternoon we were on our way 175 miles north to what was rapidly becoming the oil capital of Canada. With a fifteen-minute stopover at Red Deere, Ray raced over to the liquor store and bought a bottle of whiskey to ease the pain of the slow trip over icy roads. I'd met a nurse, Diane, aboard, and we made a date for dinner providing Edmonton was reached in reasonable time.

Alberta's capital city is on two levels, the lower level divided by the Saskatchewan River. We were directed to the lower level for reasonably priced hotels. The cab driver took us to the Devon Hotel, and needing two rooms, I suggested Ray and Trawna share one, as I was taking Diane out for the evening. Forever the optimist, I wanted to be ready for all possibilities. It turned out to be a bad gamble, although the young lady and I had an enjoyable evening.

The three of us lazed around for two days drinking, sightseeing and relaxing. The second night Ray and I went to supper at the Silver Dell restaurant on Jasper Avenue, the main thoroughfare through the city. Ray was trying to date a waitress there. While dining, Ray informed me Trawna was broke, and he had loaned him twenty bucks.

"How the hell is that possible, Ray?" I asked increduously. "We were all paid almost $150 three days ago."

"Apparently he'd already drawn some of his wages from the Mc-Donald's for clothes and sundries. Then last night he got involved with a broad, and she took him for a bundle. I'm not too flush myself, Slim," he continued, "so tomorrow we better look for work."

The following morning we decided to go three separate directions searching for employment. I hitchhiked 15 miles to Leduc where the new oil fields were located. The stink of gas fumes was almost unbearable, but there were plenty of jobs for Ray and Trawna. A physical was required, however, which would be impossible for me to pass. I spent the day at Leduc and didn't return to Edmonton until 5 p.m. Our rooms were on the ground floor of the small Devon Hotel, and when I walked inside the front door, the lady proprietor, in tears, grabbed my arm and pulled me into her little office.

"I didn't know he was a thief, Mr. Phillips. I can't be responsible," she was babbling.

"What in hell are you talking about?" I asked. "Who's a thief?"

"Your partner," she replied, still sobbing. "Seeing him leaving with his suitcase this morning, I stopped him and asked for money. He said he was broke and paid me with a 21-jewel Hamilton wrist watch. I can't be blamed. I didn't know he stole it," she continued.

Jumping up and running down the corridor, I had no idea to whom she was referring, though I was quite certain it was Trawna. Ray's door was open, and he was sitting dejectedly on his bed, head in hands with the contents of his packsack strewn across the room.

Ray, returning about 3 p.m., discovered Trawna had broken into his luggage and stolen diesel tools, his wrist watch, a wallet with $50 cash, his "pinks" (Air Force dress pants), and several other items. The police had already investigated and left.

"To think I assisted the ungrateful little bastard," Ray snarled. "Some of those things are irreplaceable."

The police confiscated as evidence the inscribed wrist watch Trawna had given the proprietress. It was a gift from Ray's mother and apparently quite dear to him.

After a few shots of whiskey, Ray was getting the affair in better perspective. The police phoned to say his tools and other items had been picked up at a pawn shop, but Trawna had not been apprehended. Although the police would hold the articles for a while, at least Ray would get them back at little cost. The hotel proprietress should have contacted the police on suspicion, but the fact she stopped Trawna was the only reason Ray would eventually get his watch back. I was grateful to Diane for being responsible I had separate quarters, thereby keeping me out of the fiasco.

We decided to go back to the Silver Dell for evening dinner. To reach the upper level you either taxied a circular route or climbed over 200 wooden steps up a steep hillside. Choosing the stairway to clear our heads and perk our appetite, we were astonished to find Ray's billfold lying on the snowy hillside torn into sections. Trawna must have been broke, or he never would have scaled the precipitous steps with his suitcase if he could have afforded a taxi. The $50 in Ray's wallet was obviously not discovered until Trawna was halfway up the staircase. Drug problems were not common in the late forties, but Trawna evidently had a monkey on his back of some kind.

The Silver Dell was a large establishment with many booths and a long counter that zigzagged in a circular fashion through the center of the restaurant. Ray's heartthrob worked behind the counter, so that is where we sat. Seated fifty feet from us at the counter were a half dozen U.S. Air Force officers. This wasn't unusual, because Edmonton, the nearest city to Alaska, was where American airmen flew to spend their short leaves. Returning from the washroom, I had to pass the boys in uniform. One of them stopped me and asked, "Hey, Mack! Who's the guy you're sitting with?"

Ray usually wore a heavy grey jumbo knit sweather with a large collar. He had a habit of keeping his head scrunched down in the garment resembling a turtle, partially withdrawn into its shell.

Glancing over at Ray, who was teasing his lady friend, and recalling he was in the American Air Force, I figured they must have thought they recognized him. "He's Ray Dunc," I replied. They then asked me to sit and have a coffee.

"Do you know him well?" one of the boys inquired.

"We've been knocking around together for a month. Why?"

"Did he tell you he was an ex-American Air Force officer?"

"He mentioned it," I said. "It isn't a big deal."

"Ray Dunc is a genuine highly decorated war hero," the fellow said. "He was sole survivor of a bomber crew that went down in the South Pacific. Ray reached a small island inhabited with Japanese. He lived off the jungle for three months and was credited with killing seven Japs. Never captured, he was rescued when our forces retook the island. We understand he avoids pomp or publicity about his exploits. Because he has glanced over, he knows we're here, so if he prefers anonymity, we'll leave him alone. But we sure as hell would like to take the pair of you to a house we have rented where we're having a little party. We just came over for some mix and elected to have a cup of coffee."

Sitting there dumbfounded for a few seconds as the story sank in, I finally said, "I'll have a word with him and see what he says."

Ray looked at me square in the face when I sat beside him. It was obvious when he saw me chatting with the others that I'd learned something.

So you're a war hero and wouldn't tell me," I began.

"Slim, I figured that's what it was about, and it's all water under the bridge; it's past history, and I want to forget the whole gawddamn horrible mess."

"Ray, I'm not as old as you, but there is one thing I'm sure of. You don't have to talk about the war, but you sure as hell won't forget it. These boys want us to join them at a party, but will leave you alone if that's what you prefer."

Ray spent a few moments in deep thought, then looking across at the six airmen, gave a little wave. That was all the signal needed. They leaped in unison off their stools and came over. Introducing themselves, they soon persuaded Ray to attend the party. Ray held up his hand to speak, "Gentlemen," he said, "If Bill and I are going with you for an evening's fun and frivolity, it has to be understood I am not joining you to swap war stories."

It was mutually agreed, so for ten wild hilarious, enjoyable hours I consorted with twenty officers of the American Air Force with ranks ranging to Lieutenant Colonel. The Yanks had rented a two-story house on a permanent basis with five or six bedrooms in one of the better residential sectors of the city. Booze, broads and the banquet were the finest Edmonton had to offer, and the quantity of all components was unlimited. At 6 a.m. an officer hollered a warning that they had an hour before cabs arrived to return them to the airport. Unshaven, dishevelled and partially hung over, they looked anything but the crack military unit that they were. Like an ugly caterpillar suddenly transformed into a graceful butterfly, the boys made an amazing metamorphosis within an hour. I don't know how they felt, but they looked remarkable.

Ray had an enjoyable time, and somehow it seemed to take a load off his mind getting back with his comrades-in-arms. The boys dropped us off at our hotel, and as we headed for our rooms and to bed, Ray put his hand on my shoulder, "Thanks, Bill," he said simply. "If it hadn't been for you, I wouldn't have talked to them."

Arousing myself after several hours' sleep, I saw a paper under my door. Ray left a note saying he decided to let me sleep while he went job hunting and would meet me at the Silver Dell at 6 p.m. I went directly to the government employment office where huge posters on the wall proclaimed, "Beware! Do not go to Vancouver; the streets are jammed with the unemployed." So at least my association with Ray Dunc had saved me a useless trip to the Coast.

Another notice on the bulletin board said: "Cutters wanted by Imperial Lumber. Fare paid to the camps." I inquired and was urged to sign up immediately because a train was leaving in the morning. The thought of returning to the woods for the winter excited me. I was eager to get into northern Alberta with its stands of virgin timber and hoped Ray would join me.

Ray, waiting for me at the Silver Dell when I arrived, was bubbling with enthusiasm. He had been offered a diesel mechanic's job at Yellowknife Transport in the Northwest Territories. Yellowknife was 700 air miles north of Edmonton.

"Slim, they are flying me at their expense and starting me at two bucks per hour, and I can leave tomorrow," he said. "I told them if you weren't included it was no deal, but they won't have room on a plane for you until next week."

"What in hell do you expect me to do in Yellowknife, Ray?"

"Look, Slim, I know you've got money, so you just cuddle up with Diane for a few days, and I'll arrange everything. I'll wire you at the Devon Hotel when to proceed to Yellowknife's office here in the city."

I told him about Imperial Lumber and my predilection for the bush. The thought of going to the Northwest Territories was fascinating, I admitted, but to commit myself before knowing what my task would be in Yellowknife was preposterous.

We had a few beers, walked the streets and talked, returned to a beverage room for more beer, and more conversation, trying to reach a compromise.

"Hell, Slim, you get settled up there with Imperial Lumber, and you'll be there for the winter," Ray insisted.

"Look, friend, you get something confirmed for me that you know is authentic and I can handle. Write my mother immediately, because she will have my address as soon as I have one. It's only a short day's train ride for me back to Edmonton, and I can join you posthaste."

We retired with that thought. Ray had to be at Yellowknife Transport's office at 10 a.m. and I accompanied him in the taxi. Just before arriving at his destination, he called for the cab driver to stop.

"Slim, you son of a bitch, we were meant to be partners, and if we separate today, we will not see each other again. I'm going back to the Devon, and we're heading for the bush."

I felt the same way, but I knew Ray was not a lumberjack, and probably wouldn't be successful in big timber country. Also, two bucks per hour was a helluva lot of money.

"Ray," I said earnestly. "Our few weeks together has been enjoyable, and I want our friendship to continue, but with your opportunity, it's more logical for you to get settled and send for me than for the two of us to go into an uncertain future. You'd be crazy to pass up this chance to get back at your old trade."

"Bill, I suppose you're right, but you'd better answer my call."

I assured him I would, and as we gripped each other's hand, I had a lump in my throat, as I know he had. Although at the moment we were both sincere about our reunion, we were both itinerants whose destinies changed with the phases of the moon.

I heard from Ray but never saw him again. For a five-week relationship, we had become extraordinarily fond of each other. Lifetime friendships are often cemented in short acquaintances; so it would have been with us in slightly different circumstances. As it was, I headed for Imperial Lumber's operations in northern Alberta and another exceedingly interesting chapter in my book of life.

As the train swayed, clickety-clacked and groaned slowly through the seemingly nonending swamplands of northern Alberta, I was relieved to be returning to the bush. It was a way of life I now understood and enjoyed.

The N.A.R., or Northern Alberta Railroad, servicing that sector of the province, was legendary. One could buy bootleg whiskey, pick up a Cree Indian girlfriend, or get involved in a table stakes poker game. The engineer halted the train on any pretext—for someone walking the railway line, thumbing a ride, any settlement—regardless of size—that placed a red flag a mile before its juncture, or a slow moving moose. Due to the snail's pace motion of the locomotive, grinding to a stop wasn't all that difficult.

The journey wouldn't have been so tiresome if the scenery was enjoyable, but it was mostly flat, featureless swampland with pockets of spindly fir trees. It was ideal moose pasture, although I never spotted one.

There was a long stopover at Lac La Biche, 90 miles northeast of Edmonton, a town of 1200 which, except for Fort McMurray on the mighty Athabaskan River, was the last sizeable settlement before the vast reaches of mostly uninhabited northern Alberta.

An Imperial Lumber settlement known as Mile 134, my destination, was finally reached at four o'clock in the afternoon, six and one half hours after leaving Edmonton.

Mile 134, approximately fifty miles northwest of Lac La Biche, was the main dispatch depot for Imperial Lumber. Hundreds of bush camps fanned out from that point covering a wide expanse of virgin timber country. Huge warehouses containing all necessary supplies including mill equipment, were distributed from there to the camps by truck or four wheeled drive vehicles. Rough 2 inch lumber, produced by the mills in the bush, was trucked back to Mile 134 during the winter when the rough bulldozed roads constructed over marshy terrain were frozen. Imperial Lumber operated a huge planing mill at the siding where rough lumber was dressed into the finished product and shipped by freight to the head office in Edmonton.

Reporting to the office upon arrival, I was introduced to Jim Fisher, supervisor of bush operations. A strapping six foot, two inch, broad shouldered man, wearing a heavy red plaid mackinaw jacket, leather knee boots, and with a roaring voice that barked authority, Jim Fisher looked capable of handling his responsibility. It was too late in the afternoon to head out to camp, so Jim directed me to a large company bunkhouse for the night and pointed out the mess hall for dinner and breakfast. I was to meet him at the office at 10 a.m. when he would transport me to Camp 11 where they needed cutters.

The smell of fresh cut timber, an atmosphere of bustling activity, and the unexplainable camaraderie of transients suddenly bunched together, gave me the same sense of unbridled freedom on that October evening that I felt the year before when first arriving at Camp 47 of Brompton Pulp and Paper. I was back in the bush and delighted with my resolution to join Imperial Lumber for the winter. Unfortunately, however, that decision was not going to result in all milk and honey, as later events would bear out.

Jim Fisher drove a four wheel drive Land Rover, and as we bounced along the spongy, rutted roadway he explained the newly opened camps were almost exclusively operated by independent contractors. Although Imperial Lumber controlled the timber lease from the Alberta government, they found it more profitable to financially support individual entrepreneurs rather than set the camps up with company managers. It was a marvelous example of private enterprise in action.

The terrain, flat with spacious marshy areas, was principally covered with virgin softwoods—white pine, spruce and balsam predominating. Camp 11 where Fisher left me (about 25 miles from the siding at Mile 134) was more like what I'd expected to see the previous year in Ontario. A small bunkhouse nestled in a grove of scraggly spruce was a hundred feet from an equally undersized combination kitchen/dining hall, and that was it. A far cry from the village atmosphere of Camp 47 in the Ontario pulp woods. Having absolutely no experience in the lumber industry, I decided after lunch to hike into the bush and watch cutters in action to evaluate the money making possibilities. The operation, though comparable to pulp cutting, had several dissimilarities. On the average, trees were considerably larger with butts up to two feet in diameter. Felled timber was cut into log lengths from eight to twenty feet, the length being determined by each individual cutter who made his decision based on the circumference of the tree and straightness of the trunk. No piling was required, and limbs and tops were left where severed. An assigned number was marked on the end of each log so the scaler who measured each piece could credit it on a tally sheet to the appropriate cutter.

Hearing falling timber, I approached the activity and came upon a three man crew from Camp 11, who had been at the lunch table with me. Chatting as they felled a sizeable white pine, I was paying no attention to the falling tree and didn't see it snap a "widow maker". As a consequence, when one of the boys hollered "look out!", I didn't know which way to jump, and a half rotten balsam crashed across the fore part of my head knocking me unconscious. One of the concerned three-some revived me by tossing cold water in my face, and all were relieved when I regained consciousness. Luckily, except for an egg on my head, I was not injured. "Widow makers" (small trees or limbs snapped off by falling timber) have killed or injured many bushmen over the years because of the difficulty in knowing which direction the wooden missile will fly.

A little woozy, I returned to camp, and whether it was the knock on the head, or just one of those twinges of fate that seems to direct human lives, I suddenly made up my mind to leave Camp 11. Grabbing my gear, I caught the first passing truck to Camp 12 two miles up the road.

There were only two frame buildings at this site also—a twelve man bunkhouse and a small dwelling that was a combination kitchen and eating quarters. It was 5 p.m., and the cook, the only man in camp, told me there were two men in the bush and, yes, they needed cutters. He also instructed me to choose a bunk.

The first evening in camp turned out to be unusual and thoroughly disconcerting, making me second guess my choice of camps. Harry, one of the cutters, was a happy-go-lucky Irishman who played an accordion rather poorly. The other chap was a mute lunatic who constantly stared at the ceiling with a stupid grin, and every half hour or so would break out in a maniacal laugh which continued on into the night.

The following morning Duncan McFarlane, the cook, persuaded me to stay for two days until Ed Carlson, the contractor, arrived from Edmonton. Providing me with a swede saw, ax and other necessary equipment, he pointed out where to start cutting. The terrain where the lumber camps were located was more distinctive than anything I'd encountered in northern Alberta. It was rolling country with undulations of two and three hundred feet. A variety of hardwoods graced the slopes while pockets of softwoods flourished in the valleys and flatlands.

Locating good timber to fell wasn't a problem, though knowing what money I was earning was impossible, because I didn't know how to scale logs.

Ed Carlson, of Swedish parentage, arrived on schedule. A man in his late thirties, he was tall and slim like myself with fair receding hair brushed straight back. He had an infectious smile that illuminated his ruddy complexion, and we liked each other on our initial encounter. Ed inspected and measured my two days' output and informed me I was earning about $12 daily.

As there were no other accommodations, Ed had to share our bunkhouse giving us a chance to become better acquainted and for him to hear firsthand the weird cackling from his mute employee. The next day, Sunday, Carlson asked me to join him on a walk through his territory to evaluate the timber potential and hunt moose. He carried a 30.06 calibre Winchester.

Walking back for supper Ed suggested we sit on a log for a cigarette break.

"How do you manage in the snow with that leg?" he inquired.

"I manage just fine. Why do you ask?"

"Bill, you have some education, and I need a General Manager. Someone who can keep books and handle authority while I'm not here. Until the mill is set up, I will be continuously travelling between here, Lac La Biche, and Edmonton where my wife and little boy are located. Would you be interested in the position, and do you think you could handle the responsibility?"

"Look, Ed, I'm here to make money," I replied, "so, what is your offer?"

"I'll pay $250 a month and no meal deduction, plus to earn extra dollars you can cut logs near camp or work on the mill when it's operating if it doesn't interfere with other duties. Besides that you can have complete control of the commissary and make whatever profit you can."

Nearing the bunkhouse I stopped, "Ed, I have a disability, so should be the first to have compassion for anyone with an affliction. However, if I accept your offer, the mute will have to go. There is no way men in that bunkhouse can either be comfortable or sleep properly in that environment," I said, looking him squarely in the face.

"You're talking like a G.M. already, so I know I made a good choice. I'll take him back to the siding when I leave next week," Ed responded eagerly.

Before Carlson left camp he began my education on lumber camp management dealing with several pertinent points—how to scale truckloads of 2 inch lumber; order kitchen supplies with Dunc's assistance; list the men required for our operation such as cutters, teamsters, truck drivers and a mill crew; and know their pay scale. Also plans to begin immediate construction of our necessary buildings: an office, two more bunkhouses, and eventually, a small bungalow on a nearby hill for Ed's wife and family.

So again, without desire, planning or intention, I was back in a position of administration. Power I didn't covet, but the chance to earn good money looked outstanding, and either I exercised authority or lost what appeared to be a golden opportunity. Therefore, I accepted the commitment.

Ed Carlson took the mute and Harry when he left camp, but hired a young chap from Saskatchewan, Paul Oproski, and instructed him to work with me constructing an office. Paul, of Polish descent, stood as tall as I, was a little heavier and a few years older. He had pitch black hair and a sullen disposition. The first morning as we worked together erecting the office, I asked him to do some small task. Dropping his hammer he walked over, stuck his chin six inches from my face, and in an acidic tone said, "Look, Phillips, let's get something straight. I'm not taking any bull shit from you."

Neither of us moved for a few seconds, like a pair of bulldogs sizing each other up, but I was getting angrier by the moment.

"Look, you dumb bastard," I finally exploded, "get your ass off this building, grab your gear, and get the f--k out of camp before I slug you with this hammer."

Paul didn't run or even hurry; he just sidled away. "And don't wait for lunch cause you're getting none," I hollered, at the slowly departing Pole.

Fifteen minutes later Paul came ambling back. I was sure a brawl was imminent, and at that moment it suited me fine.

"Phillips, I was wrong. I really didn't know you were in charge," he said quietly. "Dunc, the cook, just told me."

"Then pick up your hammer and get to work, and don't give me no more crap," I snarled.

And he didn't. For the following five months of turmoil at Camp 12 Paul the Pole, as I called him, was my staunchest and most loyal supporter.

New men streamed into camp, some already hired by Carlson, and others sent by Jim Fisher. Before the end of October we had ten men cutting logs, a half dozen building bunkhouses, and more helping Ed set up the mill. My completed 20 foot by 24 foot office was divided into two sections. The front part, 20 feet by 14 feet, contained an 8 foot by 14 foot storeroom where, locked behind heavy page wire, were commissary items plus camp records. I planned on using the 20 foot by 20 foot section, completely divided from the front by a lumber partition and with its own entrance, as my sleeping area, but decided to keep my bed and personal quarters in the front beside the commissary.

I went into Mile 134 at least twice weekly to stock my store with necessities: tobacco, toiletries, confectionary, a variety of clothing, cards and games, bush equipment, etc. There was a good markup on most items, so profits were mounting. However, keeping inventory and recording every article acquired against each man's wages was time consuming.

Ed Carlson constantly drifted in and out of camp as he brought in necessities to get the mill in production.

One early November day Ed said, "Slim, I want you to go to Lac La Biche to pick up a team of horses for skidding logs."

He gave me a $200 check payable to Cash on a bank in Lac La Biche, a branch of the bank that contained our main account in Edmonton. Ed told me to see Harry Blair in Lac La Biche, a local representative of Imperial Lumber. Ed also informed me he would have a truck and driver meet me at Blair's the following day. That afternoon I received a long letter from Ray Dunc. In part, it read, "Get your ass down to Edmonton and over to the Yellowknife Transport office for travel arrangements. You are the new head warehouseman in Yellowknife at $400 per month. Don't worry. I'll look after everything." There was a glowing description of the town and how much I would enjoy the region. The letter had gone from Yellowknife to Monominto where Mom readdressed it to Camp 12, so the missive was nearly three weeks in transit.

I had a dilemma. It would be pleasant to be with Ray Dunc again, I sincerely wanted to visit the Northwest Territories, plus it was an excellent salary. On the other hand, I was well set up to make even larger earnings, Ed Carlson was depending on me, and I was enjoying the challenge. The determining factor in my decision to stay at Camp 12 was the uncertainty of whether the job at Yellowknife would still be available when I reached Edmonton. I wrote to Ray and explained my situation and suggested when either of us left our position, we should contact the other. However, due to the unforeseen but weird circumstances at the time I left Edmonton, any attempt at contacting Dunc became impossible. I never heard from this unforgettable character again.

I arrived in Lac La Biche to purchase horses on one of the happiest days in Alberta's history. The Calgary Stampeders won the Grey Cup for the first time. The Grey Cup, symbolic of football supremacy in Canada, is hotly contested between the football champs of the Eastern League against the winners in the Western League. The West, represented by the Winnipeg Blue Bombers, had only won the trophy once in 1935 until Calgary accomplished a remarkable upset in 1948, and the province went beserk, including the town of Lac La Biche. I heard the game by radio at Harry Blair's. The oil exploration boom dominated mostly by large American corporations, made hotel accommodations in Lac La Biche almost impossible to obtain, so Harry Blair directed me to the Puzak's, a private home that was renting out two spare bedrooms. It was a neat frame bungalow near the town's center, and though it lacked inside facilities (an inconvenience I was accustomed to) it was quite suitable. What made it especially appealing was Irene Puzak, the twenty year old daughter. Irene had flaxen hair, and though plump, was pretty and friendly. She joined me in the town's celebration of the Grey Cup victory.

Strolling home late that night Irene directed me to a nearby livery stable where in the loft a couple of horse blankets were spread across a mound of hay. Irene was a passionate girl, and it was obvious I wasn't her only suitor. I was grateful to the Americans for confiscating all the hotel space.

Bill Smith, the truck driver Ed sent down, was a diminutive lad about 5'6", but the cockiest kid I'd met in a long time, especially when drunk. Finally, after some physical persuasion with "Little Bill", we got the horses loaded and began the torturous four hour journey back to camp. I was carrying a dozen bottles of assorted booze ordered by different boys in camp, and shortly after leaving Lac La Biche opened a quart of rum but didn't give a mouthful to my obstreperous truck driver. A half mile from camp I killed the bottle, and drunker than any time in my life, made a fool of myself in camp. With an ax I chopped a crude opening between two wall studs supporting the partition that separated the sections of my office building, ordered some boys to bring over two cots, and invited Ralph Long and Ed Davis to move over from the general bunkhouse. They accepted, and eventually I would pay dearly for this drunken proposal.

Ralph, a tall, rangy cowboy from central Alberta, was our head teamster in hauling logs; and Ed Davis, a Cape Breton Islander, one of the strongest, toughest characters I'd ever met, our bush foreman. One day while doing business at Mile 134, I heard one hell of a shouting match outside the office. Ed Davis, quite drunk, was blasting Jim Fisher for some company inconsideration in a voice that would have caused lesser men a heart attack. Even Big Jim was handling him with caution. Ed stood slightly less than six feet, was barrel chested with massive arms and shoulders, and a squat neck nearly as thick as my body.

As Ed Carlson was still absent from camp much of the time, I needed assistance keeping track of our operations in the bush and decided this powerful man might make a good foreman, so I hired him. Ed Davis had a hearty laugh that rocked his entire body and a great sense of humor, so he laughed frequently. His physical strength was evident when one day in camp I asked him to help me carry a quarter of beef into the cookhouse. Ed threw it over his shoulder and handled it himself as easily as if it was no heavier than a 100 pound sack of flour. Looking at the bill later, I was amazed to discover it weighed 235 pounds.

Jim Fisher was increasingly critical of the tortoise like pace of Ed Carlson in getting the mill into production. Most of the other camps were already shipping lumber, but we were still weeks from being set up. Our cutters had felled an abundance of timber; the skidders, who operate with one horse and dragged the logs into small piles, were keeping up with the cutters; and the haulers with two horse teams had a mountainous pile of logs waiting at the mill site. Ed Davis and I had a smooth running operation, but neither of us had experience in setting up a mill, so the end result was entirely at the mercy of Ed Carlson, who never appeared the least concerned.

The mill was erected on a side hill, so that many aspects of the operation could take advantage of gravity. The logs heaped on the crest were rolled down onto a framework where two men with pike hooks fed them to the sawyer and his helper. The sawyer, the highest paid man in camp, controlled the speed and production of the entire mill operation. A good sawyer was crucial to success. By looking at the circumference and crooks, it was his sole judgment to determine the maximum yield he could procure from each log, and he positioned it on the carriage accordingly. All waste, including sawdust, bark and slabs, were pitched or blown down the slope into a fire that burned all winter.

The boards sawn two and one quarter inches thick were cut in widths of from four to twelve inches in two inch increments. From the sawyer the rough hewn boards were transported on rollers to the edgerman, who, if a board had too much bark, ran it through the edger removing the objectionable bark and reducing its width by two inches. As an example, a 2 inch by 10 inch board would then become a 2 inch by 8 inch board, and the trimmings were also heaved downhill into the burning pile of waste material. From the edger the board was manually forced over another rollered platform to the trim sawyer, who had foot pedals that thrust a stopper up through the rollered carriage every two feet from eight to twenty feet. As the board went rolling past, he stepped on the appropriate pedal, depending on the board's length, and trimmed off any tag ends so that the final product was of a precise thickness, width and length. This was the only way lumber was accepted at Mile 134.

The trim sawyer shoved the finished boards from the rollered carriage onto a wooden chute where they slid down to the pilers who placed them in individual racks, depending on their width, so each truckload had boards of the same dimensions except for length. Trucks transported the rough lumber to Mile 134 where Imperial Lumber's scaler checked my scaling slip and, if in accord, the load was then credited to the contractor's account. Our entire mill crew consisted of a dozen men.

Ed Carlson, our boss, was the weak link in the chain of production. He couldn't separate himself from his family, so I had a small bungalow constructed by the camp; and he brought his young wife and five year old boy, Terry, a fine youngster, to live with him. This helped, but Ed still never grasped the urgency of getting our output into high gear.

Baron Munchausen, the 17th century character of literary fame, was a noted teller of tall tales. Ed Carlson, however, was his master and loved to gather an audience and tell wild yarns always insisting they were the absolute truth, regardless of how ridiculous. I often regretted I never wrote down many of these outrageous, but comical, stories, but I only recall one example. Someone remarked he knew an individual who was a remarkable walker. Ed countered, "Had a fellow working for me once who knew I like the daily paper, but the nearest point was at a village twenty-two miles distance. Every night, however, after eating, this chap would dash through the snow covered woods to fetch the daily for me." Even when someone pointed out the physical impossibility of such a feat, Ed would remain unfazed and absolutely guaranteed the accuracy of the tale. "I don't know how the man performed the act, but he always produced the paper," Ed maintained. An astounding prevaricator, Ed was entertaining and popular with the crew.

One day he came into the office, gave me three names to put on the payroll and said these new men were cutters. Not recognizing unfamiliar faces at the dinner table, I asked Ed to point them out. "I'll see you at the office after supper," he replied.

"Slim," he said in a confidential tone later that evening, "Those three names are dead horses."

"What the hell are dead horses?" I asked quite puzzled.

"Well, it's not unusual in this business to have a few bogus names on the payroll. Make out the paychecks, enter the amount on the tally sheet and include them on your monthly payroll request to Fisher. I'll have them endorsed, cashed and I'll deposit the money in a special account in Lac La Biche that can be used for emergencies if the company cuts back on our draws."

"Seems crooked to me, Ed," I snapped.

"What the hell, Slim, you've got enough logs cut and stacked to more than cover double the amount we owe Imperial Lumber, and it's only a precautionary measure."

Although I had no idea how much Carlson was overdrawn at that time, it didn't seem terribly dishonest, because of our large inventory of piled logs. I rationalized that it was like a temporary loan. Fisher, definitely getting snoopy, was carefully perusing and questioning each detailed request for money. He was aware we had an account in Lac La Biche as a convenience for business transacted in that town.

Carlson finally got the mill in operation in early December, and though a capable sawyer himself, hired Henry Rowbottom, who proved to be excellent. Henry hailed from central Saskatchewan and arrived with two younger brothers, one strangely called Hank, and Freddie, the youngest.

With the huge surplus of logs piled, both at the mill and in the bush, and because he wanted me to manage the camp between Christmas and New Year's while he returned to Edmonton to be with his wife's parents, Carlson suggested Ed Davis and I take a four day break and visit Lac La Biche.

Davis and I left camp on a bitter cold night on top of a load of lumber. Paul the Pole gave us forty ounces of whiskey he had saved for Christmas on the promise we would replace it from the liquor store in Lac La Biche. With several blankets we survived the torturous two hour journey to Mile 134 with the help of alcohol.

The train wasn't due to arrive until 4:30 a.m., so to keep the party going, I persuaded my laundry lady to loan us a quart of brandy until our return. As soon as we boarded, I went to sleep, but Davis picked up a little Cree Indian girl.

Arriving at Lac La Biche at 9 a.m. we went directly to Puzak's and obtained two adjoining rooms. Ed deposited his girl friend in bed; then we both went to the liquor store and each bought twelve bottles of assorted booze.

After lunch I decided to see if our bank in Lac La Biche had sufficient funds in the account to cash my October pay check. I changed the name of the branch from Edmonton to Lac La Biche, and as there were no computerized numbers in those days, it was quite negotiable. The bank remembered me from my November horse purchasing trip, and Harry Blair vouched for me, so they cashed my check without question. At least I now knew Ed Carlson wasn't withdrawing all the embezzled funds.

With the extra cash in my pocket I decided to thoroughly relax for a few days. Lac La Biche was still overrun with American oil men, who jammed every beverage room, creating a free spending environment, and money was flowing freely.

Each time Ed Davis heard me enter my room he would rouse himself, come over with a fresh bottle of booze and throw away the cork, as we never stopped until the quart was empty. Although frequently sick, I was in such perfect physical and mental condition, I would bounce back with a short rest.

The stench in Ed's room of vomit and stale sex and the filth of the little Indian girl, who never left Ed's bed, was unbearable and I avoided the room like the plague.

Irene Puzak and I went out for a party on the first evening, and afterwards stopped at a restaurant for coffee and a sandwich. Sitting at the counter and chatting with Irene, I inadvertently started tapping my coffee cup with a spoon. Suddenly, the proprietor, a smallish man, came over and shouted, "For Christ's sake, you got nothing better to do than make that infernal racket."

Embarrassed and aggravated by his unnecessary outburst, I jumped the counter, grabbed his shirt and demanded an apology. Irene, in a shrill voice, demanded I let him go. As a local girl, I guess she was frightened of any consequences. Once released, the proprietor moved back to his cash register.

Much later when Irene and I returned to the house, Ed came into my room for his usual chat and bottle opening ritual. During our conversation, I made mention of the episode at the cafe. Ed jumped up. "Do you mean to tell me you let the son of a bitch get away with talking to you that way?" he demanded.

"Relax, Ed, the guy lost his cool, but no harm was done," I answered.

But Davis had already gone to his room and in five minutes was fully dressed, the first time since we'd arrived.

"Come on, Slim. I want to see this guy that scared the crap out of you."

Walking through the winter night, I explained the whole affair and insisted I hadn't been terribly abused. It was the early hours of Saturday morning, and though the eating place was busy, there was a small table where a waitress escorted us and asked if we wanted to order. Before sitting down, Ed, looking around the room, said in a booming voice, "Where is this mouthy bastard, Slim?"

I pointed over to the proprietor, who, looking at Davis and myself, knew trouble was brewing.

Tell that guy behind the cash register, we want *him* to wait on us," Ed told the frightened waitress, who went and spoke quietly to the man, now visibly shaken.

"Can I help you?" the fellow asked when he reached our table.

"Yes," Ed said, in his usual demanding, overpowering voice. "We want two orders of roast beef, mashed potatoes, peas and gravy, and don't let anyone serve it but you."

Giving in to this troublemaker, I guess, seemed the easiest way out of the dilemma for the proprietor. Saying nothing, he went away with our order.

Except for some sandwiches Ed had brought from the Puzaks I knew he hadn't eaten since we'd left camp. I assumed after a good meal he would refuse to pay until I'd received an apology. I was hungry and looking forward to the dinner.

The cafe owner, without a liquor license, had no bouncers—only waitresses. The one R.C.M.P. officer stationed in town could be anywhere, so he had no place to turn for assistance.

As the owner approached our table with two steaming platefuls of food, my taste buds were working overtime, and I thought perhaps a decent meal might knock the chip off Davis's shoulder. That proved to be a pipe dream. Once the dishes hit the table, Ed stood up, clutched the man with one of his massive hands, grabbed the meal with the other and slammed the hot food into the proprietor's startled face.

"Now let that be a lesson, you no good bastard, and don't ever talk to my buddy like that again. Come on, Slim, let's get out of this pig pen," Davis bawled in his usual sergeant-major manner.

As I slowly left the table, the poor little guy was standing with his mouth open, mashed potatoes, gravy and peas running down his anatomy from the top of his head to his shoes. Obviously, I never entered the establishment again, but was forever mystified how Ed Davis could get away with such blatant bullying without a finger being lifted to stop him.

Like Beardmore, Ontario, Lac La Biche was a tough town, but probably not much different from any bustling mining or lumbering center where outside elements helped contribute to the breakdown in law and morality. In Lac La Biche, the extensive influx of American oil exploration teams directly competing with the increasingly prosperous lumberjacks for lodging, women and whiskey caused the majority of the trouble. The culture most affected were the Cree Indians who abounded in the area.

One example of the degradation of these once grand people occurred the second night I was in town. When away from my room, I generally wore a heavy mackinaw jacket with deep pockets in which I toted a bottle of whiskey. On the second afternoon while seated in a beverage room, I met a pleasant young chap, Rene Martel, who worked for the railroad. Although illegal, many patrons poured whiskey in a glass and used the beer as a chaser. Rene and I had a couple of drinks from my bottle, and before parting, he invited me to a house party in the evening. His fiance, Mary Petroff, from Redwater, a little town near Edmonton, was down visiting cousins in Lac La Biche; and she had an unattached sister, Laura. Rene asked if I would make up a foursome for the affair. Having nothing planned, I gladly accepted.

An Indian male, standing just inside the beverage room entrance, had been watching Rene and me with the whiskey. He followed me out the door when I left the hotel and immediately harassed me about taking the liquor to his shack for a party. As an inducement he insisted I could have my way with his beautiful young sister, and he gave her quite a build up. The little Cree, quite drunk, was persistent. Though I pushed him roughly away several times, he still followed me to the Puzak's. Ed came into my room for our drinking ceremony just as the Indian began rapping on my window and beckoning for me to come outside.

"Who the hell is that?" Davis bellowed.

I explained the situation, and Ed, in a fit of laughter, said, "Slim, get the hell out there and give him a boot in the ass, or I will."

Half disrobed as I was changing for my blind date, I slipped on trousers, heavy boots, and a jacket and stepped out the back door to get rough with the drunken Cree if persuasion wouldn't work. As I charged around the corner of the building, a female leaped from the shadows and flung herself at me like a charging rugby defensive tackle. With her legs wrapped around my middle, and arms clutching my neck, she clung as tenaciously as though drowning, and I was her only salvation.

I peeled her off limb by limb as if getting untangled from an octopus. Seeing the female's face was stomach churning. A toothless lady in her fifties and drunk as a hoot owl, she was the ugliest and dirtiest individual I ever laid eyes on. Hustling both of them through the front gate, I warned the fellow if he bothered me again there would be some rough stuff. Walking to the house I turned just at the moment the Indian drove a wicked right cross into the woman's face, knocking her into the snow. Furious at the viciousness of the blow, I made a dash towards them to prevent a reoccurrence, but he was already running, and she was stumbling through the snow, blood pouring from her mouth. I assumed he thumped her as penalty for not making a sale. I was grieved with the scene and distressed with the degradation of those sectors of our society whose living standards sink so low when money begins to flow. Without any previous experience throughout their history to prepare them, many can't adjust to the abrupt change in their lifestyles. Happily, my fortunes improved as the hours progressed.

When I entered the neat bungalow where the evening's festivities were to be held, I was greeted by Rene and saw seated around the room a dozen young people drinking, listening to music and chatting. One dark haired beauty, sitting alone, I assumed was Rene's finance, but was delighted to discover it was Laura Petroff, and not Mary, who was also attractive. Except for the fact she wasn't enamored with my partially drunken condition, we hit it off well from the beginning. Laura, of Russian descent, endowed with a well proportioned figure, plus flashing black eyes, ready wit and sophisticated manner, didn't seem to belong in the rough and tumble of Lac La Biche. After a delightful evening we became quite friendly and spent the following two days continuously in each other's company. Laura and her sister Mary were staying with her aunt.

During the second evening as we dined with Rene and Mary, Laura asked me quite suddenly.

"Bill, where are you spending the holidays?"

"Babysitting a dozen lumberjacks in Camp 12 so my boss can be with his family in Edmonton," I responded. "Why do you ask?"

"Why don't you come to Redwater with Rene and spend Christmas at our house? We have plenty of room, and my parents would welcome you," Laura said, sweetly putting her hand on my arm.

I thought I'd died and arrived in heaven as I contemplated the invitation.

Rene and Mary both rapidly endorsed the proposal, and in the euphoria of the moment I thought to hell with Carlson and Camp 12. With an opportunity to enjoy a few days with this beauteous Russian princess, Carlson's problems instantly became as insignificant as last year's holiday dinner.

"It's a deal," I said. "It sounds fantastic. I'll arrive on the afternoon train on Christmas eve."

Laura gave me her phone number and said she would meet me at the station.

Ed Davis, completely loved out, gave no trouble the following morning when I hustled him out of bed to return to camp.

Walking on air, I couldn't wait to tell Carlson about my change in plans, but wasn't quite prepared for his impassioned reaction. He pleaded, threatened, and appealed to my sympathy, and, lastly, to my moral responsibility because I had given my word. He finally wore down my determination when he promised to phone Laura from Edmonton, explain my sacrifice in his interests and tell her I would arrange for a visit in January when mutually convenient.

All the Albertans, including the Carlson's, left camp three days before Christmas. For the dozen men left in camp, Carlson shipped in two cases of whiskey, fourteen cases of beer and all the Christmas trimmings for the table. Henry Rowbottom, the sawyer, was still in camp, so I kept the mill operating until noon on Christmas eve. The boys claimed my Scrooge attitude was due to the fact I wasn't in Redwater with Laura. Although I was grieving a little over that unhappy circumstance, I knew the camp's finances were desperate and worsening, and I had substantial money at stake.

The Carlson's didn't return until a few days after New Year's; and though sawing lumber, we were shortstaffed and not in full production.

Jim Fisher was furious and told me Ed Carlson was so far in the red that Imperial Lumber was getting nervous about further draws. I tried to persuade Carlson to run the mill for two shifts, as he was also a capable sawyer. However, the threat of a financial shutdown by Imperial Lumber didn't seem to worry him.

In latter January I came down with a terrible cold which was to prove more damaging from side effects than from the virus itself. Ed Davis, the hardrock, had been in the Canadian Navy for six years and often boasted he had spent more time in the brig than on deck of the ship as a result of brawling. Ed always bragged that when he put a man down, the fight was finished, because he used his Cape Breton boxing gloves, referring to his heavy leather boots which guaranteed his adversary never got back up for a while. Ed wore the same footwear in camp and had the habit of frequently doing an impromptu tap dance which rocked our small dwelling like it was caught in the midst of a minor earthquake.

Feeling lousy when retiring one evening, I told Ralph Long and Ed Davis not to be concerned if I didn't show for breakfast, as I had taken medication and was going to try to shake my bout with the flu.

After breakfast the following morning, Ed came in my door and right beside my bed did one of his patented jigs startling me out of a dead sleep, just as suddenly as if he'd fired a double barrelled shotgun in my ear.

Jumping up, I yelled, "You ignorant son of a bitch. Don't you have consideration for anyone but yourself, you stupid bastard?" Ed just stood and stared at me for a moment, then whirled and walked out.

Feeling a little better by mid morning, I went for breakfast. Dunc, the cook, who had become a good friend, sat down while I ate and said, "Slim, did you have words with Davis this morning?"

I told Dunc what happened and said if a baseball bat had been handy, I'd have crowned the ignorant oaf.

"You'd better get the bat, Slim. Davis went to town on the first load of lumber and told everyone he is going to clean your clock when he returns tonight."

During the three months in camp I'd made a number of good friends, several of whom I'd hired. Stewart and Ronald Campbell, Ralph Long, Herman Luger, whom we called "Herman the German"; Henri and Pierre Carpentier (two powerful half breed brothers); "One Eyed Kelly", who was married to a squaw; and Ed Obleman, Kelly's closest friend. There were others, but my closest friend was Obelman, a lanky Scotchman, who had spent four years in the Canadian Provost Corps where he'd had considerable experience in physical combat. Ed Obleman did a great deal of trapping with One Eyed Kelly, and they lived near Lac

La Biche. We spent hours discussing the pleasure and excitement of operating a professional trap line. *Rolf in the Woods,* a novel written by Ernest Thomas Seaton, one of the finest writers of the out-of-doors, was our favorite reading, and we often discussed our fervent desire to ape Rolf's exploits on the trapline.

Returning to camp after Christmas, Obleman excitely informed me of an excellent 100 mile registered trap line we could purchase which included several line camps. Although it was too late in the season for 1948 trapping, Ed asked me to be his partner in the venture for the ensuing year and asked if I'd put up half the money. I enthusiastically agreed, but when Ed returned to Lac La Biche to bind the deal, the trap line had been sold. We were both deeply disappointed. Obleman, though a few years older than I, was a fine individual. As I had always dreamed of devoting part of my life to the trapping industry, it had looked like a perfect situation. But it was never meant to be. At supper Ed Obleman, who sat at my table, looked over and in a quiet voice said, "Bill, I understand Davis might be drunk and looking for trouble when he returns tonight, so I'm bringing over a cot and spending the night in the office."

"Hell, Eddie," I replied. "I'm not concerned about Davis. I'll handle him O.K."

Still miserable with the cold, I took more aspirins and retired early; but as a precaution, placed a kerosene lantern close to my bed and went to sleep.

I awoke to hear a loud voice in the room occupied by Ralph Long and Davis, and rubbing the sleep from my eyes, realized it was a drunken Davis talking to Ralph and Stewart Campbell. "There's a skunk in camp, and I can't stand the smell," I heard Ed mumble in his barroom whisper.

Listening for a few minutes to see if he would simmer down, I realized he was getting uglier, so I considered my strategy. First, I decided to attempt to reason with him, as I was no match for him physically, but if that didn't appease him, I was determined to get in the initial blow, because I outreached him by six inches. Slipping on bush trousers, heavy boots, and lighting the lantern, I stuck my head through the hole in the wall I'd created a couple of months before. In a quiet voice, I remarked, "Look, Ed, cool it; we're too good of friends to do battle. Go to bed, and we'll discuss it in the morning."

"The skunk is awake," Ed roared, jumping off his bed. "Now I'm going to chase him from camp."

When I'd hacked the opening between the rear section and my own quarters several weeks before, I left intact the bottom two eight inch boards, which meant anyone entering my living quarters had to step over a sixteen inch sill.

Putting on my heavy leather mitts to protect my hands, I decided to take my best shot if Ed stepped across that sill. On he came bellowing like a mad bull, and as he crossed the threshold, I threw a left haymaker catching him square on the side of the face. Ed went down like I'd pole-axed him, and as he crumpled to the floor, he accidently kicked over my stove still half filled with burning wood. Ralph and Stewart came rushing in with gloves and threw stove, chimney sections and flaming logs out the front door.

Ed, still dazed, slowly rose to his feet with murder in his eyes. Though he was much heavier, I knew if we swung simultaneously, I would land first again because of my reach advantage. The strategy worked perfect, except as my right cross crashed into his face, he didn't swing. Instead, as I followed through, he grabbed me by the throat, and, like I was an old shirt, tossed me on my cot.

Landing on top, Ed wrapped one of my arms across my chest with his left hand in a vice like grip, then proceeded to give me a savage beating to the face with his right. It took several seconds before I wriggled free, and once on my feet, lashed two hard blows to his face before he knocked me to the floor in a lunging tackle. Before I could regain my footing, Ed came kicking with his heavy leather boots, and landed one on my rib cage. I grasped the leg with both arms and sent him sprawling. We reached our feet simultaneously, and at that moment, I only had one thing on my mind—justifiable homicide. In a fury I leaped towards him with little thought of any logical plan of action. My wash basin stand was a rectangular board nailed to the wall near the door. As Ed staggered backwards from my charge, the corner of the shelf caught him in the small of his back. I grabbed the open door jamb with one hand and an open wall stud with the other. Bent over backwards and unable to get leverage, Davis was, at least for a moment, in a powerless position. While on the floor when Ed attacked with his boots, I'd spotted a small piece of firewood two inches in diameter near where we were standing. During the few seconds Davis was incapacitated, I planned my revenge. The moment I released him I decided to lunge for the wood and beat him into insensibility. Again, my strategy almost worked, but as I swung the wooden club at Ed's skull, his hand shot out and grabbed my wrist forcing me to release the murder weapon. He then flung me back across my bed and grabbed both wrists. For a second or two, he just looked at me, then in a sober voice spoke, "Slim, you were going to kill me." Releasing me and backing away, he continued, "If you get off that bed and continue the battle, you're going to get badly hurt. You'd better think about it."

I was whipped and knew it. Blood was pouring from my mouth and face, and my ribs ached terribly. The coward in me was rapidly overcoming the bravado, so I didn't budge but placated myself by cogitating on how and when I would get revenge.

Ralph and Stewart were assembling my stove, and Stewart brought a face cloth and basin of snow to apply to my rapidly swelling face.

As Davis stepped back into his room, he turned and spoke, "Phillips," he said, "you deserve what you got. I've told you a dozen times, when you put a man down, don't let him ever get up. You had me at your mercy."

Bathing my badly bruised face, I considered his remarks and knew for a positive certainty that the only way I could have kept Ed Davis down permanently and avoided another eventual showdown would have been to have killed him on the spot. At that moment I sincerely wished I had.

That brawl taught me just how simple it is to kill when fighting for your own survival.

While applying snow to my puffed and blackening eyes, and sensing pain in many places, I still appreciated, nonetheless, how fortunate I really was. My nose wasn't broken, and I hadn't lost any teeth. Taking a few aspirin, I finally crawled into bed and could hear Ed snoring soundly, completely unconscious, and unconcerned about his vulnerability. It amazed me how flexible are our emotions. Only an hour before I was eager to snuff out Ed's life; but now he was no longer a threat, and I'd lost my urge to kill.

I slept soundly and was roused by Dunc violently shaking my shoulder.

"Slim, hurry, get up! There's a bad situation developing in the kitchen."

Pulling on my trousers and boots, I dashed behind Dunc to the cook house. Ed Davis, his back to a corner, one of Dunc's large butcher knives in his hand, was crouched like a panther ready to spring. In a semicircle around him were Henry and Pierre Carpentier, Paul the Pole, little One Eyed Kelly, and the ringleader, Ed Obleman.

When Ed Davis arrived for breakfast with a black eye and assorted cuts and bruises, Obleman, unbeknown to me, had slipped over to the office, and seeing my battered face, informed the others who were now determined to take justice into their own hands. What particularly riled the group was when Ralph or Stewart told one of them of Davis's attack with his Cape Breton boxing gloves.

"What the hell is going on, Obleman?" I yelled.

"Keep out of it, Slim," Obleman shouted, "If this bastard wants to fight, let him thrown away the knife and tackle me."

I stepped in between the group, and in as tough a voice as I could muster, turned to Obleman and said, "Ed, I told you yesterday this was my fight, and I don't need you as a bodyguard."

Ed Carlson, hearing the ruckus from his house, had dashed into the dining hall. Sizing up the situation, he put up his hands to speak.

"Slim, go to the office and make up Davis's time check. I want him out of camp in an hour."

That defused the situation, and all the men went to work except Ralph Long. Ralph was leaving with Davis, because he believed he should have intervened, especially when Ed began using his boots. Several members of the group had openly accused him and Stewart of being cowards.

"Ralph, I hold you in no way responsible," I replied, "and will make that abundantly clear to the others."

But Ralph's conscience was bothering him, and I couldn't convince him to change his mind.

When I returned to Monominto several weeks later, a letter was waiting from Ralph with a snapshot of him and his sister, and an update on his brief association with Davis.

Shortly after arriving in Edmonton, Ed, drunk, got involved in a barroom fiasco, and the last Ralph saw was the city police handcuffing Davis and throwing him in a paddywagon. Ralph was particularly anxious to know how I'd survived the melee. I thanked him for his concern, told him my ribs had been cracked and not broken. The doctor had taped them for a couple of weeks. I then filled Ralph in on the final tumultuous weeks of Camp 12.

Ed Carlson had used ten bogus names over a three month period, kept them on the payroll records for two to three weeks, then had me make out their checks. The total he embezzled from Imperial Lumber was less than $2,000. I was almost as guilty as Carlson, but until I began to be suspicious he might go bankrupt, it seemed like good business, because of the source of emergency funds. As I became more involved in the subterfuge, it became easier to understand how many moral Germans actively participated in hideous war atrocities on the belief and pretense they were explicitly following orders. It is quite simple to get embroiled in a web of wrong doing if taken one unconstrained step at a time.

One afternoon Jim Fisher visited for an entire afternoon. He had a long chat with Henry Rowbottom to estimate our production, then talked with Carlson, and finally spent two gruelling hours going over our payroll to see where each employee came from. It was apparent the company suspected "dead horses". When Fisher left he stated the Edmonton bank account was probably frozen. I was in shock. Every pay check had been written on that account since we'd opened camp over four months before. I had three months' pay from November to February totalling $750 plus another $100 from 100 hours working as a trim sawyer. Suddenly I remembered Lac La Biche and wondered how much, if any, was in that account.

When piles of milled lumber were getting ahead of the truckers, they would frequently haul until midnight, as there was no curfew when they could unload at the siding. Also a company checker remained on duty all night. A load was leaving at 9 p.m., so I decided after scaling it I'd ride with the load of lumber to Mile 134 and catch the 4 a.m. train to Lac La Biche. Waiting for the trucker to pull in front of the office, and with my heavy mackinaw already on, I was surprised when Henry Rowbottom walked into the office.

"Going someplace, Slim?" he inquired.

"Oh, I thought I might keep the truck driver company," I replied offhandedly. Henry, a pretty intelligent chap, knew different.

"Look, Bill, I had a long talk with Fisher and know we're in financial grief," Henry stated. "If there is any possibility of cashing a paycheck, only you and Carlson would know where. I suspected if you had any ideas, you'd be leaving camp tonight. If you know where there is money, I would appreciate it if you could cash a couple of mine which I've already endorsed. Certainly my two brothers and I are deserving of some consideration."

I stood looking at this man I'd worked side by side with for three months and sensed the desperation he felt.

"Henry, I don't know if there is any money in the bank I'm heading for, and, if so, how much; but if there is enough to cash my checks, I really don't have to return.

"You aren't taking you suitcase. Are you coming back?" Henry asked.

"Yes," I replied. "Give me your checks and say nothing to Carlson."

I arrived in Lac La Biche at 9 a.m. and was at the bank when it opened at ten. The same head teller was in, and I told him Henry Rowbottom and I were buying a trapline in the vicinity and wanted to cash our checks. The teller cashed them without question. As the account was lying on the counter, I saw there was less than $100 left on deposit after the payout.

I stashed the $1500 mostly in tens and twenties in my zippered mackinaw jacket pocket and waited for the afternoon train back to Mile 134. Luckily, one of our trucks had just unloaded, so I arrived back at camp in time for the evening meal. As I often went to Mile 134 for supplies, no one was suspicious by my absence. Ed Carlson came in during the meal, walked over and said flatly, "Go to town today, Slim?"

"I'll meet you in the office in fifteen minutes, Ed," I responded, shutting off further conversation.

On my way from the dining room I walked over to Henry Rowbottom and suggested he accompany me to meet Carlson.

Ed, waiting for me as I entered my building, was sitting on my bed with a woebegone expression, and he got right to the point.

"Did you clean it out, Slim?"

"Pretty well, Ed," I replied, as I began counting out nearly $700 for Henry. "And I feel no remorse. I worked gawd-damned hard for my money, as did Henry, and if this operation gets bogged down in a boondoggle, there is no reason for us to have labored all winter for nothing. If anyone is to blame, it is Ed Carlson."

"I'm bitter, but not surprised," Ed said dolefully. "If I'd been in your place, I would have done the same, but will you stay, and let's see if we can work ourselves out of it."

"Perhaps, but first there has to be a solemn agreement that nothing leaks out about the money I just cashed, or we are all in trouble, and especially you, Ed." I stated as positively as possible. "And Henry, I did you one helluva favor, so you must guarantee not to mention it even to your brothers."

Henry, knowing nothing of "dead horses" wasn't certain why it had to be kept quiet, but he was intelligent enough to grasp the importance of my request. "Bill," he said, "keep the money locked in the commissary tonight, and I'll get it tomorrow when the bunkhouse is empty."

For the next three weeks we worked with a skeleton crew, none of them aware they might be working for nothing. I hated to be a party to the conspiracy, because the men were all my friends, but keeping the mill operating looked like the best chance for the men to get paid their winter's wages. At any rate I kept hoping something would work out.

We sawed a lot of lumber, but, unfortunately, it was all for naught. Jim Fisher came one afternoon in early March and met with me for three hours. He claimed Carlson had taken them for a bundle in early draws, and as it was impossible to cut enough lumber to get even with Imperial Lumber, the company had made the decision to take over the operation. Fisher said they were suspicious that Carlson had put a number of "dead horses" on the payroll, and if they could prove it, I was in a bundle of trouble as well.

"I don't know what the hell you're talking about, Jim. What's a 'dead horse'?" I asked looking him straight in the eyes. "And besides that, where do we cash our winter's pay checks? I doubt if we could raise $100 cash among the lot of us."

"The company has Carlson's Edmonton account frozen," he responded, "so I have no idea how you'll get paid."

It was a Friday afternoon. Before leaving, Fisher informed the men of the situation. When he jumped into his Land Rover, he hollered, "You all might as well come to Mile 134 after supper, and we'll see what can be done."

I couldn't understand why the company hadn't checked the Lac La Biche account where it would have been simple to have dug out Henry's and my cancelled pay checks, at which point they would have had Carlson and me at their mercy, because it would have been impossible to show where the funds came from. The only reason I could figure was that Fisher had failed to tell Imperial Lumber that such a bank account existed, or assumed Ed Carlson was cashing the "dead horse" checks as he received them and depositing them elsewhere.

Carlson's family had returned to Edmonton a couple of weeks before the final collapse. Excluding Carlson, there were thirteen men left in camp. Paul the Pole, three Rowbottoms, Pierre and Henry Carpentier, Ed Obleman, One Eyed Kelly, Ron and Stewart Campbell, Herman Luger, whom we called Herman the German, Dunc McFarlane, the cook, and myself. It was a downcast group that ate their last meal at Camp 12 and jumped on the back of the truck for our trip to the siding.

I recognized how important it might become for Ed Carlson and I to be able to make comparable descriptions of the so called "dead horses." We had devoted a couple of sessions to associating hair color, approximate height, stature, age, and the residences of our fictitious employees. It was well that we did.

Fisher put our group in the company bunkhouse and asked Carlson to meet with him a while. At midnight he sent for me, and for two hours Jim Fisher and I had a mental duel that covered the books, payroll records, scaling slips and partial descriptions of the men who had been in camp. Finally, Jim said, "Phillips, you will have to meet with the head office in Edmonton on Monday."

Leaping to my feet and thumping his desk with my fist, I spoke sharply. "Let me tell you something, Fisher, and listen carefully. This is Friday night, and the thirteen of us together couldn't raise fifty dollars cash. By the time we pay our fare to Lac La Biche, we will be broke. The bank there is open from 9 a.m. to 11 a.m., and we need $11,500 to cover the payroll of the thirteen. If we continue to Edmonton, the banks will be closed by the time we arrive. If you want to insist there are bogus names on the payroll, you'll have to prove it, but the twelve men in the bunkhouse, plus myself, are real people. Most of us have worked since October and don't have a red cent to show for it. What do you expect thirteen of us to do without money in this bitter cold weather?"

Jim was listening intently, and when I'd finished, asked, "And, what do you expect me to do?"

"Call an executive in Edmonton, get him to hell out of bed and tell him to get our payroll money into Lac La Biche by 9 a.m., or there will be trouble," I shouted.

"What in hell kind of trouble do you think you can cause?" he inquired derisively.

"Before I meet with Imperial, I'll visit the Department of Labor, the newspapers and the union. Up to now you have had no union problems. Well, let me tell you something. I'm a professional union organizer, and you might suggest to our executive in Edmonton if Imperial wants my union background, I'll supply it," I bluffed. "Furthermore," I continued, "if you have a beef with Carlson, it makes no sense to penalize men who worked indirectly for Imperial Lumber and did a damn good job. You don't even know how many logs are piled in the woods, because you never got off your ass to find out. The Department of Labor will insist we get paid regardless, so they may as well pay us tomorrow and save one hell of a pile of bad publicity."

Fisher was taken back with my outburst, and I had no idea what concerned him most, though he flinched when the subject of unions was broached.

"Go back to the other men, and I'll be over in a half hour," Fisher said quietly.

"Don't forget the train leaves at 4 a.m. which is only an hour," I warned, slamming the door as I left his office.

Not one of the boys was even napping when I entered the bunkhouse, and it was easy to understand the agony in their hearts at the possibility of working the winter for zilch. I was sorry there was no encouraging news, and Ed Carlson, the most dejected of the group, looked like a whipped dog.

A half hour before train time Jim Fisher entered the room. "Imperial Lumber has agreed to fund the bank in Lac La Biche by 9 a.m. tomorrow to cover your pay checks," he announced triumphantly. "But, Phillips, they want to meet with you on Monday morning."

"With bells on," I said, lying through my teeth.

A happier group of men never existed, and they clambered aboard the train like spirited school kids. As we assembled in one coach, I stated emphatically, "Gentlemen, we haven't succeeded until the cash is in our pockets. Don't anyone buy a bottle of booze or have a drink."

At that moment the boys would have done anything I asked.

Ed Carlson was ecstatic about Imperial Lumber's decision to release the money and wanted to know what I had said to Fisher, so I filled him in on what had transpired. "Ed," I said, "if we get paid, and, as you know, all I have coming is $250, it will be better for both of us if I don't meet with Imperial Lumber.

Ed wasn't stopping in Lac La Biche, and he wrote down his Edmonton telephone number.

"Slim, for Christ's sake, phone me before you leave Lac La Biche," he stated emphatically.

We arrived in Lac La Biche on time, and I asked our group to wait in the hotel two blocks from the bank while I investigated if the account had been funded. It was 9:15 a.m., and there was no money, nor was there any when I checked at 9:30, 9:45, 10:00, or 10:15. Getting nervous, I phoned Imperial Lumber's office on the perchance someone was there, although it was Saturday morning. It was obvious Imperial was expecting my call, as I was promptly connected to some executive who, thoroughly familiar with the predicament, began by telling me they weren't going to wire the money.

I went through all the arguments I'd used with Fisher seven hours before, but to no avail. Finally in desperation, and in a frenzy, I concluded my diatribe by yelling, "Let me tell you bastards sitting on your fat asses something you'd better think about. There are thirteen desperate men here without five dollars cash between them, and the temperatrure tonight is supposed to drop to thirty below. I guarantee to have a story in the Edmonton papers next week that will curdle Imperial Lumber's blood. You'll have great publicity for hiring men in the future."

"Hang on for a minute, Phillips," he ordered curtly.

About ten minutes later he came back on the phone and said Imperial had wired the payroll money but wanted to see me on Monday. It was now ten minutes before the bank's official closing time. Returning to our somber group, I said gravely, "Boys, we have a problem. There is still nothing in the account, though a company executive has assured me the money is on its way. Each man has to follow his own conscience, but I am going into the bank, and I'm not leaving until either I get my pay checks cashed or end up in jail."

As one, the dozen men arose and followed me to the bank. Before entering, I stopped, "Men, there must be no rough stuff, but on the other hand, if and when we are ordered to leave, don't move or even flinch unless I do."

We were no sooner inside when the alarm went off ending banking transactions for the day. The head teller came over and informed us the money hadn't arrived. He was apologetic but insisted there was nothing he could do, and we must vacate the building. I thanked him for his courtesy, then explained we certainly realized it wasn't their responsibility, but we were broke and had no alternative but to wait, as we were promised the funds had been telegraphed. The teller fetched the manager, who stated flatly, "Mr. Phillips, I'm sorry, but you and the others will have to leave the bank. We are not insured after 11:00 a.m.

"Sir," I replied as politely as I could. "Everyone has their own problems, and if we don't get paid, Lac La Biche is going to have major problems this weekend. I just got off the phone at 10:45 a.m. with executives of Imperial, and they guaranteed the money was on its way. If I didn't believe them, we would leave without an argument."

The manager then pleaded with the other twelve men who were all seated on the floor in the tiny anteroom. Henry Rowbottom spoke, "It's a lot warmer in here than outside, so I guess I will stay with Phillips." The others nodded their approval.

The manager invited me to his private office where for fifteen minutes he pleaded with me to be reasonable, then threatened me with police action. When I explained for the umpteenth time the funds were supposed to be sent, so why not phone Imperial Lumber, he donned his hat and coat and rapidly left the bank. I was delighted, because I thought he was finally going to phone Edmonton. But in ten minutes he returned with an R.C.M.P. officer. The constable took me into the manager's private office and explained the seriousness of my action as ringleader.

I said, "Officer, if your jail is big enough to hold the thirteen of us, at least we'll be warm and get fed. What I don't understand is why you don't have some empathy for our position and phone Imperial Lumber to find out why they haven't fulfilled their promise."

The officer went back out where the group was sitting. They were a glum, defiant, tough looking dozen. After a few moments of obvious consideration, the officer spoke quietly to the manager, and though the two said nothing to us, they departed. It was noon. Barely a word was spoken, as we all sat entranced with our own thoughts. I pondered what the boys would have said, or done, if they'd known I had over a thousand dollars cash in a money belt strapped around my middle, and also if Henry had informed Hank and Freddie, his brothers, that he had at least seven hundred.

At 12:45 p.m. the manager re-entered the bank, and before removing his coat, ordered the head teller, "Honor all checks."

The emotion that surged through the small room during the next few minutes, as that cross section of humanity realized the consequences of those three words is indescribable.

"Boys," I said, "stay where you are until Henry and I get cashed out." I knew at that moment they would obey any order I gave, and it was imperative no one see my total collection was only $250. Ironically, the teller paid me $20 too much, the only time I was overpaid in my life; but I had to leave the window before the others crowded around, so couldn't draw it to the teller's attention.

By 1:15 p.m. every check was cashed; I went and earnestly thanked the manager for his cooperation. Shaking hands, he said quietly, "You've got one hell of a pile of nerve, Mr. Phillips."

Due to the euphoria of our victory, and the utter glee and relief of my cohorts, I completely forgot the $20 overpayment. It was a terrible embarrassment when the teller came up to me a half hour later in the hotel where the celebration was just getting under way.

"Mr. Phillips, didn't I overpay you by $20? It comes out of my pay, so I'll split it with you if that's O.K."

So gawd damned ashamed, I could barely talk, I handed him the twenty and tried to explain it wasn't my intention to keep it, but in the excitement forgot the error. I don't know if he believed me, but I hope he did.

Henry and I phoned Carlson and explained the tremendous asperity in getting the money. Ed was fully aware of our travail, because he was in Imperial Lumber's office when I phoned. He wasn't certain what it was I finally said that shook them up, but whatever it was, it thoroughly disturbed them, and they succumbed to our demands.

"Slim," he said, "they are expecting you to arrive on this afternoon's bus and will likely have someone there to establish where to contact you Monday. You must avoid a meeting with them, if possible. I have two personal friends, both big boys, who will greet you as you step off the bus. I told them you'd be wearing a bright red mackinaw. They will take you to a hotel where I have five rooms reserved. Let Henry and the others bring your luggage. Good luck, and I'll see you at the hotel tonight."

He then spoke with Henry giving him the name of the hotel and warned him to tell no one until they were leaving the Edmonton bus depot by cab.

Whiskey was flowing freely, and the victory spree was flourishing when the bus arrived at 4 p.m. Ed Obleman, One Eyed Kelly, and the Carpentier brothers were staying in Lac La Biche. I was particularly sorry to part company with Obleman, and we vowed to keep in touch and get together in a few months.

We had a ten minute stopover in Redwater, and I was determined to remain, but there was no answer at the Petroff's. Laura had written a long and passionate letter in January, and I had assured her that no later than February I would pay a visit. With all the drama since Christmas, I hadn't forgotten the stunning beauty and had every intention of keeping my promise to continue our relationship. But like Ed Obleman and the others, she was soon to become just another pleasant memory in life's manuscript.

Things worked to perfection at Edmonton. One minute after stepping off the bus, Ed's friends had whisked me away. Henry said later two men from Imperial Lumber were inquiring of my whereabouts, and he told them I was visiting friends in Redwater and would be in Edmonton on Monday.

The remaining eight were determined to spare no expense at rejoicing at our triumph, so we had a gala celebration. Ed Carlson joined the happy affair and was extremely grateful for the part I played in getting the winter's wages for the men. He insisted he had nothing to show for his winter's efforts, and though he felt responsible for our failure, was disappointed he hadn't inveigled some cash for himself and family, as they were financially strapped. Ed Carlson had no reason to deposit any of the "dead horse" pay checks in the Lac La Biche account, unless he earnestly meant to use them for emergencies, as he had originally claimed. Therefore, I always felt a little guilty I'd beaten him in cleaning out the account, so I was delighted to make him aware of a simple fact he had overlooked in the confusion.

"Ed, my friend. You're not thinking so good," I said, slapping him on the back. "There is fifteen hundred bucks lying in the bank at Lac La Biche."

"What the hell are you talking about, Slim?" he asked in puzzlement.

"I got the money for the entire winter's payroll including the 'dead horses', didn't I?" I responded. There was no way we could draw it out, so unless Imperial has discovered or remembered the account, the money is there for the taking. I think it would be better if all the money is withdrawn and the account closed."

Ed suddenly realized to what I was referring. He chortled, danced around, hugged me, then went someplace and bought six bottles of whiskey. "I'll be at Lac La Biche 9 a.m. Monday morning, Slim, and I'll write you in Manitoba to let you know how I made out."

My memory of the following 36 hours has many blank spots, and I know my plans changed frequently. At times I was determined to go into Imperial Lumber and try to clear my name. At other moments, feeling more romantic and less righteous, I made plans to rendezvous with Laura in Redwater.

I wanted to reach Vancouver and apply for a job as shipper on a tramp steamer, but on Monday afternoon found myself at the railway station with the Rowbottoms, Paul the Pole, and Herman the German with a ticket to Winnipeg. To this day I'm not certain who made the final decision. Someone had arranged a lower berth for me, and I took full advantage and slept until we were halfway across Saskatchewan.

When my head cleared, and I recollected the happenings of the previous five months, I was ashamed of my actions involving Imperial Lumber, but proud of my role in obtaining the winter's wages for the men, who were innocent of any wrongdoing. By allowing myself to get entangled in Ed Carlson's nefarious scheme, I was a criminal by complicity. At the beginning, it seemed so innocent, but ended up making me a fraud and a liar. Fortunately, there wasn't a substantial amount of money at stake, and I have no doubt Imperial Lumber easily recouped their loss, as plenty of logs were stacked near the mill. It was an unpleasant experience and taught me well how easily and innocently an individual can become enmeshed in criminal activities.

A few weeks after arriving home I received a letter from Ed Carlson with pictures of his family. He did acquire the $1500 and closed the Lac La Biche account. Also the Carlson's had moved to Dawson Creek, B.C., and he had a good job driving a semi-trailer on the Alcan Highway. Ed was particularly delighted to inform me that Imperial Lumber had absolved him of any wrongdoing, and seriously doubted they had any further interest in me. He fully recognized it was me who had kept us from serious trouble and thought we'd make outstanding partners in the lumber industry. I never responded to his letter. It was a section of my personal history I wanted to forget.

Part II
The East

Chapter 1

Change of Life/ Change of Scene

Racing across the prairies towards Winnipeg and peering through the frosted coach windows, watching indications of spring diffusing the severity of the prairie winter, gave me ample time for contemplating my next adventure.

I was determined first to have a short vacation and perhaps ask Betty Rasmussen, who was entering my thoughts quite frequently, if she would accompany me to the occasional dance. Even after replenishing my wardrobe and making the usual contribution to father's financial well being, I figured there should still be sufficient funds to afford some relaxation. I, however, was thoroughly bewildered as to what to tackle following my holiday. The resolution to give up harvesting was still definite, and the wild experiences of the winter with Imperial Lumber had cooled my ardor for lumberjacking as well, and I had an immense yearning to travel.

Ed Davis and I had planned to go to Vancouver after finishing with Ed Carlson and apply for a job on a tramp steamer. Davis had a connection of some sort with the Merchant Navy and was certain with my Grade XI education I could land a job as clerk or checker. Our brawl put an end to those plans, but he had mentioned that Halifax was an ideal port for such a venture. Thus I contemplated travelling to the Canadian east coast to apply for a position on a cargo vessel. If successful, I could begin satisfying my urge to see the world while earning a livelihood. As things were to turn out, all of my tentative schemes were to dematerialize and my mode of living soon to take a dramatic shift.

251

Moments after being greeted by Mother, she took a close look at me and asked who had taken a club to my face. I was astonished the after effects of the battle were still visible. The family was as delighted to see me as I to be reunited with them, but perhaps Jack's greeting was the most enthusiastic.

"By gawd, you're just the man I hoped to see!" He said grasping my hand.

"What the hell is your hurry?" I responded, "The snow is not even off the ground, and the ball season can't possibly start for two months at least."

"No, it's not baseball," Jack interrupted, "I just signed a contract to cut two railroad cars of four foot pulpwood fifty miles east of here, and though I've cut plenty of cordwood, you're the expert on pulpwood. We leave by train Monday morning." He concluded as though that settled the issue.

"Good luck, and you'll find sawing pulp identical to cutting cordwood except it's softwood instead of hardwood," I answered slapping him on the back. "I retired the pitchfork last fall, the swede saw this spring, and after a short vacation I'll be looking for a new career."

With a determined glint in his eyes, Jack closed the topic by saying, "We'll kick it around for a day or two."

At the Saturday night Monominto shindig, I had a great reunion with all the gang but was disappointed to learn Jack had also become attracted to the beauty of Betty Rasmussen and was dating her steadily.

Throughout the weekend my brother kept urging me to reconsider his proposal to become a partner in the pulpwood project, and just as adamantly I turned him down. On Sunday evening he invited me to the local bootlegger for a few bottles of brew and a final crack at convincing me to join him for two weeks in the bush. His decisive line of reasoning to change my mind was a suggestion that if we worked like hell at cutting pulp and cordwood until the end of April, we would have sufficient funds to purchase our own car. It was an exciting prospect, so I agreed to return to the bush for a final fling.

The chainsaw was new on the market, and it was still considered more of a play toy than a genuine replacement for the reliable, but back breaking swede saw. So with gear becoming as expeditiously outdated as the threshing machine, we boarded the gas car on the GWWD on Monday morning and travelled halfway to the Ontario border to fulfill the pulpwood contract. Our accommodation was an old log cabin greatly resembling the dilapidated old shack I wintered in at the Brokenhead River. As we also had to do our own cooking, the entire setup was a tremendous comedown from my previous two sessions as a lumberjack. A good stand of spruce and balsam near camp yielded sufficient pulp to speedily fulfill Jack's obligation, and within two weeks we were back in Monominto.

During April we returned to the farm to cut cordwood for which there was still a Winnipeg market, though the steady influx of gas and oil furnaces was speedily diminishing the need for wood as a fuel.

We worked like demons throughout April, and with assistance from Ed Barham with his tractor and buzz saw, had a huge pile totalling 75 cords ready for sale by month's end. It would be the last crop I would ever take part in harvesting from land that had been a predominant part of my early existence.

We sold our wood to a Winnipeg dealer for $5.75 a cord realizing slightly more than $400. With that money, plus a little added to it, we went car shopping. After careful price comparison, a 1935 dark blue Dodge was purchased. Jack and I took turns driving our prized possession back to Monominto, and it stands as one of the proudest and happiest days in my life. It was the first sizable asset either of us had ever owned.

At the time, neither Jack nor I had formulated any definite plans for the immediate future. However, a few days after our automobile acquisition, an incident occurred that was a direct result of that purchase and would become a major factor in changing both of our destinies forever.

Jack, Ruth and I usually went to the local social functions together in the Graham Paige, although at the Saturday night dances, we frequently returned home separately. These were prosperous times, and most young people not only had a few dollars in their pocket, but also the availability of a car, whether their own or one belonging to their parents. Therefore, we were no longer restricted to the Monominto Dance Hall, but could attend barn dances or other shindigs of which there were several within a radius of ten miles. This range allowed a much greater opportunity for young people to meet a larger number of the opposite sex. As a result, mixed marriages were becoming common: French, Danish, Ukrainian and Anglo Saxons were intermarrying at a rate unheard of only a decade before.

It was a joyful time with a steady outpouring and excellent selection of music. There were ballads: "Dance Ballerina Dance" and "My Happiness", sprightly airs: "Candy Kisses" and "Enjoy Yourself", the popular "Too Fat Polka" and songs that remained popular for years such as "On a Slow Boat to China" and "The Tennessee Waltz".

Though I cavorted with several of the local belles, I hadn't lost my liking for Betty and danced with her far more than all the others combined. Whenever "The Tennessee Waltz" was played, I automatically looked for Betty as my partner, as she taught me to waltz.

One Saturday night in early May, Jack and Betty had a spat, and a chap from another village was making a play for her with the intention of escorting her home. With the availability now of two cars, we had much greater independence; and on this particular Saturday night, I had the Dodge and Jack the Graham Paige. I asked Betty if she would allow me the privilege of driving her home, and she readily agreed. When I left Monominto Hall arm in arm with Betty, my brother and sister were glaring at me in a very unfriendly manner. I had a delightful evening and didn't return home until 4 a.m.

Mom, Dad, Jack and Ruth were having a cup of tea as I entered, and they looked at me like I'd just stolen the crutches from a cripple. I never stopped walking and began climbing the stairway to my bedroom when Jack spoke up, "Bill, come and sit down for a minute. I'd like to discuss this evening with you."

"I've nothing to discuss." I snapped and continued to my bed.

The following morning at breakfast, Jack asked in a pleasant voice, "Bill, how about you and I going over to Rasmussen's and see if Betty and Asta are free this afternoon and want to go for a car ride?" Asta, Betty's sister, was three or four years older than Betty.

"Sounds like a great idea," I responded, "Let's go."

As there was no phone service, we had to drive over to Rasmussen's to see if the girls were willing to join us. Delighted, they were ready in a few minutes. When the two girls approached the car, Betty slid in the front beside me, leaving Jack no alternative but to sit with Asta in the rear seat.

The day went by pleasantly enough, but whenever we switched driving, and Jack took the controls, Betty jumped into the back with me. Jack was obviously disturbed, and I didn't know if Betty preferred sitting with me, or was just trying to annoy Jack.

Late in the afternoon as we stopped for refreshments, Betty sitting in the booth beside me quietly whispered, "Bill, let's run away and get married." I know she was teasing, but the sudden thought of marriage shocked me like I'd seen a ghost, and Betty was giggling with glee at my discomfort.

I never did ask her, but often wondered what she would have said if I replied, "O.K., I'll pick you up tomorrow afternoon." At the time, I was enough in love with her to have considered the invitation, but the uncertainty of whether she was just trying to get even with Jack for something kept me from seriously considering her remark. When we returned the girls to their home, I asked Betty if I could see her the following afternoon, and she agreed.

On Sunday evening at home I asked Mom if she would prepare my clothes, as I was leaving Tuesday for points east. Jack inquired about my plans.

"Jack, you're as miserable as hell," I stated, "and I don't know if Betty Rasmussen is interested in me, you or either of us, but when I take her out tomorrow afternoon, I will tell her I'm definitely leaving for the east and will contact her when I settle down to a permanent address. Meanwhile, the field is open for you. Although you own half the car, I will drive it east and remit your half as soon as I am able."

Jack said nothing for a while, and about a half hour later came over and said, "Let's go over to the bootleggers for a beer. I want to talk this over."

We kicked the situation around for a while, and finally Jack said, "No one has ever stepped between us before, and no woman is going to separate us now. So if you're agreeable, I'm going east with you Tuesday morning. Besides," he added, "it's half my car."

The following afternoon Betty and I went for a long ride and had an enjoyable discussion. Her plans were to leave Monominto in six weeks to begin teaching. We decided to correspond, and she gave me a beautiful enlarged photograph of herself, but neither of us made a commitment.

That evening Father and I got into a final argument over the disposition of the farm, but he held tenaciously to the position that it was his exclusive asset, and he had no intention of relinquishing ownership.

Packing our Dodge the following morning was not a happy occasion. There were lumps in everyones' throats, as it was evident this was more than a temporary parting. I had made it clear I was searching for an identity and wouldn't stop until I discovered my niche in life. However, the saddest aspect of our departure was the condition of Ruth. She had been feeling poorly for several weeks, and the doctors had been unable to diagnose her ailment. Her healthy complexion had taken on a pallid appearance, and she lost a considerable amount of weight. When we embraced goodbye, a feeling of great sadness swept over me.

Jack and I both loved to travel and observe new country, and the depression we felt at our joyless departure gradually dissipated as we traversed the sparkling lakes, and heavily forested rollercoaster countryside of Eastern Manitoba and Western Ontario.

Critically short of cash, we decided to cook our meals on the shores of secluded lakes and sleep in the car. Because it was still early May, the nights were cold in northern Ontario and in some cases we were so miserably chilled, we'd simply keep driving. The Dodge's small "South Bend Heater" gave off a little warmth, so we were more comfortable while moving.

When reaching Port Arthur-Fort William, now called Thunder Bay, we inquired about the best route east and were informed the northern route consisted mostly of narrow gravel roads frequently rough and rutted with only occasional patches of pavement. We were aware it might be shorter by circling back southwest around Lake Superior, crossing the U.S. border and taking the American route, but I had reservations about travelling in the U.S. Having never been out of Canada, I had a certain apprehension of confronting these Americans about whom I had mixed emotions, particularly when desperately short of funds. To hear them on the radio was one thing, but to associate with them on their own territory was an entirely different cup of tea. We therefore chose the northern Ontario route.

The sharp stones covering the roadway punctured our tires, and we were forced to purchase new rubber. That, together with gas and food, soon depleted our meager money supply, as the plastic credit card was still years from being introduced. We slept a while in the car Friday night, our fourth on the road, just south of North Bay and 200 miles from Toronto. After filling with gas and having breakfast, we were flabbergasted to realize our total cash had dwindled to under ten dollars.

At 4 p.m. Saturday, May 13, we reached the northern boundary of Toronto. Highway #11 connects North Bay with Toronto, and at the city outskirts becomes Yonge Street which is known as the longest street in the world. Streetcars travelled down the center of Yonge Street, flanked on both sides by two lanes for automobile traffic. I was driving and didn't realize vehicles had to stop and give the right of way to passengers jumping off the trams at designated stops. After swerving, braking and barely missing several cursing transit riders, it suddenly struck Jack, who had spent a few days in the city in the early years of his Air Force training, that Toronto law required us to halt behind trams while discharging passengers. Waiting for pedestrians slowed down our rate of movement, and it took one and a half hours to cross the city, but I never stopped until reaching the end of Yonge Street at Lake Ontario. It was a gorgeous, sunny, spring afternoon and the enormous lake dotted with islands looked picturesque and enchanting.

With a half a tank of gas, a total of five dollars, and dog tired from the five day crossing with little sleep, we considered our options.

"Should we find a cheap hotel room?" Jack suggested wearily.

"With so little cash, I think we'd be better off locating a boarding house." I replied.

I bought a paper and checked off several places advertising for boarders, then went to a pay phone, which still cost a nickel, and made some calls. One lady, Mrs. Jowett, who lived in the east end of the city said she was asking $14 per week including room and board, and would like us to come over. She gave directions to reach her Sammon Avenue home in east Toronto. On the way Jack said to me, "Sport, if they want $14 per week each, won't they want it in advance?"

"It's a gamble," I responded, "but you smile a lot, turn on the charm, and I'll deal with the money situation when I think the time is appropriate."

The Jowett's greeted us warmly, and spying our Manitoba license plates, immediately inquired about our journey. Inviting us into the living room they introduced us to Al Richard, another boarder; their son Ted, in our age bracket; and a twelve year old daughter, Marlene. Both Jowett's were English born and seemed delighted with the prospects of having Jack and I as their new boarders. After showing us the lovely bedroom, nicely appointed with ample furniture, I decided it was time to drop the bombshell.

"Mrs. Jowett," I said quietly, "everything is perfect, but the fact of the matter is we are broke. The car is paid for, and we can probably arrange a small loan on Monday. Also, we will both be getting jobs the first of the week."

After a brief huddle, they told us to unpack, and at that moment two more relieved young men didn't exist in Toronto.

We searched for work on Monday without success, but in Monday afternoon's paper I phoned in response to an advertisement for lumber shippers at T.H. Hancock in the west end of Toronto. On Tuesday morning I applied and was hired to start at once, although the pay was only 75 cents per hour. While I was in Hancock's, Jack walked across the street to a large hardware wholesale distributor, Cochrane Dunlop, and landed a job paying approximately $65, twice monthly. The low remuneration was a disappointment, but at least it would pay room and board, plus give us gas and tobacco money until we could improve our circumstances. Our friendly co-roomer, Al Richard, loaned us $10 for immediate expenses until our first paycheck. So in 1949 for the first and only time in my life I joined the 9-5 crowd of blue collar workers. At the time I didn't remotely envision that Toronto, would be my domicile and principal place of business for thirty fascinating and exciting years.

The world in the late forties was going through a metamorphosis which affected North Americans, perhaps more than other nations. Prosperity and civil peace was general. Production, employment and income reached new highs, but a new wave of strikes in 1948 brought a third round of inflationary wage boosts. General Motors granted an 11 cents per hour wage increase, and the United Auto Workers got a cost of living clause based on the Consumer Price Index included in their settlement. The American cost of living had reached an all time high. Early in 1949 a new minimum wage act raised the minimum hourly wage from 40 cents to 75 cents.

The developing welfare state in Canada was well described by author William Kilbourn. "The expanding federal civil service now administrating the welfare state introduced in the 1940's, continued to exhibit its customary professional skill and competence. Its lifestyle remained that of the archetypal Ottawa man who did nothing by halves which could be done by quarters!" Unquote. In 1949 the burgeoning growth of government was only a trickle, but in a quarter century it would reach cataract proportions.

Canadians were also becoming disturbed about the increased percentage of U.S. involvement in their industry. In fact, Canada's economy as a whole had acquired a steadily increasing dependence on their giant neighbor, who now had displaced Great Britain as the chief non-resident investor in the country. By 1949, 40% of Canadian manufacturing industry was controlled by U.S. residents.

A major cause of the inflationary spiral in North America in the post war period was the competition among the different unions. By trying to surpass each other in wage structures and increased benefits, they drove the cost of manufacturing and resource production to an all-time high. Subsequently, prices to the consumer began to skyrocket.

In Canada it was the automobile, steel and asbestos industries. In the U.S. in 1948, 360,000 soft coal miners struck for $100 per month retirement benefits at age 62. In the same year President Truman ordered the Army to operate the railroads to prevent a nationwide rail strike. In 1949 coal workers struck again, and Truman invoked the Taft-Hartley Act. The steel workers also struck and won company paid pensions. Unions, however, were not the only culprit in fueling the fires of inflation.

Money hungry industrialists, and an exploding government bureaucracy were also responsible. It would take several years, but this avaricious and potent combination would eventually precipitate an inflationary rate of over double digit figures annually. Noted economists and financial writers of the day were predicting that unless business and labor reached a compromise on wage increases and benefits, and if the different levels of government didn't slow their pace of soaring growth, North America would ultimately price itself out of world markets, with the obvious dire consequences of lost industrial jobs and a wrecked economy. No one listened because the human race has a history of never interfering with, or amending political, economical or sociological problems until catastrophe strikes, even though those perplexities are plainly evident. They either become so ponderous that even with a complete policy reversal it takes years to correct, or the situation becomes insurmountable altogether and a complete collapse is the final outcome.

The average citizen expects his country's leaders, whether government, union or industrial, to steer the nation on the most propitious path toward prosperity and happiness. Those leaders, however, whether elected or appointed, when forced to make unpopular decisions for the long term good are faced with a dilemma. If they only maintain the status quo or can be held accountable for even a slight drop in the standard of living for a short while, though it may be highly beneficial in the long run, that leader will lose the confidence, and therefore the patronage of those citizens. Without that support under our democratic system, he would lose his power base, fat salary and hence reduce his mode of living. So for self preservation he has little alternative but to approve a short term fix, regardless of whether it requires mortgaging the future.

Other areas of the planet were also in a state of flux; 1948 and 1949 saw a substantial increase in tension between the East and West. In the summer of 1948, Soviet occupation forces in Germany blockaded rail and highway traffic between West Germany and Berlin. Britain and the U.S. began an airlift that continued for over twelve months until the Russians lifted the blockade. The Allies made almost 300,000 flights carrying up to 45,000 tons of food and supplies per day.

The State of Israel was proclaimed in 1948 as the British mandate over Palestine expired. Although the struggling nation would eventually obtain enormous financial support from the U.S., few people expected the Israelis to withstand the constant pressure and animosity from the surrounding Arab countries that numerically outnumbered them by such a huge proportion. The creation of the seemingly insignificant new nation of Israel would become one of the world's greatest headaches for the next half century and a constant source of tension due to continuous attempts at political favoritism by the East and West with Israel and different Arab factions.

There was an enormous world power shift to the Communist camp in 1949 when Mao-Tse-Tung became leader of the most populous country in the world. Chiang Kai-shek moved his Nationalist forces to Taiwan where, only with U.S. aid, did the courageous Non-Communist island hold off their giant Red brothers on the mainland and become one of the show pieces of capitalism on the face of the globe.

The average North American watched these enormous shifts in the world's affairs with far more interest than they did a dozen years earlier when Hitler was gaining power. However, the innumerable new products pouring onto the marketplace mostly as a result of increased technology accelerated by the war, were helping keep peoples' minds on other things. The transistor, developed at Bell Telephone laboratories, would revolutionize the electronics industry, especially radios, computers, television and lead to the development of guided missiles. Diesel locomotives were replacing coal fired steam engines that had played such an impressive role in opening up the vast expanses of North America, resulting in the loss of a major market for coal. Air conditioners were being placed in automobiles for the first time, and it is unimaginable now that people survived in the hot months without this device in cars, homes and offices.

Perhaps the most enormous change in our way of life during those years was television. Although screens were still quite tiny, and reception was often terrible, new TV stations were springing up at a rapid rate, and programming was beginning to improve. "Ted Mack's Amateur Hour," "The Ed Sullivan Show," "Hopalong Cassidy" and "The Colgate Comedy Hour" were some of the favorites of the late forties. Though television was rapidly becoming a booming industry, only slightly over one million homes boasted a TV at the time.

Movie theaters were thriving, and John Wayne continued as a Matinee idol. "Red River" produced in 1948 would help make him a box office favorite for over thirty years.

North America was not the only part of the free world, during those years, experiencing labor trouble and creeping socialism. In 1949 the Australian government sent in troops to work the coal mines when coal workers refused to settle their dispute.

Dock workers struck in Britain, which resulted in closing the ports and partially paralyzing many industries. Britain's Labor Government began the National Health Insurance Program in 1948, and in the same year nationalized the railways. In 1949 they nationalized the iron and steel mills. Britain had proved it was a gutsy nation but now by constantly bowing to the whims of the union led masses, and Labor Government, their history as leader of the free world was rapidly diminishing, and the socialistic whirlwind was the cause of their downfall.

While the incessant struggle continued between labor, industry and government throughout the free world, I went to work at T.H. Hancock as an hourly worker. It was a position I would not retain long, though, as I was destined in the near future to change sides in this continuous battle between the three great divisions of society.

Chapter 2

Salesman!

Joining the masses struggling to and from work came as a tremendous shock to my system. I had known little restraint on my movements since a teenager. No cross city throughways existed in Toronto in 1949, and living in the eastern sector while working in the extreme west, required a full one and one-half hour traffic entangled, torturous journey twice each day.

Not only was the trip vexatious, but the job itself aggravated the hell out of me. Stacks of lumber and other highly inflammable materials covering the premises made smoking taboo. For an individual like myself who smoked heavily, this restriction made an unpleasant situation intolerable. Now I understood why a wild bronco that spent years on the range unhampered, found difficulty adjusting to harness and kicked over the traces when forced to pull a plow. Freedom of movement, a precious liberty, is too often taken for granted by those blessed with it, but when that independence is suddenly disrupted, it comes as a terrible jolt. Jack wasn't particularly enthralled with his regimen either.

We decided to tough it out until the July 1 long weekend. By then our debts would be discharged and we'd have a few dollars saved with which to escape the city. Al Richard had a brother in Welland, Ontario, whom we decided to visit. Welland, seventy miles south of Toronto and only thirty miles from Niagara Falls and Buffalo, made an ideal circuit for the holiday weekend.

The Welland Canal, connecting Lake Erie with Lake Ontario, runs through the center of the picturesque town. Blessed with gorgeous summer weather, Jack and I opted to spend the night on the grassy banks of the waterway while Al visited his relatives. Relieved to be back in the open air, we slept like new born kittens until 6 a.m. when the

261

first lake steamer bypassed our stake out. Without forethought we had picked our location fifty feet from a lift bridge and were lying no further than ten feet from the canal. To alert the bridge operator, the ship's captain let go a blast from his steamer's whistle. This unexpected din, shattering the morning stillness only twenty feet from where we slumbered, was a rude awakening. Bolting out of our bedding, we almost leaped into the water before realizing what caused the dream shattering racket. Although shaken, we watched with delight the huge ship, its sides almost within touching distance, quietly gliding down the vital waterway in what was once again a tranquil setting.

We spent a pleasurable next day at Niagara Falls marvelling at that spectacular attraction and thoroughly enjoying our probation from the travails of big city living. In the evening we elected to visit Buffalo.

A strange emotion encompassed me when we bypassed the Union Jack on the Rainbow Bridge and came under the domination of the Stars and Stripes. All my life I had been influenced by uncomplimentary remarks and articles dealing with our huge Southern neighbor. In the thirties it was regarding their stand on free trade; during the early war years it dealt with their isolationist stance while the free world fought for survival. Now it was the steady influx of American capital into the manufacturing sector that displeased many Canadians. Another irritant was the blatant attitude of many Yanks that they alone had won the war. This inflamed Canadians who had entered the conflict of their own free will and were totally involved more than two years before the Americans were forced into the fray as a result of Pearl Harbor. On the other hand, every song, movie or book that entertained us was almost exclusively American, and I was as knowledgeable of their history and culture as their citizens and took great pride in their nation's present power and spectacular accomplishments.

When we reached the outskirts of Buffalo, billboards and signs blanketed the city advertising the Barnum & Bailey Circus, yet another prime example of how American institutions affected our lives. Jack and I were so anxious to view the famous circus that racing to the site, we almost had a half dozen automobile accidents. The show was nearly over with many of the huge tents already being dismantled, but we snuck into the main arena and caught the final few acts. It made the entire trip worthwhile.

Jack and I revelled in our hiatus from slave labor, and it was apparent from joint conversations that neither could long accept the status quo. In fact, Jack stated that if he could hitchhike a ride to Winnipeg, he would leave immediately. I decided to earn another weekly paycheck, then take an afternoon off and visit the local government unemployment office. Mr. Hill, a pleasant elderly gentleman was my interviewer. After getting a little history on my background and experience, he asked, "Where have you been working since your arrival in Toronto, Bill?"

"T.H. Hancock as a lumber shipper," I replied.

"My gawd, if you smoke, no wonder you want to leave," he said earnestly. "Have you thought of trying something new?"

"Such as what, Mr. Hill?"

"Selling!"

"Selling what?" I asked.

"Well, perhaps Fuller Brush if you have a car. They pay no salary, but if you are willing to work diligently, a lot more money can be earned selling their products than you'll ever make piling lumber." Mr. Hill responded with conviction.

I tried to picture myself knocking on doors, or what it would do to my dignity to have them slammed in my face. On the other hand, I considered the freedom the job would allow a definite plus, as once again I'd be in charge of my daily existence.

Mr. Hill interrupted my thoughts. "There is a crew manager in the east end of the city named Gus Webber. I'm getting good reports on the job he is doing with his sales people. Let me call to see if he has an opening, and if so, go and have a chat and then decide."

Gus Webber lived only a few blocks from the Jowetts, and I dropped in for an interview on my way home. A territory was available almost at my back door, and with Gus's enthusiastic encouragement, I elected to try my hand at door to door sales. Gus gave me a sample case, product information sheets, price lists and a pamphlet on the techniques used to sell their products. When parting, he said if I studied over the week-end he would take me out cold canvassing on Monday morning. I devoted the next two days to the task of becoming a knowledgeable Fuller Brush salesman.

It was a brilliant hot July morning when we approached the first house. Gus turned to me, "Bill, for the next three hours, I'm working for you. Do not say one word unless spoken to. Watch intently and listen carefully to everything I say or do."

By noon Gus had written orders for $42 worth of goods! At 40 percent commission that was earnings equalling four days' salary at T.H. Hancock. I was totally flabbergasted.

"Well, do you think you can operate on your own?" Gus asked.

"I sure as hell am game to give it a whirl," I replied.

Although nervous and occasionally embarrassed due to lack of experience in dealing with prices and procedure, by 5 p.m. my total sales, including the $42 from the morning session, totalled over $100. That represented earned commission of $42, $12 more than forty hours work as a lumber clerk, and I was my own boss.

That evening I ecstatically tried to convince Jack to join me and give it a try, but he was determined to return west, in fact, had already made arrangements. By mid-July he left for Winnipeg.

Toronto's summer of 1949 was unseasonably hot, so pounding pavement and knocking on doors in sweltering temperatures was physically demanding. Nevertheless, I was damned successful. Fuller Brush has changed its "modus operandi" considerably since my stint with the company.

During my limited period of employment, salesmen were responsible for all deliveries and collections. The first week's order was sent direct to the Fuller factory, and the goods delivered to your residence for redelivery. With each succeeding requisition, you remitted payment for the previous one less whatever percentage discount you were entitled. The amount of discount was based on the total selling value of the order, and 42 percent was the highest deduction attainable. During my ten week tenure with the company, I never received less than the maximum discount.

It was a hard driving occupation. Gus Webber held at least two sales meetings per week with members of his crew, and each Monday evening, the city's 200 salesmen and managers assembled in a large hall in downtown Toronto for a two hour orientation session. They had a song book with two dozen old favorites such as "Old Oaken Bucket," with the lyrics converted to lauding the merits of Fuller Brush articles and technique. Those men with the largest weekly and monthly orders were heralded and invited to the dais to expound on the reasons for their outstanding success. It was a rare week when I wasn't the leader, or at least within the top five in the city. The job itself and the training was magnificent tutelage for any aspect of the selling profession, but it was also equally beneficial for building confidence and erasing self doubts in dealing with people in general.

My exceptional success with Fuller Brush was due to several factors. Financially hungry, I worked like hell, because to me earning between two and three hundred dollars per week was incredible. Also, several products in the inventory were hot items at the time. For example, the "Squeegee" mop; of which Fuller Brush produced an excellent model, was constantly advertised and promoted by all major stores, which made it a must item for every housewife, so I used it as a door opener. In addition, my territory located in a better than average income neighborhood in East York, was inhabited mostly by affluent, young married couples who were not hesitant to spend a dollar. But, perhaps the principal reason for my high achievement was due to a current hit movie, "The Fuller Brush Man", starring Red Skelton, which provided a great deal of excellent publicity, and I used it to maximum advantage. Despite my success, I only remained with Fuller Brush until early September.

The Jowetts lived in a semi-detached home. Semi-detached houses share one common wall and usually a front porch separated only by a small balustrade. An elderly bachelor, Cecil Holden, lived with our next door neighbors, and frequently in the evenings, while sitting on our shared veranda, we got into conversation. Cec, a real estate broker, showed a keen interest in my selling proficiency and oftentimes suggested I should try my hand at selling real estate which provided a superb opportunity to earn large amounts of money.

One hot day in early September, knocking on doors suddenly became onerous, so I elected to drive to Danforth Avenue, the main east-west Toronto thoroughfare, and apply for a position in real estate. The name of A.W. Farlinger stood out in my mind because of seeing their extensive daily newspaper advertising for men. They had seven offices located in various parts of the city, including one on Danforth Avenue, to which I applied.

After some general questioning, the manager looked over my seedy suit, then asked what type of car I owned. I answered. After only a moment's hesitation he said, "Mr. Phillips, we are not hiring right now, however, George Farr, a new broker, is just opening an office a few doors up the street. I suggest you go and see him."

I knew he was lying, because of the constant ad running in the sales help wanted section of the paper. I could understand his reluctance, however, with an old car, my lack of knowledge of the city's geography, deficiency of real estate experience, plus a shabby appearance made me a rather poor looking prospect to successfully sell property. Undaunted, nevertheless, I decided to walk the few doors to George Farr and find out if he would be interested in hiring me. It would turn out to be one of the most consequential decisions of my life.

Stepping inside the door of the small office there was no one except a short man with a greying crew cut and huge moustache sitting behind a desk reading the paper. Before I took two steps he spoke up in a cheerful voice, "Can I help you?"

"My name is Bill Phillips, and I wondered if you're looking for salesmen," I said in a nonchalant manner.

Leaping up, he grabbed my hand, "You're damn right I am, Bill. Do you know where Sammon Avenue is located?" He responded all in one breath.

"Yes, I live on it."

"Well, jump in your car, drive over to (and he gave me a number), there is a young couple standing outside, show them through the house

and have them follow you back to the office. Here's a key, get going."
He said impatiently.

"Mr. Farr, I don't have a license." I hurriedly explained.

"Don't worry about that; just do what I tell you." He stated emphatically as he urged me to the door.

No more than five minutes had elapsed from the moment I entered his office until I was in my car driving to show clients through the house. The couple were waiting on the veranda. While inspecting the property, they inquired about taxes, mortgages, etc., and I could only inform them that all information was available at the office. As a result of the incident, I inadvertently learned a vital lesson in inducing prospective purchasers to return to headquarters where there was a better chance a contract might be written. The young couple, unable to obtain replies to their queries, had no alternative but to come back to the office where George Farr rapidly convinced them to sign a contract. Had I been able to provide answers, they would simply have driven away and said if interested they would phone the broker later. Most purchasers have buyers jitters when it approaches the point of signing a contract, but are less reluctant when in the atmosphere of a private office.

During those early years in the profession, acquiring a real estate salesman's license was simple. Providing you were bondable, the license was issued within twenty-four hours. So in forty-eight hours after my sudden impulse to inquire about the vocation, I was a full fledged licensed salesman; within seventy-two hours I sold my first house; and, except for delivering the last of my orders, Fuller Brush was just another memory.

Although I earned outstanding commissions immediately, George Farr's office was a bad environment, not only to learn the trade, but also because George and the other two salesmen were not only horse racing fanatics, but were imbued with other personal problems as well. George had been a drummer and a band leader for several years in the Detroit/Windsor area performing under the name of Tony Farr and Orchestra. Alcohol became a problem, and his wife persuaded him to give up the music business and move to Toronto. George, Madeleine his spouse, and a growing young family had also located on Sammon Avenue. I was mystified as to how George procured his broker's license without owning a car, because before applying to take the broker's exam, you had to sell real estate successfully for a minimum of a year. Perhaps due to his drinking problem, it was decided he was better off without an automobile.

Lloyd Ayers, one of the other two members of the sales staff, a unique individual, was one of the most accomplished salesmen I ever worked with. A complete alcoholic, he had joined Alcoholics Anonymous one week before I became associated with the firm. Lloyd had been a bomber pilot in the R.C.A.F., and like numerous others, acquired the liquor habit between missions over Europe. After wrecking his car and losing his wife and daughter, who walked out, he decided to rehabilitate himself. It was strange to hear people in the surrounding area such as restaurant patrons, beer parlor regulars, and other real estate personnel comment about what a drunken slob Lloyd had been. During the quarter of a century that I knew him, alcohol never touched his lips. His wife and daughter returned, and the Ayers eventually increased their brood to four.

Lloyd, however, like George Farr and Vic Dawson, the other member of the force, had a great affection for the horses and little else was ever discussed in the office, particularly during the day while the races were being run. They bet with a local bookmaker and had a radio blaring out the race results. Also they attended the track several times weekly. Before long I, too, became involved and soon was nearly as addicted as they. The whole atmosphere wasn't conducive to the real estate business.

Steve Theodoru, a Macedonian, and his father, fondly known as Pop, operated a small restaurant in the same block as Farr's office. Steve, also a devotee of the ponies, handled all the local action. He had been a full fledged bookie a year or two before, but got into a tangle with the local mob, and they tossed a brick through the cafe window as a warning. This incident badly frightened Steve's parents who then forced him to give up his lucrative sideline. Steve also got married to a Macedonian beauty named Sophie that summer, and she wanted no part of a racketeer as a husband. None of this, however, dampened Steve's ardor for the horses, and there was rarely any other topic discussed among the patrons of his establishment.

Shortly after entering the real estate profession, I left Jowett's and took a room without meals on Hertle Avenue at Greenwood and Gerrard. The move was necessary because it wasn't possible to maintain regular meal hours in my new career. Most of my repasts were now eaten at Steve's, so I was bombarded with race horse lingo all day long and well into the evenings.

Despite all this interference, I was selling houses at a tremendous clip, and before September's end, had traded my trusty and reliable 1935 Dodge for a 1941 Ford Sedan. This move was a step in the wrong direction, as that vehicle was the worst lemon I ever owned. First, the front seat broke, and I had to prop it up with a 2 x 4, then the transmission started to disintegrate and I couldn't use first gear. After a week, the gear shift froze into second gear, and although it seems unbelievable, I sold property for a week with the automobile in that mode. When backing up was necessary, I got out and shoved. I didn't have sufficient money for repairs until my commission checks started arriving in late October and early November. A garage offering a replacement vehicle while repairing yours, loaned me an old Model B Ford which turned out to be a memorable experience. Never having had much aptitude with motors, I didn't understand their many idiosyncrasies, so don't know what caused the Model B to backfire. But when the engine was the slightest bit cold, it would cough and explode several minutes before settling down. Jolting down the street like an untamed bronco with a severe case of colic, the thunderous backfires, rivet-loosening jerks and shudders were so hilarious I couldn't drive for laughing and would pull over to the curb until the engine warmed. My clients usually saw the humor in the situation, and I sold four houses during the week I drove the cantankerous old Model B. My car was ready before my first commission check was due, and the garage took back the Ford, so for another week I hired taxis during which period I sold two more properties despite the inconvenience.

Although cash poor temporarily, I'd earned nearly five thousand dollars by mid-December. A large portion had gone to purchase and repair the Ford, but I was still affluent enough to return home for the holidays. Ruth's condition, which had steadily worsened, was diagnosed as a type of leukemia, so I was anxious to spend some time with my sister. Also Betty and I had corresponded regularly throughout the summer, and though she was teaching school in a small village seventy-five miles northwest of Winnipeg, she too would be home with her family for Christmas, so we would have a chance to discuss whether we had, or wanted a future together.

The long, tedious bus trip to Winnipeg through Chicago and Minneapolis-St. Paul totalled 1700 miles. Returning to the frozen prairies as a respectable businessman contrasted to previous arrivals as a rugged lumberjack or itinerant harvester. My wardrobe had improved, and either city living or associating with a less boisterous class of people had worn away a few of the rough edges I'd picked up as a homeless adventurer.

In Winnipeg I rented a new automobile for the holidays and had gifts for everyone, so my homecoming was quite ostentatious.

Ruth was indeed failing badly. From a robust young lady of 140 pounds she had wasted away to 100. Her hair was falling out, she had an anemic complexion and a totally atrophic appearance. The doctors were unable to offer any comfort or reassurance to the folks, although Ruth, the gutsy gal she was, had complete confidence she would overcome her illness. Certainly my determination to go home for the holidays was a decision I never regretted. It would be the last Christmas we would celebrate as a complete family, and despite Ruth's condition, we enjoyed a happy get-together.

Betty Rasmussen and I dated several times. More charming and attractive than ever, she was enjoying her new career as an elementary school teacher. We spent the afternoon and evening together in Winnipeg before I boarded a midnight bus for my return to Toronto. She mentioned her steady boyfriend where she taught school of who she was quite fond. I was in no position to offer much competition, and when we parted, I sensed our romance had ended. Betty married the following spring and enjoyed many years of successful marital bliss and was blessed with three daughters.

The forty below zero temperature when I left Winnipeg was typical of a Manitoba winter night with a multitude of stars and crackling aurora borealis illuminating a cloudless sky. Before traversing the sixty miles to the U.S. border and entering North Dakota, the weather changed dramatically. Though still bitter cold, snow began falling, and an escalating wind soon created severe blizzard conditions. Driving became hazardous because of limited visibility, slippery roads and the occasional drifts. Suddenly the big Greyhound lurched into a substantial snow bank, and we were stuck. The driver burned out the vehicle's transmission trying to free it from the snow. While waiting in the swirling blizzard, the operator ran the motor at intervals to prevent the passengers from freezing. Another bus, beckoned by radio, rescued us after a two hour delay. By this time our route east to Minneapolis-St. Paul was impassable, so we headed south. At 9 a.m. we crawled into Fargo, North Dakota, which was almost totally snowbound. A multitude of families returning home after the holidays from numerous parts of the country were stranded in the little prairie town waiting for roads to be opened. Radio stations had reporters interviewing the disgruntled, travel weary people. In late afternoon I was put on a bus for Chicago where I arrived the following morning, dog weary.

Mother's oldest brother Tom and his wife, Ethel, had settled in Chicago before I was born. I had never met them or their three children: Ethel, the eldest, slightly older than I; Alice in my age bracket; and Tommy, about twelve. Searching the phone book I discovered a T. Rodd in Harvey, Illinois which was a suburb of Chicago. I was delighted to reach Uncle Tom immediately. He gave me instructions to catch the Loop Train to Harvey, and met me at the station. Uncle Tom and I hit it off instantly. Though periodically hearing he was an inventive genius, I was positively stunned with his creative mind and practical inventions; of which there were several. The most notable of these was the first practical aluminum storm sash which he had perfected, patented and designed a small factory to mass produce. All efforts to market the sash had met with outstanding success, and he was swamped with orders, however, he lacked the organizational desire or ability to coordinate a labor force or sales department. We spent hours going over his production costs in relation to a realistic selling price. The money making possibilities were tremendous. I tried to induce Uncle Tom to hire personnel and get into full production, but he was cut from a different block of wood. He patiently explained that making a heap of money was unimportant to him. Instead, inventing useful articles was his forte. We became so fascinated with each other's personal philosophies and business acumen that Uncle Tom asked me to return to Chicago, assume the sales and organizational responsibilities, and he would give me an equitable position in his company. Enchanted with the prospects, I sincerely intended giving it serious consideration, but other circumstances prevailed, and I never saw Uncle Tom again. Of all the mixed opportunities in my business career, losing the chance to work with this unsung genius, I often thought, was the most regrettable.

As the bus rolled through the Ontario fruit belt towards Toronto, I was mesmerized by the unbelievable change in weather conditions since leaving the West five days before. A gentle rain was falling, the lawns were green, and there wasn't a sign of snow. Although an unseasonal warm spell, it wasn't record breaking, and to me it seemed like I was traveling in the tropics as the temperature was 80 to 90 degrees warmer than when I left Winnipeg.

Once back in harness and making sales, Chicago was promptly forgotten and other considerations came to the fore. George Farr, frequently short of money, had begun dabbling in his trust account. He didn't touch clients' funds, but often borrowed his salesmens' commissions before deals actually closed. George reasoned he could cover any deficit in his trust account with future sales deposits. Aware of this habit I was concerned because a large portion of the funds would eventually be due to me.

One March day upon entering the office, Lloyd Ayers informed me George was across the street at a used car lot negotiating the purchase of an automobile. I dashed over just as the car salesman was filling out the papers.

"Watcha doing, George?" I asked quietly.

"Getting a helluva buy on a '49 Meteor sedan," he enthusiastically replied.

"Perhaps before you sign the documents, we should go over to the pub and quaff a beer," I stated emphatically.

I turned to the car dealer who looked a trifle astonished and said, "If the automobile is as good as George claims, we'll be back to consumate a deal within the hour."

George was aggravated as we walked two blocks over to the Acadian House, our favorite watering hole. "What the hell is this all about, young fella?" George hotly inquired.

"My friend, the dough you're going to buy that vehicle with is more mine than yours, and I desperately need improved transportation." I responded, in my most positive manner. "So you can write the check for the car, but we'll put the ownership in my name after I find out what they will allow for my '41 Ford." "Anyhow George," I added, "I'll make more money with it than you, and if you'll leave the horses alone and keep your fingers out of your trust account, there will soon be sufficient dough for you to obtain transportation."

"Phillips, you're a bastard." How do you know I'm into the trust account?"

"You talk too much when you're drunk," I said, closing the conversation. The thrill of acquiring that '49 car (A Meteor in Canada was a model between an ordinary Ford and Mercury), was greater than any of my other automobile purchases over the years. Only a few months old, it was a dark blue sedan with all modern attachments and I was the proudest Real Estate salesman on the Danforth.

As spring approached, the boys in Farr's office, including George, could talk of little else than the opening of the racing season and I was resolute about not being immersed in that environment for another year.

My proficiency as a Real Estate salesman had become common knowledge amongst the local brokers and I was constantly being persuaded to change offices. A.W. Farlinger was the most progressive and businesslike realtor in the area. The manager who refused me a job several months before, had been transferred to a different part of the city and Vic Gidden, the new manager, had become a friend with whom I frequently lunched. Farlinger's had a large inventory of new houses exclusively listed which was another motivating factor in compelling me to switch allegiance. George Farr was bitterly disappointed, not only because I was a top producer, but we had become close friends.

My ability in Real Estate selling had considerably altered my style of living. For the first time I could sense a more continuous prosperity and this turned my head. Sudden affluence and the knowledge I could earn huge commissions almost at will released all concern about saving, and the dollars were squandered nearly as fast as I cashed my commission checks.

With a flashy new car, chic wardrobe and pocketful of cash, my social life was flourishing. Bill Blue, a full blooded Hawaiian, and guitar teacher, and his wife Connie, a delightful, red-haired, young Irish girl had become intimate friends. They lived in a house trailer in East Toronto. Bill, an ardent fisherman, soon had me a real devotee of the sport. His hot temper clashed with mine, resulting in several physical bouts, but we never remained enemies long and many of my weekends were spent with the Blues either at their trailer home or with Bill on a fishing trip in the Kawartha Lake sector of Central Ontario. Connie often became upset when we didn't return at the agreed time, especially if she had prepared a sumptuous meal. One Saturday evening returning two hours late, Bill knew Connie would be furious. Turning into the street leading to their trailer park, Bill spotted Connie standing by the bus stop all dressed up just as if she was off to attend a royal wedding.

"Pull the car over beside her," Bill requested.

As I came to a stop, Connie put her head in the air, as if suddenly smelling a bad odor and pretended not to recognize us. Bill rolled down the window and from the side of his mouth in a kind of stage whisper asked, "Where you goin' Con?" Connie didn't acknowledge our presence at all, but as if talking to a passing sparrow replied, "Goin' fishing."

It was hilarious, but she wasn't trying to be funny. We persuaded her to join us for a beer followed by dinner out so she soon forgave us. Throughout our acquaintanceship, Connie called me her big brother and whenever she faced a personal problem or had a spat with Bill, she would call me for consolation or advice.

Although I no longer lived at the Jowetts, Al Richard and I remained close friends. He was engaged to Rita, a wonderful girl, also from the east coast. Rita introduced me to her close friend Kay McDonald, a very attractive brunette, and the four of us socialized at regular intervals. Kay, an intelligent girl, was an excellent companion and though a year or two older than I, had not tasted much of the fruits of life. She lived in Rosedale, an exclusive residential sector of the metropolis with her mother, a strict, straight-laced and conservative lady. Kay, though twenty-five was expected home by midnight; but in spite of this restriction, I introduced the young lady to many aspects of life she hadn't experienced before. Whether I escorted her to ball games, Chinese restaurants or bars, all firsts for Kay, she accepted my boorish ways and always enjoyed herself. She would do most anything for me, and on one occasion after hearing me tell Al I required $250 for a small business transaction, immediately wrote me out a check.

Kay wasn't my only feminine companion. The city had a surplus of beautiful young ladies, probably as a result of the war when many country girls moved to cities for war time work. I was delighted to take advantage of the situation and spread myself around. Shirley Jones, a pretty dark haired brunette, and secretary in one of the nearby realty offices was another of my favorites. Shirley and I loved to drive to Niagara Falls, then cross over to Buffalo, the swinging city of the fifties, where we spent several pleasant weekends.

This whirlwind lifestyle frittered away my large commission checks and I was usually broke by Friday's payday. However, making dough was simple and my new mode of living pleasant, so little thought was given to saving for a rainy day.

Arriving at my boarding house after 1:00 a.m. one Wednesday night, Mr. and Mrs. Rogers, my landlord and his wife, a wonderful couple, were waiting up for me. Dad had sent a telegram which the Rogers had accepted and they gave me the unhappy news. Ruth's situation was critical and she had asked the folks to call and see if I could pay a visit. My wallet contained less than a hundred dollars, an amount certainly insufficient to begin a fifteen hundred mile journey through the wilds of Northern Ontario. I decided therefore there was no alternative except to wait and try to rustle up some cash in the morning. Tossing, turning and tortured by the thought I might miss seeing my lovable young sister alive if I delayed, was unbearable. Unable to sleep, I leaped out of bed with a plan of action. After packing my bag, and informing the Rogers of my decision to immediately strike out for Winnipeg, I jumped in my Meteor and hi-tailed over to Steve Theodorou's restaurant.

Though closed, Steve was inside cleaning up. He let me in, and listened sympathetically to my dilemma. Vic Giddens, my manager, lived only a few blocks away. If he was home, I thought he would give me a personal check in return for a note to A.W. Farlinger to deduct the amount from my Friday commissions. My problem was, however, I needed someone to cash Vic's check.

"Get the hell over there and see what you can do and I'll wait." Steve said immediately. "I've got cash here from the day's take."

Luck was with me. Vic was home, though fast asleep. After hearing my plight, he wrote a check for $150 and I raced back to Steve, gratified with the empathy of my two friends.

Cashing the check Steve looked at me and inquired, "How much cash you got altogether?"

"About $250." I replied.

"Better take another $100, it's a long trip."

There were tears in my eyes as I pocketed the extra cash and headed for my car. It was an outstanding gesture of friendship and compassion from a man I'd known such a short period of time.

At 3:30 a.m. I left the city lights and headed for a long, lonely 1500 mile journey through the desolate regions of Northern Ontario for Winnipeg, on primarily gravel topped, secondary highways. Being unfamiliar with the route through the U.S., I didn't realize it was 200 miles shorter and paved 80% of the way.

With Ruth constantly on my mind, the night passed slowly, but with little traffic and the highway paved the initial 200 miles to North Bay, permitting me to keep the accelerator to the floor, I covered the initial leg in a hurry. At dawn I picked up a couple of soldiers hitchhiking to Manitoba which improved the loneliness aspect, but neither had a drivers license so I gained no relief from the wheel. We stopped only for food and fuel and at one of the gas stations some idiot attendant found my gas tank cap missing, and installed a radiator cap. Without a hole to breath through, a vaccum was created which sucked in the sides of the gas tank, making the fuel gauge useless. Having never experienced such a situation, I couldn't understand why I kept running out of gas. In Port Arthur I located a garage still open, though it was 10:00 p.m. Thursday evening. They diagnosed the problem and advised me that the collapsed tank was holding less than half its proper capacity of fuel and would have to be removed requiring at least a 24 hour layover to repair. I was completely exhausted after nineteen hours of tedious driving over horrible, washboardy rutted roads plus it had been 38 hours since I'd had any sleep. Nevertheless, I elected to push on to Winnipeg, now less than 500 miles away, and have the gas tank problem remedied while visiting Ruth.

Someone advised me, when facing a wearisome drive to take an occasional sip of straight whiskey and it would alert your system. That afternoon I bought a bottle of booze and on leaving Port Arthur had a swig. It worked and I felt refreshed, however, after a half hour I needed another, which also perked me up. Before long I was reaching for my stimulant every fifteen minutes. Not only was I now getting cockeyed and becoming a highway hazard, but also finding it difficult to keep my eyes open at all.

My passengers generally were asleep. Fortunately, however, one of them regained consciousness as the car tilted nearly 45 degrees and, half off the road, was on the verge of rolling into the huge ditch paralleling our route. He awakened me with a shout and through sheer luck I righted the automobile before we overturned. The two boys evacuated at the next village.

Scared by the near accident, I vowed if staying awake became intolerable again, I'd pull over and have a nap because remaining conscious wasn't my only dilemma. The gas tank held less than ten gallons with no more service stations on the route until I reached Dryden, Ontario. At 4 a.m. approximately 35 miles from the village of Dryden in one of the most desolate stretches of countryside anywhere, I ran out of fuel for the fourth time.

Completely exhausted I didn't take the trouble to move over and lie down on the seat, but simply collapsed across the steering wheel and was asleep in a split second. A rapping at the window roused me out of insensibility. It was daylight. Lifting my head I heard a voice hollering through the locked door.

"Are you alright?" Had I been stretched out on the seat instead of sprawled across the steering wheel, the considerate stranger would have known I was asleep, but due to my awkward position, he figured I'd taken a heartattack. Spotting a Michigan license plate on the other car, I stepped out to meet the good samaritan. It was 6 a.m. and my two hour respite had passed in a trice. After assuring the American I wasn't ill and explaining my fuel tank predicament, he completely overwhelmed me when from his trunk he produced a three gallon can of gas, for which he absolutely refused payment. My image of Americans skyrocketed. I reached Winnipeg shortly after noon, completely exhausted from the 33 hour endurance test.

Uncle Geordie, Dad's youngest brother, was the most convenient relative to reach so I headed directly for their residence. Unshaven, bleary-eyed and with unkempt clothes, I looked like anything but a successful businessman. Aunt Peg insisted I bathe, shave, eat and have a few hours shut eye before visiting Ruth, and I gratefully concurred. Entering the hospital later that evening I felt like a different person, but was unprepared for the pitiful sight that greeted me. Though smiling bravely, Ruth's appearance had deteriorated immensely since Christmas. Her athletic body was now totally emaciated, a few scraggly hairs hung from her shapely head, and a worn haggard mien etched her 21 year old face. As we embraced, the tears rolled unashamedly down my cheeks, and I who had driven 1500 miles to comfort my young sister was instead being consoled by her. Nothing was said by either for a few moments until we both were recomposed.

"Bill," she said opening the conversation, "I wanted to see you, not because I think I'm going to die, but the truth of my condition is something I must know. Jack and the folks love me as much as you, but I think you will find out and tell me the truth while I'm not sure they will." I promised the next day to have a talk with her doctor, but first wanted to drive to Monominto for the night and see what information the rest of the family had obtained about her debilitating ailment. We had a wonderful visit, but Ruth was so weak the nurse chased me from her ward after an hour. Assuring my ailing sibling I would return the next day, I drove the final 35 miles to the solace of my family, and never did Monominto look so appealing.

Mom and I returned to the hospital the following day. Leaving Mom with Ruth, I tracked down her specialist. He admitted not being absolutely certain of her malady, but believed it was a form of leukemia which they hoped to control with Cortisone. Cortisone had only been on the market commercially less than a year, and because of overwhelming demand the cost per ounce was so prohibitive that in fact it was almost priceless.

Ruth had received a few small doses and the doctor thought she was showing slight improvement. My major concern while conversing with the medical expert, was if more Cortisone was either used or available would it increase her chance of recovery. A youngish man, he reached over and put his hand on my shoulder and looked me square in the eye, "Mr. Phillips," he stated in a very direct manner. "The world is looking at Cortisone as a miracle cure for several diseases. The present supply is so limited it wouldn't matter if you were a multi-millionaire, we would be unable to procure more than we are now getting to assist us in curing your sister. We will do what we can, but all the money in the world will not obtain more Cortisone." It was a frustrating answer. I was confident of being able to earn vast sums of money selling real estate for the purchase of Cortisone, if it was obtainable. I refused to accept his response as the final word, but after hours of investigating the situation with doctors and administrators in other Winnipeg hospitals, and always receiving basically the same information, I finally had to admit defeat. There was simply no place it could be bought for any amount of money.

I remained in the West for ten days and enjoyed numerous tete-a-tetes with Ruth. We discussed her doctor's diagnosis and his remarks about the scarcity of Cortisone. I assured her I would inquire in Toronto as to its availability, or if there was a possibility of obtaining it anywhere in the world.

Thank heavens someone convinced me to return East via the U.S., not only considerably shorter and almost entirely on pavement, but the route was more scenic by a wide margin than its Canadian counterpart.

After visiting three hospitals in Toronto and talking with several medical people, I received the same affirmation of the scarcity of Cortisone. Money was simply not a factor in its procurement.

I returned to work with gusto. The residential real estate market was brisk, business was booming, and it didn't take long to get back in the swing and start producing sales. An associate of mine at Farlingers, Jack Cutler, an English architect, was an outstanding salesman and particularly successful in dealing with new homes, a phase of residential sales giving me a problem. Most new subdivisions had no streets or services at the time the new homes were being constructed, so the buyers required a vivid imagination differing from resales where everything was on view. Also with new construction, if it had been raining, prospective purchasers had to trudge through mud to reach model homes. Therefore, I found it difficult to presume after considerable inconvenience they would immediately return to the office, sit down and sign a contract. Cutler, aware that my sales output of new houses didn't compare with my proficiency in handling resales; came to me one day.

"Bill, why do you always bring your clients back to the office when you show an older home usually resulting in a contract, but rarely bring people into the office when you return from the developments?" I explained that most prospective new home buyers always had a number of questions about when power, natural gas, telephone service, etc. . . . would be available. After receiving the information, they would generally request I call them at home later as they wanted to consider if they were prepared to put up with the inconvenience, and I didn't blame them.

"Don't give the next client you take to the subdivision all the information. Tell them those details are in the office," Jack instructed, then added, "If I'm in, bring them to my office and introduce me as the assistant manager."

"I have an appointment this afternoon Jack," I said, "and I'll do just that."

It was raining and not only did my people, a young married couple and the wife's mother get covered in mud, but I also got my car stuck and had to get a tow truck. Nevertheless, I took them into Jack's office and introduced them as he suggested.

"Have a seat folks and the secretary will bring you some hot coffee." "In what house were they interested Mr. Phillips?" Jack inquired. I gave Jack the street and the house number of the dwelling in which my clients showed the greatest interest, then added. "Mr. Cutler, they want some information about the area, services and mortgage set-up."

"That is fine Mr. Phillips," Jack said pleasantly, "you and Norma, (one of our secretaries), type out the contract and I'll provide Mr. and Mrs. Jones with the information." I fully expected the threesome to bolt out the door but to my amazement they sat still not saying a word. Within ten minutes I returned with the documents. Jack handed a copy to each of the three, then proceeded to read and explain the various clauses, patiently answering their questions. When he had completely gone over the offer to purchase, he immediately handed the young man a pen and in a polite voice said, "You sign here Mr. Jones, and your wife can endorse the contract below your signature."

I was flabbergasted at the ease with which Jack completed the transaction and I congratulated him on the effort.

"The only difference between what you do and what I did," Jack stated, "was that I assumed they wanted to purchase the house and you have been taking it for granted they wished to think it over." Suddenly, I recalled an identical example a year before, when showing the house on Sammon Ave. for George Farr. I vowed not to forget the lesson a second time. In the ensuing years I sold a multitude of new homes and in addition successfully applied the same philosophy to other types of marketing.

Although my sales production was steadily increasing, my gregarious mode of living was also flourishing and again I was spending my commission as promptly as I received the checks. Life indeed was just a bowl of cherries and I never considered there could come an end to the good times. Though there was an abundance of feminine companions and I thoroughly enjoyed playing the field, at least once a week I escorted Kay to a function of some kind. In early August I was astonished when she reminded me we had been dating for a year. Perhaps I should have read more into the innocent remark, because a few evenings later, she made another statement that rearranged the balance of my entire existence.

Sunnyside in the western environs of Toronto had been a miniature Coney Island for many years, with games of chance, side shows and a variety of carnival type rides. By 1950, it had dropped tremendously in popularity and many of the concessions had disappeared, but it was still a pleasant place to end an evening. The amusement park stretched along the fringe of Lake Ontario within a quarter of a mile of an exquisite hard packed sand beach, where you could park your car right at the water's edge. Tranquility and privacy made it a favorite spot for Kay and I, so frequently we dawdled there awhile following an evening out.

Sitting quietly one evening in the romantic setting, her head resting on my shoulder, Kay suddenly broke the silence by looking over and in a quiet voice asked. "Bill, have you ever considered marriage?" Had she doused me with a bucket of ice water, she couldn't have shocked me more and it was several seconds before the impact of her remark completely sank in.

Turning on the ignition, I replied quietly, "No Kay, I guess I haven't thought of it too seriously." Not a word was spoken as we motored to her residence though thoughts were churning through my noggin, like a sheaf of wheat in the middle of a threshing machine. I felt terrible and helpless both at the same time. Marrying Kay or any other Toronto girl had never crossed my mind, but it was now apparent Kay was looking at me as a potential husband. As we drove, I particularly recalled the plight of Aunt Muriel, Mom's sister, undoubtedly one of the most loving people in the world and also exceedingly attractive. Frank Kelly, who dated her for fifteen years was considered by us to be part of the family and was considered affectionately by everyone. He never asked Aunt Muriel's hand in marriage, however, for whatever reason I never understood. She finally dumped him and married another, but not until she was in her forties and too late to start a family which she dearly wanted.

Dear old Frank Kelly was abruptly castigated by all those he had been so close to for many years, and I, like most of the family, considered the whole affair a personal tragedy especially for Aunt Muriel. Not wanting to be another Kelly and seriously doubting if I loved Kay enough to propose marriage, I realized the relationship had to end.

Approaching her home, I heard her sobbing and because I didn't know what to say, said nothing. Walking hand in hand to the front door, I kissed her gently on a tear stained cheek and whispered in a cracked voice, "Goodbye Kay, I'm dreadfully sorry." I never saw nor talked to her again.

Bars in Toronto had only been licensed since 1949 and the first "The Pilot Tavern" which Jack and I visited the odd time during his tenure in the city, was not far from Kay's home in Rosedale and I needed a drink. I didn't second guess my decision to terminate the association, but my respect and admiration for the girl caused me much grief as it was obvious I'd hurt her considerably. A major error was in not informing her I wasn't marriageable material for the present, at least. How fickle are our emotions when we're young, I was soon to learn.

After several drinks, I headed home and though feeling more at peace with myself was still quite upset. The only tavern in the east end, The Orchard Park Hotel, was not far from my Hertle Ave. home. It was the favorite watering hole for all the local real estate agents, lawyers, and builders, so I decided to drop in for another quick drink with the thought in mind I might run into a friend or acquaintance. Undoubtedly I felt like talking to someone. The lounge area of the premises was in a lower level. Walking in and adjusting my eyes to the dim lights, I noticed a stunning blonde sitting with two other girls and a man at the furthest end of the establishment. Without taking my eyes off her attractive face, I kept walking towards their niche. Fate intervened as a small table was available a few feet from where this girl sat chatting with her friends.

Sipping my drink, I rarely removed my eyes from her features, but she never once glanced in my direction. Encouraged by the whiskey and determined to make an effort to get acquainted before she got up and left, I reached over and quietly asked, "Miss, could I borrow a cigarette?" She glanced over, smiled, said nothing, but passed her package of cigarettes. At full visage I was certain she was the prettiest girl on earth and was instantly smitten to the core of my soul. Considering my romantic entanglement earlier in the evening, it was indeed an unusual turn of events. From that moment, my life and Joyce Fine's would swiftly become enmeshed as one, proving the old adage "Truth is stranger than fiction."

Chapter 3
Settling Down/ Settling Up

Our destinies operate in mysterious ways, and these ways give the human race a special quality. Every individual's life is subject to abrupt changes, and these changes are an abomination to those who seek no surprises. To others, however, this ignorance of what tomorrow will bring is a unique and stimulating characteristic of mankind. To me it's this ignorance that gives life its distinct and provocative spark. How could a warrior fervently enter battle if he were aware that death was inescapable, or an athlete enthusiastically participate in competition knowing his defeat was inevitable.

Each life is like an unwritten autobiography, with each day representing a page, and the volume's size varying from a single sheet to over thirty-thousand. For the initial three-thousand pages, the author has little mastery over its contents. Following that period, however, the autobiographer takes charge and fills each sentence, paragraph, and chapter with his or her own standard of morality and quality of thought, except for those unknown twists of fate that then make it a mystery, even to its author.

My book of life would contain a multitude of unanticipated curves in nearly every chapter, because I have always been eager and susceptible to change. My conscious self has craved variety, and my subconscious has provided it. The status-quo was generally abhorrent to me.

Certainly one of the great unknowns and incontrollable factors in life's pages is the date of one's death. Less dramatic examples are the unexpected effects of natural disasters: tornadoes, blizzards, earthquakes, hurricanes, and floods.

When we awake each morning, the future consequences of those we meet directly or indirectly throughout the day is a total mystery. So it was that August night when I walked into the Orchard Park Tavern and met a beautiful blonde, named Joyce Fine. People meet their life mates in a score of ways. The majority have some association for extended periods of time before becoming serious. Schools, churches, colleges, and offices are leading locations for the meeting of men and women that might ultimately lead to matrimony. Daily association on subways, at eating establishments, or other locales frequented by marriageable singles are also prime areas where casual encounters sometimes evolve into everlasting vows. But the odds against two strangers meeting like Joyce and I were millions to one, because it was Joyce's first visit to the Orchard Park Tavern. Whether it was merely kismet, love at first sight, or a combination of both, our chance encounter soon became a life long commitment.

Immediately after receiving a cigarette from Joyce, I bought a round of drinks for her foursome and inveigled an invitation to their table. The other three included two girlfriends, Joyce Armstrong and Mary Wysoki, plus Mary's father, Joe. Joyce insists I convinced her I was an Indian with a wooden leg, and this fascinated her to such a degree that she allowed me to escort her home. On the way I persuaded her to join me for a few minutes at a house party at the Brannings.

Lorne and Edna Branning, who moved into an apartment a few doors from Farlinger's two months earlier, were soon to play a predominant role in our lives. Both Brannings had been born and raised in Saskatchewan, though they met and married in Toronto. Lorne had two attractive teenage daughters, Carol and Louise, from a previous marriage who lived with them. I had attended several functions with the Brannings, including a couple of weekend fishing jaunts around Peterboro, Ontario. They didn't have a car, so Bill Blue and I would drive them to their lake country cabin, party awhile, then go fishing on our own. Lorne and Edna were a fun-loving couple and would do most anything for a laugh. Lorne, a plasterer by trade, had a sparkling personality but drank too much. Akin to his trade, he was frequently plastered. Edna, a waitress, though not as outgoing, was engaging. Perhaps due to our common western heritage, the Brannings and I rapidly established a friendship; and, though Joyce and I only attended the Branning's party for a short time, Edna and Joyce began a relationship that was to last a lifetime.

If a swift courtship is a whirlwind romance, then ours would be properly described as a hurricane. An overpowering magnetism attracted us as a honeybee is drawn to a wild rose. Following our first date, never once did the earth completely revolve on its axis without our spending time in each other's arms. It was an impassioned courtship, but not all love and kisses. We both were endowed with similar characteristics, including quick tempers and a streak of stubbornness; but fortunately we also possessed a willingness to forgive and forget. Our tempestuous romance was filled with fights and fun-filled forgiveness and though we had many explosive spats, our relationship was soon welded into an inseparable link which made parting at the finish of each rendezvous increasingly painful.

At the beginning of our acquaintanceship, I related to Joyce my unhappy experience with Kaye, and finished the sad tale by explaining that I was not marriageable material for a few years. She understood, and assured me that she had no desire to reach the altar herself before the age of twenty-one (at the time she was only five months past nineteen). How fickle are our solemn vows when passion rules the roost!

Within eight weeks of our first embrace, we were planning wedlock. Joyce insists I proposed, which may be so, but I only recall a conversation one evening which began, "Bill, which do you think is the best Saturday for our wedding, November the 4th or the 11th?"

It made little difference to me. Completely captivated, I was totally miserable when separated, and soon realized that living without her was unthinkable. She held the same feelings for me, so a formal proposal was unnecessary. Almost from our first meeting, we both instinctively knew and accepted that our destinies were charted along the same path—a path which would contain numerous mountains and valleys.

In a letter to Mother in late October, I mentioned in the final paragraph my marriage plans, also that Joyce's mother was English-Irish and her father Jewish. I got a prompt response. Shocked at the sudden news of my impending nuptials, they probably figured I'd gotten Joyce in trouble due to the brevity of the courtship, and wanted to caution me about doing something rash without sufficient thought. Almost as an afterthought, Mother wondered if I'd considered the implications of getting involved with someone of the Jewish faith, and whether I was converting to Judaism or being wed in a Christian church. Having never been subjected to anti-Semitism in my upbringing, the query surprised me. I related Mother's concern to Joyce. She smiled smugly, then informed me that her paternal grandparents had been thoroughly aggravated when informed she was marrying an unknown gentile from God-knows-where, when there were so many outstanding young Jewish boys available from Toronto. Life can become complex where mixed marriages are involved, especially among the older generation with whom religion is a far more serious matter.

Though zooming toward married life with all its attendant responsibilities, my bankroll was still lacking substance. Total absorption with Joyce removed me from circulation regarding other female companions;

but my freespending lifestyle hadn't changed, although I had now to pay rent for an apartment and scrounge a down payment to purchase furniture and buy an engagement ring. Joyce, working as a sales clerk at Burrough's Furniture, was exhausting her paycheck as fast as it was received in preparation for the big day, so I couldn't count on her for financial support.

We chose a tiny, unfurnished, two-room apartment in a private house on Rhodes Avenue, near Joyce's parents. It contained a tiny kitchen with an adjoining bed-sitting room. Due to my limited budget, our total furnishings consisted of a chrome kitchen suite, plus a davenport and two chairs, all bought on time. I moved into our new living quarters in late October, rather than pay rent on two places. After paying $75 dollars for an engagement ring at a pawn shop, I was stone broke. In addition, my car payments were two months in arrears.

Bill Watson, a friend from a used car lot, listening to me moan about my financial situation, offered a miraculous solution to one aspect of the dilemma. Equity on my '49 Meteor was negligible, but somehow Bill traded it for a 1950 Ford and extended the first payment of the new car two months from the date of the transaction. Not only did I gain a new automobile plus four month's payments, but was assured of wheels for our honeymoon.

Acquiring money for a week's honeymoon was a predicament also solved in unique fashion. Steve Theodoru threw a stag party, sold over one hundred tickets, and presented me with a fifty dollar bill. Joyce's Uncle Martin from Detroit sent fifty dollars for a wedding present. Another of her relatives presented her with twenty-five, and John McIntyre, a real estate friend of mine, gave us ten silver dollars. Joyce wanted to keep the silver dollars as a momento of November 4th—a proposal to which I reluctantly agreed, but suggested she keep them in her purse until we returned from our honeymoon.

The incessant cash deficiency, plus my impending marital obligations, forced me to take a hard look at my status. Paying 50% of my commissions to A.W. Farlinger seemed senseless, when, by acquiring a broker's license, I could keep the entire earnings. I also possessed a great hankering to be in business for myself; so, when an opportunity presented itself, I seized it like a drowning man grabbing a life jacket. Lorne Branning wanted to get out of plastering and try his hand at selling real estate, and Edna was anxious for him to make the attempt, so she arranged an eight hundred dollar loan from her parents who owned a large farm at Wapella, Saskatchewan, for Lorne and I to go into business together. We bought out George Farr on the basis of a fifty-fifty partnership. I wouldn't take the broker's test until the week following our honeymoon, but, completely confident of passing, I handed Vic Giddens my resignation.

After our engagement, I constantly teased Joyce that it was against my religion to marry a heathen. She finally consented to being baptised at St. Bartholemews Anglican Church ten days before our nuptials at the same chapel. I didn't inform Joyce until several years later that it was her mother who put me up to the baptismal harassment, as I had no religious fervor in my soul.

November 4, 1950, was a cold, blustery day with snowflurries. I chose Roy Reid, a co-worker from Farlingers as my best man, and Steve Theodoru and Lorne Branning as ushers. Joyce's bridesmaids were Joyce Armstrong and Madeline Nunziato. Her cousin, Barbara Francis, was a junior bridesmaid.

Roy and I had ordered new suits for the wedding from a local entrepreneur three weeks before the ceremony. The fact that my right leg was more than two inches shorter than my left gave the tailor a special problem. The new attire arrived at Branning's apartment the morning of the 4th, thus precluding any final fitting. Pulling on my trousers an hour before my appointment at St. Bartholemews, I was absolutely shocked to discover the tailor had gotten mixed up. The right pant's leg hung down past my foot, while the left cuff was well above my ankle. In stunned disbelief I yelled, "Edna, for Christ's sake come here!" Staring at me a few moments, and doing her utmost not to break out into hysterical laughter, Edna, in a compassionate voice, said, "Peel them off and I'll see what can be done." What a blessing Edna was handy with a needle and thread, and there was sufficient material in the cuff to permit an alteration. They were quite presentable when she handed them back, but it was an episode during the big day never to be forgotten.

The High Anglican 4 p.m. ceremony went off without a hitch, and my gorgeous bride resembled a Christmas doll. Joyce's mother, Etta, (fondly called Eddy), had seven brothers and sisters, and Martin, her father, had five. Most of these aunts and uncles were married with families, so Joyce was well represented with relations. Though I had an excellent contingent of friends and business associates, nary a Phillips nor Rodd was present. Joyce's folks arranged a spectacular reception at Bader's Hall, attended by over two hundred guests.

A memorable moment came during the speeches, when A.W. Farlinger, known affectionately as "Bud," spoke eloquently about my association with his firm, and talked about my extremely successful eighteen months in Toronto in general and my accomplishments with his real estate firm in particular. In conclusion, he passionately stressed the long and rewarding affiliation we were bound to enjoy together. Unfortunately, he hadn't been informed that I'd handed in my resignation two days before. Bud left the party shortly after one of his managers advised him of my imminent departure.

We spent our first night as man and wife in the bridal suite of the Park Plaza Hotel. Joyce looked ravishing and I was delighted to be her husband, lover and provider. The first morning, while breakfasting in our room and gazing out the window at the lazily floating snowflakes, I felt an unusual sensation of permanency; it was a new era which I was eager to begin. Accepting the responsibility of marriage afforded me pleasing thoughts, and the challenge of finally going into business for myself, even with a partner, was a dream come true, though I knew from childhood that self-employment would be my eventual fate.

After a brief visit with the Brannings, we left the city for a few days' holiday. Driving was hazardous, so we stopped in London, Ontario, for the night. We continued on to Detroit the following day, where we enjoyed a pleasant visit with Joyce's Uncle Martin, a relation of her father. From Michigan we drove to Cincinnati, then circled back to Buffalo and across the Rainbow Bridge to Niagara Falls, Ontario, where it's tradition for newlyweds to spend some time. The four nights on the road had depleted our finances, and I regretted having to dip into Joyce's purse for six silver dollars from John McIntyre's wedding gift in order to buy gas for our return to Toronto.

Financially destitute, we settled into our Rhodes Avenue rooms in early November with payments owing on furniture and car, with rent soon due on our residence and new office, and with Christmas rapidly approaching.

Looking back now it seems as if I possessed a lot of nerve and Joyce a heap of confidence. That is partially true, but I had absolutely no doubt about my capability quickly to earn commissions once my license was obtained. The major problem would be in surviving until the first closings, so I borrowed a few dollars for groceries.

I passed the broker's exam with a ninety-plus percentage, and there wasn't a prouder human being in the city when I had painted on my new office window: WILLIAM G. PHILLIPS; REAL ESTATE BROKER. Within a period of ten days, I had obtained a wife and a business. The former would outlast the latter by many years.

Phillips Real Estate, at 1751 Danforth Avenue, was surrounded by competitors. Located within a few doors were A. Harvey & Co., A.W. Farlinger, and Don McConnell, all progressive realtors who employed over fifty sales people. Within two blocks were three additional agencies, also with extensive staffs. In comparison, the office I purchased from George Farr was miniscule, having a total square footage of no more than 450', including one cramped private office. The entire layout was dingy and needed a complete renovation; as a consequence, I thought it would be difficult to attract men, but such was not the case. My first employee was Val Lovering, a young filling station attendant who wanted to try his hand at sales. Lorne Branning readily obtained his license, Roy Reid came over from Farlingers, Charlie Crawford—a magazine salesman who had been interviewed by Farr in the early fall—joined us, as well as George Farr. Thus by Christmas I was searching for a way to obtain more space.

Sales were good from the moment I opened the door, but the majority of closings were not made until mid-January or later, so by the time the holidays rolled around, Joyce and I were destitute. To ease the situation, Joyce took a job for four weeks as a sales clerk, which work paid the rent and put a little food on the table. My gambling luck hadn't diminished and I was making ends meet by playing poker and cribbage. One bottle of gin constituted our Christmas liquor, but that didn't even last until Christmas Eve. Hank Sharpe, a new acquaintance who worked at A. Harvey & Co. came over two days before the holidays for a cocktail and didn't depart until the booze was gone. Each time he gulped down a drink and the contents shrank, my stomach churned, though I didn't interfere. Hank eventually played a prominent role in my affairs and we joked about the incident numerous times afterwards.

A pair of bedroom slippers was the best I could afford for Joyce's Christmas present. She presented me with a gold wedding band and said, though it was a gift, it was also a warning to all females that I was no longer available. The ring strengthened our bond, and the news that she was pregnant solidified our union even more firmly. Not having planned such early parenthood, our enthusiasm wasn't overwhelming; but as we shared the responsibility, we resolved to make the most of it.

Next door to our office and part of the same building, Irving Perlman sold chrome kitchen sets. He purchased the component parts and assembled them in his store. Shortly after New Years, I made a deal with Irving to let me take over his lease. Behind the store were two floors of living quarters, including a kitchen and combination dining-living room on the main floor, and three bedrooms on the second level. Consequently, Joyce and I left Rhodes Avenue and took possession. As I was unable to meet the payments on our kitchen suite, the furniture company repossessed it prior to our move, but, as part of the deal with Perlman, I got a new six-piece kitchen set. On the immediate left of our premises, a fish-and-chip shop attracted cockroaches by the droves. These pesky insects spilled over and invaded our new living quarters, thus requiring our completely saturating the place with D.D.T. bombs. Though an unpleasant situation, this setback showed that my new bride was quite capable of dealing with adversity.

Money from closings relieved our critical lack of cash. So desperately needing office space, I removed the wall dividing our quarters from Perlman's, completely refurnished the interior, and installed one of the most modern store fronts on the Danforth including a huge picture window. PHILLIPS REAL ESTATE was now as attractive as any office in the neighborhood.

Sales remained brisk until late spring, when the market temporarily dried up. Waiting for things to happen, I succumbed to the old wanderlust and, again unable to control my patience, embarked on another of my half-baked schemes. Directly across Danforth Avenue from Phillips Real Estate was the used car and truck lot at which I had purchased the Meteor. Going out of business, they were having an outstanding sale on used trucks which spawned a brain wave. One day while idly chatting with Charlie Crawford, I quietly expressed my thoughts, "You know, Chuck, I was just thinking that second hand trucks with solid boxes sell for a high price on the prairies at harvest time. At this time of year, many farmers are searching for vehicles suitable for grain hauling."

Charlie, anxious to turn over a fast buck, responded immediately. "Let's hop over and see what kind of deal we can make."

Within twenty four hours we were the owners of one three-ton plus a pair of two ton, second-hand trucks. $2,000 was required to purchase the vehicles, and $600 needed for estimated expenses; so we each put up five hundred dollars and borrowed an additional sixteen hundred from a finance company on a sixty-day note.

In addition to the possibility of making a fast profit, the truck project allowed me to visit the family. Ruth, still quite frail, was back home with the folks, and, health permitting, had been corresponding with Joyce about a visit to Toronto the following year. Jack had married Shirley Campbell, a schoolteacher, who, while teaching Monominto school, boarded with Mother. They were farming at Niverville, thirty miles from Monominto.

Roy Reid and I switched cars for two weeks. His Volkswagen Bug, which would provide cheap return transportation, was loaded on the back of the three-ton I would drive. The two-tons were piggybacked, and we hired a local chap, Lloyd Russel, to drive the tandem for $75. Admittedly, that was a minor remuneration, but Lloyd considered it a fine opportunity to see the country. Charlie's son, Ken, also accompanied us to provide companionship for Lloyd during the long drive, and to give him an occasional break at the wheel.

No Arab chieftan with a caravan of camels, and leaving on a desert safari with valuable cargo, could have been any more cavalier than Crawford and I as we jumped into the cabs of our truck fleet and headed for Winnipeg. The departure turned out to be the high point in the entire adventure. Problems began almost immediately.

Attempting to cross the U.S. border at Port Huron, Michigan, we were halted and forced to acquire a bond, guaranteeing that the trucks wouldn't remain in the U.S.A. longer than 72 hours. We lost a half day plus a portion of our expense funds as a result of the unexpected bond fee. Travelling on the two-lane highways was slow and tedious, but due to our limited cash, we dared not luxuriate in motel accommodations, and so slept in the truck cabs.

Then, hilly terrain in Western Michigan and Northern Wisconsin caused the Ford truck Lloyd was driving to heat up, forcing us constantly to stop and add water to the radiator. But the worst delay was yet to come. On a bright hot Sunday afternoon, crawling along with weekend traffic through Duluth, Minnesota, I was following Lloyd in case of another breakdown. Leaving the city from the southwest suburbs, we had to climb a precipitous grade for three miles before reaching the prairie flats. Halfway up the incline, Lloyd leaned on his horn and pointed to a warning sign on the side of our route. It read, NO TRUCKS ALLOWED ON THIS ROUTE FROM 6 AM TO 12 PM ON SUNDAYS. CITY ORDINANCE NO. 70036. Unable to pull over in the bumper-to-bumper traffic, we had no alternative but to continue the ascent. Pulling up at a roadside tavern on level highway, surrounded by grain fields, we got the impression that Duluth was now behind. Sipping a cold beer, I asked the bartender the significance of the warning sign.

"Oh hell," he replied, "that was intended for pulp trucks. An occasional pulp log used to slide off during the steep incline. That was considered dangerous to heavy weekend traffic, so they passed the law. I wouldn't worry about it."

Before he finished his statement, a Minnesota State Trooper went barreling up our route.

"They won't bother you," the proprietor assured us. "The city limits are only five miles along the highway."

Wearily, we clambered aboard our vehicles, hopeful of reaching the Manitoba border by midnight. It wasn't to be. As we neared the western boundary of Duluth, the State Patrol, in waiting, pulled us over.

"You boys not aware it's against the law to drive trucks in Duluth on Sunday?" one officer asked.

"We saw a sign halfway up the big hill, but couldn't stop until we reached the plateau." I replied. "The bar owner back five miles said it was primarily for pulp trucks."

"I don't give a damn what a bartender told you," the officer exploded. "You're in violation of the law. Park these piggybacked trucks and follow me with the other."

For eighteen miles we trailed the State trooper through the extreme western suburbs of Duluth, pulling up in the parking lot of a country restaurant, where the officer put me into his patrol car and drove another two miles to a dilapidated hovel in the middle of a hay field. Approaching the dwelling, we were greeted by a bewhiskered old man.

"Good day, son," the man addressed the officer.

"Good afternoon, judge," the cop responded.

"What we got here?" the old timer asked the trooper.

"This man is in violation of ordinance number 70036: driving trucks through Duluth on Sunday, judge," the officer responded.

"Oh my, that is serious. Come into the house and we'll discuss the infraction." The shabbily dressed old man muttered, stepping inside his shack.

In shocked disbelief, I entered the tumbledown house full of chickens and goats. Seated at a small table in the corner of a screened porch, the Judge demanded I take an oath on the Bible to tell the truth, then asked, "How do you plead, son?"

"Well, I was certainly on the highway with trucks, but I've come from a thousand miles away. How could I possibly know there was a law? There is no warning, except on the steep hill when you are already leaving the city."

"Ignorance of the law is no excuse, son," the old guy stated. "If you plead not guilty, I'll have to lock you up until court convenes in the morning."

"Judge," the state trooper interjected, "because this man is from another country and was obviously ignorant of the ordinance upon reaching Duluth, I would like to recommend clemency."

"All right, son," the judge drawled. Then speaking to me, "If you plead guilty, I'll fine you $25 plus $20 court costs."

I was caught between a rock and a hard place. Certainly spending a night in jail wouldn't help the situation, because I would still probably be found guilty in the morning. However, the $45 would put another tremendous dent in our expense money. Without any realistic alternative, I paid the penalty but my opinion of American justice plummeted. Coincidently, the month following the ordeal, *Readers Digest* published a major article condemning the practice of allowing county judges to be elected without salary; and, instead, being allowed to retain a large percentage of all court costs collected as remuneration. This travesty of justice persists in some states to this day, and many American motorists can relate horror stories of being fleeced by unscrupulous judges at one time or another.

Not only did that incident sap our financial reserves even further; it also caused an additional eight-hour delay, as the cop instructed us not to leave the parking lot until after midnight or gamble on paying another fine. So we stayed put. Winnipeg was reached without further interruptions, but three days and four nights on the highway had thoroughly depleted our enthusiasm and grubstake. We then headed directly to Monominto for recuperation and advice. Dad recommended our taking our trucks to the Winnipeg Truck Exchange on Portage Avenue. Up to this point, Charlie and I had been expecting to divide a thousand dollars clear profit on the deal. We therefore didn't eagerly jump at an offer of twenty-eight hundred dollars from the Truck Exchange for the three vehicles. That would leave us less than $300 to split after expenses. A used truck lot in St. Boniface offered to sell them on consignment assuring us they would realize the profit we expected within three weeks. So, after transferring the ownerships to Dad, the four of us headed back in the Volkswagen. Unfortunately, however, our troubles hadn't ended.

In Central Michigan, the car's clutch went kaput, and the local mechanics, who had yet to be inundated with Japanese or European automobiles, had no wrenches in millimeter sizes. The operation of removing nuts and installing a home-made plate for a clutch was horrendous, as pliers and other adjustable tools were all that could be used for the chore.

Another day-and-one-half expired, and we arrived home broke and totally aggravated. What was intended to have been a pleasant respite from the rigors of real estate, plus a means of making a few fast dollars, had swiftly turned into a nightmare.

Business was still slow, forcing George Farr, Val Lovering, and Ray Reid to find other employment. When the interest payment on the sixty-day note didn't arrive, the lending institution decided to investigate the whereabouts of the trucks. Discovering they were fifteen hundred miles away, the lenders threatened to charge us with theft. To compound our difficulties, the truck market had collapsed. Not only was the St. Boniface dealer unable to obtain bids on the vehicles, but the Winnipeg Truck Exchange was no longer interested. It was painfully obvious I had to return west to somehow dispose of what was now an anathema.

Lorne and Edna purchased a new Chevrolet sedan in the spring and were leaving in late July to visit their Saskatchewan relations. Accompanying them were Lorne's two daughters, a niece, plus a lady friend of Edna's—making six without me. Nevertheless, I persuaded them to let me join them.

Preparing to leave Toronto on that journey made me completely dejected. Joyce, who returned from the hospital with Michael, our first son, two days prior to my departure, looked at me with keen disappointment and utter disbelief when she learned of my decision to return west.

Unable to leave much money for groceries, I cursed the day I had spawned the brainwave to disrupt a prosperous real estate enterprise and get involved in running trucks. However, if I didn't sell the vehicles and discharge the finance company note, I was apt to end up in jail facing a fraud charge; so, dejectedly, I once again found myself behind the wheel on a non-stop fifteen-hundred-mile dash to Winnipeg. Though jammed into the small sedan, like the popcorn in a box of Cracker Jack, everyone slept except Edna, who didn't drive, but sat beside me to make certain I didn't fall asleep at the wheel. We crossed the border into Manitoba within twenty-four hours after leaving Toronto.

Edna's brother, Bernard, operated a Ford agency in Wapella, Saskatchewan, and Bernard was the first relative Lorne and Edna were going to visit. It was arranged between Lorne and myself that if a truck market existed in Wapella, he would phone and I would hustle the vehicles through to Saskatchewan. The day following their Winnipeg departure, Lorne called excitedly, "Bring the trucks. Bernard insists there is an excellent market."

Jack assisted me in re-piggybacking the two vehicles, and we drove the three of them four-hundred miles farther west into Saskatchewan.

Delighted with their condition, Bernard, an immense Finlander, convinced me he would sell the trucks within a week and suggested that I accompany the Brannings, while Lorne called on his three brothers located in various parts of the province. Jack returned to Winnipeg.

Returning to Wapella a week later, I was disappointed to find that Bernard hadn't sold the vehicles; but he assured me again that I had nothing to worry about. He absolutely guaranteed me that they would be disposed of, and that the money would be in Toronto before I got there. He advanced me $75 expense money and I transferred the ownership to him, hoping he was an honest man. He wasn't.

It was well into August before I was back at Phillips Real Estate and open for business, but still no money had arrived from Bernard. After two months of absentee ownership, Phillips Real Estate was in shambles. Several men who had joined the firm enjoyed variable degrees of success, but my sporadic presence had discouraged them, and due to lack of direction and leadership only Charlie, Lorne, Fred Hagen, and Don Blackburn had remained.

Blackburn, a pleasant chap, was responsible for altering the design of my signature, thus adding to my financial dilemma. Returning from the first trip west with the trucks, I tried to balance my bank account one day, and couldn't locate $100. Going through cancelled checks, I discovered one to Don Blackburn for $100 which I hadn't written. When confronted with this, Don sheepishly explained, "Bill, I was broke, couldn't pay my rent, and, certain you'd help me out, wrote and endorsed the check myself. I intended to tell you as soon as you came home, but forgot."

It was almost impossible to distinguish Don's forged signature from my own, so the bank manager recommended I adopt more of a scribble. To this day, my signature, resembling a set of turkey tracks, is amusing to those who are not familiar with it, but since 1951, it has never been successfully copied again. I didn't press charges against Don, who died a few months later, but also never recovered the $100, which weakened my cash shortfall even more.

Toronto newspapers wouldn't allow me to advertise until their bill was paid; office rent was overdue; payments on telephone, household furniture, and car were in arrears; and the finance company, with the sixty-day note now due, was livid. Not only was I on the bottom of the heap, but I was being smothered by an avalanche of indebtedness.

Joyce was heavy-hearted when we moved in with her parents in order to rent our living quarters and to assist in paying the arrears on our overall lease. But even more depressing to me was having to barter down on automobiles in order to retain transportation. Driving out of the car lot with a 1946 Dodge, which I'd traded for my 1950 Ford, seemed like suddenly being delegated to riding a bicycle. The greatest challenge, nonetheless, was raising cash to pay off our trade bills and get back into production.

Few families had their own attorney. Most engage the legal firm recommended by their real estate broker. A referred lawyer usually assures the closing of the transaction, hence the payment of commission. John Walsh, an attorney I'd met through George Farr, acted for both parties on a large percentage of Phillips Real Estate deals. The Law Society frowned on this practice due to obvious conflict of interest, and most law firms including Walsh, stopped representing both vendor and purchaser on the same transaction by the late fifties.

Some brokers got a kick back for providing clients and, though I had neither requested nor received fees from Walsh, he clearly owed me a favor. So I approached him for a $1200 loan to get Phillips Real Estate out of the red. Pointing out the lack of equity in anything I owned, John said that, nevertheless, he had a client who would gamble a $1200, sixty-day note on our office furniture for a three-hundred-dollar bonus plus interest. A deal was consummated, my debts were discharged, and we were back in business. I went to the company which had financed our disastrous truck escapade and pleaded for time, explaining that I wasn't aware it was illegal to take the vehicles from the province. I said if they would grant us a few weeks extension, we would soon earn enough money to discharge their note—something we couldn't do if locked up in prison. They agreed to a sixty-day extension, provided the interest payments were made when due.

In early September, now able to advertise, we went earnestly back to work. With a degree of financial freedom and an improved mental attitude, though still lacking a report from Wapella regarding our trucks, we wrote business immediately. Unfortunately, towards the end of September a tragic occurrence temporarily interfered with my concentration. Sister Ruth, who had courageously battled her debilitating disease for almost three years, suddenly died of a blood clot. Jack and the folks were as broken-hearted as I, but because of the sorry state of my finances, my attending the funeral was impossible.

Religion had always been a contradiction, but Ruth's death finally convinced me there was no overpowering deity who controlled our destinies. Mother, an Anglican, was not a religious fanatic; but she enjoyed attending church whenever possible and listening to sermons on the radio. She never preached religion to her family, although she frequently discussed it. Dad was more of an agnostic than a believer.

I don't doubt that Jesus Christ existed as an outstanding mortal who devoted His life to the benefit of mankind. However, I seriously question the magic He supposedly performed at "The Miracle on the Mount," His ability to cure afflictions with a wave of His hand, or His rising from the dead. Earthlings, since man first stood upright, have always been terrified of the unknown, and particularly of death. Any promise, therefore, of everlasting life or salvation from suspected evils, was bound to elicit their reflection, whether logical or not.

Those religions with tenets based on the Old or New Testament, the Koran or Torah, and which insist they are absolutely authentic, are bewildering. There are innumerable instances where historical writings of events only two or three hundred years old have been proven farfetched and inaccurate. Consequently, how can we be convinced that writings thousands of years old are truthful accounts of happenings, rather than the figment of those writers' imaginations?

Regarding God as a Supreme Being Who controls the universe, Who punishes evil but rewards virtue, or Whose will we are not supposed to question, is also confusing. If He was responsible for giving me a brain to think, then how do I switch it off when it insists on questioning His methods; or doubting that He has the power to give everlasting life to a chosen group.

Psychiatrists and doctors enlighten us with the knowledge that all individuals' traits and characteristics are molded into our nature when we are extremely young. A simple bump on the head of a new born baby will have a bearing on his future intrinsic characteristics. It would seem logical that twin boys, born, reared, and loved in identical fashion, should grow up similar in nature. This is not the case, however. If either twin, while a baby, accidentally fell from his crib, inadvertently went hungry or thirsty, burned his finger, or experienced any of a thousand accidents babies frequently suffer, then according to research, those mishaps will have a strong bearing on that child's future behavior. Consequently, if those occurrences somehow warped his infantile mind, how could he justifiably be thrust into Purgatory to expiate evil caused by events he didn't have the power to avoid? How can anyone be responsible for how he thinks and acts when traits were etched into his character at a time when he had no control over what happened? All logically thinking human beings are confronted with living their lives by a moral code they themselves believe to be within the bounds of propriety. When asked if I believe in God, I usually reply, "Describe your God and I will tell you whether I believe in Him."

If my questioners are referring to a Supreme Being who created heaven and earth, who controls and records our every moment, who has the power to give us everlasting life or banish us to an eternal hell, I admit to having serious misgivings. However, whether we credit earth's existence to the 'Big Bang' and subsequent evolution theory (which I believe), or the instant creation dogma espoused by ecclesiastics, something or someone had to be responsible for our beginning; and if that something or someone is to be designated a Supreme Being or God, then I have no problem accepting such a philosophy.

As a result of this philosophy, I found little comfort in the thought that, because Ruth had lived a pure and sin-free existence and would be blessed with an eternal heavenly hereafter, that sometime in the future our souls might meet up again. Like hundreds of millions before, she was dead through no doings of her own and had passed out of any future contact with those she loved and who loved her, simply because that's the way it is. Her untimely demise in the prime of life convinced me even more to live life to its fullest, each conscious instant.

Every precious moment must be appreciated with the knowledge that once passed, it has elapsed forever. I pity those individuals who see but never look, hear but never listen, or feel but never sense the wonders of our planet. Many have smelled a wild rose but never inhaled its alluring fragrance; have noticed a Baltimore Oriole or a wild Canary, but never admired the brilliance of their plummage nor marvelled at their graceful flight. Some mortals hear a chorus of frogs, but do not heed the medley of voices contributing to the delightful aria; or are aware of the ocean's roar, but never listen to the melancholy music pounded out by one of nature's most powerful forces.

The only solace I could find in Ruth's existence, albeit she died prematurely, was the joy she brought into her family's life and the pleasant memories she left behind. Nevertheless, she would have been the first to tell me to get back to matters at hand, because life is strictly for the living.

The residential market had improved and Phillips Real Estate was making sales, though again it was a case of surviving until the deals closed. When the due date on the sixty-day note extension drew near, Charlie and I, still without word from Wapella, were thoroughly agitated and insisted that Edna get a satisfactory answer from Bernard about the status of our investment. She spoke to her brother, but got no reasonable explanation for his delay in selling the trucks. In desperation, I phoned Jack to request that he and Dad take a bus to Saskatchewan and return the vehicles to Winnipeg. A few days later Jack phoned from Bernard's office.

"Bill, my boy," Jack said, "you have been thoroughly screwed. Your three trucks have been hauling coal and wheat, obviously for several months. Bernard, who holds the ownership, says he advanced you money and won't release the trucks."

In a combined state of shock and fury, I exploded. "Put that son-of-a-bitch on the phone!"

After some muffled conversation, Bernard came on the speaker, "How are you doing, Bill. Good to hear from you," he said in a matter-of-fact tone of voice.

"Listen you ignorant bastard," I screamed. "What kind of a rotten deal are you trying to pull on your brother-in-law's partner. We are at our wits end to meet the sixteen-hundred-dollar note at the finance company to keep us out of jail. Let me tell you something, and pay careful attention. If you don't sign those trucks back to my brother and they aren't leaving Wapella in half an hour, I swear I will be there in two days and blow your f---ing head off your shoulders! Let me talk to Jack you no good son-of-a-bitch."

A few minutes elapsed before Jack returned to the phone. "Bill, Bernard has indicated he will release them. If there is no further problem we will phone tomorrow from Winnipeg. It is twenty below zero here and there is no heater in one cab, so it will be a torturous journey."

Jack phoned the following afternoon to inform us that our trucks were back in Winnipeg, and that he and Dad had almost perished during the return trip.

"Bill, I have no idea what you said to Bernard, but after he finished talking to you, he quickly decided to transfer ownership," Jack said.

"I seriously threatened to murder him," I responded, "and that was a definite possibility had he not relented."

Dad immediately sold the two-tons, financed the three-ton and mailed us a check for sixteen hundred dollars to discharge our obligation. Although we lost our personal investment, two or three months valuable time, and almost my real estate business, Charlie and I were greatly relieved to get the finance company off our backs. I vowed to stick to my own trade forevermore, though I should have known, that for me, such a promise would be impossible to keep.

With the sordid truck adventure behind, our sales volume skyrocketed and a much happier holiday season was enjoyed by Joyce and me, though we were anxious to get back into our own place. Songs often remind us of a specific time in our lives. "Rudolph the Red Nosed Reindeer" and "Silver Bells", introduced in 1949 and 1950 respectively, remind me of Christmas during those difficult days.

During that festive period, I invited John Walsh down for lunch, as closings allowed me to pay off his client's note. While eating, I took a shot in the dark. "John, my friend, I don't believe anyone would loan twelve hundred dollars on our furniture, so it's my guess you put up the money yourself as an investment to keep us in business. If that is the case, you have a helluva nerve requesting a three-hundred-dollar bonus."

John couldn't keep a straight face. "Sometimes you're too smart for your own good, young fellow," he responded with a grin. "I won't admit you're right, but we wouldn't have accepted the bonus even if it was offered. We are all happy you are back in business."

In January 1952, two new men, Jack Harlow, and Eric Marrett, joined the firm; so, with a sales force of seven, Phillips Real Estate was again a force with which to be reckoned.

Once commissions were spendable, I corrected two serious aggravations: the '46 Dodge was traded for a sparkling new 1952 Pontiac two-door, and Joyce and I moved into a rented house. To this day, the six-room, two-story brick building on Malvern Avenue, remains one of Joyce's favorite residences. Perhaps her attachment was because the dwelling represented our first real home, though we were forced to sublet the second floor to a war widow and her child to help defray expenses. Our furnishings were meager, but, though still without a television or refrigerator, we had our independence and sufficient money for some social life.

Charlie and Marge Crawford became close friends; and Ken and Helen Watson, acquaintances of the Crawfords, also joined our inner circle. Most Saturday nights were spent in their company, together with the Brannings. We also frequently socialized with the Blues and Theodorus. Steve joined the Loyal Order of Moose and persuaded Lorne and I also to affiliate. The Moose held a Saturday night dance at the Byng Hall in East Toronto, and it was there we usually congregated. Although we drank too much, those were happy times and the music of the era depicted this lighthearted spirit: "Tzena, Tzena, Tzena"; "A Bushel and A Peck"; "Hoop de Doo"; "I'd 'Ave Baked a Cake"; "Goodnight, Irene"; "Music! Music! Music!"; "Chattanoogie Shoe Shine Boy"; and "Rag Mop" were lively tunes that filled the air waves. Several romantic ballads of those years remained popular for decades: "My Foolish Heart"; "Autumn Leaves"; "Sentimental Me"; "La Vi en Rose"; "Cold, Cold Heart"; "Till I Waltz Again with You"; plus numerous others.

Joyce and I were completely devoted to each other, though I worked seven days a week and most evenings, which allowed us little time together. At one Saturday night dance, Joyce went beyond the call of love and chanced a serious injury to come to my assistance. A group of local toughs frequently hung around the Byng Hall and harassed the patrons as they were leaving the establishment. The leader, an enormous young bully about 6'8" and weighing close to 300 pounds, was well known in the local community as a trouble maker. One evening a group, including this giant, were standing in the vestibule as several of us were leaving for home one evening. When I stepped past, the bully tripped me for no reason, sending me sprawling out the door and into the snow. In a rage, I dashed back to do battle, but lost the initial skirmish when one gang member held me in a tight embrace while another whacked me in the face. Meanwhile, the titan came charging over to tear me apart. Quite obviously, as I was no match in a slugfest, I plowed into him like a bulldozer and we crashed to the ground. Wrestling like lumberjacks, he held me in a vicious bear hug, as I struggled to get my hands on his throat, believing that to be my only chance for survival. The fellow was so enormous I couldn't understand why he didn't toss me like a rag doll instead of groaning and squirming as if I were causing him pain. Suddenly I realized Joyce, holding him by the hair, was giving him the boots with her spike heels, and he was trying harder to avoid her attack than mine. Someone shouted that the police were coming and the bevy of bullies, including my antagonist, scattered like a covey of quail. We came out of the skirmish in good shape, though I got a black eye from the initial punch. Charlie Crawford evened that score by soundly thrashing the culprit, and the big ox who started the melee must have had sore ribs for a month from Joyce's high heels.

Joyce, criticized for getting involved because she chanced getting clobbered from another gang member, replied, "Pooh, I've just spent two tough years getting a new husband trained, and don't relish the thought of losing him and having to start all over again."

Although my family and I corresponded regularly, we were mutually eager for a get-together. By July of '52, with finances straightened out and the company running smoothly, I decided to drive west for a surprise visit, to acquaint my kin with my beautiful young wife and Michael, our year-old son.

The folks had moved to Elmwood, an eastern suburb of Winnipeg, shortly after Ruth's burial. That must have been a traumatic period for the two of them. Being forced to sell the farm he had clung to so tenaciously for nearly a quarter century was a heartbreaker for Dad; and even then, those funds weren't sufficient to discharge the huge debt accumulated by Ruth's protracted illness. Consequently, the store was disposed of also. When they moved to the city, they moved with little more than the clothes on their back. Dad, then in his early sixties, drove a truck for the Blind Institute, while Mother worked as a sales clerk in a Winnipeg department store. Although it appeared like a pitiful situation, they both seemed happy and contented with their lot. Sister Joyce, then in her late teens, though not a burden, was morose and withdrawn. Music was her only real interest; she would listen to it for hours on end. She was of little comfort during my parents' period of bereavement. Jack, his bride Shirley, and their new son Bill, were still farming at Niverville. Struggling financially, they were also looking forward to more prosperous times.

We had an outstanding family reunion, particularly during the few delightful days we spent together in the lake country of Eastern Manitoba and Western Ontario. A few miles west of Seven Sisters Falls, we picnicked beside the highway. It was at the exact spot our construction trailer was located when I had worked as an oiler on the dragline that contributed to building the roadway. With modern tackle and the latest in fishing lures, Jack and I fished from the identical rock upon which I'd fished several years earlier with a piece of rough cord and a silver spoon. Ten-pound Northern Pike had been brought in with every fourth toss of the crude contraption at that time; but neither Jack nor I got a nibble, indicating to me that fish eventually learn the fallacy of attacking mechanical baits and pass this information on to their relations. Luckily the message wasn't received by the fish in a small lake outside Kenora, where we rented a cabin for a few days and caught more fish than we could eat. It was our first joint family fishing experience, so it made for a successful holiday. A few days later we were still vividly reliving our angling experiences.

Shortly after returning to Winnipeg from our recreational respite, Joyce and I headed for home. The weather was torrid and after a few hours driving, we became nauseated from inhaling a terrible odor permeating our automobile's interior. Several times we stopped and inspected the trunk, but we were unable to locate the cause of the stink. Finally, in desperation, we completely unloaded our belongings and, under the spare tire, located a putrid Northern Pike. Disposing of the

decaying carcass afforded us relief, but Joyce had to spray the uphol-
stery for a month before the smell completely disappeared.

I was delighted to find business flourishing at the office on our return,
so Joyce's surprising news that she again was expecting wasn't too
serious a shock. We wanted companionship for Michael, though we
hadn't intended having another child quite so soon. Notwithstanding
our attachment to the Malvern Avenue home, the high rent and preposterous fuel bills, which required keeping the upstairs rented, was utterly
disagreeable; so we moved into a three-room second-story apartment
on Danforth Avenue, a few blocks west of my office. There, at last, we
had complete privacy.

Shortly after moving into our new quarters, I went out to buy Joyce
a new washing machine, but arrived home instead with our first television. What an unbelievably exciting moment when I set up a pair of
rabbit ears on the roof and our first fuzzy picture became partially
visible. Our life together was never the same afterwards, as Joyce
became a T.V. devotee, an addiction she never overcame.

Though our Danforth apartment was enjoyable, we both yearned for
our own home, so in May of '53 an opportunity presented itself which I
grabbed onto with gusto. A lovely two-bedroom bungalow became available at a price we could afford, so, borrowing the down payment from
the bank, I made my first real estate acquisition. At 86 Westview Boulevard, in the township of East York, and approximately two miles from
my Danforth Ave. office stood our Taj Mahal. Shortly before taking
possession, Joyce delivered Gary, our second son. As delighted as Joyce
was over our new residence, she insists our first refrigerator was an
even bigger thrill. Though there was no food inside, she opened and
closed the door a hundred times the day it arrived.

In early summer of '53, Jack Harlow and Eric Marrett went into
business for themselves; Charlie Crawford bought a tourist establishment at the Bay of Quinte, a hundred and twenty-five miles east of the
city; and Fred Hagen moved to Vancouver. The abrupt departure of my
sales force made me restless; thus, as an insect is attracted to a fly trap,
I once more abandoned the security of my successful enterprise to chase
gold at the end of another rainbow.

Television didn't intrigue me so much for its entertainment value,
as its fantastic money-making potential. The T.V. craze was spreading
across North America as rapidly as the bubonic plague struck Europe
during the seventeenth century. Huge regions without T.V. signals were
awaiting relay stations which were springing up at an accelerating rate,
so, it was obvious to me that within two years all major North American
centres would be receiving some transmission. A financial killing was
going to be made in television, and I wanted in on the bonanza. The

most logical sector for me to secure a toehold was Western Canada, where television was as eagerly awaited as a child for Christmas. I contacted all major television manufacturers about obtaining Manitoba as an exclusive territory, and Coronet, one of the smaller and newer corporations, offered me a proposal.

Coronet, owned by Bill Harewitz, designed its models after a low-priced model being marketed in Chicago by a colorful character named Mad Man Muntz. The Coronet T.V. like its American counterpart had fewer tubes than other sets; but providing it wasn't too far from a transmissions signal, it performed as well as its competitors. Not only the manufacturing of the sets, but also the marketing was unique. A seven-day-free-home trial was the ingenious system adopted from Muntz. T.V.'s were installed in peoples' homes on the theory that, after a week's exposure, the newly addicted family wouldn't allow the set to leave the premises, and that generally was the case. Harewitz brought Charlie Stillman in from Chicago as general manager, as well as a young sales manager. Both were familiar with Muntz's methods. They set up a boiler room operation, with a bevy of phone girls arranging house appointments for a small army of salesmen. At a meeting in early summer, Stillman enthusiastically endorsed my proposition and indicated I could tie up Manitoba, Saskatchewan, and Alberta as the exclusive agent for Coronet. First however, I had to join the company in Toronto to learn their marketing technique. I couldn't wait to get started.

During the previous several months, I had become acquainted with Harold Thomas, another real estate broker. Harold had been partners with Lionel Faust, but they had split up on friendly terms and gone their separate ways. Harold and his wife Eilleen had socialized with Joyce and I; and, on a few occasions, Harold and I had discussed the possibility of joining forces.

When I plunged into the television industry, Harold suggested we jump into my new 1953 Ford Monarch sedan for a quick visit to Winnipeg to investigate the market potential. Uncle George, who had worked for the Hudson Bay Company as a radio technician since the depression, was an excellent contact, because he was in the groundswell of T.V. mania. The first transmission, scheduled to reach Winnipeg in the autumn of '53, had the populace impatient to enter the television era.

The lowest retail price per set advertised in Winnipeg was in the $500 range. Stillman assured me that the Coronet would cost less than $200 delivered to Manitoba. This would allow ample room for profit, so it appeared we were on to a good thing. Harold and I enjoyed a pleasant few days with my folks. Then, convinced we'd soon be relocating in the west, we scooted back to Toronto.

It was mutually agreed that Thomas should remain in real estate until we had something more definite with Coronet; then, if negotiations broke down for any reason, we would have the framework of a realty business to fall back on. It was a wise decision.

Our Phillips Real Estate office was converted into a television retail outlet, with a 75-foot antenna installed on the roof. Twelve men operated from my store, both as floor salesmen and house callers for the seven-day-free-home-trial appointments. I earned an overriding commission on all sales from East Toronto. Stillman showed little compassion for his own sales force when he devised a plan to guarantee that I earned sufficient money to keep me happy. He ran a contest every two weeks with a two-hundred-dollar-cash first prize for the man selling the most T.V.'s. I won every contest by a wide margin, because, unknown to the sales staff, every unit sold from my store was credited to my total. The weekly income from Coronet compared favorably with my previous real estate earnings, but I was fervently looking forward to accumulating a fortune in the west with an exclusive Coronet agency.

Finally, the world was my oyster—at least until one day in late November when, without warning, Coronet went bankrupt. Sales were excellent, but any amount of down payment had been accepted and credit checks were nonexistent, so the chattel mortgage paper wasn't marketable. All this resulted in a negative cash flow. Coronet was also experiencing technical difficulties in the manufacturing; hence, warehouses were full of broken-down sets. Hundreds of Toronto firms, as well as people, lost considerable money. I was lucky that all I lost was another delusion of opulence. Once again I had painted on my office door: WILLIAM PHILLIPS REAL ESTATE.

Approaching the holidays, Harold Thomas came to my office to plan our amalgamation which would become effective January 2, 1954. His ex-partner, Lionel Faust, wanted to join and make it a three-way partnership. I reluctantly agreed, provided that Lionel obtained his general insurance license and had no voice in the operation of the real estate division. That was agreed to, so Homeland Realty Limited was formed; and, after three years, William Phillips Real Estate became history.

Lagniappe
The Korean War

Joyce and I experienced an ebb-and-flow existence from 1950 to 1954, but no more than the world itself. Someone once said there would always be wars and rumors of wars, and more prophetic words were never spoken. Until earthlings accept one another as equal partners on planet earth regardless of race, religion or political beliefs, conflicts will be as much a part of our legacy to future generations as they were our heritage from generations of the past.

In early eras of recorded history, Egyptians battled the Sea Peoples; later, Greeks, Persians, and Romans fought for world supremacy. During the eleventh, twelfth, and thirteenth centuries, Crusaders campaigned against the Moslems. For 200 years, French, English, Dutch, and Spanish struggled for control of Europe and the New World. These are only trickles in the torrents of turmoil that have plagued mankind since the invention of military arms.

In our time, those weapons of death that had been improved for hundreds of years gradually became obsolete and were replaced by more ghastly tools of war, which served their grisly purpose when the whole world became enmeshed in combat as the Allies stamped out Nazism and Fascism. When peace was finally restored, it was hoped that mortals had learned the futility of war and would halt the constant stupid loss of needless bloodshed; instead, a new power struggle appeared. Communism and Capitalism, two entirely opposite philosophies that couldn't abide each other's political tenets, once again divided the world into two camps.

After sparring in several corners of the globe following the conclusion of World War II, the main bout between these two new gigantic antagonists began in the summer of 1950, when forces of Communist

302

North Korea invaded the Republic of South Korea, starting a conflict that continued until the summer of 1953. The U.N. authorized the creation of a United Nations command to direct military operations against North Korea, and General Douglas MacArthur was appointed Supreme Commander over the sixteen member nations sending forces to South Korea in order to resist aggression. Canada's contribution of 22,000 men was exceeded only by those of Britain and the United States.

Seoul, the South Korean capital, captured from the Communists in September of 1950 by U.N. forces, again fell in January of 1951 to North Korean soldiers, this time aided by Chinese troops who had joined the struggle a few months earlier. Seoul was recaptured a final time during the summer of 1951. The action swung back and forth across the 38th parallel until an armistice was signed in July of 1951. Casualties were heavy, with U.S. losses placed at over 54,000 dead, plus 103,000 wounded; while North and South Korean casualties were at least ten times as high. Little was gained except the possibility that Reds around the world finally realized that the free world was prepared to fight to stop the spread of Communism. I wonder how many young men who died for either cause really gave a damn!

At the conclusion of the Korean conflict, North Americans sighed with relief and hoped their sons and loved ones would be returning home to heart and hearth for good. Rumblings, however, from another troubled Asian area were already being heard that would eventually leave much deeper wounds in the United States than any war in which they'd ever been involved.

In 1950, the United States recognized Vietnam, sold military equipment to Saigon, and dispatched a mission to advise the Vietnamese how to use the arms. Vietnam, a French colony which obtained its independence in 1946, was still defended by French forces against Communist aggression until the fall of Dien-Bienphu in 1954, when a 250,000-man French army fell to a Communist army only half that size.

Shortly after the defeat of the French, a Geneva conference of world powers divided Vietnam into North and South. After a decade of leading guerilla forces, Ho Chi Minh became president of the Communistic "Democratic Republic of North Vietnam." President Eisenhower, though deeply concerned with the Communist threat in Vietnam, adamantly refused to send American troops. It wasn't until 1965 that President Lyndon Johnson dispatched American forces in large numbers to prevent further aggression by the Communist North and "to avoid humiliation."

As a result of the hatred existing between Communism and the Western Democracies, it was obvious that our generation, and those in the foreseeable future, would not be exempt from living under a shadow of constant conflict, as our ancestors had done since the early ages of the human race. Mentally accepting the inevitability of hatred among nations, we turned our minds to other topics.

Labor management strife continued unabated through the early fifties. General Motors signed a new five-year contract granting United Auto Workers' employees increased pensions and substantial pay boosts. The U.S. auto industry wasn't the least concerned about imminent competition from European and Japanese manufacturers—a grave miscalculation, as bloated salaries of American workers would soon make it impossible for U.S. industry to compete on world markets, thus causing a loss of jobs that eventually would become catastrophic. United States railroads, placed under army control in 1948, were finally returned to the private sector in 1952, after two years of actual operation by government troops. Even with Federal intervention preventing unions from rapidly escalating railway salaries, the railroad industry couldn't compete with the burgeoning trucking business, causing railway company failures and the loss of thousands of other laboring positions.

The U.S. Government was still wooing voters with socialistic capriciousness. In 1952, Congress amended the Social Security Act, increasing benefits to the elderly by 12.5 percent, and allowing pension recipients to earn up to $75 monthly without a loss in benefits.

President Eisenhower, at least conscious of the pitfalls of deficit financing, ordered all Federal agencies to curtail new requests for personnel and construction, and demanded that all Federal tax reductions be postponed until the budget was balanced. What a shame this philosophy wasn't adopted, together with clamping a tight lid on government spending; perhaps then the ravages of inflation wouldn't have become the ogre of the next generation.

Canadian industry, also experiencing labor problems, resolved them by steadily increasing wages, then upping the price of goods to make up for the higher labor costs. At the time, no one gave a damn, because the country wasn't yet competing with the swiftly improving Japanese and West German industrialists, who, not facing North America's escalating union wage scales, were turning out products at a fraction of North America's cost.

Though Canada lacked certain attributes of sovereign nationhood, both legally and psychologically, and possessed less than half of one percent of the world's population, the country nevertheless stood as the fourth most powerful state on earth. More than ever before, however, Canada's economic destiny had become tied to that of the United States. Many people regarded the growing integration of Canadian and American economics as a big step towards the inevitable disappearance of

Canadian independence. There was growing public debate about ways and means of preventing Canada from being totally absorbed into the American sphere of influence, but they were attacking their problems at the wrong source. It wasn't the steady influx of American capital that would destroy Canada's position in the economic power structure of world nations, but burgeoning labor costs, advancing prices, and an expanding government that would make the cost of manufactured products too high to compete with those from Europe and Asia. Only the enormous natural resources of Canada kept it from sinking completely out of sight in an economic quagmire, but this reliance on nature's beauty in lieu of intelligent business practice, eventually forced Canadians to become, as someone remarked, "Hewers of wood and carriers of water."

The Korean conflict, nuclear fission proliferation, labor struggles, increased government intervention in private affairs, and the death of Stalin—all these contributed to an apprehensive outlook by North Americans in the early fifties. Many positive happenings, though, also made it an exciting period. United States auto production passed seven million annually, and surfaced highways exceeded two million miles.

The automobile, one of the prime symbols in the vast economic and social change of mid-century, stood for the aspiration of everyone to a life of affluence and leisure, for private rights over public, for the dissolution of old communities and traditional values. But it was also killing North Americans at a rate that would soon surpass the total of North Americans killed during the entire second World War. Besides being a murder weapon, the cars demand for space and pavement was a voracious consumer of government budgets and urban land. Improvements were creeping into new models. The Chrysler Corporation, for instance, installed power steering in 1951. In 1952 an insignificant news release would have more ominous overtones within a decade: German Volkswagons were sold in Great Britain for the first time. Although they had been introduced into the U.S. in 1949, "the Bug" had not been accepted by the buying public. This would change dramatically within ten years.

Although automobiles changed North American lifestyles in sensational fashion during the early '50's, television had an even greater impact. Canada adopted the new medium more quickly than any other country. By 1955, the nation had become second only to the U.S. in terms of programs, number of stations, network service, extent of coverage, and per capita ownership of sets. Television sales in the U.S. soared and T.V. stations sprung up faster than dandelions after a spring rain. Popular programs such as *What's My Line; Your Show of Shows; I Love Lucy; Kukla, Fran and Ollie;* and *Dennis The Menace* were as much a part of daily living as breakfast and dinner. Color television was introduced in 1951, and, as conventional sets were unable to pick up the signals, a whole new surge in the industry began, though it would take several years for color to saturate the market.

It would be the late fifties before Japan's Sony Corporation infiltrated the North American market with television sets, but in 1950 they introduced the first tape recorder, which weighed nearly forty pounds; then, in 1952 they brought out the first pocket-size transistor radio. Japanese products were considered inferior and "Made in Japan" was a mark of substandard quality, though that stigma swiftly reversed itself and the "Made in Japan" label soon became a symbol of excellence.

Still too unknowledgeable in economic global matters thoroughly to understand the extent to which North Americans were undermining their future prosperity, I watched nonetheless with growing concern the labor unions' movement for increased wages and benefits being constantly applauded by the proletariat. My inner instincts told me we were spiralling toward financial trouble in spite of the fact that many believed only good times lie ahead.

As an independent entrepreneur, my interest lay in prognosticating the implications and their ultimate effect on the overall real estate business in the event of a substantial down turn in any sector of our society. After all, if the working class were financially unable to purchase homes, the real estate market would collapse.

Lionel Faust, Harold Thomas, and I had great plans for Homeland Realty, which officially opened its doors on January 2, 1954. We realized, however, that every shift in the manufacturing industry's prosperity would greatly affect ours.

Chapter 4

From Rags to Riches to Rags

Homeland Realty Limited took off in spectacular fashion, with two dozen experienced salesmen and a booming residential market. Harold, as President, was responsible for outside activities; Lionel, as Vice President, operated our General Insurance Division; while I, as Secretary/Treasurer, managed the office, as well as assisting our agents in closing deals. The $100 weekly draw we each took was a pleasant switch for Joyce and me after three years of impatiently waiting for closings.

Harold, though intelligent and good company, was also a bombastic, overbearing type of person who got on a lot of people's nerves, including Joyce's. When visiting, for example, he might tell his hostess that she should change the pattern of her wallpaper because it didn't match the furniture, or instruct her to get rid of her wall paintings because they didn't suit the wallpaper. Joyce was fond of Harold's wife, Eilleen, an English war bride, so we frequently went out together. On one such occasion, Joyce's clear thinking and quick action saved us some serious injuries or perhaps even lives, including her own. We four, plus another couple, Jack and Pat Scougall, were heading for a square dance in Harold's new Cadillac when a drunk drove through a red light and crashed into the driver's side of our car. The impact spun our vehicle on the icy roads a complete 180 degrees before slamming into a high curb, causing a 180 degree reverse spin which left the badly damaged automobile heading in its original direction. The force of the double whip sprung the driver's door open, and Harold, Jack, and I sailed past the steering wheel and through the open door, landing on the street in the path of the careening Cadillac. Eilleen and Pat in the back seat with Joyce both fainted; and Joyce, who had never driven nor even taken a driving lesson, but who sensed the seriousness of the situation, clambered over the back of the front seat in her long gown and somehow halted the wildly oscillating automobile, thus preventing an even more serious mishap.

Several phenomenal things occurred during that accident. First and foremost, none of us six were seriously injured, though Harold, knocked unconscious when he hit the pavement, received a bump on his head and was severely shaken up. Also strange was how big Harold, fat Jack Scougall, and I, who am over six-feet-three inches in height, floated out of the open door like crows leaving a corn field, and, though totally conscious, were unable to grab the steering wheel or any other part of the car to prevent ourselves from being hurled onto the icy pavement. Also, due to a mix-up in communications, which made us late, it was the first time we had ever left home without anyone's having had a cocktail or two. But perhaps the greatest miracle was Joyce's presence of mind in stopping an uncontrollable missile. Once again fate had intervened in our lives.

Mother and Dad, anxious to become acquainted with their third grandson, took a bus trip to Toronto in the late summer of '54 and were indirectly responsible for bringing into the world their first granddaughter. Mother had travelled through the East when she immigrated from England as a child, but neither she nor Dad had ever visited Eastern Ontario, and they both fell in love with the area and its people.

We visited Niagara Falls with the intention of spending a night, but as it was the peak of the tourist season, accommodations were impossible to locate. We had to drive all the way to Rochester before locating a satisfactory motel. Perfect weather plus my parents' delight with the countryside persuaded me to take them on a four-day tour. We motored along the southern shore of Lake Ontario to the picturesque Thousand Islands, and through Cornwall to Ottawa where we spent an interesting day. We then crossed the Ottawa River and returned to Toronto through the Laurentian Highlands.

Our original intent of spending only one night on the road meant we took few personal belongings and no protective devices. The relaxing atmosphere, the tranquil surroundings, and the cool evenings were all partially responsible for our daughter's entrance into the world nine months later. Most people's initial claim to joining the ranks of the human race is arbitrary at best, as it is a published fact that over 60% of all pregnancies are unplanned. Following Gary's birth, Joyce's doctor had advised her to limit our family to the two boys, and we had intended to abide by his recommendation. However, my parent's visit plus subsequent events which had contributed to Joyce's conceiving were responsible for one of the happiest occurrences in our marriage. Though Sherree was born by Caesarean, Joyce suffered no ill effects; nevertheless, we were doubly cautious about avoiding such accidents in the future.

Harold Thomas and I spent a considerable part of our leisure time together in the out-of-doors. Troubled with chronic appendicitis, I had it removed in early winter at Thomas's insistence, because of our concern that it might flare up at a time when reaching a hospital would be difficult. We bought a small boat and motor, which provided hours of relaxation on weekend fishing jaunts. Hank Sharpe, also a regular crony of mine on fishing and hunting excursions, located a fascinating but rustic tourist camp on the York River at Boulter, Ontario, 140 miles northwest of Toronto. Hank, Harold Thomas, Lionel Faust, Lorne Branning, I, and several others frequented the area for fishing and for duck, partridge, and deer hunting. The captivating forested and lake country attracted me tremendously, and Joyce, who had become an ardent angler, also joined me on occasional fishing jaunts into the region. Although we didn't realize it at the time, the bewitching terrain, so unlike the prairies in every physical detail, would be the general locale for one of the greatest challenges of my business life before the end of the decade.

Harold, an infantry veteran and a fair marksman, had never hunted big game until joining me in 1953 at our Boulter retreat, where he bagged a fine buck. This fanned the ember in Harold's innards into a burning desire to hunt. One weekend in late Autumn, he persuaded me to pack a little gear for a five-hundred-mile automobile journey north to Cochrane, Ontario, to try our luck at moose for three days. George Prue, manager of our Central Toronto office and one of the most unique characters with whom I'd ever be associated, accompanied us on the expedition. Though I'd shot numerous deer, I'd only seen two moose in the wild, and the immensity of the animal made the prospects an exciting challenge. If successful, it would also provide us with a large quantity of excellent meat. Not one of us had the slightest knowledge of the complexities of moose hunting. Our ignorance became obvious shortly after our arrival in Cochrane. The original plan of simply roaming the bush as we did when stalking deer was swiftly pooh poohed by the local populace. They maintained that it was very unlikely moose would be found near any road accessible by Harold's Cadillac. Moose were in the rutting season; therefore, our only reasonable hope of bagging them necessitated our hiring an Indian guide, who, mimicking the mating call, could lure the animals within shooting range. Dave Black, an Ojibway Indian guide from the Low Bush River Country fifty miles farther North, had just arrived in Cochrane with a group of ecstatic American sportsmen who had bagged a fine bull. The Americans strongly recommended we hire the Indian, whose one hundred dollar fee guaranteed at least shooting at a moose. We agreed, but Dave was so drunk it was impossible to arrange a deal. With Black still incoherent the following morning, someone suggested we take the train to Low Bush, where his son might be induced to guide us until Dave sobered up—which event wouldn't likely be until Dave was stone broke.

Cochrane, on the main transcontinental Canadian National Railway line running from Vancouver to Halifax, was also the hub for a spur line running to Low Bush, then East into Northern Quebec's mining and lumbering towns. A tiny Ojibway Indian village, Low Bush, Ontario, huddled along the railroad and straddling the Low Bush River, typified the poverty and degradation so rampant in Northern Canadian Indian settlements.

We swiftly established ourselves with Paul, Dave Black's son, and Joe Nardone, his brother-in-law. Joe, half Indian and half French, a massive and friendly man, suggested we set up camp in the area Dave generally hunted, and where he and Paul would guide us until Dave returned.

The Low Bush River, a sluggish stream, ran into Lake Abitibi, a huge, shallow, treacherous body of water over eighty miles long, twenty miles wide, and indented with hundreds of marshy bays and inlets— all ideal haunts for moose. Both the general shallowness and huge uninterrupted expanse of open lake caused rough water conditions, with only the slightest breeze. Most families in Low Bush, only two miles off the lake, had lost at least one male member at one time or another in a boating mishap.

The typical mode of water transportation was in a flat-bottom home-made craft up to thirty-two feet long and five-feet wide. It was generally driven with a ten to fifteen horsepower outboard motor, which meant it didn't attain much speed. Called a "Longboat," the Ojibways had de-signed it as a cargo carrier for transporting canoes, tents, and other gear plus up to a half ton of moose meat across the dangerous Lake Abitibi. Having towed our own outfit, including the 7½ horsepower Mercury, from Toronto, we attached our motor beside Joe Nardone's ten-horse, Johnson, thus substantially improving our speed.

In late afternoon two tents were erected on Windy Bay on Lake Abitibi at the mouth of a narrow marshy, winding creek—one for our use and the other for Joe, his Indian wife, and Paul. A cold blustery north wind, together with a raw, bone-chilling drizzle, kept us huddled in our sleeping bags waiting for the hunt to begin. As dusk engulfed the forlorn encampment, Joe entered our tent.

"We go hunting now, one man with me, one man with Paul, other have to wait."

"What the hell are you talking about? It will be pitch black outside in a half hour. How will we see to shoot?" I asked in disbelief.

"We call moose, they come to creek bank near canoe then we put on flashlight," Joe replied.

"Isn't that illegal?" Harold questioned.

"Makes no difference, that's how we hunt." Joe snorted, leaving the tent.

On the initial sally, I went with Joe and George accompanied Paul. The hunters were placed on the bottom at the bow of the twelve foot birch bark canoe, while the guide sat or kneeled in the rear. From this position he could paddle and steer the craft, plus swiftly snap on the "Hunter's Lantern," aiming the powerful beam along the rifle barrel to the quarry. I hunted with a 32 calibre Winchester lever-action I'd purchased second-hand for forty dollars. Similar to Father's 30-30 Winchester, it was light in weight, ideal for carrying in the bush, and an excellent deer rifle, but not quite powerful enough for large game such as moose.

A half mile from the encampment, in total darkness, Joe pulled the canoe over to the stream's bank, put the birch bark moose horn to his mouth, and exploded with a bellow that reverberated miles across the swampy terrain and surrounding water. Joe called two or three times at an interval of five minutes; then we sat silent and motionless for a half hour listening for anything resembling an answer before Joe repeated the procedure. Though not jubilant about this method of hunting—I had always considered jacklighting for any game extremely unsportsmanlike—sitting at the bottom of that frail canoe with night winds whistling through the evergreens, and trying to picture a fifteen hundred pound animal charging from the bush, which I was supposed to shoot by the ray of a flashlight, was not just a little spine tingling.

Alternating with the two guides through the damp chilly night, then catching a little shut eye on our sleeping shift, I thought the night would never end. By daybreak neither Joe nor Paul had received any response to their untiring efforts, so we all hit the sack for a few hours sleep. Dave still hadn't arrived. At noon Joe recommended we split up. I went with Joe and his wife in their longboat directly to the Nardone's residence in another tiny Indian village located near the railroad and approximately ten miles along the lake. Joe and I would hunt the night in his area, and I would catch the train back to Low Bush the following afternoon. George, Harold, and I would rendezvous there, then continue on to Cochrane and home.

The Nardones and their seven children, ranging from two to fifteen years of age, shared a tiny frame dwelling consisting of two small bedrooms, plus one larger chamber which functioned as a combined kitchen, living, and dining room. Their meager furnishings explained Joe's determination to get me a moose and thereby earn a hundred dollar fee, plus the opportunity to establish himself as a successful guide. He frequently asked about the possibility of getting him other hunters, and Hank Sharpe came to mind in particular. He was not only an ardent hunter, but affluent enough to afford the trip. Hank was the type of individual who would be fascinated with the lonely, wild, and desolate environment.

Although the rain ceased, a biting north wind made sitting motionless in a canoe for hours on end a real test of perseverance. Joe and I hunted from five o'clock in the afternoon until five the following morning, and, albeit oftimes miserable and never hearing one answer to Joe's incessant calling, I got a kick out of those unforgettable twelve hours. Paddling along the shores of Lake Abitibi, slithering up rivulets and streams, and investigating bays or inlets off the main body of water intrigued me to no end. And Joe's ability noiselessly to maneuver his craft with one powerful arm gripping the paddle, while holding his moose horn with the other and forcing the vessel to obey his every whim with a simple flick of his wrist was also fascinating. Every couple of hours we'd land the canoe, light a fire, boil tea, stretch our chilled limbs and chat. Joe, terribly disappointed and apologetic at his inability to locate moose, was nevertheless enjoyable company. Unfortunately I didn't have the cash to give him much renumeration for his fruitless efforts.

Beaching the canoe in front of his residence at daybreak, a bedraggled disillusioned duo, we crawled into bed for a little shut eye. My sleeping accommodation consisted of a cot in the living area. Within an hour, being awakened by Joe's chattering offsprings, I had definite reservations about the "joie de vivre" of moose hunting.

At 2 o'clock in the afternoon, I boarded the train heading back to Low Bush. The conductor, while arranging my fare, asked, "Didn't you get off at Low Bush from Cochrane a couple days ago with two other fellows?"

"Yes," I replied.

"Your two buddies are in the next coach," he continued.

"How in hell can that be?" I retorted, heading back where he pointed. Sure enough, there sat Harold and George, drinks in hand and a half bottle of whiskey on the seat.

"Have a shot partner," Harold said, handing me a glass. "And don't look so stunned. Out of booze we caught the morning train to La Sarre, Quebec, the nearest liquor outlet, because we want you to go back into

My mother in Grandmother Rodd's arms. Taken in 1899 in England.

Grandmother and Grandfather Phillips arrive in Winnipeg, 1903.

My dad working in construction in Winnipeg in 1911.

Grandfather Phillips, an enormously powerful man, with Aunt Doll in his Winnipeg garden. (1912)

The Rodd family, 1913. Back row, left to right: Edith (my mother), Grandmother Rodd and Tom. Front row, left to right: Muriel, George and Ben.

Uncle Ernie overseas in 1914 with 1st Canadian Contingent. He was wounded 3 times, and gassed at Ypres.

My dad driving a grocery wagon in Winnipeg in 1916. He couldn't get in the army due to a leg injury he suffered while playing hockey.

My mother, in front, working in Eaton's Mail Order. Winnipeg, 1922.

My dad, 1922, in Manitoba grain fields. Note the old steam engine.

My brother Jack, two and a half, and myself
at six months. Taken in 1927.

The Phillips clan (no relation) who lived on an adjacent farm and played a big
part in our lives. Taken in 1926 before we moved to Monominto. Left to right: Jim,
Rose Higgins, Alex, Aunt Sadie and Alf.

Jack and I in Winnipeg shortly before I got polio and the family moved to Monominto. (1928)

First year on the farm, 1929. Pop didn't really shoot the bear with a twenty-two calibre rifle.

Taken in 1930 shortly after I contracted polio. That's our big pet St. Bernard, Paddy. Jack is standing in the back with a neighbor, Mom holding Ruth, and myself sitting in the front.

Joyce Fine only a few months old. (1931)

Ruth and I, 1932, in front of our farm house.

Granddad Phillips shortly before he died. Taken in 1935 in his garden at 663 Maryland Street, the Phillips family home.

Uncle Ben Rodd with the Round up Rangers, 1934. Ben is standing on the left. Charlie Herald, sitting in the center, was responsible for getting me into The Shriners' Hospital.

Ed Barham with his three sisters and a cousin, 1936. The Barhams farmed one mile from us but we went to different schools. I had just begun to know Ed.

I'm out hunting rabbits at age 11, 1937.

The entire enrollment of Pinewood School in 1937. In front at the extreme right is my sister Ruth and I am directly behind her, to the left.

Mom with our pet deer
Candy, 1937.

Grandfather Rodd in Florida in his
American Home Guard uniform,
1941.

Maisey and Sparky—my favorite team. (1942)

Jack on embarkation leave. Left to right: Ruth, Jack, Mom, me, and Pop.
Sister Joyce is standing in front of Mom. (1945)

Charlie Fryza, 1945, in the grain fields in Montmartre, Saskatchewan.

Me loading sheaves in Montmartre, 1945.

The trapping cabin on the Brokenhead River, spring of 1946.

The last deer I shot on the farm and the largest. It dressed at 275 pounds. (1946)

A great picture of the big buck with our farm house in the background, 1946.

The Kruchak brothers, 1947. Left to right: Paul, Roman, Mike, Johnny and Bill with Joe sitting in front.

Walking down my strip at Camp #47 between piles of pulpwood I had sawn by hand. This was in 1947—before power saws.

Looking over Camp #47 Brompton Pulp and Paper. 1947, Beardmore, Ontario.

My sleigh loaded with eight foot pulp. In 1947 we were paid $1.15 per cord on the haul.

I'm standing third from the left with Harry, my half-breed partner, on the haul. (1947)

In front of the bunkhouse, Camp #47 Brompton Pulp and Paper, Beardmore, Ontario, 1947. Left to right: Old Man Rentz—in his eighties, I fired him as night watchman; I stand beside Andy, (4th in), the strip boss with whom I had a fisticuffs. Gus Rentz stands to extreme right with the others, the kitchen staff.

Harry and I shovelling snow off of the pulp piles in 1947. It was officially sixty-five degrees below zero—too cold to use the horses.

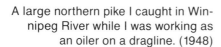
A large northern pike I caught in Winnipeg River while I was working as an oiler on a dragline. (1948)

In my baseball uniform in 1948. I used to catch for Monominto.

The town of Dugald the morning following the terrible train disaster, 1948.

Betty Rasmussen, my first girlfriend, and my sister Ruth with Betty's youngest sister. (1948)

Ed Davis and I before the "battle". Camp #12 Imperial Lumber, northern Alberta, 1948.

A few days after I returned from Imperial Lumber in northern Alberta I am helping Jack cut two carloads of pulp in eastern Manitoba. (1949)

Jack cutting pulpwood in eastern Manitoba in 1949.

Seventy-five cords of poplar cordwood Jack and I cut by hand during the month of April, 1949. We bought a '35 Dodge and headed east.

Jack and I driving our '35 Dodge from Winnipeg to Toronto (May, 1949). We drove through northern Ontario.

Joyce Fine when I met her, August, 1950.

Joyce and I leaving the church. (November 1950)

November 4th, 1950. Our wedding day.

Jack and Shirley Campbell on their wedding day. (January, 1951)

Mom and Pop in front of the Monominto store and post office which they owned and operated, 1951.

Joyce with Michael standing in front of her parents house on Woodfield Road in Toronto, 1951.

July, 1951, in front of the Monominto store when Charlie Crawford and I ran three trucks from Toronto to Winnipeg through the States. Charlie is on the extreme right with his hand on my shoulder. My last visit with Sister Ruth, sitting in front of Mom, she died of leukemia within two months.

A fishing jaunt into Lake Temagami in 1952. Left to right: Lionel Faust, Hank Sharpe, me, Harold Thomas and John Bradley, another real estate broker friend.

Feeding deer in Algonquin
Provincial Park, 1953.
Edna Branning in the
background.

Our first trip to Florida,
1955.

In Dempsey's Bar in New York City, January, 1955, with Jack Dempsey.

Sherree when she was only a few months old—December 25, 1955.

The final photo of the first generation of Phillips, taken in Winnipeg in 1956. Left to right: Jim, Geordie, Ernie, Pop and Harry.

My three children: Michael, Sherree and Gary. January 2, 1956.

Joyce with a string of bass from Bay of Quinte, Ontario, 1956.

Moose hunting on Lake Abitibi,
northern Ontario, 1956.

A good sized smallmouth bass
taken in Bay of Quinte, 1957.

Joyce with large northern pike
caught in Bay of Quinte, 1957.

Large bull moose Hank Sharpe and I shot in 1957 at Lake Muska-cenda, northern Ontario.

Excellent catch of walleyes and northern pike, Lake Muskacenda, 1957.

A boat load of deer shot at Mc-Kenzie Lake in 1957 in central Ontario. I shot two, Art Coltham (standing in the boat) shot one.

Pop and Joyce. In 1958 Pop, now 65, packed up his meagre belongings and with Mom and Joyce moved from Winnipeg to Toronto to go to work for me.

Michael, Gary and Sherree with me. (1958)

Pop with Ed Bourdan, a friend of Jack's, the day we opened Harcourt Park in 1959. Speckled trout fishing was phenomenal.

Harcourt Park, an enormous development that eventually included seventeen lakes and covered 7,000 acres. We began to prepare the property at this site in 1959 and didn't complete the entire development until seventeen years later.

Our Harcourt Park cottage on Allen Lake where our family spent many years. (1959)

East Lake in Harcourt Park, one of the finest speckled trout lakes in Canada. Totally enclosed in Harcourt Park. (1959)

Harcourt Park, 1960. Fogging equipment on one of Sumcot's four-wheel drives. We tried to cut down on insects, particularly black flies.

Harcourt Park, 1960. We constructed forty miles of roadway through the rugged terrain. Ted Sheehy shown here operating the bulldozer.

Fred Oram, Sumcot's first sales manager, with me in our Danforth Avenue, Toronto office in 1961.

Our home at 40 Shediac in Scarboro where we lived for ten years. (1960)

A sixty foot booth at the 1962 Toronto Sportsmen Show. We exhibited in Toronto, other Ontario cities, plus Cleveland and Columbus, Ohio.

An eight pound two ounce speckled trout caught in Allen Lake, Harcourt Park, 1962.

Harcourt Park, 1962. We hunted deer in the park for nine consecutive years. We usually did well and I rarely missed not shooting one or more.

Jim Hay, a Sumcot salesman, addressing a bus load of our clients in front of our Toronto office before leaving on a trip of nine hundred plus miles to Wilmington, North Carolina. (1963)

A small stretch of Sumcot's lake front lot property at Boiling Spring Lakes, North Carolina, 1963.

Bowling champs in East Toronto Bowling League in 1963. Don Sears is on my left. Fred Oram, Sumcot Sales Manager is on my right. Seated, from the left, are Jim Hay, Howard Tustin, and Eddie Jones. Howard worked for me close to nine years.

Deer hunting in Harcourt Park in 1963. Left to right: Me, Gerry Delaney, Ken Williams, Fred Oram, Hank Sharpe, Ken Watson, and Keith Tallman. Louie Rodrigue is sitting in front.

Pinewood School which I had attended for ten years. This picture was taken in August of 1964—twenty-seven years after the picture taken of Ruth and I with the entire class of fourteen students enrolled in 1937.

In 1964 we took our three children from Toronto to Winnipeg. We visited the Barhams in Monominto. Here we are with our three and five of Ed and Sheila's six children.

Hollywood, Florida, 1965. From left to right: Hans Schramm, Homer Grace, me, Joyce and Homer's wife Dot.

94 Banstock in North York, 1965. A 3500 square foot, back to front, split level where we lived from 1965 until we got our green card as U.S. immigrants.

1965 Oak Shores Estate, Bobcaygeon, Ontario. Sumcot's second major development where I installed an olympic sized swimming pool right beside Bald Lake. It was extremely popular.

Sherree, Michael and Gary growing up. (1965)

the wilds with Dave Black to get us a moose, and you don't have any whiskey."

"Not me, buddy," I immediately stated. "I'm going back to Toronto tonight, either with you or by train. I have no fresh clothes and am already a day past when Joyce expected me home."

"Look, Bill," Harold pleaded, "relax, have a drink, and listen to our proposition; we only have ten minutes before reaching Low Bush."

I quietly listened to their story. Dave Black had arrived in camp shortly after I departed with Joe. During the night he had called three animals to the river bank within fifty feet of their canoe, at which they both got to shoot at but didn't connect. After paying him fifty dollars, they made Dave a proposition. If he guided me back into his territory and I got to shoot, we'd pay him an additional seventy-five bucks. Flushed not only with the alcohol, but with the vivid recollection of their thrilling night's action, they were quite persuasive. Harold believed that, due to my hunting experience, and having Dave as my guide, our chances were excellent. Both he and George desperately wanted moose meat to show for our effort and absence.

"Here is what I'll do, Harold," I said, as the train screeched to a halt at the Low Bush station. "I'm going to Cochrane with you two this afternoon, phone Joyce, and have a bath; then I'll return to Low Bush on the morning train."

Introducing me to Dave Black, Harold explained the arrangements and assured him I had the additional seventy-five bucks if I got to shoot. We also left our Mercury outboard as a guarantee of my return.

Joyce, not pleased to hear that I wouldn't be returning for a few more days, nevertheless, wasn't too surprised, as my frequent and sudden changes of plans were not uncommon. I also phoned Hank Sharpe, who often discussed his desire to hunt moose. Hank enthusiastically assured me he would be at Low Bush within forty-eight hours, so I instructed him to meet Paul Black for a message if I wasn't at the station to greet him.

Harold, George, and I drank all afternoon and, after arranging my hotel accommodation, continued the party in my room. They planned on leaving for Toronto following an eight o'clock dinner. Harold had his automobile packed and ready to roll immediately after eating. George, however, wasn't in a mood to be hurried, and relayed this sentiment to Harold more than once. An hour after the meal, Harold still hadn't persuaded our manager to leave the dining room. Finally in exasperation, Harold stalked from the hotel, warning George to be aboard in ten minutes or be left behind.

George just laughed, "He'll be back," he said, and he was right.

Within fifteen minutes Harold returned and roared another warning before again storming out the door.

"George, my friend, Harold is a strong-willed individual. If I were you I'd get into that Cadillac," I stated very strongly.

"Bullshit!" George responded, "Do you believe for one moment he is going to drive five hundred miles by himself? He'll be back."

"Don't count on it chum." I replied.

A half hour elapsed before George showed signs of losing confidence in his positive attitude, and after an hour with no sign of Harold he took a stroll around the village. Bone-weary I hit the sack and passed out like a light, to be rudely awakened when George came pounding at my door after midnight—a thoroughly disgruntled individual.

"Bill, can you believe that ignorant son of a bitch left me without even a sweater or a coat?"

After raging a few minutes, George pulled off his clothes and climbed into my three-quarter sized bed. A roly-poly chap, he left me scant mattress area; and, what I'd hoped would be a restful night before striking back into the wilds, turned into a comical nightmare.

At times he avowed to buy clothes the next morning, borrow or steal a rifle, and return with me to Low Bush; then, after awhile he'd have a change of heart and decide to grab the next train to Toronto, so he could tell Thomas "to shove his job where it would hurt most." George altered his mind a dozen times during the night, but went back to Toronto the following day, by which point he'd cooled off and didn't resign. I, tired but excited with the prospects of impending action, returned to Low Bush on a chilly, rainy day with steadily increasing winds, which made any attempt at venturing across Lake Abitibi an impossibility and created a real dilemma for me.

Dave Black's home was a ramshackle frame dwelling on the river bank. The surrounding grounds, littered with old boats, rotting fish, and fleshy moose bones created a stench that fouled the air over most of the village. Outside, however, smelled like a rose garden in comparison to inside Dave's residence. Filthy pots of simmering meat, combined with every other conceivable household stink, nauseated me even as I stepped over the threshold. The prospect of either eating or sleeping in that environment until we went hunting was a torturous thought. Anxious not to insult him, but positive there had to be a solution, I informed Dave that I felt like going for a walk. Before leaving, I mentioned my reluctance to hunt by flashlight; however, I said if he knew no other way, I'd try it, though I probably wouldn't use his services in the future. I also apprised him of Hank's impending arrival, and requested that Paul meet the train if we were not there. Dave, preparing his longboat for a rapid take off once the weather cleared, said nothing but wore a puzzled expression as I strode away.

A hundred yards from the Blacks, I encountered two hunters by the river waiting for another guide. After chatting a few minutes I mentioned my predicament.

"Good heavens, Bill," one of them said, "I fully understand your concern, but that two-story frame building across the river is an old hotel of sorts, and clean as a whip. It's owned by a Frenchman, Henri Lacroix, who really doesn't operate it as a going concern, but I'm certain he would be sympathetic about your position." Thanking them profusely, I dashed over. Henri greeted me warmly and listened patiently to my predicament.

"Beel, this ees no problem," Henri spoke with a thick French Canadian accent. "Dave Black ees veree accustom' to 'aving his 'unters stay wit me. Pick up your gear and tell Dave to pick you up 'ere when he ees readee to go."

If I'd just won the Second World War singlehanded, I couldn't have been happier. With unbelievable relief I collected my rifle, duffel bag, and informed Dave of my new arrangements. Not the slightest upset, he said we would leave shortly after the wind died down. Instead of an exceedingly unpleasant ordeal of being forced to eat and bunk with the Blacks, the afternoon and evening turned out to be the most enjoyable of the entire hunt. The two boys who directed me to Henri's came back to the hotel when their guide refused to go across the lake in the high wind. Henri, a bachelor, put out a delicious dinner; then we played cards and listened to a hockey game. For the complete package, including the tiny, sparsely furnished, but spotlessly clean bedroom, Henri charged me five dollars—a deal comparing favorably with the purchase of Manhattan Island from the Indians for $12 and some beads. Delighted with the outlook of finally getting a sound night's sleep between clean sheets, I retired at 10 o'clock, but not for long. A powerful hand jostling my shoulder awakened me, and I sprung up to find Dave standing by the bed with a kerosene lantern.

"Come, Bill," he whispered, "the wind has dropped. Meet me at the boat in ten minutes."

Donning my clothes, I was astonished to see my watch registering 2 a.m., so I automatically assumed we were heading for another session of moose calling. It would be hard to imagine a more perfect night—completely calm and significantly warmer. The sky, now totally clear, was filled with a myriad of stars, a brilliant moon, and flashing northern lights.

With the Mercury motor attached to the longboat, together with his own 10 h.p., Dave maneuvered the long craft carefully along the winding river until he reached the open waters of Lake Abitibi, where he fully opened the throttle of both outboards. Barely a ripple wrinkled the enormous lake, and moonbeams richocheted off the shimmering water like dancing ghosts. Except for the drone of the motors, no sound disturbed the tranquility. Dave headed directly into the open expanse of the lake and, as the treed shoreline gradually faded from sight, it seemed as if he and I were the only individuals in the entire universe. Dawn slowly crept over the peaceful scene as Dave headed directly toward a long peninsula protecting a large open bay. Not cutting the engines until we were ten yards from the broad sandy shoreline, Dave forced the longboat to beach itself on the hard sand. Instructing me to grab my rifle, knapsack, and cushion, while we hastily heaved his canoe into the water, we leaped into the bobbing craft and took off across the bay.

These were the first words Dave had uttered since leaving Low Bush over four hours before. He paddled furiously to the mouth of a large creek, a full two miles from where we had landed. Entering the mouth of the stream, he stopped, listened intently, and suddenly a look crossed his sharp features as though he was about to witness the second coming of Jesus Christ. "Moose," he whispered, his finger to his lips. He then began paddling silently down the stream. The sun was just clearing the tree tops when I heard a distinct splash, similar to a startled beaver whacking the water with his tail as a warning to his family of impending danger. Glancing back at my guide, I saw from his demeanor that the sound came from our quarry and not a beaver, so I quietly snapped a shell into the barrel and prepared for action. Nearing the sloshing sound, I realized that the animal walking slowly among the willows fringing the waterway would remain hidden from view, despite the fact that only two or three hundred feet separated us, unless he wandered back out to the river bank. Without warning, Dave emitted a low cow call and I lurched around, almost upsetting the canoe. The bull grunted a response, but made no attempt to investigate the source of the call. For a half hour, Dave and the bull talked to each other, as Dave kept quietly paddling to match the animal's slow amble through the thick browse; but, though tantalizingly close, the beast remained completely hidden from view. Finally Dave quietly wheeled the canoe about, paddled back along the route we'd just travelled, not speaking until we reached the open bay; then, with obvious glee in his voice, said, "We'll get him this afternoon, Bill, you can bet. He's a huge bull judging from his hoof prints along the stream. Rutting is over for him, and his only interest is eating and sleeping, which is the reason he didn't come out of the willows after getting a belly full of lily pads. Now he's heading back to high ground for a few hours nap, but he'll return to the creek by late afternoon, and we'll be waiting." Dave, now a different person, hummed all the way to the longboat. While he set up the tent, I fried a huge pan of bacon and eggs, toasted a pile of bread, and brewed a can of tea. After devouring breakfast, we lazed about, chatting awhile in the bright autumn sun and pleasant surroundings. Finally, Dave slowly arose from his seat on a fallen spruce, then, stretching and yawning, asked, "Bill you want to bring your gun and come with me up a different stream? This is my trapping area, and I want to check for animal signs and perhaps set some traps."

"You bet" I replied, "there is nothing I would sooner do."

I was eager to see an Indian determine the presence of animals and prepare his sets. Paddling back across the bay, we entered a much larger river near the mouth of the stream where Dave first detected our moose. This waterway, however, immediately veered off in an entirely different direction. Suddenly, Dave stopped paddling. Disrupting the quiet of the exquisite morning, like discordant chords in a symphony, came the roar of a sizeable outboard motor from across the water. Not moving a muscle, Dave sat as transfixed as his cigar store counterpart while a speed boat barrelled out of the main lake, crossed our bay and zoomed into the river in which we were canoeing. Dave furiously paddled back to where the motor had stopped, and the ring of axes and falling trees now shattered the tranquility. On the river bank near the bay, three men, one an Indian, were setting up camp. Dave began loudly cursing the other Ojibway the moment we were within shouting distance; then, jumping out of the beached canoe, he charged over and unmercifully berated him. The other two men, like myself, remained out of the squabble because the heated conversation was in Ojibway. It was a miracle there wasn't physical violence due to Dave's ferocious attack, though the other chap appeared frightened of my guide's rage. Following a ten minute exchange, Dave leaped into the canoe, motioned me to follow, and paddled violently back to camp.

"Got to move," Dave snarled. "That son of a bitch scared our moose."

"Who is he?" I enquired cautiously.

"Jim Gantner from Low Bush. He has two prospectors with permits to stake claims. Jim knew I was coming here and should have waited. He is supposed to be my friend, but by gawd I'll get even with that bastard."

Thinking that if Dave reacted like that with a friend, I certainly was delighted he wasn't my enemy. But I remained mum. Few words were spoken as we dismantled camp, reloaded the longboat, and headed back out to open Lake Abitibi. A stiff breeze began riling up the water which had been as placid as a mill pond all morning.

Dave pointed our vessel further away from Low Bush in an easterly direction, stayed within a mile of Abitibi's northern shoreline, then veered toward another long finger of land jutting out into the open lake. The wind, rapidly reaching gale velocity, had the lake stirred up in a frightful frenzy as Dave beached his vessel on the point of the peninsula. Jumping out, I was astonished but pleased to see a little log cabin nestled in the woods. Still in Dave's trapping territory, it turned out to be his base camp, and, though dirty, it was one hell of an improvement over the tent, his own residence at Low Bush, or the trapping shack back on the Brokehead. Now I could cook our food with my own utensils.

The thin spit of land separated a large estuary from the two-mile-wide mouth of the Abitibi River. Gazing out over the wind-whipped water, we were astounded to see a cruiser heading up river towards the open lake. We watched dumbfounded when the party didn't immediately turn back the moment they realized the turmoil of the lake, even though they were driving a 16′ cruiser with a 25 h.p. engine. The craft, bobbing like a cork, made little headway against the pounding waves.

"Crazy son of a bitch!" Dave yelled, grabbing his rifle and firing three rapid shots across their bow. If the lake didn't deter them, the warning shots certainly did. Cautiously turning their boat, they came roaring directly over to the cabin. My jaw dropped two inches when out jumped three rangers in uniform.

"Did you fire at us?" one of them yelled.

"You're gawd damn right I did!" Dave hollered back, as he helped pull their launch onto the sand. "You bastards must be crazy trying to cross that water. Would you like to know how many Indian bones are lying on the bottom of Lake Abitibi because men weren't afraid of it?" He stormed.

They were taken back by Dave's verbal onslaught. Then one of them interrupted the indignant Ojibway.

"Are you Dave Black?"

"Yes," the Indian responded, "and nobody knows this lake better than I."

Instead of remaining angry, the rangers calmed down and apologized for their stupidity, maintaining, nevertheless, that they were about to give up the unequal struggle at the time Dave fired. On vacation, they were heading for a ranger's camp several miles across the lake for a three-day moose hunt. At Dave's invitation, they elected to join us awhile to see if the wind would calm down. Using some of their victuals and ours, we cooked up a feast which, together with a few drinks of whiskey, made the afternoon and evening pass pleasantly and swiftly. I warned Dave that if he took so much as one sip of booze, our deal was off and, though a glum look spread across his rugged countenance, he offered no argument.

By midnight, a howling gale and cold drizzle convinced the boys to return to their home base 25 miles down the Abitibi River. Crawling onto a bunk, I fell asleep again, being awakened a few hours later by Dave's heavy hand on my shoulder.

"Let's go, Bill. The water is not too rough and I know a creek we can reach with no danger."

My watch read 5 a.m. as we boarded the longboat. Dave promptly swung into the big bay, hugging the barely visible shoreline to gain relief from the turbulent water. Nevertheless, waves splashing into our vessel forced us to keep the outboards throttled back, greatly diminishing our forward motion.

A heavy overcast sky blotted out any rays of the rising sun, so dawn spread slowly across the desolate terrain. However, as my guide nosed the longboat onto a hard sand beach nestled in a tiny cove, sufficient light revealed fresh moose tracks imprinted along the sandy shoreline. Dave quietly carried the canoe two hundred feet across a narrow strip of land, dividing a marshy creek from the small estuary where we'd landed. My heart pounded as we slowly and silently moved down the waterway, stopping every few seconds to listen. The brisk breeze rattling the willows and causing water to lap against our canoe made it difficult to distinguish whether splashing sounds were moose feeding in the river ahead, or one of a dozen other customary noises of early morning in a swamp. Rifle at the ready, and intently watching every movement and straining to discern each sound, I was startled when Dave tapped me on the shoulder with the paddle. Jerking my head around, the Indian's beaming expression told me he'd spotted an animal as he pointed to a dark grey object two hundred yards ahead on the bank of the stream. It didn't remotely resemble my expectation of the moose I had visualized; nevertheless, I threw the gun to my shoulder.

"No, no," Dave frantically whispered, "don't shoot until I say."

Lowering the rifle, I watched in complete fascination as our craft glided noiselessly through the water like a snake slithering through mud, rapidly closing the distance to the motionless object. Suddenly, our inanimate target exploded into life, and the huge bull threw up his massive head and looked directly at the swiftly approaching would-be assassins, who at this point had closed to within 400 feet.

"Shoot!" Dave blurted.

Jerking the Winchester to my shoulder I sighted behind our quarry's front shoulders, but didn't pull the trigger. Awe-struck by the immensity of the magnificent creature, standing over seven feet to the top of his immense antlers, which themselves spanned almost six feet, I remained motionless gazing at the majestic sight, my rifle barrel pointed at his heart.

"Shoot!" Dave urged, and I squeezed the trigger. The long hair on a moose spreads markedly upon the impact of a bullet, allowing a hunter actually to see where his projectile strikes. My aim was true, though it didn't require an expert marksman to hit such an immense unmoving target. The stricken animal instantly leaped into the stream, submerging most of his body, except for his gargantuan head, horns, and neck. Two more shots found their mark in his massive neck, causing the mortally wounded creature to turn, swim back toward the river bank where he had originally stood, and try to escape into the evergreens from his tormentors. Another two bullets penetrated his flesh as he valiantly clambered up the steep bank, with blood streaking down his flanks, and with his gigantic head held high toward the Heavens as though pleading for help.

"Hit him in the head!" Dave screamed.

My sixth and last bullet struck the fatally injured beast directly behind the left ear. Upon impact, the huge bull froze for an instant, reared on his hind legs, then toppled backwards—already dead when he hit the creek. We were so close that water from his death plunge splashed the canoe. Dave ecstatically shouted, "Way to go boy! Way to go! Beautiful shooting, Bill! Hurray!"

My flushed face and trembling hands attested to the thrill of the action; nevertheless, I felt unquestionably ashamed that the premature death of such a glorious beast was my sole responsibility.

Humans, predominantly a carnivorous species, kill animals for their meat one way or another, and not a pound of my moose would be wasted. Most of earth's creatures satisfy their needs by preying on others. It is an integral part of the balancing of nature. Those facts, though true, didn't entirely salve my conscience. What bothered me was the inequality of the struggle. The ability to inflict pain and death at a distance was solely responsible for my victory.

"Have you got whiskey?" Dave impatiently asked. "Let's have a drink."

"What time does the afternoon train leave Low Bush for Cochrane?" I inquired.

"Four fifteen," he said.

"Look, Dave, if we hurry and butcher this animal, I should be able to catch that train. I'm eager to return to Toronto. On our long journey back across the lake, we'll have a drink from the bottle of rum that is back at your cabin."

Nothing further had to be said. Working like demons, we butchered the enormous beast in the water, wrestled each quarter one at a time into the canoe, then paddled it over to deposit the meat in the longboat, this strenuous maneuver required five trips, as the immense head, neck and antlers made a full load by itself. Returning to the cabin for our supplies, I speedily cooked a large breakfast, which we greedily devoured. Then, by eleven-thirty we headed for Low Bush.

A stiff wind plus a dark cloudy sky, which sent occasional snowflakes scudding across the lake, made it a dreary return trip. A few swigs of rum, though, kept a little warmth circulating in our bodies. Dave, taking advantage of the leeward side of all islands and peninsulas offering protection from the increasingly rough lake, slowed our progress considerably. Waves splashing over the sides of our vessel caused some concern, but I bailed the water out as fast as it sloshed in, so we were in no real danger. Nonetheless, when our boat entered the Low Bush River at 3 p.m. and Dave had taken on an entirely different disposition as a result of the alcohol, I heaved a sigh of relief. He placed the trophy head with its massive rack on the front gunwale, and, when we approached the village, began a series of war whoops. Ojibway males came pouring out of their shacks, lining both sides of the waterway. Dave, with waving arms, hailed them to his residence, where Hank, one of my great concerns, stood watching our triumphant entrance.

A dozen of Dave's neighbors arrived within ten minutes, equipped with knives. In less than a half hour, the crude butchering procedure had completely boned out the moose—the meat being heaved into sugar sacks and delivered to the station. Hank, mesmerized by the sight of the gigantic head, was eager to get out to hunt. It took a heap of careful explaining to convince him of the ridiculousness of my accompanying the pair of them back into the wilds. Though disappointed that we wouldn't be hunting together, Hank soon grasped the logic of the situation and agreed to make the most of the circumstances.

Dave, delighted with his $75 fee plus ten dollar tip, swiftly acquired whiskey to give me a victory toast. I didn't realize at the time the grave injustice I'd done Hank by starting Dave on another drunken spree, as it meant a few days would elapse before he sobered up. It wasn't a serious imposition as matters turned out, because ferocious weather rapidly moving North delayed hunting for over forty-eight hours. Luckily I remembered to tell Hank about Henri La Croix and his haven across the river from the Blacks.

My eight sacks of meat, the 110 lb. head, and I reached Cochrane an hour ahead of a transcontinental from Winnipeg, which was scheduled to arrive in Toronto at 8 a.m. the following day. Not only did I fortunately make connections, but also arranged for a sleeping compartment. Several passengers who saw the moose head transferred at Cochrane from one baggage car to another, went back to ogle the trophy; and, as the successful hunter, I became a bit of a celebrity. A trio of Canadian soldiers eager to hear details of the hunt invited me for a drink. As a result, I enjoyed some excellent company complete with a couple of highballs, and even borrowed a razor to make myself presentable for my wife in the morning—or so I believed.

It seemed like forever since I had enjoyed eight or nine uninterrupted hours of sleep, so I retired before ten, instructing the porter to awaken me at seven forty-five, fifteen minutes before our expected arrival in Toronto. Sleeping on a train is an automatic tranquilizer for me, and I slumbered like a hibernating bear. Awakening with a start, I grabbed my watch, which read eight-fifteen then, glancing through the blinds, was astonished to see rocks, evergreens, and lakes passing by, none of which were to be found in the Toronto vicinity. Also, we were crawling at a snail's pace. Heading for the washroom, I ran into the porter.

"Where the hell are we?" I asked incredibly.

"Somewhere between North Bay and Ottawa," he responded.

"Did I somehow get on the wrong train, or what happened?"

"Well, sir," he quietly replied, "a hurricane swept through Toronto yesterday afternoon killing dozens of people. It continued north, knocking out seventeen bridges between Toronto and North Bay. Unfortunately, the dining car was removed from our train, and there isn't a thing aboard to eat or drink. However, we expect to arrive in Ottawa by noon."

Thanking the man for his information, I sat down in a daze. Hurricanes don't strike Ontario I thought, but that was incorrect. Hurricane Hazel had in fact raged in from the southeast killing scores of people and causing millions of dollars in damage. Confirmed reports received aboard our train said most of the death and destruction occurred in West Toronto, so I relaxed somewhat, grateful that we lived in the extreme east end of the city. In Ottawa, the Canadian National Railways provided an excellent free meal. They also loaded other refreshments aboard, which made the slow trip to Toronto more bearable. We arrived in the stricken and soggy city at 7 p.m.

Joyce, delighted to see me safe and sound, was no more ecstatic than I about her and the kids having come to no harm. During the height of the storm, Joyce had thought our house might collapse, so placing the boys in the center of the living room, she had locked all doors and windows. The terrifying experience, plus my absence, dampened Joyce's enthusiasm over attending a house party the night of my arrival at Bill Reids, Homeland Realty's attorney. Calling Harold at Reids' affair and telling him about the moose, I suggested we pick up the meat at the depot, as it had been butchered almost forty hours. Harold, Lionel, George, and I took Harold's Cadillac, hooked up our boat and trailer, picked up the meat, placed the monstrous moose head in a prominent position hanging over the boat's transom, then drove around downtown

Toronto. At every stop, goggle-eyed pedestrians swarmed around, gazing at the mighty moose's sightless stare, while gawking motorists almost ran over pedestrians, while jockeying for a better view of the animal's ponderous head. Neither pride nor joy filled my breast, however. In fact, my conscience pricked me constantly as I pictured the noble beast only two days before crashing through the forest like a Sherman Tank in an environment as contrary to his present surroundings as a whale in a wheat field. And I was his executioner.

Hank remained in Low Bush until the weather settled. Then Dave took him to the creek where Hank shot the big bull which Dave believed had been spooked by his Indian friend. As a result of his triumph, Hank became a zealous moosehunter, and my love of the tasty meat convinced me to overcome the reluctance I felt at killing this aristocratic animal. Therefore, I shared numerous adventures with a variety of companions, including Hank, in pursuit of the noble moose over the ensuing years.

Sitting quietly in a canoe hours on end allowed plenty of time for reflection. Homeland Realty had expanded to three offices with over fifty salespeople, business was fair, and I was taking home a sizable weekly paycheck. Joyce and I had spent more time together on vacations, weekends, and evenings out over the ensuing nine months than we had over the previous three years. Everything looked rosy, except that I wasn't happy. There were several reasons: Lionel Faust and I were not getting along. His constant interference in the real estate division kept us at loggerheads, which nearly ended in physical violence more than once. Lionel, whose investment in the corporation paralleled mine in time and money, wanted an equal voice in administering its affairs. Foreseeing at our incorporation the problem of too many cooks spoiling the broth, I insisted that each of our responsibilities be specifically outlined in our initial internal management agreement. In that agreement, Lionel had no voice in real estate, and I insisted we strictly adhere to that aspect of our pact.

Also, the three way split in profits diluted our potential income enormously, making it painfully apparent that our living standard wouldn't improve substantially without a huge boost in sales volume. As usual, my patience was wearing thin while waiting for my star to shine. Perhaps, though, my unswerving predilection to be my own taskmaster caused me the greatest irritation, because I had swiftly learned that no partnership would ever satisfy that burning desire for complete independence.

Being a stubborn, opinionated free spirit, interference in matters when my decisions were obviously correct infuriated me. As a result, I wouldn't discuss certain corporate affairs even with my partners. Harold, aware of my discontentment, approached Lionel in mid summer about the possibility of our buying out his third interest in the corporation. Lionel point blank refused. A week after my return from the moose hunt, I called a meeting with my two associates and insisted we either adopt a resolution to disband Homeland Realty or come to a satisfactory plan for two partners to purchase the interest of the third. Lionel again refused to sell. As he and I couldn't possibly function as business partners, it left only one alternative. Harold and Lionel, therefore, offered me $4,500 for my one-third interest, and I accepted with gratitude. The company's total assets included our second-hand office furniture plus a few unclosed deals. Also, the accounts payable were greater than the accounts receivable, so I knew the price was right.

A great weight fell from my shoulders when the papers were signed and the check was in the bank, because, though unemployed, Joyce and I were once again affluent. Homeland's top producers, with Joyce's permission, arranged a surprise party at our Westview house, where the boys let me know that, if I planned on reopening Phillips Real Estate, they would transfer their licenses immediately. I thanked them for their fine gesture of support and friendship, but explained I hadn't decided my future course of action at the time, albeit I had some ideas.

An east end builder, Richard R. Newman, had been an acquaintance of mine since I sold his houses when employed by A.W. Farlinger. Also, Phillips Real Estate had acted as his exclusive agent for three years. Thus, we'd built up a great deal of respect for each other's business acumen. In 1953 Newman purchased an apartment site on Kennedy Road in Scarboro, suitable for two three-story, sixteen-unit buildings. But by late '54 the first structure, though completed, didn't have one tenant. Concerned at his inability to rent the units, Dick phoned for a meeting a few days following my departure from Homeland. Newman pleaded with me to take over the building one way or another, to get him off the hook with the mortgage company. We made a unique deal. I assumed the Huron and Erie Insurance Company's first mortgage on the property for $75,000. Dick arranged and co-signed an $18,000 loan for me at his own bank, which I used as total down payment. He then took back a second mortgage for $14,000, bringing the total purchase price to $107,000, of which I didn't have a penny of my own cash invested. Closing date was set for April '55, but any rental income after the signing of the contract would belong to me, while Dick would pay all direct building expenses such as mortgage payments, taxes, and insurance. I insisted on this arrangement because I required revenue from rented units to pay for an advertising campaign, and a five-month delay before closing to allow time to get the building at least partially rented before taking possession.

I thoroughly understood the magnitude of my venture, as did Joyce;

but gambling was swiftly becoming my life's pursuit. On the $18,000 bank loan I pledged everything: house, car, kids, cats, and dog; but Joyce never hesitated nor flinched when asked to sign the documents putting everything on the line.

The apartment's location created the principal obstacle in renting, because, situated in a newly built up sector of residential Scarboro, inadequate transportation and lack of decent shopping made it inconvenient for most would-be tenants. Nevertheless, with sufficient advertising plus an all-out commitment to the task, I felt certain the units would be leased. We placed large ads in the three Toronto newspapers, offering one month's free rent. Joyce arranged appointments on the phone and I did the running. If a party wanted a unit, I immediately signed them up either at the apartment building or in their home and collected two months advanced rent. If in the form of a check, it was promptly certified. Many couples had a change of heart and requested the return of their deposit; but, with so much at stake, I adamantly refused refunds. Unable to afford the loss of their money, most people moved into their new home. Within three weeks the building was completely filled, at rents ranging from $175 to $275. This brought us an income of approximately $3,000 monthly, with absolutely no outgo. With the apartment complex fully leased, I went to work for A. Harvey and Co. Realtors and listed the property for sale. Ray Gilbert, a Harvey and Co. salesman, who with his wife Dory had been friends of ours since Ray was discharged from the Canadian Army shortly after our marriage, promptly sold the building for $132,000. The deal was closed on the same date in April as my contract with Newman.

Besides earning a net profit of $20,000 after commissions and expenses, I had substantial rental income without encumbrances for five months. Finally, believing my fortune was assured, I bought a new Buick, persuaded Eddie (Joyce's mother) to babysit her two grandsons for five weeks, then, with Joyce, plus Ray and Dory Gilbert, left for our first Florida vacation. Ah! Life was sweet.

With the exception of travelling through a few North Central states between Toronto and Winnipeg, my limited exposure to Americans had aroused my curiosity about our southern neighbors, and I was anxious to become better acquainted. Nevertheless, the thought of soft ocean breezes and lazing around in Florida's semi-tropical climate while Canada shivered in blowing snow, icy streets, and frigid temperatures, provided the major incentive for the trip. In my new Buick we headed south three days after Christmas in a rain and sleet storm. Four-lane highways were uncommon, turnpikes almost non-existent, and speed limits ranged from fifty to ninety miles per hour in different states. So progress depended on traffic conditions.

The cold rain enveloped the countryside through New York, Pennsylvania, and all the way into the southern sector of Virginia, where we motelled the second night. Dawn the following morning showed promise of a better day, so under a brilliant warm sun, I went hiking for my first real glimpse of the south. Harvested tobacco, cotton fields, long leaved pines, and colored people provided ample evidence that I walked in an alien land. Blacks were almost a non-entity in Canada in the early fifties, and my only knowledge of their history or conditions came from American Books, television, and movies—none of which truly depicted their pitiful plight. We gazed in disbelief at the signs over public rest rooms pronouncing: MEN, WOMEN, and COLOREDS. Virginia, the Carolinas, and Georgia turned into an incredible revelation for the four of us. The girls were particularly shocked at the reaction of black people whenever approached or spoken to for directions or information. Without answering, a look of terror usually spread across their faces, and they would bolt away as though jolted with electricity. Another intriguing discovery in southern towns and cities was the numerous states glorifying Civil War heroes, in lieu of World War I or II leaders that graced the public squares of our country. Ideal weather remained, however, and we basked in sunshine on a delightful visit to Georgia's Okefenokee Swamp, then continued to Jacksonville for New Year's Eve. Remnants of a Gator Bowl crowd jammed the city, but fortunately we located a double motel unit only two hundred feet from the Atlantic. Few love affairs are more genuine than my infatuation with the ocean. Pounding surf, a boundless view, and its pungent smell of fish, salt, and seaweed attracts me as iron filings to a magnet. Ever since that first night, I dreamed of one day permanently living in the spray of the sea.

Our entertaining tour along Florida's East Coast included a delightful day at historic and quaint St. Augustine, plus stop overs at Marineland and Daytona Beach. We reveled in excursions up rural roads, where ripening oranges and grapefruit could be plucked from laden branches through our open car windows. Suitable accommodations for a three-week stay in Hollywood Beach was chosen a hundred yards from my beloved ocean. Glorious blue skies remained throughout our vacation, and we took full advantage while ocean fishing, gambling on the horses at Tropical Park, or just lolling in the shade of the whispering palms. Dog racing at Hollywood Park occupied many evenings, and the weeks slipped by with lightning speed, but not before the sand in our shoes insured that we would return in coming years.

Joyce, expecting our third child in May, suffered some discomfort during the journey but perked up whenever she remembered that we had to buy a new house on our return to Toronto. Before leaving on our Florida vacation, we had sold our Westview home which would soon have been too small for our expanding family. Joyce chose a new three-bedroom bungalow at 40 Shediac Boulevard in East Scarboro. We moved there in late February. Shediac, in the Hunter's Glen Subdivision, and lacking in paved streets, sidewalks, and phone service, invoked a pioneering attitude among our neighbors, and we thoroughly enjoyed the experience. The birth of our daughter Sherree made it a significant summer, particularly when through sheer stupidity I made horrible business decisions and rapidly slid back down the ladder of success I had only begun to climb.

After the apartment building deal closed, and we'd moved into our suburban home with new furniture, the twenty thousand dollars still remaining in the bank made me feel like a gold prospector who'd struck the mother lode. Although planning on returning to real estate, I first wanted to invest our bankroll in a venture that would start us on a route of financial independence. With ads in "The Money For Investment" section of three Toronto newspapers, we waited for the opportunities to flood our mailbox, and certainly weren't disappointed. A deluge of responses poured in with a broad diversity of proposals, including real estate and stock promotions, capital for business from manufacturing embalming fluid to hockey pucks, and partnerships in every imaginable enterprise. Joyce and I enjoyed perusing the letters, but had difficulty separating phony requests for money from authentic business proposals. I investigated several propositions, but eventually narrowed the myriad of overtures down to Bill Lunan, a canny old Scotsman who owned Plastics Plating Limited, an electroplating business. The company, though idle and heavily in debt due to its inactivity caused by the death of one of the principals and the prolonged illness of Lunan, showed excellent potential. There were no employees except Bill, who occasionally plated a small amount of costume jewelry in three antiquated gold and silver tanks still usable in the factory. He was one of the few men in Canada who could successfully perform this delicate application. As the moneymaking possibilities looked splendid and after intensively investigating Plastics Plating and Lunan, I bought half the company's stock for ten thousand dollars. We used the money to pay off debts, and loaned another ten thousand for working capital. Plastics Plating's factory, situated near Broadview Avenue in the East Central sector of the city, was 150′ long, 40′ feet wide, and had 12′ ceilings. This allowed us plenty of space to set up an extensive operation, while still allowing room for future expansion. A substantial inventory of old equipment, including plating tanks, electric wiring, polishing equipment, etc., already existed; but we purchased huge new copper and chrome plating vats to handle everything from car bumpers to electric kettles. While Bill set up the factory with new equipment in an assembly-line type of operation, I went out to find products to plate. With our plant ready for operation in June, truckloads of articles, primarily for copper and chrome plating, already were stacked in the factory. Figuring the charge for the plating service to our customers and deducting all labor and material expenses, I estimated our net profit should average 50% on all production. Fifteen men, mostly German immigrants, were hired to operate our assembly-line system. Each article was thoroughly buffered in the polishing division by high speed machines before being placed on racks in a huge copper vat. Those items requiring only a copper finish went directly back to the polishing department for a finishing gloss. Products requiring a chrome exterior were also copper-plated first before the chrome application; then these articles were burnished as well for a final luster. Metals are plated on a base metal, usually steel, by a combination of acid and electricity. An acid solution, together with electric current combines to remove elements from solid bars of metal hanging in the solution tanks, and transplants this thin layer of metal to the items to be plated, which items are suspended in the same large vats.

Plastics Plating looked as if it couldn't miss becoming an exceedingly profitable enterprise. To a greenhorn like myself, my investment looked brilliant, at least until two weeks after we got operating. Walking into our polishing department one day, I spied dozens of electric kettles, plus numerous car bumpers, lying on the floor. Closer inspection showed they were chrome-plated, but covered with ugly blisters. I charged over to Lunan, "What the hell is going on with those bumpers and kettles?" I demanded.

"Take it easy, William," Bill replied in his broad Scottish brogue.

"Take it easy, for Christ sake!" I exploded. "I guaranteed the company a truck load of those kettles would be delivered this week. Have you any idea how tough it was to convince that company we could do a perfect job and do it cheaper than our competitors?"

"I understand, William," old Bill patiently replied. "Too much electric current caused the problem, but I think I can judge the flow correctly from here on."

"Think? What the hell do you mean, think?" I stormed. "Do you mean you simply guess how much electric current goes into the tanks?"

"Yes, William, that is the case, perhaps we'd better go into the office and have a chat."

My partner slowly trudged toward our little office tucked in a corner of the immense building. In his quiet manner, Bill explained the dilemma. To properly control the electric current input, he needed rheostats in every tank, for which the total cost would approximate ten thousand dollars. Apparently when initially discussing my buying into

Plastics Plating, Bill judged that if he included the cost of rheostats in his estimate of setting up the plant, it would frighten me off. With many years of plating experience, he thought he could function without them, but found it more complicated in our new larger tanks than he expected. Although angry, I immediately went and borrowed $8,000 from John Walsh and a young chap, John Longo, who had worked for me at Homeland Realty. A month elapsed before the rheostats were connected, and during that four week period Plastics Plating had disintegrated into a shambles. Attaching copper plate on steel is a slow process, and plating chrome on copper is a much longer procedure; but to reverse the entire procedure is a tortuous time-consuming operation. Stripping off the plate with an acid solution left many of the articles pock-marked and unusable. Hence, plated goods were being shipped back to the manufacturers with up to a twenty-five percent shortage. After the value of damaged articles was subtracted from our total invoice, Plastics Plating usually owed our customers money. Our company slid into financial ruin almost as swiftly as the Titanic sank beneath the waves of the Atlantic, and there was little I could do to halt the fiasco. For several months I struggled to save my investment against insurmountable odds, but Plastics Plating's name had become an imprecation in manufacturing circles, so new business became impossible to find. John Walsh and I decided in December that further struggling would simply delay the inevitable, so John, as a substantial past-due creditor, put a lock on Plastics Plating's door, thus forcing it into bankruptcy. Broke, out of credit, with more liens against house and car than either were worth, and with Christmas rapidly approaching, I was forced to embark on a nefarious scheme.

Ingots of silver sold on a quota basis to plating companies at a cost much lower than market price lay gathering dust in our storage room. Racketeers had contacted me several times about obtaining raw silver. They had offered me a substantial price and I had retained their number. The afternoon prior to Plastics Platings' demise, I had arranged with the silver buyers to meet me that night in a garage off Spadina Avenue in central Toronto. A cold gusty wind, spraying a mixture of rain and sleet, made my illicit affair seem even more sinister as I snuck the silver bars into my trunk and rendezvoused with my felonious conspirators. Perhaps I chanced taking a bullet in the back, as I pocketed the $1800 in large bills without another person being present; but I wanted no witnesses to the crime. My conscience never twinged at the illegal transaction; in fact, I gained some satisfaction from knowing that Plastics Plating had at least provided for my family until I was re-established. Plastics Plating, a disastrous experience, afforded me one of the most nerve-wracking periods of my life, especially during the summer when Jack, Shirley, Mom, and Dad paid us a visit, and I was too busy to spend much time with them. Following the debacle and reflecting on the previous twenty-four months, during which time we had vacillated from pauper to tycoon and back to pauper, it was again obvious to me that my constant meddling in ventures of which I knew nothing always led to my downfall.

During Christmas of 1953, we were poor but comfortable; in 1954 we were rich as an Arab sheik; now, twelve months later, we owed far more than the complete equity in our total assets. Every name was included in our list of creditors when we filed for bankruptcy, but I assured John Walsh and Johnny Longo I would pay them back. The Mercantile Bank and the Bank of Nova Scotia, both with unsecured loans totalling ten thousand dollars, were given the same guarantee, though I point-blank refused to sign personal notes, as I had no idea how long it would take to earn that much money. My rationale was simple: the lending institutions and my associates had loaned the money because of my part ownership in the company and their faith in my business ability. All other creditors were the responsibility of Lunan, who could salve his conscience the best way he could.

Bill, completely responsible for the fiasco, died shortly after Plastics Plating's collapse. I never hated the old Scotsman, though it was unfortunate he hadn't put all the cards on the table at the beginning of the game. If we'd borrowed money for the rheostats at the start, we undoubtedly would have been a successful enterprise. But he didn't, and that's the way it was. When I advertised for a good investment, I searched for a sharp deal or a mark; but I turned out to be the dupe, so I had no one to blame except myself.

Without a real estate business and under an almost insurmountable load of debt, I eagerly sought a means of earning a pile of money in a hurry. My old friend George Farr, who was working in the mortgage division of A. Harvey & Company Real Estate, and who was aware of my business failure in the plating industry, approached me with a proposition.

"Bill, my boy, if you want to make big money fast, get into the mortgage business. It's a bonanza," he assured me.

I discussed his suggestion with John Walsh, who concurred with George's assessment. Phillips and Farr Investments was incorporated in late 1955 with me, as President, owning 40% of the stock; George Farr, as Vice President, owning 40%; and John Walsh, as Financier, owning the balance. PHILLIPS AND FARR INVESTMENTS LIMITED opened its doors for business on January 2, 1956, directly across the Danforth from the original Phillips Real Estate.

Chapter 5

Potpourri

Phillips and Farr Investments Ltd. opened in a windowless basement office not particularly pretentious, but adequate for our early requirements. Vera Johnson, chief secretary at Homeland Realty, and an outstanding office manager joined the firm. Homeland folded early in 1956 when Harold immigrated to Phoenix, Arizona and Lionel went back to the life insurance business, so Howard Tustin, one of the company's top salesmen, also came to work for us.

On January 2nd, Phillips and Farr Investments Ltd.'s first day in business, I made a $100 commission for selling a mortgage and from that minuscule but successful beginning, the company swiftly burgeoned into prominence. George Farr didn't misrepresent the splendid money making opportunities available in the industry, except he hadn't realized nor taken full advantage of its extraordinary potential, and I swiftly corrected that oversight.

Mortgages are the life blood of the real estate business, hence every builder, broker or real estate salesman require the services of mortgage brokers or money lenders. Arranging first mortgages for builders on their housing projects with major lending institutions constituted an important aspect of our function as we earned commissions on the total loans arranged, and by providing this service for builders, we usually handled their second mortgage take backs as well. This arranging fee also applied to first mortgage loans set up on resale homes. The big bucks, however, were realized from trafficking in mortgages which required the availability of substantial short term funds and George didn't have the connections or resources to raise the money for that purpose. John Walsh had known Farr longer than I, but he didn't have sufficient confidence in George's business judgement.

331

When an agent presented an offer to purchase contract on a residential home, which included a second mortgage, the seller generally wanted a written guarantee on the cash value of the second and wouldn't accept the contract without one, so the real estate person contacted a mortgage broker to obtain a commitment. The normal procedure required the mortgage broker to offer the second on the open mortgage market, and upon receipt of an acceptable bid, he would charge the real estate agent a fee for his service. The procedure took time as the potential mortgage buyer had to inspect the property, etc. The impatient agent unable to finalize his sale without the commitment, would present any offer because neither he nor the owner knew the market value of the mortgage, and simply based their evaluation of the purchase contract on the total cash that would be received on closing. As an example: A five thousand dollar second mortgage became available which I believed could be marketed for at least three thousand five hundred, I'd give the real estate agent a guarantee of three thousand dollars and if the offer was acceptable, we had until closing to sell it at a profit or if not, we'd buy the mortgage and sell it after closing. Providing I assessed its value correctly, Phillips and Farr Investments earned five hundred dollars less legal expenses instead of the normal one hundred dollar commission. When agents became aware our company guaranteed a price or outright purchased first and second mortgages thereby immediately solidifying their deals, they flocked to our door, and business not only boomed, but the operation opened up a whole new venture. Real estates with listings on unencumbered houses where the owner insisted on receiving his complete equity, would arrange with me to purchase the house for cash and then promptly resell it at a much higher price with a low down payment. As an example: With a property listed for ten thousand cash, a salesman would bring a purchase contract for the cash asking price plus a second selling agreement on the same house for fourteen thousand with a two thousand down payment. I would, therefore, become the buyer and seller within five minutes. By arranging a non-bonused first mortgage for five thousand, selling the seven thousand second mortgage for five thousand, our firm grossed two thousand dollars on the exchange and everyone was happy. The original owner received his ten thousand cash, the new buyer obtained the dwelling with only two thousand down, the agent earned two commissions and I ended up with a substantial profit.

John Walsh arranged the funds for closing all mortgage and house deals, and because George had nothing to do with the house speculating aspect of our business, John wanted a larger share of profit for his responsibility in raising the operating capital, so we formed Philjon Ltd. of which I became president and 50% owner with John Walsh controlling the balance of the stock. Interest charges billed to Philjon Ltd. for borrowing funds plus John's legal costs were matched by an equal sum paid to me for management which amounted to substantial remuneration. Within sixty days of opening our office, all business ventures flourished allowing me to keep up the numerous personal payments resulting from the Plastics Plating debacle. To add to my financial improvement, my friend John McIntyre who also speculated in buying and selling houses, often had difficulty arranging cash to close his deals, so he and I teamed up on properties which he'd located and we also earned several thousand dollars apiece. Our prospering ventures forced us to locate a larger and more dignified headquarters and we leased the entire second floor over the Bank of Commerce at the corner of Coxwell and Danforth. Due to our increasing mortgage relationship with builders and real estate brokers, I decided to get into general insurance as we could build an agency quite rapidly with our contacts. Provincial Law wouldn't allow a mortgage broker to also hold a general insurance license, so I approached Herb Richards about heading up the company.

Herb Richards, nicknamed Rick, who worked at A. Harvey and Company for several years, became a friend of mine mostly through our association at poker games which we played for reasonably high stakes. H.W. Richards Insurance Agency Ltd. was formed in late 1956, with Rick as Vice President, I as President, each with 40% of the stock and John Walsh who again became the financier held 20%. Rick worked in the mortgage field, plus general insurance, but had a hankering to build houses which would fit perfectly into our conglomerate, as a result, we incorporated Philrick Ltd. in the spring of '57 which had the identical share structure and slate of officers as H.W. Richards Insurance Agency Ltd. I now held the position of President in four small interrelated corporations which was possibly responsible for an unusual, non-related scenario during the summer of '57.

Steve Theodoru, one of my closest buddies, never lost his fascination for the sport of horse racing. Many of his cafe patrons involved in betting the ponies would leave money with Steve for a local bookmaker, who also frequented the restaurant. If the bettors were lucky, they'd pick up their winnings at the same place. Although Steve didn't gain financially, he became the patsy for an illicit operation. The Morality Squad of the Toronto Police Department, aware Steve practiced bookmaking several years before, and suspicious he still had a hand in the unlawful enterprise, planted a stooge. After a few months of befriending Steve, a plain clothes detective gave Steve money to put on a horse and my unsuspecting friend believing he was doing the chap a favor, placed the bet. One evening during dinner, I got a call from Steve's mother, whom I affectionately called 'Ma.' Born and raised in Macedonia, Ma spoke poor

English and in a tearful voice wailed, "Beel, Stevie in jail." Finding it difficult to understand the problem, I persuaded her to put Sophie on the phone who, also distraught, explained what happened. Three officers from the Morality Squad had arrested Steve at the restaurant and charged him with four offences: Bookmaking, aiding and abetting bookmaking, illegal sale of Irish Sweepstake tickets and having liquor in a public place without a license. A room adjacent to the restaurant, but no part of the eatery, contained a sofa, refrigerator and other minor furnishings so he or Pop, his father, had a retreat in which to relax during their slack periods. A part bottle of whiskey found in the room, constituted an illegality under the Ontario Liquor Act. Steve's popularity with the local retailers and businessmen, plus the pettiness of the charges, caused the lot of us to become incensed with Steve's incarceration and between the group, we swiftly raised bail money and had Steve released. Bill Reid, his lawyer, realizing all charges were technically true, decided to base Steve's defense on his excellent standing in the community and so enlisted two dozen local business leaders to go to court as character witnesses. These individuals included proprietors of butcher shops, clothing salons, drug stores, hotels, real estate brokers and salesmen, plus attorneys from other legal firms or, in fact, anyone willing to vouch for Steve's fine qualities. In court, Reid summoned these men to the stand one by one throughout one entire session and then continued the same tactics during the second. He called me on the second day as the twelfth witness and the judge obviously impatient with the proceedings, looked at me intently as I approached the stand. After the usual preliminaries Bill Reid asked, "Mr. Phillips, what is your position with Phillips and Farr Investments Ltd.?"

"President." I replied.

"Are you also President of Philrick Ltd.?"

"Yes."

"How about H.W. Richards Insurance Agency?"

"President." I again responded.

"And are you not also President of Philjon Ltd.?" Bill continued.

"Yes sir, that is correct."

At this point, the judge interrupted the questioning, turned to me and said, "Mr. Phillips, you are obviously an esteemed member of the community, and yet you come up here and regardless of the established fact that a police officer actually gave and received money from this man, you insist he is innocent? Please explain that to me."

Looking the magistrate straight in the face and speaking as earnestly as I inwardly felt, I answered, "Your honor, several years ago Steve was an usher at my wedding; my wife and I socialize once or twice weekly with the Theodorus; Steve and I frequently go fishing together and we also belong to the same fraternities, besides all that I've eaten in his establishment almost every day for six years. If you and I enjoyed the same relationship, wouldn't I know if you were an unsavory character, because that is what is at stake here, a man's reputation in the community. I don't deny Steve knows bookmakers as do many of us, but he was duped by the officer because he simply tried to do a favor for a man he considered a friend and for which he would receive absolutely no remuneration. It seems like a petty way to besmirch the reputation of a fine citizen."

The judge thanked me, pondered a few moments, instructed Reid not to call more witnesses, then dismissed all charges except the aiding and abetting indictment to which Steve previously had admitted his guilt. He fined Steve the paltry sum of ten dollars. Although my rank as President of four corporations sounded exceptionally impressive in court, I didn't enjoy the same measure of financial success at the time as several others who testified, but I was credited with playing a major role in the magistrate's favorable decision. The judge's compassion reinstated some of my faith in our courts and criminal justice system which had been severely tested six years before.

During the period of Phillips Real Estate when most of our social life revolved around the Moose Club dance, Francis and Elaine Rechaud, members of the club, joined our circle of friends. The Rechauds with three children, approached me about selling their small bungalow and getting them a three bedroom home more suitable for their growing family. I arranged a trade, but the Rechauds with little equity in their original property, were going to be financially squeezed when closing time arrived. To add to their dilemma, Francis lost his job. A week before the exchange of properties was to take place, I received a call from sobbing Elaine Rechaud.

"Bill, Francis is in jail."

"What the hell happened?" I asked.

"He went into a lumber office looking for a job, there was no one in sight and seeing a wad of bills jutting from a cash register drawer, couldn't resist the temptation and scooped up the money just as a clerk entered the building. Francis panicked and ran, but was caught by the police fleeing across that open field at Main and Danforth. I don't know what to do Bill." She wailed.

"Have you contacted a lawyer?" I inquired.

"Yes, Wally Scott, who is acting for us in the real estate transaction."

"I'll speak to Wally and get back to you." I promised.

By a rare coincidence, Lloyd Ayers and his friend Bill Johnson, were visiting in my office when Elaine Rechaud phoned.

"What was that all about?" Lloyd asked.

After I explained the situation, Bill Johnson inquired, "Are they friends of yours, do you want to get him sprung?"

He went on to explain he had a court connection and for the payment of a fee, could perhaps arrange Francis's release.

"They are not close friends," I replied, "however, they appear like a pleasant couple with three children and I do have a couple of commissions involved. How much would the payment amount to?" I questioned.

"I don't know but will call you back in a few hours." Bill stated.

Johnson phoned later in the afternoon, informed me to be at court the following morning when Rechaud came up for sentencing and to have $150 in cash. He inquired as to what I'd be wearing, instructed me to do nothing until contacted and insisted I not tell Rechaud's lawyer. When I informed Elaine of the development, she maintained that all the cash she could get together was $75 so we agreed to meet at court the next morning and I would furnish the additional $75 until their deal closed.

Wally Scott, Bill Reid's law partner and I were well acquainted and it was uncomfortable sitting in the courtroom listening to him discuss strategy which I knew would play no part in the drama. The first bombshell burst when Wally informed me Francis Rechaud had broken into the lumber company's office with a jimmying device which was found on him. Secondly, this was his third robbery offense and once Francis had served five years for armed robbery in the United States. Elaine, terribly embarrassed when she saw the look of horror cross my face blurted, "Bill, I didn't think you'd help if you knew the truth." She was one hundred percent correct with that statement but being numbstruck, I didn't reply. At mid-morning the judge called for a recess and cleared the court. As I left the room, a man approached, inquired if I was Phillips and instructed me to follow him. Down a corridor from the courtroom, I suddenly found myself in a tiny office where behind a desk sat the crown's prosecuting attorney.

"Jesus Christ, Phillips," the man exploded, "I didn't have any idea this character had a record. He should be sentenced to ten years!"

Not knowing what to say, I said nothing, just stood trembling like an oak leaf in a thunderstorm.

"You got the money?" The man demanded.

Nodding my head, I rapidly reached for the bills and counted them out on the desk without having an inkling whether Rechaud would get ten years, if they'd hang him, or set him free, all I wanted at that moment was to escape the sordid mess.

Allowing no one back in the courtroom except Elaine, Wally Scott, and myself, the judge called Francis to the bench. Wally began to speak but the prosecuting attorney motioned him to be quiet, then mumbled a few words to the judge about Francis Rechaud being a father of three, his despondency due to his unemployment and recommended clemency and a suspended sentence. For reasons I'll never comprehend, the judge concurred and within ten minutes we were on the street with Francis a free man. A more confused, though jubilant quartet never left a courtroom and all for different reasons. Francis walking on air but stunned by his release as he was still ignorant of the payoff, Wally Scott bewildered by the turn of events but convinced he had done something brilliant, and therefore had a great future as a criminal lawyer, Elaine overjoyed at the outcome and grateful for my participation, and I, well at that moment I was positive a thousand dollars could get anyone freed from any charge including murder providing the same crown prosecutor would be assigned to the case, moreover, I'd lost a heap of respect for the law.

The crooked attorney retired shortly following the episode and disappeared from public view. I suspect he lived out the balance of his life in a villa on the Riviera, but it took a while before I regained any faith in the fairness of our criminal judicial system. Many years later when I divulged to several close lawyer friends my experience with the Rechauds, I was assured that the dishonest crown prosecutor represented a rare breed in what otherwise remained a fairly honest modus operandi. Though not entirely in disagreement with this assessment, I nonetheless pointed out to my legal cohorts the value of service provided to the taxpayer, the ultimate employer, by the judiciary as well as all forms of government is dependent on the integrity of those in power. When that rigid adherence to an acceptable code of behavior becomes impaired, not only do we all suffer but I question whether our system has sufficient warning lights to prevent a simple snow slide from occasionally reaching avalanche proportions.

Though the two incidents were not remotely connected, the end results were both positive. Francis Rechaud, guilty as sin, who should have done ten years, but for the payment of a paltry $150 and a dishonest crown attorney got a job, and at my last communication with the family many years later, had advanced with his company into a responsible position, and the Rechauds were prospering. Steve Theodoru, also technically guilty because of his involvement in circumstances that violated some of our more stupid and archaic laws, was released by a logically thinking compassionate civil servant. As everyone who went to bat believed, he would, Steve remained a steadfast citizen and continued to lead a moral and contented life. Steve and I swapped personal favors for numerous years, but perhaps my biggest service to him was as the president of four insignificant corporations that when announced in court gave me the stature to gain the good judges attention.

Philrick constructed several houses in Scarboro which sold slowly but returned a reasonable profit, Rick, however, owned 300' of highway property at Fenelon Falls, a resort town less than a hundred miles northeast of Toronto. We subdivided the land into six fifty foot lots, erected small frame cabins and offered each package for sale at less than three thousand dollars apiece. The unbelievable response and ease with which we made the six sales plus earning a handsome profit, shaped the course of my business career for the next quarter century. The major obstacle in marketing rural property was financing, as lending institutions were not interested in placing first mortgage funds outside the metropolitan area. This encouraged formation of SUMCOT INVEST-MENTS LTD., our fifth corporation whose name derived from the first syllables of summer and cottages. Again I became president with 40% of the stock, John Walsh held 40% and Rick, the balance. The company's principal aim was to provide first mortgage money for summer cottages built by Philrick Ltd. To obtain funding, I intended to attract investors who would purchase preferred shares and receive not only dividends, but a percentage of the company profits. All corporate money would be matched with bank loans who would hold the mortgage portfolio as security. Several investors had pledged a total of thirty thousand dollars by the summer of 1958, so Sumcot Investments Ltd. with over fifty thousand available dollars including bank money, was ready to roll as a finance company though fate intervened and it never made a loan.

The outstanding response to our advertising while successfully selling the six units at Fenelon Falls, encouraged Rick and I to greatly expand our vacation property operations. The Fenelon Falls property facing the highway approximately a half mile from Cameron Lake sold rapidly due to the low price, but majority of our potential customers eagerly desired to be located directly on the water, so Rick and I decided to purchase only waterfront lots. We spent an exceedingly strenuous winter walking numberless miles through deep snow while examining frontage for sale on a multitude of lakes, finally settling on two locations. On Chemung Lake, commonly called Little Mud in the Kawartha Lake region of Ontario, eighty miles from the city we purchased fifty lots, and at Four Mile Lake a few miles east of Coboconk and ninety miles from the city we bought twenty more. By the spring of 1958, my personal impetus had shifted from the mortgage and house speculation field toward cottage building and development. Several reasons caused the transition, though my constant search for new challenges probably provided the greatest motivation to again alter course.

Trafficking in mortgages and speculating in properties had provided a lucrative income beyond my wildest dreams for eighteen months, allowing me to discharge our heavy burden of debts. Any successful enterprise in the business community, though, is difficult to hide, hence mortgage and residential house speculators sprang up at an enormous rate and began bidding up the price for every loan and property on the market to such an extent, that earning a profit commensurate with the investment risk became imponderable. To add to the problems, the real estate market sagged badly in '57 and '58, and Philjon Ltd. got caught holding several houses that wouldn't sell.

A personal reason also played an important role in my decision to become active in vacation property development. Jack and Shirley gave up on farming in the early fifties and Jack began a career with Memorial Gardens in Winnipeg selling cemetary plots. He enjoyed marvelous success, and in November 1956, the company transferred him to London, Ontario as sales manager. The folks now alone in Winnipeg, except for sister Joyce, paid us a visit by train in the summer of 1957. They spent a few days with Joyce and I at Charlie Crawford's fishing lodge at Picton, Ontario, then visited Jack and Shirley in London for a week. During their vacation, it became obvious they would consider moving East, providing there was some assurance of being able to earn a living. Uncle George's wife Gladys died suddenly in January of 1958, and being extremely close to both she and Uncle George, I made my first airplane flight to attend the funeral. The atrocious weather with a wind chill factor ranging to fifty degrees, convinced me to try and persuade Father to move to Toronto where the winters were considerably less severe. Although neither of us had any idea what he would do on his arrival, particularly as he had now reached sixty five years of age, I assured him we would either feast or starve together, so we shook hands on a pact that guaranteed he would immigrate east in the spring. Dad's imminent arrival and our mutual love of the outdoors, increased my resolve to expand our vacation property development activity because he and Mother's talents were well suited to various applications in that particular field. Again fate seemed to intercede when a property became available at that particular time in West Hill on the extreme eastern fringe of the city. It included a hundred feet of highway frontage, two hundred feet of depth and contained a quaint little four room frame cottage, ideally suited for a permanent residence for the folks. A real bargain at ten thousand dollars cash, it allowed me to solve the problem of providing low cost accommodation for my parents. Dividing the lot in two, I sold the 50 foot vacant portion to Philrick Ltd. for $3500 on which we built and sold a frame bungalow for a small profit. An elderly lady investor client of mine placed a $6500 first mortgage on the half containing the house and although insisting I sign personally, she arranged the repayments to work out to a low $75 monthly including taxes. Mother and Dad arrived in May with little more than their personal belongings, and I signed the title of the property over to them for the closing costs of $275. Though I could have sold the property for a minimum of $12,000 thereby achieving an excellent profit, my parents immediate contentment outweighed any possible financial gain. Father, in particular, gained self respect and dignity from owning his own hearth and home. The huge lot covered with a variety of fruit trees, evergreens and hardwoods, provided an emotional outlet allowing him to plant, transplant or remove entirely any bush, shrub or tree he so desired. Mother loved gardening, especially flowers, and also delighted in interior decorating, so, between the two, they rapidly converted their drab little bungalow into a homey, cozy retreat. For a decade it provided an enjoyable residence for them, sister Joyce, frequently Grandmother Rodd, and "old" Bob, their mongrel dog who loved the spacious grounds as much as other members of the family. Within two weeks of becoming permanent Ontario residents, they both were employed by Philrick Ltd. and spent the summer painting cottages both at Four Mile Lake and Chemung, supervising development work, plus assisting in sales at Chemung Lake. All this responsibility kept them busy as bees, but those first few months in Ontario were considered by them to be one of the most enjoyable summers of their lives.

Gypsy blood must flow in the veins of the lot of us. On the farm in the thirties, our parents and we youngsters frequently piled into our bumpity old wagon in the morning after chores and with a team of plodding farm horses, travel miles into back country, not returning home until well past dark. Perhaps the pretext for the journey was to search for lost livestock, hunt game or possibly visit distant villages to dicker at auction sales, but in every instance a delicious picnic spread awaited a suitable campsite. We were never happier as a family unit than when gathered around a campfire in some secluded niche devouring our delicious repast in an atmosphere of total solitude spiced by the pungent smell of burning birch bark. This inherent fondness for camping out in strange habitats is what fascinated Mom and Dad that first summer in the east.

A three bedroom model cottage constructed by Philrick on the shores of Chemung Lake in a superb setting overlooking the lake became their main headquarters, and when painting cottages at Four Mile Lake they either moved into another lakeside model or pitched their tent beside the water cooking meals over their beloved campfire. Independently motivated, they both preferred working with no one gazing over their shoulder, and this added to their contentment. However, the actuality of being back amongst their own devoted family was a decided plus in the overall satisfaction with their move. Joyce, the children and I went to Chemung Lake each weekend for sales, but Jack, Shirley and their clan also visited frequently. Both parents became proficient sales people as well as handling other responsibilities and we enjoyed a reasonably successful season our first full year in the vacation property industry, particularly at Chemung Lake. Unfortunately, partnerships rarely run smoothly, and Philrick proved no exception.

Throughout the summer I constantly came into conflict with Rick. Our advertising was designed exclusively to attract prospects to the two developments on weekends. It being Rick's responsibility to handle Four Mile Lake while I managed Chemung, Rick, however, rarely spent time at his designated location, relying mostly on calls from "Property For Sale" signs while I labored every Saturday and Sunday until dark at Chemung. The rupture in our relationship reached a complete severance by late summer when I informed him I wanted out at season's end. Real Estate agents from nearby towns and cities frequented the developments, first to offer their services in selling our product and second to investigate the possibilities of selling us more property. One chap, Herb Mason, from the nearby city of Peterborough dropped in one day to offer me 700 acres of land including a large quantity of water frontage on two lakes in the Habiburton Highlands, approximately 140 miles Northwest of Toronto. The property, no more than thirty miles from the Boulter country where I'd hunted and fished for several years, was terrain with which I had grown increasingly infatuated. Mother, Dad, Bill Morrow, a salesman for Herb Mason, plus Elmer Aldred, the property owner, and I, drove back to inspect the property the final day of October 1958.

My 32nd birthday had just been celebrated and over the previous two decades I'd been involved in a multitude of schemes, but this trip would spark the embryo of an idea that would rapidly gather momentum until I was embroiled in another consequential gamble and venture not reaching its conclusion for another two decades. The uniqueness of the undertaking revolved around my adoration of the outdoors including a passion for hunting and fishing. But a constant search for privacy as a result of the immense influx of sportsmen into remote areas which hitherto had been considered private domain by a select few, probably was the biggest factor in the creation of the huge development we were about to assemble. My penchant for outdoor activities steadily increased until most of my leisure hours were spent either fishing with Joyce at the Bay of Quinte, or on various hunting expeditions with a diversity of companions. Lorne Branning plus several others and myself, frequently roamed the woods and fields during the fall and winter months for partridge, jackrabbit or pheasant. Deer hunting usually found me in a party of a dozen or more, and moose hunting depended on the type of hunt to determine the numbers in the group. The general affluence of the masses since the end of the war tremendously increased the number of individuals who could afford to hunt, and it became almost impossible to locate deer hunting territories where there wasn't more guns than game. That plus the dwindling deer population around Boulter, Ontario, our favorite hunting grounds, forced us to locate more remote areas to stalk the elusive white tail. Rarely did I get skunked, although my hunting partners and I made some strenuous journeys into back country portaging canoes and equipment to reach areas with a reasonable population of deer, and trigger-happy hunters not hiding behind every tree.

In 1957, Lorne Branning, George Prue plus another acquaintance, Art Coltham, arranged with an outfitter to take us to MacKenzie Lake, south of Algonquin Park where we hunted on the fringe of that enormous game preserve. To reach our destination, we labored over three portages each nearly a mile in length. Toting on our backs food supplies, tent, canoes, hunting paraphernalia and personal gear over the slippery, hilly trails was a heart pounding accomplishment. On the return trip, we backpacked the same loads with the exception of food and liquor, but now we also transported four deer. The exhausting trip encouraged me even more to search for an exclusive hunting territory, because except for the arduous effort, I now enjoyed hunting deer with dogs more than the methods used in the west. At first, this style of hunting seemed repulsive, because in Manitoba, not only illegal, it was also considered outrageously unsportsmanlike and if you saw a dog chasing a deer, you shot the dog, not the deer. The extreme difference in terrain between Manitoba and Ontario, was responsible for the dissimilarity in custom and laws. In the flat field and bluff country of the prairies, a group of men walking a few hundred feet abreast through bush, could easily rout animals into open terrain and an ambush. If hunting alone, an individual could wait quietly in the deer's habitat for the animals to stir for food, etc. In the rugged hill and lake regions of Central Ontario, however, there were few openings in the dense forests and the deer could simply hide in cedar bogs, high precipitous ridges or swampy terrain where only dogs could flush them out. Hunting with hounds, though not as humane, was nevertheless more thrilling. In the west, the elapsed time between sighting your prey and making the kill seldom took more than two minutes, allowing your excitement little chance to mount. But dogs created an entirely different set of circumstances. Hunters placed on known deer runs, were generally in position at least an hour before the dogger released the animals. On still frosty mornings, barking hounds could be heard two miles away and their style of baying changed dramatically from short yelps when searching for sign or scent, until they came upon fresh spoor, at which time they kept up a steady baying as they chased their quarry. Frequently it took dogs a half hour to drive the fleeing whitetail into a waiting line of hunters. As yelping hound and bounding deer zig-zagged through densely wooded valleys and up heavily forested slopes, no one in ambush had the slightest idea where the animals would appear. A few moments could seem like an eternity as the chase approached. Then either the drama ended with an explosion of shooting by companions or the sudden snap of broken branches and a familiar thump, thump of a fast moving deer indicated you would promptly be in the limelight. Again at this point, little similarity existed between the two hunting patterns. Majority of deer are shot while standing or walking in a field or clearing in the west. Ontario terrain on the other hand, offer hunters only a brief glimpse of an animal stretched out in full flight and it requires an accurate marksman to bag his prey. The difficulty in locating suitable deer country away from throngs of city men with high powered rifles who knew little of the nuances of hunting, or worse still the lethal danger of firearms made chasing moose a desirable alternative, though I usually spent a week at both. In 1955 while I fought my losing battle with Plastics Plating, Hank Sharpe returned to Low Bush with Dave Black as guide and bagged a fine bull not far from Dave's trapping cabin at the mouth of the Abitibi River. Though delighted, Hank suggested we change our method the following year and try our luck without a guide, especially as neither of us were interested in night hunting.

In 1956 Hank and I bought two canoes: A twelve foot sponson, ideal as a two man hunting craft not easily upset, and an eighteen foot square stern portage canoe capable of carrying a substantial load. Both fascinated with the wilderness regions of the Abitibi, we elected to test our ability in that area with our own outfit. We drove to Iroquois Falls on the Abitibi River, attached our 7½ h.p. Mercury motor on the portage canoe, and towing the sponson, made our way slowly the thirty miles up river to Lake Abitibi, then headed for the huge wetlands where Hank shot his moose the previous year. The voyage proved to be far more formidable than we imagined, as the Abitibi River up to three miles in width, twisted and turned along its route making it often impossible to determine whether to veer right, left, or go straight ahead to remain on the river's flow. An incorrect turn could find us in a dead end bay, miles off our intended course. Fortunately Hank, quite handy with a compass, and guided by our topographic maps, could generally keep us heading in the proper direction. Another problem in the expansive sections of open water particularly in the gusty wind, was to prevent splashing waves from swamping either of our vessels. We reached our destination safely, however, and set up our tent on a hardwood ridge beside a small stream that drained from the huge marsh we intended to hunt. Having planned a weeks' vacation, and as the weather had turned unseasonably warm, we decided not to shoot a moose that day even if offered the opportunity because if the temperature didn't drop, there would be no alternative but return to the city with the meat or take a chance it would spoil. Loading our fishing gear, guns and flashlights, we trolled quietly up the creek and caught a couple of Walleyes before camouflaging ourselves amongst willows and cattails in the huge open marsh, and settled down to determine if game inhabited our chosen hunting locale. Dusk swiftly enveloped the barren swampland and moonlight dancing off the rippling water silhouettes dozens of muskrat and beaver swimming silently around our hideaway. Whenever we lit a cigarette or made a sudden move, several instantaneous loud splashes would break the silence of the ideal night like an unexpected thunderclap, nevertheless, knowing the source of the noise, we sat quietly and patiently waited for sound of moose. We tingled with excitement when suddenly the distinct calls of two distant bulls were answered by at least one cow. Then from across the swampy bay, a throaty roar indicated a third bull was heading in our general direction. An electrifying few minutes elapsed as that huge beast, lumbering through the marsh on a fast trot and grunting with every stride came directly towards our frail canoe. When the excited animal plunged into the stream a hundred feet from where we sat, the icy water suddenly hitting his steaming body, forced him to release an enormous explosion of wind. Unable to control ourselves, we burst out laughing and Hank snapped the powerful beam of our hunter's flashlight on the lovesick bull who now relieved, changed course and we caught a brief glimpse of the magnificent beast as he galloped heavily into the blackness. The evening's activity convinced us we could bag a moose at our leisure, so silently paddling back to our encampment, we were a confident pair of huntsmen. Unfortunately, a task that sometimes appears simple at first is often the one causing the greatest disappointment, and so it was, in the Autumn of '56. Three days of constant hunting never produced another sign nor sound of moose, and to complicate matters, several individuals with powerful outboards and large cruisers went roaring around the bay as if expecting the animals to stand stalk still in the swamp awaiting their execution. These novice hunters drove to Iroquois Falls as we did, then raced up the river to the lake which didn't require much know how, so we decided to move from the proximity of the river's mouth and search for a more remote and inaccessible territory. Our topographic maps showed a marshy region surrounding the mouth of a small river twenty miles directly across the dangerous lake, so at daylight one morning with not a trace of breeze and the water mirror flat, we struck out fearlessly across the open water. Several miles offshore, two rangers in a helicopter dropped down beside us and after checking licenses and determining our destination, tried to dissuade us from continuing due to the frailty of our equipment in such an immense body of water. Almost halfway across and with the weather remaining ideal, we threw caution to the wind, maintained our course and reached our objective without incident. Luckily an old fisherman (or trappers) cabin sat snuggled in a grove of evergreens at the entrance to the stream, and the rapidly changing weather made that one of few positive happenings on the trip as it proved to be considerably more comfortable than our tent. With no sign of other hunters, and exuding confidence in our new location, we seriously dedicated ourselves to finding game, rarely leaving our canoe from daylight to dark for three days. Unfortunately, we were to taste our first defeat at moose hunting, which in our final camp wasn't due to interference from other hunters. We only heard one motor during our stay on an afternoon while paddling up the waterway, and returning to the cabin, found a pleasant note pinned to the door. "Came to use camp and hunt creek, but will move to different site. Good luck, Joe and Nettie Nardone." I was sorry to have missed them. It would have been pleasant to have renewed our acquaintanceship, and perhaps got some pointers on why we couldn't locate the elusive moose.

Although disappointed and tired, Hank and I exchanged few unpleasant words. Hank standing at 5'11" with a thick neck and barrel chested, was a strong man. Fifteen years older than I, he had an earnest, pleasant face with a heavy moustache and spoke with an authoritative voice which combined with his military background earned my respect in most cases. We usually worked well as a team, though his constant orders frequently got under my skin. He earned his Captain's rank in the Canadian Army in the field, so giving commands came natural as he'd worked his way through the ranks from Sergeant. Hank always shrugged it off when told by myself and others, aggravated by his abrasive attitude, that while army privates had to take his bullshit, we didn't, but he never seemed to realize how he sounded. Nevertheless, under certain conditions he couldn't restrain himself, and without hesitation would begin barking out directions. Several of our mutual acquaintances amazed at our relationship, frequently asked why I hunted with him. The answer, though easy for me to understand, was not as simple to explain. Hank and I shared many adventures in the wilderness while fishing, hunting ducks, partridge, deer and now moose. Though irritated occasionally by his brusque manner, I nevertheless recognized a reliable, clear thinking individual. Two men alone in back country, miles from outside help, must have faith and a feeling of dependability with each other in the event of an accident or there would be no peace of mind. Hank no doubt had the same confidence in me as I did with him, that in an emergency, neither would panic. A case in point occurred on this particular trip. The afternoon before leaving the original camp-site, Hank desirous for a change in menu, decided to go to an island a hundred yards off the main lake and shoot some partridges which had been roosting in the trees. A stiff breeze severely roiling the water didn't deter him, and with hip waders he jumped into the sponson canoe and struck out across the turbulent stretch between the mainland and the island. He placed me out of sight on the mainland where he believed the birds would scatter after he fired. Hearing what sounded like a splash and muffled call for help, I sprang into the portage canoe and in less than a minute reached Hank, who had upset in the rough water and sank like a stone when his waders filled with water. Luckily the accident happened near the island and by struggling to the surface and grabbing the side of the larger craft, his feet soon reached lake bottom and he dragged himself ashore. Although a dangerous and thoughtless action on Hank's part, neither of us panicked and the incident taught a valuable lesson on the rapidity with which a serious mishap can take place. However, despite the regard I held Hank, his constant babbling, under trying conditions finally caused me to explode.

Our 7½ h.p. Mercury had been balking from the start, and as the outboard motor operator, I faced the problem of coaxing the motor to run, or when it stopped to yank the starter rope, however, many pulls it took to get the engine started again. Also keeping our portage canoe headed in the intended direction while trying to prevent the loaded sponson in tow from overturning the entire outfit, at times was exasperating. When the motor suddenly stopped and the sponson having no brakes went veering off in a direction of its own, it would cause the entire outfit to lurch wildly when it reached the end of its tow rope. Hank, watching from the bow could do nothing to help, but instead of sitting quietly, kept up a steady stream of advice. "Bill, watch where you're going!" "Bill, for Christ sake, look out for the sponson!" "Bill, use the choke on the motor!" "Hey! For gawds sake, keep the nose of the canoe into the wind!" "Bill, Jesus Christ, water's splashing into the boat!" This incessant chatter went on all week, and on three occasions after being at the controls non-stop for up to 5 and 6 hours, my nerves were as taut as violin strings on a bass fiddle by the end of the session, nevertheless, I gritted my teeth and said nothing. The day prior to returning home, we traversed a large stretch of open water to explore another creek in a final futile effort to locate game. Heading back to camp, our motor began acting up again, and once more Hank started his harangue of advice. A week of unsuccessful hunting, our lack of sleep or perhaps my head just couldn't cope no more, but with the outboard stalled, both motors pitching wildly in the rolling waves, my nerves cracked, I jumped up, grabbed an oar and screamed, "Hank, if you don't shut your f---ing yap, I'll slice your head right off your gawd damn shoulders!" "One more word out of that clucking tongue and so help me Jesus Christ I'll upset the whole gawdamn outfit and we'll swim for shore!"

Hank never said a word, just looked straight ahead as I sat back down, adjusted our motor, got it started and nursed the crippled equipment back to the sanctity of our own creek. I had no remorse for blasting Hank, in fact, felt quite relieved for getting it off my chest, but appreciated a miracle occurred when I didn't upset our canoe or at least fall overboard in my rage. Hank secured both canoes when we landed, then coming directly over, laid a hand on my shoulder. "I'm sorry," he said, "I just don't realize sometimes how aggravating it must sound, unfortunately I never got the Sergeant-Major out of my system." We experienced many a tough situation after that incident, but he never barked another order at me, though he had plenty of opportunity the following day.

Hank roused me at daylight. "The lake is calm Bill, let's load and attempt to reach the Abitibi River before a wind comes up."

By the time we left the shelter of our bay and reached the broad expanse of the main lake, a breeze not only struck up, but rapidly increased in velocity and we had one section where a fifteen mile sweep of open water would be perilous. A few islands with sheer rocky shorelines jutted out of the lake, but our canoes would be dashed to pieces if we attempted a landing. The lead canoe had to be headed in a precise direction into the rolling waves or water splashed in faster than Hank could bail it out, and twice we passed within a hundred feet of an island where if the motor had struck a submerged rock or log, we would not likely have survived the disaster. Travelling at a speed of about 4 miles per hour, it seemed like we'd been on the tossing, churning water for an eternity when a peninsula of land slicing an enormous bay off the main lake called Long Point came into view. Slowly and carefully, I veered toward its shelter where after four harrowing hours of near tragedy, we found a sandy cove and beached our outfit. Neither said a word through the ordeal, but when we were safely in the shelter of Long Point, Hank looked over with a triumphant smile and said, "Let's have a drink of rum." Eight torturous miles of Lake Abitibi still lay ahead before reaching the Abitibi River's mouth, and then thirty five miles down river to our car, but the most dangerous sector had been crossed, so we relaxed awhile. At six o'clock in the evening we reached Iroquois Falls after twelve agonizing hours on the water and we were returning with empty canoes. What an impossible journey had we been loaded with moose meat.

We chose to drive the five hundred miles home that night, making it a tiresome return trip, though we both took turns at the wheel. Discussing the week, we mostly blamed the failure of the hunt on the sudden appearance of the huge horsepower motors and stupidity of their operators who roared around our initial campsite frightening all the moose in the surrounding marshland. Resolved to locate a more exclusive moose hunting territory for the future not accessible to the average hunter, we considered hiring an outfitter to fly us into some remote region. And that is exactly what we did in 1957.

Hank arranged for he and I to join four other Toronto men on our first fly in moose hunt the following fall. Temagami Airways operated out of the village of the same name situated three hundred miles north of Toronto. In Temagami, we picked up three local guides, then drove another 150 miles over second class roads to Grassy River Landing not far from Gowganda, where we rendezvoused with the Cessna aircraft, our transportation for the final fifty miles to our Grassy Lake campsite. Each two hunters and guide operated as a separate entity, responsible for their own food, liquor and territory and any game bagged belonged to the marksman rather than the group as a whole. Don Mackenzie, a Cree and the only Indian, was assigned to guide Hank and me. The small Cessna aircraft required six trips to transport the nine men plus all the gear to the Grassy Lake encampment, which situated on a pine studded point of land jutting out into the water, was a superb location. The brilliant autumn weather helped create a tranquil setting, and at nightfall with kerosene lanterns illuminating the four tents huddled together, our attractive layout looked quite captivating for our week's hunt. Dave McConnell, the young bush pilot, who operated the Cessna, was a friend of mine. A nephew of Don McConnell, the real estate broker who operated near Phillips Real Estate, Dave worked for his uncle during the winter months when demand was limited for his services as a bush pilot.

Temagami Airways, just getting into the business of outfitting moose hunters, didn't realize they needed a Provincial dropping permit from the Department of Lands and Forests to set up hunting camps. The rangers not only forced Dave to fly to Gogama to pick up a permit, but fined him $65 for his ignorance of the law. Before returning to his Temagami base, Dave joined me for a drink in our tent and confided he would be relieved to leave Grassy Lake behind for a week before returning to take us back out to civilization, but he had a big surprise coming.

A gorgeous morning greeted us though quite chilly, and the scene and atmosphere of three campfires, sizzling pans of bacon, sausage, eggs, toast and coffee, plus the solitude made me clearly relish and understand my great attachment to wilderness where throngs of careless individuals couldn't disturb the tranquility. Being of English parentage, I thoroughly understood how fortunate we were in comparison to our ancestors on the British Isles who could be jailed for shooting a rabbit. Where only royalty and the elite could roam the limited forests at their leisure. I could also comprehend why Canadian Federal and Provincial governments protected large tracts of water and land for the use of all citizenry, because as taxpayers, everyone was entitled to this consideration. What I disliked, however, was the careless disregard a high percentage of my countrymen had for their unparalleled privilege of being able to roam, hunt or fish this immense area of public domain. Their carelessness with guns meant chancing having your head blown off and many had no compunction of desecrating the beauty of lands they had the liberty to enjoy. Littering trash, carelessly starting forest fires, needlessly massacring wildlife, making unnecessary noise and generally showing no respect for mother nature as a whole, aggravated me greatly. Though I detested the thoughtlessness of many fellow Canadians, I understood they had equal rights to the bounty of the land. On the other hand, my personal philosophy dictated if I amassed more wealth than my neighbors, allowing me to reach regions they couldn't afford or acquire property where they couldn't trespass, it was my inalienable rights. If blessed with good fortune, or possessed with the ability to make more money than others, I also had the prerogative of spending that wealth on that which pleased me under the law. So sitting around the campfire overlooking the sparkling lake, with no sound except the gab of my companions, chattering red squirrels or raucous cries of raven, I felt like a lucky man.

The following day would be the season opening and the three guides having never been near Grassy Lake before, were as unfamiliar with the country as the hunters, so they mutually agreed to scatter in three directions to look for moose sign and decide where to hunt in the morning. Don Mackenzie and I departed by canoe at midmorning on a five hour scouting mission. Don, though in his seventies, was equally adept at handling a canoe as his Ojibway cousins in Low Bush. We paddled up and down creeks and streams, around bays and inlets, then occasionally beached our craft and walked the woods. Not a sign of moose could be found anywhere and by mid afternoon we headed back for camp. A half mile from our bivouac as it began to rain, Don suggested I throw a line in the water and see if we could catch fish for supper. Within twenty minutes I caught six walleys ranging from two to four pounds and a five pound Northern Pike. Lorne Lankin, one of our group and an ardent fisherman was standing on the bank watching me reel in fish after fish as promptly as I tossed out the lure. Lorne nearly went berserk before we reached shore, and without fishing gear of his own, asked to borrow mine. Within a hundred yards of our tent in pouring rain, Lorne caught a dozen fine pickerel and a ten pound Northern Pike. One of the guides cleaned and scaled the pike, filled it with onions, potatoes, carrots, added salt and pepper, wrapped it in tin foil, then wrapped it again in wet newspapers and buried it beneath an inch of dirt. He then lit a huge campfire over the cache and continued adding fuel until a pile of flowing embers baked the fish. A more palatable dinner was never prepared, and the walleyes were delicious also.

Similar to Don and I, the other guides didn't locate one fresh moose track throughout their travels either, and between the three, had covered an immense territory over the course of the day. Having no means of communicating with Temagami Airways or anyone else for that matter, and no method of travel other than by canoe, we were in fact marooned until the scheduled arrival of Dave McConnell in seven days. As afternoon waned, the mood in camp became ugly. Guides and hunters paced around the encampment, drinks in hand cursing the colossal gall of Temagami Airways sending us into this barren land on a fools errand. Suddenly the drone of an approaching Cessna halted the babble. Several of the boys jumped onto a ledge of rock in the hope of attracting the pilot's attention, but needn't have bothered as the light aircraft landed on Grassy Lake a half mile from our camp. Two guides leaped into a canoe, frantically paddled to the plane and persuaded the pilot to taxi over for a palaver. Like squawking geese, our group finally got the point across to the pilot who was from GowGanda to phone Temagami Airways, explain our predicament and demand Dave return to Grassy Lake bright and early to transfer us into moose-country. Fortunately the next morning, though cloudy and cold, was suitable flying weather and Dave arrived before 10 a.m. He hadn't deplaned before facing a barrage of abusive language which continued throughout the day. First he had to fly to Gogama and change dropping permits then make two trips for each party to their new locations. He loaded two men with some gear on the first, then one man, canoe and the balance of equipment on the second. I remained at Grassy Lake until the final trip around 4 p.m. While loading food and paraphernalia, Dave explained the three parties were now separated by twenty miles of barren terrain and our location at Lake Muskacenda had an old lumber camp where Don Mackenzie and Hank were already cozily settled in.

"I've never experienced such an ordeal." Dave moaned, "What with everyone grousing, they won't pay for the move, and bellyaching because they lost the first day of the hunt." "Christ, it isn't my fault, I don't own the airway." He grumbled. "I don't understand it, we were assured from a reliable source this was an excellent moose hunting location." Dave taxied across the lake, whirled around and took off into the stiff breeze flying directly over our disbanded encampment.

In a tiny meadow surrounded by evergreens no more than a hundred yards from where the tents sat, an enormous bull moose with a fine looking cow stood watching as we passed a hundred feet over their upturned heads. We stared back in utter disbelief.

"Dave!" I screamed, "Turn back for Christ sake, I've got my gun!"

"Not on your life buddy," Dave replied. "Those can't be moose because there are none in the area remember, and also we don't have a dropping permit for Grassy Lake."

Those two stupid animals cost our group a pile of money as we couldn't refuse to pay for the transfer on the basis there wasn't a moose within miles as we claimed.

Hank and Don huddled beside a roaring fire in an old stove left inside the log cabin which was nestled by Lake Muskacenda, our new headquarters, and were absolutely stunned by the news of two moose almost trampling our previous campsite. The plummeting temperature and a driving snowstorm made us appreciate the comfort of the log cabin rather than shivering in tents like the other two parties. Awakening in the morning to three inches of snow on the ground plus a thin layer of ice on shallow bays, gave ample indication of the swift approach of winter. Nevertheless, the three of us left camp in the fourteen foot canoe and went exploring for several hours. With three paddlers, the small canoe covered a lot of territory in a short time and about five miles from camp, we located a large marshy bay at the mouth of a narrow stream. It looked ideal as a moose hangout. Lumber companies had dammed main outlets of the lake, raising the water level several feet, making it difficult to discern moose sign along the banks. It appeared to be prime moose territory, however, so we returned to camp for warmth, sustenance, and to prepare for the evening hunt. Returning to the bay at 4 p.m. and silently paddling a hundred yards off the heavily treed shoreline, I was jarred out of my reverie by a nearby moose bellow. Wheeling around with my Winchester to my shoulder, and noticing Hank in the same mode, I saw for a fleeting second the head and antlers of a large bull before he whirled and went crashing through the woods in full retreat. Don, though quite deaf, heard and saw the animal and quickly whispered loudly, "Don't shoot." Paddling furiously in the opposite direction from that of the fleeing bull until he reached the creek mouth where he stopped, grabbed his moose horn and gave a long cow call. "Listen carefully boys." Don ordered. Within a minute he called again. Suddenly, though a long way in the distance, I heard the sound of breaking branches. "He's coming!" I yelled excitedly. Crashing through the woods directly towards us and sounding like a ten ton truck, came our moose. Don quickly moved the canoe back around the point of land into the open bay giving us a clear view of the entire shoreline. Making another cow call toward the opposite side of the inlet, Don warned, "Get ready! He'll plunge through those trees ahead of us and dive into the bay." The bull exploded from the heavy underbrush exactly where Don had pointed and before he hit the water both rifles spit death. Though less than a hundred yards away, the bobbing, swaying 14' craft made accurate shooting impossible. After swimming twenty yards, the wounded bull turned and struggling back to shore clambered up the bank when two more bullets struck him in the region of the heart and the huge beast died before he hit the ground. It had been an unbelievable example of an expert moose caller and we congratulated Don on his ability as he obviously was the hero of the victory. It required all the next day to butcher the carcass and canoe the meat back to our cabin, and we were a proud and happy trio. Although we had two licenses, the big bull would provide ample meat for the two of us and we couldn't hunt for our cohorts as we had no idea whether they had bagged their own game.

As it would be four more days before Dave's arrival, Hank decided to try and fulfill his lifelong ambition to shoot a wild black bear. On every deer and moose hunt since I'd been associated with Hank, he carted along a bag of fish for bear bait which he hung in trees a half mile from camp. Bear season paralleled deer and moose, and a large population of these mammals inhabited most of the terrain we hunted and many were bagged by his companions. Hank shot his share of game, but seemed jinxed with bear having never drawn a bead on one in the wilds. I had numerous opportunities over the years and sighted several down my rifle barrel, but having no desire for the meat, never pulled the trigger. Hank felt certain his luck would change at Lake Muskacenda because Don pointed to numerous signs and Hank not only had distributed sacks of fish plus entrails from the moose, but would also be free for three days to devote all his energy to the task.

Improved weather with soaring temperature soon melted most of the snow. Don and I explored by canoe for hours and fished successfully both for leisure and the frying pan. Late one balmy afternoon, entering the bay where our animal had been shot, I heard a tremendous moose call from a hill a full mile to our left.

"Did you hear that bellow?" I asked Don.

"Yes." The old Indian replied, "Let's paddle over, beach the canoe, and I'll see if I can call him down."

A clearing, long and narrow, probably an old bush road, hugged the lake where we landed our canoe, and a dense cedar swamp lay between the opening and the hill where I'd heard the ear splitting bull moose call. Don gave a long, loud bull wail on his horn and got an immediate response. A few seconds later, the animal raced toward us like a roaring tornado, issuing loud snorts and grunts as he charged. Standing behind a large white pine, trembling with anticipation of the titanic beast bursting through the cedars a few feet from my ambush, I wished either I had a more powerful firearm or that Mackenzie carried a rifle, but he like Dave Black, travelled only with a knife. The rushing beast smashed trees and brush until he reached a distance no further than two hundred feet from where I stood, then for no apparent reason, stopped and gave vent to the most powerful, frightening blast I've ever heard before, or since from any animal in the wilds. Don responded with a repeat of his earlier call and the bull again replied with a thunderous roar that shook the earth and echoed and re-echoed across the Muskacenda. Regardless of the bull moose's obvious fury, he came no closer. Ten minutes elapsed while Don tried other calls attempting to entice the animal into the opening. Not only now was there complete silence from the bull, but I never even heard the cracking of a twig. Suddenly from the ridge a half mile away, the animal again bawled a warning and I'll never understand how he left the cedar swamp in complete silence. Don leading me through the dense thicket of cedar bushes gave his interpretation of the episode.

"He huge bull with massive horns and also has cow on hill. He willing to fight, but only if necessary because with wide antlers, can't maneuver good in heavy bush, so when no challenge from other bull, he return to his mate."

Don's explanation made sense when we reached the spot where the big moose issued his warning. Turf was torn a foot deep where he pawed in his rage and scarred saplings attested to the height and spread of his antlers.

"Bill, I only met a mad moose like him once before in my life." Don said as we climbed back into the canoe, "While tearing up the ground with his hooves, his head lowered and swaying back and forth, he makes that ear splitting roar from the back of his throat."

Dave Black in Low Bush no doubt was good and could communicate with moose, but Don Mackenzie actually talked to them. Blessed with a calm unseasonably warm moonlit evening, we paddled the canoe up and down the creek and around the bay for several hours. Don called three more animals within two hundred yards of the shoreline and enticed two bulls into a fight as we distinctly heard the clash of horns and severe grunting until one fled the battle ground. Returning to camp, I couldn't wait to relate the episode to Hank, who listened patiently. "What time did your bull make those calls?" Hank inquired.

"About 5:30." I replied.

"Then, believe it or not, though five miles away, I heard him," Hank said in disbelief. "I thought it was a train until realizing there is no railroad within thirty miles, I simply couldn't figure what produced such a racket."

"Hank, I'm not disappointed that bastard never came out of the cedars, we don't need more meat, and I wasn't anxious to take him on at fifty feet with my .32 Winchester," I said, closing the subject.

Meanwhile, Hank hadn't seen a bear, but figured it was only a matter of time as one bruin had torn a sack of fish from the tree where he had it wired. Then his quarry came closer. The next morning, a sugar bag containing our pork chops, steak and bacon which had been hanging on a nail outside our cabin was missing, and closer inspection indicated while we slept, Hank's bear paid a visit and stole our provisions. Fortunately, while clawing it off the wall, he ripped the sack, allowing a pound of bacon to fall through the tear which was sufficient for our breakfast, while moose meat would suffice for other meals, but my hunting partner had been thoroughly insulted. He filled a sizeable cardboard carton with empty tin cans wired together, and stuffed with fish and moose entrails, then placed the bait a hundred feet from the cabin door. Hank reckoned when the bruin returned during the night, he would make such a clamor we would have to be awakened, and he glowed about his chances. When it got dark, he had me race to the door several times to snap on the strong beam of the flashlight so he could practice his strategy. Shortly after retiring, we experienced one genuine thrill when a rustling convinced us his prey had reached the trap. Springing to action stations, we were disappointed with no sign of bear. Sitting back on our bunks a little bewildered, we soon ascertained the cause of the false alarm. A field mouse having discovered our cheese wrapped in wax paper was the noise causing culprit, so we returned to our sleeping bags. Disillusioned the next morning when Mister Bruin hadn't returned, Hank decided to join Don and I for a few hours in the canoe. He reckoned either to get his prey in late afternoon at his set up in the woods, or shoot the animal at his booby trap by the camp that night. Though in either case it would be his final opportunity, as Dave was scheduled to arrive the following morning. Returning to our cabin after a few hours on the lake, we were astonished to be greeted by four men who had driven in a four-wheeled drive Land Rover from Timmins, a large mining town, forty miles north for a weekend moose hunt. We were mortified to realize these individuals had driven two hours over bush roads by land vehicles at a cost of a few dollars, while we invested hundreds to fly into a region supposedly inaccessible to other hunters. They were happy-go-lucky French Canadians and after admiring our trophy moose, pouring a drink all around and teasing us about our cost of reaching the so-called exclusive territory, one of the boys called André said, "You lucky fellows by gar, but if not for hus, maybe you don' 'ave such good luck." The four were obviously enjoying a huge joke.

"What the hell is so funny?" I inquired.

"We came 'ere cause we 'ave used dis camp before." André responded. "When we pull up in front of your door, one huge son-a-bitch black bear raising hell inside de cabin. I shoot 'im when 'ees come out."

Sure enough, the bear Hank spent four days luring to within shooting range, and which came within five feet of sitting on his bunk, was lying dead two hundred feet from the cabin.

Hank, disappointed about the bruin episode and both a little disillusioned when learning we could have reached Muskacenda with a four-wheeled drive, we agreed, nevertheless, it had been an exciting and exceedingly fortunate week of hunting for several reasons: We bagged the only game; unquestionably had the superior guide, and our log cabin accommodation outclassed our cohorts' tents like a rooming house to the Waldorf Astoria. Perhaps my relationship with Dave McConnell was our ace in the hole.

The incident of the Timmins' hunters reaching our fly-in camp, induced Hank and I to re-examine Lake Abitibi for 1958. After buying topographic maps of the entire region, we discovered a new secondary road had been constructed which spurred east off the main highway at Matheson, and ran south of the giant lake crossing the Ghost River, a narrow stream which wound several miles through marshy terrain before reaching an entirely different section of Lake Abitibi. Joyce and I owned a fifteen foot cruiser with full centre deck, steering wheel and controls which I operated with an 18 h.p. Johnson Outboard. With a wide beam and tremendous depth, it provided safety, comfort and could haul quite a load, so we elected to take my launch and tow the sponson for hunting. Upon reaching the Ghost, we were startled to find three dozen other vehicles parked beside the waterway, signifying we weren't the only hunters to know of the new route. Our disappointment was short lived, however, as threading our way along the winding river we found most hunters tented along the banks of the stream, rather than tackle crossing the huge lake. We headed for a large clearly marked marsh fifteen miles across a section of the Abitibi thoroughly unfamiliar to us where our topographic map indicated there was also an old log cabin. Though the lake was choppy, we made good time in beautiful autumn weather and about five miles from our destination, spied another outfit away to our left, obviously heading toward the same marsh. Whoever reached the shack first would claim possession, and though a tight finish, we won the race and already had several cartons of provisions in the old log cabin when the other boat came roaring into the bay. Racing up to the camp, two brothers from Kitchener, a city forty miles west of Toronto, insisted it should be their accommodation because they'd used it the previous two seasons. Offering the boys a drink and commiserating with them for being a minute late, we nevertheless patiently explained the old adage of possession being nine tenths of the law, after which we bade them adieu. Not being any match physically, the brothers had little choice but leave. They informed us, however, they were setting up a tent at the opposite end of the colossal marsh, and we'd be competing for the same animals. The season opened the next morning and Hank and I were in the swamp before daylight. A sluggish stream snaked through cattails and marsh grass with various sized bays ballooning off the creek. Some of these inlets interconnected with other bays which eventually dead ended. Exploring one of these chain like waterways at daybreak, the unexpected call of a cow moose deep in the centre of the enormous swamp followed immediately by the bawl of a calf, spurred us into a flurry of activity. Our bull moose meat of previous years had been excellent, but calf meat was considered a delicacy and hunting for meat rather than trophies made us both anxious to return with a yearling. Paddling frantically back into and along the main stream towards the sound of the calls, we couldn't see over the tall reeds and grasses from our seats low in the canoe, so spotting a dead cedar jutting out of the bog, I suggested we use it as a support, allowing me to stand up in the wobbly canoe. Pulling myself cautiously into an upright position, I almost fell overboard when less than a hundred yards stood a magnificent bull staring directly at me.

"Christ, Hank." I whispered, "You won't believe it, but a gigantic bull moose is peering at me that I could hit with a sling shot."

"Sit down and let me have a look." Hank stammered.

The gigantic beast never flinched, just stood and glared at us. Because he wallowed in marsh at least a mile from high ground, we decided not to shoot, as butchering three quarters of a ton of moose in that location would be next to impossible. After ogling each other for five minutes, the bull turned and in a fast trot, headed toward the tree line. Paddling furiously, we tried to get in position to shoot when our quarry neared the fringe of the swamp. Rounding a bend in the creek, we reached a wider expanse of open water and our bull galloping through the quagmire at a rapid pace 150 yards on our left, was in full view. It appeared we would get clear shooting and the animal should be in range when he reached high ground. Suddenly in the midst of the exciting chase, a barrage of rifle shots shattered the early morning stillness. To our complete surprise and amazement, the Kitchener boys standing atop a beaver house two hundred yards on our right, were firing over our heads at the fleeing animal. This blatant interference in shooting at a moose we clearly were chasing, plus the realization they'd hit and downed the bull, completely infuriated us, so we paddled over to the wounded beast with the intention of finishing him off and claiming the prize. Approaching the edge of the creek where the stricken moose lay thrashing in the cattails, another dead cedar again allowed Hank to steady the canoe while I stood and surveyed the scene. Not only the wounded bull was visible at less than a hundred feet, but within a hundred yards stood the cow and calf. Hank jumped up excitedly and we both began firing from the 12 foot sponson. Not only impossible to retain ones balance, it was like shooting from a bucking bronco, and bullets exploded all over the marsh. After loading and reloading several times, we finally knocked down both animals, but not before firing nearly forty shots, which together with the Kitchener boys' barrage must have made it sound to anyone within earshot like the opening of the second front on D-Day. Our joy at bagging the cow and calf cooled our beligerence toward the pair of brothers, though we bawled hell out of them and made it abundantly clear if we hadn't killed the cow and calf, they would have had one bitch of a battle claiming the bull. Butchering the animals in two feet of water while standing in hip waders, then wrestling the carcasses into our small canoe and paddling the half ton of meat back to the cabin, was a strenuous, time consuming chore, but it was opening day and being in no panic to return to the city, we took our time. Also the lake buffeted by high winds was in a turmoil. Our boat much more stable than the portage canoe offered some comfort, but by the time we loaded our meat aboard, both vessels would be sitting quite low in the water. During the few days we waited for the weather to calm, a number of sizeable craft from cruisers to house boats came into the enormous marsh in search of game. It soon became apparent we were damn lucky bagging our moose opening morning because from that point forward we would have faced fierce competition. Once again the influx of other hunters made it obvious if we wanted privacy we would no longer find it at the Abitibi. New roads constructed into what had been unreachable territory, plus new high powered outboard motors that could drive large craft great distances and which were also ideal for accommodation allowing individuals to anchor in the heart of hunting areas and wait for animals to come to them, meant our method of hunting was now out-moded. So, for the final time we crossed Lake Abitibi and were blessed with a serene, though bitter cold morning as the thermometer had dropped to near zero. Icicles decorated our equipment and during the torturous, slow journey due to our heavy load of meat, the two of us nearly froze to death before reaching the mouth of the Ghost River where a benevolent moose camp operator allowed us to thaw out while pouring hot coffee into our chilled bodies. Although we again arrived home with meat and agreed our deer and moose hunting expeditions were usually enjoyable, the increasing difficulty in finding solitude and privacy removed some of the pleasure, so we were constantly on the lookout for a secluded territory inaccessible to the general public.

Another example of a new road causing the disappearance of what certain individuals considered their own private preserve, occurred during the spring of 1958 on a trout fishing jaunt. Les Knox, a chap I'd met in '53 at Coronet T.V., who subsequently worked for me both in television and at Homeland Realty Ltd., had remained a good friend. He and another excellent salesman, Bob Taylor, who also worked for Homeland, joined forces under the name Knox and Taylor Real Estate Ltd. and were doing exceptionally well. Les, an enthusiastic trout fisherman, invited me to join him, his brother Huey and Bob Taylor for the opening of the season at Fletcher Lake, Les's favorite trout waters. Motoring to Dorset 140 miles north of Toronto, Les explained since his last visit in May of '57, the local municipality had constructed a secondary gravel road to the lake. "In the past," Les said, "we parked our car at Dorset where the farmer who operates the lodge met us with horses and wagon to transport our group the ten agonizing miles to his home, because the trail was unusable by any type of motor vehicle." Les continued, "However, with the new road, the farmer is meeting us at the bottom of Fletcher with a boat and motor, so it will be much more pleasant this year." Or so he thought.

Being the last day of April and a late spring, the snow hadn't completely vanished from the deep bush and the new thoroughfare was rutted and slippery. Nearing the lake, the boys were flabbergasted when dozens of cars and trucks lined each side of the narrow trail, making it almost impossible to find a parking spot. Ben Johnson, our host, waiting for us in his old boat and motor, looked anything but ecstatic. Old campfires surrounded by empty beer and whiskey cartons, bottles, cans, cigarette packages, and other trash, had transformed what clearly had been a picturesque setting into an abandoned garbage dump. What might have been a serenic tableau, instead buzzed with a hodge podge of noise and activity. Boats whizzed around the lake, their occupants shouting and laughing, entirely unlike the usual trout fishing scene where avid anglers converse in subdued whispers and paddle silently while casting their lures towards the shoreline. We enjoyed a pleasant and rewarding few days only because a small lake a half mile and a couple of hills over from Fletcher, and teeming with fish had not yet been discovered by the hordes. Conversation between the Johnsons and my companions invariably revolved around the opening of the new road and the future of Fletcher Lake as a trout fishing haven. They were a sad and disheartened group. While loading our belongings into Johnson's boat for our departure, a seaplane landed, taxied over and discharged four Cleveland doctors with their fishing gear. Gazing around the lake where outboards and craft of every description still disturbed the natural tranquility, one of the new arrivals with a look of horror asked in an incredulous tone, "What the hell is going on Ben?" Ben Johnson explained how delighted he and his wife were when first learning of the construction of the new road as it made travelling to Dorset much simpler, however, he admitted their joy was short lived as the past few days proved easy access had turned their peaceful Shangri-la into a carnival.

"Ben," the doctor stated sadly, "we've been coming here for nearly a quarter of a century, but if that scene out there on our beloved Fletcher is an indication of the lake's future, we will have no alternative but to fly a few miles further over a few more hills where roads haven't yet been constructed."

My experiences while searching for privacy and constantly being disturbed by individuals with as much right to the territory as I, irritated me exactly in the same manner as the American doctors were annoyed by the sudden transformation of Fletcher Lake. Though regrettable, there was damned all anyone could do about the situation. Sort of like listening to the quiet strains of a Viennese Waltz, when suddenly someone switches the dial to a blast of rock and roll.

Progress means change, and generally most people profit from advancement, but when it greatly upsets our own little world, we get our shackles up, particularly when there isn't a damn thing we can do to retain the status quo. These aggravating incidents had a profound effect on my thinking and when the opportunity presented itself, I took advantage and embarked on a colossal venture where privacy became the entire soul of the endeavor. Though I readily admit the day my parents, Elmer Aldred, Bill Morrow and I headed into the depths of the Haliburton Highlands to investigate Elmer's 700 acres of wilderness, I never imagined it would be chapter one of that undertaking.

From the dark days following the collapse of Plastics Plating Ltd. in December 1955, until our sojourn into Elmer Aldred's acreage in October 1958, numerous changes in our lifestyle had taken place. Steve Theodoru joined the Masons in the early fifties and rapidly earned his degrees to become a Shriner. Having never forgotten my promise to Miss McClaren when discharged from the Shriner's Hospital to repay the benevolence shown me by that group of dedicated men, I asked Steve to sponsor me into freemasonry, and became a Master Mason in 1954 with Coronati as my mother lodge. I advanced to the Shrine by way of the York Right, and in May 1956, became the first Canadian patient from a Shriner's hospital to join the elite fraternity of men known as the Ancient Arabic Order of Nobles of the Mystic Shrine. With the red fez and silky black tassle perched jauntily on my head, not only did I sense great pride because of fulfilling a solemn obligation, but knew I had joined the greatest philanthropy on earth, though it would be a few years before attaining a position to partially repay the enormous benefits I received from the Shriners twenty years before.

The period from January '56 to late '58 witnessed great changes sweep across not only North America, but several other sectors of the world as well. Certainly the enormous movement in the United States to improve the lot of the blacks captured the attention of peoples in all nations. In 1954, the Supreme Court handed down a landmark decision when they declared unanimously that racial segregation in public schools was unconstitutional and all states were ordered to proceed "with all deliberate speed" to integrate educational facilities. Although repercussions reverberated through the nation for a quarter century as the edict was gradually enforced, nonetheless, it provided the blacks with their first major step towards equality since the Civil War. In 1956, Martin Luther King, Jr. who organized a black boycott of public transportation in Montgomery, Alabama as a protest against racial discrimination, was a name soon to become synonymous in the black's struggle.

Nuclear power swiftly gained prominence during the era as the first submarine driven by nuclear fission was launched in 1954, the same year as the first nuclear power station to produce electricity, opened in Russia a few miles outside of Moscow. In 1956 the Soviet Union launched Sputnik I and Sputnik II, the world's first man-made earth satellites and the battle for the heavens began.

Several other discoveries in that span of three years produced electrifying results. One in particular came a quarter of a century too late for me as the first polio immunization shots were administered in 1954. Later that year, dramatic evidence of the danger of smoking were presented by U.S. epidemiologists who claimed a high percentage of coronary heart disease and cancer deaths were caused by that unhealthy habit. I smoked three packets per day, plus cigars and occasionally a pipe. A new oral contraceptive known as "the pill" became available in 1955 and who knows if this new method of planned parenthood had been available two years earlier, whether our daughter Sherree would have made the scene. Also the American Express Card came into existence and plastic money swiftly replaced cash as a means of paying bills.

World turmoil didn't diminish during the mid fifties as major disputes erupted all over the globe. Civil war broke out in Vietnam. Polish workers rioted to protest social and economic conditions under the Communist regime and Polish troops were called in to quell the disorder, but not before 100 demonstrators were killed. Hungarian students encouraged by the situation in Poland, congregated in a rally of 100,000 and demanded democratic government. After a chaotic ten days in Budapest when the nation almost regained its freedom from the Communistic yolk, the defiance was crushed by 16 Soviet divisions supported by 2000 tanks. Hungarian freedom fighters pleaded for western assistance in their unequal struggle, but unfortunately were denied succor and Poland and Hungary remained satellite nations and puppets of Moscow. Russian's premier Nikita Kruschchev then warned western ambassadors, "History is on our side!" "We will bury you!" In the Middle East in 1956, a major conflict exploded when Egypt's President Nassar refused to renew the Suez Canal Company's claim to the vital canal. Britain and France sent in troops to regain control of the indispensable waterway, but with world opinion against them (including Canada and the United States), the two countries accepted a cease fire, agreed to a United Nations force to police the area and the famous Suez Canal remained in Egyptian hands. At the same time, Israel withdrew her troops from the Gaza Strip and Gulf of Agaba, leaving the U.N. Emergency Force to administer the troubled region, but it was only a short term solution to a long term problem.

Throughout this three year potpourri of personal business fluctuations and universal turmoil, our recreational activities also dramatically altered course. No longer did we go to dances surrounded by local thugs, but instead attended Masonic or Shriner's functions where alcoholic beverages still flowed, but we were amidst more congenial company.

Although the old rhythms and romantic ballads still predominated the top ten music charts during the mid fifties, rock 'n' roll was rapidly taking over. Such songs as: Alleghany Moon, Around the World in 80 Days, Bells are Ringing, Blueberry Hill, I Could Have Danced All Night, Whatever Will Be Will Be. Young Love and Mack the Knife had stiff competition from rock 'n' roll favorites like Elvis Presley's: Blue Suede Shoes, All Shook Up, and Hound Dog, plus other artist's hits such as Be-Bop Baby, Whole Lot-ta Shakin' Going On and The Purple People Eater. After the advent of rock 'n' roll, the air waves were never the same again as the music trend veered wildly toward loud noise and a heavily accented beat. As usual, we lived in rapidly changing times and in the autumn of 1958, heading for new adventure in my greatest personal gamble to date, not only did I again swerve into a completely new arena of endeavor, but was also accompanied by a rhythm of a different age.

Chapter 6

Harcourt Park

Blessed with a perfect autumn day, Mom, Pop and I rendezvoused with Bill Morrow and Elmer Aldred in Peterboro for our journey to Wilberforce, then continued on into the backwoods to view the lake frontage and seven hundred acres owned by Aldred. Elmer's battered old 1948 Chev. Sedan operated smoothly on the highway, which was surprising because he ramrodded it over the bush trails like a four-wheel drive.

Wilberforce, Ontario, a little town with a population of three hundred, boasted one main industry, Wilberforce Lumber and Veneer Ltd., the only major employer for a radius of fifty miles. The company owned eighteen thousand acres of forests which supplied their veneer mills, and it was through this land we had to travel at least eight miles to reach Elmer Aldred's property.

The initial six miles, known as the Burleigh Road, was one of the first trails used by pioneers when large European land companies purchased vast acreages and shipped in immigrants during the middle 19th century to settle their holdings. The Federal Government considered using the Burleigh to send troops from Ontario and Quebec through to Manitoba to quell the Riel Rebellion in the 1880's. Bouncing along over protruding rocks and through mud holes, I could readily understand why the plan to transport the army over this route didn't materialize as they would have faced about 1200 miles of similar terrain. After six miles, the Burleigh Road disintegrated into a barely discernible path, but another road called the Kennaway Trail branched off to the right. The Kennaway opened up the country south of gigantic Algonquin Park at the turn of the present century and had been used exclusively by lumbermen, except for the occasional rugged outdoorsman with a four-wheel drive vehicle who fought his way back into the harsh country for the excellent hunting and fishing. Some doubt existed, in fact, whether these roads were public or private, and I made it clear to Aldred that proof of unrestricted access into his acreage would be essential. He assured me old-timers in the area would vouch that public funds had been used for their maintenance in the past, establishing them as public domain.

Somehow Elmer managed to bump his car through or around the numerous obstacles until we reached the Burleigh-Kennaway corners where he suggested we walk the balance of the way. It had been 17 years since Elmer lumbered the property, and so he had little idea of conditions ahead. Plodding along the Kennaway Trail, the folks and I were especially enchanted with the variety of growth covering the rocky, hilly land. In western Canada it would be unusual to find more than four or five types of trees in any given sector. Ontario, however, produced as many as three dozen different species on the same acre, contrasting in size from cherry trees with a diameter of less than an inch, to enormous beech, yellow birch and basswood that Dad and I with our arms fully outstretched and touching fingertip to fingertip still couldn't completely reach around their circumference. Many, such as basswood, beech, hemlock, ironwood, highland cedar and numerous others, were completely alien to us. Certain areas of the Haliburtons, including where we walked, had produced an abundance of white pine that had been almost entirely harvested for lumber a century before and were replaced by nature with hardwoods, except for small clusters of hemlock, balsam, and a few scraggly spruce.

After walking an hour or more, we reached a magnificent stand of virgin hemlock bordering a sparkling, pretty little lake approximately ¾ of a mile in length and ½ mile wide. Calling it Fitzgerald, Elmer proudly pointed out the excellent shoreline, explaining he owned every inch. Although picturesque, the size of the lake disappointed me and I said, "Christ, Elmer, this is a long way from Toronto for people to come and buy property on such a pond." Elmer, a unique individual, and an enjoyable conversationalist with a positive point of view on all subjects passed no comment, but he insisted we continue our journey because he wanted to show us some speckled trout spawning beds.

"Hold it." I said, "If Fitzgerald is the main lake on your property, then I want to look at shoreline."

Elmer, looking at me quizzically replied, "Bill, spawning speckled trout are a beautiful sight, and I don't want you to miss the spectacle."

"Look Elmer, we've come a long way and I want to inspect lake shore, not watch fish lay eggs," I responded, a little aggravated.

Paying no need to my request, Elmer proceeded slowly down the bush trail with Bill Morrow following, leaving little alternative for the folks and me but to tail along.

Another two-mile march over a trail partially overgrown with willows and small berry bushes, which probably hadn't seen more than a dozen vehicles since Elmer's departure, led us to a much larger lake. We had to struggle through an enormous entanglement of deadfalls to reach the shoreline, but nevertheless, I was impressed with the over-all beauty of this body of water. Elmer said it used to be called Cross Lake but had been officially changed to Allen by the Department of Lands and Forests. Considerably larger than Fitzgerald, it stretched two miles in length, nearly a mile in width, displayed a beautiful sandy shoreline, and with bays in four corners, resembled a giant X which explained its original name.

Enthusiastically I remarked, "Elmer, this is more like it. Is it included in your acreage?"

"Some of it." He replied. "But let's move on, I want to see if the speckled trout are spawning."

"For Gawd sake, Elmer, show me how much of this shoreline you own, then take Bill Morrow to look at the trout while I walk around the lake," I stormed.

"Go ahead and try it," he responded with a smirk.

About a hundred yards of climbing over criss-crossed dead trees and debris that had accumulated since the beginning of time without any type of path was painstakingly slow, and so conceding defeat, I joined the others.

We continued around a couple of major hills to another bay on Allen Lake where Elmer stated all the shoreline we'd skirted was included in his 700-acre parcel. An old camp—Aldred's headquarters while lumbering—nestled in a grove of hardwoods—appeared suitable for a temporary shelter if we bought the tract. My interest mounted in the beautiful though exceedingly rugged property except for my concern about its distance from the highway, which would be a major stumbling block in attracting prospective purchasers.

Elmer persisted on visiting yet another lake to see the speckled trout spawn, and in spite of the fact the rapidly sinking sun guaranteed our return to his car would be partly in the dark, we followed him over a narrow portage trail and across a couple of more hills to a small lake called East. Peering into the placid water, we were rewarded with one of the most fascinating sights to be witnessed in the wilds. At the lake edge and two inches below the surface, dozens of enormous speckled trout lay almost motionless. Two- or three-pound speckleds are usually considered sizable trout, but these were in the seven- to ten-pound range. In complete amazement, I shot one with the shotgun I'd carried.

Though trout fishing was out of season, I was determined to take one of those monsters back to the city. Then to our complete astonishment, Father squatting on his haunches cautiously slipped his hand under one's belly and flipped a six-pounder onto the shore.

Sitting in that tranquil setting, awed by the spectacular panorama, and fascinated by the egg-laying, beautifully colored trout, I recalled Fletcher Lake and tried to visualize this area a few weeks after a road opened up the unbelievable paradise to just anyone. The scene that flashed across my mind wasn't pleasant. The unthinking general public with no investment would deplete a small lake like East of fish within one season and completely desecrate the property as well. Explaining my concern to the others, I told Bill Morrow that unless substantially more land was available other than what Elmer owned and if there wasn't some legal method of keeping out the non-investors I wouldn't be interested.

During the long jaunt back to Peterboro, we chatted about the possibility of developing a large tract of land in some way to keep it private, but no one had any idea what would be entailed in such a venture. Traveling home, the folks and I discussed the liability of Elmer's property because it was such a long way from Toronto, our principal market, and wondered whether Toronto families would travel 140 miles into the area for their exclusive enjoyment. We concluded it should be a good gamble. Joyce cooked up my trout at midnight, and though I could visualize many difficulties, I'd almost decided if sufficient acreage could be accumulated and a method found to retain its seclusion, I would attempt to transform the captivating terrain into an enormous private park and hope to convince prospective customers the area's attributes were worth the extra driving time.

The fact that Aldred's holdings were situated in Harcourt Township in the municipality of Dysart et al played an important role in our plans. Different methods of subdividing townships were used in eastern and western Canada. In the west a township comprised 36 sections. Each section a mile square and containing 640 acres was bounded by a 66-foot public right-of-way which assured access for construction of roads. In the east, townships were divided into 1000-acre parcels a mile and a quarter square bounded by 66-foot public right-of-ways. Each square in the east consisted of ten 100 acre lots a quarter of a mile wide and five eighths of a mile long.

Municipalities in both parts of the country consisted of varying numbers of townships depending on the density of population. If a township contained sufficient taxpayers to justify municipal government, then one township could constitute a municipality. In the rural agricultural sectors of western Canada with the land mostly inhabited by farmers, numerous townships were generally incorporated into each municipality, while in Ontario single townships frequently formed a municipality. In the Haliburtons, where Elmer's land was situated, however, the sparse population dictated that nine townships including Harcourt Township be incorporated in the municipality of Dysart et al.

Shortly after our tour of the 700-acre tract, Herb Mason, Bill Morrow's broker, came to see me with a Harcourt Township map showing the ownership of every 100-acre lot surrounding Aldred's property. J. J. White, a rubber manufacturer in Cleveland, Ohio, owned massive acreage immediately north of Elmer's and stretching to the southern extension of Algonquin Park. White agreed to sell 1200 acres adjacent to Aldred's land with water frontage on Fishtail Lake, the largest single body of water in Harcourt Township. His tract also included most of East Lake, where the whole idea had begun to take shape, plus 90 percent of McRae's, another picturesque little lake similar to Fitzgerald. The balance of White's property containing marketable timber but no lake shore, was not important to my plans. Stanley Mann, a Toronto real estate broker residing in Florida, owned 800 acres including the major portion of Allen Lake not encompassed in Elmer's tract. Herb Mason flew to Florida to see Mann, who agreed to sell the 400 acres which included all his Allen Lake frontage.

White's, Mann's, and Aldred's contracts were each contingent on the acquisition of all three parcels and also in having an accessible route to the perimeter of the properties. The three deals scheduled to close in the spring of 1959 had a total purchase price of $46,000. Having sold my interest in Philrick Ltd. to Herb Richards, I bought the land in the name of Sumcot Investments Lmt., which I immediately changed to Sumcot Development Corporation Lmt. John Walsh and his brother Buzz controlled 50 percent of the company stock, and I owned the balance. After tentatively assembling the land, we began investigating some method of keeping private our 2300-acre tract that contained either all or part of seven bodies of water. John and I were directed to Colonel Stanley Nash, an executive director of the Provincial Department of Municipal Affairs, to discuss ways of developing land in a manner that would permit complete privacy.

Colonel Nash explained that although municipalities were in fact under the direct control of the Department of Municipal Affairs the development of property remained under the jurisdiction of Municipal Government unless they had adopted subdivision control. In those municipalities where subdivision control had been adopted, however, development plans had to be submitted to the Department of Municipal Affairs for distribution to all affected federal, provincial, or municipal agencies for approval. Final ratification could take from six months to six years depending on the complexities of the plan. Colonel Nash further explained if a municipality had adopted subdivision control, then the land could be leased for a term not exceeding twenty years and privacy maintained. In that case, all roads inside the development would be private responsibility and not maintained by the local municipality. There were many other ramifications, but that gave us the necessary information and now a great deal depended on whether Dysart et al had adopted subdivision control.

In the late 50's, property values in most urban centers skyrocketed, escalating beyond the reach of many would-be purchasers. This created a stampede for lands outside these cities due to the intense craving of most individuals for personal property ownership. As usual, this type of demand brought out of the woodwork, sharp and ruthless operators who frequently sold unsurveyed lots where proper legal descriptions were impossible to obtain. In several instances, crooks took deposits on land they didn't even own, then disappeared with the money. Newspapers contained reports of swindles plus articles constantly warning people of the danger of purchasing property before making a full investigation. As a result of these fraudulent practices, Dysart et al, with such a large area of responsibility, decided subdivision control was their best safeguard in regulating land development and so became one of the only municipal governments in Central Ontario to adopt that measure. Unfortunately, this meant to continue with our plans for a private park, the waterfront lots could only be offered to the public on the basis of a maximum twenty-year lease.

For an agonizing six months during the winter, John Walsh and I strived to design a concept that would protect the investment of our customers as well as guaranteeing the prime intent of creating a private park where only lease holders and their guests would be allowed to enter. Patience never a virtue of mine, was severely tested during the countless hours spent in painstaking research and meetings trying to determine a method of satisfying both major problems. The task became easier once we realized a second corporation had to be formed which would eventually be made up of the prospective lessees who would have a contractual agreement with Sumcot Development Limited. At first I intended calling the development Golden Trout Park. After some persuasion, however, I named it after the township where it would be located, and so it became known as Harcourt Park and the new corporation, Harcourt Park, Inc. Draft after draft of an acceptable format was designed, altered then redesigned until eventually we chose a setup which is best described by the wording in our initial brochure under the heading "WHY LEASES?"

Quote "We believe the parcel of land called Harcourt Park, consisting of 2300 acres with numerous lakes, creeks and rivers, abounding with fish and wildlife, must be kept for the private use of the maximum 200 families who will be investing their money in the development. With proper conservation control, these families, and their descendants for generations to come, will enjoy summer living unsurpassed by any of the many vacation spots in Ontario. We also believe that these lands, if opened to the public, would soon be overrun and become devoid of the many attractive features it now possesses, seriously detracting from its value to the families who are making it their permanent summer home.

"The Planning Act of Ontario provides that if lands are to be sub-divided, and deeds given, and we quote from the Act 'land to an amount determined by the minister, but not to exceed 5 percent of the land included in the plan shall be conveyed to the municipality for public purposes other than highways,' and the Act further provides that all roads must be public roads and open to the public at any time.

"In order to retain the land for private use so that it will not be open to the public, SUMCOT DEVELOPMENTS is selling leases for the lots which cannot exceed a term of twenty years. This provision is also contained in the Planning Act of Ontario.

"When all lots have been leased, or not later than May 31, 1969, Sumcot Development Corporation will transfer all lands and leases (as described in the bylaws) to Harcourt Park Inc. clear of encumbrance for the sum of $1.00. At the expiration of the leases, members, who would then be owners of the park including the leased lots, can decide whether to renew their leases for a further twenty year period or register a plan of subdivision and issue individual deeds.

"The bylaws further provide that any decision dealing with the leases must apply to all leases and be approved by 100 percent of the membership." Unquote.

We not only limited ourselves to leasing 200 lake-front parcels but also added a clause to Harcourt Park Inc.'s by-laws controlling the amount of guests each member could have at any given time. Lessees of each waterfront lot were limited, on their membership card, to their own immediate family including only children under the ages of 18 years of age. They also received two guest cards, each card admitting one adult or a complete family unit. All individuals while on the property had to carry their guest or membership card and could be challenged to produce it by any other member. This allowed policing by the members themselves. It guaranteed that only legitimate residents and their friends would be allowed into Harcourt Park. Besides the infinite amount of time required to put together the necessary legal documentation including leases, by-laws and an agreement between Sumcot Development Corp., Ltd., and Harcourt Park Inc. to insure our intentions would be carried through, we also had to travel the north country to locate old-timers who would swear with affidavits that the Burleigh and Kennaway Roads were public roads.

During the winter of '58, Central Ontario received record amounts of snow, and John and I found ourselves traveling highways lined with 8-foot snow banks. To locate Bill Curry, whose affidavit was considered consequential, we automobiled several miles over severe bush roads to contact him at his lumber camp. Jim Robinson, another man whose signature was deemed essential, worked for Curry Bishop, a Haliburton land surveyor. We were told by good authority that due to these men's knowledge of the country's history their signed affidavits would not be questioned, and would remove any doubt about the disputed status of the two old trails. As a result of acquiring both signatures, we felt confident no one would question our right to use the access roads.

On one of our winter journeys into Wilberforce, we met three men who operated a small lumber mill beside the Burleigh Road a hundred yards off the main highway that ran through town. Keith Cameron, a long-time resident of the village, offered to provide whatever laboring help we would require at $1.25 per hour plus an hourly fee for chainsaws, horses or whatever equipment we rented. Cameron's two partners were Jack and Murray Linkart. Murray, who had just retired from the Canadian Air Force as a jet pilot, seemed like a real fireball, and he and his brother Jack wanted the opportunity to provide a loader, small crawler, trucks, and other equipment for lot clearing and road construction. Delighted with their enthusiasm, I said they would be contacted when the snow disappeared.

In early spring I received a call from an excited Keith Cameron, informing me that the township of Dysart had just passed a by-law closing the Burleigh Road to the public. Jack Wallace and Harold Hurlahey, the two principals of Wilberforce Lumber and Veneer who had pleaded with the municipality to close it for several years, were spurred into action by news of our impending plans. As two of the most influential men in the area, they carried a lot of weight with the local council, who finally acceded to their demands. We had not closed our deals and, therefore, weren't the registered owners, so I contacted Herb Mason in Peterborough about the dilemma, and he passed the news to Aldred, White, and Mann.

Ontario Municipal Law requires that an ordinance such as closing public right-of-ways has to be advertised in local papers and posted in public places for thirty days. If sufficient objections are raised, the impending statute is thrown out. Many local people were unhappy with the prospect of the Burleigh Road being closed and joined my sellers in protest. They raised sufficient hullabaloo to squelch the by-law. I didn't know it at the time, but Hurlahey and Wallace in a rage at their failure in having the roads closed blamed me exclusively for their defeat. As owners of a huge acreage surrounding the route, they greatly feared the ravages of forest fires caused by careless city people driving through their property, which would be a disaster to their industry. Jack Wallace also detested our moving into the area, because of the competition he would suddenly face in the local labor market. Cameron had been inquiring in town and the surrounding neighborhood for men available to work for Sumcot once we opened in the spring, and several who were employed by Wilberforce Lumber and Veneer, had accepted his offer of $1.25 an hour, which topped their mill wages by 40 cents per hour. We had no option but to pay higher rates because the men were forced to travel ten miles over horrible roads without any travel allowance.

During the spring and summer of 1958, I had been taking flying lessons out of the Toronto Island Flying School to get my private pilot's license. I soloed in late summer, and during the winter, I made two cross-country trips to Wilberforce to inspect our newly acquired possessions from the air. On one flight with Dad and Howard Tustin, my flight instructor, unfamiliar with the topography, almost crashed. Flying a few feet above the surface of Allen to examine the lake shore, we underestimated the height of a steep incline at the south end of the lake and barely had room to gain sufficient altitude to clear trees at the crest of the hill. On the second journey with John Walsh and Tustin as passengers, we got lost due to severe cloudiness. Each time we dropped below the cloud cover to get our bearings, our Cessna was dangerously close to hilltops, leaving no alternative but to climb above the heavy weather and return to the city by compass. Both instances gave us an excellent example of the tremendous variation in elevation between the city and the Haliburton Highlands. Toronto, just over 50 feet above sea level, was about two thousand feet lower than Harcourt Park. This enormous difference plus Harcourt's location being 140 miles further north, caused much colder temperatures and considerably higher annual snowfall. Spring didn't reach that country until a minimum of three weeks after the dandelions were blooming in Toronto, but it would require more than one season to adjust our thinking to this fact.

Father and I decided after two or three weeks of spring weather in Toronto to get our new adventure underway, and so we left for Wilberforce the next to last day of April, 1958, driving both of our cars. With absolutely no idea of conditions on our property, we arrived prepared for almost any contingency but were nevertheless amazed to find snow still in the woods. Keith Cameron immediately explained the absolute impossibility of reaching our destination without a four-wheel drive. Ron Mumford, who lived in the little village of Harcourt four miles west of Wilberforce, loved to barter and dealt in anything from wheelbarrows to waffle irons, and so we drove over to see if he had any suitable vehicles. Fortunately, Mumford had an old Land Rover that we acquired for $500. We bought enough food to last three weeks or more and loaded it in the back of our Land Rover that came equipped with a truck box covered with a canvas roof. Atop our groceries and other perishables, we placed the mattresses plus our clothing and sleeping bags. My launch and motor was hooked to the four-wheel drive, and Keith Cameron, who accompanied us with his small farm tractor, pulled a trailor loaded with stove, tables, chairs, beds and other furniture that Dad had hauled from the city behind his car for setting up camp.

Before striking back into the hinterland and unaware of any animosity, I elected to make myself acquainted with Jack Wallace and dropped into his office for a brief visit. Had I walked into the path of an on-coming tornado, I couldn't have received a more explosively hostile reception. He began by calling me a fool for believing Harcourt Park could be kept private. He insisted that no conceivable method except erecting a 30-foot barbed wire fence around the entire property would prevent the general public from trespassing. He continued his tirade by warning me that certain parts of the Kennaway Road were private and that I had no rights on a particular section which traversed a portion of their property. He produced maps to show where he claimed the road wasn't public and never had been public, I had no right to travel on it, and if caught, he would charge me with trespassing. Stunned by the vicious verbal attack, I stood with my mouth agape for a few moments, then looking him directly in the eye, responded, "Mr. Wallace, as you probably know, I have two signed affidavits from men who have lived in this area much longer than you. Both claim the road leading to Aldred's property is public domain because municipal funds were spent on repair and maintenance over the course of several years. Let me warn you that if you so much as cause me one small bit of inconvenience, don't forget you have 18,000 acres of valuable forests and are therefore far more vulnerable to my retaliation than I ever will be to yours!" With that I stormed out and slammed the door.

At 11 a.m. under threatening skies, Keith Cameron, Father and I took off with our caravan to begin our trek into the hinterland and new adventure. The severest incline on the journey began a few hundred yards from the village of Wilberforce, and by the time we reached the crest, not more than a mile from town, it was already midafternoon. Due to inexperience with conditions in the Haliburtons, we were unprepared for the incredible state of the road, and if we had been more knowledgeable, we would have delayed our first trip into Harcourt Park for at least three weeks.

During severe winters, frost is driven several feet into the ground, and when spring weather draws this frost back out, an upward pressure forces rocks to the surface, cracking and heaving the entire road bed. Then the melting winter snow pours into these newly formed crevices forming underground springs that wash out entire sectors. To add to their deterioration, the severe undulations of the terrain causes rapidly melting snow cascading down hills to become temporary small rivers that obliterate huge chunks of the trail. The condition and appearances of a bush road in summer and fall has no bearing on how that same route will appear during the spring break up.

When reaching the Burleigh-Kennaway corners around 8 p.m., a raw, cold spring drizzle added to our miseries, and though Dad and I were comfortable enough in the cab, Keith Cameron had no protection on his tractor. We expected, however, to reach Elmer's old camp within an hour. Over the nine tedious hours, both vehicles had been mired in mud numerous times, but with back-breaking effort, we had extricated ourselves. Turning back, though considered, seemed impractical, and so we headed stubbornly toward our destination. Road conditions unfortunately didn't improve, and by 10 p.m. in pouring rain, just past Fitzgerald Lake, two miles from our target, both vehicles became completely bogged down on an incline known as Beaver Lake Hill, leaving us no alternative but to wait for daylight. Keith Cameron climbed into the heated cab of the four-wheel drive to attempt to dry out and warm up, while Pop and I removed our muddy rubber boots and gingerly climbed onto the mattresses in the back of the vehicle and curled up in our sleeping bags to keep warm. Although we were hungry, digging out food and utensils buried beneath mattresses and other paraphernalia with no place in the wet and muck to set anything up seemed unrealistic. We decided to wait until daylight.

At dawn we returned to the task of trying to get both vehicles up the hill, but after another onerous four hours, we hadn't moved ten feet. Although it was cold, the rain had stopped. In disgust, Dad finally suggested we halt our seemingly futile efforts, unload the back of the Land Rover, and cook a meal of bacon and eggs. The first thing Pop layed his hands on among our cartons of provisions was a bottle of rum, and the three of us took hearty swigs that picked up our spirits, though not to the same degree as the delicious breakfast. With renewed spirits we returned to our problem, but at 2 p.m., reaching the top of the rise still looked impossible. We decided one of us should walk eight miles back out and hire a bulldozer. Suddenly, the sound of an approaching vehicle broke the stillness, and we watched in amazement when a jeep with three men came skidding around a bend in the trail and pulled behind our mired vehicles. My boat and motor had been left behind three miles back, and the trailer with the furniture sat beside the trail at the bottom of the Beaver Lake Hill. The smaller of the three men, a scruffy young chap with scraggly long hair, walked up and said, "Are one of you men Bill Phillips?"

"Yes." I replied. "I am he."

"My name is Fred Williams. At the Department of Lands and Forests in Lindsey, we were told you had purchased this property and were planning on turning it into a private park." Williams stated in a challenging manner.

"Your information is correct," I responded. "That is our intention."

"Well, look," Williams snapped. "I have been fishing trout in East Lake for three years, which is where we're headed, and if you want help out of your predicament, then I want a guarantee we'll be allowed to fish."

"Look you stupid son-of-a-bitch!" I yelled. "You and your companions get in that vehicle and get the hell out of here because you're already on private property, and there is no gawd damn way you're going to fish East Lake. Now get moving before I lose my temper properly!" I stormed.

With this outburst, the other two men came slowly forward. One chap offering his hand said, "I'm Ken Williams, no relation to Fred, and this is my friend Al Weighel. We would like to offer our help in getting you to the old camp where perhaps you'd allow us to spend the night as we have been fighting this road since daylight. If you refuse us permission to fish, we will abide by your decision."

"Okay, Mr. Williams," I replied. "That's a more acceptable request. But let me warn you, I'm giving no assurance you will be allowed to fish in East Lake. If I hear anymore bullshit from your friend, I'll personally throw him off the property."

Within an hour the three vehicles were finally over the Beaver Lake Hill, but several other washouts and mud holes still confronted us. The worst obstacle was Allen Creek where, with no bridge, we encountered a widely gushing stream of water two feet deep and thirty feet across. After fashioning a temporary bridge out of old logs, we finally reached Aldred's camp at dusk. Although it was dark, Keith Cameron chose to return to Wilberforce over a much shorter and more accessible route that we didn't use because it crossed private property and we couldn't afford to be accused of trespassing. Cameron said in parting he would return with a work force within a week. The weather rapidly turned colder, and with no stove, we spent an uncomfortable night either huddled in sleeping bags or cooking our meals over a Coleman stove. During the evening the conversation repeatedly returned to our development plans, and all three men suggested they might be our first purchasers. Not necessarily believing their sincerity but having cooled off from our original encounter, I made the boys an offer.

"You can fish for the week end if you'll give Dad and me a hand in retrieving our furniture, plus the boat, motor, and trailer following your morning fishing session," I said. Delighted, they agreed to my terms.

Three inches of snow fell overnight and the temperature plummeted. Nevertheless, at the crack of dawn the boys went to East Lake, the opening of the season to try their luck. They returned within three hours with the greatest catch of speckled trout I ever saw. Each had his limit of fish, some of them weighing as much as eight pounds. Fred Williams soon proved his expertise with four-wheel drive vehicles, obviously having had much previous experience, and shortly after lunch all of our equipment finally reached the old camp. What a relief when our huge cook stove swiftly warmed our rough living quarters. Dad and I sectioned off a third of the old dwelling with sheets of plywood torn from interior partitions, built a makeshift floor, and replaced several missing windows. By nightfall we had a cozy headquarters, and the first chapter of our twenty-year involvement became history.

The second afternoon after our arrival in nature's wonderland we were astonished to hear Cameron's tractor putt-putt-putting back along the trail. Temporarily puzzled for the purpose of this sudden long-return journey, we were delighted when Jack and his business associate, Ed Bourdan, came trotting behind the vehicle with their suitcases and other gear loaded on the tractor. Jack, as great a devotee of the marvels of nature as I, could wait no longer to personally inspect our enormous acquisition, so hired Keith to guide him and Bourdan into our hideaway.

Balmy weather finally dissipated the frigid remains of winter, and the next few days were some of the most pleasant spent during the twenty years I dedicated to the production of Harcourt Park. Jack, Pop, and I explored the shoreline, making decisions where to begin developing the mind-boggling scheme, plus examining construction sites for the first cottages to be used both as models and for our own accommodations. Brilliant sunshine swiftly converted the vanishing snow into a myriad of swirling streams and cascading waterfalls that dispersed the layers of lake ice like magic. Wandering over the heavily forested hills and valleys, bursting back to life following their harsh winter hibernation, the realization that other human beings couldn't disturb the serenity without tremendous effort gave me a sense of exquisite exhilaration. Huge V's of honking Canada geese, some flocks landing in Allen Lake and birds of many species suddenly announcing their arrival with songs of greeting added to the enchantment.

Two surveyors, Bill Rennie and Jim Robinson, arrived by Jeep the first week to begin laying out the shoreline. These two affable and conscientious gentlemen spent many, many months over a period of several years before completing the final layout of lake-front lots that eventually provided the building sites for all Harcourt Park members. Our boat and motor assisted us enormously in examining the different waterfront locales for their adaptability as a permanent headquarters. Great consideration had to be given to our choice of site due to its importance in appealing to prospective purchasers, because models, sales office and living accommodations were to be congregated in one area. A small cove at the north end of Allen Lake was selected, due to its view, picturesque beauty plus accessibility to the old bush road we would use as a base to open up the massive expanse of wilderness.

Don Garbut, from Peterboro, who owned and operated a powerful D-6 bulldozer, came to work on road construction and dragged several truck loads of lumber through muck and mud so that by late May, our first cottages were ready for occupancy. Mother, Sister Joyce and Grandmother Rodd, moved down to remain until early winter, which they would do each year for the next decade. The small bay around which our chosen administrative center hugged the Allen Lake shoreline was completely filled with old logs and dead heads, and we couldn't use our outboard motor within a hundred yards of land due to the enormous amount of debris in the water. When the first crew of a dozen men with horses, chainsaws, plus a small bulldozer began clearing out the cove, we were astounded when a prodigious quantity of pine logs came gradually surfacing from the lake bottom. Jim Robinson, thoroughly familiar with the history of the area, recalled that when the major stand of pine had been cut along the Allen Lake shoreline at the turn of the century and piled on the ice, as is common practice, they met with catastrophe. Due to an early spring break-up followed by an unusually wet summer, the logs were never retrieved. Subsequently water-logged, they had settled to the bottom of the lake. The prevailing south winds eventually pushed the pines plus all other dead trees to the north bay, requiring two weeks of strenuous labor to clear. The piles of pine logs originally appeared quite sound and usable for lumber, which would have saved us thousands of dollars. When they dried, however, tiny lines and cracks appeared in their butts, meaning the wood would swiftly rot. We enjoyed a giant bonfire when it all dried out.

While one gang cleared shoreline, the Linkart brothers with three trucks, a loader and small crawler bulldozer were fighting to open the road from Wilberforce to Allen Lake. We now realized that had we waited two or three weeks for the frost to leave the ground allowing the old road bed to dry and settle the whole operation would have been considerably less expensive. But, because the spring market was by far the strongest and we desperately needed sales, we forged ahead. Road construction required vast quantities of usable fill for the base and gravel for topping, but because of the rocky nature of the terrain, both were scarce. Fortunately, Beaver Lake Hill, where we spent our first night in such misery, turned into a blessing in disguise, for it provided an enormous mountain of sand with veins of course gravel. One day Keith Cameron mentioned that an old gravel pit existed on the continuation of the Burleigh Road approximately 200 yards beyond the Kennaway Road turn off. We were working in that area, and so I instructed the Linkarts to move their equipment over. It would save several miles of hauling as well as conserve the Beaver Lake pit for when we arrived in that area. When I mentioned this new find to Jim Robinson that evening, Jim immediately and emphatically stated, "Bill, I signed an affidavit declaring my belief that both the Burleigh and Kennaway are public roads. I must explain, however, that I do a lot of work for Wilberforce Lumber and Veneer and consider them friends. The gravel pit you refer to is on Wilberforce Lumber and Veneer's land, and so you are stealing gravel from Jack Wallace."

"Well," I said to Pop, "we don't want further problems with that company. I am going to Jack Wallace's after supper, apologize for our mistake, and offer to pay for the few loads of material that have been used." Dad agreed this was probably the best procedure.

After an hour and a half struggle in our Land Rover over roads still next to impassable, I pulled up in front of Wallace's house about 8 p.m. where Jack and his wife were sitting on the front lawn sipping cocktails.

"Mr. Wallace, I drove out to tell you that inadvertently we began drawing gravel from a pit we believed was on public property. Jim Robinson explained, however, that it was on your land, and I came to apologize and offer to pay for the five loads of material that were taken."

"You son of a bitch," he stormed. "This will cost you plenty! I knew you were stealing from me, and I've already contacted the Ontario Provincial Police! You can't buy the material you stole from my pit at any price! Just be prepared to be charged as a common thief!" Jack raged.

Astounded with his outburst, I simply got back into my vehicle and went back to Harcourt Park without opening my mouth. No Provincials arrived, so I assumed Jack only bluffed about the threat. Despite the fact that Wallace caused me a lot of aggravation during the time I shared a section of country where for many years he'd reigned as king, at no time did we face any unnecessary financial expenditures as a result of his actions. Jack Wallace was upset because Bill Phillips, the new kid on the block, was usurping his domain, and because he wanted me and the neighborhood to know he was upset, he would blast off at every opportunity. His partner, Harold Hurlihey, who became a Shriner and a friend in later years, explained one day their annoyance at Sumcot's interference in what for a long time had been their personal sphere of operations. Although selfish on their part, I could easily sympathize with their point of view. With all their harassment, however, in this one instance when they could have severely obstructed our plans, they not only didn't interfere, but also gave the situation their blessing.

For Harcourt Park to be successful probably the most important matter next to acquiring the property was arranging a deal with Ontario Hydro to provide electric power to the project. People might put up with terrible road conditions, black flies or a three-hour journey from their Toronto home, but they would insist on electricity when they arrived at their cottage. Ontario Hydro's headquarters for the Harcourt Park region was situated in the village of Bancroft, thirty miles east of Wilberforce. On one of my trips with John Walsh into the Haliburtons during the winter, we visited Charlie Hunt, Ontario Hydro's regional manager in Bancroft. Listening patiently while I outlined our plans for Harcourt Park and the desperate need for electricity, Charlie nodded his head in agreement with the importance of power for the success of my development. Then he said, "Mr. Phillips, Ontario Hydro requires a capital contribution for the construction of the service."

Aware of this stipulation because Philrick had to put up a sizable amount of cash to get power into Four Mile Lake and concerned as to the amount of capital contribution required, I cautiously asked, "How far away is the nearest line to our property Mr. Hunt, and what do you estimate would be the cost?"

After some map studying he replied. "Providing we can get permission to cross the property of Wilberforce Lumber and Veneer, the shortest distance would appear to be about eight miles and the cost of construction could easily exceed $8,000 per mile."

"Well," I said in complete dejection, "that finishes our plans for Harcourt Park. I simply don't have that kind of available cash."

"There might be another alternative," Charlie stated in a more positive manner. "If I am convinced your project will succeed, what I really require is a guarantee there will be eight hookups for every mile of line constructed at the time it reaches your development."

With my mind working at breakneck speed and looking at Charlie in a casual manner, I quietly inquired. "Supposing, Mr. Hunt, I supplied you with 64 applications for service, but at the time the power line arrived, all 64 families hadn't constructed their cottages, could they then not pay your minimum charge until such time as they do build?"

"I'll tell you, Mr. Phillips," Charlie said confidentially. "We have a large crew of men here and not a lot of work lined up for the spring, so I might try to work such a plan. However, Sumcot will have to guarantee the payment of the minimum charge, and when the families take possession of their cottages, we will transfer the service contract to them."

Ecstatic with joy at the possibility of such an agreement because to my knowledge no other developer had ever engineered a comparable deal with Ontario Hydro and also because it indicated Charlie Hunt had confidence in our plan, I thanked him warmly for his cooperation and promised to have the 64 signed applications on his desk within a month.

The significance of the arrangements didn't strike John until we left Bancroft, and I explained the deal. Ontario Hydro's minimum charge of $20 per unit every six months, would only cost Sumcot $1,280 semi-annually, even if we had no hookups, instead of perhaps a $75,000 cash contribution for the construction of the line.

Wilberforce Lumber and Veneer gave Ontario Hydro a one hundred foot right-of-way across six miles of their property to the perimeter of Harcourt Park. The new hydro line bypassed two large lakes on their land, greatly increasing the property value, so it was understandable why Wallace readily approved the line. Nevertheless, had he balked, it certainly would have thrown a monkey wrench into our plans.

Ontario Hydro's survey crew slashed the cross-country route to Allen Lake almost before we began developing. Then throughout spring and summer, they employed a crew and equipment comparable to Sumcot's in constructing the power line across terrain almost impossible to describe due to its severity. Heavy growth, including softwoods and hardwoods up to three feet in diameter, had to be felled and burned over the entire expanse of eight miles in a strip a hundred feet wide that roller-coasted up and down enormous inclines, some a thousand feet in elevation, across valleys, swamps and streams. Every single hole for the two hundred hydro poles planted six feet deep had to be dynamited because the bedrock lay so close to the surface. When the lights were finally turned on in September of '59, the families in Harcourt Park, including Mom and Joyce, celebrated for a week. Truly a difficult and magnificent feat, the power line's completion played a significant role in our success.

Charlie confided in later years that the cost of the original eight miles exceeded his eight thousand dollars per mile estimate. Throughout the two decades we developed Harcourt Park, Ontario Hydro under the management of Charlie Hunt, provided service to the six hundred lots on eight lakes over a distance that eventually spanned twenty-five miles. To a great degree, the eventual triumph of the development was due to the major involvement of Ontario Hydro. Charlie and his wife became close friends of Sumcot personnel over that period, and we all agreed that Ontario Hydro originally took a substantial risk, but it was a gamble that paid off handsomely for all parties concerned.

Many battles were waged over the initial months, but no aspect of the struggle appeared more important to win than the fight for privacy. Ken Williams, Al Weighel, and Fred Williams returned in early May to inspect lots and asked permission to fish East Lake during their visit. The surveyors had already plotted one section of shoreline, so I allowed them a couple of weeks to bring in their wives or family to approve their lot choice during which time they were welcome to trout fish. The following weekend, Ken Williams accompanied by his wife Jessie, and Al Weighel with his father and brother, came and chose their lake-front sites. Though still fighting the roads with four-wheel drives, Joyce made her first trip in the middle of May with Bill and Thelma Fyshe, some real estate friends of ours. Not ardent outdoors people, the Fyshes had a delightful time roughing it in the old lumber camp, and to our great surprise, they also purchased a lot and cottage. Fred Williams, however, kept procrastinating about signing a contract or putting up a check, and one day when he arrived with his mother, I gave him an ultimatum: put up or get out. Ken Williams informed me that Fred had six children and on a milk-man's pay, he was apprehensive about Fred's financial ability to acquire a cottage and lot.

One summer morning, John and Buzz Walsh drove into Harcourt Park on their first visit to see what they owned. Piling them into our Land Rover, I started out to give them a tour of the original property, and a glimpse at a huge tract we hoped to acquire from Chester Schwandt. Passing East Lake on the south end, which we didn't own, I recognized diminutive Freddie Williams with three other more sizable companions unloading canoes and other equipment from his Jeep. Flying out of my vehicle, I went charging over. "For Christ sake Williams, how many times must I tell you, you can't fish East Lake."

"Look Phillips, this is Chester Schwandt's property, which he gave me permission to cross, and you don't own the water," Fred chortled. "So go to hell."

White with rage, I stormed back at him and his cronies. "Listen you bastards and listen good, within an hour I will have written permission from Schwandt to throw you out on your ass. If you are on the lake when I return, I'll confiscate your Jeep by hauling it away with my bulldozer, so you'd better be patient.

The Walsh brothers never left the Land Rover cab, which didn't give me much confidence they would provide any physical support in the event of a donnybrook. Nevertheless, they sympathized with my position and so were rewarded with a flying, bumpy trip through the back country to the village of Harcourt where I rapidly obtained Chester Schwandt's authorization to evict the Williams' party plus any other trespassers.

Fred Williams and his companions were still waiting by their equipment when I returned with the letter, and after realizing it was for real, they prepared to do battle.

"Better give the situation careful consideration," I warned. "Within fifteen minutes I can be back with a dozen men, and if you are not gone, we will be less than gentle with you and your equipment. Also, Tustin will be sent out to notify the Ontario Provincial Police." I whirled and started for my vehicle.

"Hold it, Phillips!" Fred yelled. "Give us five minutes to talk among ourselves."

Before two minutes elapsed, they began to load their paraphernalia back on the Jeep, and I fervently hoped it would be Fred's final resistance to the new order in the area. But I was still underestimating the stubbornness of the little pipsqueak.

Another quartet from St. Catherines driving a Jeep outfitted with a rack to carry two large aluminum canoes arrived the week following trout opening. Stopping them on the road, I patiently explained the concept of Harcourt Park and that they would have to become members to fish the lakes. A rough-looking group, they gave me quite an argument about their rights to fish East Lake because the Provincial Government had spent public money to put trout fry in the water. They made a good point, but I had no alternative but to stand my ground. The leader, a fellow named Bill, was adamant and said they were going fishing. With only Pop and me to stop them, I resorted to persuasion.

"Bill, I appreciate this is excellent trout country," I stated quietly. "It is our intention, however, to turn it into a private development strictly for members. If you or others in your party are interested in investing, then we're willing to let you do some fishing after you've chosen your lakefront site and given me a check."

He countered with the argument that first he would have to fetch his wife to help in picking their cottage site. This was difficult reasoning to counter, and since we needed sales badly, I again relented and allowed them to fish on the assurance they were bona fide prospects. One of the men got drunk the first afternoon and fell in the lake. Frightened the chap would get pneumonia from the frigid dunking, Father brought him in and put him on my bunk. Arriving back at camp in late afternoon, I went over to see who occupied my bed before Dad had a chance to advise me of the mishap. Upset because the fellow had given him a hard time all day, Pop watched carefully as I approached the snoozing drunk. Startled when I touched him, the man lurched to his feet, and thinking he had taken a swing at me, Dad leaped forward and slugged him in the face. When the others saw their friend with a bloody nose, the incident rapidly escalated into a hostile confrontation. Before any further blows could be struck, I warned them to remember they were trespassing on our private property, and I wouldn't hesitate to prosecute. Without further commotion they loaded their canoes and disappeared. They returned the following week end without their wives, and I stopped them immediately. In a violent manner, Bill screamed, "I've been informed by my lawyers and the Department of Lands and Forests that you can't keep us out!"

In an equally threatening voice I hollered, "If you so much as get out of your vehicle at East Lake, I'll slash all four of your tires! Now, I'm telling you for the last time, turn around and skedaddle!"

The four glared at me trying to decide whether I would really do what I'd threatened, and after a few tense moments, Bill must have come to the conclusion I meant business because he swung his Jeep around and we never saw that foursome again.

Perhaps the most embarrassing enforcement of our privacy during that first spring was with the Cross Lake Hunting and Fishing Club that owned 400 acres at the extreme south end of Allen Lake. Affluent business people from Hamilton and Burlington, Ontario, they had enjoyed unbelievable serenity and the almost exclusive use of the entire area since building their lodge thirteen years earlier. It wasn't difficult to understand their disenchantment with our arrival, for we not only disrupted a quietude they'd known for many years but also, and worse, prohibited them from entering waters and lands they had used any time at their leisure. After I halted a pair of their members portaging a canoe from Allen Lake to East, they sent an envoy over to discuss their future with trout fishing in that lake. Again I patiently explained Harcourt Park's concept and our obligations to the new members, stating emphatically no way existed in which they could use East or any other lake on our property except Allen unless they became members of Harcourt Park.

During the following few weeks, in a complete frenzy they wrote menacing letters, threatened lawsuits, and used any form of intimidation they believed would make me yield. I remained steadfast, though I thoroughly understood and sympathized with their feelings. It would have been a great disappointment to me, for example, if the tables were reversed and if someone informed me I could no longer visit the Brokenhead. One day two of their members came to my cottage, told me of their financial status, and added that one of their members, of which there was a total of twelve, owned one of the largest highway construction companies in Ontario. They warned that if I didn't back away from my position and allow them uninhibited access to Harcourt Park they would bring in bulldozers and other necessary equipment to slash a main road from the Burleigh, three miles across to their cottage site, thereby opening up Allen Lake to the general public. Knowing that the three miles they would be forced to traverse included swamps, valleys, and hills with elevation shifts ranging up a thousand feet and was also crisscrossed with substantial creeks and waterways, I knew it would require an enormous sum of money to construct such a road. Also I didn't believe they would open a route that would dump the general public at their own back door, so I wished them good luck and told them to proceed.

One day to our great astonishment, a fleet of flat beds loaded with bulldozers, trucks and other road building equipment came rumbling up the Burleigh. Plenty of money was spent just transporting the enormous outfit all the way from Hamilton to the Haliburtons. Then from daylight to dark throughout the entire week end, they roared around their camp like they were constructing the Alcan Highway. Undoubtedly they expected me to jump in my boat and come racing down the lake pleading with them to stop. Ken Williams and other members who had now purchased became frantic, frightened they had invested in what might now become a public recreation center. Perhaps I suffered some apprehension, but still didn't seriously believe the Cross Lake Hunting and Fishing Club planned to build a road that would cost more money than the purchase price of Harcourt Park. Fortunately, I surmised correctly, and after three days they loaded the equipment back on the flat beds and, like thieves in the night, silently left the country—a complete contrast to their noisy arrival. I never discovered what they tore up or mutilated while blasting around the bush attempting to convince us they were constructing a highway, but it proved to be their final effort in trying to force a compromise. It must have been frustrating for them, because their Allen Lake Shangri-la required parking their autos on the Burleigh Road, then walking a rugged three-mile portage trail.

Occasionally during the summer months, several of the men brought their wives, and as most members were in advanced years, this cross-country hike was a difficult journey. In early summer, one lady had an accident at their lodge, severely slashing her leg, and they came racing down the lake for permission to bring a car all the way around to our landing to be able to rush the injured woman to the doctor. Dad piled them in his vehicle and rushed them out to the parking lot on the Burleigh, saving crucial time in getting the lady medical attention. Grateful for Dad's assistance, they never gave us further trouble, always remaining on their side of the dividing line in the bush while deer hunting and never trespassing to East, Fitzgerald, or any other lake they had used almost exclusively for thirteen years. I admired them for respecting our privacy and understood their aggravation at having to trudge three formidable miles to their lodge while every other cottager on Allen Lake drove a car to his front door.

Another hilly three-mile portage connected Fishtail Lake on our northern boundary to East, where several families with cottages on Fishtail owned boats. During speckled trout season, these ardent fishermen would trudge across this rough portage path to use their boats stashed on the East Lake shoreline. I hiked over to Fishtail in early May, posted a large sign proclaiming it now as private property and placed another prominent "No Trespassing" sign at their boats. During the first week of the season, I caught several of them on East and paddled over to explain the circumstances courteously. When they returned the second week, however, I issued a stern warning. "Don't come back because I will take an axe and smash your boats." Satisfied they had tested my determination to the limit, they asked permission to bring a truck around our roads to haul out their vessels. Mostly Japanese Canadians and pleasant people, I granted this request plus inviting them to become members of Harcourt Park. Over the next decade, several families did join the club which proved that our steadfast determination in keeping out poachers did pay off in some instances. Another notable example occurred a week or two later.

One spring morning while patrolling East Lake, I spied a canoe containing two men I didn't recognize. Brother Jack was visiting at the time, and we jumped into my canoe and paddled over to challenge these two strangers. Already with three fine trout, they introduced themselves as Roy Miles and Nels Couvier and insisted that though they'd crossed the Fishtail portage route they had never encountered any "No Trespassing" signs. Knowing they were lying, I nevertheless took into consideration they wouldn't have seen our sign until they had paddled down Fishtail Lake and up Fishtail Creek to the portage entrance. Also, they had carried their canoe on their shoulders over three tough miles, and so I agreed to allow them to fish the balance of the day, if they would be willing to leave that evening and give us no further trouble. The two readily agreed and they seemed genuinely intrigued with our plans for the area. They explained that they belonged to a little fishing club of six members from Orno, Ontario, about ten miles from Oshawa, and indicated that the group might be interested in becoming members of Harcourt Park. They wondered how our rules would affect them. I told them that to be in accord with our bylaws, they would be required to purchase two lots and cottages with two partners designated as Harcourt Park voting members. The other four would be guests, and except for their immediate families, no additional guests would be permitted at any one time. They seemed astounded at this notification, but they said they would probably be back to see us within a week or two.

Although they had accepted my ultimatum to leave that evening with no visible anger and had enthusiastically discussed our development plans, I didn't honestly expect to see them again. I was pleasantly surprised two weeks later when the six members arrived, and with little persuasion, they purchased two lots and cottages. Roy Miles, his two brothers Howard and Lloyd, Nels Couvier and the two other younger men in the fishing club became long-time and esteemed members of Harcourt Park, and were also responsible for numerous other sales.

The many confrontations during that first year not only established our reputation and resolve in keeping Harcourt Park private but also gave courage to our members who now began to challenge those on the lakes whom they didn't recognize. The war to retain our seclusion, though far from won, put the country on notice that no one was welcome in Harcourt Park except Sumcot personnel, Harcourt Park members, guests or prospective purchasers.

Another problem causing great discomfort and mental anguish that initial spring was black flies. Although occasionally plagued with mosquitoes in Manitoba, we were thoroughly ignorant and unprepared for the terrible onslaught of black flies. Swarms drove the horses almost insane, and local workmen, although accustomed to the blood-sucking monsters, found it impossible to work at times without smudges or insect repellents that only provided partial relief. Throughout the ten years Pop supervised in Harcourt Park, the black-fly plague in early spring probably caused him more suffering than any other perplexity. At first completely unfamiliar with their cycle and not knowing when they abated, I couldn't see prospective purchasers buying property when attacked by hordes of these insects. In May and early June, therefore, I spent most of our remaining cash attempting to control or eradicate this menace, but soon found it would have been simpler to convert the world to Judaism.

Fearing the pestilence would be the end of my dream, I contacted every source that might have an answer. A university professor recommended spraying pesticide from the air as the only logical means of control. Black fly larvae hatched only in fast-moving waters, and Ontario Hydro specialists informed me they had experienced success in certain areas by placing DDT pellets in rapidly moving creeks. Both methods would have been too costly for Sumcot in trying to control our 2,300 acre area, and so I opted for a cheaper alternative. At the cost of a thousand dollars, we acquired a "fogger," a machine designed to heat a mixture of DDT and diesel fuel into a gas before expelling it in a heavy, dense fog. When discharged early in the morning or during periods when there was no wind, the weight of the heavy ominous mist hugged the earth and rolled across the land including creeks and streams, killing both larvae and adult black flies—or so went the theory. Not only did I purchase a large machine but also two small models that could be handled by one man to fog around cottage construction sites or where workmen were concentrated in lot clearing or other jobs.

For the main development we placed the huge fogging apparatus on our four-wheel drive, and at the crack of dawn on week ends, we travelled the development's main roads spreading immense clouds of the poisonous mixture across the serenic land, hoping to eradicate the pest before our customers arrived. The level of relief from the insects wasn't terribly noticeable, and several of our members came screaming their disapproval when they found a few dead birds in the woods. We couldn't determine whether the demise of our feathered friends was caused by inhaling deadly fumes or from eating the insects. The general outcry, over the destruction of wildlife, which also concerned me, became more exasperating than our annoyance with black flies, and so the plan was eventually aborted. Thereafter, we only fogged around the sales area and model cottages.

One day in mid-June as a warm summer sun chased away the last vestiges of spring, I arrived from Toronto with the paychecks as usual. When Father met me on the road to pick up his crew's wages, he said, "Bill, get out of your car and see whether the black flies bother you." To my amazement, not a fly landed on either of us. Local people told Dad that the insects cannot tolerate heat. They must have moisture and cool temperatures to thrive, hence are only a menace in the early spring. So although we spent considerable money and suffered psychological distress trying to control the pests, they simply disappeared when the summer sun dried out the bush and evaporated the rivulets that ran down the hillsides and provided them with breeding grounds.

A high percentage of our original purchasers were people familiar with the area. Nonetheless, the very first official member of Harcourt Park was a man by the name of John Gordon, who came in with his family from our first newspaper advertising and bought from Howard Tustin. The Gordons, probably the most unusual buyers during 1959, had four children, from a baby in arms to a six-year-old boy. Jo, John's lovely wife, had never been in the backwoods in her life, and John had little outdoor experience himself. They simply liked the idea of privacy. While Jo minded the children in their auto, John without leaving the boat, picked out a gorgeous white birch point lot, two lots from where Joyce and I selected our cottage site and next door to Ken and Jesse Williams. The Gordons, who became close friends, epitomized our perception of Harcourt Park's future. Neither hunters nor ardent fishermen, they sought a retreat where their children could learn the wondrous ways of nature in an environment of peace and tranquility.

Although in some ways enjoyable, 1959 proved to be a strenuous ordeal. Fighting for privacy, battling insects, constructing roads over terrain far more rugged than ever anticipated, and struggling for sales meant working seven days a week, and I found few moments to relax. No lots were sold without a cottage, and service roads leading to each dwelling, which usually were situated close to the water's edge, frequently had to be built down severe inclines. The sandy clay soil caused all these service roads to become slippery after only a sprinkle of rain, and so from early morning to midnight, anyone stuck or unable to get his car up a hill had no alternative but come for our assistance with the Land Rover, the only vehicle in the vicinity capable of getting them extricated from their dilemma. Trying to avoid adverse publicity about road conditions inside the development in wet weather, we put up with the terrible aggravation and charged no fee, but rarely did we enjoy many consecutive hours of relaxation without interruption.

Another principal irritation centered around the constant policing of the park. Our members, adamant about retaining the development's privacy, were reluctant to become actively engaged in enforcing the edict, and so the surveillance fell almost exclusively on my father, myself and Howard Tustin. Still a further provocation centered around the bylaw that restricted only two guest cards per membership. Finally we relented and modified it to allow a family to apply for special guest cards on a specific date for distinctive occasions but insisted nevertheless that without limiting or controlling the number of guests brought into the park the entire concept would lose its principal ingredient. The fact that Roy Miles, Nels Couvier and partners purchased two cottages and lots as the only means of permitting their six members the benefits of Harcourt Park and who never attempted to take advantage of the rules made it imperative we implement this particular aspect of the overall scheme.

My partners, the Walshes, believed the enormity of the development required professional advertising and promotion to get it off the ground and suggested we spend a portion of our budget on contracting with a large advertising agency. We selected a large Toronto firm who designated Jack McNeil as our personal representative. Jack, a huge man and former Canadian amateur wrestling champion, wrote a press release on our unique project that was printed in three Toronto dailies, several weeklies across the province, plus the *Financial Post,* Canada's principal business periodical. This publicity conceivably did more to getting Harcourt Park accepted than any other single promotion.

The year ended with 23 units sold, totalling $35,000 in land sales and $56,000 in cottages. We considered it a reasonably successful beginning, but advertising and promotional costs, including the preparation of brochures and printing that we would use for several years, left only a small profit. This plus the many difficulties experienced during the season worried the Walsh brothers, who became increasingly concerned about their investment and wanted to bail out. My old friend Hank Sharpe, absolutely fascinated with the area, pestered John throughout the late '59 season to devise a way he could take over their 50 percent interest. In spite of my great apprehension about Hank as a partner, I had no alternative but to go along with any arrangements, and in late summer they finally came up with a workable plan. Hank owned several houses and mortgages which he transferred to Philjon Ltd. John Walsh then arranged a $50,000 loan against the combined assets in Philjon Ltd. and Sumcot Development Corp. Ltd. Hank bought the Walshes share in both corporations from his portion of the loan, but my share had to be left in the company for working capital. So, in '60 I found myself with a new partner, a complete change in working arrangements, and severe doubts about the future with Hank Sharpe as my partner.

When it became apparent Sumcot would have insufficient funds to pay Howard Tustin, Mom, Dad and myself a living wage until Harcourt Park sales began closing in the spring of 1960, I had to come up with a means of increasing our income. Having never lost my admiration for Fuller Brush's method and technique in door-to-door selling, I tried to think of a product people could carry in a sample case suitable for direct sales but not conflicting with Fuller Brush's operation. After considering numerous items, I decided costume jewelry with its enormous markup might be the most desirable product to offer housewives, and as a result, Gold Star Jewelry was born. Several costume jewelry wholesalers offered us bulk articles at unbelievably low prices. For example: cultured pearl earrings could be purchased wholesale in large quantities for as little as .2¢ per earring. We couldn't understand how the Japanese manufactured the earrings, paid customs duty, and still showed a profit at such a ridiculous low figure. Earrings costing us .4¢ per pair were retailed at .99¢. Besides earrings, we bought a vast assortment of necklaces, bracelets, rings and other items, then designed a sample case to display each piece of jewelry handsomely when the case was opened. We hired sales ladies, and after a short sales training and product knowledge session, provided them with a caseful of jewelry to offer at residences, businesses, or wherever they chose to market our product. The girls sold articles directly from the case for cash or took orders which were filled from inventory. Our advertising for prospective sales ladies with a chance to earn commissions of 40 percent, deluged us with applicants, but with only 25 sample cases, we were limited to starting two dozen. Candidates ranged from housewives to hookers. Unfortunately, many of them didn't have enough cash for a suitable deposit to protect our investment, but if they appeared to be live wires, we let them take the cases anyhow.

Although enjoying some initial success, our loss from theft became too high, and so we decided to try the method of selling at house parties, practiced successfully by Tupperware. At this point I had the good fortune to hire Violet Marlowe, one of the cleverest, most competent sales ladies and administrators with whom I have ever had the pleasure to work. She immediately suggested we locate a manufacturer who would produce an exclusive line of Gold Star Jewelry. A woman named Heddi Hill, successfully selling her own personally designed jewelry to retail stores in the city, used an east-end manufacturer whom we contacted. He agreed to produce a completely different line of about four dozen distinctive items for Gold Star Jewelry that wouldn't conflict with Heddi Hill. Vi Marlow designed an outstanding training program, and then we hired and trained a dozen attractive and intelligent young ladies to hold combination house parties and fashion shows with the sale of our product the prime consideration. Operating from our basement at Shediac, we set up our huge recreation room as a combined office, sales training headquarters and stockroom. Mother and Dad helped pack orders, but due to our severe cash shortage, Howard Tustin, after years of faithfully and successfully working for several companies under my control, had to return to the real estate business to earn a livelihood.

Gold Star Jewelry provided sufficient money to keep us eating, but whereas on the surface it seemed we should have been earning a small fortune, there were really too many pitfalls to make such success possible. Each article in our inventory had to be ordered in quantities of a gross or more to obtain a suitable wholesale price. Items that customers didn't buy at house parties were swiftly removed from the kits, and so although the enormous mark-up on certain jewelry earned big dividends, the huge inventory laying in our basement diluted the profit enormously. There seemed to be no way of knowing in advance what colors or style at any particular time might be popular with our customers. Joyce's heart broke when I bought and gave away a mink stole at the Thornecliff Park Shopping Center as her outer apparel never consisted of more than a single, cheap cloth coat. One of Toronto's leading radio disc jockeys made the presentation, and being highly publicized, it supplied us with a huge list of women interested in holding house parties. Our spendable profit, however, remained minimal. Another downfall in the jewelry undertaking was its seasonal value. Six weeks prior to Christmas, sales were excellent with Valentine's, Easter and other special occasions quite satisfactory. During great stretches of the year, though, our sales staff experienced difficulty arranging showings. Although Gold Star Jewelry provided sufficient income to survive the winter, we were anxious and delighted to return to Harcourt Park at spring breakup.

In the fall of '59, Hank Sharpe and I went moose hunting in a secluded region 75 miles northwest of Elk Lake. This lay in the same general area as Grassy Lake Landing where we had flown to Lake Muskacenda two years before. Having heard about the location from some acquaintances, Hank understood that although there would be three long and tedious portages, we would get into back country unlikely to be reached by many hunters, and it would be considerably less expensive than hiring an outfitter with an aircraft. It turned out to be the most unpleasant and most difficult of all our moose jaunts. The three portages, one over a mile in length, required several trips to transport all of our equipment, including the 18-foot portage canoe with its outboard and our sponson which weighed over a hundred pounds in itself.

Nevertheless, the most bitter disappointment developed when even after the final portage that found us untold miles from the nearest road, there were groups of hunters with Indian guides still going past us. Luckily, we located an old log cabin, because the weather turned bitterly cold and our tent would have provided miserable accommodation. Within three days, the lake began to freeze over, and having found no sign of moose and afraid we might get frozen in and marooned if the frigid conditions heralded an unseasonably early winter, we broke camp and headed back. In several instances we had to break ice with our oars to get our equipment through, and as the early freeze-up continued, I often wondered how these hunters, who passed us, ever got back to civilization.

The few days spent with my new partner provided an opportunity to hear his ideas for promoting Harcourt Park and its future development. Not liking several of his plans, I made it abundantly clear that first as President of Sumcot, and second because Harcourt Park was my scheme, it would be developed exactly as originally proposed. Hank requested that he be assigned as general manager at the development to assist Pop and look after prospects through the week while I operated in the city, managing Philjon's mortgage and house portfolio and handling the advertising and promotion for Sumcot. We would both work at the development on week ends in sales.

When first assembling the acreage for Harcourt Park, I desperately wanted to purchase the two or three one hundred acre lots with frontage on the east end of East Lake to close off that small body of water which seemed crucial to our over-all plans. Chester Schwandt, who operated a sawmill in the village of Harcourt, not only owned those lots but also hundreds of additional acres as well. In the spring of '59, Schwandt indicated an interest in working out a deal provided he retain timber rights to his property and the timber rights on our 2300 acres to boot. He had an option to buy a large tract in the center of his acreage containing Big and Little Straggle lakes that together had over ten miles of shoreline including some picturesque islands. The total land Schwandt either owned or had under option totalled 4,400 acres and embraced all or part of another nine lakes. This added to our present holdings would add up to an enormous total acreage of 6,700 acres comprising all or part of 16 lakes, plus innumerable streams, creeks, ponds, and marshes. The elevation over the undulating terrain would vary in excess of 1500 feet, and the perimeter of Harcourt Park would expand to twenty-five miles.

Throughout the spring and early summer while negotiating with Schwandt, I had not the foggiest notion where to borrow the purchase price except to hope sales would provide the necessary funds. One brilliant summer day, Chester drove Howard Tustin and me to within two miles of Big Straggle and then we walked through dense bush country to where he had a small boat and motor stashed at the lake's edge. The mile after mile of beautiful shoreline held me in a trance, and it seemed that if we consummated a deal it would take at least fifty years to sell all the 100 foot in width waterfront lots that could be developed along the gorgeous lakeshore. A multitude of smallmouth bass populating the lake were so lively it seemed they would attack idle fingers dabbling in the water. After viewing the Straggles, I became more determined than ever to arrange a deal.

Raising the required downpayment wasn't the only stumbling block because we also had to get 100 percent approval of the members to alter both the existing leases, and bylaw #27 of Harcourt Park Inc. bylaws which read:

All leases acquired or made by the Corporation are to expire on the 31st day of March, 1979.

Any decision respecting leasehold interests at their termination must be made at a special general meeting of members duly called for such purpose at least three months prior to the expiration thereof. Such decision must be confirmed by a resolution passed by at least 51 percent of the votes cast at such meeting, at which meeting at least 51 percent of the members are present or represented by proxy. Any decision reached at such meeting respecting leasehold interests must be applicable to all leasehold interests and all members having a leasehold interest must have the opportunity, equally with each other, to obtain the benefit of such decision.

Section #10 of the same bylaws outlining the powers of the directors, which I helped design and absolutely insisted be incorporated against the recommendation of several attorneys including the Walsh's, prohibited those of us who were still directors of Harcourt Park Inc. from changing bylaw #27 because bylaw #10 read:

POWERS

The directors of the Corporation may administer the affairs of the Corporation in all things and make or cause to be made for the Corporation, in its name, any kind of contract which the Corporation may lawfully enter into and, generally may exercise all such other powers and do all such other acts and things as the Corporation is by its Charter or otherwise authorized to do; provided, however, that no by-law repealing, amending or in any way affecting or modifying the operation of Section 27 of this By-Law Number 1 shall be effective unless and until the same has been sanctioned and confirmed by a resolution passed by all of the votes cast at a general meeting of the members of the Corporation duly called for the purpose of considering such by-law, at which meeting all of the members are present or represented by proxy.

This 100 percent required approval by the members to alter the leases or change by-law #27, incorporated entirely at my insistence, now became a brick wall. I felt that if bylaw #27 did in fact protect the interests of Harcourt Park members for all time, then no reason existed for it ever to be changed without at least unanimous approval. The attorneys believed more flexibility should be allowed in the directors' powers to deal with the leases. Perhaps they were right because now not only would the bylaws need changing if we acquired the Schwandt property but also all sold leases would have to be replaced. They contained clauses making any amalgamation impossible unless modified. Among them, the limit of 200 members would need to be increased to 600; transfer of land ownership from Sumcot to Harcourt Park Inc. would have to be extended seven years from 1969 to 1976, allowing a reasonable length of time to develop and sell all memberships; Schwandt's timbering rights would have to be included; and the legal description would include 67 hundred-acre township lots rather than the 23 described in the original leases.

Luckily, the thirty families who were members of Harcourt Park Inc. at the time were in full accord with our expansion plans, and at a special meeting held beside the old lumber camp in late 1960, they unanimously approved the changes. New leases were then exchanged for the originals, and bylaw #27 now read:

"All leases acquired or made by the Corporation are to expire on the 31st day of March, 1982."

As a result I could proceed with negotiations to buy Chester Schwandt's vast holdings, provided I could find the downpayment.

Hank's forceful demeanor at the development in the spring was at first an asset when he acted in the capacity of a watchdog and policeman, removing considerable responsibility from Dad's shoulders in maintaining our seclusion. The war to protect Harcourt Park's privacy abated the second spring due partly to Hank's patrol, plus the fact members were on the lakes and roads much of the time and were taking a more responsible role in challenging strangers. Several groups tested our determination, but when Hank informed them of our private club status and gave them the two alternatives—become members or vamoose—they left without incident.

We weren't completely out of the woods, however, because East Lake's fame as a trout fisherman's dream, attracted those who knew of its proliferous fish population like a siren lures sailors. Arriving at the development one Friday afternoon in early spring, Pop greeted me with, "Guess who is fishing on East Lake?"

"Not Williams." I asked increduously.

"The same," Dad replied. "A couple of hours ago, a float plane landed on Allen, taxied over to the old camp and discharged Williams and that big, burly German friend. I challenged them, but they claimed they were walking over to East on the 66-foot public right-of-way and couldn't leave because their transportation had already departed."

Hank, who just returned from a business trip to Wilberforce, listened to Pop's account with the same degree of disbelief as I.

"What do you suggest?" Hank inquired.

"We'll jump in our canoe, go over and throw them to hell out." I responded. "There is no other choice."

Fred and his big pal had set up their camp on the east shoreline and watched as we paddled across the picturesque body of water. Jumping out of the craft, I charged over to where the two boys were standing.

"I'll give you five minutes to get your tent and belongings into your canoe before I put my foot through both!" I raged.

The big blond German lad, about my height and several pounds heavier, put his chest and face beside mine and spat out, "Ve ain't movin.' "

Hank, with arms folded, moved to within ten feet and sat nonchalantly on a fallen log.

"Look, Phillips," Williams snarled. "We crossed from Allen Lake to East on the 66-foot road allowance and are now camped on the public

66-foot reserve strip running around the lake. We are definitely not trespassing, and we are absolutely not moving."

"That leaves Hank and me with two courses of action," I growled. "Either we go for the police and charge you with trespassing because you have no idea where the right-of-way is located from Allen to East, but I do, as it has already been surveyed. Or we throw you and your belongings into the lake, and you can sue us for malicious damage. As we already have made our decision, I'm giving you and your goon friend two minutes to get the equipment into that canoe before I begin swinging a big club." I then went and sat on the log beside Hank.

"We have no means of getting out," Fred snarled. "You know we came in by plane."

"You should have thought of that before you arranged the trip," I responded, as I began breaking the twigs off a large stick.

Fred stepped into the tent and came out with a double-barrelled shotgun. He opened the breach and then in front of us, to make certain we didn't miss the implication, inserted two cartridges. Watching us carefully, he circled around behind our backs, the loaded firearm cradled in his arms. Then in the swiftly encroaching twilight, he closed the breach with a menacing snap. No one moved for what seemed like an eternity. Premeditated murder seemed very unlikely, and so standing up slowly, I turned around and in a quiet but firm voice said, "Either pull the trigger or get your gear into your boat. I'm at the end of my patience."

Fred and his friend glared at Hank and me for a few moments, and then the young German prepared to fight. But Fred removed the shells from the firearm, suddenly lost his look of hatred, and shoving his buddy away, looked me square in the eye.

"You win, Bill, you son-of-a-bitch. I give up. Will you please give us a lift to the highway if I guarantee never to step foot inside Harcourt Park again except as a full-fledged member?"

His whole manner changed when he reached the decision to resist no further, and sharing a bottle of whiskey to seal the pact, I drove the pair forty miles to Fred's cottage on Loon Lake. We met occasionally over the years, and as far as I know, he kept his word and never again trespassed into Harcourt Park. But he also never joined our exclusive club.

Our aggravation with property transgressors thankfully subsided except for one notable exception in the summer of '60. Ken Gullis, a superior of Jack's at Memorial Gardens, paid me a visit one day at my Toronto office.

"Have you any idea, Bill," he said, "of the terrible embarrassment and abuse your folks are confronted with at the development?"

"Explain yourself." I replied.

"The wife and I decided to have a look at your holdings, and also spend a few hours with your Mom and Dad, so we drove up to Harcourt Park yesterday. The four of us piled into your Land Rover for a tour of the property, and at Fitzgerald Lake, three men were out on the lake in your boat. Pop hollered at them to come in as they had no rights with your boat and were trespassing on private property. Drunk as hoot owls, the trio came roaring back to the docks like demons, cursing with horrible language and threatening us all with bodily damage. We jumped into our vehicle and got the hell out of there. One mouthy guy kept screaming he would fish Fitzgerald, East, Allen, or any other lake in Harcourt Park he chose, and he'd like to see Bill Phillips try to stop him. Not only was I embarrassed, but your folks are too old for that kind of abuse," Ken concluded.

Stunned by his report, I inquired if they got any names or where the intruders came from.

"No names, but they were local toughs, I'm certain," Gullis responded.

Jack and I had put a small 12-foot rowboat on Fitzgerald the first summer and were astounded at the smallmouth bass population. Whether we used live bait or plugs, they attacked every single cast, and we landed lunkers weighing up to five pounds. Neither of us had experienced bass fishing to match it, and so we left the small craft tied up at the dock. Fitzgerald, on the outer fringe of Harcourt Park near the main entrance road, was the most difficult to police, and it didn't surprise me that poachers were using our boat. But Pop was approaching his late sixties and had already helped enough in defense of our privacy. I was outraged at any attack on him personally.

Gullis' account of the incident related on Wednesday, two days before my normal weekly sojourn to the development, allowed me forty-eight hours to devise strategy. Jack and his family were going to be at the park on the week end as well as Harold Thomas up from Arizona and Lionel Faust, both planning to spend a couple of days at our cottage. That meant at least three good men would be on hand to back me up if I located the culprits and it ended up in a free for all. In my growing anger, I decided this situation called for more than a warning, and I mentally prepared myself for war.

At the park on Friday afternoon the folks confirmed Gullis' account of the occurrence and added that the ringleader was a young tough named Roberts from Wilberforce. Hank returned to Toronto to spend the weekend with his wife, but his son Glen remained behind. Late in the afternoon the lad came racing into the folks cottage while we were discussing the ugly situation. My blood pressure was already soaring, and it really skyrocketed when Glen yelled, "Mr. Phillips, Mr. Phillips, there are four men on Fitzgerald Lake. They just kicked my friend and me out of your boat and told us to scram!"

Ten minutes before Glen's announcement, Jack with his family plus Harold and Lionel all arrived. As I scrambled to get into our Land Rover with Pop beside me, I hollered to Jack to grab Harold, Lionel, and other members of the park and high-tail it to the Fitzgerald landing where there were four toughs that had to be taught a lesson. Jack recommended I wait a few minutes until he got organized, but I was in too much of a rage to stall. Father was also in a furor and insisted on accompanying me. Our battered old four-wheel drive never moved faster than covering the two miles back to Fitzgerald. In a few bounds I reached the lake, and sure enough a hundred yards off shore, four men sat unconcernedly in my dinky boat casting into the lily pads.

"OK, you bastards!" I screamed. "You want Bill Phillips, you got him! Get back here with that boat, or I'll put a bullet hole through its bow!"

One chap immediately grabbed the oars and headed the craft directly to where we stood. When the nose of the boat touched the shore, I said, "OK, Pop, who is Roberts?"

"The guy with the oars," Dad responded.

As soon as Roberts stepped ashore, I swung a vicious haymaker catching the unsuspecting chap flush in the mouth and then continued with a flurry of poorly aimed punches. Roberts sagged under the fury of my onslaught. I turned, expecting to be jumped by one or all of the other three, but they simply stood there with mouths agape. Almost at this instant, Jack, Harold, Lionel, and half a dozen others came sprinting down the trail to our aid. Encouraged by the success of the initial skirmish, I charged over to where the other three men stood in a state of shock.

"Which one of you ass holes is next?" I challenged.

"Hold it!" one of them yelled. "What is going on?"

"Don't give me that bullshit, you local punks know f---ing what's going on. If you think we can't keep this property private, now is your chance to challenge us!" I stormed.

"I don't know what you mean," one of the men moaned. "We're visitors from Calgary. I had no idea this was private property. We hired this man as our guide," he wailed.

Surrounded by a dozen irate men, blood gushing out of Roberts' mouth, the scene must have resembled a nightmare to the three young tourists who at that moment were certain they were going to suffer the same fate as Roberts. Completely taken back by the sudden change in developments but still in a frenzy, I screamed at Roberts. "You told my folks we couldn't keep you out of Harcourt Park. Well, if I catch you in here again, one of us will end up in the hospital, now get the hell out of here and don't ever return!"

They wasted precious little time leaving our sanctity, and I felt Father had been avenged to some degree. News of the episode soon spread around, and any locals considering trespassing on our property now realized we were a tightly knit group who would stand shoulder to shoulder against intruders. There were other minor incidents over the years, but that confrontation did more to establish our reputation for tenacity as well as stiffen the determination of other members to enforce our privacy than any other act in the early years of our growth.

As summer waned, our relationship with Hank deteriorated. His abrasive ways aggravated Dad and all the men who worked for Sumcot. Another irritation was his refusal to get dressed as a businessman when prospective purchasers arrived to look at lots. He would greet them with a week's growth of beard, barefooted, and wearing a pair of tattered old army shorts. The only sales made, which totalled four, were written on the week end when Joyce and I arrived. By midsummer, we were rapidly running out of finances. The entire labor force, including the cottage construction workers, was threatening to quit, and I knew a change had to be made soon. One Friday afternoon in early August when I arrived with the payroll, Keith Cameron was waiting for me by the sales office, and I knew from his face that decision time was at hand. "Bill," he said glumly, "no one is left who will work for Sumcot while Sharpe is here, and I want to warn you that Pop just told me he's returning to Toronto also."

Hank was waiting for me at my cottage, already aware a crisis existed. There were no bad words or ugly scenes when I said no choice remained but for us to split up. A buy-sell clause included in our agreement demanded that whatever offer one partner made, the other must be willing to accept, and so I offered Hank two alternatives— either he could have Sumcot Development Corporation Ltd. and I would take Philjon Lmt., or vice versa. He asked to be allowed the week end to consider the situation and would give me his decision Monday morning. At the Toronto office after the week end, Hank admitted the men wouldn't work for him in Harcourt Park. This left him no alternative but to take Philjon Lmt. Within a week, Sumcot Development Corporation Lmt. became entirely mine for the first time since its inception, but it was like owning a Cadillac without a motor. Our deal with Schwandt had now been signed, and so the company's assets consisted of a heavily mortgaged, slightly developed huge tract of land, totalling 6,700 acres with no working capital.

Autumn colors heralded the swiftly approaching winter, and facing a bleak spring with no money for advertising and promotion and having no employees except Vera Johnson and my folks, I personally went to work at sales making phone calls to every prospect who ever contacted us regarding Harcourt Park. Fortunately, before the first snows, we sold an additional seven leases, making a total of 11 for the year. Although the lot selling price only averaged $1,500, it provided sufficient income for Mom, Pop and my family to survive until spring with assistance from Gold Star Jewelry which still operated full blast.

Coming up with sufficient cash to consummate my deal with Chester Schwandt became my greatest dilemma during the winter of '60. The total purchase price of $124,000 didn't frighten me, but the downpayment presented a problem. Fortunately, Mr. George Drew, a wealthy old gentleman and a client from my mortgage broker days, had confidence in my ability to produce and loaned me sufficient money on our model cottages to complete the Schwandt acquisition. Our financial instability tempered our excitement at tackling the enormous expansion of Harcourt Park, and we eagerly hoped additional financing could be arranged allowing us to proceed in an orderly manner. Again fate intervened, as a very unusual character entered my life who would play an important role in the saga of Harcourt Park for the ensuing four years.

Chapter 7

A Cast of Characters

When we refer to an individual as a character in present day-jargon, it usually means we consider that person an oddball or eccentric. According to the dictionary, this interpretation of the word is an informal usage. The true definition of a character when used as a noun is: "The combination of qualities or features that distinguishes one person, group or things from another." Therefore, when I make reference to people with whom I became associated throughout this chapter, I am intending the real meaning of the word, not the informal usage.

Recollecting almost any incident of our past, regardless of whether it brings back sad or happy memories, an individual who shared those times with us usually flashes to mind. The place, time, and circumstances are often important, but it would be a rare case when another person wasn't involved in the recalled event. Whenever I think of the Brokenhead River, I immediately associate "Oh Gee" Cullhane and Ed Barham; Imperial Lumber in northern Alberta brings to mind Ed Carlson and Ed Davis. Whenever I recollect my days with Brompton Pulp and Paper, Russ Claxton, Andy Melnyk and Joe Levesque flash into my consciousness.

Throughout life we are all constantly confronted with new people. Many play no prominent roles in our over-all existence, but every now and then, an individual will stand out in memory due to prevailing circumstances or that person's special qualities and mannerisms. So it happened to me during the early 1960s when a cast of several characters became enplaned in my personal orbit, some for only days but others for the balance of my life.

In January 1961, I moved my headquarters when Less Knox and Bob Taylor went their separate ways and sold me, at a good price, their two-story office building at 2652 Danforth Avenue near Homeland Realty's old head office and two miles east of my Coxwell-Danforth location. Vera Johnson, who had been with me since leaving Homeland in 1955, wasn't just an employee, but more like an older sister. She and her husband Herb socialized with Joyce and me on many occasions. Vera was not only an excellent typist, but also took shorthand with speed and precision, did all my preliminary bookkeeping, and kept abreast of every transaction to be able to deal intelligently with all matters that arose whether I worked in or out of the office. It came as a blow, therefore, when she informed me that due to Herb's retirement and their wish to travel she would be leaving, though not before finding a satisfactory successor. After interviewing several prospects, she recommended Theresa Mackey, who proved to be more than a suitable replacement. None of us imagined at the time that the new relationship between Terry and me would continue for a quarter of a century. Terry's education and business experience allowed her to perform not only as a capable secretary but as an outstanding administrator as well.

Surviving on the limited income from Gold Star Jewelry and with no idea of where to raise funds for an advertising campaign, I decided nonetheless that it would be impossible to operate without sales help. In midwinter, I made a deal with a hot-tempered redhead named Fred Oram. Coincidentally, Oram had been a partner with Jack Harlow in the real estate business but had severed that relationship after his 12-year-old son was killed in a car-bicycle collision. Fred, close to his boy, became unbearable to live with, and so he ended up with a divorce and an alcohol problem. Making an effort to straighten himself out and wanting a change of environment, he applied to me for an opportunity to sell property out of the city. After discussing the situation with Harlow, I decided to give Fred a crack at the job. Jack felt that Fred ably fit my requirements of being an able salesman, ardent outdoorsman, and a hard worker. His major downfall was his quick temper, and so I warned him of my habit of flying off the handle often with limited provocation. We elected to give it a trial nevertheless, and Terry, Fred and I put our noses to the grindstone and began advertising before our spring opening of Harcourt Park.

All respondents indicated an intense desire to visit the development, and so for the third straight year, Dad and I returned to fight the Burleigh-Kennaway roads before the frost had left the ground. We purchased a new crawler bulldozer on time, and after mastering the operation of the new machine, I drove it proudly into the development. Dad still got stuck with the Land Rover, but now the crawler equipped with a winch attachment made short shrift of extricating him from mudholes. We were in ecstasy, as it meant we could finally move around the development at our leisure without the fear of getting mired in mud. With gorgeous spring weather blessing the delightful countryside but too early for the arrival of the black fly hordes and again isolated from the hodgepodge of city life, Pop and I were enjoying our few days alone before facing the rigors of a strenuous summer. Leisurely draining blocked culverts, repairing washouts, and building small bridges in the brilliant sunshine made us wish the easy going lifestyle could last a while longer. Unfortunately, it came to an unpleasant and dramatic end far too soon. One morning Dad wrapped the crawler winch cable around a half dozen two-by-tens and asked me to tow them a couple of miles up the road where he wanted to build a wooden culvert. At the location, he experienced difficulty releasing the grab hook on the end of the cable, and so scrambling off the bulldozer to give him a hand, I inadvertently kicked the winch into gear. The hook caught Dad's gloved hand and jammed it into the winch drum, stopping the idling engine but not before Pop's entire left hand had become wedged into the mechanism. After getting his mitt released and gingerly removing the mangled glove, it was painfully obvious I had to rush him to a doctor as his little finger dangled uselessly from the badly battered hand.

"Don't panic, I'm OK," Pop insisted, as he looked at my queasy face. "Just get me back to the cottage so I can wrap it in a towel."

After a couple of fortifying belts of rum, we headed for Wilberforce and were blessed when I never got mired or delayed as Dad lost quite a pile of blood. A nurse bandaged the wounded hand and sent me scurrying 25 miles to a doctor in Haliburton who insisted Dad spend the night in the hospital. Pop lost half his little finger and received dozens of stitches in the rest of his hand but came through the ordeal in fine spirit and continued his duties as superintendent without a moment's sick leave. Workman's Compensation eventually paid $150 for the loss of his appendage, which Pop said wasn't such a bad deal because the finger was pretty old and wasn't used much except to stuff tobacco into the paper when he rolled his own. The hill where the accident occurred became known as "Pop's Little Finger Hill." It taught me a valuable lesson known by all experienced operators, which is always to switch off the ignition before getting down from the machine.

Sales progressed dismally due to our limited advertising and promotional budget, and by early summer, Sumcot balanced precariously on the brink of bankruptcy. Though Jack McNeil only worked for me on a fee basis, he had a great interest in our financial well-being, and he accompanied me as I laboriously pounded doors in the downtown financial sector of Toronto searching for a lending institution that would loan money on Sumcot's land, our only asset. Big Jack, excellent at preparing a suitable presentation and a first rate conversationalist, also provided comic relief during those dismal days of constant turn-downs. One day in desperation, I visited John Walsh to see if he had any worthwhile ideas, and he supplied me with a name that just came to his attention. J.B. (Ben) Brien would not only provide financial succor in my topsy-turvy and teeter-tottering business career but also became deeply involved in my on-going business adventures. Unfortunately, this association would sever my relationship with McNeil for a year or two.

Brien didn't appear at first glance to be a burgeoning business tycoon. A tall thin French Canadian with thinning red hair, he had a ready pleasant smile and seemed more like he should be out selling encyclopedias. The Canadian Independent Business Federation, of which he was president, had their offices on two floors at King and Yonge in the financial core of the city. The bustling activity resembled a scurrying hive of bees and gave an indication of his company's vibrant enthusiastic attitude toward business. Already operating several weeks, their prime pursuit was locating concerns in financial straits, loaning money to make them healthy, then by charging high interest rates plus factoring fees, earning large profits. In certain cases they also took a percentage of the company's common stock as a further stipulation to their becoming involved. Only hours elapsed before Terry and I were back at their offices with the necessary signed documents, and by the end of the day, checks were being issued to pay off our creditors. Although Brien had me pledge everything I possessed as security, he never requested any Sumcot shares, and for that I was particularly grateful as I fervently hoped never to have another partner as long as I remained in business.

Shortly after siphoning sufficient cash into Sumcot to get us moving again, Ben Brien called a meeting and suggested we invest a heap of money in a major advertising and promotional campaign. Marketing Methods, another small company with whom he had become financially associated, had three employees; Tom Baker, Norma Jones and Danny Mau, who were also the sole owners. Ben requested they be used as the promotional agency. A live-wire trio, they soon conjured up some wild but expensive promotional schemes and began by designing a four-page pamphlet called "The Harcourt Park Gazette," which we produced in 100,000 printing lots to be used for direct mail plus door-to-door distribution. After visiting the property, Marketing Methods prepared a half hour, 35mm slide presentation for showing in private homes or at larger gatherings of interested prospects. Finally, Ben persuaded me to drop our lakefront lot prices and follow the lead of the Florida Land Companies by offering the sites at $10 down with the balance at moderate monthly charges, including a low interest rate. Brien would then purchase these first mortgages at a discount and apply the funds to our indebtedness with him. We didn't think this type of promotion exactly fit the mold of Harcourt Park as originally intended, but broke and desperate, we were prepared to grab any straw in the wind. With all our novel advertising expenditures, however, people still weren't flocking into the development, and so a strategy was devised allowing our sales staff to meet families face to face.

A team of oxen trucked in from Quebec at a cost of $1,700 was hitched to a Conestoga wagon, and with a driver and two female models dressed in mid-1800s garb were sent lumbering through the city to neighborhood shopping malls where we set up for a four-day stay. Plaza owners gave us space in their parking lots to set up our attraction and were delighted by the impressive show that attracted throngs of curious families. We chose three major centers: Cloverdale Mall in the extreme west end of the city; Nortown located in the north central area; and Eglington Square in the east. The promotion started at the first part of August, and a week prior to arriving at each mall, we saturated the surrounding area with our new brochures, advertising both the oxen and Harcourt Park. At each location we either rented an air-conditioned store or set up huge tents where we could seat people to view our slide presentation of the development. We lacked one detail, however, to complete the atmosphere and provide assistance at our set up. Needing a rugged-looking male dressed like a settler in the 19th century and who could converse with families about Harcourt Park and entice them to visit our slide presentation where the sales staff would take over brought Louie Rodrigue immediately to mind.

Rodrigue, 6 feet 2 inches tall and weighing 225 pounds, was an entertaining conversationalist and an ideal candidate for the position. Louie, who lived in the village of Harcourt with his lovely wife Mary and six children, worked for Dad on the brushing crew. I was quite fond of the big brash French Canadian, though Father didn't exactly share my feelings. Ten years older than I, Louie had experienced an interesting life. Raised in the farming area of northern Ontario, he joined the Canadian Army Provost Corp., and spent six years during the war as a sergeant searching the northern woods of Ontario and Quebec for draft dodgers who were frequently his own neighbors and countrymen. Many French Canadians were opposed to serving in the Canadian Armed Forces to fight in Europe as they felt no loyalty toward the British and disliked France for not offering them any assistance for almost two hundred years. After the army, Louie became a Peterborough Policeman for twelve years before giving up law enforcement to move to Harcourt where he intended to make his fortune in the lumber industry.

An extroverted individual, Rodrigue had high hopes for his enterprise and did everything in grand style. He purchased thousands of dollars worth of new equipment on time, then took a contract with a local mill to cut and haul a large amount of timber. Unfortunately, before removing his logs from the bush, the owner of the timber tract was accidentally killed, and suddenly everything was tied up in an estate battle. Louie, unable to obtain money for his logs, watched the finance company repossess all his machinery and put him in hock far beyond his ability ever to repay. To provide bread and milk for his young family, he went to work with an axe for Sumcot at $1.40 per hour, but in Pop's opinion, he wasn't worth half that amount. I rarely interfered when Father wanted to fire one of his crew, but with Louie, I admitted having a soft spot in my heart, though Pop said the soft spot was in my head. With no more than four years elementary education, Louie's horizons were definitely limited but I could understand that after his spending many years in a position of authority and importance, he was reluctant to get excited with dull manual labor. The unbelievable debt load he faced together with constant dunning by creditors was a situation with which I could easily sympathize, and I hated to see him lose the only source of income available as jobs were hard to come by. The Rodrigues did own and operate a small cafe in Harcourt, but with six children, it didn't provide much financial relief. No question about it, the big Frenchman was lazy when it came to swinging an axe for an hourly wage, but if an endeavor suited him, no one could match his physical ability or enthusiasm. He absolutely adored fishing and hunting, and whenever we needed a guide to take newspaper people or photographers into some remote lake for snapshots or a fishing safari, I always hired Big Louie who would trot through the woods with the canoe and all the gear at such a speed it was next to impossible for the rest of the party carrying nothing to keep up.

Dad's annoyance at frequently finding the big lug hiding behind brush piles either reading or sleeping gradually reached a crisis point. On several occasions when I reprimanded Louie for his lackadaisical ways, he always offered an excuse about bad health or an old war injury causing him grief. I would relent and persuade Pop to give him another chance. Although aggravated, Dad deep down also liked the guy and would agree to keep him on the payroll if he'd mend his ways. That is until Friday when Pop reached the limit of his patience. "Bill, that son-of-a-bitch of a Frenchman has got to go, or I'll lose the rest of my men!" he stormed. Then proceeded to tell me once again of Louie's slovenly work habits. We were widening the Burleigh and Kennaway roads at the time, and Dad had a crew including Louie brushing back the trees and shrubs. This gave me an idea.

"Pop, on Monday morning put Rodrigue on a stretch of road by himself, mark where he starts without letting him be aware of the trap, and next Friday let's see how far he has brushed. If we're not satisfied, I'll fire him myself."

Seeing the end to his problem, Father agreed. The following week end Dad couldn't wait to race back to show me Louie's performance over the previous five days. "See what he's accomplished for forty hours pay!" Pop stormed. "Any of the others would easily have done the same amount in half the time."

"OK," I responded. "When he comes in for his pay, let him go."

Shortly after supper Louie came rolling up to the cottage in his old car for his check. "Evening, Pop," he offered. "Got my check?"

"Yes," Dad stormed, "and it will be your last because you're fired."

"What in the world is wrong Pop?" Louie asked, as innocent as a young lamb.

"I'll tell you what's wrong," Father raged. "I marked the spot where you started Monday morning, and I just showed Bill what you performed in forty hours. It isn't half what the other men brush in a week."

"Oh, Pop" Louie said, looking like a whipped puppy. "Did you think I worked all week? I've been sick and laying by the brush pile most days. You never asked for my time, and I never gave it to you. I was waiting until I saw you tonight to tell you I only worked fifteen hours and to tell you to dock my next week's wages."

Dad stood with his mouth open looking as if someone had just doused him with a pail of cold water. We both knew the Frenchman was lying through his teeth but had to admit it constituted powerful fast thinking. With little alternative, Dad retained Rodrigue, and he produced satisfactorily until I rescued him from the bush crew and put him to work with the oxen.

Louie fit into our sales promotion like a well-formed glove and performed admirably. A natural ham, he loved talking with people and easily persuaded interested families to visit our slide showing where the sales staff attempted to take $10 deposits and make appointments to visit the development. Within forty-eight hours Louie began taking deposits himself, and before the end of the week, he became a permanent member of our sales department.

Jim Hay, the manufacturer's representative who supplied Gold Star Jewelry, was a quiet, reserved chap in his mid thirties. Upon learning of our other activities during our business relations, he became interested in selling Harcourt Park. I put him on as a part-time salesman during the oxen promotion, and when he proved capable at deposit taking and dealing with customers, he also joined our ranks on a full-time basis. Lionel Faust and several others worked part-time for Sumcot at shows and other promotions, but Oram, Hay, Rodrigue and I, with assistance from Mom and Joyce, did almost all the selling for Sumcot for four years. This included not only Harcourt Park but also Oak Shores Estate on Bald Lake, a second development purchased in late 1961 but not opened until the following summer. Throughout the two decades that Sumcot offered vacation property in Ontario, no succeeding sales squad had a more effective or successful record than we did in writing cottage and lot business, but none came as close to matching our quartet in inner company animosity.

Jim and Fred agreed on very little and constantly bickered, but neither of them had any use for the happy-go-lucky Louie who due to his enormous size and physical ability didn't back down for one minute and on more than one occasion traded blows with quick-tempered Fred. Following the oxen promotion, Hay, Oram and I handled the city operations during the week while Rodrigue remained at Harcourt Park to look after drive-in traffic or week-day appointments. All four of us handled week-end prospects. Louie's slothful ways still aggravated Pop who complained bitterly about the big guy sleeping during the day in full view of everyone passing the sales office. He did an excellent job of getting contracts signed, however, and so I didn't give a damn how much he dozed if he became alert at the appropriate time. Jim and Fred's main agitation toward Louie centered around Louie's enormous ego. Rodrigue wouldn't hesitate to inform clients confidentially or anyone who would listen that he was Sumcot's sales manager, general manager or even president, depending on his mood at the time and that he worked in sales only to help out. This infuriated the other two.

One warm autumn afternoon during the week, I made a surprise visit to Harcourt Park and discovered Louie sound asleep in the office chair, his feet propped up on the desk and unaware of my presence. Not only did I do a double take at the hand-printed sign on the desk but at the moment found it so amusing I broke into a guffaw, awakening the big guy from his siesta. In crudely printed letters the sign read: "Louis Rodrigue Sales Meneger." Slightly embarrassed, Louie nonetheless insisted the title gave him a little prestige and helped him close deals. Though comical, the sign, which he must have kept hidden in his car, forced me to put my foot down. I explained that despite the fact the appellation may have added status to his position it didn't do much for the dignity of the corporation when people discerned the company's sales manager couldn't even spell and proceeded to show him copies of contracts he had drawn where the spelling and mathematics were atrocious and had to be redone in the city. As a result, Louie devised a clever sales pitch that encouraged each customer to print his own contract and credit application. Though highly irregular, it worked well for him, and this deviation from the norm just aggravated Hay and Oram that much more.

In spite of all the antagonism, we reversed our disastrous beginning and enjoyed a very successful year, ending with a total of 52 sales averaging slightly less than $1,700 per lake-front lot. The unusual aspect of our accomplishment was that all but four of those sales were written after the beginning of August when the vacation lot industry's season is deemed to be almost finished. The oxen promotion got us started, but later sales were attributed to our first promotion at the Canadian National Exhibition where we set up a booth in the Electrical Building. The C.N.E. success whet our appetite for more trade shows, and we immediately arranged for booth space at both the Toronto Sportsman Show and the Toronto Home Show the following spring. This new approach of offering our product to the public at trade shows instigated the idea of stretching our horizons beyond Ontario. Ohio provides more summer tourists to Ontario than any other American state, and so I made my second airplane flight ever to investigate the prospects in Cleveland. After interviewing several interested realtors, I settled on one large enthusiastic firm who advised me that before we could offer Ontario real estate in Ohio I would first have to be approved by the state. This would necessitate a trip to Columbus, the state capital. An appointment was arranged the following week, and so I returned to Toronto.

Joyce, who had never been in the air, vowed she never would fly, and I did nothing to change her mind. Informing her I had to return to Cleveland in a few days and continue on to Columbus, she assumed I would be driving and indicated an interest in accompanying me. I told her to pack her things. It wasn't until Oram picked us up to go to the airport that she realized we were taking a commercial flight. A little late to back out, she reluctantly went along, and like a duck taking to water, she rapidly became a more avid flier than I.

Joyce remained in Cleveland with the realtor's wife while he and I automobiled to Columbus to meet with the state hierarchy, a trip that proved to be a complete waste of eight hours of strenuous driving, and that also thrust us into an unnecessary, nasty, and embarrassing scene as well. After the usual preliminaries and we were seated in front of a panel of state representatives, one attorney asked in a sharp tone of voice, "Phillips, are you requesting we consider approving your Ontario company to sell your land in the State of Ohio?"

"Yes," I said. "That is our desire and this was explained carefully to your office when we arranged the appointment."

Harrumphing a couple of times while perusing our application, he suddenly looked up and in a sarcastic manner said, "For Christ sake man, do you think we are going to approve a Canadian company to do business in our country when you still have to get the Queen of England to OK everything you do?"

"What in the world are you talking about?" I demanded.

"What I mean is," he retorted, "your Federal or Provincial governments are still required to obtain the Queen's approval before any legislation becomes law."

"In the first place," I said bluntly, "I have no idea what this has to do with getting sanction to offer Ontario property in the State of Ohio. Secondly your facts might be correct, but your implication is utterly stupid. Canada has been an independent country since July 1st, 1867, and whereas it is true the Governor General of Canada is the Queen's official representative in the Federal Government and her Provincial representatives are the Lieutenant Governors, they are strictly figure-heads. Since Confederation, they haven't vetoed legislation passed by the Canadian Parliament, nor would they in the future under any circumstances. How long has it been since a reigning monarch in Britain interfered with the ways of that nation's government?" I asked in disgust. "Canada belongs to the Commonwealth of Nations, all of whom are ex-colonies of Great Britain, the same as the United States, and if all your citizens are as narrow-minded as you, I am personally damn thankful you had a revolution and no longer are part of that worth-while organization." With that off my chest, I got up and prepared to leave.

Other panel members offered some words of consolation, but by and large, the attorney appeared to hold sway. As it seemed obvious I would only be wasting my time and perhaps become even more irritated, if that were possible, I stomped from the room.

Though not certain of the value of being able to advertise and promote in Ohio, the incident infuriated me to such an extent that upon returning to Toronto, I hastened to inform Brien of my disappointment. "It's time you met Peter Betts," he remarked, and an appointment was immediately arranged.

Peter Betts, a senior partner of a large London, Ontario law firm, handled all of Brien's political problems and with sound reasoning. John Robarts, the present Premier of Ontario, was also a member of that firm, and their connections were widespread and powerful. London remained one of the staunchest British strongholds in the province, and Betts resembled the epitome of those roots. Thinning hair brushed straight back, a bristly moustache like that worn by most British army majors, and speaking in a clipped though precise manner resembling David Niven, Peter Betts appeared more like an English aristocrat than a Canadian barrister. He listened intently to my report of the Columbus meeting and showed extreme provocation at my account of the Ohio attorney's snotty attitude. After mentioning their firm's personal relationship with the State of Ohio's Attorney General, he suggested I leave it in his hands and they would attempt to remove the roadblocks, warning it would probably be a long, costly process.

Taking advantage of Betts' counsel and political affiliations, I decided to discuss an even more pressing problem dealing with Harcourt Park. As the development had grown and prospered making it increasingly evident we were for real and wouldn't disappear, many individuals who had either been refused permission to fish or hunt or, even more significant, had been unceremoniously thrown out, went storming to the Department of Lands and Forests complaining of our intransigence. Members of that department, always the champion of the people, were irritated about our isolation and harassed us by frequently visiting to inspect member's catches and raving we had no rights to alter Provincial game laws even though we stocked the lakes ourselves. We retorted with equal vehemence that we had absolutely no intention of breaking those game laws. Nonetheless when they were unable to catch any of our people with more than their legal limit, it seemed to make them even more determined to open Harcourt Park to the public. Most game wardens and other department personnel hated the private signs on our roads and lakes, and this added to their resolve to do something about what they considered an intolerable situation. In late 1961, the Department of Lands and Forests notified us that all 66-foot right-of-ways leading into Harcourt Park would be blazed so anyone could find our private lake shore without difficulty and be safe from prosecution. If they followed through on their threat, though the portages would be difficult to traverse, it would become legally impossible to keep interlopers out of the development. Peter Betts offered no solution to this conundrum but arranged to meet me in Harcourt Park the following week end.

Peter brought Mrs. Betts, and they spent a day visiting with Joyce and me while going over the huge tracts. Before leaving Betts informed me he was impressed with our development and thoroughly condoned the plan. Both he and Robarts owned cottages on Weslemkoon Lake, a few miles east, and were definitely concerned about the ravages caused by an unthinking general public. Before departing, Peter told me not to worry about having Harcourt Park opened to the public, as he and the Deputy Minister of Lands and Forests were well acquainted and they would work something out. We heard no more of the province's intention to open the right-of-ways, but it wasn't until a few months later I learned how Betts had halted the intrusion.

The Deputy Minister operated a government aircraft, and he and Betts often flew together on official business. One day after covering a vast area of Northern Ontario, Betts apparently mentioned the rumor of the department's plans to interfere with the privacy of Harcourt Park. When the minister admitted his department was considering such a move, Peter Betts said, "My friend, if you open one 66-foot right-of-way into Harcourt Park, then be prepared to open every right-of-way in the Province of Ontario. As we've seen today, that will constitute a heap of work and ought to keep you out of mischief for the balance of the century. No judge in this land will allow you to discriminate against Sumcot, which is operating within the framework of the law." To my knowledge the issue died with that threat and another obstacle in Harcourt Park's continuous fight for privacy was overcome. Peter Betts had become an important ally.

Though delighted with the progress of Harcourt Park, the number of families who didn't purchase for one reason or another disturbed me. Many were discouraged by their lawyers who dare not charge sufficient fees to investigate thoroughly all aspects of our bylaws, leases, and agreements relating to the 21-year lease arrangement. It was simpler and less embarrassing to dissuade their customers from acquiring property in Sumcot's private development. Another major deterrent was not only the distance from Toronto but also the rugged ten miles of winding narrow road from Wilberforce to the development gates. We tried to keep their minds off the objectionable route by nailing signs on trees every few hundred yards such as: DON'T DRIVE LIKE THE DEVIL, THIS IS GOD'S COUNTRY; CAUTION MOOSE CROSSING, or SPECKLED TROUT UP TO NINE POUNDS. They did help. Nevertheless many of our prospects still turned around and drove out without even getting out of their vehicles. Those clients unnerved by the harrowing trail from Wilberforce were usually too nervous to make any attempt at turning around until they reached the parking lot by our sales office. At that point and thoroughly aggravated, they'd blast off at the first person they saw before taking off in a cloud of dust. Unfortunately those prospects didn't stop to consider that the long tedious road traversing the huge stretch of wilderness between Harcourt Park and Wilberforce provided the buffer enabling us to maintain our seclusion.

This steady loss of customers convinced me to locate another piece of land nearer the city which we could develop in a conventional manner. J.B. Brien reluctantly agreed to provide the money for the new acquisition, and so I began to search. One day while inspecting property near Bobcaygeon, 90 miles northeast of Toronto, I heard of a piece of property owned by Roy Kennedy, a local businessman, that included large frontage on Little Bald Lake plus an additional three miles of frontage on both sides of the Squaw River. Bald Lake, adjacent to Pigeon Lake had access to the famous 240-mile Trent Waterway, connecting Lake Ontario with the Georgian Bay on Lake Huron. Kennedy, anxious to sell, agreed to show me the property in late November, but since it was not accessible by a land vehicle, I had to arrange water transportation. I went to my close buddy, Ken Watson.

Over the previous ten years, my association with the Watson family had become extremely close, and Ken and I shared many adventures, especially while fishing or hunting. The Watson's had two boys and two girls, slightly older than our youngsters. Comparing the responsibility of child rearing helped cement our relationship because though attached to our offsprings, we were both bullies when it came to discipline due to our explosive natures. English born, Ken came to Canada as a penniless orphan, and as a young man with little education, he earned his livelihood by using his wits. He spent several seasons in his early years traveling across Canada as a roustabout with the carnival, and as a result of those connections he frequently supplemented his income from selling magazine subscriptions or working as a barker at the C.N.E. sideshows. Both my parents loved him, and he affectionately called them Mom and Pop. Their first meeting, which remained a fond memory, occurred during my folks' 1954 visit when we spent a few hours exploring the Canadian National Exhibition. Strolling down the midway jammed with people, Pop and I were walking a few feet behind Mom and Joyce when above the din of the throng I heard someone holler, "La-d-ies and gen-tel---men, don't miss the greatest attraction of the midway. A gen--u--ine Bill Phillips production. Y--e--s la--di--es and gen--tel--men, an original Bill Phillips production just brought in from Winnipeg."

Giving me a whack, Pop stammered, "Listen Bill, did you hear that?" Glancing over the heads of the slowly moving crowd, I spotted Ken Watson standing on a box in front of the Snake Charmers' tent and he was doubled over in hysterics. That ridiculous incident endeared Ken in Dad's heart as Pop loved that type of tomfoolery, and Ken soon proved to be his type of man. Ken and I deer hunted together occasionally before I opened Harcourt Park. Though he loved the camaraderie of the deer camp, Ken was anything but a polished hunter, and it appeared unlikely he would ever bag his own venison. In the winter of 1959, six of us—Pop, Brother Jack, Ken Watson, Ken Williams and a friend, Jerry Delaney, and myself—formed a small party to hunt deer in our own private preserve. Mom did the cooking though we stayed in my cottage. The group enjoyed a delightful week which included bagging three animals, one shot by each of the Phillips'. The six of us, with rare exceptions, hunted together for nine consecutive years, and we rarely bagged less than 50 percent of our limit. A couple of the others were erratic marksmen, and Watson couldn't hit a barn at twenty paces. I rarely missed getting my animal and more than once shot two or three.

These annual get-togethers helped weld the warm relationship between Ken and the Phillips clan more than any other endeavor in which we all participated.

In the early 1960s, Ken and Helen sold their Toronto residence to purchase a fishing camp on Pigeon Lake in partnership with another man. The arrangement didn't work, and so they sold out and went their separate ways. But the experience of being independent and fishing whenever he chose, at which he was both ardent and competent, made Ken reluctant to return to Toronto.

At this time, Outboard Marine Corporation had acquired a beautiful stretch of lake frontage at Gannons Narrows, an isthmus of water dividing Pigeon and Buckhorn lakes. The property contained a lodge called Oak Orchard that could more aptly be described as a castle. Each of the eight bedrooms contained its own private bathroom, and the one-story structure included an enormous living room with open fireplace, expansive dining room and kitchen, and a huge, wrap-around, screened balcony overlooking the picturesque lake and beautifully manicured front lawn. Outboard Marine purchased the gorgeous holdings for several purposes including its use as a private haven for both their Canadian and American executives including Ralph Evinrude and his wife Frances Langford. Another purpose for acquiring the deluxe estate was to provide a test site for the boats, motors, chainsaws, and other products being manufactured in Peterborough, only nine miles from the property. They also used the facilities for entertaining sports writers and politicians, and as a headquarters for advertising agency personnel when preparing television commercials or other promotions.

Outboard Marine sought a personable couple to manage the maintenance of the grounds, buildings, and valuable equipment, plus, to oversee the cooking and supervision of the kitchen staff. Ken and Helen fit the requirements perfectly and landed the excellent position which paid a handsome salary, provided free accommodations and food and all the booze they could drink. Taking advantage of my relationship with the Watsons, I usually stopped in a couple of times monthly when passing, either to spend the night or to relax with a few drinks and enjoy a hearty meal, as a more deluxe Shangri-La didn't exist in Ontario. With a variety of water transportation available only ten miles from Bald Lake, I went directly to Ken to take me for a water inspection of the Kennedy property.

An icy November wind whipped a mixture of rain and sleet across the land as Ken and I prepared to cross whitecapped Pigeon Lake to reach Bald. As a result we changed plans and lugged the boat and motor by car to Pluard's Landing at the north end of Big Bald which spared us the danger and discomfort of crossing the large body of open water on

Pigeon in such inclement weather. Roy Kennedy met us at Pluard's Landing in late afternoon dressed only in a light jacket and trousers. This seemed inadequate clothing considering we still faced a ten-mile round trip in open water at the mercy of the blustery north wind and cold rain which was already forming icicles on the sides of our craft. He insisted his apparel was satisfactory, and so we continued with the inspection.

Kennedy's property covered the entire north shore of Little Bald Lake and though we cruised slowly, the shoreline wasn't easy to assess through the driving sleet. We passed two or three marshy bays bordered by groves of picturesque evergreens, and I visualized tremendous potential for the property, especially if the coves were dredgeable. After an hour in the boat, we reached the Squaw River, and Roy Kennedy, who was miserably cold, requested we pull to shore. Luckily we found some burnable wood and somehow got a fire started. Sitting in the shade of some cedar trees around our warming fire, Roy produced a quart of whiskey that swiftly put warmth and life back into our innards. The improved environment plus the alcohol induced Roy to become more talkative, and before long he indicated an anxiety to dispose of the shoreline only. His complete holdings consisting of 2,000 acres extending three miles west from the lake to the #36 Highway.

"Why do you only want to sell the lake shore?" I asked.

"Well, Bill," Roy responded, "I am still timbering the balance of the land and so will only sell three hundred feet along the lake."

"How about the Squaw River?" I inquired.

"There is three miles of river or approximately six miles of river frontage including both banks. It is useless for developing however, as there is no access to Bald Lake due to the numerous waterfalls and rapids along its course, making it impassable for boating. That, plus the fact I want to cut all that marketable hardwood standing close to the Squaw," Kennedy concluded.

Taking another slug of booze before passing the bottle back, I looked him square in the eye and with conviction said, "Roy, here's my proposition. You're asking price of $48,000 for the property is too high, but, I'm certain you are willing to negotiate. Instead of any discount in your price however, I want six hundred feet back from the lake rather than the three hundred you have offered. And though you believe it may be worthless for vacation property, I also want all of the Squaw which is to be measured a maximum of three hundred feet on both sides from the river's center and running from the lake to the #36 Highway."

Roy, swallowing hard, polished off the rye whiskey and within a few moments replied, "Let's go back. We've got a deal."

And so one of the most profitable land acquisitions of my developing career was consumated over a bottle of whiskey, a campfire and one of the severest days of miserable weather to which I've ever been exposed in the North Woods. Roy's inadequate attire was also a factor as it was his misery that induced the tete-a-tete on the bank of the Squaw River.

Returning to Oak Orchard after dropping off Kennedy, Ken asked, "What the hell are you going to do with the Squaw River, cut timber?"

"Times are changing Ken," I replied, "and the vacation property industry is facing a major transformation. Low-priced lake frontage is disappearing like the whooping crane, forcing people to go further and further from the city to pay increasingly more and more money for less and less land. Also many townships adopting subdivision control are forcing developers to install services such as water systems as a condition of approval. Therefore we have to start thinking of a greater density of lots per acre to be able to compete. I believe many families would purchase a lot and cottage along that picturesque river and keep their boat at a commercial marina, providing the marina has ample parking and isn't located too far away. If river property with the same amenities only cost the buyer a third as much as lake frontage, then it might even outsell the traditional lake-shore cottage site."

"Well you got it cheap enough," Ken chortled, "You got it for nothing."

"That is not the only thing I got for nothing," I replied. "I requested six hundred feet back from the lake instead of three hundred, because I visualize a low-priced row of back lots with a view of the lake. These second-tier sites can easily be hooked into a water line installed along the main road that will service both them and the lake front. A road, water system and power line all have to be constructed for the use of the lake shore, and so the extra cost of servicing a second row of lots will be negligible, allowing us to market them at a very low price."

"How many sites do you estimate you might get from the property?" Ken inquired.

"Philrick, my old company, is developing that stretch of lake shore which abuts Kennedy's land on the north and includes the entire north shore of Big Bald Lake. Rick Richards paid $90,000 and obtained a total of only ninety lots, and so I'll never understand why he didn't grab the property we just inspected. Unquestionably there are several swampy sections in Kennedy's property, but I believe they can be dredged out back to high ground. The severe indentation of the lake shore makes map measurement misleading, and I believe there is considerably more actual shoreline than Kennedy thinks he owns. We will probably develop three times the number of lots Philrick procured at half the price."

"It should be a sweet deal then," Ken concluded.

Neither of us dreamed how far my estimate was out and in our favor.

During the ensuing eighteen years, Sumcot developed and sold a total of 550 lots from the complete Kennedy acquisition.

Delighted with my new land purchase and confident Sumcot would now capture a larger percentage of the market plus not having any corporate financial worries prompted me to make two decisions that early winter which again altered our style of living. With regret, especially because of the hard work and loyalty of several of our female employees, I decided to close down the Gold Star Jewelry operation which was floundering mostly due to my lack of attention. Jim Hay and Fred Oram collected all the inventory and conducted a successful half-price sale at our Danforth office three weeks prior to Christmas. They surprised Joyce and me with a presentation of two thousand dollars cash as a result of their efforts, instigating my second resolution which had a far more lasting effect on our future. Now that our living depended exclusively on the vacation property industry requiring a continuous seven-day-a-week effort for ten months out of each twelve and with money in our pockets, we returned to Florida for a three-week vacation. Adding to our enthusiasm for our second journey to the Sunshine State was the 1962 Oldsmobile 98 I'd just leased. Renting a new automobile every two years in lieu of owning one was recommended by our firm's accountant and was a custom I continuously used for twenty years, though within four I switched to Cadillacs.

One significant upshot of our second Florida vacation centered around the people we met who soon became an integral part of our existence. Another consequence was our resolve to one day become Florida residents. My fantasy of staying on the ocean, nearly as important as the trip itself, was fulfilled when we obtained accommodations at The Diane Apartments in Hollywood, a complex directly overlooking the fascinating sea, The friendly group from all over the American northeast with whom we shared the Diane added to our enjoyment, but two couples soon became more than acquaintances. By the end of the first week we accompanied the Schramms and Graces in most of their endeavors including meals, card games, plus gambling trips to horses, dogs and jai-alai. Hans and Magda Schramm, though several years older, developed a warm relationship with Joyce and me that lasted throughout our lives. They were business associates and long-time companions of Dot and Homer Grace who were also to become intimate friends. In fact, within two years Dot, Homer, Joyce and I communicated almost as a family. The Schramms owned a Carvel Ice Cream franchise in Poughkeepsie, New York, but the Graces who worked for them were in the process of purchasing the operation.

My friendship with Hans at first seemed strange. Being a pronounced patriot in my earlier years and having listened to Uncle Ernie's accounts of the terrible conditions in the trenches during World War I, it almost seemed blasphemous to become buddies with Hans Schramm who fought for the Germans in that conflict. Hans assured me, however, that he couldn't have been responsible for my uncle's wounds or problems resulting from the German gas attack because shortly after the beginning of actual combat he became a British prisoner of war. Magda, also German born, was a matronly lady who dearly loved a card game, especially pinochle. The camaraderie enjoyed by the six of us meant rarely a day of our vacation passed when we weren't together for at least some portion.

Our intimacy with the Graces meant Joyce and I could now include Yankees among our personal friends, and we enjoyed the new-found relationship tremendously. Homer, an ex-musician from the big band era, dragged his a's like all upstate New Yorkers, and when pronouncing a word such as bass, it came out as baaaas, sounding more like a bleating ewe. Homer loved to gamble, particularly at jai-alai, and when excited he would holler at the athletes in his Yankee accent. I constantly teased both him and Dot about their foreign accents. Dot, a blond who always wore her hair in an upsweep, reminded me of the flappers of the 1920s. Our three-week togetherness with the Schramms and Graces turned into a lifelong companionship and played an important role in our returning to Florida at every opportunity.

With large booth space in both the Toronto Sportsman Show and the Toronto Home Show, I looked forward to a banner year. The major attraction in our exhibit, a continuous sound slide showing of Harcourt Park, drove our neighboring exhibitors to distraction but drew a continuous flow of traffic to our booth. We continued the selling technique of requesting ten-dollar deposits from prospects interested in visiting the development but added a new wrinkle. Constant objections to the distance convinced us to offer our clients one night free accommodations at Wilberforce to give them more time to inspect the property as well as allowing our sales staff a greater opportunity to control the inspection. Deposit taking flourished, and when it became evident we would be deluged with prospects, I decided to revert to our original plan of selling mostly package deals. To increase our cottage building capacity, however, necessitated a building manager, and as a result Len Nordin joined the firm.

Nordin, a Swede who took on the huge responsibility, unfortunately didn't have a personality to match that duty. Nevertheless over a span covering two decades he became one of the most trusted employees ever to work for Sumcot. An exceedingly ambitious and conscientious individual, Len never asked one of his crew to perform an assignment he himself wouldn't or couldn't do better, making him a tough taskmaster

and well respected by his charges. Without architectural plans or specifications and with each unit constructed on a different shaped lot in
the rugged undulating terrain made the actual erection a carpenter's
nightmare. Unfortunately, that only scratched the surface of the problems faced by Nordin. Due to the near impossibility of controlling theft,
we stockpiled very little lumber inventory in Harcourt Park. This required that each cottage unit be shipped complete on one truck load.
This system worked satisfactorily if there were no deficiencies on the
load, which rarely happened. When shortages did occur, it meant delaying the job until a load arrived for another site, and was perhaps
dumped at a different lake several miles from the cottage short of
material. The use of inexperienced construction crews instead of jour-
neymen carpenters, also caused considerable headaches.

Price competition in the industry wouldn't allow wages remotely
near the union pay scale, and so most cottages were constructed on a
contract basis by local farmers and handymen anxious to improve their
living standard. Each three- to five-man building crew worked from
daylight to dark to earn worth-while money, and some wouldn't hesitate
to cut corners if they thought their sloppy workmanship wouldn't be
detected. All these problems forced Nordin to work unbelievably long
and strenuous hours because Sumcot personnel constantly badgered
him to have the buildings completed for closings, our only source of
funds. Buyers eager to take possession of their newly acquired property
to enjoy the balance of the summer season also harassed the building
department unmercifully. Len moved into one of the Sumcot models
and ate his meals with Mom and Dad, which probably provided one of
the few bright spots in his employment and kept him on the job when
things got especially hectic. Most Saturday nights throughout the long
eight month season found Len and me polishing off a bottle or two of
whiskey to relieve the enormous pressure.

Oak Shores Estate, our new development on Little Bald Lake, could
only be reached with a land vehicle by traveling two miles down the
narrow gravel-topped Nicols Cove Road and then following an old log-
ging trail two miles to the property. This bush path, equally as formidable to improve as anything we faced in Harcourt Park, wound through
hilly, heavily treed terrain. Having no one else with road building or
heavy equipment experience forced me to send Rodrigue temporarily
down to supervise and look out for Sumcot's interests when we began
construction of the new road in July of 1962. Arriving in Bobcaygeon,
the nearest town, nine miles from Oak Shores Estate a few days after
we began to work, I discovered the big Frenchman had opened accounts
in nearly every store in the village, and the local citizens understood
that Louie was Sumcot's General Manager. Concerned that costs might

get out of hand, I sent my egotistical employee back to Harcourt Park and hired Len Thompson as our Oak Shores Development Manager. A bulldozer operator, Len had excellent experience in road building and did an outstanding job in all aspects of the tough assignment at Oak Shores Estate. Unfortunately he had a major alcohol problem and didn't remain too many years with the company.

Although pleased with Sumcot's progress I still faced a substantial dilemma if the firm was to prosper. As our staff steadily increased to handle sales and administration of the expanding operations, our payroll obviously skyrocketed. This was acceptable while doing business and making profits, but as our season only lasted seven months at most, keeping these employees productively occupied during the off season became a problem. Otherwise they became an intolerable drain on our resources. In search of an answer, I left the North American mainland for the first time. If Sumcot's people were capable of successfully selling and developing vacation property in Canada, I reasoned they ought to also operate successfully in the sun belt during winter months. Competition in Florida was intense, particularly between Gulf American and General Development Corporation, both offering a wide range of lots in several locations for ten dollars down, minimal interest rates, and exceedingly low monthly payments. These two companies operated large booths in all Toronto shows and would be tough for a small corporation like Sumcot to try to rival, and so I decided to spend a few weeks investigating the potential for developing in the Caribbean.

Another factor prompting me to look south to expand our selling season was our impending approval in the State of Ohio. What compelled the Columbus boys to change their attitude never came to my attention, but I was delighted when notified that a Herb Sifferlin from the Ohio State government would be visiting Ontario for the purpose of approving our land for sale. Herb proved to be the opposite of those ignoramuses with whom I originally had the misfortune of being cross-examined in Columbus. An affable, intelligent and open-minded individual, Herb became enchanted with our developments and spent several days in Harcourt Park visiting with Mom and Pop. They became such good friends that Herb arranged to bring his wife back for a visit the following summer. Finding no problem, Sifferlin approved both developments which meant we could promote Ontario land in Cleveland the following spring, the first time in that state's history that foreign property could be offered for sale within its borders. This expansion of our selling base then became another inducement to visit the sunny south to seek a suitable area for winter selling.

On a cold blustery day in early October, I left for Nassau and my initial exposure to tropical weather other than winters in Florida. When

I stepped out of the air-conditioned airline cabin, the first blast of hot humid air shocked my system almost the same as an unexpected surge of cold, and within minutes perspiration soaked my clothing. Although it was unpleasant, I decided the discomfort was much more bearable than an icy north wind which besides being disagreeable is also painful. Therefore, I again promised myself that one day Joyce and I would spend our winters perspiring in the South rather than shivering in the North.

The British Colonial, Nassau's oldest hotel, became my temporary headquarters, and the aura of British tradition pervading that century-old hostelry was overwhelming. The enormous selection of cutlery at the dinner table baffled me, and so I called over the maitre-de to receive a lesson in their proper usage. After dinner I went for a stroll through the tropical gardens ablaze with late blooms and couldn't imagine any-one not being enthralled with the allurement of the surroundings. On our two trips through the American South, the percentage of black people surprised me, but their preponderance in the Bahamas came as a complete shock. Happy people with a ready smile, they soon made me feel comfortable though I had difficulty understanding their dialect. Ambling down the main thoroughfare that first evening, the differences between Nassau and other cities in North America I had visited were quite evident. Young pimps by the dozens tried to entice me with the service of a young black girl and regardless of my vehement rejection, they persisted in attempting to sell their product. They dispersed only when I threatened to summon a policeman. The police officers were a complete antithesis of the pimps. Dressed in starchy white uniforms with red stripes and adorned with pith helmets and black gloves, the officers gave the city a truly British atmosphere. Another startling con-trast to the norm were automobiles driving on the left side of the streets.

The most successful development in the Bahama Islands, Lyford Cay, was owned by E.P. Taylor, one of Canada's most eminent indus-trialists. He purchased the property through Harold Christie, a local, wealthy, real estate operator and member of the Bahamian House of Assembly. Christie had a home and office not far from the British Colonial Hotel, and so I decided to begin my education by visiting this known personality. A well-publicized murder had taken place on the island a few years before my arrival when Sir Harry Oakes, a multi-millionaire, Canadian gold-mining industrialist had been found slain in his home. Harold Christie, a house guest at the time, became a prime suspect. Though soon cleared of any implication in the tragedy, Harold Christie's name appeared in Canadian news stories for several weeks as a result of his involvement in the drama. Christie wasn't at his office, but his affable manager after perusing my credentials suggested I visit the House of Assembly to meet both Harold and his brother Frank. When the manager introduced me to the two brothers, I no doubt looked a little astonished. Both were adorned in attire straight from seventeenth century England, including long-haired wigs, heavily starched shirts complete with bow ties, and flowing tails on their formal jackets.

Harold scanned some of Sumcot's material including our impressive four-page color brochure that seemed to clear up any doubts about my authenticity. He instructed his manager to show me the complete island of New Providence including all large parcels of land that he either owned or controlled. The tour was enjoyable, but the offerings unimpressive. I decided to spend the next day on my own inspecting other properties and getting a feel of the area with the consideration of attracting to Ontario or Ohio residents who might be interested in acquiring developed lots in Nassau for retirement, investment, or winter vacationing. At the conclusion of my fact-finding mission, a different problem began to surface. Labor costs would unquestionably be much higher because of the inexperience of Bahamians in our method of building and developing plus their habit of not working at the same frantic pace as Canadians, due undoubtedly to the intense heat and humidity that prevailed throughout much of the year.

The fact that Canada and the Bahamas were both members of the British Commonwealth of Nations allowed Canadians certain import tax advantages over U.S. corporations, but the Bahamian government was adamant about not allowing outside labor including Canadians into their country and would permit only a restricted number of managers. This could entail a lengthy and costly training program for adequate employees. Another concern was that equipment and materials had to be brought directly from Canada to be eligible for the special import tax. This meant that shipping charges would be considerably higher than if the items were simply brought across from Florida. Becoming disillusioned, I planned to leave for Jamaica and see if the same road blocks applied in that country, but that night I received a telephone call from Marcus Francis, Harold Christie's private secretary, requesting that I meet Harold at Cascadilla, his residence, at 9 a.m.

Cascadilla sounded like the title of a romantic novel, and Christie's vine-covered dwelling and expansive grounds belonged in that type of setting. The huge old brick mansion, a short block off Nassau's main thoroughfare, and surrounded by exquisite tropical gardens, appeared like a small storybook castle, though I never determined how many actual rooms were enclosed within its hoary interior. An elderly servant escorted me to Harold's private bedroom where the solemn old gentleman sat in his pajamas enjoying a morning cup of tea. Neither his wife nor children were present, but a male servant bustled around laying out Christie's clothes while preparing the master's bath in an adjoining bathroom. After inquiring about my initial impression of New Providence Island and the property I had been shown, then listening intently to my concerns regarding labor problems and shipping costs, he invited me to join him for two or three days on a tour of some of the other islands. I leaped at the opportunity and within an hour we were airborne in Christie's private plane.

Harold instructed the pilot to fly low over the numerous uninhabited islands dotting the tranquil and multi-colored waters of the fascinating Caribbean before landing at Exuma. While he attended to personal business, I was escorted around that attractive island and shown another large tract of ocean front property owned by Christies. That evening we flew to Cat Island, Harold's personal constituency, where he had a multi-bedroom bungalow. The spacious dwelling with all modern conveniences sat on the highest point in the center of the narrow island with a spectacular view of both coasts. Marcus Francis, his athletic and American educated private secretary, joined us for dinner that evening in "the castle on the hill" and remained the night.

Harold and I were the only white people on the island, and Harold's comfortably appointed retreat was the only dwelling of more than two rooms. The purpose for the visit besides showing me another stretch of ocean frontage owned by Christie was to allow Harold to do some electioneering, for the next election was just around the corner. The morning dawned calm and beautiful, and I insisted on walking to Christie's property situated approximately three miles from his residence on the uninhabited eastern shore. I agreed to let Marcus pick me up in three hours with the Land Rover. Cat Island, about 85 miles long and with no elevations higher than 200 feet above the sea, provided a meager living to a few hundred impoverished Bahamians who resided almost exclusively along the western coast. They eked out an existence by fishing, growing a little corn, and raising a few chickens and pigs. Coral and limestone predominated the surface which when broken down and mixed with a little top soil provided a rich base in which a fine assortment of fruits and vegetables flourished. Strolling down the path toward Christie's holdings, not a human within sight nor sound, I couldn't believe my geographic ignorance of the Western Hemisphere. It came as a complete surprise to discover a Caribbean Island so thoroughly remote and uncivilized. My astonishment, however, increased tenfold upon reaching the magnificent stretch of ocean shoreline included in the Christie estate. Altogether he owned ten miles of marvelous beach, and as far as I could behold in either direction, not a human footprint disturbed the endless sand. Even more astounding is that even now, twenty-three years later, the same stretch of ocean shoreline still remains in its virgin state. Returning to the house on the hill for lunch with Marcus Francis, I remarked about the solitude of the island.

Marcus, looking at me with a smile on his good natured face said, "Bill, this island is crowded compared to some in the Bahamian Archipelago."

I accompanied Harold for a few hours while he visited with his constituents and still vividly recall the pitiful chitchat that went something like this:

"Afternoon, John," Christie would say, "How you doin'?"

"I'se againin' Mr. Christie," John would drawl, ending the conversation.

This type of dialogue typified Harold's electioneering exercise. I tried to imagine Canadian politicians using a similar simple approach and decided it might be far superior to some of the nonsensical tirades we are bombarded with in my country.

During the two days Harold visited with constituents, I spent considerable time chatting with Marcus, who was full of information and opinions regarding the future of his homeland. An extremely knowledgeable pleasant man and obviously quite fond of his employer, Marcus played an important role in my journey by unwittingly divulging his point of view about the political situation in the Bahamas that discouraged me from considering the tropical paradise for our southern development.

Marcus remarked that Christie's United Bahamian Party, comprised mostly of whites, would undoubtedly get majority of seats in the election taking place in a few days, but in his opinion it would be the last time. He didn't suggest that a switch to an all-black government would necessarily be beneficial but regarded it as inevitable. The predominately black Progressive Liberal Party wanted to wrest control of the country from the white minority population who had ruled since their independence. Marcus Francis' prognostication proved accurate as the Progressive Liberal Party took over the government five years later at the next election, and whether the black populace improved their living standards over the ensuing two decades is debatable. The new government made it even more difficult to import white supervisors or laboring help in the mistaken belief this would guarantee more jobs for their own people. It is unlikely that this approach, which mirrored the thinking of many third-world nations, was effective. Trying to improve their citizens' living standards by forbidding entry to those individuals who could teach badly needed trades was like attempting to operate a university without professors.

On our final night Harold asked me to join him on his private yacht which he'd just purchased from Britain's Lord Beaverbrook and was being sailed down to Cat Island from Nassau by his captain and crew. This provided another unforgettable incident I would treasure for the rest of my life.

Having never been aboard a deluxe cruiser, I looked forward to spending a night on the yacht anchored a half mile off Cat Island. In late afternoon under cloudless skies we boarded the sleek craft sitting motionless in the turquoise waters of the calm Caribbean, a scene resembling a toy boat in a back-yard swimming pool. After being introduced to the captain and his mate, I met two of Christie's guests, Sam Griffith, a renowned American speedboat racer and his mechanic, Bob, a South Carolinian. Both were well advanced in enjoying the afternoon's happy hour. Griffith, a retired U.S. Air Force colonel who held several speedboat records and owned a yachting business in Miami, Florida, invited me to join him and his mechanic for a cocktail. I enjoyed myself immensely, and by dinnertime I was not only getting tipsy but also quite intimate with the likable colonel and his equally amiable assistant.

The unfortunate Bay of Pigs fiasco of late 1961 when President Kennedy held back the American Air Force from supporting Cuban assault troops who had landed on Cuban soil rankled many American Air Force officers, and Colonel Sam was no exception. Frequently during our cocktail party the Bay of Pigs failure entered the conversation, and the freer the whiskey flowed, the more intense became the discussion. The Canadian government had officially recognized Castro's Cuba, a situation most Americans resented, as they considered it an act of giving comfort to the enemy. Although I held no sympathy with my country's position, being a Canadian put me on the wrong side of the fence with Colonel Griffith, and he constantly inquired about my personal feelings regarding the Communist Cuban government.

"Sam," I said with sincerity, "I'm every bit as anti-communistic as you and just as disappointed at the lack of success with the Bay of Pigs operation."

"All right," Sam replied. "After we've finished eating, come back to my stateroom, and I'll give you a chance to prove your statement."

Once in the colonel's cabin, the mechanic produced a huge blueprint of a water craft and Colonel Sam in a hushed voice began to describe the details of the vessel. "This is a special type of torpedo boat," he explained. "It is being constructed somewhere in Florida right now and will be used to enter Havana Harbor for the purpose of blowing up Castro's major oil depot. The reason for the low silhouette is so we can ride between the waves and not be detected by the U.S. Coast Guard's radar, and the purpose for its length is so it will be heavy and stable enough to withstand the thrust of the projected missiles.

No doubt the incredulous expression on my face spoke louder than mere words because Griffith hesitated and then asked, "What's the matter, Bill? Are you shocked?"

"A little," I replied hesitatingly, "but where do I fit into the picture?"

"Well, I figure if you are as sympathetic to our cause as you claim, then you'd like to be a part of the attack. There is little chance we'll be stopped or captured, but there is that risk. If we do get caught and a Canadian is involved, it will help show the world it isn't only Americans that are pissed off with Castro."

My head was spinning from the combination of whiskey and the sudden revelation of an impending attack on Havana, Cuba of which I was expected to take part. Nevertheless I tingled at the contemplation of the daring enterprise and felt absolutely no compunction about getting involved.

"When do you expect the incursion to take place Colonel?" I asked in my finest military tone, just as though I was already part of the covert operation.

"Within six months, I hope," Sam responded. "Give me your Toronto phone number, and when you get a call from me, fly to Florida immediately. Until then, though, don't mention it to a soul. Harold Christie is unaware of our plans, and I'm frightened to tell him because of the proximity of the Bahamas to Cuba. He might not like the idea being so close to home."

Colonel Sam gave me his personal card so I could reach him in Miami if I got impatient.

After our secret rendezvous in the closed stateroom and the incriminating drawings had been stored away, we returned to the yacht's spacious living quarters for a cigar and brandy. Seldom have I experienced more ideal weather conditions than we encountered that evening. A radiant moon bathed the tranquil sea where not a ripple disturbed the reflection of the gorgeous white sand lying thirty feet below the anchored yacht.

"A perfect night for an ocean swim," the captain suggested, and within minutes we all disrobed and plunged into the tepid water. With no females aboard, swimming attire was unnecessary, and the sensation of lazily paddling in the nude with so little effort needed to remain afloat, was a completely new and unique opportunity. I took full advantage. Swimming in the placid salt water was so effortless that before realizing it, I had moved a couple of hundred yards from our craft. Looking back I noticed no one else in the ocean. They were either standing on deck or on the steel stairway that had been dropped for our easy access to the sea and were gazing across the water in my direction. Making my way back, I hollered "What in hell is the matter with you guys? Why aren't you swimming?"

"Come on out for a minute," Colonel Sam shouted.

"We didn't want to alarm you Bill, but these waters are heavily infested with sharks," Sam stated. "Bob and I were scuba diving this afternoon not far from here, and we spotted several rather large specimens. You were in no danger because we would have spotted one in the calm moonlit water, but it's safer around the yacht. Let's go back in and have a leisurely dip."

"No thanks, Sam," I responded in a quavering voice. "I think I'll just retire."

I left the following day for Kingston, Jamaica, and I never heard from Colonel Sam Griffith again. Given the opportunity I definitely would have accompanied them on the escapade, not only because of the thrill of the adventure, but if successful, the raid would at least have been some measure of revenge for the gallant Cubans who lost their lives at the Bay of Pigs, in our never-ending confrontation with Communism. I never knew what happened to the planned foray until two or three years later. Traveling on a commercial airliner one day, by strange coincidence I happened to be seated beside a middle-aged American Air Force officer. During our conversation I offhandedly asked if he'd ever heard of Colonel Sam Griffith.

"I know him quite well," was the reply. "Why do you ask?"

"Oh, I met him once," I remarked nonchalantly, "it was shortly after the tragic Bay of Pigs disaster, and I recall he was terribly upset."

My acquaintance looked at me and smiled. "Yes," he said, "Colonel Sam Griffith was indeed upset, like most of us, and he made an honest attempt to even the score. Sam planned on blowing up Havana Harbor and had a ship almost ready for the attack when unfortunately the plot was discovered by the CIA or the FBI. The Colonel was forbidden to leave the American mainland and is still under strict surveillance as far as I know."

"I'll be damned," I retorted, and dropped the subject.

Kingston, Jamaica was my first outright exposure to abject poverty. No matter what is read in newspapers or witnessed on television, one has to see first hand the dire conditions to which some of our fellow humans are subjected to appreciate fully the tragedy of their situation. A short distance from the affluent beach area surrounded by luxury hotels where I stayed were huge sectors of utter degradation. People were living in shelters far less spacious or comfortable than we used on the farm for pigs or chickens; children were wallowing in raw sewage with little more than a gunny sack to cover their nakedness. A look of utter despair on the faces of the inhabitants brought their pitiful plight into its proper perspective. Suddenly those years of deprivation on the farm during the Depression when I thought we had been hard up made me feel stupid. We lived like millionaires compared to these wretched human beings.

Sumcot's colorful brochures again got me the attention of the right people, and a meeting was duly arranged with several top government officials. Jamaica had opened a tract of land near Montego Bay on the northwestern tip of the island, and at the time of my visit they were luring Canadian and American companies to get involved with the promotion and further development of the government-owned property. Attending the assemblage were two white attorneys and half a dozen blacks, all members of the Jamaican government. Several times during the course of the meeting I was emphatically warned by both races that Jamaica, thoroughly integrated, would not allow any separation of the races in the development, on the work force, or anywhere. They were also adamant about refusing to allow outside labor into the country, explaining that their purpose in encouraging outsiders to participate in the Montego Bay project was to create jobs for the local populace, not for foreigners.

Following the interesting get-together, one of the attorneys invited me for lunch, and I joined him and the other white member of the assemblage to a private club in the affluent section of the city. The impressive club provided delicious food, served exclusively by black waiters, the only black people visible in the premises. Curious, I asked my host, "Are there any black members in this club?"

"Heavens no," was his startled response.

Before getting further involved with government officialdom, I chose to hire a taxi and explore the coast line on the opposite side of the island and visit Montego Bay. Lord Ronald Graham, an English nobleman owned and operated a lucrative real estate business in Ocho Rios, a picturesque town on the northeastern coast, and I headed for his office.

My talkative cab driver, with whom I spent the biggest part of a day, went to great lengths to explain the philosophy of the local population. According to his figures, less than 30 percent of all men lived constantly with one woman, but had mistresses throughout the island depending on the man's ability to provide financial assistance to the inevitable growing family. A happy individual, he introduced me to at least three of his stable of females who all seemed happy to see him so I had to admit the arrangements had a certain joi-de-vivre lacking in our culture. The taxi ride through the mountains separating the two coasts was both breathtaking and heart stopping. Luxurious tropical foliage lined both sides of the twisty, winding narrow road, which reached elevations in excess of 5000 feet. Constant near misses with fast-moving oncoming traffic, however, allowed little time to admire the scenery, and I was relieved to reach the other coast. Lord Ronald Graham, a personable and knowledgeable individual showed me several properties but admitted that the government-sponsored Montego Bay project would be hard to beat as far as the initial purchase price was concerned. When we went into building expenses I again was flabbergasted at the high labor costs in relation to the overall sales price. Graham also didn't believe there would be any relaxation of government regulations prohibiting the importation of outside skilled labor. I visited beautiful Montego Bay which showed great potential but my mind constantly returned to my grave concern about labor costs.

The north coastline was breathtakingly beautiful with verdant mountain slopes so near the water that at times they seemed to sprout directly from the turquoise sea. Jamaica unquestionably had many physical attributes to attract northerners, but my reservations about the immediate political future of the island nation urged me to search further. Before departing Kingston for St. Johns, Antigua, however, I had one further opportunity to obtain a knowledgeable opinion regarding the country's future.

Joyce Armstrong, Joyce's girl friend and bridesmaid, married shortly after our wedding and was blessed with twin boys. Unfortunately a tragic traffic accident took the life of her young husband and after collecting the insurance, she took her two sons and immigrated to Jamaica where she eventually remarried Pat Stewart. I recalled from letters Joyce had received that the Stewarts owned and operated a Texaco service station in Kingston. Miraculously after a couple of phone calls I located Pat, and on my final evening in the city, he and Joyce joined me for dinner. The night club the Stewarts recommended, situated on a heavily wooded mountain slope on the outskirts of Kingston, gave no indication of the poverty through which we traveled to reach the deluxe premises. Again the only blacks in sight either waited on tables or were the entertainers. I mentioned to Pat, a native Jamaican, my earlier conversations with government members who insisted the country didn't have any racial problems. Pat soon dispelled that notion from my mind. In fact, he said there was tremendous animosity between the 85 percent black population and the white minority who owned and controlled most of the wealth and property in the nation. When I inquired about labor costs, Joyce said, "Bill, compared to Toronto they are atrocious. We built our own home with local labor, and it took almost two years to construct what would have taken Canadians four months."

"Is it because they are slow, or do they lack the skills?" I asked.

"Both," Joyce quickly responded. "Many things were done incorrectly and had to be torn down and rebuilt. There simply are not enough craftsmen on the island to take care of demand. It is too bad an arrangement couldn't be made to send thousands of them to Canada to attend vocational school because they are willing and eager to learn."

"That settles it then," I concluded. "If I can't bring in qualified help then I will go to Antigua tomorrow and see if their government possesses the same rigid outlook regarding the importation of skilled labor."

The Stewarts immigrated to Toronto a few years later.

Antigua, a link of the Leeward Islands chain in the British West Indies, lay 800 miles southeast of Jamaica. If nothing else, the trip had expanded my perception of our planet's expanse. I was dumbfounded to learn Antigua was over two thousand miles from Toronto or nearly as far as Toronto is from the European coast, and I hadn't left the Western Hemisphere. The 108 square miles of Antigua is partially comprised of picturesque hills, a heavily indented coastline and a profusion of gorgeous white sandy beaches surrounded by groves of stately royal palms. After devoting two days to roaming the tropical paradise with different real estate agents out of Saint Johns, the capital city, I came to the conclusion the price tag on most large acreages put them out of Sumcot's financial reach. Therefore, I arranged a meeting with two Antigua cabinet ministers to discuss the possibility of acquiring state-owned land such as that offered by Jamaican officials at Montego Bay. The two ministers were interested in attracting Sumcot to their country, but their government neither owned nor controlled property on the island. They had an alternate suggestion however. Barbuda, an island ten miles long and six miles wide, lying 30 miles east, was administered by Antigua and according to the officials, more suited to Sumcot's style of development. They claimed the island boasted splendid white sand beaches and the mountainous interior gave it greater physical beauty. A major problem existed, however, about the rightful ownership of the land, and this would have to be resolved before negotiations could begin. They explained that Barbuda had been a British slave-breeding colony for many years. When Great Britain abolished slavery in 1834, the island was reputedly given to those people who lived there. Unfortunately no proof of this grant ever turned up, and so when the island came under the jurisdiction of Antigua, that country assuming the land to be state property. The Barbuda residents strongly objected and appealed to Great Britain where the matter sat unresolved.

"Mr. Phillips, would you be interested in meeting with council members from Barbuda together with representatives from Antigua to discuss the possibility of Sumcot taking ownership of a large tract of land on Barbuda with a proviso that you would create housing developments for the exclusive use and at no cost to the local inhabitants for which we would give them clear title? Perhaps by getting fee simple to some of the land they might be willing to cooperate, especially if it also means employment for their people."

"My first concern, Mr. Minister," I replied, "is your government's attitude in allowing skilled labor to be brought in for the purpose of getting a development started."

"We would allow you to hire Antigua residents," he responded, "but only a skeleton staff of Canadians would be admitted. The whole purpose of our considering such a move would be to provide jobs for both Antiguans and Barbudians."

"For a development company to make money, they must have qualified sales help, administrators, and skilled labor. Otherwise they can't possibly compete with Florida developers," I said emphatically. "This is the identical problem I faced in the Bahamas and Jamaica and will be the stumbling block in negotiations between Sumcot and Antigua toward acquiring property on Barbuda unless there is some loosening of those restrictions."

They said they would discuss the dilemma with Prime Minister Lady Byrd and contact me in Toronto if there was any interest in my proposal. I elected to postpone further consideration at the exciting prospect of doing business on the impressive sounding Barbuda until I received some encouragement from their government on the labor problem, but I never heard from them again.

On a clear day the island of Montserrat, another British dependency in the West Indies, can be seen from Antigua. A group of Toronto businessmen had been promoting a development on Montserrat for two years and were claiming great success. Since I was within 50 miles, I decided to visit. If Torontonians could be induced to buy on a tiny island like Montserrat where they had to transfer from Antigua, then Barbuda might be worth considering. I took one of the daily flights between the two neighboring island nations to make a first-hand inspection.

The tiny scenic country of volcanic origin had a total population of only 14,000, most of them residing in Plymouth, the capital, located on the opposite side of the island to the airport. A clamoring mob of cab drivers met the plane and pleaded for the opportunity to be my chauffeur. I chose Jim, with whom I thought I could understand and converse as their pidgin dialect was not easy to comprehend. Leaving the air terminal shack which sat out in an open field, I inquired from Jim if he knew the location of the Canadian development. He took me directly to another clearing adjacent to the airstrip where a lone bulldozer sat beside a scratched-up piece of coral rock that he insisted constituted the Canadian's complete property. An oasis in the Sahara Desert would have been more appealing. Jim explained the only hotels were located on the opposite coast, and I would have to cross the high hills which separated the island. With no return flight to Antigua until the following day I had no alternative but to find lodging. The road crossing the mountain range in Jamaica was a superhighway compared to the primitive snakelike trail we zigzagged over to reach the town of Plymouth in Montserrat.

Most of the island's inhabitants lived within a half mile of the ocean in both directions from Plymouth, and I was astonished at the richness of the black volcanic soil in comparison to the coral and limestone rock on the opposite coast. Agriculture flourished, with large plantations of cotton and tomatoes blanketing the plateau dividing the green-clad mountain slopes and the sea. My driver informed me that Canadians managed one of the more prosperous acreages, and so I asked him to take me to their residence. Charlie and Sue Roberts, an engaging young English couple, had immigrated to Toronto and then taken the position to oversee a 4,000-acre plantation not far from Plymouth. They offered to drive me to the hotel and join me for dinner, and so I discharged Jim.

The huge rambling hotel buildings and the sumptuous seven-course dinner served in the spacious dining room with a glorious panoramic view of the Caribbean were not what I expected. The owner, a large elderly black gentleman, joined us for dinner and recommended for my island stay one of the private villas located in the spacious and gorgeously manicured grounds beside the main hotel building. The entire complex had a spectacular vista. Situated on a grassy slope overlooking the glistening black sand beaches that edged the azure sea and a luxuriant mountain range for a backdrop made it one of the most desirable sites I'd seen on my trip. I wondered if the Canadians weren't developing the wrong side of the island.

Only a handful of whites inhabited the island nation, and they stuck together like ants in an anthill, with most of their social life centered around the gracious old hotel. A single American male staying at the hotel taught elementary school in Plymouth and offered a revelation about the sexual wonts of the female natives. Every Montserrat girl desired to have a baby with a white man, he claimed, because they believed the child would have a better opportunity in life. Therefore if I was walking the road, I should not be surprised if a young lady openly made a pass, as they would flirt without compunction. He said they were quite religious and generally carried a Bible, and it wasn't unusual for them to invite a white man to take a stroll in the jungle so they could make love while caressing their beloved Catechism.

"Do you take advantage of this situation?" I inquired.

"You bet," he replied. "The government requires you to pay five dollars per month to support any youngsters where you admit to being the father, and at that rate I can afford quite a harem."

Not certain whether to believe the cocky young American, I mentioned the conversation a while later to Chuck Roberts who immediately invited me to accompany him for a drive along the ocean trail which provided the only access to the villages scattered along the coast. Our narrow jungle path was overhung with foliage that almost brushed the simple shacks of the locals. Young ladies sitting or strolling along the trail were obviously familiar with my fellow Canadian, and they laughed, teased, and made sensual gestures as we moved slowly between their primitive hamlets. Charlie said if we gave then the slightest encouragement his Jeep would be filled with females. I remarked about the red hair and exceptional beauty of many of the girls, and Charlie said the phenomenon was due to a historical occurrence dating back four hundred years.

"In the sixteenth century," he explained, "Oliver Cromwell reputedly banished to Montserrat for life several hundred Irish prisoners, and because of all the willing and comely lasses on the island, it is said the Irishmen all died with smiles on their faces. I think you can see proof of their fertility as these girls undoubtedly have a trace of Irish blood. What the young American told you is true," Chuck continued. "This is the only place in the world I know where you can boast when you leave that you never made love to a native, because I don't quite uphold the morality of the young American school teacher and can't see how it can be good for the future of the island."

Although the young ladies did look desirable and I'd been away from home a long time, I had to agree with him. The Roberts' had become friends, and Charlie spent most of his time with me while I was on the island.

One day, the Roberts' together with their two children invited me aboard an old flat-bottomed scow for a beach picnic and a scenic cruise along a stretch of the magnificent coastline. The outstanding beauty of black sand coves surrounded by cliffs of pink coral and backdropped with steep emerald-hued mountain slopes reaching to the sky making each lagoon a private tropical sanctuary was an enchanting picture. The plantation which the Roberts' managed was owned by a Toronto corporation which, they understood, would be interested in a proposition to develop the acreage into a prestigious development or tourist resort. Montserrat with its outstanding natural physical beauty plus the fact the island had been widely publicized already in Toronto made it appear the most logical solution in my search for a southern development. That brought me back to the question of skilled labor, and so I sought the old gentleman who owned the hotel, whose name I've long since forgotten but who was highly knowledgeable about the political situation on the island.

"If I were to purchase land on the Montserrat for developing, what are my chances of bringing in adequate skilled help?" I inquired.

"None," he replied. "You would be lucky if the government approved visas for more than a half dozen."

"That is the response I received in three other Caribbean countries, and I don't think it makes much sense," I retorted. "In my humble opinion they are cutting off their nose to spite their face. By refusing to allow mainland developers, industrialists, or manufacturers to bring in adequately trained labor, they close the door on companies who would otherwise have come in and provided badly needed jobs plus government income. As an example, if Sumcot were allowed to bring from Canada up to 50 percent of its labor force, with the balance hired locally, we would be less apprehensive about the move. Under these arrangements, the 50 percent local labor would learn and adapt to our methods much faster if actually working side by side with our technicians rather than being tutored by a supervisor. People learn much faster by doing than by being taught to do. Within a few years all these island countries would have a substantial inventory of trained craftsmen, and the need to bring in outside help would be eliminated."

"An interesting approach to a touchy problem," my friend remarked. "I have several confreres in the present government and will pass along your thoughts. If there is any movement along those lines, I will send you a letter."

I never heard from him again either.

I learned a lot while visiting the beautiful Caribbean Islands, but doubted they provided an answer to the problem of annual employment for our burgeoning staff. Upon arriving home, however, I found a new possibility had begun to unfold.

Sumcot operated a lavish booth in the Governments Building at the Canadian National Exhibition, which had concluded a few weeks prior to my Caribbean jaunt. The State of Georgia had an exhibit adjacent to ours, and during the three-week tenure of the show, we befriended several of the people operating that booth. I discussed our interest in locating a southern development with their state executives who flew up for a two-day visit to the C.N.E. Returning home, these officials spread the word about our possible interest in locating a tract of land in the South, and when I arrived back in Toronto, several calls were waiting for me from realtors and land owners. One group from North Carolina insisted on setting up a meeting to discuss their development, Boiling Spring Lakes, a huge 10,000-acre property 25 miles south of Wilmington. Joyce and I planned to spend a few winter weeks in Florida to renew our energies and rekindle the warm friendship we'd established the previous year with the Graces and Schramms, and so we arranged to meet officials of the Boiling Spring Lakes development on our drive south.

Reeves Broadcasting, a large corporation listed on the New York Stock Exchange, owned television and radio stations from Bakersfield, California across the nation to Charleston, South Carolina where they'd purchased a television station owned by Drayton Hastie. The Hasties, a renowned family of several generations in South Carolina, owned considerable real estate including Magnolia Gardens a well-known plantation and botanical gardens a few miles outside the city of Charleston. Following the sale of his Charleston TV station, Drayton became president of Reeves Broadcasting. Reeves, Sr., the founder of the corporation bearing his name, had won several awards for his innovations with sound, and the firm searched for other communication depots to cash in on their publicity. When none were available, they decided to enter the lucrative land development business, and so in 1960 they purchased the large tract of land at Boiling Springs. Their interest in Sumcot centered around their belief we could be of considerable supervisory assistance due to our expertise as rural developers. We could be their sales representative in Canada and the State of Ohio. Drayton Hastie, headquartered in New York, though maintaining a residence in Charleston, met us at the property in early January 1963.

Driving through North Carolina on our way to the rendezvous, we saw huge signs along the highway advertising lots at Boiling Spring Lakes for as low as $495.00, with $10.00 down and low monthly carrying charges. I couldn't for the life of me figure how Sumcot could make any money selling land at such a low price and therefore approached my meeting with Reeves' officials in a very dubious frame of mind. Numerous tiny spring-fed ponds dotted the property, and larger lakes were being created by damming a small river. Also used for filling the man-made lakes was the flow from a spring that boiled and belched thousands of gallons daily from somewhere in the earth's interior, hence the name of the development. Large stands of long leaf pine surrounding the lakes, interspersed with holly and dogwood bushes plus an assortment of other attractive shrubs, made the lots more physically desirable than many of our Ontario properties. A nine-hole golf course had already been completed, an elegant club house constructed, and a small tract of ocean frontage acquired five miles from the project for the exclusive use of the Boiling Spring residents. The natural beauty and large capital outlay already invested plus the property's proximity to the Atlantic Coast encouraged me to at least listen to their proposal.

Over a two-day period Drayton Hastie and his development managers met with me several times, and I tried desperately to persuade them to sell only fully serviced lots and increase the price structure allowing substantially more money for advertising and promotion. They did have a small section serviced with roads, sewers, water and electric power reserved for those buyers who wished to build immediately. These lots were priced in the more realistic three to four thousand dollar range but were limited to about three dozen. Highway signs advertising lots at $495 concerned me the most because they would thoroughly confuse our customers if we sent them down by bus, and particularly if we exclusively offered the more expensive serviced lots around the largest lake as Drayton had suggested. Despite my pleadings, the Carolinians were adamant about continuing to promote low priced lots in competition with the large Florida developers, so deciding nothing more could be accomplished we continued our journey to Florida. Drayton accompanied us to Charleston where we met his charming wife and spent a pleasant evening with them at the local yacht club. Throughout the few hours spent both on the highway and during our time in Charleston, Drayton and I argued fiercely between the merits of his system of selling unserviced property at bargain basement prices or adding frills to the development and selling only fully serviced lots at a more realistic figure. Before parting I agreed to consider a compromise. Sumcot would option a block of the prime lots, many of which fronted directly on Boiling Spring Lake—the largest body of water—and adjacent to the already constructed sewer and water lines. In return, the developers would follow my suggestions of improving the selling area facade including planting rows of palmetto palms and large concentrations of azaleas and camelias to give the area a more southern look. Drayton also agreed to dress up the ocean frontage with cabanas and picnic facilities.

Joyce and I enjoyed a pleasant Florida vacation that included a delightful reunion with our four New York friends and an additional couple, Dot's sister Hazel and husband Joe Ross. We encountered a stretch of extraordinary gambling luck at the dogs, horses, and jai-alai, and though we spent freely, we left with more money than we had on our arrival. I fervently hoped it indicated a successful year for Sumcot especially as I had now decided to expand our operations to North Carolina by early summer.

Since arriving in Toronto in 1949, I generally worked long hours, but beginning with the spring of 1963, those earlier years were like a holiday. Our approval in Ohio allowed us to set up an exhibit in the Coliseum at the huge Cleveland Sportsman Show. Unfortunately their date coincided with the Toronto Sportsman Show and Home Show with only a few days separating each exhibition. Needing help, I enlarged our management and sales staff. Jack McNeil came to work full time to handle advertising and promotion, and I hired a chap, Bud Henley as

General Manager. Uncle George, who remarried following the death of Aunt Gladys, just got divorced and wanted to leave Winnipeg and The Hudson Bay Company where he'd worked for twenty-five years to begin a new life in Toronto. I put him to work on the sales force together with two new men, Gary Van and Von Vondette. Our new personnel eased the burden to some extent, but when I signed a deal with Reeves Broadcasting to option a large section of Boiling Spring Lakes, it meant Sumcot now operated on three fronts over a radius of a thousand miles. To reach Boiling Spring Lakes by commercial airlines required time and patience. The only connections were Toronto to New York to Washington, then by a twin-engine aircraft which stopped at several Virginia and North Carolina cities before reaching Wilmington. As a result of the cost and time involved by air travel, I sent Sumcot's staff to inspect our new holdings by automobile as our summer schedule permitted. Uncle George accompanied Fred Oram, Jim Hay, and Len Nordin. Gary Van plus Louie Rodrigue went with Mom and Pop. Bud Henley, Jack McNeil, and I paid a visit in midsummer as we prepared to offer our new southern property at the Canadian National Exhibition in August. I made another trip by car in early September with Joyce and our three kids, who were now a rambunctious trio from eight to twelve years of age. Joyce never drove an automobile until the spring of 1963 when she took lessons. I bought her a 1953 Dodge for $100, which proved the old adage that "you only get what you pay for," as it spent more time in the garage waiting for repairs than moving on the street. Joyce desperately needed transportation to squire our three offsprings to all those places youngsters have to go, especially as I was away so often. On our return from Wilmington I bought a 1956 Dodge for $300, which lasted a little longer.

Reeves Broadcasting replaced their Boiling Spring Lakes sales manager with Art Greene, a middle-aged man, originally from the Bronx but who had immigrated to the South shortly after World War II. Art, with considerable experience in selling and promoting vacation properties from Florida to the Carolinas, provided considerable expertise to the operation. He flew to Toronto and visited our two Ontario developments in the summer of 1963, and he, Jack McNeil and I devised a promotion for Canadian Shores, our new North Carolina development for presentation at the C.N.E. We elected to offer four-day bus trips from Toronto to Boiling Spring Lakes for $49.50 including meals, transportation and accommodations, and the money would be applied to their land purchase if they bought. Our C.N.E. promotion proved moderately successful, and in October the first bus loads of Canadians left Toronto for Dixie under the responsibility of Jim Hay. Although the buses were 90 percent full, we should have become suspicious of the motives of several of our transients when before they even left the city an assortment of musical instruments suddenly appeared plus a wide assortment of alcoholic beverages. The price for the return journey was a bargain, but we weren't prepared for the large amount of freeloaders the first two bus loads had aboard. Only three families signed a contract with Sumcot, though Jim suspected several others would go back and purchase directly from Art Greene. Justifying Sumcot's higher-priced lots although they included all public utilities in comparison to the $495 unserviced properties advertised so openly by Boiling Spring Lakes was impossible if the buyers didn't wish to build immediately. Nevertheless, because of the interest generated in Toronto as a result of our fall campaign, I decided to persevere another year.

In January, 1964, Joyce and I flew to Florida for our annual respite and the continuation of our love affair with the Schramms and Graces. We stayed at the Bimini on the intercoastal waterway so the girls could fish from the balcony but I missed the ocean and vowed never to spend time in Florida away from it again. When we returned to Toronto, I faced my first dilemma regarding the race problem that had plagued the United States for centuries.

Canada had eased the immigration laws allowing a massive influx of people from other Commonwealth countries. The West Indies, in particular, took advantage of the situation and thousands of their citizens poured into the country with Toronto a prime target because of the large concentration of industry and job prospects. Sumcot had mailed brochures across the city offering the $49.50 bus trip to our Canadiana Shores Development in North Carolina. Interested parties were given a 35 mm colored slide show of the area and its highlights, and couples wishing to book on one of the tours were requested to register with a ten-dollar deposit. The land purchase contract used by Boiling Spring Lakes contained a clause that purchasers must belong to the Caucasian race. All these unattached realities combined to create an embarrassing situation for Sumcot when Gary Van showed up at a house appointment where the occupants were black. Gary unquestionably panicked a little at the awkward situation, but nonetheless continued with the slide show and took a ten-dollar deposit for the trip to the Carolinas. Sumcot's staff decided to do nothing until I returned from Florida, at which time the following article written by Ron Haggart, one of Toronto's premier columnists, appeared in the editorial page of the *Toronto Daily Star*:

"THE SOFTEST SELL IN REAL ESTATE

 "With high pressure salesmen running around the country putting the arm on the innocent for food freezers, aluminum storm windows, health plans and cemetery plots, it's certainly a pleasure to find a company whose salesmanship is so low key as to be almost imperceptible. In fact, if the Sumcot Development Corp. Ltd., of 2652 Danforth Ave., treats all its prospective customers as lackadaisically as it treated Barbara Mercury, I'm surprised the poor fellows are able to make any money at all.

"If you live in Scarboro, where Barbara Mercury lives in a substantial five-bedroom house, you may have received one of Sumcot's luscious, full-color brochures a few months ago.

"They were selling real estate in North Carolina.

" 'Want to invest wisely for your retirement in the Sunny South?" the pamphlet asked. "Here's your chance to see the glorious Golden Zone and investigate before you invest.... Take a four-day all-expense tour to North Carolina for $49.50, and your trip is free if you decide to buy a homesite at beautiful Canadiana Shores!'

"WHY NOT TRY HALIBURTON?

"Mrs. Mercury was intrigued by the bright brochure and phoned the Sumcot office to ask for some more literature, and to arrange for a salesman to come to see her husband and herself. She phoned on Jan. 13 and the next bus tour, she learned, would be leaving Toronto on Feb. 19. On the night of Jan. 29, a salesman named Gary Van arrived at the Mercury's house with some slides to show them of the Sumcot land at a place called Boiling Spring Lakes, North Carolina.

"The Mercurys, somehow, were not bowled over with the forcefulness of Mr. Van's sales pitch. He didn't push the February tour from Toronto to Boiling Spring Lakes—he mentioned it was nearly full—and he told them there would be another bus trip in March.

"The Mercurys said March would be just fine with them and gave Gary Van a cheque for $10 as a deposit for their bus trip. Van said he'd have to check with his boss, who was in Florida just then, to see if everything was all right.

"Before he left, however, salesman Van tried to switch the Mercurys to another real estate development his company had in Haliburton. You can go to Haliburton for the weekend, Van pointed out, but North Carolina is pretty far away.

"No, Barbara Mercury said, they were the pioneering type and would like to see the North Carolina property.

"So Gary Van left with the Mercury's $10 cheque, promising to phone them back to confirm that everything was all right for the March 31 bus trip that was more than a month away.

"HARD TO FIND A SALESMAN

"When she didn't hear from the Sumcot people, Mrs. Mercury phoned their office on Feb. 4 and left a message for salesman Van. When, three days later, he still hadn't phoned back, Mrs. Mercury called again, and again left a message for Mr. Van. When, four days after that, the salesman still hadn't phoned back, she called again. She also noticed that the Sumcot people hadn't cashed their $10 cheque.

"Between then and March 31, which Mrs. Mercury had been told was the date of the next bus tour to the real estate in North Carolina, Barbara Mercury made about 15 phone calls to the Sumcot office.

"Sometimes Mr. Van was out for coffee. Then he was on two-week holiday. His holiday was then extended to three weeks. Then she was told Mr. Van was no longer with the company. She was not switched to another salesman, which Mrs. Mercury thought an enterprising real estate company might do. The March 31 date for the bus trip came and passed. The Mercury's cheque still wasn't cashed. No one tried to put the arm on them to buy real estate again.

"The Sumcot Development Corp. Ltd. is, I guess, just a kindly outfit that doesn't like to bother people. None of this, I'm sure, has anything to do with the fact that Barbara Mercury is a Negro."

The story had one major discrepancy. The check had been deposited and returned, stamped Non-Sufficient Funds. Regardless of the people's color or the clauses in the contract, if they couldn't honor a ten-dollar check, what hope did we have of selling them property? I phoned the Mercurys, who openly admitted they wanted to make an issue out of the segregation policies existing in the South and wanted to raise hell on the bus when it arrived in North Carolina. When I asked about their NSF check, they laughed and hung up. In a rage I phoned Mr. Charles Templeton the editor of the *Toronto Star* and explained our side of the story. Absolutely amazed that Haggart hadn't checked the accuracy of Mercury's report with Sumcot, Templeton promised to print a retraction and apology. Unfortunately before a repudiation of the damaging article appeared in the newspaper, Templeton resigned to run for leadership of The Ontario Liberal Party, and his successor would have nothing to do with our demand for amends. I ordered our attorneys to start a lawsuit for slander, but they advised careful consideration before beginning an action. We would probably win the case they said, but would unlikely receive any punitive damages and conceivably could be refused permission to advertise in the paper until the case was settled. The *Toronto Star,* crucial to our advertising program, won the battle without a fight, but all Sumcot personnel lost respect for the integrity of columnists. A few years earlier I had been exposed to a similar circumstance where a group of newspapers showed greater concern for readership than accuracy in writing.

In the late 1950s when John Walsh and I operated Philjon Limited as a real estate investment company, we acquired a number of old shacks on Williamston Place and Funston Avenue in the industrial heart of the city. Our intention was to obtain the entire block, then tear down the 100-year-old hovels and convert the property into an industrial warehouse complex. As they were mostly owned by different individuals, the acquisition of the numerous properties became a slow process. The majority of the units were occupied by tenants, and so we continued to collect rent which gave us a source of revenue to offset the mortgage payments. The occupants were the human dregs of the city—alcoholics, drug users, low class prostitutes and other riffraff of society. They were the only people interested in paying the low rents, and nearly all of the rent checks were issued by the city's Department of Welfare. At least two dozen children ranging in age from babies in arms to teenagers also resided in the one-story frame shanties. Howard Tustin and I felt tremendous sympathy for their deplorable state. The dwellings were so decrepit that any attempt at significant repair would have been tantamount to throwing our money down the sewer. To salve our conscience we did the occasional secondary improvement like cheap redecorating, fixing a roof leak, or patching a hole in the wall, but we might as well have burned the money.

One family who moved in with two youngsters got Howard's sympathy, and he proceeded to do some minor decorating to make the dwelling appear slightly more livable. Within two days Howard disgustedly reported that the fresh wallpaper was covered with human excrement. In another instance we freshened up a two-bedroom shack and a week later found one of the bedrooms three feet deep in old clothes. We discovered the clothes were supplied by the Salvation Army, and instead of laundering the apparel after it was used, the lady just heaved them into the youngsters' bedroom and went out to beg for more.

Perhaps the most disheartening episode occurred at Christmas. Again feeling dreadfully sorry for the children, Howard and I started a campaign to provide Christmas toys for our tenants' offspring as well as those in the neighbouring slums. Howard organized local service stations as drop offs and compiled a list with the sex and age of the kids for whom we were collecting so we could make an equitable distribution. A week before the holidays we collected the gifts, separated them into different piles according to age brackets, and took off on our errand of compassion with the trunk and complete back seat of Howard's car filled to capacity. I went with Howard because we felt it would require the two of us to get suitable presents into the hands of the grateful parents—or so we believed. Howard parked near the middle of the blighted area and remained by his vehicle to ward off nosy youngsters while I went house to house and asked the parents to come to the car to choose the appropriate parcels.

The following few minutes went past like a crazy nightmare. Someone shouted, "Hey kids, look at all the f---ing presents." Suddenly adults and children alike grabbed at the stack of parcels like vultures at a fresh carcass. They tore off the wrapping, and in less time than it takes to tell about the sordid affair, with the exception of a few pieces of Christmas wrapping fluttering in the breeze, very little trace remained of our Christmas give-away program. Disillusioned at the sight and particularly disgusted at not receiving one word of thanks for our efforts, we slithered away determined to mind our own business in the future. I have learned many times since, at least in North America, that the majority of society's impoverished riffraff are beyond redemption. The more assistance these people receive, the more they believe they are entitled to—a fact of life that will never change. The only logical answer in stamping out this scourge would be to spay the females and castrate the males so that further generations of degenerates would be eliminated. Society, however, frowns on this type of solution to its social problems.

Jean Newman, a member of the Toronto City Council, decided to run for the mayor's chair at the time we owned the Cabbage Town hovels. Like the majority of politicians, she searched for all possible means of obtaining newspaper publicity. There being no better way to get media attention than to take on the plight of the poor, she visited the city's slums. Unfortunately for Philjon Ltd., she began her crusade at Williamson Place. One morning I received a frantic call from a Toronto building inspector demanding I meet him at the property immediately. He had a list of required renovations on each of our tumbledown shacks that would have cost more to implement than the original outlay for construction. Newman made certain she had a bevy of newspaper reporters present at her inspection, and so the fat was in the fire, so to speak. By the time I returned to my office, reporters from the three Toronto dailies had either called for an appointment or were waiting for me to arrive. Being naive about their tactics I willingly granted an interview to all and tried to explain our side of the controversy. I showed proof of our low rents, scaled at half the rate available elsewhere in the city, elucidated on the fact that some of our tenants didn't have a roof over their heads until we allowed them into our shanties, and produced Toronto Welfare Department checks as evidence Philjon Ltd. was doing business with a City Hall agency, fully aware of the condition of the property. Finally, I patiently expounded on our efforts at improving, albeit only slightly, the dire living conditions in the hovels.

In spite of my disclosures, every article in the press during the furor, maligned me as a merciless slum landlord, and I was either misquoted about the facts presented in my office or the information wasn't used at all. Andy McFarlane, a *Globe and Mail* reporter sympathized with me during our interview and he said he originally came from Scotland and had first-hand experience with our type of situation. McFarlane claimed he knew of cases in Britain where families were moved from slums into newly constructed apartment buildings which shortly thereafter became the new slums and tenement houses. Regardless of his understanding of my position while chatting with me personally, his article depicted me just as hardhearted as the others. From that initial encounter with the press I realized that newspaper people were more interested in selling newspapers than in reporting an unbiased story, and so in the future I avoided all interviews if it were possible.

The whole incident puzzled me as to who benefited as a result of Newman's crusade except perhaps a few more newspapers sold. Unable to meet the standards demanded from the City Building Department, I sold our holdings to Coopers Iron and Metal, a scrapyard dealer who adjoined the property. Knowing we were either forced to sell or demolish the dwellings, they bought them for less than Philjon paid, and so we lost money. Most of the derelicts who resided in our shacks were moved to far more expensive accommodations, paid for by the Department of Welfare—or in the long run, the Toronto taxpayers. So the Toronto people as a whole lost money. City building inspectors told me years later that new housing constructed by the city for the impoverished frequently became a shambles on the inside in a very short period of time, and so neither the city nor the tenants gained much from the incident. Jean Newman? Well, she lost her bid to be the first female mayor of Toronto and so didn't benefit from her attempt at improving the lot of the poverty stricken. She did send a letter several months later, however, when the houses had been demolished, congratulating me on being an outstanding and upright citizen of the city, providing an ironic but pleasant touch to the inane episode.

It would be asinine to suggest that the article by Haggart played anything but an insignificant role in our failure to make money at Boiling Spring Lakes, but it did play a part in demoralizing our sales department as they felt caught between a new order in Toronto and the established attitudes in the Old American South. A total of five bus loads were dispatched over eighteen months, and eight families purchased a total of $17,000 worth of land at Boiling Spring Lakes. We did discover, too, that several of our customers returned later and bought less expensive lots directly from the developer. Before year's end, I cancelled our option agreement with Reeves Broadcasting, and though we all adored the area, it didn't provide an answer to my quandary of finding year-round employment for Sumcot's staff. The North Carolina escapade, in fact, cost the company considerable time and money and the services of two of its top producers.

Ben Brien, slightly disenchanted with my lack of success in the South and facing his own financial dilemma, forced me to cut weekly draws to our sales department. Fiery tempered Oram had done an excellent job over the four years even though he antagonized everyone in the corporation at one time or another, but unable to subsist without an income over the winter, he was forced to take a position with one of my competitors. Within a year Fred went into business for himself and developed some lake front property a mile from Wilberforce on the road to Harcourt Park. Sumcot's massive promotional campaign directed a steady stream of traffic into the park, which Oram got first crack at, thereby saving him extensive advertising outlay and allowing him to rapidly accumulate a pile of money. To add insult to injury he lured Len Nordin away from Sumcot in 1966. Oram's prosperity blossomed for a few years, but eventually his obstinate ways and ugly temper overcame his good fortune. The last I heard, he had emigrated to Calgary a poor man.

Jim Hay, who also established himself as an outstanding land sales-man over the four years of our association, left the company for a different reason, though the severance of his weekly paycheck accel-erated his decision. While escorting our clients into the Carolinas, Jim discovered a group of Wilmington people making big money selling ordinary candy but in a unique manner. Their sales people were attired in costumes of the Old South, the candy shop was dressed up in century-old decor, and they charged an astronomical price for the confectionary. During the 1964 C.N.E. I entered our booth one morning to find Jim in a state of exhaustion. When I asked for an explanation he recounted his discovery in the South and admitted to operating three booths in the exhibition grounds that were selling candy successfully with the same theme. Money was pouring in at such a rate that he had to work most of the night rolling dimes and quarters in order to make his bank deposits. Although it left me crucially short of experienced staff, I insisted he resign and pay full attention to his new enterprise.

Jim cleared five thousand dollars at that show, and believing he'd finally found the mother lode, he immediately opened candy stores in Toronto shopping malls. Unfortunately sales were too seasonal, the same ailment that hampered Sumcot and impeded Gold Star Jewelry. By spring he had closed all his establishments and moved to the United

States. Many years later Jim returned to Toronto and applied for a job with Sumcot at a time when no openings were available, which was regrettable as he did a splendid job in the company's formative years.

The loss of Oram and Hay caused me to search for replacements and as a result, a number of new characters entered the scene.

Merv Roberts, though not entirely new, certainly fit the modern usage of the word "character." After our hostile confrontation on the shores of Fitzgerald Lake in 1960, I never laid eyes on the harum-scarum individual until the summer of 1962 when Nordin asked permission for Roberts to work in the Park on one of our building crews. Desperate to have our cottages completed I reluctantly agreed, but whenever Merv and I chanced to meet, we either ignored the other's presence or bristled at each other like a pair of stray dogs. Circumstances, however, engendered an abrupt change in our relationship. Mom and Pop visited Wilberforce a couple of times weekly to shop and play bingo. Merv ran the bingo operation for the town and therefore got on a first-name basis with the folks. While playing cards one night at the cottage Mother suddenly put down her hand, looked over at me, and said, "You know, son, that fellow Merv Roberts has a kind face."

"What in hell are you talking about Mom?" I replied.

"Well, he was obviously drunk that afternoon at Fitzgerald Lake, and I think he now regrets that episode and wants to be friends. You ought to forget the past and have a talk with him," Mother rejoindered in that all-forgiving attitude most mothers have a habit of embracing.

"For Christ sake, Mom," I stormed. "How about the second time when you were as much in favor of physically throwing him off the property as anyone?"

"I know, son," she said, "but I think we ought to let bygones be bygones."

Whether my "bury the hatchet" Mother discussed our conversation with Roberts, I don't know, but a week or two later he showed up at our cottage with a bottle of whiskey, drunk as a hoot owl and insisting on a chat. Apprehensive at first to reach for the olive branch, due to my long-standing animosity, I finally agreed to share a drink and discuss our mutual ill feelings. Merv described his bitterness when first informed he would be barred from hunting or fishing the rest of his life in an area he'd enjoyed since a boy. His immediate determination he said was not to accept that situation without a fight. While Roberts described his personal antagonism, I again considered my own feelings if advised as a young man I could no longer set foot in the Brokenhead River country. As a result of my musings it wasn't difficult for me to envision the local peoples' hostility when we closed off the enormous tract. Merv also talked about his embarrassment at being slugged in front of strangers, then going around town with a black eye and how he plotted the destruction of Harcourt Park for several weeks—a complete conflagration being foremost in his thoughts. As time elapsed, however, he saw the development being beneficial to the town's merchants as well as to those employed by Sumcot. Gradually, he confessed, his animosity diminished. A personable chap with the ability to converse intelligently made me wonder if he wouldn't be a natural-born salesman. Following Mother's wishes, we buried the hatchet that night and throughout the following months became friends. When Sumcot desperately needed sales personnel at the C.N.E. following the departure of Jim and Fred, I put in an urgent call to Roberts who came directly to the city and worked the balance of the show. Although erratic, Merv proved capable of successfully selling real estate as I had surmised, and throughout the following four years, he produced as well as anyone on the staff.

The fact that Brien refused to fund further sales department draws concerned me greatly, and at the completion of the C.N.E. I went to him for a showdown. "Bill," he said glumly, "Our financial situation is critical. If it's within your power, get the quarter of a million dollars you owe me as rapidly as possible."

"Where in hell can I obtain that kind of money with only land security?" I asked incredulously.

"I have no idea, but remember everything you own is on demand to my company. If it is ever forced into bankruptcy, then your holdings will collapse like the proverbial house of cards," Ben answered looking severely shaken. I left his office in a state of shock and bewilderment. Where in this entire world would I find anyone willing to loan $250,000 on land I pondered? My fifteen years of experience both as a real estate and mortgage broker had taught me the hopelessness of such a task. Miracles do come to pass nonetheless, and it's an unbelievable sensation when something happens in your favor entirely opposed to what you believe can happen. Scanning the financial section of the *Toronto Star* within a week of my meeting with Brien, I noticed an advertisement offering to loan sums of money in blocks of $50,000 or more on real estate security. The man who responded to my phone inquiry turned out to be president of American Music plus the director of Atlantic Acceptance, an enormous lending institution headquartered in Toronto. When I outlined my requirements and assets the man asked, "How much do you need?"

"Three hundred thousand dollars would pay off our debts and give us a little badly needed working capital," I answered.

Without a moment's hesitation the man shot back, "Well then, Phillips, you better apply for $310,000 because my fee will be ten thousand bucks."

"Get me the loan and your fee will be no problem, " I retorted in an unbelieving tone of voice.

I'm not certain whether they ever visited our developments or just inspected the individual surveys, but within a month a new mortgage had been arranged and Brien completely removed from the picture. Interest at 12 percent, though high, was a bargain compared to the 18 percent rate I paid Brien plus factoring and management charges, which had totaled over $100,000 during the four years of our affiliation. At first I couldn't believe my good fortune in arranging the sensational loan so easily, but within a year, it would all become quite clear.

For the first time since 1954, Joyce and I visited Florida without a financial care in the world, and though we had a depleted management and sales staff, I looked forward eagerly to 1965. Sumcot showed little profit since incorporation, but our continuous growth pattern gave us ample reason to be optimistic about the future. Numerous unique individuals had been involved in our first six years of operations. Some I would never see again—such as Harold Christie, Colonel Sam Griffith and Charlie and Sue Roberts, all from a different world. Fred Oram, Jim Hay, Bud Henley and others who left Sumcot for various reasons would gradually disappear from our sphere of influence. A few would continue to play an interesting role in our affairs, among them J.B. Brien, Merv Roberts, and Louie Rodrigue. Newcomers just entering the scene, particularly Doug Prue and Edwina Seddon, would have a great effect on Sumcot's future and play a prominent part in our personal lives as well.

Chapter 8

The Times They Were A'Changin': the 60's

Events of the 1960s brought enormous changes to our North American way of life and in many ways we would never be quite the same again. Major wars or minor skirmishes continued their historical course and erupted in several sections of the world. Women's rights became a prominent topic, as did continued labor unrest plus increased government spending. Perhaps one of the greatest transitions during this decade occurred in our musical tastes and entertainment values. The root cause of most of the upheaval, however, centered around the never-ending world turmoil, and the conflict with the greatest impact on our affairs occurred on the opposite side of the world.

The Vietnam situation smoldered like a sleeping volcano for several years before erupting into a paramount struggle which eventually divided Americans into two camps, reminiscent of the Civil War. It had a serious effect on life in Canada as well, though Canadians didn't provide any combat troops for the horrible fray. An influx of conscientious objectors from the United States crossed the border in droves seeking sanctuary in our country to avoid military service in their own. Many Canadians believed these young Americans should be treated as illegal aliens and shipped back across the line either to do their military duty or to face the consequences. Those Canadians opposed to the Southeast Asian conflict not only sheltered these draft dodgers but encouraged the exodus. For several years an underground system similar to that used to help escaped slaves reach Canada during the Civil War was set up to allow U.S. draftees a chance to avoid the Vietnam War. Thousands of these young Americans eventually became Canadian citizens when they thought their hopes were dashed of ever receiving amnesty in their own nation. Canadians were divided in their feelings toward the Vietnam upheaval and they faced political unrest in their own country that would divide then just as decisively as the Vietnam War split the Americans.

Since Confederation in 1867, the Province of Quebec had primarily been an agricultural, clerically controlled society with little enthusiasm for federal politics. Suddenly, however, this attitude changed and a tremendous surge in soul-searching began as a huge percentage of Quebec's population began to rethink their way of life and reassess their relationship between Church and State. Socially many French Canadians felt they were second-class citizens in their own country and decided the alliance established in 1867 wouldn't satisfy their new ambitions. At the very least, they wanted the articles of confederation enforced as originally agreed upon by the founding fathers. Most of the misunderstandings and bitterness revolved around the immense changes that had occurred in the country since Quebec joined the confederation as one of four original provinces. Numerous factors inspired the Canadian people to form a united nation, but fear of attack from the United States was the prime motivator. The War of 1812, the American Civil War just concluded, and the Fenian raids in the mid 1860s greatly concerned those inhabitants north of the border who felt extremely vulnerable in their scattered provinces. They decided that a union was the only way to assure the survival of a separate British North American nation.

Quebec, known at the time as Canada East, was essential for such a venture to succeed, and so to entice them into the union, the founding fathers acquiesced to the demands of the French-speaking province. Quebec's traditional institutions were written into the Canadian constitution. English and French were made the official languages of both Quebec and the Canadian Parliament, and a dual school system was established within the province. The 100 years following Confederation saw six new provinces join the alliance, and Quebec, instead of being one in four with 40 percent of the total population, was now one in ten with less than 20 percent. The western provinces in particular, with no historical attachment to Quebec, refused to accept French willingly as a founding language or to acknowledge that Canada by its constitution was a bilingual and bicultural country. Many non-French in Ontario and the maritime provinces also conveniently forgot their forefathers' promises of a century before. A partial result of this divergent view of Quebec's rightful place in the federation was that the province became polarized and frequently found itself entirely separated in political philosophy from other sections of the country. This segregation of the

French and English was particularly emphasized during the era from 1960 to 1965 when Canada faced three federal elections, all held before the expiration of the usual four-year term.

In 1958 John Diefenbaker, a Saskatchewan native, was re-elected to power with the largest majority ever recorded in the annals of Canadian political history—208 seats out of a total of 265. The 1962 election left him with 118 seats, and the election in 1963 reduced his Conservative party's holdings to 95. There are numerous reasons for Diefenbaker's downfall, but in the last two elections, Quebec, with the second largest block of seats in the House of Commons, voted entirely against him. This antagonized the western provinces and created further animosity. Another incident that created considerable ill feeling between the two cultures occurred when President DeGaulle of France visited EXPO '67, Montreal's World Fair. "VIVE LE QUEBEC LIBRE," he shouted as he openly promised French support for an independent Quebec. Although rebuked by much of Canada, DeGaulle's remarks are credited with encouraging separation to flourish in the province under the leadership of Rene Levesque. Realizing that the animosity existing between the French and the English would forever disrupt the smooth running of the country started me thinking of immigrating to the United States in the middle 1960s.

The widening rift between the provinces and the Vietnam fiasco weren't the only situations dividing Canadians throughout that turbulent decade. In the early 1960s, Prime Minister Pearson gave the country its own distinctive flag, but great numbers of Canadians, including my mother, hated to see the Union Jack excluded from the final design. Many still refuse to accept, salute, or fly the new Canadian banner. Diefenbaker contributed to the decline of Canadian federalism and prestige during this period, but Mike Pearson, leader of the Liberal Party, did little to reverse the trend. Walter Gordon, Pearson's Minister of Finance, laid down measures to prevent the persistent take over of Canadian industries by Americans. Most of this attempt at limited U.S. control disappeared in a barrage of loud criticism from various sources, but the Pearson government still enacted legislation to protect Canadian banks against foreign ownership and issued guidelines to shape the behavior of U.S. companies as good Canadian citizens, advice not popularly received by Washington. The continuous extension of U.S. control over Canadian industry alarmed many Canadians who criticized this economic dependence and complained that no other nation allowed another power so much influence and profit within its borders. The opposing arguments favored the large and growing American investment in our country as the only means of reaching economic parity with our giant neighbor.

Several other issues became stumbling blocks to the normal good relations between the two neighboring nations. Canada's wheat sales to China plus increasing exports to Cuba rankled the U.S. State Department, while Canadians were constantly irritated by the Americans' insistence on their right to use Canada's natural resources, particularly water. After lengthy negotiations, the federal government signed an agreement with Washington allowing waters from the Columbia River to be diverted south of the border for American use, but British Columbia's parliament immediately rejected the treaty. Americans, impatient with Canadian ignorance of their problems and the benefits of a mutual solution, became thoroughly agitated. The situation was ironical in that the sale of Canadian water provoked lively comment and distress to its citizens while the exploitation of Canadian forest, iron and oil resources was not seriously disputed by anyone. Despite these other differences, the question of whether those Canadians should be punished who encouraged young American males to cross our border illegally to avoid the draft became the most critical issue. Also, the fact that Canadian authorities never interned nor returned these men caused a further fester between the two countries. The same conflict, however, created even more animosity in the United States.

Vietnam, an old French colony, gained independence in 1954 when the French were unceremoniously booted out after their disastrous defeat at Dien Bien Phu. The country was then divided into North and South Vietnam, and Ho Chi Minh, the Communist leader of the revolutionary war, became president of North Vietnam. The south, though recognized by western powers as a free democratic republic, more closely resembled a military dictatorship. Ho Chi Minh, intent on unifying the nation under a Communist-controlled government, organized a guerilla movement that became known as the Viet Cong. At first the Viet Cong used subversive tactics to overthrow the South Vietnamese regime but resorted to open warfare after they had strengthened their position.

The U.S. became financially involved in Vietnam as early as 1954 when in an effort to stave off a Communist take-over they paid up to 80 percent of the French war costs. After France's catastrophic collapse at Dien Bien Phu, the United States got further tangled in the civil war by attempting to prevent the Communist North from overthrowing the corrupt though supposedly democratic South. The Viet Cong swiftly became masters of guerilla warfare, and despite massive infusions of American aid and advice, the armies of the South were unable to suppress The National Liberation Front (NLF). The NLF comprised not only the Viet Cong but also seasoned troops from Ho Chi Minh's soviet equipped army. In 1961, South Vietnam signed a military and economic aid treaty with the United States which led to the arrival of the first

American support troops. The ineffective and profligate government of South Vietnam collapsed in 1963 with the aid of a military coup, and no person or group could establish complete control in the country until 1965. Meanwhile the civil war continued, and the Communists rapidly gained a dominant position, particularly in the rural areas.

The Tonkin Gulf Resolution, approved by the United States Congress in 1964, authorized President Johnson to "take all necessary measures to repel any armed attack against forces of the United States and to prevent further aggression in South East Asia." When North Vietnamese gunboats allegedly fired on a U.S. destroyer that summer, President Johnson immediately ordered air strikes against North Vietnam and Communist-controlled areas in the South. Defense Secretary J.T. McNaughton claimed that the U.S. objective in Vietnam was not "to save a friend but to avoid humiliation." In 1966, 190,000 American troops were stationed in South Vietnam, and these numbers skyrocketed to 550,000 by 1969. Before the official end of hostilities in 1973, American casualties reached more than 50,000. South Vietnamese dead totalled 400,000, and the Viet Cong and North Vietnamese lost over 900,000, many of whom were civilian victims of U.S. bombing attacks.

In 1965, "doves" across the world strenuously objecting to American participation held "Days of Protest" in several major world cities. Adding to the furor, the American people got restless. The length of the war, high U.S. casualties, and exposure of American involvement in war crimes, particularly after the My Lai massacre, soured many in the United States against the conflict. Popular sentiment turned obstreperous in 1967, and 150,000 antiwar demonstrators staged massive protests in New York and San Francisco. These were promptly followed by outcries in numerous other North American cities. College campuses also showed their disapproval and formed an association called Students for a Democratic Society. Weathermen, a splinter group of radicals, broke from the main body of students and planted bombs to express their protest. Even comic strips got involved in the controversy when Gary Trudeau, creator of Doonesbury, constantly lampooned American entanglement in the messy Vietnamese situation.

Peace wasn't officially declared until 1973 when a final accord provided for the withdrawal of American troops and the formation of a four-nation international control commission to assure peace. It wasn't effective, however, and fighting soon broke out again between the Communists and South Vietnamese who without U.S. support quickly succumbed to the Commies. On the surface, therefore, it appeared that the terrible price paid by the nation as a whole and particularly by American servicemen in their valiant effort to keep South Vietnam out of the Communist camp had ended as a complete failure. As a result of the defeat, most people accepted that all the bleeding hearts in North America who clamored for an end to hostilities were right in their undying efforts to halt American involvement. Only history will provide the final verdict, but in the long run, I don't believe those brave men died in vain.

There are no clear-cut answers as to when a country should take up arms to stop a threatening alien force, but history records numerous instances of nations who successfully halted an aggressor before they reached its borders. In 1191 B.C., Ramses II decided to take the initiative against the marauding Sea Peoples, and his resounding victory justified this strategy. The Greek triumph over the Persians at Salamis and Plataea in 479-80 B.C. is considered by historians a principal reason that democracy, as we know it today, had a chance to survive and flourish. If Attila, King of the Huns and legendary "scourge of God" had not been halted in 451 A.D. by the Gauls and the following year by the Romans, European civilization would not likely have progressed and possibly may not have developed at all. In 1588, England, not certain it could defend its shores against the mighty Spanish Army, sent Sir Francis Drake to engage the Spanish Navy at sea, and the defeat of the Spanish Armada perhaps made the difference as to whether my forefathers were Spanish or English.

Certainly World War II is an outstanding example of the tragedy of allowing an aggressor nation to prepare for full-scale war without interference from those the nation aims to destroy. If Britain and France had prepared for battle, instead of disarming in the early 1930s, World War II may not have happened, and millions of innocent lives might have been spared. Or if the American isolationists hadn't prevailed and the United States had entered the war at its beginning, there is little doubt the slaughter of human lives, including Americans, would have been a small fraction of the loss that actually occurred. Weakness encourages aggression, and there are many examples throughout the ages of states that waited and watched with trepidation, mercifully hoping to be spared from an onrushing enemy. That rarely happened, and those weak-kneed nations were generally swallowed up and their citizens enslaved. Not only realms and empires but whole continents were overrun by Visigoths, Huns, Mongols, Vikings, Turks, Spaniards, Germans, and others.

History shows that the only countries not subjected to alien rule when intimidated were either too strong or too well prepared to be vanquished or attacked before the aggressor reached their borders. If the United States had provided air power and other military assistance at the Bay of Pigs, Castro might today be only a bad dream. Cuba as a friendly democracy instead of a Russian pawn wouldn't be providing

Soviet arms and equipment to Central America. At this suggestion bleeding hearts will ask, "What about the rights of the Cuban people?" A
consideration, no doubt, but in the first place, how can an autocracy be
better than a freely elected government, and secondly if Russian troops
were suddenly marching down Broadway in New York, how many of
those pacifists would then be concerned about the plight of the Cubans?
Although too late, they would rue the day they didn't take action while
still controlling their destiny. Vietnam may have been a military catastrophe, but it sent the Communists a message. Americans would fight
to preserve their freedom and not hesitate until marauding forces were
knocking down the barriers.

What happened in Czechoslovakia in 1968 should have been a bell
ringer to all appeasers. The Czech people made a noble effort to ease
the yoke of Communism by being less restrictive on the press and
allowing profit considerations to apply to their sluggish economy. The
USSR and other satellite communistic countries had other ideas, however, and sent 200,000 troops to quell Czechoslovakia's endeavor to live
under a little less constraining form of government. The Czechs hated
their oppressors but were not strong enough to resist.

I wonder if those millions of isolationists who argued so diligently
to keep the United States out of World War II have ever considered that
their actions were indirectly responsible for the deaths of great numbers
of their own countrymen who were forced to stem the tide of Fascism
when it threatened to engulf the world, including themselves. Hawks
and doves will always permeate a democratic society, and when doves
are faced with the reality of either fighting or being enslaved, they will
often fight—at a time much more favorable to their enemies. The Berlin
Wall, erected in the summer of 1961, divided not only a city but also a
multitude of families and should stand as a warning beacon to all
freedom-loving peoples that the right of self determination cannot be
preserved by mere words. Hundreds of thousands of German families
who escaped into West Berlin before creation of the horrible Wall or
the thousands that intended to flee but didn't will certainly confirm that
naked aggression cannot be appeased with simple conversation.
Whoever said that the pen is mightier than the sword wasn't a student
of history.

The non-ending struggle between Communism and the free world
wasn't limited to Vietnam. Several incidents from secondary irritations
to major confrontations created tension between the two superpowers
throughout the 1960s. In 1960, a Soviet ground-to-air projectile knocked
down a U.S. supersonic U-2 spy plane piloted by Gary Powers, causing
considerable name calling, and the construction of the Berlin Wall
produced intense ill feeling. These two examples, however, were noth-

ing compared to the Cuban missile crisis of 1962 when U.S. surveillance discovered Soviet offensive weapons and bomber bases in Cuba. President Kennedy immediately ordered an air and sea quarantine, and the United States braced for war as the world teetered on the brink of a near holocaust. Only when Russia's Premier Khrushchev backed down and agreed to remove the offensive missiles could earthlings relax. The nearness of disaster was instrumental in creating a "hot line" emergency communication link between Washington and Moscow in the hope of reducing the risk of accidental war. Fortunately the tough stance taken by John Kennedy didn't allow Castro's Cuba to be quite the provocation that the Kremlin had hoped, although the little Caribbean country would remain a thorn in the side of the American people. Despite the apparent U.S. victory, the Cuban missile crisis could have been averted. Spawned by the American failure at the Bay of Pigs, it provided another excellent example of the hazard of avoiding a hostile encounter when all evidence portends to an eventual eruption and perhaps at a more inopportune time.

World tension wasn't solely confined to the superpowers. When another Arab-Israeli war broke out in 1967 in Africa, it left Australia as the only continent not to face open hostility during those turbulent years. After numerous incidents and provocations over many months, Israeli military forces attacked Egypt, Jordan, and Syria in June 1967 in what has become known as The Six Day War. In those six days Arab armies using Russian equipment were severely thrashed while Israel captured Arab Jerusalem, the West Bank of the Jordan River, and the Golan Heights. No finer example exists throughout the annals of our forefathers of the advantage of attacking a threatening force rather than waiting for an inevitable invasion. Since Israel became a state in 1949, its people have fiercely defended their borders by expanding them at each Arab provocation. Surrounding Arab nations numerically outnumber this tiny enclave of democracy by an enormous margin, and only the aggressive posture of the Israeli people has permitted them to retain independence and the grudging respect of their enemies.

Not only did international events cause great dislocations with North American life styles throughout this chaotic period but also national affairs severely affected us in many ways. The massive movement from farms to urban living continued, and this migration severely altered the face of North America. Rapidly expanding suburbs frequently grew larger and politically stronger than the city core which they surrounded. This created unimaginable traffic problems in most cities as the arteries leading to the downtown offices and factories were unable to handle the twice-daily flow of automobiles. People were suddenly spending half as much time reaching their jobs and returning home as they did actually working. Steadily increasing living standards meant that a two-car family became commonplace, and this just intensified the traffic dilemma. Eighty-two million motor cars were travelling North American roads by the early 1960s, an increase of more than two and one half times the numbers in 1940.

Another important crisis of the decade involved the centuries-old problem of segregation when that simmering cauldron of racial bitterness came to a boil as the black population finally determined to improve their individual rights and living standards without further delay. Several groups contributed to the success of the civil rights movement, but the Southern Christian Leadership Conference headed by Martin Luther King swiftly gained the most prominence. King's philosophy of advocating a policy of passive resistance gained a considerable amount of white sympathy and support, and so the crusade for equal rights mushroomed across the South. In 1960, blacks in Greensboro, North Carolina began sit-ins at eating places, and within months all restaurants were desegregated. Freedom riders forced their way onto buses in Birmingham, Alabama in 1961, and this set off similar demonstrations in Louisiana and several other states. Racial tensions escalated in 1962 when James Meredith attempted to enter the University of Mississippi which had been ordered by the federal government to admit the black Air Force veteran. There had been little civil rights legislation since the Civil Rights Act of 1875 except for minor changes in 1957 and 1960. In 1964, however, and at the urging of President Johnson, the most comprehensive civil rights legislation since 1875 was finally approved. The act prohibited discrimination for reason of race, color, religion, or national origin in places of public accommodation covered by interstate commerce: that is, in restaurants, motels, hotels, theaters, and similar places. Besides dealing with the desegregation of public schools, it also forbade discrimination in employment. In 1965, the Voting Rights Act provided for federal observers at polls to assure equal voting rights, while the Civil Rights Act of 1968 dealt with housing and real estate discrimination.

Desegregation would be a slow, torturous process, but the social position of blacks would gradually improve. The country would never be completely ruled by a white supremacy again. Martin Luther King's words, "I have a dream," contained in a speech he delivered at the Lincoln Memorial in Washington in 1963, became famous as a black slogan in their search for personal liberty and respect. Part of King's discourse said, "I have a dream that one day, on the red hills of Georgia, sons of former slaves and the sons of former slave owners will be able to sit down together at the table of brotherhood." Martin Luther King, Jr. was ruthlessly shot and killed in 1968 by an assassin, his dream far from being realized. Progress had been made nevertheless, and much of the improvement in the blacks' pursuit of social justice in our society must be credited to the dedicated efforts of this one individual.

Another significant action in world affairs occurring in the 1960s centered around the race to outer space between the USSR and the United States. As early as 1959, the Soviet Union released into space four missiles carrying four dogs and a rabbit, and this same year they launched the first projectile to reach the moon. Space triumphs by the USSR were responsible for the frantic effort put forth by the United States in an attempt to overtake the Russian's apparent lead in the race to put the first man on the moon. American space missiles had such code names as Titan, Pioneer, and Discoverer, and in 1959, the American Army launched Pioneer IV, the first U.S. man-made satellite to be placed in orbit. In 1961, Gagarin of the Soviet Union became the first astronaut to orbit the earth. That same year Alan Shepard and Virgil Grissom, two Americans, escaped the earth's atmosphere, but both experienced only fifteen-minute suborbital flights. Also in 1961, an American chimpanzee named Enos made two complete revolutions around the earth and was safely recovered from the Atlantic, no worse for the thrilling adventure.

In 1962, the U.S. leaped forward in the space race when Scott Carpenter circled the earth three times and Walter Shirra completed six orbits. The fierce competition to reach a lunar orbit was not without tragedy unfortunately, as three Americans, including Virgil Grissom, were killed when the spacecraft Apollo caught fire at Cape Kennedy, Florida. A few months later, Russian astronaut Komarov tragically died when his craft crash landed during re-entry. These mishaps did not dampen the enthusiasm to reach the moon, however, and in 1969, American astronauts Neil Armstrong and Buzz Aldrin were seen on television by millions of thrilled earthlings when they stepped out of their space module and became the first mortals to reach an alien body in our intriguing universe. Man's landing on the earth's only satellite left us with mixed emotions. We would never again be able to look at the moon with the same romantic attachment, but on the other hand, our scientists now looked far beyond—to other planets in our solar system and even to the exploration of the universe itself. The Space Age had certainly arrived in earnest.

Nuclear power, crucial for our space program, rapidly mushroomed into a major new source of energy, and by 1963 the first commercial nuclear reactor was installed in New Jersey. Before the end of the decade dozens more were ordered, becoming an important source of energy production in direct competition with coal and oil fuel. The public's general fear of nuclear accidents and subsequent disasters created a massive outpouring of human emotion, and groups condemning the new nuclear plants formed across the continent and participated in large-scale protests.

Another great achievement of the times, though not so controversial as nuclear power, was the St. Lawrence Seaway, officially opened in the summer of 1959. Swiftly expanding port facilities over the ensuing few years reached deep into the continent's interior, and though it proved costly to maintain, mostly due to the ravages of winter, the new waterway opened Great Lake ports from Toronto, Ontario to Duluth, Minnesota to ocean-going vessels. A personal upshot of the seaway was that the Toronto Harbor Commission provided Marty Fine, my father-in-law, with the most prestigious job of his business career.

Accomplishments in trade and commerce were at times sensational, but labor and management still reached for each other's throats. In several ways it turned out to be an important decade in this relationship. In 1959, the U.S. Congress invoked the Taft-Hartley Act to halt a long and bitter steel strike. The United Steel Workers Union challenged its validity, but the Supreme Court upheld the injunction. Although the Supreme Court decision seemed at the time like a slap in the face to the unionized steel workers, in reality it preserved some of their jobs for a few years. By halting the strike, the government indirectly prevented a substantial increase in wages and thereby granted the steel companies a few more years to be competitive on world markets. Unfortunately, this reprieve wouldn't last for long. In 1964, the largest iron-ore contract in world history was signed between the Australian Government and Japanese steel firms. By the end of 1967 over five million tons of the valuable ore was shipped to the Orient. This gigantic infusion of iron ore into Japanese steel mills made that country an industrial super power and before long American steel mills couldn't compete on world markets due primarily to their higher cost of production. As a result thousands of steel workers lost their jobs.

The North American automobile industry faced the same dilemma, although at this point, neither management nor labor was intelligent enough to see the storm clouds gathering on the horizon and therefore did nothing to prevent the oncoming calamity. Japanese Toyotas and Datsuns were flooding the country, and Volkswagens plus several other European models were steadily increasing their percentage of the market. Despite ominous signs of decreasing sales, neither U.S. automobile manufacturers nor the Automobile Worker's Union made any attempt to improve production or to cut costs to allow American cars to be more competitive. In fact, the unions still harassed the industry for even higher wages and improved benefits. Before the end of the 1960s, European and Japanese cars were outselling standard American models, and the automobile industry, like the steel business, found itself in serious trouble.

Disclosures throughout the 1950s and 1960s of improper activities by union bosses, such as collusion between dishonest employees and union officials, extortions, and the use of violence by certain segments of labor leadership, was possibly one reason that union membership peaked in the late 1960s. Total trade union membership by 1970 of approximately seventeen million had remained substantially unchanged since 1955.

Governments, like unions, hadn't learned any lessons on financial management but continued to spend taxpayers' money without restraint. Elected bodies both in Canada and the United States raced toward attaining some type of social equality for their citizens, and new legislation eventually had far-reaching detrimental effects on our future economic well-being. Lester Pearson's Liberal Government in Canada enacted a comprehensive social security program, including free medical aid for all citizens. Besides draining the country's coffers, this no-cost medical insurance greatly affected one of my own personal endeavors. Wishing to fulfill a pledge made twenty-five years earlier to Miss McClaren, superintendent of the Winnipeg Shriner's hospital, to repay the Shriners for their remarkable assistance in my early years, I requested an appointment to the Shriner's Crippled Children's Committee. Fred McBrien, Potentate of Rameses Temple in the early 1960s, arranged to have me placed on that prestigious and worthwhile board that was comprised mostly of doctors. My reponsibilities included investigating cases for admittance to our Montreal hospital or arranging for such assistance as crutches, wheel chairs, and orthopedic footwear for crippled and needy children. When free medical aid became available to all Canadians, the services of the Shriners lessened, and though I remained a member of the committee for a quarter century, my duties were significantly reduced. Free medical aid and hospitalization, the most costly social program ever enacted by a Canadian government, was unquestionably a godsend to many families including my own. Unfortunately, due to increased government spending, it also became one of the greatest causes of inflation and the principal reason Canada would never again be capable of balancing their federal budget.

The United States Government steadily pursued the same course as Canada toward social benefits for its citizens but stopped short of a completely free medical program. President Johnson said in his 1965 State of the Union address that he intended to create a "Great Society, that will eliminate poverty in America." Before the year ended, he signed into law a 1 ½ billion dollar program of federal-state economic aid. The Medicare Act set up the first U.S. government operated health insurance program, but strictly for the elderly, and was supported by payroll taxes and federal subsidies. Legislation to assist the underprivileged became a boon to many, including the deserving and undeserving, but as the government poured money into relief for the destitute, welfare rolls skyrocketed. The government suddenly became responsible for gigantic and ever-increasing handouts. North America seemed incapable of learning from the dilemma of the British, the first to inaugurate massive social programs and now facing run-away inflation. In 1965, Great Britain froze salaries and prices in an effort to check inflation and improve the nation's worsening trade deficit.

Another matter that affected our thinking during those shuffling 1960s was a constant warning from the medical profession of the dangers of eating, drinking, or doing things humans had taken for granted for ages. The most explosive news being the Surgeon General's Report in 1964 about the perils of smoking. The announcement positively claimed that lung cancer and heart-related diseases were considerably higher in smokers. After listening to the dire warnings and reading about the ominous dangers, I decided to give up the smoking habit I had nurtured for twenty-five years. This took more raw courage than any other single thing I would ever do in my life, as I now smoked three packets of cigarettes per day plus cigars, and occasionally a pipe. As if to counterbalance the bad news of cigarette smoke in relation to heart disease, the world's first heart transplant was performed in South Africa by surgeon Christian Barnard in 1967. The news I could possibly obtain a new heart if I ruined the old with the nicotine habit never induced me to return to cigarettes.

Certainly of all the changes shaping our lives during this decisive decade, none were more pronounced than our sudden deviation in entertainment and music. Rapidly disappearing were movies that could be seen by the entire family. Most Hollywood films were now designated as PG (Parental Guidance) or R (Restricted), which meant that a person had to be at least 18 years old to be admitted into those theaters with such a designation. Sex, violence, and four-letter words were now as common in books, movies, and television programs as "gosh darn" or "a straight right to the jaw" had been for a half century of movie-goers preceding this revolution. Not only were books and movies filled with risque language considered taboo a few short years earlier but also many of the current songs had suggestive passages that would have banned them from the airwaves before this enormous transformation in our musical moods.

The first real shift away from the sentimental ballads that had prevailed for scores of years was "Rock Around The Clock" by Bill Haley and his Comets, recorded in 1955. Known as "rock 'n roll," the new beat included elements of several music styles: blues, prominent with the black musicians; black and white gospel music; plus country and western. Numerous other groups followed Haley's success, and rock music soon became the predominant rhythm of the times. Other great rock 'n roll favorites of those early years included "Shake, Rattle and Roll," "Keep A-Knockin," and "Whole Lotta Shakin." The primary instruments of early rock 'n roll were guitar, piano, drums, and saxophone, although by the middle 1960s the electric guitar came into its own and frequently overpowered the others. All aspects of the music—its heavy beat loudness, self-absorbed lyrics, and raving delivery—indicated a teen-age defiance of adult values and authority. Elvis Presley rapidly became the greatest representative of the new music style during those initial years, and his plaintive wailing, dynamic delivery, and uninhibited sexuality appealed particularly to young audiences while horrifying and offending older people.

Rock music's popularity waned awhile but surged back into prominence in 1962 with the emergence of The Beatles, a British group whose songs, "I Want To Hold Your Hand," "Please, Please, Please Me," "Yellow Submarine," and "Lucy In The Sky With Diamonds" became all-time favorites, especially with the younger generation. Some Beatles' songs, but more particularly The Rolling Stones whose recording of "I Can't Get No Satisfaction" became a great success, were filled with words or incantations of violence, sadism, or sex. Beatles songs were frequently suggestive, but The Rolling Stones made the Beatles sound like choir boys in comparison. The long hair and strange attire of The Beatles and other bands had tremendous influence on styles of the younger generation, including my oldest son. Some groups, including Jefferson Airplane, tried to approximate in music the aural experience of psychedelic drugs by producing long, repetitive and occasionally exquisite songs with abstruse lyrics. Other bands contributing to the rock music craze were The Bee Gees and later Led Zeppelin. Another individual, greatly influencing musical tastes at the time was Chubby Checker, who introduced "The Twist" and launched an international dance craze. The celebrated twist led to the popularity of discotheques where patrons "twisted" the night away to a pulse provided by phonograph records.

Without question rock music ruled the airwaves throughout this period of our lives, although a few old-style ballads still filtered through the constant and blatant pandemonium of the rock beat. The few sentimental ballads and old style songs of the era, including "Put Your Head On My Shoulder," "Moon River," "Rambling Rose," "I Left My Heart In San Francisco," "Hello Dolly," "Red Roses For A Blue Lady," and "Raindrops Keep Falling On My Head," seem to have survived however, and are played today with much more regularity than those such as "Lucy In The Sky With Diamonds" or "I Can't Get No Satisfaction."

By the latter part of the decade a new style began edging out the rock craze. Country and western, always popular with a segment of the population, gradually became accepted as the music of the 1970s, although numerous western rhythms would incorporate the same instruments and even a similar beat and tempo to that of rock. "Witchita Lineman," "Ode To Billy Joe," "Gentle On My Mind," "Folsom Prison Blues," and "Harper Valley P.T.A." were a few of the new songs that replaced the stentorian sounds of the rocking 1960s.

Certainly this era witnessed enormous transitions in the attitude and awareness of North Americans as well as a majority of the world's population. The rapid expansion of satellite communications made individuals in every corner of the globe immediately cognizant of all new or startling developments. This new consciousness signified a slow awakening of many ignorant or oppressed people as it was now impossible to keep them completely in the dark about daily occurrences that were affecting their personal lives. Regardless of the tumultuous tempo of the times, and the effect on my family's existence, my own personal struggle for financial independence and survival continued unabated.

Chapter 9

Sumcot: the Growth Years

Joyce and I returned from Florida in midwinter of 1965 in high spirits. Our few weeks spent with the Schramms, Graces, and Dot's brother George and wife Peg were delightful as usual, and our stay at the ocean front Bel-Aire Motel convinced me that the extra cost of being located directly on the fascinating sea was money well spent. Rested and ready for action, I gave little thought to Sumcot's finances which seemed in excellent shape as a result of my unexpected good fortune in discovering Atlantic Acceptance and their subsequent loan of a $310,000 first mortgage on our properties. The picture was rosy. I still hadn't learned that when life's highway looks smoothest you had better start looking for cracks in the pavement. A few months elapsed before disaster struck Atlantic Acceptance and ultimately turned into one of the highest stake poker games of my business career.

We expanded our spring exhibition schedule to include a ten-day show at Columbus, Ohio which began in the middle of February, and so I had little time to relax upon returning home. Sumcot's shortage of trained sales representatives left me no alternative but to work and oversee the show myself. Jack McNeil set up our Columbus booth but rushed home to prepare for Toronto's spring exhibitions plus the Cleveland Sportsman Show. For staff at Columbus I used Mom, Pop, Len Nordin, Louie Rodrigue, and Merv Roberts. The twelve-hour-per day ten-day show held in the draughty old Coliseum in the State Fair grounds proved to be a test of endurance except for a four-day spell when Ohio's State Capital experienced one of the worst blizzards and record snowfall in their history. This greatly reduced attendance. During the height of the storm few individuals with the exception of the exhibitors ventured into the bleary barnlike atmosphere of the Colliseum. This slack period allowed us considerable time to get acquainted with our neighbours, and a golden opportunity to watch two master salesmen ply their trade.

Directly across the aisle from our display, Bob Forest and Jim Tucker, two encyclopedia hucksters, had set up a booth so simple in design that they carried most of their layout and sales tools in two suitcases and were ready for action within fifteen minutes of their arrival. I watched with a combined feeling of amusement and contempt at their simple set up in comparison to our elaborate and costly arrangement. On small stands beside each of their stools, they placed in casual array several volumes of encyclopedias plus pencils and application forms for a drawing to be held before the end of the show, the winner to receive a free set of books. My contempt turned to complete scorn when Bob and Jim began playing gin rummy and seemingly paid scant attention to prospects strolling past their display. As the show progressed, however, I realized they were frequently writing orders, and my puzzlement as to how they determined whether to make a sales pitch or to ignore the prospective customers and continue playing cards forced me to pay closer attention to their strategy. As a result I learned lessons in selling psychology that were incorporated into Sumcot's training techniques and used for as long as I remained in business. We sophisticated their rather crude methods to some extent, but watching their tactics in action was hilarious and unforgettable.

When a couple ambled past their ungarnished stand, one of the two boys would turn his head away from his cards and holler, "Put your name down for a free set of encyclopedias folks." If the people ignored the command and continued walking, the boys rarely made a second plea. Even those who came over and began filling out the draw form received little attention at first. Continuing the rummy game, one of the lads speaking out of the side of his mouth would instruct them to print their name and address carefully and then casually inquire, "Got any children folks?" An affirmative answer was swiftly followed by three or four other leading questions. At this point, providing the people hadn't left the booth, the chap doing the interrogating would leap off his stool and enter into a lengthy sales presentation. To my astonishment over half the prospects to whom they made a prolonged pitch were sold an expensive set of books. My disdain rapidly turned to admiration and during the great snowstorm I befriended the two personable pitchmen and asked the secret to their high percentage of proficiency.

"Bill, you and your staff should learn to differentiate between potential customers and deadbeats," Bob responded. "If I worked for Sumcot selling high-priced vacation property, I wouldn't talk to anyone with a square haircut who wears white socks or smokes a pipe."

All of my group listened to this astounding advice, and Merv with an amused expression asked him to explain the remark. "Well, in the first place," Bob said, a wide grin spreading across his face. "A man wearing white socks is more than likely a blue collar worker who can't afford luxury items. Any individual with a square haircut would never be interested in anything as sophisticated as vacation property or encyclopedias, and the pipe smoker will just sit there sucking on the stem of his pacifier saying 'hmmm, hmmm, hmmm,' looking very interested, but he will never make a decision."

Bob's statement sounded ludicrous and uproariously funny, but nevertheless we began to pay close attention and were amazed to find considerable accuracy in his advice. Our display booth had a little theater closed on three sides with a continuous 35 mm slide presentation of Harcourt Park. People attracted to the voice over descriptions with a musical background would glance into the enclosure where the beauty of the slides soon fascinated them, and they would be seated. When half a dozen couples sat watching our show, it was always a matter of pure conjecture as to which of them our available salespersons should approach. After the recommendations from Bob and Jim, we began to be more selective. Instead of wasting time conversing with those who wanted to talk about the gorgeous country but with little realistic hope of ever purchasing, we devoted our efforts to more promising looking buyers and even made our own list of the dress and attitudes of likely prospects. A comical consequence of the incident occurred whenever a couple sat in the theater where Louie or Merv couldn't see whether the man wore white socks or had a pipe on his person. While giving the man close scrutiny, they would attempt to find a means of getting him to stretch his pant leg upward to look at the color of his hose or open his jacket to see if a pipe protruded from the pocket.

Another valuable lesson learned from the two encyclopedia salesmen was their expertise at keeping control in selling situations by being positive and straight forward while talking and cajoling listeners to agree with their statements. They practiced this proficiency at every opportunity. Neither Bob nor Jim uttered another word to a couple who kept walking when they were ordered to, "Put their name down for a free set of encyclopedias." They felt that if people didn't obey that simple command they wouldn't have control on future conversation and were therefore wasting their time. An emergency door to the parking lot opened beside our booth and occasionally someone would sneak in to avoid paying the admission fee. Whenever Bob or Jim noticed this incursion, even though the culprits were halfway across the convention hall, they would shout, "Hey you, go back out and use the front door."

The offenders would stop and stare for a moment, but then seeing the determined look on the spokesman's face would usually retrace their steps and go back out the forbidden entrance. They also taught us another novel twist that added a little levity to otherwise disappointing sales situations. When a salesman makes a prolonged pitch to a customer who is not prepared to sign an order or make a positive commitment for whatever reason, it is unusual for that person to admit openly why he won't make a decision at that moment. Invariably the person will say, "I'll be at the show for a while, and I want to think it over. I'll be back. Yes, it will either be today or before the end of the week, but I'll be back."

Whenever Bob or Jim were unsuccessful in one of their protracted presentations and their uncooperative customer offered the alibi that they wanted to consider the proposition but would be back, the boys would shout, "Hey, I've got a member for our BEE BACK CLUB." They then handed the startled prospect a card, officially admitting the individual to the BEE BACK CLUB. One day we were all busy with customers when Bob let out a whoop, "Hey everybody, I have a BEE BACKER." To my amazememt the surprised couple nearing the booth didn't flee in embarrassment but laughed and proceeded to sign the order. Although a rather crass business practice, it gave a frustrated salesman the chance to vent his disappointment at an unproductive sales presentation without actually insulting the client, and some members of Sumcot's staff used the BEE BACK CLUB cards for as long as we exhibited at shows.

Partly due to the inclement weather, the Columbus Show proved completely unproductive as far as sales of Ontario properties were concerned. Nevertheless the teachings of the two encyclopedia salesmen probably earned more money for the company in the ensuing years than any remuneration we might have received from land sales.

We had a dramatic return to Toronto following the show. During the final shift Louie suddenly turned violently ill with intensive internal pains and so I sent him back to the hotel by taxi. Merv left for home immediately after the show's completion, but Mom, Pop, Len and I decided to spend the night in Columbus and get an early start in the morning. At the hotel we found Louie on his hands and knees on the floor of his room suffering terribly. I rushed him to a hospital. The attending physician heavily sedated Louie, then put him in bed for a couple of hours for observation. The diagnosis was a severe case of kidney stones. At midnight the doctor recommended I make a dash for Canada as Louie's hospitalization plan didn't cover him in the U.S., and if an operation became necessary, the Ohio specialist wasn't certain how long Louie would be hospitalized.

With a handful of pain pills, we rushed back to the hotel, rousted the folks out of bed, and swiftly packed our bags. By 2 a.m. the five of us were on the highway headed home. Things proceeded favorably for an hour or two until the sedation wore off, and then despite the fact Lou took several pills, the pain progressively worsened. Whenever he got an intense attack, he moaned in agony. We would stop the car on the side of the highway to allow him to be sick, and Rodrigue would roll in the snow flailing his arms and legs in misery until Len and I would force him back into the car so we could continue. Nearing Erie, Pennsylvania at 9 a.m. it became obvious the tormented Louie couldn't make the border, and so I rushed him over to another hospital. Again they determined his ailment as severe kidney stones, heavily sedated him and put him back to bed for further examination. Before noon the Erie doctor informed us there was no indication the stone was moving and surgery would likely be required. Like the Columbus specialist, he advised us to try and get him home.

The drugs held Louie steady until we reached Buffalo where again he was beset with pain. By this time Louie, getting accustomed to his distress, beseeched me to make a bolt for Toronto. Mary Rodrigue met us in Toronto and rushed her ailing husband to Peterborough and his own family physician. Louie remained in the hospital and in convalescence for several weeks. This created further strain on our depleted sales force and was especially critical as it occurred during the hectic show season. This, however, was a minor aspect of the unfortunate incident. The big likable Frenchman never fully recovered for a long period, and though he worked for Sumcot off and on over the following two years, he never again reached his former effectiveness. He sold his Harcourt home, and returned with his family to Peterborough where he went to work for that city's Board of Education as a maintenance man and janitor.

Louie Rodrigue's personal problems preceded my own by about six months. Since leaving the Winnipeg Shriner's Hospital in the late 1930s, I had never been examined for any physical deficiency except for an appendectomy in 1954. My lower left torso had compensated to a great extent for my right leg, hip, and foot, and although I remained constantly involved in strenuous physical endeavors, I rarely experienced any unbearable effects from polio. I golfed, bowled and could walk as far as any man, though perhaps not as fast and also with a noticeable limp. The only major discomfort was the big toe on my polioed limb. It curved almost entirely under the foot and had now grown a large bunion on the top of the first joint. Not only did this growth force my shoe out of shape, but the constant rubbing against the top of my footwear had become intolerable. A Dr. Johnson who had a family practice a few doors from our Danforth office took a look at the problem when I asked him to recommend a surgeon who would remove the aching toe. Dr. Johnson aghast at my request, said, "Bill, you don't realize the importance of that appendage in your forward mobility. I have an acquaintance, Dr. Edward Simmons, who is renowned as an orthopedic surgeon not only in North America but also other parts of the world. Dr. Simmons specializes in rehabilitating old polio cases, and I'd like to make an appointment for you to see him, but I believe he'll take a fit if you suggest you want to chop off your big toe."

Indeed Dr. Ed Simmons was adamant about my not losing that particular digit. After numerous x-rays and examinations, the brilliant surgeon called me in for a consultation, and his words will forever remain imbedded in my memory. "I can reestablish the complete use of your right side," he said, in an emphatic manner. "By inserting a piece of bone in your foreleg to regain its proper length and by transplanting muscle from your left leg to your right, I could build up the muscle deficiency in your thigh, calf, and foot. There would be some suffering, but you could regain almost complete mobility. The only problem is your age."

My mind swam at the remarks as suddenly I envisioned running like a deer, swimming like a fish, or perhaps being able to play baseball and football with the best. I always accepted my disability as the luck of the draw and was grateful I could maneuver without too much difficulty in comparison to the many who were in far worse condition. Nevertheless, the unexpected disclosure that I might experience a normal existence shed a different light on my affliction.

"Dr. Simmons," I asked incredulously, "I am not yet thirty-nine, so couldn't you still perform the same miracles?"

"I won't say we can't, although I might recommend against it at your age," he responded. "However, first you require two major operations to repair that toe, plus straighten out and put forward mobility in your foot. These operations will require several months, and I suggest we see how well you adjust to a new foot before we consider rehabilitating the balance of your limb. Thirty-nine may seem young to you, but it is an advanced age to begin reshaping your body." The accuracy of those words would soon become apparent.

Dr. E.H. Simmons performed the first operation in November, 1965, in the East York Orthopedic Hospital and the second in late December the following year. I remained in a cast until March, took physiotherapy treatments three times a week, and never enjoyed pain-free walking until midsummer. Dr. Simmons performed a miracle on my foot. I now had considerable forward mobility, and my big toe finally remained straight like the others. I moved with more ease and limped a little less, and so I considered going back to discuss the other operations and perhaps have my entire limb returned to normal as the good surgeon had suggested might be possible. Before the summer waned however, I began to experience pains in my good knee and then my ankle. Dr. Simmons explained the problem. My physically active lifestyle had forced my left side to compensate for the deficiency of the right, and now the left had to readjust to the change in my gait and maneuverability.

The aggravation in my left limb gradually worsened even though I constantly exercised. I also received several shots of cortisone to remove inflammation from the knee and ankle, but with little success. Finally in November, 1966, I returned to the hospital for a patellectomy or removal of the kneecap. Over the following three years I sustained three more operations on my left limb: removal of knee cartilage, repair of torn ligaments in the side of the knee, and cutting away of a bone spur in my ankle. At this point arthritic and rheumatic pains frequently aggravated my joints, and so all thoughts of further rehabilitation were forgotten. Despite the pain I endured for 4½ years and continue to tolerate as a result of my second bout with surgeons in the correction of my polio disability, I consider it a small price to pay for personal locomotion. Every time I experience a flash of pain while moving, I reflect on the multitudes who never left a wheel chair or who were once active but then lost their mobility through war or some accident. They would gladly bear a little pain and inconvenience to have the same amount of movement as I.

These physical difficulties kept me partially immobilized during what turned out to be a very hectic period in my business career. At the time, I believed our immediate financial woes were finally at an end but should have realized that in the world of finance and big business nothing is for certain. In the late summer of 1965, the Atlantic Acceptance Corporation went bankrupt without warning, causing an enormous scandal in Toronto's business community. Atlantic, one of the country's largest financial institutions, had been loaning massive amounts of money on questionable security, and when their cash flow began to dry up, they were unable to meet payments on several of their own commitments. This forced them into insolvency. Certain principals of the company were suspected of fraud. Thousands of investors lost a sizable stake in the company, while an unfortunate few had their life savings wiped out. General Acceptance Corporation in Pennsylvania and Montreal Trust in Canada were appointed trustees to straighten out Atlantic's muddled affairs and to attempt a salvage of as much cash as possible from the loans and mortgages that had been recklessly advanced. Sumcot's original $310,000 mortgage had been reduced to $275,000 but was included in the supposedly bad debts. Our mortgage still had an additional four years to run before maturity, but when I read in the newspaper about other encumbrances being settled at fifty cents on the dollar or less, the wheels started spinning in my head, and I swiftly perceived the importance of making the trustees believe the Sumcot mortgage was also a disastrous advance.

Shortly after digesting the implications of the company's collapse, I stopped sending monthly interest payments to the trustees. When officials inquired about the reason for the delinquency, I explained that Sumcot did not have the funds available, which wasn't exactly a lie as we were constantly short of cash. I clearly understood the risk, because the trustees could have immediately called the entire loan due to a delinquency clause in the contract. I felt positive they would not resort to such a drastic measure. My intuition told me to take the enormous gamble for two reasons: first, foreclosure wasn't the course of action the trustees had been following, and second, they had no idea the actual value of Sumcot's property. Accurate appraisals of vacation property were difficult and expensive to obtain. The battle of wits went on while I recovered from foot surgery. At every opportunity when speaking to the trustees I insisted that if they would restructure our mortgage I probably could borrow sufficient money to keep up the interest payments. Finally, in desperation, they signed a new agreement with Sumcot in February, 1966, which included waiving interest from October to April (a savings of over $75,000), reducing the rate from 12 percent to 6 percent over the balance of the loan, and extending the maturity date an additional two years. The lot discharge rate increased from $500 to $800 per lot, but this added cost of discharging wasn't a terrible ordeal as the retail price of our lots had spiralled upwards.

Though delighted with the new arrangements, I nevertheless instructed Terry Mackey to continue making monthly interest payments sixty to ninety days in arrears to keep the trustees nervous about our ability to repay the loan. To add to their concern, I frequently phoned Montreal Trust about borrowing additional monies for operating capital—a request always flatly refused, of course. In the fall of 1966, I began a new campaign with the trustees regarding the possibility of discounting the mortgage if I could locate a suitable replacement. This started another round of critical financial maneuvering which continued for several months. Then in April, 1967, they informed me they would consider selling our mortgage at a discount. Having no idea where I might borrow another enormous sum of money with only land security, I placed ads in the "money wanted" columns of the local papers. The only response was Mr. Jack Young, who called to inquire about our needs and agreed to visit the developments and examine our security. I decided to be completely honest with Jack Young about my war of nerves with the trustees of Atlantic Acceptance.

I felt no compunction regarding the methods I used to reduce Sumcot's debt because the thousands I hoped to save would only be a pittance in the over-all total loss of millions which the company had suffered. It might mean the difference whether creditors received 10¢ or 9½¢ on the dollar in the final settlement, but a substantial reduction in our mortgage represented one hell of a triumph for Sumcot. Fortunately Jack Young believed in my personal business acumen and Sumcot's ability to repay the loan. In July we closed a deal whereby Young placed a $135,000 mortgage on our land, and we discharged the Atlantic Mortgage at a $100,000 discount. This transaction in addition to the cash saved the previous year by the waiving of six months interest and the 6 percent interest reduction until the date of discharge put Sumcot in the black to stay and gained the corporation more profit than it had earned in almost a decade of developing. Just as important, the episode acquainted me with Jack Young, formulating a business association that would make the two of us substantial money over the next twenty years.

While the nerve-tingling, nail-biting deal with Atlantic put Sumcot on the profit side of the ledger, it didn't improve our incessant cash shortfall to any great degree, and throughout 1966-67, Terry and I fought a never-ending battle to pay our bills and keep our creditors from closing the company's doors. This inability to build up a cash reserve wasn't due to lack of sales but rather to over expansion, and the fact that the company had a shoestring start with no substantial cash base at its inception. Banks were not the answer because they considered land development companies too risky. In the beginning of 1966, I started a daily journal that I have continued to this day, and only by perusing those diaries did I determine the unbelievable amount of time and effort I expended those years in search of financing.

I had no qualms about approaching business associates, customers in our developments, friends, relatives or strangers because of my utmost confidence in our capability to repay the money, but the answer was invariably a doubtful No. The Bank of Nova Scotia, my bank since the mid-1950s, gave me little help or consideration even though I repaid the Plastics Plating loan, an obligation I wasn't legally required to assume. They were exceedingly wary about establishing a decent line of credit for Sumcot, but after non-ending persuasion, in early 1967 they finally increased our lending capacity to $10,000, an entirely inadequate amount. Desperate for an increased credit line I began negotiating with the Royal Bank of Canada in the summer of 1967. In October of that year the Royal agreed to loan our company $30,000, and so after thirteen years I left The Bank of Nova Scotia, a move that turned out to be one of the most important decisions in Sumcot's troubled financial history. In November, 1968, the Royal Bank increased Sumcot's credit line to $50,000; in February, 1969, to $100,000. As my company prospered our borrowing capacity spiralled upward, and before long we dealt in sums of seven digits.

This constant cash deficiency, mainly due to our rapid expansion, was also partially due to the nature of the industry. Whenever we opened a new stretch of shore line in either Harcourt Park or Oak Shores Estate, it usually contained upwards of fifty lots. These new surveys required the installation of all services, and the preparation of the lots themselves, requiring men and machinery to clear water frontage, brush back heavily wooded areas, install service roads, and prepare building sites. During the course of the selling season, perhaps only a dozen of the newly developed lots on each new survey would be sold. By year's end we would have built up our inventory of fully prepared lots, but our cash income would not nearly match our expenditures. To add to Sumcot's difficulties, I incorporated a new concept in vacation property development by adding recreational facilities to our summer communities. In Harcourt Park we installed docks and boat launching sites at most of the lakes, carved walking trails through miles of dense bush and created playgrounds including regulation-size softball diamonds that required enormous clearing and filling in the rugged terrain. At Oak Shores we built an Olympic-size swimming pool, and also installed most of the amenities included at Harcourt Park. These additional facilities had to be built in the early stages of development, not only to be effective for the sales department but also to satisfy the customers who had already purchased and were demanding that these promised supplements be constructed immediately. Luckily for Sumcot, lot and cottage sales were booming. In 1966, total sales reached $450,000, and in 1967 sales went over a half million for the first time. This surge in business meant a prodigious increase in personnel, and Sumcot's days as a single digit employer now faded rapidly into the past.

During our hectic years of expansion, Sumcot had a tremendous turnover in staff, especially in the sales department although the building division also experienced a steady rotation of supervisors. Terry Mackey, the only skilled executive assistant I had, proved to be a strong and intelligent internal manager, but I needed help in the field. In January, 1966, Don Fevreau joined the firm. Two employees who started in the spring of 1965, Doug Prue and Edwina Seddon, had not reached supervisory status and wouldn't for several years although they would ultimately become two of the corporation's longest employed individuals. Don Fevreau came to Sumcot as General Sales Manager and provided energetic, capable, and desperately needed support in sales and development, a service he continued to render for several years. Don experienced a personality problem which frequently interfered in his communicating with fellow employees, but this conflict usually occurred when others simply didn't measure up to his high standards.

Our greatest perplexity continuously centered around the sales department where it seemed impossible to build up any continuity in personnel. Maintaining a competent sales force required full-time application as well as nerves of steel, and Fevreau proved worthy of the thankless task. Even though we hired and trained upwards of twenty men every season, the company generally finished with two or three at most. Several factors contributed to this annual problem. Selling land is a unique art, and vacation property falling into the same bracket is totally unlike selling city real estate or other high-priced luxury items. Interested prospects who visited our development were signed to a contract when the inspection period ended; otherwise they rarely bought. Our statistics proved that less than 10 percent of our customers ever purchased if they didn't make a decision at the time of their visit. Vacation or retirement property didn't fall into the category of necessity buying, and so the majority of people preferred to think over this major acquisition before signing on the dotted line. Hence, salesmen were thoroughly trained to get a check and signature at the time of inspection.

Sumcot's purchasers usually made an excellent profit on their investment as vacation property prices spiralled steadily upwards for several years, and so no one's conscience twitched if high-pressured salesmanship was applied. Being proficient at closing deals on site, therefore, became the prime requisite whether a sales person could survive in our industry. Unfortunately, people with this talent were few and far between. Those who did prove capable of earning good commissions rarely saved any money for the idle winter months that stretched from November until April before closings again provided an income. This long period of inactivity proved too much for the majority of our commissioned staff, and by spring Don and I would have to start training a new sales department all over again. The time and patience required in teaching new recruits the technique of selling Harcout Park leases also provided its share of headaches. Interested clients were frequently suspicious of the leasehold arrangement, and it required a particularly astute and dedicated salesperson to convince people of the authenticity of the deal. An expensive aspect of our dilemma involved paying various size draws to qualified sales personnel in an effort to keep them in the fold. This strategy generally backfired, and most indebted men left the company owing anywhere from hundreds to thousands of dollars. Working every summer week end and most evenings discouraged numerous potential salesmen, especially if they had a family, and a car in good repair, an absolute requirement, prevented others from remaining with the company. Sound physical condition due to the amount of walking over hilly and rugged terrain further reduced the ranks of Sumcot salesmen. So in the day-to-day predicaments faced by the corporation, the sales department encountered its share.

Although in the minority, the company did attract a handful of competent dedicated men who remained for various periods of time and sold the bulk of Sumcot's property during this era. The foremost producer other, than Edwina Seddon was Al Chrysler, though Wayne Pirie, Andy Andrews, Dick Rolls, John Jackson and Norv Starling all contributed greatly to Sumcot's successful years from the mid-1960s to the early 1970s when an entirely different regime took over.

The cottage division also constantly provided a great proportion of Sumcot's troubles. I mentioned earlier the considerable difficulty and numerous problems of building cottages in our developments. Len Nordin who performed splendidly for four years reached the end of his rope one week end when he discovered one of his carpentry crews at Oak Shores had constructed the wrong interior design in a large cottage. When he arrived at Harcourt Park, he found another of his building gangs well advanced in erecting a pretentious building on the wrong lot. Both errors cost the company a sizable sum of money to rectify, and Nordin resigned due to embarrassment and the inability to cope with the unrelenting pressure. Several managers were hired to replace the hard-working and dedicated Swede with excellent remuneration offered as their reward, but they faired no better. Peter Brantin, following Len, lasted only a few months, then Jim Fairfield failed his opportunity. In the spring of 1967, Harry Adams joined the company with excellent credentials, but he also couldn't manage the knotty problems in the department. All were knowledgeable construction men with years of experience in building, but they were incapable of controlling the intricacies of our particular industry.

In the summer of 1967 after discharging the likable Harry Adams, I hired Gerry Cluff, a Toronto builder whose houses I sold throughout the early 1950s. Gerry was a competent and experienced general contractor, and I was delighted to add him to our staff, hoping he could finally overcome the multitude of obstacles. Unfortunately he proved no more capable of unraveling the dilemma in cottage construction than were the others. Gerry did persuade me, however, to get involved in Toronto house building as a logical means of extending our selling season. As a result, Sumcot constructed $800,000 worth of two-story brick homes in Mississauga in the late 1960s. This new venture cost the corporation a huge dollar loss and enormous inconvenience as manning the houses on week ends frequently tied up our sales department at a time when they were desperately needed in the summer property developments. Hindsight always allows us to observe mistakes in judgement taken in the course of business, but it soon became apparent that our incursion into the Toronto housing market was ill-timed and that our building location site was poorly chosen. Spiralling interest rates increased financial requirements to purchase new homes out of the reach of most people, and houses already constructed, being offered with old rate mortgages, were tough competition. Cluff chose our lot location close to Malton's expanding airport and bad publicity regarding the intolerable noise frightened people from house looking in that area, therefore limiting our traffic.

Perhaps the most important reason for slack sales resulted from what would now be considered a trivial incident. A black family purchased a house directly across the street from our model homes. At this time, Toronto people were unaccustomed to integrating with blacks in residential sectors, mainly because only a handful of blacks resided in the city and Torontonians were indoctrinated through all forms of media about racial unpleasantries south of the border. Invariably when we placed major week-end advertising, a large assemblage of blacks would be congregated at the house across the street, a situation that lost our company an unbelievable number of house sales. Through no fault of anyone, we were caught up in a thoroughly frustrating predicament that has plagued many neighborhoods in the world due to unrealistic racial prejudices.

Gerry Cluff, completely involved with our houses in the Forestwood subdivision, couldn't oversee cottage construction in the lake regions, and Len Nordin, after a two-year hiatus, returned to Sumcot to resume his old duties. Uncle George left Sumcot for a few months in the spring of 1966 to try his luck at managing a Becker's Milk Store. This turned out to be a poor move, and so he came back to Sumcot and worked as Len's assistant. The two managed the cottage division with as much success as we were to experience for all the years Sumcot remained involved with that aggravating aspect of our industry. Cluff left the company in early 1969.

The developing aspect of our business also became exceedingly vexatious as the sixties decade progressed. I personally supervised every department of the company, though overseeing sales and direct development took up most of my time and efforts. Adding to our pandemonium, in the summer of 1966 I purchased a third development which we named High View Acres, because it offered a gorgeous panoramic view of Pigeon Lake. We didn't officially put High View on the market until 1968. In 1969, I obtained Hyckes Haven, which included a developable island as well as substantial mainland acreage including shoreline. It was located near the town of Hastings, 90 miles east of Toronto. In the same year I acquired a development on Diamond Lake, and a few weeks later purchased the final 400 acres of Harcourt Park, increasing that immense development's expanse to 7,000 acres. These five subdivisions gave Sumcot a total inventory of 800 unsold lots in different phases of development at a total retail value of five million dollars when all services had been completed.

Like a mother with a half dozen children who decides six more won't add much to her general state of disorder, I figured additional sites couldn't cause me too much more mental anguish, an assessment that didn't turn out to be entirely accurate. Constant meetings with local councils and provincial authorities, a dreadfully time-consuming chore and also personally demeaning, swiftly became one of the most irritating responsibilities of the business. Environmentalists and families who couldn't afford vacation property constantly pressured government bureaus to halt lake-front development, and these agencies listened because the country's mood was to protect the non-affluent. I felt unbelievably frustrated and thoroughly dejected with the constant array of road blocks from government departments that seemed intent on impeding our progress. Making a profit was undoubtedly my aim, but Sumcot created jobs in areas that were otherwise sadly lacking in employment opportunities. Our customers brought some prosperity to towns and villages situated in the vicinity of our developments. These same people were also far more cognizant and careful with the environment than the loud mouths and public do-gooders who constantly voiced objections to Sumcot's endeavors and too frequently were included on the staffs of the government agencies themselves. It became unbearable at times to be halted by some young government official, thoroughly ignorant of the issues at stake but with the power of God to stop Sumcot in its tracks.

Standards for road construction had increased tenfold. Slopes and hills on access routes that used to be considered attractive as well as a splendid way to keep traffic traveling at a reasonable pace now had to be dynamited and levelled almost to the same degree as provincial highways. Eighteen-foot tops on roads, an ample width for our limited development traffic, was increased to thirty feet. Sloping, draining, and culverting had to conform to the identical engineering standards as provincial highways. Septic field requirements for cottages surged, and weeping tile specifications increased from fifty feet to five hundred feet in less than five years. This not only forced a dramatic increase in installation costs, but also meant that heavily treed lots were 50 percent denuded before a septic tank could be buried. An engineering report from the Ontario Department of Health claimed that the effluent from cottage developments reaching lakes and waterways was minimal in comparison to the toxides used by farmers in fertilizers. As a result of heavy rains or spring run-offs, these poisons flowed freely into ditches, brooks and streams and eventually reached the lakes that cottage developers were blamed for polluting. This massive increase in development costs obviously had to be passed on to the buyers. This meant that the $3,000 lots of the early 1960s were marketed at $6,000 by the end of the decade, yet Sumcot was not earning as much profit on their land as they had ten years before.

Despite all these new regulations, Sumcot operated without professional engineering assistance in the field, with the exception of Curry Bishop from Haliburton who provided all surveying and engineering reports to satisfy government agencies. We installed a 72-foot steel bridge (bought second hand from the Department of Highways) to span the Squaw River and constructed two concrete dams on the same stream to hold the water level at a height to provide our river-front customers with some semblance of a waterway during summer dry spells when the river became a trickle. In Harcourt Park, a steel-reinforced concrete bridge built over the narrows between Big and Little Straggle Lakes spanned a 30-foot stretch at a height of eight feet above water level. Intricate water systems were installed both above the ground and below frost level, depending on specifications, and with complex pumping stations to meet the standards of the Ontario Department of Water Resources. Whenever an engineer's signature was required to satisfy government red tape, Curry Bishop inspected the installations and signed the documents. Many of our field men had some expertise in dealing with the numerous hurdles which the company faced, and we muddled through in fine fashion.

One of the significant quandries encountered in the initial phase at Oak Shores Estate involved the heavy growth of greenery that sprouted above the water in midsummer, making shallow Little Bald Lake resemble an unmown hay meadow. Like the black-fly pestilence in Harcourt Park that caused such tremendous concern a few years earlier, the situation at Oak Shores frightened the hell out of me. I couldn't envision our customers purchasing lake-front lots when they couldn't even maneuver a boat through the dense growth of aquatic weeds. At enormous cost, I employed a contractor with a dragline operating from a barge and a huge vacuum cleaner type of machine that sucked up debris from the lake bottom and blew it several hundred feet away from the shoreline. This expensive procedure did provide canals at the water's edge, allowing our so-called lake-front lot owners to reach open water, but did nothing to discourage the growth from the lake bottom. I contacted Dow Chemical to devise a method of killing the weeds without poisoning the fish, but this idea proved impractical due to the time required to obtain government approval.

Union Carbide and I worked out intricate plans to cover the entire lake bottom with a layer of polyethelene to smother the growth, but after several unsuccessful attempts to force the plastic sheets through the water to settle smoothly on the lake floor, I gave up that plan. Mowing machines that cut below the surface of the water were purchased, but these tactics also turned out to be ineffective because the following morning the aquatic growth blooming above the lake looked even denser than before the time-consuming cutting operation. In desperation, I devised a new scheme. We constructed a raft powered with an outboard motor. Two men were set to work pulling the grass and weeds out by the roots. They were tossed aboard the raft and taken ashore for later burning. After one week, the two men assigned to the onerous chore hadn't cleared three square yards, and at that rate I determined it would require roughly 72 years to make any noticeable difference. The two workmen were bored to death and embarrassed to tears, and I had become the laughing stock of Sumcot. We also abandoned that program. Before the end of two years every lot overlooking the sea of green had been sold, and I finally decided to stop chasing imaginary dragons.

Although we had managed without professional engineering since our inception, except as outlined, I had no qualms about using their services when it became obviously necessary. The acquisition of High View Acres so close to Toronto made me decide to submit a plan to the Provincial government applying for status as a permanent community rather than as a vacation development. This would necessitate a sewer system with a lagoon and also other city amenities. The intricacy of such a venture left no alternative but to employ knowledgeable people, and so I went to Marshall Macklen and Monaghan, a large Toronto architectural and engineering firm that prepared all designs and submissions for the various government agencies. Provincial government officials flatly refused the concept because they believed it required at least five thousand people to support a permanent community and provide a tax base to allow for fire and police protection, school buses, and other essential services. That government decision left no choice but to proceed with an application for the normal summer cottage development status which meant residents were only supposed to inhabit their dwellings for six months of the year according to the Provincial Department of Municipal Affairs.

Even though we couldn't get permanent status approval, the Ontario

Water Resources Commission demanded that a year-round water system be installed, and the Department of Health insisted that our septic systems be imbedded so they would not be affected by winter weather usage and capable of handling sewage treatment twelve months of the year. Both of these departments were Provincial government agencies. The Municipal Government of Emily, the township where the development was located, had different ideas. They wanted the water system to operate the entire year instead of six months as outlined in our approval, and the local officials would have no part in forcing residents to leave their property at any time of the year to satisfy the Provincial government. The end result of this normal bureaucratic screw-up was that Sumcot sold the land for considerably less than if it had received permanent status, and installed services with only half the capacity that were needed for year-round living. Our purchasers paid no attention to the Ontario government but lived in their new vacation retirement homes as long as they pleased. Many, including my mother, made it one of the largest permanent communities in the general area, sans police and fire protection, though the local municipality did provide school bus service.

As government regulations became increasingly burdensome and attending council meetings and preparing cumbersome reports for rapidly expanding departments a regular affair, I decided in the fall of 1969 to employ a full-time professional engineer. Ron McMillan, a man with a wealth of experience in many areas similar to our industry joined the firm and removed much of the burden of demanding detail off of my shoulders. Also Doug Prue, who joined the firm in early 1965 now devoted full time to direct developing and the three of us worked in close harmony on all our projects.

Doug, the oldest son of George Prue, who worked for Homeland Realty in 1954, became connected with Sumcot by coincidence. I first met Doug as a lad of fifteen at Homeland when he came to see George, but never encountered him again until 1963 at Harcourt Park. Doug became a womanizer akin to his personable father at an early age. He married while quite young, had a daughter, then left his wife to live with an attractive young lady named Pat. They settled a short distance from the village of Harcourt and also had a daughter. Doug worked for a young German contractor who built cottages for Sumcot under Len Nordin's supervision. One day while making an inspection tour of the development, Doug approached and asked if I knew his name. The facial resemblance to his father made him instantly recognizable, and I was surprised to see the pudgy boy had grown into a muscular young man with a ready smile and pleasing personality. Over the next two years we often spoke to each other and discussed his unique father who had divorced Doug's mother, remarried, separated and now lived with yet another woman.

Doug somehow felt that as a friend of his father, whom he admired and cursed all in the same breath, we had a special relationship. Before the conclusion of the second season at Harcourt Park, Doug asked for a job because he wished to return permanently to Toronto but wanted to avoid a factory position or inside work. I started him in April 1965 as a sales trainee, and he struggled for a year attempting to make a success at the selling profession. His timid character prevented him from mastering the technique of closing land sales. With a tremendous ego, Doug couldn't stand the thought of anyone disliking him, and therefore he found it impossible to put pressure on a prospective buyer if that individual seemed the slightest bit uncomfortable. Having grown fond of the congenial young man, I took him off sales in 1966 and appointed him as my field assistant in the developments.

The new position threw Doug into close contact with me, particularly on week ends when we shared the same cottage or motel on development inspections and work layouts for the coming week. During evenings or other available opportunities the lad discussed many of his intimate fears and confidences. Although he showed an outer braggadocia, his inner emotions didn't match his cocky manner, and it also became obvious his days with Pat were numbered because he felt inferior to that intelligent young lady. One topic Doug preferred to discuss other than sex or women was outdoor activities. An ardent fisherman and an avid hunter, he never tired of listening to my moose hunting exploits and frequently expressed a great desire to join me in a moose-hunting jaunt. As it had been several years since my last crack at this exciting game animal, I arranged to take young Prue in the fall of 1966 for a week in the North Woods. This turned out to be a delightful vacation and it also provided a golden opportunity to get more personally acquainted with Doug, forging a bond of friendship that remained unbroken.

We drove to Sudbury, Ontario where we spent the night and arranged the next day for a small Cessna to fly us into Kettle Lake, a hundred miles north and completely separated from civilization. A dense overcast day with occasional snow flurries hampered low-level flying, and as the afternoon waned, it appeared we might have to spend another night in a motel. Disappointed at the news, because the season opened the following morning, we were suddenly delighted at 4:30 when the pilot instructed us to heave our equipment into the aircraft as there appeared to be a break in the clouds. When we landed on Kettle Lake, the weather began to close in again, and darkness wasn't far off. In his haste to get airborne while he could still see, the pilot heaved our gear on a rock jutting into the water that anchored his Cessna, pointed into a grove of evergreens where a tent, stove and canoe was supposedly stashed, and clambered aboard his craft. Waving good-bye and good luck, he yelled he would be back in a week and took off, soon to be swallowed up by low hanging clouds and the rapidly approaching night.

The exhilarated feeling some men cherish from pitting themselves against nature never before or in the future seemed as imbedded in my soul as at that moment. Clouds scudding low across the bleak landscape, snowflakes whipping our faces, gear piled on a rock in the middle of nowhere, and a greenhorn kid as my companion gave me a sense of challenge that forever became unmatchable. Doug accepted the situation like a seasoned trooper and followed my every instruction with unmistakable enthusiasm and without question. We soon located the tent and stove, and though the tent had no floor, it was spacious, in good condition, and easy to erect. Darkness rapidly spread across the desolate though enchanting scene, and we had to light our Coleman lantern to fell spruce trees to trim small branches for mattresses and also cut sufficient firewood to last for what promised to be a cold night. Sharing a shot of whiskey while Doug cooked steaks over an open fire, I began to feel confidence in my new hunting mate and encouraged that in an emergency he might be as reliable as Hank Sharpe. Though chilly, we spent a comfortable night, arose early, devoured a hearty breakfast and were on the water by the break of day.

Doug had limited experience in a canoe, and because we were paddling across large stretches of open water, I did have some reservations about our safety. Again though, my young companion followed instructions, and we were soon maneuvering our 12-foot craft through the murky gray morning stillness like a couple of stealthy Indians, the only sound the lapping of small waves against the slithering vessel. Searching the shoreline without uttering a word, we paddled for a couple of hours before pulling into a little cove for a hot cup of coffee from our thermos. A trapper's portage trail took off into the woods, and Doug inquired if we could follow it a ways to stretch our cramped limbs. Shucking our heavy outer garments we quietly took off over the rugged path, and within a quarter of a mile we arrived at another small lake. The beauty and tranquility of the surroundings inspired us to stop, light a cigarette, and relax for a few moments. A huge flock of Canadian geese, honking farewell, sailed gracefully overhead with a steadily increasing north breeze fanning their tail feathers.

I was enchanted by the placid surroundings, and Doug's sudden hoarse whisper seemed strangely out of place. Recognizing an urgency in his voice, I glanced over.

"A moose," he sputtered, pointing across the pond. Sure enough, two hundred yards across the lake stood our quarry with its head lowered into the water for a morning drink. Neither of us used a scope on our rifle, and so it required careful aiming to have any hope of bagging the distant target. As swiftly as we could pull the trigger and pump shells into the barrel, we emptied our guns. At the first shots the animal turned and fled from sight, and we had no idea whether either of us had connected. Stumbling over deadfalls and dead underbrush rimming the picturesque pond, we raced to the site where we believed the beast had been standing. Great disappointment surged over me when I saw no trace of our prey, well aware we wouldn't get too many chances. Though a long shot at a relatively small target, because we could see no more than the head and shoulders, I felt we should have downed our prey. All at once I heard the low groan of a wounded animal, and within a hundred feet found a mortally wounded young cow moose. Doug, searching elsewhere, came rushing over at my call, and a look of triumph spread across his face when he witnessed the slain animal. To be successful on our first hunt was indeed a victory, but bagging game on the first morning of that hunt made it especially appealing. We would have the balance of the week to butcher the meat, canoe it to our encampment and spend the rest of the holiday in a more relaxed atmosphere.

Perhaps the knee operations I required in the following two years were a direct result of that trip. The half mile from where we shot and butchered the carcass to the cove on Kettle Lake where we beached our canoe was an exceedingly rough and irregular stretch of territory. Though we slashed out a narrow trail, the walking remained treacherous. Unable to remove many of the large deadfalls left no alternative but to climb over them, and the undulating terrain was slippery and dangerous. Simply walking back and forth required considerable stamina, but with a hundred pounds of moose meat swaying on a pole slung between the two of us made it a real test of endurance. By the time we'd made the eighth and final journey, we were both exhausted. It required two days to get our meat back to camp, and although Doug had a strong, healthy body, I was impressed with his dedication to the herculean task and insistence on shouldering a larger share of the load when possible. With the exhausting chore completed, I vowed never to shoot another moose unless I could get within a hundred yards of the execution site by canoe.

After hanging our game in trees, we still had three days in which to fish and explore the fascinating country, and we made the most of the opportunity. Our topographic maps showed numerous small bodies of water within easy portaging distance of Kettle and so each day we headed off in a different direction. With fishing tackle, guns, boiling up kettle, frying pan, and enough food for a picnic, we lazed the days away investigating new areas. Fish weren't biting exceptionally well, but we caught sufficient walleyes and northern pike for savory lunches cooked over an aromatic birch fire. With no sounds to interrupt the serenity except squawking Canada jays, the lonesome wail of the loons, or the slap of a beaver's tail, we felt the world belonged to us. The golden days passed by in a flash, and before we knew it, the Cessna returned to pick us up. He had to radio for another aircraft to transport our moose meat.

Doug and I hunted together for several seasons, usually successfully, but from time to time we would be skunked. We always enjoyed each other's company and shared a multitude of thrills. That first afternoon on Kettle Lake and the following few days were always considered the high point of our mutual hunting adventures. More important, the few days spent with the young man provided me with an excellent opportunity to test his mettle and compatibility. He didn't fail in either category. Getting too friendly with an employee is generally considered unwise, but in Doug Prue's case it appeared to do no harm.

Sumcot acquired a vast amount of machinery and equipment, and Doug soon proved his value as a development assistant, particularly in the day-to-day field operations. Before the end of the 1960s he took on most of the responsibility of direct developing, albeit under my tutelage. Our separate equipment division with over a hundred thousand dollars worth of machinery and gear required continuous maintenance and service. We had four large house trailers from 36 to 50 feet in length set up in Harcourt Park to provide overnight accommodations for our customers. Independent contractors proved unreliable and costly and so we bought three dump trucks, a loader, small bulldozer, compressor for dynamiting (for which we had plenty of applications), backhoe, and a grader and float. The cost of contracting outside dredging equipment also became prohibitive for the immense job of cleaning the shallow, grassy bays and sloughs at Oak Shores, and so I purchased our own dragline. To allow the new machine to operate efficiently, I contracted to have built one of the largest barges in the entire country, and a huge scow with an automatic dumping feature so we could load the debris scooped from the lake and dump it at a site of our choosing. The dragline, barge, and scow were unique in the country for their ability to do that specific job.

In addition to all the machinery, we provided six half-ton trucks, painted blue and adorned with the Sumcot logo, for development managers and supervisors and four automobiles for the sales department. We still employed private contractors for a majority of cottage building, but most of the plumbing and electrical wiring was installed with regular Sumcot personnel. By the turn of the seventies, Sumcot had over sixty people on the direct payroll including sales staff, and an additional two dozen or more as independent contractors. Our payroll zoomed to nearly a half million annually. At this point Don Fevreau, Terry Mackey, and Doug Prue had accepted and proved capable of handling the added responsibility. Doug had several supervisors, including the hard-working and diligent Ralph Bate, Grant Austin and Pop in the day-to-day surveillance of our developing operations.

Our surge of growth demanded larger headquarters, and in the spring of 1968, I left Danforth for the first time in almost twenty years. Sumcot located its new offices on Midland Avenue in Scarborough in a brand new building with two floors and 6,000 feet of space laid out to our own design. At the office opening, 150 associates gathered to celebrate the elaborate new setup. Terry expanded the front office to eight, including Joyce's cousin Georgie, an extremely capable secretary, Fred Martin, our own accountant, and a receptionist, payroll clerk, and bookkeepers. One of the surprising additions to Sumcot's staff during that era was my brother Jack, who decided to make a change after fifteen years with Memorial Gardens. At first Jack joined the sales department and did an excellent job under the leadership of Don Fevreau. Later I appointed him as New Projects Manager. Although Jack and I remained close as brothers, we fought like hell on many occasions when we bumped heads in day-to-day affairs. His joining Sumcot wasn't always a happy arrangement for either of us. Perhaps because he had kept personally involved and interested in all Sumcot's accomplishments since its incorporation, he found it belittling to take orders from individuals who joined the firm in later years. Having been closely associated with me through all my financial struggles—even to putting up his Harcourt Park cottage as security for a desperately needed loan— he probably felt deserving of a more independent or authoritative position. Despite his feelings, I had no alternative in our fight for survival but to keep men in administrative positions where I believed they could do the best job. Though I endured numerous headaches from managers who complained about Jack's intransigence in internal affairs as well as my own chief grievance about the touch of socialism he seemed to have in his soul (he was forever trying to improve the lot of our common salespeople), he remained generally popular with Sumcot personnel. Jack and I never remained at odds for more than twenty-four hours.

Jack wasn't the only Sumcot member with whom I had frequent confrontations, during those hectic days of expansion. Edwina Seddon, the heart and soul of our sales department, gave me as much cause to scream, of which I did plenty, as any member of our permanent staff. Edwina, a robust English woman, had served with the Royal Air Force during World War II and immigrated to Canada with her husband Fred shortly after the cessation of hostilities. They had three youngsters, two girls and a boy. Laura was the youngest and only a baby in arms in the fall of 1964 when Edwina applied for a job as a telephone solicitor. A tireless worker, she nevertheless received little fruit from her labors the first year. The following spring while continuing to work the phones from her home she became extremely frustrated when her supposedly confirmed appointments never showed at the developments, for her entire remuneration was based on commission for clients that turned up and a much larger commission if they bought. She found the situation even more exasperating when the sales force didn't close what she felt were surefire sales when her customers did arrive. Disgusted, Edwina threatened to throw in the sponge. Impressed with her tenacity, I invited her to go to Oak Shores and handle her own clients, and she accepted my offer.

Edwina had some previous selling experience with jewelry but absolutely none in real estate or land. I gave her little chance for success but admired her spunk. Despite her age and lack of physical preparedness for hiking over hills and through dense growth with prospects and although she had less training than anyone on our sales staff, she began to click almost immediately and embarrassed most other members of the salesforce with her high percentage of closings. In all the years I remained in business, Edwina out-performed all others, not only in Sumcot but also our opposition as well. She became renowned as the expert salesperson in our industry.

My twenty years of selling experience at this point included Fuller Brush, Coronet T.V., real estate, and land. I had attended numerous sales seminars, read a multitude of books on the subject, and proven my ability in the field of selling. My competency in training salespeople had also been demonstrated in the success of Phillips Real Estate and Sumcot. When it came to closing land sales, however, I took a back seat to Edwina Seddon, who threw away all the books and used her own methods to achieve her outstanding rate of efficiency. She used her pleasing personality to its fullest and refused to accept a prospect's excuse for not signing a contract, if they had shown an interest in the property. To my constant amazement after several dozen flat refusals, a high percentage of her clients eventually succumbed and signed on the dotted line.

Edwina and I fought about the same degree as Jack and I—and often for similar reasons. Sumcot frequently gave away boats, motors, canoes, dishware, and other merchandise to customers who followed a certain procedure. At times when Edwina encountered a tough closing, she would offer one of the above items as an inducement, even though the prospect didn't qualify. She felt the sale justified her decision. Although delighted with the sale, I would blow my stack, as I felt it was unfair to those clients who had followed the rules. Also, I didn't want to provide expensive gifts to all our buyers. Edwina and I would jump in my car and retreat to a deserted spot where I could get the aggravation off my chest. She would argue vehemently about the logic of her giveaway. With the air cleared for a little while, at least, we would go back to business as usual. I no doubt had more personal altercations with Jack and Edwina than any other members of my growing staff, but I also enjoyed a personal intimacy with the two of them that overcame the irritations we so frequently encountered. The Seddon family friendship didn't apply only to me but to Joyce and our kids as well, and our long and fruitful relationship remained a positive plus in Sumcot's turbulent history.

With the inclusion of three new developments: High View Acres, Diamond Lake, and Hyckes Haven added to our inventory, total sales exceeded one million in 1968 and, including our houses at Forestwood, skyrocketed to one and a half million in 1969. Sales didn't come cheaply. Sumcot spent more dollars on advertising and promotion than all our competitors combined. We operated huge display booths at major Toronto shows plus numerous exhibitions in neighboring towns and cities. The Ohio market hadn't produced up to our expectations, and so after six years of continuous exhibiting at Cleveland we finally gave up the ghost in 1968. We continued advertising in Ohio newspapers, however. Sumcot purchased a 42-foot house trailer, accumulated a spectacular collection of stuffed animals, birds, and fish from all over the country and had them professionally displayed in beautifully appointed glass cases fixed permanently in the trailer. This Sumcot Nature Museum cost the company $15,000 and it promoted our properties in shopping malls throughout the city for several seasons. Another permanent display of Sumcot Developments was located in the Skylon at Niagara Falls, and it produced hundreds of inquiries, especially from Americans.

Due to the amount of time required to set up shows, write advertising, prepare promotional releases, and the thousand and one other duties indispensable to our operation, I hired Reginald Folk as our new advertising and promotional manager. Jack McNeil had long since departed Sumcot to take an executive position in a publishing company. The addition of Reg now gave me an able assistant in every department of the company and allowed me time to do things other than constantly fret about business.

For most of the year I still worked six and seven days a week with some of my days beginning at 5 a.m. Leaving the city at daylight on Friday, I would drive 250 miles to inspect our developments scattered across southcentral Ontario and arrive at Harcourt Park, the fifth and last, before 5 p.m. with the weekly payroll. Prior to school summer holidays, Joyce and the three youngsters would frequently drive to our

Harcourt Park cottage on a Friday evening with friends. All three kids loved the park, but the pressure of my existence and the desire to relax awhile induced me to drink heavily most week ends, and this revelry ruined Joyce's pleasure. Our cottage resembled a noisy honky-tonk when salesmen and other staff members joined the party.

Greg Hilton, who purchased the Harcourt Park Marina, swiftly became a buddy and willing accomplice to my drinking bouts. Greg, a professional ski instructor with a delightful sense of humor and ready smile, worked hard all week as did I, and we reverted to my old lumberjack life style of boozing and playing cards well into the night on week ends. Though most of our "wing dings" drove Joyce to distraction, my friendship with Greg Hilton during those frantic years perhaps prevented me from getting ulcers. It certainly provided an escape from reality during a stressful period of my business career, and Greg and I remained close friends. Long after selling his Harcourt Park operation, Greg remained a regular hunting partner with Doug Prue, brother Jack, and myself, and the four of us spent several thrilling seasons in Ontario's North Woods hunting elusive whitetails and the magnificent moose.

When business took an upward swing in the mid-1960s, I resolved to change residences and move to a more pretentious sector of the city. Joyce chose a huge new five-level front-to-back split home on Banstock Drive in the lovely Bayview and Finch area of North York. We bought our exciting new nine-room house plus four bathrooms for less than $50,000 in 1965, and it proved to be not only a delightful family residence but also a bargain. It contained a private den, which Joyce had nicely appointed, and finally I had a private lair to spend my leisure hours.

Though drinking heavily, I did have other means of relaxation. Television provided little entertainment value to me except for sports and an occasional comedy program, and so I devoted my spare time to other endeavors. My interests included trying to master the guitar, learning to type by a home typing manual, taking the Evelyn Wood speed reading course, and practicing writing with the Famous Writers Course, which I only half completed. The most time-consuming venture of all involved the collection and preparation of a family album, which I called "The Continuity of Life." An old picture of my mother in her mother's arms taken in Europe before the turn of the century graced the first page, followed by hundreds of snapshots of family, friends, places and events. All pictures were pasted in albums in chronological order with each photograph captioned as to persons, place, or circumstances. It turned out to be an enormous undertaking and one I continue to this day. Turning the pages slowly you can watch each family member, including myself, age at a gradual and graceful rate. My away-from-home pleasures included rubber bridge two or three times a week, a game at which I'd become a devotee and at which I loved to gamble. I golfed when time allowed, generally with other members of Sumcot, and our company operated a little curling league through the dreary winter months which proved to be a great form of relaxation and exercise.

With Jack and Shirley living in Toronto only a short distance from Mom and Pop's West Hill home, our family found itself quite closely interwoven again except that sister Joyce and Grandmother Rodd were causing Mom some anxiety. Mother, a broad-minded and concerned parent felt strongly that Joyce should never be a burden to either Jack or me or our wives, and so she believed the most suitable place for my young sibling was a home for the mentally retarded. The Ontario government operated several institutions where these unfortunate individuals were cared for professionally, and the patients were surrounded by people of their own mentality. The prohibitive waiting list prompted me to seek help from political associates, and with their assistance we had Joyce admitted to one of these homes where she remains to this day. Mother takes Joyce out for Christmas week and other holidays. She thoroughly enjoys the visit with her family, but she is always anxious to return to the hospital to be back with her friends. We never regretted the decision to have her placed in a home.

Grandmother Rodd, nearing ninety and with her mental faculties operating in forward gear, had a problem moving about, and Mother grew increasingly concerned about her well being during the summers at Harcourt Park. In the event she had an accident or suddenly became ill, getting medical help would be painfully slow. Political friends in Toronto assisted me in getting my hard-nosed grandmother placed in the cheerful and well-managed Bendale Old Folks Home where she remained until she died at the age of ninety-four.

My most aggravating family perplexity centered around my own three children, although as a family group we generally took pleasure in each other's company at this stage of their adolescent lives. Michael caused me the most anguish because he appeared to possess the highest degree of intelligence. Despite his high I.Q., he refused to apply himself at school and drove teachers to distraction with his slothful ways. No amount of lecturing by me or his tutors could motivate him from his dreamworld, and it became thoroughly agonizing to see his school years slip away and realize that though he possessed the mental capacity to accomplish great things he lacked any drive whatsoever. Finally at the age of eighteen and only in Grade X, he left school for good, and the only possibility that one of my offspring would ever go to a university departed with him.

Gary, an extremely likable lad, simply didn't have the same intelligence as his brother Mike, and I had to make numerous trips to see his teachers about minor offenses generally as a result of his inability to cope. Unfortunately, greater problems with this boy were still around the corner. Gary struggled through school until he managed to pass Grade VIII and then worked at menial jobs like pumping gas and anything else his limited education would permit him to do. At one time I investigated the possibility of placing Michael and Gary in a military school or hiring a private tutor but was discouraged by their principal. I often regretted not proceeding with that plan of action.

Sherree rarely brought home a poor report card and handled her school assignments with ease. Though two years younger, she ended up in Grade VIII the same year as Gary, and this embarrassment had a bearing on his decision to leave school completely. Sherree had the mental capacity to breeze through college, but like Michael, she lacked the motivation. Though disappointment at my children's failure to be university graduates caused me tremendous heartaches at the time, the principal importance to Joyce and me was that they would live happy and contented lives. Thomas Richard Henry, a columnist for the *Toronto Globe and Mail* once wrote an article dealing with the role a parent plays in their children's success or failure through life. He remarked that when a youngster goes wrong the world generally looks at his parents to place the blame, but if a child becomes a genius, the parents are rarely given a second look. Perhaps I remembered those words to use as a balm for my concern regarding the inadequacies of my offspring. Nonetheless I never agonized over the possibility that either Joyce or I should bear the responsibility for their actions.

Sumcot with all its complex affairs kept me away from home a great deal of time, but whenever possible, I spent some of my available leisure hours with the family. In the spring and summer the three young ones and I would occasionally tramp the nearby woods or fields as I tried to educate and interest them in the miracles of nature. Throughout school vacations either the entire family or the two boys would accompany me on my weekly tour of the developments. In winter I took the boys ice fishing, a sport they both loved. Perhaps my greatest contribution to their childhood memories involved Christmas. From the moment they could appreciate the wonders and excitement of Christmas I provided all three with the finest toys and gifts money could buy. Joyce and I also made Halloween, Easter, Valentine's Day, and July 1st (Canada's national holiday) a special day by providing candy, costumes, or firecrackers as the celebration demanded. We traveled as a family unit by automobile on three long trips: to North Carolina, Winnipeg, and in 1967 toured Expo '67 in Montreal and then continued to explore the balance of eastern Canada. We didn't recognize it at the time, but that journey would be our final long stretch of family togetherness.

The eastern jaunt proved to be pleasant and educational. Our off-spring ranged from 12 to 16 years, ideal ages to appreciate each other's company. Like all parents with growing children, I suddenly became aware that each day they seemed to sprout new growth and adopt new mannerisms. During that journey I also came to comprehend the extremely short span in a normal lifetime we spend in innocent childhood. The World's Fair at Montreal, though exciting and pleasant, didn't provide as much fascination as other places in the 5,000-mile journey. Besides Montreal and Quebec City in Quebec Province, we visited every city in the Maritimes, including; Fredricton, Moncton, Halifax, Dartmouth, Sydney, Charlottetown and St. Johns.

Many highlights were experienced in the tour. The bright red soil and emerald blue Atlantic waters at Prince Edward Island intrigued us, and so we spent a few days cod fishing and swimming in the alluring sea surrounding that picturesque province. Outstanding scenery along the Cabot Trail in New Brunswick provided a beautiful backdrop for our outdoor barbecues and picnics. The long car ferry crossing of the enormous Gulf of St. Lawrence to reach Newfoundland provided a thrill when approaching land in pitch darkness through a pea soup fog, fog-horns blaring their forlorn warnings. Later that night we experienced greater excitement when nearing Cornerbrook our automobile brushed the flanks of a huge caribou standing in the middle of the highway. Returning home through charming New England with its variety of scenery furnished a fitting finale to our long journey. We planned to spend our final night in New York State until I discovered our cash reserves had dwindled to $22. Those were the days before plastic money, and so with accommodations out of our financial grasp we sped home. The lengthy trip proved to be a wise decision, for within two years both boys had flown the coop for good.

During this turbulent era, Joyce and I had our share of marital squabbles, but with each personal adversity, business victory, or defeat, we grew closer together and more tolerable of the other's weaknesses. Joyce too lived a tempestuous existence. Due to my frequent absence she handled much of the responsibility of raising our youngsters and drove them to all the places youngsters are forever clamoring to go. She wouldn't allow me to leave the house no matter how early nor regardless of the reason without preparing breakfast and remaining with me until I departed. The kids never returned home from school when Joyce wasn't there to greet them and to provide a snack to fill their constantly ravenous bellies. Sumcot personnel frequently used Joyce as a sounding board if something or someone disturbed them. She would provide a buffer, particularly if the problem concerned me. She worked all shows and development parties, frequently ending up the top deposit taker on the crew. At Harcourt Park she filled in as a runner when required and could close as well as most. Our dinner table at the cottage generally sat from two to ten salesmen or supervisors, all craving one of her delicious home-cooked meals, and she never turned one of them away. Though most of our staff respected me, they loved and admired Joyce as much as I. Whenever the opportunity presented itself, we flew to our beloved Florida for a few weeks in the winter months where we replenished our failing reserves and spent our money gambling at jai-alai and the dogs. The Schramms had moved permanently to Pompano Beach, and so we saw them frequently, but the Graces were unable to join us for the final few years of the 1960s.

During this period Joyce and I found another mutual love. In 1968 we discovered Las Vegas, and from that day forward, our life took on a new dimension. Upon arrival, we found a taxi strike had tied up the gambling capital of the U.S. in a horrendous knot which only added to the excitement that we continuously felt throughout our stay. We arranged a lovely room at the Desert Inn with a panoramic view of the bustling Strip lined with hotels and other establishments ablaze with a myriad of multicolored neon and backdropped with the alluring mountains. Though I found it unbearably hot, Joyce preferred the intense dry heat in Nevada to the humid weather so common during a Toronto summer. Like all first-time visitors, the perpetual around-the-clock activity mesmerized us, and we could barely distinguish day from night.

Las Vegas left a lasting impression on me for a multitude of reasons, but one incident in particular remained vividly etched in my memory. Playing blackjack in the Desert Inn, I became aware of music advancing toward me. Turning my head I did a double take to see a dozen beautiful young ladies dressed in long white evening gowns marching through the casino playing lively melodies on violins. Taking seats in a small bistro adjoining the casino, they entertained the patrons for an hour with their pleasing tunes. Glancing at my watch I suddenly came to a momentous realization. Nowhere else on earth could you gamble while being serenaded by a bevy of attractive girls at 10 a.m. on the morning of the Sabbath.

Another episode that always reminded us of our naive attitude on that initial visit concerned Joyce's gambling habits. Casinos had yet to be equipped with many multi-coined slot machines, and Joyce had a ball playing the single nickel slots. The hundred dollars in her purse seemed like a small fortune at the time, and we believed it ample spending money for the few days of our stay. Toward the end of the first evening while I was playing cards I noticed Joyce standing behind watching me gamble. Believing she was interested in learning the game as an alternative to slot machines, I paid her no mind, but when she hadn't moved after a few minutes, I turned and asked, "How are things going, Kiddo?"

"Not too good," she responded glumly.

"How's your money holding out?"

"What money? I'm busted," she replied.

"How in the hell could you blow a hundred bucks at nickel slots?" I demanded.

"I don't know, but I'm broke," she insisted.

Going to our room I inquired how many jackpots she had won, and she estimated well over a hundred dollars in total. This meant that in less than eight hours she pulled the slot-machine lever over five thousand times, which became immediately apparent when she showed her swollen ankles and sore and aching arms. Although never losing her love for the one-arm bandits, she learned to play blackjack at the one dollar tables, and from that point forward her money stretched considerably further.

Harold Tomas, with his new wife Helen, joined us for two days in Vegas, then we visited Hoover Dam and continued to their home at Lake Havasu City for a short visit and to get a first-hand look at that outstanding McCullock development. Harold worked for the realty company that sold the lots, and so he gave me a knowledgeable tour of the rapidly growing city being created along the bank of the Colorado River directly opposite California. It appeared to be the most successful development in the entire country—and in my opinion, for an obvious reason. When McCullock made the deal with the Arizona government to acquire the land, he agreed to build factories and create jobs. Unlike other prefabricated communities, Lake Havasu City had a nucleus of permanent working people that gave the development a vibrant heartbeat, sadly lacking in retirement and vacation developments in other parts of Canada and the U.S. I vowed not to forget the lesson.

Joyce and I returned to Vegas after a couple of pleasant days with the Thomases to continue our vacation. The fascinating city hadn't lost any of its glitter, and we visited several top shows that intrigued us almost as much as the gaming tables. We were hooked on this tinsel town mecca in the desert and resolved to return at our first opportunity, which we did the following summer and thereafter as often as we could get away. Our Vegas trips cost a little money, but I considered it a small price to pay for the tremendous enjoyment of getting completely away from reality for awhile.

Joyce never complained about lack of money nor asked for any, unless she had a serious need, and I strived to give her some of the finer things which were now finally coming within my financial grasp. In 1967 I presented her with a mink stole for Christmas, and the following year purchased our first color TV. In 1969 she received her first new car, a Chevy II. That same year I got my first Cadillac. I also bought her another gift in 1969 that remained closer to her heart than all the other high-priced presents combined; a purebred poodle named Charlie Brown but nicknamed "Bisto," an English word for gravy, because of his rich brown coat. Few dogs on earth are 100 percent one-person dogs, but though Bisto put up with the rest of the family, he exclusively belonged to Joyce and did so throughout his fourteen years.

So our existence at this time, though frantic, offered much pleasure. The restlessness that haunted me all my life still persisted but had been quieted to some extent with the acquisition of each new development. Winter trips to Florida, our summer jaunts to Nevada, and automobile tours with the family also helped to relieve my wanderlust spirit. Nevertheless I still couldn't stand the status quo for a long period of time. In the ten years I'd operated Sumcot, we had risen from a single operation to a corporation with sales nearing two million, with a hundred employees (direct and indirect), and with complexities and troubles to match our growth. My personal income had increased tenfold. Each time I placed a competent manager in a division of the corporation, I provided myself with more free time, and with insufficient propositions or problems to occupy my mind, I'd immediately begin to consider what mountain to scale next.

Due to immense advertising and promotion, Sumcot had become a well-known name in Toronto. This brought a number of inquiries regarding my desire to dispose of the company's stock. They usually fell in one of three categories; an outright purchase, a merger with a similar type of company, or being swallowed up by a conglomerate with an exchange of stock and going public. Certain offers were in the million-dollar range with varying amounts of cash up front and the balance payable in cash or stock over a period of years. In all instances, however, a condition of the purchase required that I remain as general manager of the company for not less than five years. This arrangement appeared dubious to me because, in effect, I was earning my own pay out. Figuring if I had to remain and run the operation I might as well own it, I turned down all such propositions. On the other hand, going public meant opening my private life to the nation's auditors, and that didn't appeal to me either, although it had certain advantages over other types of sales. I decided to continue on my own for awhile and perhaps try to grow large enough through expansion into other areas to go public on my own. Then eventually I would pull back even further from the daily operation of the corporation's affairs.

The Honorable Sir Alexander Geddes, a member of one of the richest and most renowned families in England, heard of Sumcot and myself through Lord Ronald Graham, a real estate broker in Ocho Rios who showed me property on my visit to enchanting Jamaica in 1962. Looking for individuals and companies with expertise in developing areas where local services were not readily available, he wrote to arrange a meeting with me in Toronto to discuss several propositions. His imagination and plans for developing in South America, The Middle East, and other exotic world sites impressed me. The globe-hopping entrepreneur particularly envisioned an exclusive condominium set-up to satisfy the residential requirements of the embassy staff in the capitals of the world. Accommodations for these people in numerous countries lacked proper amenities and sophistication, and he claimed governments would pay well for someone to provide it. I certainly received a thrill whenever Sir Alexander phoned from his private jet while flying over the Atlantic to discuss his projects or arrange further meetings with me, and his schemes with detailed plans were exciting. Nevertheless I felt they were too risky for my limited reserves at that time, and so I turned down the opportunity to become involved.

The Brokenhead River country in Manitoba, property closer to home, constantly came to my mind, and I decided to find out if that enormous acreage could be converted somehow into a money-making project. Through Peter Betts, I arranged to meet members of Manitoba's Cabinet to discuss the purchase of the 44,000-acre tract of land, and they suggested we do a feasibility study on the property. W.L. Wardrop & Associates, a large engineering consulting firm in Winnipeg, charged $5,000 for an in-depth study which, though not especially encouraging, did indicate that money could possibly be made from certain grass crops. My plans included deepening the Brokenhead River to properly drain the swampy sectors, then construct a dam where the stream left the property at the north end to create a man-made lake, thereby providing two methods of making money. Once drained I believed the land would be useful for some type of agricultural purpose as outlined in the Wardrop report, and lake-front sites so near the city should sell rapidly.

Negotiations with the Manitoba government collapsed when they insisted Sumcot take complete responsibility for flooding north of the tract, which might result from our dredging and deepening of the Brokenhead. Control dams could have provided protection most normal years, but in exceptionally wet springs or during a rapid melt and subsequent run-off, anything could happen. I figured the risk was too great. Therefore, another possibility of expanding Sumcot's field of operations fell through. Nevertheless the dream of developing the Brokenhead River country stuck in my mind throughout the 1960s and with only the slightest excuse, I would scoot to Winnipeg. My old companion, Ed Barham, and I would invariably trek back by tractor, truck, or on foot to cook a steak dinner beside the dribbling little stream that we both loved so much.

Still another proposition came to my attention during this period that almost cost my life together with five others. The Department of Indian Affairs contacted Sumcot in 1969 about developing Christian Island in the Georgian Bay section of Lake Huron, situated 75 miles northwest of Toronto. The large land mass, owned by a small band of Indians, constituted several thousand acres of prime property with large stands of virgin bush and 25 miles of lake frontage including stretches of gorgeous white sand beach. On inspection day, Jack, Doug Prue, Don Fevreau, two professional engineers, and myself got together at a point on the mainland approximately a mile directly across the ice from the Indian village on Christian where we had scheduled a brief meeting with the Indian Council before investigating the property. Little snow covered the ice, but we could easily follow the trail the Indians used to reach the mainland. Driving one of the two snowmobiles which carried three men each, I motioned to Doug Prue who handled the second snow cruiser to pull over halfway to the island. Early for our meeting with the Indians, I suggested we veer south to a point jutting into the lake and explore the shoreline as we worked our way back to the Indian village therefore saving time.

Going full throttle and less than a quarter mile from shore, I passed over a crack in the ice and to my horror saw water bubbling through the open fissure. The ice's thickness appeared scarcely strong enough to hold up one man walking let alone six on two weighty machines. Fortunately, I had the presence of mind not to slow down but continued racing for shore which, through sheer luck, we reached without mishap. The others having also seen the wafer thin ice were ashen when we dismounted on terra firma. Indians at the village who witnessed our sudden diversion from their path told us it was a miracle we survived, as three days before it had been open water where we had traveled. Only certain sections of the lake could be used as a bridge they explained, and even then daily checks were made to determine its safety. My lack of experience with the treacherous waters of Lake Huron, plus sheer stupidity almost cost the lives of six. We would have dropped into 20 feet of water had we broken through and escape would have been unlikely. Only the buoyancy created by speed which minimized our weight on the thin ice saved our lives. Any slow down or stop would undoubtedly have proven fatal. Doug and I contracted a small Cessna to fly the area and allow us to see elevations from the air. We both turned green when open water rippled over the area we had traveled by snowmobiles three days earlier.

Despite our narrow escape, we continued negotiations with the Indians and the Federal Government advisors. My principal interest in acquiring the property, assuming I could interest commercial enterprises and industries to move into the area, was to create a development similar to Lake Havasu City in Arizona. There were several positive aspects to obtaining the large island which would accommodate many times the five thousand people demanded by the Provincial authorities to be given year-round development status. Being located on the Great Lakes allowed the possibility of harbor facilities. An annual climate warmer than most of Canada plus excellent soil conditions for either uncomplicated developing or providing excellent growing conditions existed throughout the tract. There were also indications both Federal and Provincial financial assistance might be obtainable for construction of a causeway between Christian Island and the mainland. In fact, some feasibility studies had already been completed.

I believed a tremendous market existed for a retirement city located not too far from Toronto because a multitude of retirees were reluctant to leave their families and move into southern United States yet they wanted to escape the high cost of living in the big city. Several of Ontario's top planners suggested the best method to prevent overcrowding of burgeoning cities such as Toronto was to encourage the older generation to leave. My scheme for Christian Island seemed to fit that strategy. Unfortunately the Indians saw it differently and, regardless of their desperate need for jobs and money, would only give Sumcot a ninety-nine year lease to the land, instead of fee simple. Approval by banks and other lending institutions, absolutely vital to the grand scheme I envisioned, would be reluctant to lend money unless we had clear title, and so the deal fell through after weeks of planning and meetings. I did examine a few other similar propositions, though I steadily lost my taste for fighting government agencies. All civil servants have a similar approach to propositions that appear out of the ordinary. Approving documents that contain their signature might come back to haunt them, and so they simply turn them down. Bureaucrats, civil servants, or their flunkies rarely take chances. An emphatic "No" means there may not be progress, but they won't suffer any consequences. Only a "yes" can get them into hot water.

Reaching my mid-forties by the late 1960s, I gradually became more philosophical about my personal role in the universal struggle. Like most rational beings, I accepted death's inevitability, though up to now it had affected me very little. As I aged however, it logically would play an increasingly larger part in my life, which it did. In 1966 "Pop" Theodoru passed away, and since my arrival in Toronto he had become an integral part of my daily routine as I constantly visited his and Steve's small restaurant until they sold out. The old gentleman used to take Michael as a toddler and his oldest grandson Billy for daily hikes when we lived on the Danforth behind the office. Later in 1966 Uncle Harry and Uncle Jim died within a week of each other. Though sad at their passing, I accepted the news stoically as I hadn't been too personally involved with either for many years.

In 1968, Lionel Faust, a comparatively young man, dropped dead with a heart attack. Even though we knew he suffered with angina and lived a precarious existence, his sudden demise came as a tremendous shock. Since our stormy days in Homeland Realty, Lionel and I had become exceedingly close buddies and enjoyed each other's company a great deal, particularly functions with the Shriners. We also golfed, played poker, and visited socially with our wives, and as in many relationships, the small incidents are often the longest remembered. Late one evening Lionel and I were returning from a friendly poker game in Hamilton. Lionel was driving a secondhand Cadillac he had just purchased, and he got into a shouting hassle about 2 a.m. in downtown Toronto with two young fellows in a sports car who had apparently cut him off somehow, or vice versa. The two young punks kept racing up beside our car, screaming obscenities and motioning for us to pull over. Seeing Lionel getting really perturbed, I elected to intervene, and so I rolled down my window and shouted at the two tormentors to take off or we'd call the police. Halfway across the Bloor Street Viaduct, we had to stop for a red light, and the other two, almost side-swiping the Cadillac, pulled up on the passenger side and continued to scream and swear. Now losing my temper, I jumped out, catching the driver off guard and smashed a backhand across his mouth through the open window. Lionel raced to the opposite side of the stopped vehicle to get at the other youth but discovered that window closed. He sped around to the driver's side and whacked the unsuspecting young tough another shot in the face. The entire incident lasted less than a minute, and before the light even turned green, our two antagonizers took off with tires screeching and blood streaming down the driver's face.

Lionel and I stopped at his house for a late nightcap, and although we laughed about the silly episode, we discussed the unhappy fact that we were getting too old for such foolishness. A few days later Lionel passed away, and for the first time, death had reached out and touched me where everyone is vulnerable—in the depths of the heart. The fragility of our existence came rushing into my conscious mind as well as the cold hard fact that all the money in the world will not make a farthing of difference when it comes your turn to lie in that wooden box.

The sixties decade had been strenuous, but financially I had progressed steadily. Despite our greatly improved living standard, however, I had become gradually aware that I wanted more out of life than the almighty dollar. Death hadn't been as easy for me to cope with as I had imagined, and the next one would prove the wisdom of my determination to live each day to its fullest.

Chapter 10

Pop

The warm affection my parents and I felt toward each other played a significant role in my personal life during the period of Sumcot's expansion throughout the action packed 1960s. From the time they joined the firm in 1958 until Pop's retirement at Christmas of 1968, they never complained about finances. Though frequently receiving little remuneration for their services, the company earned sufficient money to keep them living comfortably. Because their tastes were simple and overhead extremely low, they were even able to save a few dollars. Except for the occasional rift between Pop and me due to our equally quick tempers, we all got along with little aggravation. Whenever Dad and I did have a blow up over some misunderstanding in the course of our daily affairs, we never allowed hard feelings to last long or to interfere with the performance of our responsibilities. Also, though constantly facing financial disaster, we never permitted this exasperating predicament to interfere with our daily enjoyment of life or each other.

During their tenure at Harcourt Park, the folks played bingo in Wilberforce twice weekly, a game they both enjoyed. On week ends a lively card game always provided the entertainment, and usually several of Sumcot's staff participated in the fun. This fondness for cards has always been a family idiosyncracy. In the midst of the Depression a penny ante poker game was a Sunday evening ritual in the farm's old log kitchen. Our relatives visiting from Winnipeg joined my parents and the neighboring farmers in the game that invariably lasted until the early morning hours. Card games provided pleasant relief from the wear and tear of daily existence in those troubled times and contributed the same levity to our lifestyle in the sixties. Both father and mother were loved and respected by all members of Sumcot plus a majority of our customers, and they were known to us all as simply Mom and Pop.

Except as a young man when he worked as a roustabout across the prairie provinces, Dad had travelled very little, and with the exception of her early jaunts as a child in Europe, Mother had also not ventured far from Winnipeg since her arrival. They both longed to see new country, but lack of finances and the burden of raising a family had prevented any such enjoyment. It delighted me, therefore, to be partially responsible for their visiting parts of North America during their employment with Sumcot. In 1967, I sent the two of them together with sister Joyce and Uncle George by automobile to Boiling Spring Lakes. They not only thoroughly enjoyed the tour, but Mom and Unk purchased a lot in the Canadiana Shores sector of the development.

In 1968, when my financial circumstances had somewhat improved, Joyce and I took Mom, Pop and Unk on a memorable four-week journey. We left Toronto January 7th with the temperature hovering in the 20-below-zero range, and when we crossed the border at Buffalo, a blizzard sweeping across New York State made driving on the freeway almost impossible. Hundreds of vehicles stranded in ditches or criss-crossed on the ice-covered highway made our continuation look stupid, but despite the hazardous conditions I moved slowly towards metropolitan New York City where the situation hadn't improved. Disappointed at first because I thought the inclement weather might prevent us from doing the things I'd planned for our one night stay in the Big Apple turned out instead to be a blessing in disguise as it discouraged many people from leaving their homes. As a result I procured tickets to the New York Ranger–Toronto Maple Leaf hockey game in Madison Square Garden that otherwise would have been unobtainable. For over thirty years listening to Foster Hewitt and the Saturday night hockey broadcast had almost been a family solemnity, and so viewing the spectacle in person produced a thrill for the lot of us, even though the Leafs lost the game. The bitter winter storm also allowed us to obtain excellent seats at the famous Copacabana Night Club for the Sammy Davis, Jr. show and a late dinner.

The splendid evening was marred only by a frightening incident that related to the horrible weather conditions which occurred when we left the Copacabana. Taxis were next to impossible to engage although Unk and the folks were able to hop in one that had other passengers. For fifteen painful minutes I made a staunch effort to halt a passing cabbie, but with fares in their vehicles they refused to stop. The nightclub door had already been locked, making it impossible to get back inside, and with Joyce dressed only in an evening gown and light wrap, the biting wind and whipping snow made standing in the street a serious situation.

Realizing my young wife couldn't stand the frigid conditions for too long in her scanty attire and beginning to get mighty cold myself, I jumped in front of a taxi, forcing him either to come to a sliding halt or run over me. Though irate at my dangerous tactic he nevertheless consented to drive us to our hotel, and I remained forever grateful to New York taxi drivers.

We had an enjoyable but uneventful trip along the Atlantic coast with continuously improving weather conditions, and when we reached Florida, it seemed like we'd arrived at a strange planet. At Daytona Beach we spent an unforgettable night with our motel units located directly on the ocean. While driving our car along the famous sand beach at midnight, glittering moon beams ricocheting off the tranquil sea, we recalled the strenuous years we had all experienced to be able to get into our enviable position.

Two pleasant weeks in Hollywood Beach were spent gambling on horses, dogs, jai-alai, and bingo. We spent little and lost little but enjoyed ourselves immensely before continuing our journey into alien territory for all. Though it was January, the weather remained unseasonably warm as we autoed through northern Florida searching without success for some trace of Mother's stepmother Daisy and stepsister Dolly. New Orleans provided another memorable evening when we took a nightclub tour including Bourbon and Basin streets and other famous sites in that beautiful and historic city. Father showed enormous enthusiasm when we crossed eastern Texas, and he gazed fondly across the cactus-covered mesquite flats and massive stretches of farmland that we had often dreamed we would help to harvest one day. Crossing into Mexico from Laredo, Texas the night of his 75th birthday, we celebrated his three-quarters of a century on earth with toasts of tequila. Arriving back in Toronto in early February completely refreshed from our long tour and ready for another hectic season, Pop informed me it would be his final session working for Sumcot. He had certainly earned his retirement.

Mom and Pop had labored faithfully at Harcourt Park for seven seasons and were considered by many Harcourt Park members to have been crucial to its ultimate success. They performed a splendid task of liaison between any of our disgruntled buyers and the company over the many difficulties faced in the enormous development, particularly in its early stages. I knew they loved their summer home on Allen Lake, surrounded by forest-clad hills, but I also was aware that at times Pop found the lack of visibility oppressive and the dense bush overpowering. One summer day the two of us were returning to Toronto in my car after a lengthy stay at the Park, and when we reached a point south of Lindsey where open fields suddenly replaced heavy bush, Pop asked me to pull over for a moment. He stepped out of the vehicle and heaved an immense sigh as though a weight were suddenly removed from his shoulders. When he jumped back into the automobile, I asked the reason for the interlude.

"Although I like the Haliburton Highlands," he said, "I always feel a sense of deliverance when I get back to the open spaces. I suppose being prairie born and bred where the view seems to go on forever will never entirely leave my system."

"You know, Pop," I responded, "I can easily sympathize with your emotions because I feel identically the same when I've been in Harcourt Park any length of time. I often think the reason I love the sea so fervently is because of its unlimited view."

From the moment Mother and Dad saw High View Acres in 1966, they fell in love with the magnificent panoramic vista across Pigeon Lake and the surrounding hills. I wasn't surprised, therefore, when both parents asked me to consider Pop as supervisor for our third subdivision when it opened the following spring. The bulk of road construction and other major developing had been completed at Harcourt Park, and with High View Acres so much smaller in area, Pop wouldn't have to work so hard or travel such great distances to oversee his crews. Nevertheless I hated to see them leave our first development. Dad managed High View for two years before retiring at the end of the 1968 season.

One of the greatest disappointments to Father while employed with Sumcot was our lost opportunity of developing the 44,000 acres at the Brokenhead River. In 1967, when Sam, Uncle Ernie's oldest son, got married, Mom, Pop, Joyce, and I flew out for a few days to attend the wedding. Negotiations for purchasing the huge tract from the Manitoba Government were in progress and the four of us drove out to the edge of the property to picnic beside its perimeter and get a bird's view of the area around the village of Vivian where I hoped to create the lake. On that ideal summer day, we lolled beside a winnow of freshly raked hay and discussed the intricacies and excitement of opening and then bringing the massive tract of barren land to profitable production. Not more than ten miles from our old farm where we strived for years to make a living on 160 acres, the enormity of 44,000 acres was difficult to comprehend. As the folks had just taken on the responsibility of High View Acres, which they both adored, I was astonished when Pop suddenly asked, "Bill, will there be a place for me in this gigantic operation if the deal goes through?"

"Christ, Pop," I replied. "You are approaching your mid-seventies and have just taken on the burden of a new development. Do you mean to tell me you are interested in getting even further involved?"

Pop looked at me for a moment with a quizzical expression covering his lined old face before answering. "My boy, we didn't amount to a hell of a lot in Monominto during our stay, though we had nothing to be ashamed of. Nevertheless don't you think it would be one hell of a thrill for me to come back and be part of this colossal undertaking?"

"It would be a thrill for all of us, there's no doubt," I said. "And Pop, you can be sure that you can have whatever position you desire if the project gets off the drawing board."

Unfortunately my plans for the Brokenhead River turned out to be one of the enterprises that never reached fruition for reasons completely out of my control. My disappointment matched Father's especially as I had spent considerable money in its planning and wanted to attempt the project in the worst way.

Despite the fact that they were staunch supporters of my endeavors, they nevertheless amazed me one day in the mid-1960s during one of my worst financial predicaments when Pop offered me $1,500, which represented the total savings from their meager salaries. I refused the money because it wouldn't have gone far in avoiding any of the embarrassing financial situations with which I so often found myself entangled, but the generous offer further cemented the bond that had been forged between us.

Another example of their willingness to help in any way they could, came in the spring of 1967 in rather bizarre and unhappy circumstances.

After Atlantic Acceptance loaned the $310,000 to discharge my indebtedness to J.B. Brien, I really had no reason to remain in contact with the high-flying Frenchman. I had paid him more than $100,000 in factoring charges and loan interest, but I still recognized that his initial financial assistance when Sumcot teetered on the brink of bankruptcy in 1961 was the sole reason we survived. I kept in contact with him on a weekly basis and frequently discussed the possibility of one of his companies financing another of Sumcot's projects, including the Brokenhead River scheme. In December, 1966, it came as a tremendous shock when he was suddenly arrested and charged on five counts of corporate mismanagement including theft of company stock. Within thirty days his companies were insolvent. This disaster following so close on the heels of the Atlantic Acceptance fiasco had the Toronto business community in a trauma, and the Justice Department decided to make Brien pay for the mistakes of both failures. Although all of Ben's assets were seized, he had a farm in Brampton, Ontario in a family trust which kept it exempt from confiscation, and while waiting for trial, that is where he sequestered himself and his family. He contacted me shortly after the debacle to come and pay him a visit, which I did willingly.

Brien didn't confide all the details of his downfall to me but insisted he wasn't a thief in the actual sense of the word but more a victim of circumstances. He declared that a fine line existed in business between success and failure and that timing had a great deal to do with whether you win or lose. How well I knew the truth of those words, as I had used a balancing pole numerous times myself on that thin wire that represents the difference between plunging into financial ruin or reaching safety and success. Like so many in a similar position, he claimed that if his creditors had not panicked his debts would eventually have been covered and all investors repaid. Unfortunately, one of his principal lending institutions became nervous when he couldn't meet a deadline, and this caused his flimsy deck of cards to collapse like a straw hat in a tornado. I felt great empathy towards this man who had played a big part in my financial salvation and who only two years before had been hailed as Toronto's new pecuniary wizard or the next Canadian E.P. Taylor. The climb to the top of the business ladder is generally slow and painful while the drop to oblivion happens overnight. I intended to learn from Brien's unfortunate situation in that he probably tried to attain success too fast.

The enormous public outcry over the money lost by a multitude of investors caused the Justice Department to increase Ben's bail to $25,000. Unable to raise the money, he was thrown back into the Don Jail. Toronto newspapers had a heyday playing up the hapless incarceration of the fallen magnate and speculated on whether anyone would come forward to post bond for his release.

After Ben spent two nights in jail without any sign of a benefactor, Mrs. Brien phoned and asked if I could do anything to assist her imprisoned husband, and I promised to try. I contacted O'Driscoll, Brien's lawyer, and requested a meeting with Ben. O'Driscoll advised that such an encounter would require special permission from the Governor of the Don Jail, but if I was considering posting bond, he would attempt to arrange the meeting. Putting up sufficient property to satisfy the court would stretch our credit limit so I wanted to hear Ben tell me to my face he wouldn't leave the country if I went surety. I told O'Driscoll I would decide my course of action after speaking with Brien, and he arranged the visit for the following morning.

During Brien's initial imprisonment, the name of the large firm of London attorneys of which Peter Betts was a senior partner came out as being connected to the sordid affair in some fashion, and all members of that organization were bitter.

On the eve of my visit to the Don Jail I received a long-distance phone call from Peter Betts in London, Ontario. "Bill, it suddenly struck me you might be considering releasing J.B. Brien. If so, forget it. We want him right where he is."

Shocked by the abruptness of the command, I undoubtedly stammered for a moment or two. "But Peter, this man is probably responsible for my financial survival," I implored.

"Don't forget, my boy, that I have also done some personal favors for you and your family, and now I want one in return. Leave that man in jail," he again demanded.

"I'm sorry, sir," I apologized, "but I can't make that promise."

Betts hung up the phone in an obvious snit.

I felt tremendous loyalty to Peter Betts for the service he had rendered to Sumcot and myself, but I also sympathized with Brien's dilemma. Agonizing over my quandary, I decided to wait until my encounter with Ben in the morning before making a decision.

When the jailer accompanied me to the cell, Brien sat on a chair, his head in his hands in obvious dejection. Aware I was coming, he greeted me warmly, and before I could open my mouth, he looked me square in the eye and in a calm voice said, "Bill, I know why you wished to see me, and I'll make it easy for you. You are considering posting bond and want to know if I'll vamoose. Well, let me tell you this, I wouldn't run from those bastards if they give me twenty years, and yes I would like to get out of this stinking jail."

I couldn't help but laugh at Ben's sincerity, and I instantly knew that, regardless of future consequences, my conscience would give me no peace if I didn't have him released. Grabbing his hand I acknowledged he had hit the nail on the head. I said I was satisfied with his words and would arrange to post bond as soon as possible.

At this point I discovered the equity in our Banstock home wasn't enough to satisfy the courts, and so I had to call on my parents' assistance. After explaining the circumstances, Pop without a quiver of emotion or a moment's hesitation instructed me to count on his complete support. So $18,000 was liened against our Banstock home and $7,000 on Mom and Dad's residence. Within twenty-four hours, Brien again breathed the air of freedom.

Life often has a strange way of bringing certain relationships through a complete circle. Before coming to trial, Ben found himself excruciatingly short of cash, and he came to me for a $2,000 loan that, due to our usual shortage of money, imposed a strain on our cash flow. Reluctantly, I loaned the paltry sum which he promised to repay within thirty days. Unfortunately, he couldn't return the $2,000 for six months, and though he felt terribly embarrassed, it didn't help our financial shortage. It seemed such a bizarre incident when for several years we had dealt in sums of six figures.

At his trial in October of 1968, all charges against him were dropped with the exception of stealing company stock. He received a three-year sentence to be served at Warkworth, a minimum security prison in Central Ontario. An indication of the trust the Justice Department placed in his integrity occurred when they allowed him a two-week compassionate leave in 1969 to attend to his lovely wife who was dying of cancer. Ben corresponded with me while in Warkworth, and we were both delighted when he obtained an early release. He immediately formed a small enterprise which included three "quick snack" trucks to service the construction industry and came to me for financing. Still desperately short of funds, I refused to get involved and thereby closed the book on our turbulent but unforgettable association. The last I heard of the likable French Canadian, who almost became a financial czar, was that he got remarried to a wealthy lady and had moved to Peterborough, Ontario. J.B. Brien had chosen a much more pleasant method of obtaining gold than all of his previous struggles which had landed him in the penitentiary, and I fervently hope he enjoyed the balance of his existence.

My parents' relationship with J.B. Brien wasn't intimate in any way, but as an associate of mine they were prepared to assist him as a favor to me. Their affection for Ken Watson, another of my confreres, was a completely different affair. Almost from their first encounter, Pop and Ken became buddies, and during our years of deer hunting together, they thoroughly enjoyed each other's company. Ken's magnetic personality, outstanding sense of humor, and ready wit made our deer camps thoroughly enjoyable. Both Mom and Pop looked forward to the fun-filled week each fall. Over the years we put numerous whitetails within shooting range of his hideout, and he fired quite a few rounds of ammunition in their general direction without ever drawing blood, or I suspect even frightening them too badly. Frequently, in fact, we found traces of his wayward shells twenty feet high in the surrounding trees, indicating that an immense case of buck fever overwhelmed him whenever game came his way. He never lied about these opportunities of bagging his first animal, but instead kept the hunting crew in stitches with detailed accounts of each screw up.

On one occasion, he missed a doe and buck at ten yards with a full clip of ammunition, and again we discovered his spent shells imbedded in evergreens two dozen feet above the ground. Describing to the group the hectic few minutes from when he first spied the deer until I came through the woods to see if he'd finally connected was a prime example of his drollery. "You know," he explained in complete seriousness, "I saw those two animals slowly approaching a full minute before I fired, and so I had plenty of time to make my plans and get prepared. I figured to knock the two of them over, grab the empty cartridges, then dash a hundred and fifty yards to drop the casings in a conspicuous place and show you guys what a hell of a shot I really was. Missing those animals at twenty feet," he confided, "seems next to impossible."

Pop teased him unmercifully, and the two of them got a great kick out of all those foiled chances. I suspected nevertheless that if he had begun to do some thinking before pulling the trigger, then eventually he would likely settle down and start aiming toward his target.

Another humorous incident involved a black bear. Laying out the hunt and placing the men in a semi-circle a mile from where our dogs were to be released, I sent Ken a hundred yards into the woods off the main road and told him to sit quietly on a stump or fallen tree. Shortly after the dogs went yelping into the bush, an enormous barrage from a half dozen of our guns signified the dogger and his animals had roused something. So, with the hunt obviously over, I jumped into our Land Rover to pick up the hidden men and determine what we had bagged. Ken Watson, the first hunter I reached, stood out on the road white as a sheet and shaking like a leaf in a wind storm.

"What caused all the commotion, Ken?" I asked. "You look as though you just saw a ghost."

"Christ, Bill," he replied through trembling lips. "No ghost, but a bear as big as an elephant. I found a stump like you suggested, and after half an hour when I heard no dogs barking, I decided to light a cigarette. A big black mound ten feet to my right, which I thought to be an old log covered with dirt, suddenly began to move and up jumped this massive bear."

"Didn't you shoot?" I inquired.

"Hell no, I didn't shoot," Ken exploded. "That big bastard went racing past me in one direction, and I took off in the other. The son-of-a-bitch couldn't run too fast for slipping on what I was dropping, and I'm not certain who was most terrified."

When Ken saw the small black bear the boys had downed, he jokingly insisted it had to be a younger brother to the enormous brute that frightened him, and the comical incident soon became another legend of our hunting days in Harcourt Park.

Eight years elapsed before Ken finally connected. As though to make up for all his lost opportunities, he shot an enormous buck that won him a new rifle from an Ontario Gun Club. Jack, however, may have been just as instrumental in the ultimate success. Sitting on the adjoining watch a quarter mile from where Ken did the shooting, I reached him first and wasn't the slightest bit surprised to see no deer. Standing in a daze, Ken looked thoroughly dejected. "Bill, I'm going to throw this frigging gun away, or I'll shoot myself in disgust," he announced. "An enormous buck again went past me at no more than twenty feet, and for the first time I thought I'd aimed." The animal's footprints in the

Les Knox and his son Kent with fine catch of smallmouth bass taken in Straggle Lake in Harcourt Park, 1966.

A cow moose I shot at Kettle Lake in 1966, north of Sudbury, Ontario while hunting with Doug Prue.

Doug Prue with a beautiful speckled trout caught in Allen Lake, Harcourt Park, 1967.

In 1967 Tex Bloye, who used to sing with Pee Wee King and his band, entertains Sumcot employees and friends at our annual Sumcot Christmas Party where over two hundred guests always enjoyed the year end bash.

Joyce and I took the three kids on a long auto trip to Expo '67 and to the Maritime Provinces. We went cod fishing in Prince Edward Island.

Muriel Roberts, wife of Merv Roberts, who now worked for me (1967). Also Kaye and Chester Schwandt from whom I purchased over half of Harcourt Park. We remain particularly close friends to this day.

Joyce on Christmas morning, 1967, with her first mink stole.

Midland Avenue, Scarboro, 1968. Our new 6000 square foot head office with some of the office staff standing in front.

Staff meeting in our new boardroom, 1968. Jack, in the back and to my left, now worked for Sumcot.

Moose hunting camp at Marquette Lake, northern Ontario, 1968. Left to right: Grant Austin, a development supervisor; Greg Hilton, a hunting buddy for several years; and myself.

Pop retired at the end of the 1968 season. This picture was taken in Bermuda in 1969, a few months before he died of cancer.

My last deer hunt. We shot seven-teen deer for twenty hunters, 1969.

Sumcot sales staff with various trophies. Edwina Seddon, the star of the force, is third from the left. Fourth is John Jackson, fifth is Wayne Pirie and seventh is Norv Starling. (1969)

1969: Sherree and Michael with Joyce holding Bisto, her pet poodle that she had for fifteen years.

By the Seine River, 1970, in Paris.

Joyce by Zulu huts a few miles outside of Pretoria, South Africa in 1970.

Joyce feeding a wild monkey on an island in the Zambezi River, 1970.

Joyce standing beside our four-wheel drive in the beautiful Ngorengora Crater, 1970.

Dhutu tent camp in the Serengeti Plain in Tanzania, Africa, 1970.

My first visit to South Padre Island, Texas in 1970.

On one of our numerous automobile trips across the continent we visited "Old Faithful," Yellowstone National Park, in 1970. Sue Williams, a friend of Sherree's; Joyce and Sherree in the foreground.

Uncle Ernie, the Old Warrior, with Aunt Alena in his retirement home in Miami, Manitoba. (1970)

Mom and Sadie Phillips, our old neighbor. (1970)

Visiting Ed and Sheila at their farm in 1970. Fifteen years later our Manitoba "escape" would be directly across the field.

On a visit to the old farm, 1970, I discovered an old seed drill I bought for Pop in the mid '40's for $40 at an auction sale.

The old Monominto dance hall, now unused, where we caroused on most Saturday nights. (Taken in 1970.)

Theresa Mackey, who was a key Sumcot employee for nearly a quarter century, 1970.

Jack, 1970, in his private office as Sumcot's new Projects Manager.

Ron McMillan, 1970, Sumcot's engineer.

Sitting in my luxurious new office in Scarboro, 1970.

Most of the Winnipeg Phillips—cousins and their wives at the 1970 reunion.

Grandmother Rodd, 1970, at age 95. She died shortly after.

Greg Hilton and I cooking our lunch during a moose hunt, 1970, in northern Ontario.

Greg Hilton and I on a successful moose hunt, 1970, in northern Ontario.

Jack and I, 1970, butchering the big bull.

We "bagpipe" Ed and Sheila Barham through Toronto Airport, 1970, on their first visit to Toronto.

Joyce and I greet the Barhams at the airport in farm clothes, 1970.

Sheila looks on with mock surprise at the "Bunny Girl" reception, 1970.

From left to right: Me, Sophie Theodoru, Joyce, Mom, Shirley and Steve Theodoru at Steve's oldest son Bill's wedding, 1972

Steve Theodoru in 1972. He sponsored me right through Masonry and remains a close friend to this day.

Ed Barham and I spent a week together in 1972 with my brother Jack camping and fishing on The Lake of the Woods, Ontario.

Ed Barham and I at our favorite pastime—having a cookout over an open fire. (1972)

I spent a lot of time in Las Vegas and love to gamble. This was in 1972.

With the kids now adults Joyce and I spent a lot of time in Las Vegas. We took a break from the crap tables to visit Lake Mead in 1973.

My old buddy Ken Watson helps us celebrate Sherree's eighteenth birthday in 1973.

Mom and Uncle George in their garden in 1973 at Highview Acres. Another Sumcot development where Mom and Unk' resided in one of my houses.

I returned to Winnipeg at every opportunity to visit old friends and neighbors. Left to right: Ed and Sheila Barham, Verna and Roman Kruchak and myself in 1973.

Jim and Mary Wylie in 1973. The Wylie farm was adjacent to ours and Mary taught me at Pinewood for six years.

From Toronto I drove solo 14,000 miles through Canada, the Yukon and Alaska, back down the Pacific Coast and through the USA. I flew into Kotzebue, inside the Arctic Circle, and spent a couple of days visiting the Eskimos in 1973.

Jack, Greg Hilton, Doug Prue and I took our last fly-in moose hunt into the White River Country of northern Ontario in 1973.

Jack and I plan the day's hunt in our White River hunting camp while Greg and Doug catch up on some sleep.

Having a sukiyaki dinner in Kyoto on our visit to the Orient in 1974.

Joyce loves animals and found this stray on the Hong Kong beach. (1974)

Joyce and Kaye Schwandt on a shopping spree in Hong Kong in 1974.

Having a rickshaw ride in 1974 in downtown Hong Kong.

Henry, my pedicab driver, in 1974 on my Macao jaunt.

Farewell party in Honolulu for our Orient tour. Chester and Kaye Schwandt, and I plus long time buddy Ed Miller, the 1974 potentate of Ramses Temple.

Me, Joyce and Marty (Joyce's dad) having a farewell drink with Sherree before our daughter left for Europe for six months in 1974.

Our Poughkeepsie, New York friends visited Toronto in 1974. Left to right: Joyce, Magda Schramm, myself, Kate Peitchek, Dot with Bisto, and Hans Schramm.

Joyce in our luxurious suite in the Thunderbird in Las Vegas. (1974)

Jack, Eddy and I enjoying each other's company on another fishing excursion in 1974 which took us into Lake of the Woods, Ontario.

Ed, Jack and I thoroughly enjoyed cooking our fish over an open fire. (1974)

Billy, Jacqueline and Tim. Jack and Shirley's three children had now grown up. (1974)

Sumcot managers and spouses celebrate Jack's fiftieth birthday in 1974. Left to right, standing: Barry and Marylyn Ervin, Tom and Terry Mackey, Doug and Holly Prue, Fred and Edwina Seddon with Jack and Shirley and Joyce and I sitting in front.

Having dinner in Prague Czechoslovakia, 1974, with new friend General Bruce Legge.

A joyous reunion in Vienna with Sherree. Fran Deck, a noted restauranteur, stands beside her.

Al Jessop, a long time buddy. We traveled to many parts of the world together. Here he stands in a wine cellar in Brasou, Roumania in 1974.

Having a ball in Brasou. (1974)

Caesar's Chariot, a jet converted into a pleasure palace. (1975)

A friend and I aboard the luxurious Chariot. It carried about three dozen high rollers per trip.

Close friend, Fred McBrien, was parade marshal for the 1962 and 1975 imperial council sessions. We organized two of the longest parades ever held in any North American city.

In 1975 Fred appointed me as one of his deputy parade marshals.

I worked from a side car with a Toronto city motorcycle policeman. Here, after a seven and a half hour parade, I enter Varsity Stadium, the termination of the extravaganza.

The Pompano Plaza Shopping Centre I bought in a distress sale for $1,900,000 and sold a few years later for $3,200,000.

Having a party with my Monominto buddies on Ed Barham's front lawn, 1975. Left to right: Roman Kruchak, me, Dode Bell and Bill Kruchak with John Kruchak kneeling in front.

On one of the numerous cross country trips from Toronto to Winnipeg to Las Vegas to Padre Island, Texas, then to Florida and back to Toronto. (1975)

Though not one of Joyce's favorite pastimes, we ate most of our lunches in roadside parks. (1975)

Goose hunting at Kapiskow in James Bay, Ontario, with Cree Indian guide.

After seventeen years the six hundredth and final lot was sold to this family in Harcourt Park. In the background, from left to right, are Doug Prue, Edwina Seddon and Jack—1975.

Our twenty-fifth wedding anniversary, 1975. Jack, Jacqueline, and Shirley standing. Left to right, sitting: Sherree, Uncle George, Marty, me and Mom with Joyce standing on the extreme right.

The Sumcot staff threw a magnificent party for our twenty-fifth wedding anniversary. Here I share a joke with Bill Blue, my very first real fishing and drinking buddy when I first arrived in Toronto.

I took three dozen members of our staff, their spouses and people associated with Sumcot to Nassau in 1975 for one week to celebrate the selling out of Harcourt Park.

Mom shocked everyone when at the age of seventy-six she went parasailing in Nassau. (1975)

Joyce, Magda, Mom and Hans in front of the Schramm's house in Pompano Beach which Gary and Tandy purchased seven years later.

I rented a houseboat on four occasions for three to four days and nights at a time. We took our Florida friends on a cruise through the Everglades. (1976)

Joyce and a friend, Evie, with a small shark on our Everglades houseboat jaunt. (1976)

The depth of ancient history at Chitzen Itza in Mexico amazed me. (1976)

Joyce and I loved to take Caribbean cruises. Seated here, in 1976, with Jane, a New York nurse, and the Callan's, fellow Canadians with whom we enjoyed our repast.

In Frobisher's Bay in the northwest territories of Arctic Canada. It was late June, 1976.

Another get together with our Monominto friends in 1976. Left to right, back row: Tom Fryza, Bill Kruchak, Ed Barham, Roman Kruchak and Sheila Barham. Front row: Flora Fryza, Polly (Bill's wife), Joyce and Verna (Roman's wife).

We took our old friend Edna Branning, now a widow, along on our 10,000 mile jaunt across America in 1976. She is standing by the monument at the Battle of the Little Bighorn in Montana.

Edna, Helen Thomas and Joyce with Roosevelt Lake, Arizona in the background. (1976)

I purchased the two lots pictured above at Fountain Hills, a few miles east of Scottsdale, on this visit in 1976. We eventually built a permanent home.

In 1976 I toured South America and fell in love with the Iguassu Falls Region in Brazil.

A party in 1976 in Santiago, Chile with my travelling companions. Walter and Gertrude Baues, the smiling couple on the left, remain friends to this day. The Canadian flag was for my benefit.

I will never forget the enchantment of the San Carlos de Bariloche area of Southern Argentina. (1976)

A true descendent of the Incas with his llama. Cuzco, Peru, 1976.

The mystery and beauty of Machu Picchu will forever remain a highlight of my world travels. (1976)

I will also never forget the charm and intrigue of the Galapagos Islands. (1976)

Enjoying New Years in our renaissance condo in 1977. Our first ocean front Florida home. Left to right: Sherree, George Leo—a long time friend from Pough-keepsie, New York, Len Nordin—Sumcot's building manager for fifteen years, Len's friend Doris Erikson, Frieda Seddon—Edwina's oldest daughter and Wilfred whom Sherree promised to marry for the biggest part of a week.

Wilf, me and Eddy Wojic, a long time Florida buddy, at the New Years dinner table. Eddy, who held a horse trainers license, and I were going into thoroughbred horse racing but Eddy was working as a cashier at the Hollywood dog track and absconded with several hundred dollars and I never saw him again.

Gary brought his new girlfriend Tandy to visit us in Florida. (1977)

Ed and Sheila Barham and Tom and Flora Fryza spent ten days with us in Florida in 1977. We visited the Everglades National Park in Flamingo. Chester and Kaye Schwandt joined us.

I spent a week on a yacht in the Georgian Bay with several friends in 1977. Fishing was excellent and I caught an eleven and a half pound walleye. Left to right: Me, Bert Kessler, Carl Wilson—owner of the yacht, and Buel Manning.

In my private office on Midland Avenue, Scarboro. (1977)

Camel riding near the Sphynx, "Cheops," in 1977.

Man's achievements at Abu Simbel near the Soudan border overwhelmed me.

In 1977 at the "Wailing Wall" in Jerusalem—a
dramatic spectacle.

In Istanbul with the Bosphorous in the background. I sit with a member of my travel group. (1977)

The Parthenon in Athens, considered by many to be the most magnificent ancient ruin in the world. (1977)

On our ocean front balcony in Pompano Beach. From left to right: Marty, Tim (Jack's youngest), Sherree, Gary and Tandy. (1978)

B. J. Legge, Q. C., partner in the law firm of Legge & Legge, was appointed secretary general of the Confederation of Inter-Allied Reserve Officers of NATO in 1978. He was the first Canadian to hold this appointment. General Legge's military career spans forty years and membership on the Board of Trade's Tours Committee. Bruce and I remain good friends today.

Fred McBrien and I in front of the Imperial Palace in Peking in 1978. I spent three weeks touring China two weeks before the Chinese government announced normalizing relations with the West.

I took this picture in 1978 at a commune outside of Shanghai, where we Canadians met with the top officials of the commune. My good companion Tom O'Connor is seated at the far end of the table.

Canoeing down the rampaging Pagsanjan River in the central Philippines.

Harold and Helen Thomas flew from Phoenix and joined Joyce and I on a Caribbean cruise in 1979.

Our new South Padre Island office which we opened in 1979. Left to right: Gary Handin our new general manager, Adita Claire, Larry White and Tricia Skinner.

A great picture of our old farm house taken in 1980, abandoned but still standing.

Joyce and I picnicking on one of our many trips across North America. (1980)

Joyce and I persuaded Michael to cut his hair while she nursed him back to health in 1981.

I rented this fifty-two-foot houseboat on Lake of the Woods in Ontario in 1981 and took some of my Monominto buddies and their wives on a one week fishing cruise.

Ed Barham, Roman Kruchak and Jack during our Lake of the Woods jaunt.

In the summer of 1981 Monominto held a successful two day reunion. I flew Ken Watson and his wife Alice out to Winnipeg for the week's fishing on Lake of the Woods and the reunion. Left to right: Ed Barham, Ken Watson, Mom, Jack, Alice and Sheila Barham.

The entire family got together for the holidays in our new Florida ocean front townhouse in 1981.

Another Caribbean cruise, 1982.

Playing bridge with Larry Blum (extreme left) and two of his cronies in 1983—one of my favorite pastimes.

Christmas dinner, 1983 with the family. Margaret Leo is sitting next to Joyce.

Charlie Crawford, one of my first employees, whom we hadn't seen for eighteen years—July of 1984.

Groundbreaking ceremonies for Ocean Vista Towers were held Saturday, November 15, 1979 at 4:30 p.m. at the site. From left to right are: Gene Hurt, project attorney; Bill Phillips, President, Sumcot of America, Inc. Larry White, Texas Sumcot Manager; Dee Lyda, President, Carta Blanca Corp.; J. Thomas Pope, Vice-President, First National Bank of Brownsville; Rick Labunski, architect; and Glenn Theriac, Vice-President, United Savings of Brownsville.

The Ocean Vista Towers under construction in 1981.

Artist's rendering of the Ocean Vista Towers, completed in 1982.

Sherree with the three racing greyhounds we imported from Ireland in December of 1984.

Our new Manitoba home. (1985)

In the spring of 1985—looking toward our new one and a half million dollar ocean front home from the back yard.

mud sure enough verified the big buck had almost trampled Ken in its flight.

Keith Tallman and brother Jack soon reached the disgruntled hunter, and I reiterated Ken's remarks about shooting himself. Keith, a very dry individual, murmured, "Well, we've nothing to worry about on that score because he'd probably miss anyhow."

Jokes on Watson's marksmanship were at an end, however. Going over the episode Jack asked Ken to point out where he last saw the fleeing animal disappear into the dense brush. Within a minute Jack shouted out in jubilation. Not more than two hundred feet lay a big buck with a splendid rack of antlers, shot through the heart. Ken treated his accomplishment with as much buffoonery as during his years of failure, though it meant the end of Pop's good-natured needling.

For the first time in our long and warm relationship, Ken Watson and I had a serious argument during the final night of our last Harcourt Park deer hunt, and we parted camp thoroughly irritated with each other. Our disassociation didn't last long. Ken had been experiencing heart trouble, and a few months after our tiff, Helen phoned frantically for me to rush her to the hospital where Ken had suffered another attack. Swiftly forgetting our petty differences I picked up Helen and hastened to my stricken companion. Although he survived that bout, his ailing heart required a bypass operation that slowed him down considerably for the balance of his life. We resumed our friendship, and he became a tower of strength during a most sorrowful month of my life, though it wouldn't be the first time we shared personal tragedy. In the mid-1960s, Ken and Helen's eldest daughter Lorraine was killed in a freak car accident at the age of sixteen.

The Watsons frequently visited Joyce and me in our Toronto home, and rarely a month passed that I didn't spend a night or two at Oak Orchard Lodge which they still managed for Outboard Marine. At every Sumcot social function Ken and Helen, both extremely popular with my staff, were included. Invariably they sat close to Mom and Pop, as they did at the 1968 Annual Sumcot Christmas Party and the night Pop officially retired. Following dinner and before the dancing, I generally made a short speech thanking our two hundred guests who were mostly Sumcot employees, suppliers and associates, for their part in Sumcot's success and ended by handing out trophies to the top sales people and by making any other presentations that were in order. Handing Pop a beautiful clock radio and a pension check, I thanked him earnestly for the important role he had played in Sumcot's formative years. Approaching the head table to accept his gift, tears rolling down his gnarled old features, he mumbled, "Bill, they have been ten of the happiest years of my life." Those simple words meant more to me than a ten minute thank you speech. The standing ovation Dad received from his fellow employees and Sumcot associates didn't improve his emotional state and tears gushed from his eyes. Ken Watson soon had him smiling again, though others at their table told me later that for a few moments Ken wept as emotionally as my father.

Sentimentality, a significant ingredient in Dad's personal make-up frequently caused him to shed a tear or become overly despondent. In the spring of 1966 when Uncle Harry and Uncle Jim passed away within a few days of each other, Dad's dejection remained at low ebb for several days and only after we persuaded him to phone his remaining brothers Ernie and Geordie did he begin to snap out of his deep depression.

When the family reached a decision to have sister Joyce placed in an Ontario hospital, it was Father who held out to the last before agreeing to having her committed. Then, an unfortunate incident which occurred when he headed to the home for the retarded almost convinced him it wasn't meant to be. Joyce and I with our three kids had just arrived home from the Expo '67 excursion when we received a frantic phone call from Dad.

"Bill, for Christ's sake come over here," he wailed. "I think I've killed your mother."

In a few moments he calmed down a little and explained they had been in a terrible automobile accident, and both Mom and sister Joyce were in the Whitby Hospital. Joyce and I raced over to his West Hill home to find him and Uncle George guzzling whiskey, with Pop in a terrible state of despair. His car had been totally wrecked, and he wasn't certain the seriousness of Mom or Joyce's injuries. The four of us sped to the hospital, and although badly shaken up, it was a great relief to find they had no broken bones and would be all right after a couple of weeks.

When Uncle Geordie died suddenly in March, 1968, Mother and Dad flew out to Winnipeg for the funeral, and on his return it took several weeks for Pop to regain his normal good humor. Despite the fact he loved Ontario and lived close to his offspring, he sorely missed the separation from his remaining family. His roots were still deeply imbedded in the western prairies.

Though Pop had passed his 76th birthday, he drove a vehicle without difficulty, and he and Mom planned on trading their automobile for a camper truck and spending their declining years touring the country, giving in to the gypsy blood so rampant in their veins. Dad especially wanted to see those areas in the West where he had rambled and worked as a young man. It appeared he should be able to fulfill his wish as his health had generally remained quite stable, with one exception. Like many old-timers, Pop stubbornly refused to visit a doctor regularly and usually went only when I insisted he go for a check-up. In 1966, a Scarborough practitioner detected a spot on his lung, but after a careful diagnosis released him with a warning that he smoked too much. If the doctor instructed him to come back for further testing, which seemed likely, Pop never informed Mom or his sons. Avoiding a simple doctor's visit might have been responsible for shortening his life by several years.

In the winter weeks following his retirement Mom and Pop, together with Uncle George, spent a month in Bermuda and arrived back in Toronto a few days before Joyce and I returned from Florida. Jack picked us up at the airport and expressed concern about Dad's health as he seemed terribly lethargic, which Pop blamed on a bad cold. Within twenty-four hours, Joyce and I paid the folks a visit, and indeed Father appeared in ill health. I made an appointment for him to see Jim Whan, a doctor and our next door neighbor, the following day. No one suspected anything seriously wrong, and therefore Doctor Whan took his time taking tests and having him examined by a specialist. Early one morning a week later, Jim phoned with the startling news that Pop had an enormous tumor and appeared to be in the late stages of lung cancer. They rushed him to Scarborough General Hospital and after the fluid had been drained off his lung, Dad felt so much improved he believed his ailment had been cured and wanted to return home. Jack and I chose not to tell Mom immediately of Pop's critical condition. We did phone Uncle Ernie in Winnipeg who arrived within ten days accompanied by Aunt Lena, a truly compassionate act. Uncle Ernie, always a favorite of mine, did us a great favor by coming at such a trying time, especially since he hadn't made a long trip in over fifty years.

When the specialist decided to send Pop to Princess Margaret, Toronto's famous cancer hospital, it left no alternative but for either the doctor or me to advise Dad of his cancerous condition. He still had no notion of his perilous plight. Jack and I took on the unpleasant task, and Dad's reaction to the news, though calm, will always remain one of the most wretched few moments of my existence.

Jack and I sat on opposite sides of his bed. Grabbing him gently by the arm I spoke as composedly as my distressed demeanor would allow. "Pop," I mumbled, "it appears you don't have the flu but a touch of cancer in your lungs. The doctor doesn't believe it is too serious," I lied, "but you will have to go to Princess Margaret for tests and treatment."

He looked at his two sons with an unbelievable and shocked expression, then reaching over he immediately butted out his cigarette. "Cancer, you say! Lung cancer?" he repeated incredulously.

"Yes," I replied, with as much dignity as I could muster.

Dad sat a few moments in stunned silence while Jack and I fidgeted in agony over the awkwardness of the sad situation, then to our everlasting gratitude a middle-aged patient dying of liver sclerosis in an adjoining bed jumped up and came to our rescue. Pop called him "The Cowboy" because of his Albertan heritage, and they had become quite good buddies during the few days of sharing the same ward.

"Pop, you've got nothing to worry about," the Cowboy declared emphatically. "I heard the doctors talking while you slept one morning and they only found a cloud on your lung. You'll be out of here in no time." The Cowboy spoke with such confidence that Dad believed every word of our benefactor's marvelous fabrication, and the initial shock of the horrible ordeal passed without further distress.

Watching Pop's losing battle against impossible odds for the next two weeks is somewhat clouded by the mists of time, but the trauma of watching life drain steadily from his aged body will never completely be erased from my memory. Ken Watson, Uncle Ernie, and Uncle George helped to ease the torment we all felt and also made Dad's remaining days much more comfortable. Whenever fluid was drained from Pop's chest, he felt greatly improved and would temporarily be convinced the debilitating disease had been licked, but the vicious tumor, so far advanced, would soon have him gasping for breath again. On March 1st, almost a month after the disease had been diagnosed, Dad's specialist contacted us and recommended treating Pop with a substance quite similar to the mustard gas used in the World War I. He hoped it might be effective in temporarily drying up the tumor and allowing Pop a few months of relative comfort. The doctor also warned it could backfire and in that case would speed up his unavoidable demise. Jack and I, anxious to prolong our Father's time among us if it would be without suffering, swiftly instructed the doctor to proceed with the application. The negative reaction was the ill-fated result unfortunately, and Dad passed away five days later.

Pop never completely regained normal perception following the mustard gas treatment, but for a short while he hovered in a state of semi-consciousness suffering little as a result of drug injections but quite aware of those loving bodies that surrounded his death bed. Perhaps the most moving experience of my life, and one that would influence my course of action for many years, occurred the afternoon before his death. Jack and I again were sitting on opposite sides of his hospital cot. With eyes closed and barely able to speak, Pop nevertheless sensed the presence of his two sons, and in one motion he reached out and grabbed us by the arm as if pleading not to let him go. Many incidents that seem insignificant at the time are the ones that suddenly alter life's route. This heart-rendering gesture of supplication by my stricken father caused such an enormous shift in my philosophy that my outlook and direction would never be the same again.

Watching Pop's tenacious but futile fight for survival and later when we bade a final farewell at his graveside, I constantly recalled his cherished plans of spending a few years with Mom roaming the land in a well-earned retirement. Despite the fact he had enjoyed a full and rich existence shared with a loving wife and family and had never known real hunger or deprivation, it all ended a few yards short of his goal. After a lifetime of struggle, he had finally attained sufficient wealth to allow his final few years to be spent in a manner of his choosing. Though in the same financial position five years before, like most of us, the imminence of death never crossed his mind and therefore unfortunately he missed out on what might have been the most enjoyable era of his entire existence. I vowed at his graveside not to let this happen to Joyce and me.

Though only forty-two years of age, I fully recognized the suddenness and finality of death which had now been imprinted twice on my restive soul—first by the early demise of sister Ruth and now with the passing of Pop. I had already devoted a quarter of a century in the front trenches of industry and business. Sumcot flourished and my children had passed the crucial teenage years, except Sherree who posed no problem. My incessant drive for wealth had subsided somewhat and the importance of becoming a millionaire a little less intense. Observing and writing about other people and places on planet earth had always been of great importance to me, but I sensed no exigency to begin these adventures. Now, however, I felt a greater urgency to proceed with this segment of my life and at least temporarily to shelve my constant pursuit for riches. I never regretted this decision.

Part III
The World

Chapter 1

Into Africa

Father often remarked that one of man's greatest gifts was his ability to gradually forget the anguish of great personal sorrow. The tremendous grief I felt at his passing gradually waned to be replaced by a gnawing sadness at the unfulfillment of his dream to visit other lands and their people of which he always retained a great interest. With almost no formal education, he truly amazed me with his outstanding knowledge of man's affairs not only in North America but all over the globe. An avid reader, he had tutored himself to a degree of learning that flabbergasted those who knew of his limited early schooling. With the exception of three weeks in Bermuda shortly before his death and a couple of jaunts into the United States, Pop had lived his seventy-six years exclusively in Canada and hadn't even toured much of that immense country. As 1969 slowly passed, I frequently pondered the missed opportunity in Father's allotted time and so became more convinced each day that I should no longer delay my desire to begin a personal inspection of earth and its people.

My personal salary had increased in relation to Sumcot's expanding prosperity and that corporation had earnings after taxes in 1969 of over $125,000. Joyce and I both drove new automobiles, loved our large, prestigious Banstock home, and at Christmas I presented my devoted spouse with an expensive new diamond ring.

In addition to the sad lesson learned from Pop's untimely demise, another factor contributed to my usual restlessness. Despite Sumcot's flourish of business and continuous expansion, I, like a majority of independent businessmen, felt immense aggravation at the Federal Government's passing of the "White Paper." This new legislation would greatly increase the tax load on all private enterprises. Canada had steadily advanced toward becoming a totally socialistic state, and each year some new enactment not only reduced our personal liberties but too often transferred control of that loss of independence to some branch of the government. Prime examples of government interference in private and corporate affairs occurred continuously and particularly in our line of business. Developers had little control left on the type of development they wanted to create. From the time plans were submitted and had passed through three levels of government muddling over a period of several years, the final approved plans would retain little semblance to the original draft. The ultimate project design had become the concept of numerous bureaucratic bunglers who without any practical experience in the field believed nonetheless they knew better how to protect the interests of the general public. They were often dead wrong. I not only objected vehemently at every opportunity but also wrote letters to members of Parliament and joined any organization that made an effort to stem this tide of protective domination. I also resolved to examine other nations as possible retreats from this governmental intrusion into individual's rights which had become so commonplace in Canada.

As the world community is comprised of approximately 175 separate states with a colossal variety of governing framework, and an even larger diversity of languages and dialects, the choice of where to begin my search wasn't an easy one. The United States always lured me like a moth to a night light, but I wanted to check other countries, particularly those whose cultures and governing regimes were diverse to North America's form of democracy.

Weather was another determining factor in choosing a different area of the planet for consideration as a new home and to visit. Late 1969 and early 1970 were one of the bitterest for severe winter conditions since my arrival in Toronto, and I dreamed of a respite away from the cold and snow.

As the blizzardy frigid weather continued and the snow piled higher each day, we searched frantically for an escape. In mid-January our travel agent called about a 22-day tour of Africa. The cost of $4,000 included airfare, hotels, meals, fees, and most tips, and so I swiftly wrote a check. My longing to visit new worlds with different ways would finally be a reality.

One week later, Joyce and I left Kennedy Airport with the rest of our group at 10 p.m. for our first departure from the Western Hemisphere. Flying directly east toward Europe, I enjoyed watching the exploding sunrise somewhere over the Atlantic at 3 a.m. Landing at Orly Airport at 4:30 a.m. New York or 10:30 a.m. Paris time under a drizzly sky seemed like heaven, even though the citizens were carping about the inclement weather.

John Lloyd, an Englishman and our tour director, escorted us to the luxurious Paris Hilton Hotel where we both collapsed for a couple hours of rest, as we found it impossible to sleep on the plane.

At 3 o'clock, refreshed and anxious to see the famous French capital city, we took a leisurely stroll. The rain had passed and a brilliant sun had raised the temperature to a pleasant 50 degrees. A man gardening the hotel grounds instead of shovelling snow was a welcome sight and a fresh earthy smell resulting from the morning rain plus sprouting green lawns created the aura of spring. Approaching the Seine River, a conglomeration of crawling vehicles with blaring horns suggested that Paris suffered with traffic congestion like all major cities. Across the St. Michel Bridge, the Palace of Justice predominated the river bank while further along the Bois de Boulogne, Arc de Triomphe, Champs Elysees, Place de Concorde, Opera, Comedie de Francais and world-renowned Louvre were plainly visible. Joyce and I, strolling along the South or Left Bank, passed the Sorbonne, French Academy, Pantheon and Luxembourg Palace, but the Eiffel Tower overpowered all else.

Two lion's heads at the entrance to the St. Michel Bridge peered under the giant legs of the Eiffel Tower down the Champs de Mars, which is lined with avenues and centered by a broad boulevard flanked with flower gardens and lawns. Alexander Gustave Eiffel, a noted French engineer, constructed the tower for the French Exposition of 1889. Originally the structure was to be destroyed following the fair. Parisians fell in love with the imposing edifice, however, and so it remained and has become symbolic with the "City of Light." Although three viewing platforms at different heights are available to the public, Joyce and I had to be satisfied with the second platform as the top was closed for repairs during our visit.

During the few hours spent in the huge metropolis and particularly as I gazed across the city from the Eiffel Tower, an unusual sense of continuity seemed to envelop me. The combination of history, varied architecture, and realization that the old metropolis had for centuries been the cultural and intellectual center not only of France but of most of Europe took on a greater significance. In the distance across the Seine stood the Palace of Justice, a massive law-courts structure erected on the exact site where Roman law had been administered two thousand years ago. Spires of the Conciergerie, part of the Palace of Justice, jutted into the sky where within its grim medieval walls some of the most tragic scenes of the French Revolution were enacted. Condemned persons, including Robespierre and Marie Antoinette, had been imprisoned there before being led to the guillotine. One wing of the ancient building dates back to the early years of the fourteenth century. Further along the banks of the Seine, the Palais de Chaillot, one of France's beautiful old palaces housing several museums, enhanced the architectural splendor of the city that contained nine million Frenchmen. In the distance stood The Montmartre, hill of the martyrs at an elevation of 400 feet, the highest point in Paris and topped by the Church of Sacre-Coeur, constructed between 1875 and 1914.

Its history of violence dated back to Caesar, who conquered Paris in 52 B.C. and to the Huns who captured it in the fifth century. The metropolis successfully defended itself against the Norsemen from 885 to 887, but during the Hundred Years War, England occupied the city bringing famine and the Black Death. During World War I, though bombed as early as August, 1914, and constantly within earshot of big guns, it remained free. In World War II, the city wasn't so lucky as it fell to Hitler and his Nazi storm troopers in 1940 before being recaptured in August, 1944, by the Allies and the Free French led by de Gaulle. What a blessing to all mankind Paris wasn't destroyed over those turbulent years.

Joyce and I were fortunate in obtaining a pair of tickets for the evening performance at the famous Folies Berger. To reach the Folies we taxied down the Champs Elysees (meaning "Elysian fields," the paradise of Greek mythology), one of the most magnificent avenues in the world. Millions of white neon lights (no colored lighting is allowed), created a breathtaking vista of radiance, with horsechestnut trees bordering the boulevard completing the exquisite setting.

Our seats at the Folies were individual and elegantly upholstered easy chairs which provided ample comfort for the musical spectacular that lasted almost twice the length of any folies show in Nevada. Costumes were beautiful, and we enjoyed the performance, though in our opinion it didn't compare in over-all extravagance and scope with most Vegas shows.

The following morning we took a short city tour on our way to La Bourget Airport. I admired the ancient splendor of the exquisite statues, Cathedral of Notre Dame and Place de la Opera, before our vehicle turned up historic Champs Elysees which is terminated by the Arc de Triomphe, the greatest triumphal arch in the world. The charm, beauty and leisurely pace of Paris compared to the urgency in most North American cities impressed me, and I vowed to return as soon as possible for a longer look.

At 10:30 a.m. we boarded our plane for the long flight to Johannesburg. A malfunction in the wiring caused a lengthy delay, and then just prior to getting airborne, John Lloyd discovered one of our group had been left behind in the aerodrome. At first the pilot refused to return to the terminal, but John's threatening to jump off the taxiing aircraft changed his mind. Finally two and a quarter hours later, we were underway, but the delay caused us all considerable discomfort in the ensuing few hours.

We flew over the Pyrenees to the Mediterranean, crossed the Spanish Island of Majorca, sighted Algiers on the African mainland, and then spent countless hours looking down on the arid wastes of the mighty Sahara Desert. Reaching Gabon, Libreville at 7:15 provided a measure of relief from the long, monotonous journey. Disembarking to stretch our legs before continuing to South Africa, we were greeted by a violent tropical thunderstorm, intense heat, and high humidity which made our suit jackets and topcoats seem strangely out of place, and they were swiftly shed. Mr. and Mrs. Stephens, fellow passengers from Denver and both in excess of 75 years, were extensive world travellers. While sipping a cold beer Mr. Stephens confided to me of his great disappointment in not keeping diaries or taking more pictures of their numerous journeys over the years. I decided to heed his advice and keep detailed accounts of everything I saw plus take photographs with reckless abandon. The tedious flight continued at 8:15, and I certainly hadn't realized that 7,000 air miles separated Paris from Johannesburg. Only four days had elapsed since I left home and already the world had taken on much larger dimensions.

We landed at 2 a.m., an exhausted group of travellers. Lila Smith, our local guide, and John Lloyd whisked us rapidly through immigration and aboard our special bus to the Rand International, a beautiful modern hotel in downtown Johannesburg. The 50-degree temperature and star studded sky resembled a Canadian midsummer night but a far cry from the weather we had left behind in Toronto. Flopping wearily into bed at 4 a.m. we were mortified when informed our first tour bus departed the hotel at 8:15 a.m. Since leaving New York four days earlier, Joyce and I had slept a total of twelve hours and were rapidly reaching exhaustion.

Although physically drained from jet lag and lack of sleep, we made the 8:15 bus so as not to miss the native mine dances, the first item on the itinerary. Traveling out of the city along the Witwatersrand (an African word meaning "white water ridge") but more commonly called the Rand, we bypassed the leading gold-producing area in the world. South Africa claimed to turn out 81 percent of the free world's entire production. Along the great gold reef about five miles from Johannesburg, we passed the Geo. Harrison Mine, where Harrison, an Australian, discovered gold in 1886. Soon after the find forecasters said the precious metal would run out before the end of the century. By 1900 continuing revised forecasts predicted it would expire each succeeding decade.

Now it is conceded the supply of gold will last at least until the end of this century. Geo. Harrison, incidentally sold his entire interest for ten pounds and to compound the indignity got devoured by lions shortly thereafter.

Although the mines are thousands of feet deep, the ore is processed on the surface, and it takes three tons of ore to produce one ounce of gold, separated from the ore by heat and acid treatments. The gold mining industry employed 600,000 people, most of whom were Bantu, the black African. Bantu, an Afrikaans word meaning simply "the people," includes all the Hamite and Negroid races south of the Congo, consisting of 50 million persons with over a hundred different languages and dialects. Four million whites, or Europeans as all whites are termed, are included in South Africa's total population of 19 million. There are 13 million Bantu, originating from ten principal tribes, though the Xhosa and Zulu clans predominate, half a million Orientals, and coloreds making up the balance. Coloreds are the mixture of any of the races, although majority are descendents of intermarriage between Dutch Boers and the fairly light skinned Hottentots. Another large segment of coloreds are known as Cape Malays.

Bantu make up a vast percentage of the population in all East African countries. Most of them are much lighter skinned compared to the dark brown or black of the average American Negro. The darker African originates in Central and West Africa, the area that supplied most of American slaves. Lighter-skinned Africans from the east and south of the continent were sent primarily to India, Persia, and the Orient. Except for a few tribes native to the coastal regions, the preponderance of Bantu in South Africa are immigrants who arrived from the north of the continent between 1650 and 1680, the same era Dutch Boers and French Huguenots settled there from Europe. Over the centuries, Bantu have retained their original, simple, nomadic or pastoral way of life. As cities like Johannesburg sprang up, many younger Bantu, like people all over the world, gradually moved to the urban areas seeking employment, although they still retained their uncluttered outlook on life. The gold mining industry, requiring a large force of physical labor, became the logical source of employment. In past years Bantu suffered great cruelty and deprivation at the hands of European mine owners, but now everything is supposedly under strict government supervision. Whether or not they get a square deal would be difficult to determine, for numerous factors would have to be taken into consideration.

A Bantu immigrates from his jungle village looking for work of his own free will, and if the mine owner hires him, the man must agree to a one-year contract at a low starting salary with room, board, medical and dental care included. Most Bantu gain weight on the high protein diet. The new employee agrees to begin an uncomplex education consisting of reading, writing, and simple mathematics. At the end of the first contract, the company grants a leave of absence for the employee to visit his home. If he returns and completes four contracts (at which time he would be earning a considerably higher salary), the mine owners supply him with a small house for his wife and family.

Bantu love to dance and in their villages dance at every opportunity. To keep the workers content, mine owners construct outdoor dancing arenas in the compounds, and weekly competitions are held between groups of dancers from different mines. They dance exclusively for their own amusement but occasionally allow outsiders to watch. We were to be favored with the opportunity to witness one of these competitions. Unfortunately, a morning drizzle had cancelled the exhibition, but John Lloyd arranged a short visit inside the compound.

One-story brick dwellings attached end to end provided living quarters for a dozen men per unit, with furniture consisting only of the barest necessities. The men ate in communal dining halls, and the aroma of cooking mash made out of corn and millet definitely did not smell appetizing. The over-all setup greatly resembled a Canadian bush camp of my days in the woods with one significant exception: instead of snow drifts, lush green lawns and flower gardens enhanced the landscape. While inspecting the compound we noticed in a corner of the enclosure a group of men dressed in colorful costumes beginning to dance. Due to the dance cancellation, a few of the boys called Gum Boot Dancers decided to have a little practice. Music supplied by one cheap guitar was augmented by clapping hands or slapping thighs and rubber boots and foot stamping in tempo with the rhythm. A team consisting of eight members carefully followed the instructions of a lead dancer who directed them with a small baton. Every few minutes they stopped to take a swig of brew from one community gallon beer jug provided by the government at a few cents per gallon. Although containing an alcoholic content of about 2 percent, the beverage was rich in proteins and provided needed nourishment. The Bantu obviously enjoyed their dancing, and the five hundred workers in the compound seemed a jolly and contented group of humans. Little doubt existed among our entourage, however, that they were being manipulated by the mine owners.

Johannesburg, an unspectacular city of 1½ million, has experienced exceptional growth since its inception as a settlement. In 1886, with the discovery of gold, it didn't even qualify as a village, but fifteen years later boasted a population of 100,000. Perhaps the most distinctive characteristic of the metropolis were jacaranda trees lining the boulevards with gorgeous blue, bell-shaped flowers in full bloom. Otherwise,

Johannesburg with modern office buildings and 20th century architecture largely resembles any North American city.

After a short respite we left by bus for Pretoria, the administrative capital of South Africa and 34 miles from Johannesburg along a modern four-lane freeway traversing rolling countryside. During the trip, Lila Smith tutored us on South African history and gave a lecture on apartheid from the government's standpoint. Apartheid, which means living apart or separate development, was rigidly enforced in residential areas, hospitals, schools, and many public buildings, but all people shared the parks, playgrounds, stores, and similar places. The apartheid policy revolves around the white South Africans' refusal to acknowledge that South Africa is black man's country. Dutch and French settled in South Africa in the 1630 to 1680 era when only a handful of native blacks resided in that sector of the continent. British immigrants poured in following the Napoleonic wars, and a large German contingent followed shortly thereafter. Major African tribes that inhabit much of the country today were moving down from Central Africa over the same period as the European incursion. White Africans claim, therefore, the country belongs to all segments of the population and that they aren't going to allow one sector, referring of course to the Bantu, to take over control. A majority of African whites are solidly behind the apartheid policy.

I didn't hear the black South Africans point of view, though from general appearances they seemed a reasonably happy, contented people. Apartheid may work as all white Africans hope, but I often recalled one statement made by Lila Smith. "All whites do at least eighteen months compulsory military service," she declared, "but blacks are not trained militarily at all." That policy seems to prove without question that the Bantu aren't satisfied with the status quo, and the whites are thoroughly concerned about future trouble.

Few people are aware that the separation of races has been a domineering factor in South African politics since immediately following World War II. H. W. Verwoerd, assassinated in 1967, led the country out of the commonwealth in 1960 and into the status of a republic. Following his murder, John Vorster took over the premiership and continued the apartheid political system. The official languages of the country are English and Afrikaans. Afrikaans is a combination of Dutch and German with a smattering of French, English, and Bantu.

Pretoria, a city of half a million, is at 5,000 feet elevation—1,000 feet lower than Johannesburg and about 6 degrees warmer. The Paul Kruger monument in Kruger Park, commemorates the South African Boer who led the Boers politically against the British. Although he didn't do a lot of fighting, he is credited with being a major factor in South African independence. Because of his activities he was exiled to Switzerland, where he died in 1904. A cenotaph in the park pays tribute to the active participation of South Africa against Germany in both World Wars, although the majority of the nation's population is not particularly pro-British. Breath-taking flower gardens surround the parliament buildings located on a hill overlooking the city. South Africa's climate in July and August during their winter is similar to North Central Florida where occasionally frost and perhaps even light snow flurries occur, but palm trees and oranges flourish. Leaving Pretoria I noted with interest that Winston Churchill had been a prisoner in that country during the Boer War of 1898–1902 but escaped in 1899.

Returning to Johannesburg in our luxurious Mercedes Benz bus, we visited the Voortrekker monument memorializing another important event in South Africa's history. In 1820, when the British arrived in Africa, an agitation immediately erupted with the Boers. The rift grew rapidly as the British colony enlarged until seventy-five years later the Boer War broke out. In the early years, however, the Boers packed their belongings, and in great caravans migrated north, similar to the massive movement across our own western plains a hundred years ago. This trek across the African veldt became known as the Great Voortrekker movement. The hardy Boers encountered numerous hardships: yellow fever, malaria, and wild animals. But worst of all were the Zulu, who massacred hundreds of immigrants. In 1883, at the battle of Bloody River, four hundred Boers with their wives and children defeated 4,000 Zulu tribesmen. This last major engagement between the two peoples is commemorated by the Voortrekker Monument. It is constructed in such a manner, that only on the 16th day of December, the day of the battle, when the sun is in that particular position in the heavens, will it shine through a crevice in the roof and light up the memorial. Situated outside the monument, authentic Zulu huts, constructed out of woven grass, seemed terribly restricted for comfortable accommodation. Zulus, however, used them only for sleeping, spending the rest of their lives outside in what appeared to be idyllic surroundings.

Nearing Johannesburg we pulled into a farming community belonging to the Ndebele tribe, of which about 350,000 reside in the area. The outside walls of their one-story buildings were decorated with brilliantly painted geometric designs which provided an unusual finale to our first day of touring this strange but beautiful land. Upon our arrival back at the hotel we had twenty minutes to change clothes before attending a get acquainted cocktail party held by John Lloyd and to update us on itinerary changes. Several of our fellow travelers didn't attend due to fatigue, and finally at 9 o'clock after a brief dinner, Joyce and I gratefully fell prostrate into our bed.

We didn't awaken until 10 a.m. feeling thoroughly refreshed and ready for more adventure. After lunch we bused to the Jan Smuts Airport, for an uneventful 1½-hour flight to Salisbury where we spent a relaxing afternoon luxuriating in delightful 82-degree sunshine, though a severe summer thunderstorm raged fiercely throughout the night.

A brilliant sun greeted us for our morning tour of the Rhodesian capital, and an array of gorgeous blooms surrounding our hotel left no doubt we were on the opposite side of the planet. First we bused five miles outside Salisbury to Timbo, a village belonging to the Mashona tribe. The Mashona and Matabele tribes make up most of the native population in that region. The entire village reputedly belonged to one man, though he must have had an enormous family or a formidable number of in-laws if the two dozen thatched huts enclosed by the thatched bamboo fence were all inhabited. A plastered effect on interior walls achieved by rubbing them down with cow dung was the same procedure used on floors, and although it didn't smell as pleasant, it's a great deal more economical than Johnson's wax. The polygamous Mashona males marry as many wives as they can properly afford to support except they must pay "lobolo," which means donating a designated number of cows or goats to the parents of each lucky bride. The first wife inhabits the largest and most pretentious hut, which like most of the buildings is constructed of upright small logs topped with a grass-thatched roof. She also does the cooking for the chief and holds great influence over his choice of all future brides who must live with her as a house guest on a month's trial before the marriage. If wife number one discovers any disagreeable habits in the new fiance, she so advises her husband who is then obliged not to marry the new girl friend. All wives have their own personal abode plus side buildings for chickens, wood, grain and personal possessions.

Young ladies in the village, wearing only an animal skin skirt, were crushing maize into corn meal in crude wooden utensils. A young man perched on a high rock, drumming on a hollow log to drive away baboons, seemed more intent on the cornmeal operation, and with the physical comeliness of the bare-breasted young females, it wasn't difficult to understand why.

Like all Bantu, Masonas love to dance, but their primitive music made the guitarist for the gum boot dancers at the gold mines sound like a symphony orchestra. Hollow logs covered with animal skins and deep-toned gourds provided the rhythm, though the dancers clapped and chanted in accompaniment with the tempo. Bantu dance to celebrate every event—getting married, having a family, funerals, making it rain, making it stop raining, and an especially artistic dance for the death of a chief. The dancers' movements were lithesome and uninhibited, no doubt partially as a result of scanty attire. I couldn't help being a little envious of their apparent happy and carefree manner and wondered how concerned they might be with their white government's apartheid policy. Joyce said she didn't mind my being slightly envious of the Mashona but to forget the several wives routine or I might find myself running out of "lobolo" in a hurry. Matronly ladies wore western clothes, and I couldn't help but speculate they wouldn't have looked too seductive, even if totally naked.

Industry abounded in one section of the village with women forming pottery and styling wooden bowls while men were sculpturing soapstone. Soapstone, mineralogically a talc, is a soft stone with a greenish tint, and the workmen showed infinite patience as they meticulously formed each detail of their carvings which consisted mostly of grotesque statues depicting different phases and ages of their existence. Before leaving the village, we visited the local witch doctor who for a shilling proceeded to tell the fortune of Hubert Ritchie, one of our fellow travelers. The jungle magician's tools of the trade consisted of a conglomeration of monkey bones, shells, gourds, stones, and other assorted items. After profound conjecture, he solemnly announced, "I think you come many miles, across big water, I think you bring wife," who incidentally held Hubert's arm. All being deeply impressed with this clever display of clairvoyance, we boarded the bus and departed for Salisbury.

From the standpoint of population explosion, Salisbury equalled Johannesburg. At the time of our visit 390,000 people called it home, but in 1890, only eighty years before, not a human soul existed there. Sir Cecil Rhodes, instrumental in its colonization, lead a group of pioneers from the Transvaal that year, and we visited the "Copje," an Afrikaans word meaning "hill," where the pioneers began a settlement. The city appeared peaceful and serene even though the country already had found itself deeply imbedded in turmoil. In 1963, Rhodesia, then Southern Rhodesia, was a partner in federation consisting of Southern and Northern Rhodesia plus Nyasaland. Nyasaland left the federation that year because of its own political situation, and changed its name to Malawi. The following year, Northern Rhodesia left the fold for similar reasons. In 1965, Ian Smith, Rhodesia's Prime Minister, issued a unilateral Declaration of Independence, declaring the country an independent state. Britain immediately instituted a trade blockade, and the United Nations imposed a total travel and trade blockade. In spite of all the trade sanctions, Rhodesia survived, and in June 1969 the predominantly white electorate voted overwhelmingly in a referendum to abandon the profession of loyalty to the Queen of England and introduce a constitution that guaranteed white supremacy all but indefinitely. The total population of Rhodesia contained only 5 percent European (almost exclusively British), about 1 percent Oriental, and a whopping 94 percent Bantu. How long could less than 5 percent of the populace rule or control more than 95 percent?

Leaving the memorial commemorating the country's inception as a nation, I wondered what the future held for beautiful but troubled Rhodesia. Economic sanctions had curtailed gasoline to the crucial point, though some fuel and other essentials were arriving indirectly through Portuguese-owned Mozambique on the east, but this would stop when Mozambique gained its independence in 1975. Rhodesia, blessed with excellent soil, produced considerable tobacco, sugar, cotton, corn and tea as well as owning large reserves of gold, copper, and other natural resources. It seemed a shame so bountiful a nation should face such an uncertain future, and we couldn't entirely foresee in 1970 the turbulent decade that faced the tiny African state before becoming a black-controlled country called Zimbabwe.

An electrical storm again raged throughout the night, but a morning sun shone brilliantly. The balmy 75-degree temperature and low humidity seemed like heaven. Newspaper headlines screaming about terrorist activity on the border with Zambia, with killings occurring almost daily, tempered some of our enthusiasm because that troubled border was our next destination. Known as the city of flowering trees, Salisbury's cognomen appeared apt as boulevards were lined with magnificent tulip trees (a member of the magnolia family) aflame with brilliant orange blossoms. Our stay in the Rhodesian capital had been short but entertaining, and little did we realize the dramatic course of events that would soon envelop the African city.

The following morning we left for Victoria Falls in an old prop aircraft. The hour's flight at an altitude of 5,000 feet passed over landscape which looked peaceful, picturesque, and productive. Lush farmland bounded by strands of long-leaved pine, cypress, and mangroves was interspersed by sparkling rivers and fresh-water lakes. The pilot circled Victoria Falls for five minutes giving everyone an excellent view of that phenomenon from the air. Victoria Falls, over a mile in total width, but broken in places by islands and huge jutting rocks, plunges the astonishing depth of 420 feet. Niagara Falls in comparison is just over a half mile in width, including both the American and Canadian falls and drops a maximum of 165 feet, a third that of Victoria Falls. Viewing this natural spectacular from the air whetted our enthusiasm for a closer look.

Armed soldiers in every niche and corner provided ample evidence the airport occupied a war zone. Terrorists had shot up the terminal three days before our arrival, and machine-gun holes in the walls confirmed the attack, which came from insurgents operating out of Zambia. Victoria Falls is situated on the Zambezi, a river which forms the boundary between Rhodesia and Zambia. The fifteen-mile ride to the Victoria Falls Hotel traversed a game reserve, and a band of baboons bounding across the highway provided a thrill and our initial introduction to African wildlife. The hotel rooms weren't ready on our arrival, and so we were treated to a short bus tour of the surrounding area. Our first stop was a Matabele village. Next to the Mashona tribe, the Matabele are the most populous people in that section of East Africa. I noticed a definite similarity in the living habits between African Bantu and North American Indians, especially as I watched a young mother preparing lunch over an open fire, being carefully watched by her two youngsters with an expectant and hungry expression on their faces. In many ways the two African tribes we had visited in South Africa and Rhodesia would be analagous to going to see Cree and Ojibway encampments in different parts of Canada.

A short distance from the Matabele village we stopped to inspect a giant baobab tree (which produces cream of tartar), 65 feet in diameter and 1,500 to 2,000 years old. It had a strange stunted appearance due to being struck by lightning that halved its height. Local legend claims the devil uprooted the tree, and the branches are now really its roots. A squad of soldiers pulled up in an army truck while we examined the baobab and the officer in charge, the only white man, also drove the vehicle. Mounted machine-guns and soldiers in combat readiness created a striking contrast between the grim reality of the life-and-death struggle endured by the locals and the lighthearted vacation mood of the tourists.

After registering at our hotel, which had a superb view of Victoria Falls, we reboarded the bus for a closer look at that marvel of nature. Enroute we got more pictures of wild game when a herd of warthogs ambled across the road. Though fascinating, they are horrible looking beasts, with large warts on their faces and two enormous tusks protruding from each jaw.

Even though the bus driver parked half a mile from the falls, a heavy mist filled the air, and moisture droplets hung everywhere like morning dew. Donning raincoats and wrapping cameras in plastic sheets to protect them from saturating moisture, we only walked two hundred yards before getting our first glimpse of a small section of the famous falls. A heavy fog ascending in a cloud made it difficult, however, to discern the actual cascade of water. Mist rising in a gigantic cloud and the powerful roar of Victoria's cascade were perceptible 25 miles away. Along the pathway, a statue of Dr. Livingstone credits this famous man with discovering the falls in 1855. Despite this acknowledgement, evidence exists that they were known by earlier Portuguese explorers. A concrete walkway through the rainforest parallels the fissure carved out by the rampaging waters, and the downpour of moisture and gale-force winds generated by the ferocity of the natural wonder increased in intensity as we approached the main cascade.

The chasm only 80 to 250 feet in width provides a chute for 75 million gallons of water to plunge down every minute. It's an indescribable, unbelievable spectacle and frightening in its maddening fury. A forest of hardwoods lining the banks rarely see the sun due to the swirling fog mushrooming from the raging gorge. Concrete paths branching off the main walkway reach the edge of the chasm where gale force winds and driving drizzle actually took away your breath. Though still a half mile from the end of the pathway, everyone decided they'd had enough of the natural holocaust. I'm determined to return one day wearing only a bathing suit and follow the pathway to the Boiling Pot, the gorge just below the main cascade. I can't imagine the incredible ferocity of nature that must exist at that point. Some folks commented that Victoria Falls wasn't as pretty as its counterpart at Niagara, which may be so, but for unadulterated natural power, Victoria Falls would be hard to equal. Returning to the hotel we changed into dry clothes and within fifteen minutes were back on the bus, ready for a boat trip up the Zambezi River.

Boarding the launch a few miles above the falls, we headed up river for a picnic. The murky Zambezi varies between a half mile to a mile in width and our proximity to its tumble at Victoria caused great turbulence in the waterway. Our vessel was powered by twin hundred-horse-power Mercury motors and contained a top deck where most of us assembled because of the superior view. A blazing sun and 90-degree temperature toasted our tender skin in minutes, and sunburns were our reward. Rising vapor from Victoria Falls several miles away created puffy white clouds, the only blemish in an otherwise clear blue sky. Palm trees and dense foliage lined fertile banks, although the soil appeared almost white in color. We were warned not to dip either hands or feet into the river, as a water parasite can enter human pores and attack the liver, often fatally. Excitement mounted when someone sighted a hippopotamus, but he dove before we reached him. Within a few moments he resurfaced, stuck his nose above water, gulped some air, then again plunged so swiftly that picture taking was next to impossible. A hippopotamus can stay fully submerged for up to fifty minutes.

Numerous islands in the river, covered with dense bush had dilapidated docks protruding into the water, indicating they had been habitated at one time or used as picnic sites. At Kandahar Island we disembarked at a picnic spot in the impenetrable jungle where the boat crew served us refreshments. Leisurely sipping our tea in the tropical setting, we were startled by a rustling in the bushes, and suddenly a large troop of friendly African grey monkeys joined us for lunch. Their antics were amusing as they yanked each other's tails and gave no quarter in their frantic scramble for tidbits. The young clung to their mothers like leeches, wrapping all four limbs around her furry belly, which didn't seem to impede her maneuverability. Except for another glimpse at the hippo and a couple of fish eagles sitting in trees along the bank, the return trip offered no surprises, but the Zambezi River journey had provided a memorable afternoon.

John Lloyd, waiting at the hotel, had several forms to be filled out by each tour member for our entry into Zambia the following day. In South Africa and Rhodesia instead of having passports stamped, separate pieces of paper were used because we'd be refused entry into certain black-controlled countries if either South African or Rhodesian stamps were visible in our books. Also, luggage tags with those country's names were removed because John Lloyd claimed our bags would be torn assunder due to the intense hatred that existed in East Africa at that time.

Sipping a cocktail in front of the hotel overlooking cascading Victoria Falls in the splendid late afternoon while inhaling the fragrant smell of freshly mowed grass, frigid Toronto was barely imaginable. After dinner Joyce and I walked two hundred yards to a casino where we paid six dollars per person entry fee before realizing their blackjack rules weighed the odds heavily in favor of the house, and so we didn't give them any action. Joyce enjoyed a little luck with the slot machines, and when I made sufficient money at roulette to recoup my admission expenses, we called it a night. Strolling back to the hotel in the enchanting tropical evening under a star-studded sky and entranced by a delectable aroma of magnolias, the atmosphere of peace and contentment seemed an unbelievable paradox to the strife being waged only a few miles away for the soul of the nation.

Early the next morning we were awakened by a gentleman with a tray of coffee, a pleasant custom in most African hotels, and within a few hours, we crossed a bridge over the Zambezi into Zambia gaining one more excellent view of massive Victoria Falls. Both surprised and delighted when not detained at the border, we were nevertheless slightly disenchanted when informed our first stop would be a visit to Victoria Falls from the Zambian side of the river. Raincoats were again donned when we approached the main cataract, but air currents swept the mists towards Rhodesia so the atmosphere wasn't quite as drenching. Despite the fact that viewing the cascading cataract was perhaps slightly overdone, I departed quite convinced it was one of nature's most spectacular masterpieces. Lunching at the plush Intercontinental Hotel in Zambia, I considered the surrounding area a potential tourist paradise boasting fine weather, gorgeous scenery, exciting wild animal safaris, and fantastic Victoria Falls. What a shame, I mused, that they couldn't find a peaceful solution to their political problems. From Victoria Falls we took a six-hour 300-mile bus trip through Zambian countryside to Lasaka, the nation's capital. Thank heavens we were supplied with a comfortable vehicle equipped with air conditioning, lavatory and even a bar, easing some of the discomfort.

At first everyone remained glued to the windows, expectantly searching for wild game, but our local guide informed us the only animals we'd likely see would be cows and dogs, and so we relaxed for the long journey. Broad expanses of open, fertile savannah interspersed with picturesque rivers and lakes and tiny villages, each with a herd of scrawny cows and small, poorly maintained fields of maize, bordered our route. Zambia's population of 5 million, included 90,000 or roughly 2 percent Europeans, and when we drove past large prosperous-looking farms with well manicured fields, I knew before asking we were in the white man's limited sector of the country.

Rolling through the pastoral countryside, I reminisced about how the white man had devoted so much time and money attempting to enlighten the African, much the same as his insistence over the ages of civilizing the North American Indian. Obviously the average black African didn't have much money. I doubt if they needed much money, and they gave me the impression they didn't really give a damn for money. Watching youngsters frolicking with their pets in beautiful warm sunshine, dinner simmering on an open campfire outside the family hut, Papa sipping beer in the shade, probably wondering about the whereabouts of wife no. 3 or 4, I wondered to myself who is really ignorant and what does our civilization provide that the Bantu doesn't already possess, except money?

Long stretches of highway with a single lane of hardtop forced our driver to play "chicken" with oncoming vehicles, of which thank heavens there weren't many. Whoever left the pavement was coerced into skidding to a complete halt due to exceedingly rough shoulders, and so usually only inches separated the two vehicles when the chicken reluctantly slammed on his brakes and pulled over. The hair-raising incidents made napping next to impossible and the bar a godsend.

Zambia, the third largest producer of copper, following the United States and Russia, is one of the richest countries in Africa. Its great copper belt, lying on the border with the Congo, contains a fourth of the world's known exploitable reserves. Zambia gained independence in 1964, and in 1969, Kaunda, the Premier, announced measures for government takeover of the country's 1.2 billion dollar copper industry from foreign owners, of which the largest number were Japanese. Drastic reform in regulations affecting ownership of all foreign companies also implemented at this time forced numerous corporations to sell control to the government. These new laws significantly discouraged foreign investment and therefore seriously restricted industrial development in the nation.

We arrived at the modern Intercontinental Hotel in Lasaka at 8 p.m. relieved to vacate the bus and elated when informed we weren't leaving for Dar es Salaam until 11 a.m. the following day, allowing a little time to roam Zambia's capital city. In preparation for a visit from Yugoslavian President Tito, Lasaka, with a population of 155,000, was bedecked with flags of the East African Federation which consisted of Zambia, Tanzania, Kenya and Uganda. Except for a 25-minute stopover at Endola, Zambia, on the Congolese border, we flew directly from Lasaka to Dar es Salaam, where we landed at 4 p.m. local time. Instead of one vehicle, we were now grouped into sets of five in comfortable Volkswagon minibuses. Hot humid weather with the thermometer at an uncomfortable 92 degrees greeted us, and enroute to the hotel, we observed a vast difference in the general environment from the other three nations we had toured. Turbanned Indians, bustling Orientals, black and brown Africans, and Europeans of many backgrounds intermingled on squalid streets and residences ranged from tumbledown shacks to magnificent mansions. Industrial sections displayed signs with such familiar names as Massey Ferguson, Coca Cola, Imperial Oil, and Shell, but Dar es Salaam little resembled the western style cities we'd visited in South Africa and Rhodesia. Our hotel, the magnificent Kilamanjaro, overlooked the harbor on the Indian Ocean where a colorful array of ocean liners, freighters, and fishing boats sat anchored in the bay.

After unpacking, Joyce and I took a leisurely stroll along the palm-lined boulevard paralleling the waterfront. Dar es Salaam, Arabic for "Haven of Peace," is an enchanting city of 300,000 and is comprised of a mishmash of races and religions who with their varied apparel created an exotic atmosphere. Buibuis, worn by Moslem women, are black capes that are draped over the head and down the shoulders. Only a few years ago however, this apparel completely covered their faces, forbidden to be seen by strangers. Two young ladies sitting on the grass unconcernedly breast feeding their babies paid no heed as Joyce and I sauntered past, but seeing my camera, they instantly buried themselves and their offspring in buibuis showing nothing but a tent of black cloth. Moslem Arabs adorned in red turbans similar to a Shriner's fez without the tassle provided a sharp contrast to the black capes of the females.

Tanzania, predominantly Bantu, is comprised of 123 tribes, although in Dar es Salaam this prevalence of black African is not in the same ratio as the remainder of the nation.

The city's picturesque harbour has only a narrow passage to the Indian Ocean which allows few ocean vessels to enter but provides a haven for hundreds of colorful small fishing boats and native dhows that ply the East African coast collecting tropical produce from uncharted ports. The larger vessels trade with Arabia. Hot, large acacia trees along the boulevard shielded us from the tropical sun, and we enjoyed our pleasant afternoon jaunt.

Boarding the Volkswagen mini-buses for our city tour the following morning, we sweltered in the humid air with the thermometer already in the low nineties. Driving past World War II monuments honoring the victorious allies seemed strange when considering that only 20 years earlier during World War I, Tanzania was German East Africa. The country, mandated to Britain in 1920, changed its name to Tanganika, and all German settlers were expelled. Joining Zanzibar, it became the United Republic of Tanzania in 1964, but remained a member of the Commonwealth.

Dar es Salaam's public transportation consisting of antiquated doorless buses provided amusement as crowds of natives jostled, shoved, and showed little respect for age or gender. But though the transportation system provided humor, most of the adjectives in the dictionary wouldn't properly describe the local marketplace. Throngs of shoppers jabbering in Swahili milled about as they bartered and bargained for small quantities of food from various vendors. In the meat section, butchers carving beef and pork in the stifling heat without benefit of refrigeration, attracted hordes of flies which attacked the bonanza in a frenzy. Despite the stench from the meat counter, however, when compared to the fish and seafood division it smelled like a fresh mountain zephyr. Some so-called sea delicacies caused me to shudder just by their appearance, but the indescribable odors that permeated the air when I got downwind from those counters absolutely took my breath away, and I swiftly moved to a less reeking area of the market. A wide variety of fruits and vegetables were on display, and native women after haggling with the merchants filled their baskets for the equivalent of about seven American pennies. The chaotic scenario provided an unbelievable contrast, both in price and presentation, to supermarkets in North America. Our Dar es Salaam city excursion included an interesting tour of the University grounds and yet another visit to an African village, this time belonging to the Wazaramo tribe, but the marketplace provided the highlight of the day.

Returning to the hotel, we drove along Ocean Boulevard through a high-class residential sector where palm trees fringed the seashore which stretched from the luxury homes to the emerald blue waters of the Indian Ocean. Scanning the picturesque panorama, gentle breakers swooping over white sand beaches, made me wonder how many Canadians would exchange their winter wonderland for this tropical paradise. It seemed such a strange twist of human predestination that a multitude of Africans from this alluring continent were constantly struggling to reach our more prosperous society in a much less hospitable environment.

Zanzibar, not on the itinerary, held a romantic spot in my heart due to its historical significance, and I hated to be so near without paying a visit. The Ritchies, two of our tour mates, shared our feelings. The four of us chartered a single engine Cherokee Six at Dar es Salaam airport and flew fifty miles over the breath-taking beauty of a multi-hued Indian Ocean, studded with the rainbow-colored sails of native dhows, to Zanzibar.

Our pilot negotiated with a local taxi driver to chauffeur us on a two-hour tour of the island for 120 Tanzanian shillings, a reasonable fee. Zanzibar, 50 miles long and 25 miles wide, is low-lying, its maximum altitude 390 feet, and the climate, though tempered somewhat throughout the year with cool sea breezes, is still generally wet and hot. Stretching back from the road, groves of towering coconut palms prospered. They are harvested four times annually and provide one of Zanzibar's principal export items. Tropical fruits and copra are also produced but Zanzibar's economic mainstay is cloves, the tiny nation supplying the bulk of world demand. Clove trees stand approximately twenty feet in height, and when the leaves are mashed in the palm of the hand, a delightful aromatic perfume is obtained. Cultivated among groves of clove trees and resembling tomato plants were tapioca bushes, and our cab driver encouraged us to leave the taxi and walk over for a closer inspection. While Joyce and Cliff Ritchie stood savouring the fragrance of the clove trees, they suddenly discovered small, red, rapidly moving ants swarming over their legs. They made a dash for our nearby vehicle that gave the ants an exhibition of real speed.

Zanzibar at one time had a population of 165,000, but that had dwindled to less than 65,000 at the time of our visit due partially to their sudden Communistic political swing. The island, boasting exotic natural beauty and unique minarets and bazaars in the populated areas, presented a picturesque and intriguing scene against the backdrop of equatorial Africa. The region's history, dating back to the early Moslem era, reflects its position as a springboard to the east coast of the African continent. From ancient times Zanzibar has been closely connected with India and nations of the Persian Gulf and the Red Sea. Portugal captured the island in 1503 and controlled it for two centuries before the Arab Immams (or Muscat) seized it in 1698 and were responsible for the planting of cloves, and many of the customs that form the way of life known today. Britain gained control in 1870 and closed the slave market, on which site now stands a pretentious cathedral surrounded by attractive gardens. In 1964, Zanzibar became a republic and joined the United Republic of Tanzania that year.

Streets in the downtown core were decrepit and narrow, but a feeling of timelessness pervaded the city so that scenes of fat sultans bargaining for curvaceous slave girls flashed through my mind. A street almost too narrow even for a bicycle led to the American Consulate where flowering acacia trees and blooming gardens provided pleasant surroundings in an otherwise dismal spot. We did a little haggling in a hoary, dilapidated commercial establishment and purchased a few small items from the Arab merchants, who due to an almost complete lack of people must have found it difficult to eke out a living. Shops, though ancient and dusty, contained objects of ivory and teakwood, obtainable for next to nothing but which, in my unprofessional opinion, appeared quite valuable.

An Indian neighborhood bustled with activity but the antiquated shops and old bazaars defy accurate description. Few items on the shelves would be considered saleable by our standards, and in one small open shop the only item on display worth anything was an unrefrigerated bottle of Coca Cola.

Dr. Stanley Livingstone's old house, still standing, overlooked a section of the harbor that appeared terribly seedy and unused. Within sight of the same bay we stopped at a small, new well-appointed hotel for a refreshing drink. Government constructed and owned, the modern hostelry displayed elegant furnishing including the finest cutlery. A large staff stood rigidly at attention as if expecting an overflow crowd for dinner, but with the exception of the four of us, not another customer graced the establishment.

Returning to the airport we passed apartment buildings under construction, which were purported to be available to the local populace at no cost except for power and water, but it would be a long time before they completely replaced the traditional grass hut. Grass shacks are as synonymous with the Bantu as igloos are to the Eskimo, and in driving through African villages, I could see the economical advantages of grass compared to other building materials when weather isn't a factor, for upkeep costs are negligible. Giant breadfruit trees growing abundantly on the island bear a large, round fruit which when baked resembles bread and is a staple of the local diet. Our cab driver picked lemon grass which when scrunched up in the palm of his hand emitted a strong lemony smell and makes excellent tea. Even with such a variety of free natural living essentials available—fish, fruit, vegetables, and living accommodations—most Africans were poor in comparison to North Americans as far as cash and luxury items were concerned. Living standards established by our western civilization do not necessarily have to be the gauge by which we judge the affluence of other societies, however.

We departed Dar es Salaam the next morning for the game parks and excitement mounted at the realization we were soon to experience an actual African safari, the main objective of our trip. After landing at Tanga, Tanzania, a small picturesque, tropical coastal town, we continued on a further half-hour flight to Mombassa and our final view of the enchanting Indian Ocean because from there we proceeded inland to Moshi and our journey into the animal kingdom.

Arriving at the Moshi Airport in midafternoon, our entire party immediately boarded Volkswagon mini-buses with five passengers per vehicle. Sebastion, our chauffeur, had driven down from Nairobi, 200 miles away, with four other drivers to take us on a thousand-mile tour through the giant game parks of Tanzania and Kenya, ending up back in Nairobi. Poor visibility obscured the snow-capped peaks of Mount Kilimanjaro, the highest point on the African continent at 19,350 feet, but that didn't dampen our enthusiasm for the adventure that lay ahead.

Lake Manyara Lodge, our evening's destination, was over a hundred miles away, but I looked forward to every minute with eager anticipation. One passenger sat beside the driver, two in the center and two in back, allowing a window and ample elbow room for each person. Also a roll-back hatch in the roof provided an excellent facility for viewing or picture taking. The tar-topped highway traversed territory completely unlike anything I'd ever visualized. Africa had always conjured visions to me of hot steamy jungles with matted undergrowth, instead of rich, lush, fertile farmland flourishing with crops of cotton, coffee, tobacco, peanuts and sisal. Tanzania is the world's largest producer of sisal hemp. African grass huts surrounded by banana trees and small plots of corn plus other fruits and vegetables punctuated the route where farmers lived individually or in villages. Herds of goats and cows foraged in the flatlands, and the cattle, resembling brahmas, looked gaunt. It had to be as a result of breeding not feeding, however, as the land lay carpeted in rich luxuriant grass.

A refreshing breeze swept the plains cooling the air to a comfortable 80 degrees, and except for the lack of wild beasts, the journey was fascinating. A few miles in the distance, Mount Meru jutted from the prairie flatlands like a giant toadstool and looked out of place as if our creator had erred. Flourishing coffee plantations spread from the highway to its lower slopes. Daydreaming about the passing lush countryside I was mentally unprepared for the ecstasy of the next few moments. Having photographed and witnessed scores of wild animals I wouldn't have believed the intense rapture I sensed at my first real glimpse of African wildlife. A giraffe suddenly loomed from the grasslands a hundred yards from our slowly moving vehicle and within seconds we were in the midst of a herd. I absolutely quivered with excitement and could never properly describe the irresistible magic of those moments.

Leaving the browsing giraffes to their evening meal, we continued our trek to Mayanara. After passing Arushma, the only sizable town on the route, we traveled another thirty miles over a bumpy gravel road through flat grassy plains before spotting more of the country's unique wild creatures. We thrilled at our first glimpse of an ostrich running in the distance and then strutting beside our route saw a half dozen Maribu storks, a large ugly bird that lives off carrion much like a vulture. Nearing our destination we passed another herd of giraffes browsing on thorny bushes, their favorite diet and so prevalent on the plains. A distant herd of small deer and numerous strange birds of various shapes and colors completed our wildlife viewing for the evening, but the exciting afternoon journey had thoroughly whetted our anticipation for prospects in the morning. Lake Manyara Lodge consisted of a large, modern, attractive set of buildings situated on a cliff overlooking the Lake Manyara Wildlife Refuge, and it gave the impression we had finally left civilization behind.

After a refreshing cocktail and dinner, we retired to our room which had a spacious balcony that provided a pleasant view over the heavily wooded lowlands spread out in the valley below. In this serene setting, I settled down to do some writing when suddenly a blood-curdling scream shattered the tranquility. A prairie coyote or timber wolf with its spine-tingling lonesome howl could be no more blood-curdling than the wail that came reverberating from the dense woodlands. The weird screeching kept up at intervals throughout the night, and in the morning we were informed that a cheetah on the hunt provided the unusual shrieks.

"And the dawn came up like thunder," wrote Rudyard Kipling, an apt description of morning sunrise over Lake Manyara. Animal and bird cries from the jungle during the night and early morning created a haunting and unforgettable cacophony of creatures undisturbed, except by other creatures. At 6:30 a.m. I sat on the balcony in ecstasy as the prime morning gently spread across the tranquil countryside. However, with the temperature in the low 60's and an exhilarating breeze sweeping up from Lake Manyara, I swiftly became impatient to visit the mysterious valley below.

Following a hearty breakfast, we boarded our safari vehicles and circled the lip of the crater before proceeding to the valley floor where we reached the Mayanara Wildlife Park entrance. An interesting animal and bird museum provided entertainment while drivers picked up permits and park rangers who escorted us on our three-hour excursion.

From the park gate we travelled through a short stretch of dense jungle growth with baboons cavorting in the branches. Then in a patch of open savannah, we observed numerous zebras contentedly grazing on luxuriant grass and a large herd of impalas browsing in the brilliant morning sun. The impalas are agile, medium-sized antelopes that assemble in large herds, usually containing one ram and many hornless ewes. Reddish brown with black markings on their face and hindquarters, they are capable of making tremendous leaps when alarmed. Zigzagging down the trail through meadows and around slough holes, we passed giraffes feeding on acacia trees and several troops of baboons swinging among the branches in heavily wooded sections. Baobab, fig, and mahogany trees flourished in the sanctuary and also umbrella acacias that due to their parasol shape seemed aptly named. Huge ant hills, six to eight feet in height and resembling giant sandcastles, dotted the terrain, and among these ant colonies, we located our first elephants. What massive creatures they appear to be when first viewed at close range in their native habitat!

Weighing up to five and a half tons, the elephants congregate in family units of adult mothers together with their young and are led by the oldest and often largest of the females. The bull travels with the cow calf family unit only when the female is in heat. The remainder of the time he travels with an all-male group or meanders on his own. The African elephant can reach eleven feet in height at the shoulders and is larger than his Asiatic cousin, the species most commonly seen in circuses. When our vehicles pressed too close, the animals spread their ears and violently shook those massive heads, both signs of aggression. At this point the drivers hastily retreated. Occasionally an adult elephant would lift its gargantuan head and give forth a loud and glorious trumpet-like yell as the herd hastened away, a warning they'd had enough.

A cloudless sky with the temperature in the 70's reminded me of the Canadian West on a hot summer day, especially with the monotonous drone of the click beetle so common on our prairies and barn swallows constantly swooping around the animals. Most birds and their calls, however, were strange like the warble of the fan-tailed widowbird, who displayed a black tail eighteen inches long though the bird's body was no larger than a catbird's, or the chirping of hook-billed, pintailed whydahs. A fresh green smell of lush vegetation permeated the air, though the occasional whiff of carrion reminded us that many predators also inhabited the park. Beside Lake Manyara, water buffalo wallowed in the shallow water or lay in the shade of acacias with small tick birds feeding off the insects on their backs.

Disembarking for a few moments to stretch our legs, we delighted in the magnetism of the enchanting land including its unforgettable vista. The U-shaped waters of Lake Manyara with precipitous hills closing the gap created a natural enclosure for the animals in the fertile jungle sanctuary. Lake Manyara, a glittering soda lake, its shoreline surrounded by mudflats and reed beds also produced a natural haunt for flocks of flamingos, pelicans, geese, ducks of many species, and the rare, saddle-billed stork. Over 200 species of birds inhabited the beautiful refuge.

Circling back to the entrance gate we again viewed a multitude of animals, and the accompanying rangers claimed our group had witnessed the largest selection of game seen in several weeks. Though exhilarated by our morning safari, we nevertheless found our change of attitude in the short space of three hours quite astounding. At first we almost knocked our brains out scrambling for the roof hatch anytime animals appeared, but by noon we rarely turned our heads to glimpse through the side windows.

After lunch and a short siesta, we left Mayanara Lodge for Kimba Lodge on the rim of the legendary Ngorongora crater. The first twenty miles traversed excellent land blessed with rich, black loam, a result of lava from the Ngorongora volcano, thousands of years old. The Bemuru tribe who farmed the picturesque and prosperous-looking lowlands lived in frame houses rather than grass shacks, grew wheat and corn, and raised large herds of cattle and goats. Equated with western standards, the Bemuru appeared to be the most thriving tribe we had observed so far in Africa.

We steadily climbed out of the lush valley for seven or eight miles before parking on a ledge 200 feet in width where we enjoyed a breathtaking panoramic view of the region. On one side we looked down 3,000 feet into the valley just travelled, while the other overlooked magnificent Ngorongora, the largest extinct volcanic crater in the world. It stretches ten miles from north to south and twelve miles from east to west. From our altitude of 8,000 feet, an unbroken wall reached down 2,500 to a floor area of 102 square miles, where even at that tremendous height we could see large herds of animals on the crater floor with the aid of binoculars. We had now reached the land of the renowned Masai, nomadic herdsmen who drain blood daily from the throats of their cattle and mix it with the milk for drinking. Known for their courage and magnificent physiques, the young Masai warriors to this day, armed only with a shield and spear, are required to kill a lion to prove their masculinity.

By late afternoon we reached Kimba Lodge where tents provided our accommodation. Dining areas and bar, also under canvas, were perched on the crater rim and offered a spectacular view of the enormous depression. Due to our location at 7,000 feet above sea level, the temperature dropped as rapidly as the sun, and by 10 p.m. it registered 45 above—a change of 40 degrees in six hours.

Though decidedly chilly at dawn, the temperature soared with the rising sun, and by 8:30 it again reached 80 degrees. Breakfasting in the tent and peering down into the volcanic pit, thousands of flamingos were distinguishable on crater lakes, the delicate pink of their feathers shimmering in the morning sun providing a stunning sight despite the considerable distance.

At 9:30 a.m. we boarded four-wheel drive Land Rovers, also equipped with retractable roofs, and headed into the crater over a rough and precipitous trail. Acacia trees with birds' nests draped from their branches covered the slopes, though the crater floor spread out before us and colored in a dozen shades of green looked to be an open, grassy, treeless savannah. A horde of wildlife populated the valley, but the wildebeest predominated. This white bearded gnu, the clown of the plains and rather cow-like in appearance, its meat comparable to beef, is in fact an antelope. The Afrikaans word wildebeest even means "wild cattle." An adult male weighs up to 400 pounds, stands four feet at the shoulder, and both male and female are horned.

A constant variation of wildlife greeted us as we moved slowly along the crater floor. Secretary birds resembling tom turkeys strutted through long grass searching for snakes and other reptiles which it kills for food with a stamp of its foot. Nearby a small herd of eland were grazing. Six feet tall at the shoulders and weighing up to a ton, elands are the largest members of the antelope family. They have small humps on their back and resemble Brahma bulls. Two types of gazelles were also abundant in the giant canyon. Thompson gazelles, known as "Tommys," are reddish in color. Grant gazelles are smaller. They have white patches on their underbelly and a black band running through their middle, and they have the curious habit of continuously twitching their small black tail.

One hundred and forty thousand animals shared the Ngorongoras expansive plains which totalled 64,000 acres. Everyone thrilled with excitement on spying our first pair of lions, who unconcernedly sat panting in the morning sun like house cats. When our driver approached within a few feet, the old male threw back his shaggy head and with a menacing growl defied us to come closer. Lions, the largest flesh eaters in Africa can weigh up to 500 pounds when fully grown and measure 9½ feet from head to tail. Hidden in the brush of their tail is a claw composed of a keratinous material. Lions in national parks don't associate motor vehicles with people. Not being molested in any way, they lose their fear of man, provided he remains in the vehicle. The animals understand and trust the situation because they've become accustomed to it, but they wouldn't remain quiescent long if a person left the protection of his conveyance. All Ngorongora lions look fat—and with good reason. A total of only 60 lions lived in the crater, while literally thousands of wildebeests, elands, gazelles, zebras, and waterbucks were at their mercy. Logically, their plates should never be empty, and yet strangely enough, the lions are on the decline while other species are steadily increasing.

Zigzagging across the valley searching for different species of wildlife we were fascinated with our first close look at rhinoceros, who with its long prehensile lip adapted for browsing off thorny shrubs is indeed a strange-looking beast. Born with poor eyesight but a keen sense of hearing and scent, they constantly feint or make dummy charges in order to scare an intruder into movement, thus giving away its position. Weighing up to two tons and measuring 5½ feet at the shoulders, this dangerous and unpredictable brute will charge blindly at the slightest provocation. Rhinos obviously hold no animosity toward wildebeests who mingled with them without fear.

Different species of large birds were spotted, including European storks which were difficult to get near. A gray-headed heron, another timid bird, watched from tall grass as we neared a herd of zebras. All zebras looked sleek and well fed, but our accompanying rangers informed us they are usually heavily infested with internal parasites but are able to maintain health providing their general condition remains good. They have many of the general characteristics of horses, including a love of rolling on their backs in sand. I inquired why natives didn't draught them for domestic use and was told they are too difficult to tame. Watching them frolic around on the plains within a hundred yards of a slinking hyena seemed bizarre. Within hours that hyena as a member of a pack would likely be feeding on the carcass of one of the zebras, their favorite repast. Hyenas have the reputation of being scavengers, picking up the crumbs dropped from the lion's table. Their very name brings to mind a cowardly skulking figure. In fact, however, hyenas are powerful animals which frequently hunt and kill their own food, and it is not uncommon for lions to scavenge on their kills.

A flock of ostriches speeding across the savannah caught our attention, and we gave chase. Ostriches, the only flightless bird indigenous to Africa, are the largest birds in the world, and we were slightly disappointed when none stuck their head in the sand.

Feeding along the shore of a small brackish pond, long-legged Abbim storks were joined by numerous ducks, ibises, and plovers. Near the lake a gigantic male elephant watched with an unconcerned stare while dozens of white egrets perched on his back and fed on flies.

We stopped on a knoll for a leg stretch, and though the temperature had reached the low 90's, a delightful breeze and low humidity made it quite tolerable. Shortly after our breather we encountered a troop of baboons scrambling across the prairie. Baboons, with doglike faces, weigh up to 60 pounds and are the favorite food of leopards, though it has been known for a troop of baboons when cornered on the ground to turn on a leopard and tear it to pieces.

Further along, we saw three young lions about six months old snoozing in the grass, and they paid little heed as we approached. Lionesses usually rear from two to four cubs every second year. Hunting is carried out at night by the whole pride, with the lioness doing the actual killing by gripping the victim's throat in a strangulation hold and hauling down the prey in its futile attempt at dashing to freedom.

We went past another lake where a large flock of flamingos waded pensively in the water, while nearby a herd of waterbucks meandered into the open plain. Waterbucks weigh up to 400 pounds, stand about 4 feet in height, and are rarely found far from water. Natives claim they are poor eating, although the hide makes excellent leather.

Close to the waterbuck's habitat, all our vehicles plus those from other tours, gathered in a treed area for a picnic lunch and relaxation. A flowing well for drinking water, plenty of grass to stretch out on and a cloudless sky made it a picnic setting hard to equal. Birds in resplendent plumage added to the enchantment. Weaver birds with their brilliant yellow-gold feathers were perched in nearby acacia bushes, and brilliantly colored superb starlings, which have a white band separating the deep blue of the chest from the chestnut of the thighs, pecked away at tossed-out tidbits.

A short distance from the picnic area stood a Masai village, surrounded by a barricade of thorny bushes woven together for protection from unfriendly intruders. Except for their natural instinct to kill lions near their encampment, Masai kill wild animals only for food if they run into hard times and then usually it's a gazelle or an eland. Their encampment was off limits to us, but a few of their shy but curious females came and looked us over.

Sebastion, our regular driver, only drove mini-buses, and his replacement on the Land Rover, a pleasant affable chap, didn't speak very good English. Reboarding our vehicle after lunch, we suddenly sped across the prairie with our driver yelling what sounded like "eebo, eebo." He skidded to an abrupt halt alongside a small body of water. Believing he alluded to the many black birds swimming on the lake, I grabbed my camera and began snapping pictures of what I assumed must be a rare sight. When the driver stared at me incredulously I suddenly realized he was looking for hippo not an "eebo," and the black birds were ordinary coots. As usual, the hippos weren't posing for pictures, and so we departed the Ngornongora crater that on a per capita basis per acre, excepting zoos, has the largest concentration of wild animals in the world. We undoubtedly sighted most of them.

Late that afternoon we moved our bags eight miles up the road to the new ultramodern Ngorongora Wildlife Lodge where we spent one night and despite the exhilarating surroundings, we retired early in preparation for the following day's safari into the Serengeti plains.

Back with Sebastion and aboard our Volkswagen mini-buses, we departed the lodge at 9 a.m. and traveled a road that wound ten miles along the rim of the crater before emerging into the open. The Serengeti is mostly a vast flat, treeless plain except for occasional scraggly thorny bushes sprouting from the grass. Reputedly more than a million animals—primarily zebras, wildebeests, and gazelles—range the massive prairie sanctuary, and I don't doubt it because during our morning ride we actually witnessed hundreds of thousands. A few hilly sections do exist, but the Serengeti is essentially table flat, except for small saucer-like depressions that fill with rain water and provide excellent drinking holes for the animals. Zebras and wildebeests both require considerable drinking water, and so they migrate during the rainy season.

The trail through the sandy terrain stretched ahead of us like a ribbon into infinity. A jackal eyed us curiously when we passed within a few yards but showed no outward sign of alarm. Jackals are true scavengers, feeding mostly on the kills of others, though they do kill small creatures on their own. Foxlike in appearance, they feast on carrion, and the one we passed would likely soon be feeding on a dead zebra we spied a half mile further along. Some must die so others may live, such is the law of the wilds, a tenet quite evident in the enchanting African game parks.

Pretty white flowers carpeted the boundless grassy plains adding further to the breath-taking panoramic display constantly unravelling before our eyes. As we approached our destination, the Ndutu Tent Camp, a herd of hartebeest grazed among scattered thorny bushes. Hartebeests possess a foolish looking face, weigh up to 400 pounds, and are another species of antelope. Viewed from a sideways position, their horns resemble the letter "S," and when alarmed, they gallop off at a great pace with their head and neck held stiffly forward.

Our enchanting camp was situated in a large grove of acacias and overlooked a picturesque lake and lush meadows where herds of wildebeests grazed. Each 8 by 10 foot sleeping tent had a thatched roof above the canvas that extended eight feet over a concrete base and provided an excellent veranda. Wash basins, mirror, table and chairs were conveniently arranged on this porch. Two cots inside the tent together with our luggage allowed little room for movement, but they were comfortable and fit nicely into the spirit of our adventure. An Australian, who sported a shaggy red beard and a long, thin, waxed moustache that sprouted from his face like the twig of a tree, owned Ndutu Camp. This unique individual had resided in the area for fifty years, and I felt a trace of envy at his choice of lifestyle.

While lunching in the dining tent, also under canvas, the group decided to relax during the heat of the day and have a short evening safari beginning at 4 p.m. Not feeling like resting, I shouldered my camera and hiked across the fields to the lake, a distance of about half a mile, where thousands of flamingos inhabited the saline water. Besides the photogenic flamingos I wanted pictures of the timid hartebeest. Whenever I approached within decent camera range of those timorous creatures, however, they'd bound away a short distance, stop and stare. Then when I again got reasonably close, they would take off once more. We repeated this several times before I realized that quite a distance now separated me from the tents. Giving up the chase, I returned to camp where an excited John Lloyd sat waiting for me. Apparently I'd been roaming in an area where lions were making daily kills and if I'd chanced upon one stalking his dinner, I might have supplied the main course. What a dreadful inconvenience my demise would have been to poor old John had I been devoured by lions. The reports he would be required to fill out would have been endless, and so I promised to be more considerate in the future. Sepulchral-looking vultures roosting in nearby umbrella trees were grim reminders of the life-and-death struggle constantly being waged between members of the animal kingdom in what otherwise appeared to be a peaceful paradise, and I thanked my good fortune I hadn't been one of the victims.

Tea and biscuits were served before we boarded our buses for the afternoon jaunt and our first exciting safari into the boundless Serengeti. About a mile out of camp we bypassed a small picturesque blue lake surrounded by heavy growth. A diminutive antelope stood there twitching his tiny tail. Dik-diks weigh a maximum of eight pounds, and a more graceful or charming creature doesn't exist. Beyond the lake we entered an open section carpeted with long grass and saw a herd of waterbucks feeding, then within two hundred yards burst out into the open plains where in every direction, thousands upon thousands of animals covered the grass lands to the horizon. Our five buses spread out about a quarter of a mile apart, then drove straight forward, viewing and photographing whatever came into sight. Some large cranes eyed us reproachfully, several hyenas loped across the savannah, but constantly within view were gazelles, wildebeests, and zebras. No adjectives could aptly describe the seemingly limitless quantity of those animals. We drove ten miles straight across the prairie flats and at all times uncountable thousands remained in sight.

At one point creatures with a different stride, though barely distinguishable in the distance, attracted our attention and speeding toward them we soon recognized a flock of ostriches on the run. Taking chase we swiftly discerned the incredible speed those birds possess. Not only are they rapid runners but also have excellent endurance, maintaining their pace for considerable time. After a mile or two our driver gave up the chase because the birds hadn't slackened their remarkable gait nor showed any signs of fatigue. Despite the variety of wildlife on display, the ultimate spectacle on any safari is the lion or other member of the cat family and in that regard we were unsuccessful, so at 6:30 we returned to camp.

Sitting around a campfire sipping a cocktail and watching the brilliant jungle sunset combined to provide an unforgettable evening. Our dinner consisted of seven courses served with all the proper cutlery and an excellent wine list, a splendid "coup de maitre," considering we were 200 miles by air from the nearest village. Following dinner the Australian owner showed some intriguing 8 mm. movies he had filmed over the years including actual lion kills. At ten o'clock we retired to find lighted kerosene lanterns flickering in front of all tents. This, our driver informed me, was to frighten away wild animals. Believing it to be a little game to impress the tourists, I fearlessly meandered through the darkness a few hundred yards behind camp to see if local guides and drivers had lanterns in front of their quarters. Discovering they did I damn cautiously but rapidly made my way back. A propane gas lantern provided excellent light inside our tent and also supplied a little warmth. Although it was a gorgeous, star-filled summer night, the temperature had dropped into the low 50's, and the blankets felt good.

As dawn slowly spread across the tranquil countryside, chirping birds and strange animal calls made it a thrilling and most memorable morning. Camp boys brought a tray of tea and filled our buckets with steaming hot water. While washing and shaving outside our tent, a rising sun rapidly warming the land and herds of strange animals grazing within my view, an aura of unparalleled contentment enveloped me. I will always consider it one of the most precious memories of any of my outdoor experiences.

For our morning safari we headed in an entirely different direction than the previous afternoon. Shortly after leaving camp we spotted our first feline, a lion standing on a knoll, and this turned out to be an omen of things to come. Upon entering the open grassland we again fanned out abreast of each other approximately a quarter of a mile apart, and so our entourage covered over a mile as we swooped forward. Like the previous afternoon, hordes of wildebeests, zebras, and gazelles swarmed the prairie, but this time jackals, hyenas, warthogs, and giraffes added to the milieu of wildlife, and dusting themselves on one of the roadways was a flock of ostriches. Suddenly realizing the other vehicles had veered, Sebastion wheeled and took chase. Upon reaching our comrades and discovering they had obtained pictures of cheetahs, Sebastion established the direction the animals were last seen and sped off to search for this rare spectacle. Within two miles we located a magnificent specimen loping through the tall grass, and within minutes we spied another relaxing in the warm morning sun.

Cheetah stand about 2½ feet tall at the shoulder and weigh up to 130 pounds. They are exceptionally attractive animals, with black tear marks that almost join the corners of the eyes to the curves of the mouth. They are unlike other felines in that they are unable to retract their claws. Great speed is another of their uncatlike characteristics as they can travel between sixty and seventy miles per hour when in full stretch, a feat used regularly to run down smaller antelope. They will not attack humans, even when cornered, unlike leopards which under such circumstances would be highly dangerous. Cheetah are by no means common animals, and their wide distribution makes them difficult to locate. We were delighted with our find.

While we were still admiring the handsome cheetah, Sebastion without warning put the Volkswagen in gear and went bouncing over the plains as fast as he could accelerate. A leopard running in the distance had caught his eye and obtaining pictures of that creature would indeed be a coup and an even rarer find. The chase lasted about half a mile, and we were slowly gaining ground when the leopard sprang into an umbrella tree and in the twinkle of an eyelash disappeared from view. It seemed unbelievable that a 150-pound animal could become invisible in the scant foliage provided by the acacia. Within minutes the other vehicles came roaring up, and the commotion annoyed the big cat who began showing himself as he sized up the situation. Leopards, unlike cheetah, hunt by stealthy stalking, and after making a kill, they take the carcass up into trees away from lions, hyenas, and other scavengers. Taking refuge in a tree was thus a normal reaction. Leopards don't roar like lions but grunt, cough or make noises like sawing wood. When the mini-buses ringed his hideaway, the huge feline really got his dander up and began snarling, smashing tree limbs with his front paws and thrashing his tail. He appeared ready to leap on the roof of one of the vehicles, and so everyone remained at a respectable distance. Closing our roof hatch, Sebastion drove directly underneath the tree to see if he could persuade the animal to jump, but though annoyed, the beautiful beast chose to remain in its haven. Deciding we'd seen enough of the leopard, we continued our search for additional wildlife, and within half a mile located a pair of lionesses who showed little concern with our presence and continued to snooze in the brilliant morning sunshine, supplying us with a photographic gem.

Lions in the wild are generally magnificent specimens of vitality and good health, but we came upon one old-timer—toothless, very thin and a grim example of old age in the animal kingdom. He growled and snarled while making rapid lunges towards the buses when they pressed too close. Sebastion estimated the old warrior to be about eighteen years of age and said he would soon die of starvation.

Returning to camp we witnessed two cute young lion cubs with their mother. Attempting to hide in long grass, they seemed too innocent and lovable ever to become ferocious killers. Young lions, when first hunting for themselves, often bungle the job sadly and are not infrequently hurt in the process. Shortly before pulling into our tent site we caught a fleeting glimpse of a civet cat and so completed an unusually successful morning safari. Though thrilled with our photographic opportunities, we all agreed that animals on the Serengeti were generally wilder than those at the Ngorongora crater or Lake Manyara. The fact that plains animals saw vehicles and humans a lot less frequently probably provided the reason.

During our afternoon outing we sighted a few lions plus the usual multitude of wildebeests, gazelles, zebras, plus ostriches, and nearing our Ndutu headquarters, we saw two steinbok, still another species of antelope. The steinbok is small, reddish brown and can run like the wind.

Though it was a hot day, the temperature again sank with the setting sun, and by late evening we needed sweaters for comfort. Sitting outside our tent listening to the strange but thrilling songs of jungle birds and watching the gorgeous golden sunset fade into African twilight and finally disappear into total darkness, I sadly realized how soon it would all be just a memory.

Once again sonorous sounds of wildlife roused me at daybreak to another chilly but gorgeous morning. Scores of animals grazed in view on the open plains. I readily understood why many visitors fell in love and remained for an extended stay in the beautiful and enchanting land, but our short stopover had reached its conclusion. At 8 a.m. we left unforgettable Ndutu for a ten-hour land trip to Kericho. Within minutes we caught our first glimpse of topi when a pair leaped across the road in front of us. The topi, similar to the hartebeest though much darker in color, can weigh up to 300 pounds and reach a height of 4 feet at the shoulders. Upon reaching the Serengeti National Park entrance before 9 a.m., we already had witnessed the usual vast herds of animals, including a great number of hartebeests. For the first few miles inside the game preserve the scenery duplicated what we had viewed the previous two days with endless herds of animals, but the terrain itself had changed from prairie flatness to gently treed slopes and the grass became noticeably longer. Suddenly, as though we'd changed planets, the plains animals disappeared and only the occasional topi could be seen. The long grass plains were entirely different from the short grassy savannah, due to less alkali in the soil. At the onset of the dry season, forage in the short grass plains withers from the lack of moisture, and the water supply that collects in hollows and natural depressions dries up. Without adequate food or water, the animals are forced to move on. Despite the fact our weather for three days had been superb, the rainy season had officially started, and we'd experienced good fortune in witnessing the great migration when herds moved from long grass to short. Fires started either by accident or Masai tribes, sweep annually through the grasslands and they must be an awesome sight when fully ablaze. We passed within a few miles of the Oldupai Gorge where Dr. and Mrs. Leakey discovered the skull of the Nutcracker Man, considered at the time to be our most remote ancestor and estimated to be over 1½ million years old.

As the miles rolled by, the landscape changed again from long grassy rolling plains to hill country with rocky outcroppings and an abundance of thorny bushes. A bumpy, dusty road, combined with intense heat, made our trip long and tedious, the monotony broken only by an occasional shift in scenery. For 50 miles we hadn't sighted a single beast. Although we only had to travel 125 miles to Keekerok for lunch, the narrow road full of washouts meant we couldn't average twenty miles per hour, and the morning dragged on.

A small cement building with a thatched roof constituted the border post between Tanzania and Kenya. It seemed unbelievably unobtrusive for an entry point between two large countries. We admired a beautiful display of Masai beadwork hanging on the exterior wall of the dwelling, while drivers and border guards checked our official papers. Unfortunately, we learned later to our embarrassment, they weren't too thorough with their examination. When we finally pulled up to Keekerok

Lodge, a beautiful modern hotel with a delightful outlook over the rolling hills beyond, a massive bull elephant went lumbering along the side of a distant hill. Not one of our party stopped to take pictures, however, because all were so thirsty and travel weary that the second place rushed to was the bar for a cold beer. Despite our inclination to tarry, the lunch break was short due to the considerable distance we still had to travel before nightfall.

After passing through a final stretch of open plains country where we bade farewell to the colorful Masai, we reached an area where rolling hills and large open fields dotted with scraggly acacia trees dominated the landscape. The Nandi tribe, who use donkeys for domestic purposes as well as pack animals, inhabited that sector of Kenya. Considerably friendlier than the Masai, they waved at every opportunity. Road conditions hadn't improved and constant bumps plus choking dust made it apparent that precious little money was spent on highways, but the clothes, or rather lack of clothes, on youngsters we passed along the route indicated that money was a scarce commodity. Flimsy burlap sacks with holes for arms and head, the sole apparel on many, left nothing to the imagination in distinguishing their sex. Near the equator however, clothing wouldn't be considered too important.

Finally after twelve hours of a very displeasing vehicle ride, we reached the Tea Hotel at Kericho. Tired, dusty, and three days without running water, everyone shared the same longing for a hot bath and a cold drink. All members of our entourage, placed in one wing of the hotel, undoubtedly made a dash for the bathtub. Turning on our faucets, I discovered we had no cold water, and upon investigation found that the plumbing had abruptly gone funny. Word of the tragedy soon spread along the hallways, and we learned that some of our comrades had only cold, while others had no water at all. Despite feeling sympathy for our tourmates when beautiful boiling hot water filled our tub, Joyce and I decided to have dinner while we allowed the water to cool, then bathe. We did a little gloating while dining, and Joyce suggested I use the water first so she could spend longer in the tub. In my haste, I left her in the middle of dinner because I wasn't taking chances of letting the liquid get too cold. Racing into the bathroom entirely naked and ready to leap into my soothing bath, I suddenly realized to my horror that our tub lacked water. Apparently the house lady who came in to roll down our beds was unaware of the plumbing problem, and believing we'd left a tub of dirty water, she did us the favor of draining it. Bitterly disappointed but with no alternative, we, like the rest of our mates, wrapped our dirty bodies in clean white sheets and dreamed of a wetter day tomorrow. Joyce leaped out of bed at 7 a.m. and raced to test the plumbing situation, but the problem had not been resolved. So with neither cold nor hot water, I shaved in tea water.

Another gorgeous morning greeted us and though dirty, we were away early. Kericho, surrounded by tea plantations, owned by the Kenya Tea Co., was a beehive of activity as the leaves were ripe and native tea pickers with baskets strapped on their backs labored in the fields.

Dairy and beef farms with fields of coffee, sisal, and cotton replaced the tea plantations, and the black loam appeared as fertile as any in North America. The prosperous valley through which we travelled became significant in the Mau Mau rebellion of the 1950's. At that point in the nation's history an uprising led by a secret terrorist organization comprised of Kikuyu tribesmen, resulted in the brutal slaying of whites, Africans serving whites, and then equally brutal retaliation by the white community. The Kikuyu, led by Jomo Kenyatta, believing the land rightfully theirs were determined to recover it and become masters of their own destiny. Kenyatta, eventually apprehended and exiled, was released after peace had been restored and Kenya received its independence. Returning to his homeland, the incarcerated rebel leader eventually became premier of the nation which seemed to justify his earlier determination to wrest control of the country from the white minority. A majority of the rural area still owned and farmed by whites had African huts belonging to families working on the farms sprouting from fields like hay stacks. Many towns and villages dotted the route, but Nukuru, situated in the center of the fertile farming plateau, appeared the most prosperous. Lake Nukuru, a large body of fresh water, a few miles outside the town of the same name, boasted a flamingo population in excess of 1½ million, and at a distance of three miles they appeared to be magnificent; a slowly rolling wave of delicate pink.

We reached the Outspan Hotel at Nyeri, Kenya at 2 o'clock, just in time to catch a bus to the renowned Treetops Hotel. At Nyeri, our party of twenty-six divided, with fourteen spending the night at Treetops and the balance visiting Secret Valley. Joyce and I were included in the Treetops party. Our suitcases were stored at the Outspan, a pretentious hotel overlooking Mt. Kenya, the highest point in the country at slightly over 17,000 feet. Due to lack of room space we were each allowed only an overnight bag. Special buses drove us ten miles to an unloading zone in a dense forest where we were met by a professional hunter, complete with rifle, who escorted us along a jungle pathway the final two hundred yards to the Treetops Hotel. Once inside, we were forbidden to venture back outside until the following day's departure. In 1968 an enraged cow elephant charged a party as they approached the building and was shot by the guard after she knocked over a couple of the pilings. Numerous photographs in the hotel attested to the veracity of the episode. The Treetops, an unusual dwelling consisting of forty rooms on three floors, is constructed about ten feet above the ground on huge wooden piles. Large knots and small branches sticking out from the upright piles provided pegs inside the rooms for hanging clothes. Though clean and comfortable, the rooms were small and lacked private bathrooms, and so we had to wait another night before soaking in a hot tub. The unique structure had three viewing stations with huge windows that overlooked a water hole and salt lick which attracted the animals. An exciting atmosphere prevailed as different species of wild beasts ambled out of the surrounding dense bush to the water hole. The patrons assembled around the viewing stations intently searching with binoculars and hoping to be the first to recognize a new variety of jungle creature. Visiting animals included water buffalo, waterbuck, bushbuck, baboons and warthogs, who either congregated at the salt lick and water hole or grazed in the surrounding forest.

The original Treetops was burned to the ground by the Mau Maus in the mid-1950's and had been reconstructed on its present location in 1960. Although stifling hot in the rooms due to the sultry 90-degree temperature, we were warned to keep all windows closed until dusk because baboons, notorious thieves, might steal our personal belongings. Hubert Ritchie didn't heed the warning and opened his window a trifle while napping. He awakened just in time to see a baboon taking off with his camera. Fortunately a shout scared the thief and saved the camera, but Hubert hastily locked his windows for the duration of the afternoon. The baboon, a long sleeper, retires in the early evening and doesn't reappear until mid-morning.

During our delicious seven-course dinner, three rhinoceroses took over the water hole which at night was illuminated with enormous spotlights. Elephants were expected but failed to appear, and so bored with animal watching we retired early.

I roused twice during the night to look out the viewing stations, but only a couple of rhinos and a few water buffalo were in sight. Early the next morning when we departed intriguing Treetops, the ice cap on Mt. Kenya was clearly visible. After breakfast at the Outspan Hotel in Nyeri we reluctantly boarded our vehicles for Nairobi, and wildlife safaris had now become history. Our thousand-mile circuit through game parks had been a sensational experience and unforgettable memories of the myriad of wild animals in their natural habitat would remain forever.

Arriving at the New Stanley Hotel in Nairobi at noon, our joy knew no bounds when we found the plumbing in good working order. After lunch Joyce and I went shopping, and at one store, after an hour of stiff haggling, I purchased a zebra-skin vest, bringing the price down from

800 shillings to 500 shillings (about $70.00 U.S.). Indian merchants owned the shop, and I negotiated with two young men and a lady. Proud of my sharp trading ability, I departed with a superior air but glancing back through the window my ego took a sharp drop when I saw the three shopkeepers shaking each other's hands in a congratulatory manner. Nairobi, a modern city, had a population of slightly less than a half million, comprised of 95 percent African Bantu with the balance divided between European, Orientals, and Indians. Kenya had passed a law requiring all business people to become citizens of the country or suffer severe tax penalties. As a result, over 50,000 Indians, many from Nairobi, left the country rather than surrender their British passports. Indians are excellent business people, and their departure proved to be a big loss to Kenya's business community. Perhaps the years would prove me wrong, but in all black controlled countries it seemed they put too much emphasis on either discouraging or stopping entirely all non-black business and professional people from operating in their nations rather than trying to learn the reasons for their success.

In the evening, Joyce and I visited the local casino that due to the crowd of patrons didn't resemble the drab quietness of Victoria Falls's gambling hall. Roulette and blackjack, the two most popular games, had minimum and maximum bets at the tables both higher than in Las Vegas, and Indians in particular were gambling high stakes. The tables were jammed, and so we returned to our hotel.

At noon the following day we departed for Uganda, the last leg of our journey before returning to the frozen north. We encountered some difficulty leaving the country as the immigration officer couldn't find any documentation of our arrival. John Lloyd explained our unheralded entrance into Kenya from Tanzania through a rural outpost manned by two inept looking guards. After a hairy half hour, the distraught and confused inspector accepted the fact we were in Kenya and weren't Kenyans, and so he decided to let us continue our journey.

We reached Entebbes airport at Kampala, Uganda, after an hour's flight, mostly over Lake Victoria Nyanza, the second largest fresh-water lake in the world. The 30-mile bus trip from Entebbes to the Apolo Hotel in Kampala passed through lush farming terrain, with rich banana crops and tea plantations. At the time of our visit, Uganda was reputedly the most prosperous of the East African countries, and our journey to the hotel seemed to confirm this report as grass shacks were replaced by brick houses in most villages. Uganda was known as the runt and pearl of East Africa—runt referring to its size in comparison with Kenya and Tanzania and pearl because Uganda had the only favorable trade balance and also boasted magnificent tropical scenery and abundant wildlife. The nation had a population of over 8 million consisting of 98 percent Bantu, a friendly, industrious people noted for hard work.

The relative peace and prosperity of the lush African nation unhappily terminated not too many months after our visit. General Idi Amin, an army officer, seized power from Prime Minister Milton Obote in 1971 and began a reign of terror that reportedly took the lives of well over a quarter of a million Ugandans during the following eight years. The horror story didn't end until Tanzanian forces coupled with Ugandan exiles toppled the maniacal Amin in 1979, but by this time the country lay devastated in complete economic and social chaos, a condition that hasn't improved too much at this writing. Reflecting now on the beauty and prosperity that seemed to prevail in Kampala and its environs at the time of our tour, it now seems impossible to conceive of the tragedy and terror that has befallen those people over the past fourteen years.

In the final gorgeous sunny afternoon prior to our embarkation for the biting north winds of Ontario, I went strolling through the city park adjacent to the Apolo Hotel. Flowers bloomed in profusion and birds sang beautifully, an unbelievable paradox to the nightmare that would envelop this unfortunate nation within a year.

At midnight we left Kampala and began one of the longest and most tiresome journeys of our lives. Over the next twenty-four hours we leapfrogged from Kampala to Athens, Rome, London, New York, and finally Toronto. Jet lag and other distressing travel pains, a price paid by all world wayfarers, was an inconvenience to which I would eventually become more accustomed.

During the tedium of the flights, I spent much time reminiscing about the previous three weeks and wrote down my impressions of those African countries we had toured. Many aspects of their history, economic and political stability intrigued me. I believed South Africa's apartheid policy had an excellent chance of survival for at least a couple of decades because of that nation's enormous wealth and because Europeans, who comprised a third of the total population, were united, while the Bantu were divided by tribal bickerings. In Rhodesia, with a white population of only 5 percent of the total, a policy of apartheid seemed like an impossible proposition, and so that country's existence as an independent white community had to be numbered in years. My feelings were that, as an appeasement to the African countries to the west and north, major nations of the world wouldn't support Rhodesia—not because her apartheid policies were more restrictive than South Africa's but because she would make an excellent scapegoat. Though not well informed about apartheid, I nevertheless felt certain that much bloodshed would be splattered before Rhodesia solved her internal problems.

History soon proved my prognostications on both countries turned out to be quite accurate. I also predicted that in Zambia, Tanzania, Kenya and Uganda, already controlled by blacks, freedom and democracy often abused at the time of our visit would either worsen or vanish completely before there would be much improvement. Political permanence would be a long time coming I prophesied because generations of tribal jealousies and hatreds could not be overcome overnight. Another great difference between a majority of the Bantu and most western peoples was that the Black African's zeal for material wealth wasn't as pronounced. They seemed more interested in political control than riches or not interested in wealth or power of any description, and in ways I envied their seemingly carefree and uncluttered way of life.

Africa's ground area of 11,600,000 square miles, three times as large as continental United States, has a total population of only 80 million more. Except for the great deserts in the north, most of Africa is arable and, with little agricultural know-how, seemed capable of substantial production leaving little justification for starvation among their people. Unfortunately if the inhabitants do not have the incentive or desire for material wealth, they will only produce enough for their own individual needs, and rarely store anything for drought or an emergency. Monetary greed has its positive aspects as well as its sinister, as saving for a rainy day is second nature to most North Americans.

The sudden announcement to fasten our seat belts for a landing at New York jolted me from my mental wanderings. I glanced out the window, with the winter sun sinking behind fast-scudding snow clouds, and the thermometer registering 20 degrees Fahrenheit. Momentarily my thoughts again returned to Africa, with tropical sunsets outlining acacia trees in a halo of gold, and I knew without doubt I would return one day to the enchantment of the Dark Continent. First, however, I had a family to raise and a business to attend to, both of which would still control a great deal of my waking hours.

Chapter 2
Toil and Turmoil

There are few spans in man's tumultuous history when he didn't experience major aggravation of some sort. Certainly the first few years of the 1970s were no exception to the norm. Not only did most of the world suffer throughout this era, but I also endured considerable anguish both in business as well as with personal family problems.

A host of notable names entered the world stage during this period, and several who were responsible for the planet's unstable condition remain prominent at this writing. One man particularly annoying to the United States was Colonel Mu'ammar el-Qadhafi, who after a military coup took over as premier of Libya in 1970. A few months later, another despot, General Hafez-el-Assad, seized power in Syria. In Chile, Salvador Allende became the first Marxist to be freely elected as head of government in the Western Hemisphere. Major General Idi Amin, by far the most notorious of these new faces, gained control in Uganda in 1971 less than a year after our visit to that fascinating country. Amin immediately began liquidating political opponents which set in motion a horrible chain of events from which the ill-fated African nation wouldn't recover for 20 years. Both Qadhafi and Assad continuously played a principal role in the affairs of the volatile Middle East. At the same time, Anwar el-Sadat, elected President of Egypt in 1970, became deeply involved in the violence constantly erupting in that area.

Skirmishes and shellings seemed non-ending along the border between Syria and Israel, and in 1973 the Yom Kippur War broke out along the 100-mile Suez Canal dividing the Egyptian and Israeli forces and the Golan Heights. Israeli troops soon pushed back the Syrians to within twenty miles of Damascus even though Iraqi and Jordanian soldiers came in to support the Syrians. The Egyptians, however, crossed the Suez in several places and forced the Israelis to give up their defense line on the East Bank of the Canal. Soviet planes began air-lifting equipment to the Arabs, and the United States countered by shipping masses of military arms to Israel. Once again Planet Earth teetered on the brink of a catastrophe as the two superpowers came within a whisker of testing each other's mettle, particularly when U.S. forces were put on "precautionary alert."

Propitiously, the confrontation simmered down and the danger passed, but the Arab nations, embarrassed by their inability to stand up to the numerically inferior Israeli forces, decided to use a different attack on those supporting the Jewish nation. In 1970, the oil-producing countries primarily from the Middle East though including such other Third World states as Algeria and Venezuela, formed a cartel—The Organization of Petroleum Exporting Countries, known as OPEC. This syndicate mutually agreed to raise the posted price of Persian Gulf oil and increase taxes on the product. As a result of the U.S. supplying Israeli forces with supplies in the Yom Kippur War of 1973, OPEC placed an embargo on the shipment of oil, and suddenly most industrial countries faced a disastrous shortfall in energy supplies. To conserve their precious fuel reserves, Europe and Japan cut airline services. North America rapidly curtailed automobile driving, drastically cut office heating, and watched helplessly as the price of gasoline began an upward price spiral that wouldn't stop for a decade.

Although the Vietnam conflict gradually wound down during this period, a great deal of suffering still continued, particularly when the Vietnamese army moved into Laos. The bombing of Haiphong and Hanoi by waves of U.S. Air Force B-52s started another enormous outcry from the American public especially at universities. Rallies at several campuses protesting the widening of the war in Southeast Asia erupted into a national tragedy at Kent State University in Ohio. National Guardsmen opened fire on the rampaging students, killing five and wounding several others. This disaster kindled a wave of strikes and demonstrations at colleges throughout the nation that closed many for the balance of the 1970 spring term. Cessation of hostilities in Vietnam, though popular with most Americans, turned into an even worse calamity for millions of Vietnamese who had aided U.S. forces and were now suddenly abandoned to fend for themselves.

President Nixon gained a great deal of credit for pulling American forces out of Vietnam, but only history will conclude if this accomplishment didn't ultimately cause more deaths than it actually saved. Nixon's stature as a world leader also surged when he made a historic visit to China in 1972, ending U.S. hostility toward that communist state that had persisted since 1949. Richard Nixon's bright star soon began to fade, however, as the Watergate fiasco, already fermenting, wouldn't disappear until Nixon resigned under enormous pressure and the threat of impeachment.

Vietnam, OPEC, and Watergate were all crosses to bear for the Americans throughout these troubled times, but Canadians had their own national conundrums that had begun to rip the country asunder. The Quebec Separatist movement, gaining momentum, had attracted a bevy of radicals who were not prepared to wait for a political solution to the problem of self determination for their province. They kidnapped Pierre LaPorte, the Quebec Minister of Labor, and later murdered him. James Cross, a British diplomat also abducted was later released unharmed, but the brutal slaying of LaPorte and harsh treatment of Cross became a national embarrassment to Canadians. Concerned that further terrorist activity may be planned, Trudeau's Liberal government repealed the War Measures Act, placing the country on a war footing to deal with the emergency. Most citizens believed the Prime Minister had overreacted, as the War Measures Act curtailed certain civil rights guaranteed in the Canadian Constitution, and it was the first time such powers had been used by the federal government in peace time.

The Quebec Separatist movement steadily grew stronger under the leadership of Rene Levesque until they gained provincial power in the mid-1970s. This sudden crusade toward independence by French Canadians embittered many of their countrymen, especially in Western Canada, and so the polarization of Quebec from the rest of the country that had persisted since Confederation had now exploded into a full-scale national dilemma. Unfortunately, too few non-French Canadians really understood the Quebecois point of view. An excerpt from *The Canadians*, by Laurier L. LaPierre, aptly sums up the French Canadians' position: "The foundation of the Quebecois dissatisfaction lies in the fact that six million French-speaking Canadians of Canada form 'une nation'; they are a people who share a common heritage, speak the same language, have their own political and social institutions, live in a geographical unit that by the will of both English-speaking and French-speaking Canadians has become a sort of revere for French-speaking Canadians, and above all, possess 'un vouloir vivre collectif'—a will to live as a distinct people in North America."

Prime Minister Pierre Trudeau played an important role in keeping Quebec Province within the folds of Confederation, but that would be one of the few positive acts he ever performed for his native land. Trudeau, an avowed Socialist, constantly directed the nation on a leftist course and showed no inclination to control government expenditures. One of Trudeau's aides declared that the Prime Minister was trying to create "a human benefit society." Rather than agitate civil servants in their increasing demands for higher wages and expanding benefits, Trudeau constantly capitulated, and the country's coffers suffered as a result. The Air Controllers and Postal Workers Unions are examples of this weak attitude, because when their salaries increased Canadian industrial wages spiralled upwards. Private enterprise had no alternative but to match or better the paychecks of government workers to attract capable personnel, and inflation reaped the rewards.

Trudeau also fostered a policy of less foreign control of Canadian industry and resources. This tactic infuriated a multitude of American investors and resulted in the withdrawal of badly needed capital. Canadians in general suffered as a consequence. With wages, interest rates, and inflation rising, the economy not only cooled off but swiftly became a catastrophe. In the election of 1972, Trudeau garnered 108 seats for the Liberal party, mostly in Quebec, with 109 Conservatives being elected. Across the rest of the country, the NDP, with only 32 seats controlled the balance of power, and again Canadians watched helplessly as the party elected by a majority of the people could not properly rule without approval of the Labor Party supported by less than 20 percent of the electorate. Many Canadians called for Trudeau's resignation, but he flatly refused saying he was "in for keeps." As a result of government stagnation plus dozens of other factors, economic conditions gradually worsened until Canada plunged into a full-scale recession. Sumcot fared no better than other businesses.

Throughout 1970 and 1971, land sales were hard to come by, and Sumcot lost over $100,000, though we gained most of it back in 1972. During this period, several top men were lost to the company through resignations when forced to take salary cuts or becoming upset when they were transferred to less responsible positions. Don Fevreau, who had toiled diligently for Sumcot for six years, resigned in the spring of 1971. Others playing key roles in the corporation's fortunes and misfortunes in this era but lost due to the times included Dick Rolls, Bud Hyatt, Reg Folk, Fred Martin, and a legion of salesmen. One man, Barry Ervin, who joined the company in 1971, was destined to play an integral part for several years both in my business as well as personal affairs.

Not suspecting the depth of the coming economic downturn, Sumcot leased an additional 3,000 feet of office area just to accommodate an enlarged sales department. This space not only became entirely unnecessary, but a real liability when business took such a reversal. Despite the change in fortunes of our company, I still acquired two additional developments—Canadiana Shores on Lake Scugog and Buckhorn Lake Estates, both situated in the chain of lakes connected by the Trent Waterway. The years of intense aggravation I endured before Sumcot received approval by the numerous government agencies to offer these properties for sale forced me to capitulate to this unbelieveable provocation, and I finally took positive steps to abandon my native land.

Not having the resources to acquire more developable property when Canadiana Shores was offered, I contacted Jack Young, who had become a close business associate. Jack funded the purchase of the project, and this partnership turned out to be an excellent and remunerative deal for both. Many years elapsed, however, before Canadiana Shores reached its successful conclusion. A 300-foot width of marsh grass, cattails, and swamp separated open water from solid ground along the two-mile perimeter of lake frontage. The land rose gradually from the edge of the bog to an average elevation of forty feet, and this hill consisted of sandy fill. When first inspecting this property, I realized that if we carved ten to twenty feet off the hills and transferred this mountain of dirt to the low area we would not only create fine sandy lake shore but also improve the back land by making it less precipitous for road building and installation of other amenities. Before completing this enormous task we transported over a million cubic yards of fill by a variety of methods, including the utilization of giant bulldozers, scrapers, draglines, and fleets of trucks and loaders. When the gigantic job had been completed, Canadiana Shores provided as much personal satisfaction as any project I had created. Marsh Dudman, the general contractor who supervised most of the work and provided the bulk of machinery and expertise, would also have to be singled out as a major contributor to the successful conclusion of that development.

When business turned sour in the early 1970s, I decided to give Ohio another chance to provide badly needed sales. After interviewing several men in Cleveland, I sent them to inspect our properties and meet other staff members. For a variety of reasons they never panned out. Finally, after a six-month search, we decided on Jim Simpson who had an established record in land sales though primarily in the southern states. Over a period of several months Jim made a valiant effort to produce business, but after losing another $25,000, I finally decided that Americans would never provide a satisfactory substitute for Canadians in purchasing Sumcot properties. Cancelling our license to operate in Ohio, which had been so difficult to obtain and of which we had been so justly proud, wasn't a pleasant decision. Nonetheless, ten years of frustration plus $75,000 spent in advertising and promotion had provided us with less than a dozen sales, forcing me to give up the ghost.

Constantly searching for ways of making money south of the border, I frequently made inquiries about getting involved in a Florida real estate scheme. In 1970, an opportunity presented itself. Mr. Lee Brooks, an extremely wealthy American entrepreneur who lived in Coral Gables,

Florida but who had numerous connections in Toronto, owned huge acreage in the vicinity of the southern perimeter of Disney World. Having heard of Sumcot's substantial land promotions over the years, he instructed Milt Siegel, his general manager, to contact me about the possibility of our company becoming involved with them in the development and promotion of their property. Due to the seemingly outstanding location so near the enormous Disney World conglomerate, I grabbed the next plane to Miami. The time spent with Lee Brooks, in his mid-seventies, provided an unforgettable few hours. He had me driven to his gorgeous Coral Gables residence in a Rolls Royce where the opulence of the dwelling, beauty of his young wife and incredible elegance of a Chinese jade chess set displayed on an end table, had me goggle-eyed. I never discovered the value of his car, house, or youthful spouse, but each figurine of the chess set was worth $10,000.

Brooks' proposition appeared reasonable. His thousands of acres would be sold to a separate corporation for something in the neighborhood of $4,000 per acre, which after development costs would leave substantial profits for the other investors if selling and promotional costs weren't prohibitive. They claimed that Chuck Connors of T.V.'s "Rifleman" fame would not only be an investor but also front man for promotions, and so I eagerly accepted their invitation to go by private aircraft to inspect the holdings. Approaching Orlando, our pilot circled the countryside giving us a superb view of the surrounding area. The enormous amount of vacant land surprised me because I hadn't realized the population density in that sector of Florida would be so low. Though Disney World still remained a few months from its official opening, we were treated by the Disney people to a half-hour film on the outstanding preparation and exciting future of this new and potentially greatest tourist attraction in the Sunshine State. Lee Brooks didn't accompany us on the trip, but Milt Siegel and the other executives were ecstatic with the entire picture and more than a little annoyed when I didn't show the same exuberance. Though originally excited with the prospects, several things witnessed during our time spent in the area gnawed at me, and as the day waned my enthusiasm for the undertaking diminished.

When we had a chance to relax over cocktails and dinner with everyone in a more congenial mood, I began to voice some of my observations and concerns.

"Milt, one thing bothering me is the distance of Brooks' property from Disney World. On paper, Disney's holdings extend south to your property, but it's almost thirty miles to the actual amusement park."

Milt replied with just a touch of sarcasm, "Hell, Bill, it won't take any time for them to extend their facilities south to us, and remember we will soon be connected with superhighways."

Continuing to voice my anxieties, I stated quite emphatically, "Milt, the film shown by Disney officials mentioned that the Disney corporation had almost exclusive rights to any developing in Orange County and intimated that they intended to open large sections for single-family homes plus provide considerable accommodation for both tourists and Disney employees. This would appear to be stiff competition for anyone trying to sell property as far away from the action as we would be, even though Brooks' property is outside Orange County jurisdiction. To tell you the truth," I stressed, "as a result of our inspection of the surrounding country both by automobile and aircraft, it is apparent there is no scarcity of undeveloped land. It seems to me, therefore, that Brooks' selling price is quite high and that land equally as good might be purchased for half the price."

"Let me tell you something, Phillips," Milt snarled. "If you can locate property in the proximity of ours for anything like $2,000 per acre, Brooks will snap up all you can find."

Returning to our motel, we weren't on quite the same amicable basis we'd been all day, but we did agree that early the following morning we would head directly to a local realtor's office to check out the availability of developable acreage. Our motel, situated on Brooks' holdings, was on the outskirts of Kissimmee, and by 9 a.m. we had already breakfasted and were knocking on the door of a large real estate office in the town. Informing Milt before hand that I wished to be the spokesman, I approached the realtor with my Sumcot business card in hand. After introducing myself and the others, I went directly to the point. "As you see, I am a Toronto developer. We are considering getting involved in this area due to the excitement being generated by Disney World. Our interests lie in large tracts either near or abutting the Disney holdings that would be suitable for both single family and commercial developing."

Walking over to a huge wall map of the area, he turned and said, "We have several tracts listed, Mr. Phillips, that are immediately adjacent to or abutting Disney's holdings." Pointing to a colored section on his wall chart, he continued, "I believe this 3,000-acre block is the most suitable because there isn't any waste land on the entire acreage."

"What would be the asking price?" I inquired.

"I'm sure we can make a deal at $500 per acre," he replied.

I turned to Milt who stood with his mouth agape and just nodded in disbelief. In a sardonic low voice I said, "Well Milt, that means by buying the tract for $500 per acre and selling it to your boss for $2,000, we can turn a handsome profit."

It probably goes without saying that the incident ended any further discussion or negotiations regarding the Brooks' property. I never heard any more from them, nor did I ever see any sign of a development on the land. Perhaps the episode opened up Milt's eyes to the difficulty of his assignment, and he also withdrew.

This wasn't my only experience with getting involved in a land promotion outside of Canada, but the next time, only twelve months later, the locale was Hawaii, and the circumstances far different.

Ed Miller and his brother-in-law Fred McBrien had both worked their way to the top of the hierarchy in Toronto Shrinedom and were elected Potentates of Rameses Temple, though several years apart. As a result of our acquaintanceship in that worthy organization, I had become extremely friendly with both and frequently socialized either together with our wives or on stag outings. Ed and I loved Canadian football, and Sumcot possessed six permanent seats at midfield which our staff used throughout the 1970s. Eddie and his brother Hank had become locally celebrated for their continuous attendance at Grey Cup celebrations, the championship game of Canadian football that alternated between different cities. They hadn't missed a Grey Cup game since 1935. In the late 1960s, I joined the annual frolic, and even when it was held in Toronto, Ed Miller, Fred McBrien and I shared a hotel suite for the four-day festivities.

The Toronto Argonauts reached the Grey Cup final in 1971 for the first time in nineteen years, and the usual group of supporters, including Miller, McBrien and myself, flew to Vancouver for the big game which our Argonauts lost to the Calgary Stampeders. Owning his own equipment company that dealt mostly with the car-wash business, Eddie usually combined some work with pleasure. Having never visited the west coast, I thoroughly enjoyed my stay in Vancouver, and when Ed invited me to join him for a few hours in Victoria, I jumped at the opportunity. Though there was a heavy overcast, our plane flew below the clouds over the Strait of Georgia, and I thrilled at the outstanding beauty of that sector of our country.

In Victoria we lunched with two of Eddie's business associates, Bob McMillan and Bob Geddes. During the conversation I mentioned my occupation, and Geddes, a realtor, described a huge land sale to be held in a few days on the island of Kauai in Hawaii and said he and McMillan would be attending. A 1200-acre tea plantation situated along the coast of that island had been carved up into twenty or thirty parcels of varying sizes depending on the topography. These plots, to be offered to land developers, speculators, and realtors on a first-come basis, could not be inspected until a specific date. The two Bobs, both enthusiastic about the prospects of making a lot of money, thought I ought to join them in the venture. I hadn't left home with the intention of being away more than five days, but after due consideration and talking with Joyce, I decided to accompany the two Canadians on the potential money-making excursion. In the first place, I looked forward to seeing fabled Hawaii, and secondly, I had picked up some of the enthusiasm of making a fast buck. The Chicago-based real estate company handling the sale had widely promoted the property in Europe and North America. My two cohorts believed that if we were in Kauai opening morning we might tie up some prime parcels and resell them to later arrivals at a much higher price. They also presumed that the island, only 100 air miles from Honolulu, was prime for residential and commercial development. Having little knowledge of the area, I gave them no argument.

In Honolulu we were picked up at the airport and treated to lunch by a well-known radio personality who played the character of Ish Kabibel on the old Kay Kaiser radio show. Along with prospective buyers arriving steadily from continental United States and Europe, we were flown to Lihue, the small capital city of Kauai, and provided gratis accommodation in a gorgeous hotel. We were informed that private buses would take us to the property the following morning where a helicopter at the plantation would give each a personal inspection of the various plots. Getting the feeling of being stampeded, I told our hosts I would take advantage of the flight and accommodation if I could pay my own way as I didn't want to feel obligated. My two Canadian friends, caught up in the land-buying fever, were a little bewildered at my sudden reluctance to accept the hospitality. I informed them I wouldn't be going to the property first thing in the morning but would come later by cab or rented car and suggested they make no hasty decisions until I arrived.

At 8 a.m. before the others left on their inspection tour, I grabbed a taxi to visit both the Planning and Public Works Departments in Lihue. Managers and engineers, mostly of Oriental ancestry and all familiar with the big land promotion a few miles up the island, were equally outspoken regarding their feelings. I learned a lot from them, but the key point constantly emphasized was that the tea plantation presently zoned agricultural would remain zoned agricultural because they insisted Kauai's citizens had no desire to see their beautiful island transformed into another Honolulu. Leaving the government bureau, I visited two realtors, both Anglo-Saxon, who were also quite blunt in their opinion that the Orientals, the largest racial majority on Kauai, did not want an influx of mainland Americans and that the easiest way to halt such a migration was to prevent development.

Armed with this information, I rented a car, drove to the tea plantation, and immediately took a helicopter tour of the estate. Blue-green ocean waters, lush vegetation, and mountainous terrain blended together to give the property tremendous appeal, leaving little doubt in my mind that if it could be subdivided into residential lots it had excellent potential. Nevertheless, despite the money-making possibilities, I had no desire to begin another hassle with government agencies to obtain development approval when those agencies had already informed me they had no intention of cooperating. I quietly imparted my findings to my two new Canadian friends, but Bob McMillan, caught up in the excitement of the sale and exquisite beauty of the property, purchased a tract regardless of my warning because he felt it had unbelievable promise for future profits. I wished him well, but doubt that if even now, thirteen years later, there are any developing prospects on his acquisition.

Back in Honolulu, I spent a couple of delightful days. First I visited the site of the disastrous Pearl Harbor attack and then, in direct contrast, luxuriated along the beaches of Waikiki before returning to the frozen north to face a constant surge of business and personal dilemmas.

Business pressure from 1970 through 1972 plus nerve-wracking family problems made it a most unpleasant period. Despite personal predicaments faced with our children and though frequently we didn't see eye-to-eye on their solution, Joyce and I remained as close as the day we met. That fact alone took much of the agony out of those intimate unpleasantries.

My eldest son had considerable difficulty adjusting from adolescence to adulthood and adopted many of the slothful attitudes of the widely publicized hippie philosophy so rampant with young people in North America during that era. Michael occasionally left home and roamed different parts of the continent, but for reasons no one including himself could answer, he refused to apply his numerous talents to steady, gainful employment. His shoulder-length hair got cut only when he returned home because I refused to allow him in the house with a scraggly appearance. I explained to Michael that as a free man at the age of nineteen he could grow his hair to whatever length suited him. On the same basis, I had the right to dislike the fad, and rather than have mutual ill-feelings every time we laid eyes on each other, it would be better for the entire family if he tried to find his niche in life on his own.

Michael never quarrelled with my recommendation, and in the winter of 1970, he took a short trip into the southern United States. Unfortunately, upon his return he moved in with Joyce's parents who doted on him as grandparents frequently do their grandchildren. They provided a free room-and-board haven that allowed him to exercise his indolent lifestyle at an age when he should have been learning there is no such thing as a free ride. I spoke by telephone with Michael on such special occasions as birthdays, Christmas, and Father's Day but never laid eyes on him again for many years. Michael, a happy youngster, became a tremendous disappointment as I watched this carefree lad transform himself into a frustrated and despondent young man, a melancholia that eventually lead him like others of his nature into alcohol and drugs. If his grandparents hadn't provided a cost-free existence or if I had exerted more parental guidance, perhaps his life would have been much improved. Nevertheless I rarely anguished over his deficiency of character as it wasn't in my make-up to spend my life fretting about a situation I couldn't control.

Neither of my sons sassed me back, mostly because I wouldn't allow disobedience, but Michael often debated our difference in philosophy. Gary, on the other hand, paid little heed to any advice and gradually slipped into mischievous habits. Completely unable to cope with junior high school, my youngest son dropped out of Grade IX and made an attempt to find employment. Unlike his older brother, Gary didn't have a lazy bone in his body, but he lacked the will power to avoid obvious human temptations and soon began running afoul of the law. In early 1970, I bought him his first car, a 1964 Ford Galaxy, which he wracked up in short order. In desperation, I put him to work for Sumcot in the developments as a plumber's helper. My thinking had a twofold purpose: having him out of my hair at home would give me some mental relief and being away from the city environment might do him the world of good. The plan backfired badly. In his desire to spend evenings with his Toronto cronies, he and another lad stole a car, and when detected, they gave the police a difficult time before being apprehended. Toronto police woke me up at 5 a.m. with the joyless tidings that Gary, in the Peterborough jail, had been charged with two counts of car theft, plus stealing tires and resisting arrest. The ensuing three weeks stand out as an intense low point in my turbulent existence. Great anger overruled all other emotions until I reached Peterborough and observed my seventeen year old son facing a predicament he neither thoroughly understood nor was psychologically equipped to handle. Bail set at $5,000 made it financially impossible to have him released immediately, and so I elected to leave him in custody for a few days.

Gary hadn't bargained for this enforced confinement and begged the police clerk to phone me in Toronto each day pleading to be bailed out. Joyce felt we should bring our young son home, but I believed a few days in prison might do him more good than all the sermons I had preached about not becoming entangled with the law. After ten days I did arrange bond and had him released in my custody, but this didn't end the ordeal. John Walsh arranged for a Peterborough lawyer to defend Gary, and this counsellor suggested I obtain character witnesses as our only hope of obtaining a lighter sentence. Several people, including John Walsh and Doctor Whan, our next door neighbor, appeared on my son's behalf. Despite their favorable reports, the police department, bitter at the bad time the two boys had given at the time of their arrest, put up a strong argument for severe punishment and the judge put Gary back in jail for a week until he received a pre-sentencing report. The shocked look on Gary's face at the sudden realization he was being locked up for another week not only aroused my empathy but also a sense of helplessness at being unable to come to his aid. Nevertheless, that final week in incarceration perhaps did more to impress on my son's mind the value of freedom than any other facet of the incident. It also made me aware of the absolute lack of control we have when our offspring get into conflict with the law, and I wondered how some parents endure the torment when they have a son waiting to be hung for murder.

Gary received a two-year suspended sentence with probation, and to this writing, he has never spent another night in jail. Nonetheless he continued his erratic and stupid behavior, and on several occasions, he had border-line confrontations with the Toronto City Police. Joyce and I constantly expected to be awakened again one morning with another distressing report that our youngest boy was back in prison, but luckily this never occurred. In 1972, when Gary reached the age of nineteen, I decided I'd suffered enough from his escapades and suggested, against Joyce's wishes, that he go out on his own. He immediately moved into an apartment, and within three months wed a young girl of seventeen. This compulsive act proved to be a disaster for all concerned as the marriage lasted less than two years.

All mothers and fathers undergo a tremendous gamut of emotions when raising a family, and most parents must ask themselves at great frequency whether the struggle of parenthood is worth the heartaches. The pleasure I received from their infant years until they reached early teens was counterbalanced to some extent by the aggravation and sense of helplessness when they faced adolescence, the toughest age of their lives. Whether I could have improved our early relationship or steered them clear of later pitfalls is a matter of conjecture, but I wouldn't have missed the experience of raising a family for anything in the world. I also took into consideration that as a young teenager I had little chance to go wrong. Life's evil enticements rarely confronted me. This wasn't the situation with my children who were raised in surroundings where at every turn they faced a different siren song. Throughout these troubled times Sherree not only performed well at school but remained a delightful, well-adjusted child at home. Unknowingly at the time, the day rapidly approached when our daughter would cause as much grief as either of the boys.

Sherree sustained stricter discipline as a result of her older brothers inability to cope with the rigors of growing up. We wouldn't allow her to use make-up, have her ears pierced, or wear silk stockings until she reached sixteen. In the summer of 1970 I also insisted she accompany Joyce and me on a four-week automobile tour of the American Southwest instead of taking a job at the Canadian National Exhibition which she dearly wished to do. My unending inclination to get established in the southern U.S. inspired me to take a drive along the Mexican U.S. border from Brownsville, Texas to California. I hoped to locate an alternative to Florida where competition was too stiff in the land-development field. Convinced a massive population shift from all northern sectors of the continent to the "sun belt" was imminent due to old age and retirement pensions becoming available at an escalating rate urged me to get into a position to take advantage of this movement. In early August I loaded Joyce, Sherree and Sue Williams, a school chum of Sherree's, into our Cadillac and headed south for this journey of land inspection and whatever other excitement we might encounter.

We spent five leisurely days crossing the central plains before reaching Corpus Christi, Texas on the Gulf of Mexico, and there we got our first eyewitness look at a natural disaster. News of devastation left behind by Hurricane Celia which had struck the south Texas coastal region a few days before our arrival had shocked us like the rest of North America. The utter desolation confronting us as we drove into the stricken area, however, was far more appalling than we had ever imagined. More than two dozen Texans lost their lives and storm damage had run into hundreds of millions of dollars. Approaching the downtown core and residential sectors hardest hit by the storm, we were amazed at the few buildings left entirely unscathed. Only by observing a catastrophe of that magnitude firsthand can one actually conceive the horror of such a tragedy. It is difficult to imagine the terror families must endure when this type of disaster strikes as they watch their homes disintegrate board by shattered board. People are temporarily horrified when learning of these calamities, and assistance pours into the stricken area. But the tragedy is soon forgotten except by those affected. A government check or Red Cross parcel will fill an empty stomach or replace clothing but will do nothing to relieve the heartfelt grief caused by the loss of a loved one or bolster the courage of those who suddenly face the reality of having to start all over again.

We searched in vain for accommodation, but the influx of tradesmen who had swarmed to Corpus Christi to repair communications and clear away debris had confiscated every motel and hotel room for several miles. Bidding farewell to the hapless Texas city we motored inland to the town of Orange Grove where we had been offered some large acreage for development and wished to investigate while in the vicinity. Near our objective the closed roads and storm damage equalled that of the coast sectors, leaving us no option but continue south to Brownsville. I had intended to probe the Corpus Christi Bay area for land opportunities, but once again destiny had intervened to change my course of intended action, though several more years would elapse before evidence of this deviation would take effect.

I knew Texas had an extensive coastline but never imagined the extent nor beauty of their ocean frontage. Seashore along Padre, a barrier island paralleling the mainland from Mexico 90 miles north to Corpus Christi, would rival any beach in the world for sandy excellence. South Padre Island, reached by a two mile causeway spanning the Laguna Madre between Port Isabel and the town of South Padre, showed little sign of development. A Coast Guard station, marina, store, three unpretentious motels and numerous vacation homes straddling the sand dunes on stilt-like piers were the only indication that a handful of Texas and Mexican tourists were aware of the natural symmetry of the beach. Excited with my discovery, I approached several agents to inquire about the price of land and practicality of starting a development. Land costs starting from $400 or $500 per acre seemed ridiculously low, but real estate people generally believed that sales would be hard to come by as only a handful of people were aware of the area's magnificence. Fighting a tough economy in Canada, I wasn't in a position to gamble on acquiring property we might not sell over a reasonable period of time. Reluctantly, therefore, I departed the fascinating Texas coast, little knowing the importance that sector of the U.S. would eventually play in Sumcot's future.

Continuing our journey west, we crossed into Mexico at Brownsville and traveled a couple of hundred miles through semiarid scrub brush and mesquite covered rangeland before crossing the Rio Grande back into Texas. Traversing hundreds of miles of inhospitable country through Mexico, Texas, New Mexico, and Arizona provided a lot of time for cogitating. I tried to picture the contrast between our comfortable trip spent in an air-conditioned vehicle by day and luxurious motels at night to the hardy pioneers who covered the same territory only a century before. Fortunate to cover thirty miles per day compared to our five hundred, they traveled in a dusty, bumpy wagon and rarely found facilities to bathe themselves or wash their clothes. Comparing their meals with ours would have been totally unrealistic. Again the ease with which human beings adjust to a new environment or changed conditions astounded me.

At Disneyland in Anaheim, California, I tried to visualize the wonderment of those early settlers had they reached California after months on the trail and confronted Walt Disney's unbelievable dreamworld. In many ways Disneyland epitomizes the reason why courageous pioneers suffered hardships only a hundred years ago to reach a land of golden opportunities. To describe Disneyland is to describe America. It is an example of what is possible with the expenditure of money with profit as the motive and the result of numerous ingenious minds functioning together to produce a spectacular. Disneyland, a fantastic, magnificent money-maker, is a tribute to Walt Disney and his dramatic rise from Missouri farm boy to unbelievable fame and fortune, which is also the epitome of the United States of America.

Though I considered the long trek from eastern and central United States to California quite a venturesome feat for our ancestors, I swiftly came to the conclusion that far too many made the journey. From San Bernadino, 60 miles west to the Pacific Ocean, an unending chain of cities are connected by 900 miles of freeways. How such a profusion of people reached the Pacific Coast in such a short span of time is mind-boggling. Despite traffic congestion, we visited most important points of interest: the Hollywood Bowl, Beverly Hills, Sid Grauman's Chinese Theatre, and Universal Studios, to name a few. The overabundance of humans and vehicles quickly convinced me that California wasn't in my future plans, and so we headed back north.

We paid our annual dues during an enjoyable six-day visit to Las Vegas and then thrilled at the gorgeous scenery as we criss-crossed the Rocky Mountains through the Grand Tetons and Yellowstone National Park enroute to Winnipeg. After a pleasant visit with family and friends in Manitoba we returned home. Altogether we travelled through fifteen states and two provinces and covered over 9,000 miles. The splendid, interesting trip had taught me many things, but those beautiful, barren sand dunes and glistening golden beach of unpopulated Padre Island in southern Texas was the high point that frequently flashed to my mind.

Except for our African safari in February 1970 and our trip to California later that summer, I didn't believe I had traveled too extensively throughout this stage of my life. The actual extent of my wanderings, therefore, amazed me when I went back through my daily journals fifteen years later. A multitude of individuals had traveled a great deal further and more frequently than I. In most instances, however, this continuous movement was work related, and they despised constant travel while I relished each mile. Though never really understanding what caused my non-ending restlessness, I earned sufficient money to succumb to my incessant desire for new adventure, and so I gave in to the longing.

Following our California jaunt, I went to Florida to inspect Lee's property adjacent to Disney World. Then a few weeks later I flew to Timmins, Ontario to join brother Jack and Greg Hilton in a one-week moose hunting expedition. They had driven a half-ton truck and hauled our canoe plus a sixteen-foot cruiser with motor. From Timmins we drove a hundred miles northeast into a remote sector of Northern Ontario. A large lumbering concern that had negotiated with George Plummer to purchase Sumcot gave us permission to hunt in their private and enormous territory. Jack and Greg bagged a fine bull, making it both an enjoyable and successful week.

My right limb still hadn't readjusted to the operations performed in 1966, and this forced me back into the hospital throughout the winter and spring, of 1970-71 for further surgery. Dr. Simmons had me in a cast until early summer. As a result, I didn't do much moving about except in July, when Joyce and I spent another week in Las Vegas.

In October of 1971, Jack, Greg Hilton, Doug Prue, and I returned to the northern wilds for another moose-hunting session that turned out to be one of the most memorable of all—but not entirely because of the hunt itself. From an outfitters advertisement we chose Sparkling Lake which lay over 1,000 miles northwest of Toronto and less than 200 miles from the Manitoba border. Rather than drive a motor vehicle on a return trip over that distance, we elected to go by train to Ignace, Ontario where the outfitters would fly us into our destination. The Canadian Pacific Railroad offered a transcontinental passenger service from Halifax to Vancouver which passed through Ignace, and so we booked two back-to-back roomettes. Shortly after leaving Toronto we removed the partition to allow ample elbow room for a table to play cards and another table to act as a bar. At our invitation members of the train crew came in for drinks and to participate in the card game. Before long, our quarters had become established as a great place to enjoy some fun.

At Sudbury, Ontario, a divisional point, part of the squad had finished their stint and were replaced by others, but the cook, porters, waiters, and several others remained on the train throughout its cross-Canada journey. No doubt boredom of their daily routine played a part in their willingness to get bombed, as it isn't likely they got too many chances to let their hair down. The drunken bash lasted through the night. This didn't worry the four of us, for we didn't detrain until late in the afternoon the following day and would spend that night in a motel before flying into camp. Our railroad friends, on the other hand, had to cater to their patrons, and it mystified us how they managed. The cook and his staff kept a steady flow of delicious sandwiches and other tasty snacks coming to our roomette to show their appreciation for the fun-filled night. Other crewmen involved told us they would inform the squad who would be on duty on our homecoming a week later to give our party special attention, and they were as good as their word. Doug shot a fine cow moose, and so we were in a festive mood when reboarding at Ignace for our return to Toronto and pleased when the train crew, all different, welcomed us aboard like dignitaries. As a result, the journey home almost matched the first leg of the expedition for revelry. No doubt numerous passengers cursed the four moose hunters for interrupting the railroad line's normally splendid service. Nevertheless, the hilarious train rides helped provide me with the most memorable moose hunting trip of them all.

Another incident occurred during the week that would never be forgotten by our quartet. Doug and Jack, hunting together the afternoon Doug bagged his moose, were several miles in a different direction from Greg and me, and therefore, we didn't hear the shots. Returning to camp in late afternoon we found a note with the news of our partners' success and request for assistance, and so we immediately jumped into our boat and went in search of them because the weather showed every sign of turning dirty. As we interchanged hunting partners each day as well as hunting areas, we knew where to look and therefore located them without difficulty even though they were a full three miles from camp. Two shallow marshes littered with deadheads and shoals plus three small lakes dotted with islands and connected by narrow waterways separated our Sparkling Lake headquarters from the site of the kill. By the time the carcass had been butchered, a half mile in the dense bush from where our two small aluminum boats were beached, a dense fog enveloped the land and the final vestige of daylight had disappeared. A thunderstorm with a 40-degree temperature and a blinding fog is unusual, but that is what we faced together with a drenching rain.

At first we kept the boats in tandem. Within five minutes, however, our motor struck a submerged rock, and to our astonishment, Greg and I suddenly realized the nose of our craft had run up on the hidden shore. The fog had become so thick our strong hunter's lanterns couldn't penetrate more than a foot, and it became absolutely impossible to discern shoreline or anything in front of our boats. We faced the joyless possibility of spending a miserable night soaking wet in the woods with little likelihood of getting a fire started. Greg and I had brought a bottle of whiskey, and so after roping our craft together side by side, we discussed our perilous situation while warming our innards. Jack rarely travelled without topographic maps, and I suggested our only hope of finding camp would be to try to pick our way through the several waterways by map and compass. Our only glimpse of the tree line when a brilliant flash of lightning illuminated things for a second proved to be a godsend as we moved cautiously forward. With both outboards at trolling speed, we even astonished ourselves with our ability to slowly maneuver through the network of waterways in almost zero visibility. After a couple of hair-raising hours, the fog lifted temporarily and we jubilantly spotted the lantern Greg and I had thoughtfully left hanging in our cabin window. I consider the episode one of the finest feats of woodsmanship accomplished during my entire hunting experience. Perhaps none of us would have perished, but we certainly would have suffered during twelve hours in the bush on such a night. Although I did return to the North Woods one more time, that moose hunting jaunt turned out to be my swan song for bringing home game, but, my thirst to wander continued unabated.

In midwinter Joyce and I drove to Florida for a month's change of pace, and in June we flew to Winnipeg. Cousin Margaret Downey and husband Dave were celebrating their 25th wedding anniversary, and so Jack, Shirley, Joyce, I and our daughters flew out for the festivities. We also enjoyed a few pleasant days at Kenora with the Barhams. We made our annual junket to Las Vegas in September and took a side tour to the Grand Canyon. I went to Winnipeg by myself in October for a few days to attend the wedding of Roman Kruchak's youngest daughter. In lieu of moose hunting that fall, Jack, Greg Hilton, Barry Ervin, and I spent a week in Fort Lauderdale, Florida on a combination golfing and gambling junket. Then just before Christmas, Joyce and I drove back to Florida for twelve weeks with the intention of beating the horses with a complex betting system requiring the use of a pocket calculator. After the loss of $3,000 over a period of several weeks, I gave it up, but the trip was especially noteworthy as we discovered and stayed at the Seahorse Motel, the most luxurious ocean-front accommodation in Hollywood. Shortly after our return to Toronto in March, Joyce and I flew back to Las Vegas, and this time we took a side tour to the Hoover Dam. During our Vegas jaunts throughout the years to indulge in our love of gambling, we also never missed attending various casino shows. Over this period of time we were fortunate to see most of the Hollywood stars of yesteryear, including Jack Benny, Red Skelton, Totie Fields, Phil Harris, Jimmy Durante, and many present-day performers like Bob Newhart, Leslie Uggams, and Dolly Parton.

Because I spent considerable time away from home, I missed some of my Winnipeg relatives and Monominto buddies on their infrequent visits to Toronto. In the fall of 1970 when Ed Barham and wife Sheila decided to pay a call, I awaited their arrival with anticipation. Ed informed us by letter of his plans and expressed himself in his normal colorful manner. "I have purchased a new pair of overalls and rubber boots for the journey," he wrote. That gave Joyce and me an idea for a special reception. We arranged a party of a dozen or more including friends, relatives and Sumcot employees, to be present at the airport and to attend our following planned festivities. Canadian Pacific Airlines, the Barham's carrier, gave permission for three people to meet the plane at the arrival gate. Jack and Don Fevreau carried a huge banner emblazoned with "WELCOME TO TORONTO ED AND SHEILA" in flaming red letters. They and an excellent bagpiper in a kilt playing a sprightly Scottish tune escorted my two open-mouthed friends into the main terminal where Joyce and I dressed in bib overalls, colored shirts and knee-length rubber boots waited to greet them. From the airport the entire party, including the piper, went to the Beverly Hills Nightclub where we had reservations for dinner, dancing, and a show. I had earlier arranged with one of the scantily clad waitresses to approach Eddie when we were seated and pretend to be an old flame. Warned in advance about our plot, Sheila enjoyed the joke, and Ed handled the situation with humor and ease although he did appear a little taken back for a few seconds at the onset. Though the evening cost five hundred dollars, the unforgettable memories of the Barham's first visit to Toronto made it worth every penny.

In addition to roving around throughout these troubled times and an unflagging attempt to improve Sumcot's sales, I did have numerous other interests. As a result of my photographic foul-ups on the African safari, I resolved to master the technique of movie making, and so I acquired an expensive 16 mm movie camera and all the accessories, including a projector. I put together a short film with background music and sound effects of both the moose hunting jaunt to Sparkling Lake and our last automobile trip to Florida. The prohibitive cost of 16 mm film discouraged this new fad, but as I had found creating travelogues quite challenging, I switched to 35 mm, a top of the line Nikon with three lenses and all other accouterments required to do the job, including a highly sophisticated tape recorder. Another project that consumed considerable time and patience was a complete family snapshot collection. Collecting a multitude of photographs of family and friends from a variety of sources, I put together a series of albums which I titled "The Continuity of Life." Chronologically assembled on an annual basis, these hundreds of snapshots, each with typewritten captions, were taped into binders. At the beginning of each year I inserted an outline of special events, and world headline stories, and a list of songs, movies, books, and notable deaths that occurred during the course of that year. Although a time-consuming enterprise, it is one I keep up to this day as it furnishes an excellent record and emphasizes the importance of living each day to its fullest. Turning the pages slowly gives the viewer a vivid portrayal of the aging process. Family members and friends slowly change with the years in some cases from the cradle to the grave.

Thumbing through the albums and observing snapshots of myself as a child and perceiving the gradual transformation in my own appearance always renews my determination to derive as much pleasure out of this existence as is realistically possible.

Besides photography, I enjoyed playing bridge and not only indulged in rubber bridge at least twice weekly but also belonged to a team-of-four league and represented Toronto in inter-city competitions. Joyce and I curled when home during the winter, and I golfed at least once weekly throughout the spring and summer. The Granite Club, one of the finest family clubs in the city, admitted me in 1972, and I swam almost daily in their Olympic size pool. In conjunction with all my activities, both business and personal, I drank too much. Like most heavy drinkers I gave little consideration to any long-term effects of the habit. Despite my apathetic attitude, I had the sad opportunity during this stage of my life to be a firsthand witness to the disastrous consequences of a constant use of alcohol.

Death, a morbid subject at any time, is nevertheless a crucial part of any autobiography. When Grandmother Rodd passed away in the fall of 1970 at the age of 95, we were not that broken up as she had lived a full though not necessarily happy life. Homer Grace, our dear friend from Poughkeepsie, N.Y., died of a massive stroke in 1972, and although alcohol probably played no part in his demise, he obviously had been a heavy drinker at one time in his life. This also applied to Joyce's Uncle Frank, who died a relatively young man the same year. Then 1973 provided plenty of incentive for me to curb my habitual drinking. In early winter Lorne Branning, my first Toronto partner, cashed in his chips many years before his time, with booze clearly responsible for his untimely death. Later that summer, Uncle George Rodd, who had progressively increased his alcoholic intake to better than 150 ounces weekly, turned into a semi-recluse as a result. Unk lived with Mother, who had sold her Toronto home for $28,000 and moved permanently into Highview Acres where she and Dad lived when supervising that development. Mom was concerned not only about her brother's health due to his heavy drinking bouts but also that he might accidentally burn down their frame residence and so Jack and I finally intervened. Like most alcoholics, Unk refused to admit he had a problem and therefore gave me a very difficult time when I arranged to have him admitted to the Donwood Clinic in Toronto. The Donwood had become world famous as a combination institution and hospital in dealing with the disease of alcoholism. Jack and I exerted extraordinary coercion in persuading him to take their outstanding 30-day treatment, and to this day he has enjoyed an existence untroubled by whiskey.

The most sorrowful death directly attributable to alcohol abuse was my mother-in-law in 1973. Eddie was a gregarious, bouncy woman who loved to party, especially with her hard drinking brothers, sisters and many close friends. Extremely goodhearted and generally happy natured, she nevertheless seemed to need alcohol to keep on an even keel. Eventually the habit became addictive, and she ended up in the hospital with a serious liver condition. Eddie made a miraculous recovery, and if she could have left whiskey alone, might still be alive. Shortly after returning home, however, she went back on the bottle and died within a few months due to the failure of her liver. Eddie's passing caused us considerable grief not only due to our family relationship but also because it all seemed so unnecessary. She loved her grandchildren to excess, and although she often brought grief and aggravation to Joyce during her later stages, there appeared little reason for her inability to control the use of alcohol. Watching Eddie suffer and bring distress to Joyce at the same time as well as Unk's entanglement with booze made me do some heavy thinking, and so just prior to my mother-in-law's death, I went on the wagon for two months. My first attempt at curbing the use of alcohol proved short lived, and a lot of moons would cross the heavens before I gave it up for good. Giving up the nicotine habit in the early 1960s after twenty-five years of addiction had been extremely difficult but successful. My wont for alcohol however wasn't as easily repressed.

These untimely deaths again made me restless and urged me to accomplish more things, visit unfamiliar country or experience new adventures. Business boomed, and for the first time I put a limit on sales. Sumcot's accountants advised this action not only because we were depleting our inventory unnecessarily but also because we were forcing Sumcot into a cash-flow predicament when staggering corporate taxes came due the following year. Against the wishes of my three offspring, I sold our Harcourt Park cottage that for fourteen years had played a great part in their existence. The sale of our summer home also contributed to my longing to leave Toronto for awhile, as it removed any desire to spend week ends at the developments. Eager to put together another travelogue similar to my effort with African Safari, I wished to tour a country offering a wide variety of interesting picture-taking opportunities, and as my 35 mm equipment weighed several pounds, I wanted to travel by car. After taking everything into consideration, I chose Alaska. Joyce didn't share my enthusiasm and refused to accompany me on the 14,000-mile journey. I took off alone in late June, 1973, full of zeal and ready for whatever lay ahead.

Chapter 3

An Alaskan Odyssey

Alaska, meaning "the great land," is as large as Washington, Oregon, California, Arizona, and Nevada combined or one fifth the size of the original 48 states. Stretching 2,400 miles in width, the state boasts a general coastline that spans 6,640 miles (or 33,904 miles including islands) and is washed by two oceans and three major seas. Thirty-three of the thirty-five known strategic minerals are located within its boundaries. Bought from Russia in 1867 for $7,200,000 or about 2 cents per acre, Alaska's 586,400 square miles proved to be as great a bargain as the purchase of Manhattan Island from the Indians for a handful of trinkets.

Five thousand miles of automobiling through Canada lay ahead before I even reached Alaska's border. I planned a circular return trip down the Pacific coast to San Francisco, then northeast to Toronto for a total itinerary of 14,000 miles. Though a long route driving solo, I nevertheless looked forward to my departure date in late June with unbridled enthusiasm.

Instead of motoring west on the popular but crowded Lake Superior route, I chose the Northern Trans-Canada Highway which I hadn't travelled since 1950. In Hearst, Ontario, where pulp, paper and lumber mills operated sixteen hours a day, I paid a visit to the Arrow Lumber Company. Technological changes that had swept the industry in the past twenty-five years astounded me. In my lumberjacking days, trees were sectioned into logs where they fell. Here they were trucked from the woods full length to a central landing area where two men and one massive machine dissected them, up to six at a time, into 16-foot logs. Another huge apparatus then delivered them to the mill, a truckload at a time, and the complete operation didn't take ten minutes. This modern

573

mill, a gnashing, sawing, screaming mass of machinery, poured forth a stream of lumber that required 20 men just to remove the material from the conveyor belts. A superintendent informed me Arrow Lumber expected their timber holdings would mature rapidly enough to keep up with the insatiable demand for logs. According to my calculations, at present production, they would either have to upstage God in growing trees or have a lumber lease to the whole of Canada.

Driving up to the huge pile of trees where the immense log cutter operated out of sight of the rest of the complex provided me with a chuckle. Three French Canadian workmen repairing a hose connection in a rather lackadaisical fashion eyed me suspiciously when I approached them. They were chatting in French, and so I didn't interrupt but inadvertently glanced at my watch. One of the workers noticing me look at the time eyed the Caddy, spoke to the others in a startled manner, and then within seconds the repaired machinery began spewing logs. Undoubtedly they pegged me as one of the major shareholders or an efficiency expert, but a few more logs were produced that night as a result of my curiosity.

The highway between Hearst and Beardmore, one of the most dismal in Ontario, has a 250-mile stretch that looks out over a flat bog covered with scrub spruce, balsam, jackpine, and an occasional marshy lake. I could drive half an hour without spotting another vehicle, an indication of the route's unpopularity. I had travelled it twice before: once in 1949 when Jack and I immigrated east, and again in 1950 when I rushed home to my ailing sister Ruth. Most of the road at that time consisted of sand or gravel and was filled with potholes.

My plans of spending time in Beardmore to locate the old bush camp where I'd worked in 1946 went awry when the weather turned wet and cold, and so I just stopped for a short visit. Beardmore didn't resemble the wild brawling town of the postwar years when a permanent population of 400 swelled to over 2,000 every week end. On my stopover it looked as peaceful as any town in the country. I reached Winnipeg without incident and spent a pleasant few days with relatives and friends before continuing west.

Driving through the little town of Fleming, just inside the Saskatchewan border, I tried to picture the enormous changes in the world since my mother and her family immigrated there from England in the early years of the century. Even though Planet Earth experienced tremendous transformation over that period of time, I suspected that Fleming had changed little. Regina, Saskatchewan's capital city, emerged from the rich farmland like a jewel in an emerald sea, and I thought how romantic it first appeared to me in 1945 as only the second city I'd ever seen. While driving to Saskatoon I reflected on the many seasons I'd harvested across those prairie flatlands and fondly recalled the earthy smell of freshly cut grain, the groan of a tractor and separator while threshing the golden kernels, or the enchanting sight of a dozen burning straw-stacks at night. Despite my euphoria, the sudden recollection of blistered hands, sweaty clothes and bone weariness overcame any desire to return to a pitchfork for a livelihood.

Moving into Alberta, Canada's largest prairie province, I admired the unending sea of green stretching back from both sides of the highway. Grandiose mountain peaks or shimmering blue waters are awe-inspiring, but waving grain fields reaching to infinity are also a stirring spectacle. The tranquil landscape of the prairies suddenly boils up into an angry maze of rugged hills and deep chasms near Drumheller. Known as the Drumheller Badlands, numerous dinosaur skeletons have been found in that area. Gazing out over the rugged terrain, I could almost sense the nearness of the mountains, even though 75 miles of fertile farmland still separated me from Calgary and sight of the majestic Rockies.

Calgary had changed dramatically since my last sojourn in 1948 when the population was less than half of what it now was. For percentage of population increase, Calgary had grown more rapidly than any city in Canada throughout the 1970s. It was Stampede Week, and the burgeoning western town bulged with visitors. Without a reservation, I had a stroke of good fortune by obtaining a room for two nights at the modern York Hotel right in the downtown core. Calgary resembles a giant carnival during the Stampede with white Stetsons the badge of participation. Parades and downtown street celebrations which tied up the city every morning by 9:30 a.m. seemed to be complacently accepted by local motorists and pedestrians as a normal part of the shenanigans. Good tickets were scarce, but in the York Hotel bar I met a friendly and personable chap with an extra seat located in the finest location in the stadium. He sold it at cost, and we went together and enjoyed a pleasant and exciting afternoon.

Skill and courage are two of the main ingredients contestants must possess to compete in the rodeo. To stay aboard a bucking, whirling, enraged animal takes tremendous ability and a heap of spunk, but the Calgary Stampede's $150,000 cash purses, the largest in the world, help attract the finest North American cowboys. Each afternoon's performance is different as rivals battle it out in a variety of competitions over the nine days. Points are awarded toward the championship in each event.

Some contests border on mayhem, with the wild horse race apparently the most dangerous. A three-man team is required to rope and ride a wild bronco with time as the factor. Injuries are not uncommon, and at our performance one cowboy had to be removed in a stretcher when he was kicked in the face and stepped on by two different animals. Clowns who are expert bullfighters remain in the compound to divert bulls and broncos away from fallen riders. They put on numerous skits and were obviously crowd favorites. The internationally famous RCMP musical ride, a spectacular combination of precision and beauty, is also a highlight. Thirty-two riders attired in scarlet and gold astride satin-black horses, wheel their mounts through intricate patterns and designs to the music of the RCMP band, creating a kaleidoscope of color and movement. This impressive exercise provided a fitting finale to the day's exciting entertainment and Calgary visit.

Approaching the mighty Rockies from the east is fascinating. Gently rolling prairies are gradually replaced by foothills which steadily increase in size until majestic mountains seem to reach forward like giant magnetic pincers and attract you into their mighty jaws. Driving into the imposing Rockies I realized five weeks would elapse before I left their overpowering presence.

Clear hot weather blessed me from Winnipeg, but once I was inside the mountains, temperatures cooled considerably. By the time I reached famous Lake Louise, a chilly brisk breeze whistled down off the icy mountain slopes.

Within a few miles of Banff, Canada's oldest national park, I crossed Kicking Horse Pass into British Columbia and Yoho National Park. The Continental Divide, where all waters either flow east or west, is located just before Rogers Pass, an engineering phenomenon. Man's unbelievable ingenuity at constructing a highway through the seemingly impregnable Rockies was more perceptible when confronted with their immensity. Those hardy men responsible for the completion of the transcontinental railway line must also have felt an outstanding sense of accomplishment when they finally connected the Atlantic to the Pacific.

I drove the Okanagan Valley route to the Pacific coast, a decision I didn't regret because of its scenic beauty. Vancouver, Canada's third largest metropolis, is a cosmopolitan city with a lumberjack air. A great port, transportation terminus, cultural center, tourist destination and Canada's doorway to the Orient, Vancouver is the crown jewel of western Canada. On my only previous visit, in the late fall of 1971 during the Grey Cup festival, rain and fog shrouded the city throughout the four days of our stay. During this trip, however, the sun shone brilliantly, and the surrounding mountains jutted vividly into the blue summer sky, giving the city a majestic appearance.

During my short stay in the enchanting west-coast city, I visited the Bourdans, friends of brother Jack, who proved that the pioneering spirit in some Canadians is far from dead. Ed Bourdan and Jack both worked for Memorial Gardens in Winnipeg and Toronto. At one point I considered Ed as sales manager for Sumcot, but with a restless streak equal to mine, he moved his family west. After two years he got the itch to own a farm, and so they sold their lovely home in a Vancouver suburb and bought a ranch in the Cariboo region almost 300 miles north. Joan Bourdan gave me directions to their new spread which I could visit on my route to Prince George without detouring.

With the preliminaries now over, I thrilled at the thought of finally beginning the long trek north to the Arctic. The highway through the rugged Fraser Canyon parallels the scenic Fraser River. In places the gorge is so narrow you have to marvel at the ingenuity and imagination of the men who guided a road through the almost unconquerable mass of mountains, with canyon walls rising a sheer 3,000 feet on either side. Tunnels blasted out of the rock in the Hell's Gate region provided the only logical means of traversing that section. Cache Creek, where the highway forks east to Calgary and north to Prince George, lies in the Camelsfoot Range, northern tip of the same desert that stretches south to Arizona. An average annual precipitation of only ten inches leaves the country as arid and barren as desert regions of southwestern United States. Local inhabitants enthusiastically emphasized that although it's hot, there is no humidity. Gazing at their sun-parched surroundings, however, I thought to myself so is Hell, and I'm not looking forward to spending too much time in that spot.

The Prince George Highway follows the legendary Cariboo wagon road, a trail plodded by every prospector and gold miner hoping to strike it rich in the great Cariboo gold rush of the 1860's. Throughout the past century, the North has lured men for many reasons. Acquiring free or low priced land for homesteading and farming was one, and Ed Bourdon, who had just taken possession, gazed wistfully over his new ranch with profound anticipation. Despite his optimism, Ed had already discovered that all problems weren't left behind in Vancouver but simply exchanged for new ones in the Cariboo. The irrigation system had broken down, leaving the freshly sprouted hay badly in need of moisture; his cabin's faulty plumbing system needed repair, and neighborhood plumbers were nonexistent. Ed and I agreed that his troubles were trivial, though, compared to those faced by men who opened that sector of the country a century ago in their constant search for gold.

Today the stampede north to the Arctic Circle is for black gold or oil, but every village, town, or city from the Cariboo, 2,500 miles north to Nome, Alaska, had extensive vestiges left by the sourdoughs who trudged forward in their relentless hunt for the precious yellow metal. In the 1860s the fabulous Cariboo gold fields were a lure to thousands.

Miners, traders, and adventurers—many afoot and some with wheel-barrows—shared the pioneer route with mule trains, plodding oxen, freight wagons, and swaying stage coaches. Road-houses and stables located every 12 to 14 miles along the way provided havens for man and beast. From Soda Creek, sternwheelers travelled the Fraser River 400 miles north where they were replaced by the railway. At Quesnel, I turned off the main highway to visit Barkerville, the first gold boom town in Canadian history.

News of a gold discovery along the Fraser River near Williams Lake in 1858 soon reached San Francisco where their mining boom had col-lapsed, and by early summer the whole of California was in ferment. An estimated 31,000 hopefuls left San Francisco alone in May, June, and July of 1858, traveling by horse, steamer, or any conveyance that could move them to the Cariboo. Other strikes were made, but in August 1862, Billy Barker, a naval deserter, discovered on Williams Creek the richest paydirt anybody had ever seen. Around his diggings grew the town of Barkerville. Within a year Barkerville boasted a floating popu-lation of 10,000, and shortly thereafter it claimed to be the largest city north of San Francisco. Along its muddy, uneven, single street and back alleys strode men and women representing all types of humanity; miners (both experienced and inexperienced), doctors, nurses, dentists, judges, tamed-down gunslingers, faro bankers, dance-hall girls and many others. All were cast together in an untamed and often cruel environment.

Deep snow and crisp weather have their aesthetic appeal, but they produced plenty of hardships for those Cariboo pioneers. The elevation of 4,200 feet produces temperatures that fall below zero five months of the year. The lowest recorded is 52 below. Snowfall can exceed 200 inches annually. By 1868, Barkerville had prodigious buildings by the score, including numerous hotels, saloons, gambling establishments, and the elegant Theatre Royal, which now remodeled is doing a thriving business with today's tourists. There were also hundreds of log cabins, stores, and churches, of which St. Saviors' Anglican Church still stands. According to legend, Rev. James Reynard had the chapel built to prove "that men working underground have still some hopes which go upward and heavenward." Then on September 16, 1868, tragedy struck. A dis-astrous fire levelled the town in an hour and twenty minutes, leaving Scott's saloon the only building still standing. Most families lost their entire possessions. Though immediately rebuilt, Barkerville's glory days were passed as gold had rapidly given out. The town never regained the prominence it had known for a decade.

And what became of Billy Barker, whose personal claim produced an estimated $600,000? Well, a good percentage of Billy's gold helped polish the mahogany bars of saloons, and he was generous in grubstaking other prospectors. Perhaps Billy's biggest financial mistake was marrying a high-stepping young lady who helped him spend another large portion of his wealth. As a result, despite his unbelievable lucky strike, he died a pauper in Victoria, B.C. in 1894. Billy Barker and the town that bears his name rose to dizzying heights of fame together, and together passed away into the pages of history. The British Columbia government is doing an excellent job of renovating and restoring the Barkerville of the 1860s, hoping it may regain a measure of its former glory, but none of its notoriety. An aura of immortality is sensed in a ghost town like Barkerville, exemplifying the adventurous spirit, fortitude, and endurance of our forebearers, and I continued my journey delighted I had detoured to pay the town a visit.

Prince George, at the confluence of the Nechako and Fraser rivers, is the commercial, industrial, and transportation center for central British Columbia. From the city's perimeter huge forests extended north and supported 299 lumbermills as well as several large pulp and paper mills.

The 280-mile drive to Fort St. John provided an interesting diversification of terrain. At first, the land covered with pine and hardwood forests and punctuated by occasional scenic lakes resembled northern Ontario. Crossing over the Mt. Hulcross mountain range to Chetwynd, roses, phlox, and sweet clover adorned the countryside and filled the air with the sweet smell of summer. Then upon reaching the powerful-flowing Peace River which traverses the picturesque Peace River Valley, farmland predominated. British Columbia and Alberta lured settlers for many years with the offer of free land, with a provision that so much acreage had to be cleared and building improvement maintained before they received title to their holdings. The extent of farming amazed me because I had traveled 700 miles north of the 49th Parallel, equating with The Pas, Manitoba, which I considered to be polar bear country. My astonishment accelerated when I arrived at Fort St. John. Expecting a small Indian village, I found instead a thriving farming community of 10,000 people. Seven grain elevators in town were not only the first I'd seen since leaving the prairies but the greatest number in any town of comparable size in Canada. A North West Company post opened in 1805 was still operated by the Hudson Bay Company. The Alaska Highway officially begins at Dawson Creek, 47 miles south of Fort St. John, but I missed that 47-mile stretch because I'd reached Fort St. John by an alternate route.

Reports concerning the Alaska Highway's clouds of dust and twisty teeth-rattling, washboardy roads were no exaggeration as the first 300 miles proved. When the pavement ended at mile #87, 40 miles north of

Fort St. John, it became difficult to appreciate the passing scenic terrain. Swirling dust created by slowly moving vehicles, especially transports, blinded trailing motorists and made driving more hazardous than any snow blizzard. Heeding advice to install headlight guards plus a large protective screen over the front grill before departing Prince George proved to be wasted effort. Before I reached the Alaska Highway a large truck roared past me, his slipstream whipping the protective shield from my car and tossing it into a nearby field. I soon learned its value because before day's end, my car had sustained cracked headlights and windshield. Some 150 miles from Fort Nelson I halted at a roadside picnic area for a brief lunch and to enjoy, for a few minutes at least, the captivating mountainous landscape. Feeling slightly disenchanted due to driving conditions, I watched with some astonishment when two ladies pulled into the rest stop with six Siberian huskies which they began to water and feed. From Alaska and driving south on vacation, they could find no one to babysit their dogs, and so with no alternative, they were taking them along. Playing nursemaid to six animals on such a trip seemed like a massive undertaking, and so I continued to Fort Nelson a more contented man.

Located deep in northern British Columbia and established as a Hudson Bay Company post in 1800, Fort Nelson is now a lumbering town, and the hub of a growing petroleum exploration center. The modern homes resemble those of any town in North America, but few other places in the world are surrounded by such an expanse of sheer wilderness. A profusion of wild phlox bathed the land in a reflection of lavender and excellent stands of poplar trees equalled anything I'd seen since leaving home.

Traveling alone caused no mental discomfort even though I had now covered nearly 5,000 miles. I rarely used the radio because admiring and taking pictures of the constantly changing scenery kept me enter-tained. Hitchhikers were abundant, but only on a rare occasion did I pick them up as too frequently they looked like they hadn't seen a bathtub or shower for an extended period and I also harbored the usual concern about looneys. Loneliness only affected me after I reached my evening's destination, and usually I would locate a local bar and strike up a conversation with anyone willing to talk. This habit acquainted me with numerous fascinating individuals and gave me things to think about while driving the following day. At Fort Nelson I met a geologist Bob Johnson, whose tale of woe rivalled any I'd ever heard for intrigue.

Tired and dusty when I arrived at Fort Nelson, I quickly showered and then went to find the nearest tavern for a cold beer to quench my slaked throat. Three Americans seated at the bar seemed friendly and eager to chat, so I joined them. Headquartered in town for several months, they were involved in exploring oil and gas leases in surrounding terrain held by a corporation for whom they worked. With their own helicopter they covered an enormous region and amused me with engrossing wildlife yarns of days spent in country rarely seen by a white man. The other two men, both in their late twenties, were John, who piloted the helicopter, and Dunc, another geologist. Bob Johnson, in command and senior member of the trio by at least twenty years, was also the heaviest drinker. After several cocktails the boys suggested we relocate to an excellent family-style restaurant for dinner where we had a couple more drinks before eating. A natural consequence of our two-hour drinking session was that personal lives now entered the conversation more frequently. As a result, a story regarding Bob Johnson's personal life came forth that I considered quite unique.

The yarn came out when we began discussing our marital status, and Bob admitted in a gloomy demeanor that he was temporarily divorced.

"How many years were you married?" I inquired.

"Just over twenty-two," he responded.

"You remarked you were temporarily divorced, which I didn't understand," I continued. "Are you getting married again?"

"Perhaps to the same woman," Bob replied in a babbly voice.

Ordering another drink, Bob slowly mumbled his unusual story.

Originally from Kansas City, he and his wife were both young when they married and had two children within three years of their nuptials. Raising a young family while struggling through university put a strain on family life, and they existed on short rations. Everything came up rosy, however, when Bob graduated and landed a high-paying job, except that his work kept him away from home for long stretches at a time. In spite of these separations, their marriage apparently prospered even after their children permanently left home. Bob, assuming they had a perfect union, suggested to Sue now that their offspring had departed that she either join him in the field or he would find a position requiring less moving around. Relating this story over a continuous flow of cocktails, Bob embellished many details of their happy love affair— or so he imagined up to that point in their marriage.

"As a result of our wedded bliss over twenty-two years," Bob stated tearfully, "you can imagine my shock when without warning Sue informed me over dinner one evening she wanted a divorce."

"She had a boy friend on the side while you were in the woods, and I suppose you didn't realize it," I remarked wistfully.

"No, that is not what she claimed, Bill, and I have no reason to disbelieve her. A virgin when we married, I believe Sue remained true throughout our years together, which appeared to be the cause of her distress," Bob murmured, downing another gulp of his booze. "My wife insisted her morals wouldn't allow her to commit adultery. Nevertheless, she wanted an intimate relationship with other men before she became too old, and after months of serious consideration, she decided divorce the only answer. I couldn't dissuade her from the decision."

"With a change of heart, Sue now wants to remarry, is that it?" I questioned.

"Yes and no," Bob responded, as he struggled to refrain from breaking down completely. "That conversation with my wife took place four years ago. After our divorce, she requested a final meeting and insisted she had no boy friends but would be starting from scratch and for three years wanted absolutely no communication between us whatsoever. At the expiration of this term, Sue wanted me to reach her sister for a message as to her whereabouts and then we would decide if either wished to renew the relationship.

"So she must have wanted you after all," I remarked, somewhat sarcastically. "And you have decided to take her back."

"It wasn't all that simple. I never lost my intense love for Sue, but with no guarantee I'd ever see her again, I began living with Mary a year after my divorce. I contacted Sue as agreed, and she pleaded for a complete reconciliation as things had not turned out well for her. To be fair with Mary, I had to consider her position in the triangle, and sever our association as humanely as possible." Drunk almost to the point of incoherence, Bob held his head in his hands and softly sobbed.

"What in hell is the dilemma, Bob?" I asked. "It seems to me the whole thing turned out pretty much the way you wanted."

"Tell me, Bill," he responded. "How would you feel about going back to Joyce after a four-year separation if you had no idea who and what she went to bed with during that period of time?"

"If Joyce and I ever parted, it's doubtful whether I would have any interest in a renewed relationship at all," I replied. "Nevertheless, I admit your situation is unique."

Neither John, Dunc, nor I had drunk nearly as heavily, and so we helped Bob into my car and took him back to their hotel, during which time he mumbled constantly about his impending rendezvous with Sue which would take place in ten days.

After escorting Bob to his room, the two boys suggested we have a nightcap before parting. While sipping our cocktails I remarked that Bob's tale was indeed an unusual story.

Dunc looking at me quizzically, "Bill, I'm not sure the saddest part of the tale is Bob's concern about Sue's romance throughout the past four years. Either he will accept it or refuse to remarry. We have known Bob during the entire episode, and from a happy-go-lucky, well-adjusted human being he has changed into a morose, moody individual. I wonder if Sue expects to welcome back with open arms the same man she recklessly tossed aside. If so, she is in for a terrible disappointment because instead she is going to greet a complete alcoholic."

I often wondered what happened to Bob and Sue.

The 335-mile route to Watson Lake crossed a section of the Rockies where crystal-clear lakes backdropped by ice-covered peaks offered a panoramic spectacular. Summit Lake Pass, mile 392, at an elevation of 4,250 feet, is the highest point on the Alaska Highway. For several miles, the highway paralleled the bewitching Toad River, a swirling shallow ice-blue mountain stream where two moose were browsing on the bank. The Muncho Lake sector is equally beautiful, but the irritation of driving in a constant cloud of dust detracted from my pleasure at viewing the enchanting scenery. After the terror of almost blindly passing convoys of vehicles along the narrow dust-strewn road, I hesitated to remain long in any location and let them all go by me again. In retrospect, I wish I hadn't allowed anything so trivial to interfere with my enjoyment of the gorgeous tableau.

Just beyond Muncho Lake a herd of two dozen mountain goats congregated beside a short strip of macadam on the highway where they obtained salt or other elements from the composition. Bighorns are a rare sight, and so I headed for the Liard River Valley in a better frame of mind.

The forest-rimmed Liard River, a tributary of the mighty Mackenzie, runs for 600 miles through the Rockies in northern British Columbia. In 1942 during the frantic construction of the Alcan Highway, weary crews who had worked toward each other from north and south finally met in the Liard Valley. It had taken those dedicated army men the unbelievable short period of only nine months to complete the vital roadway to Alaska.

At mile 594 I reached the Yukon, a colossal territory covering 207,000 square miles and one of the greatest metal-producing areas in North America. The highway followed the old Yukon Trail where in 1898 a Northwest Mounted Police party blazed an overland route from Edmonton to Dawson City and the goldfields of the Klondike to prove the feasibility of an alternate route to the Skagway Trail. Watson Lake, a few miles inside the Yukon border, is a Royal Canadian Mounted Police post with a radio station and an airfield. Beyond Watson Lake the country flattens out for a hundred miles until nearing the impressive Cassiar Mountain Range. As I moved north, the size and quality of timber had gradually worsened until only scrub poplar and scraggly pine remained. At mile 804, I reached the outpost of Teslin situated on an arm of 72-mile-long Teslin Lake and less than 100 miles south of Whitehorse.

Nearing Whitehorse, I discovered the lure for gold still acted as a magnet to the foolhardy. At a running stream beside the highway, you could pay three dollars and pan for gold. Despite wet, cold weather, the suckers lined up to pay their money and take their chances. I had absolutely no luck at all.

Whitehorse, capital city of the Yukon Territory with a population around 12,000, is 850 miles west of Los Angeles and four time zones behind Toronto. Situated in a mountain range, the town is cradled on a wide bend of the majestic Yukon River which from Whitehorse flows 1,980 miles north into the Bering Sea. The Trail of '98, over which most gold stampeders traveled, began at Skagway on the coast, wound through Chilkoot and White passes to Lake Bennett, and then up the Yukon River to Dawson City. At Miles Canyon, 100 miles from Skagway and near the source of the Yukon River, treacherous rapids claimed many lives and wrecked scores of rafts and boats. A tent city sprang up as sourdoughs sought ways to transfer their freight around the turbulent waters, and Whitehorse was born.

The 335-mile Klondike Highway from Whitehorse to Dawson City follows the original stagecoach route between the two centers. Skeletal remains of old rest houses along the road gave an inkling of the joy passengers must have felt when sighting civilization, regardless of how limited, after traveling through a hundred miles of empty scrubland on a bouncing horse-drawn carriage. Few of the army of goldseekers traveling from Skagway to Dawson in the early years of the Klondike gold rush used the overland route. Once Bennett Lake had been reached, except for the five-mile rapids at Miles Canyon, the Yukon River provided easy going the remaining 500 miles to the strike zone.

The Klondike gold rush played a far more significant part in the opening of the Canadian-American Northwest than most people realize. Edmonton sprang from a village of a few hundred to a city of 10,000 in two years, while Vancouver, Victoria, Seattle, and Tacoma, the other major ports of embarkation to the goldfields, all grew and prospered. In the north, Skagway and Whitehorse were founded, and the immense territories of Yukon and Alaska, previously settled only by Indians, except for a handful of fur traders, was partially colonized from the impenetrable mountains to deep inside their interiors.

Another amazing aspect of the entire affair was the unbelievable short period of time involved from the first strike to the eclipse of Dawson City. In August 1896 George Carmack, with two Indian friends, Tagish Charlie and Skookum Jim, discovered gold on Bonanza Creek, a serenic stream unheard of except by a few prospectors. Less than four years later Dawson City had already become a fading memory. Those exciting forty-eight months changed the lifestyle of a multitude of North Americans, but only the handful there at the time of the strike participated in any significant sharing of the mineral wealth. Each person, allowed one huge 500-foot claim, meant that after 150 claims were staked, everything of value on Bonanza and Eldorado creeks in the gold-bearing area had been taken. Many claims, some of which produced in excess of a million dollars in gold dust and nuggets, were mortgaged, foreclosed on, traded, sold or subdivided numerous times during the following few years.

Dawson City must surely have experienced the most incredulous growth of any human settlement in the history of the world. In August 1896, a peaceful utopia existed where the Klondike River joins the Yukon. Human voices had rarely rustled the leaves. By the winter of 1897, upwards of 4,000 half-starved, frenzied stampeders and gold-crazed miners were ripping, gouging, and tearing the country asunder in their frantic search for gold, wood, game or timber, and a wild, sprawling tent city with less than a dozen buildings splattered the landscape. Despite this inauspicious beginning, by the summer of 1898, it had become known as the San Francisco of the North and had an unimaginable population of 30,000. Pierre Berton, noted Canadian author, claims that Dawson existed as a metropolis exactly twelve months, from July 1898 to July 1899. Berton wrote: "Although it lay in the shadow of the Arctic Circle, more than four thousand miles from civilization, and although it was the only settlement of any size in a wilderness area that occupied hundreds of thousands of square miles, Dawson was livelier, richer, and better equipped than many larger Canadian and American communities. It had a telephone service, running water, steam heat and electricity. It had dozens of hotels, many of them better appointed than those on the Pacific coast. It had motion picture theatres operating at a time when the projected motion-picture was just three years old. It had restaurants where string orchestras played the Largo from Cavalleria Rusticana for men in tailcoats who ate 'pate-de-foie-gras' and drank vintage wines. It had fashions from Paris. It had dramatic societies, church choirs, glee clubs, and vaudeville companies. It had three hospitals, seventy physicians, and uncounted platoons of lawyers. Above all, it had people."

Many of those people later became famous and part of its heritage: Tex Rickard earned a reputation as a famous fight promoter; Alex Pantages owned a string of motion picture theatres; Mack founded Mack Trucks; Sid Grauman became renowned for his Los Angeles Chinese Theatre; and Diamond Toothed Gertie, nightclub owner and entertainer who wore a diamond between her front teeth, was mostly remembered for her allowed statement: "The poor bastards have just gotta spend it, they're that scared they'll die before they have it all out of the ground." There were others, including Robert Service, the bard of the North, who didn't arrive until 1904, although his verse glorified the era and area before that.

Like Barkerville, disaster struck without warning. Fire razed Dawson City in April, 1899, destroying 117 buildings including most of the downtown core. Although the town rebuilt, it never again reached its former glory. By 1899, 8,000 had already left for a new strike at Nome, Alaska, and Dawson City slowly faded into obscurity eventually becoming a ghost village of a few hundred.

Pierre Berton stated that the statistics regarding the Klondike are diminishing ones. In his words: "One hundred thousand persons, it is estimated, actually set out on the trail; some thirty or forty thousand reached Dawson City. Only about half this number bothered to look for gold and of these only four thousand found any. Of the four thousand, a few hundred found gold in quantities large enough to call themselves rich. And out of these fortunate men only the merest handful managed to keep their wealth." Statistics show that from 1898 until 1901, the Klondike produced over 65 million dollars worth of gold.

Dawson City's turbulent history fascinated me. Ramshackle, deserted cabins and decaying old buildings seemed to whisper untold secrets about the depth and range of human emotions that existed during those hysterical few months of the Klondike gold rush.

Boarding a car ferry to cross the Yukon River for my last short stretch of driving before reaching Alaska, I noticed a row of neat new bungalows on the outskirts of Dawson, an encouraging sign that the historic old town was again rising from the dead. The population had risen to 1,100, with tourism the main reason for its insurgence although the price of gold had a few old sourdoughs again digging frantically along the Klondike.

The initial 180 miles of the 380 from Dawson City to Fairbanks, Alaska, was over a tortuous, dusty, bumpy, gravel road that wound through mountain country with deep pine-covered gorges and rocky canyons that plunged straight down from the edge of the highway. I sympathized with families pulling trailers or driving campers because they didn't average fifteen miles per hour. Eighty miles past Dawson City, I finally reached Alaska though still 100 miles to Tok and blessed pavement. What ecstasy I felt when tires hit that hard surface after 1,200 miles of Alcan misery. The final 200 miles from Tok to Fairbanks traversed flat country covered with poor growth poplars and stunted evergreens. At Fairbanks, the official end of the Alaska Highway and my furthest point north by car put me 200 miles closer to Tokyo than to New York City.

Fairbanks, a major commercial aviation center, had its beginning at the turn of the century with the discovery of gold but now resembled any North American community built up in the past half century. The balmy 80-degree temperature, much warmer than I had anticipated so close to the Arctic Circle, encouraged me to tarry for awhile, but except for the weather, Fairbanks contained little of interest. After a day I left for Anchorage.

The excellent highway to the coast offered little in scenic enchantment that I had expected in Alaska except a stretch through Mt. McKinley National Park. Unfortunately, clouds obscured Mt. McKinley, which at 20,320 feet is the highest peak in North America. The Matanuska Valley near Fairbanks, renowned for farming, got its start in 1935 when the U.S. Government resettled farmers from the drought-stricken Midwest. Due to the many hours of sunlight during the summer season, many things grow far beyond their normal size, with cabbages reaching 70 pounds in weight and turnips up to 30.

Anchorage, situated at the head of Cook Inlet with tides from 30 to 33 feet, is Alaska's largest and most sophisticated metropolis. Established in 1914 as the construction headquarters of the Alaska Railroad, it lies as far west as the Hawaiian Islands and as far north as Helsinki, Finland. The city's invigorating climate boasts temperature averages in January of 13 degrees and in July of 57, with an all-time record low of only 38 below zero.

Residents in Anchorage, as in the rest of the state, are fiercely independent and quickly aggravated with the lower 48, especially when there is interference in their local affairs. Many cars ostensibly displayed this annoyance with bumper stickers carrying messages such as: WE DON'T GIVE A DAMN HOW THEY DO IT ON THE OUTSIDE. Another irritation at the time of my visit centered around the delay of Congress in passing a bill for construction of the Alaska oil pipe line that would obviously have brought needed revenue to the state. Well aware of the possible fuel shortage in mainland America, bright bumper stickers again proclaimed this indignation with: LET THE BASTARDS FREEZE IN THE DARK. A movement in Fairbanks and Anchorage aimed at secession from the U.S. was a sign of their impatience but is not likely to gain much support.

On March 27, 1964, the worst earthquake to strike North America according to the Richter Scale, levelled much of Anchorage, killing 115 and causing property damage to reach the staggering sum of a half billion dollars. It was a terrible catastrophe, but visible scars are few.

I had intended to fly from Anchorage to the North Pole but finding it financially unrealistic, I settled for a two-day trip into the Arctic Circle to Kotzebue and Nome. We flew via Fairbanks over Mt. McKinley whose magnificent peak appeared very majestic towering above a shroud of puffy white clouds. Soaring over this vast country I really began to appreciate Alaska's impressive statistics. There are 15 mountain peaks higher than any others in the continental United States; 5,000 glaciers, one larger than the whole of Switzerland; and 3 million fresh water lakes.

Landing at Kotzebue with temperatures in the forties and a light drizzle falling didn't dampen my enthusiasm because it measured up to the summer Arctic weather that I had imagined. Kotzebue, with a summer population of 2,000 and almost exclusively Eskimo, lies 35 miles north of the Arctic Circle. An Eskimo trading center for hundreds of years, people from surrounding villages and as far away as Siberia come annually to the sand spit "Ekiktak" to trade their furs, seals, oil and hides. Captain Otto van Kotzebue, a Russian naval officer, discovered Kotzebue Sound in 1816 in an attempt to find a Northwest Passage. The town named after the Russian explorer is now the polar bear hunting capital of the world. When the ice disappears for a few weeks, families flock to the settlement for fishing and longshoring from which many derive their only income. For 36 days after June 3rd the sun remains above the horizon, and a spectacular ice breakup occurs in Kotzebue Sound, a huge bay of the Bering Sea. Excellent fishing for Arctic shee and salmon follows the breakup, and there is also hunting for the beluga whale. It is a busy and important few weeks in Eskimo existence.

On a treeless tundra, inaccessible by highway, Kotzebue had daily air service but no sidewalks. Sewers and water mains were being installed in the permafrost with four inches of insulation to keep heat in rather than cold out. Permafrost about eighteen inches below the surface is the principal reason no trees can survive, though vegetable gardens thrive.

The Eskimos, a fine looking race, were friendly, and most spoke English with a broad, though pleasant accent. An elementary school had been available for several years and a high school for the past three. Two Eskimo chaps about my age joked about their schooling 35 years earlier when they used polished stones for slates and pointed rocks for pencils. Great strides in the field of education had therefore been made over the past quarter century in Kotzebue.

Bodies are buried in permafrost, and I couldn't help wondering if corpses deteriorated or remained permanently frozen. Deciding the question was too ghoulish, I didn't inquire. Near the cemetery stood an old summer igloo constructed of hunks of sod. Although badly deteriorated, it furnished a good example of the only summer home these people knew until the turn of the century when lumber first arrived.

A variety of entertainment by the Eskimo people at the local auditorium contributed to an entertaining day. I especially enjoyed the blanket toss, a traditional sport originating from a combination of necessity and ingenuity. With no hills or rises of any kind, Eskimos had to find a way of getting a man high enough to sight whales out at sea, and so the blanket toss began. Eskimo children enjoyed themselves immensely and were adroit at landing on their feet after a toss of twenty feet or more.

Dog-sled rides, another favorite amusement with tourists, showed Eskimo resourcefulness at its best. Lacking snow, one Eskimo had affixed rubber wheels to his sled. Using a team of eight huskies, the Eskimo entrepreneur charged one dollar per individual to give them a 200-yard run up the road and back. Within an hour, he had collected fifty bucks which appeared to be one hell of a lot easier than hunting polar bear.

The old distant early warning (DEW) headquarters situated a mile from the village and less than 150 miles from Russia, was still utilized as an American Air Force outpost, and I pitied the poor service men billeted in that bleak environment for any length of time.

One morning over breakfast I had an absorbing chat with an 83-year-old Eskimo named Chester Spivak. Chester, for 47 years a government reindeer herder, wrote a book about his experiences in the Arctic wastelands and offered it for sale at $2.65. Nearly everyone purchased a copy, including myself. The simple manuscript, inexpensively bound, showed that Chester Spivak had also found a profitable enterprise that beat battling the elements. During our discussion he related interesting and exciting stories about his adventures in the frigid Arctic and numerous brushes with death. Chester continuously belittled the soft and easy lifestyle of Americans and vividly recalled his first sight of white people when still a young man living in a village of 3,000 people not too many miles from Kotzebue. A Russian whaling vessel had stopped for supplies, and within three months smallpox and diphtheria wiped out most of the settlement's inhabitants. Before the visit, an Eskimo only died by accident or old age, he claimed, again strongly denouncing the slothful ways of the white man. Enchanted by his yarns and weather-beaten face, I never interrupted the old native until certain he had concluded the conversation. Then with admiration in my voice I asked, "Chester, do you remain here during the long cold dayless winters, or do you return to your village with your people?"

He stared at me for a full minute like I was demented before replying, "My wife and I spend our winters in San Diego."

Though scheduled to visit Nome, we couldn't land due to inclement weather conditions, and so we returned to Anchorage. With little else left to see, I began my return journey south which mostly followed a different route. The Matanuska Glacier, a flowing mass of ice 100 miles from Anchorage, moves relentlessly down the side of a mountain, and confined between valley walls, it crushes everything in its course. A stunning spectacle, it provides an excellent example of nature's unbridled power. A few miles beyond the glacier the mammoth Wrangell Mountains reached into the sky with icy peaks peering down on a lonely world below like a giant watchdog. Steam from a live smoldering volcano, clearly visible on Mt. Wrangell, appeared to be solely responsible for puffy white clouds, the only blemish in an otherwise azure sky.

Rejoining the Alaska Highway at Tok, I traveled that section of road missed on my way north when I detoured up the Klondike Highway to Dawson City. As the first cloud of powdery dust hit my windshield on re-entering the Yukon, I realized how ecstatic I'd be when my wheels finally struck pavement for good somewhere in British Columbia.

A few miles inside the Yukon border, I pulled up for the night at a dingy looking settlement where shabby house trailers provided the only accommodation. Along the Alcan Highway, meals and lodging of any kind were often separated by hundreds of miles of emptiness, and so you grabbed whatever became available whenever you could find it. My stopover turned out to be another of those memorable incidents that occurred throughout my itinerary.

Having no idea what I might locate in the way of eating establishments, I elected to purchase some groceries and cook supper on the small stove included in the unit. It had been a hot, sultry day, and a violent-looking weather disturbance approached the settlement as I returned to the trailer with my supplies. A little early for dinner, I walked over to a small bar a hundred yards from my accommodation for a little libation and to have a more pleasant environment to ride out the impending storm.

Of the half dozen customers in the saloon, two were Indians and one of them wore an American Army uniform. Apparently known by the bartender and waiter due to the personal nature of the conversation, I assumed they were local boys. No sooner had I ordered my drink when the one in uniform came over, stuck out his hand and said, "Hi, I'm Ray, will you buy me a drink?"

He didn't appear inebriated, but not wishing to get involved with a drinking Indian, I decided to play it cool. Taking his hand I replied, "I'm Bill, and I'll be delighted to buy you a drink, but this is all for me. I covered a lot of ground today, and so I'm going back to my unit for some rest."

"Will you buy my buddy a drink also, Bill?" he asked politely.

"Certainly, but after this round I'm leaving."

His friend Henry ambled over in a reluctant manner. A big man with massive bull shoulders, Henry had a mean look on his face. While sipping our whiskey, Ray did most of the talking and openly discussed their predicament. Both from the Yukon, they had joined the American Army and served in Vietnam. Ray apparently had been decorated for bravery while Henry had been locked up for desertion. Out of the service for several months, both were broke, the reason for their brash approach. Ray had several hundred dollars in back pay coming from a horse ranch where he worked and desperately needed some sympathetic individual with an automobile to drive them to the spread 20 miles in the back country for the money. Declining to offer my services and after buying them a second round, I wished them luck and departed. As I left the table Henry muttered something about white men never doing anything for an Indian in need, which I let go unanswered.

Electing to have a quiet drink by myself, I hastened to my quarters just ahead of the impending storm and opened a bottle of whiskey. No sooner had I poured my drink when the heavens opened up with drenching rain and hailstones. My two Indian friends racing past at this moment and seeing my door open leaped inside. Making them stand by the door, I told them to wait until the rain eased, but I wasn't pouring anything to drink. Though Ray remained pleasant, Henry gradually became ugly and made a few detrimental remarks about lousy white men being ignorant and inconsiderate. Deciding I'd better establish myself before relinquishing any further ground, I grabbed the bottle of whiskey by the neck and strode rapidly over to where Henry stood. "Get out that door right now, you ignorant bastard," I hollered. "I buy you, a stranger, a couple of drinks and let you stay in my room out of the horrible weather and all you can do is bad mouth me!" I raved, brandishing the bottle.

"Hold on a minute, Bill," Ray yelled. "You wouldn't throw us out in that downpour would you?"

"I will if your mouthy friend doesn't keep his yap shut," I threatened.

Ray seemed able to control Henry, who began to look penitent. Feeling a little guilty about my outburst, I offered them a seat, then poured each a drink. As things usually work out, once you start socializing over booze, barriers dissolve and a more relaxed atmosphere prevails. Before long, my bottle of whiskey had been drained, and we were chatting like old friends. An hour or more had elapsed and a significant amount of rain had fallen, although it had finally eased up. Ray again did most of the talking, and I enjoyed listening to his experiences with the American forces in Vietnam. When it came time to leave, he pleaded once more for me to taxi him to the horse ranch for his money. Warmed by alcohol and in a more receptive frame of mind, I consented. Requesting ten minutes to get ready, I was astonished when they showed up with a full bottle of whiskey, mix and glasses.

"I thought you were broke, where in hell did you obtain the booze?" I demanded.

"I know the bartender," Ray responded. "When I told him you would drive us to the ranch, he trusted me with the whiskey."

From the highway we immediately struck into a narrow bush trail mostly covered with water from the intense storm. Fortunately the sandy soil, hard packed from the downpour, offered no great obstacle but potholes filled with water were treacherous. I touched bottom in numerous places and therefore traveled about ten miles per hour. After crawling eighteen torturous miles over road even worse than Harcourt Park when we first arrived, the trail came to an abrupt end beside a raging river. Surveying the 100-yard-wide stream of swirling water in the midst of dense forest, I turned to Ray standing beside me. "Now what do we do?" I asked incredulously.

"Follow me for a minute, Bill," he requested, and we took off down a path beside the waterway. Within a hundred yards we came to a landing where a cable attached to large trees on both banks stretched across the raging river. Although the sky had cleared, twilight had faded into nearly total darkness making it impossible to see the other shore. Muttering mostly to himself, Ray mumbled, "The gawd-damn boat must be on the other side. Wait at the car for me, Bill, I won't be more than an hour." With that he leaped for the cable and hand over hand maneuvered himself along its length, his feet dangling no more than three feet above the frothing foaming torrent. Whether pumped up on whiskey or not, it had to be one of the most daredevil stunts I'd ever witnessed, and when he hollered from the other bank, I breathed a huge sigh of relief.

Returning to the car, I found Henry standing beside the waterway, the newly opened bottle of whiskey clutched defiantly, and I sensed trouble. Being no physical match for the muscular individual and not relishing a struggle in that hostile environment, I again reckoned my best defense was a strong offense, and so striding up and grabbing the bottle, I spat out, "Ray said this booze is mine for making the trip, so you drink when I offer it to you and not before." The stunned Henry stood watching me for several minutes as I mixed myself a cocktail while sitting nonchalantly on the hood of my car. Finally, in a very conciliatory tone of voice, he requested a shot. Without argument I poured him one and from that moment, he removed the chip from his shoulder. An army deserter and perhaps a coward as well, Henry apparently didn't discern the fear I felt about my own personal safety in those wild Yukon woodlands.

After an hour and a half had elapsed I began wondering what I'd do if Ray didn't show up soon. Pistol shots shattering the stillness of the summer night suddenly announced someone's approach, and within minutes Ray and another Indian came rowing across the waterway in a small boat attached to the cable by a line and pulley that prevented them from being swept upstream. Ray claimed they fired to frighten off marauding bears, which seemed to fit the locale. The older man with Ray turned out to be Henry's father whom he hadn't seen since being freed from an American prison. Father and son had an emotional but restrained reunion in what I considered to be the most inhospitable surroundings on the planet. After a brief reconciliation, the older Indian jumped into the dinghy and rowed himself back across the stream.

None of us had eaten, and when we finally arrived back at the village, Ray insisted I accompany them to a restaurant that I didn't know existed. Though officially closed, the owners recognizing Ray and spotting his fistful of money opened up and prepared a choice steak dinner with all the trimmings plus a non-ending flow of booze. The happy Indian came away from the ranch with a pocketful of money but spent a good portion of it that night. This devil-may-care attitude seems to depict most Indians' philosophy of "drink and be merry for tomorrow you might be dead." At midnight, with everyone drunk, I silently slipped away to my trailer as I wanted to be on the road to Burwash Landing by 7 a.m. Although suffering with a hangover, I didn't regret the adventure because it furnished me with a different insight about the nature of our native aborigines, and I would not soon forget the courage Ray possessed in making that hair-raising trip across the rampaging river.

Burwash Landing, 100 miles inside the Yukon border was one of the first trading posts established in the territory back in 1904. On a clear day villagers can see Mt. Logan, elevation 19,850 feet, the highest peak in Canada over 70 miles away.

Kluane Lake guarded by Sheep Mountain, home of the Dall Sheep, would be hard to match for breath-taking color and outstanding beauty. I judged it to be the most eye-catching setting of the trip. Kluane, the largest lake in the Yukon at 153 square miles, parallels the Kluane Game Sanctuary and Alaska Highway for 40 miles. Silver City, on the shore of Kluane and site of the trading post, roadhouse, and Northwest Mounted Police barracks from 1902 to 1924, is now an abandoned ghost town.

On my northward jaunt I had travelled the 300-mile stretch between Whitehorse and Watson Lake, and so I hoped to find a new route as I progressed south. At Watson Lake I heard talk of a cross-country trail to Terrace B.C. that would save an unbelievable amount of miles. Despite the fact no one could confirm the existence of such a short cut, I decided the enormous saving in miles and the opportunity to go through country I had never seen made it worth the gamble. Early in the morning I took off for Terrace on a wild goose chase and traveled roads that would have compared with the most challenging automobile rallies. Magnificent scenery including beautiful mountain lakes, green-swathed ridges streaked with unmelted snow, virgin forests and crystal-clear cascading rivers made it a photographer's dream. The narrow trail with U-turns, S-turns, washboardy sections, washed-out areas and choking dust made it a driver's nightmare. The Skeena mountain range followed by the striking Stikines were exceptionally hazardous, and I motored over the final 150 miles directed by lumbermen, as most of that sector traversed private lumber roads. Two antiquated gas pumps operated by Indians who charged prices twice that of normal furnished my fuel needs, and I remained at the wheel for fifteen hours as there were no accommodations before I reached my destination. By late evening, to my everlasting gratification, I finally arrived at Terrace and heaved a huge sigh of relief when my tires finally reached blessed pavement.

Arranging for motel accommodations, I mentioned to the proprietor I'd driven from Watson Lake since 6 a.m. In a rather disdainful manner he insisted such a journey wasn't possible, and so I showed him the date on my previous night's motel receipt. Calling his wife and several others in the motel, he related my story and they looked at me in utter disbelief. The only highway to Watson Lake of which they were aware covered 1,300 miles which would have made my average speed over a hundred miles per hour. No one realized a route of any type existed through that almost impenetrable wilderness. My shortcut of 550 miles, saved 750 miles of torturous Alcan driving, and I was back on pavement, which I didn't plan leaving for a long time.

Throughout my lengthy absence from Toronto I had kept in constant touch with Joyce and the office. Either Sumcot personnel were driving her insane, or she began to get lonesome because my wife joined me in Vancouver for the southern lap of the circuit. While waiting in the west coast city for her arrival, I had my battered automobile rejuvenated. The windshield had been cracked in seven places, my headlamps were smashed, and several small dents marred the paintwork, the result of flying pebbles. To pass the time, I took another delightful tour of Victoria, which I reached this time by ferry, and a closer inspection of Vancouver itself, including a thrilling ride to the top of Grouse Mountain.

Joyce and I had a joyous reunion, and the day following her arrival crossed the border into Washington. In no hurry, we dawdled through the magnificent Oregon countryside, majestic mountain peaks ever visible, before entering California. A couple of pleasant days were spent in San Francisco where we took bus tours of the city proper and a boat tour of San Francisco Bay where a visit to fabled Alcatraz, or "The Rock," proved quite interesting. From California we crossed into Nevada and tried our luck at the Lake Tahoe casinos before continuing to Reno where we relaxed and enjoyed further success at the tables. Ecstatic at leaving Nevada winners, we automobiled across Utah and Colorado where after seven weeks I finally left the overpowering presence of the mountains. In North Platte, Nebraska we arrived during the staging of Buffalo Bill's Wild West Show, which provided an evening of thrilling entertainment. From there we angled northeast back to Canada and home.

Although a long journey, it had been an educational and interesting eight weeks. Northern Ontario with its diversity of terrain always intrigued me. In Manitoba, where my roots are deeply entrenched, I visited old friends, neighbors and relatives. The Calgary Stampede provided thrilling entertainment. Mountains springing out of prairie flats and overwhelming the landscape for thousands of miles was an awe-inspiring spectacle. Barkerville and Dawson City, gold mining towns depicting the rugged individuality of our forefathers and the boundless wilds and outstanding beauty of the vast Yukon territory, had left unforgettable memories. But most of all Alaska, which I reached without major incident, would always remain the highlight, including my hours spent in Kotzebue, within the Arctic Circle.

In the final analysis, I compared the journey to my marriage. Bumpy at times, beautiful at times, but always interesting. I'm not sure I'd endure it again, but I'm glad I did it, because I'd hate like hell to have missed the experience.

Lagniappe

Joyce: My Wife

By the middle 1970s I had been married nearly a quarter century, and life without Joyce now seemed inconceivable. We argued frequently, sometimes violently, but rarely remained angry long. Joyce forgave much more quickly than I. The stormier side of our love affair centered around strong ingredients of stubbornness and quick tempers that we both possessed in quantity, a tough combination for continuous compatibility. Despite our squabbles, she provided enormous comfort through my trying years. Before reaching our silver wedding anniversary, a crisis forced me to realistically contemplate existence without my loving spouse, a situation I found terrifying.

From the day of our marriage, Joyce devoted her life to her family but rarely put our children's interests ahead of mine. An excellent cook and homemaker, she tried to provide an environment to which all members of the household were always glad to return, and she succeeded admirably. Though close to all her offspring, she and Sherree enjoyed an especially warm bond, and in 1974 when Sherree elected to go to Europe to work and travel for several months, Joyce missed her immensely. With an affinity for people, Joyce made an excellent saleslady, and Sumcot's sales department called on her whenever they found themselves in need of assistance. We both loved to gamble regardless the size of the wager, which explained our attraction to the casinos that we visited annually. In 1973, we made two trips to Las Vegas, once as guests of Jack and Barry Ervin and their wives when they earned huge bonuses as a result of Sumcot's record-breaking year. Vegas provided a superb outlet for our frustrations, but we both retained our common affection for Florida and rarely missed spending a few weeks there each year.

596

Joyce didn't hanker to travel as much as I, but in the spring of 1974, I persuaded her to join me on a three-week tour of the Orient, a region I had dreamed for years of visiting. My good friend Ed Miller, newly elected Potentate of our temple, organized a trip to the Far East, and Joyce and I joined Ed, Ruth, and three dozen other Shriners and their wives, including Chester and Kay Schwandt.

Nippon, a Chinese symbol representing the place where day begins or "land of the rising sun," is a popular name for the enchanting, beautiful and strangely exciting Japan. It is a country whose history is lost in legend but steeped in tradition, and whose people, though vastly dissimilar in customs from our own, are a proud, considerate, courageous race with a culture as varied as the centuries that created it. Japan's geographical splendors, equal to any on earth, is a land brought vividly to mind by words such as Shinto shrines, Buddhist temples, cherry blossoms, sukiyaki, sake and geisha girls.

Hong Kong, on the other hand, has a history that spans only a century and a half but has created in that short period of time an aura of intrigue and fascination most countries never attain. Only a pinpoint on the world atlas, Hong Kong, though severely crowded, boasts physical features that are exceptionally scenic and her people represent the worst and best in capitalistic philosophies. The tiny territory, famous for poverty but also wealth and opportunity, sampans, and water-borne people as well as the finest duty-free shopping in the world, is inhabited by a race of people who are aloof but possess a toughness of character and tenacity of spirit allowing them to adjust to almost any condition. When the opportunity arose to travel with the Millers and others to the orient, my fantasy of seeing both of those fascinating lands became a reality, and I looked forward to the excursion with great anticipation.

Though it was a frigid 15 degrees when we left Toronto, mild sunny weather during our two-day stopover in San Francisco warmed our chilled bones. During the ensuing three weeks we experienced a wide variation of thermometer readings. We left San Francisco aboard Japanese Airlines for a five-hour flight to Honolulu where passengers and aircraft refueled in humid 80-degree temperatures before continuing on an eight hour flight to Tokyo. Crossing the International Date Line, we lost 24 hours which threw me into complete confusion; I couldn't figure if it was yesterday or tomorrow. When the luggage arrived at our room in the luxurious Tokyo Prince, I couldn't decide whether to retire, go gallivanting or have lunch, but common sense prevailed, meaning Joyce, so we went to bed.

Temperatures in the forties greeted us for our three-hour Tokyo tour. The second largest metropolis in the world, almost totally destroyed by constant bombing in World War II, Tokyo showed few scars of the conflict. Rebuilt during the American occupation, the city's building styles represented this foreign rule, and most architecture reflected western influence.

The Imperial Palace, an exception as it remained untouched throughout the bombardment, was heavily guarded by Japanese soldiers. The bleak but historic old buildings still seemed to occupy a reverential niche in Japanese culture, as queues of school children and scores of adults constantly approached the palace grounds which are surrounded by a series of picturesque moats.

Olympic Stadium, one of the few remaining Tokyo structures of the 1972 summer Olympics still standing, is located a few blocks from the palace. The massive pool, which can accommodate 1,200 persons, is converted into a gigantic skating rink in winter.

The immensity of the city became more apparent as we bused across endless miles of residential and commercial sectors all jumbled together in an interwoven mishmash showing little indication of zoning procedure.

Included in our morning itinerary, Asakusa Kannon Temple dedicated to the Goddess of Mercy had been restored with great splendor. The temple courtyard, entered through a huge vermillion wooden gate, had a large bronze urn containing hundreds of sticks of burning incense. Japanese visitors usually wash head, hands and clothes with the pungent fumes as an act of purification before entering the temple. The aromatic smoke is also supposed to cure arthritis, rheumatism, lumbago, and assorted other ailments. Though suspicious about the medicinal qualities of the burning incense, it smelled pleasant, and so rather than pass up a chance at such low-cost health insurance, I gave Joyce and myself a little massage. On the narrow street leading away from the temple, the Nakamise arcade, containing rows of bazaar-like little stores, offered a variety of merchandise including sweets, cakes, dolls, fans, kimonos, and a wide selection of souvenirs at remarkably low prices. Kites, tinsel, and good luck symbols gave the charming street a carnival atmosphere, and Joyce together with most of the other ladies preferred browsing in the interesting market place, than inspecting Shinto temples.

The bustling Ginza-Nihonbashi area, the city's chief shopping and entertainment center, was the termination point of the morning's sightseeing. Some of our group including Joyce returned to the hotel with the buses; others remained in the Ginza to lunch and shop. I slowly meandered by foot the mile or so back to our hotel to view more intimately the Japanese people in their colossal metropolis.

I had always found Japanese Canadians to be polite, courteous and reserved. During our morning tour, and while walking back to the hotel, this same urbane attitude seemed to prevail not only toward us but also among themselves. I found it perplexing to associate this chivalrous gentle manner to the same people responsible for the sneak attack on Pearl Harbor, the bloody razing and torture connected with assaults on China, the kamikaze suicidal raids of ships, and other atrocities of war of which they were unquestionably accountable. To gain insight or understanding of this paradox of human nature requires knowledge of the Japanese heritage. Japan's past is shrouded in the mists of time, and of all modern nations, none has a longer or more continuous history. To gain slight glimpses of those early periods requires delving into ancient mythology and archeological findings. By the fourth century A.D. the country had become sufficiently unified to be considered a state, and by the sixth century, Buddhism had been introduced from China, with Confucianism becoming a dominating factor shortly after. Religion has always been an all-pervasive force influencing practically every aspect of Japanese life, for there hasn't been any real separation of religion from philosophy, ethics, and government. By the twelfth century, a great leader, Yoritomo, who took the title of Shogun, meaning military governor, set up a military dictatorship, and for the next seven hundred years, Japan was ruled by warriors. Also in the late twelfth century, feudalism emerged and wasn't abolished until the middle of the nineteenth century.

In recorded history, Japan had not known successful foreign invasion, and they never admitted a stream of immigration. These two realities caused long periods of isolation from the rest of the world, making the Japanese a completely distinct group of people. This combination of Buddhism, Confucianism, feudalism, and almost total isolationism created a mass of people easily directed and led by feudal lords and military leaders. Samurai, the knights of feudal Japan in the twelfth century, were an aristocratic warrior class that lived by military virtues, stressing indifference to pain or death, plus complete and undivided loyalty to their overlords. They adopted "bushido," a code of honor and conduct borrowed heavily from Zen Buddhism and Confucianism which again emphasized complete loyalty to one's superior. The Samurai also practiced austerity, self sacrifice, and the scorning of commerce and the profit motive. Even after the Meiji restoration of 1868, bushido's code of ethics provided the basic foundation for emperor worship. Although abolished in the latter years of the nineteenth century, all statesmen, soldiers and businessmen who took the lead in building modern Japan were members of the Samurai or military class. Taking everything into consideration, it isn't difficult to understand how a race of people trained for eight centuries to believe their military conduct ethically proper and morally righteous would not have created the magnificent, militant warrior class that the Nipponese empire produced.

The Japanese without question are an adaptable people. Though rapidly adopting Western philosophies and technology, they didn't set the past aside, because perhaps nowhere else on earth do the present and past walk so closely together. Japan's transformation from an isolated feudal community to a great power speaks well for the vigor of the nation when considering the process was accomplished in less than a hundred years. In 1854, Admiral Perry, an American Naval officer, forced the Japanese to trade with the West, thus ending their isolationist policy, and by 1941 at Pearl Harbor, Japan had become one of the most industrialized states on earth. The country proved its resilience again in 1946. Physically and economically in ruins and occupied by a foreign power for the first time in its history, Japan again rebounded within a quarter century to a position of envy with all nations.

Tokyo's citizens in particular have proven the tenacity and staying power of the Japanese race. The earthquake of 1923 destroyed half the city and 150,000 persons lost their lives, but they rebuilt. Heavy bombing devastated most of the metropolis during World War II, damaging or destroying many famous landmarks and nearly all of Tokyo's industrial plants, but again they resurrected the city from the ashes. No one can deny the resiliency of the Japanese to spring from the canvas at the count of nine and go on to win the fight. As a former Winnipegger, the city that supplied most of the Canadian contingent at Hong Kong who were either killed, wounded, or tortured during the Japanese assault in 1941, it took a long time for me to forget old hatreds. However, after studying their history, associating with their people, and recognizing their military heritage, they have gained my respect and the debacle at Hong Kong, though no less tragic, became more understandable.

At 4:45 one afternoon we attended the Asakusa Kokusai theatre, with a seating capacity of over five thousand to see an all-girl revue. Settings were brilliant though gaudy, costumes resplendent and the male roles in the revue played by remarkable female impersonators. Japanese business people prefer their entertainment as they return home from work, which accounted for the strange hour, and many in the audience were eating prepared meals from cardboard containers similar to our take-out fish and chips.

Following the two-hour Kokusai theatre show, we bused to the Chinzanso Garden Restaurant for a Mongolian-style barbecue dinner. The Japanese, renowned for undercooking their food, eat species of fish absolutely raw, and so we were slightly apprehensive. Although the potatoes, corn, tomatoes, peppers and onions seemed slightly undercooked, the chicken, pork and beef tasted excellent, and we thoroughly enjoyed the repast.

Early one morning we took the Tobu Limited Express train to Nikko, a spectacularly scenic mountain vacation area about 90 miles north of Tokyo where the eminent Toshuga Shrine, Yomeimon Gate, and Taiyuin Mausoleum are located. Nikko is a magnificent blend of natural beauty and artificial pomp and splendor, scattered graciously among rolling hills and avenues lined with centuries-old cryptomeria. A thirty-degree temperature and swirling snow could have placed the picturesque town in almost any province in Canada, but as we neared the Rinoji Temple nestled against a backdrop of snow-drenched evergreens, an Oriental atmosphere soon replaced any semblance of an Occidental background. The Toshuga Shrine erected in 1636 combines both Shintoism and Buddhism in the art and architecture of the twenty-two buildings of various sizes and styles that complete the shrine.

Shintoism, the ancient native religion of Japan, is still practiced in a form modified by the influence of Buddhism and Confucianism and is not so much a religion as a set of traditional rituals and customs involving pilgrimages to famous shrines and the celebration of popular festivals. This Shinto custom was evident at Nikko where a constant stream of buses unloaded contingents of somber Japanese who slowly and solemnly paid their respects to the historic and beautiful temples. Visions of feudal lords in colorful processions proceeding up the cryptomeria-bordered avenue to the main gate brought the historical significance of the sacred grounds into perspective and made it easier to understand the obvious reverence perceived by the Japanese. The Toshuga Shrine, a breath-taking spectacle of Oriental artistry, was a photographer's dream, but unfortunately we were not allowed sufficient time to properly put in pictures the significant saga of history and painstaking craftsmanship on display.

After a fine lunch at the Kanaya Hotel, we boarded our buses for a thrilling ten-mile drive up the Irohazaka Highway to Lake Chuzenji. The one-way route, a bus driver's nightmare, had a total of forty-eight hairpin curves along the narrow road. Sheer precipitous banks soared skyward on one side of the trail while the other edge plunged straight down into a valley far below. Panoramic views of the forest-covered, snow-laden mountains were scenic, though not comparable in spectacular beauty with our own Canadian Rockies. Monkeys huddled in tree limbs, however, provided an unexpected sight. Somehow I didn't visualize monkeys inhabiting such an inhospitable locale. Clinging tenaciously to the deciduous hardwoods, they too conveyed the feeling they weren't enthusiastic about their environment. Unable to detect monkey footprints in the snow, I surmised they avoided contact with that part of nature's blessing if at all possible, and they had my sympathy. Lake Chuzenji, at 4,171 feet above sea level, reaches a depth of 528 feet, which probably explains why we saw no sign of ice. A combination of lake and mountain created an enchanting vista making it easy to understand the tremendous popularity of the area with local tourists in all seasons. The wind-chill factor reached zero degrees in the mountain heights, and so though an enjoyable and interesting day, we weren't unhappy to reboard our motorcoach for our return to Tokyo.

In our hotel directory, I noticed a massage service available, and so I called the front desk figuring to enjoy a pleasant rub down from a professional masseur while Joyce curled her hair. Joyce answered the door, and we both received a jolt when a small middle-aged Japanese masseuse entered the room. I was a little startled when she got on my back and rambled up and down my spine with her knees, but the massage was nevertheless excellent and relaxing.

Though scheduled to proceed from Tokyo to Kyoto by the 130 mph Bullet Train, we were forced to take the bus due to a railway workers' strike. The 350-mile journey to Kyoto, via Nagoya, traversed country-side contrasting from snow-blanketed mountains to orange groves and tea plantations.

We had a short stop-over at Nagoya, Japan's fourth largest city, before continuing to Kyoto, the cultural heart of the nation. Rich in historic associations and legendary lore, Kyoto contains the finest old relics of the country. A magnanimous decision by the United States to spare the beautiful old city from bombing devastation showered on other centers was greatly appreciated by the Japanese who travel from all corners of the country to visit the numerous shrines and temples situated there. Kyoto, the capital of Japan from 794 A.D. until transferred to Tokyo in 1868, embraces 22 percent of the nation's national treasures. Twelve hundred years of history and tradition are dispersed amongst her consecrated structures. Kinkakuji, or Temple of the Golden Pavilion, a three-story wooden structure covered with 22-carat gold foil, is situated by the edge of a large reflecting pool in a park at the foot of a wooded mountain. Nestled among evergreens, scintillating beams dancing in the morning sun off its golden surface, Kinkakuji Temple was indeed an enchanting vision and is claimed to be the most photographed subject in the country.

Nijo Castle, built in 1603, had been the Kyoto residence of the Tokugawa military regents. Not constructed as a fortress but rather as a semi-fortified park, it contained ramparts, moats, elaborate gardens, and a palace in the opulent painstaking style of the period. Before entering the castle floor area of about two acres, we were required to remove our shoes, not as a gesture of respect but simply complying with a Japanese custom to preserve floors. It's beyond their comprehension why western civilizations mark up and erode good wooden floors with a pair of clodhoppers for the sake of a few seconds to remove them. Inside the castle, authentically furnished rooms had wax dummies representing various personages of the manor from servants to the military dictator himself all clothed in the colorful dress of that period.

The magnificent Heian Shrine, surrounded by beautiful Japanese gardens was the origin of the present city of Kyoto where Emperor Kammu moved the capital of Japan in 794. Elaborate gardens at the Heian Shrine encompassing several acres are designed for strolling and featured small hills, streams, ponds, and many trees and shrubs harmoniously laid out to offer varying views. Elderly folks working in the gardens seemed a strange sight in that advanced society, but menial tasks in Japan are usually performed by older men and women. Certainly in North America it would be unusual to see senior citizens working for a city in such backbreaking endeavors. This attitude regarding physical labor emphasizes one of the tremendous differences in philosophy between East and West. The outlook of the Japanese worker towards employment, whether a factory laborer or a white-collared executive, is far removed from his counterpart in North America. It's difficult for us to accept the rationale of the Japanese who do not work for money as their chief incentive but who are motivated by pride in their work, their company, and their country. For good and loyal effort, employees may be rewarded with automobiles, apartments, paid vacations, or almost any other amenity of life.

Bart McDowell, assistant editor of *National Geographic*, reported in the March 1974 issue that 8 o'clock one morning while visiting a T.V. factory in Osaka he heard the foremen and all the workers sing the company song: "For the building of a new Japan, let's put our strength and mind together, doing our best to promote production, sending our goods to the people of the world endlessly and continuously, like water gushing from a fountain. Grow industry, grow, grow, grow." McDowell continued to say that at 8:30 a.m., when the office opened, all the office staff together with the executive personnel sang it, including the scientists in the laboratories. Our guides stressed that although unions are becoming stronger in the country, they still play a minor role in employee-employer relationships. The majority of Japanese companies pay benefits and bonuses to their employees for loyalty ahead of ability, and seniority plays a major role in the politics of Japanese industry, concepts that come into direct conflict with the policies of most unions.

Before departing Kyoto we visited a Japanese restaurant for a sukiyaki dinner with geisha-girl entertainment. Sukiyaki, a popular Japanese dish consisting of thin slices of meat fried with onions or other vegetables and seasoned with soy sauce, is washed down by warm sake. Geisha girls, heavily made up with a preponderance of white rice powder applied to accentuate the neck, that segment of a girl's anatomy the Japanese consider particularly attractive, are professional entertainers, skilled in dancing, singing and repartee. Their training begins at childhood, and after an apprenticeship, they are usually employed under contract for a number of years. Their social status varies in different cities. Many live luxuriously and have become wives of prominent Japanese. All geishas receive the same basic fee, but actual earnings rest upon a rigid classification of their beauty and accomplishments. Few Japanese girls are interested now in the ancient tradition of becoming geishas, which makes it a problem to find sufficient trainees.

An hour's drive from Kyoto, Nara the first permanent capital of Japan and founded in 706, still remains an important cultural and religious center. One of the chief attractions in that city are the multitude of deer, which roam almost everywhere. Regarded as divine messengers, they browse unmolested around parks, shrines, and temples.

Lunching at the Nara Hotel on a pleasant Sunday afternoon, we witnessed five separate wedding parties. Despite great changes in the Japanese way of life, the institution of marriage and the wedding itself has retained much of its feudalistic charm. Though some modern couples demand a Christian ceremony, the traditional Japanese wedding is usually performed by Shinto rites. The bride wears a strange headpiece supposedly to hide the horns of jealousy growing from her head. Elegant wedding gowns were worn by all brides and the magnificently attired flower girls resembled cute little dolls. Each groom scowled as if bored with the whole affair, but adopting this indifferent attitude is inherent—to show their superior position compared to their new spouse. Our female guide insisted, however, that today's Japanese brides do an excellent job of reversing this age-old belief shortly after the ceremony.

The Kasuga Shrine in Nara, painted in vermillion, is another distinguished temple situated in the midst of verdant woods. Three thousand lanterns, 2,000 stone and 1,000 metal, decorated the shrine area. In Deer Park, adjacent to Kasuga, huge herds of deer browsed everywhere, and though unique, they must become a terrible nuisance at times, particularly to the maintenance staff responsible for keeping the park clean.

Another hour's drive took us from Nara to Osaka through a heavily industrialized section of the country. Enroute we had our usual rest stop, and though amazed at Japanese proficiency in many fields, we were perplexed by their roadside urinals. Setting your feet in cement to prevent slipping, you aimed at a small hole in the floor in an enclosure with precious little privacy. Both men and women confronted similar circumstances and had to be extremely agile to avoid urinating over their feet, which may explain why Japanese take so many baths.

Osaka, the second largest city in the nation and almost obliterated by heavy bombing during World War II, bounded back like Tokyo and remains the commercial and industrial center of western Japan. Our tour of that vibrant metropolis ended the first leg of our journey.

Though excited at the prospect of visiting Hong Kong, I nevertheless regretted not having more time to spend in exotic Japan. We had packed a lot of sightseeing into our short visit but had seen only a trifle in comparison to what had gone unseen.

A complex country, Japan has over a hundred million people packed into 143,000 square miles, of which 80 percent is uninhabitable. This makes it one of the most densely populated places on earth. With the concentration of population in big cities being accelerated by the industrialization of the nation, the present crowded conditions will probably worsen. By our standards, residential areas in towns and cities are almost unimaginable. Back and front yards are nonexistent, and houses are jammed together like sardines in a can. Pollution, one of the country's major problems, makes breathing in Tokyo and other large cities quite hazardous. Electronic signs in the Ginza display air pollution readings for sulphur dioxide and carbon monoxide, just like other cities register time and temperature. Industrial pollution pouring into the sea is poisoning fish in ever-increasing quantities.

Despite these massive dilemmas, the country and its people have many pluses, not the least of which is their indominable spirit and proven ability to meet adversity and defeat it. They have an affection and respect for each other, together with a national pride that few citizens of any country possess, and Tokyo's crime rate is one-fortieth of New York City's, which means you can feel safe walking alone anywhere anytime of day or night. The Japanese are an action-oriented race where working is the important object in life, and pride in that work more meaningful than remuneration. An uncanny aptitude to learn rapidly from others is attested to by their present technological expertise in many areas, and this unique ability together with their strong-willed tenacity will pull the Japanese through most rough spots. Because of their proven power and influence in world affairs, I sincerely hope they remain in the camp of the free world.

We landed in Taipei, capital of Taiwan, for refueling and an exchange of passengers before continuing to Hong Kong where a pleasant seventy degrees greeted our arrival. Our room in the modern Furama Hotel in downtown Hong Kong looked out over a fascinating display of mansions and high-rise apartments that either nestled into or sprouted from heavily treed, precipitous mountain slopes. The impressive setting differed immensely from anything we'd witnessed in Japan, but the next few days would reveal numerous dissimilarities between those two Oriental, human-congested countries.

Hong Kong, a Cantonese word meaning "Fragrant Harbor," obtained its name from the historical fact that Chinese ships used to anchor there to take on water from a nearby spring. A British Crown colony until 1997, Hong Kong with a total land area of nearly 400 square miles, has a population over 4 million. The colony is separated into three principal areas; Hong Kong Island, 30 square miles, ceded to Great Britain by China in 1842 as a result of the Opium War of 1839; Kowloon Peninsula, three square miles ceded to Britain in 1860 as a result of the Treaty of Peking that ended new hostilities; Kowloon and the New Territories, 365 square miles leased to Britain in 1898 for ninety-nine years for the prime purpose of making Hong Kong more impregnable.

On our initial inspection of Hong Kong Island, "Gem of the Orient," it became immediately obvious the customs in the colony were vastly different from those of the reserved Japanese. Street vendors and hawkers of all ages swamped us when we left the hotel and dogged our every move whenever or wherever we debused. We drove through the Chinese commercial center at West Point, then stopped at the western tip of the Island where on December 8, 1941, Japanese troops stormed ashore and, after seventeen days of bitter fighting, overwhelmed the small garrison of Canadian, Indian, and British troops. Aberdeen, Hong Kong's main fishing village on the south shore, contained the lion's share of boat people who lived on up to 13,000 vessels in colony waters. Twenty thousand people resided on 3,000 sampans in Aberdeen Harbor alone. Deep Water Bay on the south shore boasts excellent beaches and a dazzling view of Middle Island and waters stretching beyond to the South China Sea. At Repulse Bay, mountain slopes ring the magnificent estuary and palatial mansions and high-rise apartments anchored to the rocky inclines have views across the sparkling blue ocean waters and scattered islands that would be hard to surpass for breath-taking beauty.

Tiger Balm Gardens, the local Disneyland without rides, provides quite a contrast to the natural beauty of the region. The park covers eight acres and cost 16 million Hong Kong, or 3¼ million American, dollars when constructed in 1935. Grottoes and pavilions displaying effigies from Chinese mythology predominate the grotesque setting. The founder of Tiger Balm Gardens, Aw Boon Haw, a Chinese millionaire and philanthropist, received the Order of the British Empire from King George VI in recognition of his contributions to social welfare in Malaya. The garden, constructed on a hillside facing Causeway Bay in Victoria

Harbor, contains gaudy displays of Chinese architecture, terra-cotta figures of Chinese myth and legend, and a 145-foot, seven-story pagoda, one of the landmarks of Hong Kong. Haw Par House, the most impressive structure and Aw family mansion, contains the finest collection of jade in the East but unfortunately is rarely open to the public.

The Aw brothers made their fortune manufacturing and selling Tiger Balm, a mentholated cure-all prepared from animal fat and reputed to be good for coughs, colds, headaches, rheumatism, neuralgia, gout, sciatica, lumbago, sore throat, toothache, asthma, scorpion bites, stings, cuts, cramps, all chest complaints, and other assorted maladies. Joyce bought a jar which cost one dollar because she figured we could drop our hospitalization coverage and save a bundle of money. Tiger Balm Gardens, colorful though bizarre, stirs different emotions in people. James Kirkup, noted author and traveller who wrote numerous books on different cities of the world, including Hong Kong, wrote: "It was a pity that the famed philanthropy of the Aw brothers had not devoted itself to the relief of the thousands of poverty stricken children and their parents living in cardboard and reed hovels scattered like dark scabs all over the hillsides round what now seemed to me to be the garden's wickedly cynical and self-indulgent piece of self-aggrandizement on the part of the creators. The contrast between all that bizarre ugliness, in all its hideous color and tasteless exhibitionism, with the malnutrition, disease, loneliness, destitution and child-exploitation of those miserable hovels covering the hillside around it, was too much for me to stomach. I went to the Tiger Balm Gardens once, but never went back again."

I didn't entirely agree with the sentiments of Mr. Kirkup. Impoverished people all over the world pay out their last few pennies to build or beautify a temple, church, or shrine to enable them to escape their miserable existence, albeit temporarily. All the money spent on Tiger Balm Gardens spread equally among the Hong Kong needy would amount to less than two American dollars per person. If that money would have greatly improved the shabby conditions of the poor, then Mr. Kirkup is certainly correct, but if the destitute obtain some pleasure in colorful Tiger Balm Gardens because it removes them for a short time from their hovels, then Mr. Kirkup's opinion is incorrect.

From Tiger Balm we circled Victoria peak and were rewarded with fabulous views of Hong Kong Island and Victoria Harbor, the watery crescent of commerce dividing the island from Kowloon beyond. Considered one of the finest harbors in the world, Victoria Harbor is also one of the busiest, with ships in a steady stream loading and unloading freight from a diversity of nations.

At the southern extremity of Victoria Peak, we lunched at the Tower

Peak Restaurant 1,305 feet above sea level and offering another spectacular panorama of the region. From Victoria Peak we took a tram down the seemingly perpendicular mountainside to within a few blocks of our hotel.

One afternoon while Joyce and Kaye Schwandt went shopping, Chester and I took a stroll a few blocks around the vicinity of our hotel. A wide selection of public transportation serviced Hong Kong Island, single and double-decker buses from London Transport, creaking double-decker trams, a huge fleet of mini-buses that picked up and let off passengers any place along their route at minimal fare, and a profusion of taxis. A new law prohibiting the issuance of any more rickshaw licenses because the government felt it too demeaning for one human being to transport another meant rickshaw transportation was gradually dwindling. Nearing our hotel, Chester and I encountered a rickshaw operator anything but demeaned. Spotting my camera, he motioned for Chester to get aboard his conveyance for a picture after which he positioned me in the rickshaw so that Chester could perform the photography. Pleased with the Chinaman's cooperation and courtesy, Chester handed him several coins. When the Oriental went into a tantrum, we assumed he was insulted with Chester's offer of money, but it soon became apparent he wanted a damn sight more than coins. After a little haggling, he agreed to settle for ten Hong Kong dollars. Chester and I simultaneously handed him ten dollar bills, and the cheeky buggar grabbed mine while making a lunge for the other. I jostled him enough that he missed Chester's sawbuck and the comical character went trotting up the street laughing convulsively, at which point I snapped the best picture of the lot.

It's only a ten-minute boat ride across Victoria Harbor to Kowloon, and ferries leave every ten minutes from early morning to late at night. A multitude of ocean-going vessels and smaller craft plying the harbor attested to the importance of the waterway as the principal mode of transportation in the colony, and it became even more obvious that Hong Kong belonged to the sea. A tunnel running under Victoria Harbor connects the two centers and has taken some of the strain off the ferries, but a five Hong Kong dollar toll each way on the underpass compared to the quarter fare on the ferry means boat transportation will continue to provide the chief means of passage for local pedestrians.

We boarded the Kowloon-Canton railway for a short trip to Sha-tin, passing through resettlement sections of Kowloon. Squalid sectors being resettled were indescribable hovels of human habitation which clung precariously to rocky slopes and made each new apartment building look like the Taj Mahal in comparison. But when you consider that 20 square feet or a room 10 feet by 12 feet was the total allotment for a family of six, you wonder how there could be much improvement in their lifestyle. In addition to their room, they shared communal kitchens and toilets. Some squatters preferred their self-built, makeshift shacks with horrible sanitation, hand-drawn water, and fire hazards. This was understandable, as the wretched huts did offer more privacy and a greater sense, however pathetic, of family and individual proprietorship than the standardized units. Bamboo poles thrust out each apartment window with fluttering newly washed clothes appeared like distress signals, and you couldn't help reflect on the giant rehabilitation problem Hong Kong has faced since 1945.

At its birth as a colony in 1842, five thousand Chinese farmers were Hong Kong's total inhabitants. Following the Japanese occupation in 1945, less than a half million people resided there, but after stable British rule returned, Chinese immigrants and refugees poured in at a rate often exceeding 100,000 every month, until now over 4 million inhabit the colony. Clothes-draped apartment buildings are considered a giant step forward by many Chinese, and hundreds of thousands of applicants await openings in these instant cities. At the time of our visit, 600 massive units had been constructed, housing over 1¼ million souls. Despite this herculean effort, hundreds of thousands still lived in shantytowns, and Kowloon's apartments aflutter with Hong Kong's "national flag" will be a symbol of the colony's distressed housing for generations.

Richard Hughes, an Australian, wrote in his book *Hong Kong*: "By normal western standards the Hong Kong housing blocks, even the latest, could not be termed luxurious or spacious, but they are better than Shanghai's or Peking's Communist effort at re-housing. And plenty of dwellers in Glasgow's Gorbals, London's East End and New York's Harlem would prefer them. As in Shanghai, the contrast should not be with today's standards in non-slum western cities but must be with yesterday's standards in Hong Kong and Shanghai." An interesting observation that emphasizes the old adage that beauty is in the eyes of the beholder.

The Kowloon-Canton train stopped at the Chinese border where passengers with proper credentials could walk across the boundary line and continue to Canton on the Chinese segment of the railway. Leaving Kowloon and entering the New Territories, impoverished looking tenements were replaced by lush fertile farmland in a valley surrounded by verdant hills. Sha-tin on Sha-tin Harbor appeared prosperous with tanned and healthy-looking school children smartly dressed in matching tunics, a stunning contrast to the British tommies in full battle dress patrolling the harbor.

Boarding a fishing junk for our coastal water cruise, we had a prime opportunity to witness at close quarters the lifestyle of the most interesting inhabitants of the colony—the "waterborne people." In many ways they seemed better off than their brethren who went ashore to eke out a bare existence in the steamy factories and resided in rat-infested shacks. Most families in sampans earn a reasonable living from fishing or cargo carrying, although fish in local waters are rapidly disappearing. Often now in search of fish, junk dwellers run head-on into modern politics of which they have little knowledge or concern. Their nets have always followed the fish wherever that led, and their junks have always run before a gale to shelter wherever offered, which might well be Communist China. As a result, most of the Hong Kong fishing fleet is also registered in China, and a certain portion of the catch must be landed there. Family life aboard junks has to be complex because large families have little chance for privacy, but in comparison to the cramped quarters of a Hong Kong or Kowloon tenement, they are no worse off. One of the unfortunate aspects of life on the boats is the children's lack of opportunity for education, though more and more are put ashore for learning. Education in Hong Kong is neither free nor compulsory. Youngsters aboard the sampans looked hearty, and teenagers, accustomed to hard work from an early age, appeared strong and wiry. Their parents also seemed to possess a certain gaiety and freedom of spirit lacking among Chinese on the streets. Sea people have few pleasures and entertainment, but in the evening when congregated in some sheltered harbor, there is time for visiting and gambling, and they often spend hot summer nights playing mahjong on their sampans till dawn, purchasing beverages, fruit and even cooked meals from vendor sampans that are floating delicatessens.

Heading out of sheltered Sha-tin Hoi, we moved into the open expanse of Tolo Harbor where ocean freighters shared the sea with the junks. Hamlets and villages nestled into the mountain greenery overlooking peaceful waters of the China Sea were in sharp contrast to rows of camouflaged British tanks and armored vehicles that almost invisibly hugged the mountain slopes within two miles of the Chinese border. A small contingent of British troops stationed in the barracks not more than four miles from the border seemed like an ant facing an elephant. British soldiers, or for that matter the entire English community, rarely fraternize with the Chinese, and I doubt if the Chinese feel much loyalty toward the Union Jack. The skeleton British Army stationed in the area wouldn't last as long against the Chinese Army as they did against the Japanese in 1941 if the Chinese Reds really decided they wanted to occupy Hong Kong. Maybe I'm a coward, but if Red China said they wanted the colony, I'd surrender before they crossed the hundred-yard-wide Sham Chun River boundary.

Due to shallow water, the large junk transporting our group couldn't get closer than a quarter of a mile to land and our parked buses, and so we anchored to a family sampan in a sheltered harbor. Waiting my turn to board the small vessel transporting our entourage ashore allowed me an opportunity to examine the Chinese junk more closely. Sampans are constructed with a similar hull shape to the *Santa Maria* used by Christopher Columbus. With lack of proper ballast and a high flat stern, the junk is not particularly seaworthy but is ideal for loading or hauling freight and for living space. Many junk dwellers would live no other way, and generations have known no other life. Their number is declining, however. A large percentage of younger people are leaving to work in factories, and with the gradual depletion of the fish population, it is generally conceded that waterborne people will be a memory of the past by the end of the century.

The small water craft carrying our group could only hold a half dozen at a time, and so numerous trips were required. A woman sculler, the sole power, toiled steadily and diligently while her husband stood poised on the bow like Lord Nelson aboard his flagship and barked instructions, unmoved by his wife's physical efforts.

Back aboard buses, we skirted Tolo Harbor to the village of Tai Po where we toured a Hong Kong carpet factory. Women laborers wore dour expressions and paid little heed to the tourist invasion, which perhaps reflected their inner feeling toward the obvious affluence of our group. Male factory laborers in Hong Kong worked six ten-hour days; women, six eight-hour days. This earned them sufficient income for a minimal existence. As a result of this regimen, it is not difficult to understand why their sympathies often lean toward their Communist brothers, even though their parents escaped from Chinese Communism only twenty years earlier. While old people are content to have found a haven, the younger generation want more, and people under twenty comprised more than half the total population. Few countries are left in the world where the contrast between rich and poor is as accentuated as in Hong Kong. In the past decade, the colony replaced Japan as the center for cheap labor. The government had made several noble efforts to improve the standard of living, but didn't get much cooperation from wealthy factory owners. Those owners or their offspring might regret this apathetic attitude if the giant Red Dragon on their border becomes annoyed because they can't expect much support from the impoverished masses unless a stronger effort is made to improve their lot. A genuine trade union movement in Hong Kong would improve conditions and wages. The government did attempt to train union leaders in western methods, but a majority of the local populace showed little interest in what they referred to as "obscure alien tricks."

We bused within a quarter mile of the Chinese border to the Lok Ma

Chau crossing station. A steep incline lead to a promontory with an excellent view of the Sham Chun River, the border between Communist China and the New Territories. Gazing across the flooded fields and visualizing hundreds of thousands of refugees struggling across that open plain in the past quarter century searching for a haven from Communism seemed unreal. The peaceful pastoral landscape contrasted vividly with the bustling, frantic activity of hawkers and peddlers occupying the sightseeing location on the hill. Comparing the two scenes with a simple turn of the head provided a picture of complete contradiction. Across the Sham Chun River was the tranquil countryside of the most populous nation in the world who preached and practiced a philosophy downgrading the bourgeois as conniving materialists, while a few yards from their border members of their own nationality ardently exercised the technique of capitalism with all its entrepreneuring aspects. Why Red China allows the existence of Hong Kong to practice a philosophy entirely opposite to their teachings is a mystery to many. When considering that Communist Chinese banks operate in the colony along with seventy other financial institutions belonging to most of the trading nations in the world and Chinese Communists annually dip out a full third of their nation's foreign exchange from those banks, it becomes easier to understand their indulgence. In my opinion, if the Chinese don't renew the lease for the New Territories in 1997, at the very least they won't destroy the system.

Chatting with a Hong Kong border policeman, I asked why no Chinese police were in sight. "No one tries to escape into Red China," he replied sardonically.

Returning to Hong Kong along the southern perimeter of the Territories, we had a picturesque view past Tsing Yi Island into the boundless blue reaches of the China Sea. Then, approaching Kowloon and as unexpectedly as a summer thunderstorm, we were back between rows of clothing-decorated apartment complexes. A sense of human congestion soon replaced the feeling of spaciousness we'd attained in the New Territories. Recrossing Victoria Harbor again by boat, ocean vessels visible far out into the evening mists made an impression that still stands out in my mind. The pulsating activity of commerce on the sea is most representative of bustling Hong Kong.

On a tour-free day, everyone including Joyce and the Schwandts, took advantage of the world's finest shopping at duty-free prices. Not being a shopper, I grasped the opportunity to visit Macao, the oldest permanent European settlement in the Orient, dating back to 1557 when it became a permanent Portuguese trading port.

Macao lies 40 miles west of Hong Kong across the Pearl River estuary and only 65 miles south of Canton in Red China. Portuguese-controlled

Macao was connected to Hong Kong by an impressive system of hydrofoils that left each city every half hour from 6:30 a.m. to 6:30 p.m. on a 1½ hour crossing. Each hydrofoil, carrying a hundred passengers, was nearly filled to capacity. For my Macao city tour I selected a pedicab with a guide and pedalist named Henry, a Chinese Communist by self assertion. Negotiating the fare for my 2½ hour tour, he nevertheless showed enterprising capitalistic tendencies. Henry settled for 25 Hong Kong dollars. Because he was knowledgeable and spoke fair English, he was worth every cent.

Macao, attached to Kwangtung province of China, is situated on a peninsula about 2½ miles long and 1¼ miles wide at its widest point. I spent fifteen minutes in one of the five gambling casinos in the colony but didn't test my luck because it was jammed with hundreds of wagering Chinese. Roulette, high-lo, fan tan, blackjack and chemin-de-fer tables were crowded, but one crap table and the American-manufactured slot machines were getting scant attention. The gambling crowd, almost exclusively Hong Kong Chinese, explained the busy hydrofoils.

Henry pedalled me slowly into the downtown business section over cobblestone streets where antiquated buildings and shops gave every indication of their 400 year history. A large majority of Macao residents are Chinese even though the Portuguese influence in architecture and mannerisms is apparent. Communist China did a thriving trade with Macao, and Red Chinese licensed vehicles hauling huge quantities of foodstuffs and a wide assortment of manufactured goods into the region, were a common sight on city streets. Henry hauled me up one of the seven hills that make up the colony, and I got another excellent view across the Pearl River of Macao's giant Communist neighbor. The Pearl River, dividing the colony from its titanic neighbor, is 200 yards wide, and in the 1950s, like the Sham Chun River in the New Territories, provided a major crossing point for hundreds of thousands of refugees fleeing Communism. Many remained in Macao, but a majority wound up in Hong Kong. In 1966, when Mao unleashed the Red Guards on tiny Macao, it appeared certain the colony had reached its finale. Portugal, finding it impossible to meet all demands of the Reds, requested a month's grace for its citizens to evacuate the colony with only their personal possessions. At that point the Chinese bullyboys paused, brooded, and then backed off, making it obvious they didn't yet wish to kick the Portuguese out and absorb Macao physically. The Chinese wanted to smear the Portuguese flag but not tear it down, and perhaps like Hong Kong, they considered it too valuable for providing desperately needed hard currency and outlets for trade. Approaching Barrier Gate, Henry warned me against any attempt at picture taking, and as I strolled toward the entry point with my camera strung around my neck, a burly policeman stepped by my side and remained there until I re-boarded the pedicab. My affable guide claimed the hulking guard would have torn my camera asunder if I had ventured to snap a photograph.

Henry delivered me back to the harbor in time to catch the late-afternoon hydrofoil, and I awarded him a substantial tip, being well satisfied with his informative tour. Peering into his impassive Oriental face when he gratefully accepted the money, I wondered if his pro-Communist sentiments were as strong as he indicated or whether Henry felt the inevitability of a Red Chinese take over and wasn't gambling at being found in the wrong uniform.

Joyce and I spent our last evening in Hong Kong at the Metropole, a Chinese theatrical restaurant which served delicious food. Crystal chandeliers and lavish furnishings in an Oriental decor enveloped the nightclub in a special Hong Kong atmosphere, and a galaxy of pretty Mandarin singing stars performed a variety of routines, including the popular lion dance. The excellent meal and enjoyable performance furnished a pleasant finale to our Hong Kong itinerary. Having a few hours in the morning before departure, Joyce and I strolled downtown, and both agreed a few more days in that tropical hodgepodge of contradictions would have been enjoyable. Hong Kong is without doubt an astonishing paradox. The vast majority of Hong Kong's 4 million people are Chinese who speak little English; its 50,000 Europeans speak little Chinese. By a strange osmosis they are bound together by a powerful, almost mystical desire to profit, each to his own standard. Occidentals consider Orientals as being steeped in mysticism with strange beliefs and unusual cults, but in Hong Kong all races practice the cult of making money. This blatant capitalism flourishes under the shadow and with the blessing of the giant Red Dragon, whose basic philosophy is the destruction of the bourgeois. I fervently hope Hong Kong continues to prosper as an example of the power of self-determination.

We flew back to Tokyo for refueling before continuing to Honolulu, the end of the tour, where we luxuriated for 48 hours beside beautiful and enchanting Waikiki Beach before returning to frigid Toronto.

The Orient tour provided Joyce and me with our first real opportunity to be away from Toronto for any period of time without concern for our family as Sherree had now reached nineteen. Another pleasant offshoot of the journey was the intimate friendship we developed with Chester and Kay Schwandt. Although I had known, respected, and had large business dealings with Chester over fifteen years, Joyce and Kay had been only casual acquaintances. The trip provided an opportunity for the four of us to get to know each other.

Despite the fact business boomed throughout 1974 and 1975 and our profit margin soared, Sumcot continued an incessant battle with the different government agencies to obtain final approval for the balance of the developments. I had turned much of the responsibility over to Ron MacMillan, our engineer, and then after he resigned in 1974 to Doug Prue who showed excellent ability in persuading local municipal governments to see things our way. Nevertheless, in the final stages of obtaining ratification, I had no alternative but to join the fray and suffer the usual aggravations in dealing with bungling bureaucrats.

The more commitment I demanded from my remaining managers—Barry Ervin, Terry Mackey, Doug Prue, Edwina Seddon, and my brother Jack—the less time I felt obliged to spend at the office. As a result, I seldom remained home for long stretches at a time. Joyce had no real reason to remain behind, but her aversion to constant travelling meant I frequently roamed alone. Up to this point, Las Vegas had remained the one place we always went together, but in 1974 and 1975, I visited the glittering capital of Nevada eight times, and on half of those junkets, I went solo.

Fate had determined the mid-1970s to be especially traumatic for Joyce. Due to the amount of loving effort she put into the welfare of her family and the time she devoted to working with the company, Joyce had little opportunity to meet people other than Sumcot-related individuals. As a result, her personal female friends consisted almost entirely of neighbors. Etta Dobson, in Joyce's age bracket, who lived across the street, had become particularly close to Joyce. After a painful and lingering illness, Etta died of leukemia in the early summer of 1974. Watching her close companion waste away before an untimely death played havoc with Joyce's emotions, as it was her first experience with the Grim Reaper except for the passing of her mother, another Etta. Dot Grace and the Schramms paid a visit to Toronto a week before Etta's passing, which helped considerably, and I took Joyce to Las Vegas a few days after the funeral. But her melancholy attitude didn't dissipate rapidly. In August, I joined Jack and Shirley in Winnipeg for ten days to attend several functions including the 25th wedding anniversary of my old friends Cora and Dode Bell. Jack, Ed Barham, and I also spent a fascinating few days fishing and camping in remote regions of mammoth Lake-of-the-Woods. Joyce's mental state had improved considerably upon my return from Winnipeg, and so I accompanied a hundred other male members of the Toronto Board of Trade on a month's tour of Balkan Europe, which I will deal with in the subsequent chapter.

Shortly after returning from Europe, I joined Ed Miller's entourage to Vancouver for the Grey Cup festivities, and again Joyce had no desire to go along. Her spirits lifted when we decided to sell our Banstock home and move into a deluxe two-story townhouse that she adored. When we accidentally bumped into Edna Branning working as a waitress in a Scarborough restaurant, Joyce again became slightly despondent. We had lost touch with Edna following Lorne's death. Nevertheless we both felt close to the woman who provided the first loan to get me started in business and who remained a steadfast friend to both of us. Joyce yearned to help Edna find more lucrative employment, but without any skills other than waitressing, it was impossible. Nonetheless, we decided to keep closer in touch with our old friend and include her as often as possible in any of our social functions.

Again to jolt Joyce from the doldrums, I persuaded her to join me, together with the Schwandts, Millers and two dozen other Shriners and their wives for a jaunt to California on a two-week tour that included a variety of entertainment.

Our first stop was San Francisco, which provided a fun-filled two days as we attended the East-West College football Shrine game and attendant festivities. The sudden death of beloved Jack Benny slightly tempered our felicitous mood. Chester and Kay Schwandt joined Joyce and me on a three-day side trip to Las Vegas before rejoining the rest of our group at Los Angeles for New Years, the Rose Bowl Parade, football game, and accompanying merrymaking. Before returning to Toronto, we spent a further few days at the Vegas gambling tables. Throughout the two-week journey, Joyce's health gradually deteriorated, but with little serious thought to the problem, she delayed going to see her doctor until mid-February. Our family physician recommended she visit a gynecologist who arranged to perform a D & C in April. While operating, this specialist noticed something amiss with Joyce's internal organs, and after a few days of testing, he discovered she had cancer in the cervix.

Undescribable terror must surge through a person's consciousness when initially receiving the shocking news they have contracted cancer, and the helpless feeling loved ones experience is also pretty traumatic. The following three months were a nightmare for all of us. Joyce suffered terribly for several weeks with radiation treatment which terminated with a radiation implant at which time she had to lie almost motionless for over a hundred hours. Though my tough little spouse endured the physical torment with little complaint, the mental anguish while waiting to know if the operation would be successful became difficult to bear. This period of uncertainty was also unimaginably distressing for the rest of the family and myself. When Joyce received the news she had licked the malady, our joy knew no bounds. The dreaded disease had luckily been discovered before it reached her lymph glands and perhaps this saved her life. When doctors informed Joyce the operation had been successful and no further sign of cancer could be detected, she received the tidings with joy and immense relief.

Nevertheless she would live with fear of a resurgence for the balance of her life and frequently would return to the cancer clinic for a check up. Not only would she be forced to live with the foreboding of a relapse but would also suffer with major bowel and other internal problems for the rest of her days.

If I had any suspicion of Joyce's condition in October, 1974, six months before the discovery of cancer, I unquestionably wouldn't have made the trip to Eastern Europe. Fortunately for me, this was not the case, and I thoroughly enjoyed my month's journey through those Communist countries.

Chapter 4

The Iron Curtain

Certainly the 1970s increased my knowledge of the world and its inhabitants, but no trip broadened my thinking more than the time spent in the Balkan countries. The itinerary allowed me to see first hand a part of our planet I had often thought of a great deal. My traveling companions, members of the Toronto Board of Trade, helped make the journey more interesting because they were mostly businessmen like myself and offered a great diversification of opinions about our communist counterparts.

Though thrilled to be visiting cities that contributed to our turbulent past, comparing the rigid regimes of the Balkan nations to the freedom of our own democracies provided the greatest incentive. To defend our system, I wanted to be knowledgeable in theirs, and so I prepared for my tour with an open mind and was delighted at the prospect of getting a peak behind the Iron Curtain.

Winston Churchill coined the phrase Iron Curtain, a dividing line between capitalistic western Europe and the eastern Communist Bloc countries. The expression "Iron Curtain" generally imparts a sensation of fear in people due to the heroic tales of thousands who successfully escaped or the fate of those who met a tragic death attempting to flee the confinement of communism. Although most nations attempt to poison the minds of their citizens against those countries whose ideologies are opposed to their own, a multitude of mortals did die in their courageous effort to reach the freedom of the West, which leaves little doubt about the aspiration of many of their citizens. The actual conditions of those masses forced to live in a society of secret police, rigid government controls, lack of political freedom, and the ever-present Russian Red Army would not be simple to ascertain. However, I intended to try to

618

determine if certain aspects of communism are superior to our own form of government.

The historical aspect of the region also provided a great inducement to me. Cradled in West Africa and nurtured along the shores of the Mediterranean Sea, our ancestry nevertheless matured in Europe. That continent with a heterogeneous multitude of religions, cultures, racial backgrounds, and political tenets has existed for over 4,000 years. The pages of history are filled with episodes of human suffering as well as chapters of outstanding achievements. Huge empires slowly developed, flourished, then disintegrated into individual states. By the twentieth century, no less than thirty independent countries existed, each steeped in a maze of historical events that would take a lifetime of study to completely absorb and understand. Our visit to eleven cities in ten countries over a period of a month would therefore allow only a fleeting glimpse into the variance of human existence resulting from hundreds of generations of turmoil.

Our large entourage of a hundred Toronto Board of Trade members plus a mountain of attendant baggage left Toronto one evening in late September to fly nonstop to Holland. Several hours were spent in Amsterdam touring that interesting Dutch city before continuing to West Berlin. In accordance with an agreement by the four protecting powers, aircraft are confined to three narrow air corridors through East Germany to reach West Berlin. West Berlin, a capitalistic oasis surrounded by a Communist Empire, is a fact not immediately evident by the attitude of its inhabitants but which became more obvious during the two days of our stay.

Our quarters in the Kempinski Hotel offered the common European caravansary custom of conveniently placing mini-bars in rooms. Unless you carefully scanned the price list, however, that quaint practice could become a sudden jolt to your wallet at check-out time.

On our first evening I meandered down the Kurfurstendamn, an avenue that portrays Berlin and Berliners like no other area of the city. An aisle of glittering lights and the hub of the world for most West Berliners, it reflects the lively spirit of a people separated by 110 miles of hostile territory from their West German brethren. Corner pubs and sidewalk cafes provided forums where students, philosophers, and business people discussed the topics of the day over coffee or steins of German lager beer. Several Berliners noticing my Canadian lapel pin sat down and chatted in fluent English. Teenagers in jeans simulated the scene in any comparable establishment in Canada. But separated by 72 miles of barbed wire and a system of hidden death strips from their countrymen, their outlook on life seemed more serious than their North American counterparts. As a matter of fact, thousands of the restive younger generation were constantly leaving for less restricted areas. Completely obliterated in 1945, the Kurfurstendamn had been totally reconstructed except for the jagged ruins of the old Kaiser Wilhelm Memorial Church left standing as a reminder of the horrors of war. Shops along the avenue displayed a wide range of consumer goods, and street vendors in sidewalk stalls selling souvenirs or a variety of German delicacies were well patronized. Strolling back to the Kempinski Hotel, I tried to visualize those dramatic hours of May 2nd and 3rd, 1945, just prior to the capture of the metropolis by Russian troops. For 48 hours a Soviet artillery barrage of unprecedented intensity demolished an already battered Berlin, which Hitler and his mistress had abandoned two days before by committing suicide in a bunker of his Chancellery on the Wilhelmstrasse located in East Berlin. I fervently hoped those young and happy faces I met in the pleasant open-air restaurants and along the Kudamn will never experience the terrors of a war such as their parents survived, even though their nation caused the holocaust.

After a short briefing session one morning by the Canadian Embassy staff, we boarded our buses for a tour into East Germany, one of the only Communist countries with whom Canada had not established diplomatic relations. The United States officially recognized the East German government four weeks prior to our visit. Canada's Department of External Affairs adopted a strong stand against East Germany's refusal to allow any of its citizens to be reunited with their families in Canada who migrated before the days of the Iron Curtain. East Germany's reason for this seemingly cold-hearted decision was their critical shortage of manpower.

Approaching Checkpoint Charlie to cross into the German Democratic Republic, a sense of trepidation came over me as though I was entering an unknown jungle without a weapon. Having never heard or read anything complimentary about the Iron Curtain countries, I, like most people in the West, harbored suspicions about all their ominous customs. Communists are generally believed to be waiting their opportunity to annihilate the bourgeois and fulfill the premise of Lenin, the original Russian Bolshevik who advocated an immediate and violent revolution to bring about the downfall of capitalism and establish an international socialist state. Lenin expostulated the Marxist manifestation of creating a system in which property and the means of production would be held in common by all members of society and not by individuals, a complete contradiction to capitalism. Capitalism is defined as an economic system in which the ownership of land and natural wealth, the production, distribution, exchange of goods and the operation of the system itself are controlled by private enterprise under competitive conditions and with little government interference. Although I didn't consider Canada a truly capitalistic society as originally spelled out, this would be my first glimpse into the communist world.

Due to my advancement from a penniless itinerant in 1949 to a person of some affluence, I, more than most Canadians, should extoll the virtues of our form of government and abhor any consideration or sympathy towards communistic precepts. During my travels, however, and observing the horrible conditions existing in countries where a majority of the population grovels in pitiful poverty while a fortunate few luxuriate in unbelievable splendor, I know unrestricted free enterprise is not the system that will erase the sordid conditions of those millions of unfortunate souls. Degrading conditions exist in many parts of the world that are not communistic. Among them are the Bahamas, India, Jamaica, Hong Kong, many African, Oriental and South American countries, and unfortunately, right in North America. History also reveals that Balkan European peasants had always suffered from indigence, and I wanted to see how they presently faired under a socialistic regime.

At Checkpoint Charlie, the principal entrance from the American zone into East Berlin, a brusk, young, well-spoken East German male immediately replaced our amicable West German female guide. Although exceedingly opinionated about the well being of the German Democratic Republic, he willingly answered questions or debated any point anyone wished to discuss dealing with his country or its politics.

East Berlin had a population of slightly more than a million, compared to West Berlin's 2¼ million. The city core had been entirely rebuilt since the war, and so historical buildings were few. Our tour appeared more political in essence than a sightseeing jaunt. Shortly after leaving Checkpoint Charlie, we entered the Unter der Linden, considered the most beautiful promenade in Berlin for over 200 years. The avenue's old structures, completely wiped out like most of the city were being rebuilt, with some restored to their former elegance from old detailed models that still existed. We lunched on the banks of the Spree River, which together with the Dahme bisects East Berlin and joins the Havel River in West Berlin at Spandau. Located in that area is the famous prison which housed Nazi war criminals, of which Rudolph Hess remained the lone inmate. Our guide made certain we stopped and inspected a memorial dedicated to victims of fascism, militarism, and all fallen resistance fighters against imperialist wars.

Turning off Unter der Linden, along the Friedrichstrasse and down a side street to the Platz de Academie, we visited the French Cathedral built in 1685, and directly across the square, the splendid Berlin Cathedral constructed for the reformed community. Karl Marx Allee, formerly named Stalin Allee before that man's name became an imprecation to the world and the Communists in particular, lead us to the Marx Engels Platz where we debused for a short break. Brandenburg Gate, a world-famous landmark situated in East Berlin near the Wall, can be viewed from either city. Built from 1788 to 1791 and intended to be a symbol of peace, it became one German project that seriously backfired.

In spacious Treptow Park stands the magnificent Russian memorial. At the entrance are the words: "Eternal glory to the heroes who fell for the liberty and independence of their socialist homeland." Commemorated in 1949, it has a 45-foot bronze figure of a Soviet soldier atop the mausoleum with a lowered sword looking out over a broken and trampled swastika. In his arms he holds a German child. Backdropped by stately silver firs, the front court of the monument has a stone sculpture of a mourning Soviet mother, and at the base two statues of bareheaded soldiers kneeling on stone pedestals. The striking memorial and startling statistics of Russian soldiers killed during World War II gives us cause for reflection and the Soviets ample reason to honor their dead. The *World Almanac* records that 7½ million Russian service men were killed out of the 12½ million who served, a staggering 60 percent. Not included are the many wounded. In comparison, the United States had 12¼ million men in uniform and suffered 293,000 casualties or approximately 3½ percent, an incredible difference. Another war memorial in Berlin was erected by the Russians before the division of the city ended up in the American zone, but an agreement between the two nations allows the Russians to keep an honor guard at the monument 24 hours a day.

I obtained a copy of a booklet our East German guide had for sale with substantial information about his country. Their version and explanation for the erection of the infamous Berlin Wall made interesting reading. One chapter, under the strange heading "The Wall of Peace" read in part: "In the early 1950s, West Berlin became the cold war stronghold of the Imperialists against the entire socialist camp, and more than 80 centers for agents and espionage were established. An American radio station and the western press poisoned the atmosphere and through hate propaganda deliberately set out to entice scientists and specialists away from the German Democratic Republic (G.D.R.). In 1953 armed gangs entered East Berlin with the intention of creating a civil war, however the Soviet Union and German workers formed armed groups for the protection of the republic and the expected victory did not materialize. In spite of this the GDR kept the borders to West Berlin open hoping that an understanding would be achieved in the interests of West Berlin. The contrary happened. The hate campaign of the press, the enticement and acts of sabotage increased and the cold war threatened to become the Third World War. In August 1961 the

National People's Army and worker's militia overnight secured its borders against West Berlin. According to estimates the GDR lost 100,000 million marks through the open border, money desperately required for construction work. The closing of the border brought an immediate and discernible easing to the situation and with new vigor the Berlin people started constructing their capital city." Undoubtedly the statement contains a portion of the truth because although we know the Communists are the world's finest propagandists, we're also aware of the covert activities of the American C.I.A. and their interference in foreign affairs. The Bay of Pigs fiasco in Cuba and involvement in Brazil and other Central and South American countries are prime examples.

The West Berliners also proffered a booklet and their published viewpoint differed drastically from their brethren on the east side of the wall, as shown by an excerpt from their publication: "History and contemporary political conditions endowed Berlin with a situation it did not seek and the German question has yet to be solved. Even though Berliners may now be parted by the wall, their common way of life, their community of thought and political conceptions will prove far stronger than the separation conditioned by time. The wall cannot and will not be viewed as one of the wonders of the world. Built in 1961 by German Communists in agreement with member states of the Warsaw Pact, its brutal force and repulsive ugliness are there for all to see. The wall has become a visible symbol of Germany's unnatural division. The divided capital of a divided land lies in the very heart of Europe and West Berlin serves as the link between the parts of Germany. The city symbolizes the will, both in East and West, to be free. This city tells the world that the Germans yearn to be a single nation, even though their country may still be divided."

In April, 1968, East Germany passed a new constitution, purportedly approved by 94½ percent of the electorate which reaffirmed Communist one-party rule and close ties with the USSR. This edict declared German reunification could take place only on the basis of socialism, and so only time will tell the ultimate destiny of the unfortunate divided capital city and nation.

The usual bureaucratic delay encountered at Checkpoint Charlie on re-entering West Berlin gave me the opportunity to observe the impassive faces of young German soldiers and police at the border. I wished I could have known their inner feelings about the Communist regime and their Soviet protectors. Twenty Russian divisions stationed in East Germany supposedly counterbalancing NATO forces in Europe was a presence deeply resented by many East Germans.

Our West Berlin tour began at Olympic Stadium. The giant arena erected in 1936 accommodates 100,000 fans but is still too small for the soccer enthusiasts in the city. Only a pile of rubble in 1945, West Berlin boasted 350,000 new buildings at the time of our visit, a colossal undertaking over a thirty-year period. The Reichstag, former German Parliament where Hitler got his start and also flattened, was not resurrected but converted into a park where flower gardens provide a scenic contrast to the horrors conspired there. A victory column erected in 1870 commemorating a German victory over the Turks furnished visual proof the Germans didn't lose every war. Following the last conflict, architects from many parts of the world assisted in Berlin's reconstruction resulting in a great divergence in building styles. The Tempelhof Memorial commemorates the gigantic airlift by France, England, and the United States in June, 1948, when the Soviets, in an attempt to force the Allies out of West Berlin, cut all land and water routes connecting the city to the rest of West Germany. Between June, 1948, and September, 1949, the Allies made 277,728 flights into the blockaded metropolis. At the peak, cargo aircraft landed in West Berlin at the rate of one very forty-five seconds. That massive show of power by the Allies has often been credited as the turning point in the cold war with the Soviets. Nearing our hotel we passed a section of canal that bordered the grim, nightmarish Berlin Wall. Crosses erected at several points marked where unfortunate victims had been killed by East German snipers as they crawled from the water attempting to escape into West Berlin and freedom.

During the journey I wrote my sentiments regarding the tragic Berlin situation in my personal log. I doubted if the city would be united in the foreseeable future and believed it inaccurate to condemn the East Germans for their actions over the past fifteen years without considering their point of view. An article by a noted American journalist in a 1970 edition of *National Geographic* stated: "Immediately after the war the Russians took from East Berlin entire machine factories, automobile works, chemical and power plants, everything down to cattle and timber, stripping the eastern part of the shattered Reich of fully 50 percent of its industrial capacity. Some industries, such as those producing plywood, precision machinery and optical instruments, lost more than 70 percent of their plants. The value of dismantled properties, profits and goods diverted to Russia totalled between 10 and 12 billion dollars. In contrast, the shattered economy of West Germany soon began to receive huge infusions of American funds, part of the Marshall Plan's program to restore economic health to Western Europe."

East Germany's distressed condition in early 1961, prior to the wall's construction, left little choice for those in charge but to make a determined effort to prevent desperately needed able-bodied humans from fleeing west where living conditions were much superior. East Germans, like all mortals, will improve the lot of their family or themselves at any given opportunity. Unfortunately, everyone couldn't escape, and therefore if East Germany intended to exist as a nation, drastic action had to be taken to prevent the loss of critically needed manpower. The East German Republic not only survived but increased its standard of living to heights undreamed at the time of the wall's erection. In spite of their labor shortage and exclusion from most of pre-war Germany's natural resources, except for some soft coal, they skyrocketed to 9th position in world trade, a miraculous accomplishment in such a short span of time.

Mr. Howard Sochurek, author of the *National Geographic* article referred to earlier, reported a conversation he had with Mr. Dellheim, a German who fought in the last war with the British Army against his Fatherland. In 1963 he returned to East Germany of his own volition. The managing director of an East Berlin factory, Mr. Dellheim was quoted as follows: "I receive a salary of 2,599 marks a month which equals about $625 and all my workers may receive an annual bonus of an extra month's pay as a production incentive. I am completely responsible for the development of this plant and the sale of our machines. We give the state 20 percent return annually on its invested capital. Our production is sold out for the next three years. We used to compare ourselves to the Soviet Union. Now we are striving to be the best in Europe and after that we'll look to the United States, and be better than you are."

Mr. Sochurek also reported a discussion with a Mr. Wegwerth, managing director of another East Berlin firm. He asked him to account for the boom in the G.D.R., and Mr. Wegwerth replied: "We are Germans. This boom can be attributed to the German mentality and to the indestructible optimism of the German spirit. We have had to accommodate to many kinds of government, but the only measure of merit is accomplishment."

I also left East Berlin with an opinion. I seriously doubted if they would have faired any better during the previous quarter century under any other form of government. It strikes one how unfortunate it is that Communists can't enjoy freedom with their politics, but perhaps that is one of their few strengths rather than one of their many weaknesses.

From West Germany we flew into Poland traversing the identical terrain crossed by the German Air Force on its infamous initial attack in 1939. Approaching Warsaw, I vividly recalled the fateful morning when squadrons of Nazi bombers flew that route triggering the horrible slaughter of World War II and razing the city we were now about to visit.

Driving rain combined with a temperature in the low forties produced a raw, uncomfortable environment for our circuit of historic but hapless Warsaw. Warsaw has known little else but foreign invasion and occupation by alien soldiers from its very beginning. It fell to the Swedes in the mid-1600s was captured and occupied by the Russians in the latter part of the 1700s, and then came under Prussian rule in 1795. Napoleon liberated the city in 1806, but it again came under Russian control in 1813. Warsaw, the principal center of an unsuccessful Polish insurrection against Russian occupation in 1830 was occupied by the Germans in 1915. In 1920 the city once more bore the brunt of the Russo-Polish war when Polish troops finally defeated the Russians. Regardless of the destruction endured by the metropolis over seven centuries, the appalling six years during World War II provided the greatest nightmare. Dwight D. Eisenhower, who had inspected Berlin, Cologne and other devastated cities, said as he trudged through Warsaw's shattered ruins that the 85 percent total destruction appeared far more tragic than anything he'd ever witnessed.

Slowly plodding along narrow, rain-drenched streets to the new "Old Town," I tried to visualize the scene of desolation the Russian troops beheld on entering the city in January, 1945. The only two buildings still standing in the Old Town area were roofless, but those two scarred, skeletal structures became the cornerstones of the miraculous reconstruction of Warsaw. Artisans had rebuilt the old market district with loving faithfulness from paintings by an 18th century artist. Complete with wrought-iron lanterns, cobblestone pavement, and multi-colored plaster, the square has been restored to its baroque elegance and serves as a shrine to Poland's past. Millions of zolte spent in the restoration of the old capital city caused some Poles to criticize the expenditure, believing the money could better have been used for more hospitals, apartments, and schools. The Old Town had been one of Poland's national treasures, however. For centuries, scholars, artists and patriots had lived on or near the old market square, and Marie Curie, co-discoverer of radium, lived nearby. Jozef Sigalin, the city's chief architect, speaking on behalf of a majority of Poles, expressed it adequately when he said, "Our people felt they had no birth certificate until Warsaw lived again."

Polish officials showed a short film of Warsaw produced by the French shortly after the war which left a lasting impression on all who viewed the appalling but excellent creation. It began with scenes of Warsaw's splendor prior to 1939, and then film recovered from Nazi planes displayed actual scenes of the barbarous bombing and artillery barrage preceding Warsaw's capture by German troops. Perhaps the most horrifying segments included demolition of the ghetto after the Polish-Jewish insurrection in 1943, and the systematic destruction of the city on Hitler's orders following the Polish underground rebellion in 1944, leaving the city an indescribable desert. The resurrection of Warsaw stands as a monument to Polish pride, fortitude, and determination. Groups of school children with their teachers toured the restored buildings, and their young happy faces reflected none of the abominable experiences etched vividly on the countenance of their elders.

Many notable prewar buildings had been reconstructed or were under construction, including several famous Roman Catholic churches. Holy Cross, the fifteenth century Church of our Lady, and St. Martins near the Old Town, were both piles of rubble where people sifted through debris to salvage any usable items. Hanging in the new St. Martins, a bronze statue of a headless Christ provides a grim reminder of the structure's sorrowful past. A few blocks from the old square, an ancient palace had been almost restored to its original elegance. That area witnessed the worst fighting in the 1944 uprising of the Polish underground against the Nazis. In the center of the square stood the city's oldest statue, an old Polish King dating back to 1644. Our local guide told me that his father, who fought in that section of the city with the Polish resurgents, watched in horror as German artillery fired at the historic old memorial for an hour before scoring a direct hit and toppling it to the ground.

The woeful tale of the Jews during the last conflict probably proffers the most shocking drama of Warsaw's troubled past, and the figures are staggering. At the onset of the war 1½ million Jewish citizens comprised 45 percent of the city's population. In 1940 the Germans isolated these hapless people in a ghetto where they were steadily starved to death or murdered in crematoriums. By 1943, a pitiful 70,000 remained, and they staged a heroic but hopeless uprising with homemade weapons and bombs. With no hope of victory, they only wished to kill as many Nazis as possible before being killed themselves. German troops mercilessly stormed the ghetto with tanks, planes, and artillery and then slaughtered the 40,000 survivors. Only 200 Jews remained alive at Warsaw's liberation. Scenes from the film of Warsaw showed the ravaged ghetto in 1945, a wasteless desert inhabited only by a hoard of rats. A large statue now stands in the midst of the old Jewish section in memory and as a tribute to those ill-fated victims of another nation's insanity, but it does nothing to erase the revulsion one feels at the incredible slaughter of 500,000 innocent human beings.

Mutual admiration between the Poles and Russians doesn't exist due to centuries of turmoil between the two nations, and the past 30 years did nothing to strengthen any bonds of friendship. Poles remember the Russians marching into their country from the east sixteen days after Hitler's onslaught from the West. They haven't forgotten the hundreds of thousands of their citizens sent to die in Siberia during the occupation. They also remember the German announcement in 1943 of the discovery of a mass grave of 10,000 Polish officers allegedly executed by the Russians. And finally they will always remember that the Russian Army sat idly on the banks of the Vistula in 1944 during the courageous battle waged for Warsaw by the Polish underground. However, the Polish masses also consider the other side of the coin. In 1939, neither Britain nor France came to her aid in terms with their agreement, even though those countries did declare war on Germany, nor did any of her Allies come to Warsaw's assistance during the 1944 uprising. Poland also recognizes the fact she shares a 770 mile common border with the USSR with a population only 14 percent as large. Perhaps the biggest plus in their sentiment toward their giant Soviet neighbor is that the Russians eventually liberated them from the hated Germans. Therefore when taking all things into consideration, they do not question the Soviet alliance or complain too bitterly about the Communist regime as long as their standard of living continues to improve.

Drab describes most of Warsaw's new architecture. Poles caustically referred to it as Stalinistic Gothic, vintage 1925. They pointed out, however, that they had little choice being entirely segregated from anything but Russian design and planning following the war. As a gift to Poland in the late 1940s, Stalin sent 5,000 Russian technicians and workers to erect the needle-spired Palace of Culture and Science, which dominated the city's skyline. The thirty-story skyscraper cost 34 million dollars and contains 2,300 rooms, three theaters, two motion-picture halls, museums, nightclubs, and a swimming pool. Its prominent tower, visible from almost any point in the city, is a constant irritant to many Poles and satirical stories circulated about the building. Two examples of these witticisms are: the best place to take a snapshot of Warsaw is from the Palace of Culture because from that vantage point you can eliminate the monstrosity from your pictures; and the rooms in the Palace are more expensive than other hotels because from their windows you don't have to look at the Palace of Culture. Personally I thought the edifice looked rather imposing, but then I'm not Polish.

Poland now trades extensively with western democracies and has greatly increased exports to the free world. The nation has ample resources and ten centuries of struggle have toughened its people to meet any emergency. They would therefore appear to have a bright future if they can keep the doors to the free world open and appease their Russian neighbors. Like the Japanese who rebuild after every earthquake or the Italian on the slopes of the Vesuvius plains who replants his vines after each eruption, the Polish, it seems, are also indestructible and have the will and stamina to overcome any catastrophe with which they are burdened.

After Warsaw's drizzle and chilly weather, we delighted in bright and warmer temperatures in Prague, Czechoslovakia's capital city. One of the most picturesque cities in Europe, Prague with a population of a million, has a history dating back to the 7th century. Known as the city of a hundred spires, Zlata Praha, possesses a regal beauty that has been praised down though the ages by poets, artists, royalty, and commoners. Prague spans the Vltava River, and like Rome, it is built on seven hills. As in Rome, all her varied architecture—Romanesque, Gothic, Renaissance, baroque and 19th century modern—exists together in serene harmony.

Prague lies in the center of Bohemia, the chief state that together with Moravia and Slovakia forms the Czechoslovakian nation. Bismarck, Germany's Iron Chancellor said in 1886: "Whoever is master of Bohemia is master of Europe. Europe must, therefore never allow any nation except the Czechs to rule it, since that nation does not lust for domination. The boundaries of Bohemia are the safeguard of European security, and he who moves them will plunge Europe into misery." Those immortal words proved to be a tragic prophesy from the man whom Hitler admired and imitated but nevertheless ignored, as Czechoslovakia became one of the first unfortunate victims of his abomination. At first the Fuhrer ruthlessly carved the nation into sections and handed chunks to Poland and Hungary, but within a few months he repossessed all the country and placed it under German occupation. For six years the Czechs suffered terribly, and thousands of innocent people were put to death. Miraculously though throughout the past two major conflicts, historic, magnificent, Prague received no war damage and her many hoary palaces, churches and monasteries still thrust their ancient spires heavenward as they have for over nine centuries.

Prague's history dates back to the 7th century when Slavic tribes settled among the rolling hills. Situated in the geographic center of Europe, the city has played an important role in the annals of the continent and the world. Czechoslovakia became a Communist country by free election in 1946, and although democratically oriented, the country adopted socialism willingly and remained friendly with Russia and her Balkan neighbors. Despite the nation's political turn to the left, their democratic background and love of freedom caused a liberalization movement that spread explosively throughout the country. In July, 1968, the USSR and other Warsaw Pact countries demanded an immediate end to the trend away from hard-core socialism, and a few weeks later, Russian, Polish, East German, Hungarian and Bulgarian forces invaded Czechoslovakia and ended their attempt to combine freedom with communism.

On our tour of fascinating Prague, several structures dating back hundreds of years left a lasting impression. The old Charles Bridge spanning the Vltava (Moldau in English) River originally constructed in 1357 still stands as a monument to the city's romantic history. Queen Anne's summer palace with its symmetrically landscaped grounds and punctuated with artistic fountains and statues provided an insight into the pride citizens of Prague take in their historical landmarks. Hradcany Castle is particularly memorable for more than one reason. Not just a castle, Hradcany actually comprises an entire borough of Prague. Hradcany Castle, or the Palace of Prague, is a cluster of ancient buildings where the Hapsburgs operated their empire. The massive palace complex, a many-winged structure, required two hours of walking to partially inspect. Original palace structures of the 9th century were wooden forts. In the 12th century, a newly constructed stone fortress began a long history of building that carried on into the 20th century. Within the walls are three huge courtyards, and the buildings portray every architectural style known to Prague, including Gothic, Renaissance and baroque. Wandering through the ancient chambers an essence of age permeates the air, and the Middle Ages suddenly come alive. The crack of lances and pounding hooves as knight broke lance with knight in jousting tournaments of those bygone days seem to echo down the musty hallways. The palace library contained a priceless array of ancient tomes. Authentic 500-year-old printing presses, aged woodcarvings and statues were on display in the hallways, and valuable paintings and splendid murals adorned the walls. Other elegant castles adorn the city including the Czernin Palace and Walstein but Hradcany is by far the most enchanting.

Numerous magnificent monasteries and churches also grace Prague although the Gothic Cathedral of St. Vitus remains the most historic. Built originally in the 10th century, it was destroyed and rebuilt under Charles IV and contains the tombs of Good King Wenceslaus, St. John of Nepomuk, plus other kings and emperors. St. Vitus, the church's namesake, had become famous for curing youth, both physically and mentally. When the emperor urged him to abandon Christianity, St. Vitus refused and was cast into prison where legend contends St. Vitus could be seen dancing night after night with the angels. As a result he became known as the patron saint of dancers, and therefore the connotation of the disease, St. Vitus dance.

Beautiful Prague and in particular Hradcany Castle will long linger in my memory, not only because of the area's historic elegance, but while gazing at one of the panoramic views of the city from the castle complex, I slipped and tumbled down a flight of stone steps, breaking my finger and almost my neck.

One bright afternoon I took a walking tour from our hotel to the Old Town Square and passed by the oldest Jewish synagogue in Europe, dating back to 1270 and one of Prague's finest examples of early Gothic architecture. In 1945, the town square became the scene of heavy fighting between resurgent Czechs and Germans, although the city received virtually no damage. The aged town hall boasts one of the most fascinating clocks in the world. Every hour on the hour, Christ and the twelve apostles move past a little window in the clock face, followed by several statuettes. The captivating spectacle attracts a sizable audience at each performance.

Although peace reigned during our visit, the square traditionally has been the site for public manifestation. In 1905, workers demonstrated there for the right to vote; in 1918, an uprising against political injustice occurred; and in early 1968, crowds congregated in the old plaza urging the government of Alexander Dubeck to greater democratic and liberal reforms. During August, 1968, however, Soviet and Warsaw Pact troops made it abundantly clear that liberalization was not the Communist way. Strolling through the Old Town Square surrounded by buildings featuring architectural styles of many eras, I recalled an article written by a well known American traveller and author after his visit to Prague in the early 1970's. He wrote following Russia's intervention and maintained that the most unusual aspect of the 1968 affair was that the Czechs didn't rebel against communism as many people incorrectly believed. In fact writers, intellectuals and reformers who urged the liberalization program were all staunch Communists. No one wanted to leave the Warsaw Pact and change the main tenets of the system. They simply wanted to combine positive features of socialism with those of Western-style democracy: state ownership plus freedom. Czechoslovakians have always retained close ties with their Russian Slav brothers, and even when Soviet troops entered Prague in 1968, the questions asked a thousand times by Czech students and reformers were: "Why did you come? We didn't call you. You were our greatest friends. Why did you turn into enemies?" Few alien Communist troops now occupy Czech soil, but bitterness caused by a political blunder will require generations to heal thoroughly.

We visited several of Czechoslovakia's hundreds of castles, churches, and monasteries, but historic Prague is the hub of the nation. A German novelist, Friedrich de la Notte Forque, described the city quite appropriately: "Kingly Prague, indescribable, incomparable is the splendor of thy churches, the beauty of thy palaces." Pope Pius II found Prague the equal of Florence, and the famous French sculptor Rodin called it the Northern Rome. To fully appreciate its historical grandeur, the fascinating city required a substantially longer visit, and I hope one day to return. Perhaps by then it will be enjoying the freedom it deserves and longs for.

From Prague we flew to Vienna—back into the land of the free. Vienna held a special treat for me because Sherree, touring western Europe, had arranged to coincide her Viennese visit with mine and awaited me at the modern Intercontinental Hotel when I arrived. Toronto Board of Trade executives arranged for my daughter to participate in all of the Board's activities throughout our Vienna itinerary. To add to our enjoyment, competent Chuck Minns, our accompanying travel agent and good friend, obtained a room for Sherree in the luxurious Intercontinental, and so she and I spent most of our Viennese visit together.

Three of Sherree's school mates traveling Europe and also in Vienna joined Sherree and me for an enjoyable evening in Grinsing, famous for wine cellars, cabarets and taverns where lilting Viennese melodies floated through the open doors. The following morning, in perfect weather, the two of us joined our group for a bus trip to romantic Vienna Woods, which isn't a park or forest but a geographic name given to a large range of rolling wooded hills extending from Vienna's doorstep to the outposts of the Alps. Country roads lined with a variety of trees, hoary old castles, modern lodges plus quaint little villages and hamlets punctuated the lush, hilly countryside, making it obvious why the Woods is a popular playground for Viennese citizens.

Following an interesting stopover at Heiligenkreuz Abbey, we traversed rolling meadowland to Myerling. That village contains the hunting lodge where in 1889 Archduke Rudolf, heir to the throne of Austria and Hungary, shot Maria Vetsera, his 18-year-old girlfriend, and then himself. Considered one of Europe's greatest tragedies of which the circumstances have always remained a mystery, the murder-suicide unquestionably altered the course of history in that part of the world. Just beyond Myerling, the Liechtenstein Castle surrounded by colorful softwoods, presented a picturesque scene in its preserved sanctuary in the Vienna Woods. We had a delightful two-hour lunch break at Baden, a village of 22,000 and a famous spa dating back to Roman times. Its sulphur springs have attracted the ailing from all over the world, including Franz Joseph, Peter the Great and other famous personages. Disaster struck after World War II when, until 1955, the Russians made it their military headquarters and occupied the hotels and other buildings. They left the village in a dilapidated condition, but at the time of our tour, Baden showed indications of recuperating from the wanton destruction. We returned to Vienna through miles of vineyards which produce the finest red wine in Austria. Many gallons of this exquisite nectar consumed during lunch and the return journey made it a merry and noisy bus ride.

Though it was chilly and raining, Sherree and I devoted a full day to touring charming Vienna, first with the Board tour and then on our own, absorbing as much atmosphere as time would allow. Vienna, the melting pot of Germanic, Slavic, Italian, and Hungarian peoples and cultures, has a recorded past that precedes the birth of Christ, when Roman legions encamped at the Celtic village, then called Vindabona, along the banks of the Danube. Famous for centuries as the musical capital of the world, it was the home of Gluck, Hayden, Mozart, Beethoven, Schubert, Brahms, and the two Johann Strauss'. The center of Austrian art, learning, and industry, Vienna is also renowned as a metropolis with a multitude of magnificent buildings. In its days of glory, the city had a population of over 2 million, but those numbers shrank to 1½ million as a result of World War II. One hundred thousand Viennese fell at the front, 50,000 Viennese of Jewish faith were murdered, 35,000 died in their resistance to national socialism, and 24,000 more were killed in air raids and during the Russian artillery bombardment of 1945.

Sherree and I spent most of our morning at the resplendent, luxurious Schonbrunn Palace, summer residence of the Hapsburgs. In 1696, Leopold I constructed the existing edifice but various rulers, including Maria Theresa, added vast improvements and additions, including a zoological and botanical garden. The Palace contains an unimaginable 1,441 rooms, with no bathrooms but with 139 kitchens. The building and its gardens occupy an area of over 700 acres. The incredible splendor of the castle and its multitude of rooms with their glittering history and brilliance of decoration and ornamentation would take volumes to describe thoroughly. At legendary Schonbrunn, meaning "fine spring," Marie Antoinette played as a child, and Napoleon's son grew to manhood and died as the prisoner of Metternick. The dazzling millions room which Maria Theresa had panelled in precious rosewood and decorated with gilded arabesques at a cost of 900,000 golden crowns exceeded the entire cost of construction of Votivkirche, another famous Vienna landmark. Forever imprisoned in the walls of The Hall of Mirrors are the unspoiled notes of child prodigy Mozart who played there before royalty. Another dramatic leaf from the past is Napoleon's apartment where the lordly conqueror of Vienna lived in 1805 and 1809 and where his son Reichstadt died at the age of 21. A Chinese Cabinet Room designed by Maria Theresa had a circular section of floor that could be lowered to one of the kitchens below, enabling the ministers of state to continue their deliberations uninterrupted after lunch and prevent the servants overhearing confidential conversations.

Like trying to conceive the distance to the stars, the overall opulence of Schonbrunn baffles the imagination. It would be impossible to estimate the construction cost of the gigantic castle in today's inflation-riddled world or the number of servants and workmen required to keep those massive chandeliers, thousands of gold-leaf panelled walls, and the huge magnificent tapestries and intricately inlaid floors all in immaculate condition. Fuel consumed by those unique stoves to keep the palace warm in winter would also stagger our believability. Those days of lavish splendor will never return to Vienna, and it's doubtful anyone really wants them back. Schonbrunn Palace nevertheless occupies a remarkable niche in Europe's chaotic history, and imagining the strains of Johann Strauss' "Emperor Waltz" echoing along those miles of corridors during imperial festivities of ages past will always keep that history alive.

From Schonbrunn we visited the Lower Belvedere Palace, summer home of Prince Eugene of Savoy. Completed in 1721 and though simple in appearance, it is an excellent example of Baroque architecture.

Sightseeing spectacles in Vienna seemed endless. The university built in 1873 in Italian Renaissance style includes such famous names among its scholars as Freud and Adler; Rathaus or City Hall, erected in 1872 is Gothic but also incorporates Renaissance elements; the Johann Strauss Monument, unveiled in 1923, is a tribute to one of the world's greatest composers. Perhaps the magnificent cathedrals, reflecting 1,100 years of history and changing building styles, were the most intriguing. Reprechtskirche, Vienna's oldest, is a Romanesque structure with Gothic elements; Michael's Church, founded in 1221, was repeatedly destroyed and rebuilt; Minoritenkirche, an Italian national Catholic church founded in 1276 and also used as a Protestant church, had its tower damaged during the Turkish siege in 1083; Karlskirche, built in 1716 by the Fischers Von Erlach, is one of Vienna's most impressive Baroque buildings, with a dome that reaches a height of 240 feet; the impressive twin-spired Votif Church was built in 1856 to French Neo-Gothic plans to commemorate emperor Franz Joseph's escape from attempted assassination and was the inspiration for St. Patrick's Cathedral in New York City. Despite the hoary magnificence of all others, the regal temple of the city is St. Stephen's Cathedral, acknowledged to be Austria's most prominent Gothic building and world famous as a Viennese landmark. St. Stephen's, the most important visitation on Sherree's afternoon itinerary, coerced me to dismiss our taxi and spend sufficient time to absorb the splendor of the beautiful building. St. Stephen's Cathedral for centuries embodied the concepts of Vienna as the bulwark of the Occident and furnished a focal point of epochs, cultures, and the life's work and dreams of thousands of people. After two hours of browsing through the noble edifice, Sherree and I strolled back to our hotel through a massive city park where superb statues of Vienna's famous composers nestled under towering hardwoods, a fitting finale to an impressive afternoon.

We were delighted to obtain excellent box seats to the evening's opera, as tickets were almost impossible to come by. The famous Vienna Opera House is celebrated throughout the world for its charm and beauty. Mozart, Hayden, Shubert, and Strauss were all Austrians who played a major role in creating the magnetism of the prestigious old building. Three weeks before the end of World War II, incendiary bombs struck the edifice, and fire destroyed the stage and auditorium. The restoration and rebuilding completed in 1955 was more important to the Viennese than new homes, hospitals, and schools. During the reconstruction, six modern galleries were added where opera lovers stroll and sip champagne during musical interludes.

We saw "The Devil's Bullet," a romantic opera in three acts and although the dialogue was German, an English program enabled us to follow the action. We thoroughly enjoyed the dazzling costumes and scenery.

Sherree and I gave Vienna and vicinity a thorough three-day inspection and did a lot of seeing, though both realized how much had gone unseen. Financially my daughter's visit left a dent in my pocketbook. Her three-night accommodations totaled $150, and she consumed five meals a day, three of them with wine. There was an opera ticket, money for a gift for her mother, and a few mementos for herself of our Viennese visit. Nevertheless, it could have been more expensive. At St. Stephen's Cathedral, Sherree complained bitterly to the elevator operator about being charged adult instead of student fare, and so he reluctantly refunded five shillings. Sherree appeared enormously pleased that she had saved her father 23 cents.

Squiring my daughter around Vienna highlighted my Balkan tour, and we were both grateful to the Board of Trade for their thoughtfulness in allowing her to join the group during those three days. I had a lump in my throat when we parted, she to continue her journey of Western Europe and I with the rest of our entourage to Belgrade.

Our first few hours in the Yugoslavian capital were a travelers bad dream as we waited six hours in the hotel lobby for our rooms to be prepared. The hotel itself was an architect's nightmare. Several vast, elaborate convention rooms and banquet halls were large enough to seat the Canadian Army, and the gigantic foyer was spacious enough for a regulation football field. In contrast, the majority of the rooms were so small they would have given claustrophobia to a pygmy. Following the war, Russia began constructing the building as a training headquarters for young Communists. In 1948, when the USSR and Yugoslavia had a falling out, the project was halted, and the building remained unused until the Yugoslavs converted it into a hotel. The small rooms were originally intended as dormitories without bathrooms, and the large convention rooms were designed for use as classrooms and mess halls. Despite the aggravating delay, our picturesque view from the hotel across the broad Danube towards Old Belgrade made the hours of waiting for rooms more bearable.

Yugoslavia, a nation with a mishmash of complexities, is inhabited by a jumble of strange, brooding people. No country on earth ever faced the unlimited obstacles the six major states comprising Yugoslavia today had to contend with over thirteen turbulent centuries. The historical facts stagger the believability of the most learned scholar. Yugoslavia has two alphabets, Cyrillic and Latin; three religions, Orthodox, Catholic, and Moslem; four major languages, Serbian, Croatian, Slavenian, and Macedonian; five main nationalities, Serbian, Croatian, Slavenian, Macedonian, and Montenegrin (plus another dozen minor nationalities including Turkish, Albanian, Hungarian, Rumanian, Gypsies, Vlachs, and Slovaks), six distinct republics, and seven frontiers. Twenty million independent-minded souls reside in this complex tangle of real estate that has struggled for centuries to eventually evolve into Yugoslavia. They have suffered abominations from successive overlords, century after century, as well as inflicting unbelievable atrocities against themselves.

During World War II, 1,700,000 Yugoslavians (one out of nine of the population) were killed. The majority were not slain by Germans or Italians, however, but slaughtered by each other. In March, 1941, Yugoslavia adhered to the Tripartite Pact with Hitler and Mussolini, but on the evening of the signing, the population exploded against the pact and threw the government from office. As a result Hitler ordered the country annihilated, and on April 6, 25,000 people died before lunch as 300 Nazi bombers leveled Belgrade. Within eight days, German tanks overwhelmed the Yugoslavian Army, and Germans, Italians and Hungarians trampled and plundered the country.

The redoubtable Yugoslavs took to the hills, reorganized into two main camps, and within two months re-entered the war. Unfortunately their heroic struggle wasn't always waged entirely against their occupiers. Too frequently, Serb fought against Croat, Orthodox against Catholic, Christians against Moslems, and Communists against Royalists. They did recapture, lose, and recapture again, much of their homeland, killing thousands of Germans and Italians and forcing the Axis to keep battalions of sorely needed troops in Yugoslavia. Unfortunately they also battled each other with even a greater ferocity. Mikhailovitch, the Chetniks leader first supported by the Allies, preferred to fight Tito's partisan army, often with the aid of the occupiers. Eventually Tito proved his leadership ability, and the

Allies switched their allegiance to him. Tito had Mikhailovitch tried and shot in 1948 as a traitor, though many said his only offense was believing Yugoslavia had more to fear from Communists than the Axis.

Despite their heroic actions during the last major conflict, there isn't a single cultural, religious or economic factor common to a majority of Yugoslavians. Tito from the very beginning placed his actions above the narrow conflicts of nationality and attempted to make communism the agent of unity between all races and cultures. This amazing man showed his personal, powerful independence when, in 1948, he defied the Stalinist policy of dictating the Communist line to all Communist countries. Expelled from the Comiform as a penalty for his actions, he then accepted economic and military aid from the USA and established trade links with France and Great Britain.

Still a poor nation by western standards, Yugoslavia has made remarkable headway, and if strong leadership is maintained, it will surpass the living standard of many Third World countries in the next 25 years.

The luckless old city of Belgrade, situated on the banks of the Danube, is not too auspicious from an architectural standpoint. Considering, however, that the metropolis has been thoroughly razed twelve times and partially destroyed on two dozen other occasions, it isn't difficult to understand the present lack of historic buildings. Arising after each disaster from its own ashes, it has now become one of Europe's most modern capitals. Belgrade, or Biograd, which means "White Castle," has one remaining ancient relic of its turbulent past: Kalemegdan, an old Turkish fortress that dominates the entire Vojvodina Plain and majestically looks out across the confluence of the Sava and Danube rivers.

Early one morning many of our large contingent boarded a hydrofoil for a day's excursion up the Danube to the Iron Gate, one of the natural wonders of Europe. A mile toward our destination, dense fog limited visibility to five yards, and our vessel floated helplessly in the middle of the river like a wounded duck. At 10 a.m. we arrived back at our hotel base where several of our compatriots who had remained in bed and were now pleasantly rested joined us for a hydrofoil excursion in the opposite direction, away from the engulfing fog. We lunched at Novi Sad, a city of 100,000 and the center of the old Serbian empire. Forty miles of river separates Novi Sad from Belgrade which provided a wonderful opportunity to view the legendary Danube with its constant flow of traffic, endless array of garbage, and a current far swifter than I'd imagined. The Danube rivals the Volga as the longest river in Europe. From its source in the Black Forest of Germany, it winds 1,750 miles through seven countries in central and southeastern Europe before entering the Black Sea. Few waterways in the world have contributed to as many major events in history as the mighty Danube.

Yugoslavia, an intriguing and complex country, provides a showcase for communism because western journalists or tourists can move freely throughout the country without the political hassles and entanglement of bureaucratic red tape encountered in most others. Yugoslavia has not reached the economic prosperity of East Germany or other East Bloc nations, but considering the enormous problems that confronted Tito after the war, he did a masterful job of maintaining peace inside his boundaries while improving the lot of all peasant classes during his autocratic reign. Due to the tremendous divergence in cultures, religions, and languages, he devised a plan unique in communistic ideology. By dividing the country into six sovereign republics and two autonomous regions, he achieved a thorough decentralization of power. Those eight regions were then divided into 1,500 communes of about 6,000 inhabitants, each administered by an elected peoples' committee. This concept of a freely elected council in each commune became the essential organ of the Yugoslav system. In principal, the local council is all-powerful and can take any initiative, albeit within the framework of federal legislation. Communes are not subordinate to district elected committees, assemblies of the republic, nor the nation's executive council.

This unusual plan allows authority to rise from the bottom rather than descend from the top. The fact that the living standard of common people is higher than at any time in Yugoslavia's tumultuous history proves the system must work to some extent, and if strong leadership prevails, that living standard should steadily improve. How free the Yugoslavian citizens are is a matter of conjecture. The Yugoslav regime, according to some reputable western journalists, is the most democratic on earth, with councils elected on every level and by secret ballot, although all those running for power must adhere to the communist dogma. Despite this freedom of choice during elections, in practice the regime is staunchly presidential, and federal authorities hold the party and state well in hand. Speech is free as long as it doesn't interfere with the working of the state, and whether this suppression of communication, the major objection most western democracies have with communism, is in fact a detriment only history will determine.

From Belgrade we flew to Bucharest, Rumania, where we were immediately wisked to the Baneasa Forest, ten miles outside the city and treated to an elegant luncheon. Located in a charming area of quaint old buildings, magnificent flower gardens, and acres of lawns surrounded by hardwood forests, the enchanting setting created a pleasant first impression of another Balkan country that has known little pleasure, prosperity, or peace.

Few Eastern European countries had happy histories. A noted American journalist, Robert S. Kane, reported that in his opinion the most sordid and grimmest past of all belonged to Rumania, even though the name Rumania was not known until a century ago. The country occupies the lands of ancient Dacia, a Roman province of the 2nd and 3rd centuries A.D. Its people have stubbornly retained the Romance language and accompanying rich Roman culture, but the land has known few substantial periods of tranquility, hardly any of national unity, and none whatsoever of democracy or representative government. Though a rather sad commentary on the nation's heritage, the first substantial break for the rank and file came from the current Communist government which, despite its repression of personal freedom (never known before anyway), at least concerned itself with the material well-being of the masses. Not many countries have had fewer rulers of their own. Rumania's past occupiers include Romans, Mongols, Hungarians, Turks, Greeks, Germans and Russians, both Czarist and Communist, and any period of which Rumania may be proud can be counted on the fingers of one hand. The hapless land has experienced war, greed, corruption, dictatorship, intrigues and coups as frequently as the changing seasons.

The nation is comprised of three principal regions: Walachia, Moldavia and Transylvania. After lunch we boarded buses for a 100-mile journey across the fertile plains of Walachia to the city of Brasov in the Transylvania Mountains. Although industry produced 50 percent of the country's gross national product, agriculture still employed 50 percent of the labor force. Over 95 percent of farms were state-owned, or cooperatives. The contrast in lifestyles between today's Rumanian farmer and my own agricultural experiences as a boy were quite intriguing. We began the day's work at 6 a.m. and were damn lucky to finish by 9 p.m., except on Sunday when we only labored six hours. My father had no personal control over the price received for his products, and though proud of his independence, he labored 70 to 80 hours weekly most of his life to retain it. A Rumanian state farmer, on the other hand, works the same hours as factory workers and on the same pay scale, with the size of his paycheck dependent to some degree on individual skills and work output. He lives in a nearby town or village, is driven by bus to his agricultural assignment, and returns home when his shift is finished to pursue whatever leisurely activity interests him. He doesn't own his land, however, and therefore lacks the individual independence and other questionable benefits that private ownership provides. Approaching Ploesti, I pondered what my father or those individuals today who still work extremely long hours on their farms gain from the title of their land except some satisfaction of knowing it is theirs and that they are truly self-employed. The state-owned or cooperative farming system removes a considerable amount of personal incentive, but the farmer enjoys more leisure time than many of his North American counterparts. Still, freedom is a precious commodity, its importance in men's lives difficult to truly value. I doubt if today's North American farmers, like my father, would trade their independence for regimentation and an easier lifestyle.

Ploesti, chief center of the Rumanian petroleum industry, was severely damaged during World War II by Allied bombing. We stopped to inspect a modern museum dedicated to the oil industry and were greeted by three Rumanian dignitaries who had driven from Bucharest to meet us. In addition to our official reception, an enthusiastic welcome from a contingent of school children really highlighted the stopover. Canadian-flag lapel pins presented to the kids and accompanying parents by our members were eagerly accepted and immediately attached to their apparel. One small group of youngsters waving Canadian flags gave us a boisterous horn-and-drum salute, and the spontaneous outpouring of goodwill by two small segments of our opposing cultures will always remain a memorable incident of our tour.

At the Carpati Hotel in Brasov, we were treated to dinner and a wine-tasting ceremony at the Cerbul Capatin restaurant. We reached the tasting room by walking through a hundred yards of wine cellar, stacked twelve feet high with giant hogsheads of aging wines. In a special savoring room, several small portions of various wines were served, after which we were escorted to the main dining room. The long tables had three quart bottles of wine placed at each setting which gave the tables the appearance of shimmering rivers of glass. During and following the sumptuous feast, we were entertained by local singers and dancers, and the delightful evening in Brasov provided a fine example of Rumanian hospitality.

One bright morning our entire entourage journeyed by bus to Castle Bran, purported by our hosts to be Count Dracula's castle. After an investigation, however, I discovered the whole thing to be a hoax by the Rumanian Tourist Bureau. Dracula, the bloodsucking vampirish character invented by Bram Stoker, an Irish novelist who published his book in 1897, based his fictitious Count Dracula on a real 15th century Transylvanian prince named Vlad Dracula, or Vlad The Impaler, so called because of his sadistic delight in impaling his victims on long sticks set into the ground. Most of Dracula's victims were Turkish enemies, although anyone who offended him, friend or foe, apparently received the impalement treatment. Reigning briefly from 1448 to 1462, he allegedly killed 100,000 people and was held in abject fear by the hated Turks as well as his own subjects, who assassinated him in 1476. Dracula actually constructed his fortress north of the city of Curtea-de-Arges on the peak of a remote mountain a few miles from the Bran Castle we visited. Little remains today of Dracula's castle on the Arges, but a reconstructed model is located in a military park in Bucharest. Castle Bran, a thirteenth century Teutonic fortress, belonged to Janos Hunyady. Perhaps in his early years Dracula had been a guest of Hunyady at Bran Castle, but if so, that would have been his only association with that structure.

I presumed the Rumanian Tourist Bureau realized the name Dracula would interest North American tourists far more than Hunyady, so they allowed a little innocent hanky-panky to attract good old Yankee dollars. At the foot of Bran Castle hill, a small village lay nestled amongst the Transylvanian mountains where local citizenry took advantage of the deception perpetrated by their government by selling local woolen goods and refreshments. Several bus loads of Russian tourists visiting Bran Castle at the same time made me wonder what story their Rumanian hosts offered them about the building.

Returning to Brasov, we visited the Black Church, an ancient Gothic structure dating back to the 14th century and so named because of extensive fire damage in 1689. Though not particularly impressive from the exterior, the aura of venerability inside the hallowed walls gave one a sense of timelessness. A bronze font enshrined in that sacred setting since 1472, twenty years before Columbus stumbled onto North America, provided some insight into the important role history plays in the lives of most Europeans but which a majority of North Americans consider inconsequential.

Bucharest also has a past dating to the Middle Ages when it emerged as a fortress and trade center. Not outstanding compared to the eternal beauty of Prague, the dynamism of Warsaw, or the captivating appeal of Vienna, Rumania's capital city nevertheless is an interesting modern city with many fine parks, libraries, and museums. A few old churches display distinctive styles, among them the Curtea Veche, elaborate seat of the Rumanian Orthodox Church. Although Bucharest didn't have the charm of other European capitals, it did seem to possess a certain fascination of its own, and I enjoyed my visit.

A kingdom throughout its history, Rumania became a People's Republic in 1947 with a constitution modeled after the USSR. They modified their setup in 1961, and a Grand National Assembly with 465 deputies elected for five year terms replaced the presidium. On the long return bus trip from Brasov to Bucharest, our Rumanian guide, a pleasant knowledgeable chap, freely discussed the nation's political situation and dodged no questions in relation to their so-called democracy. He readily agreed only the Communist Party runs candidates. Several party members can run for each seat in every constituency, however, and electors have the freedom to vote for whomever they believe will be the most capable administrators along a predetermined socialistic framework. He insisted the tenets of their system had proven successful for Rumania, far beyond their wildest expectations. University educated, he spoke perfect English. When asked if he earned as much money as the poorly educated bus driver who spoke no English, he replied with genuine astonishment, "Certainly not, nor should I." And then he explained his reasoning. Single and having just finished his education at the complete expense of the state, he still remained a liability to Rumania. The bus driver, a married man with five children, had labored many years for his country. He emphasized that when he had contributed considerably more to the state's welfare and also due to his superior education, he would eventually earn a much greater salary than the bus driver. His staunch support of the Communist regime, like others we'd talked to, seemed sincere enough. Despite this outward patriotism, many Rumanians, including our guide, would flee their homeland at the first opportunity if convinced they could improve their standard of living in the West. Self benefit will always remain a natural human trait. Rumanians, who trace their ancestry to the ancient Romans, have adopted an increasingly independent attitude towards the Soviet Union and have not allowed Russian troops on their soil since 1959, although they remain a loyal member of the Warsaw Pact.

From Bucharest Airport we took a 40-minute flight to Sofia, Bulgaria, a nation I felt some apprehension about entering. One of the least-known Communist East Bloc nations, Bulgaria is noted for following Russian socialistic dogma almost to the letter since becoming a People's Republic in 1946. The country remains closely bound to the Soviet Union ethnically and historically since Russia liberated them from five centuries of torturous Turkish rule.

Due to my diffident attitude toward Bulgarians, their official reception at the Sofia Airport took me by complete surprise. Young ladies garbed in gorgeous, colorful native costumes met our arriving aircraft and presented each disembarking tour member with a freshly cut rose. Waiting airport buses whisked us to the air terminal where fancily clad performers joined by a musical trio put on a splendid spirited show. They culminated the joyous, courteous affair by joining arm in arm with our surprised entourage and to the lively rhythm of a Bulgarian folk dance escorted us to the Customs and Immigration Office. The scene lasted fifteen minutes, but the memory will remain forever as the festive interlude further removed some of the repugnance I had always felt toward our Communist brethren.

Bulgaria, the smallest country both in area and population on our agenda, has its own unique history, like all the Balkan countries. In the 7th century, the Bulgars, a nomadic race, subjugated the Slavic tribes who had inhabited the area for a century, and the mixture of these two peoples are today's Bulgarians. The people suffered internal strife during the early centuries, but their history is far less tragic than most other Balkan nations.

Over the past century, Bulgaria became involved in three major conflicts, attempting to regain some of the lands within her original boundaries before Turkish domination. Unfortunately, they chose the losing side on each occasion. A monarchy like Rumania, they abolished the throne in 1946, believing the cause of Bulgaria's disastrous alliance with Germany during the previous two wars belonged on the shoulders of her sovereigns. In the second conflict, the country declared war on Great Britain and the United States but not on Russia. When it became obvious the Axis was doomed in 1944, Bulgaria declared its neutrality and withdrew from hostilities. A month later, Russia declared war on her, and within 24 hours Bulgaria declared war on Germany. This act didn't prevent the Russian Army from steam-rolling across Bulgaria, though without resistance from the inhabitants. Bulgars, with their affection for Russia together with their disgust for politicians who dragged them into the war, might have voted Communist in a free election without Russian interference, but Stalin had no intention of taking the risk and forced Bulgaria into the Communist camp.

Sofia received no damage in either of the past two world wars and fortunately escaped relatively unscathed throughout 2,000 years of recorded history, except for one major tragedy in 447 A.D. when Huns sacked the city. Rebuilt in the 6th century by the Byzantines, not too much remains today of Roman Sofia. Relics that have survived, however, are of great historical interest. St. George's Church, dating to the days of the Romans in the 5th century and originally constructed as a bath, later became a religious structure. Directly in front of St. George's are remnants of a Roman street where recent excavations have uncovered large bathing basins and other items from that distant era. Despite the disrepute religion is decreed in the nation, religious buildings provide the most interesting architecture in the metropolis. St. Sofia, a vaulted and domed basilica, is fourteen centuries old and, like St. George's, had been utilized by the Turks as a mosque. On the other hand, Cherna Djamia, or Black Mosque, constructed by Islamic Turks as a mosque, has now become utilized as a church. The Alexander Nevsky Memorial Church, built by Bulgarians in the late 19th century to honor the Russians for delivering them from the Turks, is the most unusual. With a Neo-Byzantine exterior appearance, it has imposing murals decorating the interior walls and ceiling. Displayed in the basement is the finest collection of medieval Eastern Orthodox icons and religious treasures in the world, collected over the years from churches and monasteries throughout Bulgaria and dating back to 865 when the country adopted Christianity.

An inscription on a monument in a large city park seemed ludicrous. It read: "To the 117 Sofia residents killed fighting the Nazis. Fighters against Fascism, and Bulgars who died beside the Russians for freedom and a happy socialist future." (The Nazis were their allies during 95 percent of the conflict.) A short distance away stands a grand statue of Alexander II astride his horse. Like the statue to a hundred Sofians killed fighting Germans, this magnificent memorial to a Russian Czar prominently displayed in Communist Bulgaria also seemed incongruous. Inconsistencies in Balkan Europe, however, were not unusual.

Our Sofia tour concluded with a visit to the top of Vitoshi Mountain and lunch at the Kopito Hotel. Sofia lies 1,800 feet above sea level, but at 7,000 feet, the peak of Vitoshi Mountain towers above the city and offers spectacular panoramic views of the sprawling metropolis. A winding highway zig-zagged to the hotel through a hardwood forest, but an occasional clearing allowed us to survey the magnificent scene in the valley below and to take pictures.

At a final reception for local dignitaries held in our hotel, the same convivial mood which began at the Sofia Airport continued. While mingling with our Bulgarian hosts, I wondered as I had while entertaining other East Bloc citizens what they felt regarding the affluent Canadians and if any of these sober faced Bulgars ever had second thoughts regarding their Communist ideologies.

How prosperous would Bulgarians be today if communism hadn't been adopted 28 years ago? Government brochures written in English and presented to us by our Bulgarian hosts boasted as follows: "The Peoples Republic of Bulgaria is building an advanced socialistic society. Industrial production in 1972 was 43 times as great as in the best pre-war year of 1939. Bulgaria is often cited by U.N. agencies as a model of modern farming. The cooperative farms represent a Bulgarian technique of restructuring private farming along collective lines. The country's national income including farmers has achieved an 11 fold increase over 1939." Another pamphlet reported: "The private ownership of the means of production and the exploitation of man by man have been liquidated. This has led to a rapid development of the forces of production, made possible by assistance from CMEA countries but above all by Soviet technology and aid." I noticed people lined up for blocks at fresh fruit and vegetable shops, and state-owned department stores were relatively barren of luxuries, which seemed to indicate things must have been pretty desperate prior to 1939. The majority of Bulgarian peasants are unquestionably more prosperous today with their socialistic system than they were during the pre-war corruption-filled era of their monarchy. This simply proves their socialist system is superior to the despotic conditions of past ages and actually isn't a comparison between socialism and free enterprise.

From Sofia we flew to Budapest, the last city on our itinerary. Budapest, the beautiful, glittering capital of Hungary has an exceptional quality setting it apart from other Balkan capitals. Three cities—Old Buda and Buda on the hilly west bank of the Danube and Pest on the east bank—were amalgamated to form Budapest in 1873. Buda, an ancient Roman spa known as Aquincum (meaning "abundant water" in Latin), has a history dating back to 150 A.D., but Pest is of much later origin. Magyars, the original Hungarians, were a nomadic tribe from beyond the Urals in Asia and were distantly related to the Mongols. Fierce, bold warriors, the Magyars gained control of much of Central Europe in less than a decade. Buda and Pest, in the direct path of barbaric hordes of Mongols under the savage leadership of Ghengis Khan, were both destroyed in 1241. Sacking of these cities continued sporadically throughout the centuries. Hungary's decision to join the Axis in World War II on the promise from Hitler it would receive all lands once part of ancient Hungary turned into another disastrous choice for Budapest. Allied bombs and Russian artillery destroyed 70 percent of Buda and a large section of Pest. As a result of the devastation, only a few structures remain of Buda and Pest's historic past. All eight major bridges spanning the mighty Danube and joining the two cities were either completely destroyed or heavily damaged by the retreating Germans.

In Pest, we visited stately Vajdahunyad Castle, a 19th century Italian Renaissance style Opera House, and the Old Cathedral. Pest also contains most of the commercial and business section of the metropolis, and crowded shops and offices make it the busiest area of Hungary. Parliament Buildings on the Pest bank of the Danube, of Neo-Gothic architecture and completed at the turn of the century, resemble the stately palaces of Venice, but the magnificent edifice is more picturesque from the Buda side of the river. The Danube allows landlocked Hungary to enjoy official maritime registry as a seaport despite the fact that Budapest is 850 miles from the Black Sea.

Crossing over the Danube to charming Buda, we parked in Trinity Square to inspect Mattais Church, commonly called King Mattais Cathedral. Dating back to the 13th century, the old shrine is the hallowed place of worship where Hungary crowned most of her kings. A respectful attitude of young and old when worshipping in those aged temples seemed to portray their linkage with ages past. This solemn attitude perhaps explains why many Europeans have stoically endured their wretched existence and devoted energies and desperately needed finances to the restoration of those sacrosanct old buildings.

Within walking distance of Mattais Church is Fisherman's Bastion, built in 1903 to honor medieval fishermen who defended the Buda side of the river against marrauding Turks. The Castle Hill complex adjacent to Fisherman's Bastion provided a vantage point for a panoramic view of Pest across the waters. Trying to visualize scenes of fierce battles fought over the centuries around those presently peaceful surroundings seemed out of place until I observed the blackened skeleton of the Royal Castle, formerly one of the most magnificent buildings in the city but now standing as a sacred memorial to World War II, a conflict of my generation.

Present Hungary is minute in area compared to its glory days when many parts of other Balkan countries were within its realm. Hungary is still 95 percent populated by the original Magyars, a handsome race. Females are particularly lovely, with high cheekbones and often slightly slanting Oriental eyes. The known history of Magyars can only be traced back a thousand years, but they've played an important role in world affairs since entering the European theater. During their first 100 years on the continent, they were the scourge of the Christian world and struck fear into the hearts of the bravest western warriors. Then in 973, Geza, the reigning Magyar chieftan, adopted western Christianity. From that date the valorous Magyars became the vanguard for Christians, especially against the invasion of barbarous Mongols and hordes of conquering Turks. Left alone to stem the tide, the Magyars were severely defeated by overwhelming odds, although they had been guaranteed military assistance from the West. This lack of promised military support from their western brothers was a deception never forgotten nor forgiven. Not related linguistically to any of their neighbors, the only European race remotely related to the Magyars are the Finns.

Hungarian Magyars, involved in every major European war since their arrival, have proven their resolute spirit and dogged determination in trying to retain their national independence. In October, 1956, they battled unrealistic odds to achieve that same goal. When irritated by Russian intervention in their country's affairs, they challenged the mighty USSR. With nothing but rifles and homemade bombs, they fought the fully equipped Soviet Army for several weeks before bowing to inevitable defeat. Goaded into action by radio-free Europe, they again expected assistance from western powers, but as happened 500 years earlier, no aid arrived even though in the later stages of the struggle they actually pleaded for help. They may not have received western aid under any circumstances for fear of triggering World War III, but their timing was unfortunate. Three days after the start of their uprising, war broke out in the Middle East with Britain and France sending troops into Egypt to retake the Suez Canal, creating a more explosive world situation than Hungary's rebellion. During the several weeks of bitter fighting in Hungary, more than 25,000 Hungarians and 7,000 Russians were killed and an animosity created between the two nations that will not be erased for generations. To keep the wound festering, Russia retains 40,000 troops on Hungarian soil.

In the long term of events, the rebellion might prove successful. At first Hungarians were forced to return to Orthodox Communism, but slowly the country made major departures from normal Communist dogma. Individuals can now own land, houses, or condominiums. Their government no longer fixes all prices. Television broadcasts include a few commercials, and a multitude of Hungarians work in privately owned enterprises from bakeries to small construction firms. Although farming is on a cooperative basis, each co-op member is entitled to one acre for each working member of the family, and a house with an additional plot for a personal garden. Many of these entrepreneurs sell produce from their individual holdings for substantial sums of money. None of these variations are allowed in the USSR, and Hungary's cautious movement to the right from hard-core communism has so far caused no further rift between the two countries. Maybe the Soviets have learned what most of Europe discovered in bygone centuries. It doesn't pay to step too hard on the toes of the tough tenacious Magyars.

Leaving charming Budapest to return home to our accepted way of life, I realized how easily most Canadians take the word freedom for granted but knew that my journey to the Iron Curtain countries had altered my outlook considerably. Visiting a section of the world governed by a political system suppressing individual liberty, although abhorrent to my free thinking Canadian mentality, gave me the opportunity to see more clearly the other major political regime's point of view.

Besides my interest in political modus operandi, visiting ancient structures always held a fascination for me. Buildings are symbols of man's everlasting struggle in the pursuit of happiness, fame, or fortune, and the fate of those buildings frequently mirrors the past of cities and its citizens. Scenes of the horrible destruction of gallant Warsaw provided an excellent example. Fire-gutted, ghostly structures in war-ravaged Berlin, Vienna, Budapest, and other cities furnished further evidence of the relationship between buildings and past events. Patiently and painstakingly being restored, some to their original splendor and others with a modern touch, by a populace whose forefathers did exactly the same thing numerous times before makes watching building reconstruction seem like reading pages from history.

Although the colorful past of buildings and cities is interesting, the biography of their inhabitants is even more intriguing. Slavs, Bulgars, Poles, Croats, Germans, Magyars, and other races comprising Eastern and Central Europe have experienced little peace for the past two thousand years. Only a small middle class ever existed in Balkan Europe, peasant farmers who comprised the vast majority of the population were rarely responsible for the conflicts but paid the highest price in suffering and humiliation. They rarely became involved with politics because their existence depended on long hours of hard labor allowing little time for leisure or other activities. The work syndrome so deeply imbedded in their character prevented them from acquiring a taste for life's pleasures or any interest in politics. Regardless of this difficult way of life, most placed the ownership of their individual little holdings above any desire for an improved lifestyle. Therefore those countries, forced into or adopting communism of their own free will, suddenly found a deep resentment from those farmers whose lands were confiscated and converted into cooperative or state-owned units. Although the peasants' workday shrank considerably under Communist rule and their living standard actually improved, the loss of their land meant the loss of personal freedom, generally more important to the old peasant than a less strenuous existence.

Political freedom in Canada compared to that in Communist countries appears at times to be a debatable point. In Canada, our Prime Minister, the leader of the party in power, appoints his Cabinet of thirty-odd members from his party at his own discretion and with the despotic power to dismiss them at his slightest whim. Legislation submitted to the House of Commons for approval is decided solely by that Cabinet. In the House of Commons when bills are submitted for debate and approval, the ruling party's members must vote in favor of that bill or face dismissal from the party. After three readings, which may take months of useless debate, the bill will be approved, providing the party has a majority in the House. After approval, it must be ratified by the Senate, a bigger farce than the House of Commons as it is nothing more than a private club filled with political patronage paid for by the Canadian taxpayers. Technically then, Canada is governed by the quirk of one man who, to retain power, enacts legislation pleasing to an unsophisticated electorate for the purpose of attracting votes and not necessarily for what is beneficial to the country's future.

Communists on the other hand have a one-party system with a basic doctrine that must be rigidly adhered to by all administrators. In most Balkan countries, those administrators are freely elected for four- or five-year terms, and any number of party members may be nominated to run in each constituency. Re-election depends on the satisfaction of the constituents with each member's record of administration, because the member can do little or nothing about any change in the socialistic constitution.

Therefore, the political freedom Canadians enjoy over Communists is the right to toss out the regime in power every four or five years, including the Prime Minister, and replacing it with a different party under the autocratic authority of another man. Unquestionably Communist party leaders retain a stronger individual grip on power than our Prime Minister and can usually only lose that position if other leading party members gain enough support among their peers to have him removed. But whether this political freedom to constantly oust the government on a periodic basis that Canadians possess is an advantage or is that segment of our democratic process that will be our undoing only time will tell.

In Canada the immense migration of people from agriculture into manufacturing, civil service, and office work during the past forty years has gradually reversed the balance of political power in Canada, as in most other western democracies. Before becoming influenced by union brainwashing, most farmers were similar to the European peasant in that they were independent and loathed government interference. Until their migration to the cities, those farmers together with professional people, entrepreneurs, and middle-class businessmen formed the majority of the electorate, therefore influencing election outcomes. But now fixed-salaried employees comprise the majority, and they don't give a damn who their employer is, whether it is government, a large corporation, or an individual. Human nature compels these people to demand as much remuneration and personal benefits as can possibly be attained. To remain in power, government or union heads must appease them. Corporation executives, small independent businessmen, entrepreneurs, farmers and professional people—all the employment creators and bastions of independence suddenly become the scapegoats upon whom the government must rely to pay the bills for Canada's steadily growing welfare state. Individuals or corporations starting an enterprise do so with earning a profit on the capital invested, the prime objective, but creating employment and paying taxes become important offshoots. This capitalistic concept made North America the greatest industrialized continent, with the highest standard of living the world has ever known. State intervention in all aspects of business endeavor, overtaxation, union demands and worker apathy too frequently remove the motivation from the doers and employment makers to create new enterprises. This bureaucratic involvement feeds on itself and grows because when laissez-faire capitalism lags, then governments increasingly involve themselves in affairs that historically are the sacred sanctum of private enterprise. If this present trend is not halted and reversed, Canada will soon be as socialistic as the Balkan nations, but with a tremendous disadvantage because the labor force will refuse or not know how to work.

Canada's natural resources should last long enough to maintain a reasonable standard of living for the forseeable future, but that living standard is being bought at the expense of subsequent generations. Whether Canada can halt the present rapid descent from reasonable business freedom to outright socialism is debatable. One possible solution, though difficult to organize due to its radical variation from normal democratic thinking, would be to adopt one of communism's precepts. A caucus of the nation's cleverest economists together with representative business leaders from coast to coast from all segments of society should be assembled to hammer out a course of action beneficial to the country's welfare and economic stability over a long period of time regardless of any short-term adverse effects. This large Canadian convocation should meet periodically to review and if necessary alter the existing performance, and government would have no power to alter decisions reached by the caucus but would function only in an administrative capacity. Whether such a system could be constituted or be effective once established would be hard to ascertain until tested. Nevertheless, to preserve individual liberty and personal freedom and to prevent Canada from finding itself bankrupt, the country must revolutionize past patterns and completely reverse the present trend toward a government-controlled society.

Most Canadians believe any suggestion of forcing a change in the constitution quite iconoclastic. They live with the hope that present prosperity will be non-ending. Unfortunately, people often don't realize they are on the brink of an avalanche until they are buried in thirty feet of snow.

Who would have dared suggest in the 1920s that the British Empire, the largest, richest, most influential realm in recorded history, would within 50 years be without colonies and on the verge of bankruptcy. Numerous British statesmen and economists well aware of their country's deteriorating financial situation were unwilling to intercede and were powerless to avoid catastrophe. Two world wars certainly contributed to Britain's plight, but much of her economic disaster could have been prevented. The cure, too unpleasant for the electorate to swallow, was therefore never implemented, at least not until the great nation had almost reached economic ruin. Unfortunately, the situation in most free democracies is not *how* but *who* will bell the cat. The tour of Balkan Europe had altered my complacent attitude towards communism considerably, as I now recognized a few positive aspects with their system.

Chapter 5

A Time to Decide

BUCKHORN LAKE ESTATES; Sumcot's Last Canadian Job. That headline on the front page of the business section of the *Toronto Daily Star* pretty well summed up my frustrations at trying to do business in my homeland after twenty years in the developing field. At every turn some government agency would either impose impractical conditions before approving our final plans or insist on upgrading services far beyond the realistic value of the lots being offered for sale. Obviously the principal offshoot of this constant demand for subdivision improvement was a steady increase in lot prices which put them out of range of many pocketbooks. Under pressure from environmentalists and citizens who couldn't afford to buy the higher-priced property, local municipal governments usually made the developers the scapegoat as they could cause the least trouble at polling booths. No one seemed to take into consideration the jobs created with each new development. Men were required for the installation of services, subsequent cottage construction, and the continuous chores required by those affluent enough to purchase vacation or retirement property. The *Toronto Star* newspaper article mentioned in several instances my dissatisfaction with bureaucratic bungling and interference. My unhappiness nevertheless was not unique in the industry, and the newspaper story concluded by saying that a high percentage of Canadian developers had moved their operations south of the border.

All of North America suffered a serious recession in 1975 and 1976, and in the latter year, Canada imposed wage-and-price controls in an effort to stem runaway inflation. The drastic step proved to be less than successful, and the restrictions were removed in 1977. To add to Canada's problems, union leaders in many industries demanded wage increases to match spiralling inflation. Postal workers, school teachers, garbagemen, airline personnel, including pilots and air-traffic controllers, all either went out on strike or threatened work stoppages until their demands were met. In 1975, Rene Levesque and his Separatist Party got elected in the Province of Quebec and threatened to pull out of confederation, further fueling a discontentment that had enveloped the country. Despite the difficulties faced by the nation, the Canadian dollar remained strong and brought a 2-cent premium in relation to the American dollar. Concerned about the Canadian economy and worried about rampant rumors that Trudeau's government planned imposing restrictions on outgoing capital prompted me to start transferring funds south of the border. In 1976 and 1977, I sent in excess of half a million dollars to Texas and Florida banks, and although I obtained a 2-cent premium on the first half, the balance suffered a 5-cent discount.

The initial decision to begin transferring assets actually began in 1975 when I reached my peak of dissatisfaction with government agencies. A senior official with the Provincial government's Department of Housing who had given me assistance and sympathy over the years told me confidentially that he realized doing business in Ontario as a developer had become next to impossible. He told me outright he wouldn't fault me for looking to the United States for Sumcot's future growth. A few weeks later while still searching for an answer to my dilemma of getting final subdivision plans registered, I visited John Robarts, the ex-premier of the province. Since retiring as leader of the Conservative Party, John had set up a law practice in Toronto, and due to his obvious connections to all branches of government, he acted as a consultant and mediator between the private sector and the civil service. Although sympathetic with my aggravation, he admitted the deplorable situation had reached such epidemic proportions that it had become almost impossible for even him to cut through the bureaucratic red tape that continuously hamstrung the country. He did try to get my difficulties untangled, but I continuously encountered brash, young civil servants who actually scoffed at John Roberts' efforts on Sumcot's behalf.

During my journey to Eastern Europe, I made the acquaintance of Ted Burton, one of Toronto's burgeoning young executives. The Burton family founded the Simpson stores in Canada, and Ted had worked his way to the top of the corporate ladder in the family firm before they amalgamated with Sears, Roebuck of the United States. Due to his prominent business position and personal charisma, Ted made speeches across the country in defense of the private sector and would frequently send copies of these addresses for my comments. Ted Burton's attempts at getting the attention of government as well as my own desperate plight caused me finally to sit down and try to put my thoughts to words, which I incorporated into a lengthy letter and sent to Burton. Though numerous things have changed in the past decade, the letter in no uncertain manner depicts my mood during that period.

June 18, 1976
Dear Ted:
I didn't return to the "New Society" until mid-April, and my desk was piled so high I didn't reach your welcome correspondence until a few weeks ago.

On February 3rd I was present at the Board of Trade when you delivered your rousing speech, "The Climate of Change," providing another excellent example of your ability to outline the increasing problems facing not only the business community in particular but also the nation as a whole. You have unquestionably stirred the blood of many of our business associates with your inspiring and appropriate words, and perhaps prolonged the inevitable state of socialism that will eventually envelope our beloved land.

You kindly asked for my comments, aware that we are in disagreement on the "modus operandi," although both in accord with the ultimate goals of Pierre. I suggest, however, that Trudeau, though leading us more rapidly to the state of complete government control than previous leaders is only going in the same direction all Canadian governments in the past half century have proceeded.

I realize you're not interested in mellifluous compliments on your splendid speeches, however, I congratulate you on the ability to say it like it is and thereby stir controversy and stimulate action. Hopefully, people with your capabilities and acumen, who are in the forefront of the fray, will get a message to those in power, and perhaps prolong our inevitable march to the "blissful" state of complete socialism in Canada. I choose the words "prolong" and "inevitable," knowing full well their meaning. I will therefore offer no more flattery on your excellent work but present my comments on your wisdom and my own thoughts and philosophy on our political future.

Most Canadians view the changes in our political environment from different perspectives and with dissimilar feelings, due to the divergence in our cultural, educational, financial and geographical backgrounds and the personal concern each individual feels about the political future of our nation. The majority of our fellow citizens, presently enjoying a standard of living unequalled in our history, are reluctant to concern themselves with the rapid loss of their personal freedom, and this makes it difficult to arouse a sufficiently large number of them to our cause. Those who become indignant about our country's plight and expend efforts to reverse the deteriorating situation are usually optimistic in their approach and always leave me with the feeling that they believe, eventually, all will be well. These public-spirited individuals have faith that we may eventually halt our evolutionary spiral to ultimate government take-over with inspiring speeches of logic and persuasion, confident these words will influence the electorate to eventually select a government who will reverse this propensity to government centralization. I'm not one of these optimists.

On the other hand, believing that nothing can prevent our eventual loss of personal freedom and our status as a free enterprising nation as we once knew it, yet refusing to become involved, is either pessimistic or realistic depending on the degree of despair in that person's mind. It is a moral question to me, whether it's more logical to be an activist like you and make an effort to stem our movement to ultimate communism, or be slothful like myself and accept our fate—watching with stupefaction as our country steadily moves towards its destiny.

I'm not a hero, but like many others would offer my life to Canada if convinced the remotest possibility existed of preserving our individual freedom, or returning our land to a state where the original concepts of modern democracy could be practiced. All methods or suggestions I've heard in the past ten years with respect to stemming the tide, however, would be comparable to ten thousand ants trying to prevent a twenty ton steamroller from crushing their home.

I consider myself a realist because I agree with a renowned British philosopher, whose name escapes me, but who stated at the turn of the century, that history proves the fact all democracies have devoured themselves within two hundred years of their founding and present systems would fare no better. He proved to be an excellent prognosticator, because the only circumstance temporarily delaying Great Britain's final demise to outright socialism is their propitious participation in the North Sea oil discoveries. This, however, will only provide temporary relief, because British voters will force their government into continuous overspending, causing increased taxation and a further decline in productivity from the private sector, which will trigger more government nationalization, making ultimate socialism inescapable. Canada will be no exception to this unfortunate epilogue of democracies during the past six centuries unless a miracle occurs. It appears certain our nation will reach the "ecstatic" state of communism within one hundred and fifty years of our founding, about fifty years ahead of the average.

I stated earlier I'm not a complete pessimist because I fervently hope there are solutions which will eventually preserve our business and personal freedoms. Some thoughts of mine would prove difficult to inculcate at anytime, and probably impossible to present for consideration until such time as economic conditions reach their denouement, and our citizens are either in revolt or demanding a complete renovation of our system, and willing to consider any alternative to Communism. I'll outline these bizarre and eccentric precepts after discussing the writings and speeches made during the past few months by many of our knowledgeable and renowned businessmen, including yourself. To reiterate my position: though I'm in complete agreement with the points expounded, I believe the endeavor is as futile as waving at windmills and of little consequential value in the long-term struggle against a socialistic climax. All champions of business, the principal hope for the preservation of our heritage, are saying the same thing and primarily to each other. I agree, some of it seeps through to government ears; but all governments in the past, now, and in the future ignore our pleas and continue to pass legislations they anticipate will be popular with the electorate in general.

Stephen Jarislowsky, the Montreal investment counsellor, is quoted in *The Establishment* as saying: "We're going through a change in class structure. The meek are not just inheriting the earth, they are grabbing it. While our capitalist system, to work properly, doesn't permit this, the politicians must inevitably look at the vote. About 90 percent of Canadian households earn under $14,000, so the vote of the rest doesn't count. Socialism is happening, whether we agree with it or not, and it's probably irreversible. The 10 percent of the people with funds to invest are locked out of the democratic process."

Mr. Gerald E. Pearson, president of the Canadian Chamber of Commerce, told the Empire Club, "On several occasions in recent months I have expressed some doubt as to the ability of the private sector to survive the compound impact of restrictive legislation, increasing government intervention and expansive government spending. On more than one occasion, I have suggested that, barring corrective action, it was not inconceivable business might some day be put out of business."

Mr. I. H. Asper, a Winnipeg lawyer, is quoted by the *Globe and Mail* as saying in reference to expansive government spending, "The massive increase in interest costs of government is stark evidence of the fact that citizens' demands on government, and government's accession to those demands, have forced Canada to live on the cuff on borrowed money. In the past ten years, interest on government debt has risen by 300 percent. Gross public debt itself rose from 27 billion in 1966 to 65 billion in 1976."

From an article in the *Canadian*, written by Alexander Ross, under the heading, "Popping Off at P.E.T." and subheaded, "The Frustrated Cry from the Boardrooms: Business is Getting the Business": "Business has always groused about government. Much of this grousing has a quality of incantation about it, as when Bank of Montreal chairman, Fred McNeill, in a recent speech in Vancouver, warned that Canadians were on the 'road to serfdom' unless the expansion of big government is halted. Such rhetoric has been the staple of service club luncheons for generations, and no one except businessmen has ever taken it very seriously."

From R. J. Miller's speech to the Toronto Board of Trade, which you attended, I cite in this case some excerpts which, of course, refer to his country, the U.S.A., "The question about America is not whether it will return to the pristine virtues of the early republic (no nation ever does), but whether a large, populous, affluent, people will demonstrate the flexibility to alter habits and customs to suit new conditions, and will find new interpretations of old principles appropriate to new and major problems.—Historically, the odds in favor of any nation's accomplishing this degree of change are not favorable.—Most nations have not."

R. J. Miller summed up his speech regarding his own country as follows: "We shall in the century ahead be called more to change our ways than to make new discoveries.—If we fail it will not be from external threat of some adventurous power. Rather, we shall fail because. . . . we loathe to make hard choices, because we resist planning ahead. Will Uncle Sam make it through his third century? While you and I will not live to know, I think from many recent stirrings that the odds might perhaps be at least even. As history goes, that is not too bad."

Similar remarks are expressed daily by prominent business and professional people, most of whom support my view that sniping at government and criticizing their policies will gain precious little in the long run, because each administration must perform in a similar fashion for their own continuance, and this fight for personal economic survival applies to all sectors of society. Union leaders know full well that most of their demands in the long run are ruinous to the industry they represent as well as financially unsound for the country as a whole. But they are paid to produce results, such as increases in income (even if inflation consumes it faster than the workers receive it) and other benefits, or they'll loss their position of power with its cushy income. And they like to drive Cadillacs, live in luxurious homes and travel around the world as well as anyone else. This personal ambition for money and power is the predominant driving force in all aspects of North American society, with government being only another example.

In your speech, "The Business of Change," you dealt with this attitude to some degree when you said, "The blame for the damage to private enterprise cannot be laid at the door of governments alone. It belongs mutually to business and government—government when it grants the privileges, and business when it seeks them. Should they collude albeit within the law, government and business speed the end of free enterprise." A few sentences further you continue. "Too many businessmen want to be free of government while they're doing well, but helped by government while they are doing badly. In this way they turn their backs on steady espousal of the system that might have sustained them—the market system."

Another example is contained in J. Irwin Miller's speech when he said, "Bankers are among our most vigorous proponents of free enterprise and less government interference in the market place, but bankers fight to maintain government control over the number and functions of banking offices, and the interest rate that may be paid on savings deposits. Doctors talk freedom but press for regulations, as do lawyers, real estate operators, beauty shop proprietors and truckers."

You can add to that list all segments of North American society, simply because self-preservation is the first law of nature and the precise reason democracy devours itself over a period of time. To retain power, government constantly makes concessions, and the general electorate will constantly seek government patronage when it suits their immediate requirements, even though the same public will rant and rail when government is succoring someone else. This philosophy pervading society is the reason I keep insisting that magnificent speeches to business and professional members of our nation will receive generous applause from our peers and attract occasional press coverage but do precious little to solve our dilemma.

Peter C. Newman writes in *The Establishment:* "Most members of the business establishment continue clinging to the notion that somehow, at some dim time in the not too distant future, society will return to what they like to think of as normal. However unlikely this is to happen, their faith that it is still possible feeds their souls and keeps them from the wind."

Multi-millionaire Max Meighen from Calgary once said that he had no faith in democracy and in 1944 prophesied that by the end of the century all Western nations would be under dictatorship, except the U.S.A., and it would be under military control. He said it is bound to occur because there are so many more have-nots than haves.

Bud Willmot, chairman of Molson's Companies, said, "As government legislation and regulations encroach on the economic system, affecting such prerogatives as financial resource allocation, investment in underdeveloped areas, executive compensation, and the quality-of-life-restrictions, we will see a gradual narrowing of the decision-making parameters for corporate executives. It would appear that if, and I say IF, the death of corporate enterprise occurs, it will not be a cataclysmic event such as a revolution, or the election of an avowed socialist government, but simply through the interplay of trends which are already at work. Indeed, there are those who would argue that 'free enterprise' as it is called has already expired in a historical sense and that it will simply become a label associated with the industrial era through which we have already passed."

In "The Business of Change," you quote economic historian, Robert Heilbroner, author of the *Human Prospect*, as follows: "The mood that so many people share today, a feeling in the pit of the stomach, is that great troubles and changes loom for the future of civilization as we know it. A feeling the world is coming apart at the seams. The feeling of crisis is widespread. Everyone senses that our age is one of profound turmoil, a time of deep change."

To conclude this diatribe on the prevailing attitude shared by most businessmen about the ultimate fate of our political future, I remind you of your own words, "No human endeavor can match the staying power of bureaucracy." And in the "Climate of Change," you said, "It is important that as contemporary business people we try to understand and accept as reality that it is *not* possible to go on as we are, or even to dismantle some of the government planning that is already embedded into our system." You conclude all your speeches on an optimistic and positive note, and I understand that in your position as President of the Toronto Board of Trade, you probably should; however, I don't have your responsibilities nor do I share your optimism.

Besides the concern and bewilderment prevalent among our business cohorts regarding those federal government problems already discussed, there is also considerable agitation over the confliction in facts and figures used by different government sources regarding government growth and expenditures. Jean Chretien told the Board of Trade, at which you were chairman, and I quote only excerpts: "Let me deal with specifics. The chief concern of the business community is unquestionably the recent growth in federal expenditures. Total spending increased by 25 percent in fiscal year 1973-74 and by 28 percent in 1974-75. I managed to cut the percentage rise to 16 percent during the last fiscal year; and with the assistance and support of my cabinet colleagues, I hope to maintain the increase in total spending to 16 percent in 1976-77." He proceeded to admit there has been quite a bulge since 1973, but said there were sound reasons to consider this bulge as a temporary and reversible phenomenon. He continued, "The reason is the actual long-term trend in federal spending. The National Accounts of Canada show that, contrary to popular belief, the federal government has absorbed, in the past twenty years, a fairly stable and even a slightly declining share of the national output."

Chretien continued, "In 1955 federal expenditures, excluding transfers to other governments, represented more than 15 percent of GNP. Since then, the proportion has varied marginally from year to year, but it stood at the lower level of 14.6 percent in 1973, despite the introduction of a great number of new programs and regular increases in social security payments.

"In 1974, the share of the GNP allocated to federal expenditures rose to 16.1 percent, still less than in 1961. In 1975, it rose again to 17.9 percent. But these increases largely reflect the recent slowdown in the growth of the private economy; they also result from unprecedented factors which are temporary in nature."

These statements, although exaggerated, may be mostly true, but they're principally an exercise in semantics. Anyone aware of the actual figures in government spending and growth realizes how much "crap" was contained in those paragraphs, because all he did was attempt to baffle us with figures and footwork. Compare what he said to the following facts reported in the *Globe and Mail*, April 29, 1976: "An examination of the federal spending growth is revealing, as is the study of each government's redistribution of wealth programs.

"In the current year, Ottawa will pay, out of taxes collected, over $4.6 billion in interest alone on the national debt, a cost that represents only 12 percent of the spending budget. Yet 20 years ago $4.8 billion was enough to run the entire federal government budget, including making interest payments on the national debt."

Compare that paragraph to Chretien's words which I repeat. "The National Accounts of Canada show that, contrary to public belief, the federal government has absorbed, in the past 20 years, a fairly stable and even declining share of national output."

The *Globe* article continued: "The scope of government operations has grown to the extent that in the past ten years the number of employees on the federal payroll has more than doubled, reaching 452,000 a year ago, having risen by 15,000 from the number employed the year before. Salaries have gone up even more rapidly because of pay raises. They have tripled from 2 billion in 1966 to 6 billion this year."

One set of figures doesn't exactly contradict the other, and Chretien's figures seem palatable. But the actual facts on government spending chill the blood.

Referring back to Chretien's harmless sounding remark regarding regular increases in social security payments. Once again I'll quote the *Globe and Mail* article: "More generous welfare approaches have seen the budget expanded by 300 percent since 1966, rising from $2.3 billion to the 1976 record of $12.3 billion. And family allowances alone have jumped from $555 million in 1967 to $2 billion this year. Total government spending has quintupled, going from about $10 billion 10 years ago to nearly $40 billion this year.

"In 1966 employers and employees were taxed (through premiums)

$328 million to support the unemployment insurance fund. The government had to contribute only $65 million. But because of the 1971 'reform', which forced the system on another 1.2 million workers, and regardless who is to blame for the slower economy, the private sector in 1975 had to contribute $1.6 billion, nearly a 500 percent increase. Government spending of tax revenue to support the program has jumped from the 1966 level of $65 million to $890 million last year, with the 1977 projections indicating a more than 100 percent increase over 1976, to produce a federal cost this year of $2 billion. That is a mighty jump over the $65 million of 1966. It means Canadians will, through taxation and premiums, subsidize unemployment this year by $4 billion, and leaves one to wonder if the money could not be better spent in creating permanent economic expansion."

Another of Chretien's remarks I'd like to examine is when he said, "In 1955 federal expenditures, excluding transfers to other governments, represented more than 15 percent of GNP. Since then the proportion has varied marginally from year to year, but it stood at the lower level of 14.6 percent in 1973. . . ."

Again Chretien's words sounded innocent enough, but why did he exclude transfers to other governments? The *Globe* article claims, "If any single area of increased spending leads the pack, it is federal transfer payments: taxes collected and redistributed in the form of grants, subsidies and support to individuals, businesses and other governments. This area of activity has quintupled since the 1966 figure of $3 billion was reached. It will come in at $15 billion this year."

In Chretien's concluding statement, he said: "In fiscal year 1976-77, for example, I expect total federal expenditures to reach about $42 billion. Even if we had managed to get rid of every public servant, every soldier, every R.C.M.P. officer, and still run a government, we would still be faced with expenditures of about $36 billion."

The preceding paragraph diagnoses our political disease precisely. His obvious intent was to paint a rose-tinted picture, but when you compare his statement to the situation ten years ago, his picture suddenly turns black. A $36 billion expenditure in 1976, while only *ten years ago*, in 1966, our total federal expenditure was only $10 billion which included the payroll of every public servant, every soldier, every R.C.M.P. officer, and we still ran a central government.

The *Financial Times of Canada* in an editorial following Chretien's speech, said: "Current estimates are for an increase of 16 percent. Most economists agree it will be closer to 19 percent. Assuming an inflation rate of about 9 percent, the real increase will be close to 10 percent. Real economic growth is not likely to exceed 5 percent. A two-to-one ratio of this nature makes no sense if the government is serious about restraint and the fight against inflation."

Chretien received a rousing ovation, and I assume he returned to Ottawa pleased with his performance. This reception aggravated me beyond description because instead of an ovation he should have been booed off the dais. Firstly, most of his audience didn't understand what the hell he was talking about, and secondly when you sifted the wheat from the chaff, he didn't say anything that gave us any reason for cheering. And it's this meaningless exchange of high-toned rhetoric that exasperates me. It does nothing to slow down our methodical movement to socialism. Unfortunately, it gives many of our adherents a false sense of optimism, because they suddenly believe something fruitful is being accomplished. I. H. Asper, the Winnipeg lawyer, wrote in his article: "But in the end, government is entitled to ask the critics: which program would you stop? Would you end the senior citizens' 'New Horizons' program to save $12.6 million? Would you face the 3.4 million families, *enough voters to upset a government*, and take the $7.3 million off family allowance, or cut out the $40 million to be spent on Northern roads, etc., etc.?"

Logical statements like the above must be stressed to all Canadians so they thoroughly understand only a complete reversal in our political thinking will stop the steady march to outright government takeover. Every free world nation, with the exception of the U.S.A. is governed by a minority of the general electorate, where the party in power must seek condescension from other political factions to retain power, and this system obviously won't entrench a government sufficiently stable to correct our political ills.

The purest form of democracy existing today in the free world is that of the U.S.A., because of their two-party system. Right and left wing elements and geographical splinter groups within both Republican and Democratic parties also exercise pressures to obtain legislation beneficial to those particular areas or those classes of people who are making the demands. The two-party system, however, allows more freedom to the legislators and makes them less vulnerable to the pleas of the minorities.

Ted, during our lifetime, every non-communist country has slipped gradually or rapidly towards a socialistic regime, and perhaps we must accept the possibility our descendents won't give a damn when Canada emerges as a full-fledged communistic state. Maybe we are the last generation who will ever be concerned about our nation's political future and our children, and our children's children will choose living in a government-controlled society in preference to the political, personal and business freedom that once belonged to Canada. I sincerely hope not, and fervently trust they will cherish the independence we knew and acquire a system to regain and retain that freedom for them. Many

Canadians believe free enterprise means nothing more than the freedom to profit-gouge, detesting those who are ambitious and successful. What a shock they will receive when they discover socialism won't produce the Shangri-La they anticipate and their standard of living drops out of sight. Stephen Jarislowsky's statement regarding free enterprise sums up my sentiments when he said: "I typify Trudeau's statement on the free enterprise system as an attempt to cover his incompetence. I see nothing in the world that would suggest government ownership of enterprise can compete with free enterprise. Free enterprise may have its shortcomings, but it has not failed."

Sweden is a prime example of a country that did not crawl but galloped to be the non-pareil of democratic socialism, transforming from a nation of uncluttered free enterprise to a state of torpid dependency in less than fifty years. A completely government-controlled society like Sweden's removes the everyday challenges so important to the mental welfare of an inquiring and healthy mind, which convinces me Sweden's political fortunes will change dramatically within a decade. I admit Sweden's present welfare state is much preferred to the situation presently existing in countries such as Hong Kong, India, Pakistan, Saudi Arabia, Mexico and many others, where the majority of citizenry is near starvation, while a wealthy minority luxuriates in opulence. It is therefore evident we must find an entirely different political route from either, because with all Sweden's welfare goodies, the 1973 election saw the Social Democrats, who have maintained power for 41 years and entirely responsible for that country's welfare state, suddenly retain only 50 percent of their seats in the Riksdag, with the balance going to non-socialistic parties. I don't believe humans will ever accept living as non-thinking robots, because biologically they desperately require some uncertainties in life to retain their equilibrium. How can anyone experience happiness if unhappiness is unknown to them?

I'm reminded of Homer's fabled lotus-eaters, who supposedly living in a Garden of Eden simply munched on the leaves of the lotus to survive and achieve a state of forgetfulness and happy indolence. Homer wrote his epics after the demise of the first great Grecian democracy, and I'm convinced he created the lotus-eaters as an example of what living in an atmosphere of apathy will do to the human race. I suggest the Swedes take heed.

It might be unfair to state I am more qualified than you to judge the penchant of the average Canadian in accepting significant political changes at this point in our history. I make the statement nonetheless because I've been more closely associated with the lower and middle classes throughout my lifetime. Social welfare, unemployment insurance and family allowances have steadily improved the social and economic status of most Canadians, so obviously that segment will strongly resist any decline in government handouts. If our country continues in its present political orbit and one morning we awaken with the Canadian dollar devalued like the Italian lira or British pound, the average Canuck, discovering his Utopia crumbling about his ears like a tent in a tornado, will act as rapidly and violently as any race on earth. He won't be as pacifistic as his forebearers of the 1930s, who stood for hours in line-ups for a small portion of potato soup with a thin slice of unbuttered bread. Remember, the police are now unionized, and a large percentage of the military will also be sympathetic with the plight of the have-nots. Today's citizens are far more militant and anti-establishment than were our ancestors.

Claiming my qualifications are superior to yours on this subject of our fellow citizens' reactions are based on the vast difference in our early background, both socially and economically, even while taking into consideration the tremendous amount of world travelling and business leadership you've been involved with for many years. I attained my rationale from years of associating and laboring with Canadians across our land in all walks of life, and often under deplorable working conditions. The average Canadian's outlook and opinions concerning not only politics but also sensitivity to predicaments affecting other occupations in different sections of the country can only be learned by direct involvement with those individuals. Many of our fellow citizens feel downright hatred and suspicion towards big business. I'll bore you with a few chapters of my personal life so you can understand more clearly what I'm driving at, then at least you can judge my limitations on this topic.

(I have eliminated eight pages of my letter to Burton outlining my experiences with numerous segments of working Canadians over the previous thirty years as this part of my life has been outlined quite thoroughly throughout the book.)

These personal experiences, which are reflected by numerous Canadian entrepreneurs, are why I insist a multitude of fancy speeches by our most prominent and intelligent business executives, plus a profusion of symposiums attended by masses of our corporate denizens can only temporarily retard our socialistic transition. I admit having tremendous admiration for the untiring efforts which men like to expend in attempting to correct that which is wrong. But is it morally correct to fight a battle you know you can't win? Or is it more logical, in spite of almost impossible odds, to attempt to work out a solution that might salvage some portion of our heritage? Personally I do not have the power, nor desire, to strive to reform a political situation as complex as ours. Despite my lack of political motivation, nonetheless I sincerely believe if something extremely dramatic doesn't occur in the next few years to alter our government's course, then if I die a Canadian, it might be under the red flag of Communism.

I don't know if you've read *Common Sense Economics*, by John A. Pugsley, an American who owns an investment counselling firm in California and is a U.C.L.A. graduate. I'm going to quote verbatim, the concluding chapter which summarizes the opinions of numerous knowledgeable North Americans. If you haven't read the book, I would like to point out that Pugsley arrives at his conclusion in a basic, logical study of economics which is difficult to dispute.

CONCLUSION: "Where will the economy of the United States go in the next ten or twenty years? There are many prophets around to answer that question. Some foresee a continuation of the past with minor ups and downs. These are the establishment spokesmen who say that if we can hold on, support our president, and have confidence, all the economic battles will be won: inflation will be licked, industry will prosper, unemployment will vanish, and everyone will live happily ever after. Other prophets see runaway inflation followed by catastrophic depression. After that, rioting, starvation, and anarchy. They exhort you to prepare for the holocaust: store food, guns, and plenty of silver and gold to use for barter. All would have you believe that the spectrum of possibilities lies somewhere in between these viewpoints.

"I, for one, don't believe either outcome is possible. The government, in order to survive, must pursue policies contrary to those that would solve the problems. There is no possibility that any action can or will be taken by this or any administration that would stop inflation or improve the standard of living of the nation. At best the actions of governments of the world will simply redistribute the wealth; the friction they cause while doing this will lower the productive output of the people and thereby lower their standards of living.

"Nevertheless, the failure of these policies, and the subsequent economic disruption will not result in anarchy and the return to a barter society. Those may have been reasonable possibilities had the same economic woes beset the world fifty or a hundred years ago when the power of central governments was relatively weak, transportation and communication slow, and many not governed by technology. Historically, debasement of a country's currency has always resulted in depression, the overthrow of the government, and anarchy if carried to the extreme. This is no longer a possibility. What is in store for the nation if the present policies continue unchecked is simply complete government ownership of the means of production; in other words, socialism. You have watched for years the gradual erosion of individual liberty and the strengthening of the power of the state. The root cause of the economic turmoil that robs you of the ability to become financially independent lies in the ever-growing federal and state bureaucracies. As the economic troubles compound, the strength of the state grows. Never has our government been stronger, and never more able to rule completely the lives of all individuals.

"As the economic scenario unfolds over the next twenty years, we will see an ever-increasing disruption of the productive mechanism, a gradual erosion of the standard of living of each individual, and a total collapse of the free enterprise system. As the government continues to meddle in the marketplace (i.e. wage-price controls, etc.), the devastating effects will be blamed on the inadequacy of the capitalist system to meet the needs of modern times and the unwillingness of selfish individuals and industries to live up to their responsibilities for the welfare of the nation. The profiteering businessman will be blamed for the ills befalling the people, and the people themselves, driven on by the propaganda mechanism of the state, will demand that the state itself take over control of the sagging industries. One by one they will be nationalized, either because they go bankrupt, as did Penn Central and Lockheed, or because they refuse to be responsive to the needs of the people.

"We will not be destroyed by an enemy nation. We will vote ourselves into slavery.

"Depression? If you define it as conditions of widespread unemployment and business failure, it will never happen. Does any communist nation suffer from unemployment? Everyone in the 'blissful' state of socialism has a nice full-time job. Of course, the standard of living falls to subsistence levels, for it is a law of nature that man will only produce efficiently when it is profitable for him to do so. When his profit is taken away and doled out to the non-producers, to the bureaucrats and welfare cases, to those too sick to work, too tired to work, too elite to work, and too crafty to work, then soon everyone will be crowding into the handout line, and only fools and slaves will produce anything.

"Since the need of any coercive government is, first of all, for soldiers and guns to enforce slavery, most of the work force and production will go directly to the state needs, as it now does in most Communist or Fascist countries. And if you look around, you might find the United States is not too far behind these other countries in this respect. Even today one person in six is directly employed by federal, state, or local government.

"So to believe that the U.S. is headed for the greatest depression in its history is, by my way of thinking, foolishness. We are headed first for an ever-increasing inflation, with rates of 20, 25 and 30 percent not far off. We will see an ever-increasing manipulation of business by the government. More controls, more "consumer protection," more power to the politicians. The entire regulatory mechanism of the government will smother business in megatons of paperwork, eating up the profitability of enterprise and swelling the work force of the bureaucracy. As businesses fall beneath the load, they will be subsidized and nationalized. Like England, we will go from a dynamic industrial giant with a standard of living the highest the world has ever known, to a whining ghost of former greatness. *Atlas Shrugged* will become a novel of prophesy.

"What will the economic position of the individual be? In an economy dominated by an inflating money supply, all forces act against the interest of the producer. The direct effects of the inflation create chaotic investment markets and all the economic risks discussed in Chapter 11. In addition to the speculative fever and its inherent dangers to your stored wealth, the state must survive. It has only two sources of sustenance: current production or stored wealth. It will consume both. Historically, under countries moving into the grip of socialism, the person who has stored wealth becomes the target of the people themselves.

"What can you do about the future? In regard to the state of the world today, probably very little. First educate yourself thoroughly in economics. Then set about protecting your wealth according to the principles discussed in this book. Leave the government alone. It's bigger than you, and you're not going to change it. Only don't help it along by feeding it anymore than you have to.

"Produce as much as you possibly can in the next few years, and store it away. Cut back, if possible, on your standard of living now, and store the excess production. Pay off your debts and mortgages, and get your assets liquid. In other words, make yourself as strong as possible financially.

"You might look at the future as would a person living in a primitive agricultural society if he knew a seven-year drought were coming. Rather than continue to consume his production at normal levels, he would tighten his belt and store as much as possible for the hard years ahead. Even though this year it might seem that times were good and there was more than enough to enjoy his normal standard of living, he would be careful to conserve. Furthermore, he would realize that most people weren't bothering to store up reserves, and these people would pose threats to his stored wealth when the famine came. If he's to survive, he'll need to protect that wealth. It would do him little good to try to protect the coming famine or to get the complacent government to do anything about it. His most prudent course is simply to shut up and prepare for the future. And so is yours. Good luck!"

I admit, Ted, that considering our present standard of living, those prophesies seem difficult to accept. Nevertheless, they are in accord with my present thinking and properly describe the fate of Canada, I'm convinced, except that we will arrive at the state of socialism more rapidly than our giant neighbor. Rather than constantly flailing our government to alter a course that's inevitable, we must attempt to devise an alternate plan to save our free enterprise system, regardless of how radical that scheme may appear. Individuals like yourself, with power and oratorical ability, must get our citizens roused up to plan and support a course of action that might be a salvation to our present lifestyle. Any success would depend on thoroughly familiarizing all Canadians outside the civil service and government with the immensity of the sickness ailing our society and the prompt and gargantuan effort required for a unification of all Canadians to join in the battle to save our freedom.

An article in the *Canadian*, entitled "The Big Sleep," by Jacques Grenier, should provide enough material to stir the blood and excite into action even the most dormant of our countrymen. Again in case you missed it, I'm going to quote some excerpts from that article: "Until a few months ago, a florist from Pickering, Ontario, used to drive about 250 miles every Friday afternoon just to do his job. He'd go to Ottawa, to the corner of Bank and Wellington streets in the heart of the city, and enter the Confederation Building. There he'd spend several hours tending to the plants that abound in hallways and offices. That done, he'd head back to Pickering. The annual cost to the Canadian taxpayer? Try $60,000.

"While that was still going on, it was suggested to the president of the federal Treasury Board, Jean Chretien, that such a process was wasteful, and Chretien chided the questioner not to be 'nitpicking.' He said, 'When you have a budget of $35 billion and 315,000 employees, you're bound to have some abuses.'

"The blame lies not with the florist, who was merely fortunate to land such a bountiful job but with the bureaucracy that would permit such abuses. The sad truth of the matter is that the federal civil service has reached the point where it is no longer controllable. In truth, Chretien was underguessing. For the present fiscal year there are 352,836 federal public service employees. To put that in perspective, its an increase of 31 percent over the past 8 years, whereas the entire national employed working force has risen only 22 percent in the same period. Or, in yet another manner, 10 federal employees in 1976 for every one such worker in 1940. A former senior official with External Affairs, John Starnes, recently headed a government task force looking into certain aspects of the civil service. He found: (1) the civil service is too large and growing too fast; (2) there are many employees who are being paid more than they are worth; and (3) there are many employees (mainly in the middle and lower grades) who quite simply do not have enough work to keep them busy.

"After a year of studying the federal civil service, Starnes reported last fall: 'The general attitude was a weary, sometimes cynical acceptance of a system of public administration that has grown too complex and too large to control.' Starnes spent 30 years in the civil service himself, and his patrician voice had a sad edge as it told me. 'About 10 percent of the people in the civil service shouldn't be there. They should be let go, if someone ever comes up with a way to fire them gracefully. As for the people who are just plain dissatisfied with their jobs, well, the proportion is much higher than 10 percent.' The problem, he says, is unlikely to be rectified quickly or easily.

"Because of the sheer size of the bureaucracy, a civil servant who wants to can go almost completely underground, performing little or no work. A federal employee at the National Museums of Canada admitted to me he works about an hour a week. He makes over $15,000 a year. A bright young bureaucrat with the Foreign Investment Review Agency admits working about two hours a week. His salary is $28,000.

"An acquaintance of mine who has been in the civil service for four years, with a salary in excess of $20,000, confided, 'I took this job because I wanted to make some kind of difference. Now I'm working a total of about three hours a week. It's at something I don't like, and there is no real way out of it.' He is completely disillusioned. . . .

"Because of the size of the government, the bureaucrats at the top can no longer control those in the middle and lower reaches. An assistant deputy minister recently said, 'I always knew the politicians could never control the bureaucracy, but when you reach the point where the bureaucracy can't control the bureaucracy, you know it's time to look for another job. . . .'

"On the organizational charts, the civil service looks like a wiring diagram for a color television set. The people round the table look at it in the same way that someone from RCA might look at the TV diagram, 'Ah, this is our problem right here in the lower right hand corner, down to the right there, next to the Media Impact Coordinator.' So corrective messages in the form of memoranda go out along the in-and-out basket network. On the organizational chart, a new little box appears next to the one labelled Media Impact Coordinator. In another few weeks, somebody new is added and a name goes into the little box. . . .

"Of those who cannot put up with the civil service and leave, there are others, always others, to replace them. In 1974 (the last year figures were available), 46,567 new people joined the federal civil service. Salaries are better than virtually anywhere else in Canada.

"During the eight-year span between the 1968-69 fiscal year and the 1976-77 year, when the number of federal civil servants increased by 31 percent, the average salary increased from $6,000 to $15,000. For the Canadian working force, the increase for the same years was from $4,993 to $9,468, and it is generally conceded that salary levels in the Ottawa bureaucracy now run ahead of private industry. Also to be considered is the extremely generous civil service pension program, which, apart from being a heavy burden on taxpayers, acts as an effective lure to draw people to the public service and as a strong magnet to keep them there once they realize its security.

"As well, practically no one is ever fired from the civil service. Where a television factory worker might have a bad period and lay people off, government never has a bad period. And the chances for advancement look good; there are all those boxes to fill right there on the organizational chart. And the Public Service Commission, in its never-ending search for the right raw material from which to fashion the perfect civil servant, has come up with the snappy advertising campaigns to recruit the best and the brightest."

You can't deny, Ted, when you read facts as outlined in Grenier's preceding article, that you come to realize the colossal task of reversing, let alone halting, the government treadmill we're caught up in, as we head to our doom. Even prominent federal officials don't know how to stop the trend. Consider these words from a speech Postmaster General Bryce Mackasey recently delivered to Toronto businessmen, "Everyone hates bureaucracy, yet everyone's forcing its growth . . . Out of one side of our mouth we holler at Government red tape, out of the other we make demands that binds us with it. Everyone is making demands on the state: minorities, women's and citizens' groups, environmentalists, consumers. And sometime, about 10 years ago, our demand forced the bureaucracy to grow beyond its own power to control itself."

Finally with a magnificent epitome of bureaucratic incompetence that portrays the essence of futility felt by many Canadians, I will quote a few words from an article in the *Star*, by Harry Bruce, "The real conversational passions of your federal public service are raises, promotions, transfers, pensions, re-classifications, bureaucratic boondoggles, raw deals, sweet deals, departmental sweetshops, individual rip-offs, collective indignities and the injustices, extravagances, stupidities and blazing absurdities of the effort to make public service bilingual."

Ted, I feel another dangerous myth about Canada and its future is that we are a great industrialized nation. We are not. Immediately following World War II our country was in the enviable position of being one of the world's leading manufacturing states, but that doesn't apply any longer. Prosperity that we've enjoyed in our lifetime is mostly as a result of our good fortune in being blessed with a treasury of natural resources, but as these gradually diminish (and some have already run out), our balance of payments in world trade will worsen dramatically. An article in the *Financial Post* by John Shepherd, executive director of the Science Council of Canada, was headlined, "The Dangerous Myth about Bountiful Canada." Shepherd wrote, "At the aggregate level, our trade deficit on fully manufactured goods has risen to more than $10 billion in 1975 from $3 billion in 1970. In 1975, also the surplus of exports of raw materials from this country, which have traditionally offset serious fluctuations in the manufacturing sectors, slipped by about $1 billion, mainly because of trade in crude petroleum. By the mid 1980s, Canada could very well face horrendous deficits, which could be compensated for only by significant increases in exports of raw minerals and agricultural products. We are not yet a 'developed nation.' We may not be much further along after another 15 years."

Mr. Shepherd continued, "The much-touted plethora of Canadian natural resources is similarly suspect. Existing data on mineral deposits contain huge gaps. Extraction costs and the price of processing severely limit the realization of what potential does exist. Canadians are, for the first time, contemplating the realities of rapid depletion of easily accessible resources—especially liquid hydrocarbons."

A little further in his article, Mr. Shepherd made another interesting point when he wrote, "Not many Canadians appreciate that, although we lay claim to 2.3 billion acres of land, there is actually less arable land here than in Western Europe. The myth of almost infinite agricultural potential is dangerous. Only 13 percent of Canada's land is classed as agricultural; only 42 percent of that is sustainable for commercial crops. We actually have about a third as much useful land as India, about one seventh that of the U.S.A."

On our tour of the Balkan countries, Ted, the brochure supplied by the Board, showing import-export trade between Canada and those countries alarmed me. Although the total trade figure isn't great, the proportional amount of manufactured goods is heavily balanced in their favor while we sell them mostly raw materials and agricultural products. While visiting those countries, though admittedly only on a skeleton tour, it became evident a complete reversal of our present emotional and psychological cycle is necessary to ever again be competitive in world markets as a major manufacturing export nation. Our future competition won't only come from Communist Europe but to a steadily increasing degree from all nations with similar historical backgrounds. Cuba, the majority of South American countries, Asia including China, and most African states, all have a remarkably analogous history, because they had an insignificant middle class, and a powerful minority who ruled and controlled the masses of peasants. Those nations already Communistic and a majority of others who will be Communistic or Socialistic within a few years will soon out produce us, not because of a more efficient form of government, but in spite of it. Their peasant class is gradually receiving improved education and learning arts and crafts before unknown to them. Although it may take a Russian three years to earn enough rubles to purchase an automobile, for him it's an unbelievable dream, and he will work with a fervor outproducing his Canadian counterpart because our citizens have simply lost the incentive to work.

The hopelessness of the worsening situation is well portrayed in a letter directed to you, and printed in the May issue of the Board of Trade Journal. Written by Bob McArthur, of Toronto, a man 28 years of age, he took great unction with your sketch of "the new class," described in your speech The Climate of Change. He claims to belong to that "new class," because he was born into comfort, never felt great concern with personal enrichment or the acquisition of material goods, and never worked in a situation where effort was rewarded with increased income. After several years of living off government subsidies, McArthur claims never to have received commissions, bonuses, or incentive, therefore he sarcastically suggests he must be unproductive. Bob McArthur better believe he's unproductive! Who the hell does he think pays for the social improvement programs he has dedicated his life toward? This is a blatant belief by many of the citizenry who think the government is a money fountain (just turn the tap and out comes money). They must be taught the simple laws of economics. They don't understand that a unit of money represents a unit of production; nothing more, nothing less. Instead of the barter system we use money, instead of trading a bushel of apples for a suit of clothes, we use money as a means of exchange.

I wonder what Mr. McArthur would eat and wear if he had nothing to trade except a letter confirming he'd worked at 999 Queen Street (a government mental institution). Would someone trade him an apple or a piece of cloth for it? These people don't seem to realize that 999 Queen Street exists only because the productive sector of the economy pays for its existence, and all government is non-productive in a democratic society. Someone must produce, or all those programs to which he is devoting his life will evaporate into thin air. Finally, who does McArthur think paid for his university education, due to the fact all educators are also non-productive and are paid to educate only by the will of the producing segment of society? I was surprised our Board of Trade printed such crap without at least explaining the facts of life and economics to the writer.

Bob McArthur should visit the Communist countries and learn how the profit motive is used to produce each nation's social benefits. He would undoubtedly be amazed to find that not only Communist countries but all developing nations are rapidly discovering and accepting that the individual profit motive provides the finest incentive in achieving increased production. A country's standard of living, regulated by its total output, is diluted by any non-producing element of that society, though I fully realize competent government is necessary or a state of anarchism would result.

What is the answer? I'm going to quote a few more statements by the American economist, John A. Pugsley, "Fiscal responsibility by government is as attainable as a magic wand. Anyone who thinks the next administration will be elected to office based on the promise that they will scrap the elaborate something-for-nothing welfare schemes of the previous administration, doesn't understand the problem. Government costs are rising and will continue to rise." In another chapter, he writes, "To assume that any party would, or could, have any long term answers to the country's economic problems is folly. To plan your financial future based on the belief that this administration or the next, or the next, will provide us with leadership and programs that will finally cure inflation will most certainly lead to your financial demise."

John Locke, 1632–1704, one of the philosophers of modern democracy, who greatly influenced the development of British parliamentary procedure, postulated that if a sovereign failed in his duties, then the people should take back the sovereignty with which they invested him. The policy of checks and balances followed in the American constitution was set down by Locke, plus his doctrine that revolution in some circumstances is not only virtuous but an obligation, because he strongly believed in the inalienable rights of property owners plus the important theory that each man has a right to the product of his labor. This doctrine together with J. J. Rousseau's social contract theory formed the philosophical justification for the French and American revolutions, both caused by a decaying government system. The general populace in both those instances were neither as sophisticated nor as affluent as the non-governing segment of society today. What will happen if and when our present-day financial government's pot runneth empty is interesting to contemplate, but frightening to envision.

In closing I will suggest some ludicrous solutions to our political problems, knowing full well under present conditions they would be impossible to implement even if logical. Despite the futility of the exercise, I offer them for whatever value they may have, as a possible skeleton to frame a society that might be acceptable to most Canadians and preserve our independence.

Radical thinking might perhaps be our only salvation and if I could wave a magic wand, suddenly creating a modern Utopia, it would not resemble any system I know of in today's world but would incorporate the positive features of all forms of government. Most important, we must reverse our political thinking and be prepared to relinquish that privilege we are convinced is the heart of democracy, which is the right to vote or elect a government as presently practiced in most free nations. The freedom we cherish the most, our suffrage, must be banished forever to protect our freedom. Communism's position of power to maintain one constant political direction appears to be the only major advantage they have over the free world. If Canada could determine an economical course, beneficial to most sections of our society, such a pursuit couldn't be accomplished without long-term, stable administration because it may take a decade or more of sacrifices and harsh decisions to propel us back to prosperity. If a system could be devised where we preserved our individual freedoms: the right to speak without fear, write without censorship, worship at the church of our choice, work at the avocation of our preference, or travel anywhere in the world at our whim, we would have a society far superior to the police state presently existing in most Communist nations.

To eliminate a substantial percentage of government costs, dual and overlapping authority, and patronage, provincial governments should be severely restricted and the country primarily ruled by a central autonomy elected on an entirely different basis than that used today. In addition to the Federal Government, freely elected regional and city governments would retain similar responsibilities as identical governments today, except they would have no power to tax, other than land taxation, or whatever additional levys were authorized by the central authority. The central executive would also have some jurisdiction over the percentage of land taxation assessed.

Canadians of voting age would be classified into 25 or 30 categories depending on their vocation or related occupations, i.e., farmers, school-teachers, miners, lumberjacks, lawyers, operators of small businesses, corporation executives, housewives, police, doctors, shopkeepers, civil servants, and so on. Each category would select, nominate and elect *for life* a minute but proportionate number of their group as permanent representatives to a central government. This representation would be in relation to population density, so that a proper geographical relationship would be attained, and it should be designed to provide a central government of about 600 members. These elected representatives should be highly paid, such as $100,000 per annum based on today's standards, plus generous traveling and other allowances. Being elected a member of this central government should be an honor and also highly remunerative. They could lose their exalted position in four ways: (1) retirement, (2) resignation, (3) fellow members of Parliament could oust him from his seat with a majority vote, (4) a vote of non-confidence by that group of citizens he represents in Parliament at a special election duly called and paid for by his classification. Each category of elected members would select its own leader which would constitute the cabinet, who would in turn elect a president and vice-president for a specified term and could be replaced by a majority cabinet vote. Finally, each cabinet member could be removed by a majority vote of his fellow members. I think this is what they term grassroots politics.

The central government would administer many of the same departments it does today, such as external affairs, environment control, national defense, social welfare, etc., but, crown corporations would be banished except to provide a necessary public service which the private sector was unable or unwilling to provide. Unions would also be outlawed, and it would be the central government's responsibility to arbitrate disputes between labor and management. Rational guidelines (though nothing as rigid as wage and price controls) would have to be approved by Parliament to assure the working man a fair wage in relation to company profits. This should allow industry to be competitive in world markets, because if companies were losing money, wages would automatically drop, and if they charged too high a price for their products, profits would soar and wages would have to increase accordingly which should provide a strong incentive for labor to work efficiently. Although unions would be illegal, popular and intelligent labor leaders, or today's union executives, would likely become elected members of my Utopian central government. Screams of anguish would greet my recommendation of having the central autonomy elected on a strictly representation by population basis, particularly in areas like P.E.I. where since Confederation they have enjoyed a disproportionate balance of power. To my thinking, though, a Maritime potato farmer faces the same basic problems as a potato farmer in Manitoba and the B.C. fisherman encounters many of the same issues as a Newfoundland lobsterman. If my assumption is correct, they would all obtain, in my system, better representation in Parliament than they do today.

A huge reduction in taxes would not necessarily result and such a situation would probably be unwise. If a percentage of profits is not skimmed off all phases of private enterprise, in an equitable manner, and redistributed across the country in some share-the-wealth scheme, we would ultimately reach the same result as in 1929 when a handful of American families accumulated and controlled the country's wealth resulting in a major depression. Most Canadians wouldn't object to paying a fair percentage of taxes providing they were earning a reasonable profit on their capital investment, and could rid themselves of the present overburden of bureaucracy and be allowed to conduct their affairs in an atmosphere of political continuity.

A prime requisite of the central government would be to assist all phases of industry in keeping products competitive with other world nations, and maintaining a political climate in which free enterprise could prosper. Programs aimed at offering our labor force sufficient incentive to work would replace government stipends for drones. As each classification of citizens would have representation in government, no one should object to getting rid of the present day freeloaders, provided adequate protection is available for the genuine unemployed or those citizens unable to work.

The central government would control all natural resources and mineral wealth, creating a more equitable position for all Canadians. Such a stipulation would unquestionably embitter Albertans, Quebecois and the Prince Edward Islanders. I am not a politician however, trying to entice voters but rather a concerned Canadian, making points which I believe are in the long term in the best interest of Canadians. All natural resources within our jurisdiction, whether in soil, sea, or in any section of the country, and not requiring human effort to create, should be owned and used for the benefit of all citizens, and no minority should be enriched by such a windfall. On the other hand, private individuals or public corporations extracting such resources would be allowed their profits, while the federal government would reap royalties to benefit all Canadians.

Foreign investment in Canada should be encouraged, providing the investor agrees to abide strictly by Canadian laws. Because Canadians have neither the gambling instincts, capital, nor ability to compete with Americans, Germans, Japanese, etc., in investing or developing our country, I see no reason to punish those Canadians who would reap benefits from such investment such as increased employment, etc. To hell with nationalism. Hungry people lose their nationalistic zeal in a hurry when their belly is empty. At the point we start protecting our citizens against competition, we'll weaken them. The same principle used in upgrading the strain of animals should be appropriate when applied to Canadian businessmen. If you want to raise strong buffalo, you breed the strongest and healthiest animals in the herd, a process which gradually weeds out the weak. We will not build a more durable industrial nation by adopting government protectionism, but like raising buffalo, only by forcing our strongest to survive will we eventually build a more robust Canada.

British and American money that built this country and created our present prosperity was welcomed at the time with open arms. Without that influx of investment we would presently have a standard of living comparable to Mexico, and most of our citizens would now be Americans. To change the rule of the game now, when the investor is at our mercy, would be calamitous for Canada's future. If we antagonize our giant neighbor and they stop purchasing Canadian goods, we will be in deep trouble, and if their capital is prohibited from coming into Canada by the American government, then we'll discover what a real financial calamity is all about. To survive as a viable nation, we desperately need strong ties with the United States.

Now that I've outlined my grandiose scheme for the salvation of our country, our free enterprise system plus our individual liberty and admitting my political hallucination's an exercise in futility, I will terminate this lengthy letter by praising your patience if you completed it, remarking that you're a genius if you understood it and betting that you'll twice consider asking me to comment on your speeches in the future.

Best personal regards to you and your family and looking forward to hearing your stimulating speeches in the months to come, I remain, Yours sincerely,
William G. Phillips.

Though unsettled all my life and searching new adventure I rambled almost constantly from June 1975 following Joyce's close call with the Grim Reaper until December 1977 when we received our "green cards" and became permanent United States residents. My complete disenchantment with Canadian government authorities and final decision to seek opportunities south of the border didn't occur overnight which contributed to my incessant gallivanting for either profit or pleasure. We initially contacted the American embassy in the fall of 1975 to discuss obtaining permanent visa status but didn't actually fill out the forms until June of 1977. Those months between were filled with indecision as we both had mixed sentiments about leaving our native soil. We met with our lawyers and accountants on numerous occasions to determine any tax difficulties or other consequences of such a major transformation in our lifestyle. Getting approval from the American government didn't pose a problem but subsequent tax complications frightened me to death. As a first step, we decided to live six months in Canada, six in Florida, and declare ourselves dual residents.

Despite my exasperation with Canada's bureaucrats, Sumcot prospered. A scarcity of registered lots due to the difficulties and delay in getting government approval encountered by all developers caused vacant land prices to skyrocket. Most of our inventory had been purchased many years before when land costs were low so profit on lot sales zoomed upwards. I faced the business and ethical consideration of whether to sell property at a low price and dispose of our lot inventory in a hurry giving the purchasers a break, or keeping prices on a level with our competition and paying enormous corporate taxes. I chose the latter course of action. Even though North Americans fought through a recession during this period, Sumcot's sales remained at a high level. The principal reason for success was twofold: a highly capable sales department that centered around Barry Ervin, Edwina Seddon and Jack and the commitment I had to advertising. Throughout those three years, our advertising and commissions topped a third of a million annually.

Due to the fact I had no intention of acquiring further Canadian properties and Doug Prue proved capable of overseeing the finalization of development at our remaining subdivisions, little remained for me to do except check operations from time to time to ascertain that my instructions were being carried out satisfactorily. This allowed considerable free time, and I used it with abandon. In the summer of 1975, Joyce and I took another 8,000 mile automobile trip from Toronto to Winnipeg, Las Vegas, Phoenix, Padre Island and back to Toronto. The journey proved memorable for numerous reasons. After a pleasant visit with relatives and friends in Winnipeg, we enjoyed our usual week at the casinos in Nevada. In Phoenix we renewed our long-time association with Harold and Helen Thomas and acquired two residential building lots in Fountain Hills for a total of $37,000. At South Padre Island we bought a new fully furnished two-bedroom oceanfront condominium for $54,000. That island paradise, though yet sparsely developed, continued to attract me like a fly to honey. Land prices for ocean frontage had increased dramatically from my first visit in 1970 because a new four-lane skyway bridge connecting Padre Island to the mainland at Port Isabel opened the area to tourism on a grand scale. My original assessment of the island's bright future seemed accurate, and I regretted not being financially able to purchase oceanfront vacant property five years previously. The Texas coast probably should have become less attractive due to the weather conditions encountered on that trip, but if anything, I found it more fascinating.

Approaching Padre Island from Phoenix, weather forecasters predicted that hurricane "Caroline" would strike the Brownsville area about the time of our scheduled arrival. Joyce pleaded with me to stop until the danger had passed but my curiosity at seeing one of those natural monsters close up compelled me to continue. The entire south Texas coast was braced for the onslaught, then suddenly breathed an enormous sigh of relief when a few hours before "Caroline" slammed ashore, the "eye" veered south toward Mexico, missing the American mainland by less than a hundred miles. We had reached within 200 miles of Padre Island when news of the storm's direction change came over the radio. Despite wind-whipped torrential rain plus flooded highways which made driving hazardous, I continued to head into the raging weather. Joyce, convinced I had lost my mind, beseeched me to pull into a motel but anxious to view the ocean under those conditions, I stubbornly continued. As we approached Port Isabel, the only vehicles on the road were going the opposite direction, fleeing water-logged Padre Island. Radio stations had been interviewing hotel and motel owners throughout the day, and though it was the beginning of Labor Day week end, rooms were empty as people heeding the warnings had abandoned the oceanfront community. Wading through a foot of water to reach the Sea Island Motel, I asked the receptionist if they had an available oceanfront unit. Looking at me with astonishment, the young lady replied, "You can have your pick of the entire complex, as you will be our only residents tonight."

By the time we took possession of our unit, in total darkness except for incessant lightning flashes, water up to two feet covered much of the barrier island. A howling gale with gusts up to 60 miles per hour and driving rain of which they received 14 inches in twelve hours were not the most vivid impressions of the wild night. That was supplied by the spectacular electrical display and the ear-splitting thunder that continued until early morning hours. A waiter in a bathing suit brought supper to our room, and the total experience remains an unforgettable memory of watching Nature in one of her most violent states. Gazing over the frenzied sea, continuous lightning flashes ricocheting off monstrous waves topped with dancing whitecaps gave me a great sense of man's insignificance and realization of our total lack of control over the whims of our environment. A few days prior to our arrival at Padre Island, we had visited the Grand Canyon, and for the first time the beauty and enormity of that monstrous natural phenomenon seemed to be related to the fury of "Caroline." Both infused me with humility. Mortals have proven their adaptability and power in thorny situations but will always face calamity when our planet chooses to kick over the traces.

Joyce and I arrived back in Toronto by mid-September, and in early October we flew to Florida to acquire a winter home. After a frantic one-week search from Hollywood to Boca Raton, we settled on an attractive sixteenth floor two bedroom condo in the Renaissance building in Pompano Beach. Facing the Atlantic but with a superb panoramic view in three directions, we were delighted with our purchase of the spacious unit at $85,000 and couldn't wait to take possession and furnish our new Florida residence. In late October I returned to Florida to arrange a first mortgage, and from Florida flew to Padre Island where I met Joyce, Jack, and Barry Ervin. We took possession of our new Sangria unit and devoted a few days researching the Padre Island region for possible land acquisition and development. Although we signed no contracts, I did establish the location I believed most suitable and left instructions with John Austin, a local agent, to contact me regarding deals on ocean frontage in the area I had chosen.

In early December, Joyce and I left Toronto by automobile to close our deal on the Renaissance. We decided to spend five months, and while furnishing the unit, test our inclination about living most of our remaining years in the Sunshine State. Those few months were some of the happiest of our marriage. For my part, I felt ecstatic about having purchased property in three different sectors of southern United States. Sherree stayed with us for a month, and she and her mother delighted in buying furniture and fixing up our new home as personal finances allowed Joyce to shop without having to scrimp or scrape for a change. While Joyce and Sherree feathered our new nest, I joined 75 members of the Toronto Board of Trade Golf Club and assorted guests on a one-week golfing holiday in the Bahamas. This delightful seven-day January respite in the Caribbean became a ritual for the next eight years and a highlight of the winter season. Yarns about golfing exploits and experiences at the gambling tables provided sparkling conversation for the balance of our existence, and my already close friendship with Fred McBrien, Tommy O'Connor, and Al Jessop became even closer.

Mother flew down to Florida in February to enjoy the sunshine for two weeks so our new southern retreat had become a winter escape for other members of the family. Over and above the overall elegance of our oceanfront residence, the incredible low cost during that first winter defied belief. Upon our arrival in early December to close the deal, a cloud on the title prevented us from completing the transaction. The recession plus a glut on the market of condominiums compelled the seller to plead with us not to back out, as his attorney assured everyone the title problem would be rapidly resolved. Fully aware of the market's weakness, I took a tough stance and, after negotiating, agreed not to cancel the agreement provided we could take possession of the unit at ten dollars daily until the deal could close. Believing they could rectify the problem within a week or two, the sellers consented to my terms, but the transaction didn't close until April, so for four months Joyce and I existed in luxury at the lowest priced accommodation on the entire Florida coast.

Despite our enchantment with the Renaissance condominium, the lack of meaningful activity kept me searching for additional action although I didn't relish leaving the tropical sunshine. Joyce and I rented a 36-foot houseboat and took the Schramms, Dot, Hazel and Ev (two of

Dot's sisters) on a delightful four-day cruise into the Everglades. Once leaving the dock we were confined to the vessel until our return as there was no place to land the boat. Nevertheless, the days passed quickly. Fishing, cruising and sightseeing filled the daylight hours while card playing kept us occupied during the evenings. This unique experience proved so enjoyable, we duplicated the pleasant sojourn several times in the following years.

Perhaps the Everglades adventure whet our appetite for sailing because in mid-March, Joyce and I took a ten-day cruise into Caribbean waters aboard Holland America's deluxe *Stattendam*. We enjoyed touring several small island countries I had never visited before, but the highlight of the land portion of the journey occurred for me when we bused across the Yucatan peninsula in Mexico to fabled Chichen Itza, site of extensive Mayan ruins.

Wintering in the Sunshine State, tropical cruises, and owning property in three southern states, including our beautiful new home in Pompano Beach, gave me the feeling we had finally joined the ranks of the affluent. Preparing to leave for Toronto in early April, however, the news that Howard Hughes had unexpectedly died leaving an estate estimated in the two billion dollar range put things back into their proper perspective.

During 1976, I continued my love affair with Las Vegas and visited the Nevada city several times, including one spring junket from Florida. During this period I was privileged to be included in stag groups that flew from Toronto to Caesar's Palace in Vegas aboard the "Charriot." Caesar's Corporation had converted a 707 jet into a superdeluxe pleasure craft, with the normal seating replaced by easy chairs and sofas that would handle a maximum of forty people. Picked up in Toronto, we were whisked to Philadelphia for the all-star baseball game before continuing to the glitter of Nevada. While aloft the patrons were treated like royalty with choice cuisine and abundant liquor served by attractive stewardesses. Other times, Caesar's Charriot would take a load of high rollers to National Football League games on the West Coast, then shuttle them back to the gaming tables. Al Rosen, a charming and interesting indivdual, worked as publicity director for Caesar's at the time, and he accompanied the aircraft on most flights. When he returned to baseball, his first love, and accepted a position as president of the New York Yankees, Caesar's Charriot lost a lot of its glamour.

Throughout most of these junkets I drank heavily, lost heavily, and frequently left in excess of ten thousand dollars on the tables. My drinking habit had become more and more perceptible, and I continuously went on the wagon for stretches extending to four months. In Toronto one of my drinking buddies, Fred McBrien, frequently accompanied me at our various private clubs, and in most cases, whether golfing or socializing, the day ended up in a bout of boozing. Due to our mutual inclination for alcohol, Fred and I enjoyed each other's company and shared some unique experiences as a result. One of the most bizarre incidents occurred in June of 1976 when Fred purchased two air tickets for a twenty-four hour jaunt to Frobisher's Bay in Canada's Arctic. Although I had been north of the Arctic Circle when visiting Kotzebue in Alaska, Fred had never seen "the land of the midnight sun" and got a delight out of snow cruising across the frozen waters during normal summer months.

Since reestablishing ties with Edna Branning, we included our old friend in all Sumcot's social activities. In the summer of 1976 when we once again decided to make the 8,000 mile circle to Winnipeg, Vegas, Phoenix, Padre Island and back to Toronto, Joyce insisted on taking Edna, a decision we never regretted. Sincerely grateful for the opportunity to see new country, Edna provided excellent company. As a matter of fact, Joyce grew even closer to Edna and took her for a couple of weeks to Florida in October while I began a seven-week tour of South America, a story I will tell in the subsequent chapter.

Our final year as Canadian residents—1977—didn't see me settle down too much. I made my usual quarterly jaunts to Las Vegas, traveled to Texas to acquire land for possible condominium construction, flew to Florida to buy $400,000 worth of warehouses, accompanied friends aboard their yacht into Georgian Bay on week-long fishing cruises, and made a four-week tour of the Middle East, which I will also narrate in a later chapter.

My interest in big-game hunting waned during this era except for one exciting excursion with Jack and Doug Prue to Kapiskau in the northern reaches of James Bay to try our fortunes at goose and duck hunting. For the few days we remained at the Cree hunting camp, two miles down river from the bay's salty marshes, unseasonably warm sunny weather affected bird hunting on the downside, but certainly made the hours we sat in the blinds more pleasant. Regardless of how many times I had heard about the multitude of geese that congregated along James Bay in autumn, it took the actual experience of seeing the heavens black with birds to really get across the enormity of the spectacle. Jack and I, with limited shotgun experience, had difficulty knocking down fast-flying geese, but our Cree guide rarely missed his target. We brought home our legal limit. It turned out to be my last hunting trip with Doug, one of my favorite outdoor companions, as he left Sumcot's employ in early 1977. Over the previous twelve years we had traveled Ontario's North Woods and shared many adventures. Regardless of the fact he had left Sumcot, we still planned more hunts into our beloved wilderness for the mighty moose or elusive whitetail, but sadly it wasn't meant to be.

One of the most dramatic events of the span occurred in 1975 when the sales department sold the 600th and final lot in Harcourt Park. I had mixed emotions when I signed the final contract. It seemed hardly creditable that seventeen years had elapsed since Pop and I fought our way into that virgin land. My children had grown from youngsters into adults during its development, and to them Harcourt Park represented a second home. I gave Gary and Sherree each a model cottage and lot next to our family summer residence on Allen Lake as they both loved the Park immensely. Joyce and I, on the other hand, were delighted to see its finale. Undoubtedly we had experienced a multitude of happy times within its boundaries, but the exasperation of being incessantly criticized for every problem, of which there were many, and difficulties encountered making sales, far outweighed the good moments. Throughout the summer of 1975, I spent large sums on advertising and urged our sales department to sell out the development before year's end. As an incentive I offered the entire sales and administrative departments a week's holiday in Nassau if they were successful. That November week in the enchanting Caribbean proved quite memorable for reasons other than the closing out of Harcourt Park.

Thirty people were in the celebration party including the Schwandts and some of the contractors who had worked with Sumcot in other developments. Two of the highlights, one involving pleasure and the other pain, occurred to two members of my family. Mother, at the age of 77, shocked everyone in the assemblage by taking a sky ride on a kite towed by a boat. The local lads running the concession looked genuinely amazed at her determination but nevertheless strapped her into harness and took off with their aged but eager passenger. Mother thrilled at soaring like an eagle several hundred feet over the azure blue waters, and it became apparent to all from whom my venturesome spirit had been inherited. Joyce's episode wasn't so enjoyable. Rushing into our suite in the dark one evening to prepare for a staff party, she tripped over a lamp extension cord which a maid had carelessly left in a dangerous position and went sprawling. She suffered a broken leg as a result of the mishap and remained in a cast for several weeks. Never too fussy about Harcourt Park, that accident soured Joyce completely, and she vowed never to set foot in our 7,000 acre paradise again. Despite the accident, the celebration provided a joyous ending to the finalization of the most notable and publicized development in Ontario. I felt extreme pride at the triumphant completion of my dream, but like Joyce, I had no great desire to luxuriate within its confines. As mentioned earlier, Harcourt Park had been a grand achievement, but unfortunately a financial flop.

The thirty months between Joyce's confinement in Princess Margaret Hospital and receiving our green cards on November 7, 1977, had been quite dramatic. Besides the ventures related so far in this chapter, and also two major trips abroad, other factors made it a most notable period. Our children, now adults, were shaping their own lives. Michael, whom I hadn't seen for several years, though he phoned Joyce and me occasionally and did visit his mother while she lay confined in Princess Margaret, insisted on retaining the hippie look with long hair and denims. My oldest son rarely held a meaningful job and still frequently lived off the benevolence of his grandfather. Gary, on the other hand, worked hard but also had difficulty holding a steady job and changed female companions with gay abandon. In 1976, he finally hooked up with a timid young lady who settled him down, and Tandy was destined to play a significant role in all our lives. Sherree had matured into an attractive young lady and switched suitors as habitually as Gary traded girl friends. She brought a fine young lad named Wilf to spend the holidays with the family in Florida in 1976. On New Years Day they announced their engagement, but two weeks later, Sherree, deciding it all a big mistake, cancelled the wedding plans and thereby almost made the Guinness record book for the shortest betrothal. Our young daughter undertook a modeling course and seemed on her way to finding her niche in life, but one day after a conversation with me elected to join Sumcot to see if she could learn the industry and perhaps become the Phillips mainstay in the operation. It worked well for a while, but unhappily ended in tragedy for all concerned.

A serious auto accident in early 1977 jolted us back to the fact that, though they were adults, our childrens' welfare will always be a principal concern throughout our existence. One May evening shortly before bedtime, Gary phoned from Haliburton with the shocking news that Sherree and Al, her current boy friend, and Tim, Jack's youngest son, had been involved in a head-on collision on the road into Harcourt Park. All victims were in the Haliburton Hospital, and because Gary wasn't certain of the seriousness of the situation, he suggested I had better come. Not knowing the extent of our offsprings' injuries made the 150-mile drive a nightmare for Jack and me and a frightful few hours for Joyce while waiting for news. Though Sherree and Timmy were both in their early twenties, that late night episode made us feel like they were only kids again. Luckily none had sustained anything more severe than lacerations and simple fractures, though Al, a Toronto policeman, partially lost his memory for a few days.

Several long-time friendships continued throughout this era, though a lapse of four years occurred between Ken Watson and myself following the estrangement from his family. We eventually re-contacted each other, however, and my old buddy became the same ideal company he had been for a quarter of a century. He was now divorced from Helen and lived with Alice, who seemed to adore him. We socialized with Steve and Sofie Theodorou periodically and spent time together when they visited Florida. Ed and Sheila Barham flew twice to Ontario for a visit, and Jack and I went to Winnipeg in 1975 and hosted a surprise 25th wedding party for my old childhood crony. Ed, Sheila, and Tom and Flora Fryza spent an unforgettable ten days with us in Florida shortly after we took possession of the Renaissance, and I never grew tired of my old friends from Manitoba. Tommy Fryza phoned his 90-year-old parents from our Florida home, and it seemed inconceivable that over forty years had elapsed since we had all been neighbors in Monominto shortly after they arrived from Poland.

One of the most remembered events of those years came in late 1977 when we sold our 94 Banstock home for $129,000. Although we still planned to spend six months of the year in Canada, we had to dispose of our house or face a substantial capital tax loss once we received our green cards. The profit of more than $80,000 helped ease our emotions, and the fact that we found a rental townhouse that Joyce loved even more than Banstock made the disposal of our old family home more bearable. The six weeks between moving into our newly decorated deluxe Crimson Millway townhouse until we finally crossed the border as American residents were probably the most hectic of our lives and to some extent traumatic. Though we suffered some anguish and mixed emotions about abandoning our native land, once a firm decision had been made and we received our documents, we thrilled at the thought of being American residents.

The climax of the entire affair occurred in the final twenty-four hours. I purchased a new Cadillac in Toronto rather than Detroit because by avoiding federal and provincial excise taxes and a much lower-valued Canadian dollar, I made a better deal with considerably less hassle and inconvenience. A condition of saving the excise taxes required having the automobile out of the country within twenty-four hours of receiving possession. Weather conditions turned atrocious the day I received the Caddy, forcing us to delay our departure until the last possible moment. To add to our dilemma, Sherree had agreed to drive Joyce's car, and we planned leaving Toronto together. The seven-hour drive to the border will always remain an indescribable nightmare. Fifty-mile-per-hour winds whipped falling snow into a wall of white making visibility almost negligible. Hundreds of cars and trucks, criss-crossed on the highway and in ditches added to the terror. Despite my obligation to have our vehicle stateside by nightfall, I almost gave up several times and pulled over to await the dissipation of the storm, but we inched forward and miraculously reached Detroit.

Crossing the border for the final time as Canadian residents seemed almost anti-climactic, but a short ceremony when we turned our sealed documents over to the authorities and were officially welcomed as new American immigrants gave us a great sense of relief and elation. We didn't dream that late afternoon amidst the swirling snow and confusion that our dual residence status which appeared so permanent at the time wouldn't last two years.

Chapter 6

South America

Numerous areas on our planet intrigued me, but none more than South America. A slowly awakening giant and a myth to a majority of North Americans, the colossal continent constitutes 11.8 percent of the planet's land mass but contains only 5.4 percent of the world's population, or less than 10 percent that of Asia. Only in the past quarter of a century have industrialized nations begun to recognize the untapped potential of South America.

The continent's unique history paralleled North America's early years of European conquest regarding the subjugation of the natives. Christianity, like most religions, caused more deaths and torture over the centuries than we dare imagine, and Catholicism, always a prime offender, played a principal part. In North America thousands of aborigines died resisting the blessing of the cross as Christianity was thrust upon them, but in South America, the Catholic church became a predominant factor in the Iberian conquest of that part of the world. The well-recognized work of John Bell in the South American handbook says: "The European conquerors first fell upon their knees and then upon the Indians. The pattern of their conquest was indeed determined by the Indian settlements, for it was in them only that they could find souls to save, and gold and silver to loot. In a comparatively short time, the collected stores of precious metal were exhausted, although in retrospect the Portuguese were not as ruthless as the Spanish."

The Spanish advance across the South American continent was unprecedented in the annals of man's past. With minuscule handfuls of troops, conquistadores established the rule of Spain over almost an eighth of the world's surface in a quarter of a century. They ravaged, prayed, and governed. They built monasteries, palaces, universities, and cities like Quito in 1534 and Lima in 1535 which preceded the establishment of the first North American outposts by almost a hundred years. The University of San Marcos in Peru was founded almost a century before Harvard—in 1551 as against 1636. The Indians, without firearms and peaceably inclined, put up a hopeless resistance and about 200,000 Spaniards conquered between 25 to 30 million native South Americans who belonged primarily to the Inca Empire. Not less than 20 million of those Indians were killed according to reliable estimates, making it the greatest blitz in history after Ghengis Khan.

Shortly after Columbus put the New World on the map, Spain and Portugal, both anxious to fill their coffers and develop empires, suddenly had placed on a platter before them just what they sought. Spain more than Portugal wanted to swell the ranks of Christendom and implant its culture, which it considered the greatest in the world, wherever it could by force or otherwise. Both countries wanted the wealth, power, and prestige which the New World could provide, and for three centuries, thanks to their emissaries—dedicated Jesuits and other clerics, gold-hungry adventurers, aristocratic courtiers and planters, and poor but ambitious peasants—they overran, raped, and controlled the southern half of the Western Hemisphere.

Their method and entire approach was cruel, repressive, totalitarian, and, with notable exceptions, devoid of the faintest touch of humanity. Treachery, murder, pillage, enslavement, lust and greed typified the Iberians in South America.

The Spaniards assimilated with the indigenous Americans, though subjugation would better describe their methods. They concentrated in densely populated Indian areas and ruthlessly pressed the natives into plantation and mine labor. The Portuguese found the Indians unsatisfactory as laborers, and exploiting Brazil's nearness to Africa, they brought over untold shiploads of Negro Africans whom they enslaved on their plantations.

A medieval caste system, similar to that in Spain and Portugal, evolved that, unlike England in North America, didn't possess the slightest heritage of representative or parliamentary government. European-born administrators, landowners and clergy dominated the top rung of the hierarchy. Next were the creoles, American-born descendents of Europeans, followed by the great mass of racially mixed people—mestizos (Indian-Europeans) and mulattoes (Negro-Europeans). Centuries of Moorish-Moslem occupation had erased from the Spaniards and Portuguese the racial inhibitions of the northern Europeans. At first they brought few of their own women, and so proceeded without compunction to cohabit with and later marry both Indians and Negroes. At the bottom of the social heap, the purebred Negroes and Indians, though long since freed as slaves, continued to live in poverty at the lowest economic rung of the ladder.

Tremendous differences exist now between North and South America, even though both essentially sprang from European immigration and are indissolubly part of the same western society.

Anglo-North America consists of two countries, while South America is made up of ten or more. The two nations that colonized South America never experienced the Protestant Reformation but were rather absolutist monarchies. The Roman Catholic Church controlled education, became by far the biggest landowner on the continent, which it still is, and exerted almost unlimited secular power in the service of absolutism, not democracy. The men who invaded South America had little, if any, previous experience of self government.

The motive for colonization also differed greatly in the two parts of the Western Hemisphere. Pioneers who immigrated to North America came to stay. They left Europe behind for good and carved out new lives in the wilderness, free of European bondage, under a new form of government. The early Latins, on the other hand, came to despoil, exploit, get rich, and return home again, although many stayed. They were not seeking a new world of religious freedom and representative government. They were plunderers, not colonists. The essential principle was different. Cortes phrased it well when he said, "I came for gold, not to toil like a peasant."

Canada and the United States didn't become independent nations without a struggle, but elements of cohesion were embedded that didn't exist in South America. Another paramount distinction was the rapidly created powerful middle class in the north, which only now is beginning to assert itself in the South American continent.

In the early 1800s, revolutions blazed like torches all over South America when the Spanish Dominion collapsed. Suddenly after three centuries of army, Church and oligarchy rule, the South American countries, with little opportunity for training in self government, found themselves still caught in the same web as local military dictatorships soon replaced their overturned colonial regimes.

The future looks brighter for most of South America and several of those nations will soon emerge as full-fledged industrialized giants who may very well dwarf the economies of their northern neighbors. A greater effort must be made by North Americans to understand the South American make-up. South America lies close to us physically, but we should keep in mind that the eastern tip of Brazil is nearer Africa than to Miami or to New York. Despite its prodigious importance to North America in politics, strategy, trade investment, and other economic matters, it does not lie close to us emotionally. Many North

Americans still think of South America as an alien continent and view it with a vague or even active distaste. North Americans do not feel the same community of interest and affection that they have for Europe, and the distrust felt by North Americans is fully reciprocated by plenty of South Americans in their attitude toward us.

And so with the knowledge that I would encounter a huge disparity in lifestyles, in October, 1976, I joined a tour leaving Miami on a 38-day visit to several of those intriguing nations. Our tour group comprised twenty Americans and two Canadians (Margaret Smith and myself), both from Toronto. Thirty-eight days would allow only the briefest glimpse into the complexities of nine South American nations, but it would be an informative trip.

When I received the list of travellers included in the tour, the name Margaret Smith from Toronto stood out like a sore thumb. Joyce and Edna Branning took me to the Miami air terminal where Joyce made a concentrated effort to locate Miss Smith and make herself acquainted. We both heaved a sigh of relief when Margaret turned out to be a charming but matronly world traveler in her mid sixties.

We flew nonstop to Brazilia for refuelling before continuing to Rio de Janeiro. The ten-hour trip on a crowded plane made our luxurious accommodations at the Rio Sheraton nestled in a sheltered sandy cove on the Atlantic Ocean look even more desirable.

Brazil's statistics are staggering. The huge nation, described as a continent within a continent, boasts 3,300,000 square miles, making it larger in area than the entire conterminous 48 states in the U.S. It extends an unbelievable 2,689 miles from north to south, 2,684 miles from east to west, and has a coast line on the Atlantic Ocean of 4,603 miles. The entire country lies within the tropical or temperate zones, with only a small section not habitable.

This most populous South American nation is also the largest country in the world speaking a Latin language, and it is the biggest Roman Catholic country. Within its boundaries is the most extensive river system and greatest mileage of navigable waterways on earth, and also the most prodigious swamp area and the largest, densest rain forest. The nation covers roughly half the total area of the continent, and with 14,000 miles of continuous land frontier, it impinges on every other South American country except Ecuador and Chile. Unlike her Spanish-speaking neighbors, Portuguese Brazil gained independence without warfare and has never had a revolution marked by serious bloodshed.

After a refreshing sleep, I strolled down to renowned and beautiful Copacabana Beach, the most popular of twenty separate beaches in Rio. The magnificent arc-shaped four mile stretch of sand is overlooked by towering skyscraper apartments, hotels and interspersed with discotheques, bars and small businesses. With no private cabanas, rest rooms or places to change clothes, you either arrive in your swimsuit or peel off your clothes at the beach with your bathing suit on underneath. No color line exists as the rich lie on the none-too-clean sand with the poor and peddlers walk over all with equal abandon. Numerous sundry items are for sale on the beach and salesmen wander among bathers and call attention to their wares by blowing whistles, shouting, singing or beating a small drum. Rio is beach crazy and Copacabana an unforgettable experience.

Besides bikini clad bathers, another intriguing spectacle along the ribbon of sand are volleyball and soccer games that spring up on short notice. From out of nowhere eight to a dozen or more young men and girls, arms loaded down with poles, nets, rope and a leather ball, will erect their paraphernalia and begin the game right over the bodies of unsuspecting drowsing beachgoers. When Brazilians open their eyes and find themselves in the middle of a playing field, they simply pick up their towels and move away, only foreigners get furious.

One bright morning, we bused to Petropolis, approximately 40 miles north of Rio along a steep picturesque mountain road. A fashionable resort city 3,000 feet above sea level, Petropolis boasts beautiful wooded estates, flower gardens, and tree-lined avenues. Fashionable and quaint residences largely owned by people from Rio leapfrog up surrounding hills, but they appeared to dump their sewage into open gutters winding throughout the city and eventually into the sea. In Petropolis we visited the summer residence of Dom. Pedro the Second, the only monarch to reign in the Western Hemisphere.

At a quaint restaurant called Maloca, we dined sumptuously on a variety of barbecued meats. The meat was carried on long swords, and waiters sliced generous slabs onto each dish. This was washed down with tangy Brazilian beer.

Following lunch we visited the local orquidario which displayed a dazzling array of various colored orchids and a small menagerie of tropical birds. Then as our guide fed us delicious, small, local bananas, we returned to Rio.

One afternoon I arranged with the Rio Sheraton to supply me with an English-speaking guide and car to properly visit the enchanting city. The six-hour tour cost 600 cruzeiros or approximately 55 American dollars and proved to be worth every penny.

Raphael, my Egyptian guide, arrived from Cairo in 1956 when peace in the Middle East looked hopeless. He loved his adopted city and did a marvelous job of selling the enchanting metropolis with its many attractions.

Brazil has a number of capitals, such as the political capital of

Brazilia and the industrial capital of Sao Paulo, but the real heart of Brazil is the city of Rio de Janeiro. A local Brazilian proverb says, "God made the rest of the world in six days and saved the seventh for Rio de Janeiro." The city stretches along the sandy shores of the Atlantic Ocean for fifteen miles. Its romantic quality rises from a unique combination of ocean, beach and mountain, although hills rising immediately behind the harbor contain some of the most revolting slums on earth. The downtown core or business section and much of the middle- and lower-class residential areas are separated from the affluent Copacabana, Ipanema, and Leblon residential beach sections by a mountain through which several tunnels have been constructed to tie the vast metropolis together.

Rio, a happy blending of foreign influence and Latin gaiety, has five to six million inhabitants, famous the world over by their witty, polite and conciliating manner of handling things and life. Carioca, the name for a citizen of Rio means "white man's home." Raphael headed along Atlantica Avenida passing magnificent Ipanema Beach, less crowded than others because it is frequented primarily by the upper class who reside in the luxurious high-rise apartments and hotels paralleling the ocean. Threading our way through congested traffic and a mountain pass, we reached Sugar Loaf Mountain, the best known rock mass in Brazil. It probably appears on more postcards than Niagara Falls. Raphael and I boarded a cable car up to Urca Hill, the halfway point to Sugar Loaf. While ascending, you have the pleasant sensation of being encased in space while a vivid panoramic view of Rio and her natural beauties unravels rapidly before your eyes. Several vantage points along the route allow you to absorb and appreciate the impressive beauty of the city. Through patches of fog rolling in from the sea, the ribbons of sand, swaying palm trees, and white buildings with red-tiled roofs provided a breathtaking spectacle. Another cable car whisked us from Urca Hill to the crown of Sugar Loaf, 1,200 feet above sea level, where the city's magnificent setting is even more discernible. Peninsulas like giant fingers reach into enormous Guanabara Bay dividing Botafogo and Flamengo beaches. Guanabara, an Indian word meaning "bay of the sea," is an appropriate name for that vast body of water which resembles a giant bubble of the Atlantic Ocean. Exhilarated by the natural splendor of Sugar Loaf, actually the highest peak of a low chain of mountains on the fringe of the harbor, I could understand why my guide said we should visit there first because otherwise I might consider it anticlimactic to the city's other attractions.

From Sugar Loaf we wound our way to Corcovado Summit by circling an inland lagoon before entering the downtown core. Eyecatching buildings and especially the Museum of Natural Art graced the avenues. On the slow climb to Corcovado, where an immense statue of Christ the Redeemer surveys the stunning vista, we bypassed a phenomenon in modern cities. Favellas, or shack towns, the slums of Rio, contain almost a quarter of the population and bulge from the rocks like giant sores. Unlike other slum areas in the world, however, Rio's favellas enjoy the finest view of the metropolis. This strange situation came about because developers bypassed the rocky hills for more easily developable low-lands, and as the peasants poured in, they settled on the most available ground near industrial areas where they hoped to find employment. Clinging to the rocks like leeches and completely without any amenities, they are a deplorable contrast to the surrounding oasis of prosperity and natural elegance.

Corcovado Summit can be reached by streetcars which crawl up the mountain slopes through dense jungle. The highway which we used winds among middle class dwellings and provides excellent views of the city. Corcovado Peak at 2,340 feet is 1,000 feet higher than Sugar Loaf. The statue of Christ together with its base, weighs 1,200 tons and stands 120 feet tall. Constructed in 1931, it became a world recognizable symbol of Rio. The head alone weighs 30 tons; each arm weighs 30 tons and each hand 8 tons. The views of city, sea, and surrounding hills are, if possible, even more impressive from that vantage point than from the Sugar Loaf.

Rio casts a spell of magic over visitors and returning to the hotel I read the opening chapter on Rio de Janeiro by Fodor, the renowned author of travel handbooks. He wrote: "Rio de Janeiro has been cited, by many experienced travellers, as the most beautiful city in the world. It has everything. There are long stretches of soft sandy beaches. Lines of tall palm trees. There are mountains covered with deep green un-touched jungle. Birds, butterflies, and flowers in profusion. There are great fleecy clouds floating lazily over the ocean, pushing its cool breezes and an occasional rain storm. There are warm days and cool nights and starlit skies and huge full moons." A beautiful description of a charming city.

On April 21, 1960, Brazilia became the new federal capital of the nation, replacing Rio de Janeiro. A visit to that spectacular city with its new and modern concept in city planning, is like taking a sudden leap into the 21st century. Brazilia's short history is as intriguing as its architecture.

The creation of an inland capital had been urged since the beginning of the last century. Urgent economic necessity of developing the interior, plus the fact Rio had outrun its water supply and power and had little available land to build on induced President Kubitschek to bring the dream to reality. In 1957 a new law established a date for the transfer of the Federal District, despite enormous objections to the site chosen, on the impoverished Plains of Goiaz, in the great underdeveloped "sertao" of the Brazilian interior, 600 miles northwest of beloved Rio.

In 1956, the 5,814 square miles now comprising the Federal District had exactly three inhabitants excluding Indians. Now the population exceeds 700,000. The monumental undertaking is without equal in the modern world. In less than three years they created a spanking new city which became the center of government for the biggest nation in the Western Hemisphere, with all the conveniences of light, power, telephones, sewage, housing, streets, police protection, fire protection, schools, hospitals, banks, industry, commerce, ministries, churches, theaters, and all the necessary buildings needed by the Congress, Supreme Court and the President to govern the country.

In the beginning nothing but red dust, scrub trees, and wild jaguars inhabited the region. Very few raw materials needed for the grandiose enterprise could be obtained in Brazilia, and so they had to be flown in continually from Rio and Sao Paulo until roads to the new capital could be constructed.

Literally thousands of unskilled, uneducated workers who needed money and were willing to face any hardship to get it poured into the burgeoning metropolis. Living in wooden shacks and working as much as fifteen hours a day, they built Kubitschek's dream city.

Those who first came in 1961 either braved a hostile environment or returned to Rio fast. Not a blade of grass nor a tree anywhere grew to stop the monstrous billowing clouds of red dust that rose from the bulldozers and moving trucks. On the 21st of April, 1960, the date of inauguration, and in spite of all odds, it was ready. All the trouble, haste, and bad feelings that Brazilia generated are now forgotten. Today the modern functioning capital city is a tribute to the ingenuity and courage of its planners. The people living there are happy and comfortable, and it offers many things of interest to the visitor aside from its architecture and feeling of unreality.

Few of us were prepared for the incredible metropolis that awaited us at Sao Paulo, called by its proud citizens "the locomotive that pulls the rest of Brazil." Sao Paulo, 253 miles from Rio by land, is a hundred years ahead by progress. No matter how much you've heard about Brazil, Sao Paulo will come as a startling surprise. Nothing like it exists in any other South American nation. Reputed to be the richest and fastest growing area in the world, Sao Paulo is the pride of all Brazilians. Our guide claimed ten million people inhabited the city and that the number is mushrooming at the incredible rate of 150,000 per year. It now covers four times more ground than Paris, is more widely spread out than Los Angeles, and new buildings rise at the rate of one an hour and a new house every five minutes. Sao Paulo, the greatest industrialized city in South America, uses more electricity per capita than Chicago to feed its 50,000 industrial establishments.

Blessed with a bracing climate due to its elevation of 2,700 feet and populated by ambitious people anxious to succeed, Sao Paulo thrived. A cosmopolitan city, it embraces large populations of Polish, Ukrainian, Japanese, Greek, German, Arabic, and Italian. Heavy investment from Germans, French, Swiss, Belgians, Japanese, Italians, and Americans has increased the annual income to twice the Latin American average. From my luxurious hotel room at the Sao Paulo Hilton, I gazed wondrously at the soaring skyscrapers that appeared to reach to the horizon. Then I wandered down spacious Avenida Iparanga to the 41-story Edificio Italia, the tallest building in Sao Paulo and South America. Ascending to a sightseeing balcony on the top floor, the immensity of the city became even more nerve tingling. I walked 360 degrees around the balcony, and the towering skyline seemed boundless in every direction.

A two-hour tour again emphasized the vibrant city's gargantuan growth, though we did see other interesting spectacles. Sport Stadium Pacembu, which due to its ultramodern lighting and sound system is considered one of the most up-to-date sports arenas in South America, holds 80,000 spectators in comparison to Morumbi, less elegant, that holds 120,000.

In the university grounds, the largest of any I've ever visited, the students are supplied with buses to move from one building to another.

In 1888 the state government purchased an old farmhouse and turned it over to a scientist who had some crazy notion that snake serum could be used to save the life of someone bitten by a snake. Today the Instituto Butantan, the largest snake farm in Latin America, counts more than 16,000 live snakes in its collection as well as thousands of spiders, scorpions and lizards and is the world's largest supplier of venom. Attendants removed snakes from their cages, and those in our party with no fear, held, and fondled them in their hands. Many reptiles were brightly colored and of varying lengths and diameters. Every year nearly 20,000 snakes are delivered to Butantan by planters or farmers who receive vials of serum in return. The antidote made from the venom has reduced deaths from snakebite by 80 percent in Brazil.

Our itinerary included a full day at Santos, a port on the Atlantic Ocean, 40 miles southeast of Sao Paulo on the Anchieta Highway that winds through heavily forested mountainous terrain with sparkling streams and rivers tumbling through greenery on their journey to the ocean. Santos, a lively city, is Sao Paulo's port and the greatest coffee center in the world.

Aside from having the biggest dock area in Latin America, Santos also boasts a tropical climate and beautiful sand beaches, which are popular with Sao Paulo residents.

The plain upon which Santos stands is, in fact, an island that can be circumnavigated by small boats. Originally settled in 1540, several areas in the ancient city have remained delightfully old-fashioned, architecturally and otherwise. In recent years modern apartment buildings have sprouted up along the beaches giving a contrasting but appealing atmosphere by integrating the old and new.

Along the dock, open markets with large displays of fruit, vegetables and other produce sold their goods primarily to docked ships for their crew's consumption. Numerous souvenir shops and stores selling a variety of dry goods cater mainly to the visiting sailors. The old port of Santos, which obviously relies primarily on the marine population for its economic survival, completed our visitation with Brazil's splendid Atlantic coast, and we prepared once more to journey inland.

Perfect weather blessed us for the trip to world famous Iguassu Falls. Flying over lush valleys and verdant hills demonstrated the vast territory in gigantic Brazil that lies unproductive. Approaching Iguassu, the pilot did a superb job of circling the Falls, giving everyone a wonderful panoramic view of the most overwhelming sight in South America and one of the great natural wonders of the world.

To gauge the beauty or magnificence of one of nature's masterpieces over another is often an impossibility. The three major waterfalls in the world are equally outstanding, each with a genuine fascination of its own. Iguassu Falls drops a maximum depth of 240 feet compared to Niagara's 165 feet, but both far less than the thundering plunge of massive Victoria Falls at 420 feet. Niagara Falls spans three-fifths of a mile, Victoria one mile, while Iguassu spreads out into 21 separate falls and covers three miles. Iguassu and Victoria are wilderness areas compared to the almost urban setting of picturesque Niagara Falls. They are all enchanting works of nature.

Iguassu Falls, on the Iguassu River, is at the convergence of Brazil, Argentina, and Paraguay, and the great falls can be visited from any of those three republics. The Brazilian side offered an advantage due to the location of the Das Cataratas, our hotel, from which you could almost roll out of bed into the gorge. Iguassu's wilderness setting is striking and unforgettable. Thunderous waters tumble and splash through virgin forests bright with orchids and serpentine creepers. Tropical ferns and palms decorated with myriads of magnificently colored butterflies grace the pathways, and permanently formed in the mist that rises from the cataract, is an exquisite rainbow. Adding to this concert are 400 species of jungle birds that provide color and sound everywhere. A two-mile paved walkway paralleling the rim of the falls allows pedestrians to view the spectacular scenery from a multitude of vantage points. The several falls have distinctive names: San Martin, Bossetti, Two Sisters, Mitre, Three Musketeers, and Devil's Throat. From a walkway jutting well into the river, Devil's Throat is a stupendous spectacle, though a raincoat and plastic coverings for camera equipment are needed for protection from the drenching mist. Below the cataract, receding water swirls and dances over jutting rocks and around tiny islets as it moves swiftly through a deep canyon a few miles before it joins the Parana River, chief tributary of the Amazon.

The two-mile walkway terminates at mighty Floriana Falls where the deafening roar drowns out all other sounds. From the base of Floriana an elevator hoists sightseers to the top of the chasm where an exciting adventure awaits the courageous. Local daredevils with rowboats took foolhardy passengers including myself into the circling eddies and landed us on a small island in the midst of the rushing river. From there we boarded a second boat that carried us to the brink of Devil's Throat where the Iguassu plunges two hundred feet into a raging maelstrom below. We landed on an outcropping of rock that actually juts into the incredible fury of plunging waters. Standing on our precarious perch, we watched with fascination as Brazilian rowers came within 30 feet of the edge of the mighty river's downward plunge. In retrospect, the hair-raising escapade seemed foolish because if the single rower took a heart attack or cramp prior to maneuvering the final turn, it would be good-bye Charlie to the boat load of tourists. Despite the danger, I doubt if anyone regretted participating in the foolhardy venture once they returned to terra firma. Within a few hours, a major storm front moved in and a heavy downpour raised the river sufficiently that several days of dry weather would have to elapse before boats could again tackle the raging Iguassu.

From Iguassu Falls we flew 1½ hours over the eastern and most inhabited part of Paraguay to Asuncion, the capital city. One of the two South American countries without a seacoast, Paraguay has limited access to the Atlantic 900 miles away by river and rail. About the size of California, the nation is cleft almost in equal halves by the 1,300-mile-long Paraguay River which forms the boundary with Brazil.

Paraguayan lands divided by the Paraguay River are in extreme contrast: the Chaco in the western half consists of a sparsely inhabited tract of cattle and scrub forest country, while across the river, rich land predominates and contains the majority of the population.

In contrast to other Spanish American nations, Paraguay enjoyed a reasonably pleasant era when Europeans discovered the land in 1537. The Spaniards married Indians instead of killing them, thus developing the first "mestizo" (Indians and whites) nation in Latin America with a national conscience. The country endured a tragic history after independence from Spain in 1811 which came about without bloodshed. During the War of the Triple Alliance from 1864 to 1871, which Paraguay almost won, the tiny nation took on Brazil, Argentina, and Uruguay. Paraguay's population dropped from 525,000 to 221,000, the total remaining male population consisting of old men and boys, amounting to the unbelievable total of only 28,746. Another vicious war—the Chaco War—came in 1932 with Bolivia, and Paraguay did win, but it cost both countries a total of 135,000 men. Paraguay has been slow to recover from those two disasters.

Asuncion, the only large town in Paraguay, is built on the shores of a bay cutting into the eastern bank of the Paraguay River. Founded in 1537, the city is almost thirty years older than St Augustine, Florida, and seventy-two years older than Jamestown, Virginia. Built on a low hill and laid out in the Colonial Spanish rectangular manner, Asuncion had no slums but also no storm sewers.

Few pretentious buildings existed in the business sector, but residential areas offered a wide variety of architectural styles surrounded by lovely grounds and gardens. Local guides on our interesting city excursion gave me the feeling that the military dictatorship permitted a fair degree of freedom. President Stroessner, in power since 1954 though not considered as despotic as other South American dictators, remains violently anti-communistic and will throw Communists in jail without hesitation.

An old prop aircraft transported us across lush terrain interspersed with winding rivers from Asuncion to Montevideo, Uruguay. Comparable to Missouri in size, Uruguay consists of undulating hills with scant forests except on the banks of its numerous streams. Black soil rich in potash produces grasses superior even to those in Argentina. Most land is suitable for farming, but cattle and sheep ranching, the two mainstays of the nation's economy, predominate.

The Spanish landed east of present-day Montevideo in 1515, but aborigines, the Charrua Indians, massacred the entire landing party. Other military expeditions met a similar fate. After a long and heroic resistance, the Charruas were eventually overcome and absorbed into the population of Spanish and Portuguese who fought over possession of Uruguay for 150 years. Finally in 1828 as a result of British intervention, both countries relinquished all claim and Uruguay declared independence.

Long known as the purest and most progressive democracy in South America and perhaps the world, the small agrarian republic patterned its growth and economy on Switzerland. For the first half of the 20th century Uruguay gradually evolved into the most advanced socialized welfare state on earth. They nationalized electricity, railways, tramways, and the waterworks system. Their government controlled the manufacture and distribution of such diverse products as gas, oil, alcohol, cement, and chemicals. They regulated insurance, ran their own banks, theaters, hotels, casinos, telephones and port facilities. A working man's charter provided for a work week as low as thirty hours for civil servants and bank employees plus mandatory severance pay, long annual paid vacations, family allowances, a minimum wage, workmen's compensation, unemployment insurance, free compulsory education, low-cost housing, milk co-operatives, and disability and old-age pensions of excessive generosity. Some government departments worked only a half day in summer so that employees could spend the afternoon at the beaches. As a result of this over socialization, the inevitable happened, and the country went bankrupt.

Uruguay, like nations throughout history, dating back to the city-state democracies of Greece long before the birth of Christ, when attempting to create a socialized utopia found bureaucracy became so lopsided that government simply didn't function. At its peak, in addition to other welfare benefits, anyone could retire at age fifty with a full pension, and in some cases even bonuses. Eventually three productive workers supported one pensioner, and four private sector workers supported one civil servant. When the private element lost its initiative, production fell, economic growth became stunted, and inflation skyrocketed. Uruguay's money value dropped from 250 pesos to the American dollar in 1963 to over 1200 during our visit, and inflation had increased a whopping 1200 percent over the same period. In 1973, as economic conditions worsened, the military intervened, and in 1976, they removed the president entirely and ruled the nation as a military dictatorship.

Half of Uruguay's population resides in Montevideo, which makes Uruguay like a big city with a large ranch on its outskirts. Relatively large communities of Italian, British, American, German, Hungarian, French and European Jewish, populate Montevideo making it quite cosmopolitan. Black people are almost non-existent, however. The Legislative Palace constructed of granite and marble is an immense and attractive building, otherwise architecture is not pretentious.

Of Montevideo's numerous attractive parks, Prado is the most splendid. Besides containing 850 varieties of roses, it has several interesting statues including Belloni's famous bronze statue of a covered wagon pulled by six oxen.

The "Cerro", or hill responsible for the city's name, overlooks the harbor area. An old fort on top of the rise, now a military museum, also contains the oldest lighthouse in the country. Ships lying in Horseshoe

Bay from all over the world mark Montevideo as one of the major ocean ports on the continent. Gazing across the Plata estuary, a hundred miles wide at that point, my mind wandered to the dramatic events in the early days of World War II when the German battleship *Graf Spee* sought sanctuary in the harbor from three British destroyers. After 36 hours, required by international law for wounded to be evacuated, and as the world sat by their radios, the German captain took the ship a mile off shore and scuttled it, rather than face the superior guns of the British Navy. The ship's bell from the British destroyer Ajax has been set up to commemorate the sinking of the *Graf Spee,* and the anchor of the *Graf Spee* was set up at the entrance to the harbor in 1964 to observe the 25th anniversary of the battle.

Gorgeous sea views and incomparable beaches, which reach all the way to Brazil, attract thousands of annual tourists, primarily from Argentina. Montevideo's affluent reside in the Carrasca residential section of the city, and homes and gardens indicated that wealthy families in the country were not a scarcity. Many North Americans together with upper-class Uruguayans and well-to-do Argentinians also had residences in that sector.

At the completion of the city tour we accompanied our Travcoa guide to a quaint restaurant for lunch. Due to our language difference, waiters and the maitre-de had difficulty understanding our order which resulted in a comical but colossal goof-up with delivery of the food. Those ordering chicken received fish and those requesting fish got steak while some got nothing at all. To the great embarrassment of the maitre-de, it took half an hour to straighten it out, but the hilarious incident provided one of the more memorable moments spent in the country.

Some years ago someone asked an American journalist what Uruguay needed most, and his prompt reply was threefold: "More Uruguayans, one economist and vitality." In answer to the second question as to what runs Uruguay, he replied, "Anybody close enough to a minister to be able to ask a favor of his secretary on the telephone." Uruguay, and Montevideo in particular, have a lot to offer either tourists or immigrants as far as natural beauty, climate, and friendly people are concerned. Hopefully in the not too distant future the little South American republic will correct its economic woes and rejoin the world community as a better-managed free democracy.

An Argentinian jet whisked us across the wide estuary of the Rio de la Plata on a half hour early morning flight to Buenos Aires, another of the massive, modern metropolises in the world. The Rio de la Plata, 120 miles wide at its mouth, is the focal point of one of the great river systems of the continent. Formed by the Parana and Uruguay rivers which pour a vast volume of water toward the ocean, much of the Rio de la Plata estuary is fresh or sweet water. Circling the huge metropolis, it was immediately apparent that Buenos Aires would rival Sao Paulo in size. One third of Argentina's population reside in that monstrous city, and when considering the total size of the nation, that is an astounding statistic. The eighth largest country in the world, fourth in the Western Hemisphere and second in area and population in South America, Argentina, like Brazil, is indeed colossal. Five times bigger than France, it stretches 2,150 miles north to south, and 980 miles west to east. Topographically and climatically, few nations equal its wide variation, which range from great heat in the Chaco, through a pleasant climate in the central pampas, to sub-arctic cold in Patagonia south.

Discovered in 1515 by Spanish explorers, Argentina remained under Spanish domination until the provinces revolted and established an independent republic May 25, 1810. Since then, its government has hovered between democracy and outright military dictatorship.

Spanish invaders almost completely obliterated the native Indians, resulting in a population that is now 98 percent European. A mass migration of Europeans took place in the last two decades of the 19th century and continued to accelerate for the first half of the 20th. Immigrants mostly came from Italy and Spain, but large numbers also arrived from Portugal, Germany, the Netherlands, and Great Britain. The British played an important role in transforming Argentina into a modern state, and the British community is still the largest in any country outside the Commonwealth.

Like Uruguay, the heart of Argentina is its capital city, the sixth largest metropolis on the planet. Our tour of Buenos Aires left no doubt as to the tremendous European influence in layout and architecture, and in many respects the attractive city reminded me of Paris. Its avenues, among the widest in the world, include the Avenue of the 9th of July. Four hundred and sixty feet wide including ten lanes for traffic, and with huge boulevards lined with impressive skyscrapers makes it an imposing thoroughfare.

The heart of the city as in colonial days is the Plaza de Mayo. We strolled through the historic and attractive Plaza where many of the city's more pretentious buildings are situated: Cabildo or Town Hall where the movement for independence from Spain first started and the first government formed in 1810; Casa Rosada, the Pink House or presidential palace, where sentries carry bold swords and wear uniforms reminiscent of medieval Europe, and on the rim of the Plaza, the Cathedral where General San Martin lies in state. Several other imposing edifices also grace the Plaza area.

Buenos Aires, the most advanced city in South America from the point of view of culture, contains hundreds of art galleries, 42 theaters, and more than 200 movie houses. The Colon Opera House, a municipal theater devoted to opera, is the largest and one of the most elaborate in the world with its own National Symphony orchestra, opera, and ballet companies. Modeled after the Paris Opera, it covers most of a city block and has a stage that can hold six hundred.

Buenos Aires must rank with the great cities of the world. Unlike Rio, with its beautiful but hilly terrain, Buenos Aires is a walking city, more like a series of villages, and I enjoyed strolling at leisure along the elegant Calle Florida, lined on both sides with a variety of shops and reserved for pedestrians only.

A delightful side trip to San Antonio de Areco provided an interesting and enjoyable day. It was 80 miles from Buenos Aires to San Antonio, but we traversed a section of the famous pampas that extend fanwise from the city for 300 to 400 miles. The economic well-being of Argentina depends heavily on that region as cattle rearing comprises the main industry.

We stopped at a gaucho museum layed out to typify ranch life from the early 19th century with manor house, mill, tavern and protected from the wind by rows of eucalyptus trees. Several enjoyable hours were spent at an active 400-acre ranch run by a man and his family. Our lunch, barbecued in a special building outside the main house, gave off a mouth-watering aroma, and it tasted as delicious as it smelled. Platefuls of steak, sausages, kidney and other meats topped off with delightful local desserts made it a regal feast.

After our superb repast, the rancher and his boys entertained us with local music, singing, and dancing. Their accordian, guitars and melodians produced a pleasant example of gaucho music, and though exclusively in Spanish, their singing blended in to give the old ranch house a true Argentinian atmosphere. The day provided another highlight of the many we enjoyed on the long journey.

At a very early hour we departed Buenos Aires for San Carlos de Bariloche, one of the most enchanting places on the planet. Gorgeous scenery overwhelmed us from the moment we stepped off the plane. Magnificent Andean peaks loomed on the horizon like giant soldiers topped with helmets of dazzling white. Bariloche, 1,100 miles by road from Buenos Aires and the furthest point south we would travel, equates with southern Manitoba as to distance from the equator, and so the weather and countryside simulated mid-spring on the old farm.

Bariloche, situated on the south shore of Lake Nahuel Huapi, is a village of steep streets with wooden chalets perched Swiss fashion on an old moraine. Two chocolate factories appeared to be the town's main industry. Several miles of breathtaking scenery lay between San Carlos de Bariloche and our hotel, the renowned and luxurious Llao-Llao.

Situated on the shore of Lake Nahuel Huapi, every window from the Llao-Llao overlooked stunning scenery, and the lake, a picturesque body of water 40 miles long, reflects an outstanding spectrum of color and is as pure as the mountain streams that feed it. Six million acres of wilderness parks surround the hotel. Strolling along the lakeshore with ducks quacking, birds singing and building nests, dandelions carpeting rolling hills in a blaze of yellow, apple blossoms exploding into bloom and backdropped by a range of snow-capped mountains, I felt the overall picture exposed Mother Nature at her creative best.

The Bariloche region is often likened to Switzerland, but Fodor, famous author of travel books, claims it outdoes Switzerland in natural beauty. The snow-capped Andes are more rugged than the Alps, and the lakes are more glimmering and more vivid in coloring. Tramping over grassy meadows, I suddenly realized no insects such as black flies or mosquitoes pestered me, and this made the area even more of a paradise.

Preparing to leave the Llao-Llao for our combination boat and bus trip to Chile and watching mesmerized as rays from an early morning sun ricocheted off dazzling mountain tops, I doubted anything could match the Bariloche region for eye-catching beauty. The day's journey, however, would furnish other natural spectacles that would match those at Bariloche. For the first leg of our long trek over the Andes into Chile, we took a launch 30 miles across Lake Nahuel Huapi to Puerto Blest. The captivating color combinations of deep blue water, dark green forested slopes threaded with white-frothed mountain streams tumbling from snow-capped peaks, and all under a cloudless azure sky was absolutely breathtaking.

Transferring our baggage from launch to bus and vice versa would become a monumental task as the day progressed, but at Puerto Blest the surrounding scenery helped allay our impatience. By bus we crawled along a dusty gravel road engulfed in forest greenery to Puerto Allegre where another launch waited to carry us across Lake Frias to Port Frias on the Argentina/Chilean border. Lake Frias rivaled Nahuel Huapi for splendor. Barely a ripple disturbed the placid water, and its variety of hues from blue to light silver green reflected the enchanting landscape like a giant mirror. Although only 150 miles from the Pacific, all waters we traveled during the morning flowed to the Atlantic as we hadn't crossed the hump of the Andes, our next destination.

From Fort Frias we bused at a snail's pace over a treacherous trail across the crest of the Andes. Toward the summit, snow began to appear and numerous trees in full leaf, their trunks encased in snow, provided an unusual picture. At the pinnacle, the hypothetical border between Chile and Argentina, we debused to take the kinks from our legs and inspect the unusual mountain terrain. Creeping down the mountain road, we sat transfixed by the slowly passing panorama. Splashing, dashing, frothing streams tumbled down the slopes in a jungle of lush foliage.

Following a lunch break at Puella, Chile, we boarded another launch for our trip across unique Lake Todos los Santos, which like Lake Frias has an amazing combination of dazzling colors including an emerald green that gave the lake the name of Esmerelda. On several high hills overlooking the shimmering water, farms with grazing cattle and fields of grain hugged the slopes and lake, their only means of communication with civilization. A lonesome life, it would certainly be ideal for any nature lover wanting to turn his back on modern society. Overlooking Lake Todos like a giant sentinel, Mount Ozorno, though not the loftiest peak in the Andes, is clearly one of the most imposing and resembles a giant bowl of jello topped with whipped cream. The majestic peak, visible for many miles, provides a remarkable guidepost for the surrounding country.

Arriving in Petrohue near sunset, we changed vehicles for the final leg of our long day's journey to Puerto Montt. A few miles from Petrohue, we stopped at Ensenanda and walked a quarter of a mile to Petrohue Falls and rapids. It seemed impossible for anything to surpass the natural wonders we had witnessed the previous few days, but the minutes spent at Petrohue Falls topped them all for outright enchantment. Swirling water, thundering, splashing and gurgling over rocks and through rugged terrain in the foreground, the icy peaks of Mount Ozorno masked in pink and gold by a setting sun in the background, created a rare picture no adjectives can adequately do justice. We were privileged to be part of one of those magic moments in life with which mortals are occasionally blessed.

Darkness rapidly engulfed us as we skirted Lake Llanquihue, the biggest of all Chilean lakes, and slowly headed for Puerto Montt after a long but unforgettable and dramatic day.

Puerto Montt anchors the northern end of the 900-mile chain of lakes and canals which stretch to Tierra del Fuego in the southern most regions of Chile. One of the smaller South American nations, Chile is still larger than Texas and is one of the oddest shaped countries in the world. Like a toothpick, it stretches 2,630 miles in length between the Pacific Ocean and the Andes Mountains, but only averages 125 in width and has more Pacific coastline than the USA. Someone once said you had to be thin to be a Chilean, otherwise you'd fall off. Though it does not have as many spectacular Andean peaks as Argentina, the Andes nevertheless are all over the place, covering a third of the total area and making a dramatic and formidable curtain only a few miles from the sea. Moreover, these stupendous mountains twitch and tremble, and as a result, the country is chronically afflicted with earthquakes, some quite disastrous.

Chile had a different beginning than most other Spanish/American nations. Pedro de Valdivia, one of the boldest of Pizarro's captains, marched down from Peru and brought most of Chile into the Spanish domain beginning in 1540. A previous expedition had failed because of fierce, stubborn and skillful resistance by the Araucanian and other Indians who inhabited the land. These aboriginies even resisted penetration by the Incas before the arrival of the white man. The Araucanians were the toughest warriors ever known among Indians in South America, and for 350 years they fought the invading Europeans, a longer period than any other race in the world has continuously fought for independence. They finally quit fighting at the end of the 19th century, but today many of them refuse to speak the language or associate with other than their own. The Spaniards lost more men trying to subdue the stubborn and fierce Araucanians than in all of their campaigns elsewhere on the continent. Valdivia, also a stubborn military leader, succeeded in establishing a foothold in central Chile and founded Santiago in 1541. Seeking to press south in 1553, he was captured by the Araucanians and executed by being made to swallow molten gold. Legend has it that the Indians said, "You come for gold—here it is." Today, hardy and industrious metizos (Indian and Spanish) constitute 70 percent of the population, pure whites 28 percent, and pure Indians 2 percent. There are no black people.

Chile's national hero is Bernardo O'Higgins, who together with Argentine General San Martin, delivered the country from Spain in the early 1800s. During the 160 years from its independence, Chile had many presidents under different forms of government, though mostly democratic in nature. In 1970, Salvadore Allende Gossens, a Marxist, was elected president in a free election, although he didn't have more than 39 percent of the vote. Gossens immediately began a great nationalization program and took over many private Chilean and American companies, including three American-owned copper mines. In an attack on the presidential palace in 1973, a military junta seized power and claimed Gossens had killed himself, a contention never officially confirmed. Rumors at the time suggested there had been American CIA involvement.

Before leaving for Santiago by air, we took an interesting tour of Puerto Montt. A Pacific port and southern terminus of Chile's mainland railways, and the Pan-American Highway, Puerto Montt is also the starting point for navigation through the inland waterways, some of which we had just journeyed through. Surrounding scenery of forested hills, picturesque lakes, narrow fiords, and peaks, including Mount Ozorno still visible in the distance, made the region a popular resort.

We made a short stopover at Puerto Montt's famous seafood stalls and small eating establishments along the harborfront and they offered a fantastic assortment of salt-water delicacies. Spiny green sea urchins had an oyster-like flesh. They were swallowed raw and seemed to be a popular item with the natives. One specimen called Piure appeared to be nothing more than ocean mud, but when pried open, they produced an edible substance that was gulped down with great ecstasy by local people as well as by a few members of our group—which didn't include me.

When we left Puerto Montt for Santiago, we began our steady return northward toward the equator. As in several other South American countries, a high percentage of Chile's population lives in the capital city. Situated at an altitude of 1,700 feet and surrounded with lush forested hills and snowcapped mountains, the city enjoys a distinctive locale and with warm sunny days and cool evenings most of the year, it is climatically a pleasant place to live. Several peaks up to four miles in height within 50 miles of Santiago offer some of the finest skiing on the continent. While some architectural elements of the colonial era remain, the atmosphere of Santiago is largely modern, with neo-classical government edifices, modern office buildings and sumptuous residences. Spacious parks, plazas, gardens and wide avenues are also characteristic features.

Hills dominate the city, but San Cristobal Hill, 1,200 feet in height, is adorned with a statue of the Virgin Mary, a gift from France, and when floodlit at night, it can be seen from almost any point in the metropolis. On our city tour we stopped at Club Hipico, one of the most beautiful race tracks in South America. An increasing number of Chilean thoroughbreds are being shipped to North America.

Driving through the Las Condes residential district nearing the National Congress Building, I snapped a picture of a military policeman about thirty seconds before our guide informed us we weren't allowed to take such pictures. Within half a block, soldiers halted the bus and demanded the culprit who took a picture. With no alternative, I admitted my guilt but explained that I used my camera before being informed it was tabu. They caused no further trouble, and I retained the film but for the life of me couldn't understand their concern, and I left Chile a little apprehensive about their militaristic regime.

Santiago, like most great metropolises, has a beauty of its own and an author once said, "Santiago, Chile must be visited more than once before you become enthralled with its uniqueness." I enjoyed the city but wasn't confident I would ever return.

From Peru, the Incas administered their enormous empire and in Peru the Spaniards established their vast Colonial domain. The cultures of both people are the glory of the nation as well as the bane of its existence. These two incredibly diverse ways of life have existed side by side for more than four centuries and have not yet been melded. This hodgepodge of ancient and modern civilizations was next on our agenda.

Nearly half of Peru's population are Indians, descendants of the country's ancient indigenous inhabitants. The other half are either white or mestizo. More than three times the size of California, Peru is the third largest South American republic and is divided into three distinctive areas. From the Pacific Ocean going east, this triple entity consists of a narrow strip of stark desert stretching for 1400 miles along the coast. Next is the overpowering sierra, followed by the montana or jungle lowlands that comprise half the country. The desert would be forbidding except for crossing valleys stretching down from the Andes and supplying seasonal streams which nurture green irrigated stretches of sugar and cotton plantations. It never rains in the desert, making it the driest place on earth, and this dryness has preserved intact the mummified bodies of people buried centuries ago on the slopes just outside their valley settlements.

Thousands of years before the Spanish conquest, the land now known as Peru was inhabited like Mexico by complex and sophisticated societies. They spread their form of civilization through the Andes, the coastal valley lands and deserts and part of the forested foothills in the east. The Incas were only the last, and in some ways, they were not even the most advanced of many different civilizations that had flourished in Peru. Some were primitive, others had highly distinctive cultures whose stonework, pottery, and textiles are now deemed among the finest of their kind in the world. The picture of the overlapping Peruvian cultures is still unclear. Bones and artifacts have been traced back many thousands of years and the coastal desert is littered with shell mounds which have been dated back to 3000 B.C.

Indian tribes still live in isolation and endure the same meager untouched existence their ancestors led in ancient times. Efforts are constantly being made to pierce further the barrier of mountain and forest. The Indians, underprivileged and underpaid, suffer from inadequate political representation as well as from fear, distrust, and passivity. It has frequently been said that the Spanish conquest of Peru was never finished.

Francisco Pizarro, conqueror of Peru, made his first expedition down the Pacific coast from Panama in 1527, attracted by rumors of gold to the south. In 1531 with an incredibly small contingent of 183 men, Pizarro through guile, treachery, and murder overpowered the mighty Incan

Empire and founded Lima as his capital in 1535. Lima remained the seat of Spanish viceroys until Argentine liberator, Jose de San Martin captured it in 1821. Defeated by Simon Bolivar and Antonio J. de Sucre, Spain recognized Peruvian independence in 1824. For one and a half centuries, the country suffered through a series of different forms of democratic governments. In 1968, a military coup ousted the president and took power, and in 1976, another coup replaced that with another military regime still in power at the time of our visit. Composed primarily of the middle class, the present government maintains it is neither capitalist nor Communist, but nationalist and humanist.

Lima, the fifth largest city in South America, was for 300 years the dominant Spanish city on the continent. With overtones of an imperialistic metropolis, Lima utterly dominates Peru and has been called "a city searching for a country." Despite its enormity and historical background, we spent little time in Lima except a short stopover at the Plaza de Armas, the most impressive sector which contains the Government Palace, Cathedral, Archbishops Palace, City Hall, and Union Club. Driving south out of the metropolis along the Pan-American Highway, we passed squatter or slum towns called barriadas which form a scabrous crust around two-thirds of the city and contain 700,000 very miserable persons.

About 20 miles south of Lima at Pachacamac, we visited the National Archeological Museum containing mummies, pottery, jewels, and tapestries from ancient Inca cultures. From the museum we bused a short distance to the ruins of the ancient city of Pachacamac dating back to 300 B.C. where we leisurely strolled through the methodical resurrection of that aged civilization. Built before the time of the Inca in one of the irrigable valleys of the coastal desert, Pachacamac is noted for frescoes that once adorned adobe walls. At the time of the Spanish conquest it was a major Inca shrine. Gazing around at the sun-baked sand-encircled ruins, I tried to envision the scene witnessed by Hernandez, Francisco Pizarro's brother, when he and his conquistadores rode over the sand dunes in 1553 and suddenly faced that thriving Incan settlement, the largest city at the time on the Pacific coast. Hernandez Pizarro destroyed idols, killed priests, and looted temples in the normal European conqueror's disregard for existing American civilizations. The ruins encircle the top of a low hill, the crest crowned with The Temple of the Sun, a pyramid built of sun-baked bricks in 1350. The walls were covered in frescoes of bird and animal designs, and doors were inlaid with coral, crystal and turquoise.

Roberto, our knowledgeable Latin guide, walked us into an area where only archeologists were normally permitted, and we viewed actual reclamation projects under way. Looking in one direction we saw ruins gradually becoming unearthed, and within a few yards in another direction, a huge mound covered with drifting sand completely hiding what obviously would be another intriguing temple with hidden treasures that only time would divulge. One of our group picked up a small bone in the drifting dunes and Roberto said it was human. Resurrection of the ancient city believed to have covered about four square miles is painstakingly slow due to lack of sufficient capital. Roberto complained that the USA shouldn't be spending billions of dollars in outer space exploration when such a desperate need exists for funds to unearth the remains of our ancestors. Returning to Lima we bypassed a massive city dump where literally thousands of unfortunate Indians frantically scratched among smoldering garbage for morsels of food. I wondered how Roberto could be so concerned with our early ancestors who no longer faced life's tribulations when his own countrymen suffered the indignities of starvation. Priorities often appear absurd and difficult to understand, but that condition is a world-wide phenomenon.

From Lima we took a one-hour flight to Cuzco, the ancient Incan capital of South America, where the Inca heritage is preserved and evident in almost every aspect of that enchanting old city. Most inhabitants distinctly show their Indian ancestry, and many present buildings rise from original Incan stone foundations.

The Incas' star began to rise in the 11th century in the vicinity of Cuzco, their capital in the Peruvian highlands. Among the greatest organizers of all time, the Incas were unabashedly imperialistic and aimed at creating a totally Incan continent, a goal they went a long way toward fulfilling. At its zenith their empire reached one third the size of the USA, held 6 million people, and became one of the greatest planned societies the world had known. It survived 500 years until the early 16th century when it died at the hands of a handful of Spaniards. They succeeded because of a brilliant sense of over-all planning and control, with which they evolved a smooth functioning pyramidal type dictatorship where people gave up individual liberties in exchange for full stomachs. Also their lack of pride allowed them to incorporate the best cultures of the people they conquered.

The Incas were great metallurgists, statisticians, political scientists, agriculturists, builders, and engineers as well as great artisans. They mined silver, gold and copper and were skilled at smelting, making alloys such as bronze and fashioning objects both practical and aesthetic. They counted by means of knotted ropes, which allowed them to compile statistics that even Washington would admire today. They had no cows, pigs or horses, but they domesticated the llama, alpaca and the dog.

Their thousand miles of road ranked among the wonders of the world and provided fast communications with every corner of the immense empire. Trained couriers who ran in relays with messages made overland journeys in a few days that later took the Spanish several weeks on horseback or by carriage.

Inherited from previous cultures, the clan became the groundwork of their society. Families under the jurisdiction of a village elder controlled the land, generally on behalf of the state, to whose officials he was subordinate. They believed their system, a type of socialism, though often harsh, was the only way to assure a viable state and systematic distribution of limited resources.

In Cuzco we were advised to have a couple of hours rest before moving about; otherwise we'd likely come down with "soroche" or altitude sickness caused by the ancient city's location of 11,400 feet above sea level. Following my siesta, I strolled slowly to the city square with a queasy stomach and feeling like I carried a hundred pounds on my back. It usually requires about 48 hours to acclimatize to excessive elevation, but the historic atmosphere in the old city soon overpowered my lethargy. In ages past at City Square, the Incas brought out mummies from the Temple of the Sun on feast days and arranged them in rows beside the reigning Inca. Over the centuries the square witnessed many executions of Incas in revolt, of conquistadors by conquistadors, and of rebels during the War of Independence, but now only amicable tourists loll about the city core. Around the square are colonial arcades and four churches. A cathedral constructed in 17th century Renaissance style has a painting of Christ attributed to Van Dyck. Incan stone foundations with Spanish adobe walls, steeped in legend and tradition, line the steep and narrow streets that wind down sloping hillsides from the center of the ancient capital.

The ruined fortress of Sacsayhuaman located on a rise in the northern outskirts was built in the 15th century. An imposing terraced fortress over a third of a mile long, Sacsayhuaman is a masterpiece of stone construction. Massive blocks (one 38 feet long, 18 feet high and 6 feet thick) were brought from long distances over rugged terrain without the benefit of wheeled vehicles and were fitted precisely without mortar so that you can't even stick a knife blade in the seams. The walls contain 21 bastions where Inca chieftans reviewed their armies, but nothing remains of the great fortified towers each of which would have held a thousand men. An impressive throne remains plus subterranean passages said to be the abode of oracles and where the Incas may have buried some of their treasure. A herd of llama and an alpaca went galloping through the venerable parade grounds and began to graze beside the hoary old walls. Though completely unaware of the historical significance of their pastureland and the drama that had unfolded over the eons, the animals somehow seemed to fit the environment.

Cuzco, Peru's leading tourist attraction, is noted as one of the most interesting cities in the hemisphere, and after only a one day visit, I could understand why. The fascinating blend of old and new is rarely witnessed in such magnificent surroundings.

The rise and fall of the Inca civilization, one of the most dramatic stories of mankind's constant struggle, perhaps reached its stunning climax at Machu Picchu, their lost city. To reach Machu Picchu, only 70 miles northwest of Cuzco, requires a slow 3½-hour train ride. At the onset, leaving the city of Cuzco requires an hour as the train makes four switchbacks zigzagging up the mountain slope before entering the lush green valley of the Inca Empire.

Forty-five miles north of Cuzco, the village of Ollanta ytambo contains the remnants of a fortress which sheltered the Incas when they fled from the oncoming Spaniards. On terraced hillsides are remains of lookout posts and ruins of what were once barricades for soldiers. Twenty-five miles further along the Urubamba canyon floor, beside the rushing brown waters of the Urubamba River, the train stops at what appears to be the end of civilization. The valley suddenly disappears in a maze of mountains, lush, impenetrable jungle gorges, and the rapidly moving river. Gazing up the precipitous slopes from the train station it is impossible to conceive that 1,500 feet up the mountain but completely hidden from view are the remains of the last known stronghold of the great Incan civilization. A steep road with hairpin curves ascends the mountain's forested slopes. While being borne upward in slow though relative comfort by motorized vehicle, the difficulty explorers and archaeologists face while searching in such terrain without a trail becomes obvious. A dozen mini-buses shuttling tourists from the valley floor to the ruins of Machu Picchu barely missed head-on collisions at every torturous curve. The fifteen-minute spine-tingling journey is rapidly forgotten, however, once you step from the bus and behold the incredible sight before your eyes. The unique beauty of the world-renowned site situated amidst exuberant jungle vegetation on the summit of precipitous mountains affords a scene that those who make the ascent will never forget. High upon a rocky pinnacle in a narrow saddle between two sharp mountain peaks, the aged ruins overlook the Urubamba River 2,000 feet below. Its history, though legendary, indicates the city may have been the home of the Inca prior to their migration to Cuzco as well as their last stronghold after Spanish conquest. Spanish explorers never discovered the fortress. It was found by an American, Hiram Bingham, in 1911. One of the few urban centers of pre-Colombian America in existence, Bingham found the imposing site virtually intact except for straw roofs which, of course, had rotted. For centuries the town had lay hidden under ferns and bush.

No historical documentation has ever been found to enlighten us on the purpose of the fortress. Some archaeologists claim that Machu Picchu became a final refuge for the virgins of the Sun from the conquering Spanish, because bones found were at a ratio of ten female to one male and all of the gold ornaments were women's.

Hot humid weather conditions made climbing steep stairways through the magnificent old citadel at the high altitude quite taxing. "Ancient Summit," the name Machu signifies in the Quechu language, is completely encircled by terraces constructed somewhat like gigantic staircases. Though they seem to barely hang from enormous precipices that surround the city, this type of arrangement apparently gained the vital area required for the cultivation of crops. Another section of terraces with narrower plains served not for agricultural purposes but to guarantee stability of the mountain itself. Water, so vital to life, came from the slopes of high peaks along stone canals. In the center of the city, sixteen perfectly tooled fountains distributed the water in various levels permitting easy rationing.

Slowly climbing to the summit we passed the tower, a magnificent piece of Incan architecture, the Palace of the Princess, believed to have been the residence of the high priest, the Royal Tomb and Royal Palace. The military area naturally had the finest view down the valley, while the ruling and religious leaders lived in the main plaza.

Although exceedingly tiring from the tropic sun, the tour of Machu Picchu will remain a highpoint in my South American journey. When you contemplate this splendid race of people slowly retreating up the Urubamba Valley in front of the steadily advancing Spaniards and choosing that aerie on the mountain top as perhaps their final retreat, it staggers the imagination. Archaeologists mostly agree that whatever its purpose, Machu Picchu was a military garrison, and eventually the remnants of the great Incan Empire simply melted away into the jungle, leaving Machu Picchu concealed for nearly four centuries.

From Cuzco our itinerary called for a visit to Quito Ecuador, but inclement weather prevented us from landing and caused our pilot to detour to Bogota, Colombia, where we spent the night. Leaving the Bogota airport for Quito the following morning, I underwent a terrifying experience. Passing through baggage check just prior to boarding the plane, a burly Colombian in plain clothes shouting "Policia, policia", seized my passport and grabbed my arm. Before I could open my mouth another man leaped forward, pinned my other arm behind my back, and the two men hustled me down a flight of stairs into a large room. In the frantic moments before disappearing from view, I rapidly scanned the terminal hoping to catch the attention of one of my traveling companions. Seeing no one did nothing to calm my surging panic as they would have no inkling of my whereabouts. After stripping me naked in front of five people, including a young woman, methodically searching my hand luggage, examining the scars on my leg, and comparing my passport picture with several others hanging on the wall, they indicated I should get dressed. No one spoke English, but after I had regained a little composure, the police captain grabbed me in his arms, kissed both cheeks, and said "A no prob, a no prob." He then dispatched a young lady with me and my belongings to catch the plane barely one minute before it taxied for departure. The horrifying encounter caused me to shake so violently that on our flight to Quito, Ecuador, I wore the crease out of my trousers.

Ecuador, meaning "equator," a country about the size of Arizona extends 100 miles into the Northern Hemisphere and 400 into the southern. Bounded by Colombia, Peru and the Pacific, the nation is divided into three zones by two ranges of the Andes: a hot, humid lowland area on the coast; temperate highlands between the ranges; and rainy, tropical lowlands in the east called "The Oriente" and true headwaters of the mighty Amazon.

Ecuador, continuously occupied since the dawn of recorded history, existed for many generations before the Inca Empire established their form of civilization on the land. By the 16th century it became the northern section of the Inca Empire. The Spanish had little difficulty conquering Ecuador, and it came officially into the Spanish realm in 1534. Like the rest of South America, Ecuador became restless in the early years of the 19th century, and under the able leadership of Jose de Sucre, the Spaniards were routed at the battle of Pichincha in 1822. For eight years they joined Colombia and Venezuela in La Gran Colombia, but Ecuador pulled out in 1830 and formed its own republic. Internal political unrest has troubled the nation seriously for the past 100 years, and military coups and counter-coups have caused constant instability.

Forty percent of the population is pure Indian, 40 percent mestizo, 10 percent white and 10 percent mulatto. The largest landowners and those with business interests in towns, both primarily white, fear that the Indians, if educated, will take over political and economic power. So similar to South Africa's apartheid policy, the tendency is to deny them education and other opportunities in order to keep them subjugated.

Few if any other small countries boast such a variety of geography, climate, flora and fauna as Ecuador. From the Galapagos to Guayaquil and from the colorful market at Otavalo down the steep eastern slopes of the Andes to the Oriente, Ecuador abounds with color and character.

Quito, the capital city lies at the foot of Pinchincha Volcano in the hollow of a gently sloping, fertile valley. Only a few miles below the equator but at an elevation of 9,350 feet, it has a pleasant, balmy climate, though it usually rains sometime during the afternoon. Subject to earthquakes, it has been damaged several times. The sprawling mountain capital dates back to 1534 when Sebastian Benalcazar, a Spaniard, founded the city on the site of the ancient Indian town of Shyria. Since its founding, Quito has welcomed an endless procession of the men who created Spain's Empire in the New World. The city still vividly reflects its historic past in the unmatched art and architecture that survives in abundance.

Fifty-seven churches in the small city are the principal tourist attractions. We visited three of these venerable old houses of worship. La Cathedral, a renowned treasure chest of great art, marks the city's stormy political past with mutilations marking the outside walls. Despite exterior scars, the ageless classic beauty of the interior still shines through. La Compania, one of the New World's most magnificent churches, is famous for its glittering interior, coated with gold leaf and an outstanding colonial art collection. San Francisco, the oldest religious foundation in South America, dates back to 1535.

The gilt and glitter of the churches contrasted flagrantly with the quaint but obviously destitute Indians who idled placidly outside their doors. The colorful Indians and mestizos inhabiting the capital seemed strangely out of place with the modern parks and buildings that enhance the city. Quito's physical prominence is probably its greatest attribute. The second highest capital in the world (La Paz, Bolivia is higher), it lies nestled in the lap of the noble Andes and gives the appearance from the distance of a city in the clouds.

Ecuador's centuries-old Indian markets are one of the country's outstanding attractions. Both north and south of Quito in the high Andean valleys a series of weekly fairs attract thousands of visitors annually, affording them a chance to buy native handicrafts and textiles at bargain prices. Within a radius of 100 miles of the capital, a colorful Indian fair is held every day of the week. We attended the Latacunga Fair, 55 miles south along the Pan-American Highway, romantically known as the Avenue of the Volcanoes, where no less than eleven snow-capped peaks frame the rich Latacunga-Ambato Valley.

Latacunga, a small town of 30,000 and once an Incan city, lies in a high mountain basin between the eastern and western Andean cordilleras. Towering volcanic Mount Cotapaxi overwhelms the village, and indirectly the mountain provided most of the gray lava rock with which the town's buildings are constructed. With luck and clear weather, the peaks of Cotapaxi and 8 other volcanic cones can be viewed from Latacunga. On our visit, however, heavy clouds obscured most of the mountain tops.

Our day at the market place coincided with "The Day of Death," a major religious holiday similar to North America's Memorial Day, and it proved more interesting than the Fair. Strangely enough, "The Day of Death" is a celebration when families gather in cemeteries to visit family crypts, trim grass plots, plant bulbs for spring flowers, and scrub gravestones. Some tombs, over eight feet in height and above-ground mausoleums, resemble miniature townhouses. The tombs which can accommodate ten or twelve families are used until the bodies decay, at which time the bones are removed and buried. Then the mausoleums are made ready for the next generation. Many families perched on the roofs of the crypts were enjoying a picnic complete with lunches, beer, and bottles of whiskey. The religious festival didn't deter pickpockets, who stole a wallet off one of our group containing over 200 American dollars. A fairgrounds operating full tilt near the cemetery contained ferris wheels and other paraphernalia jammed with happy, squealing youngsters and adults alike. It seemed an incongruity during the festival of the "Day of the Dead."

The Indian market, another beehive of activity, contained a conglomeration of stalls offering flowers, tropical fruits and vegetables, home embroidered fabrics, leather goods and livestock. The interesting panorama of Ecuadorian life seemed complete when I crossed the bridge over the rushing Cutuche River and, on the river bank below, saw an Indian mother washing her clothes in the river and laying them on a blanket to dry besides her sleeping spouse and frolicking children.

One sunny afternoon, Hugo, our tour director, and I hired a taxi and an excellent English-speaking guide, to take a 100-mile trip from Quito north along the Pan-American highway to Ibarra and Otavalo, within 50 miles of the Colombian border. At first we traversed arid mountainous terrain but then descended into the spectacular Guayllabamba Gorge and a fertile oasis near the equator where sheep and cattle ranching predominated. We stopped and took pictures at the equator and marvelled at the pleasant 75-degree temperature. In the province of Imbabura, we entered the land of the Otavalo Indians, a singularly lively and often prosperous group who produce commercial woolens. I watched fascinated as, with dexterity and ingenuity they wove their fabric of a combination of home-grown wool and colored spools of commercial banlon. Visiting a native market, I also enjoyed seeing Otavalenos stand stoically beside their homemade goods, but when tourists approached, they would barter with considerable emotion for the best possible dollar. Otavalo Indians are a pre-Inca tribe with a thousand-year heritage as farmer artisans. Except for necessities such as banlon and food staples like sugar and salt, they demand little of the white man, and their lives have altered only slightly in comparison to most other aborigines the world over who were conquered by and forced to live the way of the Europeans.

The two days spent at the Indian markets and countryside didn't portray the Ecuadorian Indians as prosperous individuals by our standards. Nevertheless, in comparison to most Canadian and American Indians, more often than not a degraded and demoralized race of humans, the Indians of Ecuador appear to live with a certain pride and have an immense desire to improve their financial position in life without giving in to the Europeans' idea of personal values.

From Quito we flew to Guayaquil, an excellent seaport, Ecuador's largest city and the country's commercial and financial center. We didn't take a tour but went directly to our waiting ship *The Iguana,* our home for seven nights on our exciting visit to the Galapagos Islands. A small ship as far as ocean vessels are concerned, it had three public decks which could accommodate 68 passengers, and we were filled to capacity. Our shipmates consisted of a large contingent of Dutch, a smaller group of British, a few French and the balance Americans and Canadians. The 600-mile ocean voyage across the South Pacific Ocean took 60 hours. Time at sea was devoted to slowly acclimatizing our skin to direct rays of the equatorial sun and attending lectures given twice daily on all aspects of our Galapagos Island venture by three English-speaking, competent and devoted young men, our guides during the week.

World-renowned Galapagos Island, one of the earth's most unique, truly different natural regions, is a strange place filled with life and things found nowhere else. Certainly not a typical tourist paradise, nevertheless, the unusual barren group of islands, with a variety of bizarre animals and plants cannot fail to strongly affect any visitor.

Volcanic in origin, the islands rose from lava outpourings on the bottom of the ocean and comprise an independent biological unit, distant from the South American continent and never attached to another land mass. Despite this fact, their native fauna and flora are derived principally from the equatorial American mainland. Over thousands if not millions of years, a few species arrived that were able to establish themselves and to evolve, though isolated from other members of their kind unable to cross the oceanic barrier. After they gained a foothold, they adapted to local conditions forming species endemic to the Galapagos Islands. Biologists say 37 percent of all species of shore fish and 96 percent of the reptiles are found nowhere else. An astonishing 47 percent of the plants grown are also not found anywhere but in the

Galapagos. And even within the island group itself, due to the changing character of each island, different forms have evolved on different islands. Charles Darwin began to realize all this when he visited the Galapagos in 1835 as a naturalist aboard the British survey vessel H.M.S *Beagle*. From those beginnings Darwin developed his theory of evolution—*The Origin of Species*. His visit to the islands is one of the landmarks in the history of science.

The archipelago, a territory of the Republic of Ecuador, lies astride the equator roughly 600 miles from the port of Guayaquil. There are thirteen major and six minor islands plus seventy-two inlets that have official names. The Galapagos Islands, lying at latitude zero, do not have a humid tropical climate because the Humboldt Current cools the air. Tropic birds, frigate birds and boobies are typical of tropical and subtropical waters, whereas penguins and albatross are more characteristic of subantarctic and antarctic waters, yet both groups reside in the Galapagos. Also coral reefs common in warm, tropical seas are nearly absent in the cool Galapagos waters.

No large land mammals ever reached the islands, and thus reptiles became dominant just as they were all over the world in ages past. To this extent the Galapagos fauna may be described as primitive or prehistoric, although the Galapagos reptiles are not actually the same as those that lived on the continents in past geological ages.

Having existed always without the menace of mankind, wildlife developed no instinctive fear of man, and most animals and birds are still extraordinarily tame. The exact age of the Galapagos group has been difficult to ascertain, but the oldest fossiliferous deposits yet discovered are probably Pliocene or up to 10 million years old. Those parts of the islands now exposed to view were built mainly during the last million years. Made up of basaltic lava, the islands themselves are the tops of gigantic volcanoes most of which rise from 7,000 to 10,000 feet above the ocean floor. Volcan Wolf, on Isabella Island, reaches farthest above the sea—to 5,600 feet. The Galapagos land masses total just 3,000 square miles but are dispersed over 40,000 miles of sea. Isabella, by far the largest island, is about 75 miles long, although Fernandino, San Salvador, Santa Cruz, and San Cristobal are all over 15 miles in length. Eruptions have taken place on six of the islands during historical times and several active volcanoes exist today. The last volcanic outbursts occurred in 1963 and 1968.

Discovered and called Galapagos (Spanish for tortoise) by the enterprising explorers of Spain in 1535, the archipelago was annexed by Ecuador in 1832. Despite their Latin lineage, the Galapagos bewitched so many British navigators and naturalists that English names are used for most of the islands as well as Spanish. Since their discovery, buccaneers, whalers and other visitors killed huge numbers of iguanas, birds, and other animals, wiping out some entirely. The tortoises especially were seriously threatened. Many thousands were put on board visiting ships as long-lasting sources of fresh meat as these tough reptiles can live an entire year without food or water. No extensive colonization of the islands took place until this century, although attempts were made as early as 1832 when Ecuador claimed possession.

The greatest threat to the ecology has been the domestic animals introduced to the islands over the past three centuries and allowed to run wild. Goats, the worst menace, destroy the vegetation, pigs and wild dogs attack young iguanas, and rats eat the eggs of tortoises, iguanas, and birds. Measures are under way to control such introduced animals and the unbelievable total of over 50,000 goats alone have been shot on three of the islands.

After 60 hours at sea and adequately tanned, we all excitedly anticipated our early morning landing on Hood Island. From the *Iguana*, we reached the islands by small landing boats called pungas propelled with outboard motors. Most islands lacked landing docks, and so the flat-bottomed pungas went swirling up on the sandy beach at the mercy of large ocean swells. When the boat hit the beach, everyone leaped overboard. With shoes, socks and camera equipment flung around your neck, you made a dash for dry land before the huge backwash took the boat back out to sea. Fifty percent of our shore excursions were wet landings and a constant source of amusement with our guides. In the usually violent surf many tourists, well advanced in age, had a difficult time scrambling ashore while fully dressed and clutching their personal belongings.

My immediate emotion when setting foot on Hood Island matched the exhilaration I sensed when confronted by the first herd of wild giraffes in the Serengetti Plains in Kenya. While sitting on a rock replacing my shoes and socks, sea lions from babies to bellowing old bulls swarmed nearby over rocks and sand, a small black storm petrel, the size of a sparrow, landed on my shoes, marine iguanas like miniature replicas of prehistoric dinosaurs eyed me suspiciously from a distance of two feet, and blue-footed boobies sitting on their nests only a few yards away paid me little heed. During those first enchanting moments, I sat transfixed in ecstacy at the unusual panorama of wildlife.

We strolled quietly along well-marked paths under the watchful eye of our guides who restrained any human interference with flora or fauna. Touching or feeding animals was absolutely forbidden as well as picking or mutilating vegetation in any way. Plastic garbage bags were strung around everyone's neck for all refuse from cigarette butts to empty film wrappers. After leaving our landing spot, we passed a colony of nesting blue-footed boobies, the most common seabirds in the Galapagos. Three booby species exist: red-footed, masked and blue-footed. Fluffy, white-downed chicks from previous hatches resembled walking puffballs, and we could walk within two feet of nesting females who would do no more than peck at our ankles if we didn't make any sudden movement.

Wandering among Hood Island's peculiar wildlife in an environment unlike anywhere else on the planet offered an intriguing phenomenon, especially with the apparent unconcern all creatures had for man. Along a rocky shoreline, ocean currents raced under a layer of rocks and came gushing out of a hole in the submarine lava with a loud whoosing roar resembling Old Faithful in Yellowstone National Park. A large herd of sea lions lying in the hot afternoon sun were taking advantage of the invigorating spray. Sitting near the blow hole with my camera provided a marvelous opportunity for photographing the menagerie of wildlife at close range.

The Darwin Research Center, located near Academy Bay on Santa Cruz Island, was next on our itinerary. Built in 1962, mutually financed by the Ecuadorian government, UNESCO, and other scientific organizations and staffed with scientists from around the world, the station's primary function is to conserve and study Galapagos flora and fauna. The Research Center personnel gave us an informative lecture on the reconstruction program of the Galapagos. In the tortoise house, egg incubators and rearing pens for the young of several subspecies were on display, and nearby corrals contained reptiles of various ages and sizes. Huge specimens in one pen resembled miniature tanks. Tortoises can weigh up to 550 pounds and live more than 150 years. As they are active only a few hours each day, perhaps the relationship between longevity and a relaxing existence may be a lesson for the human race.

A few miles off Santa Cruz lies South Plaza, a flat island composed of lava fault blocks and covered with sparse cacti plus thick, thorny, scrubby bushes. A large colony of land iguanas populate South Plaza. Along the north shore of the island rock-rimmed tidepools made excellent play areas for young sea lions, and the black shore rocks were dotted with huge scarlet Sally Lightfoot crabs. Among the cliffs, swallow-tailed gulls, petrels, shearwaters and a few red-billed tropicbirds had their nesting grounds. Returning to the landing area, I witnessed a female sea lion suckling a year old cub while a new offspring lay sprawled on her back—an unusual sight according to our guides.

Though it was hot and humid, a delightful ocean breeze made walking along the marked trail quite comfortable. I never lost my intrigue with the strange creatures, especially the land iguanas that can attain a length of four feet and were so tame it was not uncommon for them to walk across your feet.

After an all-night cruise we arrived one bright morning at Tagus Cove on the west side of Isabella Island. Surrounded by steep hills, the bay offers a small, deep, safe anchorage. Whalers who landed there in the early 19th century established a custom of engraving their names in the soft surface of the cliffs. Modern sailors continue the custom by daubing white paint on the banks, thus destroying the beauty of the cove.

Isabella, 75 miles long, contains more than half the total land area of the Galapagos. Six huge volcanoes, five considered still active, form Isabella, and these six constitute one of the most active volcanic regions in the world. At least thirteen eruptions have taken place since 1911. Boarding our pungas, we took an absorbing two-hour boat ride around Isabella in a tranquil sea. Hugging the shore around Cape Berkley, black basaltic lava formations showed quite plainly where layers of lava flowed down the slopes from the numerous eruptions over the centuries.

During our sea excursion we again observed a wide range of wildlife which inhabited the region along the basaltic cliffs. The flightless cormorant provided an excellent example of the theory of evolution. With no natural enemies on the island, the bird had no reason to escape, and by not exercising its wings, over the ages it lost its ability to fly. Now reduced in size, the bird's wings are rudimentary and useless for flight. When swimming, they are held close against the body, but once the bird climbs from the water to an elevated level, its wings are held out to dry in typical cormorant fashion. In those parts of the world where the bird has natural enemies, the cormorant dries its wings immediately after leaving the water in preparation for sudden take off. Though the wings of the flightless cormorant are useless, it still performs this ritual though ancestral habit. The Galapagos penguins, endemic to the island, only inhabit the cool waters along the coast of Fernandino and Isabella and are another example of the unique creatures that colonize the region. Blue-footed boobies and marine iguanas were the most prodigious species, but high in the crags we sighted a wild cat. Although originally house pets, these feral cats have been roaming the islands in some cases for more than a century.

On Isabella those who wished took a long arduous climb to the high point on the island. Clambering up the ancient crater's steep embankments with the temperature hovering in the 90 degree range provided strenuous exercise. Despite the hardship the panoramic view at the summit, including the fascinating spectacle of Isabella and Fernandino soaring from the multi-hued waters of the Pacific Ocean like giant boats, made the difficult climb more memorable.

Point Espinoza situated on a beautiful coastal sector of Fernandino Island is rimmed with a green mangrove forest and broad apron of lava and shell sand. A variety of wildlife inhabited the captivating island paradise including sea lions, marine iguanas, and colonies of penguins, flightless cormorants, and Galapagos hawks. At the landing while waiting for the pungas to return us to the Iguana, one of our Dutch lady tour companions went swimming in a sheltered bay. A young sea lion frolicked and clowned around her like a pet dog and appeared quite lovable, unlike old bulls who become vicious and attack anything that approaches their harem of cows.

Although our visits to other islands, such as San Salvador and Santiago, didn't introduce us to a large variety of new creatures, each separate land mass did contain some of its own unique inhabitants plus an environment exclusively its own.

On the final afternoon we cruised to Bartholome, a small island off the eastern tip of San Salvador. No creatures of any consequence populated Bartholome, but a strenuous climb to Pinncacle Rock offered the Galapagos Islands' most gorgeous view. The rugged terrain and stark landscape on the volcanic land mass resembled the moon's surface, with the only living thing some lichens—the first plant to get established after a volcanic eruption. Although a strenuous hike, the superb view looking back toward uninhabited Santiago Island offered a fitting finale to our fascinating Galapagos tour.

Regardless of any scientific aspirations or qualifications, most individuals would find the Galapagos Islands a source of continuous wonderment and excitement. Many things contribute to the magnetism of the strange land, but the unconcern most creatures showed for human interlopers will remain the most unforgettable aspect to me and I hope the islands will be forever protected to allow the slow evolutionary process to continue.

During the last war, a huge U.S. military base was established at Baltra Island to protect the Panama Canal. Now the old landing strip is the official Galapagos airfield from which we caught a flight back to Guayaquil and on to Quito. From Quito we flew to Bogota, Colombia, a country about which I had mixed emotions resulting from my run-in with their police when departing a week earlier. The fourth largest and only South American country with an Atlantic and Pacific coastline, Colombia is a land of contrasts, from torrid jungles to majestic snow-covered mountain crests. Long before the discovery of America, different races of natives inhabited the Colombian territory. Spain conquered the region in 1525 and governed through a system of viceroys until they were defeated by Simon Bolivar in 1819 and a new presidency began. Political violence and banditry have resulted in repeated states of emergency since the 1950s, but despite these internal problems, political and civil freedoms are respected.

Bogota lies in a steep uneven bowl of mountains. Though only a few degrees north of the equator, the city's elevation of 8,560 feet gives it a pleasant climate with cool evenings. Bogota's population explosion of more than 3 million in the past half century is illustrated by narrow colonial streets rising beside one-story shacks.

The showplace of Colombia's capital city is the Gold Museum. On display are 15,000 pre-Colombian gold pieces that by weight alone gives the collection a worth of over $30 million.

Although my traveling companions and I had the opportunity to see more of Bogota, we were all travel weary from our Galapagos jaunt with its early morning excursions, and so we chose to rest in preparation for the last lap of our South American odyssey. Though I was smiling when passing through baggage check the following morning for our departure to Panama City, as I recalled the chilling incident of ten days earlier, my lighthearted spirit soon disintegrated. The same grizzled old character grabbed me and again shouted, "Policia, policia."

While being unceremoniously hustled down the stairs for the second time and frantically trying to spot Hugo, our tour director, my mood turned ugly. Gesticulating wildly that I'd been along this route only a short time before, I somehow made them understand the reason for my annoyance. After a consultation in Spanish, they decided to my everlasting gratitude that they did recognize me and once more with genuine apologies guided me back to my waiting comrades who were beginning to wonder if perhaps I was a fugitive from justice. Our 1½-hour flight to Panama City took us within a few miles of returning to our own hemisphere.

Panama, the youngest of the Central American republics, is a curious blend of the historic, modern, and primitive. The hot humid nation has a shoreline of 477 miles on the Caribbean and 787 miles on the Pacific. In reality there are three Panamas; the landscaped town of the ten-mile wide Canal Zone, under the jurisdiction of the United States; the noisy international glitter of ultramodern Panama City; and tropical jungles where Indians perpetuate the ancient, primitive mysteries in their race. Its geographic position including the Canal has made this tiny tropical country a hub of world commerce.

Columbus discovered the isthmus in 1501 when he dropped anchor near the mouth of the Chagres River on his fourth and last voyage. Even though Spain controlled the area for centuries, they were constantly harassed by the English and particularly Francis Drake, who frequently lay in wait in Caribbean corridors for the gold-laden vessels of Spain. Henry Morgan sacked Panama City in 1671. With the decline of Spain, Panama fell into a state of lethargy but gained independence in 1819. Two years later, the country entered a federation with Colombia, Venezuela, and Ecuador, but that arrangement didn't pan out, and so they formed the Independent Republic of Panama in 1903. Panama granted the U.S. perpetual control over the Canal Zone that same year. Considerable agitation by Panamanians over the terms of that treaty the past three quarters of a century caused the U.S. Congress in the early 1980s to arrive at an agreement eventually relinquishing ownership of the Canal Zone back to Panama.

A cause of dissention between local people and the U.S. military is easily discernible when you view some of their deplorable living conditions compared to the neat and pretentious quarters of American families residing in the Canal Zone. Though interested in their politics and history, my prime purpose for visiting the country was to inspect the Panama Canal and that took up the biggest part of an afternoon, which I spent at the Miraflores Locks.

Completed in 1914 at a cost of $387 million, the history and statistics of the Canal are fascinating, and at the time of planning, the obstacles must have appeared almost insurmountable. Engineering problems involving digging through a mountain range to make a ditch wide enough to float the largest ships of the day, constructing the largest earth-dam ever built, designing the most massive canal locks ever conceived, constructing the biggest gates ever swung, and conquering huge landslides were only a few of the hurdles that had to be overcome.

Due to the geographical alignment of the isthmus, a great variation of tides occur in the two oceans at the canal terminals. The Pacific tides are diurnal—two highs and two lows a day and with an extreme variation of 22.7 feet. At the Atlantic entrance, the tide is irregular, and the extreme variation there is only 3.05 feet. Due to the winding nature of the isthmus, the Pacific terminus is 27 miles east of the Atlantic or Caribbean terminus. From Limon Bay on the Caribbean, a ship is raised at Gatum Locks by a continuous flight of three steps to an elevation of 85 feet. After traversing Satun Lake, a fresh-water lake, the waterway crosses the Continental Divide through Gaillard Cut, the deepest excavations for the canal with banks exceeding 300 feet in height. From this section alone initial excavations totalled more than 230 million cubic yards, a volume equivalent to a 12-foot-square shaft cut through the center of the earth.

The lock gates are steel structures 65 feet wide and 7 feet thick; they vary in height from 47 to 82 feet and weigh from 390 to 730 tons. Each lock chamber holds about 8,800,000 cubic feet of water or about 65,800,000 gallons. Every time a ship makes a complete transit some 52 million gallons of fresh water are spilled into the sea. The amount of fresh water consumed in the operation of the Panama Canal in one day would keep the city of Boston supplied for two weeks.

The average time for a ship in Canal waters is 16 hours. In addition to the unbelievable savings in time as opposed to going around the Horn, the financial savings are recognized to be ten times the amount of the toll. At Miraflores Locks, I watched with awe the passage of a huge British freighter and several smaller ships and was quite amazed to discover the existence of two parallel locks allowing the movement of two vessels simultaneously. The Panama Canal, an outstanding engineering feat, contributes enormously to world trade and economics, but already numerous ships are too large to use the canal's facilities. Consideration is being given to a widening of certain locks.

Our final day proved to be as interesting as any on the entire itinerary. From Panama City we took a twin-engine aircraft for a 50-mile flight over Panama's lush, fertile highlands to the Caribbean coast for a visit with the Cuna Indians on the San Blas Islands. The landing strip in the middle of the jungle was primitive by any standards but adequate for the purpose designed. An American, John Mann, who had spent 30 years among the Cuna Indians and our guide for the day, met us at the airport. John owned a sturdy 30 foot inboard covered with a palm-thatched roof. He used the craft as a water taxi from the jungle airport to whichever island he chose to escort his load of tourists.

San Blas, off the northeastern coast of Panama, also called the Mulatas Archipelago, comprises some 332 islands. Cuna Indians, the inhabitants are almost pureblooded aborigines of Carib origin, the tribe almost thoroughly wiped out in other Caribbean Islands in the 16th century. Protected by a treaty with the government of Panama, the Indians did not consent to permit scientific observation of their culture nor visits from tourists until the late 1940s. Now tours from Panama and many cruise ships plying the Caribbean have the San Blas Islands and their unique inhabitants on their itinerary.

A colorful race who spend most of their life on and in the water, the Cuna Indians are among the smallest people in the world, stick to their own dialect, and speak little English or Spanish. They also retain a strict color bar and refuse to intermarry or corrupt their ancient way of life. Cuna women adore colorful clothes and make-up, and they wear small golden rings in their noses. Though we were free to go into their homes and take pictures, we had to pay a quarter for each privilege.

Grown on the island are coconuts, mangoes, bananas, and several other tropical fruits and vegetables, but most Cunas have plantations in the mainland jungle where they grow majority of their foodstuffs. A wide variety of wild game, such as deer, wild boar, monkeys, and tapir, supply them with fresh meat, plus the salt-water fishing is as good as any place in the world. Their dugout canoes, small and primitive, are suitable in the normally calm waters to journey from their island home to the shore, a distance ranging from a mile to three or four miles. Their one-room thatched family huts offer precious little privacy, and the tiny islands themselves, scant seclusion for lovers. Couples are frequently seen leaving the island in their canoe together with a blanket, obviously for a little romance in the jungle greenery. This system is of great inconvenience to adulterers because if a married man has a female other than his spouse in the boat he might as well put up a notice on the local bulletin board.

Cuna Indians appear to be as prosperous as any tribe in the world. They live in a tropical paradise, pay no taxes, have at their fingertips a wide variety of foodstuffs and, for those necessities not available, earn ample money from the excellent handicrafts produced by the women folk and sold to tourists. The mola, the most sought-after item by outsiders, is an art creation fabricated in a reverse applique process which makes beautiful wall hangings, pillow covers or other decorations as well as attachments for blouses and dresses. Because money is neither an obsession nor a necessity with the Indians, ladies ask for their molas whatever price enters their head and frequently settle for 90 percent less than the asking price or, in other instances, won't budge a penny. The main criterion seems to be how well the lady likes her design or craftsmanship.

John, our local guide, warned us regarding the Cunas practice of demanding a quarter for each posing, and the habit provided some comical situations. If while one of our group was focusing on a village scene and a Cuna lady found herself in the field of vision, she would dash out of sight or swiftly cover her face with a mola. Deciding to fool one young lady, I put the camera up with a jerk while I suspected she wasn't watching, but she rapidly ducked behind one of the thatched huts. With the camera at the ready, I waited for her to reappear, then released the shutter. Turning and walking away quite smugly, I suddenly got a sharp kick in the shins for the deception. I hastily coughed up the quarter. Unfortunately the picture didn't turn out.

Twelve hundred people inhabited the first little ocean oasis where John took us, and the total island area wouldn't exceed five acres. The roofs of their huts almost touched each other, but despite their cramped quarters, the Cunas seemed to be happy and healthy, living a life of complete gratification. Young and old lay in their hammocks listening to music from Panama City on a transistor radio, proving they had adopted at least one of modern society's wonts. The ocean provided another principal source of entertainment as youngsters and adults alike were swimming or canoeing in the tranquil waters that surrounded their island home.

The thoroughly enjoyable visit portrayed a life as idyllic as any on earth, and John Mann, with his own private island, lived a life as carefree as the Cuna Indians.

We left Panama the following morning for Miami, the starting and termination point of our 38-day journey. Though 38 days is not a great period of time in a normal lifetime, it was surprising how much we had packed into our itinerary. Returning to Florida, I realized the importance of taking notes and pictures which would instantly recall highlights of our tour that otherwise would only be a massive jumble of pleasant memories.

Chapter 7

In the Cradle of Man

Man made his appearance on planet Earth roughly one million years ago. A half million years later he walked erect, used stone tools, had discovered fire, and almost certainly communicated with a primitive spoken language. Strangely enough, another 500,000 years elapsed or until 4000 B.C. before he began to leave any vestige of a recorded history, and for the first few centuries even that was clouded and filled with ambiguities.

Knowledge of our ancestors through those long and dim corridors of time before human thought and action began to be recorded on tablets of clay is clouded in perplexity. Undoubtedly numerous events were important milestones in the evolution of man.

Who sowed the first seed corn, made the first earthen pot, worked the first metal, sailed the first boat, or wrought the first wheel must remain forever unknown. Yet those acts, involving new concepts and technical skills to translate them into practical realities, initiated the long technological development which made possible all later achievements of civilized living. Hence though their date is unknown, many great accomplishments mark the story of man long before he reached the "cradle of civilization."

Over the past 6,000 years numerous civilizations slowly attained magnificence and flourished for awhile, then like the winter snows in spring, either suddenly or gradually disappeared into the haze of history depending on the circumstances of their demise. These thriving cultures were frequently replaced by barbarous hordes who smashed all structures and obliterated much of the new-born learning until they themselves were captured by other sprouting civilizations who replaced existing buildings with architecture of their own. In either case, surviving documents are rare, making it quite remarkable we are knowledge-able at all about those days of ages past.

By 4000 B.C. civilization had taken root from ancient Mesopotamia, including the Euphrates and Tigris river basins, westward over oceans of drifting sand to the Nile Valley, and thence eastward along the coast of the Mediterranean and across the Turkish plains. Groups of people had settled the land and were farming, tending animals, making pottery, and building towns, markets, and forts. In the deserts, mountains and steppes, nomadic tribesmen lived by herding animals and by hunting and raiding. As these tribes grew, competition for land, food, and sup-plies likely caused the first major incursion of man against his neighbor. Unfortunately attempts to settle differences by war have almost un-ceasingly continued to plague mankind to this day.

The cradle of civilization witnessed the rise and fall of many cities and cultures. Sumerians, Akkadians, Babylonians, Assyrians, Chal-deans, Persians, Romans, Crusaders, and the Ottoman Empire—all took root and flourished. Some left behind massive monuments, splen-did writings, and remarkable works of art; others vanished, leaving scant physical indication of their stay.

In those lands man came to the conclusion there was only one God and three great religions—Judaism, Islam and Christianity—origi-nated there. Unfortunately, those three religions caused and are still responsible for tremendous suffering, especially in that hallowed but tortured section of our planet.

Joyce again chose to remain in Toronto when in the late summer of 1977, I paid a three-week visit to the region that seems to be the true cradle of our civilization. In New York, I joined fourteen other members of my tour group plus Oliver Jones, our tour director, and flew directly to Paris for a ten-hour stopover before continuing to Cairo.

Geographically, the Holy Land has no beginning and no ending, although historically, the region lies on the eastern shore of the Medi-terranean between the Jordan and Nile rivers. Palestine, called Cannaan in the Bible, before the invasion of Joshua, is the Holy Land to the three principal faiths that began in the area—Jews, as promised by God; Christians, because it was the home of Christ; and Moslems, as heirs of Jews and Christians.

Judaism, the oldest of the great monotheistic religions, is a great complex of law, prophecy, tradition and doctrines, of which the Old Testament is the elder monument and the Talmus the younger. Chris-tianity and Islam are inextricably associated with Judaism not only because Jesus and all his apostles were Jews and because Mohammed claimed to have come as the last of the prophets of Israel but also and chiefly because the basic beliefs of Judaism are the foundations of the two younger faiths. Judaism cannot be stated in terms of an authoritative creed but rather the sum of the spiritual experience of Jewish people over a period of more than 4,000 years. According to Jewish tradition, Abraham is the founder of monotheism and the Jewish religion.

Christianity, of course, dates back about 2,000 years to the birth of Christ, and Islam dates back to Mohammed in the middle of the 6th century A.D. An adherent of Islam is called a Moslem, which in Arabic means "one who submits", and Islam is the principal religion of much of Asia, northwestern China, Indonesia, Malaya, Pakistan, Afghanistan, Iran, Iraq, Syria, Jordan, Egypt, the Arabian states, and Turkey as well as much of the USSR in Asia and, to a lesser degree, many other parts of the world. They have a total following of 600 million, as opposed to 1 billion Christians and 15 million Jewish. Devotion to the Koran, the principal feature of Islam, is believed to be the revelation of God to Mohammed. Since the Koran is written in Arabic, that language is used in Islam all over the world, hence the common custom of referring to God as Allah, his name in Arabic.

The history and solemnity of the three great religions preponderated not only the Holy Land portion of our tour but to some extent our stay in Turkey and Greece as well. No doubt the recorded history of man, not much older than vestiges of his religious beliefs, are both continuously intertwined.

The past sweeps across the Holy Land and in turn is swept away. Nabataens, Romans, Greeks, Crusaders, Turks, French and British have all at various times conquered it and momentarily thought it belonged to them. They built fortifications, collected taxes, pressed young men into their armies, made war, and in general made life as miserable as possible for as many people as possible, then crept away. Few traces remain of some, while others left a legacy of their visits.

On the long road to civilization, the emergence of the national state, particularly in the context of the world in which we live, is of paramount importance. Although other countries, in particular Mesopotamia, which is modern-day Iraq, developed some of the arts of civilization earlier, Egypt became the first country to draw itself together with a national identity. That nation's history reaches back 7 millenia with an antiquity that is astounding in comparison to a majority of nations that measure their recorded past in centuries. It is no exaggeration that without pyramids or Abu Simbel, no Valley of the Kings or Karnak Temple, ancient Egypt would still be one of the most interesting countries in the world to visit.

Egypt's 386,000 square miles is 96 percent desert, leaving less than 4 percent inhabited or cultivated. The Nile cuts Egypt from south to north for a distance of almost 900 miles from the Sudan border to Cairo where the river divides into two main branches, each 150 miles long. Cairo, the largest city in Africa, stands at the apex of the delta, a significant position for the capital through its long history. Founded in 969 A.D., the throbbing metropolis containing nearly 10 million people is the meeting place of Africa, Asia, and Europe.

At first Cairo comes at you like a sustained scream, so loud and terrible you wonder at first how people can possibly live there. Traffic is murderous, and everyone honks at everything incessantly so that the entire city is one constant blare of discordant honking. From 525 B.C. until the revolution of 1952, someone other than Egyptians ran Egypt, and over the centuries, Cairenes awoke to one crisis after another. Since 1952, the foreigners have gone, allowing them to be masters of their own house with little effective order imposed on them from anywhere. They now go about their affairs as chaotically as they please and honk their horns if they so choose.

Abdul, our local guide, maintained that most Egyptians were delighted about Sadat's decision in 1972 to oust the Russians from the country and obtain closer ties with the Western World, particularly the U.S.A. At the time of my visit there appeared little inclination toward communism. Most Egyptians simply wanted the freedom to go about their business in their own way and without outside interference.

Cairo evinced scant sign it was the Christian Sabbath on our Sunday morning city tour. The holy day for Moslems is Friday, for Jews Saturday, and the percentage of Christians in Egypt is quite small, with Moslems making up 92 percent of the populace. We made our first stop at the colossal Sultan Hussan Mosque, a masterpiece of Islamic architecture, with a gateway alone that measures 85 feet in height. Built in 1356 in the form of a cross, each section represents one of the four schools of Moslem jurisprudence.

Muhammed Ali Mosque, also known as the Alabaster Mosque, is situated within the Citadel on the slope of the Maqattam Hills and commands a complete view of Cairo. The Citadel started by Saladin in the 12th century as a fortress was constructed of stone taken from small pyramids at Giza. Before we entered the hallowed Muhammed Ali Mosque, coverings were placed over our shoes to protect the carpeting which blanketed the entire floor. Seated in a semi-circle around Abdul, Moslem Arabs in colorful attire kneeling in a solemn pose, a serene sense of antiquity seemed inescapable in the huge and aged house of worship. Upon leaving, Abdul emphatically explained that Mohammed Ali and the mosque were not connected in any way with the clown of the same name who fought in the heavyweight division in the U.S.A.

While busing through the city core, we passed a huge Moslem cemetery where crypts and mausoleums appeared far more pretentious than many of the dwellings which housed the Arabs during life. Known as the City of the Dead, the huge burial ground contained numerous elaborately decorated tombs considered outstanding examples of Moslem architecture. Time and money spent on death by many people when their countrymen live in abject squalor during life has always amazed me and seems to be another of the many paradoxes of most religions.

The Nile Hilton, an ultramodern caravansary, had a delightful pool area heavily patronized by airline crews from several parts of the world. English was spoken by most of the patrons. One-story motel units, quite Western in appearance, surrounded the pool. Bikini-clad bathers and modern facilities seemed not to belong in a city populated by the masses of needy people we'd witnessed on our morning excursion and which contained the Muhammed Ali Mosque.

Early one morning, a blazing sun already scorching the land, we boarded our bus for a visit to Memphis, the ancient Egyptian capital, plus the Necropolis Sakkara, which lies 20 miles southwest of Cairo. We travelled along the west bank of the Nile River, the lifeblood of the land, where families were doing laundry, children were frolicking and splashing, and bony cows, much resembling water buffalo, were swimming to avoid the pestering insects. Bordering the mud-brown river, a narrow strip of bright green vegetation, sometimes shadowed by palm groves, ended abruptly at a rim of desolation, the beginning of the western desert. A mighty pyramid built in steps rises out of the plateau of that billowing sand which stretches endlessly to the west, as sterile and hostile as in the days of the pharaohs.

Step Pyramid, built for Pharaoh Djoser in 2800 B.C., is the oldest large stone monument in the world, but is far from being the oldest tomb at Sakkara. A little to the north are ruins of a series of large mud-brick structures called mastabas, the Arabic word for "bench." One of these once contained the funerary equipment and probably the body of the first pharaoh of the first dynasty, a ruler who preceded Djoser by at least 400 hundred years. Sakkara, the "city of the dead" or necropolis of the Egyptian Pharaohs, contains over 14 pyramids, hundreds of mastabas and tombs, art objects and engravings dating from the first to the 13th dynasty.

A short walk in the broiling sun took us to the ancient mastaba of Lord Mereruka. A steep narrow staircase leads down into the small pillared rooms where every wall is covered with reliefs carved in the limestone, many of them painted in brilliant colors. Abdul explained the meaning of many of the hieroglyphics, and because the tombs contain a treasure house of early writings, our knowledge of those ages past is quite extensive.

Sakkara, the cemetery of Memphis, contains much more of interest than the ruins of Memphis itself. No king rivalled Ramses II as a builder. Uncovered at Memphis, an 80-ton alabaster statue of this famous pharaoh lies sprawled in a shed like a sleeping giant. Forty feet tall, the statue appears to be receiving little reverence amidst the ruins of Memphis, his nation's ancient capital. Dust and sand surround the sphinx with stately palms whispering of past glories and overlooking considerable areas of debris awaiting serious exploration. Egypt's golden age dates back over 3,200 years, and the surrounding grounds unquestionably contain huge reservoirs of treasure waiting for the archaeologist's spade.

An old song suggests that only mad dogs and Englishmen go out in the midday sun. Now tourists of Egypt must be included because the thermometer hovered at 100 degrees as we wound through a chaotic mass of Cairo traffic to Giza, only three miles south. Cairo's modern office buildings offered a startling contrast to Giza's sphinx and pyramids, the oldest architecture known to man.

Standing on a hill overlooking the Nile Valley, the pyramids are mute testimony to the ancient's belief in the immortality of the soul. To reach the base of Cheops, the largest pyramid in the world and which took twenty years to build, we had the choice of riding mules, horses, or camels. The intrigue of camel riding attracted most of our troop. Mounting posed no problem because they squat down on all four legs. Staying aboard, however, when those long-legged beasts stand up is a different matter. They first rise on their fore legs at which point you find yourself sitting at a precarious 45 degree angle. If you don't make a rapid adjustment and lean in the opposite direction when they hop up on their hind legs, you will go somersaulting over the camel's hump. Although they were covered with blankets, they weren't exactly as comfortable as a Cadillac to ride either. We arrived safely, but with a trifle more respect for the Bedouins who spend their life on the back of those animals.

Of the 80 pyramids in Egypt, the three at Giza are the most famous. Cheops, first in size and chronological order, was erected about 2690 B.C. and originally stood 481 feet in height with a base covering 13 acres. Cheophren, Cheops' son, built the second pyramid, slightly smaller in size, about 2650 B.C. The third pyramid, smallest of the three, was erected about 2600 B.C. and was named after Menkaru.

The great pyramid is estimated to contain 2.5 million tons of stone, each stone weighing an average 2.5 tons, but many exceeding 15 tons. Napoleon claimed it contained enough material to build a wall ten feet high and a foot thick entirely around France. Inside the pyramids lie the kings, nobles, and high officials in their coffins, their bodies preserved with rare oils and fluids and wrapped in linen. Accompanying the corpse in the burial chambers are food, clothing, jewelry, weapons, and everything considered to be a necessity in the afterlife. Near the pyramids, the Great Sphynx, carved from a knoll of limestone rock, represents a recumbent lion with the head of a king, probably symbolizing the Pharaoh Kharfa.

In late afternoon Giza resembled a blast furnace in Hell, but by 9 p.m. when we returned for the sound-and-light show under a brilliant starlit sky the temperature was in the low 70s, and a more pleasant evening could not be imagined. Recorded voices projected from the Sphinx recounted their history which together with a musical background echoed across the ageless desert in dramatic style. Floodlights playing on the ancient architecture completed the enchantment by vividly revealing their beautiful form and majesty. The late evening show provided a delightful finale for our visit to the venerable masterpieces.

Before leaving Cairo we dropped in at the Egyptian Antiquities Museum which contains the world's most important collection of Egyptian relics dating from earliest times to about the 6th century A.D. and including the famous mask of Tutankhamun, more commonly known as King Tut.

The Tutankhamen Galleries, on the second floor of the museum, display a marvellous treasury of the young pharaoh's recently discovered crypt. Howard Carter, a British archeologist, searched for the tomb the length of the Valley of the Kings. Just about to abandon the search in 1922, he came upon the first steps leading to the hiding place which we would visit on our trip to Luxor.

From Cairo we flew 600 miles south to Aswan. Our hotel, the Aswan Oberoi, an ultramodern caravansary located on the north end of the Elephantine Island in the middle of the Nile, was surrounded by lush gardens ablaze with a multitude of flowering trees and shrubs. Unfortunately, intense heat with the thermometer in the 130 degree range removed some of the pleasure of strolling through the gorgeous setting.

At Aswan we inspected granite quarries where many stones were cut for use in ancient monuments throughout Egypt. Viewing the quarry fields helps you appreciate the colossal task our aged ancestors faced in transporting the granite from Aswan to Luxor and in many cases much further.

The Temple of Kalabsha on the west bank of the Nile faced a watery grave with construction of the High Dam. In 1962, a German group dismantled the structure and moved it to its present location to salvage the temple from complete inundation. Building projects of great magnitude, the Pyramids, Suez Canal, and now the Aswan Dam, have been milestones in Egypt's unfolding. All gained international attention, but to present-day Egyptians, the New High Dam at Aswan represents the most important undertaking in their history. Started in 1960 and completed in 1970, the Aswan Dam, one of the world's largest, utilized 50 million cubic yards of rock and desert sand to create a 1½-square-mile artificial lake which will irrigate about two million acres. The huge dike, containing enough material for 17 Great Pyramids, cost 800 million dollars, of which Russia loaned 554 million and most of the technical expertise. Thirty-five thousand Egyptian laborers worked on the dam's construction which would bring scenes of Giza to mind at the building of the pyramids 5,000 years ago.

We boarded a felucca, a local sailing boat, for a trip among the islands on the Nile and to view the site of the reconstruction of the Temple of Philae, the most interesting of Aswan's antiquities. The oldest part of the edifice dates back to the fourth century B.C.

Moving slowly along the picturesque Nile in our man-powered craft, the waterway's importance in the life of the nation again appeared evident. Nubian adults and children were swimming, fishing or doing their laundry, while others plied a variety of crafts along the fast-moving current among the islands. Hieroglyphics on many rocky outcroppings along the bank dated back 2500 hundred years, and the enormous amount of ancient writing everywhere never ceased to amaze me. Overlooking the tranquil river on a hill stood a villa constructed by the late Aga Khan, where he is now buried in a handsome mausoleum.

Returning to our hotel in late afternoon, we saw several species of birds that inhabit the grassy banks, and in the evening, white ibis covered some trees like apple blossoms. The day had been enjoyable and entertaining despite the broiling sun. On our trip to Abu Simbel the following day, we would encounter no respite from the intense heat.

Although never proven, many believe that the Pharaoh Rameses II ruled Egypt at the time of Exodus when Moses led the Jews to the promised land, rightly regarded as a great milestone in human history. Nevertheless, when taken in the context of the age at which it occurred, the exodus of the Jews probably seemed trivial to the Egyptians who likely considered it at the time just one more tiresome episode in their humdrum existence.

Our trip to Abu Simbel put Moses' 42-year journey in a different perspective, particularly if it did happen during the reign of Rameses II. One of the most impressive figures of ancient history, Rameses II reigned 67 years (he lived to the age of 90), a time of great prosperity for Egypt. Resources were developed, trade and industry flourished, and a vast program of temple building carried through. In every city in Egypt and Nubia, his monuments proliferated.

Abu Simbel, 168 miles south of Aswan near the Sudan border, can only be reached by air or down the Nile by watercraft. We landed at a remote desert air strip, then bused a few miles to the historic site in such torrid heat that even the birds were walking. The huge rock-hewn temple complex is located in fiery desert sand dunes on the west bank of Lake Nasser, a body of water created by the Aswan Dam. My first glimpse of the outstanding spectacle standing majestically in a searing desert sun overpowered my physical discomfort. An awesome sight, the impressive facade has two pairs of seated statues of the king, each over 65 feet high. At the rear, facing due East toward the rising sun, stands a group of four rock-hewn statues: Rameses II himself, Ptah, Amen, and the sun god Horakhty, the individuals to whom the temple was dedicated. Scenes of complex composition cover the interior walls.

The original construction of Abu Simbel between 1300-1233 B.C., though a magnificent achievement, doesn't outrank moving the gigantic temple to its present location for physical exertion. Realizing that completion of the new Aswan Dam would inundate the area between Aswan and the Sudan border by rising Nile waters, the Egyptian government through UNESCO sent a world-wide appeal to governments, schools, archaeological foundations and cultural organizations for assistance in exploring the area and saving the most important ancient monuments which would otherwise be lost forever.

Saving the temples at Abu Simbel, the most difficult project, began in 1965. By building a wall to protect the area from rising Nile waters, the temples were dismantled (all 400,000 tons) by cutting them into parts, crating, and then reassembling them in the exact position as before at the top of the mountain cliff, 90 feet above the old site. The gigantic task was executed with such perfect precision that only an inch-by-inch examination of the stones can detect the salvage work. About 50 nations helped in the rescue operations, and millions of people around the globe who have never been to Egypt and may never have the chance to go sent contributions to help defray the cost.

A short distance downstream from the main temple is a smaller rock temple dedicated to Queen Nefertari, principal queen of Rameses II. Rameses sired over a hundred children, and so although Nefertari may have been his favorite queen, she obviously wasn't the only queen in the hive. Colossal standing statues of Nefertari and her husband flank the entrance to the smaller temple. Outside are six large statues: four of Rameses, two of his wife, and smaller ones of their children. Inside the main temple rooms, ceiling and walls throughout are beautifully decorated, the color in excellent condition and the wall carvings still preserved in exquisite detail.

While visiting Egypt's monuments from Memphis to Abu Simbel, many built by Rameses II and adorned with his colossal statues and wall paintings dedicated to his greatness, you gain the impression he was the greatest egomaniac of all time. But when you have seen Abu Simbel, you are grateful that time has preserved such a masterpiece and that efforts to maintain it for future generations were successful. You may pass this way only once in a lifetime, but certainly when you have seen Abu Simbel, you known you have seen one of the great wonders of the world.

From Abu Simbel we took a 40-minute flight back north to Luxor, situated 450 miles south of Cairo on the site of ancient Thebes, the capital of Egypt at its zenith. The actual site of Thebes on the east bank of the Nile is said to have occupied all the lands between Luxor and Karnak, a distance of several miles.

When touring the Valley of the Kings, including Tutankhamen's Tomb, Temple of Queen Hatshepsut, plus the Valley of the Nobles, and the Valley of the Queens, all situated west of the river, you cross the Nile by ferry. Cliffs and foothills on the west bank became the main cemetery for the city of Thebes, lying opposite. Sixty-four pharaohs' tombs have been found so far in the Valley of the Kings, but only the safest and most interesting are open to the public.

Seti's tomb, dating back to the 13th century B.C. and the XIX dynasty, is the largest and most impressive in the necropolis. Wall decorations beginning at the entrance continue all the way to the bottom of the tomb, and the drawings are exquisite and in excellent condition.

Tutankhamen, of the XVIII dynasty and the 14th century B.C., is the only crypt so far discovered which escaped the tomb robbers of ancient times. Inside chambers are small in comparison to other crypts, but colors of the fine drawings are remarkably well preserved. King Tut's gold-masked mummy is a world-famous masterpiece. Three caskets, one within the other, and all richly decorated, were placed in a great stone sarcophagus inside the burial chamber with objects for the after-life within easy reach. Amid the shining gold, two small amulets and a dagger, made of iron, turned out to be prognosticators of the future. Egypt was still in the Bronze Age at the time of the burial, but it was iron that would one day help bring an end to golden Egypt.

The terraced temple of Queen Hatshepsut at Deir el Bahari offers an unusually fine example of architecture fitted to a natural setting. Although only a short distance from the Valley of the Kings, the land-scape had abruptly changed. The maze of deep valleys replaced by steep and rugged cliffs 400 feet high was where the Queen chose to build three gleaming white terraces, like arms opening to the sky. From the palace at the foot of the cliff, a broad verdant plain stretched down to the Nile where tiny donkeys ambled along the lanes between fields and smoke from village huts curled into a sun-drenched sky, creating a scene that has altered little since Queen Hapshepsut erected her palace.

Upon the death of the powerful queen, her nephew and stepson, Thutmose III, attempted to obliterate all traces of her by destroying many of the pretentious wall drawings.

Fifty-seven tombs have so far been discovered in the Valley of the Queens, the most outstanding for its artwork that of Queen Nefertari, wife of Rameses II.

The Valley of the Nobles, segregated into several groupings along the edge of the desert, contains private tombs of priests and nobles who were prominent in the courts of the pharaohs. Famous for fine wall decorations and drawings depicting scenes from the daily life of the ancient Egyptians, nobles' tombs are quite small, and wall drawings appear as miniatures compared to those in the Valley of the Kings.

Considerable walking and climbing in the intense heat made the occasional rest stop where we quenched our thirst with beer or soft drinks most welcome. In spite of the searing sun, the fascination of the surrounding scenario never dulled our enthusiasm because the historic area more resembled the Egypt we'd read about than any of the other stops on our itinerary.

Back on the east side of the Nile, we took a horse-and-buggy ride at four o'clock in the afternoon along the river for our tour of Karnak. The thermometer had reached its zenith of about 130 degrees, but the local tableau would have seemed out of place in any other environment.

We passed the Temple of Luxor which less than a century ago remained completely covered under a hill of rubble and hovels. Discovered by accident, it took two years to excavate the excellently preserved ruins that are now visible. Luxor, the greatest monument of antiquity in Thebes and built in the reign of Amenhotep III as a temple to Amun, was originally 623 feet long. Succeeding pharaohs added to the structure, especially Rameses II, who had many colossal statues of himself erected on the grounds. Our guides never stopped at Luxor but continued to the unique ruins at Karnak approximately a mile further along the river.

When attempting to describe things of magnificent beauty or sites of great antiquity, the use of an overabundance of descriptive phrases or adulating adjectives is the norm. Karnak Temple, however, is unique and remarkable. It is unique because, unlike most relics of antiquity, Karnak does not belong to one man or one era, and it is remarkable because it displays 4,000 years of Egyptian history in one site. Karnak, the planet's largest columned temple, reflects 2,000 years of building, and 2,000 more of siege, fire, earthquake, and decay. Pharaohs raised it to honor Amun, patron god of their capital, and sometimes they built a new temple next to a temple already in existence. They saw no incongruity in building one temple next to another on hallowed ground and reveled in the opportunity to portray themselves on all the columns and pylons.

Tremendously impressed with the span of historical development represented by Karnak, I was also awed by our local Egyptian guide who devoted his whole self to describing the mysteries of the temple. When asked to read the hieroglyphics, he explained, "To read ancient writing one must follow whatever direction the symbols face, left to right, right to left or up and down." He then proceeded to translate several passages from the walls and pillars and emphasized their meaning with much enthusiasm. While standing by the hallowed ramparts in the quickening twilight, he suddenly asked, "How many men would be required today to move one of those massive blocks?" Before receiving a reply, he continued, "The answer makes no difference because it could be twenty or perhaps a hundred. The point is that today's man doesn't care to work. In the day of the pharaohs four men would complete the task because they worked from their hearts, proud of their part played in the glorious creations. The Great Pyramids, Abu Simbel, Luxor and Karnak were masterpieces not because the laborers were driven by whip but because of the pride they had in doing well the task they'd been assigned."

Returning to our hotel along the life-giving Nile as dusk rapidly engulfed us, I recalled the words of Shelley, who inspired by the great fallen colossus of Rameses at Thebes wrote:

Two vast and trunkless legs of stone
Stand in the desert. Near them, on the sand,
Half sunk, a shattered visage lies . . .
And on the pedestal these words appear:
. . . "Look on my works, ye Mighty, and despair."
Nothing beside remains. Round the decay
Of that colossal wreck, boundless and bare
The lone and level sands stretch far away.

Though we'd only visited areas along the mighty Nile from Sudan to the Mediterranean Sea, we'd seen almost the total inhabited portion of Egypt. On the way to Luxor Airport for our flight to Jordan, contrasting scenes summed up my sentiments regarding the ancient land. Two little boys splashed in the placid river while a bony cow stood stoically munching her morning meal on the grassy bank. Within a hundred yards of that serene picture, a barbed wire tank trap indicated the turbulence that has plagued Egypt for 60 centuries.

From Luxor our pilot followed the Nile Valley back to Cairo, and from 10,000 feet you could readily observe the waterway's vital role in the nation's well-being. Lush green vegetation parallels the mighty river on both banks until it reaches the desert rim, and then drifting sand stretches to infinity. The logical sequence of visiting those countries on our itinerary would have been from Egypt to Israel and then to Jordan which borders Israel. In 1977, however, Jordan refused entry to travelers from Israel, and so we had to travel first to Jordan and then back to Israel. Due to the declared war zone, to reach Amman we had to detour almost as far north as Cyprus, then circle back over the tip of Lebanon before reaching our destination, a trip taking 2 ½ hours instead of 50 minutes. Despite our aggravation at the inconvenience, the refreshing cool air in Ammam provided unbelievable relief from the constant scorching heat of Egypt and put us in a more receptive mood for our look at the Hashimite Kingdom.

When Lawrence of Arabia came to Amman in 1921, he found only a small village with one or two government offices. Today, the thriving city extends well into the surrounding desert. Busing through the modern metropolis en route to Madaba, 20 miles south, the morning after our arrival, Amman appeared well groomed in comparison to Cairo. Occupied since prehistoric times, Amman was the biblical Rabbath-Amman, capital of the Amonites and Jordan, part of Palestine for many centuries and the biblical lands of Gilead, Moab, Edom, and Amman.

Approaching the Gilead Mountains, the foothills were dotted with the tents of Bedouins, truly an intriguing race. Few things in this world are timeless and unchanging, nevertheless, the Bedouins of Jordan's desert still manage to live the same free, unchanging, and uncluttered life that their ancestors lived for hundreds of years. Bedouin, meaning "inhabitants of the desert," are still found throughout most of the Arab world, but today's heaviest concentration of the true Bedouin is in eastern Jordan where they are frequently seen camped along the King's Highway, the long north-and-south road that runs through the nation. Although over 40,000 still follow their old nomadic way of life, there is plenty of room because the land is 80 percent desert. These migrants do not wander aimlessly about but know exactly where they are going. Some Bedouin families have followed more or less the same migration route year after year for generations.

Near Madaba the rolling hills become a little more fertile and fields of tobacco, wheat, barley, tomatoes, and other crops flourished. We passed through Madaba to Mount Nebo, a distance of 10 miles. Standing on Mt. Nebo and looking across the Promised Land as seen by Moses many centuries ago seemed a rare privilege and gave one a feeling that the world had stood still in that sector for an eternity. Nearing the end of his heroic 42-year trek through those barren wastes from Egypt,

Moses and his followers chose the region as their new homeland. Moses was buried nearby, though no one has found his sepulchre.

A quote from the Bible describes the scene with great emotion:

And the Lord spake unto Moses that selfsame day, saying, "Get thee up into this mountain Abarim, unto Mount Nebo, which is the land of Moab, that is over against Jericho; and behold the land of Canaan, which I give unto the children of Israel for a possession: And die in the mount which thou goest up, and be gathered unto thy people; as Aaron thy brother died in Mount Hor, and was gathered unto his people."

The magnificent view cannot be changed much in those three thousand and more years. High cliffs look down on the Dead Sea which shimmered in the brilliant sun some 3,500 feet below. Palm trees could be seen nestling the town of Jericho on the Jordan River, and in the distance, though much changed since the days of Moses, the spires of Jerusalem were visible on the rise of Mount Zion. Recalling its history, no one could view the scene dispassionately.

On Mount Nebo, Franciscans have excavated a Byzantine Church, which was still in the process of restoration. Within a few yards of the reconstruction, on the highest point of the mountain, they have erected a cross outlined in electric lights which seems to add an air of unreality to the moment.

Back at Madaba we visited St. George's Greek Orthodox Church, believed to date back to the 6th century A.D., where inlaid in the mosaic floor is the earliest known map of the Holy Land. The amazing artistic achievement offers a pictorial view of the entire country of Palestine and depicts fish swimming in the Jordan River, palm trees growing, and wildlife. Names of towns and cities spelled out in Greek are represented by childish reproductions of houses and shrines. The town of Jerusalem, shown as a walled city, has two streets lined with columns. The amazing and beautiful tesserae has mostly retained its vivid colors.

Amman, mentioned many times in the Old Testament, has a known history that goes back to 1200 B.C. After Rabbath Amman, it became known as Philadelphia, and from it the American city took its name. Through the ages various peoples lived in Amman, and each group left its mark in buildings, roads, arches, and columns. A second century A.D. Roman amphitheatre which seats 6,000 people, is an impressive structure, and you can hardly tell where the historic stone wall work ends and talented Jordanian stonemasons began their fine restoration.

Amman is picturesquely layed out on a series of hills with the downtown section situated in a valley and with one main street running through the center of the city. Along the slopes are beautiful residential sections containing homes of the wealthier natives, ambassadors, and foreign personnel. King Hussein's Palace and complex occupies one entire promontory. Perhaps the most interesting of the elevations contains remains of the Citadel, dating back to the 8th century B.C. Imposing Citadel Hill towers over Amman and rulers throughout recorded history used it until modern times.

The usual absurdity between the wealth of religious institutions, particularly the numerous exquisite mosques, and the plight of the destitute so obvious in surrounding areas astonished me. Camps on the outskirts of Amman contained 60,000 impoverished refugees, mainly from the west bank of the Jordan River, who swarmed to the city during the Six Day War of 1967. Living in abject poverty, they pray to Allah five times daily and are allowed to enter the magnificent Moslem mosques and, momentarily at least, luxuriate in splendor. Returning to the hotel, a small tree laden with red blossoms attracted my attention. Because it blooms both in winter and summer, Jordanians call it "The Crazy Tree." Somehow that crazy tree summed up my sentiments towards the ludicrous contradictions that seemingly exist in most nations.

One gorgeous, bright morning we left Amman for the ancient rose-red Nabataean city of Petra, which lies 160 miles south of the capital. The drive along an excellent desert road, though flat and uninteresting, bypassed many fascinating bands of Bedouins with their herds of goats and camels. The railway parallelling the desert road once ran from Damascus to Medina, and along its tracks, Lawrence of Arabia blew up many Turkish trains.

Nearing Petra, the desert gave way to sparsely vegetated hills with rocky outcroppings where we stopped at the little village of Wady Musa for lunch. Pungent pepper trees in full bloom surrounded a nearby spring spouting from rocks reputed to be the place where Moses was instructed by the Lord to smite the rock with his sword so that his followers could quench their thirst. Moses did so and suddenly water gushed forth in great quantity. Supposedly the water, which I found quite delicious, has been running continuously for 3,000 years.

Petra, known in the Bible as Sela (both names mean "rock"), is an apt title for the hidden city. Occupied by the Edomites in an early era and Nabataens, who had their capital there from the 4th century B.C. before the Roman occupation in 106 A.D., Petra is like a mirror into history, reflecting past ages. Though for centuries the hub of a vast caravan trade, Sela nevertheless remained a religious center of Arabia. An early seat of Christianity, it was conquered by the Moslems in the 7th century, but was recaptured in the 12th century by the Crusaders, who built a citadel there. Petra remained unknown to the Western World until 1812 when J.L. Burchkhardt discovered the enchanting pink city languishing away in the desert dust.

We were supplied with saddle ponies for our thrilling trip along the trail called the Siq (Arabic for "pass") into Petra. From Wady Musa, a path winds down a hill through a rock-strewn mesa into a valley that gradually narrows until you are suddenly faced by sheer cliffs that seem to offer little promise of further progress. Suddenly a narrow cleft in the canyon wall appears. This hidden entrance to the road to Petra could be held by a handful of men against an army. The Siq follows an old river bed, now dry, the water having been diverted to an alternate route by a dam. As you penetrate deeper into the canyon, the cliffs rise higher and higher on either side until they soar 300 feet above your head. A multitude of twists and turns gives the impression of a road torturously groping its way through a mountain, and the trail is so narrow in places that two horsemen could not ride side by side. Rocks almost touch overhead in many places, causing perpetual twilight with only an occasional glint of sun on the cliff face high above. The world is silent except for the scurrying of pebbles ricocheting from the horses' hoofs or the soft sighing of winds among the oleanders that cling precariously to the sheer rock walls. Our party of 10 spread over a distance of 200 yards was frequently hidden from view of each other due to the narrow and twisting nature of the chasm. At such times you had the feeling of being completely cut off from the rest of the world.

Unexpectedly and about the moment you think the rock tunnel will be your natural home forever, there appears at the last turning the rock cut facade of a great temple, with rose-colored pillars dazzling bright in the sunlight. From the gloom of the Siq, the change is so sudden that for a moment you are almost dazed and bewildered. Then gradually your consciousness absorbs the glowing beauty and perfect proportions of a sculptured red sandstone temple. The tomb called the Khazneh, or Treasury, and Urn at the top of the aged temple, carry marks of countless bullets fired in the hope of shattering and releasing the treasure which local tradition says is hidden there. The Khazneh remains the best preserved of all monuments in Petra. Others are badly weathered as the soft sandstone quickly submits to the battering of wind-driven sand and rain, and the sharp profiles of sculptures are reduced to vague outlines.

Beyond the initial clearing, the gorge narrows again, with great tombs on either side, and still further a theater can be seen cut out of the living rock by the Romans. Then the hills recede leaving an open space about a mile long and three quarters of a mile wide where on the slopes are vestiges of the actual city—its temples, palaces, baths and private houses and with a fine paved street following the line of the stream and bridges reaching across at intervals. This was the great capital of the Nabataens, from which, at the height of their power, they ruled the country as far north as Damascus. The city extensively occupied from about the fifth century B.C. for 1000 years, reached its heyday during the first centuries A.D.

Gazing at the enchanting scene, an ancient stillness heavy in the air, it seemed impossible to credit the dramatic activity the hidden city had witnessed over the centuries. Nabataens originally discovered the site and constructed their tombs and temples. Then 2,000 years ago, Romans captured Petra, stamped it with their culture, and erected the massive amphitheater. Eight hundred years ago, Crusaders in flashing coats of mail came storming in to oust the Turks. Shortly thereafter they vanished, leaving the enchanting city for 500 years to a few local tribesmen who sought refuge in the caves that perforated the cliffs at various heights and are reached by interlacing stairways cut into the stone. Since its discovery in 1812, except for the constant and increasing incursion by tourists, little has changed. Many tombs and caves are still occupied by Arabs, and during the day the cliffs echo the strange cries with which they herd and control their flocks of goats. After sunset, fires make tiny points of flickering light, creating a fascinating scene in the enveloping darkness, and snatches of song may occasionally be heard, pitched in a high quavering tone and sounding unnaturally loud in the utter tranquility.

The number of tombs and their huge size and variety of form evokes wonder and admiration for the minds and wills of those ancient races who could conceive and bring into being such great and beautiful monuments. In some respects Petra reminded me of Machu Picchu, the last home of the Incas, because both cities were so well hidden and easily defended from the enemy.

From Amman we travelled by bus to Israel passing small settlements of Bedouin tents squatting in the blazing desert sand before again reaching the Gilead Mountains. At the Allenby Bridge on the Jordan River, our crossing point, we experienced the most rigid and thorough baggage and personal inspection by Israeli officials that could be possible. Shoes and all personal belongings that might contain weapons or explosives were X-rayed and luggage minutely scrutinized. Everyone had to fire his camera at the ceiling to prove it wouldn't explode and each traveler had to submit to personal examinations in a private cubicle. Though Israeli officials were grim-faced and sullen, we realized that traveling from Jordan into that nation's own occupied territory presented a rather bizarre situation. Also whereas Israel allowed tourists to cross into the occupied West Bank from Jordan, the Jordanian government didn't permit any travelers from Israel into their country.

Boarding our modern Israeli bus, we were slightly surprised to be welcomed by a very affable Jordanian guide rather than an Israeli. He immediately assured us he was happy, healthy, and possibly even a little more wealthy since 1967 when the Israelis took over. His home in the Jordanian section of Jerusalem before the 1967 war was also the home of his father and his father before him, suggesting that a change in national status wasn't unusual in that part of the world.

From the border post we went directly to famous Jericho, the lowest city in the world at 820 feet below sea level and possibly also the oldest. Though several dates are given, there is general acceptance among most archaeologists that the settlement had its beginnings over 10,000 years ago. Joshua, who became leader of the Jews after the death of Moses, captured Jericho from the Canaanite, then also destroyed it, a fate repeated several times in the city's turbulent history.

A huge oasis, Jericho is an inviting cluster of green rising out of the parched dry desert which completely surrounds it. Palm trees and citrus groves seem to be everywhere in rich profusion.

Tel es-Sultan, a mile from the town center covers the ruins of ancient Jericho where English archaeologist Dorothy Kenyon unearthed 23 strata going back to 7000 B.C. According to the Bible, in that site Joshua had the children of Israel circle the walls of the city seven days, and on the seventh, with the blowing of trumpets and the shout "The Lord has given us the city," the walls came tumbling down. Recent archaeological investigations, in fact, reveal that the walls of the city did apparently fall down at one time for some scientifically unexplained reason.

Looking westward from the Tel you can view the Mount of Temptation, which according to tradition, Jesus was "led up of the spirit into the wilderness to be tempted of the devil and he fasted forty days and forty nights. . ." Across the road, shaded by colorful poincianas, is where Elisha healed the waters with salt. You may still drink from the fountain which flows cool and sweet, contributing to the city's heady greenery. Six miles east of Jericho on the Jordan River, John the Baptist anointed Jesus and proclaimed Him the Saviour. On the outskirts of the city, a deserted refugee camp that prior to the war of 1967 held 100,000 Palestinian refugees, appears as a sad inconsistency to the holiness of the region.

Only a few miles separates Jericho from the Dead Sea where a modern hotel with good restaurant facilities is situated at the north end of the salt lake. Available for rent at the hotel are cubicles with showers where you can change into swimming trunks to walk the half mile out to the water. Twenty years ago the water lapped the hotel steps, but they have receded at a rapid rate over the past two decades. The low elevation plus a blazing sun had pushed the temperature to over 130 degrees; nevertheless I enthusiastically hiked to the edge of the brackish water.

Almost 1300 feet below sea level, lower than any other place on earth, the Dead Sea is 48 miles long and 11 miles wide. It is appropriately framed in barren mountains and shrouded in haze. Unseen mountain streams plus the Jordan River flow into its milky blue waters—so mineral heavy that no form of life can either live or drown in it. The lake contains half a pound of salt per quart, eight times the concentration found in ordinary sea water. Salt marshes surround the Dead Sea, and when the water evaporates from the marshes, a heavy crystaline salt layer remains, flashing and sparkling in the sunlight like polished diamonds. I didn't venture into the muddy water that appeared so clean from the distance, but one man in the salty brine appeared to be lying on a soft mass of matter.

We motored to Bethany, passing within a few miles of Quamran, the national park containing the caves where the Dead Sea scrolls were miraculously discovered and which have added immensely to a fuller understanding of the New Testament. Bethany, situated about two miles east of Jerusalem at the foot of the Mount of Olives, was the home of Mary and Martha, friends of Jesus and sisters of Lazarus. At Bethany, Jesus reputedly raised Lazarus from the dead, and we were shown the tomb from which he supposedly emerged "bound hand and foot with graveclothes: and his face . . . bound about with a napkin." Off the road a garden leads to the Roman Catholic Church built in 1953 where the marble floor is decorated with mosaics depicting the story of Lazarus. From the Mount of Olives Jesus frequently walked the few miles to Jerusalem, the next stop and high point in our Israeli sojourn.

My room at the luxurious Jerusalem Intercontinental had a panoramic view of the ancient and historic old city, which I never tired of ogling. My few days in Jerusalem were spent in mental contradiction due partly perhaps to the city's significance as the crossroads of three of the world's major religions—Moslem, Jewish and Christianity—and the overpowering presence of those faiths. I could accept certain Moslem or Jewish beliefs quite easily. I don't consider myself an atheist, who flatly denies the existence or the possibility of the existence of a Supreme Being, as no one knows who or what created the universe. Whether I'm a Christian would depend on the interpretation of a Christian. Webster's dictionary describes a Christian as one who believes, or professes to believe, in Jesus Christ and the truth taught by him. I certainly believe the man lived and devoted himself to the betterment of mankind as he saw it at the time, and he preached a gospel by and large beneficial to his fellowman. We must remember, however, few followed Christ's teachings until 313 A.D. when Constantine, a Roman General and emperor whose ancestors had crucified Jesus, claimed to have had a vision. Constantine, always sympathetic to the Christian religion, was entering a major battle at Milvian Bridge over the Tiber near Rome against Maxentius for the control of Italy when it is reported he saw in the sky a flaming cross inscribed with the words, "In this sign thou shalt conquer." He adopted the cross, killed Maxentius, and routed his troops. This bloody victory is considered by historians to be the turning point for the Christian religion. Therefore, if Constantine had not been successful at the battle, the life of Jesus Christ or his teachings would be unknown, and Christianity would not likely exist today. Following his triumph, Constantine and fellow emperor Licinius met at Milan and issued the edict of Milan, which mandated Christianity as a lawful religion to be tolerated throughout the empire.

An excellent book called *Milestones of History,* made up of the 100 most decisive events in the history of mankind and written by knowledgeable scholars from across the globe, included considerable writing about the time of Jesus Christ. From the chapter entitled "Jesus of Nazareth, Savior God of a New Religion," here are several excerpts:

"There have been thinkers who have denied that Jesus ever existed and have regarded him as a mythical figure. This view is no longer held by responsible scholars. But there is much conflict of opinion about what can reasonably be accepted as historical fact about both the person and career of Jesus . . . Ironically, the most certain fact that we know about Jesus is that he was crucified by the Romans for sedition against their government in Judaea . . . If Jesus were really a rebel against the Roman government in Judaea, he would have been very different from the gentle person Christian doctrine holds him to be. But, at the same time, he would be more intelligible historically, for among the Jews of his time there was a fierce hatred of Roman rule. That rule was an affront to their religion since they fervently believed that they were the Elect People of their God Yahweh and should not be subject to heathen lord . . . The Gospel accounts of the trial of Jesus reveal a strong apologetic motivation. The early Christian authors were obviously concerned with transferring the responsibility for the crucifixion of Jesus from the Romans to the Jews . . . The Gospel of Mark deals with the dangerous situation facing the Christians of Rome about 71 A.D. (This was due to the Jewish four year rebellion in Jerusalem against Rome, which made the Roman authorities and people suspect all Christians of being sympathetic with Jewish nationalism and Messianic fanaticism). But Mark's attempt to turn Pilate into a witness to the innocence of Jesus and make the Jews solely responsible for his death breaks down under analysis. This is also the case when the accounts of the trial of

Jesus in the other Gospels are examined. We must conclude therefore, that the Romans crucified Jesus as a rebel because they deemed him to be one . . .

"Something of the career of Jesus as a historical person can be reconstructed from a critical appraisal of the Gospels . . . By his followers and by many of the people, Jesus was recognized as the Messiah, God's chosen agent for the redemption of Israel. And he also undoubtedly so regarded himself. At this stage of his ministry, Jesus was probably more concerned with the opposition of the Jewish authorities than he was with the Romans, for Galilee was then ruled by a Jewish prince, Herod Antipas. The High Priest at Jerusalem who was Jewish was actually appointed by the Roman governor to control native affairs and maintain good order among his people. Consequently, both the High Priest and the Sadducean aristocracy, of which he was a member, were suspicious of any popular movement likely to disturb the peace. And the movement led by Jesus appeared to be just such a disturbance.

"The priestly aristocracy, headed by the High Priest, controlled the Temple of Yahweh at Jerusalem; their position gave them great authority as well as rich income. Seeing them as the chief obstacle to Israel's conversion, Jesus finally decided to challenge their control of the Temple. Accordingly, with his disciples and Galilean followers he staged a Messianic entry into Jerusalem at the feast of the Passover. Gathering support, he attacked the trading activities of the Temple. Those activities were a profitable source of revenue to the priestly aristocrats, and Jesus' attack was obviously a far more serious affair than the Gospels represent it to have been. It is even possible that Jesus intended to seize the Temple and reform the priesthood, as the Zealots were later to do in A.D. 66. The outcome of Jesus' bold move is difficult to assess. It would seem that he did not achieve complete success; but his supporters remained too numerous for the Jewish authorities to arrest him publicly.

"The crucifixion of Jesus, as a rebel, by the Romans was not an extraordinary event in the light of contemporary Jewish history. Thousands of other Jews similarly perished, either as leaders or supporters of revolt. But from this point onwards Christian tradition makes even more problematic the search for historical fact about Jesus. It was the usual practice for the bodies of executed criminals to be buried in a common grave. According to the Gospels, this did not happen to the body of Jesus. Instead, a disciple named Joseph of Arimathaea obtained the body from Pilate and buried it in a rock-hewn tomb of his own. Three days later the tomb was found to be empty. Subsequently a series of visions, in which the crucified Jesus appeared to various disciples, convinced his followers that Jesus had risen from the dead. The visions were, significantly limited to the disciples of Jesus; no one outside their fellowship is recorded to have had a similar experience. According to Christian tradition, these appearances of the Risen Jesus continued for forty days.

"It is difficult to evaluate these traditions of the Resurrection of Jesus. Although the physical reality of the Risen Jesus is stressed, it is never asserted that he resumed his life on earth; instead he is said to have ascended to heaven. But, whatever the truth from the disciples' faith about the Risen Jesus, there can be no doubt that from the disciples faith in it, Christianity was born.

"So the Christianity of the original disciples was essentially a Jewish faith. They probably never contemplated that it would lead to a new religion distinct and separate from Judaism.

"The Christian system of chronology still proclaims, even in a secular world, the decisive nature of the birth of Jesus—though ironically, it sets that event at least four years too late, as have been proven without question."

Considering that the Old Testament was written originally in ancient Jewish and the New Testament in Greek from scrolls or information passed down through the ages by word of mouth, and also taking into account those historical volumes were translated into several other languages, then one must accept that innumerable happenings were misinterpreted during those writings and translations. Today, for example, reporters from different newspapers will write contrasting accounts of the same event. Those reporters are not necessarily lying, but simply giving their own personal viewpoint. Reports about events that happened less than 200 years ago are now known to be inaccurate or entirely untrue, such as many of the American Civil War episodes. Regardless of how zealous a person is about the Bible, to believe it represents an accurate historical account of events thousands of years old defies logic, and with this attitude, I began my visit to Jerusalem and vicinity.

Winding through Jerusalem to Bethlehem, the birthplace of Jesus Christ and the most hallowed place in Christendom, my mind reflected to the holiday season on the farm, the highlight of our year. Religious fervor played a minor role. Christmas meant a few toys, an improved bill of fare for a few days, and the opportunity to shirk a little of our work load. "O Little Town of Bethlehem," one of my favorite Christmas carols, symbolized that joyful season on the farm but also solemnized the town only five miles outside Jerusalem I was on my way to visit.

I often wondered if a person were in the Holy Land at Christmas if a more religious attitude might prevail. A few excerpts from a book entitled *Journey Through the Holy Land,* by Betty Hartman Wolf, provided some of the answer: "What is it like to be in Bethlehem on Christmas? This is a question that my husband and I have been asked perhaps as often as any other. From a distance of thousands of miles, American Christians can picture in their minds that this tiny town must come alive and glow with joy on this most happy occasion, the celebration of the birth of Jesus.

"It was amusing to read in our American newspapers that the town of Bethlehem was alight with Christmas trees for the season. This was not true. The Christmas tree is a custom that has come from Western civilization . . . In sum, we saw no more than a half dozen trees decorated for Christmas. . .

"My husband and I celebrated Christmas in Bethlehem with the Western Christians on December 24th. The schedule of events was: a) at noon the Latin Patriarch arrived at the Church of the Nativity; b) at four-thirty in the afternoon, there was a service at Shepherd's Field; c) in the evening, there were church services in the various Bethlehem churches, some as early as 8 o'clock and others as late as midnight. . .

"In the late afternoon hours of Christmas Eve, we drove a short way out of Bethlehem to Shepherd's Field. . . At the Protestant section of the field, maintained by the YMCA, we were privileged to attend a carol sing and service held at dusk. We stood for about an hour for this service in the company of many other Christian tourists. The tourists stand on high ground. The service is held in a depression that leads into a cave. Following the service, the whole crowd presses down through the depression and into the cave. Why? Your ticket of admission to the Shepherd's Field entitles you to a sandwich, half a loaf of round native bread with cooked lamb and its juices tucked into the pocket of the bread. Inside the cave, men dressed as shepherds hand you a sandwich as you file by toward an exit that takes you back up to the field. Numbers of children, aware that this Christmas service ends with a small meal, are on hand to wheedle the sandwich away from you. Since many tourists are squeamish about eating except in first-class hotels, it is likely that the children have found the occasion easy pickings."

During my visit in the Jerusalem area I could easily envision the experience of Mrs. Wolf and her husband. The attachment and affection North Americans feel for Christmas are quite unlike the sentiment of those who actually live where it all happened.

The Church of Nativity, the most popular tourist attraction in Bethlehem, faces Manger Square, a large open plaza in front of the church. Empress Helena, in her 4th century search for the True Cross, decided she had found the exact spot where the manger had stood, and when Helena claimed to have discovered a major biblical site, her son, Constantine, built a church on it. Although destroyed, others came along and built more houses of worship on the ruins. Constructed by the Crusaders, the present church contains elements of Constantine's early structure.

Downstairs, in the Grotto of the Nativity, a silver star indicates the actual spot where they believe Jesus was born, and adjacent to the grotto is the Chapel of the Manger where the Virgin Mary supposedly placed the newborn Christ child. Most North Americans visualize the stable and manger that became the bed of Jesus far different from reality. Stables as we know them never existed in that region, instead rock caves adjoining caravanserai's provided a shelter for horses, and mangers were just depressions in the rock.

Milk Grotto Street on the south side of Manger Square naturally leads to the Milk Grotto where, according to legend, the Virgin Mary spilled a few drops of milk while nursing her child and it turned the dark stones milky white. Pilgrims can purchase little packets of chalky powder made from the stone to increase milk flow in nursing mothers, and I pondered what Jesus Christ might think about that commercial operation. Before returning to Jerusalem, our guide steered us to other tourist traps where religion didn't play a big part in the enterprise.

At first sight Jerusalem looks like an unfinished settlement, despite being one of the world's oldest cities still inhabited, and although not the most beautiful seen in my travels, the city of David, Jesus, and Mohammed certainly seemed the most stimulating.

It would be improper to say nothing changes in Jerusalem because it has been the scene of non-ending change due to constant wars and battles. Nevertheless, a great aura of timelessness and permanence pervades the ageless capital whose name in Hebrew is "Yerushalayim" and is mentioned by name in Egyptian hieroglyphics as early as 2375 B.C.

Over the centuries the city suffered continuous devastation from Romans, Arabs, The Crusaders, and even rebellions amongst themselves, but during Israel's War of Liberation, the city underwent siege and horrible shelling from the armies of Egypt and Jordan for many months. Their heroic defense with obsolete weapons while enduring shortages of food and water ranks as one of the great triumphs of the Jewish people. As a result of the Six Day War in 1967, Jerusalem at least temporarily is once more a united city.

Jewish lore holds that the Messiah will eventually descend down the Mount of Olives, a place of worship in the time of David. Christians believe Jesus often preached to his disciples from the Mount of Olives and first taught them the words of Pater Noster, the Lord's Prayer and also ascended to heaven from there. At the Church of Pater Noster on the summit of the famous Mount, the Lord's Prayer is set into the tiled walls in 44 different languages.

Descending the Mount of Olives into the Valley of Kidron and onto the Jericho Road to the Garden of Gethsemane, we inspected the Church of All Nations, also called the Basilica of Agony. Fransicans maintain the exquisite Garden of Gethsemane where Jesus was betrayed by Judas. The Garden contains a number of gnarled old olive trees which reputedly date back to the time of Jesus but more likely are descendants—albeit very, very old—of the original trees.

We climbed Mount Zion in the city of Old Jerusalem to what tradition says is the Tomb of David, but what archaeologists claim are remnants of a 14th century inn and Crusader's chambers. On the crown of Mount Zion beside the Tomb of David, the Church of the Dormition commemorates the Virgin Mary's death, or dormition, since it is believed she merely went to sleep. A chamber has been built on the site of Jesus' Last Supper with the disciples.

The Church of Peter in Gallicantu (meaning "cockcrow"), also on the slopes of Mt. Zion, commemorates the episode in Biblical history when Jesus told Peter: "Before the cock crows today, you shall have denied me thrice." The locale is believed to be where the Romans retained Jesus overnight before His crucifixion.

We completed our morning sightseeing tour at the Israel Museum to inspect the Dead Sea Scrolls. Except for the novelty of seeing the historic documents, they hold little interest to the average individual because hieroglyphics don't tell much of a story to the layman.

After lunch we bused back down Jericho Road to the Old Walled City of Jerusalem and entered through St. Stephen's Gate used by most Christian visitors because it follows "Via Dolorosa," the Way of The Cross. Israeli troops entered the city in 1967 at that point which is known in Hebrew as Lion's Gate. Inside the gate, the Church of St. Anne, a gem of Crusader architecture, is, according to legend, built over the spot where Joachim and Anne, the parents of Mary, had their home.

Near St. Anne's an excavation at the site where Jesus is believed to have healed a man with an infirmity of many years shows how far Jerusalem of Jesus' day lies below the street level of the present city. Supports and floors of three successive churches have been uncovered that were erected on top of each other. Far down at the bottom, about 60 feet below present street level, is water, and just above the water can be seen the tops of Roman arches and columns that date approximately to the time of Jesus.

Via Dolorosa (Latin for the "Way of Sadness"; or in English, the "Way of the Cross") is the route Christ must have followed on Good

Friday from Pilate's Judgement Hall to Calvary, though the actual sites would be layers below the present store-lined streets. The solemnized locations are marked by plaques, chapels and pillars, built mostly in the 19th century and not striking either for beauty or for their portrayal of that era. The route winds through the busy marketplace of Old Jerusalem and ends at the Holy Sepulchre, a giant church built above what is presumed to be the actual hilltop of Calvary. The first of the 14 Stations of the Cross, now the yard of an Arab school, was where Pontius Pilate questioned Jesus, washed his hands of the affair, and condemned Him. Across the narrow street, the Chapel of the Flagellation stands where Jesus was stripped of His clothes, whipped, forced to wear the Crown of Thorns plus the robe of royal purple, and started his final journey up the Via Dolorosa. The Third Station, where Christ fell the first time is marked by a pillar; the Fourth, where he spoke to his mother Mary, is outside an Armenian Church with a crypt displaying a 7th century mosaic. The Fifth Station, where Simon took the cross from Him, is marked by a Franciscan Chapel. At the Sixth, where tradition says Veronica wiped the face of Jesus whose features were miraculously imprinted on her veil, is a chapel. The veil, still reputed to carry the imprint of Jesus' face, lies in St. Peter's in Rome. A steep climb up a stepped street takes you to the Seventh Station, where Jesus fell the second time. To reach the Eighth, where Jesus foretold the destruction of Jerusalem to a group of women, you go through a market to a cross which hangs on the wall of a Greek monastery. The Ninth Station, marking Christ's third fall, is arrived by backtracking to the market, going up a street and climbing a stairway to the door of a Coptic church. From there you go down and through the marketplace to the courtyard of the Holy Sepulchre. The next four stations are inside the church on the rock of Calvary, also called Golgotha—both words meaning "skull," for that is its shape. These are where Jesus was stripped of His garments (the Tenth Station), nailed to the cross (the Eleventh), died (Twelfth), and where His body was taken down and anointed (Thirteenth). The Fourteenth and final station is the tomb.

The Church of the Holy Sepulchre, dark and gloomy and shared by several sects (Greek Orthodox, Roman Catholics, Armenian, Syrian, Coptic and Abysinians), is cluttered with their various chapels and hanging lights. Protestants are barred from holding services in the church, the holiest of holy sites to all Christians. Helena, in the year 326, divinely guided to this place reputedly discovered the true cross. If that wooden cross existed for 300 years, it outlasted almost any known element on earth and made it still another miracle of the times. To be a true Christian, you must believe in these wondrous things, however.

Our final tour of Old Jerusalem took us to the temple area which includes the Aqua Mosque and the magnificent and exquisite Dome of the Rock. With its gilt dome dazzling in the sunlight, the Dome of the Rock not only is an outstanding spectacle but also plays an important part in Old Testament history. If located on Mount Moriah, as believed, the mosque would be where Abraham took Isaac to inform him he did not have to sacrifice his first born to God. Solomon's Temple probably rested on the same spot as did Herod's Temple, more grand, more spacious, more pretentious than that of Solomon's and where Jesus came as a boy and a man. Archaeologists yearn for an opportunity to probe beneath the present house of worship, but Moslems forbid such an undertaking.

The nearby Aqua Mosque, though not nearly so stunning on the outside as the smaller Dome of the Rock, is truly lovely inside with Oriental rugs covering every inch of the floor where the faithful were praying or reading the Koran.

That holy Moslem area, second only to Mecca in importance to their religious beliefs, again offered an incongruity. Israeli soldiers with bayonets at the ready guarded every niche both inside and out of those hallowed mosques. They allowed Jews to enter, but if a Jew made any religious motion or attempted to sit down, the Israeli soldiers would unceremoniously expel them. I watched rather dumbfounded as a gruff Israeli soldier seized a young Jewish girl and ejected her quite rudely for no apparent reason. I inquired from our Moslem guide how this could happen when Jews captured the area from the Arabs ten years ago. "There would be an instant and terrible riot by all the Arabs in Jerusalem if the Jews were allowed to pray in or desecrate in any way the Moslem mosques. Israeli soldiers are simply preventing a problem before it starts," he answered.

Adding to the rather bizzare situation, a few yards outside the Moslem area is the Wailing Wall, part of the retaining and supporting wall of Herod's Temple and the most sacred Jewish section in Jerusalem. Over the ages Jews went there to pray and bewail the destruction of Solomon's Temple and the hard fate of the Jewish people, and so the name. In chinks between the stones are little rolled up papers and notes scrawled with prayers or names of loved ones. The stones themselves are worn smooth by the loving caress of millions of hands over the centuries.

Men and women pray at different sections of the Wall in accordance with Orthodox Jewish custom. Proclaimed a synagogue, men are not allowed to go to the Wall bareheaded. When Israeli troops captured the Old City in 1967, they found the Wall on one side of a narrow alleyway, facing crumbling old houses and public conveniences which have been cleared away and replaced by a plaza. On the three Jewish festivals—

Passover, Succot (the Feast of Tabernacles), and Shavuot (the Feast of Weeks)—as many as 250,000 Jews pray at the Wall.

Three days had been spent touring the enchanting and aged old city of Jerusalem, but I had barely glimpsed at the maze of historical lore on display in that crossroads of religion. Months of study and perception would be required to properly understand and sense the enormous influence the city has played in all our lives.

Traveling to Tel Aviv from Jerusalem by aircraft, though much quicker, would not have provided the pleasure received on the 200-mile circular tour we made through Israel by bus. Rafi, a personable but cocky young Israeli, replaced our affable Jordanian guide. Rafi proved to be interesting, talkative, and knowledgeable, though a strongly opinionated young man throughout the three days he remained with us.

Leaving the Holy city of Jerusalem with its message of peace and good will, we passed a mighty Israeli army convoy which wouldn't be the only reminder of the war status during our day's journey. Heading directly north we traveled many miles along the west bank of the Jordan River. Captured by the Israeli forces from Jordan during the 1967 Six Day War, the Israel government is settling the territory with Israeli farmers. Barbed-wire fences lined both sides of the highway, and there were tank traps and infantry obstacle barriers.

The richness of the soil due to its proximity to the Jordan River is one reason Israel will be reluctant to give back the fertile valley despite world pressure. In my opinion, they should struggle to retain the vital sector because it substantially shortens her border with Jordan and makes it considerably easier to defend the nation.

We made our first stop at Beit Shean in the Jordan Valley, a development town peopled by recent immigrants but built on top of 18 previous cities, (the current count) which had their beginnings 6,000 years ago. Christian tradition sets Beit Shean as the site of the healing of the leper, as told by the Evangelist.

A splendidly preserved Roman theater still stands on the outskirts of town, and while Rafi expounded on the ancient history of Beit Shean and the antiquity of the hallowed region, I conjured up visions of steel-helmeted Roman soldiers standing guard over Sumerian artisans building the amphitheater, while shepherds tended their flocks on the slopes of the nearby Mount Gilboa. Engulfed in a euphoria created by dreaming of days long ago, my reverie was promptly shattered when a squadron of Israeli jets swooshed overhead, breaking the peaceful stillness like a thunderbolt from a cloudless sky, and once again, today's problems pushed away the thoughts of yesteryear.

On route to Galilee from Beit Shean we traversed excellent farm land verdant with the growth of many crops and bypassed the old marshlands of Hula, the Lake of Tiberias, and the Ghor River that flows into the Dead Sea and beyond.

If the Middle East is the cradle of civilization, then the Galilee is certainly the nursery of Christianity, as that is where Christ performed his ministry. The lake, countryside and towns—Cana, Capernaum, Tiberias, Nazareth—are repeatedly referred to in the Gospels, and Jesus, known as the Galilean, chose his disciples from the local fishermen.

The Jordan River flows through the Sea of Galilee, a fresh-water lake, 680 feet below sea level. Called Kinneret by the ancients because from afar it has the shape of a lute, the lake is 13 miles long and 7 miles wide. Like Jerusalem and Nazareth, the Sea of Galilee is linked with Jesus Christ. Here according to the Bible, He walked on its waters, becalmed the storm, filled the empty fishing nets and, gathered His followers—Simon, Andrew, James, and John.

Several people swimming and frolicking in the placid lake made one forget that the Golan Heights, occupied by Israel the past few years, were only ten miles away, and we relaxed in the area the Syrians used to shell regularly. For all its religious significance, the Galilee has always been one of history's bloodiest battlefields. A natural trade and migration route between Europe and Asia, it has been fought over for thousands of years. The Egyptians fought there, as did the Canaanites, the tribes of Israel, the Philistines, the Romans, the Crusaders, and now the never-ending conflict between the Arabs and the Jews.

The town of Tiberias, built after the time of Christ by Herod the Great's son, enjoys a panoramic view overlooking the varied-colored lake. Tabgha, the traditional site of the miracle of loves and fishes, lies 80 lake-front miles north of Tiberias and is marked by the Church of Multiplication. Many believe that Jesus preached the Sermon on the Mount and chose the Twelve Apostles on a gentle slope above Tabgha.

After choosing his twelve apostles, legend claims that Jesus went to Capernaum, about two miles from Tabgha which became the center of His teaching. Columned ruins of a 3rd century synagogue mark the site of an earlier one where He began his ministry. At Capernaum, he supposedly wrought many miracles by healing the blind, the lame, and the leprous, but also in that city, His own people mocked Him. He proved he wasn't without temper when he lashed into them saying, "And thou, Capernaum, which art exalted unto Heaven, shall be brought down to Hell." In today's language Jesus in fact told the people of Capernaum to go to Hell.

From Capernaum we passed through Cana, an ancient town of Galilee where Jesus performed His first miracle by turning water into wine at a wedding. We lunched at the Kibbutz Nof Ginnossar, on the Sea of Galilee, where a delightful restaurant specialized in St. Peter's fish caught in the Galilee. Kibbutzim, 100 percent socialistic, originated solely as communal farms but now owns and operates other industries. Kibbutzim control a high percentage of Israel's agriculture. Although only about 5 percent of Israel's population hold membership, they wield considerable political influence.

Following lunch we headed for Nazareth via the Horns of Hittin. Of all the warfare of the Middle Ages, the battle at the Horns of Hittin in 1187, between the knights of the West and lords of the East, the Cross and the Crescent, undoubtedly had the most far-reaching consequences. There, Saladin hacked to pieces the Crusaders and that defeat tolled the bell for Christianity in the Holy Land.

Nazareth, a sprawling hilly town, is an Arab but Christian town in Jewish country, though a new Jewish settlement called Nazareth Heights sits on an upward slope to the northeast.

In Nazareth's the Basilica of Annunciation is where handed-down belief says Archangel Gabriel appeared to Mary to tell her that Jesus would be born by saying, "Hail Mary, full of grace, the Lord is with thee." These words are repeated by Catholics to this day.

We proceeded from Nazareth via the villages of Afula and Wadi Ara to Tel Aviv past fields of cotton ready for harvest, orange groves dripping with ripening fruit, and grains and vegetables of several varieties.

After a delightful evening in the Tel Aviv Intercontinental Hilton with its spectacular view over the blue Mediterranean, we took a morning bus ride 60 miles north along the coast to Haifa. Israel's Mediterranean shore stretches 100 miles in almost a straight line punctuated only by Haifa Bay. In both Old and New Testaments, references to the coastal regions are few and far between. Philistines and Phoenicians occupied the coast, whereas the events of dramas of Jewish lives and history took place in the interior of the country. Today most of Israel's population is concentrated along the shores of the Mediterranean with Tel Aviv and Haifa accounting for about a sixth of the total.

Haifa, an attractive city, rises in three tiers above the Mediterranean with Mount Carmel at the summit. On the crown of Mount Carmel, 1,800 feet high, you obtain an absolutely fantastic view across the city and harbor area. Haifa, only a way station at the turn of the century, is now Israel's third most populous city and the nation's leading seaport. Many heart-rending stories are told about refugees that landed shortly after the war almost all pitiful victims of the barbarous concentration camps. Finally placing their feet on land, most would fall sobbing on the sand. After their long and horrible experiences, arriving in Israel would seem like a miracle. With typical Jewish courage, it isn't difficult to understand how they overcame fantastic odds to defeat the Arabs in 1948 and retain their independence.

From the peak of Mount Carmel we wound our way down the slope to the Bahai Temple. The Bahai sect, headquartered in Haifa, claims several million followers including a large concentration in the United States and Canada. Persia, its founder's native country, prohibited the sect, and publicly executed Mirza Ali Mohammed in 1850. His remains have been interred in the Temple in Haifa.

The Bahai faith basically advocates unity and brotherhood, goals they believe are attainable through a common world language and religion. They view the prophets of the great religions—Moses, Christ, Buddha, and Mohammed—as messengers of God, all sent to parts of the world at different times in history. To the Bahai, all religions should preach the same basic doctrine: brotherhood, love and charity. Religion should bring men together, not raise barriers between them, they claim. The Bahai Temple topped with a large spendid golden dome is a graceful combination of East and West among Persian Gardens, both beautiful and unique in style.

Our tour along the Mediterranean coast occurred on a Saturday, a Jewish Sabbath, and the golden beaches were jammed with sun seekers. The joyous scene resembled North America with bathers in colorful swim wear and sea-side vendors peddling goodies to eat. Watching the shouting happy children frolicking in the turquoise water, I wondered if they would be allowed to spend their lives in that present peaceful atmosphere or be subjected to the horrors inflicted so often over the ages on their fathers and forefathers.

A new city, Haifa doesn't offer a lot of sightseeing attractions, and so after a short visit we left for Caesarea about halfway between Haifa and Tel Aviv. En route we passed Elijah's cave, where Elijah hid when fleeing from Ahab and where the Holy Family stayed after their flight from Egypt.

Caesarea, approximately 2,200 years old, began with Herod, who incorporated the coastal strip into his vassalized kingdom and transformed the settlement into a great metropolis. Herod built a harbor, an outstanding achievement for pioneer builders, and in the best Roman tradition, a splendid theater which still looks pretty much as it did when it was used for throwing performers to the lions. Presently, it is used for more humane purposes. During the summer, the Israel Philharmonic and visiting musicians perform there under the stars, and Rafi said the acoustics are almost perfect.

Returning to Tel Aviv, we took a short tour of the only true metropolis in Israel. Impersonal streets and neutral-looking buildings in Tel Aviv might easily belong to just any spot in the world, completely unlike the venerable and physical beauty of Jerusalem. Tel Aviv, meaning "the Hill of Spring," refers to the spring of 1909 when the first handful of houses in today's modern city were built. To those first settlers just returning to the homeland of their ancestors, the empty sand dunes adjacent to the ancient port of Jaffa was the site they chose to make their new home.

Jaffa, now officially a suburb of Tel Aviv, is recognized as one of the oldest ports in the world and Jerusalem's natural outlet to the sea. Tradition says it was founded by Noah's son, Japhet. In Jaffa, like other places in the Holy Land, are scenes of great contrast. On one side of the road, families basked in the sun under brightly colored umbrellas enjoying the sea, while directly across the road stood a garish bomb shelter, one of the many throughout the Tel Aviv area and its environs.

Of the three nations on our Middle East itinerary, I would find it difficult to choose a favorite. They each provided a rich source of knowledge and material that belongs to the past and history has always been one of my special subjects.

From the Holy Land and Tel Aviv, we flew to Istanbul on a delightful moonlight night with the air fresh and invigorating, a welcome change after the intense heat of the Middle East.

Istanbul, existing as a city for seventeen centuries, has not lost the essential vestiges of the past. Time, earthquake, fire, and conquerors (except for the Christian looters of the Fourth Crusade) have been uncommonly kind to the fabric of its monuments, and no city on earth has so many old buildings of beauty and distinction.

Divided by the Bosphorous, Istanbul is the only major metropolis to lie in two continents, and the five-mile-long Golden Horn cuts through the heart of the European side, so the huge city is dominated by water. Across the Bosphorous lies the Asian section of the city. Constantinople, changed officially to Istanbul in 1930, lies between the Black Sea in the north and the Sea of Marmara on the south, and has been the capital of three empires: Roman, Byzantine and Ottoman.

Exclusively situated on the European side of the Bosphorous, Constantinople was founded in 330 A.D. by Constantine I as the new capital of the Roman Empire. It became the largest and most splendid European city of the Middle Ages and shared the glories and vicissitudes of the Byzantine Empire. Though besieged on numerous occasions by various peoples, it fell only three times.

Like Rome, Istanbul now stands on seven hills. The north side of the Horn, mostly residential, does include some quaint mosques and interesting architecture, but the Old City across the water contains the business and industrial district plus historical buildings of interest to tourists. Three bridges carry a massive surge of traffic across the estuary from the south side to the Old City, causing the largest, longest, noisiest, most frustrating and non-ending traffic snarl that could possibly exist.

Rush hour is all hours. I didn't believe any place could match Cairo for chaotic congestion and blaring horns, but that city doesn't belong in the same league with Istanbul.

After waiting two hours the initial morning for our local guide to show, Oliver Jones, our tour director, began making frantic phone calls and discovered the man had been involved in a traffic accident. With a German guide, who spoke limited English as a replacement, we inched our way to the Old City, crossing the Golden Horn on the Galata Bridge.

The massive Topkapi Saray in old Istanbul, a charming old Sultan's palace, contains a series of courtyards surrounded by buildings, separated by gates. Topkapi means the "Gate of the Gun." Although the wooded courtyards and linked buildings are pleasant and impressive today, they have witnessed some of the most fearful incidents recorded in history.

Several of the names used for various rooms and palace fixtures such as Executioner's Fountain, Dead Man's Gate and The Cage, indicate the drama enacted within those walls four or five centuries ago. Started by Mohammed II, the aged seraglio consists of many buildings and kiosks grouped into three courts, the last of which contained the treasury, harem, and private apartments of the ruler. We passed through the Gate of Happiness to reach the third courtyard where on benches foreign ambassadors sat, sometimes for days, waiting for audience. On either side of the passage lived eunuchs—black on the left, white on the right.

The third courtyard, used only by the sultan and officials of the palace, also contained a library, pharmacy, offices, and a school for the children. One of the buildings now contains many costumes of the sultans that, kept in wooden trunks covered with felt, are marvelously well preserved. The guide claimed that moths were so busy eating the felt, regularly replaced, that they never got through to the clothes.

In the treasury, my eyes could scarcely conceive the wealth on display. Emeralds, rubies and other gemstones were as common as buttons in a haberdashery, sheet-gold lined display cases like plywood, and there were thrones of ivory and tortoiseshell, covered with cushions inlaid with pearls that would be the envy of the Queen of England. Topping off the dazzling array of precious jewels, the magnificent 86-carat Spoon Diamond lay supreme in its own cabinet, surrounded by little cut diamonds. The spectacular collection of famous sultan jewelry remains a sparkling memorial to the opulence of Ottoman royalty.

The heart of Topkapi Saray and soul of the Ottoman Empire up to the middle of the 19th century was the harem where up to 4,000 women and girls used to live. Standing in the harem area at Topkapi, the mind's eye conjures a picture of concubines at leisure, hundreds of them sitting around wondering who would be next "in the eye" of the sultan. That profession also had its drawbacks because legend claims that a 17th century sultan once ordered the 1,000 members of his harem trussed, weighted, and thrown into the sea. Gazing over the peaceful Bosphorous, I wondered where that ghastly splash took place.

For gigantic but impressive human achievement, Sultanahmet, the world renowned Blue Mosque, must compare with the greatest. Built for Sultan Ahmet I between the years 1609 and 1617, the mosque with six minarets seems to be deliberately planned to rival its famous neighbor, Santa Sophia, across the square. Besides the magnificence and enormity of the structure, another particular splendor of the Sultanahmet is the interior walls, almost entirely covered with tiles of blue and green which gives it a delicate, airy richness that is quite unique. Tour operators advise patrons if they are going to visit only one house of worship, then the Blue Mosque should be the inevitable choice.

We spent several hours one afternoon at Istanbul's renowned bazaar, the world's largest covered market. Spread over 50 walled and roofed acres, it houses 4,000 shops, at least 500 specializing in gold jewelry. Rings and other adornments could be purchased in the bazaar as high as $5,000 or kebab skewers could be bought for a nickel. The unimaginable marketplace has 92 streets each devoted to a special type of merchandise and 40,000 persons pass through the bazaar each day. At times the pedestrian traffic reached such massive proportions, that like a huge traffic snarl, it came to a complete halt. Always a cosmopolitan city, Istanbul has preserved much of its international and polyglot character, and Greeks, Armenians and Jews form a large part of the population.

For our ferry cruise up the Bosphorous, we were greeted with a gray morning and a cool drizzle, a welcome change after three weeks under a burning sun in the North African desert regions. Our craft hugged the European coast all the way to within sight of the Black Sea. About 90 percent of Turkey's population resides on the Anatolian Peninsula in the Asian portion of the country, while the remainder lives in the European sector bordered by Bulgaria and Greece. A republic since 1923, Turkey, a little larger than Texas, has extensive coastlines on the Black, Mediterranean and the Aegean seas. Its Asian neighbors are the USSR, Iran, Iraq and Syria. Though one of the oldest inhabited regions of the world, the history of Turkey as a national state began only with the collapse of the Ottoman Empire in 1918. Before World War I, the Ottoman Empire ruled what is now Syria, Lebanon, Iraq, Jordan, Israel, Arabia, Yemen, and islands in the Aegean.

The Bosphorous, a strait connecting the Black Sea and the Sea of Marmara separating Turkey in Asia from Turkey in Europe, is about 20 miles long and reaches a maximum width of 1½ miles. Dotted with ancient ruins, picturesque villages, and forested slopes, both shores appear quite scenic.

Despite the fact that swift currents make navigation difficult, the Bosphorous is always busy. Big ships come and go to the four corners of the earth, and passengers and car ferries shuttle back and forth several times an hour between Istanbul and numerous villages all the way to the Black Sea. There are also fishing vessels, small cargo-carrying Bosphorous boats, and innumerable small motorized caiques that go from one place to another with a dozen or a hundred passengers as well as row boats, barges, lighters, tugs, and dinghies toiling here and there for reasons of their own.

Settlements up and down the shores of the Bosphorous are charming in their various ways, with old wooden houses, modern villas, waterside cafes, mosques, and apartment blocks set on wooded hillsides. There are beaches, castles, and other objects of interest, including an anti-submarine boom up near the Black Sea, ready to swing into place at a moment's notice if the Russians show signs of becoming aggressive.

A mighty new bridge now leaps the Bosphorous, finally connecting the two continents. Three and one half years in the building, the 3,500 foot suspension span (only three in the world and all in the United States are longer) was completed in 1973. It marks the first bridging of the historic channel since King Darius of Persia lashed boats from shore to shore during a campaign in the 6th century B.C.

Within sight of the Black Sea we disembarked for lunch at a delightful open-air restaurant on the banks of the Bosphorous before returning to Istanbul by bus. The final attraction of our Turkish itinerary, the massive St. Sophia, onetime capital of Christendom and long time bulwark of Islam, cherishes its dual heritage. Not architecturally splendid, it nevertheless offers a prime example of Byzantine and Ottoman splendor. What it lacks in beauty, it makes up for in sheer bulk. Tombs of the sultans of the 16th and 17th centuries are buried inside. The 1400-year-old building is remarkably well preserved. Gazing around at the uncommonly huge chunk of empty space, one feels terribly insignificant in its empty vastness. Although the Blue Mosque is more aesthetically satisfying, no one visiting Istanbul should leave without a visit to Santa Sophia.

From Istanbul we flew to Bulgaria's capital city for a ten-hour stopover before continuing to Athens. While waiting in Sofia, I took my second city tour of that bulwark of communism in less than two years. Regardless of its political ideology, Sofia seemed like a breath of fresh air in comparison to the hodgepodge of human confusion that existed in Istanbul. I readily realized it wasn't necessarily a sign of economic vitality that made Sofia appear so clean and orderly. The difference may have been caused by the shortage of personal wealth and lack of freedom, but the city looked fastidiously tidy and its inhabitants healthy and well dressed.

Following our short stop-over at Sofia we made an evening flight to Athens, our final destination. Although it would only be for one day, I looked forward eagerly to a brief glimpse at the ancient capital.

In addition to being an integral part of any history dealing with the cradle of civilization, Athens was also the birthplace of democracy. Situated on the plain of Attica near the Saronic Gulf of the Aegean Sea, Athens is the administrative, economic, and cultural center of Greece and one of the most renowned cities in the world.

Its origin, lost in the voids of history, likely had its nativity in the Neolithic Age. Though we know for certain that settlers took advantage of the opportunities offered by the well-protected plain between the mountains and the sea as early as 3000 B.C. and continuously until the 6th century B.C., there were few signs of what Athens would become. It remained for the Persian Wars (500–449 B.C.) to make Athens the leading city-state of Greece. Numerous episodes involved in her dramatic past occurred at the world-famous Acropolis where we spent our first morning in the old but thriving metropolis.

Busing toward the Acropolis, we passed several interesting buildings, including the conservatorium and Olympic Stadium. Originally built in 330 B.C., rebuilt during the Roman period in 140 A.D., and again in 1894, the stadium became the site of the first Olympic Games of modern times, revived in 1896, and it holds a capacity of 60,000 persons.

The Acropolic (meaning "upper city"), one of the most majestic monuments left by our ancestors that exists on earth today, is built on a rocky hill 260 feet in height and with a flat oval top 500 feet wide and 1,150 feet long. A walled fortress on top of the promontory has existed for many millenia but the present Acropolis, with its temples and Parthenon, dates back to the 5th century B.C. Immortal marble monuments still standing and erected during the rule of Pericles are: the Parthenon, one of the most perfect architectural buildings ever created by man; the Propylaea, or "entrance," and the Erechthion, a temple dedicated to Athena.

Threading my way through a mass of visitors toward the Parthenon, I could readily understand why ancients chose the hill which enjoyed a spectacular view in every direction. Soaring into the Grecian sky in the distance, a steep cone-shaped Mount Lycabettus is a limestone rock that reaches an elevation of 1,000 feet. By day, it's only a green-and-white hill topped by a tiny, glaringly white church, but in the evening when the top half is floodlit, together with the Acropolis, the scene looks like something from a Walt Disney movie. The Parthenon, considered by many scholars the most perfect and magnificent ruin in the world, remains an outstanding architectural and artistic achievement even though an Englishman removed enough of the spoils of this one temple to fill a museum in England.

Another excellent specimen of Greek architecture, the Erechthion, stands near the north edge of the Acropolis in close proximity to the Parthenon. Constructed in 421–407 B.C. on the spot where the mythical King Cecrops was buried, the temple remains the most sacred and mythical of all the buildings in Athens.

Hundreds of tourists crowded the ancient ruins, and many simply sat in the gorgeous afternoon sun and marveled at what our ancestors had achieved so many centuries ago. I joined in the reverence.

From the Acropolis we took a short city tour to the Temple of Olympian Zeus, over two thousand years old, Hadrian's Arch erected in the 2nd century A.D. and of later vintage the former Royal Palace, home of King Constantine before he went into exile. Old Byzantine churches and modern religious structures grace the city and add to the enchanting mixture of new and old that makes Athens such a delight to visit.

The National Archaeological Museum contains an outstanding collection of masterpieces from excavations throughout Greece. All periods of antiquity are included, but new finds are now brought to Athens only when no regional museum has a prior claim.

In the afternoon we enjoyed a scenic 50-mile bus trip along the Aegean coastline to Corinth. Nowhere in Europe has prehistory been so faithfully preserved through legend as in the Peloponnese Peninsula which hangs like a leaf from the thin stem of the Corinthian Isthmus. The island or peninsula of Peloponnese contained the great cities of Sparta and Olympia as well as Corinth. The isthmus divides the Aegean Sea from the Gulf of Corinth, an inlet of the Ionian Sea. Centuries before construction of the canal which now divides the mainland from the Peloponnese, ships rolled over a four-mile roadway on huge wooden rollers, avoiding the dreaded Cape plus slicing 200 stormy miles off their passage from sea to sea. Commanding the strategic crossroads stood Corinth, enriched by tolls and trade. The canal according to legend was begun by Nero in 66 A.D. but not completed until 1893. We watched a tugboat leave the Gulf of Corinth and cruise through the placid canal requiring fifteen minutes that otherwise would have required ten hours, an enormous savings in time and money as a result of digging the ditch.

Corinth's roots can be traced to the point in history when it must have been one of the richest and most beautiful cities of Greece's golden age. Legend says that in the 7th century B.C. a thousand temple prostitutes and slave girls in the service of Aphrodite inhabited the metropolis of commerce and pleasure. Even 700 years later during his visit to sin city, St. Paul was shocked and according to the Bible, admonished the Corinthians, saying, "I speak to your shame." Guides point out the point where they claim he spoke.

The city suffered total destruction by the Romans in 146 B.C. All remaining ruins are therefore from the Roman period when Julius Caesar established his colony there. Still visible are remains of shops that lined the ancient streets, six Roman temples plus the remnants of two theaters. Ancient Corinth seemed an apt site to complete my tour of the cradle of civilization. Although anxious to return home, my abbreviated stop-over in Greece whet my appetite for a much longer visit to the nation and people reputedly responsible for democratic government.

Due to unusual circumstances, it took twenty-four hours instead of seven to return to Toronto which gave me ample time to rehash in my mind the previous few weeks. I especially pondered the significant difference in living standards between the people of Greece and inhabitants of the Holy Land, the two oldest civilizations on the planet. According to archaeologists, Greeks began adopting their civilized ways as much as 2,000 years after their brethren in the Holy Land, particularly in Egypt or the valleys of the Tigris and Euphrates. What profound secrets I wondered did the Greeks and Romans discover or possess that allowed them to bypass other sophisticated societies in streamlining the martial arts which gave them the upper hand in conquering and controlling the rest of the world for centuries? What made the Greeks and Romans more adaptable to logical reasoning, expert in philosophy, mathematics, astronomy, and other arts and sciences centuries ahead of people who had attained a fair degree of civilization hundreds of years before them? Many races over the ages who had reached their zenith of prosperity or attained a rich culture simply faded into obscurity or, at best, left scant traces of their existence. Greece, on the other hand, was not as powerful militarily as her ancestors, but still enjoys a prosperity far superior to any nation in the Holy Land with the possible exception of Israel. Perhaps the principal factor was an evolutionary quirk of nature which caused the religious fervor of the Greek people to be less than that of earlier civilizations who devoted all their time and energy to their many gods. The Greeks appear to have been more intent on improving their living standard than dedicated to the construction of temples and monuments. In the history of civilization, religion in its many facets has been the prime factor in a great deal of man's thinking and effort, often to his detriment.

Greece has the distinction of being the founder of the democratic way of life where the rights of the ordinary man were placed above those of the many gods worshipped by their neighbors and predecessors.

If the Holy Land is the birthplace of monotheistic religion, man's early attempt at writing, and the creation of empires, and Greece the spore of democracy and justice to the average citizen, then together they certainly form the cradle of civilization. My few weeks in that part of the world provided a marvelous, though small, insight into our ancient heritage.

Lagniappe
A Tale of Two Countries

Driving toward our Florida home in December, 1977, I felt elated at our determination to become American residents. Partially as a result of my travels throughout the 1970s but more probably because of extensive research following those wanderings, I had come to the definite conclusion that the United States of America offered much greater latitude to entrepreneurs. Although America seemed headed in a socialistic direction as well, they were going at it much more slowly than Canada. With Great Britain and Canada both rampant with escalating inflation and soaring deficits as examples, I hoped Uncle Sam might get the trend to the left stopped before it completely ruined their economy. My confidence mostly lay in their form of government, especially that ingredient which allowed members of Congress to vote their own mind as opposed to rigidly following a party line. Also their two-party system, the only one in the free world, offered a greater degree of efficiency at meeting the wishes and demands of the electorate.

Despite my ecstacy with our new American status, our two years as dual residents proved as emotionally, physically, and financially demanding and as difficult as any in my thirty years of marriage. In fact, it stretched that union almost to the breaking point on more than one occasion.

One of the principal causes of our numerous crises centered around the economic uncertainties existing in North America at that time. Canada's deplorable financial condition, mostly due to government mismanagement and overspending, wasn't helped by the political make-up of the country which permitted no real chance of a quick cure. In an attempt to reverse the downturn in the nation's business affairs, Pierre Trudeau promised in the summer of 1977 to cut government spending by two billion dollars including tax cuts, to stimulate the economy. This declaration seemed absolutely ludicrous coming from the main proponent of government spending for a decade and the man mostly responsible for the nation's malaise. Rene Levesque's popularity in Quebec had gradually waned, but unfortunately their loss at the polls offered the Liberal Party another chance to regain a foothold in the Province. Sixteen years of Liberal rule in Canada came to an end in 1979 when Canadians sent Joe Clark and his Conservative Party to Ottawa with a minority. This meant the national government again had to appease the left wing NDP or Labor Party to remain in power, a situation that had proven unworkable in the past. The electorate voted strictly along linguistic and regional lines, another regrettable aspect of the election that caused further polarization in an already divided country. The Liberals won 67 of their 75 seats in Quebec but only 3 of 81 west of Ontario. On the other hand, Joe Clark's Conservatives captured 60 seats in the west but only 2 in Quebec.

Throughout the final two years of the decade Canada's inflation rate hovered around the double-digit range, unemployment reached a post depression high, and the Canadian dollar plummeted to a 45-year low when it hit 83.5 U.S. in 1979. If Canada didn't swiftly and drastically curtail government expenditures, my native land faced a precarious future.

Conditions south of the border were not much better thoughout the same period, though neither inflation nor unemployment reached the same proportions as in Canada. The Carter administration had made halting the inflationary spiral its primary target. A three-month coal strike helped slow the pace of any hoped-for economic recovery, and it seemed unions were rapidly outgrowing their usefulness. In many instances, in fact, they did more harm to the workers they were trying to protect than to obtain benefits. Although the Canadian dollar had shrunk in relation to the American dollar, American money, in turn, had taken a shellacking against other world currencies, primarily blamed on the mounting world trade deficit and rising inflation. Americans were also becoming increasingly disturbed about the escalating budget deficit which had skyrocketed to over thirty billion in 1979. OPEC took advantage of the world gasoline shortage and gradually increased oil prices, not only adding fuel to the fires of inflation but also for the first time in American history causing long line-ups at gas pumps across the nation.

So despite our euphoria about becoming United States residents, we were trying to establish ourselves in a new country at a very inappropriate time. Sumcot of America incorporated in April of 1977, purchased $400,000 worth of Florida warehouses the same month. Fully rented and providing a good return on the investment, I knew they would appreciate quite rapidly but were only a minor asset in relation to what we hoped to acquire in our adopted country. I contacted Warren Lane, the realtor through whom I had purchased the warehouses, shortly after our arrival in Florida to look at other commercial properties. Due to the distressed state of the real estate market, investment opportunities were plentiful, and we carefully examined several. The market seemed ripe for condominium conversions or construction of deluxe warehouses, particularly with office availability. I examined several of these propositions, but when Warren showed me a 65,000-square-foot Pompano Beach shopping plaza in financial difficulty, I immediately liked its potential.

The recently constructed Pompano Plaza struck me as being a plum if it could be bought for two million dollars or less, and so I began negotiations. Of the 50 plus stores and offices in the complex, less than a dozen were occupied, and although the center had a destitute, bedraggled appearance, I felt that with some renovations and effort it could be made successful. Several liens had been placed against the property and Mutual Benefits, the first mortgagee, headquartered in Newark, N.J., had begun foreclosure proceedings. Both the owner and 2nd mortgagee were anxious to make a deal, but my offer of $1,850,000 made in May, 1978, didn't much more than cover the first mortgagee's equity. Joyce and I returned to Toronto for the summer and left the negotiating to Warren Lane, who eventually reported our bid had been turned down. George English, our Florida attorney, advised me to wait until Mutual Benefits completed foreclosure proceedings, which would clear all other liens off the title, before continuing to bargain for the property. The courts granted Mutual clear title June, 1978, and I increased my bid to $1,900,000 when informed they would sell at that figure. After tremendous haggling, they once more changed their mind and set the sale price at $2,200,000.

I spoke directly to one of their executive officers in Newark about the run-around.

"Phillips, we will put a management company on the site and fully rent the plaza stores in 6 months, at which point you will pay us $2,500,000," the man boasted.

"Best of luck," I replied.

Late in September, Warren phoned me in Toronto to see if I was still interested at $1,900,000.

"Warren, if Mutual Benefits will take back a $1,550,000 first mortgage for 30 years at 9 percent with the right to transfer, I will proceed," I answered.

Again after 30 days of bargaining during which time I refused to budge an inch, we finally acquired Pompano Plaza and closed the transaction December, 1978, for our first major foothold in the South.

My interest in Padre Island had never waned, and I frequently contacted John Austin about obtaining more developable land adjacent to the Gulf frontage we had previously acquired. In the summer of 1978, brother Jack and I spent a memorable three weeks when we traveled south by car to try to increase our holdings on the Texas coast. We stopped in Nashville on our way down and luckily obtained tickets to the Grand Old Opry. Being entertained by names like Hank Snow, Ernest Tubb, Roy Acuff, and others who had delighted us since our farm days provided quite a thrill.

An interesting incident happened on Padre Island. A barge had become stuck in a cut across the barrier island 30 miles north of South Padre Island's city limits. No road or trail existed to reach the barge, and so rescue equipment had to travel the hard-packed sandy seashore. A large flatbed hauling a dragline along the beach route lost its cargo when unknown to the driver a chain broke and the huge $50,000 dragline slipped off the truck and rapidly began disappearing in the soft sand. Recovery equipment, such as cherry pickers and enormous bulldozers, rushed to rescue the stricken dragline, creating quite a furor and causing the mishap to become locally the prominent event of the season. Each afternoon when Jack and I completed our day's appointments, we drove my Cadillac to the salvage site which at high tide meant often driving in the Gulf itself to avoid becoming mired in soft sand that hugged the water. After four days of strenuous effort, they finally retrieved the valuable machine. Watching the huge piece of equipment, more than 50 percent submerged in a sucking sand bed and frequently awash with ocean breakers, suddenly but slowly begin to escape its watery grave provided excellent entertainment but that wasn't necessarily the high point of the incident. Returning at dusk along the barren seashore, we always stopped to refresh ourselves from the heavy summer heat and humidity and were quite amazed that on an excellent beach in the largest state of the union we could swim stark naked in the Gulf of Mexico and be miles from another human being. Watching a coyote loping across the lonely sand dunes one evening, I remarked to Jack that I doubted if many Americans realized the extent of Texas's superb untouched ocean coastline.

Before we left the island paradise for Phoenix, we acquired a couple more parcels of Gulf frontage and began tentative arrangements to build an ocean-front condominium.

In spite of intense heat in Phoenix, we immediately contacted Harold Thomas, my old associate, and began searching for a business opportunity in that sector. Again after investigating different facets of real estate, I began dickering on a small shopping center in Paradise Valley, although I didn't actually acquire the property until September when I flew back from Toronto to finalize the transaction.

Jack and I successfully accomplished our mission to add to Sumcot's U.S. real estate portfolio and ended up in Las Vegas where Joyce met me for a few days relaxation. Jack returned by air, and Joyce accompanied me for the long drive back to Toronto.

More than anything else, to trade in real estate profitably requires good timing. Pop frequently used to say, "Get into the pig business when everyone else is getting out," a philosophy that applied to our recent acquisitions. We procured the Pompano Plaza, Texas ocean frontage and Paradise Valley property at reasonable figures due to the depressed market. Enormous effort still lay ahead, however, before we would turn any of our purchases into money makers.

Though I expended a great deal of effort at this time building up our real estate holdings in the United States, Sumcot Development in Canada still owned millions of dollars worth of land, some of it still being developed. The colossal filling job continued at Canadiana Shores and wouldn't be finished until 1979. We also hadn't completed final arrangements with various government agencies regarding the final take-over of services at Buckhorn Lake and Canadiana Shores on Lake Skugog.

If I needed further exasperation to convince me I made the right decision in transfering our assets south of the border, I received it when Sumcot personnel attempted to get the local municipality to take over the water works at Buckhorn Lake Estates. The costly system, approved and supervised by bureaucratically appointed engineers before and during its entire construction, had been a nightmare from its inception. Thousands of tons of rock had to be dynamited to get the line installed below frost level, although the colossal task of laying the pipe wasn't the only bugbear. Locating a sufficient flow of well water to meet Ontario Water Resource's specifications—always about 40 percent higher than the volume realistically required—turned out to be a difficult and extremely expensive proposition. They refused to allow Sumcot to remove water from Buckhorn Lake and treat it as we had done successfully at Oak Shores Estate several years before. Nevertheless, after months of testing, we finally located a gusher of beautiful spring water on our property, and everyone, including government engineers, was delighted. Despite the fact senior provincial engineers had approved the flow, a local municipal official got the bright idea that the source might be Buckhorn Lake itself and therefore insisted on a 90-day twenty-four-hour-a-day constant pumping test to see if the well would either dry up or eventually yield lake water.

Infuriated with the stupid request, I raced to Peterborough to confront the individual. "Few wells in Ontario that service thousands of homes could withstand such a test," I screamed, "and we only have 115 lots."

"I want to determine if your basic source is Lake Buckhorn," the man responded.

"And just suppose it is, even though your own senior officials plus the hydrologists say such a situation is almost impossible," I exploded. "What then?"

"Sumcot would have to install a treatment plant," he replied.

"Jesus Christ, man, I wanted to take water from Buckhorn and treat it eight months ago before I spent $25,000 locating the well, and your department refused. You people insisted that Sumcot must find a well. Now that we have the finest flow in the area, you want to see if you can find a way to force us to install a treatment plant."

He wouldn't relent, and so I instructed our field men to begin the pumping operation while I implored with senior provincial engineers in Toronto to intercede on Sumcot's behalf. To my everlasting gratitude they intervened, but not before we completed several days of constant pumping which showed no sign of lake water and the volume of flow fluctuated only a fraction. That preposterous episode just about concluded my dealings with Canada's bungling bureaucrats, but it left me with an unforgettable impression.

The economic slump that plagued the continent also severely affected vacation property sales. Again because we had an enormous profit margin built into our serviced lots, Sumcot could afford huge sums for advertising, and though we struggled, the Canadian corporation wound up with a substantial profit in both 1978 and 1979. Two waterfront lots at Buckhorn sold for the incredible price of $40,000 cash each. Government policies had halted waterfront developing almost completely, and so developers with an inventory of registered waterfront lots could almost name their own figure. It didn't seem possible that twenty years earlier, my first Harcourt Park lots sold for less than $1,000 per unit.

Fighting for sales in Canada and negotiating land deals and property investments in three sectors of the United States required almost constant travel. To add to this hectic pace, Joyce and I drove both automobiles, jammed with most of our personal effects every six months between our Toronto and Florida homes. Blaming pressure and turmoil, I drank heavily and frequently reached a point of complete inebriation. Joyce tolerated my bouts of drunkenness but with growing impatience that resulted in severely straining our close 30-year relationship. In spite of her annoyance at my alcoholic intake, she arranged an enormous surprise 52nd birthday party for me at which she had invited dozens of personal friends and associates, the affiliations extending all the way back to my first days in Toronto.

Sherree, who continued to work for Sumcot and spent a lot of time with us both in Toronto and Florida also detested my habit of over drinking. Joyce and I both recognized that our daughter, now reaching her mid-twenties, had her own life to live, and unless she asked our advice, we never interfered in her private affairs. A happy, gregarious individual, Sherree had many friends and indulged in an unconstrained lifestyle akin to the times. This warm affiliation we had enjoyed for so many years with our youngest exploded in our faces quite unexpectedly in 1978. Sherree, electing to take her vacation in late fall, suggested she drive her mother's car and spend six weeks in our Florida residence. Due to a three-week trip to China which I took in November, 1978, Joyce and I didn't plan on heading south until mid-December.

When I returned to Toronto from the Far East, I was informed that Barry Ervin had gone to Florida for a few days to consummate the closing of the Pompano Plaza deal. On his return he immediately requested a personal meeting with me and dropped the bombshell that he had left his wife and four young children and, instead of being in Florida, had been shacked up with Sherree in Ohio. He concluded by saying that when Sherree returned to Toronto they would be sharing an apartment and wanted Joyce's and my blessing. So shocked by his brash announcement, I said very little but went directly home to inform Joyce and Marty of the distressing news. At first Joyce wouldn't believe the sorrowful tidings, but if true, she declared her intention of shooting Ervin on sight if I didn't immediately fire my capable general manager. Although heavy hearted and moving around in a daze, we attended a Toronto Board of Trade dance that evening. I drank my usual and Joyce, substantially more than normal. By the time we left for home, neither of us would have passed a breathalizer test. Under the trying circumstance, our conversation naturally revolved around our daughter's predicament, and Joyce insisted I phone Barry when we arrived home at 2 a.m. and instantly dismiss him from the corporation. Having not made a final decision in my mind how to handle the fiasco, I hesitated to do anything so drastic that night and told my distraught wife we should wait until morning.

As a result of her anguish plus being fired up a little with alcohol, she leaped from the car in her nylon stockinged feet and went bounding down a 200-foot embankment into a heavily wooded valley a mile from our townhouse. After a half hour of persuasion and a guarantee from me that she could fire Barry the moment we stepped into the house, she reentered the vehicle and we proceeded home. Once inside the house, Joyce made a beeline for the phone, got Barry out of bed and in addition to calling him all types of pigs and several other non-flattering epithets, she informed him he no longer worked for Sumcot. Barry phoned me the following day to plead his case, insisting they would be married when his divorce became final and that Sherree was madly in love with him. Despite his plea, I made it clear that under the circumstances it would be better for all concerned that he clean out his desk and stay away from Joyce and me.

On her way through Georgia to our apartment, Sherree phoned to get our reaction concerning her liasion with our ex-general manager. Although disappointed at our vehement disapproval, she decided to continue to Florida and await our arrival in mid-December.

Joyce and I unanimously condemned the affair but argued continuously about our future relationship with Sherree. I felt she had the right to live her life as she saw fit, even though I didn't approve of living common law with a married man who had the responsibility of a wife and four children. Joyce, on the other hand, would have no part of her daughter if Sherree insisted on moving in with Barry.

We hoped the heavy gray cloud that darkened our days would gradually dissipate once we reached our southern home and had a face-to-face confrontation with our youngest. Ill fortune frequently comes in clusters, and so it did December, 1978. On each trip from Toronto to Florida, we carted an increasing amount of personal belongings as we gradually transferred our domicile into the U.S. We had not acquired two separate wardrobes, which meant all of our clothing plus articles such as cameras, recording equipment and items needed in both homes were packed in the car and transported back and forth. On this particular journey we had our Christmas gifts piled in the back seat as well and, most important of all, 2000 precious 35 mm slides taken on my jaunt to the Far East.

On our first night out of Toronto, the weather turned frigid, and we chose a Holiday Inn on the outskirts of Cincinnati. Due to the bulk of contents crammed into our car, we didn't unload but took only essentials into the motel. At 4 a.m. I awoke disturbed and went directly to the window to glance at our vehicle. For some peculiar reason, I knew before I peeked through the drapes that we had been robbed. Though a bright light shone over the Cadillac, the blustery cold night probably gave the thieves some confidence that few people would be roaming around. We called the office who had the police come over and make a report but to no avail. Joyce had one suitcase with some clothes, but I had nothing except the apparel worn the day before, and the total value of loss exceeded $25,000. On top of our despondent mood concerning Sherree, the burglary of our personal belongings, and especially my priceless slides, lowered our morale to even greater depths. Only the news that Joyce had cancer five years before could be considered a worse time in our marriage. Upon reaching Florida I placed ads in the Cincinnati newspapers offering $1,000 reward for my irreplaceable slides with no questions asked, but no one responded.

The holiday season of 1978 turned out to be quiet and gloomy, with Sherree the only family member present. We applied very little pressure regarding her association with Barry, nevertheless, the long love affair with our daughter had now become severely strained. Upon her return to Toronto in January, Sherree chose to live common law with Ervin, a relationship that only lasted six months. The hapless episode cost Sumcot a capable general manager, Joyce and I lost some esteem for our daughter, and Sherree learned a lesson in complexities of growing up and the stress of sharing your daily life with another human being. There were no winners.

My spouse and I shook the doldrums in March when we took a Caribbean cruise with Harold and Helen Thomas. During the pleasurable ten-day sea voyage, we visited Puerto Rico, St. Martaan, Antigua, Martinique and St. Thomas, bringing the number of countries I had visited in the previous two decades to sixty-five.

The tragic episode in Ohio dampened our enthusiasm for the biannual trek between our northern and southern residences, but that wasn't the only reason we began thinking of changing our chaotic lifestyle. The clincher in our ultimate decision to give up dual residency and declare ourselves full-time Americans was due to advice from our Canadian accountants and tax attorney who were having considerable difficulty toe-dancing between the Internal Revenue Departments of both nations. In the final two years of the 1970s, I met continuously with my Canadian and American tax advisors, a costly and nerve-wracking procedure. As an American resident owning a Canadian corporation, all profits from Canada were deemed personal income to me as far as Washington was concerned. I was instructed to get effective control of Sumcot Development Corporation, Limited out of my hands. After significant maneuvering, we gave voting power to the company's preferred shares and sold 50 percent to Jack Young, Chester Schwandt, Marty, Terry Mackey, and brother Jack for $100,000. This eliminated part of the tax puzzle that incessantly hounded us but by no means solved the entire problem. Finally in exasperation, Bob Friesen, our capable tax accountant, advised me either to rip up our green cards and return to Canada or to give up our Toronto town house and declare ourselves permanent U.S. residents. We chose the latter with little hesitation.

Perplexed by tax conundrums, Joyce and I frequently discussed being forced to give up our luxurious Toronto town house and move permanently to Florida. Joyce's principal concern was the exasperating thought of carting Bisto, her beloved poodle, up and down the elevator sixteen floors for twelve months of the year instead of six. Our luck promptly changed for the better in the spring of 1979 when a three-story town house located in exclusive Hillsboro Beach came to my attention. I immediately arranged to purchase the ocean-front residence, still under construction, for $272,000. Joyce loved the convenience of a house where she didn't have to use a public elevator for transporting groceries although our new purchase did have a private elevator, a unique feature. Her greatest elation nevertheless was the suitability for Bisto. My enthusiasm centered around the structure's proximity to the ocean. From Key West to New England, I doubt if any living room or bedroom lies closer to the Atlantic Ocean. I could spit from either room into high tide. Somewhat reluctantly, we gave up our Toronto town house, and by the fall of 1979, we were once again a family with one principal residence.

Notwithstanding my decision to become a full-fledged American, Sumcot Development's extensive unsold inventory forced me to keep our Toronto office operating on a full-time basis. We had five full-time employees in Canada, including Bob Marcotte whom I hired to replace Barry Ervin. Bob, Edwina, Terry, and Jack were initially interested in working for the American corporation either part or full-time, and we obtained work permits for the four of them to operate south of the border. At the beginning of 1979, I opened Sumcot of America's first office in our newly acquired Pompano Plaza. After interviewing several prospects, I hired Gary Handin as general manager of the American operation, with the intention of putting him in charge of the combined Canadian-American activities when his capability had been determined. Gary had practiced law in Long Island for ten years and recently immigrated to Florida with his young family. He soon proved his competence as a second in command and worked diligently to turn Pompano Plaza into a profitable venture. Gary and Bob Marcotte spent a fair amount of time on Padre Island throughout the summer of 1979, and both assisted me in August to staff a Texas office as we had decided to proceed with an ocean-front condominium on our Gulf of Mexico frontage. We chose Adita Clare, a bilingual lady, to head up our Texas branch, but by year's end we had replaced her with a personable young Texan, Larry White, who also could speak fluent Spanish.

Before we left Toronto in late autumn to become official permanent residents of our adopted land, I agreed to a family reunion. Michael, whom I had not laid eyes on for ten years, requested permission to attend the get-together wearing a wig to hide his shoulder-length hair.

His pony-tail attachment at age 28 when the fad had vanished many years before baffled me, but I accepted the condition. Not only did I wish to see my oldest son before our permanent move south but also I wanted to begin patching the rift with Sherree. Our private family gathering proved enjoyable, and during the evening, Gary and Tandy informed us they were planning on being married in late winter and requested that I sponsor them into the United States.

Our two years as dual residents had been taxing and nerve shattering. We had acquired substantial American real estate, opened offices in Pompano Beach and Padre Island with ten employees, and also had permanent representation in Phoenix. Joyce adored our new Hillsboro Beach town house and looked forward eagerly to having our furniture and personal belongings once again under one roof. Warren Lane had sold our Renaissance condo for $150,000 providing us another substantial profit in trading personal residences. Numerous unhappy episodes had occurred over the two-year period, particularly the unfortunate affair of Sherree's, but when we departed Toronto in early November, anxious to move into our new ocean-front home, the dark clouds that had hovered over us had finally slipped away, and plenty of sunshine began to appear.

Chapter 8

China

My final overseas journey on a Canadian passport occurred in late autumn of 1978. The three-week adventure, once again with the Toronto Board of Trade, included a visit to Seoul, Korea; ten days in China; a few days in the Philippines; and short stopovers in Tokyo and Hong Kong. My swan song with the Board of Trade turned out to be quite informational and very enjoyable. A number of personal friends—Fred McBrien, Bruce Legge, Tommy O'Connor, Al Gervais, and several acquaintances from previous tours—made the unique trip especially pleasant.

I felt certain reservations about visiting Red China, similar to those I experienced when crossing Checkpoint Charlie into East Berlin or when I first landed in Sofia, Bulgaria, another bulwark of communism. Chinese history and philosophy always intrigued me, but since Mao gained control in 1949, the thought of actually being in the midst of those inscrutable Orientals filled me with apprehension.

Eating habits including their dissimilar fare, a standard of living much beneath ours, and both sociological and political philosophies so entirely different made me wonder how we would intermingle or manage for ten days. Although I had no actual fear, lurid tales of rampaging Red Guards only a few years before our visit probably intensified my concern.

China rivals the Middle East as a sector of the planet where man had his beginnings. Remains of various manlike creatures who lived several hundred thousand years ago have been found in several parts of the country. Agricultural settlements dating back to 5,000 B.C. and metallurgy and Chinese writings to 1,500 B.C. provide ample proof of their venerable heritage. Like most Oriental countries, China experienced little immigration even though in the 19th century Russia, Japan, Britain, and other powers exercised enormous political and economic control. Due to rule by dynasties over thousands of years—Shang, 1500 to 1000 B.C.; Mongols in the Yuan Dynasty, 1271–1368; and the Manchus in the Ching Dynasty, 1644–1911–the Chinese, primarily an agricultural race, never developed a sizable middle class. Although ruled by foreigners throughout most of their history, the masses never altered their underlying culture and remain to this day rather diverse in their ways to other races. Perhaps their Oriental mystique was responsible for my reticence regarding the impending visit to the most populous nation on earth.

Our group of 80 Toronto businessmen departed by jumbo jet in late October, and except for a short refueling stop in Vancouver, we flew ten hours nonstop to Tokyo. The Japanese people always impressed me, and although we toured primarily the identical shrines and palaces I had visited four years before, I fancied the opportunity of refreshing my memory of this intriguing race before visiting the Koreans and Chinese, their Oriental cousins.

From Japan we flew to Seoul, where the close proximity of only twenty miles from the 38th parallel dividing North and South Korea surprised me. My friend and traveling companion, General Bruce Legge, used his military connections in attempting to get a pass for the two of us to visit Panmunjom and the famous boundary line on the 38th parallel. Unluckily for us, feelings between North and South Korea were at fever pitch at the time of our presence as South Korea had just accused the Communists of constructing a network of underground passageways into South Korean territory. President Chung Hee Park, assassinated a year after our visit, ordered the citizens of Seoul to a mass rally showing their displeasure at North Korea's encroachment. Like swarming ants when anything disturbs their hill, the people of Seoul took to the streets in one of the most massive displays of solidarity that ever could be imagined. An estimated two million souls jammed city streets, holding up traffic all over the metropolis for up to three hours.

Sitting in our tour bus watching the uncountable waves of Orientals moving slowly in every direction provided an impressive spectacle of the intense feelings of distrust South Koreans felt toward their Communist northern brothers. Though Japanese and Chinese influences have been strong over the centuries, the Koreans are a distinct racial and cultural group who can trace their origins back more than two thousand years. Like the Japanese and Nationalistic Chinese, they adopted and became proficient in western technology quite rapidly following the Korean War of the early 1950s. During several meetings with Canada's ambassadorial staff and with both Canadian and Korean trade officials, I was stunned by the major gains toward industrialization the diligent Koreans had actually achieved. Once again an Oriental race with a desire to work were out-producing their union oriented, socialized western cousins who no longer had the incentive.

The usual inspection of palaces and temples included in our itinerary proved interesting with several structures quite noteworthy. Gyeongbog Palace, surrounded by spacious grounds, dates back to 1395. The original buildings were destroyed by repeated warfare and fires but were replaced in the 19th century. Man-made lakes, pagodas soaring to ten stories, stone monuments and a diversity of Korean architecture gave the premises an enchanting Eastern atmosphere. Deogsu Palace, also reconstructed in the 19th century and the oldest western-style architecture in Korea, was where our entourage held their official reception for government officialdom. Changgyeung-Weon Shrine, the oldest renowned structure in Seoul and built in 1616 has attractive botanical gardens and an exotic display of birds and animals.

En route to a Korean village several miles outside the capital city, our bus traversed heavily wooded rolling hills remarkably similar to the Haliburton Highlands in Ontario. We strolled for miles through the authentic and picturesque village which had all aspects of a normal Korean lifestyle on view for entertainment and picture taking.

The afternoon before leaving for Tokyo and hence to Peking, Fred McBrien and I spent a couple of informative hours at the Seoul Trade Fair. The colossal variety of locally manufactured goods on exhibit made it unmistakably clear that Korea was swiftly gaining on Japan and Hong Kong to become another leading exporter of technical equipment as well as numerous other manufactured products.

Winging across the Yellow Sea to Peking, I again sensed a feeling of uneasiness as we approached the country that embraced one billion inhabitants. My first pleasant surprise occurred at customs which we passed through without the slightest delay or complication. Although not elaborate, our accommodations at the old Hsin Chiao Hotel were adequate and comfortable, making my initial impression of the country quite favorable.

The first real impact on any initial visit to China is the prodigious quantity of bicyclists. Early our first morning with the weather bright but chilly, Tommy O'Connor and I went for some walking exercise along a street leading to Peking's main avenue which is indeed a broad thoroughfare. A few vehicles, mostly trucks, used the route, but they had difficulty maneuvering through the throngs of bicycles. Men and women, young and old, all clad in blue or black denim pants and jackets jammed the wide street from curb to curb. Except for the odd sly glance at the colorful clothes worn by Tom and me, the masses of bicyclists pedalled to work and outwardly seemed to pay us little heed. My apprehension began to dissipate as I peered into the stoical faces of the passing Chinese who showed no sign of friendliness but also no ill will, though perhaps a trace of curiosity as Occidentals were still a rare sight in Peking. By the time we returned to our hotel for breakfast and a briefing session with Canadian ambassadorial officials, I looked eagerly forward to our ten days in Communist China.

Local guides, mostly females wearing the same drab dark denim uniforms and who spoke perfect English, soon made it clear they would attempt to answer any of our questions throughout our stay. Our first tour went directly to the Forbidden City, formerly the Emperor's residence, and the Imperial City, which housed his retinue but presently is the headquarters of the Communist government. Forbidden City, now a vast museum, contains the Imperial Palace and also smaller palaces, all replete with art treasures. Peking boasts several attractive artificial lakes surrounded by huge parks which provide a charming setting for aged edifices that complement the city. Some temples contain architecture from the Ming and Ching dynasties, as well as remains from earlier times. Since 723 B.C. several cities bearing various names have existed at the site, but the present city owes its origin to Kublai Khan who made it his capital in the 11th century. The Emperor's summer palaces on the outskirts of Imperial City were also surrounded by goregous parks and man-made waterways.

Unquestionably our tour of China's ancient temples offered an insight into the opulent lifestyle of the former emperors, but the highlight to me was our visit to Mao's Tomb in the Great Hall of the People. Literally thousands of Chinese, ten or more abreast, formed a line that stretched a mile or more and slowly snaked its way through People's Cultural Park where they could view Mao's body where it had lain since his death two years before. It seemed incredible after that lapse of time such a colossal mass of people still waited patiently for hours to catch a glimpse of their fallen hero. Our three tour buses wheeled up near the Great Hall, and we were paraded past the slowly moving line and entered the mausoleum within ten minutes. Regardless of their status, if that maneuver had occurred in North America, those receiving the preferential treatment would have been roundly hooted. Not so with the throngs of passive Chinese, however, who probably considered it just another simple annoyance in their humdrum existence. I studied the faces of those Chinese unhurriedly passing Mao's beautifully preserved corpse. Showing no outward sign of emotion, they gave the impression of people performing a meaningless but necessary chore.

The incident at the Great Hall was only a continuation of the outstanding courtesy and treatment we had been receiving from the moment of our arrival. What we didn't know nor discover until two weeks after returning to Canada was that a gigantic swing in international politics occurred during our visit in the country. The U.S. officially recognized the Peoples Republic of China, and severed diplomatic relations with Taiwan on December 15, 1978. As the first major contingent of western businessmen to tour Red China since the thawing of relations, we were the recipients of more courteousness than expected. This diplomatic attitude prevailed throughout our stay and especially at meal times or special banquets. Seated at each dinner table were eight or ten Canadians, one or two official Communist Party members and at least one interpreter.

All meals consisted of several courses and always included rice noodles or plain rice, a fish plate, and a bowl of soup. A jasmine tea was available at all times, but most of our group rapidly adopted the local custom of drinking an excellent Peking beer. At the main evening meal, our glasses of mao-tai, a strong alcoholic beverage and different types of rice and grape wines were consumed in great quantities. Our Chinese hosts, particularly government officials, imbibed at a pace at least equal to the Canadians and constantly proposed toast after toast. By the finish of the banquet most Canadians were half bombed, but the staid Orientals seemed to handle it with ease. Not knowing at the time about the change in relations between the Chinese and the West, I have often wondered just how much of our joyous welcome could be attributed to the forthcoming modification in international affairs. Regardless, the unexpected respect made our expedition a happy one.

One bright morning with the temperature in the 60's, we left by bus for an all-day journey to the Ming Tombs, Avenue of the Animals, and the fabulous Great Wall. The Ming Tombs, gigantic like the nation itself, are grouped in a special location originally chosen for its topographical features about 40 miles north of Peking. Nearing the tombs you bypass a white marble structure erected in 1540 and then proceed under a great red gate 120 feet in height before reaching the unusual Avenue of Animals, a short distance from the tombs. These intriguing marble statues consist of twelve pairs of animals on either side of the road, alternately crouching and standing erect, followed by four pairs of warriors and ministers, all guarding the entrance to the emperor's eternal resting place. The massive Ming Tombs were constructed by thirteen consecutive emperors who reigned between 1403 and 1643.

A short drive from the sepulcher we reached the fascinating Great Wall. We frequently caught glimpses of the phenomenon as we traversed the picturesque Chinese countryside as it wound like a giant serpent along the crest of distant mountain ranges. A multitude of things, both man-made and natural, have intrigued me during my travels, but none more than the Great Wall of China. Like Victoria Falls, you have to see the Great Wall in its natural setting to appreciate its enormity and splendor thoroughly. The finest photography simply does not do it justice. Built in different phases and forms from the 3rd century B.C. to 1644, over a period of 2000 years, the indescribable project stretches nearly 2000 miles across some of the most rugged terrain on the planet. It averages 25 feet in height, 15 to 30 feet in width at the base, and slopes to 12 feet at the top. Guard stations and watch towers are spaced at intervals of a few hundred yards along the crest. Several members of our group including myself, took a strenuous hike along the Wall which climbed steadily upward to a tower where we were rewarded with a spectacular view of the enormous man-made project as it stretched to the horizon through canyons and across mountaintops. Astronauts on their way to the moon have reported that the last distinguishable structure on earth was the Great Wall of China.

Before departing Peking for Shanghai, I visited an industrial trade fair where Canada and half a dozen other Western nations were exhibiting mostly farm equipment. Again the inscrutable Chinese provided a rather comical spectacle with their initial introduction to modern farm machinery, although the exhibitors were not amused. In long lines of which the Chinese are accustomed, they wound their way slowly to each display simply to pick up a brochure. Then without speaking to anyone would simply stand and gawk at the pamphlet or stare at the newfangled agricultural paraphernalia. What an interesting conversation it would have been to describe the functions of the equipment to the Chinese peasant farmers who spoke no English and obviously didn't comprehend the use or operation of most of the machinery. The exhibitors claimed that doing business proved almost impossible because of the hierarchy of control. They never seemed to reach the man who made the decisions. One disgruntled Canadian told me that after considerable haggling, the person in authority might agree to buy one or two tractors or other pieces of equipment instead of placing an expected order for hundreds. The Canadian insisted the Chinese wanted only one unit which they could dismantle, copy and then manufacture their own. I left for Shanghai convinced we had a long row to hoe before significant trade with the great Communist power would be achieved.

Our first day in Shanghai turned out to be long, amusing, and damned frustrating. Board of Trade members were forced to share accommodations in China, as single rooms, which I always used, were unavailable. (My affable friend Bruce Legge and I elected to room together.) Our initial lodging in the Shanghai Hotel, an elegant suite, included a full dining room, immense living room, and beautifully appointed furnishings. Only half a dozen of these suites were available, and Bruce and I had somehow drawn a long straw and were billeted in one. Bruce didn't come upstairs immediately due to a business appointment in the lobby. Chortling over our good fortune in being delegated the deluxe suite, I suddenly realized it only contained one three-quarter size bed. Figuring it to be an oversight by the hotel staff, I decided to have a nap and await the general's arrival. Bruce gleefully examined our elegant accommodations for several minutes before noticing the single bed.

"Where the hell is my bed?" Bruce hollered.

"I guess you'll have to sleep on the living room sofa," I responded.

"Like hell," he growled, and assuming his most militaristic pose, he demanded another bed from the little Chinese room porter who though he understood no English unmistakably got the message. Within ten minutes two men arrived with a simple army cot.

Bruce contacted our tour director and explained the dilemma. Within minutes we were whisked out of our sumptuous apartment with the explanation we would be transferred to a different unit upon its forthcoming availability. Just before midnight, after eight hours of complete frustration, we finally received our just reward, a tiny room with twin beds each about the size of the army cot we had so readily refused in our regal suite. We tried to get back the original apartment, but it had already been assigned to a Miss Smith, one of three single ladies with our group. Miss Smith later described the accommodation as most elegant, and though jealous, I knew what she meant.

Shanghai conjures visions of romance and intrigue, the lure of the Orient and far-away ports. The word shanghaied, meaning to be forced aboard a ship by devious means for sea duty on voyages to the Far East, no doubt enhanced the city's sinful image. One of the world's greatest seaports, the metropolis of 12 million people stretches along the Huang Pu and Yangtse rivers to the Yangtse estuary, a huge bulge in the East China Sea. Shanghai, the leading industrial city in China, is western in appearance with broad streets and spacious boulevards lined with imposing skyscrapers. Britain, France, and the United States played chief roles in Shanghai's turbulent past particularly from 1842 when the Treaty of Nanking opened the country to foreign trade until all three powers renounced their claims to the city in the 1940s.

A morning cruise along the Huang Pu and Yangstse portrayed river traffic on the vital waterways almost as chaotic as vehicular traffic in Istanbul. Cluttered with freighters, tankers, ferries, barges, and an unending assortment of junks, I couldn't perceive how they could all wind their way in different directions without a series of watery collisions. The vastness of the dock and harbor sectors was staggering, and somehow the scene of bustling commerce gave me a different slant on life in the Communist giant which I usually considered backward and mostly agricultural.

Despite the booming activity in Shanghai, 80 percent of the country's population is, in fact, involved in farming. China is the world's largest producer of rice, sweet potatoes, millet, barley, peanuts, and tea, and it is third largest in wheat. Throughout our China stay, especially on bus trips into farming country, the picture I most vividly recall was the countless number of peasants, both men and women, toiling in fields that appeared to reach from the edge of the highway to infinity. Except for a few tractors, the field work seemed to be accomplished mostly by back-breaking labor.

Our Shanghai itinerary included a long trip into a rural area to inspect a commune where again we received a royal welcome. The three tour buses visited separate farms to allow us to compare productivity in different locales. Twenty-four thousand people lived on the commune where our group spent several hours. Nothing seemed to be out of bounds or withheld from our inspection, and I came away with a contrasting opinion regarding their staunch socialistic system. Raising farm produce did comprise a majority of their endeavors, though small enterprises like basket weaving were included in their over-all production.

Points were issued to encourage individual incentive and increased output, though the only reward seemed to be additional time off. Communes operated something like the old English feudal system with an established percentage of produce going to the state. After the cadres got their slice, the balance of goods or profits was supposedly divided among the workers. On the surface it appeared to be a workable plan, but the Chinese themselves were discovering that a peasant averaged three times as much per acre when he operated on his own aggressiveness and when the net results went exclusively to improve his personal living standard. No matter how hard Communist countries try to make rural socialism successful, they have found free enterprise impossible to beat.

One of the most impressive aspects of the day occurred at the several open discussions arranged with all segments of the commune staff which the Chinese authorities themselves organized. A bevy of English-speaking guides interpreted our questions and gave us the Chinese officials' responses in a positive and candid manner. At the kindergarten where the delightful children put on an impromptu concert, the teachers responded to our queries without hesitation. Inside the tiny but clean workers' apartments, we quizzed old people about their private holdings being confiscated by the state. Again their answers appeared unsolicited. Some said they preferred the old system but likely could never have afforded modern equipment and therefore could see some merit in the takeover. At the conclusion of the day's inspection we were seated at a long conference table with the top commune officials and instructed to ask questions on any topic we chose. The Chinese seemed more anxious to obtain our impressions and opinions of their setup than to hide secrets of their own. Great political movements in the past or present and in any nation on earth did not or will not change the lifestyle of the proletariat too swiftly. Nevertheless, if China continues on her present course of mixing socialism with free enterprise and succeeds in combining the best qualities of both, they will become a powerhouse within a half century.

When we landed in Canton, hot humid weather greeted us, a startling change from the temperate climate in Peking and Shanghai. About half the size of Shanghai, Canton is the transportation, industrial, financial, and trade center of South China. Hong Kong, some fifty miles away is linked by the Canton-Kowloon R.R., a train on which I traveled through Hong Kong's New Territories to the Chinese border some years before. Canton has established huge trade ties with Hong Kong. The Canton Trade Fair, directly across the street from our hotel, offered a marvelous opportunity to compare China's industrial capacity with that of North America. In many aspects the colossal display proved that, rather than being a backward country, China now had the expertise to produce a wide range of technical and sophisticated equipment. One especially interesting facet of the enormous show was the elaborate signs on display throughout the huge three-storied complex dedicated to Mao and his thoughts. Hundreds of huge posters proclaimed his greatness and included phrases from his teachings. Engels, Karl Marx, and Stalin also received recognition for their roles in founding modern communism but not to the same extent as Mao Tse-Tung. This constant indoctrination of past Chairman Mao that saturated the nation puzzled me somewhat. We were bombarded at the Trade Fair and at theatrical performances including the opera and a circus that we attended, and his portrait was also on huge billboards along the avenues. By this perpetual publicity campaign glorifying their dead leader, did the Chinese hierarchy figure to control the minds of the proletariat or did those millions of Chinese peasants think for themselves?

Some historians suggest that much of Hitler's initial triumphs could be attributed to Gobel's propaganda. The uneducated masses or world nations who are either poor or poverty stricken are susceptible to any message of hope. They don't necessarily concern themselves whether the dogma is socialistic or capitalistic but only hope either to remain alive or possibly to improve their impoverished lifestyle. North Americans are also exposed to a formidable barrage of persuasion, particularly at election times, but have proven capable in some instances of opposing media whitewashing and making up their own minds. Nevertheless, some campaigns must accomplish something, or millions wouldn't be spent in the effort to manipulate peoples judgement.

Before leaving Red China for Hong Kong, we took a cruise along the Pearl River, another vital waterway in China's transportation network. I recollected on my visit to Macao several years before when gazing across the Pearl River estuary toward Red China with a camera in my hand, that I had butterflies in my stomach at being sternly warned of the dire consequences if I dared snap a picture. What a difference ten days in the nation had done to my personal view of the Chinese. Throughout our stay in the huge Communist nation, I used my camera incessantly without once being warned to desist and had a fantastic set of over 2,000 slides, which haplessly I lost a month later in Cincinnati, Ohio.

Numerous fond memories remain with me of my stay in China, but two small incidents really seemed to portray to me the mystique of the imperturbable Orientals. One day in Peking, our three tour buses were transferring us from one point of interest to another. Two had departed before our driver realized he couldn't get the engine started on our vehicle. Hundreds of somber Chinese watched from a discreet distance as they did at every point throughout the entire tour. Occasionally when our members attached Canadian flag lapel pins on children, the parents would graciously allow this small sign of friendship, but rarely did they smile or show emotion. After the driver spent twenty minutes fiddling with the motor to no avail, our pretty young female guide put her hand up to speak.

"Gentlemen," she said sweetly, "would you be so kind as to get off the bus and give a little push?"

Two dozen or so Canadians, several in their seventies, slowly made their way off the crippled vehicle and, with a combined effort, got the motor started within five yards. At once to our astonishment, we received a courteous ovation from the spectators who seemed to be tickled with our performance and perhaps decided we must be human after all. It must be remembered a great majority of Chinese had never laid eyes on an Occidental, a situation that would rapidly change beginning a few months after our departure.

The other episode that showed our hosts in a different light occurred at the commune kindergarten. Colorful clothing on the cute little tykes offered a vivid contrast to the drab shades of dark blue or black worn by all other segments of the population. People were obviously satisfying a yearning for bright clothing by dressing their tots in attire of many hues. One of the first significant modifications in Chinese behavior, especially by the females, following their move toward modernization in the early 1980s was to discard the drab denim and deck out in multicolored apparel.

Except for the food, I thoroughly enjoyed our Chinese journey. Not being a fish or seafood fancier automatically eliminated a large part of the average menu. I also never cared much for rice, a Chinese staple. Standard American fare wasn't available. I looked forward eagerly to a feast in Hong Kong, but my yearning for a good steak had to wait. The Board of Trade had arranged a delightful and informative cruise through Hong Kong waters for the afternoon we arrived. We ended up at the renowned Jumbo restaurant for a splendid Chinese dinner complete with several courses of fish accompanied with platefuls of steaming rice.

Our two-day stopover in the British Crown colony again demonstrated the tremendous dissimilarity between mainland Chinese and their Hong Kong cousins, even though most Hong Kong residents immigrated or escaped from the mainland. It seems when a person achieves freedom, he gains confidence. When the fear of reprisal against individual expression vanishes, this new self-assurance encourages them not only to think but also to speak out against those in power. Sometimes these immigrants will even strive to force their adopted land to conform to methods used in the state from which they escaped. The British protectorate enthralled me as before, but I was anxious to get to Manila for a three-day stay which would conclude our enlightening excursion to the wonders of the Far East.

The Philippines, an archipelago of volcanic origin, extends 1,100 miles north to south and consists of more than 7,000 islands. On eleven of these tropical land masses reside 95 percent of the country's entire population. The irregular coastline marked by bays, straits and inland seas, stretches for more than 10,000 miles. Manila, the nation's largest city, is located on Luzon, the nation's chief island, and it played a dramatic role in World War II.

The first Filipinos was a pygmy race, the Negritos, who are believed to have come from Borneo and Sumatra 30,000 years ago across land bridges then existing. Malay stock arrived later from the south in successive waves. Filipinos, though Asian, are unlike other Asians. Their Malayan culture influenced by 377 years of Spanish rule and 48 by American domination has developed the race into a distinct ethnic group who above everything else are fiercely independent. Unlike most Orientals, the Filipinos are outgoing and flamboyant, and the women are considered to be the most beautiful in the South Pacific.

During the Spanish-American war over Cuba in 1898, U.S. forces invaded the Philippines and, with Filipino assistance, toppled the Spanish regime that had lasted since Magellan claimed the islands for Spain in 1521. The treaty following the conflict ceded the Philippines to the U.S. Throughout the half century of American control, the Filipinos fought for independence, which likely would soon have been granted. Occupation by Japanese forces for three years in World War II, however, speeded up the granting of Filipino self-government, and when the islands were liberated, the nation finally became autonomous.

Gliding over the fortress island of Corregidor in Manila Bay in preparation for landing, I sensed similar emotions toward the Japanese as when first seeing Pearl Harbor or the hillside in Hong Kong where Canadian troops were overwhelmed. In World War II, Japan attacked the Philippines the day after Pearl Harbor. General MacArthur, facing numerically superior and much better equipped forces, withdrew his combined American and Filipino troops from Manila to Corregidor and the Bataan Peninsula where they waged a heroic struggle for three months before capitulating. The ensuing Bataan death march which took the lives of thousands of American and Filipino soldiers due to Japanese brutality became a rally cry for the Allies until the Japanese defeat. General MacArthur left the Philippines reluctantly but vowed to return, and in July, 1945, when he arrived victorious, the terrible conflict had nearly reached its triumphant conclusion. Manila, almost completely destroyed but rebuilt with American financial assistance following the war, has blossomed into an attractive metropolis. Bruce Legge, not only a military man but also a history buff like myself, tried to arrange a visit to Bataan and MacArthur's dramatic redoubt, but it couldn't be organized on such short notice.

An unforgettable sight on Manila streets are fleets of jeepneys, a minibus patterned after World War II Jeeps. Painted in vivid colors, no two the same, they provide a vital though hair-raising source of public transportation. Without specific routes, they pick up passengers anywhere and charge a quarter fare for any length of ride. We toured a small factory manufacturing the strange but colorful vehicles that are unlike any other form of public transportation on the planet.

The most interesting day in the Philippines included a long bus tour through the central plains of Luzon to Pagsanjan Falls. Mainly of volcanic origin, the Philippine island chain is traversed with picturesque mountain ranges, rich with vegetation and separated by great fertile plains watered by innumerable lakes and rivers. Our cross-country route bypassed huge sugar plantations, rice and tobacco fields, and enormous groves of coconuts. A wide variety of fruits, including bananas, mangoes, papayas, mandarins, oranges, and others, grow both domestically and wild in the humid tropical climate. Farming methods are still primitive in some sectors, with water buffalo the most common beast of burden.

A brief rest stop allowed us to take pictures of one of the most picturesque places in the country—scenic Taal Lake. Mount Taal, an active volcano rising majestically out of Volcanic Island situated in the midst of Taal Lake, provides a stunning panoramic spectacle.

The highlight of the day's outing occurred at Pagsanjan Falls where we were treated to an outstanding Polynesian barbecued dinner with all the trimmings, followed by a thrilling canoe ride up the Pagsanjan River. Pairs of our entourage were seated in the center of a canoelike watercraft with native paddlers in bow and stern. The initial two miles up stream bypassed bamboo huts and tiny tropical jungle villages hugging the river bank until human habitation disappeared and the swift-moving waterway narrowed and became overhung with lush vegetation and dense foliage. At this point the river became a series of frothing rapids and swirling eddies, and when we neared the cascading falls, our two paddlers leaped into the shallow stream to push and guide our bouncing craft to within a hundred feet of the exotic cataract plunging from out of the surrounding mountain greenery and rainforest. A blinding mist and our cameras being wrapped in cellophane to protect them from the penetrating moisture made picture-taking rather awkward. Nevertheless, I obtained several excellent shots of the natural attraction and nerve-tingling river ride. Bobbing along like a cork through the rapids on our return also provided great excitement.

We rested one complete day in Manila in preparation for our long journey home via Guam, Hawaii, and San Francisco. Throughout our stay, the Filipinos treated us with respect, but an atmosphere of rebellion could be sensed. President Marcos, who ruled the nation with an iron glove, wasn't popular with the lower classes. Common people particularly detested his suppression of certain freedoms, and U.S. authorities, who also disliked Marcos' methods, seemed frightened to withhold financial assistance until he mended his ways. This may not have worked, but it would have shown U.S. support for the oppressed masses. As usual when a country's poor and illiterate begin to rebel, they either turn or are drawn into the Communist camp. This is a natural direction, considering the impoverished want a more equitable distribution of both land and wealth. Trying to crush these movements by force only cements the people's determination for change, and it seems unfortunate a better system cannot be found to educate the masses about the shortcomings of socialism.

To my way of thinking, China has proven the advantages of communism over feudalism, most military dictatorships or other autocracies at least in the initial phase when a country has been smothered by a totalitarian regime for centuries. It would be ludicrous to believe that countries like China, Russia, and other nations that have never possessed a sizable middle class would have obtained a redistribution of their land and other resources by other means. The very tenets of democracy encourages those with property to retain it at all costs, and surely no one can perceive any country's principal real estate holders saying, "Here, we'll subdivide my holdings among the poor without remuneration." The ideal situation would be for a country like China to revert to democracy, albeit slowly after redividing the nation's resources, and they have educated the proletariat so that a stable middle class will emerge. Perhaps China is moving in that direction. At the time of this writing, those in control of the Philippines were not relaxing their iron grip, and unless they have a sudden change of heart or leadership, the future looks bleak and bloody for that outstandingly beautiful country.

As I slowly made my way north to Toronto, I again reflected on my extreme good fortune at being born a North American where political problems involving life and death didn't exist. Despite my aggravation with Canada's steady socialistic direction, principally responsible for my immigration to the U.S.A., I still recognized that my homeland had tremendous potential under the right leadership if a change in their political fortunes didn't come too late. Unquestionably Canada still offered a splendid lifestyle in comparison to most other world states. The United States, however, offered more freedom of decision for a striving businessman, and I was anxious to proceed with my affairs.

Chapter 9

Padre Island: the Last Great Adventure

Our individual lives, like world affairs, fluctuate as the seasons though not nearly as dependably. During the first three years of the 1980s, the earth's fortunes ebbed and flowed with earthlings mostly the cause and recipient of those fluctuations.

The brutal seizure of American hostages by Iranian militants in late 1979 threatened international peace and security for the entire 444 days of those unfortunate victims incarceration. That dramatic event probably played a part in the defeat of Jimmy Carter by Ronald Reagan, the first time an incumbent president had lost an election since 1932. It seemed more than coincidental that the hostages were released the day of President Reagan's inauguration. Canada also got involved with the suspenseful proceedings when their government officials in Teheran hid six U.S. embassy employees for three months and then assisted in their escape back to North America. The cruel affair, though a terrible ordeal for the hostages, their families and loved ones, likely did more to bring the American people back together than anything since the bitterness created by the Vietnam War. I traveled many sectors of the U.S. throughout the crisis and yellow ribbons and other signs showed America's concern for their fellow citizen's tribulations. A spontaneous celebration nearly matching the emotional outburst of V.E. Day spread across the jubilant nation at the triumphant return of the hostages.

Unfortunately several occurrences in that period didn't have such a happy conclusion. In fact, some ill-fated happenings are continuing at this writing. In late 1979 a number of Soviet divisions crossed into

Afghanistan in a brutal effort to subjugate that fiercely independent Moslem nation. The United States and a few other countries furnished and are continuing to provide covert assistance to Afghanistan guerillas who have courageously harassed their gigantic opponent. Most free countries condemned the barbaric invasion but didn't lift a finger to help the tiny state against a gigantic Communist belligerent. From the days of ancient history, people watch another race being brutally trampled, cower with fear hoping and praying the aggressor's appetite will be appeased before turning his hordes toward their borders. Doves who never get involved deplore or castigate those who do, but those same appeasers are the first on their knees begging for mercy when facing the impending assailant. They find an excuse for the wrong doings of an evil empire and then seem genuinely shocked when one morning they awaken to find their families being raped and murdered and their homes ablaze.

Afghan is indeed a long way from North America, but El Salvador and Nicaragua are right next door. If Soviet Russia gains a foothold in those Central American nations, our grandchildren or great-grandchildren may pay the horrible price of our apathy and lack of determination in the 1980s. A military coup in El Salvador late in 1979 failed to quell a civil war that has raged for many years. The rightist regime, now in power and widely supported by the U.S., would appear to have stalled the Communist attempt at a takeover for the time being, but such is not the case with one of her neighbors. Relations between Nicaragua and the United States, strained for some time due to Nicaragua's military aid to leftist guerillas in El Salvador and U.S. backed anti-Sandinista rebels in Nicaragua, is now a direct confrontation between communism and the free world.

Watching the U.S. Congress drag its feet in providing assistance, military or otherwise, to the Nicaraguan freedom fighters is reminiscent of the isolationists attitude at the beginning of World War II. Placaters consistently turn the other cheek or stick their head in the sand ostrich-like to see no evil. They refuse to destroy a weed when it sprouts from the ground, but instead they wait until it reaches maturity, has stifled the growth of productive plants, and becomes much more difficult and expensive to eradicate. Those pacifists who believe that hostile states will eventually disappear should study their history texts. Our past has proven the time to stop a political curse is at its inception and not wait until it has reached full-blown maturity. If free nations don't act now, they will leave their progeny to deal with a tempest when all they faced was a whirlwind. In addition to its many other facets, Communist ideology is based on patience. Every time we slacken our determination, they move an inch forward.

The Middle East experienced its usual turmoil throughout this period. Iraq attacked Iran in 1980, a war that continues at this writing. Both nations have lost a horde of men with no end of the carnage in sight. The conflict, supposedly to determine sovereignty over the Shatt-al-Arab waterway separating the two Moslem states, is in reality an extension of the enmity that has existed between these two peoples since the early ages when as Persia and Mesopotamia they warred incessantly. Like the macabre situation in Lebanon, religion is the root cause of their hostility.

In June, 1982, Israeli forces invaded southern Lebanon and for three years occupied a large portion of the captured territory. No conflict on earth throughout man's troubled past is more religious oriented than that in Lebanon where different factions of Moslems fight among themselves while also warring with Christians and Jews. If these people could be educated to believe in the same Almighty or perhaps the sanctity of man as opposed to a Supreme Being, a tremendous amount of lives could be saved and suffering avoided.

Rhodesia, a beautiful country that Joyce and I visited in 1970 and which I prognosticated would be thrown to the wolves by the Western nations before long did in fact endure that exact fate. The white minority who ruled for nearly a century and gave little consideration to the enormous black majority throughout that period finally succumbed in 1980. Due to world pressure plus the lack of economic and financial aid from Great Britain and the U.S.A., the whites relinquished control to the blacks. President Mugabe gained his position through free elections and soon changed the country's name to Zimbabwe. Shortly after his election, however, Mugabe confiscated white farms without paying compensation to the owners and the once prosperous African nation slowly moved leftward, soon to become another autocratic state where neither whites nor blacks were absolutely free. Blinded by hatred for whites, who often governed tyrannically, and the fact that blacks were never given adequate training to manage the intricate affairs of good government, a number of African countries are in dire straits since blacks gained control and some are leaning heavily toward outright Marxism.

South Africa, with a higher percentage of white population than its neighbors, has retained its apartheid policies and up to now protected its borders against leftist guerillas and insurgents. In fact, in 1981 South African forces crossed the Angolan border and attacked that Marxist nation who were backed by 25,000 Cubans, East Germans and Portuguese Communists. World pressure again intervened. As a result, the South Africans withdrew, and all the bleeding hearts applauded. South Africa's apartheid policies are immoral without question, but if the free world allows a Communist regime, either black or white, to take over, will the blacks be better off? Conditions in several African countries including Zimbabwe seem to indicate otherwise. People do not achieve the ability to govern wisely without generations of administrative training. This lack of firsthand experience and the inability to put aside tribal bickerings that have persisted unabated for centuries are the bane of the African continent. Despite the evils of apartheid, the do-gooders should consider the alternative before forcing the abdication of the South African regime.

Europe didn't get through the early 1980s unscathed. Poland in particular endured a sorrowful period when they reached for freedom by staging a series of strikes that forced the government in 1980 to allow independent trade unions. Solidarity became the first approved union movement in a Communist Bloc state. That exhilarating situation didn't last long. Under pressure from Moscow, Polish authorities declared martial law the following year, jailed numerous dissidents, and in 1982 outlawed Solidarity completely, thus ingloriously and defiantly snuffing out the flicker of independence. Do world pacifists presume those Marxist regimes now in control or struggling for domination will treat their pawns differently? They would have to be unbelievably naive to believe so. What do those individuals who advocate that the free world shouldn't interfere in the affairs of small nations do if and when the Marxists win out? Do they go back later to see if the lifestyle of the masses has improved or simply go on to their next crusade and to hell with the victims of the Communist takeover? To gain the proper perspective on the price of freedom, those people should spend a few hours at the Berlin Wall, speak to members of Polish Solidarity and Hungarian freedom fighters, or interview Cubans who fled from Havana.

Perhaps the fracas during this era with the greatest long-term significance didn't involve communism at all. The dispute between Great Britain and Argentina over the Faulkland Islands in 1982 may have influenced the political climate in Britain for decades to come plus affecting the governing philosophies of other nations who watch Britain closely. The victory, though unimportant so far as the physical value of territory is concerned, had enormous political overtones because British pride in Margaret Thatcher's handling of the fiasco got her re-elected Prime Minister. Due to high inflation and continuous unemployment in double digit figures, Thatcher's Conservative government had lost considerable popularity with the electorate. The Faulkland War changed all that as the British people loved her tough stance. Taking advantage of the situation, she dissolved Parliament, called an election, and got back into power. This five-year reprieve allowed her to continue the austerity measures to lower inflation, take a strong stand against unions, especially the coal industry, and support Reagan in his placement of missiles in Europe. These and other factors of her administration will have a profound effect on world affairs for a long time.

Despite our permanent American resident status, my considerable real estate holdings in Canada made the affairs of our native land still of great interest to me. After only six months in power, Joe Clark's minority Conservative Party lost a vote of confidence in the House of Commons, forcing the country back to the polls. Minority government, one of the curses of Canadian politics, was shown as the anathema it is during this period of political turmoil. The Social Credit Party, with a total of five members in the House of Commons, decided not to support the Conservative Party on Joe Clark's determination to increase the excise tax on gasoline. By joining the Liberals and New Democrats they were able to topple Clark's minority government. Two months later, the Canadian electorate put Trudeau back in power with a clear majority, but ousted the Social Credit party completely. Ontario and the other five eastern provinces gave the victory to the Liberals, and my bitterness at the outcome made me grateful that my intuition had prompted me to immigrate south.

Pierre Trudeau, a charismatic leader plus an internationally re-nowned statesman, showed signs of repudiating his earlier dogma of outright socialism, nevertheless the damage had been done. Trudeau did pass some positive legislation and affected Canada's destiny in other ways. Quebec overwhelmingly rejected separating from Canada a few months after the federal election. A great deal of credit for Quebec's decision to remain within the Canadian framework has to be awarded to Trudeau, a staunch federalist, due to his popularity in the French province. Transferring constitutional power from Britain to Ottawa also occurred because of Trudeau's dedication to the project. The new constitution replaced the old British North America Act of 1867 which brought into being the Canadian federation but kept control in Britain. Despite his good points, in my opinion Pierre Trudeau will go down in history as the man mostly responsible for Canada's demise as a leading industrial nation. He was a prime reason for my leaving Canada.

Despite the emotional upsurge Joyce and I felt at becoming full-fledged U.S. residents in late 1979 and our enthusiasm regarding business opportunities, the recession which plagued North America throughout this period would also cause financial havoc with us. The jobless rate soared as did inflation which reached double-digit figures and caused another round of union discontent. Continuous strikes and labor unrest only worsened the economic predicament in both countries because as wages went up, so did prices and inflation. Canadian postal workers struck for the umpteenth time. A disastrous coal strike in the U.S. delayed any hope of a rapid economic recovery in that nation. The

American automobile industry, in deep financial trouble, bartered for pay cuts rather than raises in the hopes of keeping factories open. An influx of cheaper and better-built vehicles from Japan and Europe had finally created instability in an industry that for three quarters of a century had epitomized the industrial might of the U.S.

All union victories now came with a struggle plus an incurable cost to the workers. The track record of large unions over the previous 25 years has been victory after victory, but in the process they exported or eliminated half the jobs they were paid to protect. Steel, autos, electronics, newspapers, railroads, and other industries experienced this attrition, and union victories in the past ten years should have been reported on the obituary page. The tables were slowly turning, however, and the air controllers strike may have been the turning point. American federal air traffic controllers in the summer of 1980 began an illegal nation-wide strike. President Reagan warned them to return to work or face immediate dismissal. Most scoffed and refused. The strike to such a vital service created chaotic conditions, particularly when controllers from other parts of the world supported and in some cases joined the Americans. Reagan held fast, which together with public indignation at the defiance of a presidential order spelled the death knell for the Air Controllers Union. The crushing of that strike plus attendant publicity of repentant but unemployed air controllers made a lasting impression on unionized workers, and striking as a means of forcing increasing benefits and wages began to steadily decline.

In 1980 a series of maniacs, murderers, and would be assassins were in action. One demented young man shot Ronald Reagan in the chest, another seriously wounded Pope John Paul, and Egypt's Anwar Sadat was killed outright. In the midst of these wars, killings and an escalating economic recession, I fought to gain a foothold in the American business community.

Impatience to establish Sumcot in the United States played a significant part in my roller-coaster existence in the early 1980s. Our Florida staff under the capable guidance of Gary Handin struggled with slow but continuous success to fill the Pompano Plaza with acceptable tenants. They accomplished this feat in late 1980 almost concurrent with our moving Sumcot's head office into a luxurious 3,000-square-foot suite on the second floor of the plaza. I spared no expense on the elaborate layout which contained seven private offices, a conference room, an equipped kitchen, and a huge general area. My spacious private office contained book cases and a wet bar.

Sumcot purchased a service station for $225,000, the only property at Cypress and McNab not occupied by the shopping center. We planned either to enlarge Pompano Plaza or to construct a three-story office building on the choice location. After three years of struggling with the City of Pompano Beach to obtain a building permit for a structure sufficiently large to justify the venture, we gave up and sold the site to 7-11 Convenience Stores for $315,000, a small profit when taking into consideration architects' fees and other expenditures.

While negotiating for approval to construct the Sumcot Building at Cypress and McNab, we conducted a feasibility study of the general area to determine the marketability of office space. Positive results encouraged me to acquire for $875,000 a seven-acre tract of vacant land at the corner of Sample and Powerline in central Broward County. Bounded on two sides by picturesque Crystal Lake plus easy access to route #95 and the Sunshine Parkway, two of South Florida's main north/south expressways, made it a choice location for an office complex. So we planned to build two seven story office towers with a total of 150,000 square feet of net leasable area. Constant headaches with the rental and management of the Pompano and Phoenix shopping centers, fighting for permission to erect the Sumcot Building at Cypress and McNab, designing, leasing and organizing financing for the two seven-story office towers at Sample and Powerline and my never-ending struggle to dispose of Sumcot Canadian property were minor skirmishes nevertheless to the main battle we waged on Padre Island, Texas.

Between the years of 1970 when Joyce and I first surveyed South Padre and 1979 when Jack and I flew from Toronto to sign a contract with an architect, I had been on the island paradise several times. In the ensuing thirty-six months my visits increased dramatically. Following that meeting with Rick Labunski, our appointed architect, I traveled to Padre from either Florida or Toronto on an average of once monthly. With the exception of financial problems, the seemingly endless conundrums with the Texas project were entirely different from those I had encountered in Ontario for over a quarter of a century. Raising venture capital wasn't new to me, though this time I required over 7 million for the 12 story, 84-unit condominum planned for our ocean-front property. We named our Texas enterprise Ocean Vista after our new Florida residence.

A Mexican oil spill, the world's worst, that lasted nine months and spewed three billion gallons of crude into the Gulf of Mexico, much of which threatened south Texas beaches, caused the first real annoyance. Not only did the calamity affect desperately needed sales, but bankers became cautious about lending money in the distressed area. Hurricane Allen, the second strongest Atlantic storm of the century which killed 272 persons as it tore a path of destruction across the Caribbean, Mexico, and the south Texas coast followed the oil spill by a few months, and further damaged the image of Padre Island in the minds of financiers. These two disasters as well as Sumcot's lack of a track record in either country with respect to high-rise construction made bankers very reluctant to loan such a large sum of money to our corporation. To add to these unavoidable disasters, the prime rate hovered in the unheard of 21 percent range. In my prolonged negotiations with lending institutions, the best I could arrange was two points over prime. This meant interest charges on a 7 million construction loan at 23 percent would exceed $130,000 monthly, a frightening figure to a former farm boy. Condo sales remained agonizingly slow throughout 1979 and the first half of 1980 despite a herculean effort by Larry White, the Texas manager. Our entire U.S. operation depended on Ocean Vista condominium deposits for financial survival. In accordance with Texas law, these 20 percent deposits which averaged $25,000, did not have to be escrowed but could be utilized for immediate cash. When expected sales didn't materialize and I failed in my effort to arrange a bank loan, our financial difficulties compounded. Despite $40,000 monthly income from our Florida warehouses, Pompano Plaza and the Phoenix shopping center, our cash reserves dwindled precariously low. Sumcot's financial ebb tide occurred in the fall of 1979 when I visited Padre Island with the hope of spurring sales, fully aware that we lacked sufficient cash to meet our immediate payroll. For the second time in my business career, imminent bankruptcy stared me in the face. On the evening of my arrival, Larry somewhat despondent over the dearth of contracts, came to see me at our Sangria home. "Bill," he said rather ashamedly, "I can write a deal with a $1,000 refundable deposit, but the family wants one week to think it over."

"Write the contract tonight and deposit the check in Sumcot's account in the morning," I replied, grateful it would cover the Texas payroll to be written the following day. Although my decision to gamble put the purchaser's $1,000 in jeopardy, I felt confident things were about to turn in our favor. Thank God, my intuition proved accurate. Before departing for Florida four days later, I persuaded John Austin, Rick Labunski, and another island realtor to put up $60,000 in deposits. This bonanza alleviated our immediate cash flow dilemma but did nothing to overcome my principal concern of raising a 7 million construction loan or arranging 8 million permanent mortgaging to take out the interim lender. Nevertheless, those sales to local businessmen provided the stimulus to get the project off the ground.

In the spring of 1980, Larry began to aim his advertising and promotion into Mexico, particularly Monterrey, the industrial capital of that nation. Within months Ocean Vista condominium sales soared and 70 percent of our buyers came from south of the border. This windfall of sales to Mexican nationals unfortunately became a double-edged sword before finalization of our Texas adventures.

On one hand, hundreds of thousands of dollars in condo deposits pouring in relieved our immediate cash flow, but until I organized 7 million to construct the building, the possibility existed that all the money might have to be returned if I didn't come up with a building loan. This dilemma created more pressure than I ever faced before in my life. It seems like I spent forever pleading with Florida, Toronto and Texas banks for interim financing. Finally after sixteen months of continuous effort, The Royal Bank of Canada came to my rescue through their Houston, Texas branch to fund the project together with the First National Bank in Brownsville who would administer the loan. Construction financing in the amount of $7.2 million was arranged. Following this success, I swiftly reached an agreement with United Savings of Brownsville for permanent financing, and Ocean Vista became a reality at last. With no experience in high-rise construction, however, I needed a knowledgeable manager.

Al Adkins, who worked on a contract basis for the builder of our Florida Ocean Vista townhouse, was recommended as a brilliant strategist when it came to building high-rises. His reputation proved accurate, and Al represented Sumcot of America in a general managerial capacity on a fee basis for eighteen months which included negotiations for a general contractor, construction supervision, and finalization of the 12-million dollar project. Headquartered in South Florida, Adkins flew to Padre Island whenever necessary to fulfill his obligations to Sumcot. Of all the headaches I encountered with the Ocean Vista, the actual erection turned out to be the least nerve wracking due to Al Adkin's capabilities.

High points and low points are common with all major schemes, and the Ocean Vista venture proved no exception. Due to the multitude of disappointments encountered while striving to raise financing, the day we received word from the Royal Bank of Canada in Houston that we had finally been approved for a 7.2 million dollar loan will forever remain a red-letter day. Returning from a long stroll along the beach, I found Joyce standing at our front door, tears streaming down her cheeks. This was rare with my wife, and so I momentarily froze as the thought struck me she had discovered some recurring sign of her dreaded cancer condition. She soon informed me however about the good news from Houston that ended 16 months of unbelievable frustration. Another highlight occurred in early November of 1980 when I arranged for the Toronto and Florida staffs to meet on Padre Island for the groundbreaking ceremony and following celebrations. Other exciting moments during the sixteen months of construction occurred when

I visited the building site after an absence of several weeks. I always received a surge of elation as the structure gradually soared skyward. The pride one feels at the successful conversion of block and mortar into an aesthetic building when so much personal effort has been involved is not easy to define.

Due to the incredible cost of borrowing the 7.2 million dollar construction loan, I gave no one including the general contractor from San Antonio, any peace until the 12-story condominium was ready for possession in the spring of 1982. My ruthless prodding to complete the building on or ahead of schedule to be able to discharge the high-costing construction loan was probably responsible for keeping Sumcot of America solvent, but for reasons not obvious to anyone at the time including myself.

I sent Jack to Padre Island in March, 1982, with implicit orders to be merciless in closing the Ocean Vista deals. Sumcot held a 20 percent deposit from all purchasers, and our contract required them to close within ten days of notification of their unit's readiness for occupancy or lose that deposit, and so Jack had the ammunition to be tough. Although he made a few enemies, Jack followed my instructions to the letter, and by the end of June, he had completely closed out the Ocean Vista, a scant six weeks before catastrophe struck in Mexico.

When Joyce and I bought our Texas Sangria unit in 1975, 12½ pesos equalled one American dollar. The peso had gradually weakened through the final years of the decade, and wealthy Mexicans seeing the handwriting on the wall were pouring money into Texas banks and real estate. This mostly accounted for our exceptional sales success in Monterrey. Early 1982 saw the peso begin to completely collapse as a result of an international oil glut, Mexico's principal export item. The situation became critical at the time Jack struggled to close the Ocean Vista units, and in mid-August the Mexican government passed a law prohibiting currency being transferred from that country. The peso had devaluated to 155 to the dollar which when equalled with Canadian currency would be similar to Canadians awakening one morning to find their buck worth less than 10¢ American, a terrifying thought.

Sumcot of America netted approximately 3 million dollars before taxes on the Ocean Vista, but for several reasons, we remained financially in trouble. At the start of Ocean Vista construction, condo sales on the island flourished and developable ocean frontage rapidly disappeared. Concerned that nothing would be available at the completion of the Ocean Vista in eighteen months and wanting to keep our excellent organization on Padre Island busy as they only had a dozen units left to sell, I decided to buy another large parcel of land for $2,800,000. This tract only contained 200 feet of Gulf frontage, but its seven acres would accommodate 170 units. We named the new project The Renaissance, after our original Florida home, and planned four buildings, two to be eighteen stories in height. This ambitious undertaking would take eight years to complete and produce 75 million in total sales. Serious problems plagued the new scheme from its inception. By far the largest portion of this new tract was acquired from a Tampa, Florida surgeon for 2¼ million dollars. This doctor claimed he had arranged to buy the property from a New Englander but had not closed the transaction at the point he sold it to us. Our agreement called for the seller to take back a $700,000 purchase money mortgage. On closing day, we discovered to our dismay that rather than owning the land, the man only had an option, which he couldn't exercise due to insufficient cash. We considered charging the good doctor with fraud, but he faced imminent death with a brain tumor. Besides, we really wanted the property, not a lawsuit. Some of the most brutal negotiations of my business career were required over a term of eight months before we received clear title to the tract. This bargaining went on simultaneously with the construction and completion of the Ocean Vista.

Despite getting the purchase price reduced $340,000 because we were forced to pay cash, the new acquisition nearly sounded Sumcot's death knell. Substantial sums had been spent on planning, architectural work, advertising, and promotion, and Larry White had received several hundred thousand dollars in deposits when the fatal collapse of the Mexican peso occurred in August, 1982, throwing the economy of the entire Rio Grande Valley into chaos. Sumcot had earned a handsome return on the Ocean Vista enterprise, but as a result of the Mexican financial fiasco, the profits were tied up in an unsaleable tract of vacant land. After refunding the Renaissance deposits and paying off all loans on the Ocean Vista, we again faced a serious cash short fall, and adding to our woes, we would owe Uncle Sam over $400,000 in corporation taxes in 1983.

Throughout the Padre Island venture, my fortunes shifted like the desert sands. For July and August, Joyce and I rented a Toronto bungalow in 1981 and 1982 from which I directed both country's operations with Gary Handin's competent support. Bob Marcotte resigned in the spring of 1981, and anxious to dispose of our Ontario lots, I wanted to give Jack and Edwina some moral and physical assistance. Ontario's vacation property market, like all North American real estate, was depressed due to the abnormally high interest rates. Nevertheless, we sold over 2½ million in those two years even though advertising costs soared to half a million dollars and cut deeply into Sumcot's profits. Terry managed Toronto's financial affairs and spent a couple of weeks annually in Florida helping the head office bookkeeping staff. In mid-

1982 with conditions in both countries extremely depressed and the Rio Grande Valley economy in a shambles, I sadly and reluctantly closed the Toronto and Texas offices and stopped all salaries with the exception of the Florida staff.

When Jack completed his assignment in Texas, he elected to return to Toronto and rejoin Memorial Gardens, his employer before linking up with Sumcot. We flew Larry White to Florida with the intention of putting him in charge of the Sumcot Executive Plaza, which we still planned to construct at Sample and Powerline in Broward County. After careful consideration, the likable and intelligent young man declined our proposition and returned to his native Texas. In the fall of 1982, pre-rentals of the first phase of our planned two seven-story office towers were coming in agonizingly slow. Gary Handin, who passed his Florida bar examinations, became concerned about Sumcot's future and indicated an interest in going back into private practice. For the first time I seriously considered pulling in my horns and giving up the seemingly never-ending fight for business survival.

My economic treadmill during the early 1980s would be mostly a blur except for my daily journal which I kept up religiously. My business life was bedlam, and my private life didn't do much to calm my venturesome spirit or nerve shattering existence. In fact, my personal mode of living too often even added to the pandemonium. Despite the fact I went on the wagon frequently and for long stretches, I consumed enormous quantities of alcohol when in the mood to drink. Fully aware my behaviour was rapidly reaching a point of complete alcoholism, I nevertheless used it as a crutch whenever business pressure got too much to bear—and this had become far too often. Thinking back at my frustrations during those times, I often wonder what might have happened if I hadn't relieved my tensions with whiskey. Perhaps I would have suffered a heart attack or other stress-related illness.

Several of my worst binges occurred in Las Vegas, sometimes with Joyce but often alone. On junkets to the glittering Nevada capital through that period, I lost $100,000 at the tables, mostly while stone drunk. Regrettably, I had the unique ability to function while completely inebriated to a degree that most people including the pit bosses didn't realize my actual mental condition. Dealing in prodigious sums in my business ventures had given money a new dimension in my subconscious reasoning. When paying $5,000 per day every day for interest payments alone, then a loss of $10,000 at the tables seemed like petty cash. That rationale applied until I awoke in the morning with a brutal hangover and the realization of my stupid actions the previous evening. Those casino experiences were costly, but like alcohol, provided an undeniable outlet for my frustrations.

Joyce despised my drinking habits but rarely interfered. Perhaps the real misfortune was that all three of our offspring drank to excess, often using the excuse that if it didn't harm father, then it should be all right for them.

With a U.S. labor department permit, Sherree worked as a teacher for a modeling school in New York City. Her employer, a young Canadian entrepreneur and family man who also had operations in Toronto, Hamilton and Ottawa, died of cancer in 1981. Sherree returned to Toronto but immediately applied for her permanent American status as an unmarried daughter of American residents which put her high on the preference list. She received her green card in early 1983. As the unpleasant memory of the Barry Irvin episode gradually faded, Sherree spent as much time with us as her responsibilities would allow. Joyce and I both noticed she often drank too much on these visits.

Gary, always close to his parents but especially his mother, desperately wanted to join us in Florida. I sponsored him as an ex-Sumcot employee, and he and Tandy received their green cards in 1982. Gary and Tandy both went to work for Sumcot of America, but Gary soon got himself in trouble and in less than six months was tossed in jail for drunken driving. He worked in maintenance, but after several altercations with tenants, partially as a result of his drinking on the job, I finally fired my youngest son and suggested he find work elsewhere. Tandy remained an integral part of the organization.

Michael, whom I had not seen since the 1978 family reunion in Toronto, had clung to his slovenly ways with long hair and no ambition. Now, however, he had added alcohol to his intractable habits. In the summer of 1981 while in Toronto to push lot sales, Joyce came to me one day and with great sadness in her voice said, "Bill, Michael is sick at father's apartment and needs help."

Michael was thirty years old, and I hesitated to interfere, as I had always taught him to live his life as he chose. Nevertheless, after an hour's careful consideration with empathy for his mother and concern for my eldest son, I said to Joyce, "I will go over to Marty's apartment and bring him back either over my shoulder or on his feet, the choice will be his, but you will have to get his hair cut."

"Please get him," she replied.

Marty wasn't at the apartment when I rang the bell, and after a few moments, I heard a muffled voice which I recognized as Michael's. "Yes," the voice said softly, like from a person on his death bed.

"It's your father," I barked. "Open the door."

After a moment's hesitation but without a murmur, I heard the buzzer sound indicating he had let me in.

When I reached their 12th floor apartment, the door was ajar, and upon entering, I stood for a moment shocked and appalled at the scene. Dirty clothes, foul air and a look of despair on Michael's face removed any remaining doubts I had about my decision. "Gather your personal belongings son," I ordered. "You are going with me."

Without a word of defiance or a question about our destination, he grabbed his things, and we left the suite.

With her nursing and good cooking, Joyce had him back on his feet in a week plus she persuaded him to get a hair cut, the first time in twelve years. I gave him money for new clothes, and the incredible change in his appearance made the emotional undertaking an outstanding success.

When Michael arrived in Florida with Marty a few months later to join the rest of the family in a joyous and real old-fashioned Christmas, Joyce and I were truly delighted with our efforts on behalf of our son. I purchased $600 worth of electric trains, remote-controlled toys, and games of all descriptions, and the lot of us, including my mother, Uncle George and Marty, regressed to our childhood. We had a ball.

Unfortunately Michael reverted to his old ways for a while when he returned to Toronto. Nonetheless, both father and son were rapidly coming to the conclusion that alcohol would be responsible for an early demise if we didn't get the habit under control, which we both hated to admit meant total abstinence. I rarely shouldered responsibility for the failings of my offspring but as the three of them held great respect for me and my philosophy, I felt certain their failure to control alcohol was a direct result of my continuous abuse of that curse.

Because of Michael's reluctance to keep his hair at a reasonable length or his appearance in some conformity with my lifestyle, I still didn't encourage him to join us in Florida, though gave him a few hundred dollars for clothes and traveling expenses.

With other members of my family, I was far more generous. Beside the $20,000 cottages to Gary and Sherree, I gave Gary and Tandy substantial sums for various reasons and paid $6,000 to fix Gary's teeth. I spent a similar amount on brother Jack's. To be certain Mother could afford some luxuries, I put $10,000 in her account. She and Uncle George enjoyed a pleasant existence, spending six months in a house of mine beside Pigeon Lake in Ontario and six months in their own Central Florida trailer. I also squandered money quite freely with friends and employees. Discovering my old friend Ken Watson hard up and unable to work, I presented him with a check for $5,000 which I told him was a finder's fee for telling us about the Buckhorn Lake acreage. In the summer of 1981, I also treated Watson and his new wife Alice, together with Ed and Sheila Barham, Roman and Verna Kruchak, and Jack to a vacation on a 52-foot houseboat on Lake-of-the-Woods where we passed a pleasant week loafing, fishing, and enjoying each other's company. Also in Florida each spring, I took Dot Grace, her sisters and the Schramms for a few days on a houseboat excursion into the Everglades at my expense. Money wasn't terribly important to me except for what it could provide in physical enjoyment of which I either wanted to be a participant or at least see the result of my beneficence. Michael, who couldn't bring himself to accept my philosophy therefore automatically eliminated himself from being a recipient of any gift giving because he rarely was in my presence.

At the point in 1981 when our Padre Island program was in full swing, I sincerely believed we were on our way to untold wealth, and as a result, I looked for a more pretentious residence. The Hillsboro Mile in Hillsboro Beach, Florida often referred to as "Millionaires Mile," appeared to offer the best opportunity to locate our dream home. We investigated several properties all of which fronted on the Atlantic Ocean and stretched back to the Intracoastal Waterway, as all private residences in the City of Hillsboro Beach must do. Just before Christmas in 1981, we bought an estate with 277 feet of beautiful sand beach and an equal amount of intracoastal frontage. For that 4½-acre tropical paradise, I paid $1.1 million with half a million in cash. The mortgage balance at 13½ percent and the taxes and maintenance costs totalled in excess of $7,000 monthly, a paltry sum at the time considering the huge amount of cash I dealt with weekly in my combined Canadian and American operations. Nevertheless, when conditions in Texas reversed, this monthly payment became a substantial personal burden, and so I put the attractive tract on the market expecting to make a fast and handsome profit. To my astonishment this proved incorrect, and the property just sat, helping in the erosion of our swiftly dwindling reserves.

As 1982 waned, my dreams and aspirations again changed, and with North America still locked in a recession and Sumcot of America together with Sumcot Canada in a shambles, I had to decide whether to retrench and start anew or retreat gracefully and attempt to get out from under my unbelievable burden of debt.

For the first time in our married life, Joyce and I segregated ourselves from our family for the holidays. I arranged for the finest suite available on the *Voldendam,* and we embarked on a two-week Christmas cruise to Martinique, Barbados, Trinidad, Aruba, and St. Maarten. The only association we had with our family was when Sherree came aboard the afternoon of departure and set up a Christmas tree in our cabin.

The two weeks at sea gave me time for reflection. Two months prior to the voyage I had visited Toronto for a week to be a part of the annual Grey Cup celebration. Of my many drinking sprees spanning forty years, that few days topped them all, and I returned to Florida in sorry shape. Although I didn't entirely abstain while at sea, no doubt remained in my mind that my days with whiskey were numbered. If I could somehow get rid of my monstrous financial responsibility, I knew to stop drinking would be a cinch.

One day in early 1981, Joyce and I started to reminisce of bygone days, and both of us found it difficult to recall certain places and specific dates. I began to enumerate in chronological order the many major happenings throughout our days together. When I started to elaborate on paper about certain incidents, the idea struck me to put them down in book form. After further thought I decided to write my memoirs and philosophies strictly for my own amusement and so perhaps started the toughest project of my diverse existence. Returning from our sea voyage with my autobiography well under way and facing the toughest financial predicament yet in my business career, I entered 1983 a tried but determined individual, knowing Padre Island held the key to my salvation.

This Is How It Is, 'Cause That's the Way It Was

As I near the end of my long story and approach my 59th birthday, I still wonder whether any interrelationship exists between religion and man's destiny. Are we solely responsible for plotting our own course or does an unseen hand control the steering wheel at times? If our lives are designed in advance and beyond our control to alter, who is the architect of this structuring of human existence?

Religion has played a prominent role in man's fate and too frequently in his everyday affairs. This theological interference has irritated me since childhood. Never being able to accept the theory of an afterlife or most other religious dogma, I used to deride my mother about her beliefs and involve her in debates about those nonsensical convictions which she always found difficult to defend. One day when still a young man, I realized Mother got considerable contentment from her faith, and though irrational in my mind, I had no right nor reason to interfere. From that time, I regarded religion from a different point of view. Though I now accept that a high percentage of our ancestors and for that matter our progeny did and will get solace from their faith, I still find it distressing that millions of people go through life accomplishing nothing on the mistaken assumption that life on earth is Hell and they will reap some reward in a fictitious Heaven for a meaningless existence. Human life is far too valuable for such a waste.

If an Almighty does have reign over our lot in life, I seriously question

His judgement despite the fact we are taught He works in mysterious ways. There seems to be no logical justification for taking a life like sister Ruth's, as an example, and allowing a monster like Hitler to survive and be responsible for the massacre of 50 million people.

Whether man's fate is ever predetermined can be thought-provoking. Take, for example, a simple game like golf. A tour professional who normally drops a twelve-foot putt on an average of once in every ten attempts will for some unexplainable reason suddenly start holing 50 percent of those putts. During the same tournament, his chip shots start landing inches from the cup rather than yards. Although he wins that match, he can't for the life of him come near to duplicating that feat for years or perhaps the balance of his golfing career. Another for-instance are the innumerable bridge players or professional gamblers who experience extended winning or losing streaks that last beyond all rules of averaging. Too many of these incidents contradict principles of logic not to believe something either within our subconscious or factors beyond human control actually influences certain decisions or actions.

Whether my destiny was predetermined or self inflicted, I will never know but my topsy-turvy existence often belied logical answers. Fortuitous decisions I frequently made that turned out well would be impossible to credit exclusively to conscious intelligence or good planning. A so-called "gut feeling" often was solely responsible for many of my business decisions. In most situations I felt confident my verdict would eventually turn out correct and spent little time in self recrimination if it didn't.

The final two years of my story, including 1983 and 1984, whether predetermined or otherwise saw me flounder in the depths and subsequently soar to the heights of human emotions, and several incidents entirely out of my control greatly influenced these last years.

On January 2, 1983, Dode Bell's oldest son Andy phoned me in Florida with the sad news his father had died without warning at the age of 61 from a heart attack. My close association with Dode reached back to Depression days on the farm when Mother ran the dances at the local hall. For some reason I always pictured Dode in his mid-teens prancing into the dance hall, cocky, smoking a cigar, and very spirited. During my numerous visits to Monominto I rarely passed through without dropping in on Dode and his wife Cora. Cora taught Ruth her final year at Pinewood School in the middle 1940s. Jack and I had the pleasure to attend a Monominto reunion in 1981. When some of the old gang got into a ball game, Dode, full of his usual zest for life played on Jack's and my team, and it didn't seem possible that now he was dead. Unfortunately this turned out to be only a harbinger of the appalling events of the ensuing six months.

A few weeks after Dode's untimely demise, Joyce went to a local radiologist for her annual checkup rather than flying to Toronto for her normal examination at Princess Margaret. Our family doctor, after receiving the X-ray report, phoned Joyce and advised her to fly to Toronto immediately and see the gynecologist who had attended her at the initial discovery of cancer. The horror she went through for several days until the Toronto specialists informed her they could find nothing wrong, could not be aptly described by mere words. Apparently the Florida radiologist had simply misread her X-rays. Joyce's mental torment could not be measured in dollars and cents, and so we refrained from suing though the hospital swiftly refunded all her fees.

Determined not to allow alcohol to get the better of me, I remained on the wagon throughout the spring of 1982. In late March, Tandy and I flew to Padre Island to arrange financing on two Ocean Vista units in default on which we were cosigners and hence responsible. On the first evening Jack phoned with the deplorable news that my close buddy Ken Watson had just perished with a heart attack. That night I got drunk. No friend was more personally associated with me throughout my thirty years in Toronto. Always a great supporter of mine and a sounding post for my tribulations, he seemed synonomous with my life in that city. Though fully aware of his serious heart condition, it never really occurred to me that Ken Watson would not be available one day when I called to go on a hunting or fishing excursion. Few men are ever closer nor shared more intimate moments of joy and misery than he and I. I would miss him terribly.

Two months later, an evening phone call shocked me with the unbelievable tidings that Doug Prue, age 43, had just succumbed to a massive stroke and heart attack. I flew out to the funeral, attended by numerous ex-Sumcot employees, some of whom I hadn't seen for several years. Though I hadn't seen Doug for a year or more, he always kept in touch and had phoned me in Florida a few months earlier when we planned one more moose hunt for the fall of 1984. Now he too would be only a memory. Always like a younger brother, Doug would be irreplaceable in my heart, especially as an outdoor companion. The loss of Doug and Ken Watson would make hunting or fishing sojourns into Ontario an empty adventure.

While in Toronto at Doug's funeral, I learned Don Filsinger, our next door neighbor at Shediac for five years, had also become a victim of a heart attack plus Harry Bray, a friend in my age bracket from the Toronto Board of Trade. Feeling despondent, I flew to Winnipeg to see some of my remaining friends before tragedy befell either them or me. Two hours after landing, I drove to Barhams in Monominto, and before

I reached the front door, Sheila informed me Mike Kruchak was dying with cancer. This seemed almost too incredible to be believable.

I visited Mike at home and despite his bravado and courage, death was stamped on his face. For several years on my Winnipeg trips Bill Kruchak, Mike's oldest brother, Roman, a younger brother, plus Ed Barham, and all their wives would join Joyce and me or me by myself for an evening get-together, including dinner. Although almost too ill to eat, I persuaded Mike and his wife Gladys to join us for our usual gathering. We spent a delightful evening reminiscing about our days together as chainmen on a survey crew, oilers on the same dragline, and as a battery on the old Monominto baseball team. In the parking lot following our pleasant dinner as we slowly approached our separate automobiles, Mike hesitated momentarily before entering his car. With a big smile he waved farewell which we both knew would be our final salutation on this earth.

With despair in my heart from the incredible series of events since the turn of the year, I departed Winnipeg to meet Tandy on Padre Island for a couple of days to negotiate a pending deal on our property. Following my business in Texas and needing a break to combat my terrible despondency, I arranged to meet Joyce, who hadn't left Florida, in Las Vegas. Tandy returned to her Florida duties, and when Joyce and I arrived at our Riviera suite a message to call Tandy made my heart sink. "Dad," she said sadly, "I almost didn't call but decided I must. Al Jessup just phoned to let you know Tom O'Connor suffered a fatal heart attack last night." Stunned with these final woeful tidings, I almost returned to Florida.

Tommy, exactly my age, a constant jogger and the picture of health, had been my golfing companion for the years we were both members of the same Toronto Club and had taken eight consecutive junkets to the Bahamas. Close associates on journeys abroad and during Toronto Board of Trade functions, I would especially miss his brilliant mind and ready wit. Tommy's unexpected passing on top of the others forced me to stop and cogitate about the time still left on my life's calendar and how I wished to spend those cherished days.

Over and above the unbelievable series of tragedies befalling my closest friends, in early 1982 I suffered the most stressful few months of my entire business career. Shortly after the new year, Gary Handin confirmed his desire to go back into private law practice which he did on April 1st. Due to the closing of Sumcot's affairs in Toronto and Texas, no one with managerial expertise now remained in the corporation. I therefore decided that after nearly forty years in the front lines of industry, the time had come to call it quits. Packing it in with the enormous debt load I carried in both countries, however, made that conclusion easier said than done. We sold the warehouses in 1982, but most of the $400,000 profit had been taken back in a second mortgage that only generated $3,000 in cash monthly. Gary had negotiated to sell Pompano Plaza before leaving the company, though nothing resulted, and so our assets were tied up in the shopping center and 7 million dollars worth of raw land in Canada, Texas, and Florida. I put everything on the market, confident we would dispose of something before huge interest payments forced us into insolvency. My business career for thirty-five years had resembled a trolley car out of control on a giant roller coaster. Once in 1955 with Plastic Plating it crashed, and on numerous occasions it looked as though the wheels might come off. As 1983 progressed, another total collapse appeared inevitable.

Our most salable asset, the Pompano Plaza, caused us the biggest and most prolonged headache. Over a period of one year we answered thousands of phone calls, handled hundreds of appointments and perused dozens of contracts or letters of intent. I accepted five offers to purchase which didn't go through for various reasons—such as accountants not approving the shopping center's income, lawyers not endorsing mortgage clauses, the roof leaked badly, and others. In October we finally arranged a 3.2 million dollar deal. Not scheduled to close until January, 1984, it didn't alleviate our immediate cash shortage. As our financial woes accelerated, I strove incessantly to find some way to salvage my 35 years of effort. For ten years Joyce and I had retained $45,000 in municipal bonds as a little nest egg. I borrowed $37,000 against them which kept us afloat for a few weeks. High interest rates plus borrowing costs made arranging a $75,000 2nd mortgage on our lovely Hillsboro residence an expensive loan, but it staved off bankruptcy until the Pompano Plaza closing in January, 1984. Considering I paid 1.9 million for the shopping center which produced $350,000 annual gross income when fully occupied made the 3.2 million selling price or 1.3 million capital gain an excellent profit and the five-year exercise an outstanding venture. However, $935,000 of that profit came back in a purchase money second mortgage, which meant our massive cash insufficiency didn't substantially improve. The plaza sale had therefore just provided a breathing spell.

More than once we were within hours of defaulting on payments of mortgage principal or loan interest, but somehow shuffled our limited cash flow and avoided catastrophe. The half million owed to the Internal Revenue Service gave us the most concern as they were charging interest and penalties of approximately 20 percent and also were becoming exceedingly impatient for us to settle the account. All of our Texas Ocean Vista profits in an economically depressed Padre Island neither interested the Internal Revenue Service, nor did they offer any sympathy. Plain and simple they demanded their money or threatened to lock our door and begin foreclosure proceedings. An inglorious finale to my exciting business adventures appeared imminent. Nevertheless, despite the horrible prospect of being forced to start all over again, I really never gave up hope of finding a solution to the crisis, and I had a deep seated conviction everything would somehow turn out all right. Every lending institution in Florida, Texas, and Toronto that I had contacted to borrow money against our vacant land flatly refused our plea for financial assistance. This rejection didn't surprise me because as a Toronto mortgage broker in 1956 I had discovered that mortgaging undeveloped land almost equalled trying to grow wings on a horse.

In the opening paragraphs of this chapter, I mentioned my uncertainty about whether certain actions are predetermined, controlled by an unseen hand, or instigated by our subconscious. A perfect example of an unconscious decision of mine that resulted in long-term implications was tumbling into the Orchard Park tavern thirty-three years earlier and meeting Joyce on a million-to-one shot chance encounter. Doing things on the spur of the moment occurred frequently throughout my existence, and the spontaneous action I took one morning at the pinnacle of our fiscal misery is also unaccountable.

The Walter Heller Mortgage Company, one of the largest and toughest lending institutions in North America, had arranged a large loan for Sumcot to assist in acquiring the Texas Renaissance property two years earlier. Unable to discharge the complete loan at the closing of the Ocean Vista, they still held a $600,000 first mortgage on the ocean-front parcel of that tract. When I contacted them two months earlier about the possibility of increasing their loan, they not only refused my request outright but indicated they wanted the $600,000 repaid as rapidly as possible. Herb Gruber, president of Heller's southeastern division, had become acquainted with me during extensive and difficult negotiations on the Padre Island agreement. Familiar with Padre Island and the economic slump due to the enormous devaluation of the peso, Herb had been instrumental in refusing assistance on my earlier plea. I therefore had no reason at the height of my crisis to return to him for help.

Sitting at my desk one morning early in 1984, deep in gloom and trying to figure a means of keeping my little real estate empire from collapsing like a deck of cards, I suddenly found my fingers dialing Gruber's number. Without forethought, as if commanded by an unseen voice before Herb answered my call, I felt a surge of confidence as though I already knew Herb would now be receptive to a proposition. From that moment the gray clouds that had hung over us for so long began to dissipate and the sun came out at last.

A huge Japanese corporation had just acquired the Walter Heller

Mortgage Company, reportedly making them the largest lending institution in the world. As a result of this merger, Heller was anxious for business and the reason my request received a positive response. For reasons I will never understand, I recontacted them at a very auspicious time, otherwise my story may have had an entirely different ending. But instead we had a slow but steady climb to fiscal prosperity from that unexplainable phone call.

Herb invited me to present a proposal that would not only put us in a sound cash position but also allow a reasonable amount of time to sell our holdings. Tandy and I carefully outlined our needs, and Herb arranged a total loan of 3.1 million, discharging all outstanding indebtedness, including the I.R.S., plus allowing sufficient capital to operate without further property sales until 1986. Heller held a first charge on all our lands and other assets except our personal properties in Hillsboro Beach. Our unnerving ordeal, now over, meant my rocketing trolley car had reached the bottom of the roller coaster ride without losing its wheels. Now it began a steady ascent to the top where I planned to disembark if it ever made the trip successfully.

The loss of my friends in 1983 (I attended Mike Kruchak's funeral in October), inconceivable business pressure, and the soul-searching decision to close Sumcot's offices and disband the staff, didn't create a favorable atmosphere for me to curb my alcoholic consumption. Though I stopped for intervals varying from three days to three months, the emotional highs and lows gave me an excuse to have a drink and drown my sorrows or toast a triumph. I considered joining Alcoholics Anonymous and went so far as phoning them one morning, but I never attended a meeting. Our family doctor recommended antibuse which I tried for a brief spell. Antibuse provided a crutch, but I knew that in the long run an ultimate commitment had to come from me. If I didn't give it up, my liver would give out, and Joyce's health and peace of mind were also affected by my boozing. In December, 1983, after a particularly heavy session, I finally halted the debilitating habit. To say I regretted my drinking days would be untrue. Like everything else in my life, whiskey played a part. At times it made me act stupid, but often alcohol provided a needed panacea to my mental strain. Regardless of the purpose, for forty years I drank because that is the way I was, though I am grateful I had the will power to stop.

When the Heller deal closed in April, 1984, and our business affairs were in order for the first time since our arrival in the U.S. as residents, Joyce and I elected to take another extended automobile journey, and as usual, we combined business with pleasure. To claim I had complete peace of mind as a result of our 3.1 million loan would not be entirely true. Interest payments alone totalled over half a million annually—or

$1,500 per day for 365 days of the year. I simply hoped our property would sell before interest payments completely eroded our equity.

We specifically wanted to spend a month in Toronto to take another crack at disposing of our remaining Ontario lots. Jack and Edwina, working on a part-time basis through spring and early summer, had been unsuccessful in selling any of our real estate as the market remained depressed. Terry had achieved a marvelous legal victory over the Canadian Department of Internal Revenue, saving Sumcot Development Ltd. $120,000. This windfall gave me the confidence and money to gamble on a small but expensive advertising campaign in an attempt to sell our property.

Before reaching Canada, Joyce and I spent three weeks on a well-earned vacation. A few pleasant days at Disney World and Epcot, followed by a short stay at Nashville where we enjoyed a night at the Grand Old Opry and a day at Opryland took up the first week. When our financial position improved sufficiently, we planned to locate a summer retreat to escape the intense Florida heat. Advised to consider the North Carolina mountains, we passed three delightful days around Asheville but decided that region didn't suit our requirements. We visited my old cohort, Art Greene at Boiling Spring Lakes Development on the North Carolina coast. Reminiscing with the Greenes, now retired, it seemed impossible to believe over twenty years had elapsed since our association with that flop.

Caesar's Palace in Atlantic City invited us to be their guests, and we spent five relaxing and profitable days in their casino while luxuriating at night in a suite so deluxe it would have charmed English royalty.

On our first evening in Ontario we stayed at a Trenton area motel near where we knew the Crawfords had retired. Charlie worked for Phillips Real Estate in the early 1950s. He and Marge had remained bosom friends of ours for a long time, but we'd had no contact with them for 17 years. I located their residence without difficulty, but sorrowfully, Marge had passed away four months before. Delighted to see us, Charlie suggested the next day we look up our mutual friend Helen Watson, Ken's ex-wife, who lived in Peterborough. We hadn't seen her for 14 years. After a happy reunion, we congregated at Mother's for a pleasing get-together and rehash of old times.

Our thirty-day stay in Toronto proved successful beyond my wildest dreams. I carefully designed a $7,000 display ad based on experience gained over a 30-year span of real estate promotions. Accepting a low down payment and less than average interest rate on mortgage take backs greatly assisted us in selling out both Buckhorn Lake and Canadiana Shore before the season ended. In lieu of non-productive raw land, I now held over $300,000 of interest-producing mortgages. Though delighted, the disposal of our Canadian land didn't hold a candle to our ecstasy when during our Toronto stay a parcel of our Texas holdings sold for $1,660,000 cash.

Not certain if we would ever make this long automobile journey through North America again, we planned to look up as many old friends as possible. Social get-togethers with the Theodorus, Legges, Walshs, Millers, and numerous family members made us realize how many good friends we had left behind in Toronto. Despite this unhappy fact, neither of us had any regrets regarding our move to Florida.

While visiting the Schwandts in Harcourt, Ontario, Chester, Mother and I took a two-hour drive through Harcourt Park. It seemed incredible twenty-five years had elapsed since Pop and I first opened up that gigantic development. Time has a way of removing unpleasantness out of irksome situations, but though Harcourt Park looked beautiful, I didn't rue not seeing my old dream world more frequently. Our success in selling the Canadian lots and the Texas transaction allowed us to leave Toronto for Winnipeg via Chicago on "cloud nine." Our good fortune in seeing old friends and relatives continued as we moved westward.

I had not seen nor heard from Uncle Tom's offspring since I accidentally arrived in the Windy City during the blizzard of January, 1950. Mother gave me the phone numbers of Alice and Ethel, the two oldest girls. Joyce and I registered at a motel in the Harvey sector of Chicago around 3 p.m., and I immediately phoned my two female cousins. Alice lived 40 miles west of Harvey, Ethel 40 miles east in Indiana. The two boys, Tommy and Bill, resided in the vicinity of Harvey. Almost miraculously, at 7:30 p.m. all four cousins together with their spouses—except Ethel's husband, Red, who worked a night shift—sat down with Joyce and me at an exciting reunion dinner. We continued our westward journey elated with reestablishing a kinship with our Chicago cousins.

Our week stay in Winnipeg turned out just as pleasant as we renewed our association with relatives and friends alike. Ed Barham and I made our usual trek back to the barren Brokenhead. Though farmers had steadily encroached on our childhood sanctuary, we spent a perfect afternoon hiking, chatting, and cooking steaks over an open fire surrounded by an environment we both loved, found difficult to explain, yet understood that the strange enchantment was simply because that is the way we were.

En route to Las Vegas our luck continued at locating old companions when we found Edna Branning in a rural sector of Saskatchewan happily married to a gentleman she knew long before she met Lorne. We also ferreted out the Thomas' who had moved to Kingman, Arizona just east of the Nevada border. My old partner had sustained a bout with cancer, but nevertheless he and Helen appeared contented in their retirement. Our success in renewing ties with the past reached its pinnacle shortly after returning to our Florida home.

My search for Dolly, Mother's half sister, had taken up a lot of my time and effort over an extended period of time. Two years earlier Mother discovered and gave me an old address of Dolly's which showed her living in Nashville, Tennessee. During our brief stay in that city in the summer, I phoned every Helms (Dolly's first husband's name) in the telephone directory without chancing upon any trace of my missing aunt. Joyce and I drove over to the address and found a new wing of Vanderbilt Hospital where apartments used to stand, which meant I'd reached another dead end. While chatting with cousin Ethel in Chicago, I happened to inquire if any of them including Uncle Tom had ever communicated with Granddad Rodd or other members of that branch of the family.

Sounding a trifle surprised Ethel said, "Bill, my Dad never forgave Grandpa Rodd for abandoning his family, and so those ties were rarely discussed. But a lad by the name of Brent Helms phoned from O'Hare Airport a couple of years ago, and he inquired if we might be first cousins."

"My gawd, Ethel, that is who I've been trying to locate for many years. Did he mention where he lived?"

"Yes, Jackson, Mississippi. I took down his address which I'll bring to our get-together tonight," she replied.

Before leaving our motel the following morning, I tried to reach Brent by phone but to my dismay, no listing could be found at the given address. Joyce suggested I write to Brent and mark on the envelope: "Urgent, please forward if possible." I did that as soon as we reached home.

Still recuperating from our 12,000 mile journey a week later, Joyce came racing breathlessly into the room. "Brent Helms is on the phone," she cried excitedly.

I couldn't believe my ears and answered with a quiver in my voice. The soft southern drawl on the line didn't even slightly resemble what I expected to hear, but he sounded enthusiastic about the communication. I almost choked when he informed me Dolly, now divorced the second time, also lived in Jackson. She didn't have a home phone, but he said he would have his mother contact me shortly. As Brent promised, Dolly phoned within twenty-four hours. After a lengthy and exciting conversation, my long lost aunt agreed to join me on a trip to Toronto in October for a rendezvous with Mother. I called Jack and Mom with the electrifying news which injudiciously proved unwise. Dolly, an admitted introvert and frightened at possibly discovering old skeletons in the family closet, backed out of the date. Several following attempts to set up a tete-a-tete of any kind ended in failure until 1985 when on another of our lengthy road trips Joyce and I drove to Jackson and finally met Brent but not the elusive Dolly. The gist of conversation was inconsequential to our jubilation that we had finally contacted our blood relatives of whom we knew so little but wished to know so much.

Our turn of good fortune didn't waiver when we returned from our lengthy wandering in 1984. One of my principal concerns, other than the huge interest payments to Heller, was the $7,500 monthly costs on the vacant tract we personally owned in Hillsboro Beach. For two years I tried desperately to sell the property privately and through agents, but in spite of tremendous interest including numerous showings we never received a serious offer. My original investment of 1.1 million had now mushroomed to over 1.3 million.

Shortly after getting home, I said to Joyce, "I have traded in real estate for thirty-five years, in most cases successfully. Our Hillsboro holding, however, appears to be a white elephant, and I'm prepared to lose $200,000 and get rid of the headache."

"Before you offer it at a discount," Joyce responded, "why not contact the agent who last spring had someone willing to trade another Hillsboro property for ours?"

"He only has 120 feet of ocean frontage in comparison to our 277 feet," I remarked acidly.

"That's true, but his property includes a beautiful house while we have two that must be destroyed."

"I'll give the agent a call," I answered tiredly, feeling the effort would be a waste of time.

Once more our destiny took a sharp turnaround as a result of that insignificant chat. For whatever reason, our timing again was perfect. The owner of the other property had communicated with the agent a few days earlier, expressing a keen interest in our large tract. A wealthy young entrepreneur, he required property with our dimensions to erect a private castle of 14,000 square feet.

He offered us $300,000 in addition to his estate which, though appraised at one million, would bring 1.5 million on a good market according to the agent. Therefore I received $300,000 plus a property worth near 1.5 million for our parcel which I would have sold for 1.1 million. A rambling 4,000-square-foot ocean-front mansion sat in the middle of 1½ acres of newly installed tropical foliage and landscaping with a large outdoor pool and a huge jacuzzi whirlpool. The 120 feet of expensive docks along the intracoastal would berth the most luxurious yacht—which I expected to own one day. Joyce, in love with the spacious rooms, ultramodern kitchen, four bathrooms, and other amenities, begged me to move in. Reluctant at first due to the huge debt I still owed and recognizing those obligations could be substantially reduced by selling our new estate, I decided to linger until positive the Texas deal would close.

Before year's end, Sumcot's tract at Sample and Powerline sold for 1.6 million. This together with the sale of the Padre Island parcel reduced Heller's debt to 1.5 million. On the plus side of the ledger we now held over 1.8 million in mortgages and still had unsold Texas real estate valued in the 4 million dollar range. As a result of our greatly improved financial position, I agreed to move into our luxurious new ocean-front villa, and did so two weeks before Christmas. Joyce and I reveled in our deluxe new domicile, with its panoramic view across my beloved sea and reflected on our first apartment that totaled 300 square feet. Joyce admitted in those early days she hoped that eventually we would be able to afford a more pretentious residence than the bare two-room flat we started out with, but never in her wildest imagination had she dreamed of anything as sumptuous as our new home on millionaire's row. I recalled the ramshackle outhouse on the farm where we used Eaton's catalogue for toilet paper and at that point in life never envisioned owning a mansion by the sea with four deluxe bathrooms. We had come a long way.

The impact of the tragic loss in 1982 of my five personal companions had dramatically altered my outlook. The enormous amount of money that had passed through my hands in forty years had never brought me great contentment or satisfaction, but on the other hand, it caused no misery. I thoroughly enjoyed what money could provide but also recognized most things in life that gave me pleasure didn't involve dollars. All five of my dead friends had future plans about how they would enjoy their remaining years, which revolved around spending money, but those intentions went for naught and the dollars will be spent by someone else. I was determined this wouldn't happen to Joyce and me.

The reasons for my financial successes often eluded me, although I thought about it frequently. On the positive side I knew my greatest personal asset was determination. Like most humans, I often dreamed, but I also struggled to fulfill those dreams. Many individuals who dream do nothing to reach their goal, while others put forth some effort but lack persistence to overcome obstacles that begin to cloud their visions. Unquestionably luck played a role in my achievements, but luck only comes to those who try. As stated earlier, certain spontaneous decisions I made seemed to be as a result of a predetermined fate or the guiding hand of a Divine Being. Unfortunately those identical factors often seem to be responsible for some people's evil decisions. This means that if our destiny is predetermined then the one charting our life's direction is no more moral than immoral. Whatever the justification for my financial well being, Joyce and I appeared to have more money than we could ever reasonably expect to spend. Though I arrived at the conclusion I no longer needed to strive for wealth, I still planned to continue on the same course of positive action for fulfilling our fantasies in future years.

Sherree joined us in Florida for sixteen months, still searching for her own niche in life. While she worked for Sumcot, we went into greyhound racing and imported three dogs from Ireland at a cost of $16,000. Since 1954, Joyce and I had gambled at dog tracks on countless occasions and enjoyed ourselves most times, but watching our own dogs run provided us with more amusement than I ever could have imagined and opened up another exciting venture to fill our days. Sherree loved the challenge of the greyhound business, but when offered an outstanding opportunity in the modeling field, she returned to Toronto in January, 1985. With Tandy the sole remaining employee, I closed down Sumcot's Florida office, and for the first time in 36 years had no place to hang my hat other than at home. Gary and Tandy sold their Harcourt Park cottage, and with that money plus some assistance from me, they acquired the Schramm's Pompano Beach residence. Hans and Magda, approaching their late eighties, had moved in with their son Kurt on the Gulf Coast. We moved all corporate and my personal affairs into a spare bedroom, and Sumcot paid a monthly rental to the kids to help carry their payments. Tandy capably administered both the corporations and my personal matters. Not since Pop started me milking cows and cutting stove wood at age six did I awaken in the morning with no responsibilities, but I didn't lack schemes to take care of my leisure hours.

Many of my actions in life often baffled our friends and acquaintances. They couldn't understand why we wished to maintain four separate residences in different regions of North America as we planned. I thoroughly believed, however, in the long term value of good real estate and felt it offered better protection against inflation than gold or currency. It also gave us four places to rearrange furniture which kept our existence from becoming boring.

Another resolution that irritated some of our Canadian friends was our determination to become U.S. citizens, which we did proudly in early 1985. We didn't drop our Canadian heritage without some remorse, but my adopted country suited my political philosophy, and I was delighted to be an American.

Besides my love of reading, writing, gambling, golfing and playing bridge, numerous places in the world, especially those I hadn't yet visited held a great attraction for me, and so I didn't expect my future years would be wasted in idleness. I simply did not wish to be involved with money-making schemes.

In spite of our rapture with the Hillsboro Beach villa, we both loved to relax a few days each year in our tiny but exquisite beach-front condominium on Padre Island. Phoenix also held an attachment, and the two lots I purchased at Fountain Hills in 1975 for $18,000 each had now skyrocketed in value to $60,000 per lot. We decided to build two houses on these properties, one for sale and the other for our personal use.

The view from our Fountain Hills site was a mesmerizing spectacle, though a complete contrast to Florida. Our Hillsboro home outlook offered constant movement. Watercraft passing on display day and night ranged from giant freighters, passenger liners and tugboats towing their loaded barges to pleasure craft of all descriptions and especially sailboats with their gaily colored canvas. The sea's ever-changing colors and temperament ranging from a tranquil pond to a raging uncontrollable fury kept me forever fascinated. On the other hand, the scene from our Arizona property included majestic mountains, and overlooking the tenth tee of the Fountain Hills golf course, it included a pleasant vista of rolling green fairways bordered by desert cactus. Both perspectives were beautiful in their own way.

Last but by *no* means least, I wanted a place to escape the intense seasonal heat of the South, and after months of careful deliberation, I elected to establish a summer home in Monominto. Several factors prompted me to return to my roots, other than cool summer evenings. For fishing and hunting, no area of North America offered the diversity of terrain and abundance of wildlife as Northern Ontario and Manitoba. To reach some of that rugged region would require a four-wheeled drive, but I planned to acquire such a vehicle outfitted with every available modern convenience. Though I adored the wilds, I also cherished all the comforts money could procure and resolved to pamper myself. Perhaps the most important motive for wishing to pass some of my remaining time in Manitoba revolved around the many people with whom I had a close association during my first twenty years, a bond that had never been broken.

Joyce, impressed with the luxurious trailer home Thomases had purchased in Arizona, suggested a similar structure would be ideal for our Manitoba retreat. I flew to Winnipeg in early 1985, and for $40,000 purchased a deluxe trailer home 16 feet wide and 76 feet long, complete with sunken living room, an open fireplace, and a master bedroom almost as large as in our Florida mansion. Where to locate our northern escape became the next crucial decision. Numerous possibilities existed, but many elements had to be taken into consideration, such as services, telephone, and power, proximity to year-around residences to cut down on the possibility of vandalism during our absence, and, because Joyce, a city girl, would be left alone on occasions when I went on a stag fishing party, the nearness to compatible people. Our old farm attracted me like a hound to a rabbit. The original frame and log house still stood, though it was badly dilapidated beyond hope of restoration. It nevertheless occupied a prime location—at least to me. The view across the fields and meadows seemed unchanged in half a century and brought peace and tranquility to my soul. Manitoba maples planted by Mother as saplings, flourished as towering shade trees. Lilac, choke-cherry and rose bushes still bloomed, and the fresh smell of an unpolluted land still filled the air. Despite my longing for the past, common sense overcame my nostalgia, and I went back to my second choice, the most logical site in Monominto to fit my requirements.

One evening while chatting with Ed and Sheila, I explained my quandry.

"Ed, old friend, would you consider selling me three or four acres of your holdings, across the field in sight of your house?"

"Let's grab a tape measure and mark out your plot," Ed replied enthusiastically.

Everything suddenly seemed too simple, we swiftly arrived at a satisfactory price and made arrangements to prepare for the amenities including driveway, power, telephone, TV dish, drilled well, and foundation for the trailer.

"Eddie, do you anticipate any trouble getting a severance from the municipality?" I inquired.

"Hell no, they permit them all the time. I'll call tomorrow," he responded.

When I arrived at the Barham household the following morning, Ed was on the phone with his local councilman. After he hung up he turned to me, "Bill, what the hell is subdivision control?"

"Don't tell me Tache municipality has adopted subdivision control," I answered anxiously, my mind swirling back to the problems of getting deeds for Harcourt Park 27 years earlier.

"Yes," Eddie replied. "That fellow said we will have to submit a plan of subdivision."

"How many acres are left on the farm?" I inquired.

"Two hundred and seventy-five including the plot where my house sits. Why do you ask?"

"You never made much money farming the land (Ed had toiled 25 years in the railway yards in Winnipeg). Perhaps you ought to consider subdividing the entire tract and make some real dough."

"Bill, I have neither the money, the knowledge, nor the inclination for such an undertaking, but would you consider taking on the venture? That might be the only way Sheila and I will get our money out so I can retire and join you on those fishing jaunts we've talked and dreamed about for fifty years."

"Ed," I pensively responded, "After our mutual cronies, Dode Bell, Mike Kruchak, and three of my Toronto pals kicked the bucket so unexpectedly two years ago, I took an oath to quit trying to make money and just spend it for a change. Nevertheless, your farm would make an ideal rural residential development, and no doubt if we could obtain municipal and provincial approval, we could design an attractive sub-division and probably make a ton of money, if . . . ."